Handbook of
Counseling Psychology

Handbook of
Counseling Psychology

Second Edition

Edited by

STEVEN D. BROWN
Loyola University Chicago

ROBERT W. LENT
Michigan State University

A Wiley-Interscience Publication

JOHN WILEY & SONS, INC.

New York • Chichester • Brisbane • Toronto • Singapore

Library of Congress Cataloging-in-Publication Data

Handbook of counseling psychology / edited by Steven D. Brown, Robert
   W. Lent. — 2nd ed.
        p.   cm.
   Includes bibliographical references and index.
   ISBN 0-471-51254-0 (cloth : alk. paper)
   1. Counseling. 2. Psychology, Applied. I. Brown, Steven D.
   (Steven Douglas), 1947–   . II. Lent, Robert W. (Robert William),
   1953–   .
   [DNLM: 1. Counseling. 2. Psychology, Applied.   WM55 H235]
   BF637.C6H315   1992
   158′.3—dc20
DNLM/DLC
for Library of Congress   91-30150
                                                                      CIP

To Linda, Zachary, Kathryn, Ellen, and Jeremy

CONTRIBUTORS

Elizabeth M. Altmaier, Ph.D.
Professor
Division of Psychological
  and Quantitative Foundations
University of Iowa
Iowa City, IA

Donald R. Atkinson, Ph.D.
Professor
School of Education
University of California
Santa Barbara, CA

Nancy E. Betz, Ph.D.
Professor
Department of Psychology
Ohio State University
Columbus, OH

Fred H. Borgen, Ph.D.
Professor
Department of Psychology
Iowa State University
Ames, IA

Steven D. Brown, Ph.D.
Professor and Director,
Counseling Psychology Program
Department of Counseling
  and Educational Psychology
Loyola University Chicago
Chicago, IL

Monroe A. Bruch, Ph.D.
Associate Professor
Department of Counseling Psychology
State University of New York
  at Albany
Albany, NY

Peter C. Cairo, Ph.D.
Associate Professor and Director,
Counseling Psychology Program
Department of Social, Organizational
  and Counseling Psychology
Teachers College,
Columbia University
New York, NY

Jerry L. Deffenbacher, Ph.D.
Professor
Department of Psychology
Colorado State University
Fort Collins, CO

Ruth E. Fassinger, Ph.D.
Assistant Professor
Department of Counseling and
  Personnel Services
University of Maryland
College Park, MD

Patricia A. Frazier, Ph.D.
Assistant Professor
Department of Psychology
University of Minnesota
Minneapolis, MN

Bruce R. Fretz, Ph.D.
Professor
Department of Psychology
University of Maryland
College Park, MD

John P. Galassi, Ph.D.
Professor
School of Education
University of North Carolina
Chapel Hill, NC

Lawrence H. Gerstein, Ph.D.
Professor
Department of Counseling Psychology
  and Guidance Services
Ball State University
Muncie, IN

John Gibson, M.A.
Doctoral Candidate
Department of Counseling
  and Educational Psychology
Loyola University Chicago
Chicago, IL

Lucia Albino Gilbert, Ph.D.
Professor
Department of Educational Psychology
University of Texas
Austin, TX

Gail Hackett, Ph.D.
Professor
Division of Psychology in Education
Arizona State University
Tempe, AZ

P. Paul Heppner, Ph.D.
Professor
Department of Psychology
University of Missouri
Columbia, MO

Elizabeth L. Holloway, Ph.D.
Associate Professor
Division of Counseling
  and Educational Psychology
University of Oregon
Eugene, OR

John J. Horan, Ph.D.
Professor
Division of Psychology in Education
Arizona State University
Tempe, AZ

Brian D. Johnson, B.S.
Doctoral Candidate
Division of Psychological
  and Quantitative Foundations
University of Iowa
Iowa City, IA

Robert W. Lent, Ph.D.
Associate Professor
Department of Counseling, Educational
  Psychology and Special Education
Michigan State University
East Lansing, MI

Frederick G. Lopez, Ph.D.
Associate Professor
Department of Counseling, Educational
  Psychology and Special Education
Michigan State University
East Lansing, MI

Michael J. Mahoney, Ph.D.
Professor
Department of Psychology
University of North Texas
Denton, TX

Kathleen McNamara, Ph.D.
Associate Professor
Department of Psychology
Colorado State University
Fort Collins, CO

Roger A. Myers, Ph.D.
Professor
Department of Social, Organizational
  and Counseling Psychology
Teachers College
Columbia University
New York, NY

Christine M. Olson, M.A.
Doctoral Candidate
Division of Psychology in Education
Arizona State University
Tempe, AZ

Kathleen McCray Patterson, M.A.
Doctoral Candidate
School of Education
University of California
Santa Barbara, CA

Trent A. Petrie, Ph.D.
Assistant Professor
Department of Psychology
University of North Texas
Denton, TX

Susan D. Phillips, Ph.D.
Associate Professor
Department of Counseling Psychology
State University of New York
  at Albany
Albany, NY

Joan Polansky, M.A.
Doctoral Candidate
Division of Psychology in Education
Arizona State University
Tempe, AZ

Karen L. Poulin, M.Ed.
Doctoral Candidate
Division of Counseling and
  Educational Psychology
University of Oregon
Eugene, OR

Richard K. Russell, Ph.D.
Associate Professor
Department of Psychology
Ohio State University
Columbus, OH

Nancy K. Schlossberg, Ph.D.
Professor
Department of Counseling and
  Personnel Services
University of Maryland
College Park, MD

Mary J. Schwendener-Holt, M.A.
Employee Assistance Counselor
Personnel Development Group
Indianapolis, IN

Sandra L. Shullman, Ph.D.
Director, Organizational
  Consultation Services
Organizational Horizons, Inc.
Columbus, OH

Norma P. Simon, Ph.D.
Psychologist, Independent Practice
New York, NY

Chalmer E. Thompson, Ph.D.
Assistant Professor
Division of Counseling and
  Educational Psychology
University of Southern California
Los Angeles, CA

Diane J. Tinsley, Ph.D.
Senior Counseling Psychologist and
  Adjunct Associate Professor
Career Development Center
Southern Illinois University
Carbondale, IL

Howard E. A. Tinsley, Ph.D.
Professor and Director, Counseling
  Psychology Program
Department of Psychology
Southern Illinois University
Carbondale, IL

Bruce E. Wampold, Ph.D.
Professor
Division of Counseling and
  Educational Psychology
University of Oregon
Eugene, OR

PREFACE

In our Preface to the first edition of the *Handbook of Counseling Psychology,* we observed:

> *Counseling psychology is a field notable for its diversity and vigorous evolution. Influenced by diverse political and social forces as well as by developments from within mainstream psychology, it has expanded from an initial concern with educational and vocational guidance to the remediation and prevention of personal, interpersonal, vocational, and educational concerns. Further reflecting counseling psychology's growth is the great diversity in work settings, types of services performed, and theoretical orientations that characterize today's counseling psychologists.*

This depiction of the field, particularly its growth and flux, strikes us as still accurate today, eight years after the *Handbook*'s debut. Happily, the counseling psychology profession and its scientific base have continued to evolve. At the same time, counseling psychologists continue to embrace a coherent, yet flexible, core identity and a stable set of human service and scientific values that lend continuity to the specialty. This second edition of the *Handbook* attempts to keep pace with the field's change, chronicling key developments since the first edition and charting potential future directions.

We have designed this revision to maintain consistency with the first edition in several ways. First, it is based on a definition of counseling psychology as an "applied psychological discipline devoted to scientifically generating, applying, and disseminating knowledge on the remediation and prevention of vocational, educational, and personal adjustment difficulties" (Preface to the first edition). Second, we have continued to survey the field broadly, to reflect its diversity as well as its distinctiveness. Third, the *Handbook* attempts to synthesize inquiry on key counseling psychology-related topics, providing a critical analysis of the field's knowledge base along with implications for practice and future research. Included are topical areas in which counseling psychology has made seminal contributions (e.g., career choice, counselor training) as well as topics that, despite their relevance to the field's mission, have not always received sustained empirical attention from counseling psychologists (e.g., organizational dynamics, substance abuse).

Fourth, we have tried to encourage a cross-disciplinary perspective on the field's subject matter, with the goal of furthering dialogue and collaboration among related specialties that seek to promote psychological wellness. Thus, we have asked our authors to draw liberally on theory and research from other areas of psychology and the social sciences. Finally, as before, we have aimed this edition at a broad audience of both students and professionals in counseling psychology and related fields; our overarching goal is for the *Handbook* to contribute to science-based practice *and* practice-based science in counseling psychology. We believe it contains something of value for those who are primarily either service providers or researcher-academics, but that its greatest utility will be for those who identify as *scientist-practitioners.*

Despite these similarities to the first edition, this revision departs substantially from its predecessor in some crucial respects. The major headings have been revised to better reflect what we believe to be the definitional distinctiveness of counseling psychology. Thus, after the opening chapters on scientific and professional developments, the *Handbook* turns to developmental/preventive issues and educational/career development concerns—areas that have historically been considered central to the profession's definition. The *Handbook* ends with a collection of chapters devoted to counseling for personal and interpersonal problems. This latter domain represents a fruitful area of counseling psychology practice, one in which counseling psychologists' interests and expertise increasingly converge with those of professionals in related mental health fields.

A more fundamental change involves the chapter content and thematic organization of this edition. In particular, we have tried to feature theoretical advances and developmental themes to a greater degree than in the first edition. In keeping with these objectives, the lead chapters in Parts Two through Four are devoted to reviewing theoretical developments, respectively, in life-span psychological development, career development, and personal/interpersonal counseling. Part Two is aimed at counseling psychology's mission of promoting psychological and physical health across the life span and with sensitivity to issues of gender and culture. Chapters in this Part highlight family dynamics and psychological individuation in late adolescence, counseling for life transitions, the promotion of physical wellness, multicultural counseling, and gender-related counseling topics. These chapters reflect counseling psychologists' diverse involvement in developmental, preventive, and/or advocacy efforts. Part Three takes a life-span view of the career/educational development process, complementing the field's traditional focus on career entry issues with coverage of both earlier and later developmental tasks, including adjustment to college, work, and retirement. Rounding out coverage in this Part are chapters devoted to selected developments in career assessment and workplace/organizational issues such as consultation.

Another important thematic change involves this second edition's coverage of counseling for personal and interpersonal concerns (Part Four). Our strategy in the first edition was to address major research and practice issues (e.g., the status of prescriptive counseling, pantheoretical counseling ingredients, maintenance and transfer of client gains) that cut across specific client problems. In the current edition, we decided instead to organize our coverage primarily around common problems for which clients seek counseling. Rather than abandoning the focus on cross-problem treatment issues, however, we simply asked the current authors to address such topics as assessment, treatment prescription, and maintenance of gains within the context of their separate chapters on counseling for affective, anxiety, interpersonal, and substance abuse problems. The lead chapter in this Part surveys broad developments in theories of counseling and client change. The intent of the organization of Part Four is to make the *Handbook* more immediately responsive to the needs of service providers.

Another organizational change is the expansion of Part One of the *Handbook* to reflect the many exciting professional, training, and scientific developments that have occurred in counseling psychology in recent years. The topics in these opening chapters were chosen for their broad relevance to counseling psychologists. They include an update on professional, ethical, legal, and policy issues; overviews of advances in counseling-related measurement technology, research methods, and philosophy of science; the application of social psychological theory to counseling phenomena; and new developments in counselor training and supervision.

To ensure that this edition would convey a "fresh perspective" on the field, we elected to invite an almost entirely different set of contributors. This proved to be our single most difficult and painful editorial decision: we respect immensely the many outstanding psychologists who authored chapters for the first edition, and we are grateful to have worked with them. However, we wanted to encourage a diversity of views and a lively exchange of ideas, and felt that a fresh group of authors would best promote these ends. A very few authors do remain from the first edition, but they have written on different topics this time around. We believe that, collectively, the changes noted above make the current edition a substantially new volume rather than a simple update of the first edition.

In addition to relying on our own sense of the field's evolution in designing this second edition, we were fortunate to have received helpful feedback and suggestions from many colleagues around the country. We have tried to incorporate much of their feedback into the current *Handbook*. In future editions of the *Handbook,* we would like to devote coverage to important and evolving counseling psychology topics, including some that are not covered fully herein.

Once again, we have many people to thank for their crucial help throughout this project, including our colleagues and students at Loyola University Chicago and Michigan State University, and Herb Reich, our editor at Wiley. We are especially grateful to our contributors for their dedicated work and gracious responses to our editorial suggestions. In an attempt to make the *Handbook* affordable and accessible to as many users as possible, we developed strict length requirements for all chapters. We sincerely appreciate the authors' herculean efforts to keep their chapters within these page restrictions.

Finally, we warmly acknowledge the incredible support and encouragement of our spouses (Linda Heath and Ellen B. Lent) and the inspiration provided by the new additions to our families (Zachary and Kathryn Brown and Jeremy Lent). To them, this volume is lovingly dedicated.

STEVEN D. BROWN
ROBERT W. LENT

Chicago, Illinois
East Lansing, Michigan
March, 1992

CONTENTS

PART ONE
PROFESSIONAL AND SCIENTIFIC ISSUES

CHAPTER 1

PROFESSIONAL ISSUES IN COUNSELING PSYCHOLOGY: CONTINUITY, CHANGE, AND CHALLENGE

BRUCE R. FRETZ
NORMA P. SIMON

Counseling psychology is now midway between reports of prospects for the 1980s (Whiteley, Kagan, Harmon, Fretz, & Tanney, 1984) and projected views of the profession for the year 2000 (Whiteley & Fretz, 1980). In rereading those reports, one can find much about the profession that seems unchanged; yet, some developments that were predicted for the year 2000 have already occurred. Both the continuities and the changes in the training settings and work roles of counseling psychologists are reviewed in the first section following this introduction.

A more than ample supply of challenges is now provided for counseling psychologists. Competing demands for changes in training and in new career opportunities continue, as our society attempts to address and finance health care. In the 1980s, numerous conferences and ad hoc groups of psychologists developed recommendations that called for radical changes in the curricular and experiential components of academic training at the predoctoral, internship, and postdoctoral levels. These recommendations followed an unprecedented amount of change, during the late 1970s and early 1980s, regarding requirements for licensure. An entire section of this chapter reports on the major conferences. Their recommendations are identified and compared to recommendations from the Third National Conference for Counseling Psychology ("the Georgia Conference"; Gazda, Rude, & Weissberg, 1988). Counseling psychology is, in some ways, a microcosm of psychology at large: it encompasses a very broad range of scientific professional researchers and practitioners. The profession will be challenged to develop a workable consensus on many of these training issues and will need to maintain active leadership in an increasingly diverse array of emerging psychological organizations and groups of psychologists intent on influencing the future of psychology.

As the data and issues reviewed in the early part of the chapter will make clear, significant changes are occurring in the professional organization of mental health services in this country. These changes are leading to both new opportunities and increased challenges for counseling psychologists. This chapter reviews the recent literature describing the ever expanding range of career opportunities for counseling psychologists, especially those that build on skills traditionally found in counseling

3

psychology training. The growth of these opportunities will be partly determined by how well practicing psychologists (whether clinical, school, counseling, or other health service providers) confront a number of challenges to psychology—restricted licenses, insurance companies' definitions of reimbursable psychologists, and relationships with psychiatry regarding hospital and prescription privileges.

Another major purpose of the chapter is to acquaint readers with the broad range of identity issues that currently face *all* professional psychologists and, in particular, the identity issues for counseling psychology in the 1990s. The waxing and waning of concerns about identity are almost as interesting as the content of the identity issues themselves.

The chapter also reviews the developments in ethical and legal issues that most affect counseling psychologists. Because our profession is involved in providing services to vulnerable and distressed persons, understanding the issues involved in ethical practice is an ongoing responsibility. Psychologists also need to become increasingly aware of their own vulnerability to ethical and legal entanglements, as well as how to deal with colleagues whose ethical behavior fails to meet prevailing standards.

The final brief section on legislative and public policy issues builds on the foundations provided by Schmidt and Meara (1984) and Brammer et al. (1988), who identified important roles that counseling psychologists need to fulfill if our profession is to achieve its potential for promoting human welfare.

COUNSELING PSYCHOLOGISTS: CHANGING WORK ROLES AND TRAINING SETTINGS

The results of several surveys in the past decade concur in finding notable changes in the places where counseling psychologists work as well as what they do in those workplaces. Watkins and Campbell (1987) compared current counseling psychology work settings with those found in surveys conducted since 1949. They found continuity in the percentage (50 to 60%) of counseling psychologists working in the college/university setting. They also found, however, significant evidence of change: a marked decrease in the number of hospital placements and a lesser decrease in the number of those working in community mental health centers were both offset by a huge increase (300–400%) in the number of counseling psychologists working primarily in private practice. (The term private practice was the "generic" term used in these surveys to include psychologists in independent, solo practice and those in group or managed care practice.)

The latter results were echoed by Cameron, Galassi, Birk, and Waggener (1989) in their review of placements of new doctoral-level counseling psychologists between 1975 and 1987. Their data were derived from the annual survey conducted by the Council of Counseling Psychology Training Programs (CCPTP). By the late 1980s, private practice regularly ranked second or third as a source of employment for new doctorates. Moreover, the authors found "counseling psychology graduates seeking their first jobs entered academic and university counseling center positions in decreasing proportions during the 15 year period of these CCPTP surveys" (p. 310). Further, in contrast to earlier decades, by the 1980s, those taking positions in general hospitals regularly exceeded the number of those taking positions in Veterans Administration (VA) hospitals. Extrapolation of these trends suggests that, for the first time in the history of counseling psychology, less than 50% of all counseling psychologists will soon be in academic settings *and* private practice will be the most frequent first placement of new doctorates in counseling psychology.

Two studies have taken an in-depth look at how counseling psychologists spend their professional time (Fitzgerald & Osipow, 1986; Watkins, Lopez, Campbell, & Himmell, 1986). Fitzgerald and Osipow used a carefully developed task-based job analysis instrument including 64 work behaviors (e.g., personal adjustment counseling, data analysis, needs assessment) classified into seven dimensions. Respondents indicated what they actually did on their jobs, which behaviors they considered most important in the proper performance of their job, which behaviors were most central to their professional identities, and on which behaviors they spent most of their time. The authors received 351 completed returns (56% return rate), with a distribution of men and women equal to that of the Division of Counseling Psychology (Division 17) at the time of the survey (80% men, 20% women). The five work behaviors in which counseling psychologists were most frequently involved included: collecting data about clients, personal adjustment counseling, problem identification/diagnosis, vocational counseling, and long-term psychotherapy. The highest ratings on importance, identity, and amount of time spent were all assigned to the work behavior of long-term psychotherapy. Considering the other work domains of research, supervision, administration, counseling, writing/editing, and teaching/training, the authors' concluded that "when actual work domains and work behaviors are examined, the data suggest that counseling psychologists are primarily involved in counseling and secondarily in teaching and training. Few counseling psychologists were involved in research, consultation, administration, writing/editing, or even supervision" (Fitzgerald & Osipow, 1986, p. 540).

The only significant sex difference obtained was that male counselors were more likely to use tests than were female counselors. When older versus younger respondents were compared, many more significant findings were obtained. From an extensive array of such analyses, the authors' summation was that "in general the older and younger groups engaged in essentially similar activities. They did, however, appear to feel quite differently about them. The older counseling psychologists considered vocational counseling and its associated activities . . . to be a more salient part of their professional identity, and they spent more time on these activities than did their younger colleagues" (p. 542).

Watkins et al. (1986) obtained similar findings using a somewhat different survey instrument. Their sample of 716 respondents (73% return rate) indicated, from a list of 11 professional activities, that psychotherapy was their most frequent task. Somewhat in contrast to the Fitzgerald and Osipow results, the Watkins et al. study found that vocational counseling and vocational assessment were among the least preferred activities. The only significant sex difference they obtained was that men were found to spend a greater percentage of time doing personality diagnosis and assessment. In looking at the research activities of their sample, they found that approximately 80% had published at least one article; the mean and median were 13.1 and 4, respectively. In looking at professional self-views, they found that "clinical practitioner" was the most endorsed primary view (47.7%), followed by academician (28.4%). The most frequently endorsed theoretical orientations were eclectic (40.2%), cognitive (11.0%), psychodynamic (10.4%), Rogerian (7.9%), and behavior therapy and learning (6.2%).

In all of these surveys, there is consistent evidence that far more time is being spent on remedial, therapeutic activities than on the preventive and developmental/educational activities that have long been identified as major themes in the profession. Moreover, employment in the types of setting associated with preventive and developmental services is decreasing, especially among the younger generation of counseling psychologists. The survey authors concluded that there is little empirical basis for distinguishing counseling psychologists from their colleagues in clinical psychology in terms of actual professional activities.

Fitzgerald and Osipow (1988) went on to survey the vocational aspirations of graduate students in counseling psychology. Using the items from their occupational analysis study (1986), replies from 210 graduate students (58% response rate) indicated even greater movement toward psychotherapy and private practice settings. Students' ideal choices were in private practice (27%), academic positions (24%), counseling centers (13%), and community mental health centers (13%). The authors concluded that graduate students' aspirations took them further away from academia and vocational psychology and toward private practice. Moreover, "students prefer to conduct long-term psychotherapy and group, couples, or family therapy rather than the more traditional counseling tasks of vocational counseling, interest and aptitude testing, job search counseling, and so forth" (p. 581).

Some 15 years of data on training programs in counseling psychology also yielded indications of both continuity and change (Cameron et al., 1989). The number of applicants to APA-approved programs remained steady throughout the 1980s at around 100 per program per year. The number of applicants to non-APA-approved programs showed a significant decrease. The longitudinal analysis of these data is somewhat confounded by the fact that, during the 1980s, there was a rapidly changing balance of non-APA to APA-approved programs. When the CCPTP surveys were started, nearly half of all respondents were not APA-approved; by the late 1980s, only 20% were not APA-approved. In both types of programs, the percentage of females steadily increased during the 1980s to around 60%. Throughout the 1980s, approximately 10% of the students enrolled in graduate training in counseling psychology were minorities. No increase was noted in this percentage over the decade. Kunkel and Meara (1987) explored differences in students enrolled in counseling psychology programs housed in schools or departments of education as compared with those housed elsewhere. They found no significant differences in Graduate Record Examination (GRE) scores or grade point averages, but they did find that programs housed in colleges of education admitted a notably higher percentage of their applicants.

Yet another perspective on the characteristics of graduate students in counseling psychology was provided by Tipton and White (1988) in their survey of 232 beginning graduate students. From their study of respondents' salient demographic characteristics and motivational factors in choosing counseling psychology, they described the typical beginning graduate student as a 25- to 35-year-old white female with prior mental health-related work experience who was influenced to enter counseling psychology by interests in helping people and being able to enter private practice.

The Cameron et al. (1989) study also reviewed patterns of internship placements from 1973 to 1987:

> *Although the percentages of students from all programs at the five principal types of sites (university counseling centers, VA hospitals, community mental health centers, other hospitals, and other) were rank ordered the same in 1987 as they were in 1975, there were several shifts during the intervening years. Veterans Administration hospitals, after a decline in the late 1970s, climbed back to a solid second place behind university counseling centers. Community mental health centers, on the other hand, followed a late 1970s increase in placements with a rapid decline in the early 1980s before assuming a more stable third place. Other hospitals, in fourth place, made sizable gains since 1983, whereas other placements,*

such as child guidance clinics, schools, and private practice, noticeably lost ground
since then. [pp. 306–307]

Notice the contrast of internship placements with the new-position data reviewed earlier. The much higher use of hospitals for internships while private practice internships declined is most probably attributable to the importance that emerged, in the 1980s, of having APA-approved internships. Almost no private practices offer approved internships, whereas many VA and other hospital internships had obtained accreditation by the mid-1980s.

Responding to Myers' (1982) observation that insufficient efforts have been made to address the adequacy of training in counseling psychology, Birk and Brooks (1986) surveyed recent counseling psychology graduates to determine their perceptions of the adequacy of their training relevant to the skills required on their current jobs. The 217 respondents (72% return rate) indicated that they felt more than adequately trained in areas such as objective assessment, career counseling, data analysis, and process and outcome research, but insufficiently trained in areas such as consultation, program development, special populations, administration, legal issues, individual/staff accountability, and marriage and family counseling. Looking at training emphases from another perspective, Schneider, Watkins, and Gelso (1988) compared the views of program directors in 1986 to those in 1971. The directors did not differ, during this time period, in their emphasis on such topics as social/emotional and educational/vocational counseling, group work, or research skills, although they perceived that counseling psychology students' interests in the 1980s were focused more on other areas such as marriage and family counseling.

One aspect of training programs received more attention in the 1980s than in any other decade—research training in counseling psychology (Gelso et al., 1988). For example, an entire issue of *The Counseling Psychologist* (Vol. 14, January, 1986) was devoted to that topic, as were major parts of an issue of the *Journal of Counseling Psychology* (Vol. 34 (4), 1987), an issue of the *Journal of Counseling and Development* (Vol. 66 (1), 1987), and a chapter in the first edition of the *Handbook of Counseling Psychology* (Magoon & Holland, 1984).

FUTURE TRAINING OF COUNSELING PSYCHOLOGISTS

The late 1980s witnessed more national conferences, task forces, and ad hoc groups concerned with the training and practice of psychology than did any other period in the history of the profession. Both prior to and following counseling psychology's own Third National Conference in 1987, other groups held national conferences that generated recommendations about curricula and internships for all of professional psychology. The Task Force on the Scope and Criteria for Accreditation of the APA and the Joint Commission on Professional Education in Psychology generated recommendations of their own regarding predoctoral and postdoctoral training for all professional psychologists. Not only were there frequent disagreements regarding the recommendations of these groups, but the thrust of the more professionally oriented recommendations was completely antithetical to the views of traditional academic and scientific psychologists. Such incompatibilities between scientists and professional practitioners were part of what led, in 1988, to the defeat of a reorganization of the APA and the subsequent establishment of the more scientifically oriented American Psychological Society (APS).

By 1990, the Council of Graduate Departments of Psychology, after long years of working closely with the APA, reacted so strongly to the 1989 recommendations of the report of the Task Force on Scope and Criteria for Accreditation that they wrote to the Council on Post-Secondary Accreditation suggesting that the APA no longer be certified to provide accreditation in psychology. Dissension has also extended to such groups as the Association of Psychology Internship Centers (APIC), the National Council of Schools of Professional Psychology, and even counseling psychology, where there are strongly competing viewpoints about the acceptability of the various training recommendations.

The purposes of this section are to (a) identify some of the fundamental issues underlying these conferences and task forces; (b) describe the major recommendations that, if implemented, will have significant implications for the training and practice of counseling psychology; (c) compare congruences and incongruences of those groups' recommendations with the recommendations of the Georgia Conference on counseling psychology; and (d) identify some major initiatives counseling psychology needs to undertake if it is to maintain reasonable control of its own destiny.

Three Fundamental Issues

Any description of the myriad issues underlying the numerous recommendations that have come forth from diverse groups during the past few years is, in a sense, an interpretive act. We see the fundamental issues as involving (a) the definition of professional psychology, (b) the definition of professional specializations within psychology, and (c) the balancing of practice and scientific emphases. Each of these issues has implications for counseling psychology, but each is also truly an issue of the entire profession of psychology. Diverse segments of psychology are differentially impacted by each issue.

Defining Professional Psychology

Why does professional psychology need further "definition"? The most critical impetus is competition with the medical profession in terms of achieving insurance reimbursements and hospital privileges. Many psychology professionals view attacks by psychiatry on the definition and curriculum of psychology as a way of precluding psychologists from more direct access to patients and from reimbursement for services without supervision by an M.D. (Capp v. Rank is overturned, 1990). Because many states have generic licensing of psychologists, an experimental psychologist with no therapy training could be licensed and apply for hospital privileges. How then, it is asked, can psychologists be seen as qualified health service providers?

An increasing number of psychology practitioners, understandably, are calling for a much more regulated curriculum similar to the standardized medical school curriculum. Also, in accordance with the typical patterns in medical schools and law schools, they call for licensing to be restricted to those who are completing APA-approved programs. Such recommendations go significantly beyond the credentialing conference recommendations of the 1970s (Wellner, 1978), which primarily emphasized that programs educating psychologists had to be clearly labeled "psychology," in distinction to the many other labels that were in use at that time, for example, human development, counselor education, human ecology.

Efforts to define professional psychology reflect substantive as well as economic and political concerns. For those in most direct competition with medical specialties, the issue is paramount; for other practitioners, especially those in well-established service centers, such as counseling centers, and for all academic and research psychologists, the issue appears nonessential. The immediate and profound implication for all of psychology is that, whereas there have traditionally been extremely diverse curricular emphases in psychology programs, many of the proposed changes would lead to greatly increased uniformity in curricular requirements. Moreover, program requirements would be defined by external agencies, not by the department or university. Because APA accreditation is currently limited to school, counseling, and clinical psychology, all other areas of psychology would be excluded from licensing if the proposals noted above were implemented.

Defining Specialization Within Psychology

A somewhat more internally driven controversy concerns the lack of accreditation for other specialties. As more and more licensing stipulations and employment opportunities have been linked to graduation from accredited programs, a larger percentage of psychologists in areas such as neuropsychology, applied developmental psychology, forensic psychology, and applied behavior modification have felt themselves disenfranchised. In the early 1980s, the APA made significant efforts to develop procedures for recognizing additional specialties within psychology, with the expectation that those specialties could then become accredited.

How does one legitimize new specializations, and are they co-equal with the present ones? Are the new specializations built on the traditional accredited ones of counseling, clinical, and school, or are they "freestanding"? Concerns have been raised about the possibility of multiple accredited programs in a given academic department and about the substantive basis on which distinctions can be made between newer versus older specialties. All of these issues remain at this writing. The APA Task Force on the Scope and Criteria of Accreditation was constituted largely to resolve such issues. By the late 1980s, there was an emerging emphasis on a more standardized *generic* predoctoral curriculum; such a change would then require that *specialized* training occur at the internship and/or postdoctoral level. The Task Force has, over the past several years, vacillated from one position to another with regard to the generic curriculum. Many psychologists involved in both the traditional and the new specializations are anxious to maintain *predoctoral* emphases. Those who are involved in the more externally driven issue of parity with medicine are arguing for the generic curriculum.

Balance of Practice and Science

Many of the antithetical recommendations coming out of the various groups and conferences reflect differing concerns about the balance of practice and science in the training of psychologists. For many years, psychologists involved primarily in practitioner settings (and especially those in independent practice) have expressed their dismay over the traditional scientist/practitioner model of training. They have objected to the amount of time spent in training in the basic science of psychology—training that they do not see as translating directly into their practice. At the same time, they find themselves not as well-prepared as they would like for the practice of psychology. The main argument is not to eliminate a core of science but rather to emphasize the application of psychological knowledge as compared to acquiring the research skills needed for producing that knowledge. A second emphasis of the practitioners is to greatly increase the minimum specifications for the number of practicum hours, including clients seen, amount of supervision, and so forth.

Concern over these issues led to the emergence of many professional schools of psychology during the 1970s and 1980s. In these schools, there has been continued dismay that the criteria for accreditation have not reflected shifts toward practitioner priorities. By the mid-1980s, when psychologists who were in health service provider positions began to significantly outnumber psychologists of all other types, the balance of power shifted in the APA: there was much more opportunity for practitioners to have an impact on APA policy, including accreditation criteria. This power shift led to the numerous attempts to reorganize the APA during the late 1980s. When all attempts for reorganization failed, the more scientifically oriented psychologists formed the American Psychological Society.

Recommendations Most Affecting Counseling Psychology

Before describing the recommendations that have the most implications for counseling psychology, it is important to cite the conferences and committees that have generated relevant recommendations and to briefly identify the *scope* of their recommendations. There have been at least four pertinent conferences within the past several years.

1. The National Conference of Graduate Education in Psychology, held in Salt Lake City in 1987, generated 11 sets of recommendations encompassing the full range of issues in graduate education, such as whether the psychology doctoral curriculum should be individualized or standardized; what should be the structure and content of prerequisite undergraduate, graduate, and postgraduate instruction; and in what kinds of settings (e.g., freestanding schools, types of colleges) should graduate education occur. A full description of the conference's resolutions, plus six background papers, appeared in the *American Psychologist* (Bickman, 1987).

2. The National Conference on Internship Training was also held in 1987 (Belar et al., 1989). The primary product of that conference was an internship policy statement addressing issues such as which psychologists needed internships; when the internship should occur; and what should be the entrance criteria, core requirements, outcome criteria, and characteristics of an internship. The conference also recommended changes in criteria for APA-approved internships. As will be seen in a subsequent section, a number of these recommendations were found unacceptable by participants in counseling psychology's Georgia Conference, held a few months after the internship conference.

3. A conference that may, at first, seem less relevant to counseling psychology was that of the National Council of Schools of Professional Psychology, in 1986. There are no counseling psychology programs in any of the member schools of that council, but their resolutions, which involve a much greater specification of curriculum for practitioner training, have the potential to affect APA accreditation criteria. This conference produced recommendations for a competency-based approach to graduate education, requiring basic proficiency in six areas: interpersonal relationships, assessment, intervention, research/evaluation, consultation/training, and management/supervision (Bourg, Bent, McHolland, & Stricker, 1989).

4. Early in 1990, over 20 organizations within the field of psychology, including many associations of directors of psychological training, took part in the National Conference on Scientist Practitioner Education and Training for the Professional Practice of Psychology. The conference was hosted by the Assembly of Scientists/Practitioner Psychologists and the Department of Clinical and Health Psychology of the

University of Florida. The former group had been created during the last throes of the attempts to reorganize the APA. The primary recommendations of this conference gave new impetus to an integration of science and practice through attention to didactic *and* experiential components for *both* the scientific and practice parts of training. According to one of the seven counseling psychology participants (E. M. Altmaier, personal communication, February 28, 1990), the conference generated "little with which most programs would disagree . . . counseling psychology programs seem more "clustered" on the scientific-practitioner continuum than do clinical psychology programs . . . many of our views regarding optimal development as opposed to pathology were well represented."

Major concerns have also been raised by the recommendations from the APA Task Force on the Scope and Criteria of Accreditation. In a widely distributed report submitted to the APA Education and Training Board in the spring of 1989, the task force recommended that accreditation be made available to all doctoral programs in the fields of professional psychology and to both predoctoral and postdoctoral programs in recognized specialty areas of professional psychology. Although the report did not mandate a generic predoctoral education program and still left to the university primary responsibilities for how the educational goals of its program were achieved, the recommendation that accreditation should now become available to every area in psychology has raised a huge number of organizational issues for universities. Many universities have five to ten "specialties" within psychology, such as biopsychology, social psychology, and developmental psychology. Additionally, the possibility for accreditation of postdoctoral programs in recognized specialty areas requires the development of some way of defining coherent specialty areas. The strongly competing "forces" unleashed by this report (see below) has resulted in diverse organizational initiatives to move control of accreditation outside of the APA. The 1990s will clearly see much more debate about the scope, criteria, and administration of accreditation. Counseling psychology will need to continue to maintain an active voice in these discussions.

The debates about accreditation just described underlie the continuing work of another group, formed outside of any recognized organization. In the summer of 1988, a group of professionals concerned about these issues created the Joint Commission on Professional Education in Psychology to work "toward creating a core curriculum or generic training program for psychologists" (Joint group seeks uniform standards, 1988). One of the founding members of the group stated that "we need to do a better job of homogenizing the product . . . individual programs will have electives, but specializations will go on at the postdoctoral level" (p. 42). The group has been meeting with representatives from most of the APA practice divisions, including counseling psychology, and various groups of training directors. An implicit agenda of this group is to have a stronger impact on accreditation criteria, either by affecting policy in the APA or by challenging the APA's authority for accreditation and thereby taking more direct control. One of the consequences of the fractionation of the APA has been a much more explicit attempt by various groups to build a "power base." As of this writing, other groups continue to emerge both within and outside of the APA and the APS, and these groups take various positions on these issues. The presence of these groups and their diverse agendas makes for a constantly shifting pattern of alliances, ensuring that resolution of the conflicts will be a slow process.

From the broad range of recommendations coming from these diverse conferences and groups, three interrelated issues can probably be identified as having the most direct implications for counseling psychology. In terms of potential effects on the viability and philosophical components of the profession, perhaps the most salient recommendation involves a *generic predoctoral curriculum*. There is much concern, in both old and potentially new specialties, that a generic predoctoral curriculum would look most like practice-oriented clinical programs, with a primary emphasis on individual psychotherapy. Philosophically, such a position is incongruent with the emphasis on prevention in both counseling psychology and community psychology and with counseling psychology's emphasis on educational/developmental interventions. Other areas of psychology, such as industrial/organizational (I/O) and social, can also identify significant philosophical concerns regarding a generic approach that emphasizes remediation of pathology through psychotherapy. Moreover, regarding counseling psychology's traditions in career psychology, it is of interest to note that, in a 1989 survey of over 30 members of the National Council of Schools of Professional Psychology, only two required the study of career assessment and only three additional member schools offered it as an elective (Morrison & Williams, 1990).

From a pragmatic viewpoint, a generic predoctoral curriculum raises significant concerns about the viability of multiple programs on one campus. At the present time, the majority of counseling psychology programs exist in administrative units other than departments of psychology. If a generic predoctoral curriculum is approved, how does one justify the existence of similar training programs in different departments? Currently, it is rare for more than two administrative units on a campus to ask for accreditation. If accreditation is extended to other areas in psychology, then requests may also come from, for example, a College of Business wanting an accredited program in I/O psychology, or a College of Physical Education seeking an accredited program in sports psychology. Unless the various administrative units on a campus can work together collaboratively, these proposals obviously raise the possibility of internecine warfare!

The second major pertinent recommendation that can affect counseling psychology involves *recognition of other specialties within psychology*. As the criteria are set for defining what is a new specialty, will those criteria have implications for the viability of the long existing "de facto" specialties of counseling, school, clinical, and I/O? In terms of public image, counseling psychology probably has a more difficult time distinguishing itself from clinical psychology, at least in today's world, than do, for example, I/O and social. Much of the effort of the Georgia Conference work groups on public image and organizational and political structures addressed this issue by identifying the need for documentation and "advertisement" of those differences. The Professional Affairs Committee of Division 17 subsequently prepared such documentation (reviewed below in the section on identity issues).

A third significant recommendation is the Association of Psychology Internship Centers' (APIC) call for a *two-year internship* with a core curriculum in the first year and a specialized curriculum in the second year; the latter would be a postdoctoral internship. How would such a plan fit with the traditions of university counseling center internships? There is evidence (Watkins & Campbell, 1989) of the divergence of counseling centers from many of the other internship centers, for example, on use of psychological assessment instruments. Would a core curriculum for the predoctoral internship now require assessment training that is not congruent with counseling centers' missions? Would there be a greater emphasis on pathology and remediation as compared to some of the outreach and consultation thrusts of counseling centers? In short, one can see the potential for a core curriculum of a predoctoral internship to look much more like the modal hospital internship than the typical counseling center internship. Relatedly, if all specialties are relegated to postdoctoral training, what would a postdoctoral internship in counseling psychology look like? Can it occur in hospital or clinic settings as well as counseling centers? If so, what would its content be in those settings? Can counseling centers offer postdoctoral internships in specialties other than counseling psychology? The specialty as it has been known and practiced for half a century does not readily fit such an internship model.

Congruences and Incongruences with Georgia Conference Recommendations

There is clear agreement on only two sets of recommendations from the various conferences and groups. In almost all of the recommendations, one finds specific comments about the need for increased attention to issues of cultural diversity in curriculum as well as in recruitment and retention of students and faculty. There is also agreement that the education of professional psychologists should have some core that acquaints students with the knowledge base of psychology. However, there is no clear agreement as to exactly what that knowledge base should include and how it should be taught. Among the more scientifically focused groups' recommendations, the description of this common educational core is left up to the institution. The more professionally oriented groups exhibit a concern with teaching this knowledge base in an applied fashion as compared to emphasizing basic theoretical and methodological content.

Some other areas of agreement among recommendations from the various conferences, as reviewed by Fox and Barclay (1989), include diversity of models of training, legitimization of the doctor of psychology (Psy.D.) degree, university-based education, and immediate licensure after graduation. Fox and Barclay's review, however, did not include the results of the Georgia Conference, which firmly reiterated counseling psychology's commitment to the scientist-practitioner model of training. As elaborated by Meara et al. (1988):

> [T]he terms scientist and professional . . . represent the broad and integrative nature of the concepts of research and practice and emphasize the many possible roles and job placements for well-trained counseling psychologists. Some programs may wish to train primarily health service providers in psychology; others, researchers; others, academics or consultants; and some, the combination of two or more of these roles. Whatever the intent of the program, all students need to be trained in a scientist-professional model. (p. 368)

Thus, for counseling psychology, neither the pure research training model nor the general practitioner model as espoused by Psy.D. programs is seen as acceptable. The Georgia Conference was not in agreement with other conferences in legitimizing the Psy.D. degree (at least in counseling psychology); however, it did agree on the need for university-based education of professional psychologists.

Although the concept of a generic predoctoral curriculum was not directly addressed in the Georgia Conference, Gallessich and Olmstead (1987) found a large majority of training directors opposed to the concept of a generic curriculum. In response to such proposals from the APA, Division 17 presidents in 1988 and 1989 (Meara and Goldman, respectively) wrote strong letters of concern to the APA regarding the pragmatic and philosophical implications for counseling psychology, as well as for a variety of other specialties, if generic predoctoral training is implemented.

The Georgia Conference was held after the APIC conference and objected to the latter's proposals for a two-year internship and for *doubling* the amount of prerequisite practicum and supervision hours. The Georgia Conference endorsed the present APA requirements of a one-year internship with a prerequisite of 400 hours of practicum. The Georgia Conference participants also objected to another APIC-proposed requirement that students *complete* their dissertation prior to the *beginning* of an internship, noting that this would pose an undue hardship for many students. Resolving conflicting recommendations among the various conferences and task force reports will be a major agenda for all of professional psychology in the 1990s.

Essential Initiatives

Three of the five work groups at the Georgia Conference drafted recommendations that were concerned with the promotion of counseling psychology's viewpoint for both public and professional purposes. These work groups emphasized the importance of advertising the identity and strengths of counseling psychology to consumers and the public. They particularly encouraged academic counseling psychologists to (a) become involved in state psychological associations, (b) more effectively disseminate research and practice findings, (c) address visibility concerns by promoting individual members for positions on APA boards and other organizational committees, (d) support and encourage faculty members' efforts to monitor license-related legislation, and (e) promote efforts to safeguard the interests, aims, and objectives of counseling psychology. The needs and tasks have been well-identified. Involving a larger number of counseling psychologists in these multiple assertive initiatives is perhaps the most fundamental challenge to counseling psychology in the 1990s.

OPPORTUNITIES AND CHALLENGES FOR PRACTICE IN THE 1990S

By 1990, a greater number of counseling psychologists were working in employee assistance programs, athletic departments, medical hospitals, nursing homes, consulting firms, and various kinds of group practices than at any time in the profession's history. The Georgia Conference work group task force on professional practice (Kagan et al., 1988) was correct in stating:

> *During the past quarter century, counseling psychologists have increasingly shown that they are, first and foremost, professional psychologists who have been able to practice anywhere they have demonstrated the competence to practice. It is apparent from the success of counseling psychologists in various settings that we are able to make unique contributions affecting diverse client populations and issues. (pp. 348–349)*

From this perspective, the *range* of opportunities for counseling psychologists is limited only by our resourcefulness in translating our skills into services relevant to particular organizations or individuals, whether these services be preventive, educational/developmental, or remedial. Resourcefulness typically means "moving out of the office" to provide nontraditional services. Opportunities for all mental health professionals, even in independent practice, will be notably proscribed if the only services delivered are individual or group therapy in the practitioner's office.

Resourcefulness in nontraditional areas provides an almost unlimited range of opportunities in practice, but rapidly changing patterns of how mental (and physical) health care is defined and provided in this country are affecting the professional opportunities and services offered in different practice settings. The primary purpose of this section is to indicate how such changes are expected to affect what counseling psychologists do, including where they work (setting) and with whom (clientele). We will also review the particular challenges that all health service psychologists, including counseling psychology practitioners, need to confront in order both to maintain and expand present practice opportunities.

The Georgia Conference work group on professional practice focused largely on the major settings in which counseling psychologists now practice and described the nature of services and the types of clientele in those settings, including university counseling centers, business and industry, schools, medical settings, VA hospitals, community mental health centers, and independent practice. Further descriptions of opportunities in several of these settings can be found in the major papers and the reactions published in issues of *The Counseling Psychologist* regarding university counseling centers (Vol. 18 (4), 1990), behavioral medicine and health psychology (Vol. 13 (1), 1985; Vol. 19 (3), 1991), and business and industry (Vol. 10 (3), 1982; also see Chapter 18, by Gerstein and Shullman). These settings have proven particularly suitable for applying counseling psychologists' skills to the normal-range population, that is, those without clearly diagnosed psychological dysfunction. These settings also call for prevention services, such as wellness clinics offered by hospitals and businesses, and for the use of educational strategies, such as stress management.

Private practice, the setting that is growing fastest in its employment of new counseling psychologists, has not received equally extensive treatment in the counseling psychology literature. Yet, as was made clear by the Georgia Conference task force, there is need for more information on this option, such as marketing and managing strategies. Space does not permit extensive coverage of independent practice issues here, but several points may be made regarding such practice in the 1990s. In particular, the nature of private or independent practice may soon change noticeably. The vast majority of psychologists in independent practice up until the 1980s were in business for themselves (solo practice), but the rapid emergence of managed care in the 1980s began to change this pattern. For example, from 1981 to 1986, the number of Health Maintenance Organizations (HMO) offering comprehensive mental health services increased by 300% (Belar, 1989). By 1990, an increasing number of major companies, as well as the Civilian Health and Medical Program of the Uniformed Services (CHAMPUS), were contracting with local and national group practitioners for specified services at set fees. Employees or dependents have their mental health services covered only if they use the contracted providers.

The effects of these developments vary greatly both by geographic region and by the experience level of the practitioner. In areas with, for example, large numbers of military employees or a large number of union employees, where almost all services are provided through an HMO, there may be limited opportunity for psychologists to practice independently. Most of the clients in the area have to go to the designated providers if they wish to have any of their mental health care costs covered by insurance. In areas where there are not heavy concentrations of such employees or dependents, there may be little change in the opportunities available for independent practitioners. Moreover, well-established practitioners often have sufficient clientele aside from those employees, and may even see some employees who prefer to pay their own fees rather than change to the insurance-designated provider. In such situations, however, new psychologists have difficulty establishing an independent practice because fewer clients are on the "open market." Moldawsky argues that, contrary to the predictions of many psychologists, solo practice is not dead (Despite managed care, 1989).

The increasing trend toward managed care may limit opportunities for independent practice, especially among new psychologists, but it has opened up numerous new group practice opportunities for health service psychologists. Such opportunities are, no doubt, the primary reason why private-sector practice is rapidly becoming one of the most popular employment options of new counseling psychology doctoral recipients. Although opportunities to join a group practice were almost nonexistent for counseling psychologists a decade ago, a current graduate may find several such opportunities available in any given metropolitan area.

Ideologically, the concept of managed care should provide more unique opportunities for using the strengths of counseling psychologists in emphasizing prevention and short-term treatment as well as in teaching, training, and research. Belar (1989) has described how psychologists are unique among the mental health professions in the services they can provide HMOs. On the other hand, a number of critics of managed care have argued that the emphasis on cost containment means that there is more rhetoric than actuality in prevention services and that more severe disturbances often have to be treated much less thoroughly than the professional deems necessary. Additionally, cost-containment emphasis may mean that mental health professionals are sought at the lowest dollar cost, implying that the doctoral psychologist is less preferred than various master's-level mental health professionals. The debate continues as to whether managed care is a bane or boon for psychologists; some see managed care as a source of important new opportunities, and others see it as a major obstacle to the delivery of adequate psychological services (DeLeon, Uyeda, & Welch, 1985).

Just as changing developments in society affect those settings in which mental health services are offered, so too can societal changes affect which clientele will receive services. Changes in federal laws and in sensitivities to social issues are having an impact on the clients of counseling psychologists in the 1990s. Recent changes in federal rehabilitation laws and in Medicare have major implications for the potential clientele of counseling psychologists. Farkas (1989) reviewed changes in rehabilitation laws that can greatly enhance the opportunities for psychologists working in employee assistance programs, especially because these laws expand the occupational options for mentally and physically impaired employees, including those impaired by alcoholism and drug abuse. Further, the inclusion of psychologists as service providers in the 1989 revisions of Medicare makes possible direct coverage for psychological services for the millions of elderly covered by Medicare.

Developing practice opportunities with these new populations will take active outreach on the part of counseling psychologists. The elderly, in particular, often feel stigmatized by utilizing psychological services, yet respond very enthusiastically to educational outreach programs on topics such as retirement, normal aging, and Alzheimer's disease. Following such educational interventions, the elderly and/or their families frequently seek services that can now be offered through their Medicare coverage. Counseling psychologists in independent practice or in fee-based clinics thus have significant new opportunities in response to these changes in federal policy.

In recent years, it has become increasingly apparent that service opportunities in independent practice and in various hospital clinics and counseling centers are greatly affected by the cultivation of specialized skills for working with particular clientele. Given the special requirements associated with, for example, counseling ethnic minorities, gays and lesbians, victims of family abuse, substance abusers, and AIDS patients, many counseling psychologists have developed thriving practices by focusing on those groups for which they have special expertise. In short, counseling psychologists wanting to expand practice opportunities need to think as much about types of clientele as about setting.

Counseling psychology already provides basic training and preparation for many specialized services. To maximize the range of opportunities for counseling psychologists, however, the Georgia Conference recommended that students should attain, as part of their doctoral-level training, the following competencies: individual and group counseling with diverse populations, consultation, developmental interventions, system and environmental interventions and reformulations, policy formation, assessment, supervision, program development, and program evaluation (Kagan et al., 1988).

Challenges to Implementing Practice Opportunities

As professional psychology has evolved over the past several decades, the public has acquired new expectations of the standards by which professionals in any field are supposed to conduct themselves. Because of this development and the multiplicity of functions that psychologists perform, it is now more difficult to determine who is or is not qualified to provide psychological services. Licensing boards have been involved in such determinations, as have insurance companies that provide mental health payments. Furthermore, other professions, especially psychiatry, have challenged many of the new roles taken on by counseling psychologists and other professional psychologists. Each of these groups has presented significant challenges to professional psychology, especially in implementing new practice opportunities and often simply in maintaining present practice roles.

Recent Developments in Licensing

During the past decade, a great many licensure changes have taken place for counseling psychologists. In 1984, Simon and Osipow reported that counseling psychology candidates for licensure had experienced difficulties in at least two distinct spheres: the names of their training programs and the content of their programs. There were lawsuits from a number of psychologists, in counseling and other specialties, to rectify what they believed to be an untenable situation: new regulations, promulgated in the late 1970s and early 1980s, suddenly precluded licensure for large numbers of doctoral-level graduates from programs that had previously been accepted for licensure, even though not explicitly labeled as psychology. Soon, most programs that had offered counseling psychology as a distinct specialty began to change the title of their training programs from Counseling, or Guidance, to Counseling Psychology, and to ensure adequate emphasis in their programs on the core areas of psychology, such as biological and cognitive—areas that previously had been lacking in many counseling programs.

A brief survey made in preparation for this chapter indicated that counseling psychology programs no longer are experiencing major difficulties in having their graduates sit for the licensing examination. In addition, it is noteworthy that in the late 1970s there were only 16 counseling psychologists serving on 15 licensing boards (Simon & Osipow, 1984) but by 1985 that number had increased to 52 counseling psychologists serving on 35 boards (Packard, 1987). Many counseling psychologists now serve as chairs of state boards and several have recently served as presidents of the American Association of State Psychology Boards (AASPB).

A newer licensing issue is that many state associations and boards have attempted to narrow the scope of generic licensure by a variety of means. In New York, for example, there is a "compatibility clause" limiting the applicant to practice that is compatible with one's education. This would, for example, prevent an experimental psychologist with supervised postdoctoral clinical experience from using such experience to qualify for the licensing examination because his or her doctoral "education" was not compatible with clinical psychology. This educational compatibility requirement is also included in the APA Model Act for State Licensure of Psychologists (American Psychological Association, 1987). Where specialty licensure is available or required in order to receive third-party reimbursement (e.g., in Virginia and Hawaii), entry into the examination in the specialty is even more closely proscribed. Thus, the ethical issue (practice within the area of competence) has been taken out of the hands of the psychologist and placed in the hands of legislators and licensing boards. Another means of controlling practice is the "attestation of competencies," in which each candidate for licensure must attest to being competent in his or her practice of modalities and techniques; this statement is then updated at each license renewal.

Another point of contention in the 1990s is the issue of requiring continuing education for licensure renewal. The APA's continuing education committee recommended that the APA support, in principle, the efforts of state psychology boards to require continuing education. A majority of state associations require continuing education, but various professional and educational committees in the APA remain convinced that continuing education should remain a state-by-state decision and not become APA policy. The data to support the efficacy of continuing education in improving practice are simply not available (APA weighs value of required CE, 1990).

Insurance

The ERISA law (Employee Retirement Income Security Act), intended in part to protect the elderly, has been a source of difficulty for all of psychology with respect to third-party reimbursements. Even with favorable judicial precedent (e.g., in Massachusetts and Missouri), many self-insured companies are exempt under ERISA, which permits them to exclude whomever they wish from reimbursement. Thus, General Motors Corporation, one of the largest self-insured companies in the country, excludes psychologists from reimbursement for mental health services. Although APA, through its Practice Directorate, has been negotiating with the auto workers' union to get GM to recognize psychologists, it once again becomes the task of psychology to prove its worth. The laws of most states stipulate that an individual has the right to choose his or her own practitioner. Because most people probably give little thought to mental health benefits when commencing employment, unions and companies have little incentive to change the status quo.

Hewlett-Packard is the latest example of a self-insured company that has changed the provisions specified under the law. The company's benefits package, beginning in 1989, excluded psychologists with Ed.D. degrees. As of late 1990, the APA Practice Directorate continued to work with the company, to understand the reason for the exclusion and to attempt to remedy it. Hewlett-Packard has indicated that its *medical* consultants were instrumental in the decision (A. Lev, personal communication, March 29, 1989). We are not yet "out of the woods" with the medical establishment.

Relationship with Psychiatry

The 1989 legislative hearings regarding the inclusion of psychologists as service providers for Medicare recipients were, perhaps, the best example of psychiatry's determination to ensure that psychology remains in a powerless and noncompetitive position vis-à-vis psychiatry. Thanks to the efforts of the APA Practice Directorate and a "grass roots" network of psychologists all across the country, psychiatry failed and psychology was written into the Medicare statutes. Organized psychology is now thoroughly aware of the need for facts and figures to present to legislators. Little by little, psychologists are learning how to change the way psychology is viewed *and* that psychiatry does not speak for the entire medical profession in its view of psychology. In rural areas of the country, for example, medical professionals rely on psychologists for information about mental health, psychopharmacology, and treatment (Egli, 1989; LaCrosse, 1989). These psychologists are often the only available mental health consultants.

Other battles between medicine and psychology, already under way, have to do with hospital and prescription privileges. Hospital privileges for psychologists have been obtained in the District of Columbia and in California, after an extensive legal battle (Capp v. Rank is overturned, 1990). As more and more states grant such privileges, there will be fewer restrictions on the practice of psychology. Beginning in 1991, the National Register of Health Service Providers in Psychology will list psychologists who have approved hospital privileges.

Prescription privileges will most likely become the major psychology–medicine controversy in the 1990s. The Department of Defense (DoD) had been ordered by the Senate Appropriations Committee to develop a special training program to teach psychopharmacology to psychologists in all branches of the military, enabling these psychologists to prescribe limited medication for depression and anxiety. The APA Board of Professional Affairs (BPA) held a historic retreat on this subject, attended by representatives from the armed forces and psychologists with expertise in pertinent areas. At the conclusion of the retreat, the BPA passed a resolution calling for the development of a model curriculum in psychopharmacology for psychologists, in order to address more effectively the public's psychological and mental health needs.

Any new legislation dealing with prescription privileges, hospital privileges, and Medicare will affect counseling psychology. Whether counseling psychologists enjoy new practice opportunities as these changes come to pass will depend on whether doctoral programs provide training in the skills, techniques, and theories necessary for graduates to work within these new areas. This impact on counseling psychology will be as great in the 1990s as that of the licensure and accreditation issues was in the 1980s.

IDENTITY ISSUES

Revisiting Identity Issues

Many counseling psychologists may understandably react to another reading on professional identity by exclaiming "Not again!" Some might argue that if we paid as much attention to implementing our identity as we do to discussing it, there would be no problem! Before dealing with recent developments on the identity of counseling psychology, at least three points should be made.

1. Identity issues are always present for any profession or occupation. Their immediate salience will wax and wane, depending on dynamic changes in society. Consider the history of activism in various trade unions in establishing the "identity" of, for example, garment makers or steel makers, when imports threatened the viability of such jobs. In short, when there is no competition, identity issues lack salience; whenever conditions develop that lead to increased competition, then identity issues rise in prominence. Relatedly, the more focused a professional or occupational identity, the more specific the competitive "threat" must be to make identity issues salient. Conversely, a broader professional definition greatly increases the range of overlap with competitive professions, thereby increasing identity issues. As will be seen in succeeding paragraphs, counseling psychology's choice to maintain a fairly inclusive definition, with considerable overlap

with many other specialties within and outside of psychology, almost guarantees continuing concern with identity.

2. Numerous fields within psychology are experiencing significant identity "problems" (Fretz, 1984). The identity problems of all specialties in psychology are now being exacerbated by the broader identity problem of psychology as a profession as it seeks simultaneously to achieve parity with psychiatry in the practice domain and to maintain its place as a scientific discipline. Counseling psychologists must acknowledge that continued action and vigilance are needed in response to the various external forces that have the potential to affect the licensure and professional roles of all psychologists.

3. The identity problems of the profession are not isomorphic with identity problems as felt by individual counseling psychologists. Countless counseling psychologists have followed the career paths they wished and have experienced no handicaps because of identity concerns. Gelso and Fretz (1992) recently suggested that, for counseling psychology, ontogeny recapitulates phylogeny, that is, as individual counseling psychologists progress from graduate school to professional status, they may experience heightened and then decreased identity crises.

These three points are intended to provide a context for maintaining some equanimity about the possibly discomforting controversies in the following paragraphs.

The Identity Problem: Chronic or Acute?

The above subtitle is telling. It includes only the terms "chronic" or "acute"; the option of "cured" is not provided. In the past decade, almost as much attention has been given to whether counseling psychology does or does not have an identity problem as has been given to further explicating a professional identity. Authors have disagreed among themselves as to the implications of the data presented earlier, regarding how counseling psychology should define itself, "market" itself for potential consumers, insurers, and credentialing authorities, train its students, and relate to other specialties both in and outside of psychology.

One might argue that there has been a shift in perceptions from an acute to a chronic problem in the past ten years. The identity problem was acute in the early 1960s, when Berg, Pepinsky, and Shoben (1980) argued for the dissolution of counseling psychology, given the strong overlap with clinical psychology that emerged in the 1950s, when clinical psychologists shifted their primary function from psychological testing to psychotherapy. The profession of counseling psychology survived this "acute" crisis of the 1960s with strong reactions from Tyler, Tiedeman, and Wrenn (1980), and then entered a decade or two of plateau, at least in terms of the growth of counseling psychology programs and the involvement of counseling psychologists in professional psychology.

By the end of the 1970s, another potential identity crisis had emerged. Counseling psychologists emphasizing career counseling, prevention, and educational/developmental interventions saw these areas receiving less and less attention in contrast to remedial, psychotherapeutic interventions; counseling psychologists in service delivery settings, especially outside of universities, felt increasingly isolated from the profession that had trained them. The committees working on *The Coming Decade in Counseling Psychology* project (Whiteley et al., 1984) encountered several strong, and often contradictory, arguments for excluding or downplaying certain professional functions in the definition of counseling psychology. Despite a variety of pleas, the Committee on Definition, and subsequently the Division of Counseling Psychology Executive Committee, approved a more inclusive position:

> *Counseling psychology is a specialty in the field of psychology whose practitioners help people improve their well-being, alleviate their distress, resolve their crises, and increase their ability to solve problems and make decisions. Counseling psychologists utilize scientific approaches in their development of solutions to the variety of human problems resulting from interactions of intrapersonal, interpersonal, and environmental forces. Counseling psychologists conduct research, apply interventions, and evaluate services in order to stimulate personal and group development, and prevent and remedy developmental, educational, emotional, health, organizational, social, and/or vocational problems. The specialty adheres to the standards and ethics established by the American Psychological Association. (Division of Counseling Psychology, 1985, p. 141)*

By the end of the 1980s, the leaders of Division 17 were affirming this diversity of roles as a unique strength of the profession (Hurst, 1989; Meara, 1990). Moreover, Division 17 members, through their increased participation and leadership in a variety of psychological credentialing organizations, have seen to it that the term counseling psychology is included in pertinent documents. As noted in an earlier section, there is now a lessened sense of concern about counseling psychologists' rights regarding licensing and professional practice.

There is one other issue regarding identity about which little has been written, despite strong feelings on the part of many counseling psychologists. Among those entering independent practice, many have felt they have not been provided "full citizenship" within counseling psychology. Some practitioners have felt that direct service provided outside of agency or institutional settings is seen as a less acceptable career alternative by many of the profession's leaders. Elected officers, committee chairs, and editorial appointments have not yet reflected the increased percentage of counseling psychologists in independent practice. It seems likely that, unless the programming, publications, and activities of Division 17 reflect increased attention to the concerns of those in practice outside of agency settings, there will be new articles on this area of "identity" and possibly defections of counseling psychologists, both old and new, from membership in Division 17 (Corrigan, 1985).

In sum, many counseling psychologists feel there is less "acuteness" to the identity crisis now. However, the 1990s bring the continuation of several "chronic" identity problems caused by at least three different sets of external factors: (a) the public's "image" of counseling psychology, (b) similarities to and differences from other specialties in psychology, and (c) relationships with other counseling professions.

Public Image

The work group on public image at the Georgia Conference (Zytowski, Casas, Gilbert, Lent, & Simon, 1988) concluded that the public's view of counseling psychology was based on inadequate information or on misconceptions. This group carefully described how psychology in general has many public image problems and only recently has begun to address them. The public by and large does not discriminate among psychiatrists, psychologists, marriage and family counselors, and myriad other counselors. All are "shrinks" of one sort or another. Trying to help the public understand the differences *within* psychology has often been perceived as an almost hopeless task.

Somewhat ironically, even in the one instance where a reasonable segment of the public is being educated (through introductory psychology texts), descriptions are typically limited to distinguishing psychologists from other mental health professionals. Where different kinds of psychologists are described, most textbooks separate "clinical" from other types such as social, developmental, and experimental; if distinctions are made between clinical and counseling, they often only involve counseling psychology's focus on vocational issues.

Similarly, attempts to educate legislators about differences within psychology, for reasons concerning licensure and insurance payments, have typically only distinguished clinical psychologists from other psychologists. Such lobbying began most seriously in the 1960s and 1970s, when large percentages of clinical psychologists were moving into independent practice. Only a small percentage of counseling psychologists were involved in private practice at that time, given that there were more than ample positions for counseling psychologists in counseling centers, VA hospitals, and universities. Thus, counseling psychologists paid little attention to the implications of the insertion of the word "clinical" in a variety of legislative acts. Some counseling psychologists did not find such titles obstructive because the argument was made that the term clinical was made with a "small c," meaning generic health service providers as distinct from nonapplied psychologists.

However, in the 1970s, certain counseling psychologists experienced significant obstacles in obtaining licenses, positions, or third-party payments in some states, because of lack of clarity about the scope of the term "clinical psychology." Activism by a few key leaders in counseling psychology, with significant help from legislative aides and credentialing authorities, resulted in several key pieces of legislation explicitly stating "clinical and counseling psychologists" or defining clinical as those psychologists who had preparation as health service providers. Issues of potential exclusion recurred in the 1989 Medicare legislation regarding psychologists and required clarification by concerned counseling psychologists (and Psy.D. and Ed.D. degree holders, who were also initially excluded from the bill).

Although counseling psychologists gained "legitimacy" through such acts, there was still no really distinct public image of counseling psychology. Most of the recommendations from the public image group at the Georgia Conference have received little concerted attention. In fact, many counseling psychologists are uncomfortable with the thought of "self-promotion." Unless the leadership of the profession can generate enough support for active promotion of the profession, it is unlikely that the public will ever perceive counseling psychology's unique identity (Lent, 1990).

Similarities and Differences Compared to Other Psychology Specialties

The most visible identity problem throughout the history of counseling psychology has been how to differentiate counseling psychology from clinical psychology. Ever since the mid-1950s, it can be argued, the overlap of clinical and counseling psychology has been increasing. Watkins (1983, 1985, 1987) argued persistently throughout the 1980s that counseling psychology was failing to recognize the increasing overlap of the two specialties regarding functions, despite possible differences in training, job titles, or professional identities. Tyler (1980), Delworth (1984), and others foresaw less attention to differentiation among health service providers and suggested the "demise" of all current applied specialties; from a more skeptical viewpoint, such a change could mean the demise of counseling and school psychology under the hegemony of clinical psychology.

Watkins (1987, p. 334) argues that "it seems increasingly important that we identify and market our specialty as one that substantively addresses remedial functions." Zook (1987), Drum (1987), Hamilton (1987), and Troy (1987) all acknowledged Watkins' observations about similarities, yet they highlighted important differences that they believed would most likely be nurtured only through the maintenance of a separate identity for counseling psychology. In preparing documentation for the APA regarding the specialization of counseling psychology, E. T. Dowd (personal communication, July 5, 1988) outlined differences from clinical, school, and I/O psychology in terms of a life-span developmental and contextual orientation to viewing and working with clients. Counseling psychology attends to developmental and adjustment issues as they pertain to career development and adjustment, as well as to educational concerns throughout the life span, and it advocates a preventive and psychoeducational *as well as* a remedial approach to human psychological difficulties.

With all the attention to the overlap between counseling and clinical psychology, little attention has been paid to the overlap between I/O psychology and counseling psychology. As counseling psychologists move into employee assistance programs, and I/O psychologists pay more attention to career development as a factor in organizational effectiveness, there is ever increasing overlap. On the other hand, one could argue that the specific skills of I/O and counseling are more complementary and less overlapping than those of counseling and clinical psychology and, thus, there is much less acrimony about the overlap.

Relationships with Other Professions

As the storms have raged recently around the clinical–counseling psychology differentiation, earlier identity issues vis-à-vis other counseling professions have been almost completely overshadowed. In the 1970s, relationships between counseling psychology and other counseling organizations, for example, the American Association of Counseling and Development (formerly the American Personnel and Guidance Association), underwent periods of strain as new rules for licensing of psychologists suddenly eliminated the practice possibilities for many master's-level counselors, many of whom had long identified themselves as counseling psychologists.

With the new stipulations for eligibility as psychologists, which emerged from the various credentialing conferences of the late 1970s (Fretz & Mills, 1981), there were rapid developments in the counseling profession for licensing of master's-level mental health counselors. By the early 1990s, over one-third of the states had such licensing, greatly alleviating the earlier tension between counselors and counseling psychologists. On the other hand, the rapid growth of managed health care will mean that there will be increasing "competition" between master's- and doctoral-level mental health professionals, especially to the extent that the former make available similar mental health services at a lower fee.

Ideally, attention will continue to be devoted to recognizing the legitimate overlap of functions of various levels and specialties of counselors and psychologists, as well as the meaningful differences in philosophy and practice that can support the continuing viability of the variety of mental health professions. A high degree of overlap in professional role functioning does not have to lead to hegemony by one profession; a clear specification of both unique and complementary professional roles can lead to a collaboration of professions that can benefit consumers as well as acknowledge unique professional competencies.

CONTEMPORARY ETHICAL AND LEGAL ISSUES IN COUNSELING PSYCHOLOGY

Within psychology generally, as well as in counseling psychology, there have probably been more publications about ethical and legal issues in the past ten years than in the entire prior history of psychology. By the late 1980s, over 100 such articles were being published *each year* in journals included in the abstracting services of the APA. In earlier decades, most attention was directed at issues such as confidentiality and mis-representation of professional qualifications. Currently, whole new domains of ethical issues have emerged, involving, for example, dual relationships, radio talk shows, and computer technology. A variety of ethical dilemmas have become inextricably bound with legal issues, such as ethical standards for maintaining confidentiality versus laws requiring therapists to warn others of potential harm and to report evidence of physical or substance abuse. An excellent introduction to the emergence of many of these ethical and legal issues was provided by Schmidt and Meara (1984). One purpose of this section is to outline new developments in the past decade that have further shaped certain ethical issues.

Another type of literature began to emerge in the mid-1980s: the philosophical, theoretical, and empirical foundations for understanding how one becomes (and re-mains!) an ethical psychologist. The purposes, then of this section are to (a) describe the inadequacies, identified in the literature, regarding the teaching and implementation of ethical guidelines; (b) present the concepts underlying development of an ethical profes-sion (i.e., going beyond identifying duties to observe ethical guidelines); (c) present a brief update on the most frequent types of ethical charges; (d) describe emerging legal–ethical dilemmas; (e) present a brief compendium of the major resources available to the professional psychologist who needs more information on contemporary develop-ments in ethical and legal issues; and (f) describe developments in two areas of legal and ethical concern which psychologists, like all professionals, prefer to keep "out of sight, out of mind"—professional misconduct and impaired psychologists.

Ethical Practice: Failure to Learn or Failure to Apply?

"There has been a striking increase in the number of people who contact the ethics office expressing an intent to file a complaint. . . . In the space of two years there has been an increase of 76 percent" (Ethics Committee of the APA, 1988, p. 564). Welfel and Lipsitz (1984), in reviewing surveys of psychologists, concluded that approximately 5% to 10% of practitioners appear substantially insensitive to the ethical dimensions of their work.

The work level of both national and state psychological association ethics commit-tees increased radically during the 1980s, especially in terms of complaints filed by *clients*. The number of complaints filed by psychologists against other psychologists actually decreased (Ethics Committee of the APA, 1988). One can speculate on a variety of reasons for this rapid growth of ethical complaints in the 1980s, including the increased access of the public to psychological services through third-party payments; changing social and legal norms regarding topics such as dual relationships and duty to warn; and the increasing litigiousness of our society. Whatever the reason for such a rapid increase, a few investigators began to look at how well contemporary psycholo-gists understand ethical issues and what effects their knowledge has on the observance of ethical guidelines. Welfel and Lipsitz (1984) reviewed the few studies on ethics training published between the 1950s and the 1970s and found a rapid increase in formal ethics training requirements during the 1970s. However, Hall (1987) reported that, as of the mid-1980s, 5% of APA-approved programs still did not offer any ethics courses or have procedures for incorporating ethical issues in required courses. More optimistically, she found that 25% of the programs had a required course on ethics and incorporated ethics into a variety of other required courses and practica.

Is there any evidence that varying levels of education about ethics have any effect on the ethical behavior of psychologists? Welfel and Lipsitz (1984) concluded that the meaning of research findings on this topic "is lost in the inconsistency of methods and samples and the general lack of rigor in research design" (p. 37). There is at least some meager evidence to suggest that more exposure to ethics leads students to score some-what higher on measures of sensitivity to ethical issues (Baldick, 1980; Welfel & Lipsitz, 1983). There are, however, no definitive studies on whether training will lead to more adequate observation of ethical guidelines. Bernard and Jara (1986) and Bernard, Murphy, and Little (1987), in their studies of graduate students and practicing professionals in clinical psychology, found that one-third to one-half of each group would probably *not* do what they believed a situation demanded when a peer was behaving unethically. In other words, knowledge of what *should* be done was often not related to what the psychologist *would* probably do. (No similar studies have been reported for counseling psychologists.) Ironically, such data suggest that psychologists are adding to the level of "unethical behavior" by not fulfilling principle 7G of the APA ethical principles, which states: "If the violation does not seem amenable to an informal solution or is of a more serious nature, psychologists bring it to the attention of the appropriate local, state, and/or national committee on professional ethics and conduct" (American Psychological Association, 1990, p. 394). Unfortunately, a small but significant minority of practicing therapists think that it is always, or under most circumstances, unethical to file an ethics complaint against a colleague (Pope, Tabachnick, & Keith-Spiegel, 1987).

Concerning characteristics of those who commit ethical violations, there are as yet no sufficiently replicated findings on which to rely. Welfel and Lipsitz (1984) reported three types of such studies: analogue studies, interviews with those who have admitted to inappropriate professional behavior, and tests of theories of the differences in ethical decision making. The few studies of these types (e.g., Haas, Malouf, & Mayerson, 1988) have yielded, at best, even in analogue studies, only very modest relationships between professional or personal characteristics and ethical decision making.

On Being Ethical

In recent years, the profession has shown an increased awareness that even thorough familiarity with the code and powerful sanctions against non-conforming psychologists are insufficient in themselves to guarantee ethical practice . . . it appears that effective self-regulation entails more than clearly written, widely disseminated, frequently taught and strictly enforced ethical codes. What appears to be necessary is a membership capable of making sophisticated judgements about which course of action may be ethical in situations in which no one behavior seems entirely ethical or unethical. (Welfel & Lipsitz, 1984, p. 31)

A number of thoughtful writers have begun to give more attention to the foundations of ethics—foundations that have a written history dating back into antiquity (e.g., Aristotle's Nicomachean Ethics). Biggs and Blocher (1987) and Beauchamp and Childress (1983) described a variety of philosophical positions that have emerged during the evolution of ethical codes. The concepts range from "God's will" to the authority of duty to various utilitarian theories. At this level of discussion, the development of ethics is inextricably related to fundamental philosophical issues such as the basic nature of humans, free will versus determinism, and "social contracts." From this more foundational level, at least three areas of thought have been pursued. Beauchamp and Childress (1983), with a focus on biomedical ethics, provided a widely cited explication of five foundational principles (autonomy, nonmalfeasance, beneficence, justice, and fidelity) which they believe underlie an ethical analysis of dilemmas. Fitting (1984), Kitchener (1984), Lindsey (1984), and Powell (1984) provided valuable contributions by translating these fundamental principles from biomedical ethics into situations specific to counseling psychology.

A second approach to ensuring that counseling psychologists are capable of making sophisticated judgments has been identified as "virtue" ethics. Jordan and Meara (1990) contrasted virtue ethics, which focus on the "decider," with principle ethics, as described above, which emphasize the cognitive analyses needed for rational decision making. Jordan and Meara argued that a heavy reliance on principle ethics underestimates affective dimensions such as human pain, pathos, and historical particularity. They built a case for a careful examination of the contributions of virtue ethics as a way of reaching greater consensus about what psychologists ought to *be* versus what psychologists ought to *do*. "From this perspective, professionals would do well to focus on the kinds of persons whom they recruit for their training programs and the kinds of experiences that they seek throughout their careers to enhance their personal and professional integrity" (Jordan & Meara, 1990, p. 109). In short, they argue that professional character needs to be looked at as seriously as ethical principles in the process of improving the ethical behavior of psychologists.

Rest (1984) integrated social and developmental psychology research in developing a model of moral behavior applicable to psychologists. His model identified four component processes: (a) interpreting the situation in terms of how one's actions affect the welfare of others, (b) formulating a moral course of action, (c) selecting among competing value alternatives, and (d) executing and implementing what one intends to do. What is most interesting to note about Rest's model is that the use of a code of ethics is primarily related only to the second component, that is, identifying the moral ideal for a specific situation. All the other components involve responsibilities that transcend ethical codes. The third component forces the recognition of a fact that is too often covert in psychology: there is always a choice to act in a way that serves only one's self-interests. As Rest noted, perceptual distortions and other psychological processes may prompt actions antithetical to one's moral ideal.

Each of these views of ethical professional behavior suggests that much more attention needs to be given to both the professional person making the decision *and* the decision-making process, as compared to mere acquaintance with a set of ethical principles. Instruction about ethics should, therefore, involve extensive use of cases, dialogue about the principles involved, *and* identification of several possible courses of action, of which several may be equally justified by a variety of conscientious and ethical psychologists.

The need for ethical decision-making skills is clearest when considering common ethical dilemmas. The term dilemma is used here to describe those situations in which one finds the honoring of one ethical principle results in a "violation" of another. Perhaps one of the most frequent dilemmas psychologists face is that of maintaining patient confidentiality after the patient has informed the psychologist of intentions to harm self or others. Although ethically obligated to maintain confidentiality, the psychologist also must "avoid any action that will violate or diminish the legal and civil rights of clients or others who may be affected by their action" (American Psychological Association, 1990, p. 391). Both principles cannot be honored simultaneously. In coping with such dilemmas, the "judgment" qualities of psychologists become as crucial a part of ethics as is an awareness of APA ethical principles.

Patterns of Ethical Violations and Legal Developments

According to the Ethics Committee of the APA (1988), the largest number of ethical violations involve dual relationships, especially sexual intimacy between therapists and patients, even though such relationships are now explicitly precluded by the Ethical Principles of Psychologists (American Psychological Association, 1990). There is now a considerable literature on both the extent and damaging effects of sexual intimacy between psychotherapists and patients (Bouhoutsos, Holroyd, Lerman, Forer, & Greenberg, 1983). One-third of the premiums of the APA's professional liability insurance go directly to the costs involved in such cases. Such actions have also resulted in legal developments in Wisconsin and Minnesota, where sexual intimacies with clients are now considered a felony. The issue of sexual relationships with *former* clients is also receiving increasing attention (Akamatsu, 1988; Ethics Committee of the APA, 1988; Gottlieb, Sell, & Schoenfeld, 1988).

Somewhat surprisingly, although the principle of confidentiality has received extensive attention in writings about ethics, only 4% of the ethics complaints involve failure to preserve appropriate confidentiality. A larger number of ethical complaints arise from failure to observe professional standards, institutional regulations, and governmental laws. Fee practices have been an increasing source of ethical and even criminal charges. Ignorance or a lack of agreement with insurance companies' billing regulations is no defense against ethical or criminal charges; fee-based practitioners need to keep abreast of the most current professional literature.

Legal changes have increased in number and complexity. Laws passed in many states limit the confidentiality rights of psychologists (and other professionals) when it appears to be in the best interest of the client or a third party for the professional to break confidentiality. Child abuse, substance abuse, and "unsafe sex" practices by HIV-positive clients are all examples of new areas where this conflict has spread beyond the "duty to warn" principles described by Schmidt and Meara (1984).

Few state laws are specific about what concrete evidence has to be obtained in order to compel such a report. Some professionals have stated openly that they believe their judgment to be better than the law. Because the laws are often general in their wording (e.g., "a reasonable suspicion"), it is difficult to convince psychologists that they must obey the law. A Michigan case, *People v. Cavaiani,* provides a good example of the confusion and difficulty faced by a professional, and the many judgment errors that are possible in determining whether to report. Cavaiani, a professional working with a family in which the identified offender (the father) was part of the family being seen in therapy, decided not to report suspected child abuse to the authorities. The family had been sent to him by the courts after an earlier incident of child abuse had been reported. During the sessions, the child told Cavaiani that the father had continued to abuse her. Conflicting evidence was provided by the mother. Cavaiani decided that, because the Michigan statute requires "a reasonable cause to suspect," there was not enough evidence to file a report. He was prosecuted for not reporting the information but was subsequently exonerated because a claim "without any supporting evidence did not constitute reasonable suspicion, because of a complete lack of objectivity and concreteness" (Kavanaugh, 1989). Thus, the issue of when to report is simultaneously an ethical dilemma, a moral issue, and a legal vulnerability.

Legal and ethical issues regarding confidentiality are moving beyond psychotherapy into the areas of supervision, research, and professional writing. What are the guidelines for writing a case for publication? How much should the client know of the research or writing? Should the client see the material prior to publication? What happens if the client recognizes himself or herself in a presentation or written piece? What rights does the client have if he or she is the subject of a publication? Could a professional be sued for breach of confidentiality if a member of a group talks outside the group? What are the protections afforded the client in peer supervision groups? Graduate school seminars? These questions require concerted thought and discussion to ensure ethical conduct.

The issue of obtaining informed consent in psychological research also has become more broadly applied than previously. Stromberg (1988) reported that, because the National Commission for the Protection of Human Subjects defines research as "a systematic investigation designed to contribute to generalizable knowledge," demonstration and service projects offering psychological services may require informed consent from participants, even though few currently obtain such consent.

A Compendium of Resources

The escalating attention to ethical issues in the 1980s was, fortunately, accompanied by an increase in bibliographic resources for educating both psychologists and the public. For counseling psychologists, two basic resources regarding ethics are the special issues of *The Counseling Psychologist* (Vol. 12 (3), 1984) and *The Journal of Counseling and Development* (Vol. 64 (5), 1986). Two valuable bibliographic lists were also published by Haas and Fennimore (1983) and Haas, Fennimore, and Warburton (1983). Models for teaching ethics have been provided by Abeles (1980), Eberline (1987), and McGovern (1988).

Contemporary ethics case material has been provided by the APA Board of Professional Affairs Committee on Professional Standards in the case materials published in each year's archival issue of *The American Psychologist* (usually the June issue). By the end of the 1980s, six or more cases had been published in each of the following areas: counseling, clinical, industrial, and school psychology. Keith-Spiegel and Koocher (1985) provided a comprehensive text with cases illustrating the APA ethical guidelines. Biggs and Blocher's (1987) brief text included coverage of cognitive foundations of ethical counseling, major professional issues, cases, and methods of analysis.

Given the extent of concerns about sexual relationships between clients and therapists, several special documents have been published on this topic. Pope (1987) described a set of principles for conduct of therapy by therapists at risk for therapist–patient sexual intimacy. Focusing more on clients' needs, the Committee on Women in Psychology (1989) published a document, "If Sex Enters into the Psychotherapy Relationship." Hall's (1987) article on gender-related ethical dilemmas also provided useful illustrations and pertinent resources.

The recent literature on ethics has focused on newer problem areas that seem likely to receive increased attention in the 1990s. The unique dilemmas regarding confidentiality when treating AIDS patients have been reviewed by Morrison (1989). Ethical issues for dealing with the elderly (Rabins & Mace, 1986) and rational suicide (Snipe, 1988) will probably receive greater attention in the years ahead, especially given the recent changes in Medicare that allow older persons more direct access to psychologists. Sampson

(1983) and Eberly and Cech (1986) identified a range of ethical issues when using computers in assessment and counseling roles. Roman and Blum's (1987) article on ethics in worksite health programming is valuable for those working in employee assistance programs, as is Lowman's (1985) casebook on ethical issues in I/O practice.

An area that is not yet routinely incorporated in ethical guidelines but which doubtless will receive more attention in the 1990s is that of psychologists' ethical responsibilities regarding practice and research with culturally diverse persons. Scarr (1988) called attention to ethical issues in the study of race and gender. Ivey (1987) described what he saw as ethical issues regarding the competence of psychologists who are engaged in the multicultural practice of psychotherapy. Other ethical issues in research, especially related to deception and treatment, also continue to receive important discussion (Aubrey, 1987; Howard, 1987; Robinson & Gross, 1986; Stanley, Sieber, & Melton, 1987).

Because of the inextricable relationships between ethics and law, the APA, the National Register for Health Service Providers in Psychology ("the Register"), and the American Association of State Psychology Boards (AASPB) have all published numerous articles about such issues in their respective publications. The Register also has published *The Psychologist's Legal Handbook* (Stromberg, 1988), which includes information on such topics as licensure, offering testimony in court, and business issues. Cohen and Mariano's (1984) *Legal Guidebook in Mental Health* has a narrower focus, concentrating on malpractice and other professional liability issues. The increase in scope evident between the 1984 and 1988 volumes dramatically illustrates the expansion of legal issues to which psychologists need to attend.

Another major resource for psychologists concerned about licensing and legal issues is *The Law of Professional Licensing and Certification Quarterly,* published by the AASPB. This publication reports recent court decisions pertinent to licensing in a broad range of professions and covers such topics as statutes, regulations, and grounds for disciplinary actions against professionals. The *Quarterly* contains a fascinating look at the regulatory bodies of various professions and what legal precedents might affect psychology.

Professional Conduct Regulations

Over the past decade, state licensing codes have become increasingly stringent in regulating the behavior of psychologists. Some now have a Code of Conduct that is part of state law or of the rules and regulations of the licensing board. For many years, psychologists have been marginally aware that a code of conduct is in existence, that certain behaviors are acceptable and others are not, and that an individual can be brought up on charges before a state licensing board for various forms of misconduct. However, most practitioners have not been intimately conversant with such codes.

The AASPB recently issued a model professional conduct code for psychologists. This is a detailed and far more encompassing code than any now existing in state laws. The APA Model Act for State Licensure also now defines the rights of a psychologist who has been charged with misconduct, and defines hearing panels and penalties. There is also a list of behaviors that would be grounds for suspension, probation, revocation of license, or remediation programs. The list includes fraud, immoral conduct, endangering the welfare of clients, felony conviction, a conviction that would impair the ability of the practitioner to practice with due regard to the safety of clients, harassment, sexual contact with a client, aiding or abetting the practice of psychology by unlicensed persons, Medicare or Medicaid fraud, and exploiting clients, students, or supervisees for financial or other personal advantage. As the public becomes more aware of client rights, more professionals in all fields are being charged with misconduct.

A very tricky emergent issue concerns psychologists' choice of treatment for a given client and whether that choice falls within chargeable offenses of professional conduct regulations. The Board of Scientific Affairs of the APA, with the Board of Professional Affairs, is undertaking a long-term study of the "Evidentiary Basis of Treatment." The purpose of this study is to survey research on the effects of various treatment procedures on specific disorders. The 1990s might bring psychology closer to understanding the types of treatment that are helpful for specific problems; however, the danger in this movement is that treatment could become so rigid as to limit creativity and judgment. The threat is that unless an individual uses the exact treatment indicated, in exactly the indicated manner, the psychologist could be charged with misconduct. There will likely be many controversial positions taken, for example, between behavioral and psychodynamic therapists, and this issue may remain unresolved for quite some time.

The Distressed Psychologist

The term "distressed psychologist" represents an evolution of terms for describing psychologists who are at risk for committing a variety of ethical violations. In the past decade, one finds a broadening of terms, from "the alcoholic psychologist" (Thoreson, Nathan, Skorina, & Kilburg, 1983), to impaired practitioners (Wood, Klein, Cross, Lammers, & Elliott, 1985), to distressed psychologists (Thoreson, Miller, & Krauskopf, 1989). The latter terms include an array of personal problems beyond abuse of alcohol.

A survey by Thoreson et al. (1989) found 10% of their random sample of psychologists expressing distress in the areas of depression, marital relations, physical illness, loneliness, or alcohol use. In another survey of 749 psychologists, Guy, Poelstra, and Stark (1989) found that "74.3 percent reported experiencing personal distress during the previous three years; of those, 36.7 percent indicated that it decreased the quality of patient care, and 4.6 percent admitted that it resulted in inadequate treatment" (p. 48) of their patients. Ackerley, Burnell, Holder, and Kurdek (1988), in studying professional "burnout," found that more than one-third of their sample of over 500 practicing psychologists reported experiencing high levels of emotional exhaustion and depersonalization. The modal "burned out" clinician in their sample was young, had a low income, engaged in little actual psychotherapy, felt a lack of control in the therapeutic setting, and felt overcommitted to clients.

These survey data raise significant questions about psychologists' fulfillment of their first ethical principle, that of professional responsibility. Moreover, as Thoreson et al. (1989, p. 153) reported, there is now a considerable literature indicating "substantial resistance to confronting, directing, or reporting an impaired colleague to treatment or licensing boards." Such situations present immense difficulties. For example, ethical charges against a colleague can have damaging financial consequences and result in litigation against the person making the charge. Moreover, evidence of psychologists' doing harm to their clients may often be only inferential, even though the harm to the psychologist may be clearly manifest in terms of both physical and mental health symptoms or problems. Ironically, most psychologists are probably poorly prepared to make observations about substance abuse among colleagues, given that, except for those who specialize in substance abuse counseling, professional psychologists generally receive scant training in alcohol and substance abuse (Lubin, Brady, Woodward, & Thomas, 1984).

Responding to reports that efforts to aid impaired psychologists were woefully inadequate (Laliotis & Grayson, 1985), the APA has provided a manual for use by state associations in their work with distressed psychologists. Such materials can be useful for understanding the range of sanctions *and* rehabilitation efforts that can be utilized, but there still seem to be notable lacunae in efforts to educate all psychologists about their ethical responsibilities in this area. If the 1980s were a time when the profession began a more explicit confrontation of the problem and consideration of treatment alternatives, perhaps the 1990s can be the era for an increasing amount of research on the predisposing factors and early warning signs such that *prevention* of psychologist distress receives as much attention as do sanction and rehabilitation.

LEGISLATIVE AND PUBLIC POLICY ISSUES

The 1980s saw a marked change in psychologists' concern with legislative and public policy issues. Schmidt and Meara (1984) cogently described how public policy, especially legislation, affects psychology and how psychology can influence such policies. The most significant developments have been at the national organization level. In the APA, the development of the Science and Practice central office directorates narrowed the focus of interest for each area of psychology, and resulted in both positive and negative changes. The positive change is that each directorate could and did choose areas of immediate concern on which to concentrate lobbying and educational efforts. The negative change is that the separation between practitioners and scientists seems to have become more of a chasm than a division; one result has been the splitting off of many scientists into the American Psychological Society (APS) in August, 1988.

The APA has long concerned itself with legislative issues, but did not involve itself in many major lobbying efforts until the formation of the directorates and the imposition of a special assessment levied on licensed practitioners to help support the legislative initiatives of the Practice Directorate. With the availability of these new resources, the APA's focus shifted from committee-based efforts to a more "central government" approach. For example, legal, marketing, lobbying, and financial experts were hired by the directorates. These experts play an important part in expanding the lobbying repertoire of the APA; with them, the APA is no longer dependent on psychologists to perform functions for which they were not trained, were less capable, or had less time and inclination to perform.

With the creation of directorates at the APA, public policy issues are dealt with primarily by the Public Interest Directorate. However, because many of the issues before this directorate overlap those of the other directorates, they typically work together to assist legislators in drafting beneficial regulations. Concerns such as AIDS, child care, child abuse, homelessness, and civil rights have been foci of all the directorates. The APS has also concerned itself with lobbying efforts.

Psychology's contribution to matters that deeply affect the public has greatly increased during the past decade; this development speaks to the continuing maturity of the profession. Instead of spending large quantities of time proving the legitimacy of the profession, there now is a focus on the profession's many contributions to the public good. Increasingly, professional and scientific commitments in the public arena provide psychology with much needed credibility and give the public necessary information and expertise.

All psychologists need to contribute toward these goals. Counseling psychologists, with an emphasis on developing human potential, are well-poised to spearhead efforts to use psychological knowledge in improving social welfare. To do this, counseling psychologists need much more strategic planning (Brammer et al., 1988). Such plans can ensure that counseling psychologists regularly work with other professional organizations, public advisory groups, and offices of the APA and APS to see that our expertise as both researchers and practitioners is more often utilized for the enhancement of the public good.

REFERENCES

Abeles, N. (1980). Teaching ethical principles by means of value confrontation. *Psychotherapy: Theory, Research, and Practice, 17,* 384–391.

Ackerley, G. D., Burnell, J., Holder, D. C., & Kurdek, L. (1988). Burnout among licensed psychologists. *Professional Psychology: Research and Practice, 19,* 624–631.

Akamatsu, T. J. (1988). Intimate relationships with former clients: National survey of attitudes and behavior among practitioners. *Professional Psychology: Research and Practice, 19,* 454–558.

American Psychological Association. (1987). Model Act for State Licensure of Psychologists. *American Psychologist, 42,* 696–703.

American Psychological Association. (1990). Ethical principles of psychologists. *American Psychologist, 45,* 390–395.

APA weighs value of required CE. (1990, March). *APA Monitor,* pp. 1, 26.

Aubrey, R. F. (1987). Ethical issues in psychotherapy research. *Counseling and Values, 31,* 139–140.

Baldick, T. (1980). Ethical discrimination ability of intern psychologists: A function of training in ethics. *Professional Psychology: Research and Practice, 11,* 276–282.

Beauchamp, T. L., & Childress, J. S. (1983). *Principles of biomedical ethics* (2nd ed.). New York: Oxford University Press.

Belar, C. D. (1989). Opportunities for psychologists in health maintenance organizations: Implications for graduate education and training. *Professional Psychology: Research and Practice, 20,* 390.

Belar, C. D., Bieliauskas, L. A., Larsen, K. G., Mensh, I. N., Poey, K., & Roehlke, H. J. (1989). The national conference on internship training in psychology. *American Psychologist, 44,* 60–65.

Berg, I. A., Pepinsky, H. D., & Shoben, E. J. (1980). The status of counseling psychology: 1960. In J. Whiteley (Ed.), *The history of counseling psychology* (pp. 105–113). Monterey, CA: Brooks/Cole.

Bernard, J. L., & Jara, C. S. (1986). The failure of clinical psychology graduate students to apply understood principles. *Professional Psychology: Research and Practice, 17,* 313–331.

Bernard, J. L., Murphy, M., & Little, M. (1987). The failure of clinical psychologists to apply ethical principles. *Professional Psychology: Research and Practice, 18,* 489–491.

Bickman, L. (Ed.). (1987). Proceedings of the National Conference on Graduate Education in Psychology, University of Utah, Salt Lake City, June 13–19, 1987. *American Psychologist, 42,* 1041–1085.

Biggs, D., & Blocher, D. (1987). *Foundations of ethical counseling.* New York: Springer.

Birk, J. M. & Brooks, L. (1986). Required skills and training needs of recent counseling psychology graduates. *Journal of Counseling Psychology, 33,* 320–325.

Bouhoutsos, J., Holroyd, J., Lerman, H., Forer, B., & Greenberg, M. (1983). Sexual intimacy between psychotherapist and patients. *Professional Psychology: Research and Practice, 14,* 185–196.

Bourg, E. F., Bent, R. J., McHolland, J., & Stricker, G. (1989). Standards and evaluation in the education and training of professional psychologists. *American Psychologist, 44,* 66–72.

Brammer, L., Alcorn, J., Birk, J., Gazda, G., Hurst, J., LaFromboise, T., Newman, R., Osipow, S., Packard, T., Romaro, D., & Scott, N. (1988). Organizational and political issues in counseling psychology: Recommendations for change. *The Counseling Psychologist, 16,* 407–422.

Cameron, A. S., Galassi, J. P., Birk, J. M., & Waggener, N. M. (1989). Trends in counseling psychology training program: The Council of Counseling Psychology Training Programs Survey, 1975–1987. *The Counseling Psychologist, 17,* 301–313.

Capp v. Rank is overturned. (1990, August). *APA Monitor,* p. 1.

Cohen, R., & Mariano, W. (1984). *Legal guidebook in mental health.* New York: Free Press.

Committee on Women in Psychology. (1989). If sex enters into the psychotherapy relationship. *Professional Psychology: Research and Practice, 20,* 112–115.

Corrigan, J. D. (1985, August). Current status of the practice of counseling psychology. Paper presented at the APA meeting, Los Angeles, CA.

DeLeon, P. H., Uyeda, M. K., & Welch, B. L. (1985). Psychology and HMOs: New partnership or new adversary? *American Psychologist, 40,* 1122–1124.

Delworth, U. (1984). Present realities and future scenarios. *The Counseling Psychologist, 12*(4), 183–185.

Despite managed care, solo practice isn't dead. (1989, November). *APA Monitor,* p. 22.

Division of Counseling Psychology. (1985). Minutes of Midwinter Executive Committee Meeting. *The Counseling Psychologist, 13,* 139–149.

Drum, D. J. (1987). Do we have a multiple personality? *The Counseling Psychologist, 15,* 337–340.

Eberline, L. (1987). Introducing ethics to beginning psychologists? A problem-solving approach. *Professional Psychology: Research and Practice, 18,* 353–419.

Eberly, C. G., & Cech, E. J. (1986). Integrating computer-assisted testing and assessment into the counseling process. *Measurement and Evaluation in Counseling and Development, 19,* 18–26.

Egli, D. (1989, November). Prescription privileges: Rural perspective update. Board of Professional Affairs Retreat, American Psychological Association, Washington, DC.

Ethics Committee of the American Psychological Association. (1988). Trends in ethics cases, common pitfalls, and published resources. *American Psychologist, 43,* 564–572.

Farkas, G. M. (1989). The impact of federal rehabilitation laws on the expanding role of the employee assistance programs in business and industry. *American Psychologist, 44,* 1482–1490.

Fitting, M. D. (1984). Professional and ethical responsibilities for psychologists working with the elderly. *The Counseling Psychologist, 12*(3), 69–78.

Fitzgerald, L. M., & Osipow, S. H. (1986). Occupational analysis of counseling psychology: How special is the specialty? *American Psychologist, 41,* 535–544.

Fitzgerald, L. M., & Osipow, S. H. (1988). We have seen the future, but is it us? The vocational aspirations of graduate students in counseling psychology. *Professional Psychology: Research and Practice, 19,* 575–583.

Fox, R. E., & Barclay, A. (1989). Let a thousand flowers bloom or weed the garden? *American Psychologist, 44,* 55–59.

Fretz, B. R. (1984). Beyond vigilance. In J. M. Whiteley, N. Kagan, L. W. Harmon, B. R. Fretz, & F. Tanney (Eds.), *The coming decade in counseling psychology* (pp. 343–354). Schenectady, NY: Character Research Press.

Fretz, B. R., & Mills, P. H. (1981). *Licensing and certification of psychologists and counselors.* San Francisco: Jossey-Bass.

Gallessich, J., & Olmstead, K. M. (1987). Training in counseling psychology: Issues and trends in 1986. *The Counseling Psychologist, 15,* 596–600.

Gazda, G. M., Rude, S. S., Weissberg, M. (1988). Third National Conference for Counseling Psychology: Planning the future—Introduction. *The Counseling Psychologist, 16,* 323–324.

Gelso, C. J., Betz, N. E., Friedlander, M. L., Helms, J. E., Hill, C. E., Patton, M. J., Super, D. E., Wampold, B. E. (1988). Research in counseling psychology: Prospects and recommendations. *The Counseling Psychologist, 16,* 385–406.

Gelso, C. J., & Fretz, B. R. (1992). *Counseling psychology.* Fort Worth: Harcourt Brace Jovanovich.

Gottlieb, M. C., Sell, J. M., & Schoenfeld, L. S. (1988). Social/romantic relationships with present and former clients. *Professional Psychology: Research and Practice, 19,* 459–462.

Guy, J. D., Poelstra, P. L., & Stark, M. J. (1989). Personal distress and therapeutic effectiveness: National survey of psychologists practicing psychotherapy. *Professional Psychology: Research and Practice, 20,* 48–50.

Haas, L. J., & Fennimore, D. (1983). Ethical and legal issues of professional psychology: Selected works, 1970–1981. *Professional Psychology: Research and Practice, 14,* 540–548.

Haas, L. J., Fennimore, D., & Warburton, J. R. (1983). A bibliography on ethical and legal issues in psychotherapy, 1970–1982. *Professional Psychology: Research and Practice, 14,* 771–779.

Haas, L. J., Malouf, J. L., & Mayerson, L. H. (1988). Personal and professional characteristics as factors in psychologists' ethical decision making. *Professional Psychology: Research and Practice, 19,* 35–42.

Hall, J. E. (1987). Gender-related ethical dilemmas and ethics education. *Professional Psychology: Research and Practice, 18,* 573–579.

Hamilton, M. K. (1987). Some suggestions for our chronic problem. *The Counseling Psychologist, 15,* 341–346.

Howard, E. S. (1987). Ethical issues in research on psychotherapy: Comment. *Counseling and Values, 31,* 130–152.

Hurst, J. C. (1989). Counseling psychology—a source of strength and pride in the ties that bind. *The Counseling Psychologist, 17,* 147–160.

Ivey, A. E. (1987). The multicultural practice of therapy: Ethics, empathy, and dialectics. *Journal of Social and Clinical Psychology, 5,* 195–204.

Joint group seeks uniform standards. (1988, October). *APA Monitor,* p. 42.

Jordan, A. E., & Meara, N. M. (1990). Ethics and the professional practice of psychologists: The role of virtues and principles. *Professional Psychology: Research and Practice, 21,* 107–114.

Kagan, M., Armsworth, M. W., Altmaier, E. M., Dowd, E. G., Hansen, J. C., Mills, D. H., Schlossberg, N., Sprinthall, N. A., Tanney, M. F., & Vasquez, N. J. T. (1988). Professional practice of counseling psychology in various settings. *The Counseling Psychologist, 16,* 347–365.

Kavanaugh, P. (1989). People v. Cavaiani: Cavaiani wins! *Michigan Psychologist, 14.*

Keith-Spiegel, P., & Koocher, G. P. (1985). *Ethics in psychology.* New York: Random House.

Kitchener, K. S. (1984). Intuition, critical evaluation and ethical principles: The foundations of ethical decisions in counseling psychology. *The Counseling Psychologist, 12*(3), 42–56.

Kunkel, N. A., & Meara, N. M. (1987). Selected characteristics of counseling psychology applicants, training programs and host departments as a function of administrative housing. *Journal of Counseling Psychology, 34,* 333–338.

LaCrosse, M. (1989, March). *Drugging the elderly: The other drug problem.* Paper presented at Board of Professional Affairs Hearing, American Psychological Association, Washington, DC.

Laliotis, D. A., & Grayson, J. H. (1985). Psychologist, heal thyself: What is available for the impaired psychologist? *American Psychologist, 40,* 84–96.

Lent, R. W. (1990). Further reflections on the public image of counseling psychology. *The Counseling Psychologist, 18,* 324–332.

Lindsey, R. D. (1984). Informed consent and deception in psychotherapy research: An ethical analysis. *The Counseling Psychologist, 12*(3), 79–86.

Lowman, R. L. (Ed.). (1985). *Casebook on ethics and standards for practice of psychology in organizations.* College Park, MD: Society for Industrial/Organizational Psychology.

Lubin, B., Brady, K., Woodward, L., & Thomas, E. A. (1984). Graduate professional psychology training in alcoholism and substance abuse. *Professional Psychology: Research and Practice, 17,* 151–154.

Magoon, T. M., & Holland, J. L. (1984). Research training and supervision. In S. D. Brown & R. W. Lent (Eds.), *Handbook of counseling psychology* (pp. 682–715). New York: Wiley.

McGovern, T. B. (1988). Teaching the ethical principles of psychology. *Teaching of Psychology, 15,* 22–26.

Meara, N. M. (1990). Science, practice, and politics. *The Counseling Psychologist, 18,* 144–167.

Meara, N. M., Schmidt, L. D., Carrington, C. H., Davis, K. L., Dixon, D. N., Fretz, B. R., Myers, R. A., Ridley, C. K., & Suinn, R. M. (1988). Training and accreditation in counseling psychology. *The Counseling Psychologist, 16,* 366–384.

Morrison, A., & Williams, B. (1990, January). *National Council of Schools of Professional Psychology core curriculum survey.* Paper presented at NCSPP midwinter conference on the core curriculum in professional psychology, San Antonio, TX.

Morrison, C. F. (1989). AIDS: Ethical implications for psychological interventions. *Professional Psychology: Research and Practice, 20,* 16.

Myers, R. A. (1982). Education and training—the next decade. *The Counseling Psychologist, 2*(4), 117–122.

Packard, T. (1987, April). *Counseling psychology and the licensure/certification system.* Paper presented at the National Conference on Counseling Psychology, Atlanta, GA.

Pope, K. S. (1987). Preventing therapist–patient sexual intimacy: Therapy for therapists at risk. *Professional Psychology: Research and Practice, 18,* 624–628.

Pope, K. S., Tabachnick, B. F., & Keith-Spiegel, P. (1987). Ethics of practice: The beliefs and behaviors of psychologists and therapists. *American Psychologist, 42,* 993–1006.

Powell, C. D. (1984). Ethical principles and issues of competence in counseling adolescents. *The Counseling Psychologist, 12*(3), 57–68.

Rabins, P. B., & Mace, M. L. (1986). Some ethical issues in dementia care. *Clinical Gerontologist, 5,* 503–512.

Rest, J. R. (1984). Research on moral development: Implications for training counseling psychologists. *The Counseling Psychologist, 12*(3), 19–30.

Robinson, S. E., & Gross, D. R. (1986). Counseling research: Ethics and issues. *Journal of Counseling and Development, 64,* 331–333.

Roman, P. N., & Blum, T. C. (1987). Ethics in worksite health programming. *Health Education Quarterly, 14,* 57–70.

Sampson, J. P. (1983). An integrated approach to computer application in counseling psychology. *The Counseling Psychologist, 11*(4), 65–74.

Scarr, S. (1988). Race and gender as psychological variables: Social and ethical issues. *American Psychologist, 43,* 56–59.

Schmidt, L. D., & Meara, N. M. (1984). Ethical, professional, and legal issues in counseling psychology. In S. D. Brown & R. W. Lent (Eds.), *Handbook of counseling psychology* (pp. 56–98). New York: Wiley.

Schneider, L. J., Watkins, C. E., Jr., & Gelso, C. J. (1988). Counseling from 1971 to 1986: Perspective on and appraisal of current training emphases. *Professional Psychology: Research and Practice, 19,* 584–588.

Simon, N., & Osipow, S. (1984). State boards of psychology. In J. M. Whiteley, N. Kagan, L. W. Harmon, B. R. Fretz, & F. Tanney (Eds.), *The coming decade in counseling psychology* (pp. 233–241). Schenectady, NY: Character Research Press.

Snipe, R. E. (1988). Ethical issues in the assessment and treatment of a rational suicidal client. *The Counseling Psychologist, 16,* 128–138.

Stanley, B., Sieber, J. E., & Melton, G. B. (1987). Empirical studies of ethical issues in research: The research agenda. *American Psychologist, 42,* 735–741.

Stromberg, C. (1988). *The psychologist's legal handbook.* Washington, DC: The Council for the National Register of Health Service Providers in Psychology.

Thoreson, R. W., Miller, M., & Krauskopf, C. J. (1989). The distressed psychologist: Prevalence and treatment considerations. *Professional Psychology: Research and Practice, 20,* 153–158.

Thoreson, R. W., Nathan, E. P., Skorina, J. K., & Kilburg, R. R. (1983). The alcoholic psychologist: Issues, problems and implications for the profession. *Professional Psychology: Research and Practice, 14,* 670–684.

Tipton, R. M., & White, G. L. (1988). Factors related to professional development of beginning students in counseling psychology. *The Counseling Psychologist, 16,* 111–127.

Troy, W. G. (1987). Right diagnosis: Wrong treatment. *The Counseling Psychologist, 15,* 347–350.

Tyler, L. E. (1980). The next 20 years. In J. M. Whiteley & B. R. Fretz (Eds.), *The present and future of counseling psychology* (pp. 132–135). Monterey, CA: Brooks/Cole.

Tyler, L., Tiedeman, D., & Wrenn, C. G. (1980). The current status of counseling psychology: 1961. In J. Whiteley (Ed.), *The history of counseling psychology* (pp. 114–124). Monterey, CA: Brooks/Cole.

Watkins, C. E., Jr. (1983). Counseling psychology versus clinical psychology: Further explorations on a theme or once more around the "identity" maypole—with gusto. *The Counseling Psychologist, 11*(4), 76–92.

Watkins, C. E., Jr. (1985). Counseling psychology, clinical psychology, and human services psychology: Where the twain shall meet? *American Psychologist, 41,* 1054–1056.

Watkins, C. E., Jr. (1987). On myopia, rhetoric, and reality in counseling psychology. *The Counseling Psychologist, 15,* 332–356.

Watkins, C. E., Jr., & Campbell, V. L. (1987). Counseling psychology: Considering retrospective data from the past 36 years. *Professional Psychology: Research and Practice, 18,* 293–295.

Watkins, C. E., Jr., & Campbell, V. L. (1989). Personality assessment in counseling psychology. *Journal of Personality Assessment, 53,* 296–307.

Watkins, C. E., Jr., Lopez, F. G., Campbell, V. L., & Himmell, C. D. (1986). Contemporary counseling psychology: Results of a national survey. *Journal of Counseling Psychology, 33,* 301–309.

Welfel, E. R., & Lipsitz, M. E. (1983). Ethical orientation of counselors: Its relationship to moral reasoning and level of training. *Counselor Education and Supervision, 23,* 35–45.

Welfel, E. R., & Lipsitz, M. E. (1984). The ethical behavior of professional psychologists: A critical analysis of the research. *The Counseling Psychologist, 12*(3), 31–42.

Wellner, A. M. (1978). *Education and credentialing in psychology.* Washington, DC: American Psychological Association.

Whiteley, J. M., & Fretz, B. R. (1980). *The present and future of counseling psychology.* Monterey, CA: Brooks/Cole.

Whiteley, J. M., Kagan, N., Harmon, L. W., Fretz, B. R., & Tanney, F. (1984). *The coming decade in counseling psychology.* Schenectady, NY: Character Research Press.

Wood, B. J., Klein, S., Cross, H. J., Lammers, C. J., & Elliott, J. K. (1985). Impaired practitioners? Psychologists' opinions about prevalence and proposals for intervention. *Professional Psychology: Research and Practice, 16,* 843–850.

Zook, A., II. (1987). On the merger of clinical and counseling psychology. *Professional Psychology: Research and Practice, 18,* 4–5.

Zytowski, D. G., Casas, J. M., Gilbert, L. A., Lent, R. W., & Simon, N. P. (1988). Counseling psychology's public image. *The Counseling Psychologist, 16,* 332–346.

CHAPTER 2
PSYCHOMETRIC THEORY AND COUNSELING PSYCHOLOGY RESEARCH

HOWARD E. A. TINSLEY

Counseling psychologists are frequently called on to deal with fuzzy concepts. Most would agree that empathy is an important counselor behavior, that congruence is an important attribute of the interview, and that self-esteem is an important attribute of the client, but these are intangible attributes. Measuring units, such as inches, furlongs, stones, gills, and hectares, are of little use in quantifying constructs such as empathy, congruence, and self-esteem. We are suitably impressed by physicists' ability to measure the speed of particles in nanoseconds, but we seldom consider that physicists do not measure particles that way for fun. They do it because it is necessary. Skill and precision in measuring relevant constructs are equally necessary in counseling psychology research.

Good counseling practice is dependent on our ability to evaluate theories and potential interventions. The quality of our evaluations depends on the quality of our measurements. Improvements in practice must come either as a result of sound research based on skillful measurements or pure, serendipitous, hit-or-miss luck.

Most counseling psychologists are familiar with the terms "reliability" and "validity" and know that good measuring instruments need these qualities. Fewer practitioners understand that these are not qualities of instruments. Reliability is a quality of the data that result from the complex interaction of the instrument, the respondents, and the situation in which they interact. Validity is concerned with the appropriateness and adequacy of the interpretative and action inferences drawn from the data. Most counseling psychologists are familiar with indexes of reliability and validity such as "internal consistency reliability" and "construct validity," but may not understand that these indexes do not reveal universal truths about measuring instruments. Instead, the interpretation of these indexes depends on the theory that defines and gives meaning to the construct being measured and explains how the construct is similar to and different from other important constructs. The indexes that characterize measuring instruments are ambiguous at best; more likely, they are meaningless unless the theory that defines the construct being measured is understood.

This chapter provides an overview of basic principles of psychological measurement; recent advances in our understanding of the development and use of measurement

The author thanks Karen Rains for her invaluable assistance in the preparation of this chapter.

techniques are integrated throughout. It should be acknowledged, however, that developments treated as recent advances may not have occurred so recently and, in many instances, are well back from the cutting edge of the field. For example, much of what is covered under item response theory was at the cutting edge 20 years ago (see Tinsley, 1971). Psychometricians continue to introduce new concepts, models, and techniques, but a substantial period of evaluation and refinement is needed before the practical usefulness of the innovations is apparent. In this chapter, I have attempted to highlight some developments that I believe are on the verge of practical usefulness for counseling psychology researchers.

Specific topics to be covered include theories of mental organization and personality structure; reliability in the context of classical test theory, domain sampling theory, generalizability theory, and item response theory; factors that influence reliability; and validity. In rendering a conceptual rather than mathematical treatment of these issues, I have avoided statistical formula almost completely, but more mathematically oriented treatments of these issues are identified for those desiring further information. Counseling psychologists who are relatively unfamiliar with measurement should find this chapter to be a useful introduction. Those who are knowledgeable and experienced in psychological measurement should find useful information about recent advances.

THEORIES OF TRAIT ORGANIZATION

The mathematical basis of factor analysis was derived well in advance of computers' capacity to do the computations. Measurement theorists began to consider the number and nature of the latent dimensions underlying psychological constructs long before practical means were available to investigate the issue. Development of the first practical intelligence test by Binet, and its translation to English by Terman, focused much of this attention on the nature and organization of intellectual abilities. The advent of mechanical calculating machines allowed scholars such as Spearman to begin empirical investigation of the dimensionality of intellectual abilities. Later, the availability of computers allowed Lewis and Thelma Thurstone to use more refined techniques. These historical developments are among the factors that led to the development of conflicting conceptualizations of the structure of human intellectual abilities and, to a lesser extent, personality structure. The psychological measures used today owe their philosophical underpinnings to these theories, which have influenced the structure of tests, the properties that tests are expected to possess, and the way in which tests need to be evaluated.

Spearman's Two-Factor Theory

Spearman (1904) conceptualized mental ability as consisting of two factors, G or general mental ability, and a large number of highly specific factors. Any specific mental activity is attributable to G, plus a sample of the specific factors, and all correlations among tests are attributable to G. The more extensively two tests measure G (i.e., the less the tests are contaminated with specific factors), the higher the tests will correlate. For example, Spearman's theory suggests that the correlation between scores on the Miller Analogies Test (MAT) and the Information scale of the Wechsler Adult Intelligence Scale—Revised (WAIS-R) is due exclusively to the fact that both tests measure G.

Spearman's G is a conceptual notion that reflects the individual's ability to deal with abstract relations. Verbal, numerical, and graphic analogy items come the closest to representing what Spearman meant. Tests such as Raven's Progressive Matrices and the MAT are highly saturated in G. Intelligence tests such as the Stanford–Binet Intelligence Scale and the WAIS-R yield global intelligence scores that might also be thought of as representations of G.

Spearman's theory suggests that tests should be developed to be as highly saturated with G as possible. Because of their specificity, the specific factors have no use in theoretical or practical work, and their effects on test scores represent biases or errors of measurement. Tests providing a relatively pure measure of G can be used to predict performance in a wide variety of situations. This outcome is ideal for counseling psychologists. Only one test need be administered, and scores on the test can be used to predict a wide variety of criterion behaviors.

Spearman's theory may sound strange to American readers, but the theory has had widespread influence and its logic is discernible in many testing practices. The use of a single score to indicate general mental ability, as is done by the Stanford–Binet, the Army General Classification Test (AGCT), and the MAT are consistent with Spearman's theory. Other tests that yield verbal and performance IQ scores (e.g., the Wechsler scales) also provide an overall IQ score. College aptitude tests such as the American College Testing (ACT) instrument yield a single aptitude score. Although others such as the College Board Scholastic Aptitude Test (SAT) and the Graduate Records Examinations (GRE) yield verbal and numeric scores, some (the SAT) also provide an overall aptitude score.

The measurement of personality constructs developed later than the measurement of intellectual abilities; the Woodworth Personal Data Sheet (WPDS; Woodworth, 1920) is generally recognized as the first personality test. Perhaps more importantly, personality theory development preceded the development of personality instruments and explicitly recognized personality as multidimensional. Therefore, few personality instruments represent the extreme position, analogous to Spearman's, that personality consists of one construct of overriding importance. Nevertheless, some parallels to Spearman's theory of mental organization can be seen in personality assessment.

One early measure that provided a global assessment of personality in a manner reminiscent of Spearman's G was the Maudsley Medical Questionnaire. This test resulted in a single measure of neuroticism which, the test developers believed, provided all the information psychologists needed about personality in a clinical setting. The successor to this instrument, the Eysenck Personality Questionnaire (EPQ; Eysenck & Eysenck, 1975), now contains scales for neuroticism, psychoticism, and extroversion. The Embedded Figures Test (EFT; Witkin, Oltman, Raskin, & Karp, 1971), a more recently developed test, measures a single construct believed to represent a global aspect of personality. Field dependence has come to be regarded as a perceptual component of personality referred to as cognitive style. The Need for Cognition Scale (NCS; Cacioppo, Petty, & Kao, 1984) is an even more recently designed instrument that measures individual differences in the propensity to engage in and enjoy effortful thought.

Although work has long shown that the correlations among tests often exceed those that would be expected on the basis of G alone, proponents of Spearman's theory still believe that G is the most important factor accounting for cognitive abilities. Personality theorists typically regard personality as multidimensional, but much research focuses on a single salient dimension of personality. Many psychologists within the United States (e.g., Gottfredson, 1986; Hunter, 1986; Thorndike, 1986) and particularly European psychologists remain proponents of Spearman's theory.

Thompson's Sampling Theory

Thompson's (1948) sampling theory postulates that mental ability depends on an almost infinite number of ability elements so highly specific they have been described as almost on the order of single stimulus–response associations. Performance on any test depends on a large sample of ability elements. Correlations among tests depend on the proportion of ability estimates common to the two samples.

According to Thompson, these elementary units are highly situation-specific. Each test should duplicate as closely as possible the situation it is designed to predict, and a unique test must be developed for each specific situation. Test construction should begin with an analysis of the specific ability elements required for success in the criterion situation, and the test should be constructed to sample those specific ability elements.

This approach may sound somewhat foreign to counseling psychologists, but proponents argue that tests tailor-made for a specific situation tend to yield the highest predictive correlations (e.g., Wernimont & Campbell, 1968). Examples of tests constructed according to Thompson's sampling theory are the typing test, in which each applicant types a standard piece of work used for comparative purposes, and the road test required to get a driver's license. These tests closely mirror the specific ability elements required for success. Additional examples include the Minnesota Clerical Test for file clerks, and the USES General Aptitude Test Battery (GATB) Assemble and Disassemble subtests for assembly-line workers. An extensive evaluation procedure based on the premise of sampling theory is the Work Evaluation conducted by some rehabilitation agencies to determine disabled workers' areas of potential employability. In some of its forms, the Work Evaluation consists of having examinees report to a sheltered workshop, where they work for one or two days on various units—the janitorial staff, the assembly line, the office machines area. These units have been constructed to mirror as closely as possible specific situations that can be predicted for the workers. This procedure allows close observation and detailed assessment of the workers' potential in each area.

Tests developed according to sampling theory have very specific applications; they may not be useful in situations that are similar to but different in any way from the original situation. They enjoy relatively little use in counseling because counseling psychologists typically are dealing with individuals who need information about a number of alternatives. Their usefulness in research is limited because the goal typically is to learn about human behavior rather than to make a specific prediction. Tests developed according to the logic of sampling theory are most useful in selection and placement.

Some personality tests are designed to measure specific personality attributes, and their underlying conceptual basis is essentially that of Thompson's sampling theory. The Beck Depression Inventory contains 21 items for the assessment of specific symptoms or attitudes that appear to be "specific to depressed patients, and which are consistent with descriptions of . . . depression . . . in the psychiatric literature" (Beck, 1970, p. 189). The Mathematics Anxiety Rating Scale (Suinn, Edie, Nicoletti, & Spinelli, 1972) instructs respondents to report how frightened they are by 98 situations involving mathematics. Scales such as the Suicide Probability Scale (Cull & Gill, 1982) and the Hopelessness Scale (Beck, Weissman, Lester, & Trexler, 1974), which measure relatively specific aspects of personality, may be used to predict the respondent's potential to engage in a specific behavior, such as suicide.

Thurstone's Multifactor Theory

Multifactor theory holds that mental ability comprises a relatively small number of broad group factors, each of which is weighted according to its importance for performing the specific tasks at hand (Thurstone, 1933). Correlations among tests result from the fact that the tests are measuring these common factors. This theory suggests that a small number of factor-pure tests be developed to measure these broad group factors. For example, Thurstone's test of Primary Mental Abilities measures six factors: verbal comprehension, word fluency, number, special relations, associative memory, and perceptual speed. Other widely used tests that follow this model include the GATB, the Differential Aptitude Tests (DAT), and the Armed Services Vocational Aptitude Battery (ASVAB).

Research is necessary to determine how to weight scores on each test for each criterion situation prior to using these tests. The most extensive example of this approach is the research that established the norms for the GATB—the Occupational Aptitude Patterns. This approach allows predictions to be made regarding performance in a relatively large number of situations after administration of a single, relatively brief test battery. These tests typically do not achieve the level of predictive validity attainable using tailor-made tests (i.e., tests developed according to sampling theory). Nevertheless, tests designed according to this model are useful in counseling, in research, and in industrial settings in which a gain in the generalizability of the results is judged to offset the small loss in accuracy of prediction.

Numerous widely used personality instruments have been devised to measure aspects of personality that could be called broad group factors. These include the Minnesota Multiphasic Personality Inventory (MMPI), the California Psychological Inventory (CPI), and the Sixteen Personality Factors Questionnaire (16PF). After more than 50 years of research on the number and nature of personality dimensions, there is some convergence on a 5-factor model of personality. Tupes and Christal (1961) and Norman (1963) were among the early advocates of the position that 5 factors are both necessary and sufficient for describing the major features of personality. Digman (1990) recently traced the historical emergence of the 5-factor model, operationalized in the NEO Personality Inventory (NEO-PI), which measures neuroticism, extroversion, openness, agreeableness, and conscientiousness, and summarized the recent literature on the 5-factor model.

Vernon's Hierarchical Theory

As work on the organization of cognitive abilities continued, some scholars found that secondary analyses of measures of G yielded underlying factors that resembled broad group factors. Others noted that secondary analyses of the correlations among broad group factors yielded an underlying global dimension not unlike G. Thus, some reproachment of the major theoretical positions occurred.

Vernon's (1960) Hierarchical Theory represents one view of the relations among these theories (see Figure 2.1). At the top is G, a placement representing the view that G is of primary importance in explaining the important relations among tests and behaviors depending on cognitive abilities. Underlying G are two major group factors representing verbal–educational and practical (knack or mechanical) abilities. These can be further delineated into minor group factors. The minor group factors can be subdivided further to yield specific factors. Conceptually, Thurstone's broad group factors are located somewhere between the major group factors and the minor group factors, illustrating their secondary importance. Thompson's specific factors are at the very bottom and they have little importance in this view.

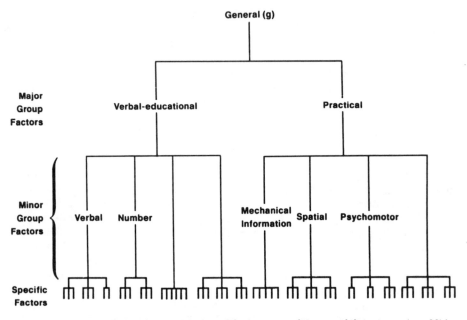

Figure 2.1   Vernon's hierarchical model. From *The Structure of Human Abilities* (rev. ed., p. 22) by P. E. Vernon. 1960. London: Methuen. Copyright 1960 by Methuen & Co. Reprinted by permission.

Guilford's Structure of Intellect

As computers became larger, faster, and more widely available, factor analyses of cognitive abilities began to proliferate and the relations among the ever increasing number of factors were obscured. Guilford's (1967) Structure of Intellect model provided an organizational scheme for intellectual traits that is analogous to the periodic table of the elements. Guilford's model suggests that the type of content or data to be analyzed, the mental operation or analysis to be performed, and the outcome or solution to be produced interact to determine the specific mental ability that will be used (see Figure 2.2).

Guilford identified four types of content or data: (a) figural content refers to information presented in the form of visual or auditory units or patterns; (b) symbolic content denotes information having to do with numerical or symbolic ideas or concepts; (c) semantic content pertains to language; and (d) behavioral content provides information related to the behavior of persons or animals. Guilford's model explicitly recognizes that test items may be presented using any of these types of content and that different cognitive abilities are required to deal with each of these types of information. Persons who perform operations using figural content might be described as having artistic ability; those who show facility with symbolic content have mathematical–spatial ability. Persons who perform operations effectively using semantic content have verbal ability, and social ability is indicated by the effective use of behavioral content.

According to Guilford, performing an operation on semantic content (i.e., answering a question expressed in words) calls on a different cognitive ability than performing the same operation on behavioral content (i.e., answering a question expressed in pictures), even when the question is the same in both instances. Tinsley and Dawis (1974) identified four attributes on which behavioral (i.e., picture) and semantic (i.e., word)

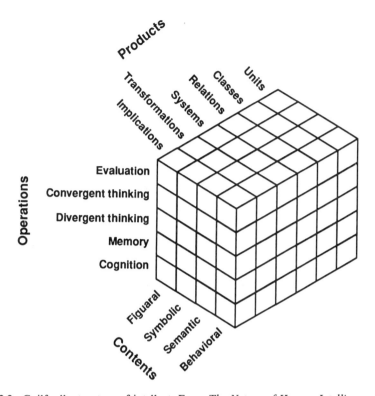

Figure 2.2 Guilford's structure of intellect. From *The Nature of Human Intelligence* by J. P. Guilford. 1967. New York: McGraw-Hill. Copyright 1967 by McGraw-Hill, Inc. Reprinted by permission.

test items may differ. First, they may differ in novelty. Most individuals would recognize a picture of a mountain goat, but few would recognize the word ibix. Conversely, most individuals would recognize the words brake drum, but few would recognize a picture of a brake drum. Second, they may differ in their complexity. Words may communicate a more specific meaning or concept than pictures. For example, the word woman stimulates in our mind a general notion reminiscent of Plato's notion of chairness. In contrast, a picture of a woman presents a complex array of attributes—a young, middle-aged, or old woman; a tall or short woman; a heavy or thin woman; a woman dressed in summer or winter clothing, to name but a few. Third, picture and word test items may differ in level of abstraction. Abstract concepts such as emotions (e.g., anger, love, and fear), times other than the present (e.g., yesterday and tomorrow), and comparative evaluations (e.g., better, best, and worst) can be communicated with words but not with pictures. Finally, because picture and word items often differ in their novelty, complexity, and abstractness, it is difficult to develop picture and word tests having identical item content. Thus, picture and word tests typically sample different specific behaviors because they do not ask exactly the same questions.

Guilford's model suggests that the mental operation the individual is required to perform also influences the ability used. Cognitions require the individual to become aware of the existence of something; memory simply requires remembering something that was once known. Convergent thinking requires the identification of a single correct answer; divergent thinking requires the production or creation of numerous alternative answers. Evaluation requires the individual to make judgments and decisions. The third dimension of Guilford's Structure of Intellect pertains to the products or outcomes of the mental operations. These were identified by Guilford as units, classes, relations, systems, transformations, and implications.

The relation of Spearman's, Thompson's, and Thurstone's theories is modeled in Guilford's Structure of Intellect. Each of the 120 cells in the model can be thought of as representing a specific factor. The entire cube represents G, and the five slices of the cube corresponding to the operations represent the broad group factors.

Comparison of Theories

The theories of Spearman and Thurstone represent what might be described as the world views of European and American psychologists. European psychologists' heritage emphasizes the search for general laws that explain human behavior. Constructs such as G, which emphasize an essential similarity in all persons, ascribe behavior to a universal cause, and explain intellectual performance in a wide variety of situations, are consistent with this world view. Although this view may seem alien to an American audience, it is the philosophy underlying numerous psychological tests that provide important insights into human behavior and continue to have important applications in contemporary psychology (see Gottfredson, 1986).

In contrast, the world view of American psychology has been essentially that of the school of differential psychology. No doubt heavily influenced by dearly held American beliefs in democracy, the worth of the individual, and rugged individualism, American psychology is most concerned with discovering the ways in which each person is unique. This task calls for a larger number of constructs, and Thurstone's multifactor theory is the result. American psychologists may acknowledge the goal of identifying universal laws, but these tend to be laws that will explain the individual's uniqueness rather than laws that explain some essential similarity. Given this world view, Spearman's G and tests that measure a single attribute of personality such as neuroticism seem too limited to many American psychologists. Instead, multifactor batteries such as the DAT and MMPI reflect the American world view.

The three major theories lead to essentially different tests. Tests modeled after Thompson's sampling theory should be exceedingly factor-complex, reflecting the reality that human behavior is factorially complex. Tests modeled after Spearman's 2-factor theory should be moderately complex; their factor complexity should not approach that of a test based on sampling theory, but several broad group factors typically will be present. Tests measuring one of Thurstone's broad group factors should be factor-pure: they should measure only 1 factor. These differences have important implications for evaluating the reliability of test scores and the validity of the inferences based on the scores.

RELIABILITY

Reliability coefficients are descriptive of certain properties of the data on which they are calculated. Attempts to generalize those properties to data obtained from other samples require an estimate of their generalizability. Selection of a measure of reliability should be based on a consideration of the theory underlying the test and what we want to know about scores on the test.

The correlation between two parallel forms was the first definition of reliability and this conception influenced the early development of classical test theory. Test–retest reliability, an early alternative to strictly parallel forms, provides a measure of the stability of the scores across time. Internal consistency measures indicate the consistency of measurement across the entire test and provide an indication of the adequacy with which the domain has been sampled. The development of internal consistency reliability was associated with adoption of the current classical test theory definition of reliability as the ratio of true score variance to observed score variance. This definition means that, given a high reliability, a large proportion of the variance in observed scores on a test results from true score differences among the examinees on the trait being measured. Many researchers appear to be unaware that internal consistency reliability indexes are not appropriate if the test is conceptualized as factor-complex or if we are concerned about the stability of the measures. Instead, many seem to view internal consistency reliability as synonymous with reliability.

Classical Test Theory

Most of what counseling psychology researchers know about reliability derives from classical test theory, sometimes referred to as true score theory or the theory of true and error scores. This theory derives from Spearman's (1904) observation that test scores are fallible measures of human traits, and his efforts to distinguish the objective true score of the individual from the fallible test score (Spearman, 1907). The assumptions and derivations that form this model were elaborated over the years by many writers, most notably Guilford (1954), Gulliksen (1950), and Lord and Novick (1968).

Classical test theory assumes that an observed score is the composite of a true score and a random error component (i.e., $X = T + E$). It follows, therefore, that the observed variance of examinees' scores on a test is a composite of true score and error variance (i.e., $\sigma_X^2 = \sigma_T^2 + \sigma_E^2$). The individual's true score is a constant that does not change, so any difference between his or her true score and observed test score is due to the error score. Because errors of measurement are random, the mean of the errors of measurement would be zero (i.e., $\mu_E = 0$) if we administered (a) a given test to a population of examinees or (b) an infinite number of parallel forms to a single examinee. Given the second scenario, the examinee's true score would remain constant and the mean of the errors of measurement would equal zero, so the mean of the observed scores would be the true score and the variance of the observed scores would equal the variance of the errors of measurement. Finally, because errors of measurement are random, they are uncorrelated with true scores (i.e., $\rho_{TE} = .00$) and with each other (i.e., $\rho_{E_1E_2} = .00$).

Parallel Forms and Test-Retest Reliability

Parallel forms reliability indicates the equivalence of two tests and the stability of test scores across time. Early formulations of classical test theory defined reliability as the correlation between scores on parallel forms. This led to the development of our notions of parallel forms and test-retest reliability and to their dominant position as measures of reliability up through the 1950s. Later developments in classical test theory still can be viewed conceptually as attempting to determine the correlation between parallel forms.

Parallel form reliability requires the administration of two tests measuring the same trait to a single sample in counterbalanced order. Scores on the two tests are then correlated using the product-moment formula. This form of reliability indicates the equivalence of the two tests and, to a lesser extent, the stability of the trait. Because errors of measurement, being random, do not correlate, the correlation between parallel forms indicates the correlation of true scores on the two tests. Parallel forms reliability indicates the reliability of both tests and requires the ready availability of two forms of the same test, a condition all too seldom satisfied. Although from a theoretical standpoint parallel forms is a most highly regarded index of reliability, it is often incompatible with practical realities and is not frequently used today.

Readministration of the same test following a suitable delay is one solution to the problem posed by the absence of a parallel form. Test–retest reliability data are obtained by administering the test to a sample of individuals, waiting a designated time, and then readministering the same test. Scores on the two administrations are then correlated using the product–moment correlations. Because the expected correlation of the random errors of measurement is zero, test–retest reliability indicates the stability of true scores on the test.

Variations Among Parallel Forms

Given the central role of parallel forms in reliability estimation, theoreticians have been concerned for most of this century with how to estimate reliability in the absence of parallel forms. This work has led to the development of split-half and internal consistency measures of reliability. The theoretical distinctions underlying these measures are not well understood by counseling psychologists, and most are unaware of the many alternative reliability indexes available. Central to understanding these distinctions is the formal definition of parallel forms and variants of that definition. In this chapter, I will distinguish among classically or strictly parallel forms, tau-equivalent forms, essentially tau-equivalent forms, and congeneric forms. Each type of parallel form requires a different procedure for estimating reliability.

Tests may be regarded as parallel only if they measure the same trait, they yield scores that have equal means and variances, and they correlate equally with each other and with any measure that is not a parallel form. In actuality, these stringent conditions are seldom satisfied. This led Lord and Novick (1968) and others to distinguish between strictly parallel forms that meet these criteria exactly, and alternative models that satisfy these equalities to varying degrees. Tau-equivalent forms have equal means but they allow for differences in the error variances, and, therefore, in the observed score variances of the two forms. Essentially tau-equivalent forms have both different means and variances. The mean difference is a constant, however, and depends solely on the two test forms (e.g., one test may be easier than the other).

Congeneric forms also have different means and variances. Differences in observed score variance are partly due to differences in error score variance, just as in tau-equivalent and essentially tau-equivalent forms, but differences in observed score variance are partly a function of true score variance. Feldt and Brennan (1989) describe the effect as similar to that obtained by lengthening or shortening the test (i.e., true score variance should be greater on longer tests than on shorter tests).

Split-Half Reliability

Data for split-half reliability are obtained by administering a single test to a single sample at one time. Once administered, the test is conceptually divided into two forms. There are several ways to divide the test, but the most commonly used method is to perform an odd/even split (i.e., the odd-numbered items constitute one form, the even-numbered items constitute the other form). Each form is scored separately, scores on the two forms are correlated, and the Spearman–Brown Formula is used to estimate the reliability of the total test. In the case of split-half reliability, the Spearman–Brown formula is two times the correlation divided by 1.0 plus the correlation (i.e., $(2 \times r)/(1.0 + r)$).

Conceptually, the Spearman–Brown coefficient estimates the extent to which two independent samples of items yield equivalent scores. Use of this formula assumes the two halves of the test are classically parallel (Feldt & Brennan, 1989). Reliability is a function of the number of items on the test, so attempts to generalize this reliability estimate involve both generalization to a new sample of respondents and estimation of the reliability of the full test from the correlation of the classical halves.

Internal Consistency Reliability

No matter how the test is divided, the method used yields only one of a large number of possible splits of the test. There is no single correct way to split the test, but alternative methods of splitting the test could result in a different reliability estimate. The most frequently used internal consistency procedures yield a reliability coefficient that is equivalent to the mean of all the possible split-half coefficients for the test.

Conceptually, the commonly used internal consistency coefficients represent an extension of the concept of parallel forms. In split-half reliability, the test is regarded as two classically parallel forms, each consisting of half of the items. Internal consistency coefficients can be thought of as conceptualizing the test as a series of 1-item parallel forms. Theoretically, this should reduce the error in estimating the reliability (i.e., the true correlation between parallel forms) because a large number of parallel forms is used. These coefficients require the assumption that the part (i.e., item) scores are essentially tau-equivalent forms (Feldt & Brennan, 1989).

The Kuder–Richardson 20 formula provides a measure of internal consistency reliability for dichotomously scored items (i.e., items that are scored right or wrong, as in ability measures, or true or false, as is typical in personality measures). Hoyt's (1941) ANOVA procedure and Cronbach's (1951) coefficient alpha are appropriate for tests consisting of items having multiple response categories (i.e., 7- or 5-point response scales). Hoyt's reliability coefficient and Cronbach's coefficient alpha are algebraically equivalent. Given a test consisting of dichotomously scored items, the Kuder–Richardson 20, Hoyt ANOVA, and Cronbach alpha coefficient formulas will yield identical results.

Cronbach (1951) explained five possible interpretations of coefficient alpha; these interpretations apply with equal validity to Kuder–Richardson 20 and Hoyt reliability. First, we noted earlier that there are many possible ways in which a test can be divided to form split halves. Each possible split can be expected to yield a somewhat different reliability estimate. These internal consistency coefficients represent the mean of all the possible split-half reliability coefficients.

Second, coefficient alpha is the value expected when two random samples of items from a pool like those in the test are correlated. That is, if we drew two random samples of items from the domain being measured, administered both samples of items to a common set of examinees, then correlated the resulting scores, coefficient alpha is the value we would expect to obtain. Thus, the internal consistency coefficients indicate the extent to which the sample of items used in the test is representative of the entire domain being measured. A high internal consistency reliability indicates that the test is a representative sample of the domain; a low reliability coefficient indicates that the test is not a representative sample.

The third and fourth interpretations of the internal consistency coefficients are that they provide a lower bound estimate of the proportion of test variance attributable to common factors among the items, and an upper bound estimate of the proportion of test variance attributable to the first factor. These coefficients give the highest possible estimate of the proportion of variance in the test attributable to a single factor, the first factor. Thus, coefficient alpha and other internal consistency estimates are most appropriate for use with factor-pure tests. As the factor complexity of the test increases, the proportion of variance accounted for by the first factor decreases. The total amount of common variance may remain stable or even increase, however, because the test will contain common variance attributable to the second and subsequent factors. Almost no test is totally factor-pure, so there will be some common variance present due to additional factors, making the internal consistency coefficients a lower bound estimate of the proportion of test variance attributable to the common factors.

Finally, the internal consistency coefficients indicate the extent to which the items in the test are consistent in their ordering of the subjects. If the test consists of a series of 1-item parallel forms, then each of the items in the test must be measuring the same factor. Regardless of the factor being measured, each individual can have only one status on that construct. Therefore, each item should order the individuals the same. As we will see, this way of viewing performance on test items is also central to item response theory.

Reliability of Congeneric Forms

Feldt and Brennan (1989) summarized work on the development of coefficients to estimate the reliability of congeneric forms. Coefficients have been derived for three-part congeneric forms and multiple-part congeneric forms, including the special case presented when the lengths of the congeneric parts are unknown (e.g., as in an essay test, where the effective length of each item is not readily discernible). Counseling psychologists will seldom have a need to use these coefficients, for two reasons. First, they make esoteric distinctions that are seldom necessary or desirable in counseling psychology research. Second, they yield reliability estimates that typically differ only .01 or .02 points from the values obtained when the Spearman–Brown and the Cronbach alpha coefficients are used (see Feldt & Brennan, 1989, pp. 114–116).

Interrater Reliability and Agreement

Hoyt's (1941) ANOVA reliability is seldom used because it is algebraically equivalent to coefficient alpha, but his work stands as an early application of analysis of variance procedures to reliability estimation. One extension of ANOVA methodology is Ebel's (1951) suggestion of the intraclass correlation as a means of calculating interrater reliability.

Counseling psychologists frequently use scales that require raters to evaluate a characteristic by assigning it to a point on a scale. Frequently, the objects to be rated are persons (e.g., a client or counselor) or aspects of the counseling process (e.g., genuineness, concreteness, or effectiveness). An extremely important distinction to make when evaluating the quality of ratings is that between interrater reliability and interrater agreement. Unfortunately, work in this area has suffered for decades from repeated failures to use these terms precisely.

Tinsley and Weiss (1975) defined interrater agreement as the extent to which judges give exactly the same ratings to the rated objects. For example, if judge 1 assigned a rating of 6 to an object, agreement occurs only if judge 2 assigns a rating of 6 to the same object. The more two ratings of a given object diverge, the less the agreement. In contrast, interrater reliability indicates the degree to which the ratings of the judges are proportional when expressed as deviations from their means. If the relationship of one rated individual to a second rated individual is the same, then the fact that the judges use different numbers to express this relationship is irrelevant. For example, if judge 1 consistently rates objects 5 points lower than does judge 2, the ratings would have high interrater reliability but interrater agreement would be virtually nonexistent.

This distinction ceases to make sense when nominal level measurements are involved. Ratings that reflect a nominal level of measurement do not differ quantitatively (i.e., the numbers in nominal measurement serve the function of names), so different types of disagreements among the ratings generally do not differ in severity. Therefore, the concept of proportionality of ratings ceases to make sense, and Tinsley and Weiss (1975) suggested that all nominal level indexes reflect interrater agreement.

The intraclass correlation is the appropriate statistic for calculating interrater reliability, but two dichotomous decisions need to be made to choose the appropriate form of the intraclass correlation. These decisions are orthogonal, yielding the possibility of four different reliability coefficients (see Tinsley & Weiss, 1975, for the formulas). Under some circumstances, these coefficients can vary from 1.0 to virtually zero.

The first question is whether the investigator should treat mean differences in the ratings of the judges as error. The answer is often, but not always, no. Generalizing the results of a reliability study to other settings requires that differences in the mean ratings of the judges be regarded as error, but this is seldom feasible. Generalization of an interrater reliability is permitted only if the results were obtained from a random sample of judges and the training given the two sets of judges was comparable. Furthermore, the cost paid in terms of a lower reliability coefficient is too great in many situations. Thus, the only circumstances under which mean differences in the rating assigned by the judges must be regarded as error are when decisions are made by comparing objects rated by different judges or different sets of judges. Suppose that applicants to graduate school are being evaluated by a panel of three judges, but, as a labor-saving device, each applicant is evaluated by only two judges (i.e., some applicants are related by judges 1 and 2, some by judges 1 and 3, and some by judges 2 and 3). In situations such as this, decisions are made by comparing objects that are rated by different sets of judges, so the mean differences in the ratings of the judges must be treated as error in evaluating the reliability of the ratings.

The second decision is whether the investigator wants to calculate the average reliability of a single judge or the reliability of the composite rating of the judges. Investigators may have theoretical reasons for wanting to know the average reliability of a single judge, so this decision is orthogonal to the previous decision. When describing the reliability of a set of ratings, however, the reliability of the composite rating of the judges is always preferred, unless decisions are to be made on the basis of a single judge's ratings. In these instances, mean differences in the ratings assigned by the judges must be regarded as error.

An important principle to understand when considering measures of interrater agreement is that all sets of ratings are expected to include some chance agreements. For example, when asked to make a dichotomous yes/no decision about each object in a set of objects, two judges who ignored the objects entirely and assigned their ratings purely at random would be expected to agree on 25% of their ratings. Frequently, psychologists ignore the possibility of chance agreements and report raw proportions of interrater agreement. This practice is unacceptable. Instead, scholars should use an index of interrater agreement that indicates the proportion of agreement after the effects of chance agreements have been removed statistically. Tinsley and Weiss (1975) developed a descriptive index (i.e., the T-index) of interrater agreement for this purpose, and they recommended Lawlis and Lu's chi-square to determine the statistical significance of the level of agreement.

Work continues in this area, but much of it is of no consequence for counseling psychologists and some of it is downright misleading. Scholars frequently derive new formulas only to find that they have a strong relation to an already well known statistic, as is the case with Cohen's (1968) weighted kappa. Kappa (Cohen, 1960) and weighted kappa were originally developed as measures of interrater agreement. However, subsequent work revealed that weighted kappa transforms nominal data to data possessing the properties of ratio measurement, and that weighted kappa is actually a measure of interrater reliability, which is identical to the intraclass correlation in most logical circumstances (Fleiss & Cohen, 1973; Tinsley & Weiss, 1975).

Writers frequently design, for special situations, new indexes that subsequently are shown to be faulty. Often, these are mislabeled as indexes of interrater reliability when in fact they measure interrater agreement. For example, James, Demaree, and Wolf (1984) suggested a method of computing interrater reliability when only one stimulus is rated. As noted earlier, classical test theory defines reliability as true score variance divided by observed variance. When only one stimulus is rated, no true score variance exists and the concept of reliability ceases to make sense. Thus, while the James et al. (1984) statistic may measure interrater agreement, it was described as a measure of interrater reliability. This is not a purely academic consideration, because Hater and Bass (1988) subsequently used this statistic as a measure of interrater reliability. Counseling psychologists would be well advised to avoid these relatively new and untried statistics until a suitable period of evaluation has revealed whether they have any advantages over well-established statistics.

Two recent efforts merit brief mention. Stine (1989) argued that interrater agreement makes sense only when using an absolute scale. Observers need to agree only on empirically meaningful relationships, but those meaningful relationships change as a function of the scale of measurement used. Stine proposed a class of measures for relational agreements at different levels of measurement. The underlying premise that not all disagreements are important was recognized long ago. The T-index and Lawlis and Lu's chi-square provide a flexible procedure that allows investigators to operationally define agreement in terms of the meaningfulness of agreements and disagreements in the ratings (Tinsley & Weiss, 1975). Furthermore, the possibility exists that some of Stine's formulations may actually measure interrater reliability instead of interrater agreement. The advantage of Stine's (1989) procedures remains to be established.

Cicchetti, Showalter, and Tyrer (1985) examined levels of interrater agreement and reliability as a function of the number of rating categories or scale points used. Interrater agreement and interrater reliability both increase as a function of the number of scale categories. The most dramatic increase occurs when the scale is increased from two to three categories, but substantial increases continue up to 7-point scales, beyond which further increases in rating scale points result only in trivial increases in interrater reliability and agreement. Counseling psychologists should consider carefully the number of meaningful distinctions that can be made. The number of points on a rating scale should not require distinctions that do not exist in the real world, but up to seven categories can be used profitably to increase interrater reliability and agreement when justified by the attribute being rated. Researchers should not use fewer than six rating scale points without carefully considering the effect of the decision on the reliability of the resulting ratings.

Domain Sampling Theory

Several alternative conceptualizations of test behavior have developed over the past 40 years, including domain sampling theory, generalizability theory, and item response theory. Each will be summarized briefly.

Domain sampling theory (Tryon, 1957) was the first serious alternative to true score theory. Domain sampling theory does not lead to new statistical formulations or alternative measures of reliability, so only a brief conceptual overview is presented here. A good primer on domain sampling theory can be found in Ghiselli, Campbell, and Zedeck (1981).

Classical test theory regards performance as influenced by an immutable true score, which remains constant over a long period of time. Tryon thought this rigidity was inconsistent with the complexity and dynamics of psychological behavior. Domain sampling theory conceives of tests as consisting of a series of items, each of which elicits one or more of the behaviors that depend on some common property. The sum total of all the behaviors that might be influenced by this trait is called the domain. Domains are hypothetical constructs, analogous to a population; they are thought of as infinite or at least tremendously large.

Domain sampling theory regards the items on a test as a sample from the domain of items relevant to the trait. Scores on the test are significant only insofar as they indicate the individual's status on the construct represented by the total domain. In evaluating tests, therefore, the main problem is to determine the extent to which each item and the total sample of items are representative of the total domain. Instead of conceiving of a total domain from which we sample items, however, domain sampling theory turns traditional logic on its head. The test defines the hypothetical domain that is of interest. Samples are used to estimate population parameters. The test provides an operational definition of the hypothetical domain, and it offers the best possible estimate of the population parameters when defensible test construction strategies have been followed. Therefore, the hypothetical domain can be expected to have the same properties as the test, and the domain to which we can generalize is whatever hypothetical domain is implied by the sample of items.

Classical test theory defines reliability in terms of parallel forms; domain sampling theory suggests a different view of reliability. Suppose we actually had parallel form measures of a domain. If we analyzed each of the components of the parallel forms, we would find that some of those components are better measures of the domain than others. Instead of correlating these parallel forms, therefore, domain sampling theory suggests that we should take the best items from each form and create a single form that would provide a superior measure of the domain. The domain then is more precisely defined by the new test than it was by the parallel forms.

In essence, the objective of domain sampling theory is to determine the reliability of the very best sample of items obtainable, not the reliability of parallel forms. The conceptual task is to estimate the correlation between our real sample of items and other hypothetical samples of items taken from the domain. Because the test is conceptualized as a random sample of items from the domain, relations among items within the test should differ from relations between the real and hypothetical sample of items only because of sampling error. Therefore, the relations among items in our real sample of items can be used to determine the correlation of our real and hypothetical sample of items (i.e., the reliability).

The formulas that result from domain sampling theory are the same as those derived from classical test theory. Reliability is still the ratio of true score variance to observed score variance. The main difference is that parallel forms and split-half reliability violate the spirit of domain sampling theory. Test–retest reliability is not inconsistent with domain sampling theory, but theoretically the internal consistency estimates are most compatible with domain sampling theory.

Generalizability Theory

Generalizability theory represents a second extension of classical test theory, achieved primarily through the application of analysis of variance procedures. Classical test theory regards error as a single entity; different measures of reliability are required to estimate the effects of errors across time (test–retest), forms (parallel forms), items (internal consistency), and raters (interrater). A unique study must be done to estimate the effects of each of these sources of error. In contrast, generalizability theory recognizes multiple sources of measurement error and replaces the single overall reliability index with variance components that indicate the magnitude of each source of error. In addition, generalizability theory distinguishes between relative and absolute decisions, and between generalizability and decision studies. Webb, Rowley, and Shavelson (1988) have written a useful primer on generalizability theory; Feldt and Brennan (1989) and Shavelson, Webb, and Rowley (1989) provided more advanced treatments; and Jones and Appelbaum (1989) reviewed recent developments.

Generalizability theory involves the conceptualization of test behavior in terms of an analysis of variance research design (Shavelson et al., 1989). Consider a typical test–retest design in which a sample of individuals completes a sample of items on more than one occasion. This represents a generalizability study in which persons are crossed with items and occasions. Analysis of variance allows the decomposition of the total score into eight variance components (mean squares for persons, items, occasions, persons by items, persons by occasions, items by occasions, total, and residual). The variance component obtained for persons is referred to as the universe score variance and is analogous to true score variance in classical test theory. Generalizability theory concentrates on the magnitude of the variance estimates instead of their statistical significance.

In the above example, a fairly large variance component for persons, relative to the other components, would show that the persons differ on the measured attribute across occasions and items. This source of variability is desirable because it represents individual differences in the measured attribute. The variance component for items indicates the amount of variability among the items in the extent to which they measure the construct of interest. The variance component for occasions indicates the extent to which the rank ordering of persons differs across occasions. In most instances, the variance attributable to items and occasions should be small relative to the variance attributable to the universe score (i.e., to persons). The variance attributable to the interactions indicates the extent to which (a) persons are rank-ordered differently by the different items (persons by items), (b) persons are rank-ordered differently on different occasions (persons by occasions), and (c) the items (i.e., mean item scores) are rank-ordered differently on different occasions (items by occasions). The residual effect (in this instance, the three-way interaction) can be interpreted as indicating a complex three-way interaction among persons, occasions, and items, or as an indication of the influence of factors that have not been systematically included in the design.

Generalizability theory introduces the concept of the universe of admissible observations, which consists of all of the possible observations that would be acceptable. For example, a score obtained by a particular individual on a particular test on a particular day is not the only acceptable indicator of that person's status on the attribute measured. A score obtained on a different day would be acceptable, so the occasion on which the measure was obtained is one of the facets of the study. A score on another test might be acceptable, so the test used is another facet. When using multiple-item tests, we can assess the generalizability of the individual's responses across the items, so items become a facet. When raters are asked to judge some attribute, raters become a facet of the generalizability study. The number of levels of each facet is called a condition. The occasions facet is assumed to be infinitely large if we could test the individual on virtually any day. The test facet is large but not infinite if we could test the individual on any one of a hundred different tests.

Generalizability theory distinguishes between relative and absolute decisions. Relative decisions concern the rank ordering of individuals. These are of interest whenever scores on the test are to be correlated with another factor or the relative performance of individuals is to be judged (e.g., determining percentile ranks). An indication of the error variance for relative decisions is obtained by summing the variance components associated with the relations among the individuals. The components summed vary, depending on whether a crossed or nested design has been used. Absolute decisions involve situations in which the absolute score of the individual is important (e.g., when cutting scores are used to determine whether an individual passes or fails the test). Regardless of whether the generalizability study uses a cross or nested design, the error variance for absolute studies consists of all variance components except the component for the universe score. The generalizability coefficient for relative (or absolute) decisions is calculated by dividing the variance attributable to persons by the variance attributable to persons plus the error variance for relative (or absolute) decisions.

Generalizability theory suggests two types of studies, generalizability studies and decision studies. Generalizability studies are analogous to the typical reliability study, but they provide much more information; they are used to determine the major sources of measurement error and their prominence. Once the relative magnitudes of the sources of measurement error are known, decision studies can be performed to obtain information for decision making. Measurement error can be minimized in decision studies by manipulating the number of occasions, items, or raters. For example, if a substantial error component is associated with items and a small error component is associated with occasions, the measure should be administered on only one occasion (because occasion does not contribute substantially to the error component), but the number of items should be increased (thereby decreasing the error component associated with the number of items).

Generalizability theory assumes random samples of subjects, items, occasions, and raters. This assumption is seldom practical; it results in nonrandomly sampled facets being fixed, and it limits the generalizations that can be made. Webb et al. (1988) suggest two means of avoiding this problem. First, they offer the concept of exchangeability; a condition can be considered random if conditions not observed in the study can be exchanged for those observed in the study. For example, we cannot administer all items measuring anxiety to an individual, but we can regard items as random if we can reasonably argue that alternative items measuring anxiety could have been substituted for the items used. Alternatively, Webb et al. suggest that the investigator should conduct a preliminary generalizability analysis on available data. Finding a very small estimated variance component for a source of error indicates that scores are affected relatively little by variation on that facet. Therefore, that facet can be regarded as random.

Certain aspects of generalizability theory have prevented its more widespread use by psychologists, notably the complexity of its calculation and interpretation. The simplicity and apparent authoritativeness of the reliability coefficient are seductive. Computer programs are readily available to calculate test–retest, parallel forms, and internal consistency reliabilities, and most psychologists would agree that a coefficient above .70 is acceptable and a coefficient of .80 or greater is good. Nevertheless, generalizability theory provides a more complex view of test behavior, which should provide useful dividends to counseling psychology researchers. Computer programs are widely available to do the analysis of variance computations, and the procedures and interpretation of the results quickly become familiar with use.

Item Response Theory

Classical test theory defines an individual's true score in terms of the test administered. Examinees can expect to obtain different true scores on two tests reportedly measuring the same trait. Reconciliation of these differing true score estimates requires a consideration of (a) the characteristics of the sample that took the tests and (b) the attributes of the two tests. Estimates of examinees' true scores and of the item parameters vary across samples and tests.

Gulliksen (1950) remarked over 40 years ago that the discovery of invariant item parameters that would remain stable as the item analysis group changed would constitute a significant contribution to item analysis theory. In the past 30 years, advances in item response theory and developments in programs to operationalize item response theory have made strides toward this objective. Item response theory models can be applied to a wide variety of instruments, including ability tests, personality measures, and attitude scales consisting of dichotomously and polychotomously scored items. Regardless of the construct being measured, item response theory terminology commonly refers to the person's score as an ability estimate. This is a convention to ease communication and is not meant to imply a limit in the applicability of item response theory models.

Item response theory (IRT) models produce item statistics that are independent of the sample to which the test was administered, and ability estimates that are independent of the items used in the test (i.e., invariant parameters). The objective of IRT models is to indicate how performance on an item varies as a function of the relevant parameters of the individual and the item. Ability (i.e., the attribute being measured) is the only examinee parameter considered by IRT models, so IRT models vary in the number of item parameters they include and in the hypothesized relation between the item parameters and ability.

The relation between the proportion of correct responses to an item and the total test score is a straight line with slope $1/K$ (where K = number of items), if all items are equivalent. IRT models specify the relation of the proportion of correct responses to an item to the latent trait under consideration instead of to total test scores. Early IRT models proposed a linear and a latent distance (i.e., stepwise) relation of the proportion of correct responses to the latent traits, but those were largely abandoned in favor of the normal-ogive model and, more recently, the logistic model (see Tinsley, 1971). The logistic model is favored because it provides a close approximation to the normal-ogive model (i.e., it is graphically indistinguishable from the normal-ogive model to the naked eye; Lord & Novick, 1968, p. 399), and it is much easier to work with mathematically.

IRT models have been proposed for use with polychotomous items with nominal response categories, graded response categories, and continuous response categories, and for items that allow partial credit for responses. Most attention has been directed to the unidimensional, nonlinear, dichotomous response models in which all responses are scored as indicating or not indicating the modeled response. Despite important differences, three fundamental ideas are common to all IRT models.

1. Most IRT models assume that the test measures only one trait. This idea of unidimensionality is the same notion as that underlying internal consistency reliability: the test is factor-pure. This may be an unrealistic assumption, in some cases, and some work is underway with multidimensional models, but it is a necessary simplification in most models. McKinley (1989) recommended that a factor analysis should be performed to assess dimensionality. Most IRT models satisfy the assumption of unidimensionality if a dominant component or factor accounts for performance on the test.

2. The responses given by the respondents to the different items are assumed to be independent. This is related to the first assumption in its implication that only the latent trait being measured influences responses to the items. In the case of a unidimensional ability, the assumptions of local independence and unidimensionality are equivalent. There are no accepted procedures for determining whether this assumption is met, but application of latent trait models should not be attempted with tests that contain obvious interitem dependencies.

3. All IRT models assume that a mathematical function can be developed that relates the probability of observing a response on a given item to the trait or traits measured by the items. In unidimensional models, the function is referred to as an item characteristic curve; more generally, these are referred to as item characteristic functions, a term that includes both unidimensional and more complex models. An item characteristic function represents the regression of item scores on the latent trait being measured, so that the probability of a particular response at a given ability level can be determined. Item characteristic functions differ in the number of parameters (i.e., 1, 2, or 3). The parameters are established on the basis of theory or philosophical orientation rather than an empirical basis.

IRT models are typically named for how many item parameters they contain. One of the most widely investigated models is the one-parameter logistic model of Rasch (1966), also referred to as the Rasch Simple Logistic Model. The single-item parameter the Rasch model considers is item difficulty, denoted as the b-parameter in IRT terminology. The Rasch model makes the following assumptions:

1. Items are scored dichotomously;
2. Speed does not influence the probability of a correct response;
3. Given the parameters for item difficulty and subject ability, all responses on a test are stochastically independent;
4. The probability of a correct response is a function of the ratio of ability to difficulty.

Rasch's one-parameter logistic model assumes that the items are all equal in discrimination and that chance factors do not affect the probability of a correct response.

Rasch's one-parameter logistic model has several properties that make it attractive. First, it is easier to work with because it involves fewer item parameters. Second, there are fewer parameter estimation problems. Finally, the model was designed for the express purpose of yielding specific objectivity. This means that unbiased ability parameters can be estimated from items that fit the model without respect to the particular sample of items, and that unbiased item parameters can be estimated independent of the distribution of abilities in the sample of examinees. It may be difficult to find items that fit the one-parameter logistic model, and specific objectivity is not obtained if the model does not fit, but Tinsley and Dawis (1975) found no such difficulty in one large-scale test of the model. Proponents of the model suggest discarding the misfitting items when the model does not fit, instead of using a more complex model.

Two-parameter IRT models typically include a parameter for item discrimination, the a-parameter. Lord (1952) proposed a two-parameter normal-ogive model, and Birnbaum (1968) proposed a two-parameter logistic model, but these models have stimulated relatively little research.

Birnbaum's (1968) three-parameter logistic model adds a pseudo-guessing parameter, the c-parameter, to the item difficulty and item discrimination parameters. The c-parameter indicates the probability of a correct response for examinees with very low ability. Typically, the curve flattens out at the lower end in the three-parameter model, indicating that, below a certain ability level, the probability of getting the item correct remains the same for all individuals. Models (e.g., Rasch's simple logistic model) that do not have a c-parameter predict that examinees with very little ability have a zero probability of giving the modeled response (i.e., guessing does not affect the probability of the modeled response).

Item response models can be used in test construction. This use requires administering a pool of items to a sample, calculating the item parameters, and then selecting items for the final test, based on these parameters. Items can be selected to optimize precision at a designated ability level or to measure ability as precisely as possible across the entire range of ability levels. This procedure is easier using the one-parameter logistic model in which the item b-parameter (i.e., difficulty) equals the information function of the item.

Information

An important feature of IRT models is the information function, an index indicating the extent to which a test or an item measures the intended region of the ability range with sufficient precision. It is well known that tests should consist primarily of items that discriminate best at the point at which maximum discrimination is desired. For example, a test intended to discriminate among high-ability subjects should contain primarily difficult items, a test intended to discriminate among low-ability examinees should contain primarily easy items, and a test intended to discriminate well across ability levels should contain a combination of hard, moderate, and easy items. The information function indicates the amount of information that would be extracted by administering an item. An item has a different information function when administered to subjects of high or low ability, so the information function must be calculated for each ability level. The item information values can be summed across all of the items in an instrument, to obtain an information function for the test. The relative efficiency of two tests is the ratio of test information values for the two tests. Relative efficiency indexes can be used to compare alternative tests that might be administered to a sample, and to compare IRT models to determine which one has the greatest efficiency in modeling the relation of performance to ability on the latent trait.

Computer-Adaptive Testing

An exciting advance made possible by item response theory is the use of IRT models in on-line computerized testing. This testing involves administering an item or a small subset of items to the examinee, using the IRT model to calculate a provisional ability estimate, and then calculating the information function of each item remaining in the pool for a person at that ability level (see Weiss, 1974, 1982, 1983, 1985). Next, the item or small subset of items that will yield the most information is administered. This process if iterated until the examinee's ability has been estimated at the desired level of precision.

The advantages of this procedure are that only those items that will provide information about the examinee's ability level are administered, and the testing procedure ceases once the examinee's ability has been estimated at a desired level of precision. Computer-adaptive tests, therefore, should be more economical (they require the administration of fewer items) and precise (testing ceases only when the desired level of precision of measurement has been obtained).

Estimating IRT model parameters is a very complex process and is not feasible without a computer. Two computer programs are available for IRT analyses. LOGIST (Wingersky, 1983; Wingersky, Barton, & Lord, 1982) uses a maximum likelihood estimation procedure to simultaneously estimate the item and person parameters of the one- or three-parameter logistics model. The program is flexible enough to accommodate other models as well. BICAL (Wright & Mead, 1977) uses a joint maximum likelihood estimation procedure for the one-parameter logistic model (i.e., Rasch Simple Logistic Model). BICAL is quicker and less complicated to use than LOGIST, but it is also less flexible.

McKinley (1989) provided a useful primer for readers desiring more information about IRT, and Hambleton (1989) offered a more technical and extensive treatment. McKinley and Hambleton reviewed procedures for estimating true scores (i.e., number correct scores), information functions, and conditional standard errors for item response models. They provided illustrations of the notions of test information and relative efficiency and of conditional standard errors of measurement. Hambleton summarized current efforts to extend these models and Jones and Appelbaum (1989) briefly reviewed recent work in this area.

FACTORS THAT INFLUENCE RELIABILITY

Method of Computing Reliability

By now it should be clear that reliability estimates describe the outcome of the complex interaction of respondents, test items, occasions, and possibly raters. Different approaches to estimating reliability have been developed in response to this complexity. Therefore, the measure of reliability used is one of the most important factors that influence the reliability estimate.

Thorndike (1951) described a conceptual scheme for considering the sources of variation in test performance. This way of viewing test performance is useful in understanding the differences among the alternative reliability measures. Whether the source of variation contributes to true score variance or to error variance depends on the measure of reliability used.

Lasting and general characteristics often are the attributes the test is designed to measure (e.g., intelligence, verbal fluency, and numerical ability). Nuisance factors such as test-taking abilities, a tendency to guess, or an ability to comprehend instructions may also be lasting and general characteristics of the person. Whatever the source, these factors exert a constant influence across many tests and across substantial periods of time, and all forms of reliability regard variation from these sources as true score variance.

Lasting but specific characteristics can be dichotomized into those that influence performance on the entire test and those that influence performance on a subset of test items. Characteristics specific to the entire test include the construct measured by the test (e.g., knowledge uniquely required by the test but not by other tests), and knowledge or skills specific to the type of test items used (e.g., skill in answering essay questions). All measures of reliability regard variation from this source as true score variance. Variation that is specific to particular test items may be related to the sample of test items. It is here that the measures of reliability begin to disagree. Test–retest reliability treats this type of variation as true score variance; the other measures of reliability treat it as error variance.

Two forms of variation account for much of the difference in the reliability estimates obtained from split-half and internal consistency estimates as opposed to parallel forms and test–retest estimates. Temporary but general characteristics influence performance on a great many tests. These include demand characteristics of the test situation (e.g., the emotional strain on the individual), external conditions (e.g., the level of background noise), and individual factors (e.g., health, fatigue, and understanding of the mechanics of testing). Temporary and specific characteristics that influence performance on the entire test may involve the comprehension of the specific task (e.g., the clarity of the instructions and the attention of the respondent). A temporary lack of attention when test directions are provided orally would influence the individual's performance only on the test being taken. Internal consistency measures of reliability treat these forms of variation as true score variance, but reliability estimates involving repeated measures across a time interval (i.e., parallel forms and test–retest) regard these as error variance.

The remaining three forms of variation are treated as error variance by all the forms of reliability. Temporary and specific characteristics that influence performance on selected test items may include fluctuations and idiosyncrasies in human memory and in the quality of measurement within the test. Systematic factors that influence test performance include adherence to the time limits, helpfulness of the examiner, and unreliability or bias in subjective rating or scoring. Finally, chance factors, such as luck in guessing the correct answer and mistakes in marking the answer sheet, also contribute to variation on the test.

Comparison of how the measures of reliability interpret these sources of variation reveals that parallel forms reliability regards the greatest number as error variance, followed by test–retest reliability. Parallel forms reliability provides the lowest estimate of reliability because it regards form-to-form and time-to-time variations as error. Test–retest reliability provides a relatively low estimate of reliability, but it allows spurious increases in reliability attributable to respondents' remembering their answers to specific questions. Parallel forms reliability eliminates this possibility. Therefore, the true reliability of a test is likely to be no lower than parallel forms reliability.

The internal consistency measures yield higher estimates of reliability because they regard relatively few of these sources of variation as error. All one-time estimates of reliability eliminate time-to-time variations (which are usually substantial) as a source of errors. In addition, consistency of performance is increased by the existence of a speed component in a test. Almost all tests have some speed component, thereby further increasing internal consistency estimates.

Split-half reliability provides the upper-bound estimate of reliability. The internal consistency (i.e., Kuder–Richardson 20, Hoyt, and coefficient alpha) reliability estimates are likely to be lower than the split-half estimate because they are lowered by the factor complexity of the test, and most tests have some factor complexity. This points to an important difference in the applicability of these estimates. Internal consistency estimates are appropriate for tests that measure a single, relatively factor-pure construct. In contrast, split-half reliability requires only that the two half-tests (i.e., the classically parallel halves) have the same factor composition. For example, a high split-half reliability coefficient could be obtained for a test having five factors, so long as the five factors are apportioned across the two halves of the test in the same manner.

Speededness

Any single trial estimate of reliability is inflated by the presence of a speed component in the test. Recall, for example, that the one-parameter IRT model assumes that speed does not influence the probability of a modeled response. In practice, time limits on standardized tests are often set so that 75% to 90% of the respondents can finish in the time allotted. Therefore, many widely used tests have some speed component, and internal consistency and split-half coefficients provide inflated estimates of the reliability of those tests.

The effects of speededness on a single trial estimate of reliability can be illustrated using the example of an odd/even split performed on a pure speed test (e.g., the circle dotting test). In a pure speed test, every item reached is answered correctly, so the maximum possible difference between scores on the two halves of the test is 1.0. Persons who answered an even number of items will have identical scores on the odd and even halves of the test, and persons who answered an odd number of items will score one point higher on the odd half than on the even half. Therefore, scores on the two halves of the test increase in lock-step fashion and the split-half procedure gives a spuriously high estimate of reliability.

Test–retest or parallel forms reliability must be used with speeded tests. In general, speeded tests tend to have higher reliabilities than power tests, even when the correct reliability estimate is used, because there is a greater consistency in the maximum rate with which humans can perform than in their quality of performance.

Test Length

Longer tests tend to be more reliable than shorter tests because increases in test length increase true score variance more rapidly than error variance. Recall that each observed score contains a true score and error score component. In relation to a shorter test (e.g., a 50-item test), a longer test (e.g., a 100-item test) can be conceptualized as consisting of the shorter test and an alternate form. Because an examinee can have only one true score on a given construct, the correlation of true scores on alternate forms is 1.0. Error scores are completely random, however, so the correlation among errors on alternate forms is zero. The variance of a composite (i.e., the sum of a set of items) is equal to the sum of the item variances plus the interitem variances. The item variances are composed of true score and error score variance, so both increase as test length increases. The interitem covariances are what allow correlations among items, however, so these contain no error variance. Therefore, when test length is increased, true score variance is increased as a result of the true score variance added by the new items and the interitem covariance (i.e., true score correlation) among the items added. In contrast, error variance increases only as a result of the error variance added by the new items. The result is that true score variance increases as a function of the square of increases in test length, but error variance increases only as a linear function of increases in test length. Because reliability is defined as the ratio of true score variance to total or observed score variance (i.e., true score variance plus error variance), increases in test length increase the proportion of total variance that is due to true score variance.

Group Heterogeneity

The greater the variability in the examinees on the trait measured, the higher the reliability. As just noted, reliability is defined as the ratio of true score variance to total or observed score variance. Total variance consists of true score and error variance, so reliability can be defined as true score variance divided by true score plus error score variance. The true score variance will be greater in a heterogeneous group and smaller in a homogeneous group, but the type of error of concern in reliability is random error, so error variance will not vary as a function of group heterogeneity. Therefore, only true score variance changes as a function of group heterogeneity.

The effect of increased variability on reliability can be seen clearly in a numerical example. Suppose we have a homogeneous sample in which observed score variance equals 5.0 and a heterogeneous sample in which it equals 10.0; error variance equals 3.0 in both samples. Taking observed score variance minus error variance reveals true score variance to be 2.0 in the homogeneous sample and 7.0 in the heterogeneous sample. The reliability for the homogeneous sample (2.0/5.0) is .40; doubling the heterogeneity of the sample raises the reliability to .70 (i.e., 7.0/10.0).

Because the heterogeneity of the group directly influences the reliability, it cannot be emphasized too strongly that reliability estimates are sample-dependent. Calculated reliability coefficients are descriptive of the sample on which they are based; they are estimates when attempting to generalize the observed value to a new sample. Therefore, the sample on which the reliability coefficient is calculated must be described in sufficient detail that potential users of the test can judge its generalizability to their intended sample, and it is crucial that reliability be established on a sample comparable to the sample with which the test will be used. Furthermore, it is necessary for researchers to document the quality of their data by reporting, for all measures used in their study, appropriate reliability estimates based on their particular sample rather than relying on inferences based on published reliability estimates.

Because reliability estimates are influenced by group heterogeneity, the reliability is an index of the relative stability of scores on the test. It indicates the degree to which persons maintain their relative position in the group. It would be useful to have available an absolute index (i.e., a measure that is independent of group heterogeneity). The standard error of measurement provides an index of the absolute stability of measurement. Expressed in test score units, the standard error of measurement is independent of the heterogeneity of the sample on which it is calculated.

One interpretation of the standard error of measurement is as the standard deviation of the errors of measurement. Because measurement errors are random deviations from respondents' true scores, the true score is defined as the mean of the observed scores obtained on successive testings with parallel measures. Because the true score would be a constant on these parallel measures, all observed score variation would be due to error variance. Therefore, the standard deviation of the observed scores obtained on successive testings with parallel measures equals the standard deviation of the errors of measurement. This index is called the standard error of measurement.

The standard error of measurement has important applications in interpreting the test score. The standard error of measurement indicates how large an error component is likely to exist in an individual's score, permitting the establishment of confidence intervals around the observed score. These confidence intervals allow the specification, at a known level of probability, of the range of scores that is likely to include the respondent's true score. Thus, the standard error measurement is helpful in answering questions about the individual's true score. An important limitation to remember, however, is that the standard deviation, which is expressed in test score units, is used as a multiplier in the formula for the standard error of measurement ($S_x\sqrt{1 - r_{xx}}$). This converts the standard error of measurement to test score units. For this reason, it is not feasible to directly compare standard errors of measurement from one test to another.

Item Characteristics

We have identified several features of reliability that have implications for the design of items. Although these features are related, it is instructive to consider them as three separate factors. I have noted repeatedly that reliability is a ratio of true score variance to observed or total score variance, which means we must attempt to maximize true score variation while minimizing error variance. IRT models specify one important consideration in accomplishing this objective: the probability of the modeled response must be influenced only by the latent trait. In the vernacular, the item must measure one factor and one factor only. Second, in discussing the effects of group heterogeneity, I emphasized the importance of obtaining a sample that is heterogeneous on the latent trait. It is important to realize that attributes of the items also influence the observed score variance. Third, whenever possible, we should eliminate factors that contribute to chance variation, because all forms of reliability treat this as error variance.

The use of trick questions, catch questions, or items that stimulate an emotional response should be avoided. These items essentially introduce another factor that influences the probability of making the modeled response. Catch questions or trick questions measure in part the examinees' ability to discern the trick in addition to the construct being measured. Responses to emotionally laden items vary as a function of individual differences in the intensity of the emotional reaction and in the ability to ignore the emotional reaction stimulated by the question in deciding on an answer. These factors introduce variation that is extraneous to the construct being measured, and thereby reduce the factor purity of the test. The effect is to lower the reliability of the test.

Interdependent items (e.g., matching items) also reduce the reliability of a test. By definition, interdependent items do not operate independently, so they have the effect of shortening the test. The result is the same as if a shorter test had been used.

Item difficulty also influences the reliability of a test. Questions that are too easy are answered correctly by most persons, thereby contributing little to variation in scores on the test. In the extreme case in which an item is answered correctly by everyone, the item variance is 0. Without variance, there can be no reliability. An item that is too difficult decreases variance in an analogous manner, but the effect is not as great because difficult items lead to an increase in guessing and to the likelihood that individuals will answer some items correctly by chance. The overall effect is to reduce total variance while increasing error variance, thereby decreasing the reliability of the test.

The probability that an item can be answered correctly by chance influences the reliability of the test: reliability decreases as the probability of answering correctly by chance increases. Therefore, the number of alternative responses in a test influences the reliability of the test. Consider a test consisting of 100 seven-response multiple-choice items with a parallel forms reliability of .91. If all other factors were held constant but the number of response options was reduced to five, the reliability would drop to .88.

Reducing the response options to two (as in a true–false test) would further reduce the reliability to .84. Symonds (1924) long ago concluded that seven-response options were optimal in rating scales. Later, Guilford (1954) expressed the opinion that this was usually lower than optimal and, in some situations, up to 25 rating scale divisions may be desirable. Research, however, has confirmed that reliability tends to increase markedly up to five points. It levels off thereafter, but increases of practical importance still occur up to seven-point scales (Garner, 1960; Nunnally, 1978). Increasing the number of response or rating scale options beyond that point probably will not yield increases in reliability that have practical significance.

VALIDITY

As with reliability, understanding of validity has matured over the years. The earliest view was that validity is concerned with the extent to which the test measures what it purports to measure (Garrett, 1937). A bewildering number of specific procedures for evaluating validity were suggested during the first half of the century, but the 1954 codification of validity into content, predictive, concurrent, and construct organized these procedures into a coherent system. Today, most psychologists think of validity as comprising content, criterion-related, and construct validity, but significant changes in the way validity is conceived have occurred since the introduction of that classification in 1974. Extensive treatments of these developments are available in Messick (1989) and Wainer and Braun (1988). My limited objective in this space is to summarize briefly the current thinking about the nature of validity and the unified view of validity. Within this context, I will review five types of evidence that can be used to evaluate construct validity. Special attention will be given to Cattell's (1966) Data Box, a conception of covariation largely overlooked by psychologists, which suggests designs having important applications in counseling psychology research.

Theory of Validity

"Validity is an integrated evaluative judgment of the degree to which empirical evidence and theoretical rationales support the adequacy and appropriateness of inferences and actions based on test scores or other modes of assessment" (Messick, 1989, p. 13). Comparison of Messick's contemporary definition of validity with Garrett's earlier view illustrates two important differences.

1. Garrett referred vaguely to the test's measuring what it purports to measure; Messick stated explicitly that the theoretical conceptualization and available empirical evidence define the construct measured by the test. The process of defining constructs is evolutionary; the precision with which a construct can be defined is limited by the extent and quality of the prior theory and research pertaining to the construct. Progress occurs by making the theoretical notions as explicit as possible, developing deliberate theoretical challenges to those notions, and then devising a study in which the alternatives lead to different predictions. Many of the constructs that counseling psychologists measure are difficult to observe directly, but the theory behind the test, the evidence that supports the theory, and the interpretations of the test that are theoretically possible must be clearly established before meaningful research on the construct validity of the test can be undertaken. Relations between scores on a test and other variables have no implications for the validity of the test unless a clear a priori basis exists for predicting what the relation should be.

2. Garrett referred to the test; Messick referred to inferences and actions based on test scores. Psychologists have come to understand that neither reliability nor validity refers to the test itself. Instead, the test is merely one element in a chain of events. First, a complex interaction occurs among the examinees, the test, the situation, and possibly the raters. This interaction results in data (i.e., test scores) that are characterized to a greater or lesser extent by the attributes we refer to as reliability. Typically, however, the chain of events continues, with interpretive and action inferences being drawn from the test scores. These interpretive and action inferences are to be validated, not the test or the test scores.

Unified View of Validity

The most significant contribution to the formulation of modern validity theory was Cronbach and Meehl's (1955) elucidation of construct validity. Today, the emerging view is that construct validity is a comprehensive approach that subsumes all forms of validity (Anastasi, 1986; Angoff, 1988; Messick, 1989). Concurrent and predictive validity data refer to specific types of construct validity data. Content validity refers to a fixed property of the test rather than to the inferences drawn from test scores, and does not qualify as a form of validity (Angoff, 1988; Messick, 1989).

Anastasi (1986) argued that validity is a quality that should be built into the test throughout the test construction process rather than an attribute of the test to be evaluated once the test is fully developed. Development of a valid test begins with the clear, explicit, and detailed definition of the construct to be measured. This definition guides the selection of procedures and interpretation of results throughout the development and validation of the test. Major sources of information that can be consulted to guide the development of constructs include personality theories, factor analytic investigations, clinical observations, research on information processing, and studies from cognitive psychology. The special context in which the test is to be used also influences the development of the test. Tests used for clinical diagnosis need to be constructed differently than tests used for an occupational testing or educational evaluation. This requires a content analysis of the particular behavioral domain, reminiscent of Thompson's sampling theory.

A careful elucidation of the construct to be measured requires a very careful assessment of the criterion. For example, individuals who wish to develop a scale to measure depression start by reviewing the theory and empirical research on depression. After a painstaking analysis of the construct, items are written to reflect the information gained. The identification of the construct in both the test performance and the criterion behavior at the time of the initial construct definition and formulation of item-writing specifications builds validity into the test.

Once the test items have been developed, empirical item analyses are performed and the most valid items from the initial pool are selected. Internal analyses are then carried out (e.g., factorial validity may be assessed). Finally, criterion-related validity and more extensive construct validity analyses are performed to validate and cross-validate the interpretations suggested for the scores.

Construct validity calls attention to the fact that the test measures a hypothetical construct having a clearly specified relation to a number of other hypothetical constructs. The theory guiding the development of the test should specify factors to which the construct is highly and moderately related, and factors to which the construct is not related. The latter must not be overlooked in establishing the validity of a test. All too often, tests have been found to be heavily loaded with a personality or intellectual ability factor unrelated to the intended construct (see, for example, Betz's discussion of career maturity in Chapter 14 of this *Handbook*). Furthermore, it is important to specify, on the basis of theoretical and empirical expectations, whether the construct should be related to demographic characteristics such as gender and race.

The interpretation of negative results in a construct validity study is ambiguous because construct validity involves the mutual evaluation of theory and the inferences that can be drawn from the test. Three possibilities exist when the results fail to support the interpretation that the test possesses construct validity. First, the test may not be a valid measure of the hypothetical construct. Often, this is the issue the investigator set out to study, and therefore many investigators seize on this conclusion immediately. Two additional possibilities are that the theory describing the hypothetical construct is incorrect, or the experimental design failed to test the hypothesis properly. This ambiguity is best avoided by skillfully designing the validity study. Ideally, investigators should include only one untried element in each study. Manipulation checks should be included to assess the effectiveness of any manipulation. When the test is relatively untried, some well-established aspect of the theory can be investigated and possibly a better established alternative measure of the construct can be included. When some relatively untested feature of the theory is to be examined, the measurement of pertinent constructs must be performed adequately.

Evidence of Construct Validity

Five types of evidence can be used to evaluate the validity of a test. First, group differences can be examined in a cross-sectional analysis of validity. This approach compares the scores of groups postulated to differ on the construct measured by the test. The groups selected must correspond to some well-established a priori basis for postulating how they will relate. The groups might differ diagnostically (e.g., schizophrenics vs. depressives), developmentally (e.g., freshmen vs. seniors), demographically (e.g., women vs. men), or experientially (e.g., experts vs. novices).

Second, changes in scores over time can be evaluated using a longitudinal design. The resulting information about the stability of the scores must be evaluated in terms of the theoretically expected changes in the level and variability of the scores. Issues that can be evaluated using longitudinal designs include the stability of supposedly stable traits, the sensitivity of mood scales, the occurrence of expected maturational changes, and the occurrence of anticipated changes in response to experimental manipulations.

Third, evidence pertaining to validity can be obtained by examining internal consistency. The anticipated degree of item homogeneity should be specified by the theory underlying the test. A high degree of internal consistency is desirable in a test measuring one of Thurstone's broad group factors, but not desirable in many other situations. Some researchers seem to have the mistaken view that a high degree of internal consistency is desirable in all situations.

Study of the test-taking process is the fourth procedure that can be used to evaluate construct validity. Stimulated by developments in the study of cognitive information processing, a variety of techniques have been proposed for this purpose (see Messick, 1989). An example of this approach is Tinsley and Westcot's (1990) validation study of the Expectations About Counseling—Brief Form (EAC-B). They asked respondents to say out loud every thought that occurred to them while they were completing the EAC-B. A content analysis was performed and it determined that the EAC-B elicited primarily cognitions about expectations as opposed to thoughts concerning preferences, perceptions, the clarity of the items, or the degree of involvement in the research.

Finally, correlational analyses are the most widely used approach to studying construct validity. Following shortly after Cronbach and Meehl's (1955) seminal work on construct validity, Campbell and Fiske (1959) described a procedure for analyzing a multitrait–multimethod correlation matrix to determine the convergent and discriminant validity of a test. Factor analysis provides another powerful technique for evaluating the extent to which the items in a test load on factors in a manner consistent with the definition of the construct. Simultaneously factor-analyzing item responses and scores on other tests of known factor composition, or test scores and criterion behaviors provide evidence of construct validity.

Cattell's Data Box

Typically, correlational analyses focus on the relation between two columns of numbers (i.e., test scores, item responses, ratings) within a sample. Suppose, for example, Tinsley's (1982) 17-scale EAC-B was administered to a sample of college students. Calculating the correlation between scores on the first two scales, Motivation and Openness, would involve computations on two columns of numbers (i.e., the scores of respondents on those two scales). This procedure is so thoroughly familiar that the actual existence of additional data is not confusing. We readily understand that we ignore the respondents' scores on the other 15 scales when calculating the correlation between the Motivation and Openness scales. However, having calculated this correlation, we could ignore the Openness scores and calculate the correlation between Motivation and Responsibility. In this manner, we could proceed through the data calculating every possible pairwise correlation.

Modifying our example, suppose we wished to investigate changes in clients' expectations across a series of 10 counseling interviews. To do this, we administer the EAC-B before each of the 10 counseling sessions. The resulting data would now form a clients × EAC-B scales × testing occasions cube (i.e., Cattell's Data Box; Cattell, 1966). Although we now have data on 17 EAC-B scales obtained at 10 different times, we ignore most of the data in calculating any single correlation, and use only the data needed (e.g., scores on the Motivation and Openness scale prior to the third counseling session).

Cattell's Data Box alerts us to possible relations many counseling psychologists might not have considered previously (see Table 2.1). There have been numerous calls in recent years for the use of more varied research designs (e.g., see Howard, 1984).

Table 2.1 Cattell's Data Box

Letter Name	Persons	Variables	Occasions	Descriptor	Randomly Sampled	Factors
O	1	N	2	Single case	Variables	Occasions
P	1	2	N	Single case	Occasions	Variables
Q	2	N	1	Static	Variables	Persons
R	N	2	1	Static	Persons	Variables
S	2	1	N	Monovariate	Occasions	Persons
T	N	1	2	Monovariate	Persons	Occasions

Note: N designates the attribute randomly sampled; 2 designates the attribute correlated; 1 designates the locus of the correlation. Factor analysis reveals the latent dimensions underlying the correlated attribute (i.e., designated by 2).

These calls have gone largely unheeded, perhaps because of counseling psychologists' concerns about small sample designs and their uncertainty about how to analyze the data obtained from these studies. Cattell's Data Box suggests several useful strategies.

O Correlations

These correlations indicate the association between occasion 1 and occasion 2 across a sample of variables for one person and the degree to which the relation among the variables within one person is stable across the two occasions. Factor analysis of 0 correlations reveals latent dimensions underlying occasions because each 0 correlation indicates the relation between two occasions (see Table 2.1).

O correlations are of interest in research that focuses on the intensive study of the single individual across time (e.g., examination of an individual's personality structure across time or of relations occurring in the counseling process). Because counseling occurs across time, O correlations have much greater potential applicability in counseling research than has been realized. Issues such as changes in the individual's self-esteem, self-confidence, or level of anxiety as a function of some attribute of the intervention can be analyzed using O correlations. Hypotheses specifying processes that occur as a function of the phase of counseling may be investigated by O correlations. One barrier to the use of case study designs has been the belief that these data are not amenable to analysis. The O correlation is one statistic that can be used for describing relations within these data, and for making these data amenable to multivariate analysis.

P Correlations

P correlations, the transpose of O correlations, represent the correlation between two variables across a sample of times for a single person (see Table 2.1). Factor analysis of P correlations reveals latent dimensions underlying the variables. As with O correlations, the locus of the relation is in the single individual. The previous observations about the potential for application to the analysis of case study data and the study of the counseling relationship therefore apply to the P correlation also. Instead of examining relations among occasions, however, P correlations sample occasions and examine relations among variables. P correlations are ideal for examining issues pertaining to developmental processes, including developments occurring within the counseling process. For example, the hypothesis that the client's ego strength should increase and the client's neuroticism should decrease as counseling progresses would be supported by the finding of a significant negative P correlation. Beyond that, however, counseling psychology researchers often investigate developmental processes occurring across the college years (e.g., moral development, vocational self-concept crystallization). P correlations provide a means of studying these processes as they occur within the individual.

Q and R Correlations

Q correlations indicate the association between two individuals across a sample of variables at one time. These are the transpose of the more familiar R correlation; they indicate the relation between two variables across a sample of persons on one occasion. Both Q and R correlations indicate the strength of association at a single point in time (see Table 2.1). They differ in that the familiar R correlation indicates the relations among variables, but the Q correlation indicates similarities and differences among persons. Because factor analysis of Q correlations reveals the latent dimensions underlying the persons, Q correlations are used in typology studies to identify "people types." For example, a counseling center could administer the 90-item version of the Symptom Check List (SCL-90) to potential clients at intake. After sufficient data have been obtained, cluster analysis of the Q correlations (calculated between every possible pair of clients) would reveal relatively homogeneous subgroups (i.e., types) of clients.

Note that the second column in Table 2.1 (Persons) conceptually represents entities of interest. Q correlations have been used to examine the relations among entities such as occupations and leisure activities. For example, my associates and I have obtained descriptions of more than 80 leisure activities, each measured only once, using the 46-scale Paragraphs About Leisure (PAL). Q correlations calculated on these data reveal how similar the two correlated leisure activities are across the 46 PAL scales. Efforts to develop occupational typologies have used Q methodology in a similar manner.

S Correlations

S correlations indicate the relation between two persons across occasions for a single variable (see Table 2.1). Like Q correlations, S correlations may be used in typology studies to reveal similarities and differences among persons. Like P correlations, S correlations reveal information about developmental processes. P correlations focus on developmental processes occurring within the single individual; S correlations depict developmental processes as illustrated by a single attribute. In counseling psychology research, S correlations can be used to test hypotheses about patterns of development across the counseling process and across the college years. Counseling theories reveal numerous variables that might be thought to vary in a predictable manner across counseling sessions (e.g., ego strength, level of involvement, or frequency of irrational thoughts) and across other developmental time spans (e.g., vocational realism, psychological individuation, and fear of success).

T Correlations

T correlations, the transpose of S correlations, indicate the relation between two occasions, across a sample of people, for a single variable (see Table 2.1). Test–retest reliability coefficients are T correlations, so it is clear that T correlations indicate the temporal stability of scores on a single variable. T correlations have much broader applicability in developmental studies, however, and many of the earlier points about potential applications in testing hypotheses about counseling as a developmental process apply to T correlations also. As with the O correlations, factor analysis of T correlations identifies latent dimensions underlying pairs of times.

Usefulness of Cattell's Data Box

Counseling psychologists use R correlations almost exclusively. Q correlations have been used by counseling psychologists studying occupations or leisure activities, or in isolated attempts to develop a typology. T correlations have been used in assessing test–retest reliability. These uses of Q and T correlations seemingly have occurred almost without the realization that they represent different types of correlations than does the R correlation. Cattell's Data Box describes a greater range of possibilities, many of which hold special interest for counseling psychologists. Especially relevant are the possibilities for studying developmental changes across the counseling process.

CONCLUDING REMARKS

Reliability is a quality of the data that result from the interaction of the test, the examinees, and the situation in which they interact. Construct validity is a mutual evaluation of the theory defining the construct and the interpretive and action inferences drawn from the test. Contemporary psychometric theory regards all data pertinent to the theory establishing the construct as relevant to construct validity. Development of a valid test requires the application of techniques or procedures we have come to identify with content, criterion-related, and construct validity at different stages in the test construction process. Neither reliability nor validity refers to properties of the test, per se, and neither can be evaluated adequately without a detailed understanding of the theory defining the construct.

REFERENCES

Anastasi, A. (1986). Evolving concepts of test variation. *Annual Review of Psychology, 37,* 1–15.

Angoff, W. H. (1988). Validity: An evolving concept. In H. Wainer & H. I. Braun (Eds.), *Test validity* (pp. 19–32). Hillsdale, NJ: Erlbaum.

Beck, A. T. (1970). *Depression: Causes and treatment.* Philadelphia: University of Pennsylvania Press.

Beck, A. T., Weissman, A., Lester, D., & Trexler, L. (1974). The measurement of pessimism: The Hopelessness Scale. *Journal of Consulting and Clinical Psychology, 42,* 861–865.

Birnbaum, A. (1968). Some latent trait models and their use in inferring an examinee's ability. In F. M. Lord & M. R. Novick, *Statistical theories of mental test scores.* Reading, MA: Addison-Wesley.

Cacioppo, J. T., Petty, R. E., & Kao, C. F. (1984). The efficient assessment of need for cognition. *Journal of Personality Assessment, 48,* 306–307.

Campbell, D. T., & Fiske, D. W. (1959). Convergent and discriminant validation by the multitrait-multimethod matrix. *Psychological Bulletin, 56,* 81–105.

Cattell, R. B. (1966). The data box: Its ordering of total resources in terms of possible relational systems. In R. B. Cattell (Ed.), *Handbook of multivariate experimental psychology* (pp. 67–128). Chicago: Rand McNally.

Cicchetti, D. V., Showalter, D., & Tyrer, P. J. (1985). The effect of number of rating scale categories on levels of interrater reliability: A Monte Carlo investigation. *Applied Psychological Measurement, 9,* 31–36.

Cohen, J. (1960). A coefficient of agreement for nominal scales. *Educational and Psychological Measurement, 20,* 37–46.

Cohen, J. (1968). Weighted kappa: Nominal scale agreement with provision for scaled disagreements or partial credit. *Psychological Bulletin, 70,* 213–220.

Cronbach, L. J. (1951). Coefficient alpha and the internal structure of tests. *Psychometrika, 16,* 297–334.

Cronbach, L. J., & Meehl, P. E. (1955). Construct validity in psychological tests. *Psychological Bulletin, 52,* 281–302.

Cull, J. G., & Gill, W. S. (1982). *Suicide Probability Scale.* Los Angeles: Western Psychological Services.

Digman, J. M. (1990). Personality structure: Emergence of the five-factor model. *Annual Review of Psychology, 41,* 417–440.

Ebel, R. L. (1951). Estimation of the reliability of ratings. *Psychometrika, 16,* 407–424.

Eysenck, H. J., & Eysenck, S. B. G. (1975). *Manual: Eysenck Personality Questionnaire (Junior & Adult).* San Diego: Educational and Industrial Testing Service, Inc.

Feldt, L. S., & Brennan, R. L. (1989). Reliability. In R. L. Linn (Ed.), *Educational measurement* (3rd ed.). New York: Macmillan.

Fleiss, J. L., & Cohen, J. (1973). The equivalence of weighted kappa and the intraclass correlation coefficient as measures of reliability. *Educational and Psychological Measurement, 33,* 613–619.

Garner, W. R. (1960). Rating scales, discriminability, and information transmission. *Psychological Review, 67,* 343–352.

Garrett, H. E. (1937). *Statistics in psychology and education.* New York: Longman.

Ghiselli, E. E., Campbell, J. P., & Zedeck, S. (1981). *Measurement theory for the behavioral sciences.* San Francisco: Freeman.

Gottfredson, L. S. (Ed.). (1986). The G factor in employment [Special issue]. *Journal of Vocational Behavior, 29*(3).

Guilford, J. P. (1954). *Psychometric methods* (2d ed.). New York: McGraw-Hill.

Guilford, J. P. (1967). *The nature of human intelligence.* New York: McGraw-Hill.

Gulliksen, H. (1950). *Theory of mental tests.* New York: Wiley.

Hambleton, R. K. (1989). Principles and selected applications of item response theory. In R. L. Linn (Ed.), *Educational measurement* (3rd ed.). New York: Macmillan.

Hater, J. J., & Bass, B. M. (1988). Supervisors' evaluations of subordinates' perceptions of transformational and transactional leadership. *Journal of Applied Psychology, 73,* 695–702.

Howard, G. S. (1984). A modest proposal for a revision of strategies for counseling research. *Journal of Counseling Psychology, 31,* 430–441.

Hoyt, C. (1941). Test reliability obtained by analysis of variance. *Psychometrika, 6,* 153–160.

Hunter, J. E. (1986). Cognitive ability, cognitive aptitudes, job knowledge, and job performance. *Journal of Vocational Behavior, 29,* 340–362.

James, L. R., Demaree, R. G., & Wolf, G. (1984). Estimating within-group interrater reliability with and without response bias. *Journal of Applied Psychology, 69,* 85–98.

Jones, L. V., & Appelbaum, M. I. (1989). Psychometric methods. *Annual Review of Psychology, 40,* 23–43.

Lord, F. M. (1952). A theory of test scores. *Psychometric Monograph, 7.*

Lord, F. M., & Novick, M. R. (1968). *Statistical theories of mental test scores.* Reading, MA: Addison-Wesley.

McKinley, R. L. (1989). An introduction to item response theory. *Measurement and Evaluation in Counseling and Development, 22,* 37–57.

Messick, S. (1989). Validity. In R. L. Linn (Ed.), *Educational measurement* (3rd ed.; pp. 13–103). New York: Macmillan.

Norman, W. T. (1963). Toward an adequate taxonomy of personality attributes: Replicated factor structure in peer nomination personality ratings. *Journal of Abnormal and Social Psychology, 66,* 574–583.

Nunnally, J. C. (1978). *Psychometric theory* (2nd ed.). New York: McGraw-Hill.

Rasch, G. (1966). An item analysis which takes individual differences into account. *British Journal of Mathematical and Statistical Psychology, 19,* 49–57.

Shavelson, R. J., Webb, N. M., & Rowley, G. L. (1989). Generalizability theory. *American Psychologist, 44,* 922–932.

Spearman, C. (1904). "General intelligence," objectively determined and measured. *The American Journal of Psychology, 15,* 201–292.

Spearman, C. (1907). Demonstration of formulae for true measurement of correlation. *American Journal of Psychology, 18,* 161–169.

Stine, W. W. (1989). Interobserver relational agreement. *Psychological Bulletin, 106,* 341–347.

Suinn, R. M., Edie, C. A., Nicoletti, J., & Spinelli, P. R. (1972). The MARS, a measure of mathematics anxiety: Psychometric data. *Journal of Clinical Psychology, 28,* 373–375.

Symonds, P. M. (1924). On the loss of reliability in ratings due to coarseness of the scale. *Journal of Experimental Psychology, 7,* 456–461.

Thompson, G. H. (1948). *The factorial analysis of human ability* (3rd ed.). Boston: Houghton Mifflin.

Thorndike, R. L. (1951). Reliability. In E. F. Lindquist (Ed.), *Educational measurement.* Washington, DC: American Council on Education.

Thorndike, R. L. (1986). The role of general ability in prediction. *Journal of Vocational Behavior, 29,* 332–339.

Thurstone, L. L. (1933). *The theory of multiple factors.* Chicago: Author.

Tinsley, H. E. A. (1971). An investigation of the Rasch simple logistic model for tests of intelligence or attainment. (Doctoral dissertation, University of Minnesota.) Ann Arbor, MI: University Microfilms, 1972, No. 72–14, 387.

Tinsley, H. E. A. (1982). *Expectations about counseling* [Test manual]. Unpublished manuscript, Southern Illinois University, Department of Psychology, Carbondale, IL.

Tinsley, H. E. A., & Dawis, R. V. (1974). The equivalence of semantic and figural test presentation of the same items. *Educational and Psychological Measurement, 34,* 607–615.

Tinsley, H. E. A., & Dawis, R. V. (1975). An investigation of the Rasch simple logistic model: Sample free item and test calibration. *Educational and Psychological Measurement, 35,* 325–339.

Tinsley, H. E. A., & Weiss, D. J. (1975). Interrater reliability and agreement of subjective judgments. *Journal of Counseling Psychology, 22,* 358–376.

Tinsley, H. E. A., & Westcot, A. M. (1990). Analysis of the cognitions stimulated by the items on the Expectations About Counseling—Brief Form: An analysis of construct validity. *Journal of Counseling Psychology, 37,* 223–226.

Tryon, R. C. (1957). Reliability and behavior domain validity: Reformation and historical critique. *Psychological Bulletin, 54,* 229–249.

Tupes, E. C., & Christal, R. E. (1961). Recurrent personality factors based on trait ratings. USAF ASD Technical Report No. 61–97.

Vernon, P. E. (1960). *The structure of human abilities* (rev. ed.). London: Methuen.

Wainer, H., & Braun, H. I. (Eds.). (1988). *Test validity.* Hillsdale, NJ: Erlbaum.

Webb, N. M., Rowley, G. L., & Shavelson, R. J. (1988). Using generalizability theory in counseling and development. *Measurement and Evaluation in Counseling and Development, 21,* 81–90.

Weiss, D. J. (1974). Strategies of adaptive ability measurement (Research Report 74–5). Minneapolis: University of Minnesota.

Weiss, D. J. (1982). Improving measurement quality and efficiency with adaptive testing. *Applied Psychological Measurement, 6,* 379–396.

Weiss, D. J. (Ed.). (1983). *New horizons in testing.* New York: Academic Press.

Weiss, D. J. (1985). Adaptive testing by computer. *Journal of Consulting and Clinical Psychology, 53,* 774–789.

Wernimont, P. F., & Campbell, J. (1968). Signs, samples, and criteria. *Journal of Applied Psychology, 52,* 372–376.

Wingersky, M. S. (1983). LOGIST: A program for computing maximum likelihood procedures for logistic models. In R. K. Hambleton (Ed.), *Applications of item response theory* (pp. 45–56). Vancouver: Educational Research Institute of British Columbia.

Wingersky, M. S., Barton, M. A., & Lord, F. M. (1982). *LOGIST user's guide.* Princeton, NJ: Educational Testing Service.

Witkin, H. A., Oltman, P. K., Raskin, E., & Karp, S. A. (1971). *A manual for the Embedded Figures Text.* Palo Alto, CA: Consulting Psychologists Press.

Woodworth, R. S. (1920). *Personal Data Sheet.* Chicago: Stoelting.

Wright, B. D., & Mead, R. J. (1977). BICAL: Calibrating items and scales with the Rasch model (Research Memorandum No. 23). Chicago: University of Chicago.

CHAPTER 3

COUNSELING RESEARCH METHODS: ART AND ARTIFACT

BRUCE E. WAMPOLD
KAREN L. POULIN

There is no single research method for counseling psychology. Research in counseling psychology spans a wide range of applied areas and uses many different methods. Even within a specific topical area, various research methods will be used to investigate the nature of the phenomena being studied. For example, consider the many ways in which the cognitive activity of counselors in a counseling session has been studied (Hill & O'Grady, 1985; Martin, Martin, & Slemon, 1987; McCarthy, Shaw, & Schmeck, 1986; Morran, Kurpius, & Brack, 1989). Journal articles and books presenting new methods appear daily. The researcher faced with designing an experiment must match the method to the area being investigated and the specific questions being asked. However, determining the optimal method is not a prescriptive technology; designing good research is a challenging and creative process. Background knowledge in research methods is essential, but an investigation that illuminates our knowledge is often a work of art.

The utility of a research method depends on whether the inferences made about knowledge are appropriate and whether the conclusions reached are important. In other words, is the research valid? If the research is not valid, then the conclusions are artifacts. From our perspective, art and artifact are central to research in counseling psychology. The investigator needs to creatively design and conduct a study and, in the process, take great pains to avoid reaching false conclusions.

Some comments about how we will discuss art and artifact are in order. An art is not learned by systematically acquiring skills or knowledge in an area. Research artistry is no more a collective knowledge of design and statistics than is psychotherapy the application of individual counseling skills. Similarly, avoiding artifact is more complicated than avoiding violations of rules (although certain violations will certainly lead to artifact). Because the research process is complex (*and* nonlinear), in this chapter we will avoid systematically reviewing advances in research methods or rules. (Various sources do this; for example, see the special issue of the *Journal of Counseling Psychology,* on advances in statistical methods related to counseling psychology research; Wampold, 1987b.) Rather, we will explore selected counseling research domains that reveal creative solutions to difficult problems.

In choosing to organize the chapter in this way, we faced the dilemma of selecting the particular research domains to emphasize. Arbitrarily, but not capriciously, counseling process and treatment outcome were selected for discussion. This typology obviously does not capture other dimensions of counseling research and thus does not directly address areas such as developmental models, treatment of specific disorders, model building, and a number of other areas for which specific methods exist. Although the process/outcome distinction is arbitrary, this division provides a useful way to discuss various methods. As we began our review of methods used in counseling research, we realized that many advances in methods have occurred in process research and that these methods are more allied with counseling psychology than with other applied psychology areas. Consequently, we have stressed counseling process research.

To understand what makes one study art and another artifact, it is important to examine the concept of research validity. Therefore, before we focus on process and outcome, we will briefly review research validity.

RESEARCH VALIDITY

Validity refers to the degree to which inferences drawn reflect the actual state of affairs (Cook & Campbell, 1979; Heppner, Kivlighan, & Wampold, 1992). There are many stages of research that require critical inferences. Consider the following process of hypothesis testing. First, the research hypotheses are derived from applicable theory, practice, and/or previous results. A research hypothesis is a statement about the relationships among psychological constructs. Second, operations are chosen to represent the constructs. The operations may involve manipulations of the independent variable or selection of an instrument or instruments to yield measures of outcome. Third, the study is designed so that the covariation of the operations can be examined. For instance, the independent variable is manipulated so that its effect on the dependent variable can be assessed. Fourth, it is determined whether the measured variables do indeed covary as expected.

Having designed and conducted the study, the investigator reverses the direction of the sequence described above, making inferences along the way: The measured variables do indeed covary; the independent variable was the cause of the concomitant covariation in the dependent variable; the independent variable and the dependent variable accurately reflect the constructs of interest; the results apply to various persons, settings, and times; and the results have implications for theory and/or practice. Keep in mind that each of the inferences made may or may not be proper. If the validity of the study is high, there are few rival interpretations and they are relatively implausible; if the validity is low, there are many alternative and veridical explanations for an obtained result.

The seminal work of Campbell and Stanley (1966) explicated two types of validity, internal and external. Bracht and Glass (1968) expanded on the external validity theme. Concerned about drawing inferences in field settings, Cook and Campbell (1979) later divided both internal validity and external validity, yielding four types: statistical conclusion validity, internal validity, construct validity of putative causes and effects, and external validity. Recently, Wampold, Davis, and Good (1990), who expanded the concept of validity by considering the theoretical context of research, coined the term "hypothesis validity."

Each of these validities will be discussed briefly. Campbell and Stanley (1966) began the tradition of considering the conditions that threaten validity. Threats are alternatives to the inference made by the researcher. Each of the validities and its related threats are listed in Table 3.1.

Table 3.1   Threats to Research Validity

Statistical conclusion validity
    Low statistical power
    Violated assumptions of statistical tests
    Fishing and error rate problem
    Reliability of measures
    Reliability of treatment implementation
    Random irrelevancies in the experimental setting
    Random heterogeneity of respondents

Internal validity
    History
    Maturation
    Testing
    Instrumentation
    Statistical regression
    Selection
    Mortality
    Interactions with selection
    Ambiguity about the direction of causal influence
    Diffusion or imitation of treatments
    Compensatory equalization of treatments
    Compensatory rivalry by respondents receiving less desirable treatments
    Resentful demoralization of respondents receiving less desirable treatments

Construct validity of putative causes and effects
    Inadequate preoperational explication of constructs
    Mono-operation bias
    Mono-method bias
    Hypothesis-guessing within experimental conditions
    Evaluation apprehension
    Experimenter expectancies
    Confounding constructs and levels of constructs
    Interaction of different treatments
    Interaction of testing and treatment
    Restricted generalizability across constructs

External validity
    Interaction of selection and treatment
    Interaction of setting and treatment
    Interaction of history and treatment

Hypothesis validity
    Inconsequential research hypotheses
    Ambiguous research hypotheses
    Noncongruence of research hypotheses and statistical hypotheses
    Diffuse statistical hypotheses and tests

Note: Threats to statistical conclusion, internal, construct, and external validity are discussed by Cook and Campbell (1979); threats to hypothesis validity are discussed by Wampold, Davis, and Good (1990).

Statistical Conclusion Validity

The first inference typically made in a study is whether the variables truly covary. Typically, statistical tests are used to make this inference. When statistical tests are employed, the null hypothesis is that there is no relationship between (or among) variables in the population. When the null hypothesis is rejected, the decision is made that, in the relevant population, the two variables covary. For example, in a radomized treatment design, a statistically significant t-test indicates that scores on the dependent variable covaried with the manipulation to the extent that it was unlikely that the obtained result would have occurred by chance had there been no true population relationship. In a passive design (i.e., passive in the sense that there is no experimental manipulation; see Cook & Campbell, 1979), a statistically significant Pearson correlation coefficient indicates that the observed linear relationship was sufficiently large to conclude that it did not occur by chance and thus there is a true linear relation between these two variables.

The rub with statistical inferences is that one is never sure whether they are true. Type I Error involves deciding that variables are related (i.e., rejecting the null hypothesis of no relationship), when in fact there is no relationship. Type II Error involves deciding that there is no relationship (i.e., variables do not covary), when in fact there is a relationship. Alpha, the probability of making a Type I Error, and beta, the probability of making a Type II Error, are indicators of the statistical conclusion validity. If a study is designed so that alpha equals .05, then there are fewer than 5 chances out of 100 that the investigator has made an incorrect inference by concluding that the variables covary.

Threats to statistical conclusion validities are conditions that inflate the error rates. For example, if the assumptions of a statistical test are violated, the chances of falsely concluding that variables covary may be much greater than the nominal alpha set by the investigator. Similarly, if power is low, the probability of falsely concluding that there is no covariation is high. Table 3.1 summarizes threats to statistical conclusion validity.

Statistical conclusion validity applies to inferences about covariation whether or not inferential statistics per se are used. For example, single-subject designs often are used to establish the *functional* relation between an intervention and a behavior (Barlow & Hersen, 1984). Essentially, functional relation means that the independent variable (baseline vs. intervention) covaries with the dependent variable (typically, some behavior). In this context, Type I and Type II Errors continue to exist; for example, one might falsely conclude that there is a true functional relation.

Internal Validity

If it has been determined that two variables covary, a causal attribution typically is made. For example, in a randomized treatment design, when the manipulation of the independent variable results in a concomitant change in the dependent variable, the treatment is said to be the cause of the change. However, the causal inference may be incorrect. For example, the clients who were not benefiting from treatment may have dropped out of the treatment group, raising the mean for this group; mortality is then an alternative explanation for the results. Internal validity refers to the degree to which an attribution of causality for a given relationship between variables is correct. Threats to internal validity are listed in Table 3.1.

Internal validity is highest when subjects are randomly assigned to conditions, the conditions differ on only one dimension, and all treatments and assessments are given to the groups simultaneously. However, even under the best conditions (e.g., laboratory studies), threats to internal validity creep in. Nonrandomization presents special problems in that groups may not be comparable before the treatments are administered (this is a selection threat). Passive designs present special challenges to causal inferences because variables are not manipulated. However, in any context in which causation is attributed, the trick is to rule out as many threats to internal validity as possible.

An important aspect of internal validity is that it is related to the design of the study and not to the statistical procedure used. Statistical procedures are not design-specific (Cohen, 1968). For example, a regression analysis can be used just as well to analyze the data from a purely experimental design as it can to analyze the data from a passive design (Wampold & Freund, 1987). In a randomized treatment design, a correlational analysis can be used if the control group subjects are assigned a 0 on the independent variable and the treatment group is assigned a 1. In fact, the statistical inference made from conducting a t-test or a correlational analysis with coding will be exactly the same. The purpose of the statistical test is to establish covariation; causation is inferred from the design of the experiment.

Construct Validity of Putative Causes and Effects

Presumably, the measured or manipulated variables in a study are reflective of psychological constructs. When measured variable X is thought to be the cause of measured variable Y, then one wants to infer that the construct operationalized by X is the cause of the construct operationalized by Y. Construct validity refers to both the independent and dependent variables. The manipulation of the independent variable should reflect some construct. For example, Ponce and Atkinson (1989) manipulated the ethnicity of counselors by using surnames that reflect ethnicity as well as pictures of the counselors. It was inferred that this manipulation adequately reflected ethnicity. The dependent variable should also operationalize a construct. If a treatment is intended to affect depression, then any measures of the dependent variable used should reflect depression and not some other construct, such as social desirability.

When it is not clear whether the variable or variables in a study reflect one construct or another construct, a confound is said to exist. In essence, a confound involves an alternative construct that cannot be logically or statistically differentiated from a hypothesized construct. Ponce and Atkinson operationalized ethnicity with surnames and pictures. Because pictures of counselors were used, an alternative construct for the obtained results was personal attractiveness; that is, the effect on the dependent variable may have been due to the attractiveness of the counselors in the pictures rather than the ethnicity of the counselors. Fortunately, Ponce and Atkinson controlled for this confound by matching photographs on personal attractiveness. If an instrument intended to measure depression actually measures, to some degree, social desirability, then depression and social desirability are confounded. The threats to construct validity are presented in Table 3.1.

External Validity

Cook and Campbell's (1979) explication of external validity differs subtly from the popular conception of this validity. Most frequently, external validity is meant to imply generalizability *to* a population. Observations are randomly selected from a population and then the results are generalizable to that population. Generalizability to populations has been discussed in detail by Bracht and Glass (1968). Random sampling from a population is extremely rare in counseling psychology research.

Because the implications of using nonrandomly selected samples in counseling research have been discussed thoroughly elsewhere (Heppner et al., 1992; Serlin 1987), we will not dwell on this type of external validity.

Cook and Campbell (1979) focused their discussion on generalizability *across* types of persons, settings, and times. In the context of treatment studies, external validity of this type refers to questions about which treatments work with which types of clients in which settings when delivered by which type of counselors (Krumboltz, 1966; Paul, 1967, Williamson, 1939). Threats to external validity are stated as interactions between the treatment and persons, settings, and times (see Table 3.1). Suppose, for example, that two treatments of depression interact with gender in such a way that treatment A is most effective with women and treatment B is most effective with men. If the design of the study ignores gender (and both genders are included in the sample), averaging across gender will result in the misleading conclusion that treatment A and treatment B are equally effective. More pernicious would be a study that contained only men or only women, leading to the conclusion that one or the other treatment was superior, generally. These misleading conclusions would be the result of an (unexamined) interaction between treatment and persons (see Heppner et al., 1992).

Hypothesis Validity

Wampold et al. (1990), concerned about the relation of method to theory, discussed hypothesis validity. Hypothesis validity refers to the extent to which results elucidate theoretically derived predictions about the relations between or among constructs. Hypothesis validity involves four steps. First, the research hypotheses, which are statements about presumed relations among constructs, should be crucial to extending knowledge. This is the "who cares?" factor. Research may be beautifully designed and conducted, but unless it has important implications for the field of counseling psychology, few will be interested in the results.

The second step inherent in designing a study with high hypothesis validity is to state the research hypothesis unambiguously and in a form that is falsifiable. If the hypothesis is ambiguous, it will be impossible to determine whether the obtained results are consistent with the hypothesis.

The third step involves the congruence of statistical hypotheses and research hypotheses. For example, if the research hypothesis refers to mean differences, then the statistical hypotheses should be stated in terms of μ. However, if differences in variances are expected, the statistical hypothesis should be stated in terms of σ^2.

The final step involves using statistical hypotheses and tests that focus on the research hypothesis. Ideally, there would be one and only one statistical test for each research hypothesis; the results of the test would provide evidence about the truth of the research hypothesis. Multiple statistical tests cause confusion because some may support the hypothesis and others may not (to wit, the ubiquitous "the results lend partial support to the hypothesis"). Lack of clarity results when a study contains multiple statistical tests, omnibus tests, or extraneous variables (Rosnow & Rosenthal, 1988; Serlin, 1987).

The threats to hypothesis validity are presented in Table 3.1.

Comment on Validities

The validities presented here are useful ways to determine whether inferences made in research are appropriate. However, partitioning them into five categories is somewhat arbitrary. It is not important whether some aspect of a study is a threat to internal validity or construct validity; most important is that the threat be recognized, and, to the extent possible, minimized.

A second point is that there is no perfectly valid study. As Gelso (1979) noted, if one tries to eliminate all threats to one type of validity, threats to other validities will emerge elsewhere (called the "bubble hypothesis"). However, programmatic research will accrue robust findings because threats to one study will be ruled out by other studies. Take the case of smoking and disease. Because it is unethical to randomly assign subjects to a smoking condition, no single study has "scientifically proved" (much to the delight of the Tobacco Institute) that smoking causes disease. However, over many studies, using a variety of designs, the link between smoking and disease has been unequivocally established.

Our discussion of research validity has been necessarily brief. However, this discussion provides a framework within which to examine the art and artifacts of counseling research. More detailed examination of research validities is found elsewhere (Bracht & Glass, 1968; Campbell & Stanley, 1966; Cook & Campbell, 1979; Heppner et al., 1992; Wampold et al., 1990).

UNDERSTANDING COUNSELING PROCESS

Without a doubt, one of the most conspicuous foci of counseling research in the past decade has been on the process of counseling. Although other periods have witnessed interest in what transpires during the counseling session, recently a number of dedicated and imaginative researchers *systematically* investigated this interesting and informative area (Gelso & Fassinger, 1990). The general goal of process research is to determine (a) what happens within the counseling session, (b) how in-session events and interactions change over time or are related to various other factors, and (c) how what happens in the session leads to client change (Hill, 1982; Martin, Martin, & Slemon, 1989). In this discussion, we are using the term "counseling process" generically so that it includes related interpersonal interactions, such as supervision.

Several models for conceptualizing process research have been discussed. The simplest model and the one that underlaid early process research is the process–product model (Martin, 1984). This model, presented in Figure 3.1, assumes that in-session counselor behaviors affect client behaviors, leading to immediate and long-term change or growth in the client. The case study presented by Hill, Carter, and O'Farrell (1983) was based on this model.

Martin (1984) noted that the process–product model is deficient for two reasons: (a) reciprocal causal connection is absent (i.e., the client affects the counselor, as well as vice versa), and (b) the model does not account for the cognitive activity of the counselor or client. Martin proposed a paradigm shift to a cognitive mediational model, which is also presented in Figure 3.1. This model reflects two general trends in psychology: reciprocal influences in interpersonal relations and the cognitive activity of persons in a variety of contexts. Since Martin proposed this model, many process researchers have attempted programmatically to asses counselor and client cognitions and to investigate their interrelations with behavior and outcomes.

This section discusses various research methods used to study process. The focus will be on method and the relation of the method of the two models discussed previously, although we will also note some exciting findings accruing from process research. We begin by discussing how overt and covert events in counseling are assessed. Next, we address how process studies are designed and how the data are analyzed. Finally, we examine the validity of process research.

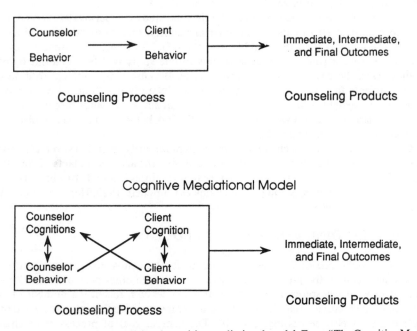

Figure 3.1 Process–product model and cognitive mediational model. From "The Cognitive Mediational Paradigm for Research on Counseling" by J. Martin, 1984, *Journal of Counseling Psychology, 31*, p. 561. Copyright 1984 by the American Psychological Association. Adapted by permission.

Coding Overt Events in the Counseling Session

During the counseling session, counselors and clients exhibit a wide range of overt behaviors. Those investigating counseling events need some way to categorize the events into discrete classes that can be investigated. Development of coding systems is a complicated process. What is the unit of analysis? What type of event should be coded? How can the categories be developed? What theoretical aspects are considered? These decisions should be made with awareness that the purpose of developing (or choosing) a coding system is to capture the essence of some phenomenon. This is a construct validity question. Generally, determination of the construct being studied should precede development or choice of a coding system. (We will return to this issue later in this section.) As discussed below, several issues are related to coding counseling behaviors.

Structure of Coding Systems

Essentially, coding systems assign behaviors to nominal categories. Each category in the system is given a name that represents an overt event. For instance, the Hill Client Verbal Response Category System (HCVRS; Hill, 1986; Hill et al., 1981) contains nine categories: Simple Response, Requests, Description, Experiencing, Insight, Discussion of Plans, Discussion of Client–Counselor Relationships, Silence, and Other. Most systems for coding client and counselor behavior contain categories that are mutually exclusive and exhaustive; that is, each behavior is assigned to one and only one category. Although mutually exclusive and exhaustive category systems are not required, data analysis is complicated when categories overlap. To facilitate reliable coding of the data, definitions and exemplars of each category typically are provided. Often, extensive manuals accompany well-developed systems (Hill et al., 1981).

Unit of Analysis

The unit of analysis involves determination of what constitutes an event. Counseling research in this area has utilized several units, the most prevalent of which are the speaking turn and the grammatical unit. A speaking turn represents a unit of continuous speech by one participant that is uninterrupted by the other participant (or participants). When a speaking turn is used, a single behavioral code typically is assigned to the entire turn. For example, if a system included the category Discussion of Plans, then this code would be assigned to the speaking turn (according to the rules of the system).

The second popular unit of analysis is the grammatical (or thought) unit. Generically, a grammatical unit—a speech act that communicates a thought—is roughly equivalent to a grammatical clause. Penman (1980, p. 63) defined a unit as "one in which there is a connected flow of behavior in which a single intent of an elocutionary 'form' can be identified." Similar definitions are provided by Bakeman and Gottman (1986), Hill et al. (1981), and Gottman (1979).

Although speaking turns and thought units are the most frequently used units of analysis, many others exist. For example, duration of events may be of interest and can be coded by noting onset and offset in real time. Thorough discussions of behavioral coding in terms of sequences of behaviors are found elsewhere (Bakeman & Gottman, 1986; Wampold, in press; Wampold & Margolin, 1982).

Coding Systems

Because there are many coding systems for overt events that have been used in counseling research—we counted over 15 used in the past 5 years in the *Journal of Counseling Psychology (JCP)*—we will not review all of them. Rather, we will briefly present some of the major systems and discuss their key differences.

From our review of process studies in the *JCP*, it appears that the Hill Counselor Verbal Response System (Hill, 1978; Hill et al., 1981) and subsequent revisions (e.g., Friedlander, 1982) have been most frequently used for coding counselor behaviors (e.g., Cummings, 1989; Kivlighan, 1989; Lee, Uhlemann, & Haase, 1985) and that the Hill Client Verbal Response Category System (Hill, 1986; Hill et al., 1981) has been the most frequently used system for coding client behaviors (e.g., Hill et al., 1983; Kivlighan, 1989). The categories used in these systems refer to the grammatical structure of counselor and client speech and are independent of the content of the verbal behavior. For example, the Interpretation category in the counselor system indicates that the counselor made an interpretation, but does not indicate the substance of the interpretation (i.e., content) or whether the interpretation was delivered skillfully (i.e., the quality). Although Hill's categories were derived from a number of sources (e.g., counseling skill texts, experienced counselors) and refined empirically, they are essentially atheoretical in the sense that they are not intended to operationalize any constructs.

A number of coding systems are comprised of theoretically derived categories. The Penman (1980) system operationalizes the constructs of power and involvement at both the manifest and latent levels of communication. Each thought unit of the counselor and client is coded at the manifest and the latent levels and each of the codes is represented along the dimensions of power and involvement. Power and involvement are consistent themes in theoretical conceptualizations of interpersonal communication (Leary, 1957; Sullivan, 1953). The manifest level refers to the surface description of a message, and the latent level refers to a deeper structure that depends on the context of the manifest message (Holloway, Freund, Gardner, Nelson, & Walker, 1989; Penman, 1980; Watzlawick, Beavin, & Jackson, 1967). Thus, the Penman system is useful for investigating the constructs of power and involvement as well as the congruence of manifest and latent levels of communication (Holloway et al., 1989; Nelson & Holloway, 1990; Reandeau & Wampold, 1991).

Another theoretically derived system is the Relational Communication Control Coding System, originally proposed by Sluzki and Beavin (1965/1977). Counselor and client behaviors are coded as Up, Down, or Across, depending on whether the message attempts to exert control or to give up control, or is neutral with respect to control, respectively. Pairing a message with a subsequent message allows the determination of whether the relationship is complementary or symmetrical (Bateson, 1936/1958; Rogers & Farace, 1975). This system or variations of it have been used to study individual and family counseling (Friedlander & Heatherington, 1989; Heatherington, 1988; Heatherington & Allen, 1984; Lichtenberg & Barke, 1981).

Coding Covert Events in the Counseling Session

As Martin (1984) noted, limiting investigations of the counseling session to overt events ignores other psychological processes. Mirroring the general zeitgeist in psychology, process researchers have, with vigor, turned to investigating the cognitions of both the counselor and the client in the counseling session. Assessing cognitions raises methodological questions because thoughts are not directly observable. Although there are numerous methods to assess cognitions (e.g., Ericsson & Simon, 1980; Merluzzi, Glass, & Genest, 1981), counseling process investigators typically have made inferences about cognitions from the verbal reports of the participants. When verbal reports are used, some method of obtaining the reports is needed, as well as some method of making sense of the reports. Reports of cognitions usually are obtained after stimulating the participant in some manner (e.g., after viewing a videotape). Sense is made of the reports either by having participants structure their report according to some system (i.e., the reports are made by selecting a cognition from a list of cognitions) or by coding unstructured reports.

In this section, we will discuss a few of the more commonly used methods used to study cognition in the counseling process. Keeping in mind that there are many types of cognitive processes (e.g., encoding, recall, retrieval, problem solving, storage) and structures (e.g., short-term memory, long-term memory, working memory), the emphasis of this discussion is on the method for operationalizing the particular cognitive construct of interest. For a discussion of cognitive assessment strategies relevant to process research, see Martin (1984).

Hill and her colleagues have investigated both counselor and client cognitions. Hill has defined the counselor cognitive activity responsible for choice of an intervention as an *intention*. Intentions are the "therapist's rationale for selecting a specific behavior, response mode, technique, or intervention to use with a client at any given moment within the session" (Hill & O'Grady, 1985, p. 3). Intentions are assessed by using interpersonal process recall methods (Kagan, 1975). Specifically, after completion of the session, the counselor reviews a videotape or audiotape of the session. The tape is stopped after each counselor statement, and the counselor retrospectively indicates his or her rationale for making the statement by selecting one or more intentions from a list of intentions (Hill & O'Grady, 1985). The intentions were derived rationally by having experienced counselors indicate their intentions and then refining them iteratively until 19 categories with "minimal overlap" were obtained (Hill & O'Grady, 1985). Hill's procedure of determining the rationale for counselor statements has been used widely (e.g., Fuller & Hill, 1985; Kivlighan, 1989).

An alternative to the structured recall procedure used by Hill and her colleagues is the less structured stimulated recall procedure used by Martin and his colleagues (Martin et al., 1987, 1989; Martin, Martin, Meyer, & Slemon, 1986). This procedure differs in that, instead of choosing a category for each statement, the participant is asked to describe what he or she was thinking (see Martin et al., 1986, for a description of a structured interview schedule for this purpose). The verbal reports are then coded using a system of cognitive operations (Martin et al., 1986). Each of the cognitive operations in Martin's system is based on an information-processing construct.

A variant of the less structured stimulated recall has been developed by Kurpius, Morran, and their colleagues (Kurpius, Benjamin, & Morran, 1985; Morran et al., 1989), who used a thought listing technique (Cacioppo & Petty, 1981) to obtain verbal descriptions of covert thoughts about stimulus videotapes of sessions. Subjects view the stimulus tapes, which are stopped periodically, and write their thoughts about the most recent segment of the tape. Although the verbal reports can be coded to obtain information relevant to specific research questions, Morran et al. (1989) have developed an atheoretical system for categorizing the verbal reports of thoughts.

Martin and his colleagues (Martin, Pavio, & Labadie, 1990; Martin & Stelmaczonek, 1988) have also developed a procedure to assess clients' and counselors' perceptions of important events in counseling. The assumption is that events perceived to be important will remain in memory. The procedure consists of simply asking the participant: "What were the most important things that happened during this session?" Follow-up questions are used if necessary. Each event reported by the client is then coded in a number of ways. For example, Martin and Stelmaczonek (1988) classified each event on the basis of a typology of important moments in counseling (Mahrer & Nadler, 1986; Martin et al., 1987) and then rated it on five information-processing dimensions (deep–shallow; elaborative–nonelaborative; personal–impersonal; clear–vague; conclusion oriented–descriptive oriented; McCarthy et al., 1986).

Affect is another of the covert processes in counseling sessions that are of interest to researchers. Affect may or may not result in demonstrable behavior. Historically, counseling psychology research has been interested in affect; consequently, there are many scales to rate sessions on affective dimensions (e.g., The Experiencing Scale; Klein, Mathieu-Coughlan, & Kiesler, 1986). However, process researchers currently are interested in the affective reactions as they occur on a moment-to-moment basis. Hill and her colleagues (Hill, Helms, Spiegel, & Tichenor, 1988) have developed a system for assessing client affective reactions to counselor interventions. Client reactions are defined as covert feelings about counselor statements (Hill, Helms, Spiegel, & Tichenor, 1988). As was the case with Hill and O'Grady's (1985) assessment of intention, a structured recall procedure is used to assess client reactions. Procedurally, clients are informed of the reactions list and then view a videotape of the session; the tape is stopped after each therapist thought and the client selects one or more reactions from a list of reactions. The list was derived by revising Elliott's (1985) categories and by brainstorming. The final list contained 21 reactions, which are then further classified as positive or negative.

Design and Analysis

Design and analysis of any research depend on the research hypotheses. It is rare that any two studies, especially process studies, will share a common design and analysis. However, there are some designs and analyses relevant to various aspects of the process–product model and the cognitive mediational model (Martin, 1984) that have been successfully used in process research.

Description of Counselor and Client Behaviors, Cognitions, and Affect

The most elementary analysis of counseling process involves describing the behavior, cognition, and affect of the counselor and the client during the course of the session. This may be accomplished simply by counting various counselor and client behaviors. Although it is rare that the sole purpose of an investigation is to examine the relative frequency of various behaviors, determination of which counselor and client behaviors are used most and least frequently can provide interesting information. For example, Hill, Helms, Spiegel, and Tichenor (1988) presented the relative frequency of 21 client reactions in 5 cases. No Reaction and Understood occurred most frequently; Unstuck, New Ways, and Misunderstood occurred least frequently. Similarly, Morran et al., (1989) determined the relative frequency of various counselor thought categories and found that Client-Focused Questions, Summarizations, and Inferences occurred most frequently.

Process researchers have used the occurrences of various categories to empirically develop or refine coding systems and to understand the basic structure of such systems. The basic goal of these investigations is to determine whether various categories in a coding system tend to occur simultaneously or are similar in some way. Based on these co-occurrences or similarities, various types of analyses that reveal clusters of categories (e.g., cluster analysis; see Borgen & Barnett, 1987) or underlying dimensions (e.g., multidimensional scaling; see Fitzgerald & Hubert, 1987) can be conducted. Elliott (1985) created a taxonomy of helpful and unhelpful events in counseling by examining similarities of events. First, he generated helpful and unhelpful events through an Interpersonal Process Recall procedure; he then had judges free-sort these events (i.e., place similar events in the same group). Based on the similarities produced by the free sort, a cluster analysis was used to produce homogeneous groups of events, thus creating a taxonomy of helpful and unhelpful events. Morran et al. (1989) used a variation of this process to examine cognitions in counseling. They used a thought-listing procedure to generate counselor cognitions, which were then classified into 14 categories. Based on the co-occurrences of the categories within interviews, a multidimensional scaling procedure was used to examine dimensions underlying the category system. Morran et al. found two dimensions, Information Seeking—Attending/Assessing and Integrative Understanding—Intervention Planning. These methods have also been used by Hill and her associates to refine and validate coding systems (e.g., Hill & O'Grady, 1985).

Descriptions of client behaviors, cognitions, and affect have limited utility in understanding counseling process, because the interactions between counselor and client are ignored. For example, descriptions of counselor and client behaviors provide information about two components of the process–product model (see Figure 3.1), but not about the relationship between these two components. To answer the question of how counselor behavior affects client behavior, the sequencing of behaviors needs to be examined.

Unidirectional Sequencing

Both the process–product model and the cognitive mediational model posit interactive effects between the participants in the counseling relationship. Typically, process researchers have investigated the interactions between counselor and client by examining the moment-to-moment sequencing of events in the counseling session. A simple way to represent the interaction is to identify sequential patterns that occur frequently. Martin et al. (1989) identified patterns involving both cognitions and behavior. For example, they found that Feelings (counselor intention) was followed by Open Question (counselor behavior), which in turn was followed by Recalling Something (client cognitive operation).

One problem, however, is that frequency of patterns ignores the base rates of behaviors. Event B may follow event A frequently; however, if event B occurs often in the counseling session, then the fact that it follows event A frequently may be due entirely to chance. An entire statistical area, generically known as sequential analysis, has been developed to investigate whether one event follows another more often (or less often) than would be expected by chance (Allison & Liker, 1982; Bakeman & Gottman, 1986; Gottman & Roy, 1990; Lichtenberg & Heck, 1986; Wampold, in press). In this way, patterns of interaction can be identified that are departures from random interactions. In essence, sequential analyses focus on the timing of responses in a social interaction and thus appear to be particularly well-suited for investigating counseling (Lichtenberg & Heck, 1986; Russell & Trull, 1986). Sequential analyses frequently have been used by process researchers (Friedlander & Phillips, 1984; Hill et al., 1983; Hill, Helms, Spiegel, & Tichenor, 1988; Hill & O'Grady, 1985; Holloway et al., 1989; Holloway & Wampold, 1983; Lichtenberg & Heck, 1986; Tracey, 1985; Tracey & Ray, 1984; Wampold & Kim, 1989). As an example of a pattern identified by a sequential analysis, consider Hill et al.'s (1983) case study, which was further analyzed by Wampold and Kim (1989). Wampold and Kim found that counselor Minimal Encouragers followed client Description more often than would be expected by chance. This was particularly revealing because it appeared that Minimal Encouragers were reinforcing Description, a client behavior that included maladaptive storytelling.

On a more global level, Hill and her colleagues have used sequential analyses to establish the validity of her process model (Hill & O'Grady, 1985). The model hypothesizes that

therapist intentions → therapist response modes →
client reactions → client overt behavior

Sequential analyses have shown a dependence between therapist intentions and therapist response modes (Hill & O'Grady, 1985), therapist intentions and client reactions (Hill, Helms, Spiegel, & Tichenor, 1988), and therapist response modes and client reactions (Hill, Helms, Tichenor, et al., 1988).

The term unidirectional dependence has been used to describe one event's effect on another (Wampold & Margolin, 1982); however, a number of more complex and substantively interesting patterns can be examined with sequential analyses.

Other Sequential Patterns

As Martin (1984) pointed out, the process–product model is limited because it examines only the influence of the counselor on the client. However, reciprocal influences in social interaction are salient aspects and need to be examined. Two particular patterns of interaction seem particularly well suited to examining higher order patterns of counseling interactions.

Bidirectional dependence refers to patterns operating from counselor to client and client to counselor. For example, in Wampold and Kim's (1989) analysis of Hill et al.'s (1983) case study, not only did counselor Minimal Encourager follow client Description more often than would be expected by chance, but client Description followed counselor Minimal Encourager more often than would be expected by chance, creating a circular pattern, which has been labeled a *circuit* (Holloway et al., 1989). Tests for circular patterns have been discussed by Wampold (in press; Wampold & Margolin, 1982).

Another sequential pattern of interest to process researchers is related to dominance. In this context, dominance refers to unequal influence. Specifically, dominance is defined as an *"asymmetry in predictability;* that is, if B's behavior is more predictable from A's past than conversely, A is said to be dominant"* (Gottman & Ringland, 1981, p. 395). Constructs related to dominance have been identified theoretically as important determinants of successful counseling (e.g., Haley, 1963). Statistical methods related to dominance have been developed (Allison & Liker, 1982; Budescu, 1984; Gottman & Ringland, 1981; Wampold, 1984, in press) and applied to counseling process (e.g., Tracey, 1985; Wampold & Kim, 1989). For example, Tracey (1985) found that the counselor is dominant in the middle stage of successful counseling.

Another question related to patterning is whether one participant's behavior is more predictable from the other participant's behavior or from one's own behavior. This question poses some difficult statistical issues (Dumas, 1986; Wampold, in press) and has particular implications for understanding counseling process (Tracey, 1987).

Linking Process and Outcome

In both of the models discussed by Martin (1984; see Figure 3.1), counseling process is linked to counseling outcomes. This linkage is the critical step to establishing the mechanisms of effective counseling (Greenberg & Pinsof, 1986a). Investigating this linkage presents special problems for the process researcher. In this section, several strategies for linking process and outcome are discussed.

To obtain some linkage between process and outcome, adequate measures of outcome are needed (a construct validity issue). An important distinction for process research has been made by Greenberg (1986), who discussed final, intermediate, and immediate therapeutic outcomes. Operations for final therapeutic outcomes typically would consist of the dependent measures in a treatment study (i.e., some measure of psychological function or dysfunction, such as depression, anxiety, or achievement of psychotherapeutic goals).

Operational definitions for intermediate outcomes typically consist of some measure of session characteristics or satisfaction with counseling interactions. One of the most popular measures of the characteristics of a session is the Session Evaluation Questionnaire (SEQ; Stiles & Snow, 1984b). The SEQ has been found to be sensitive to what transpired in the session and not to characteristics of the counselor or client, and to be composed of two relatively orthogonal factors, depth and smoothness (Stiles & Snow, 1984b). Other measures of session quality used by process researchers include the Therapy Session Report (Elliott, 1980; Orlinsky & Howard, 1975), Supervision Perception Form (Heppner & Roehlke, 1984), Supervisor and Trainee Personal Reaction Scales (Holloway & Wampold, 1985), and the Working Alliance Inventory (Horvath & Greenberg, 1986, 1989). Some scales have been developed for a particular investigation (e.g., Martin et al., 1986).

Immediate outcomes encompass indicants of quality assessed on a moment-to-moment basis. For example, the Helpfulness Rating Scale (Elliott, 1985, 1986) is used to rate the client's perception of the helpfulness of each counselor's speaking turn. Various immediate and intermediate outcomes measures are discussed in Greenberg and Pinsof (1986b).

The most direct way to link process and outcome is to investigate the relationship between various measures of each, for example, by correlating a process measure with an outcome measure. Much of the process research in counseling psychology has been devoted to examining the correlation among frequencies (or proportions) of events in the session with intermediate outcomes. For example, Hill, Helms, Spiegel, and Tichenor (1988) correlated the proportions of client reactions with the depth and smoothness subscales of the SEQ, as well as with a composite final outcome measure. For the SEQ, these correlations were calculated across and within cases. When calculated across cases, mean proportions and SEQ scores were calculated for each case and then the correlation of the mean values was determined. Within-case correlations were determined by correlating proportion of intentions and SEQ scores across sessions. In this study, the across-cases correlations were generally nonsignificant; however, the within-case correlations showed that sessions in which the clients felt Misunderstood (i.e., high proportion of this client reaction) were perceived as less valuable (low scores on outcome).

In terms of the process–product model, correlation between frequencies (or proportions) of events and outcomes ignores the interaction between the counselor and client (Shoham-Salomon, 1990). Diagrammatically, these correlations are represented as relations between counselor behavior and outcome and as relations between client behavior and outcome, as presented in Figure 3.2. Direct inquiries of the process–product model would require that indexes of the interaction between counselor and client be related to outcome, as depicted in Figure 3.2.

Wampold (1989, in press) has developed a method for indexing sequential patterns; these indexes can then be correlated with various outcomes. Interesting differences between correlating outcome with base rates of behavior and correlating outcome with indexes of sequential patterns are often found. For example, Wampold and Kim (1989) found that client satisfaction was positively correlated with client Description (i.e., the more the client described, the more satisfied she was with the session), whereas client satisfaction was negatively correlated with an interaction variable that indexed the degree to which the counselor reinforced the client's description with a Minimal Encourager (i.e., the greater the degree to which the counselor followed a client Description with a Minimal Encourager, the less satisfied the client was with the session). Thus, it may be that the client was satisfied describing, but did not like being reinforced for it.

Another example relating indexes of counselor–client interactions with outcomes was provided by Martin et al. (1986). Martin (1984) predicted that "the degree of correspondence between a client's cognitive perceptions of and reactions to a counselor's behavior and intentions will mediate the client's immediate and longer-term learning from counseling, thus determining how effective counseling will be" (p. 562). Martin et al. (1986) tested this hypothesis by investigating the relation between cognitive-behavioral matches and ratings of effectiveness and found that, indeed, various types of matches were highly correlated with participants' perceptions of effectiveness.

Another way to link process and outcome is to examine the differences between process variables for various groupings of counselor–client interactions, where the groups are formed on the basis of some outcome variable. Tracey (1985) provided an illustrative example of this strategy. From a pool of 15 counseling dyads, he selected

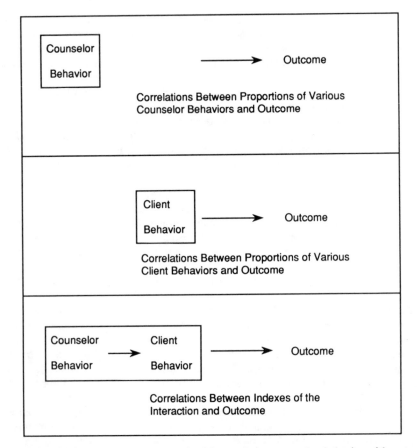

Figure 3.2 Linking process to outcome by (a) correlating counselor behavior with outcome, (b) correlating client behavior with outcome, and (c) correlating indexes of the intereaction between counselor and client with outcome.

the three best and worst dyads based on counselor- and client-rated outcome. Tracey found the counselors of the best dyads were dominant in the middle stage of counseling (i.e., clients' behavior was more predictable from the counselors' than conversely; see discussion of dominance above), whereas there were no asymmetries of influence in the worst cases.

Not every study linking process and outcome fits neatly into one of these designs. Examination of two studies linking process and outcome will provide some sense of the variation in approaches. Barkham and Shapiro (1986) studied the relation of verbal responses of counselors to the occurrence of perceived empathy. In this study, clients were instructed to push a button when they felt that the counselor was understanding their point of view particularly well (a measure of immediate outcome). Rather than correlating frequency of events and perceptions of empathy, they looked for changes in frequency (i.e., trends) of response modes preceding perceptions of empathy. They found that, in the 15 seconds preceding the empathic event, the rates of Interpretation, Reflection, and especially Exploration increased significantly.

Another example of a study that examined change over the course of a session is Holloway, Wampold, and Nelson's (1990) examination of a paradoxical intervention with a couple for which the female's insomnia was the presenting problem. Their purpose was to determine the immediate impact of the intervention on the couple's system. The interview was divided into three phases representing before, during, and after the intervention; base rate and sequential analyses were used to examine changes in interactive patterns across the phases. The results indicated that, following the intervention, many patterns showed significant changes. For example, the woman's use of high power and symmetrical behaviors with her partner emerged during the intervention; the man expanded his use of positive, supportive behaviors; and the symmetrical, negative, involving patterns between the partners were eliminated after the intervention.

Relation Between Process Variables and Other Variables

Studies that investigate the relation between process variables and theoretical orientations, stage of counseling, gender, and other variables use similar strategies to those that link process and outcome. The major difference is that the nonprocess (e.g., gender or theoretical orientation) variable is not an outcome variable. For example, Hill and O'Grady (1985) used this strategy successfully to study the use of intentions by therapists of varying theoretical orientations. They found, for example, that psychoanalytic orientations were related to the intentions Focus, Feelings, and Insight, whereas behavioral orientations were related to intentions Set Limits, Change, Reinforce, and Reinforce Change.

Investigators have examined the relation between process variables and a number of interesting variables, including the stages of counseling (Martin et al., 1986; Tracey, 1985, 1987), levels of counselor experience (Martin et al., 1986; Sipps, Sugden, & Faiver, 1988; Tracey, Hays, Malone, & Herman, 1988), gender (Nelson & Holloway, 1990), theoretical orientation (Hill & O'Grady, 1985; Holloway et al., 1989), level of working alliance between counselor and client (Reandeau & Wampold, 1991), client problem type (Cummings, 1989), type of training (Kivlighan, 1989), perceived expertness, trustworthiness, and attractiveness (Lee et al., 1985), and portions of a session (Friedlander et al., 1988; Hill et al., 1983; Holloway et al., 1990).

Validity of Process Research

The purpose of this chapter is not to review substantive results. However, from an epistemological vantage point, a critical review of process research strategies is needed to judge the validity of findings from this important area of counseling psychology research. The sections that follow examine the statistical, internal, construct, external, and hypothesis validity of process research.

Statistical Conclusion Validity

Because the statistical analysis of process research data is particularly complex, it is not surprising that there are a number of threats to statistical conclusion validity in this research. Although all of the possible threats to statistical conclusion validity discussed by Cook and Campbell (1979) can be problematic in process research, two seem to be particularly pernicious in this context: violation of assumptions of statistical tests and the fishing and error rate problem. Cognizance of these threats will avoid creating artifacts rather than art.

Violation of the assumptions of statistical tests detracts from a number of conclusions reached by process researchers. One of the ubiquitous assumptions of commonly used statistical tests is independence of observations. Although these tests are arguably robust with regard to violation of other assumptions (e.g., normality or homogeneity of variance), violation of the independence assumption is especially pernicious (Darlington & Carlson, 1987; Hopkins, 1982; Wampold & Drew, 1990). Nevertheless, process researchers frequently analyze their data as if the observations were independent, when clearly they are not. For example, repeated measurements of the same individual (or dyad) are not independent and probably should not be treated as such. This problem is most apparent when each event (e.g., speaking turn) in a session is considered a unit of observation and when the events are assumed to be independent of each other. Hill, Helms, Spiegel, and Tichenor (1988) compared helpfulness ratings of two clusters of client reactions generated from five clients with an analysis of variance with 12,221 degrees of freedom in the denominator; the impact of dependence on the F test is unknown. Dependence is also a problem when counseling dyads are sampled in such a way that each counselor is paired with several clients (i.e., clients are nested within counselors). Imaginative statistical solutions to the dependent observation problem have been presented, involving either using groups of subjects as units (e.g., a classroom or a therapeutic group) or modeling the dependence (see Darlington & Carlson, 1987; Hopkins, 1982).

Multicollinearity is another violation of an assumption that causes particular problems in process research. Because there are a fixed number of events in a session, frequencies of categories in a coding system are linearly dependent (i.e., if the frequencies of $k - 1$ of the k categories are given, the frequency of the kth category is determined). Thus, many procedures that analyze the frequencies of all categories will result in indeterminate solutions. Eliminating one category from the analysis eliminates the statistical problem but the conceptual problem remains: if one category has a high frequency, another has to have a low frequency, which confuses attributions of causality (i.e., is some outcome related to the high or to the low frequency event?). This problem is attenuated when particular events are examined because of their theoretical or practical significance (Wampold, 1986).

Statistical procedures unique to the analysis of social interactions have special and often misunderstood assumptions. For example, common assumptions of most sequential analyses are that (a) any behavior can follow itself and (b) the probability of an event is stationary across the session. Violation of the first assumption can lead to detection of artifactual patterns that reflect only the structure of the data rather than of the interaction (Wampold, 1986). The second assumption may be untenable because there are ebbs and flows within a counseling session, an observation supported both logically and empirically (Friedlander et al., 1988; Hill et al., 1983).

Another deleterious threat to the statistical conclusion validity of process research is the fishing and error rate problem. When there are numerous statistical tests, several will be significant by chance, and interpretations of these findings will be misguided. Although this is a problem for any research, it seems to be particularly problematic for process research, for two reasons. First, statistical tests are often calculated on each category of a coding system and on the transitions from one category to another. Second, because much process research is atheoretical, all possible relations between variables are legitimate objects for inquiry (Martin, 1991a), a point that we will discuss later in more detail. Consider Hill, Helms, Spiegel, and Tichenor's (1988) investigation of client reactions, which contained more than 300 statistical tests; most probably, many of the statistically significant tests were due to Type I Error rather than true relationships among the variables of interest.

Internal Validity

Threats to internal validity are particularly relevant to process research because only rarely are subjects randomly assigned to conditions. One of the major purposes of process research is to determine how what goes on in the session affects client outcomes. Without random assignment, obtained relationships between process variables and outcome may not represent causation. Consider Tracey's (1985) study of dominance, in which he found that the best cases in terms of outcome were characterized by counselor dominance in the middle stage of therapy, whereas no dominance was exhibited in the worst cases in any stage. Is counselor influence the cause of better outcomes? Because dyads were not randomly assigned to conditions, several alternative explanations become possible:

1. Resistant and difficult clients refuse to be influenced by the counselor, causing both a lack of dominance and poorer outcomes (client characteristics);
2. More prestigious appearing counselors lead to client attributions of counselor expertness, which cause the client to be more acquiescent and to improve (counselor characteristics);
3. Clients with better final outcomes saw improvement in the beginning stage of therapy and thus were willing to give up control to the counselor in the middle stage (contextual explanation).

Essentially, the passive nature of process research makes it virtually impossible to attribute causality to observed covariation between process and outcome variables for any particular study. However, the hope is that, over many studies, a persuasive case may be built for causal patterns (see earlier discussion of the link between smoking and disease). Suppose that the following can be obtained. Process measure A is correlated with outcome measure B over many studies, across theoretical orientations, and with clients with various problems and levels of dysfunction. Untrained counselors conduct sessions that are not characterized by the process measure and also have poorer outcomes, whereas trained counselors display the opposite pattern. Further, the process measure temporally precedes immediate and important outcomes, such as critical events, ratings of helpfulness, or highly memorial events. Moreover, counselors indicate that the process variable is an important aspect of their strategies. As well, suppose that there are well-articulated theoretical bases for the mechanisms of change involved (Martin, 1991a) and that the outcome variable reflects that mechanism (Brown & Heath, 1984). Finally, the research results are obtained by various methodologies and by various researchers (Shoham-Salomon, 1990). These convergent findings would establish, with a fairly high degree of certainty, the causal connection between process and outcome.

Construct Validity

Of the validities discussed, construct validity may pose the most troublesome threats to process research. What are the constructs being studied, and are they being properly and consistently operationalized? As an example of the difficulty in operationalizing constructs, consider the construct of control. Haley (1963) indicated that counselor control is a vital ingredient in successful counseling. Control can be defined as the emission of powerful statements and operationalized as the frequencies of various categories in coding systems. For example, the Relational Communication Control Coding System (Sluzki & Beavin, 1965/1977) contains the code UP, which indicates that the participant is attempting to exert control. Similarly, the Penman Coding System (1980) is constructed around the dimensions of power and involvement. Emission of codes that represent powerful behaviors has been labeled *expressed power* (Holloway et al., 1989). However, emission of a powerful behavior does not imply that it had an impact on the recipient. Often, an innocuous behavior will have a dramatic influence on another's behavior, depending on the relationship (e.g., a furtive glance by an explosive spouse). Therefore, an alternative way to define control is to examine the influence of a behavior. As discussed previously, if a client's behavior is more predictable from the counselor's than conversely, the counselor is said to be dominant (Tracey, 1985; Wampold & Kim, 1989). Control defined in this way has been called *achieved power* (Holloway et al., 1989). Still another way to operationalize control is to examine Topic Following and Topic Initiation, to assess who is determining the topic (Tracey & Ray, 1984). The role of control in counseling will not be clarified until the construct of control is understood (Tracey, 1991).

Ambiguity about constructs also arises in the area of counselor cognitions. Hill and O'Grady (1985) defined intentions as "a therapist's rationale for selecting a specific behavior, response mode, technique, or intervention" (p. 3). Because the counselor's rationale is covert, intentions must be assessed by means other than observation. A popular means used to assess intentions is through interpersonal process recall (Kagan, 1975), in which the counselor reviews a tape and stops after each statement to indicate his or her rationale for making the statement. Hill and O'Grady assessed intentions by having the counselor select a statement from a list of intentions. Hill and O'Grady (1985) developed the list without theoretical bases, so that theory would not direct the inquiry and the results would be open to interpretation from various perspectives (Hill, 1990; this issue is discussed in more detail below). In spite of the nontheoretical nature of the intentions list, there is confusion about the construct validity of the results. At a basic level, there are differences in how the intentions should be generated. Hill and O'Grady (1985) had counselors select intentions from a list, for each counselor statement; Martin et al. (1989) had counselors describe as completely as possible their thoughts, and then coded these thoughts by using the list of intentions developed by Hill and O'Grady. The former strategy places a structure on the responses that the latter does not. Whether this methodological difference affects the results is an empirical question. On a conceptual level, Stiles (1987) argued that a nontheoretical investigation of intentions ignores relevant psycholinguistic theory about verbal discourse. With regard to construct validity, clarity about the nature of intentions and their operations is needed.

Another problem related to construct validity is the variety of measures used to study process. As noted earlier, over the past 5 years, we found in the *JCP* 15 different systems for coding overt counselor and client events. More troubling was that it was extremely rare for any two groups of researchers to use the same system. The issues are whether the same or different constructs are being measured by these systems and whether this diffusion of methods prevents convergence of findings across laboratories. In the case of theoretically derived coding systems, different constructs are being operationalized and comparison of results of studies using different constructs is conceptually inappropriate. Nevertheless, some data show that there is a modicum of convergence in process research results. For example, Elliott et al. (1987) compared six systems designed to categorize counselor responses and found agreement for the six behaviors that the systems had in common (question, information, advisement, reflection, interpretation, and self-disclosure). Martin et al. (1989) identified action-act sequences that were similar to those identified earlier by Hill and O'Grady (1985), although the methods used were different in several important ways.

Construct validity becomes an issue when one examines the source of data in process research. If several variables are measuring the same construct, then they should be at least moderately consistent. However, a number of studies have found that consequential differences exist for data generated from various sources, even though the same phenomenon was purportedly being assessed. For example, differences have been found between counselor and client evaluations of sessions (Stiles & Snow, 1984a); counselor and client ratings of helpfulness (Hill, Helms, Tichenor, et al., 1988); correlations of process and outcome variables for counselors, clients, and observers (Hill, Helms, Tichenor, et al., 1988; Wampold & Kim, 1989); judge and client ratings of nonverbal behavior (Lee et al., 1985); counselor and client perceptions of intentions and their relationship to session effectiveness (Fuller & Hill, 1985); and counselor and client ratings of empathic statements and their relation to response modes (Barkham & Shapiro, 1986). As an example of the confusion that can result from ignoring the source, consider a study by Lee et al. (1985), who found that client perceptions of counselor expertness, trustworthiness, and attractiveness were not predicted by independent judges' ratings of the counselor's verbal and nonverbal behavior but rather were predicted by the *client's perceptions* of the counselor's nonverbal behavior.

The source of the data is an important consideration in any process investigation (see Holloway, 1984, for a discussion of this issue in the context of supervision). It should be noted that Martin has explicitly examined how the match between client and counselor cognitions would be related to outcome (Martin et al., 1987). Surprisingly, Martin et al. (1987) fond that accurate client perceptions of counselor intentions negatively correlated with ratings of effectiveness, raising the possibility that discrepancies among sources may be related to successful outcomes. In any event, it should not be assumed that process and outcome constructs are unrelated to the source from which they are derived.

Most studies linking counseling process and outcome have used intermediate measures of outcome, such as the Session Evaluation Questionnaire (SEQ; Stiles & Snow, 1984b). The presumption is that intermediate outcomes are related to final outcomes (and thus may be a proxy for final outcome measures), although this certainly may not be the case (Garfield, 1990). Garfield (1990) criticized process research for its inability to tie process to final outcome. On the positive side, Hill and her colleagues (Hill et al., 1983; Hill, Helms, Spiegel, & Tichenor, 1988; Hill, Helms, Tichenor, et al., 1988) have been especially diligent to include final outcome measures.

External Validity

External validity poses a problem for process researchers because the intensive nature of the research typically requires small sample sizes. Hill et al.'s (1983) intensive case study of 12 sessions illustrates the effort required to study process comprehensively and to link it to outcome. Nevertheless, the small sample sizes raise the issue of generalizability. Hill and her colleagues (e.g., Hill et al., 1983; Hill, Helms, Tichenor, et al., 1988; Hill & O'Grady, 1985) have used a variety of case studies—small n and large n—to investigate counseling process. Tracey (1986) found in a small n study (2 successful dyads, 2 unsuccessful dyads, and 2 dyads that were terminated prematurely) that dyads that terminated prematurely had lower levels of topic determination. This investigation was then followed by a large n study (18 dyads) that confirmed the relationship between termination and topic determination, thereby increasing the generalizability of the findings.

On the one hand, there has been a hope that the processes in counseling would be uniform; that is, interactive patterns would be related to outcome consistently across theoretical orientations, experience, gender, and so forth (Martin et al., 1989). However, increasingly, there has been a recognition that process may be specific for various types of clients, counselors, and matches. Martin et al. (1990) developed and tested a model that specifies differences in information processing of clients with counselors of various theoretical orientations. Others also have found differences in process variables for theoretical orientations (e.g., Hill & O'Grady, 1985).

One variable conspicuously missing, with few exceptions, from investigations of counseling process is the gender of the counselor and client. In the context of supervision, Nelson and Holloway (1990) found that (a) male and female trainees used a significantly greater number of high-power messages with female supervisors than with male supervisors, (b) male and female supervisors reinforced their female trainees' high-power messages with low power, and (c) female trainees responded to supervisor low-power encouraging messages with high-power messages significantly less often than did male trainees. Nelson and Holloway's findings raise the specter that we have again fallen into the uniformity myth (Kiesler, 1966) by assuming that we can identify a "process" that is optimal for clients, regardless of their gender, presenting problems, education, previous counseling experience, and other characteristics. To strengthen the external validity of process research, we must examine the interaction of the results with various client characteristics, counselor characteristics, settings, and so forth.

Hypothesis Validity

Hypothesis validity refers to deriving crucial research hypotheses from theory, stating the research hypotheses clearly, matching statistical hypotheses to research hypotheses, and conducting focused statistical tests (Wampold et al., 1990). Hypothesis validity is relevant to inquiries shaped by theory. Although the need for theory-driven psychotherapy research has often been stated (Martin, 1991a; Meehl, 1978), others have made the case for exploratory or discovery-oriented research (Elliott, 1984; Hill, 1990; Mahrer, 1988). The distinction between these approaches to process research clarifies various issues related to hypothesis validity.

Ideally, theory-driven research results in strategic tests of theoretical propositions (Meehl, 1978; Serlin, 1987; Wampold et al., 1990). The constructs selected for study and the hypothesized relation between or among them are derived from theory. Elegant theoretical studies will result in focused tests of a statistical hypothesis; the result of the statistical test will provide information about the research hypothesis, which in turn will inform theory. Theory will be revised to accommodate new findings or be discarded if sufficiently at variance with obtained results. Although such a neat enterprise is not often achieved in applied psychology (see, for example, Meehl, 1978), many argue that this conception should guide our inquiry (Martin, 1991a; Wampold et al., 1990).

The advocates of discovery-oriented research claim that theory-driven research has not advanced our knowledge in counseling process because (a) theory-driven research has not and really cannot succeed in confirming or disconfirming theoretical propositions, and (b) research results from programs of theory-based research have not resulted in an accumulation of knowledge (Hill, 1990; Mahrer, 1988). Discovery-oriented research is not guided by theory and thus avoids the restrictions of theory-based research. The short-term objective of discovery-oriented process research is to "describe what occurs within psychotherapy sessions from a nontheoretical stance" (Hill, 1990, p. 288). Discovery-oriented research is the first step in the scientific method: observation, hypothesis formulation, hypothesis testing, replication, and development of theory (Hill, 1990).

Hill (1990) argued that research endeavors are often a blend of theory-driven and discovery-oriented strategies. Nevertheless, it will be instructive to examine lines of research emanating from these two approaches. Hill and her colleagues (Hill, 1978; 1986; Hill, Helms, Spiegel, & Tichenor, 1988; Hill & O'Grady, 1985) conducted a series of studies that are essentially nontheoretical. The basic model underlying these investigations is that "therapist intentions lead to therapist response modes that in turn lead to client reactions and to overt behavior" (Hill, Helms, Spiegel, & Tichenor, 1988, p. 27). Hill's efforts have focused on developing systems for categorizing the four components and on investigating how the four components relate to each other. The exploratory nature of the research has consequences for the method. First, because theory is not invoked to make predictions about the relations among the components, all possible permutations are examined (Martin, 1991a). For example, Hill and O'Grady (1985) performed a sequential analysis of all transitions from therapist intentions to therapist response modes and from therapist intentions to client response modes. A second implication of exploratory research is that there is no attempt to reference underlying constructs. Intentions and reactions are defined primarily by their operations.

The research of Martin and his colleagues (Martin et al., 1986, 1987, 1989, 1990) provides a good example of research driven by theory, namely the cognitive mediational paradigm (Martin, 1984). Martin (1984) predicted that "the degree of correspondence between a client's cognitive perceptions of and reactions to a counselor's behaviors and intentions will mediate the client's immediate and longer-term learning from counseling, thus determining how effective counseling will be" (p. 562). Accordingly, Martin et al. (1986) developed a measure of matches between client behavior and cognitions and counselor behavior and cognitions, and related this matching variable to outcome. Based on results of this work, Martin (Martin et al., 1987; Martin et al., 1990) altered the cognitive mediational paradigm (Martin, 1984) to make specific predictions about how counseling process, and particularly the information processing of clients, will differ according to differing theoretical orientations. Both methodologically and conceptually, Martin's program of research has also moved from an earlier emphasis on participants' cognitive processes to focusing on participants' memories of important therapeutic events (Martin et al., 1990).

There are important differences between discovery-oriented and theory-driven approaches. Discovery-oriented research does not limit the inquiry to those questions that are theoretically interesting, and thus leaves open the door to serendipitous findings. Serendipity has had a splendid place in the history of the natural sciences. On the other hand, theory results in questions that may have never occurred to the discovery-oriented researcher. For example, Tracey et al. (1988) considered two types of response learning—response acquisition and strategy acquisition—to hypothesize that experienced counselors, who focus on strategies rather than responses, would demonstrate increased response flexibility. Response flexibility was defined as the standard deviation of each counselor's responses around his or her mean number of responses. Without theoretical considerations, it is doubtful that this variable would have been examined.

The challenge to theory-driven researchers is to show that empirical investigations do result in revision or rejection of theory and that there is a convergence to tenable theoretical propositions regarding counseling process. The challenge to discovery-oriented researchers is to identify consequential and consistent processes and to develop theories of counseling that are novel and conceptually tenable.

In spite of the differences between theory-driven and discovery-oriented research, it is interesting to note that one of the most conspicuous convergences in process research is between the results of Hill and O'Grady's (1985) counselor intentions–therapist response mode–client response mode sequences and Martin et al.'s (1989) action–act sequences. Such congruence adds credence to Hill's (1990) discussion of the blending of the two research strategies.

It could be argued that no study is truly nontheoretical; that is, there is an implicit theory behind any inquiry. For example, both Hill and O'Grady's (1985) and Martin's (1984) sequences of therapist intention–therapist response mode–client reaction–client response mode assume that behaviors and cognitions are discrete, linear, and unidirectional. The linearity of behavior is reasonable because behaviors are observable and unfold over time. However, questions can be raised as to whether cognitions are similarly discrete and linear (Martin, 1984). Cognitions, especially higher-order processes, likely are continuous and interconnected and may surround and permeate behavior in complex ways. Both the Hill and O'Grady model and the Martin model tend to assume that behavior and cognitions are of the same order. The metaphysical status of these variables needs to be carefully considered. Martin (1991b) and Patton (1982, 1989) have made a convincing case that exhibited behaviors are actually outcomes (i.e., they are observable results of internal processes) and that process is covert and can only be inferred from the observables. This is not a meaningless semantic debate; the implications for research methods are real (Patton, 1989). For example, sequential analyses of behavior–cognition sequences assume that the two types of variables have equal status and occur in linear fashion.

Comments on Process Research

Counseling process research is characterized by a diversity of methods, strategies, and goals. We have imposed a structure on this literature, realizing that many important issues would fall between the cracks. The discussion here was focused on unique issues raised in counseling process research; other sources contain discussion of general issues related to understanding social interactions. For example, we have omitted a discussion of interrater agreement for coding systems because that topic is covered elsewhere (e.g., Bakeman & Gottman, 1986).

The diversity of methods in counseling process research represents both a strength and a weakness. The strength lies in the fact that results will not be unique to a particular methodological approach. The weakness involves the subsequent difficulty in integrating findings. Can the divergent findings be integrated into a coherent picture of what happens in the counseling session and how this leads to client improvement?

DETERMINING TREATMENT EFFECTIVENESS

Without a doubt, determining the effectiveness of interventions is one of the most important, if not the most important, general goals of research on counseling. Which interventions are most effective with which type of clients in which settings (Krumboltz, 1966; Paul, 1967; Williamson, 1939)? Prototypically, outcome studies are amenable to experimental designs in which subjects are randomly assigned to treatment and control conditions, treatments are administered, and posttreatment functioning is assessed. Data from these designs typically are analyzed with analyses of variance or other traditional parametric statistical tests. However appealing, this prototype often is not possible or even desirable. Institutional constraints, ethical issues, design problems, unusual research questions, and other issues more often than not place limitations on the design and analysis of outcome studies.

There have been numerous discussions of design and analysis of outcome studies in counseling and psychotherapy (Gottman & Markman, 1978; Kazdin, 1980, 1986a, 1986b; Lambert, Christensen, & DeJulio, 1983). Therefore, we will highlight several methodological issues related to outcome research, specifically (a) size of treatment effect, (b) meta-analyses, (c) multiple dependent variables, and (d) repeated measures. Each of these issues represents some deficiency in the prototypical model or some extension of this model to improve the validity of the inferences drawn. Incidentally, many of the issues discussed here have applications to research areas other than outcome research, and these will be noted.

Size of the Treatment Effect

Statistical tests determine whether there is sufficient evidence to reject the null hypothesis; that is, if the magnitude of the test statistic is sufficiently large, the null hypothesis is rejected in favor of some alternative. In the case of treatment studies, the alternative hypothesis reflects the effectiveness of the treatment (e.g., the mean of treated persons is greater than the mean of untreated persons). Basically, statistical tests indicate whether an observed relationship between the independent and dependent variable is reliable: If the experiment were repeated, would the treatment effect be observed again? Thus, statistical tests provide information about whether a true effect exists.

It is important to understand what information statistical tests do *not* provide. Statistical tests do not index the size or the clinical significance of the treatment effect. Rejection of the null hypothesis indicates good reason to believe that there is a nonzero effect, but it does not indicate whether the effect is small or large. The size of the effect is important because it answers the question: *How* effective or clinically important is the treatment? Essentially, an effect size is a measure of the magnitude of the relationship between the independent and dependent variables. A statistically significant result may be the consequence of a treatment that is minimally effective; similarly, the treatment may be very effective and the result statistically nonsignificant (Fagley, 1985; Paquin, 1983, Rosnow & Rosenthal, 1988; Wampold, Furlong, & Atkinson, 1983).

In the simplest treatment study, the researcher is interested in the difference between the treated population and the untreated population. The most direct way to index the effect size in such a case is to contrast the means of the two populations. When expressed in terms of standard deviation units, the effect size would thus be $(\mu_T - \mu_C)/\sigma$, where μ_T is the population mean for treated individuals, μ_C is the population mean for untreated individuals, and σ is the standard deviation of the populations (under the assumption of homogeneity of variance).

To be useful to the researcher, estimators of the population effect size are needed. A straightforward estimator of the effect size between a treated and untreated population is

$$(M_T - M_C)/s_{pooled}$$

where M_T is the obtained mean of the treated subjects, M_C is the obtained mean for the untreated subjects and s_{pooled} is the unbiased estimator of the population variance found by pooling the scores of all subjects. (For simplicity, we will use "effect size" to refer to the sample rather than the population value.) Several variants of this formula, based on different variances and corrections for bias, have been discussed in the technical literature (Cohen, 1988; Glass, McGaw, & Smith, 1981; Hedges & Olkin, 1985). Because this discussion is focused on conceptual and nontechnical issues, the differences between

these variants will not be discussed here, although technical issues do become important in several contexts (Hedges & Olkin, 1985; Mitchell & Hartmann, 1981; Murray &
Dosser, 1987; O'Grady, 1982). There are many other forms of effect size that do not
rely on the differences between means (Cohen, 1988; Glass et al., 1981; Hedges &
Olkin, 1985; Rosenthal, 1984); some of them will be discussed as necessary below.

A primary issue involves the interpretation of the obtained effect size. For example,
if the effect size was .75, should the researcher be excited? In this section, several ways
to interpret effect sizes will be discussed. Smith and Glass (1977), in their meta-analysis
of outcome studies, displayed a particularly useful way to understand effect sizes in the
context of treatment studies. If normality is assumed, then the distributions for the
treated and untreated populations can be superimposed to compare treated and untreated individuals. For example, if an effect size of .75 (using the formula discussed
above) is obtained, then the average treated individual is better off than 77% of the
untreated individuals, as shown in Figure 3.3. This method provides a convenient and
understandable way to present and explain effect size.

Another way to assess the size of an effect is to compare it to effect sizes obtained in
a particular area of inquiry. Haase, Waechter, and Solomon (1982) surveyed research
published in the *Journal of Counseling Psychology* for the years 1970 to 1979 to determine the size of effects in counseling psychology. In their analysis, Haase et al. (1982)
used the index η^2, which is equivalent to R^2, the sample proportion of variance accounted for in the dependent variable by the independent variables (Wampold & Drew,
1990). Measures that index proportion of variance accounted for are used frequently to
describe the size of an effect. For the years 1970 to 1979, the median η^2 was .0830. The
effect size referenced above ($M_1 - M_2)/s_{pooled} = .75$) is equivalent to an η^2 of .14, a value
that exceeds Haase et al.'s median value for counseling research. Comparison to Haase
et al.'s distribution can be problematic because effect sizes in counseling research are
unlikely to be homogeneous across the various topical areas of counseling research. For
example, the effect sizes for vocational and personal counseling may be different.
However, a researcher investigating treatment efficacy in a specified area (e.g., social
anxiety of adolescents) may find it useful to compare obtained effect sizes with established effect sizes in this specific area.

To facilitate the calculation of power, Cohen (1988) created a taxonomy of effect
sizes. Based on numerous examples from many fields, he classified effect sizes as small,
medium, or large (effect sizes of .2, .5, and .8, respectively, calculated as differences in
means divided by standard deviation). Classification of effects into these three classes
provides a description of the obtained effects. However, it should be realized that
Cohen's taxonomy has been considered arbitrary (Glass et al., 1981) and certainly does
not apply equally well to all specific areas of research inquiry. The effect size of .75
discussed above is slightly smaller than a large effect.

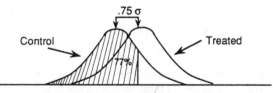

Figure 3.3 Distributions for control and treated subjects for an effect size of .75 standard deviation units.

Another intriguing method for interpreting effect size is discussed by Rosenthal (1984; Rosenthal & Rubin, 1982; Rosnow & Rosenthal, 1988), who used the correlation coefficient r to assess practical significance. When used with focused tests (tests that are used to answer specific questions; see Rosnow & Rosenthal, 1988), r can be conveniently tied to outcomes in an understandable way. Essentially, the effect size is displayed as a 2 (treatment, control) by 2 (improved, not improved) Binomial Effect-Size Display (BESD; Rosenthal & Rubin, 1982). For the continuing example, the original effect size of .75 is equivalent to an r of .37, which then results in the BESD shown in Table 3.2, illustrating that the success rate increased from .31 to .69. It should be noted that the BESD assumes that overall 50% improve; Wampold and Brown (1992) altered the BESD to reflect other improvement rates.

Rosenthal (1990; Rosnow & Rosenthal, 1988) made a cogent argument that focusing on proportion of variance is misleading and that attention to the correlation coefficient leads to more meaningful conclusions. For example, Rosnow and Rosenthal pointed out that the correlation coefficient for the effect of aspirin on heart attacks was .03; for Vietnam service and alcohol consumption, .07; for AZT and survival with AIDS, .23, and for counseling/psychotherapy and outcome, .32. Thus, while counseling/psychotherapy accounts for "only" 10% of the variance in outcome (i.e., $(.32)^2$), the size of this effect exceeds that of several well-known and important results (aspirin and heart attacks, Vietnam service and alcohol consumption, and AZT and AIDS survival)!

Another way to examine effect size is to determine the clinical significance of a result. Until recently, clinical significance was defined qualitatively, for example, as a large change, an improvement in everyday functioning, a change recognizable by peers and significant others, elimination of the presenting problem, and posttreatment functioning that is similar to functional peers (Jacobson, Follette, & Revenstorf, 1984; Kazdin, 1977). Jacobson, Follette, and Revenstorf (1984) developed statistical procedures to determine whether individual clients were clinically improved. Clinical significance is obtained when "the client moves from the dysfunctional to the functional range during the course of therapy" (p. 340). Using the distributions of the normal and dysfunctional populations, they developed formulas for determining whether a client has clinically improved. To determine, as well, that the change is reliable (i.e., not due to chance), Jacobson, Follette, and Revenstorf (1984) also proposed a "reliable change index." Errors in the original reliable change index (Christensen & Mendoza, 1986) led to some modifications (Jacobson & Revenstorf, 1988). Indexes of clinical significance and reliable change could be used in individual studies to determine the proportion of subjects who were clinically and reliably improved, as well as to establish the efficacy of various treatments. With regard to the latter strategy, these methods have been used to establish the efficacy of behavioral marital therapy (Jacobson, Follette, Revenstorf, Baucom, et al., 1984), exposure-based interventions for agoraphobia (Jacobson,

Table 3.2 Binomial Effect–Size Display (BESD) for r = .37

| Condition | Success Rate | | Total |
	Improved	Not Improved	
Treatment	68.5	31.5	100
Control	31.5	68.5	100
Total	100.0	100.0	

Wilson, & Tupper, 1988), and interventions designed to increase satisfaction with social support (Brown, Brady, Lent, Wolfert, & Hall, 1987).

As with any method to examine efficacy, effect size measures have their own problems (Hollon & Flick, 1988; Mitchell & Hartmann, 1981; Murray & Dosser, 1987; Nietzel & Trull, 1988; O'Grady, 1982, Wampold & Jenson, 1986). Nevertheless, effect size does provide information unavailable from statistical tests; many recommend that effect sizes be routinely reported (Cohen, 1988; Fagley, 1985; Folger, 1989). Ellis, Robbins, Shult, Ladany, and Banker (1990) provided a nice example of the utility of examining effect size. Besides using effect size to establish the strength of their findings (although not in the context of a treatment study), they also used effect size to corroborate a theoretical model of errors in clinical judgment. The correlation between the predicted effect sizes (under a mitigation hypothesis) and the obtained effect sizes was .93, very strong evidence indeed.

Meta-Analyses

Because individual studies inevitably have threats to their validity, drawing conclusions from many studies leads to a more accurate representation of the true relation among psychological constructs (Heppner et al., 1992). Meta-analyses are quantitative means to integrate the findings from studies investigating the same or similar research questions and have the capacity to establish the efficacy of treatments, to determine what factors influence this efficacy, and to corroborate theoretical predictions. Essentially, meta-analysis involves calculating the effect size for a treatment for all the studies (or for a sample of the studies) in a given area, and then analyzing these effects to determine the average effect size and to relate the effect sizes to such moderating variables as therapist experience, type of study, type of control group, setting, and so forth (Glass et al., 1981; Hedges & Olkin, 1985; Hunter, Schmidt, & Jackson, 1982; Rosenthal, 1984).

Meta-analyses became popular with Smith and Glass's (1977) meta-analysis of psychotherapy outcome studies. Their meta-analysis of 375 studies with 833 effect sizes of about 25,000 subjects yielded an average effect size of .68 (calculated as difference between treatment and control mean in control standard deviation units), indicating that the average treated subject was better off than 75% of untreated subjects. Furthermore, they found that generally there were few differences in effect size among diverse approaches to counseling and psychotherapy. Finally, a number of variables mediated effect size, including intelligence of subjects, similarity of therapists and clients, internal validity of the study, and reactivity of the outcome measure.

Meta-analytic methods are beginning to appear in specific areas of counseling. For example, Baker, Daniels, and Greeley (1990) meta-analyzed the studies investigating three counselor training modalities: human resource training/human resource development (HRT/HRD), interpersonal process recall (IPR), and microcounseling (MC). They found that mean effect sizes (expressed as differences between means in standard deviation units) for HRT/HRD, IPR, and MC were 1.15, 0.20, and 0.69, respectively. According to Cohen's taxonomy, these results correspond to a large effect for HRT/HRD, a small effect for IPR, and a medium-size effect for MC. Baker et al. (1990) found that moderating variables, such as methodological characteristics, nature of the comparison groups, length of the training program, and complexity of the skills taught, generally had little effect on the size of the effect for any of the training modalities.

Holloway and Wampold (1986) examined studies of conceptual level and counseling-related tasks, as well as studies of the interaction between conceptual level and structure of the environment. Their meta-analysis of 24 studies (and 176 effects) demonstrated that

(a) high conceptual level thinkers performed better in counseling-related tasks than did low conceptual level thinkers, and (b) counselors matched with a compatible environment (low conceptual thinkers in relatively structured environments and high conceptual thinkers in relatively unstructured environments) performed better than did subjects in incompatible environments (low conceptual thinkers in relatively unstructured environments and high conceptual thinkers in relatively structured environments), as predicted by conceptual systems theory. Various moderating variables were found to affect the results; for example, the quality of the design was inversely related to the effect size for studies investigating conceptual level and performance.

Multiple Dependent Variables

One of the threats to construct validity is mono-operation bias (Cook & Campbell, 1979). Mono-operation bias refers to, in part, conclusions drawn from single measures of an outcome construct, such as depression. Single operations underrepresent the construct and contain irrelevancies; consequently, the construct is poorly operationalized. To avoid mono-operation threats, it is often recommended that multiple measures be used to represent an outcome construct (Cook & Campbell, 1979; Heppner et al., 1992; Kazdin, 1980; Lambert, Shapiro, & Bergin, 1986). In treatment studies, the number of outcome measures can become large because there will likely be several constructs targeted for change (e.g., depression, anxiety, and self-concept) and possibly several constructs related to side effects. Counseling researchers have heeded the advice and are using multiple dependent measures in their studies (Wampold, 1987a). (See Lambert et al., 1986, for a comprehensive discussion of outcome variables in psychotherapy and counseling.)

Although using multiple dependent measures has the potential to increase the construct validity of a study, this practice also complicates the analysis used and the inferences made (Wampold et al., 1990). The question is raised: How should multiple dependent measures be analyzed? For illustration, consider a study with three groups (treatment, placebo control group, and wait-list control group) and several outcome measures. A separate analysis of variance could be conducted for each of the outcome measures. This univariate approach is flawed, for two reasons. First, the probability of making a Type I Error is increased dramatically (Haase & Ellis, 1987; Hays, 1988; Leary & Altmaier, 1980). Second, the inferences made are confused because measures of the same construct may not yield similar results (e.g., some measures of a construct may yield statistically significant results whereas others may not; see Wampold et al., 1990). Multivariate approaches are needed when multiple dependent variables are utilized.

The most often used multivariate procedure for analyzing multiple outcome measures is the multivariate analysis of variance (MANOVA; Haase & Ellis, 1987). The MANOVA simultaneously tests the outcome measures and thus provides a single test of significance. Although this procedure protects against inflated Type I Error rates (but see Huberty & Morris, 1989), the inferential ambiguity remains:

> The omnibus null hypothesis in multivariate analysis of variance subsumes an even larger [than the univariate omnibus F test] set of mostly uninterpretable [italics added] contrasts performed on mostly uninterpretable [italics added] linear combinations of the dependent variables. (Serlin, 1987, p. 370)

To aid in interpretation, significant MANOVAs are often followed up with univariate analyses of variance for each outcome measure. However, this too leads to inferential confusion because the pattern of results may be partially consistent with theoretical predictions, reducing the hypothesis validity of the study (Wampold et al., 1990).

The trick in multivariate methods is to perform an analysis that is interpretable. Although there is no unanimity about how to approach this problem, procedures for interpreting results with multiple dependent measures that preserve both the construct and hypothesis validity of the study have been suggested. Bray and Maxwell (1982) recommended following up significant MANOVAs with a discriminant analysis (Betz, 1987). Examination of the discriminant function provides information about the linear combinations of the outcome measures that contribute to the significant MANOVA.

Another suggestion for analyzing multiple dependent variables is to separate conceptually independent outcome variables (Biskin, 1980; Huberty & Morris, 1989; Wampold et al., 1990). Conceptually independent variables are variables that either measure different constructs or are referenced in separate research hypotheses. Horan and his colleagues (Cianni & Horan, 1990; McNamara & Horan, 1986) separated cognitive and behavioral variables to examine the construct validity of treatments for depression and assertiveness training. In the depression study, it was expected that cognitive and behavioral therapies would affect the cognitive and behavioral variables differently (McNamara & Horan, 1986). They found that the cognitive treatment affected the cognitive outcomes measures with some generalization to behavioral measures, although the behavioral treatment affected neither the behavioral nor the cognitive measures.

The use of latent variables offers a propitious alternative for analyzing multiple dependent variables. Latent variables are statistical entities that underlie observed variables. If five outcome measures are hypothesized to measure a construct, then the latent variable formed from these five observed variables constitutes the redundancies within the observed variables and excludes the irrelevancies, thereby increasing the construct validity. The latent variables can then be analyzed as if they were entities in and of themselves. The statistical procedures for forming latent variables (called the measurement model) and relating the latent variables (called the structural model) are encompassed in statistical procedures called structural equation modeling. Application of these methods to counseling psychology research has been discussed by Fassinger (1987).

Repeated Measures

In the simplest outcome study, the subjects are assessed solely at the end of treatment. There are obvious limitations to a single assessment of posttreatment functioning; for example, subjects may relapse (at various times), the effects of treatment may not be immediate, the pattern of change is ignored, the statistical power of such designs is relatively low, and attrition results in missing data. The use of assessments over time (e.g., follow-up data) is not unusual in treatment studies. The typical means to analyze data from measures obtained over time is the repeated measures analysis of variance, a topic covered in most elementary statistics texts. The focus of this discussion will be on alternative procedures that offer certain advantages.

There are instances in which a variable of interest is the amount of time after treatment that elapses before a stipulated outcome occurs. For example, the researcher may be interested in the number of months that pass before a relapse, the number of minutes of playground activity before a targeted child exhibits an aggressive behavior, the number of sessions until termination, and so on. There are two straightforward, although misleading and/or not powerful, means to analyze such data. One method would be to compare the proportion of those that respond in each group in a given period of time; the other method would be to compare the median response times.

A method that is more powerful and informative than examining proportions or response times involves survival analysis. Survival analysis compares the cumulative proportion of cases "surviving" (i.e., those who have not exhibited the targeted outcome) in each group at frequent time periods. For example, Figure 3.4 presents the (fictitious) survival curves for two approaches to brief therapy, where "survival" indicates that the client has not dropped out of therapy before the 15th and final session. It appears that approach A is more effective in preventing premature termination, although statistical tests are needed to confirm this inference made from the survival curves. Greenhouse, Stangl, and Bromberg (1989) presented an overview of survival analysis for clinical trials.

Kraemer and Thiemann (1989) discussed a method for analyzing data from randomized treatment studies that relies on indexes of slope as outcome measures rather than posttest assessments. The method involves assessing functioning at several time points during the treatment and calculating the slope at each time point using baseline (pretest) as the origin. The greater the magnitude of the slope, the greater the effect of treatment for a particular subject (in fact, posttest assessment and slope are perfectly correlated). The advantage of Kraemer and Thiemann's (1989) method is that the use of slope calculated from multiple measurements yields a more powerful statistical test and accommodates missing data.

Often, data on two or more variables are assessed at various time points, to investigate change. In these designs, it is difficult to assess whether X causes Y, Y causes X, or both are caused by some third variable. Consider the case of marital therapy, where two measures of interest are communication pattern and self-reported marital satisfaction; suppose that these two variables are measured over time. An important research question involves determining whether the therapy affects (a) the communication patterns, which in turn affect marital satisfaction; (b) marital satisfaction, which in turn affects the communication patterns; or (c) communication patterns and marital satisfaction directly and independently. Linear panel analysis (Kessler & Greenberg, 1981) is a collection of methods intended to answer these questions and other related questions.

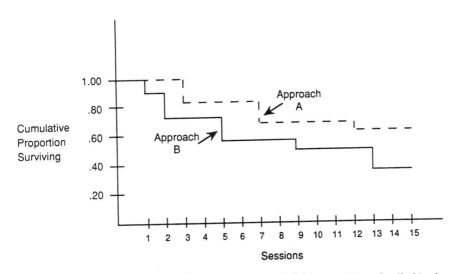

Figure 3.4 Fictitious survival curves for two approaches to brief therapy (15-session limit), where survival indicates that the client is still in therapy at a given session.

Other quantitative methods for assessing change in equivalent and nonequivalent designs have been recently discussed and have potential for counseling researchers (Bryk & Raudenbush, 1987; Bryk & Weisberg, 1977; Porter & Raudenbush, 1987; Rogosa, Brand, & Zimowski, 1982).

Comments on Outcome Research

Problematic areas of outcome studies have been examined here, to indicate how treatment effectiveness may be assessed. First, the size of the effect needs to be substantial enough to justify the expense of treatment. Several options for judging the size of an effect were discussed. If, over many studies, a reliable and sizable effect can be associated with a treatment, the efficacy of the treatment is established. However, care must be taken to ensure that the outcome measures are sensitive to the constructs being operationalized. The warning to avoid mono-operation bias has resulted in multiple outcome measures, raising many issues about how such data should be analyzed. Analysis of multiple measures must contend with threats to statistical conclusion validity, construct validity, and hypothesis validity. Finally, change is a process that unfolds over time and varies across clients; consequently, examination of repeated measures of outcome is appropriate.

DISCUSSION

Presenting an overview of counseling psychology research is a formidable challenge. Although we discussed the major trends in process research and examined some innovative ways to analyze outcomes, there are many modern developments in statistics, measurement, and research design that were beyond the scope of this chapter (Aiken, West, Sechrest, & Reno, 1990). The purpose of this chapter has been to discuss the state of the art in counseling psychology research. The frontiers of scientific research in counseling psychology, however, will be expanded by adapting new methods and refining old ones. We have purposefully not listed a series of recommendations for future research; advances in science originate from the creative and deductive processes of individual researchers (Platt, 1964).

An important caveat to the expanding frontier analogy is that it is based on a traditional research model. The methods discussed in this chapter rely, for the most part, on a positivistic base. That is, it is assumed that the laws of nature can be induced from data, that the process of helping clients can be understood by examining the component parts, that the knower and known are independent, that laws of behavior and behavior change are universal, and that the inquiry is value-free. It may well be that this positivistic strategy has obscured the real frontiers and that alternative research paradigms may yield a dimension not yet visible (Borgen, 1992; Gelso, 1984; Lincoln & Guba, 1985; Patton, 1989). Again, it is not the method, but rather the creative use of the method, that will expand frontiers and discover new worlds.

REFERENCES

Aiken, L. S., West, S. G., Sechrest, L., & Reno, R. R. (1990). Graduate training in statistics, methodology, and measurement in psychology: A survey of Ph.D. programs in North America. *American Psychologist, 45,* 721–734.

Allison, P. D., & Liker, J. K. (1982). Analyzing sequential categorical data on dyadic interaction: Comment on Gottman. *Psychological Bulletin, 91,* 393–403.

Bakeman, R., & Gottman, J. M. (1986). *Observing interaction: An introduction to sequential analysis.* Cambridge: Cambridge University Press.

Baker, S. B., Daniels, T. G., & Greeley, A. T. (1990). Systematic training of graduate-level counselors: Narrative and meta-analytic reviews of three major programs. *The Counseling Psychologist, 18,* 355–421.

Barkham, M., & Shapiro, D. A. (1986). Counselor verbal response modes and experienced empathy. *Journal of Counseling Psychology, 33,* 3–10.

Barlow, D. H., & Hersen, M. (1984). *Single case experimental designs: Strategies for studying behavior change* (2nd ed.). New York: Pergamom Press.

Bateson, G. (1958). *Naven.* Stanford, CA: Stanford University Press. (Original work published 1936)

Betz, N. E. (1987). Use of discriminant analysis in counseling psychology research. *Journal of Counseling Psychology, 34,* 393–403.

Biskin, B. H. (1980). Multivariate analysis in experimental counseling research. *The Counseling Psychologist, 8,* 69–72.

Borgen, F. H. (1992). Changing scientific paradigms and directions in counseling psychology. In S. D. Brown & R. W. Lent (Eds.), *Handbook of counseling psychology* (2nd ed., ch. 4). New York: Wiley.

Borgen, F. H., & Barnett, D. C. (1987). Applying cluster analysis in counseling psychology research. *Journal of Counseling Psychology, 34,* 456–468.

Bracht, G. H., & Glass, G. V. (1968). The external validity of experiments. *American Educational Research Journal, 5,* 437–474.

Bray, J. H., & Maxwell, S. E. (1982). Analyzing and interpreting significant MANOVAs. *Review of Educational Research, 52,* 340–367.

Brown, S. D., Brady, T., Lent, R. W., Wolfert, J., & Hall, S. (1987). Perceived social support among college students: Three studies of the psychometric characteristics and counseling uses of the Social Support Inventory. *Journal of Counseling Psychology, 34,* 337–354.

Brown, S. D., & Heath, L. (1984). Coping with critical life events: An integrative cognitive-behavioral model for research and practice. In S. D. Brown & R. W. Lent (Eds.), *Handbook of counseling psychology* (pp. 545–578). New York: Wiley.

Bryk, A. S., & Raudenbush, S. W. (1987). Application of hierarchical linear models to assessing change. *Psychological Bulletin, 101,* 147–158.

Bryk, A. S., & Weisberg, H. I. (1977). Use of the nonequivalent control group design when subjects are growing. *Psychological Bulletin, 84,* 950–962.

Budescu, D. V. (1984). Tests of lagged dominance in sequential dyadic interaction. *Psychological Bulletin, 96,* 402–414.

Cacioppo, J. T., & Petty, R. E. (1981). Social psychology procedures for cognitive assessment: The thought-listing technique. In T. V. Merluzzi, C. R. Glass, & M. Genest (Eds.), *Cognitive assessment* (pp. 309–342). New York: Guilford Press.

Campbell, D. T., & Stanley, J. C. (1966). *Experimental and quasi-experimental designs for research.* Chicago: Rand McNally.

Christensen, L., & Mendoza, J. L. (1986). A method of assessing change in a single subject: An alteration of the RC Index. *Behavior Therapy, 17,* 305–308.

Cianni, M., & Horan, J. J. (1990). An attempt to establish the experimental construct validity of cognitive and behavioral approaches to assertiveness training. *Journal of Counseling Psychology, 37,* 243–247.

Cohen, J. (1968). Multiple regression as a general data-analytic strategy. *Psychological Bulletin, 70,* 426–443.

Cohen, J. (1988). *Statistical power analysis for the behavioral sciences* (2nd ed). Hillsdale, NJ: Erlbaum.

Cook, T. D., & Campbell, D. T. (1979). *Quasi-experimentation: Design and analysis issues for field settings.* Boston: Houghton Mifflin.

Cummings, A. L. (1989). Relationship of client problem type to novice counselor response modes. *Journal of Counseling Psychology, 36,* 331–335.

Darlington, R. B., & Carlson, P. M. (1987). *Behavioral statistics: Logic and methods.* New York: Free Press.

Dumas, J. E. (1986). Controlling for autocorrelation in social interaction analysis. *Psychological Bulletin, 100,* 125–127.

Elliott, R. (1980). *Therapy session report: Short forms for client and therapist.* Unpublished manuscript, University of Toledo.

Elliott, R. (1984). A discovery-oriented approach to significant change events in psychotherapy: Interpersonal process recall and comprehensive process analysis. In L. N. Rice & L. S. Greenberg (Eds.), *Patterns of change: Intensive analysis of psychotherapy process* (pp. 249–286). New York: Guilford Press.

Elliott, R. (1985). Helpful and nonhelpful events in brief counseling interviews: An empirical taxonomy. *Journal of Counseling Psychology, 32,* 307–322.

Elliott, R. (1986). Interpersonal process recall as a research tool. In L. S. Greenberg & W. M. Pinsof (Eds.), *The psychotherapeutic process: A research handbook* (pp. 503–528). New York: Guilford Press.

Elliott, R., Hill, C. E., Stiles, W. B., Friedlander, M. C., Mahrer, A. R., & Margison, F. R. (1987). Primary therapist response modes: Comparison of six rating systems. *Journal of Consulting and Clinical Psychology, 55,* 218–223.

Ellis, J. V., Robbins, E. S., Shult, D., Ladany, N., & Banker, J. (1990). Anchoring errors in clinical judgments: Type I Error, adjustment, or mitigation. *Journal of Counseling Psychology, 37,* 343–351.

Ericsson, K. A., & Simon, H. A. (1980). Verbal reports as data. *Psychological Review, 87,* 215–251.

Fagley, N. S. (1985). Applied statistical power analysis and the interpretation of nonsignificant results by research consumers. *Journal of Counseling Psychology, 32,* 391–396.

Fassinger, R. E. (1987). Use of structural equation modeling in counseling psychology research. *Journal of Counseling Psychology, 34,* 425–436.

Fitzgerald, L. F., & Hubert. L. J. (1987). Multidimensional scaling: Some possibilities for counseling psychology. *Journal of Counseling Psychology, 34,* 469–480.

Folger, R. (1989). Significance tests and the duplicity of binary decisions. *Psychological Bulletin, 106,* 155–160.

Friedlander, M. L. (1982). Counseling discourse as a speech event: Revision and extension of the Hill Counselor Verbal Response Category System. *Journal of Counseling Psychology, 29,* 425–429.

Friedlander, M. L., Ellis, M. V., Siegel, S. M., Raymond, L., Haase, R. F., & Highlen, P. S. (1988). Generalizing from segments to sessions: Should it be done? *Journal of Counseling Psychology, 35,* 243–250.

Friedlander, M. L., & Heatherington, L. (1989). Analyzing relational control in family therapy interviews. *Journal of Counseling Psychology, 36,* 139–148.

Friedlander, M. L., & Phillips, S. D. (1984). Stochastic process analysis of interactive discourse in early counseling interviews. *Journal of Counseling Psychology, 31,* 139–148.

Fuller, F., & Hill, C. E. (1985). Counselor and helpee perceptions of counselor intentions in relation to outcome in a single counseling session. *Journal of Counseling Psychology, 32,* 329–338.

Garfield, S. L. (1990). Issues and methods in psychotherapy process research. *Journal of Consulting and Clinical Psychology, 58,* 273–280.

Gelso, C. J. (1979). Research in counseling: Methodological and professional issues. *The Counseling Psychologist, 8,* 7–35.

Gelso, C. J. (1984). Special section: Philosophy of science and counseling research. [Special Section]. *Journal of Counseling Psychology, 31*(4).

Gelso, C. J., & Fassinger, R. E. (1990). Counseling psychology: Theory and research on interventions. In *Annual review of psychology* (Vol. 41, pp. 355–386). Annual Reviews.

Glass, G. V, McGaw, B., & Smith, M. L. (1981). *Meta-analysis in social research.* Beverly Hills: Sage.

Gottman, J. M. (1979). *Marital interaction: Experimental investigations.* New York: Academic Press.

Gottman, J., & Markman, H. J. (1978). Experimental designs in psychotherapy research. In S. L. Garfield & A. E. Bergin (Eds.), *Handbook of psychotherapy and behavior change* (pp. 23–62). New York: Wiley.

Gottman, J. M., & Ringland, J. T. (1981). The analysis of dominance and bidirectionality in social development. *Child Development, 52,* 393–412.

Gottman, J. M., & Roy, A. K. (1990). *Sequential analysis: A guide for behavioral researchers.* Cambridge: Cambridge University Press.

Greenberg, L. S. (1986). Change process research. *Journal of Consulting and Clinical Psychology, 54,* 4–9.

Greenberg, L. S., & Pinsof, W. M. (1986a). Process research: Current trends and future perspectives. In L. S. Greenberg & W. M. Pinsof (Eds.), *The psychotherapeutic process: A research handbook* (pp. 3–20). New York: Guilford Press.

Greenberg, L. S., & Pinsof, W. M. (Eds.). (1986b). *The psychotherapeutic process: A research handbook.* New York: Guilford Press.

Greenhouse, J. B., Stangl, D., & Bromberg, J. (1989). An introduction to survival analysis: Statistical methods for analysis of clinical trial data. *Journal of Consulting and Clinical Psychology, 57,* 536–544.

Haase, R. F., & Ellis, M. V. (1987). Multivariate analysis of variance. *Journal of Counseling Psychology, 34,* 404–413.

Haase, R. F., Waechter, D. M., & Solomon, G. S. (1982). How significant is a significant difference? Average effect size of research in counseling psychology. *Journal of Counseling Psychology, 29,* 58–65.

Haley, J. (1963). *Strategies of psychotherapy.* New York: Grune & Stratton.

Hays, W. L. (1988). *Statistics* (4th ed.). New York: Holt, Rinehart, and Winston.

Heatherington, L. (1988). Coding relational communication control in counseling: Criterion validity. *Journal of Counseling Psychology, 35,* 41–46.

Heatherington, L., & Allen, G. J. (1984). Sex and relational communication patterns in counseling. *Journal of Counseling Psychology, 31,* 287–294.

Hedges, L. V., & Olkin, I. (1985). *Statistical methods for meta-analysis.* San Diego: Academic Press.

Heppner, P. P., Kivlighan, D. M., Jr., & Wampold, B. E. (1992). *Research design in counseling.* Pacific Grove, CA: Brooks/Cole.

Heppner, P. P., & Roehlke, H. J. (1984). Differences among supervisees at different levels of training: Implications for a developmental model of supervision. *Journal of Counseling Psychology, 31,* 76–90.

Hill, C. E. (1978). Development of a counselor verbal category system. *Journal of Counseling Psychology, 25,* 461–468.

Hill, C. E. (1982). Counseling process researcher: Philosophical and methodological dilemmas. *The Counseling Psychologist, 10*(4), 7–20.

Hill, C. E. (1986). An overview of the Hill Counselor and Client Verbal Response Modes Category Systems. In L. S. Greenberg & W. M. Pinsof (Eds.), *The psychotherapeutic process: A research handbook* (pp. 131–159). New York: Guilford Press.

Hill, C. E. (1990). Exploratory in-session process research in individual psychotherapy: A review. *Journal of Consulting and Clinical Psychology, 58,* 288–294.

Hill, C. E., Carter, J. A., & O'Farrell, M. K. (1983). A case study of the process and outcome of time-limited counseling. *Journal of Counseling Psychology, 30,* 3–18.

Hill, C. E., Greenwald, C., Reed, K. R., Charles, D., O'Farrell, M., & Carter, J. (1981). *Manual for Counselor and Client Verbal Response Category Systems.* Columbus, OH: Marathon Consulting Press.

Hill, C. E., Helms, J. E., Spiegel, S. B., & Tichenor, V. (1988). Development of a system for categorizing client reactions to therapist interventions. *Journal of Counseling Psychology, 35,* 27–36.

Hill, C. E., Helms J. E., Tichenor, V., Spiegel, S. B., O'Grady, K. E., & Perry, E. S. (1988). Effects of therapist response modes in brief psychotherapy. *Journal of Counseling Psychology, 35,* 222–233.

Hill, C. E., & O'Grady, K. E. (1985). List of therapist intentions illustrated in a case study and with therapists of varying theoretical orientations. *Journal of Counseling Psychology, 32,* 3–22.

Hollon, S. D., & Flick, S. N. (1988). On the meaning and methods of clinical significance. *Behavioral Assessment, 10,* 197–206.

Holloway, E. L. (1984). Outcome evaluation in supervision research. *The Counseling Psychologist, 12,* 167–174.

Holloway, E. L., Freund, R. D., Gardner, S. L., Nelson, M. L., & Walker, B. R. (1989). Relation of power and involvement to theoretical orientation in supervision: An analysis of discourse. *Journal of Counseling Psychology, 36,* 88–102.

Holloway, E. L., & Wampold, B. E. (1983). Patterns of verbal behavior and judgments of satisfaction in the supervision interview. *Journal of Counseling Psychology, 30,* 227–234.

Holloway, E. L., & Wampold, B. E. (1985, May). Dimensions of satisfaction in the supervision interview. *Resources in Education* (ERIC Document Reproduction Service No. ED 251 757).

Holloway, E. L., & Wampold, B. E. (1986). The relationship between conceptual level and counseling related tasks: A meta-analysis. *Journal of Counseling Psychology, 33,* 289–319.

Holloway, E. L., Wampold, B. E., & Nelson, M. L. (1990). Use of paradoxical intervention with a couple: An interactional analysis. *Journal of Family Psychology, 3,* 385–402.

Hopkins, K. D. (1982). The unit of analysis: Group means versus individual classrooms. *American Educational Research Journal, 19,* 5–18.

Horvath, A. O., & Greenberg, L. S. (1986). The development of the working alliance inventory. In L. S. Greenberg & W. M. Pinsof (Eds.), *The psychotherapeutic process: A research handbook* (pp. 529–556). New York: Guilford Press.

Horvath, A. O., & Greenberg, L. S. (1989). Development and validation of the Working Alliance Inventory. *Journal of Counseling Psychology, 36,* 223–233.

Huberty, C. J., & Morris, J. D. (1989). Multivariate analysis versus multiple univariate analyses. *Psychological Bulletin, 105,* 302–308.

Hunter, J. E., Schmidt, F. L., & Jackson, G. B. (1982). *Meta-analysis: Cumulating research findings across studies.* Beverly Hills: Sage.

Jacobson, N. S., Follette, W. C., & Revenstorf, D. (1984). Psychotherapy outcome research: Methods for reporting variability and evaluating clinical significance. *Behavior Therapy, 17,* 336–352.

Jacobson, N. S., Follette, W. C., Revenstorf, D., Baucom, D. H., Hahlweg, K., & Margolin, G. (1984). Variability in outcome and clinical significance of behavioral marital therapy: A reanalysis of outcome data. *Journal of Consulting and Clinical Psychology, 52,* 497–504.

Jacobson, N. S., & Revenstorf, D. (1988). Statistics for assessing the clinical significance of psychotherapy techniques: Issues, problems, and new developments. *Behavioral Assessment,* 133–145.

Jacobson, N. S., Wilson, L., & Tupper, C. (1988). The clinical significance of treatment gains resulting from exposure based interventions for agoraphobia: A reanalysis of outcome data. *Behavioral Therapy, 19,* 539–554.

Kagan, N. (1975). Influencing human interaction: Eleven years with IPR. *Canadian Counselor, 9,* 44–51.

Kazdin, A. E. (1977). Assessing the clinical or applied importance of behavior change through social validation. *Behavior Modification, 54,* 95–105.

Kazdin, A. E. (1980). *Research design in clinical psychology.* New York: Harper & Row.

Kazdin, A. E. (1986a). Comparative outcome studies of psychotherapy: Methodological issues and strategies. *Journal of Consulting and Clinical Psychology, 54,* 95–105.

Kazdin, A. E. (1986b). Research designs and methodology. In S. L. Garfield & A. E. Bergin (Eds.), *Handbook of psychotherapy and behavior change* (pp. 23–68). New York: Wiley.

Kessler, R. C., & Greenberg, D. F. (1981). *Linear panel analysis: Models of quantitative change.* New York: Academic Press.

Kiesler, D. J. (1966). Some myths of psychotherapy research and the search for a paradigm. *Psychological Bulletin, 65,* 110–136.

Kivlighan, D. M., Jr. (1989). Changes in counselor intentions and response modes in client reactions and session evaluation after training. *Journal of Counseling Psychology, 36,* 471–476.

Klein, M. H., Mathieu-Coughlan, P., & Kiesler, D. J. (1986). The Experiencing Scales. In L. Greenberg & W. Pinsof (Eds.), *The psychotherapeutic process* (pp. 21–77). New York: Guilford Press.

Kraemer, H. C., & Thiemann, S. (1989). A strategy to use soft data effectively in randomized controlled clinical trials. *Journal of Consulting and Clinical Psychology, 57,* 148–154.

Krumboltz, J. D. (Ed.). (1966). *Revolution in counseling: Implications of behavioral science.* Boston: Houghton Mifflin.

Kurpius, D. J., Benjamin, D., & Morran, D. K. (1985). Effect of teaching a cognitive strategy on counselor trainee internal dialogue and clinical hypothesis formation. *Journal of Counseling Psychology, 32,* 263–271.

Lambert, M. J., Christensen, E. R., & DeJulio, S. S. (1983). *The assessment of psychotherapy outcome.* New York: Wiley.

Lambert, M. J., Shapiro, D. A., & Bergin, A. E. (1986). The effectiveness of psychotherapy. In S. L. Garfield & A. E. Bergin (Eds.), *Handbook of psychotherapy and behavior change* (pp. 157–211). New York: Wiley.

Leary, M. R., & Altmaier, E. M. (1980). Type I Error in counseling research: A plea for multivariate analyses. *Journal of Counseling Psychology, 27,* 611–615.

Leary, T. (1957). *Interpersonal diagnosis of personality: A functional theory and methodology for personality evaluation.* New York: Ronald Press.

Lee, D. Y., Uhlemann, M. R., & Haase, R. F. (1985). Counselor verbal and nonverbal responses and perceived expertness, trustworthiness, and attractiveness. *Journal of Counseling Psychology, 32,* 181–187.

Lichtenberg, J., & Barke, K. (1981). Investigation of transactional communication relationship patterns in counseling. *Journal of Counseling Psychology, 28,* 471–481.

Lichtenberg, J. W., & Heck, E. J. (1986). Analysis of sequence and pattern in process research. *Journal of Counseling Psychology, 33,* 170–181.

Lincoln, Y. S., & Guba, E. G. (1985). *Naturalistic inquiry.* Newbury Park, CA: Sage.

Mahrer, A. R. (1988). Discovery-oriented psychotherapy research: Rationale, aims, and methods. *American Psychologist, 43,* 694–702.

Mahrer, A. R., & Nadler, W. P. (1986). Good moments in psychotherapy: A preliminary review, a list, and some promising research avenues. *Journal of Consulting and Clinical Psychology, 54,* 10–15.

Martin, J. (1984). The cognitive mediational paradigm for research on counseling. *Journal of Counseling Psychology, 31,* 558–571.

Martin, J. (1991a). To hypothesize or not to hypothesize. *American Psychologist, 46,* 651–652.

Martin, J. (1991b). The perils of "process talk" in counseling and counselor education. *The Counseling Psychologist, 19,* 260–272.

Martin, J., Martin, W., Meyer, M., & Slemon, A. (1986). Empirical investigation of the cognitive mediational paradigm for research on counseling. *Journal of Counseling Psychology, 33,* 115–123.

Martin, J., Martin, W., & Slemon, A. G. (1987). Cognitive mediation in person-centered and rational-emotive therapy. *Journal of Counseling Psychology, 34,* 251–260.

Martin, J., Martin, W., & Slemon, A. G. (1989). Cognitive-mediational models of action–act sequences in counseling. *Journal of Counseling Psychology, 36,* 8–16.

Martin, J., Pavio, S., & Labadie, D. (1990). Memory enhancing characteristics of client-recalled important events in cognitive and experimental therapy: Integrating cognitive experimental and therapeutic psychology. *Counseling Psychology Quarterly, 3,* 239–256.

Martin, J., & Stelmaczonek, K. (1988). Participants' identification and recall of important events in counseling. *Journal of Counseling Psychology, 35,* 385–390.

McCarthy, P. R., Shaw, T., & Schmeck, R. R. (1986). Behavioral analysis of client learning style during counseling. *Journal of Counseling Psychology, 33,* 249–254.

McNamara, K., & Horan, J. J. (1986). Experimental construct validity in the evaluation of cognitive and behavioral treatments for depression. *Journal of Counseling Psychology, 33,* 23–30.

Meehl, P. E. (1978). Theoretical risks and tabular asterisks: Sir Karl, Sir Ronald, and the slow progress of soft psychology. *Journal of Consulting and Clinical Psychology, 46,* 806–834.

Merluzzi, T., Glass, C. R., & Genest, M. (Eds.). (1981). *Cognitive assessment.* New York: Guilford Press.

Mitchell, C., & Hartmann, D. P. (1981). A cautionary note on the use of omega squared to evaluate the effectiveness of behavioral treatments. *Behavioral Assessment, 3,* 93–100.

Morran, D. K., Kurpius, D. J., & Brack, G. (1989). Empirical investigation of counselor self-talk categories. *Journal of Counseling Psychology, 36,* 505–510.

Murray, L. W., & Dosser, D. A., Jr. (1987). How significant is a significant difference? Problems with the measurement of magnitude of effect. *Journal of Counseling Psychology, 34,* 68–72.

Nelson, M. L., & Holloway, E. L. (1990). Relation of gender and power and involvement in supervision. *Journal of Counseling Psychology, 37,* 473–481.

Nietzel, M. T., & Trull, T. J. (1988). Meta-analytic approaches to social comparisons: A method for measuring clinical significance. *Behavioral Assessment, 10,* 159–169.

O'Grady, K. E. (1982). Measures of explained variance: Caution and limitations. *Psychological Bulletin, 92,* 766–777.

Orlinsky, D. E., & Howard, K. I. (1975). Varieties of psychotherapeutic experience. New York: Teachers College Press.

Paquin, M. J. R. (1983). Beyond significant yet meaningless results in psychotherapy research. *Psychotherapy: Theory, Research and Practice, 20,* 38–40.

Patton, M. J. (1982). A methodological preface to research on counseling. *The Counseling Psychologist, 10(4),* 23–26.

Patton, M. J. (1989). Problems and alternatives to the use of coding schemes in research on counseling. *The Counseling Psychologist, 17,* 490–506.

Paul, G. L. (1967). Strategy of outcome research in psychotherapy. *Journal of Consulting Psychology, 31,* 104–118.

Penman, R. (1980). *Communication processes and relationships.* London: Academic Press.

Platt, J. R. (1964). Strong inference. *Science, 146,* 347–353.

Ponce, F. Q., & Atkinson, D. R. (1989). Mexican-American acculturation, counselor ethnicity, counseling style, and perceived credibility. *Journal of Counseling Psychology, 36,* 203–208.

Porter, A. C., & Raudenbush, S. W. (1987). Analysis of covariance: Its model and use in psychological research. *Journal of Counseling Psychology, 34,* 383–392.

Reandeau, S. G., & Wampold, B. E. (1991). Relationship of power and involvement to working alliance: A multiple-case sequential analysis of brief therapy. *Journal of Counseling Psychology, 12,* 107–114.

Rogers, L. E., & Farace, R. (1975). Relational communication analysis: New measurement procedures. *Human Communication Research, 5,* 222–239.

Rogosa, D. R., Brand, D., & Zimowski, M. (1982). A growth curve approach to the measurement of change. *Psychological Bulletin, 90,* 728–748.

Rosenthal, R. (1984). *Meta-analytic procedures for social research.* Beverly Hills: Sage.

Rosenthal, R. (1990). How are we doing in soft psychology? *American Psychologist, 45,* 775–777.

Rosenthal, R., & Rubin, D. B. (1982). A simple, general-purpose display of magnitude of experimental effects. *Journal of Educational Psychology, 74,* 166–169.

Rosnow, R. L., & Rosenthal, R. (1988). Focused tests of significance and effect size estimation in counseling psychology. *Journal of Counseling Psychology, 35,* 203–208.

Russell, R. L., & Trull, T. J. (1986). Sequential analyses of language variables in psychotherapy process research. *Journal of Consulting and Clinical Psychology, 54,* 16–21.

Serlin, R. C. (1987). Hypothesis testing, theory building, and the philosophy of science. *Journal of Counseling Psychology, 34,* 365–371.

Shoham-Salomon, V. (1990). Interrelating research process of process research. *Journal of Consulting and Clinical Psychology, 58,* 295–303.

Sipps, G. J., Sugden, G. J., & Faiver, C. M. (1988). Counselor training level and verbal response type: Their relationship to efficacy and outcome. *Journal of Counseling Psychology, 35,* 397–401.

Sluzki, C. E., & Beavin, J. (1977). Symmetry and complementarity: An operational definition and a typology of dyads. In P. Watzlawick & J. H. Weakland (Eds. and Trans.), *The interactional view* (pp. 71–87). New York: Norton. (Reprinted from *Acta Psiquiatrics y Psicologica de America Latina,* 1965, *11,* 321–330)

Smith, M. L., & Glass, G. V. (1977). Meta-analysis of psychotherapy outcome studies. *American Psychologist, 32,* 752–760.

Stiles, W. B. (1987). Some intentions are observable. *Journal of Counseling Psychology, 34,* 236–239.

Stiles, W. B., & Snow, J. S. (1984a). Counseling session impact as viewed by novice counselors and their clients. *Journal of Counseling Psychology, 31,* 3–12.

Stiles, W. B., & Snow, J. S. (1984b). Dimensions of psychotherapy session impact across sessions and across clients. *British Journal of Clinical Psychology, 23,* 59–63.

Sullivan, H. S. (1953). *Conceptions of modern psychiatry.* New York: Norton.

Tracey, T. J. (1985). Dominance and outcome: A sequential examination. *Journal of Counseling Psychology, 32,* 119–122.

Tracey, T. J. (1986). Interactional correlates of premature termination. *Journal of Consulting and Clinical Psychology, 54,* 784–788.

Tracey, T. J. (1987). Stage differences in the dependencies of topic initiation and topic following behavior. *Journal of Counseling Psychology, 34,* 123–131.

Tracey, T. J. (1991). The structure of control and influence in counseling and psychotherapy: A comparison of several definitions and measures. *Journal of Counseling Psychology, 38,* 265–278.

Tracey, T. J., Hays, K. A., Malone J., & Herman, B. (1988). Changes in counselor response as a function of experience. *Journal of Counseling Psychology, 35,* 119–126.

Tracey, T. J., & Ray, P. B. (1984). Stages of successful time-limited counseling: An interactional examination. *Journal of Counseling Psychology, 31,* 13–27.

Wampold, B. E. (1984). Tests of dominance in sequential categorical data. *Psychological Bulletin, 96,* 424–429.

Wampold, B. E. (1986). The state of the art in sequential analysis: Comment on Lichtenberg and Heck. *Journal of Counseling Psychology, 33,* 182–185.

Wampold, B. E. (1987a). Covariance structure analysis: Seduced by sophistication? *The Counseling Psychologist, 15,* 311–315.

Wampold, B. E. (Ed.). (1987b). Quantitative foundations of counseling psychology research [Special issue]. *Journal of Counseling Psychology, 34*(4).

Wampold, B. E. (1989). Kappa as a measure of pattern in sequential data. *Quality & Quantity, 23,* 171–187.

Wampold, B. E. (in press). The intensive examination of social interactions. In T. R. Kratochwill & J. R. Levin, *Analysis of single-case research.* Hillsdale, NJ: Earlbaum.

Wampold, B. E., & Brown, S. D. (1992). *Binomial effect size displays with various base rates.* Unpublished manuscript.

Wampold, B. E., Davis, B., Good, R. H., III. (1990). Hypothesis validity of clinical research. *Journal of Consulting and Clinical Psychology, 58,* 360–367.

Wampold, B. E., & Drew, C. J. (1990). *Theory and application of statistics.* New York: McGraw-Hill.

Wampold, B. E., & Freund, R. D. (1987). Use of multiple regression in counseling psychology research: A flexible data-analytic strategy. *Journal of Counseling Psychology, 34,* 372–382.

Wampold, B. E., Furlong, M. J., & Atkinson, D. R. (1983). Statistical significance, power, and effect size: A response to the reexamination of reviewer bias. *Journal of Counseling Psychology, 30,* 459–463.

Wampold, B. E., & Jenson, W. R. (1986). Clinical significance revisited. *Behavioral Therapy, 17,* 302–305.

Wampold, B. E., & Kim, K. H. (1989). Sequential analysis applied to counseling process and outcomes: A case study revisited. *Journal of Counseling Psychology, 36,* 357–364.

Wampold, B. E., & Margolin, G. (1982). Nonparametric strategies to test the independence of behavioral states in sequential data. *Psychological Bulletin, 92,* 755–765.

Watzlawick, P., Beavin, J. H., & Jackson, D. D. (1967). *Pragmatics of human communication: A study of interactional patterns, pathologies, and paradoxes.* New York: Norton.

Williamson, E. G. (1939). *How to counsel students: A manual of techniques for clinical counselors.* New York: McGraw-Hill.

CHAPTER 4

EXPANDING SCIENTIFIC PARADIGMS IN COUNSELING PSYCHOLOGY

FRED H. BORGEN

In psychology fresh winds are blowing, sweeping away overly restrictive assumptions, dusting off concepts that had been covered over and neglected, picking up and juxtaposing separate ideas to produce novel combinations. A dynasty of dominant theories has been overthrown. No longer does a rigid hypothetico-deductive model hold exclusive sway in the laboratory. No longer is a rigid adherence to Freudian or Rogerian doctrine required of psychotherapists. . . . Pluralism is the order of the day. Underlying these liberating changes are some liberalizing assumptions about what it means to be a scientist. (Tyler, 1978, p. 1)

Viewing psychology from the vantage point of a 40-year distinguished career, Leona Tyler (1978) began her stimulating book *Individuality* with the optimistic commentary above. Although her comments are now 14 years old, they continue to have a freshness and prescience that aptly introduce this discussion of expanding and changing scientific paradigms.

OVERVIEW

The paradigmatic expansion within psychology generally, and counseling psychology specifically, has been huge over the past three decades. Especially profound have been our public appraisals of our implicit epistemology. We have courageously asked the epistemologist's question: "What do we know and how do we know it?" Psychologists generally have increasingly addressed these "deep structure" issues in penetrating and radical ways, as exemplified by numerous articles in the *American Psychologist* (Gendlin, 1986; Gergen, 1985; Hare-Mustin & Maracek, 1988, 1989; Koch, 1981; Mahoney, 1985, 1989; Manicas & Secord, 1983; Packer, 1985; Scarr, 1985; Sperry, 1988; Wachtel, 1980). Counseling psychology, in particular, has addressed these issues with vigor and visibility (Ford, 1984, 1987; Forsyth & Strong, 1986; Gelso, 1979, 1985; Hill, 1982, 1984; Hoshmand, 1989; Howard, 1984, 1985, 1986a, 1986b, 1989, 1991; Howard & Conway, 1986, 1987; LaCrosse, 1986; Polkinghorne, 1983, 1984, 1988, 1991).

For their helpful comments on earlier drafts of this chapter, I thank Gregg Bieber, Steve Brown, Bob Lent, Rhonda Lovell, Lon Olsen, Sara Sundstrom, and Mary Ann Swiatek.

It is as if we have been applying the ethnographer's lens to ourselves and our scientific enterprise. We have publicly reflected on some very basic questions: How can we best do inquiry in psychology? What are our assumptions, world views, and metagoals? What are the implications for scientific progress and counseling practice? Our willingness to indulge in this often distressing self-appraisal reflects both a maturity in the discipline and a discontent with pursuing the status quo (Borgen, 1984a). As Maracek (1989, pp. 374–375) observed, "The emergence of competing epistemologies is not a sign of disarray, but of healthy intellectual ferment."

A Science of Both Insight and Action

Wachtel (1987) aptly captured the dialectic tension between behavior therapy and psychodynamic therapy with his book title *Action and Insight*. Emerging integrative work in therapy shows the necessity of both action and insight components. This metaphor also might well be useful for thinking about counseling research, where *action* refers to the doing of research and *insight* refers to thoughtfulness about the assumptions, goals, and methods of one's research. Ultimately, our best scholarship merges insight and action. Insight in research, as in therapy, means understanding the deep structure and embedded meanings, not just the surface structure. For the aware researcher, insight accesses not the preconscious, but the paradigm. Meehl (1978) and others have observed that, too often in doing "rigorous" research, "our energy is misinvested with narrow operationism wedded to ever more skilled applications of Fisherian designs that do not fit our subject matter" (Borgen, 1984a, p. 594). As Glass and Kliegl (1983, p. 35) lamented:

> *It is a regrettable egocentric failing of many scientists that they are unable to reflect self-consciously on the historical choices that have bequeathed to them their particular "science," but instead believe that logic demands that they pursue their inquiries precisely as they are pursuing them.*

We have put our discipline on the couch. At the same time, the goals of this change enterprise are often unclear, at least insofar as the "patient's" awareness and acquiescence of the goals are concerned. The goals for some reformers aim toward restructuring psychology's epistemology completely; for others, a brief checkup and a little fine-tuning seem to be sufficient. Not surprisingly, there is some turmoil and resistance when the goals of some reformers do not match those of others in the discipline.

Counseling psychology research of the 1980s showed promising examples that merged insight and action. The real heroes were those who aggressively questioned old traditions, modified assumptions to fit their subject matter, and then, most importantly, proceeded to apply these new looks in research examples. We are now seeing products of such renewed endeavors in several areas that will be highlighted later in this chapter: self-efficacy, volition, and counseling process task analysis.

Goals for This Chapter

My primary goal in this chapter is to describe and comment on this disciplinary change process as I observed it during the 1970s and 1980s. I confess at the outset that I have no clear idea what the ultimate outcomes of this change process will be. I hope that we will continue to have greater awareness of implicit epistemological issues, and thus have greater ultimate control in selecting and achieving outcomes. Making explicit the implicit culture of science is intrinsically valuable. I also hold the bias that, for counseling psychology, the ultimate outcome for our science enterprise should be improvement of the service we are able to provide our clients.

This chapter examines paradigmatic expansion under three general themes:

- Expanding philosophy of science
- Expanding conceptual paradigms
- Expanding methodological paradigms

I chose this organization because I wished to begin with more general and abstract knowledge issues and then move to more specific and concrete examples of the work of everyday science. The trichotomy is artificial to the extent that many issues and writers often touch to some degree on all three themes. Thus, because many recent writers address epistemology, concepts, and methods, their contributions cannot be covered adequately under any one of the major headings I am using. Nonetheless, I hope that my structure will provide relatively separate foci to issues that I believe merit independent evaluation. Concurrently, I am acutely aware of the strong natural overlap among these three topics. The coverage of materials within these topics is necessarily selective and to some degree idiosyncratic. The potential breadth of the topic is wide indeed, and readers will likely see topics neglected that they might readily weave into this broad tapestry.

The initial plan was to title this chapter Changing Scientific Paradigms in Counseling Psychology. While thinking and writing about these issues, I realized it was appropriate to amend the chapter focus and title from "changing" paradigms to "expanding" paradigms. Changing paradigms might imply that old paradigms have been discarded in favor of the new. My interpretation is that this kind of revolution has not occurred in psychology. Rather, new paradigms have tended to evolve and to coexist—sometimes peaceably, sometimes not—with the old. Thus, my emphasis on expanding paradigms is meant to focus on the growth points in the scientific enterprise. Traditional paradigms are very much alive and active in counseling psychology, despite my relative lack of attention to that theme in this chapter. Just as therapists have become increasingly eclectic (Norcross, 1986; Norcross & Prochaska, 1988; Smith, 1982), there are signs of researchers engaging in epistemic eclecticism (Borgen, 1984a, 1984b, 1989), and that unfolding is a focus of this chapter.

Two Contexts for Knowledge: Discovery and Justification

Philosopher of science Hans Reichenbach (1938) usefully differentiated two kinds of knowledge: knowledge derived in the *context of discovery* and knowledge derived in the *context of justification*. Typically, the discovery context is the source for our concepts and hypotheses, and the justification context is the warrant for their confirmation or disconfirmation. Many of the leading epistemic edges covered in this chapter fit predominantly within Reichenbach's context of discovery. The notion of paradigm itself can be interpreted to mean the lens that causes us to look in new directions and thus to reframe new possibilities. The discovery context can be as dramatic as Archimedes exclaiming "Eureka!" or it can be as subdued as Clara Hill (1984) quietly concluding that past outcome and process research missed the mark in capturing what she knows as a clinician about the counseling process. In either case, the discovery insight leads to a new way of approaching science. In a refreshing essay written for industrial and organizational psychologists, McCall and Bobko (1990) argued for a greater openness to nonconventional research methods that may abet the discovery process.

The distinction between contexts of discovery and justification parallels our distinction between insight and action. Both modes are necessary for a fully developed science. I tend to neglect the justification side in this chapter, but I have previously argued for the justification position in psychology's well-developed received tradition of research (Borgen, 1984a, 1984b, 1989). It is precisely because of the strengths and maturity of our ongoing research community that we are able to consider productive self-renewal of our enterprise. Thus, openness to new thinking in the contexts of both discovery and justification should be our goal, while thoughtfully building on the strengths of the old.

People as Active Rather Than Passive Agents

Many of the contemporary trends noted in this chapter reflect the ascendance of the view that people are active rather than passive agents. The human mind, with its special capacity for verbalizing and thinking, is increasingly recognized for its active role in shaping concepts and in planning and directing behavior. The human mind has the capacity to think about itself, and in doing so actually changes the concept of the human mind. These resurgent trends toward seeing people as active agents are quite different from psychology's once dominant view of people as passive agents. This rethinking of thinking is deeply affecting not only our core theories of human behavior, but also our metatheory, our concepts about doing science, and our views of the appropriate research methods for a human science.

Tyler (1978) described this paradigmatic shifting of the focus of human inquiry from *reaction* to *action.* Dowd and Pace (1989, p. 213) observed that "the view that people are active participants in the construction of their own reality" stands in contrast to the dominant empiricist trends of modern psychology. They noted that both behaviorism (Skinner, 1987) and its prime competitor, information-processing psychology, "are tied to empiricist philosophy that holds that reality exists independently of the perceiver and that knowledge is acquired only through sensory experience" (p. 213). The commonality of both models is that causal influences are seen as moving from the outside inward. Buss (1978) took a related but somewhat different view, observing that psychology has shifted between two dominant paradigms with opposing assumptions: Either reality constructs the person or the person constructs reality. The person as constructor of reality is currently vying with the opposite metaphor. Several writers are working to meld both in theoretical systems (Buss, 1989; Wachtel, 1977, 1987). These newer trends are placing the active mind at center stage and seeing it as directing the human drama. No longer does the shibboleth "What do the data say?" dominate our science. The emerging constructivist metaphor is more "I will see it when I believe it."

The raw data of empiricism are increasingly seen as not speaking with singular clarity but as selectively perceived and interpreted through our alternate paradigmatic spectacles (Highlen & Hill, 1984). This view of the rising salience of active thinking in human knowing will be evident throughout this chapter. It has affected how we think about science, with the Kuhnian perspective especially debunking our faith that data per se lead inexorably to scientific progress. The reemergence of the mind in psychology has deeply affected our paradigms for conceptualizing human behavior. Much of the vigor and excitement in psychology derives from the liberating assumptions of cognitive theory and therapy, constructivist perspectives, and a focus on human agency. Finally, there is an increasing openness toward examining the methods we use in human inquiry. This focus on a *human* science has led to a demystifying of vestigial recipes for a narrow empiricism and its associated philosophy of logical positivism. A renewed energy prevails for expanding our methods to build a knowledge base that more fully maps human experience and that guides more effective counseling practice.

The Person as Central

The net effect of the shift outlined above is that our theory, research, and practice have all become more *person-centered*. There is more valuing of the mind, the individual's experience and perspective, and the needs of the individual person. Carl Rogers (1985) was often frustrated by his apparent lack of success in influencing American academic psychology toward a more phenomenological view of the person. In many ways the themes of this chapter, especially the renewed valuing of the person's active perceptions and agency, as well as expanding methods of science, promise to achieve many of the goals Rogers espoused. His ultimate goal was facilitating clients' self-actualization, and the liberalizing themes of this chapter have that potential.

EXPANDING PHILOSOPHY OF SCIENCE

Changing Views of Science

Science in the early 20th century was a continuing technological success. Psychology's growth proceeded in a parallel fashion. Psychology viewed itself as having the map to travel the royal road to truth and believing that continued use of that map would bring us closer and closer to the truth. However, for many observers of the past three decades (e.g., Fiske & Shweder, 1986; Meehl, 1978), there has not been the cumulative progress that many expected. In 1984, I commented as follows about this epistemological unease:

> *Empistemology is in disarray in much of psychology. The resulting malaise over method is evident in anguished and thoughtful appraisals of the "slow progress of soft psychology." . . . The key lament (in my partly clinical interpretation) is that the vision for psychology in the 1950s, as exemplified in such advances as construct validation and the building of nomological nets (Cronbach & Meehl, 1955), has not been achieved. (Borgen, 1984a, pp. 593–594)*

Today, Fiske and Shweder's (1986) edited volume is a revealing, and even disturbing, treatment of epistemological unease in the social sciences. Especially poignant to psychology are the separate chapters by Campbell (1986), Cronbach (1986), and Meehl (1986). These major figures in psychology, our visionaries of the 1950s, have been methodological mentors without peer in extending quantitative inference beyond a narrow positivism. Most prominent are their creations of construct validity (Cronbach & Meehl, 1955) and the multitrait–multimethod matrix (Campbell & Fiske, 1959). Yet, in commenting on our cumulative progress toward generalized knowledge, Campbell, Cronbach, and Meehl are not especially sanguine. On the other hand, they share with others in the Fiske and Shweder (1986) book commitments to methodological openness and pluralism. This book is highly recommended for additional reading on the topics of this chapter, especially to gain varied perspectives about qualitative methods, and methodological openness. Also recommended is a review by Hall (1990), who outlined how far some sociologists have moved from the epistemology of logical positivism.

Kuhn and Expanding Views of Science

Without Thomas Kuhn, this chapter would not have been written. His book on *The Structure of Scientific Revolutions* (1962, 1970) revolutionized the way we think about science. His singular contribution to our lexicon is his special use of the word "paradigm." In the past two decades, as Kuhn's ideas have been widely disseminated, there have been major changes in the way we think about science. Perhaps it has been a coincidence of the zeitgeist—others were beginning to be affected by developments as had Kuhn—and he was only expressing what others had already come to believe. But I believe his impact has been distinctive, giving clarity and authority to an increasing self-awareness and self-examination of how we do science. As Mahoney (1980) suggested, intriguing parallels exist between Kuhn's analysis of scientific revolution and the cognitive insight and reframing in counseling change.

There are legitimate technical debates about whether Kuhn's ideas of paradigm shifts and scientific revolutions should be applied to the social sciences. Kuhn himself, in his initial 1962 presentation, believed the social sciences to be undeveloped and thus preparadigmatic and not subject to the sea changes of scientific revolution. Nonetheless, I am exercising the temerity to use the term paradigm in this chapter as I examine changes in the science of counseling psychology. Although in some crucial particulars Kuhn's analysis does not fit the social sciences, there are substantial practical ways in which Kuhn's analysis does apply. One is simply usage. Social scientists have widely adopted the Kuhnian framework, or at least parts of it (Mahoney, 1976, 1980; Suppe, 1984). The question of whether the Kuhnian analogue is a tight logical fit to the social sciences has not made a large practical difference in its impact on our thinking. As a metaphor, it has been powerful.

Kuhn clearly showed that science does not progress merely by accretion. To continue doing more of the same normal science is not enough. At some point, science profits from radical reconceptualization—a paradigm shift equivalent to a conversion experience. Unlike logical positivists, Kuhn did not presume that research becomes closer and closer to the truth. There is no teleology. Science is not a simple accumulation process; instead, it moves through shifts, without the next stage being superior on some metric, other than passage of time. Moreover, Kuhn debunked the naive question "What do the data say?" Although a physicist, Kuhn's analysis was largely sociological and psychological, and he thus demonstrated how science is largely a human and social creation.

Kuhn's Conversion Experience

It is shocking to reread Kuhn (1970) and see how profoundly his insights were the product of exposure to psychologists who laid a foundation for the active agent–constructivist camp of today's psychology. In his introduction, Kuhn noted (p. vi) how his early insights about science were the product of exposure to psychologists' ideas: Piaget's stages, gestalt psychologists, and Whorf's speculations about the effect of language on world view. Kuhn wrote (p. viii):

> *Yet, somehow, the practice of astronomy, physics, chemistry, or biology normally fails to evoke the controversies over fundamentals that today often seem endemic among, say, psychologists or sociologists. Attempting to discover the source of that difference led me to recognize the role in scientific research of what I have*

since called "paradigms." These I take to be universally recognized scientific achievements that for a time provide model problems and solutions to a community of practitioners. Once that piece of my puzzle fell into place, a draft of this essay emerged rapidly.

Using the concepts of gestalt psychologists, Kuhn saw that scientific paradigms provide new lenses, like a gestalt switch in the perception of an ambiguous figure. He saw that normal science proceeds as puzzle solving until it reaches an impasse with data that cannot fit the current paradigm. Then the science is thrown into crisis, and a scientific revolution ensues as a new paradigm or world view is framed to accommodate the new discrepant data. In his chapter on "Revolutions as Changes of World View," he observed "paradigm changes do cause scientists to see the world of their research-engagement differently. . . . Only after a number of such transformations of vision does the student become an inhabitant of the scientist's world, seeing what the scientist sees and responding as the scientist does" (p. 111).

In Kuhn's view, one scientific paradigm must ultimately prevail within a discipline—at least until another crisis occurs.

These examples point to the third and most fundamental aspect of the incommensurability of competing paradigms. . . . The proponents of competing paradigms practice their trades in different worlds. . . . Practicing in two different worlds, the two groups of scientists see different things when they look from the same point in the same direction. . . . That is why a law that cannot even be demonstrated to one group of scientists may occasionally seem intuitively obvious to another. Equally, it is why, before they can hope to communicate fully, one group or the other must experience the conversion that we have been calling a paradigm shift. Just because it is a transition between incommensurables, the transition between competing paradigms cannot be made a step at a time, forced by logic and neutral experience. Like the gestalt switch, it must occur all at once (though not necessarily in an instant) or not at all. . . . The transfer of allegiance from paradigm to paradigm is a conversion experience that cannot be forced. (Kuhn, 1970, pp. 150–151)

A reasonable implication of Kuhn's analysis is that eclecticism is impossible. He is saying that normal science, at least within subdisciplines, is monolithic and always has a singular world view. This Kuhnian presupposition is a popular one and probably reflects psychology's historic resistance to eclecticism. It reflects a need to seek a singular truth, to follow logic and cognitive coherence, and to batten down the hatches and proceed full speed ahead to get one's own team to win.

Kuhn as Social Scientist

The ultimate irony is that Kuhn engaged in *social* science to reach his conclusions about how science operates. He used the methods of Freud, Piaget, and Frank—anecdotal observation, insight, analysis, and creativity—and worked within Reichenbach's context of discovery. Kuhn's analytic techniques were qualitative and ethnographic; his landmark book contains not a single test of statistical significance. Kuhn's dissonance led to his insight. Having been trained as a physicist and then exposed to courses on how science was supposed to occur, he was acutely aware of a chasm. This led him to build a new conceptual map that has become known as the Kuhnian view. He observed, through the lens of his new paradigm, how science actually operates. The impact of Kuhn has been profound, rivaling any position in epistemology of this century; yet the evidentiary base for his largely psychological and sociological analysis does not follow the revered canons of modern social science. Things that affect science need not be scientific. Thus, Kuhnian notions have thrust themselves on the thinking of scientists, but the bases of Kuhn's hypotheses are fragile reeds indeed, by the standards of modern empirical psychology.

Rethinking Kuhn

One can benefit from Kuhnian thinking without buying all of his conclusions. Psychology as a discipline can be interpreted in all of Kuhn's analyses, with the exception of his conclusion that a science abhors inconsistency and must always move toward a singular, monolithic paradigm. If we apply Kuhn's ethnographic methods, we may justifiably reach this conclusion. Following are Kuhnian insights that apply equally well to the social sciences and the physical sciences:

- Science does not proceed with the pure logic of logical empiricism.
- Science is not always cumulative; it often moves with shifts.
- Science is not wholly objective, but operates with an implicit world view.
- Science proceeds in a sociological context.
- Scientific advances emerge from scientific failures and cul de sacs.

Kuhn forced a procrustean fit of all sciences to his analysis of the natural sciences. Why can't an alternative analysis of the social sciences be made that reflects their realities? Kuhn did not anticipate the ability of social scientists (and practitioners) to hold more than one world view. As Highlen and Hill (1984, p. 339) noted, "numerous models abound for effecting client change in individual counseling. An interpretation of recent events within counseling therefore must take into account this important difference between the social and physical sciences."

Physical scientists, perhaps because they are wedded strongly to traditional notions of a single truth, may need to operate within a logically consistent world view. However, in psychology, the strong eclectic trend of the past 20 years, especially in counseling and psychotherapy, shows the value of being able to take multiple viewpoints (Beutler & Clarkin, 1990; Borgen, 1984a, 1984b, 1989; Norcross, 1986). The essence of eclecticism is to argue for the value of not locking into one gestalt. The eclectic viewpoint, by definition, states that multiple world views, and the flexibility to move among them, have many desirable consequences. Eclecticism and empathy are partners. It should not surprise us that the field of psychotherapy, where empathic relationships are now implicitly essential, should be overwhelmed by the new eclecticism. People who practice taking the other's viewpoint get good at it, and begin to do it routinely.

We need a Kuhnian analysis of the social sciences that examines their unique features. In Kuhn's view, a scientific revolution follows a realization that things have gone wrong. Rarely does that occur with clarity in the social sciences. Old theories never die, they just accumulate. Perhaps the key is that the social sciences do not operate primarily in the mode of puzzle solving. Rather, it seems that much of what social scientists do is template or model matching: "We have these general gestalt explanations for events and we tend to run competitive races to determine which of the models better matches the data."

Consciousness Raising: Toward Permeable Paradigms

The metaphor of consciousness raising is a better metaphor than Kuhn's "conversion experience." Consciousness raising does not imply replacing one dogma with another dogma. Rather, it implies the possibilities for holding multiple world views and operating from multiple paradigms. One can have one's consciousness raised about sexism, but also have one's consciousness raised about racism. New views on one do not preclude new views on the other. In fact, learning to raise one's consciousness, to adopt alternate world views, may make one better able to experience a gestalt switch in other areas. It may be that the more consciousness-raising experiences one has, the smaller the core of rigid beliefs that one holds. One develops more permeable constructs of the world, increasing potentialities for seeing many more options.

Tyler's (1983) analysis and reformulation of Kuhn is similar to my description of paradigms as consciousness raising or to Highlen and Hill's (1984) alternate spectacles. Tyler reframed Kuhn's idea of paradigms as the concept of alternate realities of science, with the scientist having choices among varied intellectual habitats. Similarly, Thompson (1989) advocated postparadigmatic thinking to transcend the limits of single paradigms.

There are implicit paradigms of the counseling process. They tell us where to focus, what to see, and where to go within the complexity of the counseling hour. We do not have easy recipes for these counseling schemata, as the ready anxiety of new counseling trainees reflects. As Kuhn (1970, p. 113) wrote, "In the absence of such training there can only be, in William James' phrase, a 'bloomin' buzzin' confusion.'"

As in counseling, scientific paradigms that are permeable, open, and flexible, rather than rigid, closed, and reactionary, will serve us best (Ivey, Ivey, & Simek-Downing, 1987). Beginning especially with Kuhn, social scientists seem to be sensitized to the irrational and rigid down sides of operating within a single paradigm. Mahoney (1980, 1985, 1989) and Coyne (1989) well exemplified this emerging view. Many are now alert to the pitfalls of paradigms, and willing to monitor themselves and their scientific thinking. In comparison to the scientist, the clinician has less epistemic risk when focusing on what works, or what is in the best interests of the client.

If what Kuhn was describing as the process of science is primarily a psychological and sociological phenomenon, why *must* it fit this stochastic, gestalt-switch model? Where is the evidence that people cannot operate from more than one paradigm? Interestingly, psychology has distinctive examples of direct attempts to make paradigms commensurable (Dollard & Miller, 1950; Wachtel, 1987). It is notable that these writers also were clinicians, practiced in the art of looking at things from different perspectives.

Kuhn's Legacy: Expanding Epistemologies

Kuhn's analysis—and the concurrent zeitgeist—has had a substantial effect on our metatheory. In effect, he said a discipline is not always what it seems to be; rather, it operates within a paradigm, a set of often hidden assumptions and covert social cognitive sets and motivations. Kuhn (1962, 1970) created a watershed in rethinking the way logic had been equated with science. He raised our consciousness about the nonrational and covert aspects that drive science. His very analysis created a cognitive set that encouraged us to ask "What is this covert metastructure of our discipline?" New kinds of questions followed: "What does our paradigm allow the data to say?" More specific questions ensued: "Is scientific rigor always the ultimate criterion for our research; might we not want also to have relevance to our practice?" (Borgen, 1984a; Gelso, 1979, 1985).

EXPANDING CONCEPTUAL PARADIGMS

Psychology's paradigms are like paisley ties: hang on to them long enough and they will eventually come back into style. The history of psychology is rife with irony if we presume, in a pre-Kuhnian stance, that all scientific developments occur with order and tight logic. If we were to assume that progress routinely occurs in linear fashion, building logically on assumptions, we would never have expected the events we have seen in this century. How could behaviorism, founded on the rejection of mentalism and introspection, ever have given rise to cognitive behavior modification? How could Rogerian counseling, founded in opposition to other approaches, ever have become imbedded as a given within today's major approaches, which take a quality counseling relationship as a necessity?

Dogmatic behaviorism created a science of the artificial. Especially in rejecting mentalistic concepts, behaviorism rejected both the construct of the mind and everyday observations. Thus, for several decades, American psychology was not very receptive to everyday concerns. Freud's ideas about dark, unseen, and persisting forces in mental life did not fit. Rogers's ideas about caring and self-actualization were not of interest. The clinician's insights about the everyday experience of everyday people did not fit the mainstream academic paradigm.

Thus, some of the changes within academic psychology of the past quarter-century have been remarkable. Leading mainstream academics published a book entitled *The Unconscious Reconsidered* (Bowers & Meichenbaum, 1984). Albert Bandura (1977, 1982, 1989) forged a leading theory about Rogers's material: human agency and self-efficacy. Most remarkable of all was the macrorevolution of cognitive psychology—a direct disengagement from dogmatic behaviorism, yet closely linked to the research rigor of methodological behaviorism.

Constructivist Perspectives

The emerging constructivist perspective can be seen as a complementary extension of Kuhn's viewpoint. Kuhn raised our consciousness to a new way of thinking about the social sciences. The constructivist perspective likewise says we should look deeper, to see what is really going on in the science. This viewpoint asserts that our realities are *constructed* from the inside-out by our thinking. It contends that our approach to science *begins* with world views, paradigms, and alternate spectacles (Highlen & Hill, 1984; Ivey et al., 1987) that *determine* what we will look for and see at the level of data. It says that the context of discovery and human construction inevitably shapes the context of justification and scientific inference.

Gergen, a social psychologist who early expressed a crisis of confidence with established approaches in his discipline (Gergen, 1973), has been a leading articulator to psychologists of the constructivist perspective (Gergen, 1982, 1985; Gergen & Davis, 1985). The constructivist critique of traditional scientific realism is indeed radical and unsettling to many, but clearly merits our most careful thought (Chaiklin, 1986; Scarr, 1985). Some observers (Campbell, 1990) see Gergen as taking the critique of traditional science too far toward nihilism. Several writers have presented constructivist accounts of the psychotherapy change process (Dowd & Pace, 1989; Guidano, 1991; Lyddon, 1990; Mahoney, 1980, 1985, 1988, 1991; Mahoney & Lyddon, 1988; McCann & Pearlman, 1990). Hare-Mustin and Maracek (1988, 1989) demonstrated how the constructivist perspective articulates and informs a feminist rethinking of past research on gender.

Hare-Mustin and Maracek (1988) starkly contrasted the perspectives of positivism and constructivism. They wrote: Thus, whereas positivism asks what are the facts, constructivism asks what are the assumptions; whereas positivism asks what are the answers, constructivism asks what are the questions (p. 456). Mahoney and Lyddon (1988) observed: "The constructivist perspective is founded on the idea that humans actively create and construe their personal realities. . . . Central to the constructivist formulations is the idea that, rather than being a sort of template through which ongoing experience is filtered, the representational model actively creates and constrains new experience and thus determines what the individual will perceive as 'reality'" (p. 200). This view contrasts wholly with the "doctrine of immaculate perception," as Mahoney (1988) christened the traditional realism assumption that sense data emerge on their own, without need of any conceptual parentage by the observer.

A Constructivist Interpretation of Jerome Frank

I find Frank's (1973, 1987) analysis of the counseling change process to be the single best extant explanation (cf. Highlen & Hill, 1984). It is, for me, the richest and most comprehensive account of what is going on at the core of the counseling process. It has the greatest verisimilitude in capturing the clinical process and the important questions. Yet, startlingly, the empirical underpinnings of Frank's explanation are thin compared to the power it derives as a "thought experiment." Frank's account, like Kuhn's, was an insightful construction and interpretation within the context of discovery (Mahrer, 1988; Reichenbach, 1938). It hypothesized that the vagaries of therapy and its divergent schools can be reconstructed as the common factors that combat demoralization within the social context of the healing setting. Frank transcended paradigmatic schisms by reframing a new construction at a level of abstraction that finesses past debates.

Frank's analysis, though more clinical and constructivist insight than laboratory empiricism, has fared very well over the past two decades of formal research on counseling process and outcome. The questions he framed are increasingly the questions at the leading edges of today's research. Because the recent yields of outcome and process research have been disappointing, much current interest has turned to common change processes. Further, Frank's viewpoint was inherently contextual; it recognized the deep social expectations of the healing setting.

The Cognitive Revolution

The singular sea change of the past 25 years within psychology has been the cognitive revolution (Baars, 1986; Dember, 1974; Gardner, 1985; Mahoney, 1991; Seligman, 1991, pp. 8–9). At times, the tide has been slow enough to go unrecognized, but then suddenly, on reflection, psychology is awash in cognition. The change can be seen across psychology. The epicenter of the cognitive revolution was experimental psychology (Gardner, 1985; Miller, Galanter, & Pribram, 1960; Neisser, 1967), which led to a new focus on information processing. Here the change occurred as a direct assault on the traditional behavioral model, initiated by Neisser's (1967) seminal and provocative book *Cognitive Psychology* (cf. Mahoney, 1991, pp. 67–94).

The shifting of paradigms within counseling and psychotherapy has not been so simple as a behaviorist–cognitive struggle. Academic psychology was more influenced by a singular paradigm in behaviorism. In the field of practice, a larger variety of models has held center stage, and Skinner and Wolpe shared the stage with Freud and

Rogers. In counseling practice, the scientist's quest for logical consistency has given way to multiple metaphors that enhance outcomes for clients.

Coyne (1989) on Down Sides of the Cognitive Paradigm

Paradigms, rigidly pursued, are at once beacons of light telling us where to look and blinkers obscuring our vision. Coyne (1989) wrote a perceptive critical essay on the down sides of aggressively and exclusively applying the cognitive model to the analysis of depression. His commentary illustrated how a new paradigm infuses energy and activity into a problem area, but then it begins to blind vision to other promising avenues. The fact that his critical essay appeared in a major handbook on cognitive therapy reflects the healthy maturity and intellectual openness of the area.

Coyne (1989) wrote:

> *[T]he resurgence of the cognitive perspective in the early 1970s was so strong that it became widely described as the "cognitive revolution" (Dember, 1974). More than a decade later, there still has been little in the way of critical response or sober reevaluation of the enthusiastic claims and polemics that accompanied this shift in perspective. . . . Does this state of affairs demonstrate that all is well? Was this the revolution to end all such fundamental shifts in conceptual and theoretical frameworks? Has clinical psychology finally found its long-sought, general, unifying paradigm? Or is this "cognitive revolution" better seen as just another wave, soon to crash on the shore and be followed by yet another such transformation of perspective? Certainly, any suggestion of the crash of the cognitive perspective seems premature, if not grossly exaggerated. Yet, serious problems are accumulating, indicating that even if not imminent, its demise is inevitable. (p. 227)*

Coyne held: "Although cognitive theory was initially a source of great inspiration and innovation in psychotherapy, it is now a constraint on both creative and critical thinking, and the limits of its assumptions deserve careful scrutiny" (p. 228). He also argued that the cognitive approach to depression is overfocused on cognitions, to the neglect of other perspectives. It neglects environmental factors, especially the interpersonal environment of the depressed person. In becoming overfocused on thinking processes, it develops a simplistic account that lacks contextual richness. Coyne asserted that emerging data contradict much of the cognitive explanation of depression, and that measures of depressive cognitions may be seriously flawed, being confounded with semantic contents that are more likely the results of depression than causal antecedents. He interpreted the cognitive view of depression as advocating a traitlike conception of depressive cognitions that would typify depressed individuals prior to the onset of depression and after the remission of depression; he contended that the data support neither of these expectations. Finally, Coyne argued that the acknowledged success of cognitive therapy for depression does not prove the particulars of cognitive theory, for a variety of reasons.

Human Agency

When I was a graduate student in the 1960s, my wise grandmother was appalled that I studied not a wit about the human will. She could not see how any account of human behavior could approach completeness without addressing "the will." I did not try to explain to her that Skinner had made it clear that such concepts were unnecessary—and worse, unscientific. But the conflict between Skinner's and my grandmother's view of human nature has persisted as a tension. Today, she would be pleased that psychologists think seriously about something akin to her concept of the human will, although they dress it up with fancy terms such as volition, human agency, self-determination, self-efficacy, and learned optimism (Seligman, 1991).

The recent focus on human agency represents the epitome of the active agent model. Although developing from quite different perspectives, Bandura (1982, 1989) and Howard (Howard, 1986b, 1989; Howard & Conway, 1986, 1987; Howard & Myers, 1990) are leading exemplars of this perspective, publishing voluminously with both active theorizing and vigorous empirical research programs. A core concept of Bandura's theory, self-efficacy, has had major heuristic value in generating research throughout psychology. Counseling psychology in particular has been invigorated by productive research programs in topics such as career self-efficacy (Betz & Hackett, 1986; Hackett & Betz, 1981; Lent & Hackett, 1987) and academic self-efficacy (Brown, Lent, & Larkin, 1989; Lent, Brown, & Larkin, 1984, 1986, 1987).

Current thrusts in human agency reflect the confluence of many of the paradigmatic trends discussed in this chapter. Today's focus on human agency is, most of all, a product of the recent cognitive revolution and the re-emergence of concepts of people as thinking, planful agents who assess and act upon their environments (Pervin, 1989). Indubitably, this is a major paradigmatic shift from radical behaviorism, as well as from a psychoanalysis that puts strong deterministic limits on human potential. Bandura (1989) strikingly described the model of people that underlies human agency:

> People do not simply react to immediate environmental influences like weathervanes, nor are they mechanically steered by implants from their past. . . . Theories that seek to explain human behavior solely as the product of external influences or the remnants of past stimulus inputs present a truncated image of human nature. . . . The capability for intentional and purposive action is rooted in symbolic activity. (p. 1179)

Current work in human agency also gives one a sense of dèja vu. Somewhere, we have heard much of this—in Rogers's self-actualization, Kelly's personal constructs, and elsewhere. These themes of empowering clients to act in their best interests seem to be what counseling psychology has tried to do from its beginning. Counseling psychologists *have* seen their clients as active agents, although perhaps temporarily stuck and needing help in developing skills for self-assessment, choosing productive environments, and planning for successful life tasks.

The current excitement about human agency is quite justified, however; for the first time, it now has credible salience on three fronts: theory, research, and practice (cf. Sappington, 1990). In the past, theorists and practitioners such as Rogers spoke eloquently about people as active agents, but were out of step with the dominant academic paradigm of their time. Thus, the research base to buttress this position failed to develop strongly within academic psychology. Today, the assumptive world of psychologists is markedly different, and human agency is a hot topic. Consequently, active research programs are flourishing within this paradigm and are leading to a synergy among theory, research, and practice. Sappington (1990, p. 26) recently noted these major changes from the 1950s as follows: "Empirically oriented psychologists no longer routinely assume that a scientific psychology must be a deterministic psychology. They increasingly use concepts such as *conscious choice* and *purpose* to predict and account for data." Thus, there is currently productive energy in the contexts of both discovery and justification. We are effectively melding insight and action.

Tyler (1978) was one of the first to see so clearly how psychology was shifting toward human agency. In observing the changes afoot in psychology, she wrote:

> *Perhaps the most fundamental is a shift from* reaction *to* action *as the phenomenon to be studied. . . . As research findings accumulated, it became increasingly apparent that action is more fundamental than reaction. Action occurs in the absence of any identifiable stimulus; living things are* inherently *active. (p. 2)*

Similarly, Ford (1987) comprehensively reviewed human agency to build an ambitious model viewing humans as self-constructing living systems.

The exemplary human agency work of Howard and Bandura deserves the special coverage that follows.

Howard on Human Agency

In a spirited program of theory and research, George Howard recently advanced the strong stand that human action is mainly attributable to agency (or alternately, volition or self-determination). Howard and Myers (1990) described Howard's earlier work on human agency:

> *Howard . . . proposed a model that presents human beings as self-determining, story-telling, active agents. . . . From this telic, agentic perspective, the nonagentic factors . . . studied by traditional psychological research are seen in a new light. (p. 227)*

Howard appears to be motivated to operationalize the humanistic agenda within the received research tradition. Thus, he tries to use traditional research methodologies, designed within a mechanistic, linear, causal model, to access elusive volition. As Howard and Conway (1987, p. 1035) stated: "We began our work on volition with two nonnegotiable requirements: (a) the projects must be empirical, and (b) they must possess sufficient methodological rigor to be acceptable to mainstream research in psychology." Thus, although there are alternative routes to empiricism, they approached the problem with psychology's cynosure of the experiment and analysis of variance. But here may be the crucial rub, where Howard is hoist with his own petard. Volition is inherently a naturalistic concept, and to study it with experimental control may be a contradiction in terms. The quest for rigor may quixotically miss the relevant concept (Gelso, 1979, 1985) and leave all with a dissonance about the lack of verisimilitude of the product.

In trying to demonstrate one paradigm with the tools of another, Howard made himself vulnerable to critics from both sides. The phenomenologist (Ford, 1987) recoils at the use of the common methods of the "implacable experimenter" (Wachtel, 1973) to address volition; the theoretical and methodological behaviorist (Hayes, 1987) is unimpressed by the experiment because of its vulnerability to alternative interpretations. As Kuhn (1970) alerted us, the languages of different paradigms are incommensurable, and productive discourse across them is not probable.

Leapfrogging Legacies: "By George, Just Do It"

In the 1970s, when university counseling centers were more generous with unlimited contact hours, a very thoughtful client and I had spent years of intermittent counseling sessions in building insight about her life and psyche. But the real-world payoffs of her cognitive successes were thin. Then, at a turning point, perhaps borne of frustration, she suddenly grasped her most important cognition: "Just Do It." She leapfrogged the rhetorical impasses of our intellectualizing, and her real-world successes followed rapidly. Researchers can also benefit from making a gestalt switch and simply leaping to an action mode, even though their intellectual selves may feel the work of insight is incomplete.

Howard addresses volition experimentally, and to do so successfully would indeed be impressive within that major tradition of psychology. But Howard need not play only on that turf. Volition might readily and profitably be addressed in naturalistic behavior. Recent trends in counseling research, discussed later in this chapter, emphasize naturalistic behaviors in counseling. Thus, Hill's (1982, 1984, 1989, 1990) major research program takes a more aggressive approach to upending received methods. Hill, and similar researchers, can be interpreted as assuming volitional concepts as they focus on intentions in the counseling process. Hill makes a more radical departure from typical research, and in so doing achieves a gestalt switch that engenders less dissonance in merging assumptions, concepts, and methods. Which approach will have ultimate payoff is an open question. My point is that numerous research pathways address volition-like concepts, and it would be premature and limiting to equate the span of volition with Howard's vigorously pursued research paradigms.

In my view, Howard is overly pessimistic about the role of volition in past research (Ford, 1987; Sappington, 1990). He wants to demonstrate volition within the experimental paradigm, and thereby creates a perhaps insuperable hurdle at this stage. He wants to create methodological paradigms that will definitively assess the proportion of variance in behavior that is due respectively to volitional and nonvolitional factors. His reach is so broad that he risks disappointment, however heroic his efforts.

Howard seems to underestimate how successfully Bandura (1977, 1982, 1989) has finessed volitional issues and potential critics by simply assuming agency to be present in self-efficacy and related constructs. Bandura then proceeds to study such concepts in a cumulative research program, but not a program dependent on one grand, definitive, experimental test. Rather, in Bandura's program, the construct of self-efficacy is explicated and supported through a nomological net built on numerous cumulative studies.

The issues are degree of entrenchment of belief systems, and the potency of data needed to confirm a new perspective. If we assume that the discipline is strongly Skinnerian (1987), operating from the assumption that mentalistic concepts are unnecessary in the science of psychology, then one needs strong and pervasive evidence indeed for volition. But large segments of psychology, especially following the hegemony of the cognitive revolution, do not require such strong evidence for human agency and volition. The Bayesian consensus (i.e., the paradigm) is already inclined toward that conclusion. Howard is trying too hard, within the received tradition, to conduct the crucial experiment that will mightily merge the contexts of discovery and justification about volition. The context of discovery, in many quarters, has already accepted volitional concepts (Pervin, 1989; Sappington, 1990). At this stage, there is not a continued rhetorical need to justify such a research program. There may be a greater payoff in simply pursuing agency-invested research programs such as Bandura's. For those interested in research on volition, may advice is simply: "Just Do It!"

Bandura (1989): Human Agency in Social Cognitive Theory

Bandura's (1982, 1989) approach to theory and research in human agency is mature, sophisticated, elaborate, complex, heuristic, productive for research, and highly influential. Although he differs with some extreme emphases of past perspectives, he does not reject models such as the environmental. Rather, he integrates them into his models, saying that what is needed is a larger purview for adequately describing human nature. Thus, Bandura (1989) asserted: "Social cognitive theory rejects the dichotomous conception of self as agent and self as object" (p. 1181). Most reflective of his blending and integration of models is his system of triadic reciprocal determinism. Although this causal model includes external environmental factors, it also embraces the causal contributions persons make to their own motivation and action. "In this model of reciprocal causation, action, cognitive, affective, and other personal factors, and environmental events all operate as interacting determinants. Any account of the determinants of human action must, therefore, include self-generated influences as a contributing factor" (Bandura, 1989, p. 1175).

What is so amazing about Bandura is that his theorizing strikes one as so obvious. It is intriguing to consider why this is so; perhaps it is partly the zeitgeist. For example, Ellis's work considerably predated Bandura's, and his idea that the way we think affects the way we act and feel is now commonplace. Moreover, Bandura incorporated phenomena of self in a way that was predated by Rogers and other humanistic psychologists.

Perhaps Bandura's theoretical system has such high verisimilitude because it is not inconsistent with any major therapeutic paradigm, save perhaps the Freudian. It fits learning models. It fits cognitive models. It fits humanistic models. It probably even fits Freud in some ways. One linkage is the *ego,* the core cognizing agent and the manager of self-efficacy beliefs. Bandura also fits with the delay of gratification functions of the ego; he advocates persisting and sacrificing toward ultimate goals, in the face of frustration.

At first glance, Freud and Bandura appear to be on opposite poles of the pessimism–optimism world view continuum. Freud was not sanguine about possibilities for human change; Bandura is quite the opposite. However, their differences here are more surface than substance. Bandura writes about winners; Freud wrote about losers. Bandura focuses on successes, coping, and performance. Freud's focus was on human trial, distress, and neuroticism. But Bandura's model is an embedded dialectic, and, although he writes most about the mechanisms of success, as derived through self-efficacy, there is the inevitable side of explaining human misery through self-*in*efficacy. The flip sides of psychological constructs are nicely illustrated by Seligman's work on learned helplessness suddenly being presented as learned optimism (Seligman, 1991).

Bandura's account is one of the most common-sensical theories psychology has ever had. Some of its essences are the banalities of Everyperson, especially in America. One is successful because one believes in oneself and persists toward one's goals. What athletic coach would disagree with that philosophy? At the core of Bandura's theory is self-efficacy, first taught to most of us before kindergarten by the Little Engine That Could: "I think I can, I think I can."

For the clinician, the verisimilitude of Bandura's concepts is high. In working with distressed clients, it is obvious that the most distressed are lamentably lacking in self-efficacy. They do not believe that their efforts will be successful in solving their problems. But we knew this long before Bandura coined the term self-efficacy. We knew it from Rogers. We knew it from Frank's writing about demoralization. We knew it from personality assessment: the more distressed a person, the higher the demoralization the person shows on an inventory such as the MMPI; K is low, F is high, and the person is generally saying "I can't cope." We knew both from clinical work and from an extensive personological literature that one of the strongest individual difference variables is optimism–pessimism, or what Frank has called demoralization. Bandura's self-efficacy engages our clinical belief because it captures the essence of this hoary variable.

Bandura (1989, 1991) argues for the situational specificity and distinctiveness of self-efficacy as a construct, but I share the reservations of commentators such as Corcoran (1991), who have difficulty separating self-efficacy from locus of control or other related constructs. From either a personological or clinical viewpoint, it is tempting to suggest that several writers are massaging the same potent variance in individual differences, but giving it names to suggest a distinctiveness that does not exist. To an outsider and nonspecialist within these vigorous paradigms, it is hard, for example, to see how Bandura's (1989) self-efficacy and Seligman's (1991) learned optimism are not similar, especially when extrapolated outside the lab to the clinic, the home, and the rest of life. Yet they both argue for the distinctiveness of their constructs.

I have intentionally stated this commentary on Bandura in a declarative, confident style, emulating the style of Bandura's propositions. Like his, my assertions should be subjected to empirical test. Does his approach to self-efficacy say quite new things, not imbedded for some time in our knowledge claims? The answer may revolve around semantics and methodology. If we have to measure self-efficacy precisely, as Bandura has, its generality to other long-standing constructs may be constrained. But if we are able to take self-efficacy as a beginning conceptual definition and then apply it with diverse measurement strategies, we are likely to confirm more of my assertions.

Self-efficacy helps us think about what brings people to counseling and what differentiates those who respond rapidly. First, many people with high self-efficacy will not even seek professional help. Thus, of the 40 million people who have quit smoking, the majority have done it without professional help. Generally, a subset of people who believe strongly in their ability to change will not need to seek professional help. For some, seeking counseling will be part of their quest toward problem solving. A counselor in a student counseling center will often see this phenomenon; coming to counseling is part of problem solving. College students are accustomed to living with self-efficacy; they believe that their efforts and persistence will be rewarded. Thus, they may come briefly to counseling, to gain a problem-solving tool, and then be rapidly on their way toward continued action and success.

Contrast chronic mental patients and other people who are unsuccessful by our standards. Their self-esteem is nil, they have no history of success, self-inefficacy is their core belief. We clinicians can see what these persons' deficits are and what they need, but being therapeutic is often quite another matter. We do not have brain grafts of self-efficacy.

There is also much to be gained by translating more of self-efficacy into counseling theory. What are the determinants of self-efficacy? How can one therapeutically enhance self-efficacy? Are Frank's curative factors a good model for explaining how self-efficacy is addressed in therapy?

Bandura's current theory is likely to have a continuing major effect on psychology. He says much that we already believe. He gives license to assumptions that have not always had a good reception in psychology. Most central of these is the legitimacy of thinking humans as active agents. The heuristic value of Bandura's theory is huge—a prime example of ideas whose time has come.

EXPANDING METHODOLOGICAL PARADIGMS

Hoshmand's (1989) Alternate Research Methods

Hoshmand (1989) sounded the most ambitious and far-reaching call for alternative research paradigms in counseling psychology. Many past calls for research reform can be seen as coming from within the received tradition of research (Gelso, 1979; Howard, 1983, 1984), but Hoshmand's treatise advocated reform in research methods quite beyond the usual boundaries of psychological research (Gelso & Fassinger, 1990, p. 373). Thus, she presented a stimulating and scholarly summary of major alternate research approaches that are not often familiar to psychologists.

Like Polkinghorne (1983, 1984, 1991), Hoshmand (1989) looked at more qualitative research methods, such as (a) naturalistic–ethnographic, (b) phenomenological, and (c) cybernetic and other "high-context" approaches. These are typically research methods established in disciplines other than psychology. Hoshmand intended her article to be a "catalyst for more investment in teaching and development with respect to alternate research paradigms" (p. 5). Although aspects of her article have struck some commentators (Borgen, 1989; Harmon, 1989) as an overdrawn critique of customary research approaches, she temperately invited "the reader to view this article as an invitation to learn more about constructive extensions of the more established models of inquiry currently in use and not as a proposal on necessarily better alternatives or a panacea for problems of research training" (p. 5).

Hoshmand presented research models that she saw as alternates to "experimental research in the reductive-positivist tradition" (p. 5). She called the three approaches that she presented *paradigms,* or systems of inquiry, and sketched features distinguishing them from the received tradition in research. She saw researchers as having a commitment to discover the meaning and essence of human experience. Her emphasis is on description and discovery more than theory testing and verification alone.

Commentary on Hoshmand's Proposal

Goldman (1976) has long been a forceful, if sometimes lonely, voice calling for new relevance in our research approaches. His commentary on the Hoshmand (1989) treatise was highly enthusiastic:

> *Lisa Hoshmand has established a new milestone in the history of research in counseling psychology. She helps us take a step toward the opening of major new vistas in research, and with this step begins the move into the 21st century . . . her presentation is offered so modestly that it is easy to miss the great importance of her contribution. (Goldman, 1989, p. 81)*

These still waters run deep indeed. In commenting on the Hoshmand article, I observed that "it is chock-full of new ideas and references that are provocative, informative, insightful, timely, and diverse. It stretches our thinking to new ways of looking at how we know as both scientists and practitioners" (Borgen, 1989, p. 90). I saw Hoshmand's article as "a distinctly valuable contribution likely to be seen as a future classic with impact on the discipline" (Borgen, 1989, p. 91). However, like any new paradigm, the advocacy in Hoshmand's article will be controversial, especially insofar as it implied severe limitations in received research traditions.

In commenting on the Hoshmand (1989) contribution, Helms (1989) pointedly noted the ethnocentrism of our customary approaches in accessing the world views of other cultures. Thus, she welcomed the promise of Hoshmand's alternate paradigms for informing our cross-cultural research. The Helms point also speaks to feminist research, which is motivated to bring fresh and person-centered perspectives to monolithic traditional constructions (Crawford & Gentry, 1989; Maracek, 1989; Nielson, 1990). Many advocates of the feminist research approach add the principle of the value of the "feminist standpoint." The feminist standpoint means that women, as subordinates within a societal power structure, are likely to have insights that are unique and valid. Qualitative research methods, and their focus on phenomenology, may come to be increasingly visible, more through currently energetic feminist research programs than through generic calls for alternate paradigms (Maracek, 1989).

One central and practical question about the alternate research methods is whether the discipline has the will and the energy to embrace them fully and effectively (Borgen, 1989; Goldman, 1989; Harmon, 1989; Helms, 1989). Where will the time and energy be found, by faculty and students alike, to learn and become expert with them? Will the time and energy be taken from typical research methods? Are the kinds of leading edge but mainstream quantitative methods, such as those covered in Wampold's (1987) special issue of the *Journal of Counseling Psychology,* to be ignored, so that time is available to study hermeneutic inquiry (Messer, Sass, & Woolfolk, 1988; Packer, 1985)? What is the relative value of knowing how to apply and interpret MANOVA versus content analysis? MANOVA emerges from a very traditional research approach, but its purposes are quite in accord with some of those of the alternate methods—namely, to take into account a number of variables simultaneously and to avoid atomistic, reductionistic, piecemeal interpretations. Indeed, MANOVA (like other multivariate methods) has some prospects for yielding the "context-rich" information desired by the alternate methodologies—and doing it in a way that more clearly shows many important quantitative properties of the data (Haase & Ellis, 1987; Wampold, 1987).

The bottom-line reservation about qualitative methods is whether they can distinctively advance knowledge in ways that are improbable with traditional quantitative research methods. Psychologists have some of the most sophisticated training in research, designed to protect the integrity of inference. We should not casually overthrow the strengths of this legacy by engaging in an overdrawn and unproductive dialectic between "quantitative" and "qualitative" methods. Rather, we should be ecumenical and eclectic, nondefensively reaching beyond the blinders of our paradigms and incorporating new thinking. I believe there are many robust examples of this within the received tradition of research. In fact, the preceding content of this chapter is a striking testament to how mainstream psychology, using traditional research methods, is addressing some of the same metagoals Hoshmand (1989) advocated for newer qualitative methods.

Recent vigorous research within the cognitive revolution and associated work on human agency contrast with Hoshmand's characterization of a psychology dominated by extremes of positivism and reductionism. In my view (Borgen, 1989), Hoshmand seems to equate psychology too exclusively with Skinner's (1987) perspective. In fact, the themes sketched earlier in this chapter as emerging conceptual paradigms share many of the metagoals of Hoshmand's alternate qualitative methodological paradigms. One broad area of linkage is phenomenology, where the cognitive revolution signaled the re-entry of the mind and human agency into mainstream psychology. Sperry (1988, p. 607), in characterizing these changes as the new mentalist paradigm, observed:

[they] have radically reformed scientific descriptions of human nature and the conscious self. The resultant views today are less atomistic, less mechanistic, and more mentalist, contextual, subjectivist, and humanistic.

Thus, I conclude that many of the goals of qualitative research *are* being achieved within traditional quantitative research traditions. As Miles and Huberman (1984) observed, "if one looks carefully at the research actually conducted in the name of one or another epistemology, it seems that few working researchers are *not* blending the two perspectives" (p. 20). We need to be careful to differentiate the core features of quantitative and qualitative methods from those that are historical accidents or rhetorical baggage.

Many of the flaws of some past research that Hoshmand mentions are being addressed within counseling psychology as it seeks to move research closer to the complexities and subtleties of counseling practice (Borgen, 1984a, 1984b, 1989). Some additional specific examples of these are discussed in the following section.

Openness in Methods

I suspect that the greatest impact of the Hoshmand (1989) treatise will be indirectly on mainstream research rather than directly on the construction *de novo* of counseling research programs from the qualitative perspective she advocates. I believe this because the major subtext of her argument involves methodological openness, especially toward approaches likely to discover fresh constructions of clients' and counselors' worlds. In my view, these metagoals are already informing much leading edge research within our traditional sources. The zeitgeist that motivates much of Hoshmand's work also motivates many researchers in counseling psychology and psychology in general. Thus, I expect the metagoals of the Hoshmand perspective will continue to energize many current research programs that emerge from traditional research but are unfettered by traditional assumptions. These changes are most evident in the paradigm shift that occurred in counseling process research in the 1980s.

The Invigoration and Transformation of Counseling Process Research

As Gelso and Fassinger (1990) exulted, the decade of the 1980s represented a "full-fledged assault on the counseling process—finally" (p. 375). A new look now imbues counseling process research. It is led by a cadre of dynamic young researchers who are trained in traditional methods but courageously transcending old approaches by framing new questions and methods. Gelso and Fassinger noted that there are "important programs by Hill, Tracey, Martin, Stiles, and Elliott . . . others could easily be added here" (p. 375). Their work has prominently appeared in our flagship research journal, the *Journal of Counseling Psychology.*

This new assault on process research eminently illustrates the self-renewal of the discipline within the received research tradition. The new thinking about how to conceptualize counseling research is often highly radical, by psychology's traditions, but portrays how much a discipline can be moved if researchers are willing and able to think new thoughts and try new approaches. Journal gatekeepers, of course, have to be receptive to such new approaches, and it is not incidental that Gelso (1979, 1982) announced that under his editorship the *Journal of Counseling Psychology* would pursue openness as a major goal.

I will not attempt to repeat here the excellent and timely synopsis of recent counseling process research by Gelso and Fassinger (1990). Advances in this area are also discussed elsewhere in this volume (see Chapter 3, by Wampold and Poulin). Rather, I wish to highlight two seminal contributions that exemplify major rethinking of traditional research in counseling process. These are the work of Hill and colleagues (Highlen & Hill, 1984; Hill, 1982, 1984, 1989, 1990; Hill, Carter, & O'Farrell, 1983) and of Rice and Greenberg (1984; Greenberg, 1986). Their work has led, with others', to an explosion of new and demanding research in counseling process. I will not describe the expanding substantive research by them and others, but rather will suggest how their work has been motivated by a fresh set of metagoals. I hope to depict some of the ways in which the received tradition in counseling research has taken some very new turns into uncharted territory.

Hill has developed the leading process research program, and its development makes a fascinating and enlightening story. Fortunately, she has publicly shared the personal dilemmas and frustrations she has faced in forging a research program that addresses important questions (Hill, 1982, 1984). Her emerging insights about assumptions, goals, and methods can be seen as a courageous odyssey by a traditionally trained researcher to transcend the fetters of tradition and enlarge the scope of research. She stated:

> *I have grown to recognize the limitations of research, particularly the traditional models. . . . It is easy to put together an idea and run a study, but it is very difficult to do a study that says anything about counseling. . . . I have come to have more confidence in studying my own ideas in my own ways. In my early years of doing research, I felt that I had to follow established methodologies, whereas I now feel free to try out new ways of doing research, particularly qualitative means. (1984, p. 99)*

Hill's leadership is unexcelled in merging the perspectives of the scientist and practitioner. She is a prime example of a researcher actively merging insight and action. She continually tries to integrate the knowledge frames of research, practice, and teaching. Most illustrative of her change in direction is her landmark case study (Hill, Carter, & O'Farrell, 1983), in which the intensively studied therapist is Hill herself. Subsequently, Hill (1989) published eight coordinated case studies in a book. The 1983 publication of Hill et al.'s first case study is a landmark for the discipline, because it signaled the discipline's readiness to forgo its premature nomothetic needs in favor of careful and intensive idiography. The subsequent new looks in process research in the 1980s were profound—and constitute a paradigm shift. A not-incidental signal of this paradigm shift is that Hill is now the Associate Editor of the *Journal of Counseling Psychology.*

The depth of this paradigm shift is reflected in how Hill has upended several once sacrosanct assumptions of traditional research (Hill, 1984; Hill & Gronsky, 1984). Hill (1984) recounted how she was able "to put the value and potentials of research into a better perspective, primarily *by understanding that I would have to utilize new paradigms to study counseling/psychotherapy process*" (p. 105, emphasis added). Hill and Gronsky identified what they saw as bad assumptions of traditional research, and reframed a set of more appropriate assumptions:

Bad assumptions

- Behavior is governed by universal laws or truths.
- Science will ultimately be able to discover these laws and create a better world.
- The best way to seek truth is through the scientific method, generally characterized by inductive logic, linear causality, experimental research design, complex

inferential statistics, use of large samples, and measurement of change in a pre–post manner.

More appropriate assumptions

- There is no truth; rather, there are multiple realities that are dependent on the vantage points, psychological filters, and predefined contours of the mind.
- Clinical phenomena are elusive and reactive.
- Clinical problems are often intractable.
- Human behavior should be studied holistically rather than in a piecemeal fashion.
- Cause-and-effect relationships or linear causality concepts may not be useful at this point in our understanding of human behavior. (Hill & Gronsky, 1984, pp. 154–156)

The leap of Hill and Gronsky's (1984) assumptive shifts, especially the list of "bad assumptions," will make traditionalists cringe. They will react, "You cannot do that and still do science." But the liberating effect of this radical reframing on Hill's research program has been huge. It has opened exhilarating horizons in a discovery-oriented program of empirical research on counseling (Mahrer, 1988).

I suggest that the assumptive worlds of Hoshmand (1989) and Hill (1982, 1984) are very similar to each other and very different from what is often seen as traditional psychology. Both are at center stage in a newly framed human science that is "qualitative, molar, naturalistic, idiographic, field, subjective, holistic, and nondeterministic" (Gelso & Fassinger, 1990, p. 373). The best current exemplar of Hoshmand's vision for meaningful research is Hill's empirical research program. Yet, significantly, Hill's work emerges within a reframing of traditional methods rather than an adoption of the specific qualitative methods advocated by Hoshmand (1989) and Polkinghorne (1991).

The other salient turn toward the new look in counseling process research is marked by Rice and Greenberg's (1984) innovative and penetrating book. Their work is highly congruent with Hill's in powerfully rethinking process research and forging a new set of questions and methods to address the natural complexity of counseling. They have reframed the research focus as *task analysis,* and stimulated, with Hill (1984, 1989, 1990) and others, a burgeoning line of research under this rubric. Task analysis rejects the extremes of a process–outcome dichotomy and focuses on client change events. Using discovery-oriented, intensive, and rigorous studies of single cases, this approach intends to identify pivotal change events occurring in the counseling process.

Marmar (1990) observed that these second-generation process studies "signal a paradigm shift toward multidimensional, episode anchored, sequentially patterned approaches to the investigation of change" (p. 265). Similarly, Kiesler's (1985) review of the Rice and Greenberg book aptly called it a landmark that "forcefully articulates the emerging new paradigm and demonstrates its scientific utility" (p. 527). Kiesler, who sensitized us to the risks of "uniformity myths" in therapy research (Kiesler, 1966), has long led the field in asking timely questions. Like Hill (1984), he believes that, in "process" research, crystallized traditions have come to focus on issues that are too small ("micro-units") and, in "outcome" research, on issues that are too big ("macro-units"). He observed that between these two foci "is a vast unexplored terrain" of intermediate units of dyadic interchange within sessions where "we are most likely to discover the real 'action' of psychotherapy" (Kiesler, 1985, p. 528). Kiesler noted that therapy researchers are coming to believe "that we need to return to an essential first step that we bypassed in our rush to nomothetic respectability—to wit, careful naturalistic observation guided by clinical judgment" (p. 528). The energetic themes in books by Rice and Greenberg (1984) and Greenberg and Pinsof (1986) were addressed to the new perspectives and methods needed for this endeavor.

FINAL COMMENTARY

The above sketch should indicate that the past three decades have been marked by an emergence of often startling new ways of thinking about psychology and of doing research. The health and vigor of the discipline are evident in the progress we have made with the conceptual dysfunction that Thoresen (1979) dubbed "hardening of the categories." In the historically brief period of the 1980s, a sea change swept over the assumptive world and research products in counseling process research and research programs in human agency. The sea change of the cognitive revolution continues.

For counseling process researchers, the 1980s began with something of a Kuhnian crisis, in which impasse was seen in the epistemic yield from traditional research methods. An often unspoken malaise set in as the hoped-for payoffs from the "best and the brightest" of psychology's research legacy were toted up and found wanting in their capacity to inform our knowledge of the counseling process. The results failed the verisimilitude test, especially for scientists close to the practitioner's world view. The result for some has been a zero-based budgeting in research, a return to first principles to construct a new paradigm of process research.

It is important to note the function of traditional methods in this Kuhnian revolution. Without them, we would not be at the current stage of renewed enthusiasm for assault on the process research problem. The 1970s' consensus of the discipline was that we possessed the best methods for effectively addressing central problems. These approaches necessarily had to be applied before we could reach a stage of disappointment with the yield. Their limitations could not be revealed and faced by working researchers until that stage occurred. That stage of crisis has occurred, new conceptions of the very questions are emerging, and there is a huge agenda for future research.

A corollary phenomenon is occurring within the focused domain of outcome research. Beginning with the Sloane, Staples, Cristol, Yorkstown, & Whipple (1975) studies and culminating with the NIMH Collaborative Depression study (Elkin et al., 1989), we have seen a series of outcome studies applying *state-of-the-art research methods* for studying the comparative effectiveness of psychotherapies. Many observers, in watching the cumulative yield of many such rigorously designed studies, have now found the answers to the original questions disappointing. The assumptions were that substantial and nuanced differences would be found, and that they would guide counseling and psychotherapy practice. Instead, the big answer has been that there are few differences. The implications of this unease in outcome research are continuing to unfold. For some, the answer seems to be in doing a better job of conducting traditional outcome research (Kazdin, 1986; Kendall & Lipman, 1991). For others, the impasse has stimulated a major rethinking of some central questions. These newly interesting questions involve: (a) eclecticism; (b) common therapeutic mechanisms; and (c) redefinition of placebos and nonspecific effects.

The impasse in outcome research has undoubtedly played a role in rethinking process research (Hill, 1984; Kiesler, 1985). Thus, the artificial dichotomization of process–outcome research is now publicly acknowledged, and many are reframing the questions. This is most evident within counseling process research itself and best reflected in the exciting focus on *task analysis*.

The public science of psychology is typically equated with the context of justification. A typical empirical article in a research journal is tightly focused on the core of justificationist inference. There is often little revelation of the discovery context, the assumptive paradigm begetting the study, and the fits of frustration by the researcher. This chapter notes how some of this content is changing in counseling psychology. As the discipline has reached a level of self-confident maturity, we have seen a thriving public self-analysis within our major journals. We have transcended knee-jerk applications of established methodologies and have asked ourselves how we might best address our most important questions. The editors of our journals have abetted this openness by welcoming fresh approaches. Thus, much of the material discussed above is flourishing within the context of discovery. The tighter canons of established justificationist research have often been momentarily waived. We are in a process of re-evaluating which of these canons are ultimately necessary for our human science, and which may be unnecessary baggage. Ultimately, the energetic programs now being openly pursued in these discovery contexts will need to prove their mettle to many, within a revised justification context. The ultimate product will leave a new imprint, but its specific contours are not currently visible as we openly and courageously take this journey of insight and action.

Beyond Paradigms: Postparadigmatic Science

The important theme of this chapter is that the best science is ultimately science that is open. This means transcending the natural rigidities of paradigms and applying greater insight to the preconscious aspects of paradigms. Paradigms in their natural state rush toward functional autonomy and action. Although that action produces products in the short run, it ultimately creates its own down sides by its rigid and premature closure on questions and methods. The push of paradigms is tendentious; conceptual commitments are forced that preclude thinking and insight. Debate preempts dialogue.

Our maturing human science can tolerate and build on epistemological pluralism and openness. Expanding paradigms can be embraced for the new insights they bring, without adopting them so unthinkingly that they obscure our vision. Our continuing challenge is to move beyond paradigm strictures to a postparadigmatic science (Thompson, 1989) flourishing with methodological openness (Gelso, 1982) and eclectic epistemologies (Borgen, 1984a, 1984b, 1989). Mahoney (1985, 1989), in eloquently making a case for genuine intellectual openness, concluded: "The time has come to transform ideological swords into conceptual plowshares and to risk trusting in the harvest of open dialectical exchange" (1989, p. 1375). The recent growth points in counseling psychology reflect such healthy trends toward a liberating openness.

REFERENCES

Baars, B. J. (1986). *The cognitive revolution in psychology.* New York: Guilford Press.

Bandura, A. (1977). Self-efficacy: Toward a unifying theory of behavioral change. *Psychological Review, 84,* 191–215.

Bandura, A. (1982). Self-efficacy mechanism in human agency. *American Psychologist, 37,* 122–147.

Bandura, A. (1989). Human agency in social cognitive theory. *American Psychologist, 44,* 1175–1184.

Bandura, A. (1991). Human agency: The rhetoric and the reality. *American Psychologist, 46,* 157–162.

Betz, N. E., & Hackett, G. (1986). Applications of self-efficacy theory to understanding career choice behavior. *Journal of Social and Clinical Psychology, 4,* 279–289.

Beutler, L. E., & Clarkin, J. F. (1990). *Systematic treatment selection: Toward targeted therapeutic interventions.* New York: Brunner/Mazel.

Borgen, F. H. (1984a). Counseling psychology. *Annual Review of Psychology, 35,* 579–604.

Borgen, F. H. (1984b). Are there necessary linkages between research practices and the philosophy of science? *Journal of Counseling Psychology, 31,* 457–460.

Borgen, F. H. (1989). Evolution of eclectic epistemology. *The Counseling Psychologist, 17,* 90–97.

Bowers, K. S., & Meichenbaum, D. (Eds.). (1984). *The unconscious reconsidered.* New York: Wiley.

Brown, S. D., Lent, R. W., & Larkin, K. C. (1989). Self-efficacy as a moderator of scholastic aptitude–academic performance relationships. *Journal of Vocational Behavior, 35,* 64–75.

Buss, A. H. (1989). Personality as traits. *American Psychologist, 44,* 1378–1388.

Buss, A. R. (1978). The structure of psychological revolutions. *Journal of the History of the Behavioral Sciences, 14,* 57–64.

Campbell, D. T. (1986). Science's social system of validity-enhancing collective belief change and the problems of the social sciences. In D. W. Fiske & R. A. Shweder (Eds.), *Metatheory in social science.* Chicago: University of Chicago Press.

Campbell, D. T. (1990). The Meehlian corroboration–verisimilitude theory of science. *Psychological Inquiry, 1,* 142–147.

Campbell, D. T., & Fiske, D. W. (1959). Convergent and discriminant validation by the multitrait-multimethod matrix. *Psychological Bulletin, 56,* 81–105.

Chaiklin, S. (1986). Constructing productions and producing constructions: A case for nuance. *American Psychologist, 41,* 590–593.

Corcoran, K. J. (1991). Efficacy, "skills," reinforcement, and choice behavior. *American Psychologist, 46,* 155–157.

Coyne, J. C. (1989). Thinking postcognitively about depression. In A. Freeman, K. M. Simon, L. E. Beutler, & H. Arkowitz (Eds.), *Comprehensive handbook of cognitive therapy* (pp. 227–244). New York: Plenum Press.

Crawford, M., & Gentry, M. (Eds.). (1989). *Gender and thought: Psychological perspectives.* New York: Springer-Verlag.

Cronbach, L. J. (1986). Social inquiry by and for earthlings. In D. W. Fiske & R. A. Shweder (Eds.), *Metatheory in social science.* Chicago: University of Chicago Press.

Cronbach, L. J., & Meehl, P. E. (1955). Construct validity in psychological tests. *Psychological Bulletin, 52,* 281–302.

Dember, W. N. (1974). Motivation and the cognitive revolution. *American Psychologist, 29,* 161–168.

Dollard, J., & Miller, N. E. (1950). *Personality and psychotherapy.* New York: McGraw-Hill.

Dowd, E. T., & Pace, T. M. (1989). The relativity of reality: Second-order change in psychotherapy. In A. Freeman, K. M. Simon, L. E. Beutler, & H. Arkowitz (Eds.), *Comprehensive handbook of cognitive therapy* (pp. 213–226). New York: Plenum Press.

Elkin, I., Shea, T., Watkins, J. T., Imber, S. D., Sotsky, S. M., Collins, J. F., Glass, D. R., Pilkonis, P. A., Leber, W. R., Docherty, J. P., Fiester, S. J., & Parloff, M. B. (1989). National Institute of Mental Health Treatment of Depression Collaborative Research Program: General effectiveness of treatments. *Archives of General Psychiatry, 46,* 971–983.

Fiske, D. W., & Shweder, R. A. (Eds.). (1986). *Metatheory in social science: Pluralisms and subjectivities.* Chicago: University of Chicago Press.

Ford, D. H. (1984). Reexamining guiding assumptions: Theoretical and methodological implications. *Journal of Counseling Psychology, 31,* 461–466.

Ford, D. H. (1987). *Humans as self-constructing living systems: A developmental perspective on behavior and personality.* Hillsdale, NJ: Erlbaum.

Forsyth, D. R., & Strong, S. R. (1986). The scientific study of counseling and psychotherapy: A unificationist's view. *American Psychologist, 41,* 113–119.

Frank, J. D. (1973). *Persuasion and healing* (2nd ed.). Baltimore, MD: Johns Hopkins University Press.

Frank, J. D. (1987). Psychotherapy, rhetoric, and hermeneutics: Implications for practice and research. *Psychotherapy, 24,* 293–302.

Gardner, H. (1985). *The mind's new science: A history of the cognitive revolution.* New York: Basic Books.

Gelso, C. J. (1979). Research in counseling: Methodological and professional issues. *The Counseling Psychologist, 8,* 7–36.

Gelso, C. J. (1982). Editorial. *Journal of Counseling Psychology, 29*, 3–7.

Gelso, C. J. (1985). Rigor, relevance, and counseling research: On the need to maintain our course between Scylla and Charybdis. *Journal of Counseling and Development, 63*, 31–37.

Gelso, C. J., & Fassinger, R. E. (1990). Counseling psychology: Theory and research on interventions. *Annual Review of Psychology, 41*, 355–386.

Gendlin, E. T. (1986). What comes after traditional psychotherapy research? *American Psychologist, 41*, 131–136.

Gergen, K. J. (1973). Social psychology as history. *Journal of Personality and Social Psychology, 26*, 309–320.

Gergen, K. J. (1982). *Toward transformation in social knowledge.* New York: Springer-Verlag.

Gergen, K. J. (1985). The social constructionist movement in modern psychology. *American Psychologist, 40*, 266–275.

Gergen, K. J., & Davis, K. E. (Eds.). (1985). *The social construction of the person.* New York: Springer-Verlag.

Glass, G. V., & Kliegl, R. M. (1983). An apology for research integration in the study of psychotherapy. *Journal of Consulting and Clinical Psychology, 51*, 28–41.

Goldman, L. (1976). A revolution in counseling research. *Journal of Counseling Psychology, 23*, 543–552.

Goldman, L. (1989). Moving counseling research into the 21st century. *The Counseling Psychologist, 17*, 81–85.

Greenberg, L. S. (1986). Change process research. *Journal of Consulting and Clinical Psychology, 54*, 4–9.

Greenberg, L. S., & Pinsof, W. M. (Eds.). (1986). *The psychotherapeutic process: A research handbook.* New York: Guilford Press.

Guidano, V. F. (1991). *The self in process.* New York: Guilford Press.

Haase, R. F., & Ellis, M. V. (1987). Multivariate analysis of variance. *Journal of Counseling Psychology, 34*, 404–413.

Hackett, G., & Betz, N. E. (1981). A self-efficacy approach to the career development of women. *Journal of Vocational Behavior, 18*, 326–339.

Hall, J. R. (1990). Epistemology and sociohistorical inquiry. *Annual Review of Sociology, 16*, 329–351.

Hare-Mustin, R. T., & Maracek, J. (1988). The meaning of difference: Gender theory, postmodernism, and psychology. *American Psychologist, 43*, 455–464.

Hare-Mustin, R. T., & Maracek, J. (1989). Thinking about postmodernism and gender theory. *American Psychologist, 44*, 1333–1334.

Harmon, L. W. (1989). The scientist/practitioner model and choice of research paradigm. *The Counseling Psychologist, 17*, 86–89.

Hayes, S. C. (1987). Contextual determinants of "volitional action": A reply to Howard and Conway. *American Psychologist, 42*, 1029–1030.

Helms, J. E. (1989). At long last—paradigms for cultural psychology research. *The Counseling Psychologist, 17*, 98–101.

Highlen, P. S., & Hill, C. E. (1984). Factors influencing client change in individual counseling: Current status and theoretical speculations. In S. D. Brown & R. W. Lent (Eds.), *Handbook of counseling psychology* (pp. 334–396). New York: Wiley.

Hill, C. E. (1982). Counseling process research: Philosophical and methodological dilemmas. *The Counseling Psychologist, 10*, 7–19.

Hill, C. E. (1984). A personal account of the process of becoming a counseling process researcher. *The Counseling Psychologist, 12*, 99–109.

Hill, C. E. (1989). *Therapist techniques and client outcomes: Eight cases of brief psychotherapy.* Newbury Park, CA: Sage.

Hill, C. E. (1990). Exploratory in-session process research in individual psychotherapy: A review. *Journal of Consulting and Clinical Psychology, 58*, 288–294.

Hill, C. E., Carter, J. A., & O'Farrell, M. K. (1983). A case study of the process and outcome of time-limited counseling. *Journal of Counseling Psychology, 30*, 3–18.

Hill, C. E., & Gronsky, B. (1984). Research: Why and how? In J. M. Whiteley, N. Kagan, L. W. Harmon, B. R. Fretz, & F. Tanney. (Eds.), *The coming decade in counseling psychology.* Schenectady, NY: Character Research Press.

Hoshmand, L. L. S. T. (1989). Alternate research paradigms: A review and teaching proposal. *The Counseling Psychologist, 17,* 3–79.

Howard, G. S. (1983). Toward methodological pluralism. *Journal of Counseling Psychology, 30,* 19–21.

Howard, G. S. (1984). A modest proposal for a revision of strategies in counseling research. *Journal of Counseling Psychology, 31,* 430–432.

Howard, G. S. (1985). The role of values in the science of psychology. *American Psychologist, 40,* 255–265.

Howard, G. S. (1986a). The scientist-practitioner in counseling psychology: Toward a deeper integration of theory, research, and practice. *The Counseling Psychologist, 14,* 61–105.

Howard, G. S. (1986b). *Dare we develop a human science?* Notre Dame, IN: Academic Publications.

Howard, G. S. (1989). *A tale of two stories: Issues in the narrative approach to psychology.* Notre Dame, IN: Academic Publications.

Howard, G. S. (1991). Culture tales: A narrative approach to thinking, cross-cultural psychology, and psychotherapy. *American Psychologist, 46,* 187–197.

Howard, G. S., & Conway, C. G. (1986). Can there be an empirical science of volitional action? *American Psychologist, 41,* 1241–1251.

Howard, G. S., & Conway, C. G. (1987). The next steps toward a science of agency. *American Psychologist, 42,* 1034–1035.

Howard, G. S., & Myers, P. R. (1990). Predicting human behavior: Comparing idiographic, nomothetic, and agentic methodologies. *Journal of Counseling Psychology, 37,* 227–233.

Ivey, A. E., Ivey, M. B., & Simek-Downing, L. (1987). *Counseling and psychotherapy: Integrating skills, theory, and practice* (2nd ed.). Englewood Cliffs, NJ: Prentice-Hall.

Kazdin, A. E. (1986). Comparative outcome studies: Methodological issues and strategies. *Journal of Consulting and Clinical Psychology, 54,* 95–105.

Kendall, P. C., & Lipman, A. J. (1991). Psychological and pharmacological therapy: Methods and modes for comparative outcome research. *Journal of Consulting and Clinical Psychology, 59,* 78–87.

Kiesler, D. J. (1966). Some myths of psychotherapy research and the search for a paradigm. *Psychological Bulletin, 65,* 110–136.

Kiesler, D. J. (1985). The missing link in psychotherapy research [Review of *Patterns of change: Intensive analysis*]. *Contemporary Psychology, 30,* 527–529.

Koch, S. (1981). The nature and limits of psychological knowledge. *American Psychologist, 36,* 257–269.

Kuhn, T. S. (1962, 1970). *The structure of scientific revolutions.* Chicago: University of Chicago Press.

LaCrosse, M. B. (1986). Research training: In search of a human science. *The Counseling Psychologist, 14,* 147–151.

Lent, R. W., Brown, S. D., & Larkin, K. C. (1984). Relationship of self-efficacy expectations to academic achievement and persistence. *Journal of Counseling Psychology, 31,* 356–362.

Lent, R. W., Brown, S. D., & Larkin, K. C. (1986). Self-efficacy in the prediction of academic performance and perceived career options. *Journal of Counseling Psychology, 33,* 265–269.

Lent, R. W., Brown, S. D., & Larkin, K. C. (1987). Comparison of three theoretically derived variables in predicting career and academic behavior: Self-efficacy, interest congruence, and consequence thinking. *Journal of Counseling Psychology, 34,* 293–298.

Lent, R. W., & Hackett, G. (1987). Career self-efficacy: Empirical status and future directions [Monograph]. *Journal of Vocational Behavior, 30,* 347–382.

Lyddon, W. J. (1990). First- and second-order change: Implications for rationalist and constructivist cognitive therapies. *Journal of Counseling and Development, 69,* 122–127.

Mahoney, M. J. (1976). *Scientist as subject: The psychological imperative.* Cambridge, MA: Ballinger.

Mahoney, M. J. (1980). Psychotherapy and the structure of personal revolutions. In M. J. Mahoney (Ed.), *Psychotherapy process: Current issues and future directions.* New York: Plenum Press.

Mahoney, M. J. (1985). Open exchange and epistemic process. *American Psychologist, 40,* 29–39.

Mahoney, M. J. (1988). The cognitive sciences and psychotherapy: Patterns in a developing relationship. In K. S. Dobson (Ed.), *Handbook of cognitive-behavioral therapies* (pp. 131–156). New York: Guilford Press.

Mahoney, M. J. (1989). Scientific psychology and radical behaviorism: Important distinctions based in scientism and objectivism. *American Psychologist, 44,* 1372–1377.

Mahoney, M. J. (1991). *Human change processes: The scientific foundations of psychotherapy.* New York: Basic Books.

Mahoney, M. J., & Lyddon, W. J. (1988). Recent developments in cognitive approaches to counseling and psychotherapy. *The Counseling Psychologist, 16,* 190–234.

Mahrer, A. R. (1988). Discovery-oriented psychotherapy research: Rationale, aims, and methods. *American Psychologist, 43,* 694–702.

Manicas, P. T., & Secord, P. F. (1983). Implications for psychology of the new philosophy of science. *American Psychologist, 38,* 399–413.

Maracek, J. (Ed.). (1989). Theory and method in feminist psychology [Special issue]. *Psychology of Women Quarterly, 13,* 367–491.

Marmar, C. R. (1990). Psychotherapy process research: Progress, dilemmas, and future directions. *Journal of Consulting and Clinical Psychology, 58,* 265–272.

McCall, M. W., Jr., & Bobko, P. (1990). Research methods in the service of discovery. In M. D. Dunnette & L. M. Hough (Eds.), *Handbook of industrial and organizational psychology* (2nd ed.) (vol. 1, pp. 381–418). Palo Alto, CA: Consulting Psychologists Press.

McCann, I. L., & Pearlman, L. A. (1990). *Psychological trauma and the adult survivor.* New York: Brunner/Mazel.

Meehl, P. E. (1978). Theoretical risks and tabular asterisks: Sir Karl, Sir Ronald and the slow progress of soft psychology. *Journal of Consulting and Clinical Psychology, 46,* 806–834.

Meehl, P. E. (1986). What social scientists don't understand. In D. W. Fiske & R. A. Shweder (Eds.), *Metatheory in social science.* Chicago: University of Chicago Press.

Messer, S. B., Sass, L. A., & Woolfolk, R. L. (Eds.). (1988). *Hermeneutics and psychological theory: Interpretive perspectives on personality, psychotherapy, and psychopathology.* New Brunswick, NJ: Rutgers University Press.

Miles, M. B., & Huberman, A. M. (1984). Drawing valid meaning from qualitative data: Toward a shared craft. *Educational Researcher, 13*(5), 20–30.

Miller, G. A., Galanter, E., & Pribram, K. H. (1960). *Plans and the structure of behavior.* New York: Holt, Rinehart and Winston.

Neisser, U. (1967). *Cognitive psychology.* New York: Appleton-Century-Crofts.

Nielsen, J. M. (Ed.). (1990). *Feminist research methods: Exemplary readings in the social sciences.* Boulder, CO: Westview Press.

Norcross, J. C. (Ed.). (1986). *Handbook of eclectic psychotherapy.* New York: Brunner/Mazel.

Norcross, J. C., & Prochaska, J. O. (1988). A study of eclectic (and integrative) views revisited. *Professional Psychology: Research and Practice, 19,* 170–174.

Packer, M. J. (1985). Hermeneutic inquiry in the study of human conduct. *American Psychologist, 40,* 1081–1093.

Pervin, L. A. (Ed.). (1989). *Goal concepts in personality and social psychology.* Hillsdale, NJ: Erlbaum.

Polkinghorne, D. (1983). *Methodology for the human sciences.* Albany, NY: State University of New York Press.

Polkinghorne, D. E. (1984). Further extensions of methodological diversity for counseling psychology. *Journal of Counseling Psychology, 31,* 416–429.

Polkinghorne, D. E. (1988). *Narrative knowing and the human sciences.* New York: State University of New York Press.

Polkinghorne, D. E. (1991). Two conflicting calls for methodological reform. *The Counseling Psychologist, 19,* 103–114.

Reichenbach, H. (1938). *Experience and prediction.* Chicago: University of Chicago Press.

Rice, L. N., & Greenberg, L. S. (1984). *Patterns of change: Intensive analysis of psychotherapy process.* New York: Guilford Press.

Rogers, C. R. (1985). Toward a more human science of the person. *Journal of Humanistic Psychology, 25*(4), 7–24.

Sappington, A. A. (1990). Recent psychological approaches to the free will versus determinism issue. *Psychological Bulletin, 108,* 19–29.

Scarr, S. (1985). Constructing psychology: Making facts and fables for our time. *American Psychologist, 40,* 499–512.

Seligman, M. E. P. (1991). *Learned optimism.* New York: Knopf.

Skinner, B. F. (1987). Whatever happened to psychology as the science of behavior? *American Psychologist, 42,* 780–786.

Sloane, R. B., Staples, F. R., Cristol, A. H., Yorkston, N. J., & Whipple, K. (1975). *Psychotherapy versus behavior therapy.* Cambridge, MA: Harvard University Press.

Smith, D. (1982). Trends in counseling and psychotherapy. *American Psychologist, 37,* 802–809.

Sperry, R. W. (1988). Psychology's mentalist paradigm and the religion/science tension. *American Psychologist, 43,* 607–613.

Suppe, F. (1984). Beyond Skinner and Kuhn. *New Ideas in Psychology, 2,* 89–104.

Thompson, B. (1989). The place of qualitative research in contemporary social science: The importance of postparadigmatic thought. In B. Thompson (Ed.), *Advances in social science methodology* (Vol. 1). Greenwich, CT: JAI Press.

Thoresen, C. E. (1979). Counseling research: What I can't help thinking. *The Counseling Psychologist, 8*(3), 56–61.

Tyler, L. E. (1978). *Individuality: Human possibilities and personal choice in the psychological development of men and women.* San Francisco: Jossey-Bass.

Tyler, L. E. (1983). *Thinking creatively.* San Francisco: Jossey-Bass.

Wachtel, P. L. (1973). Psychodynamics, behavior therapy, and the implacable experimenter. *Journal of Abnormal Psychology, 82,* 324–334.

Wachtel, P. L. (1977). *Psychoanalysis and behavior therapy: Toward an integration.* New York: Basic Books.

Wachtel, P. L. (1980). Investigation and its discontents: Some constraints on progress in psychological research. *American Psychologist, 35,* 399–408.

Wachtel, P. L. (1987). *Action and insight.* New York: Guilford Press.

Wampold, B. R. (Ed.). (1987). Quantitative foundations of counseling psychology research [Special issue]. *Journal of Counseling Psychology, 34,* 361–489.

CHAPTER 5

SOCIAL PSYCHOLOGICAL PROCESSES IN PSYCHOTHERAPY: EXTRAPOLATING BASIC RESEARCH TO COUNSELING PSYCHOLOGY

P. PAUL HEPPNER
PATRICIA A. FRAZIER

The goal of counseling has often been conceptualized as helping clients to solve problems (Fretz, 1982; Heppner, 1978). Because many of the problems that clients bring to counseling are interpersonal in nature, basic social psychological research on interpersonal processes is quite relevant to counseling psychologists. In addition, counseling is itself a social process in which clients and therapists engage in a series of social interactions designed to help clients resolve their difficulties. In short, there is a great deal of overlap between social psychological processes and the counseling process. Unfortunately, although the utility of integrating social psychology and counseling psychology has been recognized for some time, this integration has been slow in developing.

The application of social psychology to the counseling process can be traced to the work of Kurt Lewin (1948). As Strong (1978) noted, many of Lewin's students generated social psychological constructs that are basic to the counseling process, such as cognitive dissonance (Festinger, 1957), social power (Cartwright, 1965), and causal attribution (Kelley, 1967). In the 1960s, several writers explicitly discussed and examined the applicability of these social psychological constructs to counseling (Bergin, 1962; Goldstein, 1962, 1966; Goldstein, Heller, & Sechrest, 1966). One of the most direct applications was made by Jerome Frank (1961), who suggested that psychotherapy is a social persuasion and influence process. Seven years later, Stanley Strong (1968) reiterated Frank's idea and extrapolated variables from the attitude change literature (e.g., perceived expertness, attractiveness, and trustworthiness) to the counseling process.

In the 1970s, two publications were particularly influential in promoting this trend toward integrating social and counseling/clinical psychology (Leary & Maddux, 1987):

The authors would like to thank the following people for their helpful comments on earlier drafts of this chapter: Craig A. Anderson, Jeffery Burnett, Stephen Cook, Cecelia Deidan, Ann Fischer, Paul Gold, Carol Jacquet, Laurel Kramer, David Wallace, and Deborah Wright.

Brehm's (1976) *The Application of Social Psychology to Clinical Psychology* and Strong's (1978) chapter in the *Handbook of Psychotherapy and Behavior Change*. In the 1980s, the integration of these two areas of psychology sparked even more excitement, and several more books appeared, including: *Integrations of Clinical and Social Psychology* (Weary & Mirels, 1982), *Social Perception in Clinical and Counseling Psychology* (McGlynn, Maddux, Stoltenberg, & Harvey, 1984), *Social Psychology and Dysfunctional Behavior* (Leary & Miller, 1986), *Social Processes in Clinical and Counseling Psychology* (Maddux, Stoltenberg, & Rosenwein, 1987), and *Social Cognition and Clinical Psychology* (Abramson, 1988). In addition, the *Journal of Social and Clinical Psychology* (Harvey, 1983) was established, which focuses specifically on this integration.

As the 1990s begin, there is an identifiable subspecialty in psychology that focuses on the interpersonal aspects of psychological problems and psychotherapy. Leary and Maddux (1987) described three focus areas within this subspecialty: social-dysgenic, social-diagnostic, and social-therapeutic psychology. Social-dysgenic psychology pertains to the "study of interpersonal process involved in the *development* of dysfunctional behavior" (p. 907). This area examines topics such as the role of social support in adjustment, self-presentational models of social anxiety, and attributional models of depression, shyness, and loneliness. The social-dysgenic area of psychology provides useful information for clarifying the social psychological processes involved in the etiology of clinical problems.

Social-diagnostic psychology is defined as the "study of interpersonal processes involved in the identification, classification and assessment of psychological and behavioral problems" (Leary & Maddux, 1987, p. 907). This area focuses on how information is processed and how judgments or inferences are made. Topics in this area include person perception, heuristics, and the inferential biases of counseling and clinical psychologists. Finally, social-therapeutic psychology is defined as "the study of interpersonal processes in the prevention and treatment of dysfunctional behavior" (p. 907). This area focuses on such topics as attitude change processes in counseling, socially based treatments for social anxiety, and the effects of role playing in therapy. Both the social-diagnostic and social-therapeutic areas have important implications for counselor training as well as therapeutic interventions.

The purpose of this chapter is to further stimulate thinking and research on three prominent topics within the focus areas identified by Leary and Maddux (1987): attitude change processes, attributional processes, and human inference processes. In this chapter, we examine the literature in each of these areas and make recommendations for extrapolating current social psychological research in each area to (a) assessment in counseling, (b) the change process, and (c) counseling outcomes. Our basic belief is that understanding of central cognitive, affective, and behavioral processes within counseling can be substantially increased by more integration of basic social psychological research with applied research in counseling psychology.

In the first section of the chapter, we discuss the attitude change process within counseling, which was the first area of social psychological research to be applied to the counseling process. This topic pertains directly to the social-therapeutic area of psychology. We focus on the attitude change process both because of the long-standing attention it has received in counseling and because of its centrality to the change process.

We then discuss the application of research on attributional processes to counseling. This topic pertains mostly to the social-dysgenic and social-therapeutic areas of psychology. We selected attributional processes because attribution theory is one of the leading theoretical and empirical topics with social psychology (Fiske & Taylor, 1984). Attributions have been linked to expectancies, mood, and behavioral performance, all of which are central to presenting problems of clients. Thus, attributional processes seem to have important implications for the counseling process.

Finally, the chapter focuses on human inference processes. This topic has relevance to all three areas (dysgenic, diagnostic, and therapeutic), although we focus less on diagnostic issues because of the scarcity of research in this area. We included human inference processes because this area examines complex cognitive activities involved in information processing that have not received a great deal of attention in counseling psychology. We believe this research has tremendous potential for clarifying the dynamics of clients' presenting problems, the counseling process, and counseling outcomes.

ATTITUDE CHANGE PROCESSES

The attitude change literature in social psychology is enormous. For example, Lipstein and McGuire (1978) noted that over 7,000 attitude change publications appeared within one decade. A number of theories have been proposed to describe the attitude change process, although no one theory has gained dominance (Eagly & Chaiken, 1984). Some have lamented this state of affairs (Fishbein & Azjen, 1972; Kiesler & Munson, 1975), but others have maintained that multiple theoretical perspectives are needed to adequately reflect the complexity of attitude change processes (Eagly & Chaiken, 1984). Thus, McGuire (1969) recommended, "Let a hundred flowers blossom together, let a hundred schools of thought contend" (p. 264). Given these multiple theoretical perspectives, it is not surprising that many different operational definitions of "attitudes" have been developed. For the purpose of this chapter, attitudes are broadly defined as "general and enduring positive or negative feelings about some person, object, or issue" (Petty & Cacioppo, 1981, p. 7).

Attitudes often play prominent roles in clients' presenting problems; that is, some clients hold maladaptive attitudes such as negative feelings about themselves, pessimistic attitudes about changing some behavioral pattern (e.g., high caloric food intake), or prejudicial attitudes toward a gender or race. The counselor's role is often to assist these clients in changing their maladaptive attitudes. Thus, the topic of attitude change is highly relevant for the counseling profession.

Researchers in counseling psychology have examined attitude change processes since at least the 1960s (see reviews by Corrigan, Dell, Lewis, & Schmidt, 1980; Heppner & Claiborn, 1989; Heppner & Dixon, 1981). The vast majority of this social influence literature in counseling has examined source (i.e., counselor) characteristics, such as perceived expertness, attractiveness, and trustworthiness. This focus on source characteristics is representative of research on attitude change conducted by Hovland and his colleagues in the 1950s (Hovland, Janis, & Kelley, 1953). Although major advances have been made in social psychological theories of attitude change since that time (McGuire, 1985; Petty & Cacioppo, 1986), very little of this literature has been incorporated into counseling theory and research (Heppner & Claiborn, 1989).

The purpose of this section is to discuss recent social psychological theories of attitude change that appear to have particular relevance for research and practice in counseling psychology. We first very briefly review the status of social influence research in counseling. Next, we provide a brief overview of two current attitude change models in social psychology: the Elaboration Likelihood Model (Petty & Cacioppo, 1986) and McGuire's (1985) Persuasion Matrix. Finally, we extrapolate from social psychological research some variables and processes that seem useful for increasing understanding of the attitude change process within counseling.

Social Influence in Counseling

Perhaps the most essential and yet most complex element of counseling is the process by which one person influences another to change. Three decades ago, the change process in counseling was likened to persuasion by Jerome Frank (1961). Strong (1968) elaborated on this notion in a very influential article in which he proposed a two-phase model of counseling. In the first phase, counselors need to establish themselves as a useful resource, namely as expert, attractive, and trustworthy. Once the client perceives the counselor as a useful resource, the counselor is in a position to enter the second phase, in which the attitudes, opinions, or behaviors of the client are influenced. Since the appearance of Strong's article, more than 100 empirical investigations have been conducted on the social influence or attitude change process in counseling (see Corrigan et al., 1980; Heppner & Claiborn, 1989; Heppner & Dixon, 1981).

Strong's (1968) two-phase model of social influence not only identified a new model for counseling but, more importantly, identified specific variables to examine within the change process. Researchers have focused heavily on Strong's first phase of counseling, in an effort to understand the events or variables that affect perceptions of counselor expertness, attractiveness, and trustworthiness. A wide range of variables has been identified as affecting these perceptions (Corrigan et al., 1980; Heppner & Claiborn, 1989; Heppner & Dixon, 1981). Probably the most consistent finding is that responsive nonverbal counselor behaviors (e.g., smiling, head nods, forward lean) positively affect client perceptions of the counselor. Likewise, a broad range of verbal behaviors (e.g., self-disclosure, psychological jargon, profanity) affects perceptions of the counselor, either positively or negatively.

Conversely, general counselor characteristics (e.g., gender, sexual orientation) do not consistently affect client perceptions, suggesting that such general characteristics may not be as powerful as more specific behavioral variables. Similarly, general client characteristics (e.g., gender) do not consistently affect client perceptions of counselors (Heppner & Claiborn, 1989). As Heppner and Claiborn noted, the generalizability of this research to counseling is unclear because "much of our knowledge about perceived counselor expertness, attractiveness, and trustworthiness is based on brief vignettes (e.g., 10 to 15 minute videotapes) and viewers' initial impressions, quite removed from actual counseling interactions" (p. 370). When data are collected in field settings, clients seem to perceive counselors as very expert, attractive, and trustworthy without apparent regard for status and evidential cues such as titles or diplomas (Heppner & Heesacker, 1982, 1983).

Considerably less attention has been focused on Strong's (1968) second phase of counseling, which involves influencing the client to change in some way (Heppner & Claiborn, 1989). There is some evidence that perceived counselor expertness, attractiveness, and trustworthiness are related to favorable counseling outcomes as measured by Goal Attainment Scaling (LaCrosse, 1980) or changes in client self-concept (Dorn & Day, 1985). Other studies suggest that counselor variables are related to client satisfaction (Heppner & Heesacker, 1983; Zamostny, Corrigan, & Eggert, 1981) and hypothetical decisions about seeking counseling (Freeman & Conoley, 1986), although these studies provide a weak test of influence.

Current Social Psychological Models of Persuasion

As mentioned, numerous theories of the attitude change process currently exist. Petty and Cacioppo (1986) and McGuire (1985) proposed theoretical models aimed at providing a broader conceptual framework for understanding the attitude change process. We introduce these models to highlight some of the major psychological processes that social psychologists are finding useful in understanding attitude change, and to discuss their implications for counseling psychology.

Petty and Cacioppo (1981, 1984, 1986) outlined a general theory of attitude change called the Elaboration Likelihood Model (ELM). Basically, the ELM examines interactions among source, subject, and message variables. Petty and Cacioppo suggested that there may be two distinct routes in persuasion (peripheral and central) and that they depend on the quality of the message as well as motivation and ability to process the message. Specifically, if a person lacks the motivation or the ability to think about a message, then change in an attitude may be affected by peripheral source cues (e.g., the perceived expertness of the communicator). However, if a person is motivated and able to think about a message, perhaps because the topic is personally relevant, then the person will think more carefully about the message. If the message is perceived to contain strong, compelling arguments, thinking about the message will result in favorable thoughts about the message, and attitudes will be likely to change in the direction advocated. If the arguments are perceived as weak, the person may move away from the position advocated in the message. Thus, both the amount and type of thought engaged in directly affect the attitude change process (Petty & Cacioppo, 1986). Finally, ELM research suggests that attitude change created through the central (as opposed to peripheral) route tends to persist longer and to be more predictive of subsequent behavior (Cialdini, Petty, & Cacioppo, 1981; Petty & Cacioppo, 1986).

As mentioned, in order for central route processing to occur, a person must be motivated to think about a persuasive message. According to Petty and Cacioppo, one of the most important motivational variables is personal relevance. In essence, a message has personal relevance if individuals expect a message to have significant personal consequences for them (Apsler & Sears, 1968). As personal relevance increases, people become more motivated to cognitively process specific aspects of the message (Petty & Cacioppo, 1981, 1986). For example, subjects attend more to message quality and are more likely to discriminate between strong and weak arguments as personal relevance increases (Petty & Cacioppo, 1979).

In addition to being motivated, a person must be able to process a message. Research suggests that the ability to think about a message is enhanced when (a) the message is not accompanied by distracting stimuli (Petty, Wells, & Brock, 1976), (b) there is moderate repetition of a message (Cacioppo & Petty, 1979), and (c) the subject reads (vs. hears) a message (Chaiken & Eagly, 1983). In addition, if a person has no framework for incorporating a message into his or her existing belief system, processing of the message will be less likely, even if sufficient motivation is present (Petty & Cacioppo, 1981).

Several studies have attempted to test the ELM framework within counseling (see McNeill & Stoltenberg, 1989, for a review). For example, Stoltenberg and McNeill (1984) manipulated both personal involvement (high vs. low career decisiveness) and counselor credibility in a study of attitudes toward an audiotaped career counseling session. Subjects who were undecided about their careers (i.e., highly involved) reported more favorable attitudes toward a career counseling session, but only if the counselor was highly credible. In a follow-up study in which message quality was also manipulated (McNeill & Stoltenberg, 1988), attitudes toward specific counselor recommendations were influenced by message quality but not by level of involvement or by counselor credibility. Heesacker (1986a) also manipulated personal involvement, message quality, and counselor credibility in a study of attitudes toward a counseling group being advocated in an audiotaped message. He found that attitudes were most affected by message quality, although highly involved subjects also reported more favorable attitudes.

At this point, it is difficult to evaluate the applicability of the ELM to counseling. First, the few studies that have been conducted are difficult to compare because they have operationalized the major variables in different ways. For example, message quality has been operationalized both in terms of counselor empathy (McNeill & Stoltenberg, 1988) and in terms of compelling (vs. uncompelling) interventions (Heesacker, 1986a). Second, studies have not as yet assessed the amount of issue-relevant thinking engaged in by subjects, which is a central aspect of the ELM framework. Finally, studies have used analogue designs and counseling-related issues rather than actual attitude change within counseling. Thus, the ELM appears to be a promising framework, but its relevance for counseling has yet to be adequately tested (see Heesacker, 1986b, and McNeill & Stoltenberg, 1989, for suggestions for improving research in this area).

In another attempt to organize the vast attitude change literature, McGuire (1985) proposed an input/output matrix structure as a conceptual framework for the persuasion process. This matrix consists of a number of input variables on one dimension, and a number of output variables on the other dimension. Describing all of the details of this matrix is beyond the scope of this chapter; instead, we will highlight several aspects of McGuire's model that appear to have direct implications for the attitude change process in counseling. According to McGuire, the input variables are manipulable independent variables related to the communication; the most relevant variables for counselors are source (e.g., credibility, attractiveness, power), message (e.g., types of appeals, message style, extremity of position), and channel variables (e.g., verbal, nonverbal). The output column represents a chain of 12 possible responses that can occur during a persuasion attempt:

1. Tuning-in, which produces exposure to the communication;
2. Attending to the message;
3. Liking or being interested in the message;
4. Comprehending the message;
5. Generating relevant cognitions;
6. Acquiring relevant skills;
7. Changing an attitude;
8. Storing the memory;
9. Retrieving the relevant material from memory;
10. Decision making on the basis of the retrieval material;
11. Acting in accord with the decision;
12. Postaction consolidating of the new pattern.

Although McGuire described favorable responses to attitudinal messages, it is important to note that neutral or even counterattitudinal responses are also possible at each step.

The number of variables in the matrix highlights the complexity of the attitude change process. Previous social influence research in counseling has primarily emphasized source characteristics such as expertness, attractiveness, and trustworthiness. McGuire's model suggests not only that a number of different independent variables may be useful to consider but also that there may be interactions among those variables in their effects on the dependent or output variables. In terms of dependent variables,

McGuire's model suggests that persuasion is a complex process that is not adequately depicted by a single attitude change measure. For example, a persuasion attempt may have an effect on the recipient, but perhaps only at step 3 (interest in the message); other persuasion attempts may affect step 7 (agreeing with the message) or even step 11 (acting in accord with the message). In sum, McGuire has identified a number of steps or processes that seem important to consider within the attitude change process. As yet, these processes have received little attention in counseling research.

Recommendations for Extrapolating to Attitude Change in Counseling

As noted above, a great deal of research within counseling has examined variables related to perceived counselor expertness, attractiveness, and trustworthiness. A few investigators have also examined the actual influence process (e.g., LaCrosse, 1980). In addition, the attitude change process in counseling has begun to be examined in terms of Petty and Cacioppo's (1986) Elaboration Likelihood Model (ELM) of attitude change. Although McGuire's (1985) model is promising, it has yet to be extended to counseling research.

In the most recent review of the social influence literature, Heppner and Claiborn (1989) recommended that (a) attitude change be evaluated more broadly by examining various sources of data and a wider range of change variables; (b) the client be conceptualized as an active processor of information within the influence process, with particular attention to the client's cognitive and affective processes; (c) methodological procedures be improved by reducing the overreliance on brief analogues, employing more multivariate statistical procedures, and incorporating more procedures and instruments from counseling process research; and (d) future research incorporate, and directly test, current social psychological theories of attitude change (see Heppner & Claiborn (1989) for more details). We expand on a few of these recommendations, in an effort to further stimulate attitude change research in counseling. Specifically, we offer recommendations related to (a) assessment of client motivational factors, (b) client cognitive processes in the attitude change process, and (c) multiple outcomes of attitude change within counseling.

Recommendation 1. More comprehensive assessments are needed of client motivational factors that can inhibit or facilitate client attitude change.

Attitude change research within social psychology suggests that motivational factors are important determinants of the amount of issue-relevant thinking and of subsequent attitude change. However, it is unclear at this point how motivational factors affect attitude change within a counseling context. Previous research in counseling has manipulated levels of involvement (Heesacker, 1986a), but clients who seek professional counseling assistance typically have a personal concern with which they are very involved and have struggled for some time. People usually seek help from friends, clergy, or teachers before turning to a professional counselor (Wills, 1987). If most individuals seeking counseling are already highly involved with a particular problem, then research manipulating levels of involvement may not accurately reflect the counseling setting.

In addition, it seems that particular attitudes, at least if they are personally involving and important to clients, do not exist in a vacuum. Rather, an attitude may be part of a larger psychological system that involves psychological defenses, irrational beliefs, and distorted perceptions. In other words, an individual may be personally involved in an issue but may also perceive change to have too many costs (e.g., fears, energy, time). These costs can create complex motivational issues that inhibit change.

The ways in which affective responses might inhibit cognitive processing of highly involving and psychologically painful topics appear to be an important element in the counseling process. We suspect that cognitive processes within the attitude change process are often distorted or inhibited by strong emotional reactions (e.g., anxiety, anger, depression) and by maladaptive psychological defenses. In other words, there may be motivating forces that have the effect of decreasing attention to, or elaboration of, a message in a counseling context. This viewpoint is consistent with Strong and Matross's (1973) initial conceptualization of the social influence process within counseling as involving compelling and restraining forces, although relatively few researchers have examined these restraining forces.

Recommendation 2. Research is needed to examine message and contextual variables that influence the attitude change process.

Clients typically seek counseling because they have problems they have not been able to resolve. They often are experiencing intense negative emotions and confusion. Moreover, if they are first-time clients, the counseling process is often foreign to them. They are unsure of what to expect and how to act. They meet with a stranger (the counselor) to talk about a problem that is not only confusing to them but stressful and painful as well. It is conceivable that, under these conditions, a client may not understand all of the counselor's statements nor have a way to incorporate the counselor's statements into his or her existing belief system. This perspective highlights the heavy cognitive demands made on clients in counseling and the importance of understanding the variables that affect the client's ability to think clearly.

Extrapolating from social psychology, we suspect that several message and contextual variables may affect clients' cognitive processes in counseling. For example, moderate repetition of a message has been found to increase a perceiver's ability to process a message (Cacioppo & Petty, 1979). Within counseling, it would be useful to examine whether message repetition (e.g., repeating variations of an interpretation over several counseling sessions) increases a client's ability to understand an interpretation. Social psychological research also suggests that messages that are not accompanied by distracting stimuli are processed more easily (Petty et al., 1976). This could also be examined within the counseling process in terms of the number of statements made by the counselor within a session and the client's ability to identify the central point the counselor is trying to make. To date, there has been little research within counseling that has examined variables that might affect how clients process counselors' messages (Heppner & Claiborn, 1989). Attention to such variables would enable us to more clearly understand the attitude change process as well as the larger change process in counseling.

Recommendation 3. In assessing counseling outcomes, research is needed to examine the long-term effects of changes in clients' attitudes, including how clients use new attitudes.

In his matrix model of attitude change, McGuire (1985) suggested that a number of cognitive processes are involved in changing an attitude. For example, attitude change must be examined in terms of the new information that is introduced (i.e., comprehended), thought about, agreed with, stored, retrieved, applied, and incorporated into a larger attitudinal framework. All of these activities may be usefully examined within counseling, in order to broaden understanding of attitude change in clients. Thus, in addition to examining variables that affect *how* clients change a particular attitude, it may be beneficial to examine the utility of the attitude change over time, using longitudinal designs.

For example, consider some of McGuire's steps within a counseling context. The seventh step involves attitude change (agreeing with the information provided about a topic). This has been the major variable examined in early attitude change research and is often considered to be the goal of persuasion. However, attitude change at one particular point in time does not necessarily imply permanence of the attitude change. Especially within counseling, which often focuses on complex attitudes (e.g., self-concept), it seems that clients' attitudes vacillate tremendously from week to week during the change process. For example, after some action, a client may experience positive or negative cognitions and emotions that may either strengthen or weaken the attitude change. To date, research in counseling has focused largely on measures of initial attitude change and has failed to examine relations with other attitude change processes over time, such as information storage, information utilization, and behavioral compliance. In addition, research is needed that examines the relations between attitude change and other important counseling outcomes. Finally, it should be noted that the process of attitude change may differ from the process of attitude change maintenance and may require different counseling interventions.

Conclusion: Attitude Change

Attitude change research within social psychology suggests that both type and amount of cognitive processing directly affect the attitude change process. Thus, a closer examination of client cognitive processes within counseling is warranted. For example, various message, contextual, and motivational factors that affect cognitive processing need to be examined. Within counseling, it seems essential to examine variables that both enhance and inhibit cognitive processing. Finally, it seems important to examine the multiple outcomes of attitude change, especially in relation to counseling outcomes. The vast majority of counseling research within the social influence literature has examined counselor characteristics and some single, unitary measure of attitude change (e.g., need for achievement). The extrapolations from social psychological research on attitude change suggest that additional variables need to be examined. The complexity and utility of social influence research in counseling could thereby be greatly increased.

ATTRIBUTIONAL PROCESSES

Attribution theory, which focuses on how individuals use information in the social environment to formulate causal explanations for events, has been described as the leading theoretical and empirical topic in social psychology (Fiske & Taylor, 1984). Attribution theory developed when researchers began to examine perceived *causes* rather than mere descriptions of others' behavior (Antaki, 1982). Heider (1958) initiated this change in focus by proposing that, in order to understand the world, individuals need to understand the causes of events. Heider's work set the stage for subsequent attribution theories such as Jones and Davis's (1965) correspondent inference theory and Kelley's (1967) covariation model. This work forms the basis of modern attribution theory, although several others also made significant early contributions (see Fiske & Taylor, 1984).

Attribution theory was developed to describe how people perceive the causes of others' behavior, but, like any good theory, it has applications far beyond its original purpose. Indeed, it has been one of the most widely applied theories ever developed by social psychologists (Fiske & Taylor, 1984). Many of these applications are very relevant to events in clients' lives and to the counseling process. For example, the attributions that clients make about success and failure experiences may influence their moods, their expectations regarding future success and failure, and their subsequent achievement behaviors (Weiner, 1979). Attributions about other negative life events, such as illness and victimization, have also been found to be related to postevent functioning (Frazier, 1990; Janoff-Bulman & Lang-Gunn, 1988; Turnquist, Harvey, & Andersen, 1988). Thus, the attributions clients make about events in their lives may have important implications for their adjustment to those events.

In this section, we first briefly describe two of the most influential applications of attribution theory: Weiner's (1979) attributional theory of achievement behavior, and Abramson, Seligman, and Teasdale's (1978) attributional theory of depression. We then review and critique research in which investigators have attempted to alter attributions in order to modify cognitions, affect, or behavior (i.e., attributional retraining). We conclude with recommendations for extrapolating research on attributional processes to counseling practice and research.

Applications of Attribution Theory

According to Weiner's (1979) theory, achievement-related emotions, expectations, and performance are a function of past performance and the attributions individuals make about their performance. Weiner and his colleagues postulated that attributions for success and failure vary along three dimensions (locus, stability, and controllability), each of which is related to particular outcomes. Specifically, the locus dimension is concerned with whether an individual attributes success/failure to internal or external factors and is associated with affective responses to success and failure. The stability dimension is concerned with whether the cause will change and is associated with expectations for future success or failure. The controllability dimension is concerned with whether an individual has control over the success or failure and is also associated with affective responses.

Abramson et al.'s (1978) attributional theory of depression is actually a reformulation of the learned helplessness theory of depression (Maier & Seligman, 1976), which proposed (a) that individuals "learn" to be helpless following repeated experiences of lack of control and (b) that helplessness involves motivational, cognitive, and emotional deficits (i.e., depression). Focusing on the emotional sequelae of helplessness, the attributional reformulation added the notion that the attributions individuals make about uncontrollable events will determine the amount and duration of depression that will be experienced.

According to the Abramson et al. (1978) model, three attributional dimensions are important: locus, stability, and globality. The locus (internality/externality) dimension is associated with the effects of the uncontrollable event on one's self-esteem (i.e., internal attributions for uncontrollable events are associated with lowered self-esteem). The stability dimension is associated with how long the depression will persist (i.e., stable attributions for uncontrollable events are associated with more persistent depressive symptoms). The globality dimension is associated with the pervasiveness of the depression (i.e., individuals who make global attributions for uncontrollable events should experience more generalized depressive symptoms). Thus, individuals who make internal, stable, and global attributions for uncontrollable life events are most at risk for depression.

Abramson and her colleagues have recently presented a revised model of hopelessness depression (Abramson, Metalsky, & Alloy, 1989). According to this model, the experience of hopelessness is a sufficient condition for hopelessness depression, which is thought to be a specific subtype of depression. The model also specifies a series of contributing causes that increase the likelihood of experiencing hopelessness. The first step in the hypothesized causal chain is the perceived occurrence of a negative (vs. uncontrollable) life event. Negative life events are more likely to lead to hopelessness, and thus hopelessness depression, if they are perceived as important and: (a) they are attributed to stable and global (but not necessarily internal) causes; (b) they are seen as having important negative consequences; or (c) they lead the individual to infer negative characteristics about himself or herself. Thus, the revised model places somewhat less emphasis on causal attributions and specifies other cognitive diatheses (i.e., inferences about consequences and self-characteristics) that can lead to hopelessness and hopelessness depression.

What is the evidence? Are attributions about success and failure related to subsequent moods, expectations, and performance? Are attributions about uncontrollable events associated with depression? Because these two theories are actually quite similar in their predictions, and given space limitations, we briefly discuss the research examining the relation between attributions about negative events and depression.

Since the publication of the attributional theory of depression in 1978, numerous studies have assessed the relation between attributions and depression. In addition, several reviews of these studies have appeared (Coyne & Gotlib, 1983; Peterson & Seligman, 1984; Sweeney, Anderson, & Bailey, 1986). However, reviewers have varied in their judgments regarding the extent to which the evidence supports the attributional theory of depression. For example, in their review of 20 relevant studies, Coyne and Gotlib (1983) concluded that the evidence for the model was equivocal. On the other hand, Peterson and Seligman (1984) reviewed 22 studies and concluded that the model received strong support. A meta-analysis of 104 studies (Sweeney et al., 1986) revealed that, for attributions about negative events, all three dimensions (as well as a composite score) were associated with increased depression. Correcting for the unreliability of the measures, the effect sizes were categorized as moderate (.34 to .44). Moreover, effect sizes did not appear to depend on the type of subject, event, setting, depression measure, or publication status of the research.

Attributions have also been associated with counseling-relevant outcomes other than depression. For example, attributions have been found to be associated with loneliness and shyness (Anderson & Arnoult, 1985), career motivation and aspirations (Farmer, 1985), and procrastination (Rothblum, Solomon, & Murakami, 1986). Several studies have also examined outcomes that are directly related to the counseling process. For example, Rosen and Osmo (1984) found that clients with an internal locus of control were more likely to take initiative in the initial counseling interview. In another study, clients who made internal, personal attributions for their problems were viewed by counselors as more motivated and attractive than clients who attributed their problems to external, situational factors (Schwartz, Friedlander, & Tedeschi, 1986). However, this relation depends somewhat on the nature of the client's problem (Westbrook & Nordholm, 1986).

Although attributions are generally related to various affective and behavioral responses, current research does not clearly support any one attributional model. Indeed, several criticisms of the Abramson et al. (1978) model have been raised. For example, research testing the model was criticized on methodological grounds (Brewin, 1985) and because it did not include the controllability dimension, which has been shown to be the most important of the attributional dimensions in predicting problems in living (Anderson & Arnoult, 1985). In addition, as Brown and Heath (1984) noted, although the original helplessness model stressed the importance of attributions about perceived uncontrollability, most research that tested the model assessed attributions about negative events (which may or may not be perceived as uncontrollable). The recent revision of the attributional model of depression (Abramson et al., 1989) attempted to address many of these criticisms; thus, the revised (rather than the original) model should form the basis for future work in this area.

Implications for Applied Interventions: Attributional Retraining

Because research suggests that attributions about negative life events are associated with depression and other important outcomes, investigators have attempted to alter attributions in order to modify subjects' affect and behavior. These "attributional therapy" studies fall into two broad categories: misattribution training and reattribution training (see Antaki & Brewin, 1982; Forsterling, 1985; and Harvey & Galvin, 1984, for reviews). Misattribution training typically involves persuading subjects to attribute physiological arousal to an external (vs. internal) source. In reattribution studies, attempts are made to alter subjects' attributions about some behavioral outcome (e.g., success or failure). Because the misattribution approach has not consistent been found to be effective and because reattribution procedures are more similar to approaches actually used by counselors, we focus here on attributional retraining studies primarily from the social psychological literature. Three primary questions are addressed:

1. Is attributional retraining effective?
2. Are certain techniques more effective than others?
3. Does the effectiveness of the attributional intervention depend on characteristics of the client?

Effectiveness of Attributional Retraining

In general, the available data from social psychological research suggest that attributional retraining is a promising therapeutic tool. Forsterling (1985) reviewed 15 attributional retraining studies in the achievement domain, most of which involved training subjects to attribute failure (or both success and failure) to effort (an internal, unstable, controllable cause) rather than to ability. Results of these studies indicated that attributional retraining was effective in increasing success expectancies, improving task performance, and increasing task persistence. The attributional interventions were also effective in changing subject attributions on similar tasks; however, global attributional style did not generally change. Affective changes resulting from the attributional intervention were typically not assessed in these studies. Achievement-related studies not reviewed by Forsterling also support the efficacy of an attributional approach (Brewin & Shapiro, 1985; Brockner & Guare, 1983; Miller, Brickman, & Bolen, 1975).

Studies that have attempted to alter client attributions about nonachievement-related issues have also been successful. For example, Firth-Cozens and Brewin (1988) examined changes in attributions and depression in 40 clients who were experiencing anxiety and/or depression. Each client received 8 sessions of interpersonal therapy and 8 sessions of cognitive-behavioral therapy in a crossover design. They found, first, that following both treatments, client attributions for negative events became more unstable, specific, and controllable. Second, although both treatments were effective in changing attributions and reducing depression, the cognitive-behavioral treatment was somewhat more effective in changing client attributions. Finally, attributional change was, in fact, associated with a decrease in depression. Attributional interventions have also been successfully used with individuals experiencing problems with low self-esteem (Brockner & Guare, 1983; Layden, 1982), procrastination (Claiborn, Ward, & Strong, 1981; Strong, Wambach, Lopez, & Cooper, 1979), negative emotions (Claiborn & Dowd, 1985), and social anxiety (Forsyth & Forsyth, 1982).

Effectiveness of Specific Techniques

Given that attributional retraining appears to be a promising intervention, an important question for counselors is whether there are specific techniques that appear to be more effective than others. In the 15 attributional retraining studies reviewed by Forsterling (1985), three primary techniques were used. First, investigators attempted to alter attributions by reinforcing the desired attributions (e.g., effort attributions for failure). For example, in one study (Andrews & Debus, 1978), reinforcement resulted in increased effort attributions and task persistence for up to 4 months following the training, for both similar and dissimilar tasks.

A second technique involved providing subjects with information designed to alter their attributions. For example, Wilson and Linville (1982, 1985) presented subjects (college freshmen worried about their academic performance) with information suggesting that most students' grades improve over time. Compared with subjects who did not receive this consensus information, these subjects were less likely to drop out of school and showed greater improvements in grades.

The final and most frequently used technique was persuasion or suggestion. In most of the studies using this method, subjects were persuaded to attribute their performance to effort. For example, in one study, subjects were told that their task performance was due to uncontrollable (dispositions and ability) or controllable (effort and strategies) factors. Subjects who were told that their performance was due to controllable factors had higher expectancies regarding their future performance as well as improved motivation and task performance (Anderson, 1983).

Thus, it appears that all three attributional retraining techniques (reinforcement, information, and persuasion) have shown some effectiveness. Unfortunately, very few studies have assessed the relative effectiveness of the various techniques. In one study, (Zoeller, Mahoney, & Weiner, 1983), modeling of attributions and in vivo attributional persuasion techniques were found to be equally effective; in another (Andrews & Debus, 1978), social reinforcement of attributions was as effective as social reinforcement combined with token reinforcement. Rather than comparing different ways of changing attributions, others have compared attributional retraining to nonattributional approaches. For example, Miller et al. (1975) reported that attributional retraining and positive reinforcement conditions were more effective than a nonattributional persuasion approach in improving math self-esteem. Finally, other studies have compared attributions that differed in *content*. For example, attributing successful math performance to ability was no more effective than attributing performance to motivation (Miller et al., 1975). Similarly, in a counseling analogue study, clients rated cognitive-behavioral and analytic treatment approaches as equally helpful, although the former stressed internal, controllable causes of client problems and the latter stressed external, uncontrollable causes of client problems (Hoffman & Teglasi, 1982).

Client Characteristics and Effectiveness

A final question pertains to whether some interventions may be more effective with some clients than with others. In one of the first studies within counseling to examine this issue (Altmaier, Leary, Forsyth, & Ansel, 1979), subjects (who were either internal or external in locus of control) were told that another student had evaluated them very negatively. Results suggested that the effectiveness of the intervention (an external attribution for the negative evaluation) depended both on client locus of control and the timing of the intervention (whether it occurred before or after the negative evaluation). In a subsequent study using the same paradigm, Forsyth and Forsyth (1982) found that attributing the negative evaluation to internal/controllable factors was associated with better outcomes than other attributional interventions for clients with an internal locus of control; however, clients with an external locus of control did not respond to any of the interventions.

Other studies have examined the relation between specific attributions (rather than global locus of control orientation) and intervention effectiveness. For example, providing an external attribution for failure on a task appeared to be most helpful to subjects who initially made an internal attribution for task failure (Brewin & Shapiro, 1985). Sober-Ain and Kidd (1984) also found that the effectiveness of various attributional retraining techniques depended on whether subjects attributed both success and failure or only failure to external causes prior to the intervention. Similarly, Anderson (1983) reported an interaction between subjects' initial attributional style (behavioral or characterological) and the attributional manipulation they received.

Recommendations for Extrapolating to Attributional Change in Counseling

Current social psychological research suggests that attributional retraining is a promising approach to changing attributions, emotions, and behaviors. Several attributional retraining techniques appear to be effective (i.e., reinforcement, information, and persuasion), although no one technique is clearly superior to the others. However, initial research within the counseling literature suggests that the effectiveness of an intervention may depend on characteristics of the client (e.g., locus of control). Because most of this research has not been conducted with actual clients within counseling settings, these findings must be considered suggestive. In an effort to stimulate thinking and research in this area, we offer several recommendations related to (a) assessment of client attributions, (b) attributional interventions, and (c) counseling outcomes.

Recommendation 1. More comprehensive assessments are needed of the accuracy and specificity of particular client attributions prior to the implementation of attributional interventions.

Attributional retraining models have tended to focus on the consequences, rather than the antecedents, of attributions (Forsterling, 1986). This emphasis has resulted in a tendency to ignore whether an attribution is *accurate*. For example, clients often blame themselves for failure, which leads to negative affective (e.g., sadness) and behavioral (e.g., lack of persistence) outcomes. However, for a given client, an internal attribution for failure may be accurate. A client may actually be lacking in ability in a particular area, and it would be maladaptive for that client to attribute failure to lack of effort or to an external cause.

Attributional retraining may be most appropriate in situations where a client is making an inaccurate attribution (e.g., attributing failure to a misperceived lack of ability) that is causing a dysfunctional reaction (e.g., depression). In such a case, it may be helpful for a counselor to focus on changing the inaccurate attribution. However, if a client is making an accurate attribution (e.g., attributing failure to actual lack of ability) and suffering a dysfunctional reaction (e.g., depression), it may be more appropriate to help the client change his or her goal (e.g., attending medical school) or develop requisite skills, rather than change the attribution for failure (e.g., to lack of effort).

It also seems important for future counseling research to assess specific attributions about particular events rather than, or in addition to, global attributional style. For example, several studies in the counseling literature have assessed general locus of control orientation, with the assumption that attributions about particular events will correspond to this general style. Interventions have then been targeted at the specific attribution (which is presumed to correspond to the global style). However, research on the cross-situational consistency of attributional style in social psychology suggests that the attributions individuals make about different kinds of events are only moderately correlated (Anderson, Jennings, & Arnoult, 1988). In other words, individuals may make certain attributions about interpersonal events and other attributions about achievement-related events in their lives (see Dykman & Abramson, 1990). Because measures of global attributional style may not predict attributions about a particular event, it may be more effective to assess specific attributions prior to attempting to change those attributions.

Recommendation 2. Research is needed on the process of creating attributional change in a counseling context.

In attempting attributional change, it is important to recognize the difficulty of creating long-term change in attributional patterns. Many of the attributional retraining studies conducted to date involve a one-time instruction to subjects that they should, for example, attribute failure to lack of effort rather than to lack of ability. A few studies have involved somewhat longer interventions, such as providing attributional information within the context of two brief counseling sessions (Claiborn & Dowd, 1985). However, even these are not representative of what actually takes place within counseling.

In a critique of attributional therapies for depression, Peterson (1982) outlined several reasons why simple attributional interventions were unlikely to lead to long-term change. First, research on belief perseverance suggests that simply providing individuals with new information does not necessarily change their beliefs, even if the information directly contradicts those beliefs (Ross, 1977; Slusher & Anderson, 1989). Thus, simply instructing individuals to begin making effort (rather than ability) attributions for failure is not likely to create lasting change. Second, attributions are part of an individual's entire belief system; they cannot be removed like "psychological tumors" (Peterson, 1982, p. 107). The attitude change research would suggest that more complex interventions are needed that involve central route processing. In other words, interventions should focus not simply on attributions but on the assumptions and defenses underlying the attributions. Third, the importance of the counselor–client relationship has largely been ignored in most attributional retraining research. Research on the change process in counseling has underscored the role of this relationship (Highlen & Hill, 1984); for a more complete understanding of the effects of attributional retraining within counseling, the counselor-client relationship must also be examined.

In addition to utilizing longer and more complex interventions, research is needed that compares attributional change techniques. Very few studies have compared techniques, and techniques that have been compared tend to be quite similar to one another (Andrews & Debus, 1978). Further, some of the techniques used in attributional retraining studies appear somewhat naive from a clinical standpoint. For example, simply telling a client "You should be good at math" or "You are doing well at math" (Miller et al., 1975) does not represent the kind of intervention that is likely to be used by a counselor with a client.

Recommendation 3. Client change needs to be defined more broadly in attributional retraining research.

Studies need to examine broader definitions of client change in order to more completely assess the effects of attributional retraining. For example, studies in the achievement domain (Forsterling, 1985) typically assess the effectiveness of attributional retraining in terms of changes in attributions, expectancies for success, and persistence at and performance on related tasks, but not in terms of changes in affect (e.g., depression). The measures used to assess change in counseling analogue studies are somewhat more varied and include measures of attributions, expectations for success in counseling, actual behavioral change, depression, the quality of the counselor–client relationship, and the perceived helpfulness of the intervention. Interestingly, very few studies assess changes in both attributions and depression (Claiborn & Dowd, 1985; Firth-Cozens & Brewin, 1988; Layden, 1982), and only one study has examined whether changes in attributions are, in fact, related to changes in depression (Firth-Cozens & Brewin, 1988). Thus, future research should include more comprehensive assessments of outcomes, including measures of attributions, depression, and behavior change, and particularly the relations among them.

Recommendation 4. Research is needed that attends to attributions about the change process itself.

We believe that it is important to attend to attributions that clients make about the change process itself. In this respect, it may be useful to distinguish between attributions about the *cause* of a problem and attributions about the *solution* to a problem (Brickman et al., 1982). In other words, a person may perceive that a problem (e.g., low self-esteem) was caused by uncontrollable factors (e.g., early childhood experiences), but may feel that he or she now has control over solving the problem (e.g., by seeking counseling). Although both kinds of attributions are important, much less attention has been paid to client attributions about the change process. Some research suggests that increasing internal attributions for the change process leads to greater maintenance of behavioral change (Galassi & Galassi, 1984; Sonne & Janoff, 1982). Thus, clients who attribute the changes they make to their own efforts are likely to maintain those changes longer than clients who attribute change to an external factor (e.g., the counselor). Further research is needed regarding the effects of attributions about the change process on the maintenance of change as well as on methods of facilitating internal attributions for change within counseling.

Conclusion: Attribution Theory

Attribution theory appears to have important applications to counseling psychology. Attributions have been shown to be related to important client outcomes, and attributional retraining has been shown to effectively alter attributions, emotions, and behaviors. However, the vast majority of the previous research on attributional retraining has been with subjects who have been solicited for a psychological experiment rather than clients who have sought professional counseling. At this point, the generalizability of the existing research on attributional retraining to a real-life counseling context is unclear. Given the consistent link between attributions and depression, we suspect that attributional retraining may play a useful role within counseling. However, further research might reveal additional complexity in attempting to change attributions within counseling.

Extrapolating from social psychological research, we have made several recommendations for increasing the relevance of attributional research for the counseling process. We have suggested that researchers and practitioners carefully assess whether an attributional intervention is appropriate. This hinges in large part on whether the attribution is accurate and/or adaptive. If the attribution is inaccurate and is causing a dysfunctional response in the client, it might be useful to examine the assumptions underlying the attribution. In short, it seems important that attributional interventions acknowledge the role of attributions within the client's belief system. Within the context of the counseling relationship, the counselor and client can work to change those assumptions and the resulting attributions. It also seems important to assess client change on multiple dimensions (cognitive, affective, behavioral) over an extended period of time. With regard to interventions, it might be useful to target specific attributions about both the problem and the solution to the problem. Finally, researchers might examine interventions that maximize internal attributions for change, which could facilitate the maintenance of change.

HUMAN INFERENCE PROCESSES

Human inference is a process of collecting and combining information and then making a judgment (Fiske & Taylor, 1984). As such, inferences are needed for the most mundane tasks (e.g., perceiving the intentions of a waiter approaching a restaurant table) as well as the most complex judgments (e.g., assessing client suicidal behavior). The complex cognitive tasks subsumed by human inference are often conceptualized by basic and applied psychologists within an information-processing paradigm (e.g., Anderson, 1980; Heppner & Krauskopf, 1987; Turk & Salovey, 1988).

In general terms, research on human inference processes suggests that, although individuals are capable of solving complex problems in highly creative and ingenious ways, they are also capable of a wide range of inferential errors and biases (e.g., Kahneman, Slovic, & Tversky, 1982; Nisbett & Ross, 1980; Turk & Salovey, 1988). Nisbett and Ross aptly depicted this paradox between the "great triumphs and the dramatic failures of the human mind" (p. xi) by contrasting the theories of Piaget and Freud. Whereas Piaget emphasized complex problem-solving abilities, Freud depicted adults as governed by unconscious conflicts and by primitive, often irrational, thought processes. The apparent paradox between the triumphs and failures of human inferential processes reflects the enormous complexity of these processes.

The study of human inference processes is helpful for understanding the cognitive processes of both clients and counselors. For example, clients may exhibit biases in the ways in which they process information about themselves and other people. These biases can create or maintain problems that eventually bring clients into counseling. In addition, counselors are not immune, having been shown to exhibit various biases in the way they process information and make clinical decisions (Meehl, 1954).

This section discusses research on human inference that we believe is particularly relevant for research and practice in counseling psychology. Specifically, we focus on two cognitive factors—cognitive structures and cognitive processes—that play critical roles in how information is processed (Hollon & Kriss, 1984). First, we focus on cognitive structures referred to as schemata, and specifically the powerful effects of self-schemata on behavioral, affective, and cognitive processes. Next, we discuss how self-schemata can be altered. Finally, we focus on cognitive processes, such as information sampling and heuristics, that can lead to various inferential errors, and conclude with recommendations for extrapolating this research to counseling psychology.

Cognitive Structures: Schemata

Within social psychology in the past decade, there has been a great deal of research on cognitive structures, or schemata, and the ways in which these schemata influence thoughts, feelings, and behaviors (Fiske & Taylor, 1984). In general terms, a schema is defined as a cognitive structure that represents organized knowledge about a concept and that guides how people select, remember, and make inferences about information in their environments (Fiske & Taylor, 1984). Although prior cognitive structures or schemata can help people make sense of the vast amount of information available to them, schema-guided information processing can also lead to various errors or biases. For example, research suggests that individuals tend to seek information that is consistent with their prior beliefs (e.g., confirmatory hypothesis testing; Snyder & Swann, 1978). In addition, people are more likely to remember information that is consistent with their prior beliefs or schemata (e.g., reconstructive memory; Snyder & Uranowitz, 1978). Finally, research suggests that people tend to maintain their prior beliefs well beyond what is justifiable (e.g., belief perseverance; Slusher & Anderson, 1989). For example, it appears that beliefs are maintained even when the information used to establish them is discredited (e.g., Anderson, Lepper, & Ross, 1980; Ross, Lepper, & Hubbard, 1975).

A particular type of schema that has received considerable attention in clinical applications is the self-schema (Goldfried & Robins, 1983; Hollon & Kriss, 1984; Turk & Salovey, 1985a; Turk & Speers, 1983). Self-schemata are defined as "cognitive generalizations about the self, derived from past experience, that organize and guide the processing of self-related information contained in the individual's social experience" (Markus, 1977, p. 64). Research has revealed that self-schemata, like other schemata, influence all stages of information processing (Fiske & Taylor, 1984). For example, self-schemata have been found to influence the encoding of information (Markus, 1977) as well as the retrieval of information from memory (Rogers, Kuiper, & Kirker, 1977). Self-schemata have also been found to influence perceptions of others (Catrambone & Markus, 1987). In general, these studies indicate that we are more likely to attend to and recall information that is consistent with our self-schemata (see review by Schrauger, 1982).

Much of the research on self-schemata in the social psychological literature has focused on positive self-beliefs that create various self-serving biases (Greenwald, 1980; Taylor & Brown, 1988). However, individuals who seek counseling often have negative beliefs about themselves and low self-esteem. In fact, the reason for seeking counseling is often to change such negative self-beliefs. Thus, a more clinically relevant theory was proposed by Swann (1983, 1987), who demonstrated that individuals tend to verify their self-beliefs whether those beliefs are positive or negative.

Swann (1987) outlined two general processes used by individuals to verify their self-conceptions. First, individuals engage in various behavioral strategies that maintain their self-views, such as choosing partners and settings that provide information consistent with their self-views. For example, people who have positive self-views seem to prefer others to view them positively, whereas people who have negative self-views seem to prefer others to view them negatively. This appears to be particularly true of individuals who are highly certain of their self-beliefs. Second, individuals act in ways that cause others to view them in accordance with their self-views, particularly when they think their partner's appraisal of them is discrepant from their own. Thus, subjects who saw themselves as unlikable and thought their partners liked them, acted in ways that elicited the most negative reactions from their partners (Swann & Read, 1981a).

When these behavioral strategies fail to produce confirmatory feedback, there are several cognitive strategies that individuals often use to maintain their self-views (Swann, 1987). For example, people tend to pay more attention to and have better recall for feedback that confirms their self-views (Swann & Read, 1981b), and they tend to regard confirmatory feedback as more credible (Swann, Griffin, Predmore, & Gaines, 1987). Again, this seems to be particularly true of individuals who are highly certain of their self-views (Swann & Ely, 1984).

Although most of this research has used nonclinical samples, some research has examined self-schematic processes in clinical populations, particularly depressed individuals (see reviews by Dykman & Abramson, 1990; Segal, 1988). For example, research by Kuiper and his colleagues (Derry & Kuiper, 1981; Kuiper & MacDonald, 1982) has assessed depressive self-schemata using a self-referent encoding task. These studies suggest that depressed individuals are more likely than nondepressed individuals to rate negative adjectives as self-descriptive (MacDonald & Kuiper, 1984), to rate negative adjectives more quickly than positive adjectives (MacDonald & Kuiper, 1984), and to recall more negative adjectives (Derry & Kuiper, 1981). In addition, research by Strohmer, Moilanen, and Barry (1988) suggested that depressed and nondepressed individuals exhibited confirmatory biases in testing the hypothesis that they were depressed or happy, respectively.

Schema-guided information processing is also evident in the ways in which counselors process information about clients (Faust, 1986; Hollon & Kriss, 1984; Snyder & Thomsen, 1988; Turk & Salovey, 1985b). In his classic work, Meehl (1954) was among the first to point out that clinicians are not immune to inferential biases in their clinical decision making. However, few studies have directly examined schema-guided processing in counselors. The research that does exist suggests that clinicians tend to form impressions of clients very quickly and that, once formed, these impressions may be rather resistant to change (Friedlander & Phillips, 1984; Friedlander & Stockman, 1983; Hirsch & Stone, 1984; Houts & Galante, 1985). Thus, once a counselor has made a diagnosis, he or she may not notice symptoms that are inconsistent with that diagnosis (Arkes & Harkness, 1980). Studies that have focused on the sources of initial counselor impressions suggest that the label (e.g., healthy or disturbed) a counselor is given about a client (Temerlin, 1968) and the counselor's theoretical orientation (Bishop & Richards, 1984; Houts, 1984; Langer & Abelson, 1974) can influence how a client is perceived and diagnosed. Finally, several studies have investigated whether clinicians test their hypotheses about clients in a confirmatory manner. These studies suggest that, when counselors choose questions from a prepared list, they tend toward a confirmatory approach; when they can choose their own questions, they adopt a more unbiased strategy (Dallas & Baron, 1985; Strohmer & Chiodo, 1984; Strohmer & Newman, 1983). Recent research also suggests that counselors exhibit a confirmatory bias when testing a self-generated (vs. experimenter-generated) hypothesis (Haverkamp, 1990).

Implications for Applied Interventions: Changing Self-Schemata

Individuals who seek counseling often have negative beliefs about themselves. These negative self-beliefs can influence the ways in which they process information such that those negative self-beliefs are maintained. Thus, an important question concerns how self-schemata and maladaptive ways of processing information can be altered. Unfortunately, much less research exists on changing self-schemata than on describing the effects of self-schemata. This section describes three areas of research that offer suggestions for self-schemata change.

One promising approach to changing self-beliefs was developed by Montgomery and Haemmerlie (1987). Their approach involved providing individuals with the opportunity to perform in a way that was inconsistent with their current self-beliefs. Specifically, heterosocially anxious male subjects were assigned to either a control group or an experimental group in which they interacted with 12 different partners. The partners were female undergraduates who were simply told to carry on a positive, friendly conversation with each male. Experimental subjects were told that the study involved the nature of dyadic interactions; no mention was made of counseling or anxiety. Thus, in essence, the heterosocially anxious male subjects experienced successful interactions with 12 different females. Results indicated that, following these "biased interactions," subjects in the experimental group were less socially anxious than the control group on several self-report and behavioral measures (i.e., they later initiated more conversations with a female experimental confederate, and made more personal statements in conversation). Six months later, subjects in the experimental group continued to be less anxious and had been on significantly more dates than the individuals in the control group (Haemmerlie & Montgomery, 1982). In subsequent research, this technique was found to be more effective than an imaginal exposure technique (Haemmerlie & Montgomery, 1984) and to be effective with heterosocially anxious females (Haemmerlie, 1983). In sum, this technique appeared to be effective in changing self-beliefs (e.g., social anxiety) as well as actual (e.g., conversational and dating) behaviors.

A second area that may have implications for schemata change is research on the revision of stereotypic beliefs. Weber and Crocker (1983) identified three possible models of stereotype change. First, the "bookkeeping" model views stereotype change as an incremental process whereby each piece of disconfirming evidence elicits a small change in the stereotype. Major change in the stereotype occurs after many pieces of disconfirming evidence have been encountered. Second, according to the "conversion" model, changes in stereotypes occur in response to dramatic, salient counterinstances, but are not changed by minor disconfirmations. Finally, according to the "subtyping" model, when individuals encounter group members who do not fit their stereotype, subtypes within the more general stereotype are created. Because subtyped members differ from other group members, they are regarded as exceptions and have little impact on the superordinate stereotype.

In a series of four studies that tested competing predictions of the three models, Weber and Crocker (1983) concluded that stereotype change generally followed the subtyping and bookkeeping models. Specifically, when the stereotype-inconsistent information was concentrated within a few individuals, the effects were consistent with the subtyping model. Apparently, when only a few individuals displayed inconsistent information, they were subtyped and seen as exceptions to the general stereotype. However, when stereotype-inconsistent information was dispersed throughout several individuals, stereotypes changed according to the bookkeeping model.

The effect of stereotype-inconsistent information on stereotype change may also be mediated by the attributions individuals make about the inconsistent behavior. For example, Crocker, Hannah, and Weber (1983) found that, when individuals encounter stereotype-inconsistent behavior, they are more likely to attribute that behavior to the situation than to the person. In this way, the stereotype-inconsistent information is discounted and change in the stereotype does not occur.

How does this research relate to changes in self-schemata? If we think of self-schemata as analogous to stereotypes about ourselves, schemata change may be most likely to occur when inconsistent information comes from several sources. For example, in the Haemmerlie and Montgomery (1982) study, subjects essentially encountered 12 individuals who provided them with information that was inconsistent with their stereotypes or schemata about themselves. This may have been much more effective than exposing subjects to one "biased interaction" because that one person could have been "subtyped" ("I had a pleasant encounter with that one person but, still, in general, I have trouble talking to others"). Thus, in addition to helping clients attend to stereotype-inconsistent information already available in their environments, it might be useful for counselors to create opportunities for clients to encounter schemata-inconsistent information. Although counselors are one source of such information, clients may subtype counselors as "different from other people." Constructing other opportunities to get schemata-inconsistent information provides clients with consensus data that may prevent them from attributing the counselor's feelings about them to the situation ("You only like me because it's your job as a counselor").

One final approach to changing self-schemata stems from work that combines self-verification and attitude change research. Drawing from persuasion research, Swann and his colleagues (Swann, Pelham, & Chidester, 1988) reasoned that one way to create belief change is to ask leading questions. For example, in response to a question like "Why should we change our national health care policies?", people are likely to come up with reasons why our policies should be changed, even if they do not fully believe in the position they are advocating. To create belief change in even highly certain individuals, Swann et al. developed another technique that involved "superattitudinal" (i.e., extreme) questions. For example, when asked "Why do you think women should be kept barefoot and pregnant?", even very conservative persons are unlikely to agree with the basic statement and will come up with relatively liberal responses to refute it. Then, noticing themselves providing liberal responses, they may come to believe they are more liberal than they thought.

In two studies, high-certain individuals did show more belief change when asked superattitudinal questions, and low-certain individuals showed more belief change when asked traditional leading questions (Swann et al., 1988). In both cases, once they had made statements that were inconsistent with their original beliefs, individuals inferred that they must believe what they just said. Thus, leading questions (e.g., "In what ways are you good at communicating with others?") might lead to more belief change with clients who are less certain of a negative self-view (e.g., lack of social skills); superattitudinal questions (e.g., "Why do you think you have trouble communicating with everyone you meet?") may lead to more belief change with clients who have strongly held negative self-views. In fact, the superattitudinal, paradoxical technique described by Swan et al. (1988) is similar to techniques used in Ellis's (1973) Rational Emotive Therapy.

Cognitive Processes: Utilizing Information and Heuristics

People engage in a variety of cognitive processes daily, as they form inferences and make judgments. Cognitive processes determine how incoming information is perceived, encoded, combined, and altered with respect to information already in the system. In essence, these cognitive processes are the "transformational rules for turning input into judgments" (Hollon & Kriss, 1984, p. 40). For example, when clients struggle to clarify why they feel depressed, they must decide what information to consider, what comparisons to other people are appropriate, and how much to weigh certain events. Fiske and Taylor (1984) nicely depicted the activities involved in forming inferences: (a) deciding what information is relevant to collect, (b) collecting information from samples, and (c) combining and integrating the collected information. We review below the activities involved in forming inferences, as well as errors that can arise in the process. We then describe two shortcuts in forming inferences, commonly referred to as heuristics, that can lead to various inferential errors (Nisbett & Ross, 1980).

A major activity in forming inferences is deciding what information is relevant to collect. This process is heavily influenced by preexisting expectations or theories (Fiske & Taylor, 1984; Nisbett & Ross, 1980). For example, consider a client who is deciding whether to go into teaching as a profession. According to the client's beliefs, teachers need to be very outgoing in order to be successful. Thus, in making a decision, the client may focus on collecting information about the extent to which successful teachers are extroverted. As a consequence of the use of this hypothesis-testing strategy, the client may find information that supports the hypothesis even if it is not correct.

A second activity in making judgments involves collecting information from samples. Several biases can enter into this process as well. For example, people tend to be insufficiently attentive to potential biases in samples, such as their size, extremity, or lack of representativeness (Fiske & Taylor, 1984). Thus, a client may feel inadequate because his or her performance in a highly competitive graduate school program is compared only to that of colleagues, without recognizing the biased nature of this comparative sample. To make matters worse, it appears that people do not use information about sample typicality even when it is available (Hamill, Wilson, & Nisbett, 1980). Finally, even when the sample on which the relevant information is based is adequate, people tend to prefer less valid, but more vivid, anecdotal information to base rate information (Borgida & Nisbett, 1977).

Another major activity in the inference process involves combining and integrating information. Research suggests that people often use the wrong cues, use too few cues, or improperly weigh cues in integrating information (Chapman & Chapman, 1967, 1969; Hamilton & Gifford, 1976). For example, a client may give too much weight to a small piece of negative evaluative information and too little weight to a much larger amount of positive information about himself or herself.

In sum, this research suggests that individuals often are biased in how they select information, how they draw samples and interpret sample information, and how they combine and integrate information. This is partly a function of the fact that using objective, normative strategies is too time-consuming, given the number of inferences and decisions that individuals face daily. Thus, individuals often use heuristics or shortcuts that reduce complex problem-solving tasks to more simple judgments, in essence using a "satisficing" rather than an "optimizing" approach. In other words, heuristics are quick and useful ways of reducing the vast amount of available data to manageable size. Although they often lead to accurate judgments, they can also produce inaccuracies (Tversky & Kahneman, 1974). Two of the most frequently used heuristics are representativeness and availability.

The representativeness heuristic is used when making judgments about the probability of the occurrence of an event based on the event's similarity to a more familiar category or model (Kahneman & Tversky, 1972). This heuristic is used in answering such questions as "What is the probability that a client is a member of a certain category (e.g., antisocial personality disorder)?" According to the representativeness heuristic, this probability is greater to the extent that the client is similar to the counselor's recollection of other individuals with antisocial personality disorder. Use of this heuristic often produces fairly accurate judgments because similarity is often a good basis for making probability judgments. However, overreliance on this heuristic may lead people to ignore other information relevant to the probability judgment, such as base rate information.

This heuristic may also influence the way clients think about their emotional problems. Consider a male client whose father died very unexpectedly and tragically. The client experienced this as a great loss, and became very emotionally upset, insecure, and depressed. This client had little information about mental illness and psychotic disorders, and, perceiving his emotional experiences as representative of psychotic disorders, became very fearful because he thought he was "out of control and going crazy." Thus, this client thought he was going crazy because his behavior was representative of "craziness," although other data did not support this conclusion.

The availability heuristic is a shortcut for making judgments about the frequency or probability of events based on how quickly available events are brought into working memory (e.g., specific airline crashes vs. base rate data; Tversky & Kahneman, 1973). A number of variables influence the availability of an event, such as the vividness and importance of the event (Borgida & Nisbett, 1977), the perceiver's frame of reference (Taylor & Fiske, 1978), and affective states (Clark & Teasdale, 1982). This heuristic may also affect the ways in which clients process information. For example, when asked about the probability of passing an upcoming exam, a recent failure may be highly available to a client. Thus, the client may judge the probability of failure as being higher than it actually is, based on base rates for success and failure in his or her own life.

The representativeness and availability heuristics may also influence how counselors process information about clients. For example, on the basis of representativeness, a counselor might assume that a client who is emotionally distraught has had more traumatic life experiences than someone who is less disturbed. Thus, the counselor might try to uncover these past traumas, and, if they are not uncovered, may hypothesize that they have been repressed (Faust, 1986). The availability heuristic may affect counselors' estimates of the probabilities of various diagnoses. For example, a counselor who frequently works with clients who have eating disorders may overestimate the frequency of those disorders because of the ease with which instances of individuals with such disorders come to mind.

Recommendations for Extrapolating to Inference Processes in Counseling

Research on the effects of cognitive structures and processes on human judgment clearly indicates that people often are biased in how they perceive and interpret information. Research on schema-guided information processing in general, and self-schemata in particular, suggests that self-beliefs can influence the activities individuals select, the information they attend to and recall, and their behavior toward others, all in a way that maintains current self-perceptions. Therapists constantly struggle with the tenacious, yet maladaptive, belief systems of clients. However, very little research has directly examined change in self-schemata and subsequent information processing within a counseling context. Research on forming inferences and judgmental heuristics suggests various biases that may also influence the way both clients and counselors process information. To facilitate exploration of these processes within both clients and counselors, we make the following recommendations related to clinical assessment, the change process within counseling, the evaluation of counseling outcomes, and counselor training.

Recommendation 1. Attention to both cognitive structures and processes is needed in counseling assessment.

Formal assessment in counseling psychology tends to utilize standardized inventories, such as the Minnesota Multiphasic Personality Inventory or the Strong–Campbell Interest Inventory. Research on inferential biases suggests that therapists and researchers also need to assess the ways in which clients process information about their daily experiences. First, we need to more clearly understand how clients encode their experiences with regard to their presenting problems (Heppner & Krauskopf, 1987). For example, to what extent does a client encode a particular interpersonal problem as shameful or embarrassing? Second, we need to know how clients collect and weigh information to reach their conclusions and explanations. Do they make decisions quickly (e.g., "People are always laughing at me"), perhaps based on a single piece of information (e.g., a group of students are laughing as the client walks through a hallway)? Finally, we need to know how clients' prior beliefs might bias or distort the information they seek, recall, and interpret. Perhaps a deep-seated belief ("Nobody likes me") influences the client to perceive neutral events as hostile. In short, we need to more clearly assess the extent to which reasoning and inferential biases contribute to maladaptive patterns.

In addition to assessing a client's cognitive processes, we should pay more attention to the content of the client's cognitive structures, such as specific self-efficacy expectations and irrational beliefs (see Hollon & Kriss, 1984). Individuals can also differ in the complexity of their self-concepts, which may influence their ability to cope with stressful life events (Linville, 1987). Other useful structures to assess may be the client's possible selves (Markus & Nurius, 1986), undesired self (Ogilvie, 1987), and self-discrepancies (Higgins, 1987). Several of these constructs are described in more detail in Chapter 9, by Gibson and Brown.

Recommendation 2. Research is needed on the process of changing self-schemata and reducing biases in information processing within a counseling context.

Much less research exists on changing self-schemata than on describing the effects of self-schemata. Thus, little is known about the microprocesses involved in altering maladaptive client beliefs (Winfrey & Goldfried, 1986). For example, we do not know which techniques are most effective in helping clients incorporate new information into their schemata or how much new information is needed to facilitate schemata change. Although several articles have outlined strategies for facilitating cognitive change in clients (Goldfried & Robins, 1983; Hollon & Kriss, 1984; Slusher & Anderson, 1989), very few studies have examined schemata change processes within counseling. Martin's (1984) cognitive mediational paradigm, Hill's intentions–reaction paradigm (Hill, Helms, Spiegel, & Tichenor, 1988), or Heppner and Krauskopf's (1987) information-processing paradigm might provide useful perspectives from which to examine schemata change within counseling. Several areas of research in the social psychological literature also offer promising approaches for changing self-beliefs, such as Haemmerlie and Montgomery's (1982) biased interaction treatment, Weber and Crocker's (1983) work on stereotype change, and Swann et al.'s (1988) superattitudinal approach to changing highly certain self-beliefs.

In examining the change process, we also need to conceptualize client change as involving a number of inference processes that can greatly affect the change process in both rational and seemingly nonrational ways. There is no reason to assume that clients will be free of biases as they process information in counseling. This does not imply that a focus on rational processes is inappropriate, but rather that we must also account for nonrational inferences and motivations within the change process.

For example, it might be useful to ask the following kinds of questions about the role of client inferences and reasoning in the change process:

1. What kinds of inferences inhibit or enhance counseling interventions (e.g., does client belief perseverance neutralize interventions? What can counselors do to

mitigate against client's maladaptive confirmatory bias? Do client heuristics inhibit change?)?

2. What kinds of inferences do clients make about the counselor or the counseling process (e.g., how do the client's preexisting theories about counseling affect his or her present counseling experience? Do novice (vs. experienced) clients make different inferences about counselor expertness?)?

3. What kinds of inferences do clients make about the content of counseling interventions (e.g., how do clients combine or integrate information about themselves across counseling sessions? How do clients explain the change process to themselves throughout the course of counseling?)?

Recommendation 3. Research is needed that examines the role of environmental factors in maintaining schemata change in clients.

Research from social psychology suggests that people tend to maintain their self-views by choosing partners who agree with their self-views (Swann, 1987). Research is needed to determine whether these social psychological findings regarding behavioral confirmation processes generalize to a counseling context. For example, if clients experience significant change within counseling, their partners may no longer verify their self-views. Because targets (i.e., clients) tend to act in accordance with perceivers' (i.e., significant others') expectations of them, it would seem helpful for significant others also to change their perceptions of the client in order for change to be maintained. In addition, it might be useful to (a) explain the behavioral confirmation process to clients who might not be aware that others' expectancies can influence their behavior (Hollon & Kriss, 1984); (b) help clients identify how new behaviors elicit different reactions from others; and (c) help clients choose situations and partners that will support their new self-views (Snyder & Ickes, 1985).

Recommendation 4. Changes in clients' cognitive structures and processes should be major outcomes of counseling.

Because cognitive structures and processes affect how people collect information and make judgments and ultimately how they cope with their problems (see Heppner & Krauskopf, 1987), changes in cognitive structures and inferential processes should be important outcomes of counseling. In the past, outcome researchers have been more concerned with either psychological symptoms (e.g., depression) or client perceptions of counseling (e.g., client satisfaction). There is no doubt that these variables provide useful information about counseling outcomes. However, a focus on client reasoning as a counseling outcome, particularly when maladaptive inference patterns are present, has the potential for providing considerably more information about how the client changed or what specifically changed within the client. For example, it might be useful to examine changes in (a) how clients perceive their problems at the end of counseling, (b) the content and structure of self-beliefs at the end of counseling, (c) maladaptive inference processes (e.g., overreliance on heuristics, biased sampling), and (d) clients' awareness of how they make inferences (particularly if client biases were related to their presenting problems). In addition, it might be useful to examine the maintenance of cognitive changes over time. A number of relevant methodologies are already available, such as Interpersonal Process Recall (Kagan, 1975), thought listing (Cacioppo & Petty, 1981), critical incidents (Elliott, 1983; Greenberg, 1986), client reactions (Hill et al., 1988), and schemata analysis (Martin, 1985). Nonetheless, other creative methodological approaches may also be needed to examine changes in the maladaptive reasoning patterns of clients.

Recommendation 5. Counselors need to recognize that they are not immune to biases in information processing.

The evidence suggests that therapists are not immune to various biases in information processing; at this point, however, it is unclear what needs to be done to facilitate more accurate processing of information. Turk and Salovey (1986) suggested that strategies such as focusing attention on one's own cognitive processes, careful self-interrogation, generation of competing hypotheses, and careful record keeping might decrease biases in information processing among counselors (Faust, 1986). There is, however, little empirical evidence to guide either counselors or counselor educators.

Despite the fact that Pepinsky and Pepinsky (1954) emphasized the thinking processes of therapists within the scientist-practitioner model well over 30 years ago, there has been a lack of attention given to the full range of reasoning processes of counselors. More research is needed that examines biases in counselor reasoning processes, particularly because people are generally not aware of their own inaccuracies and often place too much confidence in the accuracy of their judgments (Nisbett & Ross, 1980). In addition, educators need to develop training strategies that focus more intensively on counselor reasoning processes (Johnson & Heppner, 1989; Robinson & Halliday, 1988). For example, it might be useful to examine how increased attention to the acquisition of scientific thinking skills (Claiborn, 1987; Heppner, Kivlighan, & Wampold, 1992) might affect counselor reasoning and inferential processes.

Conclusion: Human Inference Processes

Within social psychology in the past decade, there has been a major focus on social cognition and, in particular, on the ways in which cognitive structures and processes influence subsequent thoughts, feelings, and behaviors. Research on human inference suggests that people are capable of complex problem solving as well as an array of inferential errors and biases. These biases can play important roles in clients' presenting problems and can make changing beliefs very difficult. For example, people are often insensitive to new information and perceive evidence to support their beliefs where none actually exists. Thus, "beliefs can take on a life of their own, no longer in need of the evidence that gave them birth" (Slusher & Anderson, 1989, p. 11).

The vast majority of the research on human inference has been conducted by social psychologists rather than within a counseling context with actual clients and counselors. The research on human inference processes, however, appears to hold considerable promise for the counseling process by delineating cognitive structures and processes that may affect how information is processed by both counselors and clients. In particular, we have recommended examination of (a) cognitive structures and processes in clinical assessment, (b) methods of changing self-schemata and biases within the counseling process, and (c) the role of environmental factors in facilitating and hindering the change process, (d) clients' cognitive structure and processes as a major outcome of counseling, and (e) biases and inferential errors in counselors.

CONCLUDING COMMENTS

Basic social psychological research has a great deal of relevance for the counseling process. The research on attitude change suggests that counseling psychologists might find it useful to more closely examine client cognitive processes as well as various message, contextual, and motivational factors that might affect attitude change within counseling. The research on attributional processes suggests that attributions are related to psychological well-being, and that attributional retraining is a promising approach to changing attributions, emotions, and behaviors. Finally, the research on human inference processes suggests we may increase understanding of the change process by assessing the cognitive structures and processes that affect how information is processed by both counselors and clients. We firmly believe that both researchers and practitioners in counseling psychology can be more effective if they are cognizant of basic research in these and other areas of social psychology and psychology in general.

However, it is naive to assume that basic research can be taken from a laboratory setting and directly applied to a counseling context. Rather, social psychological theories must be tested with actual clients in counseling settings, to establish their relevance for the counseling process. In doing so, it is vitally important for counseling researchers to carefully translate social psychological concepts to the counseling process. For example, in studies that have assessed the relative effectiveness of different attributional interventions (Hoffman & Teglasi, 1982; Strong et al., 1979), the interventions have not always accurately represented the intended attributional dimensions. In addition, in extrapolating social psychological theory to counseling, it is essential for counseling researchers to stay abreast of the social psychological literature. For example, research within the counseling domain should reflect current advances in research on attitude change as well as recent reformulations of attributional theories of depression (Abramson et al., 1989). Finally, it is important to recognize that not all social psychological terms directly translate to the counseling process. For example, it has been difficult to translate the concept of "personal relevance" from social psychological theories of attitude change into counseling. In sum, the advantages of an extrapolatory approach carry with them the responsibility to be true both to social psychological theory and the counseling process (Heppner & Claiborn, 1989).

In addition to stressing the relevance of social psychology to counseling, we feel it is important to note that research in counseling psychology can provide useful replications, extensions, and revisions of social psychological theory. Most importantly, counseling psychology research, because of its applied nature, can provide useful tests of the external validity of social psychological research. For example, therapists have the opportunity to directly query clients about their attitudes, attributions, and inferences, which can provide tremendous insights into the nature of these processes. In contrast to researchers, who often have difficulty obtaining repeated measurements of subjects over time, therapists often meet regularly with the same client week after week. Thus, they can continually monitor client change in various processes and the effectiveness of counseling interventions designed to alter those processes. In short, counseling psychologists are in a position to collect valuable information about basic psychological processes. In this way, counseling research can be part of a larger effort to understand basic human behavior and can contribute to the unity of basic and applied research (Forsyth & Strong, 1986).

Our understanding of counseling processes and outcomes has greatly increased in the past 40 years (Garfield & Bergin, 1986; Gelso & Fassinger, 1990; Highlen & Hill, 1984). We suspect that our understanding can now be substantially increased by more integration of counseling research with basic research in social psychology. Extrapolating from social psychological research holds a great deal of promise for increased specificity in client assessment, in understanding of the change process in counseling, in clarification of counseling outcomes, and in understanding of the inference process of therapists. Perhaps the central message is that, by drawing on basic social psychological research, we can identify much more specific cognitive, affective, and behavioral processes that both facilitate and hinder client change. We believe that both counseling psychology and psychology as a whole can be enriched by such an integration.

REFERENCES

Abramson, L. Y. (Ed.). (1988). *Social cognition and clinical psychology.* New York: Guilford Press.

Abramson, L. Y., Metalsky, G. I., & Alloy, L. B. (1989). Hopelessness depression: A theory-based subtype of depression. *Psychological Review, 96,* 358–372.

Abramson, L., Seligman, M., & Teasdale, J. (1978). Learned helplessness in humans: Critique and reformulation. *Journal of Abnormal Psychology, 87,* 49–74.

Altmaier, E., Leary, M., Forsyth, D., & Ansel, J. (1979). Attribution therapy: Effects of locus of control and timing of treatment. *Journal of Counseling Psychology, 26,* 481–486.

Anderson, C. (1983). Motivational and performance deficits in interpersonal settings: The effect of attributional style. *Journal of Personality and Social Psychology, 45,* 1136–1147.

Anderson, C., & Arnoult, L. (1985). Attributional style and everyday problems in living: Depression, loneliness, and shyness. *Social Cognition, 3,* 16–35.

Anderson, C. A., Jennings, D. L., & Arnoult, L. H. (1988). Validity and utility of the attributional style construct at a moderate level of specificity. *Journal of Personality and Social Psychology, 55,* 979–990.

Anderson, C. A., Lepper, M., & Ross, L. (1980). Perseverance of social theories: The role of explanation in the persistence of discredited information. *Journal of Personality and Social Psychology, 39,* 1037–1049.

Anderson, J. R. (1980). *Cognitive psychology and its implications.* San Francisco: Freeman.

Andrews, G., & Debus, R. (1978). Persistence and causal perception of failure: Modifying cognitive attributions. *Journal of Educational Psychology, 70,* 154–166.

Antaki, C. (1982). A brief introduction to attribution and attributional theories. In C. Antaki & C. Brewin (Eds.), *Attributions and psychological change: Applications of attributional theories to clinical and educational practice* (pp. 3–21). New York: Academic Press.

Antaki, C., & Brewin, C. (1982). *Attributions and psychological change: Attributional theories in clinical and educational practice.* London: Academic Press.

Apsler, R., & Sears, D. O. (1968). Warning, personal involvement, and attitude change. *Journal of Personality and Social Psychology, 9,* 162–168.

Arkes, H. R., & Harkness, A. R. (1980). Effect of making a diagnosis on subsequent recognition of symptoms. *Journal of Experimental Psychology: Human Learning and Memory, 6,* 568–575.

Bergin, A. E. (1962). The effect of dissonant persuasive communications upon changes in self-referring attitude. *Journal of Personality, 30,* 423–438.

Bishop, J., & Richards, T. (1984). Counselor theoretical orientation as related to intake judgments. *Journal of Counseling Psychology, 31,* 398–401.

Borgida, E., & Nisbett, R. E. (1977). The differential impact of abstract vs. concrete information on decisions. *Journal of Applied Social Psychology, 7,* 258–271.

Brehm, S. S. (1976). *The application of social psychology to clinical practice.* Washington, DC: Hemisphere.

Brewin, C. (1985). Depression and causal attributions: What is their relation? *Psychological Bulletin, 98,* 297–309.

Brewin, C., & Shapiro, D. (1985). Selective impact of reattribution of failure instructions on task performance. *British Journal of Social Psychology, 24,* 37–46.

Brickman, P., Rabinowitz, V., Karuza, J., Coates, D., Cohn, E., & Kidder, L. (1982). Models of helping and coping. *American Psychologist, 37,* 368–384.

Brockner, J., & Guare, J. (1983). Improving the performance of low self-esteem individuals: An attributional approach. *Academy of Management Journal, 26,* 642–656.

Brown, S. D., & Heath, L. (1984). Coping with critical life-events: An integrative cognitive-behavioral model for research and practice. In S. D. Brown & R. W. Lent (Eds.), *Handbook of counseling psychology* (pp. 545–578). New York: Wiley.

Cacioppo, J. T., & Petty, R. E. (1979). Effects of message repetition and position on cognitive responses, recall, and persuasion. *Journal of Personality and Social Psychology, 37*, 97–109.

Cacioppo, J. T., & Petty, R. E. (1981). Social psychological procedures for cognitive response assessment: The thought listing technique. In T. V. Merluzzi, C. R. Glass, & M. Genest (Eds.), *Cognitive assessment* (pp. 309–342). New York: Guilford Press.

Cartwright, D. (1965). Influence, leadership, control. In J. G. March (Ed.), *Handbook of organizations* (pp. 1–47). Chicago: Rand McNally.

Catrambone, R., & Markus, H. (1987). The role of self-schemas in going beyond the information given. *Social Cognition, 5*, 349–368.

Chaiken, S., & Eagly, A. H. (1983). Communication modality as a determinant of persuasion: The role of communicator salience. *Journal of Personality and Social Psychology, 45*, 241–256.

Chapman, L. J., & Chapman, J. P. (1967). Genesis of popular but erroneous diagnostic observations. *Journal of Abnormal Psychology, 72*, 193–204.

Chapman, L. J., & Chapman, J. P. (1969). Illusory correlation as an obstacle to the use of valid psychodiagnostic signs. *Journal of Abnormal Psychology, 74*, 271–280.

Cialdini, R. B., Petty, R. E., & Cacioppo, J. T. (1981). Attitude and attitude change. *Annual Review of Psychology, 32*, 357–404.

Claiborn, C. D. (1987). Science and practice: Reconsidering the Pepinskys. *Journal of Counseling and Development, 65*, 286–288.

Claiborn, C. D., & Dowd, E. T. (1985). Attributional interpretations in counseling: Content versus discrepancy. *Journal of Counseling Psychology, 32*, 188–196.

Claiborn, C. D., Ward, S. R., & Strong, S. R. (1981). Effects of congruence between counselor interpretations and client beliefs. *Journal of Counseling Psychology, 28*, 101–109.

Clark, D. M., & Teasdale, J. D. (1982). Diurnal variation of clinical depression and accessibility of memories of positive and negative experiences. *Journal of Abnormal Psychology, 91*, 87–95.

Corrigan, J. D., Dell, D. M., Lewis, K. N., & Schmidt, L. D. (1980). Counseling as a social influence process: A review [Monograph]. *Journal of Counseling Psychology, 27*, 395–441.

Coyne, J. C., & Gotlib, I. H. (1983). The role of cognition in depression: A critical appraisal. *Psychological Bulletin, 94*, 472–505.

Crocker, J., Hannah, D. B., & Weber, R. (1983). Person memory and causal attributions. *Journal of Personality and Social Psychology, 44*, 55–66.

Dallas, M., & Baron, R. (1985). Do psychotherapists use a confirmatory strategy during interviewing? *Journal of Social and Clinical Psychology, 3*, 106–122.

Derry, P., & Kuiper, N. (1981). Schematic processing and self-reference in clinical depression. *Journal of Abnormal Psychology, 90*, 286–297.

Dorn, F. J., & Day, B. J. (1985). Assessing change in self-concept: A social psychological approach. *American Mental Health Counselors Association Journal, 7*, 180–186.

Dykman, B., & Abramson, L. (1990). Contributions of basic research to cognitive theories of depression. *Personality and Social Psychology Bulletin, 16*, 42–57.

Eagly, A. H., & Chaiken, S. (1984). Cognitive theories of persuasion. In L. Berkowitz (Ed.), *Advances in experimental social psychology* (Vol. 17, pp. 267–359). New York: Academic Press.

Elliott, R. (1983). Fitting process research to the practicing psychotherapist. *Psychotherapy: Theory, Research, and Practice, 20*, 47–55.

Ellis, A. (1973). *Humanistic psychotherapy: The rational-emotive approach.* New York: McGraw-Hill.

Farmer, H. S. (1985). Model of career and achievement motivation for women and men. *Journal of Counseling Psychology, 32*, 363–390.

Faust, D. (1986). Research on human judgment and its application to clinical practice. *Professional Psychology: Research and Practice, 17*, 420–430.

Festinger, L. (1957). *A theory of cognitive dissonance.* Stanford, CA: Stanford University Press.

Firth-Cozens, J., & Brewin, C. (1988). Attributional change during psychotherapy. *British Journal of Clinical Psychology, 27*, 47–54.

Fishbein, M., & Ajzen, I. (1972). Attitudes and opinions. *Annual Review of Psychology, 23*, 487–544.

Fiske, S., & Taylor, S. (1984). *Social cognition.* New York: Random House.

Forsterling, F. (1985). Attributional retraining: A review. *Psychological Bulletin, 98*, 495–512.

Forsterling, F. (1986). Attributional conceptions in clinical psychology. *American Psychologist, 41,* 275–285.

Forsyth, D. R., & Strong, S. R. (1986). The scientific study of counseling and psychotherapy: A unificationist view. *American Psychologist, 41,* 113–119.

Forsyth, N., & Forsyth, D. (1982). Internality, controllability, and the effectiveness of attributional interpretations in counseling. *Journal of Counseling Psychology, 29,* 140–150.

Frank, J. D. (1961). *Persuasion and healing.* Baltimore, MD: Johns Hopkins University Press.

Frazier, P. (1990). Victim attributions and post-rape trauma. *Journal of Personality and Social Psychology, 59,* 298–304.

Freeman, S. T., & Conoley, C. W. (1986). Training, experience, and similarity as factors of influence in preferences of deaf students for counselors. *Journal of Counseling Psychology, 33,* 164–169.

Fretz, B. R. (1982). Perspectives and definitions. *The Counseling Psychologist, 10*(2), 15–19.

Friedlander, M. L., & Phillips, S. D. (1984). Stochastic process analysis of interactive discourse in early counseling interviews. *Journal of Counseling Psychology, 31,* 139–148.

Friedlander, M. L., & Stockman, S. J. (1983). Anchoring and publicity effects in clinical judgment. *Journal of Clinical Psychology, 39,* 637–643.

Galassi, J., & Galassi, M. (1984). Promoting transfer and maintenance of counseling outcomes: How do we do it and how do we study it? In S. D. Brown & R. W. Lent (Eds.), *Handbook of counseling psychology* (pp. 397–434). New York: Wiley.

Garfield, S. L., & Bergin, A. E. (Eds.). (1986). *Handbook of psychotherapy and behavior change: An empirical analysis* (3rd ed.). New York: Wiley.

Gelso, C. J., & Fassinger, R. E. (1990). Counseling psychology: Theory and research on interventions. *Annual Review of Psychology, 41,* 355–386.

Goldfried, M., & Robins, R. (1983). Self-schema, cognitive bias, and the processing of therapeutic experience. In P. Kendall (Ed.), *Advances in cognitive-behavioral research and therapy* (Vol. 2, pp. 33–80). New York: Academic Press.

Goldstein, A. P. (1962). *Therapist–patient expectancies in psychotherapy.* New York: Pergamon Press.

Goldstein, A. P. (1966). Psychotherapy research by extrapolation from social psychology. *Journal of Counseling Psychology, 13,* 38–45.

Goldstein, A. P., Heller, K., & Sechrest, L. B. (1966). *Psychotherapy and the psychology of behavior change.* New York: Wiley.

Greenberg, L. S. (1986). Change process research. *Journal of Consulting and Clinical Psychology, 54,* 4–9.

Greenwald, A. G. (1980). The totalitarian ego: Fabrication and revision of personal history. *American Psychologist, 35,* 603–618.

Haemmerlie, F. (1983). Heterosocial anxiety in college females: A biased interactions treatment. *Behavior Modification, 7,* 611–623.

Haemmerlie, F. M., & Montgomery, R. L. (1982). Self-perception theory and unobtrusively biased interactions: A treatment for heterosocial anxiety. *Journal of Counseling Psychology, 29,* 362–370.

Haemmerlie, F. M., & Montgomery, R. L. (1984). Purposefully biased interactions: Reducing heterosocial anxiety through self-perception theory. *Journal of Personality and Social Psychology, 47,* 900–908.

Hamill, R., Wilson, T. D., & Nisbett, R. E. (1980). Insensitivity to sample bias: Generalizing from atypical cases. *Journal of Personality and Social Psychology, 39,* 578–589.

Hamilton, D. L., & Gifford, R. K. (1976). Illusory correlation in interpersonal perception: A cognitive basis of stereotypic judgments. *Journal of Experimental Social Psychology, 12,* 392–407.

Harvey, J. H. (1983). The founding of the Journal of Social and Clinical Psychology. *Journal of Social and Clinical Psychology, 1,* 1–13.

Harvey, J. H., & Galvin, K. S. (1984). Clinical implications of attribution theory and research. *Clinical Psychology Review, 4,* 15–33.

Haverkamp, B. (1990). *Confirmatory bias in hypothesis testing for client-identified and counselor self-generated hypotheses.* Manuscript submitted for publication.

Heesacker, M. (1986a). Counseling pretreatment and the elaboration likelihood model of attitude change. *Journal of Counseling Psychology, 33,* 107–114.

Heesacker, M. (1986b). Extrapolating from the elaboration likelihood model of attitude change in counseling. In F. J. Dorn (Ed.), *Social influence processes in counseling and psychotherapy* (pp. 43–54). Springfield, IL: Thomas.

Heider, F. (1958). *The psychology of interpersonal relations.* New York: Wiley.

Heppner, P. P. (1978). A review of the problem-solving literature and its relationship to the counseling process. *Journal of Counseling Psychology, 25,* 366–375.

Heppner, P. P., & Claiborn, C. D. (1989). Social influence research in counseling: A review and critique [Monograph]. *Journal of Counseling Psychology, 36,* 365–387.

Heppner, P. P., & Dixon, D. N. (1981). A review of the interpersonal influence process in counseling. *Personnel and Guidance Journal, 59,* 542–550.

Heppner, P. P., & Heesacker, M. (1982). Interpersonal influence process in real-life counseling: Investigating client perceptions, counselor experience level, and counselor power over time. *Journal of Counseling Psychology, 29,* 215–223.

Heppner, P. P., & Heesacker, M. (1983). Perceived counselor characteristics, client expectations, and client satisfaction with counseling. *Journal of Counseling Psychology, 30,* 31–39.

Heppner, P. P., Kivlighan, D. M., Jr., & Wampold, B. E. (1992). *Research design in counseling.* Pacific Grove, CA: Brooks/Cole.

Heppner, P. P., & Krauskopf, C. J. (1987). An information processing approach to personal problem solving. *The Counseling Psychologist, 15,* 371–447.

Higgins, E. T. (1987). Self-discrepancy: A theory relating self and affect. *Psychological Review, 94,* 319–340.

Highlen, P. S., & Hill, C. E. (1984). Factors affecting client change in individual counseling: Current status and theoretical speculations. In S. D. Brown and R. W. Lent (Eds.), *Handbook of counseling psychology* (pp. 334–396). New York: Wiley.

Hill, C. E., Helms, J. E., Spiegel, S. B., & Tichenor, V. (1988). Development of a system for categorizing client reactions to therapist interventions. *Journal of Counseling Psychology, 35,* 27–36.

Hirsch, P., & Stone, G. (1983). Cognitive strategies and the client conceptualization process. *Journal of Counseling Psychology, 30,* 566–572.

Hoffman, M. A., & Teglasi, H. (1982). The role of causal attributions in counseling shy subjects. *Journal of Counseling Psychology, 29,* 132–139.

Hollon, S. D., & Kriss, M. R. (1984). Cognitive factors in clinical research and practice. *Clinical Psychology Review, 4,* 35–76.

Houts, A. C. (1984). Effects of clinician theoretical orientation and patient explanatory bias on initial clinical judgments. *Professional Psychology: Research and Practice, 15,* 284–293.

Houts, A. C., & Galante, M. (1985). The impact of evaluative disposition and subsequent information on clinical impressions. *Journal of Social and Clinical Psychology, 3,* 201–212.

Hovland, C. I., Janis, I. L., & Kelley, H. H. (1953). *Communication and persuasion.* New Haven, CT: Yale University Press.

Janoff-Bulman, R., & Lang-Gunn, L. (1988). Coping with disease, crime and accidents: The role of self-blame attributions. In L. Y. Abramson (Ed.), *Social cognition and clinical psychology: A synthesis* (pp. 116–147). New York: Guilford Press.

Johnson, W. C., Jr., & Heppner, P. P. (1989). On reasoning and cognitive demands in counseling: Implications for counselor training. *Journal of Counseling and Development, 67,* 428–429.

Jones, E., & Davis, K. (1965). From acts to dispositions: The attribution process in person perception. In L. Berkowitz (Ed.), *Advances in experimental social psychology* (Vol. 2). New York: Academic Press.

Kagan, N. (1975). *Interpersonal process recall: A method for influencing human interaction.* East Lansing, MI: Michigan State University.

Kahneman, D., Slovic, P., & Tversky, A. (Eds.). (1982). *Judgment under uncertainty: Heuristics and biases.* New York: Cambridge University Press.

Kahneman, D., & Tversky, A. (1972). A subjective probability: A judgment of representativeness. *Cognitive Psychology, 3,* 430–454.

Kelley, H. (1967). Attribution theory in social psychology. In D. Levine (Ed.), *Nebraska Symposium on Motivation* (Vol. 15). Lincoln: University of Nebraska Press.

Kiesler, C. A., & Munson, P. A. (1975). Attitudes and opinions. *Annual Review of Psychology, 26,* 415–456.

Kuiper, N., & MacDonald, M. (1982). Self and other perception in mild depressives. *Social Cognition, 1,* 223–239.

LaCrosse, M. B. (1980). Perceived counselor social influence and counseling outcomes: Validity of the Counselor Rating Form. *Journal of Counseling Psychology, 27,* 320–327.

Langer, E. J., & Abelson, R. P. (1974). The patient by any other name . . . : Clinician group difference in labeling bias. *Journal of Consulting and Clinical Psychology, 42,* 4–9.

Layden, M. (1982). Attributional style therapy. In C. Antaki & C. Brewin (Eds.), *Attributions and psychological change: Applications of attributional theories to clinical and educational practice* (pp. 63–82). New York: Academic Press.

Leary, M. R., & Maddux, J. E. (1987). Progress toward a viable interface between social and counseling–clinical psychology. *American Psychologist, 42,* 904–911.

Leary, M., & Miller, R. (1986). *Social psychology and dysfunctional behavior: Origins, diagnosis, and treatment.* New York: Springer-Verlag.

Lewin, K. (1948). *Resolving social conflicts.* New York: Harper.

Linville, P. (1987). Self-complexity as a cognitive buffer against stress-related illness and depression. *Journal of Personality and Social Psychology, 53,* 663–676.

Lipstein, B., & McGuire, W. J. (1978). *Evaluating advertising.* New York: Advertising Research Foundation.

MacDonald, M. R., & Kuiper, N. A. (1984). Self-schema decision consistency in clinical depressives. *Journal of Social and Clinical Psychology, 2,* 264–272.

Maddux, J. E., Stoltenberg, C. D., & Rosenwein, R. (1987). *Social processes in clinical and counseling psychology.* New York: Springer-Verlag.

Maier, S., & Seligman, M. (1976). Learned helplessness: Theory and evidence. *Journal of Experimental Psychology: General, 105,* 3–46.

Markus, H. (1977). Self-schemata and processing information about the self. *Journal of Personality and Social Psychology, 35,* 63–78.

Markus, H., & Nurius, P. (1986). Possible selves. *American Psychologist, 41,* 945–969.

Martin, J. (1984). The cognitive mediational paradigm for research on counseling. *Journal of Counseling Psychology, 31,* 558–571.

Martin, J. (1985). Measuring clients' cognitive competence in research on counseling. *Journal of Counseling and Development, 63,* 556–560.

McGlynn, R. P., Maddux, J. E., Stoltenberg, C. D., & Harvey, J. H. (Eds.). (1984). *Social perception in clinical and counseling psychology.* Lubbock, TX: Texas Tech Press.

McGuire, W. J. (1969). The nature of attitudes and attitude change. In G. Lindzey & E. Aronson (Eds.), *Handbook of social psychology* (2nd ed.) (Vol. 3, pp. 136–314). Reading, MA: Addison-Wesley.

McGuire, W. J. (1985). Attitudes and attitude change. In G. Lindzey & E. Aronson (Eds.), *Handbook of social psychology* (3rd ed.) (Vol. 2, pp. 233–346). New York: Random House.

McNeill, B. W., & Stoltenberg, C. D. (1988). A test of the elaboration likelihood model for therapy. *Cognitive Therapy and Research, 12,* 69–80.

McNeill, B. W., & Stoltenberg, C. D. (1989). Reconceptualizing social influence in counseling: The elaboration likelihood model. *Journal of Counseling Psychology, 36,* 24–33.

Meehl, P. E. (1954). *Clinical versus statistical prediction.* Minneapolis: University of Minnesota Press.

Miller, R., Brickman, P., & Bolen, I. (1975). Attribution versus persuasion as a means for modifying behavior. *Journal of Personality and Social Psychology, 31,* 430–441.

Montgomery, R., & Haemmerlie, F. (1987). Self-perception theory and heterosocial anxiety. In J. Maddux, C. Stoltenberg, & R. Rosenwein (Eds.), *Social processes in clinical and counseling psychology* (pp. 139–152). New York: Springer-Verlag.

Nisbett, R. E., & Ross, L. (1980). *Human inference: Strategies and shortcomings of social judgment.* Englewood Cliffs, NJ: Prentice-Hall.

Ogilvie, D. M. (1987). The undesired self: A neglected variable in personality research. *Journal of Personality and Social Psychology, 52,* 379–385.

Pepinsky, H. B., & Pepinsky, P. N. (1954). *Counseling: Theory and practice.* New York: Ronald Press.

Peterson, C. (1982). Learned helplessness and attributional interventions in depression. In C. Antaki & C. Brewin (Eds.), *Attributions and psychological change: Applications of attributional theories to clinical and educational practice* (pp. 97–115). New York: Academic Press.

Peterson, C., & Seligman, M. (1984). Causal explanations as a risk factor for depression: Theory and evidence. *Psychological Review, 91,* 347–375.

Petty, R. E., & Cacioppo, J. T. (1979). Effects of forewarning of persuasive intent and involvement on cognitive responses and persuasion. *Personality and Social Psychology Bulletin, 5,* 173–176.

Petty, R. E., & Cacioppo, J. T. (1981). *Attitudes and persuasion: Classic and contemporary approaches.* Dubuque, IA: Brown.

Petty, R. E., & Cacioppo, J. T. (1984). *Attitude change: Central and peripheral routes to persuasion.* New York: Springer-Verlag.

Petty, R. E., & Cacioppo, J. T. (1986). *Communication and persuasion: Central and peripheral routes to attitude change.* New York: Springer-Verlag.

Petty, R. E., Wells, G. L., & Brock, T. C. (1976). Distraction can enhance or reduce yielding to propaganda through disruption versus effort justification. *Journal of Personality and Social Psychology, 34,* 874–884.

Robinson, V., & Halliday, J. (1988). Relationship of counselor reasoning and data collection to problem analysis quality. *British Journal of Guidance and Counseling, 16,* 50–62.

Rogers, T., Kuiper, N., & Kirker, W. (1977). Self-reference and the encoding of personal information. *Journal of Personality and Social Psychology, 35,* 677–688.

Rosen, A., & Osmo, R. (1984). Client locus of control, problem perception, and interview behavior. *Journal of Counseling Psychology, 31,* 314–321.

Ross, L. (1977). The intuitive psychologist and his shortcomings: Distortion in the attribution process. In J. Berkowitz (Ed.), *Advances in experimental social psychology* (Vol. 10, pp. 173–220). New York: Academic Press.

Ross, L., Lepper, M., & Hubbard, M. (1975). Perseverance in self perception and social perception: Biased attributional processes in the debriefing paradigm. *Journal of Personality and Social Psychology, 32,* 880–892.

Rothblum, E., Solomon, L., & Murakami, J. (1986). Affective, cognitive, and behavioral differences between high and low procrastinators. *Journal of Counseling Psychology, 33,* 387–394.

Schrauger, J. S. (1982). Selection and processing of self-evaluative information: Experimental evidence and clinical implications. In G. Weary & H. Mirels (Eds.), *Integrations of clinical and social psychology* (pp. 128–153). New York: Oxford University Press.

Schwartz, G. S., Friedlander, M. L., & Tedeschi, J. T. (1986). Effects of clients' attributional explanations and reasons for seeking help on counselors' impressions. *Journal of Counseling Psychology, 33,* 90–93.

Segal, Z. (1988). Appraisal of the self-schema construct in cognitive models of depression. *Psychological Bulletin, 103,* 147–162.

Slusher, M. P., & Anderson, C. A. (1989). Belief perseverance and self-defeating behavior. In R. Curtis (Ed.), *Self-defeating behaviors: Experimental research, clinical impressions, and practical implications* (pp. 11–40). New York: Plenum Press.

Snyder, M., & Ickes, W. (1985). Personality and social behavior. In G. Lindzey & E. Aronson (Eds.), *Handbook of social psychology* (Vol. 1, pp. 883–948). New York: Random House.

Snyder, M., & Swann, W. B. (1978). Hypothesis-testing processes in social interaction. *Journal of Personality and Social Psychology, 36,* 1202–1212.

Snyder, M., & Thomsen, C. (1988). Interactions between therapists and clients: Hypothesis testing and behavioral confirmation. In D. Turk & P. Salovey (Eds.), *Reasoning, influence, and judgment in clinical practice* (pp. 124–152). New York: Free Press.

Snyder, M., & Uranowitz, S. W. (1978). Reconstructing the past: Some cognitive consequences of person perception. *Journal of Personality and Social Psychology, 36,* 941–950.

Sober-Ain, L., & Kidd, R. (1984). Fostering changes in self-blamers' beliefs about causality. *Cognitive Therapy and Research, 8,* 121–138.

Sonne, L., & Janoff, D. (1982). Attributions and the maintenance of behavior change. In C. Antaki & C. Brewin (Eds.), *Attributions and psychological change: Applications of attributional theories to clinical and educational practice* (pp. 83–96). New York: Academic Press.

Stoltenberg, C. D., & McNeill, B. W. (1984). Effects of expertise and issue involvement on perceptions of counseling. *Journal of Social and Clinical Psychology, 2,* 314–325.

Strohmer, D. C., & Chiodo, A. L. (1984). Counselor hypothesis testing strategies: The role of initial impressions and self-schema. *Journal of Counseling Psychology, 31,* 510–519.

Strohmer, D., Moilanen, D., & Barry, L. (1988). Personal hypothesis testing: The role of consistency and self-schema. *Journal of Counseling Psychology, 35,* 56–64.

Strohmer, D. C., & Newman, L. J. (1983). Counselor hypothesis-testing strategies. *Journal of Counseling Psychology, 30,* 557–565.

Strong, S. R. (1968). Counseling: An interpersonal influence process. *Journal of Counseling Psychology, 15,* 215–224.

Strong, S. R. (1978). Social psychological approach to psychotherapy research. In S. Garfield & A. E. Bergin (Eds.), *Handbook of psychotherapy and behavior change* (2nd ed.) (pp. 101–136). New York: Wiley.

Strong, S. R., & Matross, R. P. (1973). Change processes in counseling and psychotherapy. *Journal of Counseling Psychology, 20,* 25–37.

Strong, S. R., Wambach, C. A., Lopez, F. G., & Cooper, R. K. (1979). Motivational and equipping functions of interpretation in counseling. *Journal of Counseling Psychology, 26,* 98–107.

Swann, W. (1983). Self-verification: Bringing social reality into harmony with the self. In J. Suls & A. Greenwald (Eds.), *Social psychological perspectives on the self* (Vol. 2, pp. 33–66). Hillsdale, NJ: Erlbaum.

Swann, W. B. (1987). Identity negotiation: Where two roads meet. *Journal of Personality and Social Psychology, 53,* 1038–1051.

Swann, W. B., & Ely, R. J. (1984). A battle of wills: Self-verification versus behavioral confirmation. *Journal of Personality and Social Psychology, 46,* 1287–1302.

Swann, W. B., Griffin, J. J., Predmore, S. C., & Gaines, B. (1987). The cognitive-affective crossfire: When self-consistency confronts self-enhancement. *Journal of Personality and Social Psychology, 52,* 881–889.

Swann, W. B., Pelham, B. W., & Chidester, T. R. (1988). Change through paradox: Using self-verification to alter beliefs. *Journal of Personality and Social Psychology, 54,* 268–273.

Swann, W., & Read, S. (1981a). Self-verification processes: How we sustain our self-conceptions. *Journal of Experimental Social Psychology, 17,* 351–372.

Swann, W. B., & Read, S. J. (1981b). Acquiring self-knowledge: The search for feedback that fits. *Journal of Personality and Social Psychology, 41,* 1119–1128.

Sweeney, P., Anderson, K., & Bailey, S. (1986). Attributional style in depression: A meta-analytic review. *Journal of Personality and Social Psychology, 50,* 974–991.

Taylor, S. E., & Brown, J. D. (1988). Illusion and well-being: A social psychological perspective on mental health. *Psychological Bulletin, 103,* 193–210.

Taylor, S. E., & Fiske, S. T. (1978). Salience, attention, and attribution: Top of the head phenomena. In L. Berkowitz (Ed.), *Advances in experimental social psychology* (Vol. 11, pp. 249–288). New York: Academic Press.

Temerlin, M. (1968). Suggestion effects in psychiatric diagnoses. *Journal of Nervous and Mental Disease, 147,* 349–353.

Turk, D. C., & Salovey, P. (1985a). Cognitive structures, cognitive processes, and cognitive-behavior modification: I. Client issues. *Cognitive Therapy and Research, 9,* 1–17.

Turk, D. C., & Salovey, P. (1985b). Cognitive structures, cognitive processes, and cognitive-behavioral modification: II. Judgments and inferences of the clinician. *Cognitive Therapy and Research, 9,* 19–34.

Turk, D. C., & Salovey, P. (1986). Clinical information processing: Bias inoculation. In R. E. Ingram (Ed.), *Information processing approaches to clinical psychology* (pp. 305–323). New York: Academic Press.

Turk, D. C., & Salovey, P. (Eds.). (1988). *Reasoning, inference, and judgment in clinical psychology.* New York: Free Press.

Turk, D., & Speers, M. (1983). Cognitive schemata and cognitive processes in cognitive-behavioral interventions: Going beyond the information given. In P. C. Kendall (Ed.), *Advances in cognitive-behavioral research and therapy* (Vol. 2, pp. 1–32). New York: Academic Press.

Turnquist, D. C., Harvey, J. H., & Andersen, B. L. (1988). Attributions and adjustment to life-threatening illness. *British Journal of Clinical Psychology, 27,* 55–65.

Tversky, A., & Kahneman, D. (1973). Availability: A heuristic for judging frequency and probability. *Cognitive Psychology, 5,* 207–232.

Tversky, A., & Kahneman, D. (1974). Judgment under uncertainty: Heuristics and biases. *Science, 185,* 1124–1131.

Weary, G., & Mirels, H. J. (Eds.). (1982). *Integrations of clinical and social psychology.* New York: Oxford University Press.

Weber, R., & Crocker, J. (1983). Cognitive processes in the revision of stereotypic beliefs. *Journal of Personality and Social Psychology, 45,* 961–977.

Weiner, B. (1979). A theory of motivation for some classroom experiences. *Journal of Educational Psychology, 71,* 3–25.

Westbrook, M. T., & Nordholm, L. A. (1986). Reactions to patients' self- or chance-blaming attributions for illnesses having varying life-style involvement. *Journal of Applied Social Psychology, 16,* 428–446.

Wills, T. A. (1987). Help seeking as a coping mechanism. In C. R. Snyder & C. E. Ford (Eds.), *Coping with negative life events: Clinical and psychological perspectives* (pp. 19–50). New York: Plenum Press.

Wilson, T., & Linville, P. (1982). Improving the academic performance of college freshmen: Attributional therapy revisited. *Journal of Personality and Social Psychology, 42,* 367–376.

Wilson, T., & Linville, P. (1985). Improving the performance of college freshmen with attributional techniques. *Journal of Personality and Social Psychology, 49,* 287–293.

Winfrey, L. P. L., & Goldfried, M. R. (1986). Information processing and the human change process. In R. E. Ingram (Ed.), *Information processing approaches to clinical psychology* (pp. 241–258). New York: Academic Press.

Zamostny, K. P., Corrigan, J. D., & Eggert, M. A. (1981). Replication and extension of social influence processes in counseling: A field study. *Journal of Counseling Psychology, 28,* 481–489.

Zoeller, C. J., Mahoney, G., & Weiner, B. (1983). Effects of attribution training on the assembly task performance of mentally retarded adults. *American Journal of Mental Deficiency, 88,* 109–112.

CHAPTER 6

SUPERVISION: A WAY OF TEACHING AND LEARNING

ELIZABETH L. HOLLOWAY

A discussion of education in any professional field depends on knowledge of practice; that is, what are the methods, techniques, and skills that promote effective practice? In the specialty of counseling psychology, the sequence of practice experiences typically begins with interviewing skills, often referred to as microcounseling skills, microtraining, or microskills. These training packages are then followed with practicum experiences in which the student provides counseling services to a limited number of clients under intensive supervision by a more experienced professional. Often, these experiences take place in a "sheltered workshop" situation such as a department-run or university counseling clinic. Next, students engage in a field placement in which field-based professionals provide supervision within the context of an agency. Finally, students embark on an internship, during which they are ordinarily engaged full-time in the practice of diverse professional activities with intensive supervision. Postdegree education occurs in many forms, including residency requirements for licensure, remedial programs of learning, and respecialization programs. At each stage of this progression, supervision is the critical teaching method; professional education depends on the supervisory process to facilitate the development of the student from novice to autonomously functioning professional.

THE HISTORY OF SUPERVISION

Supervision is, literally, to "oversee," to view another's work with the eyes of the experienced clinician, the sensitive teacher, the discriminating professional. Supervision provides an opportunity for the student to capture the essence of the psychotherapeutic process as it is articulated and modeled by the supervisor, and to recreate it in the counseling relationship. However, such recreation by the supervisee is ideally not an undiscriminating adoption of the supervisor's methods and view. Rather, it is a unique improvisation of the principles and means inherent in the professional knowledge provided by the supervisor and reconstructed by the supervisee for a particular client at a specific point in the counseling process. The supervisor's challenge is to create a learning context that will enhance supervisee skill in constructing relevant frames of reference from which to devise effective strategies in work with clients. Although research-based techniques and principles of practice are an important part of the knowledge base from which the supervisee will operate, there remains the untold area of "artistry" in practice. It is in this latter kind of knowledge, "artistry as an exercise of intelligence" (Schon, 1983, p. 12), that supervision may play the most critical role.

> *[L]earning all forms of professional artistry depends, at least in part, on . . . freedom to learn by doing in a setting relatively low in risk, with access to coaches who initiate students into the "traditions of the calling" and help them, by "the right kind of telling" to see on their own behalf and in their own way what they need most to see. (Schon, 1983, p. 17)*

The first method of supervision was defined by the psychoanalytic school of psychotherapy. Analysts-in-training were expected to be in analysis themselves, with the supervising analyst. Evident in this first supervisory approach is the primacy attributed to a supervisee's awareness and understanding of self and the modeling of the analyst's methods through the direct experience of being the recipient of treatment. The art of psychotherapy was meant to be transmitted through the relationship with the teaching therapist (Ekstein and Wallerstein, 1958).

The advent of direct observational methods of counseling practice (Rogers, 1957) ushered in the second generation of supervisory practice and research. The actual behaviors of therapist and client could be observed by supervisors and used as the foundation of supervisory discussions. Further, investigation of therapeutic discourse and technique could now adopt more rigorous positivistic methodologies rather than the descriptive, anecdotal methodologies traditionally used. Translating the artistry of Rogers's facilitative attitudes—genuineness, unconditional positive regard, empathy, and congruence—into discrete and teachable units was an important development in educational programs.

Truax and Carkhuff (1967) began this process by identifying communication strategies that were used in client-centered counseling to establish the necessary facilitative conditions of the relationship as described by Rogers (1957). Research on the facilitative conditions of psychotherapy led to training programs designed to teach these skills (Matarazzo & Patterson, 1986). An emphasis on skill development was ushered in by the microskills training programs (e.g., Ivey, Normington, Miller, Morrill, & Haase, 1968). These structured, competency-based approaches contrasted with the more global, case-method approach of traditional psychotherapy training. Counseling psychology training programs incorporated microskills training as an instructional method that could be used in a classroom format to teach beginning-level counseling skills. The emergence of specific approaches to skill development resulted in a method of teaching that was distinct from the dyadic supervisory situation. However, the use of dyadic supervision continued to be utilized as an instructional method to teach more prescriptive use of counseling skills in the context of actual counseling.

Group supervision (the supervision of counselors-in-training in a group) emerged as a third component of counselor training during the 1960s. In contrast to the programmatic learning of microskills training, this method of instruction resembled the interpersonally oriented psychotherapy groups (Holloway & Johnston, 1985); groups were designed to increase counselor trainees' self-awareness of interpersonal style and behaviours, and ability to provide feedback to peers.

Thus, three components of therapeutic training evolved historically: (a) techniques training (microskills and intervention training packages), (b) dyadic supervision, including direct observation of counseling interactions to teach the individualized application of counseling techniques, and (c) group supervision that addressed the intrapersonal and interpersonal awareness of the trainee. Microskills training is frequently used in educational programming, and there have been recent comprehensive reviews of its accompanying literature (Baker & Daniels, 1989; Baker, Daniels, & Greeley, 1990; Lambert & Arnold, 1987; Matarazzo & Patterson, 1986; Russell, Crimmings, & Lent, 1984). Additionally, the use and effectiveness of intervention training packages or "manualized training in psychotherapy" have appeared in several major reviews (Beutler, 1988; Lambert, 1980; Lambert & Arnold, 1987; Matarazzo & Patterson, 1986; Russell et al., 1984).

Because of the centrality of the supervision method in the teaching and learning of psychotherapy and the availability of comprehensive reviews of microskills training and treatment packages, this review focuses on theory and research in dyadic and group supervision. The bulk of research has been on dyadic supervision; therefore, the chapter is largely devoted to this topic. There has been considerable research activity since the Russell et al. (1984) review in the first edition of this *Handbook,* but no new models of supervision have appeared. Because Russell et al. described in detail all of the major models of supervision, this review provides only a brief overview of the history of model building in dyadic supervision, offers a conceptual framework or "map" for organizing the various topics of research, and then reviews each area of research as defined by the "map." A brief discussion of approaches to group supervision follows the dyadic supervision section, and a general discussion of implications for research and training concludes the chapter.

MODEL BUILDING IN DYADIC SUPERVISION

Supervision has been the focus of considerable theoretical speculation in counseling psychology since Mueller and Kell's (1972) book on the supervisory relationship. In counseling psychology, the first approaches to supervision reflected models of supervision that were built on theories of counseling. In fact, the names of these models speak directly to their adherence to theories of counseling, for example, client-centered supervision (Patterson, 1983), social learning approach to supervision (Hosford & Barmann, 1983), and supervision in rational-emotive therapy (Wessler & Ellis, 1983). Although models are built to aid in the interpretation and description of complex phenomena and to help in the learning of complex skills, the "counseling-bound" models of supervision have provided few directions for either research or practice (Russell et al., 1984). Their parochialism has prevented them from incorporating knowledge from relevant foundational disciplines such as developmental, educational, and social psychology. Research on the process of supervision has largely revealed that supervisors do not practice supervision as they practice counseling and that the character of a supervision interview has features unique from the counseling interview (Russell et al., 1984). Thus, the fundamental assumptions of the "counseling-bound" models have been challenged and are being replaced by models that incorporate knowledge from related psychological subdisciplines and that provide frameworks for empirical inquiry.

Ekstein and Wallerstein (1958) distinguished between the practice of psychotherapy and the problem of teaching and learning psychotherapy. In their seminal text, they focused on the problem of "how to transmit these skills [of psychotherapy] to another, how to supervise rather than how to do psychotherapy" (p. xii). Recognition that the teaching of psychotherapy is different from doing supervision is reflected in the approach of "cross-theoretical" (Russell et al., 1984) models that incorporate knowledge of individual difference, social role theory, and instructional psychology. Two major cross-theoretical approaches have appeared since 1979: developmental models and social role models. Although 18 different developmental models have been described, the most comprehensive models, which have received the majority of research attention, are those of Stoltenberg (1981) and Loganbill, Hardy, and Delworth (1982). More recently, Stoltenberg and Delworth (1987) collaborated on a detailed description of the developmental approach to supervision. Critical reviews of the developmental models and related empirical studies appeared in Holloway (1987, 1988a), Stoltenberg and Delworth (1988), and Worthington (1987).

Developmental models draw from developmental psychology, including theories of Loevinger (1976), Perry (1970), Chickering (1969), and Hunt and Sullivan's (1974) person–environment matching model in education. The fundamental assumption of these models was that supervisors need to adjust their style of supervision to match the trainee's level of development as a counselor. Another approach that used a person–environment matching model of supervision was Abbey, Hunt, and Weiser's (1985) experiential learning model, which relied on Kolb's (1984) learning styles theory to conceptualize the teaching–learning processes in counseling and supervision. Abbey et al. did not include a developmental perspective in their model, but did rely on individual differences in trainees' cognitive or learning styles as a basis for structuring supervisory environments (Sugarman, 1985). These models are discussed more extensively within the context of research that has investigated their prescriptions for supervision.

Another prevalent cross-theoretical approach to supervision is that of "social role models." These models include Bartlett (1983); Bernard (1979); Boyd (1978); Hess (1980); Littrell, Lee-Borden, and Lorenz (1979). These models were reviewed in Russell et al. (1984), but have not been associated with the social psychological literature on social roles. The fundamental theoretical principle underlying these models is that the supervisor position includes a set of roles that establish a certain composite of expectations, beliefs, and attitudes about what functions the supervisor will perform. The supervisor engaging in recurring actions that are consistent with the expected role will promote an experience of behavioral consistency and certainty for the trainee. Although the role model approaches have focused almost exclusively on the supervisor as the role-sender, the trainee also has certain expected roles to play in conjunction with the supervisor (Holloway, 1984). Because of counseling psychologists' familiarity with the roles prescribed for the supervisor, these models have provided a useful heuristic tool in guiding practice (Hess, 1980). There is little research that directly tests these models; however, their contribution to research efforts is discussed in a later section.

RESEARCH IN DYADIC SUPERVISION

Often, research reviews are organized around the types of dependent and independent variables that are employed in the various studies being described. This approach has the advantage of providing a single organizing framework that matches the existing empirical literature. The disadvantage is that important researchable topics may be overlooked. I have chosen to organize the research conceptually rather than methodologically. By drawing from the literature on counselor, teacher, and administrative supervision, Holloway and Dunlap (1989) developed a scheme for identifying the various aspects of supervision and the flow of information and influence among these aspects. They called this scheme a "map" (see Figure 6.1) because it guides the investigator through the difficult terrain of knowledge in supervision.

The dynamic character of supervision is immediately obvious from the graphic display. Supervision exists in the context of the profession's requirements for training,

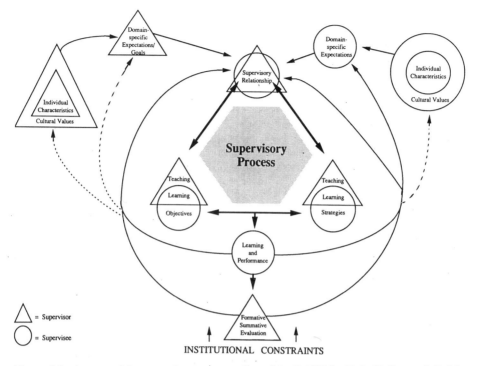

Figure 6.1   Aspects of the supervisory process. Copyright © 1990 by E. L. Holloway & D. M. Dunlap. Reprinted by permission.

the organization's policies and needs, the supervisee's learning requirements, the supervisor's teaching objectives, and the consumer's need for effective professional service. The supervisory relationship is embedded in the larger contexts of the profession and the organization, and is yoked to the actual counseling situation through the supervisee's role in both relationships. It is my hope that the map will provide the reader with easily recognizable landmarks in the quest to understand this very complex phenomenon and the research that has sought to guide the way.

The research literature is organized around the following aspects of the map: individual and cultural characteristics of the participants, domain-specific expectations and goals, supervisory relationship, teaching objectives and strategies, evaluation, and institutional factors. Each section introduces the specific area of research, reviews the findings, with emphasis on research since 1983, and summarizes the general trends.

Supervisor Characteristics

What are the qualities of the ideal supervisor? Many authors have described the ideal supervisor as a person who exhibits high levels of empathy, understanding, unconditional positive regard, flexibility, concern, attention, investment, curiosity, and openness (Carifio & Hess, 1987). Such qualities are, of course, valuable in any working relationship.

Early research focused on Rogers's (1957) ideal supervisor characteristics; however, since 1980, more attention has been given to supervisor experience, theoretical orientation, and gender. There were no studies found that examined supervisor ethnic or cultural characteristics. Dependent variables in these studies have included supervisory satisfaction, planning behaviors of supervisors, in-session verbal behaviors, and preferred interpersonal power bases. More recently, supervisor characteristics were examined in conjunction with trainee characteristics, for example, the interaction of supervisor and supervisee gender. (These studies are examined in the "Supervisee Characteristics" section.)

Supervisor Experience

Sundblad and Feinberg's (1972) analogue study examined the relationship among the core facilitative conditions (i.e., empathy, warmth, and genuineness), interpersonal attraction, and experience of the supervisor. Findings revealed that, when given a positive set about the supervisee, supervisors with more experience provided the highest levels of facilitative conditions. Conversely, when given a negative set, they provided the lowest level of facilitation. The authors concluded that interpersonal attraction to the supervisee differentially affects the supervisor's delivery of facilitative conditions. Surprisingly, more experienced supervisors were more negatively influenced and thus less attracted to the negative-set trainees. The authors suggested that, because the more experienced supervisors in this study were not trained in the experiential-didactic training model (due to historical cohort group) whereas the less experienced supervisors had been so trained and were also in closer proximity to the student role, the latter were more tolerant of the negative-set supervisees.

In another analogue study, Worthington (1984a) asked experienced and inexperienced counselors to assume a supervisor role and to rate counselors and clients, represented in a 10-minute excerpt from a counseling session, on eight personality trait labels. Experience level of supervisor, defined by the amount of counseling experience of the participants, ranged from "no experience" through postdoctoral experience. Half of the supervisors were led to believe that the counselor in the videotape vignette was at the beginning level and half were told she was at the internship level. The results indicated that supervisors with more counseling experience made fewer trait attributions to the counselor than did supervisors with little or no counseling experience. Theoretically, the argument was made that supervisors' experience in counseling promotes increased cognitive role taking (empathy) and thus they are better able to attribute the supervisee's behaviors to situational variables rather than personal traits. The "set" of counselor's level of training had no significant effect on the supervisors' judgments of counselor traits. Further, supervisors, regardless of counseling experience, did not differentially attribute trait labels to the client. The supervisor's ability to recognize interpersonal and situational factors in counseling that may influence the counselor's behavior is salient to establishing an empathic relationship and assisting the supervisee to devise different counseling strategies that respond to contextual factors. Unfortunately, the definition of experience level in this study limits the generalizability of the results. Because most supervisors have some counseling experience, it is unlikely that "no experience" in counseling is a realistic alternative as a supervisor characteristic. However, because many training programs use doctoral students to supervise beginning-level counselors, these results emphasize the importance of using more experienced counselors as supervisors and/or teaching supervisors, to focus on situational influences on the supervisee.

Stone (1980) found that more experienced supervisors focused more on counselor behavior in their before-session planning statements than did inexperienced supervisors. Marikis, Russell, and Dell ((1985) improved on Stone's study by including only participants with counseling experience and with at least a didactic course on supervision. Experience level of supervisors ranged from "no supervisory experience" to post-doctoral supervisory experience. Additionally, Marikis et al. compared planning behavior to actual in-session behavior of the supervisors. Their findings indicated that there were no differences on planning behaviors among the different experience-level groups and that the most frequent planning behaviors were counselor-oriented statements, followed by client, subject-matter, and process statements. These results contrast with Stone's findings that there were significant differences in planning behavior across the different experience groups. Marikis et al. also found that there was little relation between the planning process and in-session verbal behaviors. However, there were differences in verbal behaviors between the "no-experience" and two experienced groups. Supervisors with some experience were more verbal in session, self-disclosed more, and provided more direct instruction of counseling skills. Similar research that examines planned objectives and in-session strategies in conjunction with trainee learning and performance is needed. This type of investigation can potentially identify effective instructional methods of supervision.

Supervisor Theoretical Orientation

The influence of the supervisor's theoretical orientation on supervisory behavior has been the subject of several studies. This is not surprising, given the influence of counseling-bound supervision models in the field. Sundblad and Garfield (cited in Sundblad, 1977), and Beutler and McNabb (1981) found that students tend to adopt the theoretical orientation of supervisors and/or the director of clinical training. In an extensive study of clinical psychology graduates in a medical school practice setting, Guest and Beutler (1988) confirmed that orientations of prominent supervisors were particularly important in establishing a trainee's viewpoint, regardless of the correspondence between trainees' initial orientation and the supervisor's orientation. Further, trainee locus of control and other personality variables did not contribute to changes in orientation or values over the course of 1 training year or in follow-up 3 to 5 years after training.

Goodyear and Robyak (1982) found that, regardless of theoretical orientation, more experienced supervisors shared similar emphases in supervision; less experienced supervisors were more divergent in ways consistent with their theoretical orientation. These results supported similar studies in psychotherapy (Friedler, 1950) and an early study by Demos and Zuwaylif (1962) in supervision. In another study, Goodyear, Abadie, and Efros (1984) had experienced supervisors view supervision sessions of prominent supervision theorists working with the same supervisee (Goodyear, 1982). Findings indicated that supervisors of different theoretical orientations were rated differently in attractiveness (as measured by the Supervisor Rating Form; Heppner & Handley, 1982) and in their use of the critic, model, and nurturing roles. They also were perceived as different in their use of the counselor and teacher roles and in supervisory focus on such issues as case conceptualization, counseling skills, and transference. Holloway, Freund, Gardner, Nelson, and Walker (1989) also studied the Goodyear (1989) videotape series and concluded that, although there were prominent similarities in patterns of verbal behaviors, there were also predictable differences among the theorists. Thus, in these two studies of the same data set, theoretical orientation of the supervisor was related to perceived differences in supervisory behavior and actual differences in supervisory discourse.

Supervisor Gender

Robyak, Goodyear, and Prange (1987), drawing from the interpersonal influence model of counseling (Strong, 1968; Strong & Matross, 1973), examined the influence of supervisor's gender, experience, and supervisory focus on his or her preferences for expert, referent, and legitimate power bases (French & Raven, 1960). The expert power base stems from specialized knowledge and skills. Referent power is derived from interpersonal attraction. Legitimate power is a consequence of perceived trustworthiness, in that the professional is a socially sanctioned provider of services. In this analogue study, male and female supervisors, ranging in supervisory experience from 1 month to 40 years, read a typescript of a female supervisee's comments and then selected from three possible supervisor responses. Each response reflected the use of one of the three power bases by the supervisor. The results indicated that both gender and amount of supervisory experience had significant main effects on the supervisor's preference for the referent power base, but not on the choice of the expert or legitimate power bases. It appeared that males and inexperienced supervisors preferred the use of the referent power base. Supervisors who focused on self-awareness of the supervisee showed a greater preference for the expert power base than did the supervisors who focused on client conceptualization. The legitimate power base was not significantly related to any of the three independent variables.

Supervisee Characteristics

Who is the ideal supervisee? The psychological health and personal character of the therapist were considered to be of primary importance in the traditional training of the analyst. In-depth personal therapy was regarded as a critical element in the training process to (a) enhance the therapist's ability as an unbiased clinical observer and to mitigate the effects of countertransference; (b) demonstrate experientially the validity of therapy as a treatment; (c) model first-hand the techniques of psychotherapy; and (d) improve the psychological health of the therapist and ameliorate the stresses of practice (Wampler & Strupp, 1976). However, as training programs in counseling psychology became more competency-based in their approach to evaluating trainees' appropriateness for the counselor role, researchers focused on those characteristics of the trainee that may influence the acquisition of behaviors deemed necessary for effective counseling. In particular, the facilitative conditions, as assessed in simulated or actual counseling, became the target behaviors for assessing the influence of such personal factors as cognitive structure and experience level (Hansen, Pound, & Petro, 1976; Hansen, Robins, & Grimes, 1982; Holloway, 1984; Holloway & Wampold, 1986; Russell et al., 1984).

In the 1980s, as models of supervision began to attend to the actual process and strategy of supervision (Goodyear & Bradley, 1983; Hess, 1980; Loganbill et al., 1982; Stoltenberg, 1981), researchers became interested in characteristics of the supervisee that may influence the supervisory relationship (Holloway, 1984; Russell et al., 1984; Worthington, 1987). The cognitive structure, experience, gender, ethnicity, and race of supervisees were examined again, but now in relation to *supervision* (rather than counseling) events. This section reviews studies published since 1983 that were designed to investigate the relation of supervisee factors to supervisory needs, acquisition of counseling skills, perception of the client, and in-session cognitions of the counseling process. Research on the trainee's cognitive processes and experience level is particularly critical to the developmental models of supervision.

Cognitive Characteristics

Several measures of counselors' cognitive functioning have been of interest to researchers. In particular, conceptual systems theory (CST; Harvey, Hunt, & Schroder, 1961) has enjoyed considerable popularity since the early 1970s. Holloway and Wampold (1986) conducted a meta-analysis of the research on CST in counseling, classifying research studies into two primary types: type A studies investigated the effect of conceptual level (CL) on the performance of counseling-related tasks, and type B studies investigated the matching model hypothesis of CST. The matching model examines the effects of structured versus unstructured learning environments on the skill acquisition of high-CL (cognitively complex) and low-CL (cognitively concrete) individuals. The findings implied that cognitively complex (vs. cognitively concrete) individuals were better able to perform complex, ambiguous tasks such as those needed in counseling. However, if environmental conditions for learning were highly structured, then cognitively concrete individuals were able to perform as well as or better than cognitively complex subjects. Although the studies reviewed did not represent actual supervisory contexts, they suggested that matching learning environment to trainees' cognitive characteristics may be fruitful in creating facilitative supervisory environments.

Cognitive constructs related to CST, such as ego development, dogmatism, and locus of control, have also been investigated in relation to counseling skills and cognitions. The interest in these developmental constructs might be traced to the early work of Mosher and Sprinthall (1971) in psychoeducation and the importance of developmental characteristics in planning learning environments. Carlozzi, Campbell, and Ward (1982) investigated the trainee's dogmatism and external locus of control as they related to the facilitative conditions, and found that facilitative skill was negatively correlated to level of dogmatism. Another study (Carlozzi, Gaa, & Liberman, 1983) found that counselor scores on Loevinger's scale of ego development were positively related to empathy. Brown and Smith (1984) investigated the relation of "all-inclusive conceptualization" (AIC; Drakeford, 1967) to practicum students' empathic understanding. AIC is defined as the tendency to respond to stimuli in terms of overgeneralized language. Those trainees who scored higher in AIC tended to offer their clients lower levels of empathic understanding. Bernstein and Lecomte's (1979) earlier study on the relation between locus of control and written feedback conditions concluded that field-independent trainees agreed more with feedback and evaluated it more positively than did field-dependent trainees. Although none of these studies took place in the context of the supervisory situation, they do suggest that certain cognitive constructs may influence the learning and performance of counseling-related skills.

A series of investigations by Borders and associates examined the relation of trainees' ego development to (a) beginning- and advanced-level counseling skills (Borders & Fong, 1989), (b) perceptions of clients (Borders, Fong, & Neimeyer, 1986), and (c) in-session cognitions about actual counseling events (Borders, 1989; Borders, Fong, & Cron, 1988). In each of these studies, with the exception of Borders et al. (1986), experience level of the participants was controlled by examining only one level of counseling experience.

In two related studies, Borders and Fong (1989) examined beginning-level and advanced-level students' acquisition of counseling skills (warmth, empathy, genuineness, concreteness, self-disclosure, advanced empathy, confrontation, and immediacy), as demonstrated in a simulated counseling situation, and of more advanced process skills, as demonstrated in actual sessions and measured by the Vanderbilt Psychotherapy Process Scales (VPPS; Suh, Strupp, & O'Malley, 1986). In the first study (Borders & Fong, 1989), ego development was not related to performance on posttraining measures of counseling skills. Rather, the best predictor of posttraining performance was pretraining ability level and pretraining counseling performance. High ego development students performed better during training, but did not perform significantly better in posttraining. These results may be explained by the analogue nature of the study and the elementary-level skills being assessed. As in the CST research, the greater social perceptual skills reflected in the higher developmental levels may not be necessary in less ambiguous situations, such as responding to discrete client messages outside of actual counseling. The second study (Borders & Fong, 1989) resulted in no significant findings; however, the trends reported were that students with less training who were at higher ego levels tended to receive higher VPPS ratings than did students at lower ego levels. Because beginning-level students were not measured on the advanced skills and vice versa, the effect of experience level on more advanced counseling tasks was not apparent.

The study of in-session cognitions of counselors as assessed by recall stimulation methods has been of considerable interest in counseling process research (Hill & O'Grady, 1985; Martin, Martin, Meyer, & Slemon, 1986). Borders and associates conducted two separate studies that applied the techniques of recall stimulation with counselors-in-training. Borders et al. (1988) used a case study method and an open-ended recall procedure to determine the in-session cognitions of a first-practicum supervisee. The purpose of the study was to assess the range of cognitions that might be produced with an open-ended as opposed to a structured recall procedure. The supervisee's in-session cognitions revealed themes similar to those postulated as present in early stages of the developmental models of supervision, for example, intense self-scrutiny and self-doubt, a strong sense of responsibility, and reliance on supervisors' suggestions. This study, however, did not examine the relation of these cognitions to all levels of experience or ego development. In a multiple-subject study, Borders (1989) controlled for counselor experience level by including only first-practicum supervisees of varying levels of ego development and again asked them to report in-session cognitions of a counseling session. Audiotapes of the cognitions produced during the recall stimulation were coded according to the Dole coding system (Dole et al., 1982). Borders concluded that the trainees seemed to be at different stages relative to the various supervisory issues described by the Loganbill et al. (1982) model of supervision. However, trainees at the same level of experience produced different types of cognitions relative to their level of ego development. Thus, preexisting personality constructs seem to mitigate the influences of experience level. Friedlander and Synder (1983) and Friedlander, Keller, Peca-Baker, and Olk (1986) studied the role of trainee self-efficacy in supervision in analogue investigations. They found that self-efficacy, rather than experience level, predicted the trainees' general expectations for supervision. Trainees expected supervisors to be, in order, trustworthy, expert, attractive, evaluative, and supportive. When role conflict between the supervisor and trainee was simulated, Friedlander et al. (1986) found that trainee self-efficacy was inversely related to anxiety and anxiety was inversely related to performance. Thus, trainees' individual differences in self-efficacy were related to performance.

Experience Level[1]

The preponderance of research studies in the past decade have focused on the effect of trainees' experience level on supervisory needs. These studies were largely instigated by developmental models of supervision, especially those of Hogan (1964), Loganbill et al. (1982), and Stoltenberg (1981). Worthington (1987) reviewed the conceptual and empirical literature on the changing needs of supervisees as they gain experience in counseling. From 12 studies examining trainees at various levels of experience, he concluded that, in support of the developmental models, trainees at beginning level and internship level differed in their preferences for some supervisory activities. Holloway (1987) reviewed studies specifically related to the supervision models devised by Loganbill et al. (1982), Blocher (1983), and Stoltenberg (1981). She concluded that different preferences for supervisory behaviors are expressed by trainees at different experience levels, but such differences have not been clearly shown to result from the developmental level of the trainees. The reader is referred to both of these reviews for a more detailed, critical examination of this literature. Four subsequent studies examined the experience level of the trainee: Stoltenberg, Pierce, and McNeill (1987); Rabinowitz, Heppner, and Roehlke (1986); Krause and Allen (1988); and Tracey, Ellickson, and Sherry (1989).

The studies on experience level of the trainee were instigated primarily by the developmental models of supervision and therefore might be said to have been theory-driven. Developmental models postulate that the trainee undergoes developmental changes during the period of supervised training and that such qualitative shifts in thinking and focus demand appropriate and corresponding changes in the supervisory environment. Because trainee characteristics are fundamental to the model, it seems important to examine the implications of these findings in light of the theories from which they are derived. The experimental hypotheses of studies in this area have focused on changes that might occur in trainees' or supervisors' perceptions of the supervisory experience during the trainees' progression from neophyte to master counselor. Those studies (Cross & Brown, 1983; Friedlander & Synder, 1983; Heppner & Roehlke, 1984; Krause & Allen, 1988; McNeill, Stoltenberg, & Pierce, 1985; Rabinowitz et al., 1986; Reising & Daniels, 1983; Stoltenberg, Pierce, & McNeill, 1987; Worthington, 1984b) that have examined the trainees' perception of supervisory incidents and their own needs have used self-report questionnaires including the Supervision Questionnaire (SQ; Worthington & Roehlke, 1979), Level of Supervision Survey (Miars et al., 1983), Counselor Development Questionnaire (Reising & Daniels, 1983), Supervisory Styles Inventory (SSI; Friedlander & Ward, 1984), and Supervisee Needs Questionnaire (SNQ; Stoltenberg et al., 1987). Each of these questionnaires asks the trainee to rate on a Likert-type scale descriptions of supervisor behaviors and supervisee needs.

Supervisors' perceptions of their supervisory practice with different levels of trainees have also been assessed using the same self-report questionnaires (Krause & Allen, 1988; Miars et al., 1983; Wiley & Ray, 1986; Worthington & Stern, 1985), trainees' judgments of supervisors' behaviors in supervision (Heppner & Roehlke, 1984; Worthington, 1984b; Worthington & Stern, 1985), and supervisors' judgments of trainee behaviors (Wiley & Ray, 1986; Worthington & Stern, 1985).

Many of these studies have interpreted supervisees' expressed need for differences in supervisory environment as an indication of different developmental levels. By

---

[1]A portion of this section first appeared in "Developmental Models of Supervision: Is It Development?" by E. L. Holloway, 1987, *Professional Psychology: Research and Practice, 18,* pp. 209–216. Adapted by permission.

seeking perceptual views from both the supervisors and supervisees within the context of the supervisory relationship, researchers have attempted to understand the person–environment match postulates of developmental models—the trainee's changing needs and competencies, and the supervisor's changing supervision strategies. Trainees and supervisors have been asked to remark on events in supervision that reflect emotional, relationship, and professional needs.

The predominant findings regarding trainee characteristics across various levels of trainee experience indicate that significant differences exist only between the expressed needs of beginning-level and intern-level trainees and that these differences involve relationship characteristics (Heppner & Roehlke, 1984; Miars et al., 1983; Reising & Daniels, 1983; Wiley & Ray, 1986; Worthington, 1984b; Worthington & Stern, 1985). For example, initial-level trainees appear to require more support, encouragement, and structure in supervision; interns demonstrate increasing independence from the supervisor (Hill, Charles, & Reed, 1981; McNeill et al., 1985; Reising & Daniels, 1983; Wiley & Ray, 1986; Worthington, 1984b; Worthington & Stern, 1985) and more interest in higher-level skills and personal issues affecting counseling (Heppner & Roehlke, 1984; Hill et al., 1981; McNeill et al., 1985; Stoltenberg et al., 1987; Worthington & Stern, 1985).

However, Rabinowitz et al. (1986) found that needs for structure and support were present in the beginning of all supervisory relationships, regardless of experience level of the supervisee. Krause and Allen (1988) reported that, although supervisors thought that they behaved in a more collegial, unstructured fashion with more advanced trainees, trainees of different experience level reported no differences in their perceptions of supervisor behaviors. They concluded, as did Friedlander and Ward (1984) and Allen, Szollos, and Williams (1986), that supervisory style and attitudinal stances of supervisors outweigh the impact of such specific factors as structure, format, and technique, suggesting that factors other than trainee experience level may influence the needs and perceptions of supervisees.

Evidence of supervisory change across experience levels parallels findings regarding trainee change. Of the three studies that examined supervisors' perceptions of their behaviors with trainees of different experience levels, only distinctions between entry-level trainees and interns were found (Krause & Allen, 1988; Miars et al., 1983; Wiley & Ray, 1986; Worthington & Stern, 1985). Supervisors reported that they recognized more variable relationship needs among beginning-level students, but that interns' supervisory relationships were more stable (Worthington & Stern, 1985). Supervisors saw themselves providing a different learning environment for entry-level and intern-level trainees (Krause & Allen, 1988; Miars et al., 1983; Wiley & Ray, 1986).

The results of the studies on experience level are important and informative in devising supervisory environments. However, it is not clear that trainees are engaging in a developmental process during their supervised practice experience, despite the fact that researchers are interpreting their findings to support the developmental models. Several factors mitigate the strength of these findings with respect to developmental processes.

The most obvious problem is the absence of longitudinal data to investigate developmental change. The current reliance on cross-sectional data is not an adequate approach to the developmental issue, for the following reasons. First, because the historical and cultural development of the trainee has not been assessed, the effect of existing personality structures such as ego-, cognitive-, and moral-development levels cannot be used to understand contemporary observations. Reising and Daniels (1983) concluded that assessment of basic personality structures is a necessary step in furthering the understanding of the trainee's experience. Borders and associates (Borders,

1989; Borders et al., 1986, 1988; Borders & Fong, 1989) responded to this charge in their investigations of trainee ego development. Second, the lack of information on intraindividual changes across the course of a training program seriously weakens a developmental explanation of behavior change. Any observed group change does not necessarily represent a behavior change for a particular individual, nor does it describe the particular pattern of change experienced by an individual. Third, although long-term processes are involved in adult development, supervision, investigations have typically been limited to 4-year time spans, or have reflected the duration of training programs. Cross-sectional data assume that there are no selection biases in sampling, no differences between cohort groups entering graduate programs at different times, and no historical effects that may affect groups differentially. These assumptions cannot be made within the context of graduate training programs. There are clearly changes in curriculum, instructional personnel, and perhaps even theoretical orientation within the same program across several years.

The employment of self-report techniques is a standard practice in developmental research; however, in initial investigations, preferred methods include (in increasing order of preference) open-ended questionnaires, structured and semistructured clinical interviews, and direct observation (Rest, 1979). The use of structured questionnaires prior to more open-ended techniques unnecessarily biases the results in favor of the experimenters' understanding of what they should find and emphasizes the comparison of subjects on quantitative changes.

An assumption undergirding this approach to data collection is that the supervisory event captures the essence of the trainee's development and is the best source of information on this phenomenon. Although supervisors' observation of trainees may be valuable in certain respects, it is confounded by the supervisor's own experience of the relationship. Similarly, trainees' judgments of their own training needs are influenced by the relationship, as reflected in the studies conducted by Krause and Allen (1988), Friedlander and Ward (1984), and Allen et al. (1986). If the course of the supervisory relationship is the object of study, then current sources of information may be relevant and informative. However, because the trainee's development as a counselor is the professed target of interest, studies that examine the cognitive charac-teristics of trainees and the interactions among cognitive, personality, and experience-level factors on counseling behaviors are critical to understanding the developmental models.

Cognitive Characteristics/Experience Level Interactions

Since 1986, a few researchers have examined experience level of trainee and other personality factors, to uncover the relation of trainee characteristics and supervisory needs. These studies responded to the previously outlined methodological shortcom-ings of the research that considered only experience level.

Borders et al. (1986) examined the relation between student counselors' experience level (practicum vs. intern level) and ego development (Loevinger's scale), and percep-tions of their clients. Their results indicated that ego development levels were more pre-dictive of descriptors used by students than were experience levels. Lower ego level students tended to use more simplistic, concrete descriptors; those at higher ego levels used more sophisticated, interactive descriptors. These results are supportive of the work of Holloway and Wolleat (1980), which investigated the relation among conceptual level (CL), a construct related to social perceptual development, experience level, and clinical hypothesis formation. Although student experience level was not a significant factor, students with higher CL asked more divergent questions and had greater clarity in their clinical hypotheses than did low-CL students.

Tracey et al. (1989) designed an analogue study in an effort to examine the central tenet of developmental models of supervision; namely, that the degree of structure provided in the supervisory relationship is central to trainees' learning opportunity. Specifically, beginning-level trainees are said to need more structured environments than do more advanced trainees. Tracey et al. were interested in how counselor trainees' preferences for varying levels of supervision structure may be moderated by experience, reactance potential, and the content of supervision. Reactance potential was described as a personality variable related to an individual's need to resist or comply with imposed structure or direction in interpersonal contexts. The content of supervision was described as either a noncrisis situation or a crisis situation that involved a suicidal client. The findings of this study revealed several interactive effects of the independent variables on trainees' preferences for supervisory structure. The authors concluded the following: (a) structure was important for beginning trainees and less so for more advanced trainees; (b) urgency of the client condition had a strong moderating effect on the experience–structure preference; and (c) in the noncrisis content condition, reactance accounted for structure preferences of advanced-level trainees. These findings supported some of the previous indications that, as trainees progress through levels of practice experience, their need for supervisory structure diminishes (McNeill et al., 1985; Reising & Daniels, 1983; Stoltenberg et al., 1987; Wiley & Ray, 1986). However, the structure–experience relation is moderated by both the personality variables of the trainees (in this case, reactance potential) and the situational determinants of the supervisory focus (crisis vs. noncrisis client). This well-designed study presented a strong argument for researchers to include personality characteristics, experience level, and content conditions of supervision in studies of supervisory environments.

Winter and Holloway (in press) completed an analogue study that examined the relation of supervisees' conceptual level (CL), experience level, and perception of supervisory approach to their choice of audiotaped passages to be presented for a simulated supervisory interview. Cognitively complex supervisees were more likely to choose passages with a counseling skills focus over passages that focused on client conceptualization or personal growth. Descriptive data showed that nearly 75% of complex supervisees made explicit requests for supervisor feedback, as compared to 50% of the middle-CL group and 35% of the low-CL group. Thus, cognitively complex counselors preferred to focus on passages that would encourage the supervisor to provide feedback on their counseling skills. The authors interpreted this finding in light of the higher personal responsibility generally demonstrated by complex individuals in interpersonal situations. That is, high-CL participants selected segments that focused on their skills and actual behaviors in the counseling passages; thus, they invited the supervisor to provide direct feedback on their work and allow the trainees an opportunity to improve their skills. Experience level was a significant influence in the choice of passages. The greater the counselor experience, the less the focus on client conceptualization, the more the focus on personal growth issues such as countertransference, self-efficacy, and self-awareness, and the more the willingness to choose passages that reflected less favorably on them as counselors. There were no interactive effects of CL and experience level, nor did supervisor approach influence the choice of counseling passages. As discussed earlier, the results regarding experience level of trainees are consistent with numerous other studies that have examined supervisory needs at different levels of practical experience (Heppner & Roehlke, 1984; McNeill et al., 1985; Miars et al., 1983; Rabinowitz et al., 1986; Stoltenberg et al., 1987).

Gender/Experience Level Interactions

A study by Robyak, Goodyear, Prange, and Donham (1986) examined the relation of gender, supervised experience in counseling, and client presenting problem to students' preferences for using particular power bases to influence client change within an analogue study design. The findings indicated that experience level of the trainee was related to preferences for legitimate and referent power bases; gender and type of presenting problem had no significant effect. Students with little experience preferred the legitimate and referent power bases to a greater extent than did students with more supervised experience. The authors explained their results from the perspective of social influence theory, stating that the legitimate power base allows beginning-level trainees to use the socially sanctioned role of counselor to structure the relationship and gain credibility. Additionally, the use of the referent power base mitigates the stiffness or formality of legitimate power by seeking to gain the client's confidence through personal qualities that will enhance interpersonal attractiveness. Although this research is limited by the analogue and survey approach to data collection, it does provide information regarding the role of experience in the choice of power base in formal, working relationships such as counseling and supervision. The trainee's use of different power bases across these two relationships may be an interesting area for future research.

Cultural Characteristics

Although the investigation of cultural and racial characteristics in the counseling relationship has generated considerable research in the past decade (Helms, 1984; Parham, 1989), only one empirical study was found in the supervision literature. Cook and Helms (1988) were interested in the predictability of satisfaction with cross-cultural supervision from relationship dimensions as measured by the Barrett-Lennard Relationship Inventory (BLRI; 1962), the Supervision Questionnaire (Worthington & Roehlke, 1979), and a personal data sheet. They asked four culturally diverse groups—Black, Hispanic, Asian, and Native American—to respond to a survey regarding their supervision experiences. The results indicated that only supervisor liking and conditional liking relationship dimensions were related to satisfaction with supervision. Additionally, supervisees' perception of their supervision relationships varied according to their race or ethnicity: (a) Blacks, Hispanics, and Native Americans felt lower levels of liking from supervisors than did Asians; (b) all groups but Native Americans felt that supervisors were emotionally comfortable with them; (c) Blacks and Native Americans perceived the highest mean levels of unconditional liking; (d) Blacks perceived significantly higher levels of unconditional liking than did Hispanics; and (e) Native Americans perceived significantly higher levels of discomfort than any other group. The limitations of this study warrant mention: the sample size for Native Americans was 8, only 51% of potential participants chose to respond, and the dependent measures reflected perceptions of the supervisor's attitudes rather than actual behaviors of the supervisor. However, it is important, given the paucity of research on this topic, that future researchers use diverse methods to understand the role of ethnicity and race on relationship dimensions in supervision.

Supervisor/Supervisee Interactions

The influence of a matching of supervisor and supervisee individual characteristics on trainee satisfaction and performance has been studied by several investigators. Hester, Weitz, Anchor, and Roback (1976) looked at attitude similarity and dissimilarity, as measured by Byrne's Attitude Scale (Byrne, 1971), and trainees' attraction to the supervisor. Findings indicated that the skill level of the supervisor was a greater determinant of attraction than was attitude similarity. Lemons and Lanning (1979) found that similarity in value systems, as measured by the Rokeach Value Survey (Rokeach, 1967), was not related to the quality of the relationship or the satisfaction of the trainee; however, level of communication in supervision was related to these same variables. Kennard, Stewart, and Gluck (1987) found that theoretical similarities between supervisors and trainees enhanced trainees' perceptions of the quality of supervision.

The influence of same and mixed gender dyads has been the focus of three studies. Worthington and Stern (1985) examined a number of trainee variables, including gender matching of supervisor and trainee. They found that male supervisors and trainees thought they had better relationships than did female supervisors and trainees, and that matching of gender was more important to trainees than to supervisors. Trainees felt that they had closer relationships with same-gender supervisors, and they attributed more influence to the same-gender supervisor than to other-gender supervisors. Goodyear (1990), using an analogue design, examined the extent to which gender of supervisor and supervisee was related to interpersonal influence strategies and global skill ratings of the supervisee. Both supervisors and supervisees perceived female supervisees to be more likely to employ a "person-dependent" influence style, that is, dependent on supervisor behaviors; there were no other significant main or interaction effects for gender on global skill ratings. Nelson and Holloway (1990) studied gender effects in supervision process. (This study is reviewed below, in the "Supervisory Process" section.)

Domain-Specific Expectations and Goals

Domain-specific expectations and goals of the supervisor and supervisee include professional role expectations for the supervisor and the counselor-in-training. The supervisor's view of the requirements for autonomous professional performance as a counselor will be a part of his or her expectations of the supervisee. These expectations are broad-based criteria of competence and performance for the counselor and supervisee roles. This area does not include the prescriptive goals that a supervisor would plan for specific trainees. The supervisor also has a prescribed set of functions required of the supervisory role.

Counselor/Supervisee Role

There is little research in this area and the focus has been primarily on the counselor role, because being an effective counselor is the overriding goal of supervision. Early in the history of our profession, numerous authors addressed the question "What does a counselor need to know?" (Altrucher, 1967; Chenault, 1968; Wolleat, 1974). Many of these statements reflected a concern with the counselor as a person, a holistic view of the individual's character and of the manner in which certain personal qualities would be necessary and of benefit in the counselor role. The interest in personal analysis for the trainee was an important component of these early training programs, because such qualities could be recognized and enhanced within the context of psychotherapy.

Another approach to domain-specific expectations for the counselor was the development of behavior-oriented lists of competencies (Friedlander, Ward, & Ferrin, 1984; Hector, 1977; Jakubowski-Spector, Dustin, & George, 1971). These lists defined more precisely what was expected of the successful trainee and served as guides for the evaluation of performance in the counselor role. Menne (1975) asked 75 experienced counselors from a variety of work settings to indicate those competencies they believed necessary for effective counseling. From a list of 132 competencies, 12 factors were identified: professional ethics, self-awareness, personal characteristics, listening and communicating, testing skills, counseling comprehension, behavioral science, societal awareness, tutoring techniques, professional credentials, counselor training, and vocational guidance. The importance of these dimensions varied, depending on the respondents' work setting, professional affiliation, theoretical background, and experience.

Both supervisor and supervisee begin supervision with expectations regarding the appropriate behavior for the roles in the supervisory relationship. Although new supervisees have only a vague understanding of the supervisory relationship, supervisors usually have clear role prescriptions both for their own behavior and that of the supervisee. Hess (1983) and Holloway (1984) remarked that supervisors make judgments regarding supervisees' competence and interpersonal skill based on the supervisees' performance in that role. However, only one study was found, a thesis referred to in Hess (1983), that prescribed role behavior for the supervisee. Swain (1981, cited in Hess, 1983) identified the following dimensions as critical supervisee behaviors from the perspective of supervisors: interest in the client and client welfare; preparation for supervision; theoretical knowledge; self-exploration, disclosure, self-esteem, and self-awareness; openness to suggestions; expertise, clinical skills, and interpersonal skills; boundary management; and decision-making abilities.

Supervisor Role

Role theories of supervision outline the expectancies and behaviors that are considered to be a part of the supervisory relationship and, specifically, the role of the supervisor. A few research studies have investigated the types of roles that are typical of the supervisor (Ellis & Dell, 1986; Ellis, Dell, & Good, 1988; Gysbers & Johnston, 1965; Stenack & Dye, 1982). In an early study, Gysbers and Johnston (1965) asked supervisors and supervisees to respond to the Supervisor Role Analysis Form (SRAF). Supervisees' expectations for supervisor behaviors changed across the 6-week practicum from specific help, demonstration, and teaching behaviors to consultative and student-directed behaviors. Supervisors acknowledged their expectation to be responsible for structuring the learning experience, but disagreed on the degree of specific direction or counseling support they should offer the student. Similarly, Stenack and Dye (1982) had both faculty and graduate students with supervision experience indicate the correspondence of a list of 60 supervisor behaviors to the roles of teacher, counselor, and consultant. They found that the teacher and counselor roles were clearly distinguished but the consultant role overlapped with the teacher role. It appeared that any differences between teacher and consultant were related to issues of supervisor control of the interaction rather than to specific supervisor behaviors. A more shared approach to control was indicative of the consultant role. They concluded that specific behaviors alone cannot clearly define supervisor roles; other elements of the interaction, such as goals, control, and focus, are also determinants.

Ellis and associates conducted three related studies in which the role model theories of Bernard (1979) and Littrell et al. (1979) were examined using a multidimensional scaling methodology. In the first study (Ellis & Dell, 1986), supervisors' perceptions of the supervisor role were characterized by three dimensions: process versus conceptualization, consultant versus teacher/counselor, and cognitive versus emotional (or nonsupportive vs. supportive). The findings in the next two studies of counselor trainees' perceptions of supervisor roles (Ellis et al. 1988) corroborated the three-dimensional structure of supervision found in Ellis and Dell (1986). However, trainees differentiated between the teacher and counselor role; supervisors did not. The authors concluded that the results modestly supported Bernard's (1979) supervisor roles of teacher and counselor and supervisor functions of process, conceptualization, and personalization. However, there was little support for the developmental dimension of supervision as posited by Littrell et al. (1979), because there were no differences across experience levels of trainees. The most apparent difference in the findings with the models was the emergence of an emotional-behavioral dimension.

The research has not drawn from the rich information on social role theory that is available in organizational development literature (Katz & Kahn, 1978). The hierarchical, formal, working relationship of supervision has many of the qualities of power and affiliation that are associated with other positions of influence. The specific expectations for performance in the supervisor role are intrinsically linked to the evaluation process. Although each supervisor and supervisee will have particular idiosyncratic expectations of roles and function, there needs to be a more explicit and empirical set of competencies that are expected of the supervisor and of the counselor-in-training as both a supervisee and a counselor. As in any working relationship, the clarity of these expectations from the beginning will probably enhance the development of the relationship and the establishment of specific learning goals.

The Supervisory Relationship

Many different approaches have been taken in the study of the supervisory relationship. As previously discussed, the quality and characteristics of the relationship as perceived by both participants has been the outcome measure for many of the studies of supervisor and supervisee characteristics. This section includes those studies that seek to define the dimensions of the relationship and to examine the correlations among various characteristics of the relationship as perceived by the participants. It does not include studies that examine the actual discourse between the supervisor and supervisee; these studies are discussed in the "Supervisory Process" section.

Measuring the Relationship

Very few instruments have been developed specifically for the measurement of the supervisory relationship. The majority of instruments used to assess the quality of the supervisory relationship have been adopted from counseling research. For instance, prominent in the early literature were studies that used the facilitative conditions (Carkhuff & Berenson, 1967; Truax & Carkhuff, 1967), the Barrett-Lennard Relationship Inventory (BLRI; Barrett-Lennard, 1962), and the Counselor Rating Form (CRF; Barak & LaCrosse, 1975) to describe the relationship. The importance of having measurement devices that are specific to the supervisory context has been recognized in the ensuing years (Hansen et al., 1982; Holloway, 1984; Lambert, 1980). Three instruments that measure supervisory relationship characteristics have been developed: the Supervisor Personal Reaction Scale (SPRS) and Trainee Personal Reaction Scale (TPRS; Holloway & Wampold, 1985), the Supervisory Styles Inventory (SSI; Friedlander & Ward, 1984), and the Supervisory Working Alliance Inventory (SWAI; Efstation, Patton, & Kardash, 1990).

The Supervisor Personal Reaction Scale (SPRS) was originally developed by Sundblad and Feinberg (1972) as an adaptation of Ashby, Ford, Guerney, and Guerney's (1957) Therapist and Client Personal Reaction Scales. Subsequently, Holloway and Wampold (1983, 1985) developed the Trainee Personal Reaction Scale (TPRS) and factor analyzed the SPRS and TPRS to yield a 12-item multifactor scale to measure (a) judgment of other, (b) judgment of self, and (c) level of comfort in the supervisory interaction. Confirmatory factor analysis with supervisory dyads of differing theoretical orientation and trainee experience levels is needed to improve the psychometric qualities of these scales.

The SSI has the most adequate reliability and validity. There are two versions of the scale, one to be completed by the trainee to describe supervisory characteristics and one to be completed by the supervisor to describe his or her own behavior in supervision. Friedlander and Ward (1984) conducted a series of studies that revealed three factors describing the perceptions of heterogeneous samples of trainees and supervisors: attractiveness, interpersonal sensitivity, and task orientation. These scales have received considerable use in describing supervisory relationships since their appearance in the literature (Worthington, 1987) and they provide an excellent example of the construction of an instrument specific for supervision.

Efstation et al.'s (1990) development of an inventory to measure the relationship in supervision represents the latest effort in establishing a reliable and supervision-specific instrument. Influenced by the extensive study of the working alliance in counseling and the probable importance of the relationship in supervision process (Holloway, 1987; 1988a), the authors constructed two parallel forms of a 30-item inventory that would reflect the supervisors' and supervisees' judgment of the supervisory relationship. There are three orthogonal factors for the supervisor version: client focus, rapport, and identification. Two factors emerged for the trainee version: rapport and client focus. This instrument will be a valuable resource in uncovering the different emphases in the relationship across supervisors and trainees of varying experience levels and in different clinical contexts.

Perceptions of the Relationship and Outcome Measures. A number of studies have examined the relation among characteristics of the supervisory relationship, participants' satisfaction, and supervisee learning. Examples of early work in this area are studies by Hansen and Barker (1964) and Hansen (1965). Hansen and Barker's findings indicated that supervisees who rated the relationship high on the BLRI (Barrett-Lennard, 1962) had higher levels of experiencing in supervision, as measured by Gendlin's Experiencing Scale (Gendlin, 1962). However, this finding was not consistent with the supervisors' perceptions, because in only one supervisor group was there a positive correlation between level of experiencing and the supervisor's rating of the relationship. Hansen (1965) examined trainees' expectations of the supervisory relationship before and after their experience in supervision, as measured by the BLRI. The trainees did not expect the degree of empathy, support, and congruency they experienced from their supervisors, because they had feared the evaluation component as an overriding supervisory purpose.

Recent studies have expanded the search for relationship characteristics that may be related to trainee and supervisor outcome variables. Friedlander et al. (1986), in an analogue study designed to investigate role demands in the supervisory relationship, examined the relation of a disagreement on intervention strategy between supervisor and trainee to trainees' anxiety level, self-statements regarding experience of conflict, and plans for a counseling interview. Trainees' self-efficacy expectations were used as a covariate. They found that planning performance of beginning-level counselors did not appear to be affected when conflict situations were present. However, there was a significant inverse relation between anxiety and performance, and anxiety and self-efficacy.

Kennard et al. (1987) were interested in what variables in the supervisory relationship might best predict congruence in the supervisors' and supervisees' perceptions of the quality of the relationship. The participants represented supervisory experiences at first practicum through internship training levels. The findings suggested that trainees who reported positive supervisory experiences were evaluated more highly by supervisors than trainees who reported negative supervisory experience on two dimensions, interest in the supervisor's feedback and the supervisor's suggestions for professional development. Trainees who reported a positive experience rated their supervisors significantly higher on supportiveness and on instructional and interpretative competence than did the negative experience group. Supervisors' self-perceptions as confrontational and instructional in supervision were significant variables in the type of experience reported as well as in the match of theoretical orientation between supervisor and trainee.

In a recent study, Carey, Williams, and Wells (1988) examined the relevancy of Stron's social influence model to trainees' judgments of the supervisory relationship (as measured by the Supervisor Rating Form; Heppner & Handley, 1982) and trainees' performance (as measured by the Counselor Evaluation Rating Scale, CERS; Myrick & Kelly, 1971). The investigators asked ongoing supervisory dyads to participate after they had completed at least six sessions. Trustworthiness of the supervisor proved to be related significantly to all CERS scales and accounted for larger proportions of variance in relationship judgments than did expertness and attractiveness. Further, trustworthiness was related to trainee performance in counseling. The results supported previous research in this area by Dodenhoff (1981), Heppner and Handley (1982), and Friedlander and Synder (1983). An important element of this study is the inclusion of trainee counseling performance as an outcome variable in supervision research.

Supervision Process

This section includes those studies that examine the actual interaction that occurs in the supervision interview. Although numerous studies characterize the relationship by using self-report measures (as discussed in the previous section), few have used content analysis schemes to characterize the transactions of the interview. Rogers's work in the 1960s generated a number of studies that used measures of facilitative conditions to analyze supervisory behaviors in supervision and counseling (Karr & Geist, 1977; Lambert, 1974; Pierce, Carkhuff, & Berenson, 1967; Pierce & Schauble, 1970, 1971). These studies were primarily interested in discovering the relation between supervisors' level of facilitative functioning and trainees' ratings of satisfaction in supervision and subsequent delivery of facilitative conditions in the counseling relationship. Although these studies restricted the view of supervision interaction to conditions of empathy, respect, genuineness, concreteness, and self-disclosure, a few examined outcome variables in the counseling context. Wedeking and Scott (1976) looked beyond supervisor empathy and categorized verbal behavior patterns of the supervisor and trainee (measured by Wittmer's Counselor Activity Profile, 1971) in supervision and counseling relationships, as well as trainee competencies in counseling (measured by four of Blocher's five scales, 1968). The analyses compared the generation of verbal behaviors of the trainee in counseling sessions and of the supervisor in supervision sessions. Four 3-minute segments were taken from two sessions, one at the beginning and one at the end of a 15-week training period. Findings indicated that there were no significant changes in trainee empathy ratings during training and that supervisors provided consistently higher empathy levels than did trainees. The amount of time spent using each of the verbal categories appeared quite different for trainees and supervisors. However, intercorrelations among the verbal categories were calculated and it was noted that higher levels of information-giving activities may depress the use of other behavior such as leading or questioning. The trainees demonstrated significant improvement on role adaptation and cognitive flexibility competencies by the end of the training period.

Dodenhoff (1981) studied the effect of counselor trainees' interpersonal attraction to their supervisors and the supervisors' style of influence (characterized by direct or indirect behaviors) on counseling effectiveness, as measured by clients' and supervisors' ratings of client outcome and supervisors' ratings of counselors' effectiveness. All participants were in actual supervisory relationships. The main finding was that trainees who were highly attracted to their supervisors were rated more effective by their supervisors, but there was no difference in clients' ratings of counseling outcome. Additionally, more direct supervisors rated trainees more effective on the client outcome measurement. Dodenhoff concluded that the mutuality of the relationship and the social influence effects extend to the evaluation of the trainee. Although these investigators did not examine the interactive nature of the discourse and did not statistically examine the similarity of verbal patterns between supervision and counseling sessions, their attention to the relationship as reflected in supervisory discourse was a precursor to the process research of the 1980s.

Content Analysis of Supervision Transactions

The 1980s brought considerable interest in using content analysis schemes that categorized both supervisor and trainee verbal behaviors in the supervision interview. The examination of moment-to-moment transactions between the participants ushered in more sophisticated stochastic statistical methods to illuminate the patterns of discourse in supervision. A comprehensive review of the observation methods, analyses, and findings of microanalytic studies in supervision appears in Holloway and Poulin (in press).

Holloway and associates have completed a series of studies that describe supervisory transactions and their relation to trainee and supervisor satisfaction (Holloway & Wampold, 1983), consistency of supervisor behaviors with different trainees (Holloway & Wolleat, 1981), prevalence of recurring interactions in supervision (Holloway, 1982), the relation of power and involvement dimensions to theoretical orientation (Holloway et al., 1989), and the relation of patterns of interactions to matched and mismatched gender dyads (Nelson & Holloway, 1990). These studies represent a number of methodological approaches including analogue (Holloway et al., 1989; Holloway & Wolleat, 1981), naturalistic (Holloway, 1982; Holloway & Wampold, 1983), multiple case study (Holloway et al., 1989), and factorial designs (Nelson & Holloway, 1990).

In any analysis of discourse, the content analysis scheme is a critical component of the design because it will determine the labeling and meaning attached to verbal messages. The Blumberg Interactional Analysis (BIA; Blumberg, 1970) was used in four studies (Holloway, 1982; Holloway & Wampold, 1983; Holloway & Wolleat, 1981;

Rickards, 1984). The advantage of the BIA over the facilitative conditions coding of previous work is its inclusion of categories that reflect instructional as well as counseling behaviors and categories for trainee behaviors. The latter quality permits the use of sequential methods of statistical analysis and underscores the conceptual importance of trainee influence in the dyadic interaction. In general, the studies using the BIA found that (a) individual supervisory styles persist across two different trainees (Holloway & Wolleat, 1981), (b) a restricted repertoire of supervisor responses, although successful in eliciting affective responses from the trainee, was not effective in eliciting the trainee's cognitive-type responses (Holloway, 1982); (c) specific verbal patterns and satisfaction with the interview by supervisor and trainee were related (Holloway & Wampold, 1983), and (d) supervisors' verbal patterns of behaviors and trainees' judgments on the SRF (Rickards, 1984) were related. All four of these studies indicated that the supervisor spends more time providing information, opinions, and suggestions (task-oriented behavior) than giving emotional support or attending to the trainee's emotional life. These results contrasted with findings in counseling interviews, where social-emotional behaviors were more prevalent. Instructional strategies in supervision discourse predominated; these results lend support to Ellis and Dell's (1986) and Ellis et al.'s (1988) findings of the prominent "teacher role" in supervision.

Holloway et al. (1989) examined the relation of discourse in supervision and supervisors' theoretical orientation. Additionally, she compared her findings to Goodyear et al. (1984) and Friedlander and Ward (1984) on the same data set, in an effort to uncover the type of information gained from atomistic, content analysis approaches to more global, perceptual ratings. The Holloway et al. (1989) study used the Penman (1980) coding scheme, which was introduced to the supervision literature by Martin, Goodyear, and Newton (1987). The Penman scheme has particular advantages over the BIA because (a) it classifies behavior on both manifest and latent levels of communication, thus allowing the introduction of the latent relationship quality of the interaction, and (b) it is based on theory that defines transactions on the dimensions of power and involvement in the transaction. Both of these principles are congruent with the importance attributed to the relationship in supervision models and prior research findings. The results of this study confirmed the presence of dominant teacher–student transactions across all theoretical orientations and distinct patterns of messages evident in the different theoretical orientations. Importantly, the supervisee behaved differently even when discussing the same case with each of the supervisors, supporting the conclusion that supervisors had an important influence on the supervisee's experience of power and affiliation in the relationship. In an earlier study (Holloway & Wolleat, 1981), supervisors' frequency of categories of verbal behavior remained similar across different trainees. When Martin et al. (1987) used the Penman scheme in a case study, they found a relatively small proportion of support statements and a high proportion of advising statements by the supervisor, a result similar to other studies of supervisory discourse, but dissimilar from other studies of supervisees' perceptions of what their supervisors offered (Rabinowitz et al., 1986; Worthington & Roehlke, 1979).

The verbal behaviors of the Goodyear videotape series were also analyzed by Harris and Goodyear (1990), using the circumplex model coding scheme (Strong, Hills, & Nelson, 1988). Although reporting only preliminary analyses, the results coincide with the dominance of supervisors' leading responses and the supervisees' cooperation; the unlikelihood of the supervisors' using distrustful, self-effacing, and docile responses; and the low frequency of the supervisees' using nurturant, critical, and self-enhancing responses. Because the Penman (1980) coding scheme and the Interpersonal Communications Rating Scale (ICRS; Strong et al., 1988) are based on the same theoretical principles of Leary (1957), it is not surprising that the same kinds of conclusions have been drawn from these studies.

Friedlander, Siegel, and Brenock (1989) used the Relational Communication Control Coding System (RCCCS; Ericson & Rogers, 1973), Hill Counselor Verbal Response Category System—Revised (HCVRCS-R; Friedlander, 1984), and a rating system developed for the study (Supervisory Feedback Rating System; SFRS) to evaluate the parallel process in counseling and supervision, as manifested in one case. Friedlander et al. (1989) argued that the relationships often mirrored each other by citing the parallel nature of the self-report data and verbal communication patterns across nine concurrent supervisory and counseling sessions. They concluded that supervision and counseling seem to be reciprocal and interlocking processes and that trainees are in a highly vulnerable position as the linchpin between both relationships. This is one of a few studies (Doehrman, 1976; Wedeking & Scott, 1976) that have investigated the effects of the supervisory process on the trainees' process with their clients.

In the only study that used patterns of behavior (coded by the Penman system) as dependent variables in a factorial design, Nelson and Holloway (1990) looked at the influence of gender matches and mismatches in supervision. Three interactional patterns were conceptualized for this investigation: a deferential pattern, representing a high-to-low-power transition; an ascendancy pattern, representing a low-to-high-power transition, and an involving pattern, representing a high-to-high-involvement transition. Findings indicated that male and female trainees utilized a significantly greater number of high-power messages with female than with male supervisors. Male and female supervisors reinforced their female trainees' high-power messages with low-power, encouraging messages significantly less often than they did for male trainees. Female trainees, responding to supervisors' low-power, encouraging messages, used high-power messages significantly less often than did male trainees. If a goal of supervision is to empower the trainee to become an autonomously functioning professional, then supervisors need to promote their interpersonal power in the relationship. It would seem that supervisors may be well-advised to specifically reinforce female trainees' opinions and suggestions, encouraging them to take a more powerful role in the relationship. Otherwise, female trainees are likely to acquiesce to the more formal power of the supervisor.

Strozier, Kivlighan, and Thoreson (in press) were the first to investigate supervisors' and trainees' intentions and reactions, respectively, to each supervision interview over a 15-week relationship. The sequential analyses of supervisors' intentions and trainees' reactions (the use of sequential analysis with metacognitions is discussed by Wampold and Poulin in Chapter 3 of this *Handbook*) were described within the context of the participants' perception of the "depth" and "ease" of the session (Session Evaluation Questionnaire, SEQ), the helpfulness of the session (Helpfulness Rating Scale; Elliott, 1986), and qualitative measures, including the participants' response to an open-ended questionnaire and a video-recall procedure on each session, an in-depth clinical interview at the termination of the supervision relationship, and the researcher's written impressions from viewing all supervision sessions.

Findings of this case study indicated that the supervisor's intention to *explore* and, to a lesser degree, *restructure/change* and *assess* led to the trainee's reaction of feeling *work-challenged.* In the early microanalytic studies by Holloway (1982) and Holloway and Wampold (1983), it was unclear what supervisor interventions may lead to the trainee's offering his or her opinions or suggestions. The qualitative data from Strozier et al. (in press) describe a very intense, dynamic, and affect-oriented supervisory relationship. In fact, results of the SEQ were similar to reports of counseling relationships.

These data contradict other findings that suggest that supervision is oriented cognitively rather than affectively. However, as is common in other microanalytic studies, findings indicated that the trainee's reactions were more predictable than the supervisor's intentions.

The supervisor rated the sessions "smoother" on the Smoothness factor than did the trainee. Because this factor is described as the perceived smoothness—pleasant, easy, and safe rather than rough, unpleasant, difficult, and dangerous—it is logical that a participant who is less in control, or who has less achieved power (as defined by Holloway et al., 1989) and less certainty of what to expect in the interaction, would experience the interaction as more dangerous or uncertain. Although this study reveals differences in the frequency of support intentions and affect-oriented material when compared with previous studies, it confirms the supervisor as maintaining the "relational control" in the interaction.

Supervisory Objectives and Strategies

This section includes studies that identify different types of supervision strategies, test the effectiveness of particular strategies, or indicate methods for establishing specific objectives for particular types of trainees. More general, broad-based objectives of counselor training have been discussed under "Domain-Specific Expectations and Goals." There are numerous articles that describe rather than empirically test the advantages of using various counseling techniques in the service of supervision. A sampling of approaches described in the literature includes triadic methods of supervision (Spice & Spice, 1976), social learning approaches (Kurpius & Morran, 1988; Levine & Tilker, 1974), mental imagery (Liddle, 1982), cognitive-structural approaches (Biggs, 1988; Ellis, 1988; Holloway, 1988b; Prichard, 1988), and peer supervision (Remley, Benshoff, & Mowbray, 1987).

Russell et al. (1984) provided a comprehensive review of the studies (dated to 1983) that investigated the effects of different training techniques and packages. Most of these studies investigated comparisons of didactic versus experiential approaches, social learning principles such as modeling and reinforcement, and different instructional formats for presentation of information (Lambert & Arnold, 1987; Russell et al., 1984). In more recent years, the introduction of the developmental models of supervision initiated the investigation of different types of strategies as related to trainees' level of experience in counseling. Stoltenberg and Delworth (1988) suggested that particular learning environments should be devised by the supervisor to accommodate trainees' learning needs as defined by their level of development in counseling. Although the research on trainee experience and developmental qualities has been reviewed earlier, the research that addresses types of strategies for the supervisor to adopt is most relevant in this section.

Worthington and Roehlke (1979) were interested in developing a self-report questionnaire that would describe supervisory behaviors. Their Supervision Questionnaire (SQ) included 42 behaviors rated on a 5-point Likert-type scale and was completed by supervisors and trainees after the conclusion of their relationship or after each supervisory session. Factor analyses of the perceived frequencies of the behaviors revealed two independent factors: evaluation and support. Heppner and Handley (1982) examined the relation of the SQ to perception of supervisor expertness, attractiveness, and trustworthiness. They found that the evaluation factor was more highly correlated to these three variables than was the support factor. These results imply that beginning-level trainees view evaluative supervisory behaviors as being more consistent with effective supervisors. The SQ has since been used in numerous studies that have focused on establishing a developmental approach to supervision (Cross & Brown, 1983; Miars et al., 1983; Heppner & Roehlke, 1984; Rabinowitz et al., 1986; Wiley & Ray, 1986; Worthington, 1984b; Worthington & Stern, 1985; Zucker & Worthington, 1986).

Investigators have used the SQ to depict the supervisory strategies that trainees of different experience levels prefer. The SQ has added to our knowledge of the appropriateness of supervisory behaviors at different stages of the trainee's learning progression (Worthington, 1987). However, the match of such strategies and learning needs has relied heavily on trainee experience level and self-report preferences for supervisor behaviors. Recent findings by Borders (1989), Borders et al. (1986), and Tracey et al. (1989) indicated that trainee cognitive characteristics, interpersonal factors, and client clinical variables are also related to supervisory preferences. However, it is yet to be determined which learning objectives best match different levels of trainee experience and what supervisory environments would optimally achieve the established objectives.

Research on actual supervisory transactions also provides information on the probabilistic nature of certain supervisor strategies, as represented in verbal behaviors of trainees' responses and vice versa (Holloway, 1982; Holloway et al., 1989; Holloway & Wampold, 1983). Unfortunately, this body of research does not connect such processes with learning objectives for the trainee. Although models of supervision suggest an assessment of the trainees' learning needs, there is little in the literature to provide a means for such an assessment or to determine the strategy that will match trainee learning needs. Abbey et al.'s (1985) experiential learning-style model addresses the matching of learning styles in supervision and may be a possible framework for future research on objectives and strategy matching. In many ways, the matching of objectives with strategies in supervision is the critical component of systematizing and teaching supervision. However, without acknowledging the influence of stylistic characteristics of the supervisor, the trainee, and the relationship, such matches will remain sterile and irrelevant to the actual ongoing process.

Evaluation

In any discussion of evaluation in supervision, two contexts must be considered: the evaluation of the trainee's performance in the professional context, that is, the counselor role; and the evaluation of the supervisory process, that is, the counselor's performance in the supervisee role and the effectiveness of the supervisor. The primary focus of writing and research in supervision has been on measuring the counselor's performance. Galassi and Trent (1987) described two purposes in evaluation: decision-oriented inquiry and conclusion-oriented inquiry. Individuals such as supervisors, administrators, and teachers take a decision-oriented approach to assist them in making practical decisions in an educational setting. Research investigators use a conclusion-oriented approach to test hypotheses regarding the relationship between learning and teaching strategies, for the purpose of making broad generalizations. The literature in supervision reflects a focus on the development of measurements of counselor and supervisor performance that are relevant to conclusion-oriented evaluation. Although these instruments provide standardized methods for evaluating performance, they are often impractical or irrelevant to the practice of training. Several reviews of the literature have described the various instruments that have been used to measure trainees' acquisition of such skills as the facilitative conditions and interview behaviors (Holloway, 1984; Lambert & Arnold, 1987; Worthington, 1987). Rather than repeat the review of conclusion-oriented instruments, this section reviews the issues of evaluation in supervision and the instruments that may be useful in a decision-oriented approach.

Evaluation of Trainee's Performance in Counseling

The ultimate goal of supervision is counselor competence. The first task for the supervisor is to define what professional competence is and what specific criteria must be met if the trainee is to receive a positive evaluation. Both a formative and a summative evaluation process occur in supervision. The domain-specific goals of the profession should be directly related to the criteria for evaluation, particularly summative evaluation. "Competency refers to the adequacy or skill with which the therapist applies the procedures relative to some critical, external standard" (Beutler, Crago, & Arizmendi, 1986, p. 292). The specific learning objectives of the supervisor and trainee at different times in their work would be related to summative criteria, but would also play an important role in the formative feedback and evaluative process. Unfortunately, definitions of therapist competence have not been accompanied by clear methods for measuring this construct (Shaw & Dobson, 1988). At the very least, the level of experience and training of the student should be taken into account when determining the level and type of competence that must be demonstrated.

Although the research literature on supervision has described the supervisory needs of trainees at different training levels, there has been little research on defining what competencies the trainee must acquire at each level, other than the rudimentary skills taught in microskills training. The complexity of psychotherapy has made it very difficult to identify clear, relevant criteria for evaluation, and feasible, practical methods for implementing the evaluation.

Shaw and Dobson (1988) recommended that competency measures be developed out of particular theoretical schools and modalities. A number of standardized rating scales that correspond to particular theoretical orientations are available. For example, the Therapist Strategy Rating Form (TSRF; Chevron & Rounsaville, 1983) measures the skill of interpersonal therapists; the Cognitive Therapy Scale (CTS; Young & Beck, 1980) measures the competence of cognitive therapists; and the Vanderbilt Negative Indicators Scale (Strupp, Hadley, & Gomes-Schwartz, 1977) focuses on the dynamic components of patient–therapist interaction, therapist personal qualities, and errors in technique. Numerous scales have been developed to measure trainees' competence in facilitative conditions of client-centered theory (CERS, Myrick & Kelly, 1971; CRS, Barak & LaCrosse, 1975; BLRI, Barrett-Lennard, 1962; Carkhuff Scales, Carkhuff & Berenson, 1967).

Supervisors may well vary the criteria for competence, specificity of behavioral items, and process of evaluation, depending on many of the aspects identified, such as individual and cultural characteristics of the trainee, the counseling or supervisory relationship, or the institutional factors (see Figure 6.1). As an example of a more individualized evaluation process, Oetting and Michaels (1983) developed a detailed assessment of the trainee's skills. The authors designed it so that trainee skills on each of the competency areas can be assessed at the beginning of the practice experience and serve as an anchor for the supervisor's evaluation. In this way, the assessment is relevant to the trainee's learning needs and both provides a structure for ongoing feedback and forms the basis of the training contract.

Evaluation of Trainee's Performance in Supervision

In a survey of predoctoral training programs, Hess and Hess (1983) found that supervision was the predominant training modality. They also reported that there were few specific and direct evaluation procedures for assessing supervision quality. Norcross and Stevenson (1984), in a survey of academic clinical psychology programs, found that personal impressions and informal, qualitative evaluation methods were used most frequently. Garb (1989) concluded, from a study that compared the advantages of training versus experience in the acquisition of therapeutic skills, that training programs will advance only when evaluation of clinical performance is related to specific clinical goals for specific students. Stevenson and Norcross (1987) noted that only when training programs are better described can evaluation research lead to improvements in training programs.

Evaluation of the trainee's performance in the supervisory relationship has been considered in process research (Holloway & Wampold, 1983) and in an analogue study by Ward, Friedlander, Schoen, and Klein (1985). They examined the influence of different self-presentational styles on supervisors' judgments of counselor competence. Their study addressed an important and rarely addressed area, the evaluation of the trainee based on in-session supervisory behavior. In this analogue study, the investigators created stimulus conditions in which trainees were viewed taking a defensive or counterdefensive interpersonal style. The defensive trainee was evaluated by supervisors as more self-confident; the counterdefensive trainee was evaluated as more socially skilled. When a client was reported to have improved, trainees, regardless of style, were judged as more competent, self-confident, expert, and attractive than when the client worsened. It appeared from this study that supervisors base their judgments of trainees' professional skills on client progress. This is particularly salient, given the lack of attention to client outcome in evaluating supervisory methods.

The research to date is primarily correlational; that is, certain trainee needs or supervisory behaviors are related to satisfaction measures or, in some cases, to trainee effectiveness in counseling. Much of this research has been conclusion-oriented (Galassi & Trent, 1987) and therefore has not yet been successful in advising decision makers (i.e., supervisors) in what measures could be used to assess supervision effectiveness for counselors of varying needs. Measures that would help supervisors decide when to switch the content or strategies of supervision sessions would be helpful in matching supervisory focus to counselor needs. Although substantial gains have been made in describing the supervision process through self-report and process research, there is as yet no systematic method for incorporating this knowledge into an evaluation of supervisory effectiveness.

Institutional Influences

Training takes place in a context, such as in-house departmental clinics, university counseling centers, hospitals, or community mental health settings. The role of the training program in respect to the service demands of the organization is an important consideration for accrediting groups. Yet, the influence of organizational variables on supervision has rarely been studied. In a survey that asked interns to indicate their level of readiness for the professional demands of the internship, participants most frequently expressed concern over their lack of preparedness for dealing with organizational politics (Cole, Kolko, & Craddick, 1981). Dodds (1986) summarized the different goals and roles of training institutions that can place the supervisor and supervisee in conflict. He provided a framework to understand the stresses that emerge from the overlapping systems of a training institution and a service agency. Ekstein (1964) described the clinical rhombus as the interactions among the four roles that were necessary to ensure the effective functioning of an agency with training involvement—the agency administrator, the clinical supervisor, the supervisee-therapist, and the client. The need to maintain a relationship among all of these participants (not always face-to-face) is critical to the quality of professional training. The Director of Internship Training or the supervisor often has the responsibility of orienting the trainee to the agency, the training program, and the various personnel, service functions, and goals, as an important beginning step to integrate the intern into the agency (Holloway & Roehlke, 1987).

Although surveys of professionals suggest that institutional variables are critical to maintaining an effective supervisory program, there is no research that specifically examines the relation of certain institutional policies, procedures, or goals on trainees' learning.

Models in Group Supervision[2]

In previous reviews of supervision theory and practice, group supervision techniques have been excluded. Dyadic, or one-to-one, supervision is considered the primary training context, as evidenced by the numerous models that have described this relationship. However, in spite of the lack of models and research describing group supervision activities, the use of a group format to augment supervisory activities is included in the American Psychological Association (1986) standards for practicum and internship sites. The goals of group supervision have included case conceptualization skills, clinical practice information, peer review experience, inter- and intrapersonal awareness, and the development of cohesive cohort groups among practicum students. Since 1985, there has been no significant research in group supervision of individual practice; thus, the reader is referred to Holloway and Johnston (1985) for a detailed review of the research in group supervision.

A range of instructional practices have been labeled "group supervision," including (a) group supervision of trainees, in a practicum setting, who are learning individual counseling skills; (b) group supervision of trainees who are learning pre-practicum interviewing skills; (c) leaderless groups in which trainees provide peer supervision in a group format; and (d) group supervision of trainees, in a practicum setting, who are focusing on learning group facilitation skills. Three types of approaches to group supervision of counselors-in-training have been described. Interpersonal process groups for counselor trainees, designed to promote self-awareness and affective growth, were prevalent during the 1960s and early 1970s. By the middle 1970s, interpersonal process groups were no longer popular in training programs; however, current group supervision practices still retain some of the personal growth emphasis (Bartlett, 1983; Hess, 1980; Loganbill et al., 1982).

The second type is the case presentation approach, in which the group is used to discuss trainee cases and clinical issues as they arise from students' client caseload. The case presentation format has persisted in descriptive reports of the literature from the middle 1960s to the present, but, surprisingly, no substantive empirical information is available on this approach. However, this approach has been described, among dyadic models of supervision, as an opportunity for heightening interpersonal awareness of counselors as well as peer consultation on clinical matters (Blocher, 1983; Wessler & Ellis, 1983).

The application of a developmental framework to group supervision has been proposed by Sansbury (1982) and Yogev (1982). The developmental formats have included

---

[2]A portion of this section first appeared in "Group Supervision Widely Practiced and Poorly Understood," by E. L. Holloway and R. Johnston, 1985, *Counselor Education and Supervision, 24*, pp. 332–340. Adapted by permission.

components of didactic instruction, group process, and case conceptualization, as did the case presentation format. However, theoretically, developmental frameworks adjust the content, method of instruction, and emphasis of these components according to trainees' level of mastery. Although the empirical literature on individual models of developmental supervision has increased in the past decade, there has been virtually no research on this format in group supervision.

IMPLICATIONS FOR RESEARCH AND TRAINING

Since Russell et al.'s review (1984), there have been important developments in research on supervision. As Russell et al. predicted, the cross-theoretical models of supervision and, in particular, developmental models have played an influential role in the choice of research topics. It appears that authors and researchers have embraced the idea that cross-theoretical approaches to supervision are fruitful and informative. This development shifts the field of scientific inquiry into a new period; one that is separated from the past by its recognition of supervision as a process unique from counseling and related to knowledge gained from the foundational disciplines of psychology and sociology. The shift to theoretically related empirical questions represents an important change in the history of supervisory research. In previous years, empirical questions were largely atheoretical and represented isolated research efforts (Hansen et al., 1976; Hansen et al., 1982; Hansen & Warner, 1971). Most research studies are now tied to models of supervision, or foundational constructs in instruction, or interpersonal relationships.

Efforts in model building have been sparse in the past 8 years. The developmental models that have taken a prominent position in the field were introduced in the early 1980s (Loganbill et al., 1982; Stoltenberg, 1981). Although they have been embellished conceptually (Stoltenberg & Delworth, 1988) and empirically (Worthington, 1987), no new developmental models have appeared. The idea of "role models" of supervision has been introduced in this chapter to group together those models that have appeared in the early supervision literature and that depend on the identification of subroles to describe the activities and functions of the supervisor. These models appeared during the same period as the developmental models and have often been classified as "eclectic" because they are not bound to a particular counseling theory. They have generated only a small amount of research (Ellis and Dell, 1986; Ellis et al., 1988; Stenack & Dye, 1982), but may be a promising paradigm if the broader context of social psychological role theory is considered in their refinement and testing. An examination of the type of research conducted, from the perspective of the map devised in Figure 6.1, reveals that several aspects have dominated the literature. Trainee and supervisor characteristics, and the supervisory relationship, are the most researched aspects. Supervisory process as reflected in discourse has been of interest to a small group of researchers, but in no way reflects the abundance of studies on this topic in the counseling process literature. The most ignored aspects of supervision are supervisory objectives and strategies, learning and performance of the trainee in the counseling and supervisory relationship, and institutional variables. These areas must command the attention of researchers in the coming years, if we are to devise a prescriptive approach to supervision (Holloway & Hosford, 1983).

Evidence that trainees express different supervisory needs and, consequently, that different supervisory environments are necessary to meet these expressed needs, has been relatively well-established. The source of trainees' needs is becoming clearer as research questions and variables become more complex. The level of experience in training is an important variable, as reflected in the research on trainee experience level. More recent research has identified other critical trainee variables such as gender, reactance potential, client characteristics, and ego development. Studies that consider more complex trainee variables and their interaction may have implications for the design of supervisory strategies.

Future research questions should extend our understanding of the relationship between trainee characteristics and trainee performance in supervision and counseling. Because the proof of effectiveness in training will finally rest with the client, it is not sufficient to know only the supervisory preferences of trainees or supervisors for supervision. It is necessary to know what supervisory strategies, matched with what teaching objectives for a particular trainee, will result in effective learning and effective client change.

Perhaps the next hurdle in research is the assessment and description of the environmental characteristics of supervision. It is informative to characterize supervisory behaviors as direct–indirect in structure, supportive versus task-oriented, and as teacher, counselor, or consultant behaviors. However, these approaches must be linked to the teaching decisions a supervisor makes with a particular trainee. If the goal is ultimately to educate counselors to be effective professionals, then supervisors must be educated to be effective supervisors. Teaching supervision demands specific knowledge of instructional methods appropriate for supervision. Research has not yet provided educators with instructional principles or specific teaching methods that can guide their education of supervisors. The knowledge base of supervision could be substantially strengthened by the inclusion of research and conceptual frameworks in instructional and cognitive psychology. Clinical supervision is a substantial area of research and thinking in teacher education. The focus of work in teacher pre-service training has been on objectives, strategies, evaluation, and institutional contexts, in lieu of relationship and individual differences (Glickman & Bey, 1990). Thus, the strengths in teacher education are the deficits in counselor supervision. Both fields might do well to collaborate and promote cross-disciplinary involvement in research.

There are neither adequate models nor convincing empirical studies of group supervision approaches; only the most general rationales support their inclusion in counselor training. However, group supervision seems to be both an economical and unique contribution to trainee learning and therefore will likely persist. Thus, it is imperative that a systematic examination of the group supervision process begin. Conceptually, educators need to ask questions similar to the following: What should be the goals of group supervision? What roles should the group supervisor adopt, to promote the realization of these goals? What balance among didactic material, case conceptualization, and interpersonal process is most productive for trainee learning? What is the role of evaluation in group supervision? What unique contribution does group supervision make in a training program?

Will there ever be a manual with step-by-step procedures for the practice of supervision? I think not. The opening comments of this review reflect my belief that the best of supervision will appear in the creative moments of an accomplished supervisor with an engaged student. However, the belief that supervision involves artistry as well as skill cannot stop educators from striving to establish an epistemology of practice. A method is needed to guide the educational efforts of beginning supervisors to understand the principles of pedagogy, to learn the skill of supervision, and to apply creatively these methods with the individual learner. In the past 7 years, research in supervision has taken a long step forward in exploring the terrain of this complex instructional method. Educators of professional practice need to continue to discover new elements of relevance and interest, collaborating in their perspectives on supervision.

REFERENCES

Abbey, D. S., Hunt, D. E., & Weiser, J. C. (1985). Variations on a theme by Kolb: A new perspective for understanding counseling and supervision. *The Counseling Psychologist, 13,* 477–501.

Allen, G. J., Szollos, S. J., & Williams, B. E. (1986). Doctoral students' comparative evaluations of best and worst psychotherapy supervision. *Professional Psychology: Research and Practice, 17,* 91–99.

Altrucher, N. (1967). Constructive use of the supervisory relationship. *Journal of Counseling Psychology, 14,* 165–170.

American Psychological Association. (1986). *Accreditation handbook.* Washington, DC: American Psychological Association Committee on Accreditation.

Ashby, J. D., Ford, D. H., Guerney, B. G., & Guerney, L. (1957). Effects on clients of a reflective and leading type of psychotherapy. *Psychological Monographs, 7,* 1–32.

Baker, S. B., & Daniels, T. G. (1989). Integrating research on the microcounseling program: A meta-analysis. *Journal of Counseling Psychology, 36,* 213–222.

Baker, S. B., Daniels, T. G., & Greeley, A. T. (1990). Systematic training of graduate-level counselors: Narrative and meta-analytic reviews of three major programs. *The Counseling Psychologist, 18,* 355–421.

Barak, S. A., & LaCrosse, M. (1975). Multidimensional perceptions of counselor behavior. *Journal of Counseling Psychology, 22,* 471–476.

Barrett-Lennard, G. T. (1962). Dimensions of therapist response as causal factors in therapeutic change. *Psychological Monographs Applied, 76* (43), No. 562.

Bartlett, W. E. (1983). A multidimensional framework for the analysis of supervision of counseling. *The Counseling Psychologist, 11*(1), 9–18.

Bernard, J. M. (1979). Supervisor training: A discrimination model. *Counselor Education and Supervision, 19,* 60–68.

Bernstein, B. L., & Lecomte, C. (1979). Supervisory type feedback effects: Feedback discrepancy level, trainee psychological differentiation, and immediate responses. *Journal of Counseling Psychology, 26,* 295–303.

Beutler, L. E. (Ed.). (1988). Training to competency in psychotherapy [Special issue]. *Journal of Counseling Psychology, 56*(5).

Beutler, L. E., Crago, M., & Arizmendi, T. G. (1986). Therapist variables in psychotherapy process and emotions. In A. E. Bergin & S. L. Garfield (Eds.), *Handbook of psychotherapy and behavior changes* (pp. 257–310). New York: Wiley.

Beutler, L. E., & McNabb, C. E. (1981). Self-evaluation for the psychotherapist. In C. E. Walker (Ed.), *Clinical practice of psychology* (pp. 397–439). New York: Pergamon Press.

Biggs, D. A. (1988). The case presentation approach in clinical supervision. *Counselor Education and Supervision, 27,* 240–248.

Blocher, D. H. (1968). *A study of two types of internships for counselor training.* ERIC/CAPS No. ED 012 488. Minneapolis: University of Minnesota.

Blocher, D. H. (1983). Toward a cognitive developmental approach to counseling supervision. *The Counseling Psychologist, 11*(1), 27–34.

Blumberg, A. (1970). A system for analyzing supervisor–teacher interaction. In A. Simon & G. Boyer (Eds.), *Mirrors for behavior* (Vol. 34, pp. 34.1–34.15). Philadelphia: Research for Better Schools.

Borders, L. D. (1989). Developmental cognitions of first practicum supervisees. *Journal of Counseling Psychology, 36,* 163–169.

Borders, L. D. & Fong, M. L. (1989). Ego development and counseling ability during training. *Counselor Education and Supervision, 29,* 71–83.

Borders, L. D., Fong, M. L., & Cron, E. A. (1988). In-session cognitions of a counseling student: A case study. *Counselor Education and Supervision, 17,* 7–12.

Borders, L. D., Fong, M. L., & Neimeyer, G. J. (1986). Counseling students' level of ego development and perceptions of clients. *Counselor Education and Supervision, 26,* 37–49.

Boyd, J. (1978). *Counselor supervision: Approaches, preparation, practices.* Muncie, IN: Accelerated Development.

Brown, P. B., & Smith, H. D. (1984). All-inclusive conceptualization as a dimension of trainee empathic responding. *Counselor Education and Supervision, 23,* 341–345.

Byrne, D. (1971). *The attraction paradigm.* New York: Academic Press.

Carey, J. C., Williams, K. S., & Wells, M. (1988). Relationships between dimensions of supervisors' influence and counselor trainees' performance. *Counselor Education and Supervision, 28,* 130–139.

Carifio, M. S., & Hess, A. K. (1987). Who is the ideal supervisor? *Professional Psychology: Research and Practice, 3,* 244–250.

Carkhuff, R. R., & Berenson, B. G. (1967). *Beyond counseling and therapy.* New York: Holt, Rinehart and Winston.

Carlozzi, A. F., Campbell, N. J., & Ward, G. R. (1982). Dogmatism and externality in locus of control as related to counselor trainee skill in facilitative responding. *Counselor Education and Supervision, 21,* 227–236.

Carlozzi, A. F., Gaa, J. P., & Liberman, D. B. (1983). Empathy and ego development. *Journal of Counseling Psychology, 30,* 113–116.

Chenault, J. (1968). A proposed model for a humanistic counselor education program. *Counselor Education and Supervision, 8,* 4–7.

Chevron, E. S., & Rounsaville, B. J. (1983). Evaluating the clinical skills of psychotherapists. *Archives of General Psychiatry, 40,* 1129–1132.

Chickering, A. W. (1969). *Education and identity.* San Francisco: Jossey-Bass.

Cole, M., Kolko, D., & Craddick, R. (1981). The quality and process of the internship experience. *Professional Psychology, 12,* 377–384.

Cook, D. A., & Helms, J. E. (1988). Visible racial/ethnic group supervisees' satisfaction with cross-cultural supervision as predicted by relationship characteristics. *Journal of Counseling Psychology, 35,* 268–274.

Cross, D. G., & Brown, D. (1983). Counselor supervision as a function of trainee experience: Analysis of specific behaviors. *Counselor Education and Supervision, 22,* 333–341.

Demos, G. G., & Zuwaylif, F. (1962). Counselor attitudes in relation to the theoretical positions of their supervisors. *Counselor Education and Supervision, 2,* 280–285.

Dodds, J. B. (1986). Supervision of psychology trainees in field placements. *Professional Psychology: Research and Practice, 17,* 296–300.

Dodenhoff, J. T. (1981). Interpersonal attraction and direct–indirect supervisor influence as predictors of counselor trainee effectiveness. *Journal of Counseling Psychology, 28,* 47–62.

Doehrman, M. J. (1976). Parallel processes in supervision and psychotherapy. *Bulletin of the Menninger Clinic, 40,* 1–104.

Dole, A. A., Nissenfeld, M., Bowers, C., Herzog, M., Levitt, D., McIntyre, P., Wedemen, S., & Woodburn, P. (1982). Six dimensions of retrospections by therapists and counselors—A manual for research. *JSAS: Catalog of Selected Documents in Psychology, 12,* 23 (Ms. No. 2454).

Drakeford, G. C. (1967). *Cognitive and linguistic inclusiveness: A factor analysis.* Unpublished master's thesis, University of Calgary, Canada.

Efstation, J. F., Patton, M. J., & Kardash, C. M. (1990). Measuring the working alliance in counselor supervision. *Journal of Counseling Psychology, 37,* 322–329.

Ekstein, R. (1964). Supervision of psychotherapy: Is it teaching? Is it administration? or is it therapy? *Psychotherapy: Theory, Research and Practice, 1,* 137–138.

Ekstein, R., & Wallerstein, R. S. (1958). *The teaching and learning of psychotherapy.* New York: Basic Books.

Elliott, R. (1986). Interpersonal process recall (IPR) as process research method. In L. S. Greenberg & W. M. Pinsof (Eds.), *The psychotherapeutic process: A research handbook* (pp. 503–528). New York: Guilford.

Ellis, M. V. (1988). The cognitive development approach to case presentation in clinical supervision: A reaction and extension. *Counselor Education and Supervision, 27,* 259–264.

Ellis, M. V., & Dell, D. M. (1986). Dimensionality of supervisor roles: Supervisors' perceptions of supervision. *Journal of Counseling Psychology, 33,* 282–291.

Ellis, M. V., Dell, D. M., & Good, G. E. (1988). Counselor trainees' perceptions of supervisor roles: Two studies testing the dimensionality of supervision. *Journal of Counseling Psychology, 35,* 315–324.

Ericson, P. M., & Rogers, L. E. (1973). New procedures for analyzing relational communication. *Family Process, 12,* 245–267.

French, J. R. P., Jr., & Raven, B. H. (1960). The bases of social power. In D. Cartwright & A. Zander (Eds.), *Group dynamics: Research and theory* (2nd ed.) (pp. 607–623). New York: Peterson.

Friedlander, M. L. (1984). Hill Counselor Verbal Response Category System—Revised. *Tests in microfiche.* Princeton, NJ: Educational Testing Service. (Test collection, No. 012397, Set I.)

Friedlander, M. L., Keller, K. E., Peca-Baker, T. A., & Olk, M. E. (1986). Effects of role conflict on counselor trainees' self-statements, anxiety level, and performance. *Journal of Counseling Psychology, 33,* 1–5.

Friedlander, M. L., Siegel, S. M., & Brenock, K. (1989). Parallel processes in counseling and supervision: A case study. *Journal of Counseling Psychology, 36,* 149–157.

Friedlander, M. L., & Synder, J. (1983). Trainees' expectations for the supervisory process: Testing a developmental model. *Counselor Education and Supervision, 23,* 342–348.

Friedlander, M. L., & Ward, L. G. (1984). Development and validation of the supervisory styles inventory. *Journal of Counseling Psychology, 4,* 541–557.

Friedlander, M. L., Ward, L. G., & Ferrin, H. (1984, August). *A behavioral analytic model for evaluating counselor training programs.* Paper presented at the annual convention of the American Psychological Association, Toronto, Canada.

Friedler, F. (1950). A comparison of therapeutic relationships in psychoanalytic, nondirective, and Adlerian therapy. *Journal of Consulting Psychology, 14,* 436–445.

Galassi, J. P., & Trent, P. J. (1987). A conceptual framework for evaluating supervision effectiveness. *Counselor Education and Supervision, 26,* 260–269.

Garb, H. N. (1989). Clinical judgment, clinical training, and professional experience. *Psychological Bulletin, 105,* 387–396.

Gendlin, E. (1962). Experiencing: A variable in the process of therapeutic change. *American Journal of Psychotherapy, 15,* 233–245.

Glickman, C. D., & Bey, T. M. (1990). Supervision. In W. R. Houston (Ed.), *Handbook of research in teacher education* (pp. 549–566). New York: Macmillan.

Goodyear, R. K. (Producer). (1982). Psychotherapy supervision by major theorists [Videotape series]. Manhattan: Instructional Media Center, Kansas State University.

Goodyear, R. K. (1990). Gender configurations in supervisory dyads. Their relation to supervisee influence strategies and to skill evaluations of the supervisee. *The Clinical Supervisor, 8,* 67–79.

Goodyear, R. K., Abadie, P. D., & Efros, F. (1984). Supervisory theory into practice: Differential perception of supervision by Ekstein, Ellis, Polster, and Rogers. *Journal of Counseling Psychology, 31,* 228–237.

Goodyear, R. K., & Bradley, F. O. (1983). Theories of counselor supervision: Points of convergence and divergence. *The Counseling Psychologist, 11*(1), 59–69.

Goodyear, R. K., & Robyak, J. E. (1982). Supervisors' theory and experience in supervisory focus. *Psychological Reports, 51,* 978.

Guest, P. D., & Beutler, L. E. (1988). Impact of psychotherapy supervision on therapist orientation and values. *Journal of Consulting and Clinical Psychology, 56,* 653–658.

Gysbers, N. C., & Johnston, J. A. (1965). Expectations of a practicum supervisor's role. *Counselor Education and Supervision, 2,* 68–75.

Hansen, J. C. (1965). Trainees' expectations of supervision in the counseling program. *Counselor Education and Supervision, 2,* 75–80.

Hansen, J. C., & Barker, E. N. (1964). Experiencing and the supervisory relationship. *Journal of Counseling Psychology, 11,* 107–111.

Hansen, J. C., Pound, R., & Petro, C. (1976). Review of research on practicum supervision. *Counselor Education and Supervision, 16,* 107–116.

Hansen, J. C., Robins, T. H., & Grimes, J. (1982). Review of research on practicum supervision. *Counselor Education and Supervision, 2,* 15–24.

Hansen, J. C. & Warner, R. W. Jr. (1971). Review of research on practicum supervision. *Counselor Education and Supervision, 10,* 261–272.

Harris, D. S., & Goodyear, R. K. (1990, April). *The circumplex model in four supervisory dyads: A study of interactions.* Paper presented at the annual meeting of the American Educational Research Association, Boston, MS.

Harvey, O. J., Hunt, D. E., & Schroder, H. M. (1961). *Conceptual systems and personality organization.* New York: Wiley.

Hector, M. A. (1977, March). *Competency-based counselor supervision.* Paper presented at the annual convention of the American Personnel and Guidance Association, Dallas, TX.

Helms, J. E. (1984). Toward a theoretical explanation of the effects of race on counseling: A Black and White model. *The Counseling Psychologist, 12*(4), 153–165.

Heppner, P. P., & Handley, P. G. (1982). The relationship between supervisory expertness, attractiveness, or trustworthiness. *Counselor Education and Supervision, 22,* 23–31.

Heppner, P. P., & Roehlke, H. J. (1984). Differences among supervisees at different levels of training: Implications for a developmental model of supervision. *Journal of Counseling Psychology, 31,* 76–90.

Hess, A. K. (Ed.), (1980). *Psychotherapy supervision: Theory, research and practice.* New York: Wiley.

Hess, A. K. (1983). *Learning counseling and psychotherapy skills: A challenge in personal and professional identity.* Unpublished manuscript available from Auburn University, Montgomery, AL.

Hess, A. K. & Hess, K. A. (1983). Psychotherapy supervision: A survey of internship training practices. *Professional Psychology: Research and practice, 14,* 504–514.

Hester, L. R., Weitz, L. H., & Anchor, K. N., Roback, H. B. (1976). Supervisor attraction as a function of level of supervisor skillfulness and supervisees' perceived similarity. *Journal of Counseling Psychology, 23,* 254–258.

Hill, C. E., Charles, D., & Reed, K. G. (1981). A longitudinal analysis of changes in counseling skills during doctoral training in counseling psychology. *Journal of Counseling Psychology, 28,* 428–436.

Hill, C. E., & O'Grady, K. E. (1985). List of therapist intentions illustrated in a case study and with therapists of varying theoretical orientations. *Journal of Counseling Psychology, 32,* 3–22.

Hogan, R. A. (1964). Issues and approaches in supervision. *Psychotherapy: Theory, Research and Practice, 1,* 139–141.

Holloway, E. L. (1982). Interactional structure of the supervision interview. *Journal of Counseling Psychology, 29,* 309–317.

Holloway, E. L. (1984). Outcome evaluation in supervision research. *The Counseling Psychologist, 12*(4), 167–174.

Holloway, E. L. (1987). Developmental models of supervision: Is it development? *Professional Psychology: Research and Practice, 18,* 209–216.

Holloway, E. L. (1988a). Models of counselor development or training models for supervision: Rejoinder to Stoltenberg and Delworth. *Professional Psychology: Research and Practice, 19,* 138–140.

Holloway, E. L. (1988b). Instruction beyond the facilitative conditions: A response to Biggs. *Counselor Education and Supervision, 27,* 252–258.

Holloway, E. L., & Dunlap, D. M. (1989, April). *The power of involvement in the supervision relationship.* Paper presented at the annual meeting of the American Education Research Association, Boston, MA.

Holloway, E. L., Freund, R. D., Gardner, S. L., Nelson, M. L., & Walker, B. R. (1989). The relation of power and involvement to theoretical orientation in supervision: An analysis of discourse. *Journal of Counseling Psychology, 36,* 88–102.

Holloway, E. L., Hosford, R. E. (1983). Towards developing a prescriptive technology of counselor supervision. *The Counseling Psychologist, 11*(1), 73–76.

Holloway, E. L., & Johnston, R. (1985). Group supervision widely practiced and poorly understood. *Counselor Education and Supervision, 24,* 332–340.

Holloway, E. L. & Poulin, K. (in press). Discourse in supervision. In J. Siegfried (Ed.), *Therapeutic and everyday discourse as behavior change: Towards a micro-analysis in psychotherapy process research.* New York: Ablex.

Holloway, E. L. & Roehlke, H. J. (1987). Internship: The applied training of a counseling psychologist. *The Counseling Psychologist, 15,* 205–260.

Holloway, E. L., & Wampold, B. E. (1983). Patterns of verbal behaviors and judgments of satisfaction in the supervision interview. *Journal of Counseling Psychology, 30,* 227–234.

Holloway, E. L., & Wampold, B. E. (1985, May). Dimensions of satisfaction in the supervision interview. *Resources in Education* (ERIC/CAPS No. ED 251 757).

Holloway, E. L., & Wampold, B. E. (1986). Relation between conceptual level and counseling-related tasks: A meta-analysis. *Journal of Counseling Psychology, 33,* 310–319.

Holloway, E. L., & Wolleat, P. L. (1980). Relationship of counselor conceptual level to clinical hypothesis formation. *Journal of Counseling Psychology, 27,* 539–545.

Holloway, E. L., & Wolleat, P. L. (1981). Style differences of beginning supervisors: An interactional analysis. *Journal of Counseling Psychology, 28,* 373–376.

Hosford, R. E., & Barmann, B. (1983). A social learning approach to counselor supervision. *The Counseling Psychologist, 11*(1), 51–58.

Hunt, D. E., & Sullivan, E. V. (1974). *Between psychology and education.* Hinsdale, IL: Dryden.

Ivey, A. E., Normington, C. J., Miller, D. C., Morrill, W. H., & Haase, R. F. (1968). Microcounseling and attending behavior: An approach to prepracticum counselor training [Monograph supplement]. *Journal of Counseling Psychology, 15*(5).

Jakubowski-Spector, P., Dustin, R., & George, R. L. (1971). Toward developing a behavioral counselor education model. *Counselor Education and Supervision, 10,* 242–250.

Karr, J. T., & Geist, G. O. (1977). Facilitation in supervision as related to facilitation in therapy. *Counselor Education and Supervision, 17,* 263–268.

Katz, D., & Kahn, R. L. (1978). *The social psychology of organizations* (2nd ed.). New York: Wiley.

Kennard, B. D., Stewart, S. M., & Gluck, M. R. (1987). The supervision relationship: Variables contributing to positive versus negative experiences. *Professional Psychology: Research and Practice, 18,* 172–175.

Kolb, D. A. (1984). *Experiential learning.* Englewood Cliffs, NJ: Prentice-Hall.

Krause, A. A., & Allen, G. J. (1988). Perceptions of counselor supervision: An examination of Stoltenberg's model from the perspectives of supervisor and supervisee. *Journal of Counseling Psychology, 35,* 77–80.

Kurpius, D., & Morran, D. K. (1988). Aspects of counselor preparation. *Counselor Education and Supervision, 27,* 368–376.

Lambert, M. J. (1974). Supervisory and counseling process: a comparative study. *Counselor Education and Supervision, 14,* 54–60.

Lambert, M. J. (1980). Research and the supervisory process. In A. K. Hess (Ed.), *Psychotherapy supervision: Theory, research and practice* (pp. 423–452). New York: Wiley.

Lambert, M. J., & Arnold, R. C. (1987). Research and the supervisory process. *Professional Psychology: Research and Practice, 18,* 217–224.

Leary, T. (1957). *Interpersonal diagnosis of personality: A theory and a methodology for personality evaluation.* New York: Ronald Press.

Lemons, S., & Lanning, W. E. (1979). Value system similarity and the supervisory relationship. *Counselor Education and Supervision, 19,* 13–19.

Levine, F. M., & Tilker, H. A. (1974). A behavior modification approach to supervision of psychotherapy. *Psychotherapy: Theory, Research and Practice, 11,* 182–185.

Liddle, H. A. (1982). Using mental imagery to create therapeutic and supervisory realities. *The American Journal of Family Therapy, 10,* 68–72.

Littrell, J. M., Lee-Borden, N., & Lorenz, J. (1979). A developmental framework for counseling supervision. *Counselor Education and Supervision, 19,* 129–136.

Loevinger, J. (1976). *Ego development: Conceptions and theories.* San Francisco: Jossey-Bass.

Loganbill, C., Hardy, E., & Delworth, U. (1982). Supervision: A conceptual model. *The Counseling Psychologist, 10*(1), 3–42.

Marikis, D. A., Russell, R. K., & Dell, D. M. (1985). Effects of supervisor experience level on planning and in-session supervisor verbal behavior. *Journal of Counseling Psychology, 32,* 410–416.

Martin, J. S., Goodyear, R. K., & Newton, F. B. (1987). Clinical supervision: An intensive case study. *Professional Psychology: Research and Practice, 18,* 225–235.

Martin, J., Martin, W., Meyer, M., & Slemon, A. (1986). Empirical investigation of the cognitive mediational paradigm for research on counseling. *Journal of Counseling Psychology, 33,* 115–123.

Matarazzo, R. G., & Patterson, D. R. (1986). Methods of teaching therapeutic skill. In S. Garfield & A. Bergin (Eds.), *A handbook of psychotherapy and behavior change* (3rd ed.) (pp. 821–843). New York: Wiley.

McNeill, B. W., Stoltenberg, C. D., & Pierce, R. A. (1985). Supervisees' perceptions of their development: A test of the counselor complexity model. *Journal of Counseling Psychology, 32,* 630–633.

Menne, J. M. (1975). A comprehensive set of counselor competencies. *Journal of Counseling Psychology, 22,* 547–553.

Miars, R. D., Tracey, T. J., Ray, P. B., Cornfeld, J. L., O'Farrell, M., & Gelson, C. J. (1983). Variation in supervision process across trainee experience levels. *Journal of Counseling Psychology, 30,* 403–412.

Mosher, R. L., & Sprinthall, N. A. (1971). Psychological education: A means to promote personal development during adolescence. *The Counseling Psychologist, 2*(4), 3–82.

Mueller, W. J., & Kell, B. L. (1972). *Coping with conflict: Supervising counselors and psychotherapists.* Englewood Cliffs, NJ: Prentice-Hall.

Myrick, R. D., & Kelly, F. D. (1971). A scale for evaluating practicum students in counseling and supervision. *Counselor Education and Supervision, 10,* 330–336.

Nelson, M. L., & Holloway, E. L. (1990). Relation of gender to power and involvement in supervision. *Journal of Counseling Psychology, 37,* 473–481.

Norcross, J. C., & Stevenson, J. F. (1984). How shall we judge ourselves? Training evaluation in clinical psychology programs. *Professional Psychology: Research and Practice, 15,* 497–508.

Oetting, E. R., & Michaels, L. (1983). *The Oetting Michaels Anchored Ratings for Therapists: OMART (Preliminary Form).* Unpublished manual, Colorado State University, Western Behavioral Studies Center, Ft. Collins, CO.

Parham, T. A. (1989). Cycles of psychological nigrescence. *The Counseling Psychologist, 17,* 187–227.

Patterson, C. H. (1983). A client-centered approach to supervision. *The Counseling Psychologist, 11*(1), 21–26.

Penman, R. (1980). *Communication processes and relationships.* London: Academic Press.

Perry, W. G., Jr. (1970). *Forms of intellectual and ethical development in the college.* New York: Holt, Rinehart and Winston.

Pierce, R., Carkhuff, R. R., & Berenson, B. G. (1967). The differential effects of high and low functioning counselors upon counselors-in-training. *Journal of Clinical Psychology, 23,* 212–215.

Pierce, R. M., Schauble, P. G. (1970). Graduate training of facilitative counselors: The effects of individual supervision. *Journal of Counseling Psychology, 17,* 210–217.

Pierce, R. M., & Schauble, P. G. (1971). Study on the effects of individual supervision in graduate school training. *Journal of Counseling Psychology, 18,* 186–187.

Prichard, K. K. (1988). Reactions to "the case presentation approach in clinical supervision." *Counselor Education and Supervision, 27,* 249–251.

Rabinowitz, F. E., Heppner, P. P., & Roehlke, H. J. (1986). Descriptive study of process and outcome variables of supervision over time. *Journal of Counseling Psychology, 33,* 292–300.

Reising, G. N., & Daniels, M. H. (1983). A study of Hogan's model of counselor development and supervision. *Journal of Counseling Psychology, 30,* 235–244.

Remley, T. P., Jr., Benshoff, J. M., & Mowbray, C. A. (1987). Postgraduate peer supervision: A proposed model for peer supervision. *Counselor Education and Supervision, 27,* 53–60.

Rest, J. R. (1979). *Development in judging moral issues.* Minneapolis: University of Minnesota Press.

Rickards, L. D. (1984). Verbal interaction and supervisor perception in counselor supervision. *Journal of Counseling Psychology, 31,* 262–265.

Robyak, J. E., Goodyear, R. K., & Prange, M. (1987). Effects of supervisors' sex, focus, and experience on preferences for interpersonal power bases. *Counselor Education and Supervision, 26,* 299–309.

Robyak, J. E., Goodyear, R. K., Prange, M. E., & Donham, G. (1986). Effects of gender, supervision, and presenting problems on practicum students' preference for interpersonal power bases. *Journal of Counseling Psychology, 33,* 159–163.

Rogers, C. (1957). Training individuals to engage in the therapeutic process. In C. R. Strother (Ed.), *Psychology and mental health* (pp. 76–92). Washington, DC: American Psychological Association.

Rokeach, M. (1967). *Value survey.* Sunnyvale, CA: Halgren Tests.

Russell, R. K., Crimmings, A. M., & Lent, R. W. (1984). Counselor training and supervision: Theory and research. In S. D. Brown & R. W. Lent (Eds.), *Handbook of counseling psychology* (pp. 625–681). New York: Wiley.

Sansbury, D. L. (1982). Developmental supervision from a skills perspective. *Counseling Psychologist, 10,* 53–58.

Schon, D. A. (1983). *Educating the reflective practitioner.* San Francisco: Jossey-Bass.

Shaw, B. F., & Dobson, K. S. (1988). Competency judgments in the training and evaluation of psychotherapists. *Journal of Consulting and Clinical Psychology, 56,* 666–672.

Spice, C. G., Jr., & Spice, W. H. (1976). A triadic method of supervision in the training of counselors and counseling supervisors. *Counselor Education and Supervision, 15,* 251–258.

Stenack, R. J., & Dye, H. A. (1982). Behavioral description of counseling supervision roles. *Counselor Education and Supervision, 21,* 295–304.

Stevenson, J. R., & Norcross, J. C. (1987). Current status of training evaluation in clinical psychology. In B. A. Edelstein & E. S. Berler (Eds.), *Evaluation and accountability in clinical training* (pp. 77–115). New York: Plenum Press.

Stoltenberg, C. (1981). Approaching supervision from a developmental perspective: The counselor complexity model. *Journal of Counseling Psychology, 28,* 59–65.

Stoltenberg, C. D., & Delworth, U. (1987). *Supervising counselors and therapists: A developmental perspective.* San Francisco: Jossey-Bass.

Stoltenberg, C. D., & Delworth, U. (1988). Developmental models of supervision: It is development—response to Holloway. *Professional Psychology: Research and Practice, 2,* 134–137.

Stoltenberg, C. D., Pierce, R. A., & McNeill, B. W. (1987). Effects of experience on counselor trainees' needs. *The Clinical Supervisor, 5,* 23–32.

Stone, G. L. (1980). Effects of experience on supervisor planning. *Journal of Counseling Psychology, 27,* 84–88.

Strong, S. R. (1968). Counseling: An interpersonal influence process. *Journal of Counseling Psychology, 15,* 215–224.

Strong, S. R., Hills, H. I., & Nelson, B. N. (1988). *Interpersonal communication rating scale* (rev.). Unpublished manuscript, Department of Psychology, Virginia Commonwealth University, Richmond, VA.

Strong, S. R., & Matross, R. P. (1973). Change process in counseling and psychotherapy. *Journal of Counseling Psychology, 20,* 125–132.

Strozier, A. L., Kivlighan, D. M., & Thoreson, R. W. (in press). *Supervisor intentions, supervisee reactions, and helpfulness: A case study of the process of supervision. Psychotherapy: Theory, Research and Practice.*

Strupp, H. H., Hadley, S. W., & Gomes-Schwartz, B. (1977). *Psychotherapy for better or worse: The problem of negative effects.* New York: Aronson.

Sugarman, L. (1985). Kolb's model of experiential learning: Touchstone for trainers, students, counselors, and clients. *Journal of Counseling and Development, 64,* 264–268.

Suh, C. S., Strupp, H. H., & O'Malley, S. S. (1986). The Vanderbilt process measures: The Psychotherapy Process Scale (VPPS) and the Negative Indicators Scale (VNIS). In L. S. Greenberg & W. M. Pinsof (Eds.), *The psychotherapeutic process: A research handbook* (pp. 285–323). New York: Guilford Press.

Sundblad, D. M. (1977). Theoretical orientations of psychotherapists. In A. S. Gurman & A. M. Razin (Eds.), *Effective psychotherapy: A handbook of research* (pp. 189–222). New York: Pergamon Press.

Sundblad, L. M., & Feinberg, L. B. (1972). The relationship of interpersonal attraction, experience, and supervisors' level of functioning in dyadic counseling supervision. *Counselor Education and Supervision, 12,* 187–193.

Tracey, T. J., Ellickson, J. L., & Sherry, P. (1989). Reactance in relation to different supervisory environments and counselor development. *Journal of Counseling Psychology, 36,* 336–344.

Truax, C. B., & Carkhuff, R. R. (1967). *Toward effective counseling and psychotherapy: Training and practice.* Chicago: Aldine.

Wampler, L. D., & Strupp, H. H. (1976). Personal therapy for students in clinical psychology: A matter of faith? *Professional Psychology, 6,* 195–201.

Ward, L. G., Friedlander, M. L., Schoen, L. G., & Klein, J. C. (1985). Strategic self-presentation in supervision. *Journal of Counseling Psychology, 32,* 111–118.

Wedeking, D. F., & Scott, T. B. (1976). A study of the relationship between supervisor and trainee behaviors in counseling practicum. *Counselor Education and Supervision, 15,* 259–266.

Wessler, R. L., & Ellis, A. (1983). Supervision in counseling: Rational-emotive therapy. *The Counseling Psychologist, 11*(1), 43–50.

Wiley, M. O., & Ray, P. B. (1986). Counseling supervision by developmental level. *Journal of Counseling Psychology, 33,* 439–445.

Winter, M., & Holloway, E. L. (in press). Effects of trainee experience, conceptual level, and supervisor approach on selection of audiotaped counseling passages. *The Clinical Supervisor.*

Wittmer, J. (1971). An objective scale for content-analysis of the counselor's interview behavior. *Counselor Education and Supervision, 10,* 283–290.

Wolleat, P. L. (1974). What the counselor needs to know: Dimension of counselor behavior. In G. Farwell, N. R. Gamsky, & P. Mathieu-Coughlan, *The counselor's handbook* (pp. 123–131). New York: Intext Educational.

Worthington, E. L., Jr. (1984a). Use of trait labels in counseling supervision by experienced and inexperienced supervisors. *Professional Psychology: Research and Practice, 15,* 457–461.

Worthington, E. L., Jr. (1984b). Empirical investigation of supervision of counselors as they gain experience. *Journal of Counseling Psychology, 31,* 63–75.

Worthington, E. L., Jr. (1987). Changes in supervision as counselors and supervisors gain experience: A review. *Professional Psychology: Research and Practice, 18,* 189–208.

Worthington, E. L., Jr., & Roehlke, H. J. (1979). Effective supervision as perceived by beginning counselors-in-training. *Journal of Counseling Psychology, 26,* 64–73.

Worthington, E. L., Jr., & Stern, A. (1985). The effects of supervisor and supervisee degree level and gender on the supervisory relationship. *Journal of Counseling Psychology, 32,* 252–262.

Yogev, S. (1982). An eclectic model of supervision: A developmental sequence for beginning psychotherapy students. *Professional Psychology, 13,* 236–243.

Young, J., & Beck, A. T. (1980). *Cognitive Therapy Scale: Rating manual.* Unpublished manuscript, Center for Cognitive Therapy, Philadelphia, PA.

Zucke, P. J., & Worthington, E. L., Jr. (1986). Supervision of interns and postdoctoral applicants for licensure in university counseling centers. *Journal of Counseling Psychology, 33,* 87–89.

PART TWO

DEVELOPMENT, PREVENTION, AND ADVOCACY

CHAPTER 7

UNDERSTANDING THE ADULT YEARS: PERSPECTIVES AND IMPLICATIONS

RUTH E. FASSINGER
NANCY K. SCHLOSSBERG

The study of adulthood is a relatively new and evolving discipline. The concept of adulthood in the psychological sense did not appear in America until the late 19th century and was brought about by changes in demography (Hareven, 1982). The fertility rate fell markedly throughout the 1800s and the mortality rate declined—trends that have continued to the present. Turn-of-the-century changes such as the spread of compulsory education and the exclusion of children from the labor force established the perception of childhood as different from the rest of the life cycle, and heralded the discovery of adolescence and old age as distinct developmental periods. The recent worldwide "graying" of the population has created social, economic, and political changes that have forced attention to a more complex articulation of adulthood. This study is increasingly informed by the interdisciplinary work of psychologists, political scientists, sociologists, humanists, historians, economists, and philosophers (Datan, Rodeheaver, & Hughes, 1987).

The purpose of this chapter is to present an overview of theoretical and empirical work pertaining to the adult years. After a preliminary review of definitional and methodological issues,[1] the chapter is organized according to this purpose. First presented is an overview of different theoretical perspectives on understanding the adult years: contextual, developmental, transitional, and life-span approaches. The focus then shifts to studies of individual lives. The final section discusses trends and implications in current work, including the role of counseling psychologists in addressing the adult years. Throughout the chapter, an effort has been made to attend to diversity in terms of race/ethnicity, gender, social class, sexual orientation, geographic milieu, and other sources of variability in this population.

---

[1] It should be noted that some of the methodological information here was presented by Robert F. Rodgers in the first edition of this *Handbook*. However, because it is considered so central to understanding the theoretical and empirical work in adult development, and because it addresses oft-ignored research issues, we have chosen to include it in this chapter.

DEFINITIONAL AND METHODOLOGICAL ISSUES

A variety of terms has been used in the literature to refer to the sequence of events comprising a person's life experience. *Life span* is often used by psychologists, and *life course* is used among sociologists; psychologists tend to be interested in internal, subjective events, and sociologists focus on socially created, shared events (Hagestad & Neugarten, 1985). All societies divide the life course into two or more phases, and, although events that define the life course are particular to a culture, age provides a basis for assigning roles and resources in every society (Stevens-Long, 1988). This stratification creates a normal, predictable *life cycle* within a culture, one that implies an underlying order in the life course (Hagestad & Neugarten, 1985). These conceptualizations can be investigated from a variety of perspectives.

Some researchers focus on developmental influences on adult lives, classified into three categories of events (cf. Stevens-Long, 1988):

- *Age-graded* influences are strongly associated with chronological age, such as physical maturation or age-appropriate social behavior (e.g., military conscription);
- *History-graded* influences are strongly associated with historical time and are experienced by all those born into a culture at the same time; examples are the 1930s Depression and the Vietnam era;
- *Nonnormative* influences are events that do not occur universally or in predictable patterns, such as geographic relocation or the unexpected death of a family member.

These influences often overlap and may interact with the developmental process presumed by some researchers; for example, the early adulthood task of settling into an occupation was very different during the 1950s postwar boom than it was during the 1930s Depression. This type of variation would have dramatic effects on vocational research using those *cohorts,* that is, groups of people born in the same historical period who share similar environmental circumstances during their maturational sequence. In developmental research, *time-* and *age-related changes* are difficult to distinguish. For example, executive burnout at age 45 may seem an age-related change, but may actually occur because a person has spent 20 years on the job. Age differences may also reflect the biases of researchers, subjects, and the general culture at a particular *time of measurement;* observed memory differences between 40- and 80-year-olds, for example, may be confounded by current social stereotypes regarding mental decline in the elderly.

Part of the process of sorting out observed differences depends on choosing an appropriate research design. The three most common approaches in research on adulthood are cross-sectional, longitudinal, and sequential designs. In the *cross-sectional design,* in which people from two or more cohorts are observed at one time of measurement, individual change is apparent, but cohort differences confound age interpretation of observed differences and thus threaten internal validity (Birren & Cunningham, 1985; Nesselroade & Labouvie, 1985; Schaie, 1983b). In *longitudinal research,* in which the same people are observed over several measurement points, intraindividual change can be assessed; however, this design is plagued by the problems of test effects, cohort-specific characteristics, attrition, and substantial cost and time demands (Birren & Cunningham, 1985; Nesselroade & Labouvie, 1985).

Researchers recently have begun to combine and extend simple cross-sectional and longitudinal designs to reap the advantages of both. These combinations are termed *sequential designs* because they call for sequences of multiple age and cohort samples taken across several measurement occasions (Schaie, 1983). The increased information produced by this type of design allows the researcher to estimate the effects of age, cohort, and time of measurement separately (see Schaie, 1983, for discussion of three distinct sequential analysis designs: *cohort-sequential, time-sequential,* and *cross-sequential* strategies). Schaie and Hertzog (1985) recommended a sampling-with-replacement model, with new subjects added to each age group at each time of measurement; by comparing the behavior of retested and new subjects, researchers can begin to determine the influence of practice, test–retest, and experimental mortality effects. In addition, several researchers (Birren & Cunningham, 1985; Nesselroade & Labouvie, 1985; Schaie, 1983) recommended analyses that include linear structural equation modeling procedures (see Fassinger, 1987), in order to extend the explanatory power of these more sophisticated observational designs.

A major criticism of research on adults centers around the issue of subject selection. Random samples tend to maximize cohort differences, so investigators often try to match subjects from different age groups on characteristics that might influence the phenomenon of interest; in addition, extreme groups (groups differing widely on a variable of interest) may be used. Whatever sampling procedures are used, it is important for the researcher to describe the critical characteristics of the participants, a practice that is seldom done; even basic information about health and education is often missing (Stevens-Long, 1988). In addition, sampling decisions regarding adults must be determined conceptually rather than for convenience, and investigators must give more systematic attention to base rates, dropout analysis, and replacement possibilities in sampling procedures (Schaie, 1983).

Studying subjects of different ages raises the question of whether an instrument is measuring the same set of attributes across age groups, an issue termed *measurement equivalence* (Schaie & Hertzog, 1985). Because of vast differences that often exist among cohorts, some researchers argue that older forms of some tests are preferable in working with the cohorts upon whom those tests were originally constructed. This advice seems inconsistent with our usual press to obtain the most current measure. Because the problems of 20-year-olds are very different from those of 80-year-olds, factors predicting effective behavior in the real world may differ greatly over the life span and may not be measured accurately by the instruments chosen (Stevens-Long, 1988). Approaches to the equivalence problem include developing measures specifically designed for each age group, as well as using a set of measures rather than a single measure (a practice that lends itself particularly well to the multivariate strategies previously mentioned). Datan et al. (1987) pointed out that research in adult development is moving toward more descriptive work, including increased use of biography, autobiography, diaries, clinical case histories, storytelling, historical fiction, and the like, with an emphasis on the individual's construction of the life story rather than a more "objective" account of events.

Other methodological problems confound the interpretation of findings regarding the adult years. One issue receiving increased attention is that of *ecological validity*, based on the idea that the scientist, subject, and observational situation exist in an ongoing dialectic of continuous mutual influence (Stevens-Long, 1988). The four major sources of influence include experimenter effects, subject effects, situational effects, and the more general effects of the social and cultural context, all of which must be considered in evaluating research. For example, the widespread publicity about midlife crisis might lead middle-aged subjects being questioned about their emotional life to describe some form of discomfort or distress, a clearly undesirable situational confound in research with this population.

In summary, there are many methodological problems in studying the adult years. Despite limitations, however, theoretical and empirical work has burgeoned in recent years, as the review given in this chapter indicates.

FOUR PERSPECTIVES ON UNDERSTANDING THE ADULT YEARS

The study of adulthood has not yet produced rigorous theories; current perspectives offer interesting but largely untested predictions about the course of adult life (Stevens-Long, 1988). We present these perspectives grouped into four categories, based on the degree to which they encompass continuity or variability in the life course: the contexts in which adult life occurs, the developmental stages, the transitional events in the life course, and the life span of the individual. Although the four conceptual perspectives are discussed separately here, in actuality they overlap, interact, and build on one another.

The Contextual Perspective

The contextual perspective involves mapping factors in the social environment that affect individuals' lives. For example, in a study of bakery workers in France, Bertaux (1982) illustrated how their similar life stories were a direct result of the structure and nature of their work. Most were at their jobs six nights a week, nine hours per night, a requirement that determined most of the rest of their lives. Time use, family life, health, and activities outside work were severely restricted by work hours and chronic lack of sleep. Bertaux's approach was to use life stories in order to move from observed patterns of behavior over a number of cases to the assumed structure of underlying social relationships.

In another example of the contextual perspective, Rosenbaum (1979) provided an alternative view of the "midlife crisis" based on research on the impact of organizations on individuals. He plotted the pattern of a cohort's promotional mobility from 1962 to 1975, to study the relation between promotion and age. He found that the promotion selection system tends to withdraw active consideration after age 40, and suggested that such precipitous decreases in chances for promotion are conducive to the psychological reactions that are often attributed to midlife crisis.

Kanter (1977) corroborated Rosenbaum's position by demonstrating that people's problems stem from organizational structures rather than from intrapsychic issues. She located a large measure of responsibility for people's work behaviors and organizational fate in the structure of the work systems themselves. Occupational environment factors affecting individuals have also been identified by Kohn (1980). The most important of these is substantive complexity, the degree to which the work requires thought and independent judgment; individuals whose work is substantively complex demonstrate stronger intellectual functioning over time.

Support for a contextual view can be found in other work as well. Scheidt and Windley (1985) reviewed literature in the "ecology of aging," documenting the reciprocal interaction of the physical and social environment with the aging process. Hagestad (1985) outlined the way changing demographics have led to dramatic changes in the structure and demands of the family. Stewart and Healy (1989) proposed a framework for linking individual development and societal change; in their model, based on secondary analyses of several data sets, individuals' receptivity and response to social events were mediated by their life stage (e.g., the women's movement has affected women differently, depending on whether it was experienced in adolescence or adulthood). A similar idea was incorporated into Bardwick's (1990) model of adult development, which describes the interaction of gender, age, and historical period.

Some recent theorists have begun to examine the impact of context on individual lives within the broad perspective of the state. Mayer and Schoepflin (1989), for example, presented an analysis of the way in which the state defines the individual life course by controlling access to legal, economic, and social structures (such as education and marriage); this control leads to rigid age stratification, weakened social bonds, separation of the individual from the collectivities of family and kin, individual independence and mobility, and an external rather than individually created order throughout life. The increasing irrelevance of the person and her or his biographical contexts thus deteriorates into passive performance of specialized and anonymous social roles, ultimately leading to an inability to form comprehensive and long-term life designs.

Similar arguments have been put forth by Gutmann (1987) and Rosenmayr (1985). Gutmann argued that our modern industrialized society has pushed the elderly out of their traditional responsibilities of nurturing and passing down culture to younger generations, and of maintaining cultural supports for effective parenting. Using several cross-cultural examples, Gutmann demonstrated how urbanization and the resulting "deculturation" have led to individually rather than collectively determined lines of affiliation; usually based on similarity, these groupings give rise to racism, sexism, and, particularly, ageism.

Rosenmayr (1985) discussed the impact of technology on the social position of the elderly in Western culture (his work based on European research) and contextually defined views of aging as tied to societal division of labor. He articulated the difficulty for the elderly of finding a place in postmodern society and presented the notion of "cumulative deprivation" to describe how adverse factors (such as poverty or lack of education) interact to increase environmental lethality over time, putting lower-class elderly persons at particularly high risk for problems.

As the foregoing examples indicate, a body of literature is accumulating in which researchers examine individuals by accounting for the contextual factors that affect them. Similarity and continuity are emphasized in the contextual, as well as the developmental, perspective.

The Developmental Perspective

The developmental perspective emphasizes the sequential nature of change during adulthood and is the perspective most familiar to the lay public. Developmental theories can be categorized into three (often overlapping) types: those based on age; those based on stages; and domain-specific theories related to the unfolding of moral, cognitive, ego, or various kinds of identity development.

Development Based on Age

Levinson and colleagues (Levinson, 1986; Levinson, Darrow, Klein, Levinson, & McLee, 1978) focused on relatively universal age-linked "seasons" that unfold in an orderly sequence, with alternating stable and transitional periods. Levinson maintained that each adult builds a sequence of *life structures,* a pattern of relationships with objects, people, groups, and institutions; each one lasts 5 to 7 years and then ends in a transitional phase during which the adult reappraises the current life structure, explores alternatives, and becomes committed to whatever new choices seem required.

In 1969, Levinson began a longitudinal study with a group of 40 men, aged 35 to 45, representing a wide variety of occupational and social characteristics. Levinson explored six age-linked periods, each characterized by its own developmental tasks. Levinson's formulations, which allowed for individual variation, nonetheless emphasized an underlying sequential order and similarity. His findings claimed relatively low variability in the age at which every period begins and ends, and that the hypothesized patterns operated in women's lives as well.

However, a recent review of four studies investigating the applicability of Levinson's theory to women's lives (Roberts & Newton, 1987) indicated limited support for the theory. Despite similarity to men in the timing of the periods and the nature of the developmental tasks, both the strategies for addressing the tasks and the outcomes were very different for the women in these samples. The authors discussed the "split dreams" of these women as lending a tentative quality to the women's lives throughout much of early adulthood and into middle age. The fact that the women's choices were continually influenced by inner conflict resulted in dissatisfaction with both family and career, greater difficulty in establishing an occupation, formation of fewer mentor relationships, and perception of husbands as obstacles to development. Thus, the life structures of these women appeared less stable than those of their male counterparts, because of greater complexity in the dreams they attempted to integrate into their lives and the obstacles they encountered in doing so.

Additional work on Levinson's theory as applied to women (Harris, Ellicott, & Holmes, 1986) supported the observation of greater variety in the "seasons" of women's lives; this work found that most women did not experience Levinson's transitions, or that timing of family events was far more salient than age-related changes, underscoring the fact that each woman's transition, issues, and outcomes were unique. These findings reflected a pattern consistent in empirical work on women's development: a shift away from age-based determinants of behavior because of the greater diversity of roles held by women (relative to men) and the complexity in living out those roles (Wrightsman, 1988).

That the tasks Levinson theorizes may be closely tied to gender and race is supported in limited cross-cultural and cross-racial research. Ross (1984), for example, in a study of Mexican immigrants, found that subjects followed the general hypothesized sequence but differed dramatically in attained education (influencing occupational choices), mentoring (family members filling this role), occupational goals (focused on providing security), family (strong ties to extended family), and transition (cultural transition overshadowing later changes). In studies of Levinson's model as applied to African Americans, Ruffin (1989) and Gooden (1989) found mixed support. Ruffin's study of Black professional women found that racial identity strongly influenced the developmental phases, with the formation of intimacy especially salient during early adulthood. Support for occupational goals was sought in family and friends rather than from "mentors," and achievement aspirations were related to becoming successful in a White world. Gooden's research on professional and working-class Black men found limitations in Levinson's theory in regard to both race and socioeconomic status; the school teachers in his study, for example, fit Levinson's theory better than did the "street men." Gooden also discussed the impact of victimization in the early lives of Black men in terms of developmental difficulties in finding mentors, forming intimate relationships, and sustaining their dreams in a context of obstacles and limited opportunity. Gooden (1989) noted that research in African American adult development must ask "how individuals encounter and respond to social opportunities and restrictions in their efforts at forming a viable life" (p. 88), a reminder of the strong impact of race and class in the life course. It would seem that theories of racial identity must be incorporated into age-related conceptualizations such as Levinson's, if we are to understand the lives of racially diverse groups of adults and plan appropriate interventions.

Development Based on Stages

Another view of adulthood postulates that people pass through an invariant sequence of developmental stages, although these stages are not linked exactly with chronological age; some may move through the stages faster than others, and some may become arrested at one stage and never successfully move on. Erikson (1950), for instance, postulated a well-known eight-stage progression in psychosocial development, with each stage characterized by a crucial issue to be resolved; the adult stages involve the issues of identity, intimacy, generativity, and ego integrity.

Erikson's work provided the backdrop for Vaillant's (1977) 40-year longitudinal study of Harvard men. Vaillant found that these men progressed through the basic stages identified by Erikson as well as an additional stage of career consolidation; he also found that those men who achieved intimacy were then able to deal effectively with their careers, which in turn led to achieving generativity and integrity. Vaillant (1982) also examined longitudinal data based on men living in the inner city, and found progression through Erikson's stages despite vast differences in external circumstances. A recent follow-up of Terman's gifted women (Terman & Oden, 1959) found that creativity was associated with manifesting generativity and adjusting to old age (Vaillant & Vaillant, 1990).

Erikson's work provided a context for the well-known identity status research (Marcia, 1966), which classified individuals into four categories of identity: Achievers (those who have successfully explored and resolved identity issues); Foreclosures (those who have adopted predetermined identities); Moratoriums (those who struggle with identity but are not yet resolved); and Diffused (those who neither fully explore nor resolve identity issues). In research on men, those engaging in identity exploration (Achievers and Moratoriums) were found to possess greater self-esteem than those unable or unwilling to engage in identity exploration (Foreclosures and Diffused).

Recent work (Josselson, 1987) suggested a different pattern for women. In a longitudinal study of women first interviewed in the early 1970s and again 12 years later, Achievers and Foreclosures were found to have the highest self-esteem and lowest anxiety of the four statuses, and Josselson suggested that society may actually discourage women from extensive identity exploration. Social and religious values were found to determine identity status for women more than occupational and political decisions (as for men). Josselson asserted that women's development is tied to relational connections and their identity achievement depends on a process of differentiation within attachment, a process she terms "anchoring"; whether in the work, family, or societal arena, the central aspect of identity is the self-in-relation rather than the self alone, facing an abstract world.

Domain-Specific Development

Other stage theorists postulate domain-specific sequences of stages, each of which is characterized by a qualitative difference in the way people view the world within that particular domain. Perry (1970), for example, postulated a hierarchical model of cognitive development reflecting attitudes about knowledge and education. This model can be summarized in four epistemological positions: *Dualism,* in which the world is seen in polarities, knowledge is absolute, and authorities have the right answers; *Multiplicity,* a chaotic phase in which all values and knowledge are seen as equally valid; *Relativism,* in which all knowledge and values are contextual, with situationally determined decision rules possible; and *Commitment,* in which absolute certainty is impossible, but personal commitment and affirmation of values can be made.

A revision of Perry's scheme along gender lines (Belenky, Clinchy, Goldberger, & Tarule, 1986) postulated five epistemological perspectives to reflect women's experiences: *silence,* a voiceless position in which all knowledge is subject to external authority; *received knowledge,* in which the individual can receive and reproduce but cannot create knowledge; *subjective knowledge,* in which knowledge is personal and private, subjectively known or intuited; *procedural knowledge,* in which there is investment in objective procedures for obtaining and communicating knowledge; and *constructed knowledge,* in which knowledge is seen as contextual, objective and subjective strategies are valued, and the individual can see herself as a creator of knowledge.

Both Loevinger (1976) and Kegan (1982) posited stage theories of ego development in which individuals move from childhood stages of impulsivity, self-interest, and external control to more complex adulthood stages; in these theories, individuals become increasingly sensitive to others, tolerant of ambiguity, able to function both autonomously and interdependently, and responsive to internal standards and values.

Kohlberg (1981) developed a similar, well-known sequence of moral development stages, based primarily on research with young men, in which people move from being motivated to obey rules by fear of punishment, to later motivations of conforming to society and, finally, of being principled and autonomous. Gilligan (1982), however, argued that there are qualitative differences in the way men and women process and interpret the world, and that issues of attachment, responsibility, caring, and interdependence are central to women's moral reasoning. Gilligan wrote:

Male and female voices typically speak of the importance of different truths, the former of the role of separation as it defines and empowers the self, the latter of the ongoing process of attachment that creates and sustains the human community. Since this dialogue contains the dialectic that creates the tension of human development, the silence of women in the narrative of adult development distorts the conception of its stages and sequence. (p. 156)

Gilligan's assertion was that the view of adulthood needs a remapping in which caring and interdependence are central to experience; the view of the heroic individual marching up a sequence of stages and ladders is inadequate, and must include a view of the individual renegotiating interdependence in ever widening circles of attachment (see Enns, 1991 for a counseling-oriented discussion of relational models of women's identity).

Focusing on young adults, Chickering (1969) developed a theory of college student development that included a variety of developmental tasks along seven vectors of personal functioning: achieving competence, managing emotions, becoming autonomous, establishing identity, freeing interpersonal relationships, developing purpose, and developing integrity. In this developmental sequence, students tend to move from dualistic, egocentric, conformist approaches to the world toward increased complexity, internal responsibility, sensitivity, and multiple perspectives in evaluating problems.

Identity development theories, which incorporate one's membership in a societally oppressed group, are gaining increasing attention. In explicit recognition that identity is largely socially determined, these models attend to the interplay between the individual and the environment. Initial work focused on the development of racial identification of

Black Americans in the political upheaval of the 1960s; later work (Helms, 1985, 1990) extended this work to identity models in other racial/ethnic groups and in counseling situations (see Chapter 11, by Atkinson and Thompson).

Helms (1985) noted that most of the racial identity models posit from three to five stages and propose an ongoing conflict between internal views of two cultural groups: white and relevant minority. In addition to biculturalism, these models assume that: minority groups develop modal personality patterns in response to white racism; some styles of identity resolution are healthier than others; stages are distinguishable and can be assessed; affective, cognitive, and behavioral elements are involved; and cultural identification affects both intra- and intercultural interaction. The models begin with a lack of racial awareness and with enmeshment in a European American world view, including denigration of one's own culture, poor self-esteem, and idealization of white culture. The next stages involve confrontation with the reality of oppression and subsequent immersion in one's racial group, with rejection of the dominant white group. The final stages involve the internalization of identity, increased self-esteem, and interpersonal relationships that are not restricted by race or social group membership. In these models, identity transformation is dependent on a combination of personal readiness, prior cultural socialization experiences, and educational experiences (Helms, 1985).

As our field becomes increasingly sensitive to diversity, efforts to extend these ideas lead to generic models of the cultural identification process of any oppressed group (e.g., Highlen et al., 1988); in addition, models of women's identity (Peck, 1986), feminist identity (Downing & Rousch, 1985), and gay identity (see Fassinger, 1991) have been developed. However, unlike racial identity development, which involves attitudinal change toward the meaning of an identity already apparent and within a context of potential family and community support, other kinds of identity development (e.g., gay and feminist identity) involve a new awareness and an articulation of an identity that is often rejected in one's immediate environment. Fassinger (1991) observed of gay identity development, for example, that the confrontation of both external and internalized oppression must occur repeatedly in situations in which one's sexual orientation is not known, in the context of overt prejudice and legal discrimination, lack of family support, few if any role models, and, for gay people of many racial/ethnic groups, potential loss of primary community. Models that posit some form of public affirmation and political activism as markers of integrated identity therefore may not adequately describe the experience of some oppressed individuals in present-day society.

The limitations of these models notwithstanding, they help us understand certain aspects of creating a healthy self-identity within a context of societal oppression, prejudice, and discrimination. As Brown (1989) pointed out, truly integrating into our clinical and research paradigms the experience of people who struggle daily with marginality, biculturalism, and the need to create norms, can enrich our understanding of identity, interpersonal intimacy, family structures, and other aspects of human behavior. Recent attention to the development of White racial identity (Helms, 1990) supports the importance of cultural awareness as an integral part of any individual's identity.

A recent study (Whitbourne & Hulicka, 1990) indicated that developmental stage theories dominate the material on adulthood included in psychology texts, although they are beginning to be more critically evaluated and less reified than in the past. Whatever their theoretical limitations, it is clear that these models can be very useful in counseling. They aid both clients and professionals in understanding, predicting, and normalizing experiences, as well as in identifying difficulties that may stem from developmental processes and tasks. In addition, some stage models may help members of oppressed groups identify and articulate cultural needs and values, and aid counselors in sorting out issues that arise in the therapeutic relationship.

The Transitional Perspective

The third perspective in adulthood focuses on transitions, which can be looked at in two ways: culturally and individually.

Cultural Transitions

Cultures have normative age systems that regulate status and role occupancy across the life span. For the individual, such norms provide (a) a scheduled set of changes in social identity and (b) movement into new phases of life that have distinctive characteristics, resources, social roles, and obligations (Hagestad & Neugarten, 1985). A full understanding of these life course transitions requires an examination of cultural age norms as well as three kinds of time: individual, family, and historical time (Hareven, 1982). For example, having a baby appears to be an individual and family choice, yet the decision is dependent on the social and demographic presses regarding child bearing that operate in a culture at a particular time. The impact of historical time is highlighted by differences between U.S. Colonial and present-day responses to childhood death (Hiner, 1985). High infant mortality rates during the 18th century had profound impact on married life, particularly for women, who spent all of their adulthood bearing and raising children; marriages were more frequent and of shorter duration (because women frequently died in childbirth), and loss of a child was an expected reality of adult life. This historical context contrasts sharply with current ideologies, characterized by long-term partnerships and fewer children; today, loss of a child is unexpected and particularly traumatic.

Neugarten and Neugarten (1987) emphasized that individual lives must be viewed in historical context because social prescriptions for age-appropriate behavior change over time. For example, with increased longevity, the postparental period has lengthened considerably. Economic independence for many young people is delayed as larger proportions attend college and graduate or professional school. Patterns for women have changed—more young women are employed full-time, and more middle-aged women are returning to the labor force after children leave home—and child-rearing practices are changing as fathers slowly begin to share responsibility. Multiple marriages and improved health keep older adults engaged in activities traditionally reserved for the young.

These kinds of historical trends suggest that social norms for age-appropriate behavior are loosening up in today's society (Neugarten & Neugarten, 1987). Research suggests, for example, that responses to menopause, an age-related biological event, are closely tied to other midlife events (such as children's leaving home), which in turn are very much influenced by environmental and historical context. One recent study (Adelman, Antonucci, Crohan, & Coleman, 1989) demonstrated that cohort membership strongly affected both the "empty-nest" experience and the well-being of women at midlife; a cohort who had reached adulthood during a period of emphasis on the maternal role experienced greater distress than a cohort (matched on age, education, and marital status) who had entered young adulthood during a period of emphasis on labor force participation. A study of rural women at midlife (Finch, 1989) also found responses to midlife transitions environmentally influenced; factors such as the uncertain farm economy, strong religious values, and connectedness with their community seemed to minimize the impact of the empty-nest experience among these women, supporting the importance of cultural explanations for transitional behaviors.

The societal blurring of age-defined roles and tasks has been referred to as the "fluid life cycle" and represents flexibility and freedom for many (Neugarten & Neugarten, 1987). However, for others, uncertainties and strains may be created, with new timetables simply replacing the old. For example, because young adult transitions currently are more compressed than they have been historically (Hagestad & Neugarten, 1985), people may feel inadequate if they have not met their achievement (and, for many, family) goals by age 35, even though they are likely to live into their 80s. Because some people maintain traditionally defined internal timetables, even though their behavior is not age-stereotypic, they experience intrapsychic anxiety and conflict (Neugarten & Neugarten, 1987).

That social norms are pervasive, systemic, and powerful was illustrated by Ehrenreich and English (1979), who presented an analysis of the way women's place in American society has been manipulated through the advice of "experts," in order to preserve economic stability, labor balance, and male privilege. These kinds of proscriptive forces create a "social clock" (often masked in rhetoric about "biological clocks"), suggesting why transitions are so difficult to deal with when they are off-time according to the prevailing zeitgeist. Societal subgroups may have their own age norms, with factors such as race, socioeconomic status, disability, and sexual orientation creating systematic variations in age-defined behavior (Hagestad & Neugarten, 1985). For example, the lengthy "coming out" process for gay people (Fassinger, 1991) may delay the establishment of permanent relationships and families; occupational discrimination may impede career attainment for African Americans and some other racial groups. These kinds of variations become especially salient when we attempt to apply theory to our intervention efforts (see Chapter 9, by Gibson and Brown).

Individual Transitions

Transitional perspectives may also focus on the individual, according to life-span theorists who identify life events as markers or milestones that play a pivotal role in giving shape and direction to each individual's life. Fiske and Chiriboga (1990) conducted a longitudinal study of four groups of lower-middle-class men and women in San Francisco: graduating high school seniors, newlyweds, middle-aged parents, and preretirement couples. These groups, each on the threshold of a major transition at the start of the study, were assessed five times over a 12-year period, utilizing in-depth interviews, standardized scales, and specially developed research instruments. The researchers found that normative transitions did not predict change, but, rather, that unanticipated events most often brought upheaval and change. Furthermore, they found that people's individual circumstances reflected such diversity that a person's life could not be predicted simply by knowing his or her age or life period. They concluded that self-concept, environmental context, and progression along the life course were alone insufficient to determine stability or change in adulthood; instead, the self in transaction with life's historical and personal circumstances resulted in self-rated stability or change.

Schlossberg (1984, 1989) offered a transitional model of coping that incorporates both anticipated and unanticipated life events. In contrast to anticipated transitions, which can be planned and rehearsed, unanticipated transitions usually involve crises such as job loss or demotion, divorce, premature spousal death, or serious illness of a child. The Schlossberg model looks at the process of assimilating transitions, in which an individual moves from being enveloped and defined by the transition to eventually integrating the transition; for example, an individual is no longer a graduate but someone who has graduated.

The model also identifies variables that influence the ease with which transitions are assimilated. Schlossberg grouped the variables into three clusters: transition characteristics such as timing, source, and duration; individual characteristics such as coping and ego strength; and environmental characteristics such as support systems and options. The model, based in part on studies of the impact of geographical relocation and job elimination, is eclectic; it incorporates the work of sociologists by identifying normative cultural transitions, and the work of psychologists by examining individuals' responses to anticipated and unanticipated life events.

Another approach to transitions was developed by Whitbourne (1985), who reviewed three popular models of adaptation, noting their strengths and limitations:

1. The life events model postulates stress as a mediator between individual adaptation and life events as measured by classification systems, a tradition that dimensionalizes stressful events and moderating characteristics of individuals but ignores subjective meanings of these events.

2. The cognitive appraisal model emphasizes life events as subjective phenomena with impact on well-being; appraisal and coping occur in a transactional process, a tradition that focuses clearly on subjective reactions to events but inadequately addresses causal issues in choosing different coping strategies.

3. The subjective well-being model assumes that adaptation is reflected in satisfaction based on continuous evaluation of life experiences rather than reactions to discrete events, a tradition that focuses on positive subjective responses to events but reinforces passivity in its emphasis on intrapsychic forms of coping.

Building on these three adaptation models, Whitbourne (1985) presented a transactional model of changes in the "life-span construct" as the result of incongruent experiences. The life-span construct contains two aspects, the scenario and the life story. The scenario translates the life-span construct into a set of concrete plans influenced by both social norms and individual identity, revised as one moves through the life cycle; a person's life story gives personal meaning and continuity to these events, maintaining congruence between identity and past reality. In this model's transactional conceptualization of coping, the content of the life-span construct determines an individual's aspirations, which, in turn, form the basis for the appraisal of events. Coping may result in meanings of events being distorted toward the maintenance of self-esteem, in aspiration levels being altered toward greater congruence with actual capacities, or in the environment being changed when it is clear that failure to achieve aspirations does not stem from individual inadequacy. Thus, in this model, the adaptation process takes on different configurations, depending on the consistency of an event with the individual scenario, and reciprocally influences the life story.

Another area in which a transitional approach offers promise is that of thanatology, or death and dying. Kastenbaum (1985) presented an integrative framework for understanding the phenomena of death and bereavement in old age within a social context and as the result of a lifelong developmental process. Criticizing stage theories of dying as neither empirically valid nor theoretically adequate in their emphasis on response to immediate crisis, Kastenbaum argued that ideas of futurity and death are important from middle childhood on, well before the close prospect of death is encountered. Exploring the increasing discrepancy between social expectations and immediate reality as an individual ages, Kastenbaum asserted that current attitudes toward the elderly may arise out of the principle of compensation, in which certain psychological or spiritual qualities are ascribed to the aged to compensate for failing health, lowered status, and impending death. Kastenbaum maintained that dealing with the transitions around death and loss must occur if an aging individual is to maintain a sense of continuity and selfhood over the entire life span. Similar views were presented by Jackson (1989), who corrected societal myths regarding Blacks' attitudes toward death, offering his own life-control theory to explain transitions in individual lives where control is frequently imposed by outsiders.

The Individual Perspective

The fourth theoretical perspective focuses on individual continuity and change. Some theorists see continuity among individuals over the course of life; others see so many individual pathways that variability becomes the cornerstone of adulthood. Kagan (1980), for example, compared social scientists who search for stability and continuity to detectives who attempt to link pieces of apparently unrelated evidence into a coherent story. He questioned the premise that information about a growing child is sufficient to explain his or her life course; in examining conclusions about a Berkeley longitudinal study in which 166 people were observed from birth through adulthood, he noted: "When the subjects were seen at age 30, 12 years after their previous interviews, the researchers were shocked by the inaccuracy of their expectations. They were wrong in two-thirds of the cases, mainly because they had overestimated the damaging effects of early troubles" (p. 64).

Neugarten (1982) also emphasized variability, which she termed individual "fanning out." She pointed out that 10-year-olds are more similar to each other than are 60-year-olds, adding:

Perhaps the most consistent finding to emerge from the study of aging is that people grow old in very different ways. [There are] . . . striking variations between successive groups who reach old age . . . between ethnic, . . . urban and rural, and . . . socioeconomic groups. This is to say nothing of the idiosyncratic sequences that widen the divergence among individuals. The result is that 60-year-olds or 80-year-olds are extremely heterogeneous groups. (p. 6)

Pearlin (1982) echoed Neugarten's emphasis on variability, which he maintained is as rich as people's historical conditions, current circumstances, and individual coping responses. Thus, it is untenable to speak of either ages or stages as though undifferentiated people are following a uniform life course; in his own research on strain and coping (Pearlin, 1980), life stresses and strains were most frequently concentrated in young women of lower socioeconomic groups. The adult experience clearly differs across race, gender, socioeconomic status, age, health status, and many other dimensions; unfortunately, much of the work on adulthood to date is based on white middle-class individuals, particularly males (Schlossberg, 1984b). Pearlin also argued that one life phase or event should not be overemphasized, and cited the "midlife crisis" as a case in point. It is known that crisis can occur at any period and that young adults suffer more strains than do other age groups; yet the media and some writers continue to emphasize crisis in midlife, the inevitability of which is not corroborated by hard data. Pearlin's warning is that exclusive focus on any particular life event, period, or transition (like retirement or birth of a child) risks categorizing people as if they were all the same.

Understanding the individual perspective also requires attention to gender similarity and difference, an area of burgeoning research in the past several decades (see Chapter 12, by Gilbert). Although detailed discussion is beyond our scope here, Schlossberg (1984b) noted that differences in behavior that are ascribed to men and women are often the most striking differences among adults. In a widely cited early study of gender differences, for example, Lowenthal and colleagues (Lowenthal, Thurnher, & Chiriboga, 1975) found that the women in their sample had less positive self-images than did the men, felt less in control of their lives, and were less likely to plan for transitions; their affective lives, however, were richer and more complex, and they had a greater tolerance for ambiguity. Men anticipated placing more value on expressive and interpersonal goals as they grew older, whereas women expected to direct their interests outward toward contributing to society and doing good in the world.

More recently, Gutmann (1987) contended that there is evidence of new personality development, in both men and women in later life, that goes beyond adjustment to imposed loss. Studying people in a variety of cultures, including the Navajos in the United States, the Highland Mayas in Mexico, and the Druze in Israel and the Golan Heights, Gutmann found that men in later life acquired more affective and reflective qualities, while women moved in the opposite direction, embracing the aggressive masculinity that the older men were relinquishing. Gutmann suggested that this is a natural, universal, developmental process, confirming clinical observations made by Jung several decades earlier. The criss-crossing trajectories of men and women at successive life stages reflect different types and scheduling of developmental changes, and, although these notions have received some empirical support, gender differences must be seen in historical perspective, with views likely to change over time. Current challenges to existing theory on grounds of relevance to diverse populations remind us that "normal" depends on the researcher, the research question, and the sample, and highlight the nonconscious ideologies that drive our therapeutic and research work.

Summary of Perspectives

Preparing an overview of theoretical perspectives on adulthood is necessarily simplistic and arbitrary. However, the continuum of perspectives illustrates that, even though theorists may have opposing views of continuity and variability in adulthood, they all provide useful frameworks for conceptualizing the life course. The research conclusions depend on the samples studied and the methodologies used. For example, Levinson studied a small sample of career-successful men within a narrow age range; Neugarten studied a variety of samples at a single point in time but focused on historical and social trends. And, although the theoretical perspectives described here represent one very important index for organizing and understanding the adult experience, they may not adequately address individual differences in adulthood, which is the topic of the next section.

INDIVIDUAL DIFFERENCES: ANOTHER PERSPECTIVE ON UNDERSTANDING THE ADULT YEARS

Another index for organizing the adult experience, borrowed from Plath's (1982) description of cultural pathways, is obtained by looking at individuals (*biography*), at their "convoy" of interpersonal relationships (*co-biography*), and at the institutional and social contexts of their lives (*life course context*).

Biography: The Individual

The task of describing an individual's biography is enormously complicated. We briefly describe here only two major elements of individual biography: personality and intellectual capacity. Another crucial element, body changes and health, is covered in Chapter 10, by Altmaier and Johnson.

Personality

Troll (1982) noted that personality development is difficult to write about because it is an ambiguous, conglomerate structure. Researchers use a variety of methods and foci in their research on the adult personality, and clear conclusions become difficult. Some researchers focus on emotion or affect (Malatesta & Izard, 1984; Schultz, 1985); on adaptation and well-being (Chatters & Jackson, 1989; Whitbourne, 1985); on traits (Costa & McCrae, 1989); or on life events and coping (Lazarus & Folkman, 1984; Pearlin, 1980). Regardless of focus, most researchers who study personality in adulthood grapple with issues of stability versus change, a debate that has endured for several decades.

To make sense of the overwhelming data from an enormous number of disparate studies, the question of what is meant by personality, stability, and change must be addressed. Kagan (1980) defined *stability* as the "persistence of psychological structures and behaviors" and *continuity* as the "maintenance of psychological processes or functions" (p. 31). Kagan outlined a number of human attributes, such as cognitive structures and processes, and feeling and motivational states, each of which can be assessed in terms of change as well as stability, and suggested a framework for distinguishing among four classes of change: *enhancement,* in which a particular psychological structure or process becomes better articulated, with the essential nature of the psychological quality remaining unchanged; *derivation,* in which the structure or process that emerges from an earlier one is a transformation of the original; *replacement,* in which the earlier structure vanishes, although the conditions of occurrence may be similar; and *disappearance,* in which a structure, stage, or process vanishes and is not followed or replaced by a functionally related one. Kagan concluded that, during the early years of development, replacement and disappearance are likely to be most manifest. With growth, structures and processes come to have a longer life, and derivatives become more common.

This framework clarifies some of the discrepancies in various studies; each viewpoint may be looking at different gradations of change. For example, to document stability, McClelland compared his brilliant doctoral student, 20-year-old Richard Alpert, with Ram Das, the spiritual teacher and follower of Maharaji that Alpert became 25 years later. In physical appearance, the difference was dramatic, but McClelland concluded that the motive for power was the same, despite external differences (Schlossberg, 1984b). Other theorists would likely see change, suggesting that the conclusions that are reached depend on both the assessed and the assessor.

Costa and McCrae (1989) noted that, unlike child development research, in which investigators try to account for well-known phenomena, researchers in adult development try to identify phenomena to be explained, disclosing patterns previously unnoticed. They argued that the study of adulthood should be the study of personality, although it has been noted (Costa, McCrae, Arenberg, 1983) that there is widespread lack of agreement as to what personality traits are most useful in understanding adulthood and aging. In the long-term comprehensive Baltimore Longitudinal Study of Aging (see Costa & McCrae, 1989), personality has been studied within three broad domains that are believed to subsume most of the traits investigated in other research: neuroticism (which includes such traits as anxiety and depression), extroversion (which includes sensation seeking and activity), and openness to experience (which includes absorption and authoritarianism). Their most recent revisions of trait investigation add two traits to their taxonomy: agreeableness and conscientiousness. Using a variety of objective and projective measures on large samples of mostly advantaged adults still living in their communities, and utilizing two major kinds of change measures (mean level changes and retest stability) to review their own and others' empirical work, they concluded that, between the ages of 20 and 30, people develop a configuration of traits that will characterize them for the rest of their lives. They further concluded that the process of change after age 30 does not continue as a maturational, normative phenomenon at a perceptible pace; thus, presumed developmental phenomena such as midlife crisis are more a matter of stable personality characteristics (in this case, neuroticism) than of developmental change. In mean levels of traits, across many studies of maturational processes, there is little or no change; in stability coefficients, regardless of the instruments or sample, there is evidence of considerable stability over intervals up to 30 years (median Rs ranging from .34 to .75, with most above .50), with higher stability in studies with subjects over the age of 30. These authors also observed that, although most adults see themselves as stable in personality traits, some perceive changes; however, when perceptions are tested against objective data, little or no support for change is found. They noted that evidence for stability in longitudinal studies using different samples, measures, and methods is remarkable, and they asserted: "Dozens of theories compete to predict the course of transitions in adulthood, but the most compelling data point to continuity, despite role changes, traumatic events, biological aging, and the sheer accumulation of experience" (Costa & McCrae, 1989, p. 66).

In another comprehensive review of personality and aging, Bengston, Reedy, and Gordon (1985) attempted to draw conclusions from a wide range of research results on self-conceptions, which they proposed as a more definable construct than personality. Suggesting that self-conceptions have affective, cognitive, and conative aspects, these authors presented a typology of self-conceptions involving six dimensions (current, idealized, disvalued, and presented self-conceptions; conceptions of other's responses; and inferred self-images of those responses). Reviewing 62 studies from a wide variety of methodological, statistical, and sampling perspectives, the authors drew 15 conclusions from the research, which they labeled "propositions," to underscore their tentative nature. A few of these propositions are: (a) there is considerable stability in self-concept dimensions across the adult years, particularly on dimensions most closely related to temperament; (b) subjective self-conceptions evidence more change than "objective" measures of change; (c) there is an increased tendency with age to incorporate traditionally defined opposite-sex gender-role characteristics into self-conceptions; (d) cohort membership, sex, sociocultural trends, and life-stage experiences have greater impact on self-conceptions than does maturation; (e) determinants of age identification and self-esteem may be different in old age, and there appear to be sex differences in sources of esteem in old age; (f) global self-esteem may be as high or higher among older as compared to younger persons, but specific dimensions related to competence may decline; (g) individuals of different personality types adapt differently to age-related life events; and (h) older persons exhibiting dysfunctional personality types may demonstrate *less* change over time.

It would seem, then, that personality changes little over the adult years, with the possible exception of gender-role behaviors and global self-esteem. Datan et al. (1987) contended that the order demonstrated in adult personality is a reflection of the individual's attempt to maintain a sense of continuity, rather than the result of a linear developmental trajectory, and suggested that the personality "development" of adults is characterized by reorganization toward internal consistency, a process that resembles stability in its outward manifestations. Further, these authors asserted that more recent studies of adult personality, which increasingly focus on subjective narration of the life story as it is created by the individual (rather than "objectively" measured by the researcher) provide a conceptual and methodological unity out of the disarray of previous research. Rather than debate over stability versus change, this research attends to the contexts of change and continuity, and the individual's construction of the life course in a way that maintains internal consistency. These authors point to a similar shift toward contextual interpretation in the study of intellectual capacity in adulthood.

Intellectual Capacity

Labouvie-Vief's (1982) categorization of the numerous studies on intellectual capacity and intelligence into three models provides a way to look at change and continuity in cognitive competency. One of her models focuses on growth regression, the second on context, and the third on hierarchical life-span views.

The first model, growth regression, views growth and aging as a single-peaked function that parallels biological development, the assumption being that intellectual functioning slows down with age. Studies have long differentiated "fluid" intelligence (the ability to process new information) from "crystallized" intelligence (already acquired information) and have found the former to generally decline with age and the latter to remain stable or to improve (Salthouse, 1989). However, research on the plasticity of fluid intelligence has demonstrated that older adults can benefit dramatically from training programs in problem-solving strategies and cognitive skills (Baltes & Lindenberger, 1988). One recent study (Baltes, Sowarka, & Kliegel, 1989), comparing a structured and a self-guided training program as applied to 72 older adults, showed subjects capable of producing by themselves gains that were comparable to those obtained in tutor-guided training. This suggests that, even in the area of fluid intelligence, the oft-noted declines may not be as immutable as believed, especially when contextual variables that influence cognitive processes are considered (Labouvie-Vief, 1985).

Labouvie-Vief's second model, contextual, reflects a view of growth and aging as determined by standards that vary with social class, culture, and historical time. In illustration, she noted that ideas of decrement in aging are strongly motivated by labor market needs and the pressures to create occupational opportunities for the young, thereby creating a mythology of the deficient older worker to support an economic structure. Empirical support for a contextual view is suggested by Kohn (1980), who demonstrated that learning capacity may increase over time in certain occupational contexts. Kohn maintained that, if people of equivalent intellectual flexibility begin jobs different in substantive complexity, the person in the more complex job would experience greater intellectual growth than the person in the less complex job; thus, small initial job differences could lead to increasing differences in intellectual development.

The third model categorized by Labouvie-Vief, hierarchical life-span views, proposes a nonlinear conceptualization of life-course development in which different time periods are characterized by dominant modes that supersede and replace earlier ones, suggesting that the young and old may be *differently* (rather than *unequally*) competent

(Datan et al., 1987). Newer conceptualizations of cognitive functioning (Labouvie-Vief, 1985, 1986) posit a form of mature reasoning that is subjective and intuitive in nature. Noting that older adults tend to perform poorly on formal operational tasks because they tend to personalize such tasks, analyzing alternative interpretations and incorporating affective dimensions into their solutions, Labouvie-Vief postulated a form of complex social reasoning that adds a subjective, intuitive mode ("mythos") to the objective, rational mode ("logos") of adult reasoning. Such conceptualizations challenge existing assumptions regarding intellectual capacity in adults and suggest that intellectual performance cannot be separated from its social and cultural context (Datan et al., 1987).

In the most recent comprehensive review of cognitive stability and change in adulthood, Salthouse (1989) concluded that, although age-related differences in cognitive processes are reasonably well-established, we still cannot answer questions of scope and cause. Noting that most research in this field has focused on decline in fluid intelligence, Salthouse reviewed research according to three hypotheses of cognitive decline.

The first of these theories, the speed hypothesis, presumes that declines in test performance are due to age-related reductions in the speed of peripheral sensory or motor processes, resulting in slower perceiving or encoding of test items. This hypothesis is credible because the age-related slowing of perceptual and motor processes is one of the best documented phenomena in cognition research. Empirical evidence, however, is mixed, and peripheral slowing processes do not explain the phenomenon entirely; Salthouse suggested that a central nervous system version of the speed hypothesis may be viable.

The second hypothesis, the disuse hypothesis, suggests that decreases in test performance are due to lack of exercise of those abilities. Reviewing many different kinds of studies, Salthouse noted that disuse accounts for very little of the decline. He also noted that the apparent success of training procedures in increasing the cognitive performance of older adults suggests optimism regarding the design of effective training programs for older workers.

The third hypothesis, the changing environment hypothesis, relies on assessing cohort groups and assumes that aspects of the physical and social environment (rather than the individual) change, such that successive generations perform better on the same measure. Citing Schaie's extensive work in this area, Salthouse maintained that cohort factors are not responsible for many age-related differences observed in cross-sectional studies, because equivalent age-related differences are also evident in comparisons within same-birth-year cohorts. Salthouse also cited animal learning studies that demonstrate age-related declines in cognitive processes in the absence of changes in the external environment. Thus, the overall evidence does not support the hypothesis that age-related differences in cognitive functioning are attributable to changes in the external environment rather than to changes in the organism.

Salthouse noted two current hypotheses that are beginning to be researched in the cognitive field: componential analysis, which analyzes cognitive activities in terms of hypothesized elementary components; and health status influence, the recognition that many diseases common in older adults impede cognitive functioning. Both of these hypotheses suffer from definitional and measurement problems, however, the former in determining the appropriate level of component analysis, and the latter in creating an inexpensive, quick, valid measure of health status. With definitional and measurement problems resolved, these hypotheses might contribute to our understanding of the relationship between cognitive functioning and age. Currently, research is unable to make causal inferences regarding long-noted patterns.

In summary, in terms of individual lives, empirical findings are mixed regarding continuity versus change in adulthood. We seem to be increasingly aware of the contextual nature of these variations as defined both by the individual and by external forces. Some of the interpersonal influences on individual lives are discussed in the next section.

Co-Biography: Interpersonal Relationships

An individual operates in a network of relationships, and Plath (1982) pointed out that the study of an individual is complete only when seen in relation to others. Indeed, in a recent study of psychological well-being among adults, Ryff (1989) found that an "others orientation" (being a caring, compassionate person and having good relationships) was emphasized in definitions of well-being by both middle-aged and older adults.

Some researchers assert that each person moves through the life course surrounded by a "convoy," a set of significant others who give and receive social support (Antonucci, 1985). An individual's convoy includes those who are stable over time and not role-dependent, those who are somewhat role-related and likely to change over time, and those who are tied directly to role relationships and therefore most vulnerable to role changes.

In this section, we examine intergenerational relationships, sibling relationships, coupling and uncoupling, and friendship and support networks. Interestingly, three of these convoys concern the family, which is still very much alive despite predictions of its imminent death. Demos (1986) argued that we have, in this century, isolated family life as the primary setting for caring relations between people, suggesting that the family unit will withstand further demographic and social change. In fact, the growing number of divorces, remarriages, nontraditional living arrangements (such as nonmarried heterosexual couples and gay couples), single-parent households, and four-generation families indicate the beginning of new kinds of families.

Intergenerational Relationships

Demographic changes such as increased longevity and decreased birth rates have resulted in multigenerational, "top-heavy" families (older members outnumbering younger members), with increases in *inter*generational relationships and decreases in *intra*generational relationships (Hagestad, 1985). Of older people with children, 90% are grandparents, and 46% of that group are great-grandparents. Of those over 65, four-fifths have living children and about 10% of those have children who are also over 65 (Brody, 1990). In no other historical period have the generations overlapped as significantly as they do today; for the first time in history, a woman can be a grandmother and granddaughter at the same time (Neugarten & Neugarten, 1989).

How has this changing demography affected family patterns, interaction, and support? Despite some indication of elder abuse and neglect in our society (Datan et al., 1987), studies of intergenerational interaction generally find contact and caring as the norms. Although fewer than 10% of parents over 65 live with their children, surveys show that most people over 65 live near at least one child, that a majority report giving help when a child or grandchild was ill, and one-fourth report giving financial assistance to a child within the previous year (Neugarten & Neugarten, 1989). A survey of telephone contacts between mothers and daughters (Schlossberg & Leibowitz, 1988) found that regularity was the pattern, although parents judged the calls too infrequent, while adult children felt they spent a great deal of time keeping in touch with their parents. Most older people report high levels of life satisfaction, and fewer than 20%

(about the same percentage as the younger population) report loneliness as a serious problem (Neugarten & Neugarten, 1989).

The potential influence of grandparents is also evident. About three-fourths of people over age 65 have living grandchildren, and three-fourths of these see their grandchildren every day or so (Troll, 1982). The majority of people become grandparents in middle age, when they are still leading very active lives; the younger they are, the more likely they will be active in their grandchildren's lives. Grandparents have been referred to as "family watchdogs" (Troll, 1982) because of their role in helping to maintain the emotional and financial stability of their children's lives, particularly by supporting the mother in the child-rearing unit (Hagestad, 1985). They fill a variety of stabilizing roles, including easing the transition to parenthood, deflating the intensity of nuclear family interactions, serving as buffers for stress, attempting to influence the values and life-styles of grandchildren, and standing as symbols of family continuity (Hagestad, 1985).

As with other facets of adulthood, racial differences in grandparenting are apparent. Mexican Americans, for example, tend to have more grandchildren than other racial groups, would prefer to live closer to their grandchildren, and experience more satisfaction in the grandparenting role than do Whites and Blacks (Lacayo, 1984). Research on Black families consistently reports greater exchanges of help across generations than in White families (Mutran, 1985; Taylor & Chatters, 1989), largely attributable to economic disadvantage, which necessitates pooling resources (Taylor & Chatters, 1989), and to cultural variations in family ideology (Mutran, 1985). Gender differences exist as well: grandmothers tend to be more salient than grandfathers, because of both longevity differences and the role of women as the family "kin-keepers" (Hagestad, 1985).

Lest this discussion romanticize intergenerational interaction, some negative trends must be noted. Data indicate that caregiving to the elderly is most often provided by daughters; three-quarters of those caring for the elderly are women, although it has been noted that men will increasingly serve as caregivers (Brody, 1990; Kaye & Applegate, 1990). As the life span lengthens parallel to skyrocketing health care costs, and the young increasingly delay establishing independent lives, women in midlife often find themselves having to provide care for children, grandchildren, and parents. These women are frequently caught in a "dependency squeeze" caused by the competing pressures of employment (over half work outside the home), children (nearly 40% are still raising their own children), and their aging parents (Brody, 1990). One recent federal government report indicated that the average American woman will spend 17 years raising children and 18 years helping aging parents. A recent survey of 7,000 federal workers indicated that nearly half reported caring for dependent adults, and three-fourths had missed some work as a result; in recent years, 14% of caregivers to the elderly have switched from full-time to part-time jobs, and 12% have quit work altogether (Beck, 1990). Unlike child care, elderly care is apt to be suddenly precipitated, and only 3% of U.S. companies presently have policies that assist employees in caring for the elderly (Beck, 1990).

Demographers also point out that, within several decades, the elderly population will double and the percentage of young will decline, creating great need for attention to eldercare issues in the future (Beck, 1990; Hagestad, 1985). Brody (1990) noted that, in addition to providing intensive, long-term care for which they are not trained, and suffering guilt feelings because they believe they are providing inadequate care, today's women are also caught in societal expectations regarding career achievement—all of which create enormous stress in trying to meet competing obligations. Not only is there need for increased attention to eldercare, but supportive interventions must be provided for caregivers.

Sibling Relationships

The emerging interest in sibling relationships is rooted in the same demographic changes that affect multigenerational families. Because people live longer and are having fewer children, and because of increases in divorce, singlehood, and geographic mobility, siblings have a unique potential for enduring relationships. Life with a sibling might last as long as 80 to 90 years.

Studies of sibling relationships indicate that most adults have a living sibling whom they see or talk to regularly. Over age 60, 83% of all elderly report that they feel close to at least one sibling (Stevens-Long, 1988), and in one study of sibling relationships in a small midwestern city, even those older than 80 still had at least one sibling (Cicirelli, 1980). Troll (1982), in a study of San Francisco residents, reported that people over 65 had more siblings alive than any other relatives—38% had spouses, 61% had children, and 93% had siblings.

Paradoxically, adult sibling interaction, with its potential for being a lifelong resource, tends to be culturally ignored. Bank and Kahn (1982) noted that, in Western culture, rituals such as baptism, bar mitzvah, and graduation mark important changes between parents and children. The bonds between couples are celebrated by engagements, commitment ceremonies, and weddings, and are legalized by marriage and divorce. However, no religious or social rites celebrate sibling bonds.

In researching sibling bonds, Troll (1982) suggested concentrating on structural changes over the years. In childhood, the sibling relationship is one of daily contact and the sharing of most experiences; separation is most extreme during early adulthood, as each forms his or her own home. Caring for aging parents can bring increased interactions in adulthood, but the death of parents may mark the break of sibling ties as old rivalries impede the settlement of parents' financial affairs. As siblings get older, they may try again to renew old family loyalties and relationships. Troll's conceptualization of sibling relationships thus contains the contradictory attributes of solidarity and rivalry.

Other writers also point to the waxing and waning of sibling relationships and to the intense feelings often activated during stress periods, particularly around issues of parent care. Schlossberg (1984b) identified as critical issues the frustration of caretakers over losing the freedom of their middle years and resentment toward siblings who do not bear their share of the load. Often, the caretaker child, who gives time and attention to the parent, is also the receiver of the parent's anger and criticism, while the absent sibling receives praise. Underlying many sibling resentments is residual rivalry from childhood, which can exacerbate current conflicts.

Cicirelli (1982) pointed to differences in amount and kind of sibling interaction and affection based on sex and social class, as illustrated by the findings that siblings from working-class families are often close friends and companions, and that sisters seem to have stronger ties than do brothers or cross-sex siblings. In a recent interview study with 83 individuals aged 61 to 91, Cicirelli (1989) investigated the relationship between sibling attachment and well-being. Results indicated that a bond with a sister was associated with less depression in both women and men, and that women's perceptions of difficulty in their relationships with sisters were associated with increased depression; these results support other research suggesting the importance and effectiveness of women in maintaining family ties. Overall, research on sibling bonds is sparse, and this area is ripe for empirical investigation.

Coupling and Uncoupling

Demos (1986) asserted that couples and families in their various forms have supplanted all other contexts in which intimate ties might develop, and have constricted our capacity to form and maintain extrafamilial relationships. Demos presented historical background demonstrating that the meaning of coupling has changed dramatically in the past 100 years, from a context for economic survival and child rearing to an agent of self-growth and emotional gratification, suggesting that families are being asked to meet new challenges in personal fulfillment.

Troll (1982) emphasized the importance of studying nontraditional intimate arrangements as well as the traditional family unit living in one household. Studies on new forms of coupling (Rubin & Macklin, 1983) have demonstrated that needs for attachment are met in various ways and that the existence of intimate connections with others is far more important than the specific forms they may take. Current statistics (Stevens-Long, 1988) indicate dramatic changes in domestic arrangements over the past several decades. For example, the number of family households (related individuals living together) has grown by 19%, but the number of nonfamily households has increased by 89% and unrelated people living together now represent more than 25% of all households. Over 1 million heterosexual couples live in cohabitation, with some 250,000 children. Same-sex coupling appears to be experiencing a growth spurt, and increasing numbers of gay and lesbian couples are choosing to parent (Fassinger, 1991). One-parent families comprise 15% of White families and nearly 50% of Black families, and most of these are headed by women. Trends show increasing numbers of single people (10% of young adults, a 100% increase over the 1970s) and many of these (particularly women) are also choosing to parent.

About 95% of adults have been married at some point, and, although the marriage age is rising, Americans still marry early compared to adults in other countries. About 50% of existing marriages end in divorce, up from 38% in 1960 and 11% at the turn of the century; about 44 out of every 100 persons are divorced. Although the rising divorce rate is a complex social phenomenon, it is being experienced in almost every Western country, and can probably be attributed to such factors as increased longevity, changing expectations regarding marriage, and the emancipation of women. Stevens-Long (1988) pointed out that, at the turn of the century, the life expectancy was 45 years and most marriages ended with the early death of a spouse. A couple marrying today in their mid-20s will live another 50 to 60 years or more. Maintaining a monogamous, fulfilling relationship for that length of time may be an unrealistic expectation, and the rising divorce rate may simply balance out the declining death rate. Despite high divorce rates, however, 75 to 80% of adults will remarry (five-sixths of the men and three-fourths of the women); more than 30% of people who marry have been married before. From half to two-thirds of these remarriages last until one partner dies, and remarried people report being satisfied in their marriages, particularly sexually (Wrightsman, 1988).

In terms of uncoupling among older adults, only a small number (about 1%) of divorces occur in people over age 65, and only about 5% of people now over 65 are divorced or separated and not remarried, supporting the observation that divorce primarily occurs among younger couples. However, current divorce trends have implications for the economic and social well-being of the elderly on several levels (Stevens-Long, 1988). Being divorced oneself may significantly decrease financial resources, particularly for women (2 out of every 3 elderly persons). Many writers point to the "graying of the feminization of poverty" as a growing social problem, because half of elderly women earn less than $5,000 a year, and a full 82% of elderly Black women exist at poverty level (Datan et al., 1987). Family and kinship networks of the elderly are also affected by divorce, either of oneself or one's children, and problems in children's marriages are likely to make them unavailable for financial or social support and to disrupt grandparenting roles (Hagestad, 1985). In addition, the growing numbers of stepparents and "blended" families raise questions about the responsibility of nonbiological children for caregiving to the elderly. Looking to non-White communities may offer guidance in this regard, because caring for nonbiological elders and youngers has historically been a necessity in many of those communities (Mutran, 1985; Taylor & Chatters, 1989).

Divorce is, of course, not the only (or even primary) agent of uncoupling among the elderly, who are much more subject to death of a partner or spouse. Again, this is particularly true for elderly women, who outnumber men 5:1; by the age of 75, 70% of women have lost their spouses, compared to 39% of men, and only 5% of women widowed over age 55 ever remarry. Studies generally show that bereaved men and women report increased emotional and health problems upon the death of a spouse, but that they recover and experience satisfaction with their lives (particularly women) in the absence of other problems (Stevens-Long, 1988). However, poverty is a pernicious problem for elderly women, particularly for Black women, who tend to be widowed earlier and are often impoverished to begin with. In coping with widowhood, middle-class women have the advantage of greater social options and wider nonfamily social support systems (in addition to increased economic resources), which ease the adjustment to loss of a partner.

Thus, while the need for attachment and intimacy may be continuous throughout life, the forms of that attachment seem subject to considerable change. Generally, studies show decreased levels of satisfaction in initial stages of enduring relationships (although most research has been done on White heterosexual marriages), and particularly in the earlier stages of bearing and raising children. Satisfaction seems to increase again after children have left home, although consistent gender differences point to more dissatisfaction in women than men across all marital stages (Stevens-Long, 1988). Wrightsman (1988) suggested that these contrasts may be due to marriage being secondary to a man's self-esteem, while relationship roles are primary for women. Interestingly, women seem to be increasingly finding single life to their advantage; single women of all ages report being happier than single males, and societal pressures to couple may be easing somewhat (Stevens-Long, 1988). There are, of course, wide variations in satisfaction with and meanings of coupling across racial and socioeconomic groups, suggesting that inclusive generalizations about this social institution are impossible to make.

Friendship and Support Networks

The importance of having friends is increasingly being documented, and research suggests that friendships may be more predictive of general life satisfaction than family associations (Aizenberg & Treas, 1985). Having friends has been associated with adjustment to death of a spouse and other life transitions such as children leaving home, impact of geographical moves, and well-being in adults (Stevens-Long, 1988). Research generally finds that women have larger and more satisfying friendship networks than men, and that men's friendships tend to grow out of similar activities and interests while women's friendships are based on deep sharing and mutual support (Wrightsman, 1988). Mazur (1989) reported that although men and women differed in their manner of engaging in friendship in terms of self-disclosure and involvement, subjective outcome of satisfaction was similar across gender.

Troll (1982) outlined five developmental trends that provide a way to conceptualize the study of friendship: *turnover,* with rapid change characterizing youth and persistence typifying adulthood; *number of friends,* with newlyweds and older adults having the most friends and middle-aged adults the fewest; *importance of friends versus family,* with family more important in youth and very old age, and friends important in middle years; *reciprocity and mutuality,* both of which increase over time; and *functions,* with assistance and intimacy remaining constant over time.

Rubin (1985) noted that, like sibling bonds, friendship has no rituals that validate its existence. Friendship is a "nonevent," a relationship (primarily private) that just "becomes" over time. There are no linguistic variations to distinguish among the many kinds/degrees of friendship, nor are there clear boundaries and consensual agreement on what constitutes friendship obligations and behavior. Although we have a well-developed ideology about family (despite great variation in family arrangements across time, social class, race, life-style, and geographical location), Rubin asserted that we have failed to note the significance of friendship in our lives. She observed that, during passages of separation and individuation, friends provide a reference outside the family by which to judge the self and they give support in the adaptation to new roles; friends also compensate for deficits in other intimate relationships and encourage the development of parts of the self that cannot occur in a family context.

Rubin conducted in-depth interviews regarding friendship with 300 men and women aged 25 to 55, across a range of social classes, and found dramatic differences between men and women in the quantity and quality of their friendships. At every life stage, women had more and higher-quality friendships than did men, and were making friends even in old age. For women, friendships meant shared *intimacy* (self-revelation, nurturance); for men, friendships involved *bonding* in shared activities. Three-fourths of the single women in this study had a best friend (usually a woman) and the remaining one-fourth were troubled by the lack of a best friend; more than two-thirds of the single men, by contrast, could not name a best friend, but were not troubled by it; among those who had a best friend, the friend was usually a woman. Married men were more likely to lack a best friend, unless they named their mate; married women usually named another woman as their best friend. Rubin asserted that women need outside friendships to affirm their identity because so much identity is lost in marriage; friends fill in the missing gaps in the marriage relationship. For men, emotional needs are often satisfactorily met by their spouses.

Rubin also discussed opposite-sex friendships, most of which occurred in the college-educated middle class. Interestingly, men were more satisfied with these friendships than were women; two-thirds of the women named by men as close friends did not feel the same way and complained that they did all the emotional work. Sexual tension in these friendships was also commonly identified. According to Rubin, friendships between gay men and heterosexual or lesbian women may be the cross-gender friendships that afford the greatest equality and fewest tensions.

Rubin also pointed out that, like mates, friends must accommodate the vacillations in intimacy common in any long-standing relationship. Friendships, however, are secured by emotional bonds alone, making them the most "neglected and fragile relationships of our time" (p. 191). With the reification of the family, family bonds take precedence over friendship, and friends are deprived of the sense of entitlement that is crucial to any secure and committed relationship. Neugarten (1982) and Rubin (1985) pointed to factors such as rising divorce rates and dissolution of traditional nuclear families, increased mobility, fewer children and smaller family networks, and more leisure time as increasing the likelihood that friends will become crucial in the lives of adults in the future. Today, the exchange of services and care is within families; tomorrow, it is probable that the exchange will be among friends and in the context of a larger community, necessitating both investigative and interventive attention to extrafamilial bonds.

Life Course Context

Individuals live their lives in many arenas: they work, learn, play, and participate in family, religious, and community experiences, which make up the social and institutional contexts of people's lives. What happens in one arena affects all the others; for example, a change in work location or having a baby affects family life, education, and leisure. In this section, we look briefly at one of these arenas—education—because it has been largely neglected in work on adults.

Demographic trends reveal that people are moving away from a linear trajectory involving education for the young, work for adults, and retirement for the elderly, to a blended plan in which people of all ages are continuously working, playing, and learning (Cross, 1981). For children, who are no longer needed in the work force as they were in the 1800s, education is now almost year-long and compulsory until age 18. Continuing education for adults to update job skills has become increasingly necessary as more adults experience occupational and family shifts in their lives. Aslanian and Brickell (1988) suggested that learning tends to be stimulated by work changes for men and by family changes for women. Willis (1985) outlined a number of reasons for adults' seeking learning opportunities, including understanding one's own aging, comprehending sociocultural change, combating technological or sociocultural obsolescence, preparing for retirement roles, and changing careers.[2]

In terms of participation, adult learners grew from approximately 3.2 million in 1972 to 5.1 million in 1988 (an increase of 59%) and comprised 40% of all postsecondary enrollment (Andersen, 1990). According to a recent American Council on Education report, enrollment of the 35 to 44 age group, which more than doubled between 1974 and 1988, continues to grow; the over-45 age group has also increased, but at a slower pace. This growing enrollment stems from part-time participation.

There are, nevertheless, formidable barriers to adult learning that need to be considered. Although there has been a tremendous increase in adult education and training, only 18% of all adults are currently enrolled in structured learning experiences (part- or full-time students in credit or noncredit courses) and, among these, White, middle-class, educated, and young people predominate (Schlossberg, 1984b).

Cross (1981) surveyed potential learners (individuals who indicated a desire for but were not engaged in organized instruction) and found that situational barriers were mentioned most frequently as impediments to learning. The cost of education and not enough time were mentioned most frequently, although other situational barriers included home and job responsibilities, no child care, no transportation, no place to study or practice, and nonsupportive family and friends. Subgroups of potential learners perceived different barriers as salient; low-income adults, for example, identified costs, while young mothers mentioned lack of child care.

---

[2]For a more cynical view of educational trends, see Collins (1979), who argued that increasing levels of education necessary for occupational entry and maintenance function mainly to restrict occupational access of underrepresented groups, thereby maintaining rigid class stratification and the status quo of White privilege.

Among women, participation in adult education has increased much more than among men, but the rate of increase was smallest among women in the 35-to-54 age group, who, as we have noted, may be struggling with responsibility for children, home, and aging relatives. In addition, many of the policies, practices, and programs of higher education institutions disadvantage older adults, including age-restrictive admissions practices, credit-restrictive transfer policies, financial aid targeted at full-time students, and time limits on certain kinds of programs, which make full-time study mandatory (and therefore impossible for some potential learners). The location and time of classes can also constitute barriers, particularly for those who have to travel some distance. These adults also find it hard to make full use of academic resources such as libraries, laboratories, and computer centers, and of health and counseling centers. Faculty and staff attitudes, ranging from overt hostility and active harassment to more subtle forms of sex and age discrimination, may discourage the middle-aged and elderly from pursuing education. The lack of female role models among faculty and administrators can be a deterrent to adult women (Schlossberg, 1984b).

Feelings and personal characteristics may also create barriers to adult learning. Many older people are influenced by prevalent age stereotypes; if they accept the assumption, for example, that learning ability declines with age, they may not even consider enrolling in an educational program. In addition, women and members of particular racial groups may be affected by prevalent sex and race stereotypes. Willis (1985) pointed out that research on cognitive change in older adults indicates continued learning potential throughout the life span, although some older adults may be intellectually disadvantaged because of negative cohort trends. Race, class, and gender variables that negatively affected people in youth are apt to operate even more strongly as they age, suggesting that educational interventions for adults must be targeted directly and appropriately to specific groups.

Summary

Empirical approaches to understanding adulthood suggest the presence of both continuity and change. Whether we examine biography, co-biography, or life course context, the rich variability of adult experience reminds us that factors such as gender, race, class, culture, sexual orientation, and historical time have tremendous impact on life-span development. Whatever commonalities are noted (such as relative stability in personality traits or cognitive functioning), these must be viewed within the context of each individual's unique situation, suggesting a need for attention to individual differences in planning research and intervention.

TRENDS AND IMPLICATIONS

Although sweeping generalizations about adulthood as a field of theory and research are difficult and risky to make, a few trends and implications are notable in the work done to date.

1. *Theoretical trends* indicate increasing integration of social science fields and perspectives in understanding the complexity of adulthood. Integrative models like those of Kastenbaum (1985) and Whitbourne (1985), which attempted to link separate strands of research, are much needed in the study of adult life. There also appears to be a trend toward increased attention to ecological/contextual variables by researchers, and these perspectives are being incorporated into existing theories.

2. *Methodological trends* indicate increased statistical sophistication and greater attention to multivariate conceptualizations and analyses. There appears to be an increased use of sequential designs, with a concomitant greater capacity to define and sort out issues of age and time. Interest in more qualitative, nontraditional data-gathering approaches is burgeoning; thus, interview data, a long-time staple in this research, is being enhanced by the increasing use of individually constructed biographies, storytelling, diagrams and life lines, and other approaches. Related to this shift is an increasingly deliberate incorporation of the subjective experience of both the researcher and subject in understanding phenomena under investigation (Datan et al., 1987).

3. *Conceptual trends* indicate increased attention to the loosening of age-related norms, roles, and timing of life events, with enormous implications for counseling, research, and policy. These trends imply a need for much greater focus on individual differences in our investigative, interventive, and advocacy work with adults. Neugarten and Neugarten (1989), for example, discussed the importance of social policy based on *need* rather than *age,* given the wide diversity in functioning and resources in older adults. Research studies that continue to narrowly focus on age demarcation and differences are not likely to be particularly informative regarding the rich experiences of heterogeneous adults.

4. *Attention to diversity* indicates a general paucity of research on non-White racial groups, social-class issues, persons with disabilities (except as specifically aging-related), sexual orientation, and, in many areas, gender. This lack of empirical and theoretical attention seriously undermines the validity of what we think we "know" about adult lives. In addition, there is a need to incorporate theoretical work done on diverse groups (such as racial and sexual identity development) with "mainstream" adult development theory, an endeavor that offers tremendous heuristic promise (see McEwen, Roper, Bryant, & Langa, 1990, for an example of this kind of integrative work, focusing on theories of student development as applied to African Americans).

5. *Integrative literature reviews* that analyze trends and point out directions for research are much needed, particularly if they are able to incorporate diverse lines of inquiry on the same issue. Given the burgeoning of literature on adulthood in recent years, the field is ripe for these kinds of efforts.

6. *Interface between the individual and society* requires increased attention, particularly in regard to law and social policy issues. Current trends toward contextual perspectives on adulthood are promising, but they need to be transplanted more directly into the legal and political arenas of society.

Although detailed counseling strategies for a variety of issues common to adults are covered throughout this volume, we note in the concluding section the unique contributions that counseling psychologists can make in research and intervention with the adult population (see Ganikos & Blake, 1984; Gatz, Popkin, Pino, & VandenBos, 1985; and Myers, 1990, for detailed discussions of interventions with older adults).

Roles and Responsibilities of Counseling Psychologists

Gelso and Fassinger (1990), in a 6-year, comprehensive review of the counseling psychology empirical literature, noted the continuing emphasis of our field on research and interventions with college students. They observed that very little theoretical, conceptual, or empirical work on older adults and aging has appeared in our core journals, and urged counseling psychologists to take a more active role in reaching this population.

Furthermore, Fassinger (1991) noted some of the unique characteristics that equip counseling psychologists for serving client populations that previously have been neglected in "mainstream" therapeutic and investigative work. The needs of diverse adult populations would seem congruent with the espoused philosophy and identity of our profession.

Inherent in our philosophy is a nonpathological focus on normalcy and day-to-day problems in living, with emphasis on strengths and adaptive strategies in our clients, important perspectives for work with an elderly client population that has been the target of much stigmatization and myth. We see ourselves as educators, we emphasize the empowerment of individuals, we value preventive as well as ameliorative intervention efforts, and we work toward enhanced functioning for all people; these, too, are crucial perspectives for educating people about predictable life changes and transitions. Our scope includes environmental as well as individual interventions, promotion of mental health at the level of groups and systems, the effective use of community resources, and social and political advocacy where relevant. An environmental focus is useful in therapeutic and research work, where context is so salient, and our advocacy roles are especially valuable in helping subgroups of adults (e.g., the elderly, certain racial and ethnic groups, gay and lesbian people, women) negotiate societal barriers to effective living. We see ourselves as versatile, able to function in a wide variety of settings and to work collegially with other diverse professionals—valuable skills in providing links with a variety of needed services. We emphasize developmental approaches to working with people, including attention to their sociocultural context and the influence of gender, race, age, ethnicity, sexual orientation, (dis)ability, and sociohistory. These characteristics give us the unique opportunity to be in the forefront of sensitive investigation of and effective service delivery to adults in all their variability.

Because we pride ourselves on studying and working with diverse individuals, it may be difficult to recognize our own ageism, but it is imperative to begin asking ourselves how we feel about our own aging. For example, if we dread it, what are our implicit ideas about those who are at the age we dread? How can we help an 80-year-old create options if we believe there are none? Studies of age bias are much needed; training workshops and continuing education programs to help counseling psychologists may be warranted. Also needed are studies of age-mixed counselor–client dyads, with focus on both process and outcome. Are 25-year-old counseling psychologists seen skeptically by 60-year-old men and women contemplating retirement? Can a young individual facing a lifetime of professional possibilities relate to an older person who might be seeing closing options? As with all kinds of diversity, we need to acquire the attitudes, knowledge, and skills that will help us work effectively in mixed-age interactions.

Incorporating work on adulthood into our professional repertoire has tremendous implications for training. Most counseling psychologists will work with adults at some point; however, few current training programs offer specific courses in adult development or counseling adults, and many counseling psychologists remain unaware of the knowledge base in the field. We suggest that this dilutes our scientist-practitioner framework; we are practitioners with adults, but we are not yet scientists with adults. Lack of knowledge makes it difficult to ascertain exactly what theoretical and empirical work drives our practice, and may prevent us from truly effective work with adult clients. Deliberately incorporating this substantive base into our training is one way to begin educating ourselves for broader professional roles.

In summary, counseling psychologists have much to learn and a great deal to offer, both scientifically and therapeutically, with regard to the adult population. The heterogeneity in this population, the heuristic richness of burgeoning theoretical and empirical work, and our unique training and professional orientation provide a seemingly ideal triangulation of the attitudes, knowledge, and skills required in effective work with adults. The coming decades offer us ample opportunity to live up to our professional promise.

REFERENCES

Adelman, P. K., Antonucci, T. C., Crohan, S. E., & Coleman, L. M. (1989). Empty nest, cohort, and employment in the well-being of mid-life women. *Sex Roles, 20,* 173–189.

Aizenberg, R., & Treas, J. (1985). The family in late life: Psychosocial and demographic considerations. In J. E. Birren & K. W. Schaie (Eds.), *Handbook of the psychology of aging* (2nd ed.) (pp. 169–189). New York: Van Nostrand Reinhold.

Andersen, C. J. (1990). Enrollment by age: Distinguishing the numbers from the rates. *Research Briefs, 1.* Washington, DC: American Council on Education.

Antonucci, T. C. (1985). Personal characteristics, social support and social behavior. In R. H. Binstock & E. Shanas (Eds.), *Handbook of aging and the social sciences* (2nd ed.). New York: Van Nostrand Reinhold.

Aslanian, C. B., & Brickell, H. M. (1988). *How Americans in transition study for college credit.* New York: The College Entrance Examination Board.

Baltes, P. B., & Lindenberger, U. (1988). On the range of cognitive plasticity in old age as a function of experience: 15 years of intervention research. *Behavior Therapy, 19,* 283–300.

Baltes, P. B., Sowarka, D., & Kliegel, R. (1989). Cognitive training research on fluid intelligence in old age: What can older adults achieve by themselves? *Psychology and Aging, 4,* 217–221.

Banks, S. P., & Kahn, M. D. (1982). *The sibling bond.* New York: Basic Books.

Bardwick, J. M. (1990). Where we are and what we want: A psychological model. In R. A. Nemiroff & C. A. Colarusso (Eds.), *New dimensions in adult development* (pp. 186–210), New York: Basic Books.

Beck, M. (1990, July 16). Trading places. *Newsweek,* pp. 48–54.

Belenky, M. J., Clinchy, B. M., Goldberger, N. R., & Tarule, J. M. (1986). *Women's ways of knowing.* New York: Basic Books.

Bengston, V. L., Reedy, M. N., & Gordon, C. (1985). Aging and self-conceptions: Personality process and social contexts. In J. E. Birren & K. W. Schaie (Eds.), *Handbook of the psychology of aging* (2nd ed.) (pp. 544–593). New York: Van Nostrand Reinhold.

Bertaux, D. (1982). The life course approach as a challenge to the social sciences. In T. K. Hareven & K. J. Adams (Eds.), *Aging and life course transitions: An interdisciplinary perspective* (pp. 127–150). New York: Guilford Press.

Birren, J. E., & Cunningham, W. (1985). Research on the psychology of aging: Principles, concepts, and theory. In J. E. Birren & K. W. Schaie (Eds.), *Handbook of the psychology of aging* (2nd ed.) (pp. 3–34). New York: Van Nostrand Reinhold.

Brody, E. M. (1990). *Women in the middle: Their parent-care years.* New York: Springer.

Brown, L. S. (1989). New voices, new visions: Toward a lesbian/gay paradigm for psychology. *Psychology of Women Quarterly, 13,* 445–458.

Chatters, L. M., & Jackson, J. S. (1989). Quality of life and subjective well-being among Black adults. In R. L. Jones (Ed.), *Black development and aging* (pp. 191–214), Berkeley, CA: Cobb & Henry.

Chickering, A. W. (1969). *Education and identity.* San Francisco: Jossey-Bass.

Cicirelli, V. G. (1980). Sibling relationships in adulthood: A life span perspective. In L. W. Poon (Ed.), *Aging in the 1980's: Psychological issues* (pp. 455–462), Washington, DC: American Psychological Association.

Cicirelli, V. G. (1982). Sibling influence throughout the life span. In M. Lamb and B. Sutton-Smith (Eds.), *Sibling relationships: Their nature and significance across the lifespan* (pp. 267–284). Hillsdale, NJ: Erlbaum.

Cicirelli, V. G. (1989). Feelings of attachment to siblings and well-being in later life. *Psychology and aging, 4,* 211–216.

Collins, R. (1979). *The credential society.* New York: Academic Press.

Costa, P. T., & McCrae, R. R. (1989). Personality continuity and the changes of adult life. In M. Storandt & G. VandenBos (Eds.), *The adult years: Continuity and change* (pp. 41–78). Washington, DC: American Psychological Association.

Costa, P. T., McCrae, R. R., & Arenberg, D. (1983). Recent longitudinal research on personality and aging. In K. W. Schaie (Ed.), *Longitudinal studies of adult psychological development* (pp. 222–265), New York: Guilford Press.

Cross, K. P. (1981). *Adults as learners.* San Francisco: Jossey-Bass.

Datan, N., Rodeheaver, D., & Hughes, F. (1987). Adult development and aging. *Annual Review of Psychology, 38,* 153–180.

Demos, J. (1986). *Past, present and personal: The family and the life course in American history.* New York: Oxford University Press.

Downing, N. E., & Rousch, K. L. (1985). From passive acceptance to active commitment: A model of feminist identity development for women. *The Counseling Psychologist, 13,* 695–709.

Ehrenreich, B., & English, D. (1979). *For her own good: 150 years of the experts' advice to women.* Garden City, NY: Anchor Books.

Enns, C. Z. (1991). The "new" relationship models of women's identity: A review and critique for counselors. *Journal of Counseling and Development, 69,* 209–217.

Erikson, E. H. (1950). *Childhood and society.* New York: Norton.

Fassinger, R. E. (1987). Use of structural equation modeling in counseling psychology research. *Journal of Counseling Psychology, 34,* 425–436.

Fassinger, R. E. (1991). The hidden minority: Issues and challenges in working with lesbian women and gay men. *The Counseling Psychologist, 19,* 157–176.

Finch, J. E. C. (1989). *A qualitative paradigm reflecting potential themes in the lives of rural women at midlife.* Unpublished doctoral dissertation, University of South Dakota.

Fiske, M., & Chiriboga, D. A. (1990). *Change and continuity in adult life.* San Francisco: Jossey-Bass.

Ganikos, M., & Blake, R. (1984). Counseling the aged. [Special issue]. *The Counseling Psychologist, 12.*

Gatz, M., Popkin, S. J., Pino, C. D., & VandenBos, G. R. (1985). Psychological interventions with older adults. In J. E. Birren & K. W. Schaie (Eds.), *Handbook of the psychology of aging* (2nd ed.) (pp. 755–785). New York: Van Nostrand Reinhold.

Gelso, C. J., & Fassinger, R. E. (1990). Counseling psychology: Theory and research on interventions. *Annual Review of Psychology, 41,* 355–386.

Gilligan, C. (1982). *In a different voice.* Cambridge, MA: Harvard University Press.

Gooden, W. E. (1989). Development of Black men in early adulthood. In R. L. Jones (Ed.), *Black adult development and aging* (pp. 63–90). Berkeley, CA: Cobb & Henry.

Gutmann, D. L. (1987). *Reclaimed powers: Toward a new psychology of men and women in later life.* New York: Basic Books.

Hagestad, G. O. (1985). Vertical bonds: Intergenerational relationships. In N. K. Schlossberg (Ed.), *The adult years: Continuity and change* (pp. 133–166). International University Consortium and Ohio University, Columbia, MD.

Hagestad, G. O., & Neugarten, B. I. (1985). Age and the life course. In R. Binstock & E. Shanas (Eds.), *Handbook of aging and the social sciences* (2nd ed.). New York: Van Nostrand Reinhold.

Hareven, T. K. (1982). The life course and aging in historical perspective. In T. K. Hareven & K. J. Adams (Eds.), *Aging and life course transitions: An interdisciplinary perspective* (pp. 1–26). New York: Guilford Press.

Harris, R. L., Ellicott, A. M., & Holmes, D. S. (1986). The timing of psychosocial transitions and changes in women's lives: An examination of women aged 45 to 60. *Journal of Personality and Social Psychology, 51,* 409–416.

Helms, J. E. (1985). Cultural identity in the treatment process. In P. Pedersen (Ed.), *Handbook of cross-cultural counseling and therapy* (pp. 239–246), Westport, CT: Greenwood Press.

Helms, J. E. (1990). *Black and White racial identity: Theory, research and practice.* New York: Greenwood Press.

Highlen, P. S., Reynolds, A. L., Adams, E. M., Hanely, T. C., Myers, L. J., Cox, C., & Speight, S. (1988, August). *Self-identity development model of oppressed people: Inclusive model for all?* Paper presented at the annual meeting of the American Psychological Association, Atlanta, GA.

Hiner, N. R. (1985). Adults in historical perspective. In N. K. Schlossberg (Ed.), *The adult years: Continuity and change* (pp. 47–73). International University Consortium and Ohio University. Columbia, MD.

Jackson, M. (1989). Life control theory: A perspective on Black attitudes toward death and dying. In R. L. Jones (Ed.), *Black adult development and aging* (pp. 375–388). Berkeley, CA: Cobb & Henry.

Josselson, R. (1987). *Finding herself: Pathways to identity development in women.* San Francisco: Jossey-Bass.

Kagan, J. (1980). Perspectives on continuity. In O. G. Brim, Jr. & J. Kagan (Eds.), *Constancy and change in human development* (pp. 26–74). Cambridge, MA: Harvard University Press.

Kanter, R. M. (1977). *Men and women of the corporation.* New York: Basic Books.

Kastenbaum, R. (1965). Dying and death: A lifespan approach. In J. E. Birren & K. W. Schaie (Eds.), *Handbook of the psychology of aging* (2nd ed.) (pp. 619–646). New York: Van Nostrand Reinhold.

Kaye, L. W., & Applegate, J. S. (1990). *Men as caregivers to the elderly.* Lexington, MA: Lexington Books.

Kegan, R. (1982). *The evolving self.* Cambridge, MA: Harvard University Press.

Kohlberg, L. (1981). *The philosophy of moral development.* San Francisco: Harper & Row.

Kohn, M. L. (1980). Job complexity and adult personality. In N. J. Smelser & E. H. Erikson (Eds.), *Themes of work and love in adulthood* (pp. 193–210). Cambridge, MA: Harvard University Press.

Labouvie-Vief, G. (1982). Individual time, social time, and intellectual aging. In T. K. Hareven & K. J. Adams (Eds.), *Aging and life course transitions: An interdisciplinary perspective* (pp. 151–182). New York: Guilford Press.

Labouvie-Vief, G. (1985). Intelligence and cognition. In J. E. Birren & K. W. Schaie (Eds.), *Handbook of the psychology of aging* (2nd ed.) (pp. 500–530). New York: Van Nostrand Reinhold.

Labouvie-Vief, G. (1986). Modes of knowledge and the organization of development. In M. L. Commons, L. Kohlberg, F. A. Richards, & J. Sinnott (Eds.), *Beyond formal operations 3: Models and methods in the study of adult and adolescent thought.* New York: Praeger.

Lacayo, C. G. (1984). Hispanics. In E. B. Palmore (Ed.), *Handbook on the aged in the United States* (pp. 253–267). Westport, CT: Greenwood Press.

Lazarus, R. S., & Folkman, S. (1984). *Stress, appraisal, and coping.* New York: Springer.

Levinson, D. J., Darrow, C. N., Klein, E. B., Levinson, M. H., & McLee, B. (1978). *The seasons of a man's life.* New York: Knopf.

Levinson, D. J. (1986). A conception of adult development. *American Psychologist, 41,* 3–13.

Loevinger, J. (1976). *Ego development: Conceptions and theories.* San Francisco: Jossey-Bass.

Lowenthal, M. F., Thurnher, M., & Chiriboga, D. (1975). *Four stages of life: A comparative study of men and women facing transitions.* San Francisco: Jossey-Bass.

Malatesta, C. Z., & Izard, C. E. (Eds.). (1984). *Emotion in adult development.* Beverly Hills: Sage.

Marcia, J. E. (1966). Development and validation of ego identity status. *Journal of Personality and Social Psychology, 3,* 551–558.

Mayer, K. U., & Schoepflin, U. (1989). The state and the life course. *Annual Review of Sociology, 15,* 187–209.

Mazur, E. (1989). Predicting gender differences in same-sex friendships from affiliation motive and value. *Psychology of Women Quarterly, 13,* 277–291.

McEwen, M. K., Roper, L. D., Bryant, D. R., & Langa, M. J. (1990). Incorporating the development of African-American students into psychosocial theories of student development. *Journal of College Student Development, 31,* 429–436.

Mutran, E. (1985). Intergenerational family support among blacks and whites: Response to culture or to socioeconomic differences? *Journal of Gerontology, 40,* 382–389.

Myers, J. E. (Ed.). (1990). *Techniques for counseling older persons.* [Special issue]. *Journal of Mental Health Counseling, 12,* 245–392.

Nesselroade, J. R., & Labouvie, E. W. (1985). Experimental design in research on aging. In J. E. Birren & K. W. Schaie (Eds.), *Handbook of the psychology of aging* (2nd ed.) (pp. 36–60). New York: Van Nostrand Reinhold.

Neugarten, B. L. (1982, August). *Successful aging.* Paper presented at the Annual Meeting of the American Psychological Association, Washington, DC.

Neugarten, B. L., & Neugarten, D. A. (1987). The changing meanings of age. *Psychology Today, 21,* 29–33.

Neugarten, B. L., & Neugarten, D. A. (1989). Policy issues in an aging society. In M. Storandt & A. R. VandenBos (Eds.), *The adult years: Continuity and change* (pp. 143–167). Washington, DC: American Psychological Association.

Pearlin, L. I. (1980). Life strains and psychological distress among adults. In N. J. Smelser & E. H. Erikson (Eds.), *Themes of work and love in adulthood* (pp. 174–192). Cambridge, MA: Harvard University Press.

Pearlin, L. I. (1982). Discontinuities in the study of aging. In T. K. Hareven & K. J. Adams (Eds.), *Aging and life course transitions: An interdisciplinary perspective.* New York: Guilford Press.

Peck, T. A. (1986). Women's self-definition in adulthood: From a different model? *Psychology of Women Quarterly, 10,* 274–284.

Perry, W. G. (1970). *Forms of intellectual and ethical development in the college years.* New York: Holt, Reinhart and Winston.

Plath, D. W. (1982). Resistance at forty-eight: Old-age brinksmanship and Japanese life course pathways. In T. K. Hareven & K. J. Adams (Eds.), *Aging and life course transitions: An interdisciplinary perspective* (pp. 109–125). New York: Guilford Press.

Roberts, P., & Newton, P. M. (1987). Levinsonian studies of women's adult development. *Psychology and Aging, 2,* 154–163.

Rosenbaum, J. E. (1979). Tournament mobility: Career patterns in a corporation. *Administrative Science Quarterly, 24,* 220–241.

Rosenmayr, L. (1985). Changing values and positions of aging in Western culture. In J. E. Birren & K. W. Schaie (Eds.), *Handbook of the psychology of aging* (2nd ed.) (pp. 190–215). New York: Van Nostrand Reinhold.

Ross, D. B. (1984). A cross-cultural comparison of adult development. *Personnel and Guidance Journal, 62,* 418–421.

Rubin, L. B. (1985). *Just friends: The role of friendship in our lives.* New York: Harper & Row.

Rubin, R. H., & Macklin, E. D. (Eds.). (1983). *Contemporary families and alternative lifestyles.* Beverly Hills: Sage.

Ruffin, J. E. (1989). Stages of adult development in Black professional women. In R. L. Jones (Ed.), *Black adult development and aging* (pp. 31–62). Berkeley, CA: Cobb & Henry.

Ryff, C. D. (1989). In the eye of the beholder: Views of psychological well-being among middle-aged and older adults. *Psychology and Aging, 4,* 195–210.

Salthouse, T. (1989). Age-related changes in basic cognitive processes. In M. Storandt & G. R. VandenBos (Eds.), *The adult years: Continuity and change* (pp. 5–40). Washington, DC: American Psychological Association.

Schaie, K. W. (1983). What can we learn from the longitudinal study of adult psychological development? In K. W. Schaie (Ed.), *Longitudinal studies of adult psychological development.* New York: Guilford Press.

Schaie, K. W., & Hertzog, C. (1985). Measurement in the psychology of adulthood and aging. In J. E. Birren & K. W. Schaie (Eds.), *Handbook of the psychology of aging* (2nd ed.) (pp. 61–94). New York: Van Nostrand Reinhold.

Scheidt, R. J., & Windley, P. G. (1985). The ecology of aging. In J. E. Birren & K. W. Schaie (Eds.), *Handbook of the psychology of aging* (2nd ed.) (pp. 245–260). New York: Van Nostrand Reinhold.

Schlossberg, N. K. (1984a). *Counseling adults in transition.* New York: Springer.

Schlossberg, N. K. (1984b). Exploring the adult years. In A. M. Rogers & C. J. Scheirer (Eds.), *The G. Stanley Hall Lecture Series* (Vol. 4, pp. 101–154). Washington, DC: American Psychological Association.

Schlossberg, N. K. (1989). *Overwhelmed: Coping with life's ups and downs.* Lexington, MA: Lexington Books.

Schlossberg, N. K., & Leibowitz, Z. B. (1988). *Caught in between: Issues of adult development.* NBC-TV Knowledge Series, produced and originally aired in Washington, DC.

Schultz, R. (1985). Emotion and affect. In J. E. Birren & K. W. Schaie (Eds.), *Handbook of the psychology of aging* (2nd ed.) (pp. 531–543). New York: Van Nostrand Reinhold.

Stevens-Long, J. (1988). *Adult life* (3rd ed.). Mountain View, CA: Mayfield.

Stewart, A. J., & Healy, J. M. (1989). Linking individual development and social changes. *American Psychologist, 44,* 30–42.

Taylor, R. J., & Chatters, L. M. (1989). Family, friend, and church support networks of Black Americans. In R. P. Jones (Ed.), *Black adult development and aging* (pp. 245–272). Berkeley, CA: Cobb & Henry.

Terman, L. M., & Oden, M. (1959). *Genetic studies of genius: Vol. 5. The gifted group at midlife.* Stanford, CA: Stanford University Press.

Troll, L. E. (1982). *Continuations: Adult development and aging.* Monterey, CA: Brooks/Cole.

Vaillant, G. E. (1977). *Adaptations to life.* Boston: Little, Brown.

Vaillant, G. E. (1982, May). *Maturity over the life cycle.* Paper presented at the meeting of the Helpers of Adults, College Park, MD.

Vaillant, G. E., & Vaillant, C. O. (1990). Determinants and consequences of creativity in a cohort of gifted women. *Psychology of Women Quarterly, 14,* 607–616.

Whitbourne, S. (1985). The psychological construction of the life span. In J. E. Birren & K. W. Schaie (Eds.), *Handbook of the psychology of aging* (2nd ed.) (pp. 594–618). New York: Van Nostrand Reinhold.

Whitbourne, S. K., & Hulicka, I. M. (1990). Ageism in undergraduate psychology texts. *American Psychologist, 45,* 1127–1136.

Willis, S. L. (1985). Towards an educational psychology of the older adult learner: Intellectual and cognitive bases. In J. E. Birren & K. W. Schaie (Eds.), *Handbook of the psychology of aging* (2nd ed.) (pp. 818–847). New York: Van Nostrand Reinhold.

Wrightsman, L. S. (1988). *Personality development in adulthood.* Newbury Park, CA: Sage.

CHAPTER 8
FAMILY DYNAMICS AND LATE ADOLESCENT IDENTITY DEVELOPMENT

FREDERICK G. LOPEZ

> . . . *Your children are not your children.*
> *They are the sons and daughters of Life's longing for itself.*
> *They come through you but not from you,*
> *And though they are with you yet they belong not to you.*
> *You may give them your love but not your thoughts.*
> *For they have their own thoughts.*
> *You may house their bodies but not their souls,*
> *For their souls dwell in the house of tomorrow, which you*
> *cannot visit, not even in your dreams* . . . .
>
> From The Prophet *by Kahlil Gibran*

> *In building a life of our own, we challenge our family's myths and roles—and, of course, we challenge the rigid rules of childhood. For leaving home will not become an emotional reality until we stop seeing the world through our parents' eyes.*
>
> From Necessary Losses *by Judith Viorst*

Together, these observations speak to a unique human drama—the separation and individuation of the young adult identity—and the important transformation it demands of the parent–child relationship. What do we know about this transformation? How is it achieved? How is it impeded? How does it contribute to identity formation?

Although counseling psychologists have historically been concerned with normal human development and adjustment, particularly that of late adolescents and young adults, our appreciation of identity development as an active relationship process is only in its infancy. In order to explain this outcome, we must recognize that our preferred theories and research models have been saddled by some common epistemological constraints. For instance, our theories have generally focused attention on what is presumably happening within the individual. Contextual variables, when they are considered at all, are typically assumed to exert antecedent and unidirectional influences on the development of self.

Similarly, our traditional research models have been designed to reduce complex patterns and sequences to discrete elements and to posit causal arrows from one

element to another. Their ability to describe and measure bidirectional influences—
that is, when causal arrows may be going in opposite directions simultaneously to
produce a particular phenomenon—is inherently deficient and hence of limited value
in capturing the complexities of human transactions (Bronfenbrenner, 1979; Vondracek, Lerner, & Schulenberg, 1983).

These constraints have largely shaped our common ways of knowing, which are to
consider "figure" and "ground" separately, as though their interrelatedness was of little
consequence. Not surprisingly, our understanding of the contemporaneous influence of
family dynamics on late adolescent functioning has regrettably been neglected, despite
the widely held view that the family serves as the primary context for identity development. In particular, these limitations predispose us to accept individual (intrapsychic)
explanations of identity disturbance and developmental difficulties before considering
the interactional significance that particular dysfunctions may have within a person's
immediate family context, or how the larger person–context relationship may operate to
provoke, minimize, or maintain these disturbances. This bias, in turn, restricts our
clinical abilities to "see" problem patterns in close relationships and correspondingly
limits our capacities to devise interventions that promote individual change via relationship change.

Fortunately, significant advances have been made recently in the formulation of
systemic models of individual and family behavior—models that, among other things,
offer a distinct perspective on the process underlying late adolescent identity development by considering the impact of immediate family dynamics on individual adjustment. This paradigmatic shift, stimulated by the adoption of a cybernetic epistemology
(Bateson, 1979; Keeney, 1983), has opened up new conceptual possibilities for deepen-
ing our understanding of the complex human process that eventuates in the adolescent's
successful transition into early adult life.

This is not to say, however, that the earlier, pioneering work of theoreticians and
researchers of adolescent identity development will now or should soon pass from our
view. Quite the contrary: the careful crafting that went into personological models of
identity formation and individuation continues to offer us useful descriptions and
explanations of what may be happening *within* the adolescent as the individuation
process is engaged. An equally careful consideration of the family context in which
this intrapsychic process is embedded should, by illuminating the larger stage and
supporting cast, enrich and not diminish this story. More importantly, the coexistence
of these distinct views of the same phenomenon should stimulate present and future
generations of scholars to search further for those "patterns which connect" (Bateson,
1979) human development and change as it unfolds at the individual, familial, and
societal levels of organization.

The primary purpose of this chapter is to selectively review and critique research on
the role of family dynamics in late adolescent individuation and identity formation and
to consider some of its implications for counseling practice. To begin, I attempt to
define and discuss important constructs that form the larger topic of identity development. Then, some key psychodynamic theories of late adolescent identity development
are summarized and, wherever possible, assumptions, propositions, and constructs that
may speak to important aspects of parent–adolescent process are highlighted. Several
prominent family models of the same phenomenon are then introduced and more fully
described; an overview and critique of current research on the relation of family dynamics to late adolescent identity development and adjustment follow. The final sections of the chapter focus on the implications of these findings for counseling practice
and for future theory development and research.

INDIVIDUATION AND IDENTITY: TOWARD AN INITIAL CLARIFICATION OF CONSTRUCTS

The means by which human beings come to understand *who* they are and *how* they are unique and separate from others have been the focal point of psychology's long-standing interest in identity formation and development. Indeed, many established theories in our discipline hold that the adequate unfolding of this process is the sine qua non of psychological well-being and adjustment. It is generally assumed that the quest for selfhood begins at our earliest moments and continues throughout our lifetime; however, a crucial crossroads is reached at late adolescence.

In contemporary Western society, it is during late adolescence that the adequacy of our progress toward identity formation faces its first significant challenge. As we stand at the intersection of adolescence and young adulthood, we are expected to make adultlike decisions and to be responsible for them. Should we continue with our education? Should we work? Marry? Leave home? What should we do? What exactly do we believe? These are among the many burning questions of this period that test the mettle of our self-understanding.

Efforts to describe the journey that has brought us to this crossroads and that may predict our subsequent progress (or lack thereof) have been organized around the constructs of "individuation" and "identity." Persons who successfully advance through this period and pursue the developmental tasks of young adulthood are said to have "individuated" and formed a clear "identity."

The construct of "individuation" refers to the social, relational dialectic that permits self-formation and revision. Karpel (1976), for example, noted: "Individuation involves the subtle but crucial phenomenological shifts by which a person comes to see him/herself as separate and distinct within the relational context in which s/he is embedded" (p. 67). Individuation, then, is a particular form of self-reflection—one in which important self–other distinctions are gradually considered as informative of both our emergent sense of wholeness and our experience of separateness within the wider social network. It speaks to a complex and evolving sociodevelopmental process that furnishes us with novel fragments of self-awareness on which to construct a new self-understanding.

During infancy, our eventual recognition that a primary caregiver exists as an entity separate from our own continuous and undifferentiated experiencing marks the first significant individuation. It is a necessary distinction for the formation of a rudimentary self-concept. Individuation activity must proceed and produce many other self-percepts if the child is ultimately to achieve an autonomous and functional sense of "self." It is therefore advantageous to view individuation, not as a process limited to a particular phase of human development, but rather as a powerful activity that runs the course of the life cycle and that may set the stage for significant changes in self-understanding.

The construct of "identity," on the other hand, represents the consolidation and exposition of those aspects of self that have acquired their autonomy through the individuation process. For example, Josselson (1980) argued that identity formation "goes beyond the tasks of individuation and of the reorganization of internal experience" and is characterized by a "public declaration of the self that the individual intends to be taken seriously." Similarly, Marcia (1980) suggested that identity is both an existential self-view as well as a particular "sociopolitical stance"—in other words, "identity" describes the presence of coordinated belief–action sequences that effectively display the person's sense of separateness and differentness within the wider social surround. The construct of identity is thus more closely tied to the individual's purposeful efforts to integrate and represent his or her reorganized internal experience of self to others.

Another common thread in these perspectives of identity is the implication that identity formation is facilitated when both the individual and his or her social network realign themselves to permit and affirm the former's revised expression of self. The significance of late adolescence is that this period is marked by the confluence of such interdependent personal and social forces seeking mutual accommodation.

This presumed interdependency also suggests that identity and individuation are recursively joined processes: an increase in identity formation, while preceded and facilitated by individuation, can itself provoke further individuation of other aspects of self that in turn may serve to bolster and stabilize the emergent self-reorganization (Josselson, 1980). This integrative view is further elaborated in the epilogue to this chapter. At this juncture, however, it may be most appropriate to overview several existing psychodynamic perspectives of adolescent identity development.

PSYCHODYNAMIC PERSPECTIVES ON LATE ADOLESCENT IDENTITY DEVELOPMENT

Virtually all traditional and contemporary psychodynamic perspectives on adolescent identity development can trace their ideological roots to the seminal writings of Freud. Curiously, however, Freud himself offered few insights on human development beyond the latency period, a neglect that later compelled his daughter Anna to comment that the study of adolescence was a "stepchild" in psychoanalytic theory (Freud, 1958). Thus, efforts to employ Freudian theory in the explanation of adolescent identity development required that psychoanalytic concepts and assumptions be extended and revised in order to facilitate navigation through this largely unchartered terrain. This section summarizes the perspectives offered by several of these significant expeditions, making particular note of observations and speculations that may speak to relevant relationship processes.

The Recrudescence of the Oedipal Conflict

A core assumption of Freudian theory is that human adjustment is predicated on the ego's increasing capacity to free and to cathect (fix) libidinal energy in socially adaptive ways. The ego's adoption of more sophisticated and effective means of expressing and defending against instinctual wishes and impulses is a progressive development whose course is shaped primarily by the adequacy of earlier efforts at the same basic task. Unsuccessful or partially successful efforts are characterized by the adoption of less sophisticated, more primitive modes of ego defense requiring more costly expenditures of psychic energy, thus rendering the entire personality structure more vulnerable to particular stresses. When those stresses occur, the individual is expected to demonstrate a *regression* toward the use of these primitive defenses as the means of coping with the internal psychic struggle and to symbolically recapitulate the original, unresolved conflict.

Perhaps the most critical drama of the entire Freudian scenario is the child's confrontation and resolution of the oedipal dilemma during the genital stage of psychosexual development. During this period, the emergence and coexistence of powerful sexual feelings and longings for the opposite-sex parent, along with equally powerful fears of retribution from the same-sex parent, provoke, in most cases, the child's identification with the latter as the primary means of conflict resolution and adaptation. To arrive at the identification "solution," the child internalizes (introjects) parental values, standards, and expectations as part of his or her emergent *ego ideal,* a psychic structure that then serves as a needed internal control for curbing these libidinal wishes and impulses. This achievement, in turn, promotes the child's effective entry into the latency stage by liberating psychic resources to develop the ego ideal, thus further differentiating ego functioning.

Venturing more deeply into the territory of adolescence, Anna Freud (1958) reasoned that toward the end of the latency period the advent of puberty ushers in a new wave of libidinal forces that reawaken infantile object ties and threaten existing ego defenses. Because the internalized *parent image* acquired during the previous phase is now inadequate to stem the instinctual tide of adolescence, the individual must rework the original oedipal conflict to arrive at a more sophisticated defense. As part of this struggle, he or she may withdraw libido from parents and transfer it to others (parent substitutes, leaders, peers) or demonstrate a reversal of affect (love to hate, dependence to revolt). In salutary outcomes, this process leads once again to the incorporation of a more mature and differentiated ego ideal that is no longer anchored by the internalized parent. However, individuals for whom the original oedipal resolution was itself flawed would be expected to demonstrate less salutary outcomes, evidenced by the regressive use of more primitive defenses and accompanied by the loss of ego boundaries. Regardless of outcome, it is noteworthy that, according to this perspective, the person's internalized image of parents must be assailed and revised if the adolescent is to achieve a more mature level of defense and adjustment.

Commenting further on the traditional psychodynamic view of adolescence, Adelson and Doehrman (1980) noted that the regressive and unstable forces of this era draw the adolescent closer to the family as he or she oscillates between feelings of closeness and flight. These authors also acknowledged that these dynamics are not without their *interactional* consequences when they observed that "the child's coming into maturity will often evoke equally strong regressive feelings in the parents. The child's nubility may awaken conflicted, unconscious emotions of rivalry and desire along with a sense of time's passing and the waning of one's own power and beauty" (p. 105).

A "Second Individuation" Model of Adolescent Identity Formation

A major extension of Freudian theory to the study of late adolescent process was offered by Peter Blos (1979). Blos drew on important work on object relations during infancy and early childhood (Mahler, 1963; Mahler, Pine, & Bergman, 1975), which proposed that early child ego development was predicated on a significant individuation process occurring within the mother–infant relationship. During this individuation process, the child's psychic organization moves progressively from a poorly differentiated state to a transitional state of fusion or symbiosis with the mother, and culminates, around 3 years of age, with the achievement of sufficient self- and object constancy to permit greater internal self-regulation, physical separation from the mother, and pursuit of independent activities. Parenthetically, the view that the child's "secure attachment" with the mother and with the family in general serves to advance healthy separation–individuation processes has also been extensively developed by other theorists (Ainsworth, 1989; Bowlby, 1982).

Consistent with the traditional view, Blos proposed that adolescence initiates a "second individuation" process that, in several respects, parallels the dynamics of the "first individuation" described by Mahler. During the second individuation, the adolescent is attempting to achieve separateness from the internalized parental objects that were formed during the latency period via identification and superego development. As part of the ensuing struggle, the adolescent is forced to wrestle with observed discrepancies between idealized and more realistic views of parents and to search for new internal controls for regulating emotional equilibrium (self-esteem). Departing from the traditional view, however, Blos asserted that the emergence of regressive behavior during this transition was not indicative of a flawed process but instead could be in "the service of" normal human development. The regressive movements of adolescence are expectable responses to the confusing task of revising obsolete parental representations while, at the same time, experiencing the same real-life parents in everyday encounters.

The interpersonal consequence of the adolescent's shifting images of parents is relationship behavior that may oscillate erratically between stable and impulsive positions. In a further elaboration of the traditional view, Blos (1979) suggested that *how parents respond* to these oscillations may influence the progress of this period. In particular, he contended that normal adolescent "confusion is worsened whenever the parent participates in the shifting positions of the adolescent and proves unable to maintain the fixed position as the adult vis-à-vis the maturing child" (p. 166).

The successful resolution of this period is marked by the adolescent's "shedding of family dependencies" and achieving a capacity for maintaining a "narcissistic balance" that is not dependent on conformity to the demands of the oedipal superego and, by association, to the demands of previously introjected parental objects. Indeed, it is the disengagement from internalized (family) love and hate objects that enables the adolescent to pursue external (extrafamilial) love objects.

"Mirroring" and the Ascendance of a "Cohesive Self"

A contemporary psychodynamic perspective on adolescent identity development can be found in Heinz Kohut's "psychology of the self." In many respects, Kohut's formulations (Kohut, 1971, 1977) represented a more radical departure from the Freudian doctrine than did Blos's. For Kohut, the "self" was not a specialized ego component but rather the initiating center of the person whose growth was synchronized with the development of narcissism, or the individual's capacity for self-expression. According to Kohut, narcissism evolves along two dimensions, grandiosity and idealization. Grandiosity refers to the developing person's natural desire to express his or her distinctiveness and power vis-à-vis important others; idealization refers to the equally natural impulse to merge with the perceived perfection of powerful others. According to Kohut, the infantile self consists of two self-objects, the "grandiose self" and the "idealized parental image" (Lapan & Patton, 1986).

Progress along the grandiosity dimension is marked by movement from infantile exhibitionism to greater self-assertion and finally to mature ambition; progress along the idealization dimension evidences a transition from infantile wishes to merge with "omnipotent" parents to admiration of others and concludes with the adoption of a mature system of goal-setting ideals. The concomitant development of these naturally occurring self-expressive trends promotes the emergence of a "cohesive self." Disorders of the self, on the other hand, represent an underlying lack of self-cohesion and a corresponding vulnerability to threats to self-esteem. They are the product of inadequate development on one or both dimensions. Elaborating on the Kohutian position, Robbins and Patton (1985) stated that "without a firm sense of self . . . the person lacks the capacity to empathize fully with others, is extremely vulnerable to criticism, separation, and loss, and cannot formulate realistic life plans or sustain the striving necessary to implement them" (p. 222).

More so than Blos, Kohut emphasized the significant role that parents play as "self-objects" responsible for "mirroring," or selectively attending to and reinforcing, the child's idealizing projections. Indeed, Kohut attributed the origins of self-disorders to the chronic failure of parents in fulfilling these critical empathic functions. Such persistent parenting failures leave the child fixated at less mature, more vulnerable levels of self-development. The child then requires excessive dependence on others to maintain self-esteem or excessive reliance on defensive strategies for protecting it.

This is not to say that parental empathy must be constant and continuous in order for normal development to proceed. To the contrary, it is the "inevitable and phase-appropriate lapses in parental empathy [which] promote the gradual breakup of the infantile objects and their [eventual] reconsolidation . . . into mature, reality-based percepts" (Lapan & Patton, 1986, p. 136). For Kohut, it was not the onset of puberty but rather a change in the self caused by a transformation of the ego ideal that set the psychodynamic processes of adolescence into motion. In essence, the adolescent's increasing disillusionment with parents catalyzes both the dismantling of the ego ideal and the pursuit of a new ideal. It is through this generative process that transformations of the self occur. The primary task of adolescence is thus the consolidation of a new "cohesive self."

Identity and the Psychosocial Crisis of Adolescence

Perhaps the most influential of all psychodynamic perspectives on adolescent identity development is contained in Erikson's psychosocial theory of human development (Erikson, 1968). Erikson asserted that the traditional psychoanalytic view was inadequate to grasp the concept of identity because it had not conceptualized the environment as a "persuasive actuality." Erikson argued further that the complex interplay of psychological, social, historical, and developmental forces during the adolescent period was best conceptualized as a form of "psychosocial relativity," which prompts the individual to search for, consolidate, and affirm a sense of self.

In response to the conceptual limitations of traditional views, Erikson proposed the existence of eight hierarchically arranged life stages, each incorporating a set of unique developmental conflicts and tasks that must be confronted. These stages unfold in an invariant sequence and according to a timetable shaped by both biological and social forces. Each stage presents the person with a new "psychosocial crisis" that must be addressed whether or not earlier stage conflicts have been satisfactorily resolved; conflict resolution at one stage is in part a function of the individual's history of resolving previous stage conflicts. For Erikson, the degree and direction of conflict resolution determined the overall health of the personality.

In the Eriksonian schema, adolescence is characterized as a distinct life stage—a period of "psychological moratorium"—whose central developmental task is the formation of an identity. As part of this formative activity, the person "employs a process of simultaneous reflection and observation . . . of what he perceives to be the way in which others judge him . . . [and] how he perceives himself in comparison to them" (Erikson, 1968, pp. 23–24). The successful synthesis of this dialectical task (stage 5) is the achievement of a positive and stable "identity" or, in other words, a coherent and purposeful self-definition. This achievement facilitates the later engagement and resolution of the tasks of young adulthood, most prominently the establishment of *intimacy* (stage 6). On the other hand, a failure to master the necessary tasks and conflicts of adolescence will result in identity confusion and contribute to the individual's pervasive sense of paralysis when faced with subsequent demands for commitment to occupational choices, intimate relationships, and an ideological world view.

An "Identity Status" Model

Among the most notable and sustained efforts to operationalize, evaluate, and refine Erikson's concepts of adolescent identity formation has been the work of Marcia and his colleagues (Marcia, 1966, 1976, 1980; Orlofsky, Marcia, & Lesser, 1973; Schiedel & Marcia, 1985). Marcia (1966) reasoned that individual outcomes of the developmental tasks of adolescence can take one of four distinct forms, each resulting in a different identity status. Persons classified as *identity-achieved* are described as having undergone a crisis period and emerged committed to an occupation and ideology; individuals in the *moratorium* status are currently in a crisis period and actively struggling to make commitments. Persons in a *foreclosure* status have avoided the experience of crisis by prematurely and uncritically committing themselves to goals and values that have been espoused by significant others, usually parents; and *identity-diffused* persons have neither entered a crisis period nor made significant commitments.

Utilizing a procedure that incorporated both a semistructured interview and an incomplete sentences blank, Marcia (1966) presented results that were generally supportive of predictions from his four-status model and of his interview method of assessing identity status. For example, he anticipated that foreclosures—those individuals who had made personal commitments without having entered and emerged from a "crisis"—would be "extremely threatened" if faced with a performance "situation in which parental values were nonfunctional"; as expected, these subjects performed poorly on most task variables.

Summary of Psychodynamic Perspectives and a Comment on Current Research

This section summarizes key commonalities and divergences among the selected psychodynamic perspectives on adolescent identity formation; it also comments briefly on findings from current empirical research that has been guided by these theories. Finally, the limitations of these perspectives in describing how identity development is facilitated or impeded by ongoing relationship dynamics are discussed.

Certainly, one common theme in all of the above perspectives is that adolescence is a period of significant psychological change. Moreover, with the exception of Kohut, these theorists pointed to the biological imperatives of puberty as being either primarily or partially responsible for destabilizing earlier psychic structures and thus provoking the need for more differentiated ego functioning or self-transformation. Although the theories differ in their appraisals of how tumultuous these changes are, there seems to be little argument that adaptive errors can and do occur and that they are reflected in observable adjustment difficulties during this period. It is noteworthy that every study of adolescent development that has employed a representative (i.e., nonclinical) sample has failed to support the more tumultuous view of adolescence implied by orthodox Freudian doctrine (Adelson & Doehrman, 1980).

Relevant to the latter point, there is an important difference between traditional and contemporary psychodynamic views regarding the nature and role of "regression" in the adolescent's experience. Freudian theory holds that the appearance of regression signals the presence of a defect in the underlying psychic structure. The formulations of Blos and of Erikson, on the other hand, argue that regression during this time is not necessarily pathological and may indeed be instrumental to ego/identity development. Kohut appears to fall midway between these positions, although he may be somewhat more traditionally aligned on this issue.

Perhaps more central to the present discussion are the different theoretical emphases placed on the function of interpersonal (family) relationships in expediting the psychological changes of adolescence. Although Freud and his disciples were sensitive to the powerful shaping influence of early parent–child attachments, traditional psychodynamic theory does not grant a key role to *current* parent–adolescent relationships in the presumed reworking of the oedipal conflict near the end of the latency phase. In addition, this perspective assumes that the successful "termination" of infantile object ties during this period should propel the adolescent ego well beyond the orbit of parental influence.

Toeing the traditional line, Blos also saw the second individuation resulting in a "shedding of family dependencies." Erikson, while acknowledging the larger familial, social, and cultural pressures on identity formation, also focused predominantly on individual changes over time and tended to regard the social context as a relevant but undifferentiated background factor. Kohut, on the other hand, called some specific attention to the significant, ongoing roles parents play throughout the course of self-development in "mirroring" the child's age-appropriate grandiosity and in serving as functional "self-objects" for their offspring's idealizing projections.

These various perspectives appear to be in general agreement when they contend that, barring significant impairment, the important intrapsychic work of adolescence should result in improved emotional self-regulation, less dependence on parental and other authority figures, better reality-testing and perspective-taking capabilities, more differentiated and self-referential thinking, and greater confidence and competence in personal decision making. In short, these theories explicitly or implicitly assume that the hypothesized changes in the adolescent's psychic organization should have important cognitive, affective, phenomenological, and behavioral manifestations associated with more adult functioning.

There has been observable variation in the heuristic value of the traditional and more contemporary theories. As Robbins (1989) noted, empirical tests of hypotheses from psychoanalytic theory have been woefully lacking or confined to single case study designs. The work of Silverman and others, identifying positive relations between subliminal activation of unconscious wishes and adaptive behavior, was an exception (see Silverman & Weinberger's 1985 review), although this work has been the target of criticism (Balay & Shevrin, 1988).

Recently, Kohut's theory of the self stimulated an important line of research within counseling psychology (Lapan & Patton, 1986; Patton, Connor, & Scott, 1982; Robbins & Patton, 1985; Robbins & Tucker, 1985). These investigations largely focused on the development and validation of scales to measure the concepts of grandiosity and idealization. Robbins and Patton (1985), for example, reported that both of these scales were significant predictors of the level of career decidedness among college students.

Erikson's notions of adolescent identity development, and particularly Marcia's four-status identity model, have received the most research attention among the psychodynamic approaches. In his review of this substantial literature, Waterman (1982) concluded that "the basic hypothesis embodied in Erikson's theory—that movement from adolescence to adulthood involves changes in identity that can be characterized as progressive developmental shifts—fares very well in empirical studies" (p. 355). Waterman specifically observed that, with the exception of the moratorium status, Marcia's other identity statuses were relatively stable over the high school years, that the greatest gains in identity formation appeared to occur during the college years, and that, despite the absence of overall sex differences with regard to identity achievement, men and women appeared to differ in their pattern of interstatus similarities. Among men, identity achievers and moratoriums shared many commonalities and both were distinctive from their peers in the other status categories. Among women, identity-achieved and foreclosed individuals looked more similar on some qualities; on other dimensions, identity-achievers and moratoriums showed greater similarity.

Additionally, Waterman noted that foreclosed subjects were found to have the "closest" relationships with their parents and generally described their families as "child-centered." Identity-diffused adolescents, by contrast, reported the "most distance" from their families and most often described their parents as indifferent, inactive, detached, and rejecting.

A number of counseling psychologists continue to test hypotheses generated by Erikson's and Marcia's work (Blustein, Devenis, & Kidney, 1989; Blustein & Phillips, 1990; Larkin, 1987; Savickas, 1985) and have found support for predictions that differences in identity formation are related to differences in career decision-making styles, level of occupational commitment, and other career-related behaviors.

A major conceptual problem affecting all psychodynamic perspectives on identity development is their use of different concepts and terms to describe the same or similar processes or outcomes. The basic notion of "identity," for example, has been variously described as "ego-identity," "self-identity," and "ego development" by different theorists, with generally limited effort to relate or connect new terminology to existing terms or constructs.

The available research has generally reflected the above-mentioned biases as well as other conceptual and methodological limitations. Emphasis is more often placed on the assessment of a global outcome (e.g., has the person achieved a stable identity?) than on the study of relevant identity-forming relational processes. The widespread emphasis on interviews or semiprojective measures yielding categorical data has also been criticized (Craig-Bray & Adams, 1986). Researchers have been content to categorize persons into different identity statuses and have not chosen to deal with differences in the change processes occurring within different content domains (e.g., sex-role, occupational, political). When family influences have been studied, data gathering has typically been restricted to subjective (and sometimes retrospective) reports of adolescents themselves; parents often have not been included in these efforts. Consequently, much of the available information on the influence of family relationships is subject to errors of memory, defensive distortion, and conscious impression management (Waterman, 1982). Longitudinal designs, not surprisingly, are few, cover relatively short time intervals, and again are usually limited to changes in adolescent self-report over time (Adams & Fitch, 1982; Kroger & Haslett, 1988).

In sum, it is clear that the reviewed psychodynamic perspectives on adolescent identity development are affected by the two common epistemological constraints that were discussed earlier. First, these theories share a preferred focus on the individual as the unit of analysis. Secondly, they attempt to explain progress in identity formation as the linear effect of certain postulated causative factors, either internal or external to the individual. As a result of these constraints, attention to relational patterns associated with adolescent individuation or to the relevance of transformations in ongoing relational systems (within which the individual is embedded) to this process has been neglected. Therefore, our understanding of how one such primary context—the family—affects this developmental process has not been adequately integrated into psychodynamic theories.

FAMILY SYSTEMS: AN ALTERNATIVE PARADIGM FOR UNDERSTANDING IDENTITY DEVELOPMENT

In recent years, a number of theorists and researchers have turned their attention to the family as a significant context affecting individual behavior, development, and change. This emergent interest in family dynamics has coincided with proposals for the adoption of a cybernetic or "systemic" epistemology for understanding the change-inducing qualities of relational systems (Bateson, 1979; Keeney, 1983). Generally speaking, these models view the family as a natural "open system" containing members who reciprocally influence one another and whose interdependencies combine to form the family's unique structure. These models propose that individual behavior is better understood when viewed within the dynamic context of one's family relationships. Excellent historical accounts of the emergence of the "family systems" therapy movement and detailed discussions of the key concepts and assumptions of systemic epistemology can be found elsewhere (Becvar & Becvar, 1988; Hoffman, 1981) and are not reconsidered here. Rather, this section introduces several prominent perspectives of family functioning, underscoring those concepts and assumptions that may enhance our understanding of the relational processes involved in late adolescent individuation and identity development.

A Family Life Cycle View

Carter and McGoldrick (1980, 1989) offered a six-stage model of the family life cycle presumed to be characteristic of intact, middle-class American families during the last quarter of this century. Their model attempts to explain how, over time, the developmental agendas of younger and older family members are interconnected within a complex relational process. Each stage represents a developmental advance in the family's internal organization that is facilitated by "second-order changes" in family status. "Second-order changes" refer to the consequences of internal or external events that transform status and meaning within a system and usher in an entirely new structure (Terklesen, 1980). These changes may be engendered by "paranormative events" (i.e., parental divorce, chronic illness) but more often are precipitated by predictable normative transitions. The period of late adolescence represents one such normative transition in the family's life cycle.

During this period, which spans stages 4 ("Families with Adolescents") and 5 ("Launching Children") of their model, families must adopt flexible "boundaries," in order to permit the adolescent to "move in and out of the family system" and to develop greater independence. This transformation is facilitated in a number of ways. Parents may begin shifting their energies and attentions away from active parenting responsibilities and more toward their own midlife concerns. Among these may be somewhat greater involvement in caring for their own aging parents. The adolescent, on the other hand, advances the transformation by increasing his or her involvement with the extrafamilial world. At this juncture, parents must renegotiate their relationships with one another as well as with their increasingly mature children. These negotiations promote the emergence of a new parent–child process, one in which both parties eventually experience a less dependent and more peerlike relationship that advances the pursuit of their divergent developmental tasks.

Combrinck-Graham (1985) cautioned that the family life cycle should not be viewed as a linear event that begins with a particular stage and ends at a different stage. Focusing instead on the reciprocity between generations at any given point in the family's development, she proposed a "family life spiral" model. This model assumes that family process oscillates naturally between phases of closeness and nonpathological enmeshment (referred to as "centripetal" periods) and more distant and disengaged phases ("centrifugal" periods). The period of late adolescence, coinciding as it typically does with parents' self-absorption in the midlife reevaluation of the 40s and the grandparents' preparations for retirement, marks a centrifugal period in the family's life cycle wherein both younger and older generations are concurrently "working on issues of personal identity and personal goals" (p. 144). By independently pursuing their separate developmental tasks during the centrifugal period, the family collectively works toward redefining existing relationships and building the basis for eventual movement toward a new centripetal period characterized by a closer and qualitatively different level of family functioning.

Both life cycle frameworks clearly assume that all families must adapt to phase-appropriate changes in the levels of closeness and distance experienced in their relationships with one another, if optimal growth and adaptation are to be achieved. In addition, and most importantly, these models encourage a broadening of the concept of late adolescent identity to include the concurrent developmental efforts of other family members. Indeed, at the systemic level, it could be argued that all family members, and not just the late adolescent, may be simultaneously affected by a common process that, beyond promoting the adolescent's own personal growth, serves to change the family itself.

An Intergenerational Model

Closely allied with family development (life cycle) formulations is Bowen's multigenerational family model (Bowen, 1978; Kerr & Bowen, 1988). Bowen's model is also relevant to the present discussion in that the "differentiation of self" is a core construct in his framework. For Bowen (1978), "[a] 'differentiated self' is one who can maintain emotional objectivity while in the midst of an emotional system in turmoil, yet, at the same time, actively relate to key people in the system" (p. 485). His model assumes that there are two aspects of the differentiation process: (a) the differentiation of self from others, and (b) the differentiation of feeling processes from intellectual processes.

Bowen conceptualized differentiation as a property both of individuals and of relationship systems. Well-differentiated persons and family systems are flexible, adaptable, and self-sufficient, and can tolerate high levels of relationship stress without developing symptoms or problematic family alignments. Poorly differentiated persons and systems, on the other hand, are typically characterized by their participation in fused and symbiotic relationships wherein reactive decisions are made on the basis of emotional pressures rather than reasoned principles. A poorly differentiated family system is likely to produce one or more of the following outcomes: (a) overt marital conflict or reactive disengagement of spouses, (b) physical or emotional dysfunction in one or more spouses, and (c) projection of the problem onto one or more children.

The latter outcome is particularly salient to a Bowenian view of problems in late adolescent identity development. According to this perspective, parents transmit their lack of differentiation to their children via a multigenerational *family projection process*. This process is captured in family patterns wherein parents (who are themselves assumed to be poorly differentiated from their families of origin) seek stability and assurance from their adolescent who, in turn, seeks stability and assurance from them. Both parents and adolescent thus become locked in a "triangle" marked by mutual and intense emotional reactivity.

The late adolescent may respond to these circumstances by remaining "fused" with his or her family or by effecting an "emotional cutoff," separating (physically) from the family and minimizing subsequent contact with his or her parents. Either response is considered a failure of differentiation and will likely lead to the adolescent's development of a "pseudo-self" whose articulation is highly dependent (either positively or negatively) on the relationship with the parents. Persons who "leave" their families and have a "pseudo-self" are assumed to seek and to marry partners who are at about the same level of differentiation as themselves, thus perpetuating the transmission of differentiation problems to the next generation.

A Structural Family Model

Another useful perspective was offered by Minuchin (1974) and embodied in his structural model of family relations. Minuchin's sensitivity to the role of family functioning in promoting identity development is apparent in his observation that "in all cultures, the family imprints its members with selfhood. Human experience of identity has two elements: a sense of belonging and a sense of being separate. The laboratory in which these ingredients are mixed and dispensed is the family, the matrix of identity" (p. 47).

The belief that families possess an internal "structure" that organizes the ways in which family members interact is a key model assumption. Family transactions are presumably guided by an invisible set of "rules" or "boundaries" that determine the nature of members' participation in specific family situations. One aspect of a family's internal structure is the inherent "power hierarchy" within the parental/marital subsystem and between the parental subsystem and the sibling, or children's, subsystem. In general, Minuchin's model assumes that well-functioning families evidence clear generational boundaries—that is, there is a clear distinction with regard to the status and functions of parents and their children, wherein parents are in a hierarchically superior position. Parents are also assumed to evidence interdependent and cooperative behavior in executing their specific responsibilities.

"Boundary" is considered a dynamic relationship and is not to be confused with the notion of a "barrier." Rather, the hallmark of a clear internal boundary between members is their capacity to contact one another and exchange information while, at the same time, preserving an appropriate level of differentiated functioning. Adaptive family functioning is compromised when the internal boundaries between parents and children become closed to contact or "rigid," or when these boundaries become "diffuse" and lose their ability to sustain differentiated behavior. Different patterns of closed, open, and diffuse boundaries may exist within the same family and characterize its particular structure. For example, a parent whose relationship with her spouse is conflicted may enlist the support of one or more children in her marital struggle and thus weaken the parent-child boundary, a pattern labeled a "parent–child coalition." Alternatively, parents may attempt to manage tension arising within their own relationship by jointly blaming or attempting to enlist the support of another family member; these patterns are designated respectively as "detouring/attacking" and "triangulation." By implication, then, the late adolescent's participation in these dysfunctional alignments keeps him or her functionally and emotionally bound to the family in unhealthy ways.

A Communication Model of Relationship Transformation

Some of the earliest observational research on family dynamics formed the basis of a communication model for explaining how the presence of incongruent and "double-binding" communications within families leads to the development of psychotic behavior (Bateson, Jackson, Haley, & Weakland, 1956; Watzlawick, Beavin, & Jackson, 1967).

According to this model, human communication can be subdivided into two levels representing different orders of message. At the basic or "content" level are the words that are said or the verbal report; operating at a higher level of abstraction is the "demand" or "relationship" component of the communication, which is largely influenced by nonverbal behavior. The latter message is assumed to qualify the verbal report by indicating how the message is to be received and by indirectly suggesting what *kind* of relationship transaction the speaker wishes to establish with the recipient. Two types of relationship transactions are possible. In *complementary* transactions, there is an unequal relationship between communicants; one member assumes a "one-up" position and the other accepts a "one-down" role. By contrast, *symmetrical* transactions are more peerlike and egalitarian exchanges wherein neither party assumes a "one-down" position.

To define the nature of their relationship, participants must accurately discriminate between the levels of messages they give and receive. This discrimination is facilitated when the messages at both levels are congruent, but is obstructed when the message at one level contradicts or disqualifies the message at the other level. An example of such a communication would be the words "Of course I love you" said in a sullen and dispassionate voice. Generally speaking, persons can address such incongruencies by *metacommunicating* (i.e., commenting on the other's communication), in this case, requesting clarification. However, in close, highly disturbed communication systems wherein metacommunication is prohibited or itself disqualified, the repeated exchange of paradoxical communications is assumed to "double bind" participants by precluding relationship definition.

Given our language system's limited capacities to signal the desire for a relationship change, Rabkin (1976) argued that important relationship transformations (e.g., efforts by participants to move from more complementary to more symmetrical transactions) are often accompanied by the exchange of paradoxical injunctions. To illustrate, consider a parent-to-adolescent communication: "I want you *to want* to go to college." Presumably, this communication invites the adolescent to find his or her own reasons for attending college (a symmetrical response), yet it is delivered in the form of a directive that demands the complementary (one-down) response of compliance. Such communications are not necessarily pathological, provided that the recipient is able to metacommunicate regarding the incongruency or that the parent recognizes the adolescent's subsequent decision (to go or not to go to college) as an authentic expression of the adolescent's autonomy. Indeed, Rabkin proposed that such paradoxical exchanges may be needed to provoke a necessary relationship transformation.

The communication perspective would thus hold that late adolescent identity development is furthered by a qualitative shift in parent–adolescent communications away from predominantly complementary transactions (more characteristic of early adolescence and childhood) and toward more symmetrical exchanges where both participants mutually acknowledge their "individuality" and capacity for independent action. This view also implies that, when family members are able to metacommunicate their relationship needs to one another, the family system is best positioned to achieve such transformations.

THE RELATION OF FAMILY DYNAMICS TO LATE ADOLESCENT INDIVIDUATION AND ADJUSTMENT: CURRENT STATUS OF RESEARCH

This section reviews and critiques research examining the role of family-related variables in late adolescent individuation, identity formation, and adjustment. This review is selective, highlighting those reports that have tested hypotheses emanating from existing models of family development, process, and structure during late adolescence. In addition, this review focuses on studies that have employed normal (nonclinical) samples of adolescents from intact families (i.e., parents married and living together). The selected studies have been grouped under three subheadings: (a) correlational studies of family structure and late adolescent functioning, (b) communication studies of parent–late adolescent interactions and identity development, and (c) investigations of the relation of current family dynamics to late adolescent vocational identity and career decision making. The section concludes by underscoring consistent findings and citing unresolved questions and methodological problems in this research.

Correlational Studies of Family Structure and Late Adolescent Functioning

A number of investigators have tested the general hypothesis that features of the family's internal structure, or qualities of internal family relationships, are closely associated with late adolescent identity and adjustment. Among the most prominently considered features have been the stability of the marital alliance, the presence of inappropriate parent–late adolescent coalitions, patterns of emotional "fusion" and "triangulation" within the family, and the nature of parent–late adolescent psychological separation.

Marital Conflict and Family Coalition Patterns

Kleiman (1981) formed two groups of adolescents on the basis of their scores on a self-image questionnaire. Students scoring at least one standard deviation above the mean of a normative sample were classified as "healthy," and those scoring within one-third of a standard deviation above or below the comparison group mean constituted the "normal" group. Using both self-report and structured family interview methods, Kleiman observed that the families of "healthy" adolescents evidenced significantly stronger marital alliances and clearer generational boundaries than those exhibited by the families of "normal" adolescents.

Testing predictions from structural family theory, Bell and Bell (1982) found that female adolescents scoring highly on measures of maturity, ego development, and personality functioning reported higher scores on family-based measures of cohesion, affective expression, and flexibility than did less well-adjusted students. Moreover, high-scoring adolescents were less likely to report being "triangled" into the marital relationship either as scapegoats or as participants in a cross-generational coalition with one parent. Teyber (1983a) examined whether the quality of the marital dyad and the presence or absence of cross-generational coalitions were differentially predictive of college students' personality development and academic adjustment. The adjustment of students who reported that their parents' marital relationship was "primary" (i.e., the most important two-person unit within the family) was compared against that of their peers who reported that some other family dyad (e.g., parent–child, grandparent–parent) was "primary." Women (but not men) demonstrated a positive relationship between the primacy of the marital relationship and their own personality adjustment.

In a subsequent study using an exclusively male sample of college freshmen, Teyber (1983b) found that the primacy of the marital relationship was positively and significantly associated with students' internality scores and with objective indexes of academic success that controlled for ability differences. More recently, Lopez, Campbell, and Watkins (1989a) explored the effects of marital conflict, family coalition type, and student sex on measures of psychological separation and college student adjustment. Their operationalization of four coalition groups was based on student responses to two self-report items used to determine whether the student acknowledged participating in a secret (covert) alliance with one, both, or neither parent. They reported significant main effects for marital conflict and for student sex but not for family coalition type, on the major dependent measures. Students from maritally distressed families reported significantly more conflicted relationships with parents as well as significantly lower scores on all measures of college adjustment. A multivariate test of the interaction of marital conflict and family coalition type approached but did not reach significance. These authors contended that their method of defining coalition groups was limited and may have contributed to the mixed findings.

Intergenerational Fusion, Triangulation, and Parental Support

Other investigations have similarly explored relations among indexes of family cohesion and differentiation, parent–adolescent overinvolvement or "fusion," the adolescent's experience of "divided loyalties" to parents ("triangulation"), and parental warmth and support to late adolescent ego identity, individuation, and personal adjustment. Both structural (Minuchin, 1974) and intergenerational (Bowen, 1978) family models assume that overly involved, "enmeshed," or poorly differentiated parent–adolescent relationships impede normal separation–individuation processes. Indeed, a frequently used self-report measure assessing both "fusion" and "triangulation" patterns in families—the Personal Authority in the Family System Questionnaire (PAFS; Bray, Williamson, & Malone, 1984)—was developed from a theoretical framework integrating structural and intergenerational family concepts. Using the relevant PAFS scales, Fleming and Anderson (1986) found that adolescents who perceived themselves to be more fused or triangulated within their families of origin were more likely to experience poorer college adjustment, lower self-esteem and sense of mastery, a greater number of health-related problems, and lower grades than their more emotionally independent peers.

Anderson and Fleming (1986) found that PAFS measures of intergenerational fusion and triangulation collectively explained significant variance in college students' ego identity total scores, and especially subscale scores measuring resolution of the Eriksonian issues of autonomy/shame, initiative/guilt, and identity/identity confusion. Only triangulation scores were significantly predictive of students' "industry" scores, with triangulated students reporting a greater sense of inadequacy about themselves and their abilities.

Campbell, Adams, and Dobson (1984) gathered information from both late adolescents and their parents to test a model (Cooper, Grotevant, & Condon, 1983) postulating that measures of family "connectedness" and "individuality" would be predictive of adolescent membership in one of the four identity statuses originally defined by Marcia (1966). (The Cooper et al. model is described in greater detail in a later section.) In the Campbell et al. study, a main effect for identity status was observed, with identity-achieved and foreclosed students reporting significantly more affectionate relationships with their mothers than those reported by their peers in the moratorium and identity-diffused statuses. Support was also observed for the hypothesis that identity-achieved and moratorium youths would rate themselves as more independent from parents than their peers in the other statuses. Foreclosed students reported stronger emotional attachments to family and relatively weaker independence from parents than did their identity-achieved counterparts, a finding compatible with previous research on adolescent identity development (Waterman, 1982).

Other investigations have linked lower internal family differentiation to poorer adolescent identity development and maladaptive alcohol use (Bartle & Sabatelli, 1989) and to adolescent reports of lower peer intimacy and greater psychological distress (Harvey, Curry, & Bray, 1986). However, some researchers have challenged the view that effective adaptation during late adolescence involves a reduction in the level of intrafamily closeness and a weakening of parent–adolescent emotional ties (Kenny, 1987a; Lapsley, Rice, & FitzGerald, 1990). Kenny (1987b) concluded that research on nonclinical samples of adolescents and college students did not support theoretical expectations that excessively close parent–adolescent relationships were dysfunctional. Unfortunately, several of the studies cited earlier in this section were not included in Kenny's review. Nevertheless, there is little argument with the view that adequately differentiated late adolescents are still "connected" to their families in meaningful ways. Kunce and Priesmeyer (1985), for example, reported that among two independent samples of adolescents and their parents, perceived satisfaction with family relationships was positively associated with a sense of "togetherness" and negatively correlated with the presence of strict "rules."

More recently, Kamptner (1988) proposed a causal model of identity development incorporating measures of parental autonomy and warmth, family cohesion, and family security with adolescent autonomy; she also tested this model in explaining scores on four separate measures of identity. She found that adolescents' reports of independent (family) security (i.e., feeling secure in relations with parents while, at the same time, having confidence in one's self) was enhanced by parental autonomy (i.e., parents' acceptance of adolescent independence) but, curiously, was negatively related to parental warmth (i.e., parental expressions of affection and support). Familial security was found to enhance identity formation directly, and also indirectly via its positive impact on adolescents' social confidence and social relatedness. Kamptner's evidence also suggested that family dynamics exert a slightly stronger influence on male identity than on female identity.

Studies of Parent–Late Adolescent Psychological Separation and College Adjustment

A related yet more focused line of research was initiated by Hoffman (1984) and stimulated by his development of the Psychological Separation Inventory (PSI), a 138-item self-report measure assessing four dimensions of parent–late adolescent independence or psychological separation:

1. Emotional independence reflects the late adolescent's freedom from needs for emotional support and approval from parents;
2. Functional independence assesses freedom from needs for physical and economic assistance by parents;
3. Attitudinal independence indicates the degree to which the parents' and adolescent's attitudes, values, and beliefs are distinct;
4. Conflictual independence reflects the absence of guilt, anger, and resentment in the parent–adolescent relationship.

Higher scores on each subscale were assumed to indicate a greater level of psychological separation on that dimension. In his original report using the PSI, Hoffman found that two subscales—conflictual independence (CI) and emotional independence (EI)—

were significantly related, respectively, to better personal adjustment reported by women respondents and to less problematic love relationships reported by both men and women.

Lopez, Campbell, and Watkins (1986) explored sex differences on PSI scores and tested hypotheses that both depression and college adjustment scores would be related to overall PSI totals. Their results indicated that men did score significantly higher than women on several of the PSI subscales but that the expected relations among PSI total scores, depression (negative relation), and college adjustment (positive relation) existed only among women in their sample. They concluded that these interconstruct relations were complex and that psychological separation is best conceptualized as a multidimensional construct.

Subsequent investigations using the PSI with generally larger samples yielded additional insights into the relations among different aspects of parent–adolescent separation, other features of family functioning, and individual adjustment. Hoffman and Weiss (1987) presented evidence that, for both men and women, the greater the conflictual *dependence* (i.e., lower CI scores) of the student on either or both parents, the higher the reported frequency of psychological symptoms. They also cited a noteworthy sex difference: among men, conflictual dependence on mother and on father appeared to function additively in predicting student distress; among women, however, conflictual dependence on either parent was as predictive of distress as was conflictual dependence on both parents. Lopez, Campbell, and Watkins (1989b) also found that, compared to their nondepressed peers, depressed college students reported significantly lower conflictual independence from parents, higher attitudinal independence, and generally high levels of dysfunctional family interactions. Friedlander and Siegel (1990) found lower conflictual independence (particularly in the mother–daughter relationship) to be a significant predictor of eating disorders among college women.

Employing canonical correlation to examine relations among measures of family structure, college adjustment, and the four PSI subscales, Lopez, Campbell, and Watkins (1988) found general support for structural family theory. Their analyses revealed the presence of two significant canonical roots underlying the relations between the subscales measuring dysfunctional family structure and parent–adolescent psychological separation. The first dimension appeared to describe family process wherein high levels of marital conflict were co-occurring with other aspects of dysfunctional family interactions (i.e., parent–child role reversals, coalitions). Men scoring highly on this dimension evidenced angry–rebellious relationships with parents, whereas women scoring highly on the same dimension evidenced angry–dependent relationships with parents. The second canonical dimension appeared to describe a family process wherein high levels of marital conflict were occurring within an otherwise sound and functional family structure. In general, both men and women scoring highly on this dimension demonstrated higher psychological separation scores. Only one significant canonical root was extracted in the analysis of PSI and college adjustment subscales; this dimension appeared to underscore an important relation between conflictual independence and personal adjustment.

Lapsley, Rice, and Shadid (1989) compared relations among PSI and college adjustment subscales among samples of college underclassmen and upperclassmen and found that, as expected, freshmen reported more functional and attitudinal dependencies on both parents and more emotional dependencies on mothers than did upperclassmen. Among both age groups, higher levels of functional and emotional independence from mother were positively associated with personal–emotional adjustment. However, only among their upperclassmen sample were emotional and conflictual independence from mother and conflictual independence from father positively associated with academic adjustment.

Rice, Cole, and Lapsley (1990) sequentially employed factor analysis and structural equation modeling in analyzing college student scores on multiple measures of separation–individuation (including the PSI), family cohesion, and college adjustment. Their analyses indicated the presence of two dimensions of separation–individuation that were only moderately correlated with one another yet were quite differently correlated with measures of college adjustment. The first dimension (independence from parents), measured by the functional, emotional, and attitudinal independence subscales of the PSI, was found to be negatively related to family cohesion and unrelated to college adjustment; the second dimension (positive feelings about separation), measured in part by the conflictual independence subscale of the PSI, was unrelated to family cohesion yet strongly related to college adjustment. These authors concluded that effective late adolescent individuation "does require some separation from the family orbit and perhaps some reworking of the parent–adolescent relationship" (p. 201).

Communication Studies of Parent–Late Adolescent Interactions and Identity Development

Although family systems theories assume that important qualities of parent–adolescent interaction characterize the process by which late adolescents form stable self-views, surprisingly few investigations have attempted to directly examine and quantify patterns within actual parent–adolescent interactions and to evaluate relations between these patterns and independent indexes of adolescent identity formation. Grotevant and his colleagues (Cooper, Grotevant, & Condon, 1983; Grotevant & Cooper, 1985, 1986) are noteworthy exceptions. These investigators proposed a relational model for understanding the development of psychosocial competence during late adolescence. Their model emphasizes the significance of the family context—in particular, internal communications that typify qualities of both "individuality" and "connectedness" in relationships—as instrumental in promoting the late adolescent's identity exploration, role-taking, and perspective-taking behavior.

In their studies, Grotevant and his associates gathered data in the homes of families containing a late adolescent, including unobtrusive observation of the family's participation in a group discussion requiring them to make plans for a fictional 2-week vacation for which they had unlimited funds (Family Interaction Task). In general, these investigations yielded support for their view that the "co-occurrence of individuality and connectedness in family relations contributes to the adolescent's ability to explore identity-related choices and to coordinate multiple perspectives" (Grotevant & Cooper, 1986, p. 96).

Using a different coding system that identified "constraining" and "enabling" parent–adolescent exchanges, Hauser et al. (1984) found that these patterns were differentially associated with variations in adolescent ego development, with enabling exchanges showing a positive association. Moreover, and of particular support for a systemic view of family communication, these authors observed that constraining exchanges between parents and adolescents had reciprocally inhibiting effects on participants' subsequent interactions. A clear implication of this research is that recurrent conflictual exchanges between parents and adolescents constrain the nature of their dialogue and may directly or indirectly limit the subsequent probability of "enabling" parent–adolescent transactions.

Investigations of the Relation of Current Family Dynamics to Late Adolescent Vocational Identity and Career Decision Making

Galinsky and Fast (1966) suggested that problems in adolescent identity formation are often expressed as difficulties in choosing a career. It should not be surprising, then, that several writers have recently called for efforts to extend and test family systems models in examining the career-related behavior of late adolescents and young adults (Brachter, 1982; Lopez & Andrews, 1987; Schulenberg, Vondracek, & Crouter, 1984; Zingaro, 1983). To date, however, only a few empirical studies have directly tested predictions from family systems theories.

Eigen, Hartman, and Hartman (1987) employed Olson's circumplex model of family functioning (Olson, Sprenkle, & Russell, 1979)—which assumes that well-functioning families exhibit balanced levels of cohesion (closeness) and adaptability (capacity to change)—in differentiating college students classified as career-decided, developmentally undecided, or chronically undecided. Results did not support their specific model-related predictions, but they did suggest that chronically undecided students were more likely to describe their family environments as either (a) highly structured and emotionally connected (i.e., "too tight") or (b) having little structure and emotional attachment (i.e., "too loose").

Lopez (1989) tested a model for predicting vocational identity that was based on structural family theory and that sequentially considered information on college students' current family dynamics, trait anxiety, and academic adjustment. All three sources of information were found to contribute unique and significant variance in predicting the vocational identity scores of both men and women. Interestingly, among men, (a) low marital conflict and (b) unconflicted relationships with both mother and father emerged as significant family predictors of high vocational identity; among women, the most significant family-related predictor of high vocational identity was an unconflicted relationship with father.

Testing predictions from intergenerational family theory and using the PAFS measures of "individuation" and "triangulation," Kinnier, Brigman, and Noble (1990) found that college students' level of individuation from parents was a significant though modest predictor of their scores on a measure of career indecision, with students who reported less individuated parental relationships evidencing more career indecision.

In a two-part investigation, Blustein, Walbridge, Friedlander, and Palladino (1991) initially explored relations between the dimensions of psychological separation measured by the PSI and measures of career "outcome" (i.e., career indecision and career decision-making self-efficacy) and found no significant canonical relations among their sample of college students. In the second part of their study, PSI subscales and measures of parental attachment were jointly examined in relation to more process-oriented measures of career development, which assessed the level of vocational exploration/commitment and the student's tendency to foreclose (i.e., to adopt a closed, dogmatic, dualistic posture with regard to the career commitment process). This analysis did reveal a significant canonical function underlying variation between the family functioning and career progress measures. Subsequent analyses further revealed that the *conjoint* influence of psychological separation and attachment variables was significantly related to career progress, while the independent contributions of psychological separation and attachment variables to the career measures were inconsequential. These authors concluded that "progress in committing to career choices . . . seems to occur most readily for those persons who experience both independence from and attachment to their parents" (p. 39).

Summary and Critique of Research on the Family Dynamics of Late Adolescent Identity Development

This section provides an integrative summary of the selected studies on the relation of family dynamics to late adolescent separation–individuation and identity development. This summary highlights key findings and conclusions, underscores unresolved questions and areas for future inquiry, and considers important methodological issues and limitations in this research.

Key Findings and Preliminary Conclusions

There is ample evidence that disturbed family dynamics are significantly associated with problems in late adolescent separation–individuation and identity development. In particular, there is general support for predictions from structural and intergenerational models of family functioning that assume that the presence of marital conflict/instability, the late adolescent's participation in fused or poorly differentiated alliances or coalitions, and high levels of conflict in parent–adolescent relationships may interfere with identity development and contribute to psychological distress and poorer extrafamilial adjustment. In addition, there is emergent and preliminary support for communication models of family functioning that link separation–individuation problems to specific features of parent–adolescent interactions, specifically, the predominance of mutually "constraining" exchanges and an imbalance between family interactions evidencing tolerance/ acceptance of "individuality" (self-assertive) and "connectedness" (mutuality) responses.

Collectively, these findings challenge traditional (psychoanalytic) notions that appropriate identity development in late adolescence requires a "shedding of family dependencies" and a repudiation of parental influence. Rather, results indirectly support expectations from family development (life cycle) theories that the effective "launching" of the late adolescent/young adult is accompanied by a complex transformation of family processes, creating a climate wherein *both* the adolescent and his or her parents can acknowledge and affirm the former's increasing independence and capacity for self-direction while, at the same time, maintaining satisfactory contact.

For both late adolescent men and women, the clearest index that this family transformation has not yet been achieved is the presence of recurrent conflict, particularly within the parent–adolescent relationship. Such conflict suggests that the current level of differentiation in the parent–adolescent relationship may be insufficient to promote the latter's individuation. Efforts at expressing "differences" in these relationships become problematic and threatening, in that the "self" boundaries of each participant are excessively meshed or fused with one another. Each presumably struggles to define the relationship in his or her *own* terms, thus delaying achievement of a mutually negotiated redefinition. It seems important to note here, however, that, although parent–adolescent conflict may signal a delay in family transformation that has negative adjustment consequences, it may also be (in some families) a necessary "transitional" step toward such transformations (Karpel, 1976). Indeed, the more insidious and potentially debilitating family patterns may be those in which the distress of parent–adolescent fusion is experienced yet mutually disqualified (Held & Bellows, 1983; Richman, 1979).

Unresolved Questions and Areas for Future Inquiry

The available research has produced several conflicting and ambiguous findings that require further study; it has also neglected study of certain variables that may enhance our understanding of the family processes relevant to late adolescent identity development. Of particular note are the following issues.

The Conceptualization and Measurement of Psychological Separation.   In an earlier review of the state of family assessment, Gurman and Kniskern (1981) concluded that efforts to measure "core theoretical constructs" suffered from "serious deficiencies." The past decade has witnessed important progress on this issue, but the appropriate conceptualization and measurement of family dynamics remain vexing problems. This is no less true with respect to those family dynamics that are presumably implicated in the process of late adolescent identity development. For example, the foregoing presentation clearly suggested that "psychological separation" is a complex and multidimensional concept whose relationship to "family closeness" is not antithetical. Relevant to this point is consistent empirical evidence that the four subscales of the PSI are not uniformly correlated with each other or with independent measures of late adolescent adjustment (Baker, 1989), and that conflictual and nonconflictual PSI subscales may be tapping two relatively distinct dimensions of separation–individuation (Rice, Cole, & Lapsley, 1990).

These inconsistencies may be in part a function of the tendency of researchers to use single measures of these constructs. Cole and Jordan (1989) recently criticized this practice of "monomethodism"; they also presented evidence of important variation across family members' perspectives of the nature of cohesion and adaptability within the different "component dyads" in the family (i.e., mother–father, mother–student, father–student), with the mother's perspective appearing to be the most valid. These authors cautioned that "global assessment of molar family constructs may overlook substantial differences between family subsystems" (p. 461) that may enhance the prediction of family and individual adjustment. Their deployment of a multitrait–multimethod approach to family assessment holds promise as a strategy for clarifying the complex nature of individuation processes within the family. Benjamin's Structural Analysis of Social Behavior (SASB; Benjamin, 1979; Humphrey & Benjamin, 1986), an interactional coding scheme also based on a multitrait–multimethod strategy, may hold similar promise.

In a related vein, the use of factor analysis (of multiple family and adjustment measures) along with structural modeling techniques can be an effective method for developing and testing models of separation–individuation processes (Rice, Cole, & Lapsley, 1990). Together, these data-analytic approaches should help future research identify those aspects of parent–adolescent interaction that distinguish healthy emotional "closeness" from dysfunctional "enmeshment."

Gender Differences.   Reported interrelations among gender, family dynamics, and individuation/adjustment processes have also demonstrated inconsistencies that suggest the need for further inquiry. There is evidence that men generally score higher than women on available measures of psychological separation, but there are also indications that late adolescent men and women experience the individuation process differently, particularly when separation themes involve freedom and detachment from parents (Moore, 1987). Moreover, recent research on young adult samples of men and women (ages 22 to 32) has indicated that "competent" (i.e., independent) women are more likely to report "connected" attachments to parents than are competent men (Frank, Avery, & Laman, 1988). The latter finding lends some support for the view that men and women pursue different pathways toward psychological independence (Gilligan, 1982; Josselson, 1988). Still, the adjustment implications of these possible differences are unclear. Some investigators, for example, have concluded that women may be more sensitive and reactive to family conflict and disturbances than are men (Hoffman & Weiss, 1987; Lopez, Campbell, & Watkins, 1988); others have argued that men have greater difficulty renegotiating those family ties that are necessary for greater autonomy and self-governance and that, relative to women, they may hold less mature views of parent–adolescent separation (Moore, 1987). It has also been suggested that the identity development of men may be more highly influenced by ongoing family dynamics (Kamptner, 1988).

Individuation and Identity Development in Nonintact Families. Much of the available research has focused on families in which parents are married and living together. Given estimates that, by the year 2000, one-half of today's American children will become stepsons or stepdaughters (Glick, 1989), future research on late adolescent identity formation within these "nontraditional" families is clearly needed. Thus far, only a handful of studies have addressed this concern and, although preliminary results suggest that parental divorce may accelerate many aspects of the separation-individuation process, there are noteworthy methodological limitations in much of this work (Lopez, 1987; Lopez, 1991). Future studies would do well to evaluate specific postdivorce households (i.e., single parent, remarried), consider the concurrent influence of original-family and step-family relations, and, in general, employ designs capable of examining the relation of parent–adolescent interactions and identity development within these family structures.

Other Methodological Issues and Design Limitations

Despite their explicit efforts to test systemic views of family functioning during late adolescence, many of the studies cited in this review gathered data solely on late adolescent respondents (typically, college students), few included observations of other family members, and self-reports often served as the only source of data. As a consequence, the generalizability of many reports to actual family processes and to the individuation and identity development of non-college-bound youth is limited. The influence of ethnicity and socioeconomic status on identity development processes within families has also received insufficient attention. It thus seems reasonable to conclude that the "adolescent only" focus of much of this literature yields incomplete information, is highly limited in its ability to test systemic views and, for all intents and purposes, may have outlived its usefulness.

It would seem that, ultimately, careful and sustained observational research on ongoing family processes may hold more promise for advancing our understanding of how the family context promotes or impedes late adolescent individuation and identity development. Beyond facing the obvious logistical problems associated with conducting research on entire families, researchers must select a method of gathering and coding family transactions that is appropriate for the types of questions and theoretical models under investigation. Grotevant and Carlson (1987) provided an excellent review of 13 major coding systems in current use, noting differences among these systems on many dimensions, including level of analysis (micro vs. macro), ease versus complexity of administration and scoring instructions, availability of reliability and validity information, and theoretical foundations. Like Cole and Jordan (1989), these authors called for comparative studies of different coding systems to establish convergent and divergent validity.

On a more positive note, useful technologies (one-way mirrors, dual observing/interacting teams, videotaping) for unobtrusive observation and controlled interaction with families currently exist and will likely play a more prominent role in future family research. These technologies also have the potential for advancing serious study of how the counselor's or "observer's" perspective on the nature of family interactions may provide a more complete cybernetic description of family process (Keeney, 1983).

IMPLICATIONS FOR PRACTICE AND TRAINING

This section discusses the implications of extant research to counseling practice, and, in particular, its relevance to the future training of counseling psychologists. Specifically considered are attitudes and circumstances within our field that may unnecessarily constrain the adoption and integration of systemic models and approaches within counseling psychology training.

Implications for Practice

The above findings offer considerable support for the view that immediate family dynamics are significantly associated with the process of late adolescent identity formation and adjustment. Negative relations among specific family patterns—parent–adolescent conflict and emotional overinvolvement; coalitions; marital instability—and multiple indexes of late adolescent adjustment have been consistently observed, suggesting that counselors should think in terms of relationship systems when assessing the functioning of their late adolescent clients. The reviewed studies also affirm that certain dynamic conditions within the family—most notably, the presence of *both* "individuality" and "connectedness" responses in observed parent–adolescent interactions—are positively associated with adolescent identity formation. Presumably, these families provide the most supportive contexts for late adolescent exploration, individuation, and perspective taking. By contrast, the consistent findings linking high levels of conflict in the parent–adolescent relationship with poorer late adolescent adjustment suggest that less salutary environmental conditions are present in these families and that therapeutic efforts to address and resolve these conflicts may indeed advance healthy separation–individuation processes.

The predominantly correlational nature of much of this research does not establish that certain disturbances in current family functioning are *causally related* to problems in late adolescent individuation and identity development. Such conclusions must await the results of future studies employing longitudinal and process-oriented research designs. By the same token, however, the establishment of linear causal connections among these variables is neither a necessary nor a sufficient condition for the adoption of a family systems view of late adolescent identity development. Rather, the essence of most systemic conceptualizations is that disturbances in identity development should be considered as part of a larger *pattern* of mutually interactive family events and transactions that collectively restrain relationship (and individual) change during a time when such change may have clear adaptive consequences.

At a very basic level, counselors should recognize that an adolescent's effort to consolidate a personal identity is not a neutral or inert element in the ongoing drama of family functioning. How parents have organized their views of the adolescent, how they think about and respond to that member's expressed and/or exhibited difficulties, and whether they have altered their usual behavior toward or expectations of their offspring all become potential grist for the systemic mill. In short, how well or poorly both adolescent and parents are able to coordinate their relationship movements to achieve a higher level of differentiated functioning must be carefully assessed.

It would seem, then, that opportunities to observe, assess, and intervene in actual family interactions would create an especially useful therapeutic context for promoting late adolescent individuation and identity development (Bloom, 1987). Yet, surprisingly, the present literature review did not uncover any comparative treatment studies of individual and family therapy approaches that specifically evaluated change in late adolescent identity formation. Despite this important omission, some preliminary thoughts on the potential utility of a family-based approach to late adolescent identity development are in order.

In working with families containing a distressed late adolescent, counselors could serve important roles in heightening family awareness of the developmental pressures of this period, which portend the need for family transformation. Certain families may also require therapeutic assistance in developing the metacommunicative skills that, if consistently used, may prevent repetition of unproductive relationship struggles and weaken existing patterns of emotional overinvolvement. Other families may require substantial strengthening of the parental alliance, with the counselor directly encouraging parents to adopt flexible yet consistent parenting skills and to address and resolve their marital difficulties directly with one another and without the involvement of other family members. Similarly, the counselor may help the adolescent to recognize how he or she may be unwittingly drawn into marital disputes, and how more appropriate distance and neutrality can be maintained. One or more of these changes in family process may be necessary, in order to disengage the late adolescent from the "triangulating" emotional undercurrents within the family that may be subverting his or her individuation. In short, the family treatment context may provide all participants with the most effective venue for observing and experiencing the bidirectional relationship pressures that may be impeding family change.

Additionally, counseling psychologists (particularly those employed in college counseling centers) could potentially play important roles in designing on-campus programs and workshops for students and/or their parents, to address these topics and serve educational and preventative functions. As an example of the latter, Palmer and Cochran (1988) demonstrated the efficacy of a program designed to help parents become effective "agents" of their adolescent's career development. A primary focus of this program was assisting parents and adolescents to develop a sense of "partnership" about the latter's career development.

Individual counseling case studies that have employed systemic models and techniques have also suggested their therapeutic utility in disrupting problematic relationship struggles and in promoting adaptive behavior even when other family members are not actively involved in their therapeutic process (Lopez, 1983; Searight & Openlander, 1984). Without question, however, the potential success of such endeavors would likely depend on the counselor's skills in assessing and conceptualizing the systemic nature of maladaptive family dynamics as well as his or her skill in developing and implementing constructive interventions. Thus, the significance of appropriate training and supervision in family systems models and interventions is apparent.

Obstacles to the Integration of Systemic
Approaches in Counseling Psychology Training

Unfortunately, there are several possible barriers to the development and integration of family systems coursework and training within counseling psychology programs. To begin with, exposure to prominent systemic theories has not traditionally been part of the training of counseling psychologists, and this reality has a twofold impact. First, in many cases, existing training programs would have to develop new courses, particularly if such courses are not available elsewhere on campus, for example, through social work, clinical psychology, or family science/human ecology programs.

Second, it is doubtful that most faculty in our field have themselves developed adequate familiarity with family theories and counseling practices, a likelihood that may argue for efforts to retrain existing faculty who desire to teach relevant coursework. Sherverbush and Ward (1989) discussed how such retraining was successfully conducted within their counselor education department by soliciting the involvement of a local family therapy training institute as well as the cooperation of area practitioners and schools. Parenthetically, it appears that, relative to our discipline, counselor education departments have been much more involved in efforts to integrate marital and family therapy competencies within their training curricula (Gladding, Burggraf, & Fenell, 1987; Hovestadt, Fenell, & Piercy, 1983; Meadows & Hetrick, 1982), with approximately two-thirds of their programs now offering such courses (Peltier & Vale, 1986).

A related consideration is practicum and clinical supervision. A possible obstacle here is that many university counseling facilities (where much of our practicum training is typically done) have historically limited their services to individual students, and have directly or indirectly discouraged the therapeutic involvement of other family members. Yet, at counseling centers where family counseling has been offered, parents were found to be very willing to attend conjoint sessions, even when this commitment required several hours' travel time (Whiting, 1981). An appropriate family practicum experience should also include opportunities to experience "live" supervision using the one-way mirror, participation in team observations, and use of interactional coding systems of family assessment. The latter experiences, in particular, could further stimulate student interest in family-related research.

Expressed concerns within our profession regarding the utility and ethicality of systemic treatment approaches—most notably, the use of paradoxical and reframing interventions (Johnson, 1986; Ridley & Tan, 1986)—may also constrain support of family systems training. Both reframing and paradoxical counseling techniques have found widespread acceptance within family therapy circles as useful strategies for disrupting problematic interactions within distressed relationships. Reframing refers to counselor attempts to connote positively events or behaviors that clients view as negative and uncontrollable; paradoxical direction involves assignments to purposefully enact undesired and seemingly involuntary behaviors (West & Zarski, 1983). Such interventions could be useful in remediating those recurrent conflictual family patterns that may be impeding late adolescent individuation. To date, empirical evaluations of these techniques have yielded impressive support for their therapeutic efficacy and for the absence of reported adverse effects (DeBord, 1989; Dowd & Milne, 1986; Hill, 1987; Shoham-Salomon, 1987). Moreover, persuasive counterarguments for their ethical use have been marshalled (Hunsley, 1988).

A compelling argument for integrating family systems models and techniques into counseling psychology training is that, ready or not, many counseling psychologists are already "trying their hand" at marital and family therapy. A recent survey of counseling psychologists showed that almost 44% of all respondents currently involved in clinical work reported doing some family therapy (Watkins, Lopez, Campbell, & Himmell, 1986). Indeed, among counseling psychologists in full-time private practice, 83.7% and 68.2% reported involvement in marital and family therapy, respectively (Watkins, Lopez, Campbell, & Himmell, 1989).

EPILOGUE: TOWARD AN INTEGRATION OF INDIVIDUAL AND FAMILY SYSTEMS PERSPECTIVES OF LATE ADOLESCENT IDENTITY FORMATION

The traditional and family systems models of late adolescent individuation and identity development offer us different perspectives on how the individual forms and consolidates a stable self-view. The former models emphasize the notion of "self" as a "structure" that gradually develops *within* the person, enabling the individual to better regulate his or her emotions, assume greater agency and initiative in personal affairs, exhibit less dependency on the views and reactions of significant others, and adaptively pursue adult roles and responsibilities. This perspective further assumes that, by late adolescence, a "self-identity" has emerged and has become the centralized locus of one's sense of personal order and uniqueness.

The family models, by contrast, urge us to consider a view of "self" as a relational "process" that unfolds within the family context and expresses a particular pattern of transaction *between* parents and their maturing children. Important changes or shifts in self-views are interdependently managed and coordinated by these relationship participants and may require qualitative changes in the nature of their relationship. In a sense, this perspective suggests that "self-identity" is an oxymoron, that one cannot come to know "self" outside of one's active and continuing participation in human relationships. Instead, it proposes a "decentralized" view of one's sense of personal order and uniqueness by emphasizing the critical and inescapable bond between human experience and ongoing social transactions (Sampson, 1985).

Are these two basic perspectives necessarily incompatible or irreconcilable? Some vexing questions are clearly posed by their coexistence. For instance, if once the "self" is formed it is considered relationally independent, then by what process do persons modify or revise their self-views? Alternatively, if a "self" is at all times relationally interdependent, can a person ever truly be capable of independent, agentic behavior? Resolving these potential contradictions and effectively integrating individual and systemic views of identity development may require us to foresake models premised on a structure/process dualism and to embrace an epistemology that considers "self" as an intrapersonal "structure" *and* an interpersonal process, both of which are recursively joined (i.e., reciprocally interacting) elements in an organized pattern.

Fortunately, important conceptual work toward such integrations is already under way. Gergen (1987) and Markova (1987), for example, described important aspects of self theory within the wider framework of social constructionism, which assumes that all knowledge, including self-knowledge, is the by-product of social interchange. This perspective holds that intimate social groups (such as families) furnish their members with both the vocabulary and the semantic rules for use in self-labeling. Sabatelli and Mazor (1985) highlighted conceptual links between traditional developmental and family systems perspectives of identity formation. Specifically, they underscored the interdependency between the person-centered phenomenological shifts captured in the notion of "individuation" and the transactional and adaptational qualities of the larger social system, wherein concepts such as "differentiation" describe important systemic properties.

In a relevant effort at synthesizing the burgeoning social psychological literature on self-verification processes in human relationships, Swann (1987) argued that both perceivers *and* targets play active roles in the relational processes wherein persons form stable self-views. He proposed an "identity negotiation" framework that attempts to integrate both personological variables (e.g., goals, agendas, life histories) and social structural variables (e.g., norms, roles, social conventions); he also encouraged researchers "to consider simultaneously how the activities of both perceivers and targets are woven into the fabric of social interaction" (p. 1048).

Others have proposed conceptual models that incorporate both important psychodynamic and systemic concepts. Karpel (1976), for example, defined three "relational modes" (fusion, ambivalent fusion, and "dialogue") for describing the development of individuation processes in close relationships, for explaining the systemic nature of "projection," and for predicting individual reactions to "object-loss." Similarly, Polster's (1983) historical review of the psychoanalytic construct of "ego boundary" emphasized its unfortunate semantic association with the concept of a "barrier" between the person's psychic organization and the external world. Polster presented an alternative "systemic-contextual model," which describes ego boundary in terms of "dialectical processes of separation and inclusion which mediate a person's complex relationship with the world" (p. 247). Brighton-Cleghorn (1987) called attention to conceptual linkages between the underlying assumptions of family systems theories and Kohutian "self psychology." She especially stressed the utility of the "self–selfobject" unit for bridging the historical disjuncture between structural and process views of self-transformations, and for serving as the most meaningful unit of analysis for describing these transformations and their interactional concomitants.

Corresponding advances toward a more integrative research methodology have been slower to develop, but a number of calls for greater "methodological diversity" have already been sounded within our profession (Howard, 1984; Patton, 1984; Polkinghorne, 1984), urging enhanced sensitivity to the "systemic character" of human experience. To quote one of these writers: "The human realm is organized in a systemic manner, and for this reason investigations that isolate parts and determine their independent relations often miss the essential contextual relations that are more basic than particular relations among some of its parts" (Polkinghorne, 1984, p. 427). Echoing this theme, Claiborn and Lichtenberg (1989) discussed how stochastic process models may provide useful methods for "capturing and measuring the theoretical concepts and sequential phenomena that characterize the interactional view" (p. 444).

Perhaps, like the late adolescent within the family, counseling psychologists are enjoined in a necessary collective struggle to resolve contradictions in our current understandings of normal human growth and development and to achieve a more differentiated, higher-order perspective on this domain of human knowledge than the one we have historically embraced. How will we respond to this challenge? Will we cling tenaciously to possibly outdated images of ourselves (as scientists and practitioners) and of the objects of our inquiry (other human beings)? Or will we risk the "loss" of familiar concepts and understandings in order to pursue new understandings and integrations? Within our "community," will we co-create a supportive "climate" for risk taking or will we undermine each other's movements toward change? Answers to these questions will likely determine the pace and ease with which we are ultimately able to explain what reflective parents and philosophers have grasped for some time— that the adolescent's achievement of a personal "identity" changes both adolescent *and* parents, forever.

REFERENCES

Adams, G. R., & Fitch, S. A. (1982). Ego stage and identity status development: A cross-sequential analysis. *Journal of Personality and Social Psychology, 43,* 574–583.

Adelson, J., & Doehrman, M. J. (1980). The psychodynamic approach to adolescence. In J. Adelson (Ed.), *Handbook of adolescent psychology* (pp. 99–116). New York: Wiley.

Ainsworth, M. D. S. (1989). Attachments beyond infancy. *American Psychologist, 44,* 709–716.

Anderson, S. A., & Fleming, W. M. (1986). Late adolescents' identity formation: Individuation from the family of origin. *Adolescence, 21,* 785–796.

Baker, R. W. (1989). *An analysis of the relation between a measure of psychological separation from parents and a measure of student adjustment to college.* Unpublished manuscript.

Balay, J., & Shevrin, H. (1988). The subliminal psychodynamic activation method: A critical review. *American Psychologist, 43,* 161–174.

Bartle, S. E., & Sabatelli, R. M. (1989). Family system dynamics, identity development, and adolescent alcohol use. *Family Relations, 38,* 258–265.

Bateson, G. (1979). *Mind and nature: A necessary unity.* New York: Dutton.

Bateson, G., Jackson, D. D., Haley, J., & Weakland, J. (1956). Toward a theory of schizophrenia. *Behavioral Science, 1,* 251–264.

Becvar, D. S., & Becvar, R. J. (1988). *Family therapy: A systemic integration.* Boston: Allyn & Bacon.

Bell, L. G., & Bell, D. C. (1982). Family climate and the role of the female adolescent: Determinants of adolescent functioning. *Family Relations, 31,* 519–527.

Benjamin, L. S. (1979). Structural analysis of differentiation failure. *Psychiatry, 42,* 1–23.

Bloom, M. (1987). Leaving home: A family transition. In J. Bloom-Fesbach & S. Bloom-Fesbach (Eds.), *The psychology of separation and loss* (pp. 232–266). San Francisco: Jossey-Bass.

Blos, P. (1979). *The adolescent passage.* New York: International Universities Press.

Blustein, D. L., Devenis, L. E., & Kidney, B. K. (1989). Relationship between the identity formation process and career development. *Journal of Counseling Psychology, 36,* 196–202.

Blustein, D. L., & Phillips, S. D. (1990). Relation between ego identity statuses and decision-making styles. *Journal of Counseling Psychology, 37,* 160–168.

Blustein, D. L., Walbridge, M. M., Friedlander, M. L., & Palladino, D. E. (1991). Contributions of psychological separation and parental attachment to the career development process. *Journal of Counseling Psychology, 38,* 39–50.

Bowen, M. (1978). *Family therapy in clinical practice.* New York: Aronson.

Bowlby, J. (1982). *Attachment and loss: Vol. I. Attachment* (2nd ed.). New York: Basic Books.

Brachter, W. T. (1982). The influence of the family on career selection: A family systems perspective. *Personnel and Guidance Journal, 61,* 87–91.

Bray, J. H., Williamson, D. S., & Malone, P. E. (1984). Personal authority in the family system: Development of a questionnaire to measure personal authority in intergenerational family processes. *Journal of Marital and Family Therapy, 10,* 167–178.

Brighton-Cleghorn, J. (1987). Formulations of self and family systems. *Family Process, 26,* 185–201.

Bronfenbrenner, U. (1979). *The ecology of human development.* Cambridge, MA: Harvard University Press.

Campbell, E., Adams, G. R., & Dobson, W. R. (1984). Familial correlates of identity formation in late adolescence: A study of the predictive utility of connectedness and individuality in family relations. *Journal of Youth and Adolescence, 13,* 509–525.

Carter, E., & McGoldrick, M. (1980). *The family life cycle: A framework for family therapy.* New York: Gardner Press.

Carter, E., & McGoldrick, M. (1989). *The changing family life cycle: A framework for family therapy.* Boston: Allyn & Bacon.

Claiborn, C. D., & Lichtenberg, J. W. (1989). Interactional counseling. *Counseling Psychologist, 17,* 355–453.

Cole, D. A., & Jordan, A. E. (1989). Assessment of cohesion and adaptability in component family dyads: A question of convergent and discriminant validity. *Journal of Counseling Psychology, 36,* 456–463.

Combrinck-Graham, L. (1985). A developmental model of family systems. *Family Process, 24,* 139–150.

Cooper, C. R., Grotevant, H. D., & Condon, S. M. (1983). Individuality and connectedness in the family as context for adolescent identity formation and role-taking skill. In H. D. Grotevant &

C. R. Cooper (Eds.), *Adolescent development in the family: New directions for child development* (pp. 43–59). San Francisco: Jossey-Bass.

Craig-Bray, L., & Adams, G. R. (1986). Different methodologies in the assessment of identity: Congruence between self-report and interview techniques? *Journal of Youth and Adolescence, 15,* 191–204.

DeBord, J. B. (1989). Paradoxical interventions: A review of the recent literature. *Journal of Counseling and Development, 67,* 394–398.

Dowd, E. T., & Milne, C. R. (1986). Paradoxical interventions in counseling psychology. *The Counseling Psychologist, 14,* 237–282.

Eigen, C. A., Hartman, B. W., & Hartman, P. T. (1987). Relations between family interaction patterns and career indecision. *Psychological Reports, 60,* 87–94.

Erikson, E. H. (1968). *Identity: Youth and crisis.* New York: Norton.

Fleming, W. M., & Anderson, S. A. (1986). Individuation from the family and personal adjustment in late adolescence. *Journal of Marital and Family Therapy, 12,* 311–315.

Frank, S. J., Avery, C. B., & Laman, M. S. (1988). Young adults' perceptions of their relationships with their parents: Individual differences in connectedness, competence, and emotional autonomy. *Developmental Psychology, 24,* 729–737.

Freud, A. (1958). Adolescence. In R. S. Eissler et al. (Eds.), *Psychoanalytic study of the child* (pp. 255–278). New York: International Universities Press.

Friedlander, M. L., & Siegel, S. M. (1990). Separation–individuation difficulties and cognitive-behavioral indicators of eating disorders among college women. *Journal of Counseling Psychology, 37,* 74–78.

Galinsky, M. D., & Fast, I. (1966). Vocational choice as a focus of the identity search. *Journal of Counseling Psychology, 13,* 89–92.

Gergen, K. J. (1987). Toward self as relationship. In K. Yardley & T. Honess (Eds.), *Self and identity: Psychosocial perspectives* (pp. 53–63). Chichester, England: Wiley.

Gilligan, C. (1982). *In a different voice.* Cambridge, MA: Harvard University Press.

Gladding, S. T., Burggraf, M., & Fenell, D. L. (1987). Marriage and family counseling in counselor education: National trends and implications. *Journal of Counseling and Development, 66,* 90–92.

Glick, P. (1989). Remarried families, stepfamilies, and stepchildren: A brief demographic analysis. *Family Relations, 38,* 24–27.

Grotevant, H. D., & Carlson, C. I. (1987). Family interaction coding systems: A descriptive review. *Family Process, 26,* 49–74.

Grotevant, H. D., & Cooper, C. R. (1985). Patterns of interaction in family relationships and the development of identity exploration in adolescence. *Child Development, 56,* 415–428.

Grotevant, H. D., & Cooper, C. R. (1986). Individuation in family relationships: A perspective on individual differences in the development of identity and role-taking skill in adolescence. *Human Development, 29,* 82–100.

Gurman, A. S., & Kniskern, D. P. (1981). *Handbook of family therapy.* New York: Brunner/Mazel.

Harvey, D. M., Curry, C. J., & Bray, J. H. (1986, August). *Individuation/intimacy in intergenerational relationships and health: Patterns across two generations.* Paper presented at the annual meeting of the American Psychological Association, Washington, DC.

Hauser, S. T., Powers, S. I., Noam, G. G., Jacobson, A. M., Weiss, B., & Follansbee, D. J. (1984). Familial contexts of adolescent ego development. *Child Development, 55,* 195–213.

Held, B. S., & Bellows, D. C. (1983). A family systems approach to crisis reactions in college students. *Journal of Marital and Family Therapy, 9,* 365–373.

Hill, K. A. (1987). Meta-analysis of paradoxical interventions. *Psychotherapy, 24,* 266–270.

Hoffman, J. A. (1984). Psychological separation of late adolescents from their parents. *Journal of Counseling Psychology, 31,* 170–178.

Hoffman, J. A., & Weiss, B. (1987). Family dynamics and the presenting problems of college students. *Journal of Counseling Psychology, 34,* 157–163.

Hoffman, L. (1981). *Foundations of family therapy: A conceptual framework for systems change.* New York: Basic Books.

Hovestadt, A. J., Fenell, D. L., & Piercy, F. P. (1983). Integrating marriage and family therapy training within counselor education: A three-level model. In B. F. Okun & S. T. Gladding (Eds.), *Issues in training marriage and family therapists* (pp. 29–42). Ann Arbor, MI: ERIC/CAPS.

Howard, G. S. (1984). A modest proposal for a revision of strategies for counseling research. *Journal of Counseling Psychology, 31,* 430–441.

Humphrey, L. L., & Benjamin, L. S. (1986). Using structural analysis of social behavior to assess critical but elusive family processes. *American Psychologist, 41,* 979–989.

Hunsley, J. (1988). Conceptions and misconceptions about the context of paradoxical therapy. *Professional Psychology: Research and Practice, 19,* 553–559.

Johnson, M. (1986). Paradoxical interventions: From repugnance to cautious curiosity. *The Counseling Psychologist, 14,* 297–302.

Josselson, R. (1980). Ego development in adolescence. In J. Adelson (Ed.), *Handbook of adolescent psychology* (pp. 188–210). New York: Wiley.

Josselson, R. (1988). The embedded self: I and thou revisited. In D. K. Lapsley & F. C. Power (Eds.), *Self, ego, and identity: Integrative approaches* (pp. 91–106). New York: Springer-Verlag.

Kamptner, N. L. (1988). Identity development in late adolescence: Causal modeling of social and familial influences. *Journal of Youth and Adolescence, 17,* 493–514.

Karpel, M. (1976). Individuation: From fusion to dialogue. *Family Process, 15,* 65–82.

Keeney, B. (1983). *Aesthetics of change.* New York: Guilford Press.

Kenny, M. E. (1987a). The extent and function of parental attachment among first-year college students. *Journal of Youth and Adolescence, 16,* 17–29.

Kenny, M. E. (1987b). Family ties and leaving home for college: Recent findings and implications. *Journal of College Student Personnel, 28,* 438–442.

Kerr, M. E., & Bowen, M. (1988). *Family evaluation: An approach based on Bowen theory.* New York: Norton.

Kinnier, R. T., Brigman, S. L., & Noble, F. (1990). Career indecision and family enmeshment. *Journal of Counseling and Development, 68,* 309–312.

Kleiman, J. I. (1981). Optimal and normal family functioning. *American Journal of Family Therapy, 9,* 37–44.

Kohut, H. (1971). *The analysis of the self.* New York: International Universities Press.

Kohut, H. (1977). *The restoration of the self.* New York: International Universities Press.

Kroger, J., & Haslett, S. J. (1988). Separation–individuation and ego identity status in late adolescence: A two-year longitudinal study. *Journal of Youth and Adolescence, 17,* 59–79.

Kunce, J. T., & Priesmeyer, M. L. (1985). Measuring family dynamics. *Journal of Counseling Psychology, 32,* 40–46.

Lapan, R., & Patton, M. J. (1986). Self-psychology and the adolescent process: Measures of pseudoautonomy and peer group dependence. *Journal of Counseling Psychology, 33,* 136–142.

Lapsley, D. K., Rice, K. G., & FitzGerald, D. P. (1990). Adolescent attachment, identity, and adjustment to college: Implications for the continuity of adaptation hypothesis. *Journal of Counseling and Development, 68,* 561–565.

Lapsley, D. K., Rice, K. G., & Shadid, G. E. (1989). Psychological separation and adjustment to college. *Journal of Counseling Psychology, 36,* 286–294.

Larkin, L. (1987). Identity and fear of success. *Journal of Counseling Psychology, 34,* 38–45.

Lopez, F. G. (1983). A paradoxical approach to vocational indecision. *Personnel and Guidance Journal, 61,* 410–412.

Lopez, F. G. (1987). The impact of parental divorce on college student development. *Journal of Counseling and Development, 65,* 484–486.

Lopez, F. G. (1989). Current family dynamics, trait anxiety, and academic adjustment: Test of a family-based model of vocational identity. *Journal of Vocational Behavior, 35,* 76–87.

Lopez, F. G. (1991). The impact of parental divorce on college students. In R. Witchel (Ed.), *Dealing with students from dysfunctional families* (pp. 19–33). San Francisco: Jossey-Bass.

Lopez, F. G., & Andrews, S. (1987). Career indecision: A family systems perspective. *Journal of Counseling and Development, 65,* 304–307.

Lopez, F. G., Campbell, V. L., & Watkins, C. E. (1986). Depression, psychological separation, and college adjustment: An investigation of sex differences. *Journal of Counseling Psychology, 33,* 52–56.

Lopez, F. G., Campbell, V. L., & Watkins, C. E. (1988). Family structure, psychological separation, and college adjustment: A canonical analysis and cross-validation. *Journal of Counseling Psychology, 35,* 402–409.

Lopez, F. G., Campbell, V. L., & Watkins, C. E. (1989a). Effects of marital conflict and family coalition patterns on college student adjustment. *Journal of College Student Development, 30,* 46–52.

Lopez, F. G., Campbell, V. L., & Watkins, C. E. (1989b). Constructions of current family functioning among depressed and nondepressed college students. *Journal of College Student Development, 30,* 221–228.

Mahler, M. S. (1963). Thoughts about development and individuation. *The Psychoanalytic Study of the Child, 18,* 307–324.

Mahler, M. S., Pine, F., & Bergman, A. (1975). *The psychological birth of the human infant.* New York: Basic Books.

Marcia, J. E. (1966). Development and validation of ego identity status. *Journal of Personality and Social Psychology, 3,* 119–133.

Marcia, J. E. (1976). Identity six years after: A follow-up. *Journal of Youth and Adolescence, 5,* 145–160.

Marcia, J. E. (1980). Identity in adolescence. In J. Adelson (Ed.), *Handbook of adolescent psychology* (pp. 159–187). New York: Wiley.

Markova, I. (1987). Knowledge of self through interaction. In K. Yardley & T. Honess (Eds.), *Self and identity: Psychosocial perspectives* (pp. 65–80). Chichester, England: Wiley.

Meadows, M. E., & Hetrick, H. H. (1982). Roles for counselor education departments in marriage and family counseling: Current status and projections. *Counselor Education and Supervision, 22,* 47–54.

Minuchin, S. (1974). *Families and family therapy.* Cambridge, MA: Harvard University Press.

Moore, D. (1987). Parent–adolescent separation: The construction of adulthood by late adolescents. *Developmental Psychology, 23,* 298–307.

Olson, D. H., Sprenkle, D. H., & Russell, C. S. (1979). Circumplex model of marital and family systems: Cohesion and adaptability dimensions of family types and clinical applications. *Family Process, 18,* 3–28.

Orlofsky, J. L., Marcia, J. E., & Lesser, I. M. (1973). Ego identity status and the intimacy vs. isolation crisis of young adulthood. *Journal of Personality and Social Psychology, 27,* 211–219.

Palmer, S., & Cochran, L. (1988). Parents as agents of career development. *Journal of Counseling Psychology, 35,* 71–76.

Patton, M. J. (1984). Managing social interaction in counseling: A contribution from the philosophy of science. *Journal of Counseling Psychology, 31,* 442–456.

Patton, M. J., Connor, G., & Scott, K. J. (1982). Kohut's psychology of the self: Theory and measures of counseling outcome. *Journal of Counseling Psychology, 29,* 268–282.

Peltier, S. W., & Vale, S. O. (1986). A national survey of counselor education departments: Course offerings on marriage and family. *Counselor Education and Supervision, 25,* 313–319.

Polkinghorne, D. E. (1984). Further extensions of methodological diversity for counseling psychology. *Journal of Counseling Psychology, 31,* 416–429.

Polster, S. (1983). Ego boundary as process: A systemic-contextual approach. *Psychiatry, 46,* 247–258.

Rabkin, R. (1976). A critique of the clinical use of the double bind. In C. Sluzki & D. Ransom (Eds.), *Double bind: The communicational approach to the family* (pp. 287–306). New York: Grune & Stratton.

Rice, K. G., Cole, D. A., & Lapsley, D. K. (1990). Separation–individuation, family cohesion, and adjustment to college: Measurement validation and test of a theoretical model. *Journal of Counseling Psychology, 37,* 195–202.

Richman, J. (1979). The family therapy of attempted suicide. *Family Process, 18,* 131–142.

Ridley, C. R., & Tan, S. (1986). Unintentional paradoxes and potential pitfalls in paradoxical psychotherapy. *The Counseling Psychologist, 14,* 303–308.

Robbins, S. B. (1989). Role of contemporary psychoanalysis in counseling research. *Journal of Counseling Psychology, 36,* 267–278.

Robbins, S. B., & Patton, M. J. (1985). Self-psychology and career development: Construction of the superiority and goal instability scales. *Journal of Counseling Psychology, 32,* 221–231.

Robbins, S. B., & Tucker, K. R. (1985). Relation of goal instability to self-directed and interactional career workshops. *Journal of Counseling Psychology, 33,* 418–424.

Sabatelli, R. M., & Mazor, A. (1985). Differentiation, individuation, and identity formation: The integration of family system and individual developmental perspectives. *Adolescence, 20,* 619–633.

Sampson, E. E. (1985). The decentralization of identity: Toward a revised concept of personal and social order. *American Psychologist, 40,* 1203–1211.

Savickas, M. L. (1985). Identity in vocational development. *Journal of Vocational Behavior, 27,* 329–337.

Schiedel, D. G., & Marcia, J. E. (1985). Ego identity, sex role orientation, and gender. *Developmental Psychology, 21,* 149–160.

Schulenberg, J. E., Vondracek, F. W., & Crouter, A. C. (1984). The influence of the family on vocational development. *Journal of Marriage and the Family, 10,* 129–143.

Searight, H., & Openlander, H. (1984). Systemic therapy: A new brief intervention model. *Personnel and Guidance Journal, 62,* 387–391.

Sherverbush, R. L., & Ward, D. E. (1989). Adding a family counseling component to a community agency counseling master's degree. *Journal of Counseling and Development, 67,* 356–357.

Shoham-Salomon, V., & Rosenthal, R. (1987). Paradoxical interventions: A meta-analysis. *Journal of Consulting and Clinical Psychology, 55,* 22–28.

Silverman, L. H., & Weinberger, J. (1985). Mommy and I are one: Implications for psychotherapy. *American Psychologist, 40,* 1296–1308.

Swann, W. B. (1987). Identity negotiation: Where two roads meet. *Journal of Personality and Social Psychology, 53,* 1038–1051.

Terklesen, K. G. (1980). Toward a theory of the family life cycle. In E. Carter and M. McGoldrick (Eds.), *The family life cycle: A framework for family therapy* (pp. 21–52). New York: Gardner Press.

Teyber, E. (1983a). Effects of parental coalition on adolescent emancipation from the family. *Journal of Marital and Family Therapy, 9,* 305–310.

Teyber, E. (1983b). Structural family relations: Primary dyadic alliances and adolescent adjustment. *Journal of Marital and Family Therapy, 9,* 89–99.

Vondracek, F. W., Lerner, R. M., & Schulenberg, J. E. (1983). The concept of development in vocational theory and intervention. *Journal of Vocational Behavior, 23,* 179–202.

Waterman, A. S. (1982). Identity development from adolescence to adulthood: An extension of theory and a review of research. *Developmental Psychology, 18,* 341–358.

Watkins, C. E., Lopez, F. G., Campbell, V. L., & Himmell, C. D. (1986). Contemporary counseling psychology: Results of a national survey. *Journal of Counseling Psychology, 33,* 301–309.

Watkins, C. E., Lopez, F. G., Campbell, V. L., & Himmell, C. D. (1989). Counseling psychologists in private practice: Who are they? What do they do? What do they practice? *Psychotherapy in Private Practice, 7,* 135–150.

Watzlawick, P., Beavin, J., & Jackson, D. (1967). *Pragmatics of human communication: A study of interactional patterns, pathologies, and paradoxes.* New York: Norton.

West, J. D., & Zarski, J. J. (1983). The counselor's use of the paradoxical procedure in family therapy. *Personnel and Guidance Journal, 62,* 34–37.

Whiting, R. (1981). The practice of family therapy in a college counseling center. *Journal of College Student Personnel, 22,* 558–559.

Zingaro, J. C. (1983). A family systems approach for the career counselor. *Personnel and Guidance Journal, 62,* 24–27.

CHAPTER 9

COUNSELING ADULTS FOR LIFE TRANSITIONS

JOHN GIBSON
STEVEN D. BROWN

Adulthood is hardly a static affair. Any number of potential events—marriage, divorce, the loss of loved ones, major illness, job termination, and so on—may require us to make adjustments in the patterns of our daily living (Stewart, 1982). Because of their timing in the life cycle, many life transitions will be anticipated. But other potential events, for instance, being diagnosed as having cancer, will catch us by surprise. Not all life transitions are negative, but even positive events, when accompanied by significant changes, have the potential to be distressing.

Most people weather the stormy periods in their lives without professional assistance. Others may find that the distress and disruption of a life transition provides an occasion to consult a psychologist. In our view, counseling psychologists are especially suited to helping clients with life transition issues. The goals of counseling psychology have historically been aligned with developmental, educative, and preventive issues, and these goals are quite compatible with life transition concerns. Moreover, counseling psychologists have been keenly interested in helping their clients make the best possible use of their resources (Super, 1955). In this chapter, we attempt to show how useful the concept of *resource* is for helping clients with life transition issues. Indeed, resources serve as the chapter's organizing theme.

Life transitions can be thought of as a crossroads for several different literatures. For instance, the literatures of stress and coping, social support, personality, victimization, life-span development, stressful life events, and depression are all relevant to the study of life transitions. Although we draw from each of these topics in varying degrees, our intent is not to provide an exhaustive review of these literatures, nor is it to provide a new theory of life transitions. Instead, we view the chapter as an opportunity to review diverse findings in light of a particular counseling problem—life transitions. Thus, our aims are more toward integration and synthesis.

Drawing heavily from existing theoretical models, we begin by providing an overview of the life transition process, in a section devoted to matters concerning definition, impact, and the process of adaptation. We then review new developments and findings in the area of coping resources. This review is followed by a brief discussion of the implications that these developments might have for practice and future research.

LIFE TRANSITIONS: OVERVIEW

Definition

One of the first tasks in any discussion of life transitions is to come up with a working definition. Life transitions are commonly referred to as turning points, bridges, or passages. These words are apt metaphors; they evoke concrete images to represent the periods of change that occur in our lives as we move from one point of stability to another, but they lack the precision needed for empirical investigation.

A central feature of a life transition is change (Golan, 1981; Schlossberg, 1984). The literature is replete with different terms that refer to change in adulthood—life change (Holmes & Rahe, 1967), serious life event (Horowitz, 1979), stressful life event (Dohrenwend & Dohrenwend, 1974), crisis (Lindemann & Lindemann, 1979; Moos & Schaefer, 1986; Parry, 1990), midlife transition (Levinson, 1978), and life strain (Pearlin, 1985). These terms are often used interchangeably with the word transition. The result is a confusion over constructs, if not conceptual and empirical traditions. If a transition is a change, what other features can be used to define it?

The term transition has been used in a number of different ways. Levinson (1978), for example, used the term to mean shifts between major developmental periods (e.g., early adult transition) and life structures (e.g., age 30 transition). On the average, these shifts are assumed to last about 5 years. External events will naturally occur during these periods, but they are not explicitly tied to Levinson's conception of a transition. Similarly, Loevinger (1976) discussed the transitions between levels of ego development, and Kegan (1982) enumerated the transitional periods between eras in the development of the self. What these three theorists have in common is that they refer to transitions between stages, levels, or eras. Generally, these changes refer to a process that is internal to the individual and maturational (see Chapter 7, by Fassinger and Schlossberg, for a more complete discussion of these theories). In contrast, our use of the term transition refers to the changes individuals make as a result of experiencing external events.

Life events are frequently tied to the life span as marker events, or milestones (Brim & Kagan, 1980; Brim & Ryff, 1980; Danish, 1981; Hultsch & Plemons, 1979). For example, young adults are often faced with the changes brought about by leaving home after high school, to enter college. Other common marker events include job entry, marriage, childbirth, retirement, and so on. Such events punctuate the ongoing process of the life span and consequently have the potential to exert influence on an individual's life.

Not all life events can be neatly categorized in the predictable, developmental progression of the life span. Many events are idiosyncratic or unscheduled (Pearlin, 1985). For instance, individuals may experience a major illness (e.g., cancer) early in adulthood, an unexpected loss (e.g., a house fire), or an unexpected gain (e.g., winning a lottery). Even though these events are not markers of an underlying developmental process, we would consider them to be life transitions (assuming they are perceived as change from the individual's point of view). It is important for a definition of life transitions to be flexible enough to include events that have little direct relationship to the life span. In this regard, we do not agree with Danish (1981), who maintained that all life transitions should be understood within a life-span perspective.

Some investigators use the term crisis interchangeably with the term life transition (Moos & Schaefer, 1986; Parry, 1990). A crisis generally refers to events that are sudden, dramatic, and novel; crises are states of disequilibrium that are accompanied by heightened emotions—fear, anxiety, anger, and guilt—where habitual responses seem insufficient (Lindemann & Lindemann, 1979; Moos & Schaefer, 1986). Schlossberg (1984) made the point, however, that many transitions are not dramatic and sudden, and that some actually fail to happen. Thus, it is important that less dramatic events be included in a definition of life transitions.

In sum, our review of the literature suggests that it is helpful to make four distinctions in defining a life transition:

1. Our definition presumes that the change is in response to an external event. Individuals negotiate changes in the context of their external circumstances, and these changes require a new level of adaptation.
2. We do not, as some do (Golan, 1981; Sherman, 1987), equate life transitions with the vicissitudes of adult development, although it is certainly useful to embed many life transitions in a developmental framework.
3. We do not use the term life transition synonymously with the term crisis. In our definition, all crises, if they result in change, are life transitions, but not all life transitions are crises.
4. A life transition must be perceived as a time of change, from the individual's point of view.

Impact

We have said that a life transition is an event that, from the individual's perception, calls for change. But what changes? How will an individual's life be different after the transition is completed?

Our review suggests that there are a number of potential areas in one's life where the impact of a transition may be felt. For instance, one theoretical model maintains that routines, relationships, and roles may change (Schlossberg, 1981, 1984). This assertion has been borne out in recent research with clerical workers (Charner & Schlossberg, 1986). Recent empirical investigations of the life transition to first-time motherhood have suggested that new mothers are apt to actively revise their self-concepts to accommodate their new views of themselves as mothers (Deutsch, Ruble, Fleming, Brooks-Gunn, & Stangor, 1988). Similarly, McAdams (1988) showed that it is not uncommon for individuals to select exalted turning points in their lives and weave these into conceptions of identity via their life story.

Not all of the changes in a life transition will be benign, however, as illustrated by recent work concerning adjustment to victimization (Janoff-Bulman, 1989). Some cognitive revisions may result in what Janoff-Bulman refers to as a "cognitive crisis." Janoff-Bulman maintains that we all hold tacit assumptions about ourselves and our world. These assumptions can be placed in one of three categories:

1. Benevolence about the world, which concerns the extent to which people view the world positively or negatively;
2. Meaningfulness about the world, which involves people's beliefs about the distribution of outcomes (i.e., are outcomes distributed with justice, are they controllable, are they distributed by chance?);
3. Worthiness of self, which concerns how vulnerable one believes oneself to be.

According to Janoff-Bulman, these assumptions usually remain tacit and generally unquestioned. But if a traumatic event occurs, such as a criminal or sexual assault, a natural disaster, or a major accident, these implicit assumptions are dramatically challenged. When Janoff-Bulman compared victims with nonvictims on the World Assumptions Scale, she found that the two groups differed in their assumptions: victims perceived themselves more negatively and perceived the impersonal world as more malevolent. Moreover, male victims viewed the world as distributing outcomes more by chance, and both male and female victims were more depressed than nonvictims.

Janoff-Bulman's study does not show that the traumatic events *cause* a change in the respondents' world assumptions; it only raises this possibility. Interestingly, the respondents experienced their stressful life events several years prior to the study. It could be that some stressful life events, if traumatic enough, etch deep and lasting marks into our cognitive systems.

Finally, some types of life transitions may be linked with psychological and physical disorders. This is suggested by the large body of research, dating back to the work of Holmes and Rahe (1967), that links stressful life events with various mental and physical health outcomes (Brown & Harris, 1989; Dohrenwend & Dohrenwend, 1974). We hasten to add, however, that numerous investigators have routinely bemoaned the weak relationships that are typically found in stressful life event studies (typically around .30). Brown (1990) countered that this problem can be averted by using structured interviews to measure life events, instead of questionnaires. Indeed, Brown asserted that he and his colleagues, using their interview method, have consistently related negative life events to such disturbances as depression, anxiety and phobic disorders, and somatic disorders (Brown & Harris, 1978, 1986, 1989; Brown, Bifulco, & Harris, 1987; Murphy & Brown, 1980).

In short, the impact of a life transition may be felt through a variety of different changes. Changes may occur in routines, roles, relationships, views of self, identity, world assumptions, and perhaps even physical and mental health.

Adaptation

The impact of a transition is concerned with understanding *what* particular changes occur across a life transition; adaptation is concerned with understanding the broader psychological work that needs to be completed throughout the transition. In other words, adaptation is concerned with the *process* dimensions of the change.

The terms adaptation and coping were clarified by White (1985), who maintained that adaptation is a broad term that refers to coming to terms with the environment. It is not to be confused with happiness, contentment, or satisfaction. Rather, it refers to the constant interaction between individuals and their environments, in which realities are neither passively accepted nor completed transformed. Adaptation is a broad, ongoing process of compromise. Coping, on the other hand, is one strategy of adaptation under relatively difficult circumstances. Coping is subsumed under the broader term adaptation.

White's distinctions are useful in the context of life transitions. We have defined life transitions to mean those events that result in change. Adaptation, then, refers to the broader process of coming to terms with this change. In the spirit of White's definition, we reserve the term coping to mean those narrower sets of responses that individuals use to manage the distress associated with life transitions. However, these terms do not stand in sharp relief from one another; to some degree, they are confounded by definition. Nevertheless, we maintain that it is useful to keep these terms separate, to allow for a rendering of the life transition process with both broad and narrow brush strokes.

In general, the process of adapting to a life transition is one of assimilation (Horowitz, 1979; Janoff-Bulman, 1989; Schlossberg, 1984). The changes associated with a life transition need to be assimilated into one's life. Some researchers conceptualize this as a process of phases. For example, Hopson (1981) proposed that individuals undergo 7 phases in assimilating a life transition: immobilization, denial or minimization, self-doubt, letting go, testing out, search for meaning, and integration. Not all transitions are expected to fit neatly within these phases. Schlossberg (1984) also suggested that assimilation is a process of phases, but she preferred a more generic framework. She suggested that assimilation involves the introduction of the transition, which involves a pervasive preoccupation with the event; a middle phase, which is concerned with establishing new norms in the midst of the disruption; and a final phase, which is concerned with integration.

Adaptation during a life transition is not always characterized by phases of assimilation. Some researchers prefer to discuss the adaptive process in terms of tasks, or themes. This was illustrated by recent research with cancer patients (Taylor, 1983). Taylor proposed that successful cognitive adaptation to threatening events involves three central themes. First, individuals must search for *meaning* in the experience. This involves not only an attributional search for causality, but also a broader focus on the *implications* of the event, in terms of what the event means for one's entire life. Second, individuals attempt to regain mastery over the event itself and their lives in general. Third, individuals must exert efforts to restore self-esteem through the use of self-enhancing strategies. In particular, the women in Taylor's study used downward comparison; that is, most of the women, when they compared themselves to other women in similar situations, believed that they were doing as well as, or better than, their counterparts.

Taylor maintained that the key to successful resolution of these three themes depends on the patients' ability to sustain and modify illusions. The patients in her study developed beliefs about meaning, mastery, and self-enhancement that were frequently without any factual basis, or else they chose to view the known facts in a particular light. Taylor concluded that the ability to generate and sustain illusions is an integral component of the adaptative process because illusion provides a buffer against present threats and future setbacks. For instance, a patient might develop a belief about the cause of her cancer (frequently, patients attribute their cancer to stress), and a belief that it can be controlled in the present and avoided in the future. Although such beliefs may be erroneous, they lead to other constructive thoughts and actions, such as exerting greater control over those aspects in one's life that actually can be controlled.

Moos and Schaefer (1986) presented the following set of adaptive tasks, which closely parallel those suggested by Taylor: (a) establish the meaning and understand the personal significance of the situation; (b) confront reality and respond to the requirements of the external situation; (c) sustain relationships with family members and friends as well as with other individuals who may be helpful in resolving the crisis and its aftermath; (d) maintain a reasonable emotional balance by managing upsetting feelings aroused by the situation; and (e) preserve a satisfactory self-image and maintain a sense of competence and mastery.

Coping

Not only must individuals negotiate a new level of adaptation during a life transition, but they must also devise ways to cope with the event. Again, according to White (1985), coping is only one strategy of adaptation under relatively difficult circumstances. The overarching process of adapting to a life transition is concerned with assimilating the event, but the narrower process of coping refers to the fine-grained responses that people use to manage the distress of the event. Some types of life transitions are more difficult to adapt to than others. Yet, in adapting to similar types of events, not everyone seems equally effected. The concept of resources has been used to explain why some individuals cope and adapt effectively and others do not (Holahan & Moos, 1986, 1987; Pearlin & Schooler, 1978; Schlossberg, 1984).

Pearlin and Schooler (1978) made a meaningful distinction among three types of resources:

1. *Coping responses,* which refer to the concrete efforts that people make in dealing with distressing situations;
2. *Social resources,* which refer to the interpersonal networks that people have available to them for social support;
3. *Psychological resources,* which refer to the personality characteristics that help people manage distressing situations.

In the next sections, we review a number of new developments regarding coping resources. Following Pearlin and Schooler's (1978) lead, we divide these resources into coping responses, social resources, and psychological resources, and discuss each in turn.

COPING RESPONSES

In the past decade, there has been a burgeoning interest in understanding how people cope with stress (Aldwin & Revenson, 1987; Billings & Moos, 1981; Carver, Scheier, & Weintraub, 1989; Endler & Parker, 1990; Lazarus & Folkman, 1984). Investigations have generally sought to test the notion that coping responses—the strategies people use to manage, master, reduce, or avoid harmful encounters—mediate the relationship between stressful events and psychological and physical illnesses. In this section, we discuss conceptualization and measurement of coping, coping effectiveness, and anticipatory coping.

Conceptualization and Measurement

Coping responses have been conceptualized and classified in a variety of ways. Perhaps the most influential body of work has come from Lazarus, Folkman, and their colleagues (Cohen & Lazarus, 1973; Folkman & Lazarus, 1980; 1985; 1986; Lazarus & Folkman, 1984). Over a number of years, these researchers have refined a model that emphasizes cognitive processes in the perception of stress and coping.

A central concept in their model is appraisal, which mediates encounters between individuals and their environments. Cognitive appraisals are of two types. During *primary* appraisals, individuals evaluate what is at stake in the encounter: "Am I okay or in trouble?" During *secondary* appraisals, individuals evaluate whether anything can be done to overcome, prevent, or improve the encounter: "What can I do about it?" Essentially, secondary appraisals involve a search for the resources that one has available to manage the perceived demands of the situation. If limited resources are detected, the individual experiences stress. Primary and secondary appraisals do not need to occur in a linear fashion; indeed, Folkman and Lazarus suggested they are highly interdependent.

The Lazarus and Folkman (1984) model has three other important features. First, coping is conceptualized as having two broad dimensions. In *problem-focused coping,* coping efforts may be aimed directly at doing something to alter the source of the stress.

But coping efforts may also be directed toward regulating emotional reactions; this is *emotion-focused coping*. Most situations are complex enough to require both problem- and emotion-focused coping. Second, Lazarus and Folkman maintained that coping (and stress) is fundamentally a process; it is not static. Thus, as the stressful or problematic encounter unfolds, appraisals naturally fluctuate, as do coping responses. Third, stress and coping are best viewed within a context.

Folkman and Lazarus (1980) devised the Ways of Coping Scale to measure their conceptualization of coping. This instrument has undergone at least one revision (Folkman & Lazarus, 1985). Although its conceptual framework emphasizes two broad dimensions of coping (problem-focused and emotion-focused), factor analyses of the Ways of Coping Scale typically reveal between 6 and 9 factors, depending on the populations and situations under investigation (Aldwin & Revenson, 1987). For example, in one recent study, 8 factors were reported: confrontative coping, distancing, seeking social support, accepting responsibility, escape–avoidance, planful problem solving, and positive reappraisal (Folkman, Lazarus, Dunkel-Schetter, Delongis, & Gruen, 1986).

Although the Ways of Coping Scale has been widely adopted in the literature, some investigators have identified weaknesses in the instrument. For instance, Carver et al. (1989) charged that it is not grounded in theory (this is true of most coping scales). Consequently, they derived their own instrument (entitled COPE) to reflect Carver and Scheier's (1982) control theory. Endler and Parker (1990) identified psychometric weaknesses in the Ways of Coping Scale (most noteably, inadequate reliability for certain scales). They offered a new measure, The Multidimensional Coping Inventory.

The literature has no shortage of coping measures to choose from (for other recent scales, see Amirkhan, 1990; Rohde, Tilson, Lewinsohn, & Seeley, 1990). Indeed, Aldwin and Revenson (1987) reported that they were aware of no less than 20 coping measures that have been developed in the past 10 years. In measuring coping responses, one issue that repeatedly arises is the construct's dimensionality. Virtually all investigators agree that coping is a multifaceted construct. For instance, Amirkhan (1990) reported three factors for the Coping Strategy Indicator: problem solving, seeking social support, and avoidance coping. Likewise, Endler and Parker (1990) reported three coping factors for the Multidimensional Coping Inventory. These were labeled task-oriented, emotion-oriented, and avoidance coping. Carver et al. (1989), however, found 14 coping factors for their newly created COPE scale.

In short, there appears to be little consensus regarding the dimensionality of coping responses. Undoubtedly, new scales will continue to proliferate in the literature, and each will propose a new variation on the number and kinds of coping strategies that individuals use to mediate stressful encounters. Currently, however, it is helpful to retain the broad division suggested by Folkman and Lazarus, because problem-solving strategies and emotion-focused strategies, of one sort or another, frequently tend to emerge in measurement studies.

Effectiveness

Research tends to show that the negative impact of stressful situations and events can be reduced through the use of coping responses (Lazarus & Folkman, 1984; Pearlin & Schooler, 1978). Once we know that, can we ascertain which strategies are most effective? The answer to this question requires a bit of qualification. For instance, values play a role in deciding what strategies are effective, as do the unit of analysis (i.e., physical, psychological, sociological), the time frame (i.e., short vs. long-term impact), and the particulars of the stressful situation (Monat & Lazarus, 1985).

With these qualifiers in mind, we can make five basic points about coping effectiveness.

1. Coping is clearly a complex process, and, as one might expect, research repeatedly demonstrates that no single coping strategy works for all situations (Charner & Schlossberg, 1986; Folkman et al., 1986; Folkman & Lazarus, 1985; Pearlin & Schooler, 1978). Folkman, Lazarus, and their colleagues generally found, as their model had predicted, that most encounters require combinations of problem-focused and emotion-focused coping responses (Folkman et al., 1986; Folkman & Lazarus, 1985).

2. Lazarus and Folkman (and others) also found that coping strategies vary, depending on whether the event is appraised as changeable. Changeable events are more likely to result in problem-focused strategies, whereas nonchangeable events are more likely to result in emotion-focused coping (Carver et al., 1989; Folkman & Lazarus, 1980).

3. Avoidance coping has been consistently linked to depression in both cross-sectional and longitudinal analyses. Perhaps this is most clearly illustrated in the work of Holahan and Moos (1985, 1986, 1987), who found that avoidant coping strategies consistently predicted higher levels of depressed mood and physical symptoms, even when initial symptom levels were controlled. Conversely, subjects who were able to resist the effects of stress were more likely to rely on active or approach coping strategies. Similar findings have been recently reported by Rohde et al. (1990). Using a longitudinal design, they reported that escapism predicted not only current levels of depression, but future levels of depression as well.

4. It may be important to make a distinction between coping effectiveness and coping efficacy (Aldwin & Revenson, 1987). Aldwin and Revenson suggested that, whereas coping effectiveness is concerned with the relationship between various coping strategies and outcome measures, coping efficacy refers to how successful coping strategies are in meeting an individual's goals (from the individual's point of view). In Aldwin and Revenson's study, for example, when subjects perceived the strategy of negotiation as being effective, their perception tended to *reduce* their symptoms. But when this strategy was perceived as not working effectively, the perception was associated with *increased* distress.

5. The relationship between coping and mental health may be bidirectional (Aldwin & Revenson, 1987). In Aldwin and Revenson's study, subjects' initial levels of distress predicted the use of ineffective coping strategies. Ineffective coping strategies, in turn, predicted increased distress. Thus, distress and coping efforts may operate in a cyclical fashion.

Anticipatory Coping

Thus far we have discussed the coping process as if it were largely a matter of responding to events after, or during, their occurrence. However, many life transitions can be predicted and foreseen well in advance, and consequently prepared for (Brown & Heath, 1984). Brown and Heath asserted that persons who are faced with a life transition will ask themselves five questions:

1. Is the event probable?
2. Will the event happen to me?
3. Can I change the likelihood that the event will occur?

4. Can I prepare for the event?
5. Do I choose to prepare for the event?

These questions are categorized under the constructs of predictability, expectedness, and preparedness. The central hypothesis in the Brown and Heath model is that successful life-transition outcomes are more likely to occur when individuals predict the transition, expect it, and then prepare for it.

Preparedness requires the anticipation of potential negative consequences, the development of explicit strategies to deal with those consequences, and behavioral efforts to prevent the occurrence of the identified consequences. According to Brown and Heath's model, those individuals who reach the point of taking preparatory action are more likely to be "prepared" than those who stop short of exerting behavioral effort.

Preparedness would seem to fill a gap in the coping literature. For instance, Taylor and Schneider (1989) asserted that one limitation of many current coping models is their lack of explicit attention to mental simulation. They defined simulation as the mental construction of scenarios; these might include rehearsals of future events, reconstructions of past events, fantasies, and mixtures of real and hypothetical events. Such scenarios may be helpful in anticipatory coping, because of their role in problem-solving and emotional regulation. By replaying a past event, for instance, we may be able to detect what went wrong in the interaction, understand it better, gain some sense of mastery over it, or possibly even construct an ending that is more to our liking. Likewise, for future interactions, we may have no script or sequence of behaviors (Abelson, 1981) to call upon, but mental simulation may provide us a method of creating one, because we can construct a plan of action.

Most current models of coping imply some type of mental rehearsal that is consistent with Taylor and Schneider's notion of mental simulation. For instance, on the Ways of Coping Scale, an item on the Self-Controlling subscale reads: "I went over in my mind what I would say or do." Another item, on Escape–Avoidance subscale, reads, "Had fantasies about how things might turn out" (Folkman et al., 1986). In a similar vein, Carver et al. (1989) devised one of their scales on the COPE to reflect planning. One of their items reads: "I think hard about what steps to take." Another item reads: "I make a plan of action." Both of these scales reflect some degree of planning or cognitive rehearsal, although these concepts are not central to their respective coping models.

In contrast, mental simulation is a key component in Brown and Heath's concept of preparedness. Yet preparedness goes one step further than simulation: it requires action. Preparedness refers not only to the mental simulation of probable negative outcomes, but to behavioral responses.

One empirical foothold for preparedness comes from a recent investigation involving widows (Remondet, Hansson, Rule, & Winfrey, 1987). These researchers sought to link behavioral and cognitive rehearsal, prior to widowhood, with postwidowhood adjustment. They asked their subjects to recall their experiences prior to the loss of their husbands. Their findings showed that cognitive rehearsal was positively and significantly associated with emotional disruption. At first, this finding might seem to argue against the hypothesis that rehearsal provides a coping benefit. But behavioral rehearsal was positively and significantly related to adjustment. Moreover, one component of behavioral rehearsal (taking action) was also negatively associated with emotional disruption. These findings need to be interpreted cautiously, because of the study's retrospective design, but it is interesting that rehearsal was found to be effective only when it was brought to the level of action. This is consistent with Brown and Heath's concept of preparedness.

Summary

Our review can be condensed into the following statements: (a) people apparently use combinations of coping strategies in stressful situations, unless the situation is perceived as unchangeable, in which case emotion-focused strategies are more likely to be used; (b) measurement studies typically reveal that coping is a multifaceted construct, but there is little agreement among investigators about the number and kinds of coping dimensions that individuals use to protect themselves in stressful experiences; (c) the relationship between coping efforts and mental health may be bidirectional; and (d) it may be important to make a distinction between coping effectiveness and coping efficacy, especially for strategies that are perceived by individuals as risky (e.g., negotiation).

SOCIAL RESOURCES

In 1974, Weiss proposed that one way to think about social relationships was in terms of the "provisions" that they offer—security, sharing of concerns, nurturance, assurance of worth, alliance, guidance, and so on. Weiss hypothesized (as many others had before him) that these relational provisions were critical in the sustenance of personal well being. These relational provisions might be termed social resources or social support. Nearly two decades have passed since Weiss's seminal paper, and presently there is a large body of evidence attesting to the benefits of social support (for reviews, see Cohen & McKay, 1984; Cohen & Syme, 1985; Cohen & Wills, 1985; Wallston, Alagna, DeVellis, & DeVellis, 1983).

Benefits of Social Support

Early investigations tended to focus on three themes. The most straightforward of these was simply to document that social support did indeed have a beneficial effect for individuals who were coping with stressful events and situations. This association has been repeatedly demonstrated—so much so, in fact, that some reviewers have urged that it is now time to move forward and begin to refine the concept of social support (Heller, Swindle, & Dusenbury, 1986). A second theme was determining whether social support worked primarily through a buffering effect or a direct effect. Essentially, the buffering model posits that social support is helpful only during times of significant stress, but that it is unnecessary during times of low stress. Conversely, the direct effects model posits that social support contributes to well-being regardless of the level of stress. Reviewers typically concluded that social support has both buffering and direct effects (e.g., Cohen & Wills, 1985). The third theme has been concerned with how social support should be conceptualized and measured. Social support has been examined in terms of network characteristics (e.g., density, size, and so on), received support, and perceived support. Of these three approaches, however, it is the *perception* that one is supported by others that seems to be most important in predicting various psychological and physical outcomes (Sarason, Sarason, & Pierce, 1990; Sarason, Shearin, Pierce, & Sarason, 1987).

The above findings are encouraging, but they do little to illuminate *how* social support yields its benefits (Cohen & Syme, 1985; Cutrona, 1990; Heller et al., 1986; Thoits, 1986). For instance, do support needs vary across life transitions? Is it important to receive some types of support from some individuals, but not others? Are there traceable underlying physical mechanisms that help explain why social support provides protection against stress? With these types of questions, we find ourselves in waters that are largely uncharted. Only recently have research efforts been initiated in these directions.

Components of Social Support

One preliminary step in the process of understanding social support is to clarify and refine the construct's components. Social support is generally understood to be a multifaceted concept. For example, House (1981) proposed a four-component model that is often cited in the literature. These components are emotional support (esteem, trust, concern, listening), appraisal support (affirmation, feedback, social comparison), informational support (advice, suggestion, directives, information), and instrumental support (aid, money, labor, time, help in modifying the environment). Other investigators have proposed similar taxonomies. For instance, Cutrona (1986) proposed six social support components—attachment, nurturance, guidance, reliable alliance, social integration, and reassurance of worth. In a similar vein, Brown, Alpert, Lent, Hunt, and Brady (1988) proposed five components: acceptance and belonging, appraisal and coping assistance, behavioral and cognitive guidance, tangible assistance and material aid, and modeling.

A clear delineation of the components of social support makes it possible to examine types of support under varying adaptational demands (Cohen & Syme, 1985). One model of how components might be utilized was recently proposed by Cutrona (1990). She and her colleagues argued that previous attempts to match support needs with types of stress were hampered by treating support as a unidimensional construct. They identified common social support components from the literature (similar to those described above), as well as common dimensions of stressful life events (e.g., controllability, life domains affected by the stress). Their research is still in the preliminary phases, but, in future investigations, Cutrona and her colleagues hope to match the support components with stressful life-event dimensions. Studies of this type would be very valuable.

A similar line of investigation is provided by recent work with cancer patients. Dakof and Taylor (1990) employed a fine-grained approach toward the study of social support that included not only different kinds of components of social support, but also different sources of support. In other words, their study was designed to address the question "What is helpful from whom?" (Dakof & Taylor, 1990, p. 80). Their findings showed that patients generally valued intimate others (e.g., spouses, friends) primarily for their role in providing esteem or emotional support; informational support and tangible aid were less valued in these relationships. However, in relationships with nonintimate others (e.g., physicians, cancer patients), informational support was more valued than esteem or emotional support.

How Does Social Support Work?

It is not enough to merely show that social support leads to certain benefits. We need an explanation of how it works. However, presently we are in no position to offer anything more than a bit of conjecture and a few tentative findings.

For instance, Thoits (1986) offered an explanation of how social support works by pointing out how closely coping strategies parallel the provisions given by others. She suggested that it might be useful to reconceptualize social support as coping assistance. Her argument was that, when others provide supportive transactions, they are allowing themselves to be participants in another person's efforts to manage stress. For instance, consider two ways in which individuals might be supportive: one strategy might be to help the distressed individual by providing direct assistance in solving the immediate problem; a second strategy might be to help by reinterpreting or relabeling the stressful situation. Thoits argued that these types of supportive interactions can be easily aligned with problem- and emotion-focused coping dimensions, as discussed by Folkman and Lazarus. Moreover, the by-product of coping assistance is enhanced self-esteem or self-worth. This stands in contrast to the more common view, which assumes that one function of support is the provision of direct statements about self-esteem, self-worth, and so on.

There is also presently some evidence that ties social support to the immune system, the body's primary mechanism in defending itself against disease. This link has been recently illustrated by two studies. Jemmott & Magloire (1988) examined social support and immunoglobulin A (S-IgA) during the midst of final exams in undergraduates. S-IgA is "an antibody class that plays an important role in mucosal defense against acute respiratory tract infections" (Jemmott & Magloire, 1988, p. 803). Measures of S-IgA were collected 5 days before students' exam period, during the exam period, and 14 days after the exams were completed. Comparing students who reported adequate levels of social support with those who had less than adequate social support, they found that the former group had superior immune functioning (as reflected by S-IgA concentrations).

Jemmott and Magloire's findings parallel those of Baron, Cutrona, Hicklin, Russell, and Lubaroff (1990). These researchers examined social support and immune functioning in cancer patients. When individuals who reported greater social support were compared with those who reported lower levels of social support, those with greater social support were found to have faster T-lymphocyte proliferation (an increase in these cells aids the immune system in times of stress), and their systems were more effective in destroying target tumor cells.

Social Support and Personality

A number of dispositional characteristics have been found to be correlates of social support. For instance, research has shown links with social competence (Sarason, Sarason, Hacker, & Basham, 1985), self-esteem (Dunkel-Schetter, Folkman, & Lazarus, 1987; Hobfall & Freedy, 1990), self-mastery (Hobfall & Freedy, 1990), religiosity, interpersonal trust, values, and personal commitments (Dunkel-Schetter et al., 1987). These kinds of findings have prompted some investigators to speculate that social support—especially the *perception* of support—is perhaps more accurately conceptualized as a personality component rather than a relational provision.

This stance has been advocated by the Sarasons and their colleagues (Sarason et al., 1985, 1990; Sarason, Sarason, & Shearin, 1986). For instance, in one of their studies, they noted that levels of social support, in addition to being highly correlated with social skills, remained consistent for up to 3 years, even more so than levels of anxiety, depression, and hostility (Sarason et al., 1986). This led them to conclude that social support has traitlike properties. A similar position was suggested by Lakey and Cassady (1990), who examined perceived social support in the context of a number of other dispositional variables. Like the Sarasons, they concluded that perceived social support is perhaps better characterized as a "cognitive personality construct" than a social resource.

The Need for Theory

One consistent criticism in the literature has been that most measures of social support have seldom been embedded in theory (see Heller et al., 1986; Sarason et al., 1990;

Thoits, 1986). A recent exception to this criticism is the Social Support Inventory (SSI) developed by Brown and his associates (Brown et al., 1988; Brown, Brady, Lent, Wolfert, & Hall, 1987).

The SSI was carefully developed from a person–environment (P–E) fit conception of satisfaction. The P–E model suggests that satisfaction with support is seen as a function of the match between the strength of one's interpersonal needs and the interpersonal resources available to fulfill those needs. Dissatisfaction occurs when one's needs outweigh the available resources, and Brown et al. (1987) hypothesized that dissatisfaction would be experienced as personal strain, thereby providing a motive to improve the fit with the interpersonal environment. The SSI contains 39 interpersonal need statements that respondents rate on two scales: (a) "How much of this type of help or support have you needed in the past month?" (Need Strength), and (b) "How much of this type of help or support have you received in the past month?" (Perceived Supply). To calculate an overall Perceived Fit score (SSI-PF), Perceived Supply is subtracted from Need Strength and summed across all 39 items.

The SSI illustrates a useful point about social support and needs. An advantage of the way the SSI is designed is that it allows for Need Strength to be directly compared against Perceived Supply of social support. For example, Brown et al. (1988) tested different scoring models using the Need Strength and Perceived Supply combinations. They found that satisfaction with support plateaued when supplies matched perceived need; an oversupply of support did not generally lead to an increase in satisfaction, nor did an oversupply lead to an increase in dissatisfaction. It appears that individuals have certain support needs, but once those needs are met, more support is not necessarily better.

Summary

Perceived social support is beneficial to psychological and physical health because of its direct and buffering role in protecting against the effects of stress. This much we can say with confidence. But, as Heller et al. (1986) pointed out, it is time to move beyond the demonstration phase and begin to explore *how* social support has its effects. Recent efforts in this direction have focused on identifying and clarifying the components of social support. These efforts, in turn, have made it possible to begin examining types of social support in relation to types of stressful situations and varying sources of interpersonal aid. Future research in this area may help clarify how social support needs change—or don't change—as life transitions unfold.

Social support may be more than a relational provision; it may also be something that is appropriately located in the person. We pointed out the traitlike stability of perceived support and said that it is consistently associated with other personality variables such as social competence, self-mastery, self-esteem, and so on. Do others reflect back to us a sense that we are supported, cared for, valued, liked, and so on, in response to the various dispositional characteristics that we bring to the transaction? Or is the *perception* that we are supported a consequence of having internalized numerous supportive transactions over a lifetime? The hypothesis that social support is a personality construct needs more attention.

Social support is a construct in search of a theory (Sarason et al., 1990). However, Brown and his associates have recently developed a psychometrically sound measure— the SSI—that is solidly grounded in theory. This instrument will undoubtedly prove useful in further explicating the role of support components in relation to perceived availability and perceived need for support.

PSYCHOLOGICAL RESOURCES

Psychological resources refer to the various personality factors that help people cope with stress. Unlike coping responses, psychological resources are dispositional characteristics or traits that people *have* (Pearlin & Schooler, 1978). Pearlin and Schooler identified self-esteem, self-denigration, and self-mastery as important psychological resources. In their analysis, self-denigration (freedom from negative attitudes toward self) had the strongest relative importance with regard to stress; self-mastery followed, and then self-esteem. Schlossberg (1984), in her theoretical formulation, added to these resources and suggested that ego development, outlook (or role complexity), and commitment and values may be also important resources for coping with stress.

But what about other psychological resources? Recent developments in the stress and coping literature suggest that there may be several personality factors that protect against stress. We do not provide an exhaustive review of these factors, but instead focus on four constructs in particular: hardiness, dispositional optimism, negative affectivity, and explanatory style. Because of their role in the coping process, we argue that these constructs merit further empirical attention as psychological resources for adapting to life transitions.

Hardiness

The concept of hardiness is an appropriate starting point for a discussion of psychological resources. In the late 1970s, on the heels of a decade's worth of studies concerned with stressful life events and health, Kobasa and her colleagues (Kobasa, 1979; Kobasa, Maddi, & Courington, 1981) became interested in why some individuals do *not* become ill—despite the presence of stressful life events—as others might. They pointed out, as others had, that the literature revealed consistent correlations between stressful life events and various health outcomes, but that these relationships were generally quite weak. Kobasa (1979) suggested that it was time to examine personality as a moderator variable, and introduced the concept of hardiness.

Hardiness is comprised of three components: control, challenge, and commitment. Hardy individuals believe they have *control* or influence over their experience; they are not distressed by change so much as *challenged* by it; and they are *committed* to the activities of their lives (Kobasa, 1979, 1982; Kobasa et al., 1981). Kobasa and her associates embedded their construct in existential psychology, which emphasizes authenticity in living. The hardiness components—control, challenge, and commitment—were intended to reflect the antithesis of powerlessness, threat, and alienation.

Through a provocative series of investigations, Kobasa and her colleagues (and others) have accumulated support for the positive benefits of hardiness. The initial study was conducted with a large sample of executives (Kobasa, 1979). By using a retrospective design, Kobasa demonstrated that the hardiness concept was able to distinguish between healthy executives and ill executives who had faced stressful life events. Subsequent work extended these findings to prospective designs (Kobasa et al., 1981; Kobasa, Maddi, & Kahn, 1982). Moreover, additional investigations demonstrated that hardiness was a significant predictor of health even when type A behavior pattern and social support were included as independent predictors (Ganellen & Blaney, 1984; Kobasa, Maddi, & Zola, 1983; Kobasa & Puccetti, 1983).

Hardiness may have its effects on health through cognitive mechanisms. One focus of investigations has emphasized cognitive appraisals. Recent research has shown that, when hardy persons are compared with nonhardy persons, hardy individuals appraise their life experiences as being controllable, more positive, less negative, and requiring less adjustment (Rhodewalt & Agustsdottir, 1984; Rhodewalt & Zone, 1989). Other investigations have shown that attributional style may mediate hardiness (Hull, Van Treuren, & Propsom, 1988).

Despite the appeal of the hardiness concept, several writers have identified serious problems with the hardiness literature. These can be briefly summarized as follows. First, critics have charged that the construct has been studied inconsistently (Funk & Houston, 1987; Hull, Van Treuren, & Virnelli, 1987). For instance, the number of hardiness subscales used in the literature tends to vary, as does the manner in which some scales are employed (e.g., the same scale used to represent different components in different studies). Also, not all investigators report the same type of scoring; some researchers derive composite scores, while others use component scores (Funk & Houston, 1987).

Second, the relationship of hardiness to health is not entirely consistent with Kobasa's model. According to Kobasa (1979), hardiness is expected to show buffering (interactive) effects in predicting health-related outcomes. However, there is scant evidence for this hypothesis. Rather, most studies show evidence for direct (additive) effects in connection with health (Allred & Smith, 1989; Funk & Houston, 1987; Hull et al., 1987; Rhodewalt & Zone, 1989; Scheier & Carver, 1987). Moreover, not all of the hardiness components are equally effective in predicting health. The challenge component, in particular, typically fails as a significant predictor (Hull et al., 1987).

A third criticism of hardiness is that it has been inadequately measured. For instance, it is unclear whether hardiness is unidimensional or multidimensional. Although Kobasa initially reported a one-factor solution, others have reported two-factor solutions (Funk & Houston, 1987), and three-factor solutions (Hull et al., 1987). Also, because the hardiness components were developed as negative indicators of existential concepts, high levels of one construct (e.g., alienation) are used to index low levels of another construct (e.g., commitment) (Funk & Houston, 1987). This fact complicates the interpretation of the components.

Finally, it is unclear what is being measured by the existing hardiness scales. Some investigators have suggested that existing hardiness scales overlap substantially with negative affectivity (Allred & Smith, 1989; Funk & Houston, 1987; Hull et al., 1987; Rhodewalt & Zone, 1989). This assertion has important implications, but perhaps these are more appropriately reserved for our discussion of negative affectivity.

Dispositional Optimism

Popular writers have heralded the virtues of positive thinking for years (Cousins, 1977; Peale, 1956), but generally these claims have been ignored by the scientific community (Scheier & Carver, 1987). Recently, however, Carver and Scheier have begun to examine the effects of dispositional optimism on coping and health (Scheier et al., 1989; Scheier & Carver, 1985, 1987; Scheier, Weintraub, & Carver, 1986). Dispositional optimism is a characteristic of individuals who hold *generalized* expectations of success (Scheier et al., 1986). During times of stress, optimists, unlike pessimists, anticipate positive outcomes, so they are expected to persist in the face of difficult situations.

Optimism and pessimism are closely tied to control theory (Carver & Scheier, 1981, 1982). This theory states that, when a discrepancy is perceived between goals and situations, an assessment process is initiated. If it appears as though the discrepancy can be reduced or eliminated, goal-directed efforts are renewed (Smith, Pope, Rhodewalt, & Poulton, 1989). Conversely, if negative outcomes are expected, goal-directed efforts cease. Optimists habitually expect that such discrepancies can be reduced; pessimists do not. In theory, dispositional optimism is a significant benefit because it fosters the expectation of success, despite the presence of obstacles or challenges in the environment. Thus, in contrast to dispositional pessimists, optimists are more apt to remain engaged in constructive coping efforts.

Initial research efforts have supported the idea that dispositional optimism affords health benefits. For instance, in one study (Scheier & Carver, 1985), college undergraduates were given a physical symptom checklist and a measure of dispositional optimism at two points in time, separated by 4 weeks. These measures were given during the closing weeks of their semester, a time deemed stressful by many students. As expected, dispositional optimism was negatively correlated with symptoms at time 1. More importantly, when compared to pessimists, optimists reported fewer symptoms 4 weeks later. Moreover, this relationship remained when even initial symptom levels were controlled.

Additional beneficial effects of dispositional optimism were revealed in a study of middle-aged men who were recovering from coronary bypass surgery (Scheier et al., 1989). Data were collected at three points in time: 1 day before the surgery, 6 to 8 days postoperative, and 6 months postoperative. The findings showed that dispositional optimism was positively correlated with a faster rate of recovery during hospitalization, a faster rate of return to normal activities after discharge, and higher quality of life at 6 months after the surgery.

It is important not only to discern the benefits of optimism, but also to uncover the mechanisms of how optimism has its effects. One study suggests that optimists and pessimists rely on divergent types of coping strategies (Scheier et al., 1986). In this study, optimism was positively correlated with problem-focused coping, as measured by the Ways of Coping Scale (Folkman & Lazarus, 1985). Optimism was also correlated with seeking social support and with a greater likelihood of developing elaborated coping plans. Pessimism, in contrast, was more likely to be associated with coping strategies such as denial, distancing, and expressing feelings about stressful events. Thus, optimism—to the extent that problem-focused coping is more adaptive—may yield advantages in health through coping efforts.

Negative Affectivity

Another personality dimension that has attracted recent attention is negative affectivity (NA), or neuroticism. Negative affectivity is a stable, dispositional dimension of mood that reflects a tendency to experience negative, distressing emotions (Costa & McCrae, 1987; Watson & Clark, 1984). The terms negative affectivity and neuroticism are generally used interchangeably, although some writers prefer the term negative affectivity over neuroticism because the latter term is associated with the outdated term neurosis (Watson & Clark, 1984). It is important to point out that negative affectivity is essentially a normal and pervasive personality dimension, and does not by itself reflect psychopathology.

Watson and Clark (1984) presented an exhaustive review of the construct. They reported that individuals high in NA are more likely, when compared to those low in NA, to be distressed and upset and to have negative views of self. Persons with high NA are more likely to be dissatisfied with themselves and the world, and are sensitive to minor frustrations, failures, and irritations. Watson and Clark maintained that high NA is manifest even in the absence of overt stress, yet high NA does not preclude joy or satisfying experiences. Rather, persons with high NA are more *likely* to experience a wide range of negative affects (e.g., anxiety, anger, guilt, sadness, and so on) across time and situations.

Negative affectivity is a broad personality construct under which several other affective and cognitive concepts may be subsumed (Costa & McCrae, 1987; Watson & Clark, 1984). Watson and Clark showed that NA was reflected in a variety of diverse scales, to varying degrees; for instance, various scales on both the MMPI and the CPI are saturated with NA. A number of depression and anxiety scales (e.g., Beck Depression Inventory, Taylor Manifest Anxiety Scale) show a considerable relation to NA (see Watson & Clark, 1984, for a review).

More recently, however, NA has begun to attract attention because of its potentially confounding effects in measures of stress, coping, and health (Brief, Burke, Robinson, George, & Webster, 1988; Watson, Clark, & Carey, 1988; Watson & Pennebaker, 1989). In six samples of subjects, Watson and Pennebaker (1989) examined the relationships between NA and various symptom indexes and found that NA was consistently and significantly related to health complaints. However, NA did not predict *actual* or long-term health status (as measured by more objective health outcomes). Watson and Pennebaker concluded that subjective stress and health measures reflect a significant NA component. This conclusion implies that the true associations typically found between stress and illness are likely to be overestimates, because NA appears to be operating as a nuisance factor. These conclusions are similar to those of Costa and McCrae (1987), who studied coronary heart patients, and Brief et al. (1988), who examined the relationships between job stress and job strain.

Negative affectivity is central to the present discussion because it has also been implicated in the measurement of hardiness and optimism. For instance, in the case of hardiness, some reviewers of the construct have challenged the notion that hardy individuals are somehow resistant to the effects of stress. Rhodewalt and Zone (1989) and Allred and Smith (1989) found that existing measures of hardiness were substantially overlapped with NA, and suggested that the relationships between hardiness and health outcomes may be overestimated. Similarly, Hull et al. (1987) studied the convergent and discriminant validity of existing hardiness scales and found strong associations between hardiness and measures of depression, optimism, and distress.

The Hull et al. (1987) findings are interesting for two reasons. First, in this study, depression was measured with the Beck Depression Inventory (BDI). As we noted earlier, Watson and Clark (1984) asserted that the BDI reflects a substantial amount of negative affectivity. Second, when dispositional optimism, also discussed earlier, was measured with the Life Orientation Test (LOT), measures of hardiness were found to be related to the LOT. It is interesting to note that Smith et al. (1989) examined the LOT and found limited support for its discriminant validity. Instead, they stated that "the LOT is virtually indistinguishable from measures of neuroticism, and previously reported findings using this scale are perhaps more parsimoniously interpreted as reflecting neuroticism rather than optimism" (p. 640). What we have, then, is a problem of tangled constructs: hardiness overlaps with negative affectivity and optimism, and optimism overlaps with negative affectivity.

This is not merely a point of academic interest. Hardiness and optimism, as we stated earlier, have been shown to be important predictors in helping people resist the effects of stress. But what if the existing measures of these constructs are more appropriately interpreted as negative affectivity (i.e., hardiness and optimism are the *absence* of negative affectivity)? We said earlier that studies show that negative affectivity is related to subjective health complaints but not to objective health outcomes. Thus, it appears as though there is an NA style of interpreting bodily systems consistent with mood. In many of the studies involving hardiness and optimism, stress resistance effects are demonstrated by predicting subjective or "soft" health outcomes. If NA is being measured by hardiness and optimism measures, it may be that previously demonstrated associations are overestimated, or possibly even spurious.

Explanatory Style

Explanatory style is a personality construct that is derived from the reformulated helplessness model of depression (Abramson, Seligman, & Teasdale, 1978). This model suggests that, when individuals are faced with negative events, they will seek to explain those events, and that these causal explanations can be analyzed along three dimensions. In particular, individuals who make internal, stable, and global attributions for negative events are considered to be at risk for depression (Peterson & Seligman, 1984).

Explanatory style is generally measured with the Attributional Style Questionnaire (Seligman, Abramson, Semmel, & von Baeyer, 1979), or the Content Analysis of Verbatim Explanations (CAVE) technique (Peterson, Luborsky, & Seligman, 1983). Individuals who habitually make internal, stable, and global explanations for bad events are characterized as pessimistic (Burns & Seligman, 1989; Peterson, Seligman, & Vaillant, 1988); those who habitually make external, unstable, and specific explanations for bad events are characterized as optimistic (Seligman & Schulman, 1986; Zullow & Seligman, 1990). A recent study found that pessimistic explanatory style was remarkably stable across the life span (Burns & Seligman, 1989). As a result, these investigators concluded that pessimistic explanatory style is perhaps best viewed as a trait.

Explanatory style has been shown to be an important predictor for various outcome variables, but perhaps the largest number of studies to date have been concerned with the construct's link to depression. Recently, Sweeney, Anderson, and Bailey (1986) reported a meta-analysis of 104 studies and found a reliable and significant association with depression, as the model would suggest. In addition, explanatory style has been linked to achievement in insurance agents (Seligman & Schulman, 1986), health (Peterson et al., 1988), and, more recently, the success of presidential candidates (Zullow & Seligman, 1990).

Of particular interest to us is the relationship of explanatory style to health, which was illustrated most clearly by the Peterson et al. (1988) study. The subject pool for this investigation consisted of individuals who participated in the Grant Study of Adult Development (Vaillant, 1977). The study followed the lives of a cohort of Harvard men for several years. Explanatory style was measured with the CAVE procedure, based on responses that were given to open-ended questionnaires at various points in the study. Overall, the findings showed that men who explained bad events with stable, global, and internal causes (pessimistic explanatory style) at age 25 were less healthy from ages 45 to 60 than men who made unstable, specific, and external attributions (optimistic explanatory style). These associations were found even when initial health levels were controlled. In short, pessimistic explanatory style appears to predict health status two and three decades later.

As provocative as the Peterson et al. (1988) findings are, they shed no light on the underlying process that links explanatory style and health. However, Peterson and Seligman (1987) speculated that explanatory style presumably affects coping responses. In particular, they identified six possible pathways:

1. Pessimistic explanatory style may lead to passivity in the face of disease;
2. Health care may be neglected, making pessimistic individuals more vulnerable to health problems;

3. As a result of being poor problem solvers, pessimistic individuals may be less likely to effectively manage or avoid crises, which in turn would increase their exposure to greater numbers of life changes;

4. Pessimistic individuals may not receive as much social support, because pessimism tends to be associated with social withdrawal;

5. Pessimism may lead to depression, which in turn may lead to increased vulnerability to illnesses;

6. Pessimistic explanatory style may be associated with less competent immune systems.

Summary

Physical and mental health benefits have been associated with hardiness, dispositional optimism, and explanatory style. Moreover, dispositional optimism appears to exert its influence on stress through various coping strategies, and hardiness appears to work in a similar fashion, through the appraisal process. Explanatory style has also been hypothesized to operate via coping mechanisms, although presently we are unaware of any data to support this notion. These constructs thus appear to be important psychological resources that individuals use in coping with stress. As such, we would expect them to be of service to individuals who are coping with the stress of a life transition.

However, as we noted, negative affectivity has complicated matters. Some studies show substantial overlap between negative affectivity and hardiness, and other studies show substantial overlap between negative affectivity and dispositional optimism. One interpretation of these findings is that negative affectivity is a nuisance variable, something to be weeded out of future measures of both hardiness and dispositional optimism. From this point of view, hardiness and dispositional optimism are both viable constructs, but their measures are confounded with negative affectivity.

Another interpretation of the overlap problem is that measures of hardiness and dispositional optimism are simply weak measures of negative affectivity. From this point of view, hardiness and optimism might be thought of as new names for an old construct, which sometimes goes by the name of neuroticism, or negative affectivity, or negative emotionality. Hardiness and optimism measures might then be seen as reflecting the *absence* of negative affectivity. As we noted earlier, this interpretation is not without precedent. Watson and Clark (1984) reviewed a host of seemingly different measures and, based on their high intercorrelations, concluded that there are a number of different scales that might be better reinterpreted as measures of NA (e.g., Taylor Manifest Anxiety Scale, and Beck Depression Inventory).

Future research is needed to untangle the constructs of hardiness, dispositional optimism, and negative affectivity. This is a point of some interest. Negative affectivity has been consistently associated with the perceptions of various types of symptoms, but typically not hard health outcomes. If hardiness, for example, which has often been correlated with self-report measures of health, is more appropriately interpreted as a weak measure of negative affectivity, we may wish to rethink many of the existing findings related to that construct.

There is also the matter of the two constructs that purportedly both measure optimism. Carver and Scheier's construct refers to individuals who hold generalized expectations of success; that of Seligman and colleagues refers to individuals who make external, unstable, and specific attributions to bad events. Are we to conclude that both of these constructs define optimism? On the one hand, we are dealing with expectations; on the other hand, we are dealing with attributions of causality. Do both of them refer to the same latent dimension? This puzzle remains unsolved.

We have limited our review to four personality constructs: hardiness, optimism, explanatory style, and negative affectivity. These are not the only candidates that could be culled from the stress literature for inclusion as psychological resources for life transitions. A number of other dispositional variables have been linked to the coping process. Self-complexity (Linville, 1987), sense of humor (Nezu, Nezu, & Blissett, 1988), and self-focused attention (Pyszczynski, Holt, & Greenberg, 1987) are perhaps three other constructs that merit future attention in relation to life transition models.

Finally, we have argued that hardiness, optimism, explanatory style, and negative affectivity may be important psychological resources for predicting who will cope and adapt successfully during a life transition. It is also important to understand how these psychological resources interact with, or perhaps relate to, coping responses and social resources.

IMPLICATIONS FOR PRACTICE

Thus far, we have tried to selectively review a number of coping resources that have been found useful in helping people manage stressful encounters. First, we provided an overview of the life transition process. Then we said that adaptive efforts are facilitated by the application of coping resources, and that the concept of resources could be meaningfully classified as coping responses, social resources, and psychological resources (Pearlin & Schooler, 1978). This division has been skillfully used by others for the purposes of both theory (Schlossberg, 1984) and empirical investigation (Holahan & Moos, 1986, 1987, 1991). In this section, we discuss the implications of our review of resources for counseling adults in life transitions.

We recognized from the outset that there can be no hard and fast rules about how best to counsel clients who have life transition concerns; life transitions are as varied as the individuals who experience them, and no set of rules can be drawn up to meet the needs of all situations. However, as we suggested earlier, different types of life transitions may be similar in terms of the underlying *process* of coming to terms with the event (i.e., assimilation and adaptive tasks). We offer now a few points for consideration, based on the new developments and findings that we reviewed above.

Coping Responses

The process of adapting to a life transition provides a salient occasion for individuals to mobilize their coping behaviors. Again, we emphasize that coping responses are the things that people do to manage, avoid, or reduce the distress of a life transition. The first point we wish to make is that coping responses are learned behaviors, and, as such, it follows that they can be taught (Moos & Schaefer, 1986).

The rub is in knowing what skills to teach clients. If there is one thing that the literature repeatedly emphasizes, it is that no single coping strategy works for all situations. Lazarus and Folkman emphasized this in their conceptualization of stress and coping, and they have found it to be true in their empirical investigations. Again, they found that individuals tended to use problem-solving strategies for situations that were perceived as changeable, and emotion-focused strategies for situations that were not perceived as changeable. This might be wise counsel for our clients.

We suspect, however, that many individuals will overrely on certain strategies that might be considered emotion-focused, or perhaps avoidant. In the recent studies by

Holahan and Moos, avoidance coping strategies were repeatedly shown to be linked to depression in longitudinal analyses. It is just as plausible to suggest that depression and other types of disorders produce ineffective coping strategies as it is to say that ineffective coping produces depression. Regardless of the causal sequence, it is still advisable to help clients develop, or make use of, other coping skills that are not avoidance based. In a word, the key appears to be flexibility (Cantor & Norem, 1989).

Some life transitions can obviously be anticipated, and thus they present opportunities for anticipatory coping. Brown and Heath's model suggested that preparation may be a critical ingredient in predicting successful outcomes to expected life transitions. In the study of adjustment in widows, described earlier, it was not simply cognitive rehearsal that prepared them for the event—in fact, that alone tended to be associated with disruption and distress. Successful adjustment required behavioral rehearsal—in other words, action. Although we do not wish to make too much of this study because of its inherent design flaws, it does illustrate the point made by Brown and Heath (1984). Preparedness is perhaps most useful when clients not only identify possible negative outcomes and develop strategies, but also when they act on those strategies.

One fruitful line of inquiry might be to determine whether there are specific psychological resources that predict who will prepare and who will not. For instance, Scheier et al. (1986) examined the coping strategies of dispositional optimists and pessimists. In Study 2 of that investigation, they asked subjects to provide written descriptions of their coping efforts, which were subsequently coded for elaboration of detail. When optimists were compared with pessimists, optimists tended to produce more elaborate plans of how to handle the stressful situations. Although we would not consider this a complete operationalization of preparedness, it does suggest that dispositional optimism may be a likely candidate for predicting preparedness.

Social Resources

Individuals who perceive the availability of social support tend to be better off than those without such support in combating the effects of stress. Two decades' worth of studies make this much clear. It follows that, as interventionists, we might help clients identify and mobilize sources of support.

We must qualify this suggestion with two additional remarks. First, as new research efforts are beginning to show, different types of social support may be desired from different persons. Not just any support, from any person, will do. It is advisable to help clients determine what kind of support they need and from whom. This may also be a valuable point for clinicians who are consulting with family members and other health professionals, particularly in the case of a crisis. For instance, clinicians might encourage family members to provide emotional and esteem support, rather than informational support, which might better be provided by other health care professionals.

Our second point concerns support satisfaction. With the knowledge in hand that social support protects us against stress, it is tempting to counsel all of our clients to get more of it. This may be a mistake. Satisfaction with support has been found to occur when interpersonal supplies matched one's need for support. After the match occurs, however, the provision of more social support may be neither more helpful nor harmful. From a clinical view, this is valuable information. Although some individuals may have small interpersonal networks, this would not necessarily indicate low perceived support. The number of supportive transactions that occur is less important than whether those transactions are deemed, by the client, sufficient to meet his or her needs. Therefore, it is quite conceivable that some clients will require only a few persons in their networks to supply those supportive transactions, and additional social support may be superfluous.

We noted earlier that some investigators have taken the position that social support is, at least in part, a personality construct. This view suggests a different focus for interventions. For instance, social support may require certain interpersonal skills that some clients lack. Consequently, it may make more sense to help clients develop skills associated with social competence, self-mastery, and so on, rather than helping them to identify sources of support and then sending them off to get it.

Psychological Resources

We reviewed findings suggesting that hardiness, dispositional optimism, and explanatory style have been found to be associated with health benefits. This is encouraging news, especially if one happens to possess one or more of the traits in question. But what about people who are nonhardy or pessimistic? The available research suggests that these individuals may be more vulnerable to the effects of stress, and, by extension, we argue that these individuals may have greater difficulty adapting to life transitions. Can the counseling process promote traits such as hardiness or optimism? Presently, we are unaware of any studies that address this issue.

We are aware that Seligman and his colleagues have speculated that pessimistic explanatory style can be changed (Peterson & Seligman, 1987). Indeed, in his recent book, *Learned Optimism,* Seligman (1990) maintains that cognitive therapy can promote an optimistic outlook, at least as optimism is defined from the point of view of attributions. In light of the findings concerning cognitive psychotherapy for depression, this is not an unreasonable assertion. Yet, as we noted earlier, pessimistic explanatory style has been shown to have traitlike properties, remaining stable over several decades of adulthood. It may be that becoming undepressed is not the same thing as becoming optimistic. We know, for instance, that individuals who have been depressed tend to remain susceptible to depression. One hypothesis might be that the remnants of a pessimistic explanatory style remain, despite the absence of depression.

Dispositional optimism, and perhaps hardiness and explanatory style, may have their beneficial effects through coping efforts. The value of being, say, dispositionally optimistic is that one will presumably select strategies that are effective in reducing or avoiding stressful encounters. But what happens when clients are taught to improve their coping effectiveness (i.e., with a broader range of strategies, and less reliance on avoidance coping mechanisms)? Would these interventions, if successful, have any bearing on the client's psychological resources? Aldwin and Revenson (1987) suggested that coping responses are bidirectional. In their study, initial distress led to ineffective coping, which, in turn, led to more distress. One can see how this cycle could be perpetuated indefinitely. But suppose interventions are provided to help clients make consistently better use of their coping responses. How then might this causal mechanism work?

We do not mean to imply that our remarks about the implications of coping resources cover the full gamut of issues for counseling adults in life transitions; this is far from the case. We have said, for instance, nothing about the importance of helping the client find meaning in the life transition, and nothing about helping the client gain a sense of mastery and retain a sense of self-esteem. As we pointed out in the overview, these are important adaptive concerns that clients need to address so that the life transition can be assimilated into their lives. Our interest has been more toward highlighting the role of coping resources in light of new findings and developments.

CONCLUSION

Our review of coping responses, social resources, and psychological resources has led us to conclude that recent developments and findings concerning coping resources are converging on a theme that emphasizes the person. Although Lazarus has repeatedly denounced a trait conception of coping (Lazarus, 1990), others have made the claim that it may be time to bring personality variables back into the coping process (Ben-Porath & Tellegen, 1990; Costa & McCrae, 1990; Watson, 1990; Weber & Laux, 1990). A trait approach to personality, as it relates to stress and coping, provides one way to do this.

Our rationale for this view is as follows. First, we reviewed evidence to the effect that coping responses are a probable pathway for dispositional characteristics such as hardiness, optimism, and possibly explanatory style. Hence, it makes sense to include personality traits in stress and coping models so that the models will be more complete. A trait approach to coping can thus complement a transactional approach, as proposed by Folkman, Lazarus, and their associates. Second, we pointed out that recent work in the area of social support has suggested that social support may be, at least in part, a personality variable. It may be that (a) individuals contribute to relationships via social skills, high self-esteem, self-mastery, and so on, in such a way that they create a propensity for others to respond supportively toward them, or that (b) the perception that one feels consistently supported (recall that support has traitlike stability) is one aspect of healthy personality functioning, perhaps as a result of developmental transactions that have accumulated over a number of years (i.e., conceptions of supportive, internalized others) (Sarason et al., 1990). In either case, relational provisions appear to be closely intertwined with personality dispositions. Third, several writers have pointed out that traits such as negative affectivity may help resolve the consistent problem of confounding that occurs between measures of stress and adaptation (Ben-Porath & Tellegen, 1990; Costa & McCrae, 1990; Watson, 1990). This, too, suggests the need for the integration of traits in conceptions of stress and coping.

We believe it is desirable to take a closer look at negative affectivity (NA). This construct was linked to measures of hardiness and dispositional optimism; again, we emphasize the need for research that will help untangle these constructs. In terms of its role in stress, coping, and life transitions, NA may be more than simply a nuisance variable. Negative affectivity seems to reflect a chronic tendency for individuals to perceive dissatisfaction and experience stress. Earlier, we noted that individuals high in this trait consistently report more "soft" health complaints than those who are low in it. However, NA has also been found to predict job and life satisfaction, and to partially explain the often reported relationships among self-reported job stress, somatic complaints, and mental health outcomes (e.g., Brief et al., 1988).

Moreover, we would not be surprised if NA were also related to perceived social support. Earlier, we mentioned that perceptions of support have been consistently linked with mental and physical health outcomes. We also noted that social support—or at least the perception that one is supported—may be partly a dimension of personality. Could it be that the relationships between self-reported mental and physical health outcomes and perceived support are partially accounted for by individual differences in levels of NA?

We suggest that models of stress, coping, and life transitions place greater emphasis on the person. Specifically, we need a better understanding of how personality characteristics such as NA, dispositional optimism, hardiness, and explanatory style relate to life transitions, to each other, and to social resources and coping responses. Such research could have profound implications for how we work with clients in transition. For example, assume that future research does find that NA accounts for a substantial proportion of the variance between perceived social support and self-reported health outcomes. Could we then, as practitioners, expect to significantly modify perceptions of support without first tackling the client's disposition to perceive interpersonal relationships as negative and distressing?

Similarly, recent data suggest that some people are more genetically disposed than others to experience job dissatisfaction, regardless of work setting (Arvey, Bouchard, Segal, & Abraham, 1989). Thus, NA may also be an important target for career counseling, especially for individuals who are experiencing job transitions. Also, we wonder whether high NA would predict increased numbers (and perhaps kinds) of work-related transitions. If traits such as NA do turn out to be important explanatory and predictive constructs for life transitions, it is especially important to determine whether they can be modified.

In closing, we find it instructive to paraphrase a point made by McCrae and Costa (1990). After demonstrating that personality traits are remarkably stable in adulthood, they suggested that it might be better to ask how personality shapes life experiences, rather than how life experiences change personality. We wish to underscore this point. It is undoubtedly true that life transitions have an impact on persons. But it may be equally true that personality dispositions, or what we have termed psychological resources, do much to shape—and perhaps create—life transitions.

REFERENCES

Abelson, R. P. (1981). Psychological status of the script concept. *American Psychologist, 7,* 715–729.

Abramson, L. Y., Seligman, M. E. P., & Teasdale, J. D. (1978). Learned helplessness in humans: Critique and reformulation. *Journal of Abnormal Psychology, 37,* 49-74.

Aldwin, C. M., & Revenson, T. A. (1987). Does coping help? A reexamination of the relation between coping and mental health. *Journal of Personality and Social Psychology, 53,* 337–348.

Allred, K. D., & Smith, T. W. (1989). The hardy personality: Cognitive and physiological responses to evaluative threat. *Journal of Personality and Social Psychology, 56,* 257–266.

Amirkhan, J. H. (1990). A factor analytically derived measure of coping: The Coping Strategy Indicator. *Journal of Personality and Social Psychology, 59,* 1066–1074.

Arvey, R. D., Bouchard, T. J., Segal, N. L., & Abraham, L. M. (1989). Job satisfaction: Environmental and genetic components. *Journal of Applied Psychology, 74,* 187–192.

Baron, R., Cutrona, C. E., Hicklin, D., Russell, D. W., & Lubaroff, D. M. (1990). Social support and immune function among spouses of cancer patients. *Journal of Personality and Social Psychology, 59,* 344–352.

Ben-Porath, Y. S., & Tellegen, A. (1990). A place for traits in stress research. *Psychological Inquiry, 1,* 13–17.

Billings, A. G., & Moos, R. H. (1981). The role of coping responses and social resources in attenuating the stress of life events. *Journal of Behavioral Medicine, 4,* 139–157.

Brief, A. P., Burke, M. J., Robinson, B. S., George, J. M., & Webster, J. (1988). Should negative affectivity remain an unmeasured variable in the study of job stress? *Journal of Applied Psychology, 73,* 193–198.

Brim, O. G., & Kagan, J. (Eds.). (1980). *Constancy and change in human development.* Cambridge: MA: Harvard University Press.

Brim, O. G., & Ryff, C. D. (1980). On the properties of life events. In P. B. Baltes & O. G. Brim, Jr. (Eds.), *Life span development and behavior* (Vol. 3, pp. 368–388). New York: Academic Press.

Brown, G. W. (1990). What about the Real World? Hassles and Richard Lazarus. *Psychological Inquiry, 1,* 19–22.

Brown, G. W., Bifulco, A., & Harris, T. O. (1987). Life events, vulnerability, and the onset of depression: Some refinements. *British Journal of Psychiatry, 150,* 30–42.

Brown, G. W., & Harris, T. O. (1978). *Social origins of depression.* London: Hogarth Press.

Brown, G. W., & Harris, T. O. (1986). Establishing causal links: The Bedford College studies of depression. In H. Katschnig (Ed.), *Life events and psychiatric disorder* (pp. 107–187). Cambridge, England: Cambridge University Press.

Brown, G. W., & Harris, T. O. (1989). *Life events and illness.* New York: Guilford Press.

Brown, S. D., Alpert, D., Lent, R., Hunt, G., & Brady, T. (1988). Perceived social support among college students: Factor structure of the Social Support Inventory. *Journal of Counseling Psychology, 35,* 472–478.

Brown, S. D., Brady, T., Lent, R., Wolfert, J., & Hall, S. (1987). Perceived social support among college students: Three studies of the psychometric characteristics and counseling uses of the Social Support Inventory [Monograph]. *Journal of Counseling Psychology, 34,* 337–354.

Brown, S. D., & Heath, L. (1984). Coping with critical life events: An integrative cognitive-behavioral model for research and practice. In S. D. Brown & R. W. Lent (Eds.), *Handbook of counseling psychology* (pp. 545–578). New York: Wiley.

Burns, M. O., & Seligman, M. E. P. (1989). Explanatory style across the life span: Evidence for the stability over 52 years. *Journal of Personality and Social Psychology, 56,* 471–477.

Cantor, N., & Norem, J. K. (1989). Defensive pessimism and stress and coping. *Social Cognition, 7,* 92–112.

Carver, C. S., & Scheier, M. F. (1981). *Attention and self-regulation: A control-theory approach to human behavior.* New York: Springer-Verlag.

Carver, C. S., & Scheier, M. F. (1982). Control theory: A useful conceptual framework for personality—social, clinical, and health psychology. *Psychological Bulletin, 92,* 111–135.

Carver, C. S., Scheier, M. F., & Weintraub, J. K. (1989). Assessing coping strategies: A theoretically based approach. *Journal of Personality and Social Psychology, 56,* 267–283.

Charner, I., & Schlossberg, N. K. (1986). Variations by theme: The life transitions of clerical workers. *The Vocational Guidance Quarterly, 34,* 213–224.

Cohen, F., & Lazarus, R. S. (1973). Active coping processes, coping dispositions, and recovery from surgery. *Psychosomatic Medicine, 35,* 375-389.

Cohen, S., & McKay, G. (1984). Social support, stress, and the buffering hypothesis: A theoretical analysis. In A. Baum, J. E. Singer, & S. E. Taylor (Eds.), *Handbook of psychology and health* (Vol. 4, pp. 253–267). Hillsdale, NJ: Erlbaum.

Cohen, S., & Syme, S. L. (1985). Issues in the study and application of social support. In S. Cohen & S. L. Syme (Eds.), *Social support and health* (pp. 3–22). New York: Academic Press.

Cohen, S., & Wills, T. A. (1985). Stress, social support, and the buffering hypothesis. *Psychological Bulletin, 98,* 310–357.

Costa, P. T., & McCrae, R. R. (1987). Neuroticism, somatic complaints, and disease: Is the bark worse than the bite? *Journal of Personality, 55,* 299–316.

Costa, P. T., & McCrae, R. R. (1990). Personality: Another "hidden factor" in stress research. *Psychological Inquiry, 1,* 22–24.

Cousins, N. (1977, May 28). Anatomy of an illness (as perceived by the patient). *Saturday Review,* pp. 4–6, 48–51.

Cutrona, C. E. (1986). Objective determinants of perceived social support. *Journal of Personality and Social Psychology, 50,* 349–355.

Cutrona, C. E. (1990). Stress and social support—in search of optimal matching. *Journal of Social and Clinical Psychology, 9,* 3–14.

Dakof, G. A., & Taylor, S. E. (1990). Victims' perceptions of social support: What is helpful from whom? *Journal of Personality and Social Support, 58,* 80–89.

Danish, S. J. (1981). Life-span human development and intervention: A necessary link. *The Counseling Psychologist, 9*(2), 40–43.

Deutsch, F. M., Ruble, D. N., Fleming, A. S., Brooks-Gunn, J., & Stangor, G. S. (1988). Information-seeking and maternal self-definition during the transition to motherhood. *Journal of Personality and Social Psychology, 55,* 420–431.

Dohrenwend, B. S., & Dohrenwend, B. P. (Eds.). (1974). *Stressful life events: Their nature and effects.* New York: Wiley.

Dunkel-Schetter, C., Folkman, S. F., & Lazarus, R. S. (1987). Correlates of social support receipt. *Journal of Personality and Social Psychology, 1,* 71–80.

Endler, N. S., & Parker, J. D. A. (1990). Multidimensional assessment of coping: A critical evaluation. *Journal of Personality and Social Psychology, 58,* 844–854.

Folkman, S., & Lazarus, R. S. (1980). An analysis of coping in a middle-aged community sample. *Journal of Health and Social Behavior, 21,* 219–239.

Folkman, S., & Lazarus, R. S. (1985). If it changes it must be a process: Study of emotion and coping during three stages of a college examination. *Journal of Personality and Social Psychology, 48,* 150–170.

Folkman, S., & Lazarus, R. S. (1986). Stress processes and depressive symptomatology. *Journal of Abnormal Psychology, 95,* 107–113.

Folkman, S., Lazarus, R. S., Dunkel-Schetter, C., Delongis, A., & Gruen, R. J. (1986). Dynamics of a stressful encounter. *Journal of Personality and Social Psychology, 50,* 992–1003.

Funk, S. C., & Houston, B. K. (1987). A critical analysis of the Hardiness Scale's validity and utility. *Journal of Personality and Social Psychology, 53,* 572–578.

Ganellen, R. J., & Blaney, P. H. (1984). Hardiness and social support as moderators of the effects of stress. *Journal of Personality and Social Psychology, 47,* 156–163.

Golan, N. (1981). *Passing through transitions: A guide for practitioners.* New York: Free Press.

Heller, K., Swindle, R. W., & Dusenbury, L. (1986). Component social support processes: Comments and integration. *Journal of Consulting and Clinical Psychology, 54,* 466–470.

Hobfall, S. E., & Freedy, J. R. (1990). The availability and effective use of social support. *Journal of Social and Clinical Psychology, 9,* 91–103.

Holahan, C. J., & Moos, R. H. (1985). Life stress and health: Personality, coping, and family support in stress resistance. *Journal of Personality and Social Psychology, 49,* 739–747.

Holahan, C. J., & Moos, R. H. (1986). Personality, coping, and family resources in stress resistance: A longitudinal analysis. *Journal of Personality and Social Psychology, 51,* 389–395.

Holahan, C. J., & Moos, R. H. (1987). Personal and contextual determinants of coping strategies. *Journal of Personality and Social Psychology, 52,* 946–955.

Holahan, C. J., & Moos, R. H. (1991). Life stressors, personal and social resources, and depression: A 4-year structural model. *Journal of Abnormal Psychology, 100,* 31–38.

Holmes, T. H., & Rahe, R. H. (1967). The Social Readjustment Rating Scale. *Journal of Psychosomatic Research, 11,* 213–218.

Hopson, B. (1981). Response to the papers by Schlossberg, Brammer and Abrego. *The Counseling Psychologist, 9*(2), 36–39.

Horowitz, M. J. (1979). Psychological responses to serious life events. In V. Hamilton & D. M. Warburton (Eds.), *Human stress and cognition* (pp. 235–263). New York: Wiley.

House, J. S. (1981). *Work, stress, and social support.* Reading, MA: Addison-Wesley.

Hull, J. G., Van Treuren, R. R., & Propsom, P. M. (1988). Attributional style and the components of hardiness. *Personality and Social Psychology Bulletin, 14,* 505–513.

Hull, J. G., Van Treuren, R. R., & Virnelli, S. (1987). Hardiness and health: A critique and alternative approach. *Journal of Personality and Social Psychology, 53,* 518–530.

Hultsch, D. F., & Plemons, J. K. (1979). Life events and life-span development. In P. B. Baltes & O. G. Brim, Jr. (Eds.), *Life-span development and behavior* (Vol. 2). New York: Academic Press.

Janoff-Bulman, R. (1989). The benefits of illusions, the threat of disillusionment, and the limitations of inaccuracy. *Journal of Social and Clinical Psychology, 8,* 158–175.

Jemmott, J. B., & Magloire, K. (1988). Academic stress, social support, and secretory immunoglobulin A. *Journal of Personality and Social Psychology, 55,* 803–810.

Kegan, R. (1982). *The evolving self.* Cambridge, MA: Harvard University Press.

Kobasa, S. C. (1979). Stressful life events, personality, and health: An inquiry into hardiness. *Journal of Personality and Social Psychology, 37,* 1–11.

Kobasa, S. C. (1982). The hardy personality: Toward a social psychology of stress and health. In G. S. Sanders & J. Suls (Eds.), *Social psychology of health and illness* (pp. 3–32). Hillsdale, NJ: Erlbaum.

Kobasa, S. C., Maddi, S. R., & Courington, S. (1981). Personality and constitution as mediators in the stress–illness relationship. *Journal of Health and Social Behavior, 22,* 368–378.

Kobasa, S. C., Maddi, S. R., & Kahn, S. (1982). Hardiness and health: A prospective study. *Journal of Personality and Social Psychology, 42,* 168–177.

Kobasa, S. C., Maddi, S. R., & Zola, M. A. (1983). Type A and hardiness. *Journal of Behavioral Medicine, 6,* 41–51.

Kobasa, S. C., & Puccetti, M. C. (1983). Personality and social resources in stress resistance. *Journal of Personality and Social Psychology, 45,* 839–850.

Lakey, B., & Cassady, P. B. (1990). Cognitive processes in perceived social support. *Journal of Personality and Social Psychology, 59,* 337–343.

Lazarus, R. S. (1990). Theory-based stress measurement. *Psychological Inquiry, 1,* 3–13.

Lazarus, R. S., & Folkman, S. (1984). *Stress, appraisal, and coping.* New York: Springer.

Levinson, D. J. (1978). *The seasons of a man's life.* New York: Ballantine.

Lindemann, E., & Lindemann, E. (1979). *Beyond grief: Studies in crisis intervention.* New York: Aronson.

Linville, P. W. (1987). Self-complexity as a cognitive buffer against stress-related illness and depression. *Journal of Personality and Social Psychology, 52,* 663–676.

Loevinger, J. (1976). *Ego development.* San Francisco: Jossey-Bass.

McAdams, D. P. (1988). *Power, intimacy, and the life story.* New York: Guilford Press.

McCrae, R. R., & Costa, P. T. (1990). *Personality in adulthood.* New York: Guilford Press.

Monat, A., & Lazarus, R. S. (Eds.). (1985). *Stress and coping: An anthology.* New York: Columbia University Press.

Moos, R. H., & Schaefer, J. A. (1986). Life transitions and crises. In R. H. Moos (Ed.), *Coping with life crises: An integrated approach* (pp. 3–28). New York: Plenum Press.

Murphy, E., & Brown, G. W. (1980). Life events, psychiatric disturbance, and physical illness. *British Journal of Psychiatry, 136,* 326–338.

Nezu, A. M., Nezu, C. M., & Bissett, S. E. (1988). Sense of humor as a moderator of the relation between stressful events and psychological distress: A prospective analysis. *Journal of Personality and Social Psychology, 44,* 520–525.

Parry, G. (1990). *Coping with crises.* London: Routledge, Ltd. and British Psychological Society.

Peale, N. V. (1956). *The power of positive thinking.* Englewood Cliffs, NJ: Prentice-Hall.

Pearlin, L. I. (1985). Life strains and psychological distress among adults. In A. Monat & R. S. Lazarus (Eds.), *Stress and coping: An anthology* (pp. 192–207). New York: Columbia University Press.

Pearlin, L. I., & Schooler, C. (1978). The structure of coping. *Journal of Health and Social Behavior, 19,* 2–21.

Peterson, C., Luborsky, L., & Seligman, M. E. P. (1983). Attributions and depressive mood shifts. *Journal of Abnormal Psychology, 92,* 96–103.

Peterson, C., & Seligman, M. E. P. (1984). Causal explanations as a risk factor for depression: Theory and evidence. *Psychological Review, 91,* 347–374.

Peterson, C., & Seligman, M. E. P. (1987). Explanatory style and illness. *Journal of Personality, 55,* 237–265.

Peterson, C., Seligman, M. E. P., & Vaillant, G. (1988). Pessimistic explanatory style as a risk factor for physical illness: A 35-year longitudinal study. *Journal of Personality and Social Psychology, 55,* 23–27.

Pyszczynski, T., Holt, K., & Greenburg, J. (1987). Depression, self-focused attention, and expectancies for positive and negative future life events for self and others. *Journal of Personality and Social Psychology, 52,* 994–1001.

Remondet, J. H., Hansson, R. O., Rule, B., & Winfrey, G. (1987). Rehearsal for widowhood. *Journal of Social and Clinical Psychology, 3,* 285–297.

Rhodewalt, F., & Agustsdottir, S. (1984). On the relationship of hardiness to the Type A behavior pattern: Perceptions of life events versus coping with life events. *Journal of Research in Personality, 18,* 212–223.

Rhodewalt, F., & Zone, J. B. (1989). Appraisal of life change, depression, and illness in hardy and nonhardy women. *Journal of Personality and Social Psychology, 56,* 81–88.

Rohde, P., Tilson, M., Lewinsohn, P. M., & Seeley, J. R. (1990). Dimensionality of coping and its relation to depression. *Journal of Personality and Social Psychology, 58,* 499–511.

Sarason, I. G., Sarason, B. R., Hacker, T. A., & Basham, R. B. (1985). Concomitants of social support: Social skills, physical attractiveness, and gender. *Journal of Personality and Social Psychology, 49,* 469–480.

Sarason, I. G., Sarason, B. R., & Pierce, G. R. (1990). Social support: The search for theory. *Journal of Social and Clinical Psychology, 9,* 133–147.

Sarason, I. G., Sarason, B. R., & Shearin, E. N. (1986). Social support as an individual difference variable: Its stability, origins, and relational aspects. *Journal of Personality and Social Psychology, 50,* 845–855.

Sarason, B. R., Shearin, E. N., Pierce, G. R., & Sarason, I. G. (1987). Interrelations of social support measures: Theoretical and practical implications. *Journal of Personality and Social Psychology, 52,* 813–832.

Scheier, M. F., & Carver, C. S. (1985). Optimism, coping, and health: Assessment and implications of generalized outcome expectancies. *Health Psychology, 4,* 219–247.

Scheier, M. F., & Carver, C. S. (1987). Dispositional optimism and physical well-being: The influence of generalized outcome expectancies on health. *Journal of Personality, 55,* 169–210.

Scheier, M. F., Matthews, K. A., Owens, J. F., Magovern, G. J., Lefebvre, R. C., Abbott, R. A., & Carver, C. S. (1989). Dispositional optimism and recovery from coronary artery bypass surgery: The beneficial effects of physical and psychological well-being. *Journal of Personality and Social Psychology, 57,* 1024–1040.

Scheier, M. F., Weintraub, J. K., & Carver, C. S. (1986). Coping with stress: Divergent strategies of optimists and pessimists. *Journal of Personality and Social Psychology, 51,* 1257–1264.

Schlossberg, N. K. (1984). *Counseling adults in transitions.* New York: Springer.

Schlossberg, N. K. (1981). A model for analyzing human adaptation to transition. *The Counseling Psychologist, 9*(2), 2–17.

Seligman, M. E. P. (1990). *Learned optimism.* New York: Knopf.

Seligman, M. E. P., Abramson, L. Y., Semmel, A., & von Baeyer, C. (1979). Depressive attributional style. *Journal of Abnormal Psychology, 88,* 242–247.

Seligman, M. E. P., & Schulman, P. (1986). Explanatory style as a predictor of performance as a life insurance agent. *Journal of Personality and Social Psychology, 50,* 832–838.

Sherman, E. (1987). *Meaning in mid-life transitions.* Albany, NY: State University of New York Press.

Smith, T. W., Pope, M. K., Rhodewalt, F., & Poulton, J. L. (1989). Optimism, neuroticism, coping, and symptom reports: An alternative interpretation of the Life Orientation Test. *Journal of Personality and Social Psychology, 56,* 640–648.

Stewart, A. J. (1982). The course of individual adaptation to life changes. *Journal of Personality and Social Psychology, 42,* 1100–1113.

Super, D. E. (1955). Transition: From vocational guidance to counseling psychology. *Journal of Counseling Psychology, 2,* 3–9.

Sweeney, P. D., Anderson, K., & Bailey, S. (1986). Attributional style in depression: A meta-analytic review. *Journal of Personality and Social Psychology, 50,* 974–998.

Taylor, S. E. (1983). Adjustment to threatening events. *American Psychologist, 38,* 1161–1173.

Taylor, S. E., & Schneider, S. K. (1989). Coping and the simulation of events. *Social Cognition, 7,* 174–194.

Thoits, P. A. (1986). Social support as coping assistance. *Journal of Consulting and Clinical Psychology, 54,* 416–423.

Vaillant, G. E. (1977). *Adaptation to life.* Boston: Little, Brown.

Wallston, B. S., Alagna, S. W., DeVellis, B. M., & DeVellis, R. F. (1983). Social support and physical health. *Health Psychology, 2,* 367–391.

Watson, D. (1990). On the dispositional nature of stress measures: Stable and nonspecific influences on self-reported hassles. *Psychological Inquiry, 1,* 34–37.

Watson, D., & Clark, L. A. (1984). Negative affectivity: The disposition to experience aversive emotional states. *Psychological Bulletin, 96,* 465–490.

Watson, D., Clark, L. A., & Carey, G. (1988). Positive and negative affectivity and their relation to anxiety and depressive disorders. *Journal of Abnormal Psychology, 97,* 346–353.

Watson, D., & Pennebaker, J. (1989). Health complaints, stress, and distress: Exploring the central role of negative affectivity. *Psychological Review, 96,* 234–254.

Weber, H., & Laux, L. (1990). Bring the person back into stress and coping measurement. *Psychological Inquiry, 1,* 37–40.

Weiss, R. S., (1974). The provisions of social relationships. In Z. Rubin (Ed.), *Doing unto others* (pp. 17–26). Englewood Cliffs, NJ: Prentice-Hall.

White, R. W. (1985). Strategies of adaptation: An attempt at systematic description. In A. Monat & R. S. Lazarus (Eds.), *Stress and coping: An anthology* (pp. 121–143). New York: Columbia University Press.

Zullow, H. M., & Seligman, M. E. P. (1990). Pessimistic rumination predicts defeat of presidential candidates, 1900 to 1984. *Psychological Inquiry, 1,* 52–61.

CHAPTER 10

HEALTH-RELATED APPLICATIONS OF COUNSELING PSYCHOLOGY: TOWARD HEALTH PROMOTION AND DISEASE PREVENTION ACROSS THE LIFE SPAN

ELIZABETH M. ALTMAIER
BRIAN D. JOHNSON

There is an increasing recognition within the profession that problems of physical health and illness are potential foci of psychological research and intervention. Although psychologists have been involved in health research since the early 1900s, the recent recognition of psychology's value in dealing with health issues has a rather short history, dating to Schofield (1969), who noted the paucity of research efforts by psychologists in health-related problem areas. Since that time, among psychologists, there has been a virtual explosion of interest in physical health concerns, with counseling psychologists becoming involved in applying our specialty's traditional strengths and emphases to issues of health and illness (Thoresen & Eagleston, 1984).

With the advent of increasingly sophisticated diagnostic facilities and varieties of medical and surgical treatments, there has been a corresponding increase in the confidence of the American public that diseases can be cured. The statistics somewhat support this confidence; deaths due to acute illness have diminished over the past 50 years. However, the leading causes of death today among adults are heart disease, cancer, and stroke. These diseases, as well as other prime causes of death such as motor vehicle accidents, appear to be associated either with particular behavioral practices, such as smoking, or omissions, such as a lack of preventive health care (Matarazzo, 1980). The increasing realization among medical personnel that dealing with preventable illnesses necessitates a focus on human behaviors and attitudes will almost certainly increase the involvement of psychologists in health research and practice in the future.

The purpose of this chapter is to highlight five areas of health care that we believe illustrate the potential for increased counseling psychology involvement. The first area

Support for the preparation of this chapter was provided by the Iowa Testing Program and the Center for Health Services Research, both at The University of Iowa.

is that of preventive health. Counseling psychology has for years argued that remedial approaches in mental health need to co-exist with preventive approaches, and a parallel argument can be made regarding physical health. We chose to illustrate this area with applications in a counseling center context.

Counseling psychology also considers itself a developmentally based specialty in its view of personality development, career development, and other areas of human functioning. We have therefore chosen to examine three illnesses from varying points across the life span, to illustrate health problems that are current foci of research and treatment efforts: childhood leukemia, adult chronic pain, and Alzheimer's disease among the aged. In all of these health problems, there is a large role for the family, and we emphasize the potential of involving the family in treatment.

Our final section considers counseling psychology's potential role in health care consultation. Although many consultation efforts could be mentioned, we have chosen to discuss how we might assist physicians and other health care providers to provide the best possible care to patients. Our emphasis is on the nature of the physician–patient relationship and on research regarding patient satisfaction with medical care—areas that provide evidence of the need for efforts to increase physicians', and other health care providers', interpersonal skills and sensitivities to patient concerns.

We hope that the excitement of working in medical settings, with medical or health problems, and toward the pursuit of physical as well as mental health, is "catching." This chapter is written in the firm belief that counseling psychology is perhaps uniquely qualified among psychological specialties to deal with problems of health and illness. Our traditional emphases of identifying and building on clients' strengths and resources, of assessing and incorporating the impact of the environment into work with individuals, of considering the importance of work in adjustment, and of using psychoeducational approaches in treatment are all excellent bases for understanding and enhancing health promotion and disease prevention across the life span.

HEALTH PROMOTION AND DISEASE PREVENTION

Over the past 50 or so years, the percentage of deaths due to acute diseases has been diminishing, while the proportion of deaths due to diseases such as cardiovascular disease and cancer, and to accidents and injuries, has been increasing. These changes parallel a dramatic increase in individual and corporate spending on health. In fact, health care has become one of our country's biggest businesses: in 1987, consumers spent $280.8 billion, federal and state governments spent $207.3 billion, and industry spent $12.2 billion on health care expenses (U.S. Department of Commerce, 1989). However, along with this increased spending has come a growing gap between those who can afford health insurance and medical care and those who cannot. Recent reports (Califano, 1986) reveal that great disparity exists in medical spending: over 35 million Americans do not have medical insurance, and Medicaid covers only one-half of the people who need its coverage. An additional concern is that medical care is increasingly characterized by advanced technologies, with a corresponding increase in costs for equipment, training, and health services.

The change in the primary causes of death is also critical; many of the illnesses that are now major causes of mortality involve specific risk factors that are behavioral in nature. For example, risk factors for cardiovascular disease are smoking, hypertension, and high blood cholesterol. Fatal motor vehicle accidents increase with nonuse of seat belts and with driving under the influence of alcohol or other drugs. Ironically, these behavioral "causes" coexist with an apparent increase in health-related knowledge among the American public. The 1985 Health Interview Survey (Thornberry, Wilson, & Golden, 1986) revealed that 91% of adults knew of the link between smoking and heart disease and 77% could relate high blood pressure to increased risk of stroke. However, the same survey revealed a critical lack of preventive health behaviors, such as seat belt use (only 32% used seat belts all or most of the time) and breast self-examination among women (only 34% of women had examined their breasts more than six times during the previous year). Increased health knowledge has not been translated into more effective health practices.

Models of Preventive Health Behaviors

Preventive health behaviors have been the focus of medical sociologists and public health planners and policy makers for many years. During this time, several models of preventive health have been presented and tested. These models considered a range of variables presumed to influence persons' health actions, from medical variables (e.g., convenience and quality of health services) to economic and sociocultural variables. Several models have focused more closely on the link between attitudes about health and subsequent actions. We have chosen to present two such models, based on their research support and their relevance to interventions practiced by counseling psychologists.

Health Belief Model

The model that has received the most widespread attention, and that offers the most treatment implications, is the Health Belief Model (Becker, 1974; Rosenstock, 1974). The Health Belief Model contains the following elements: (a) the individual's readiness to take a particular action, which is determined by perceived susceptibility to the illness and perceived severity of its consequences; (b) the individual's evaluation of the benefits of the proposed action balanced against the costs of the action and barriers preventing the action; and (c) the particular "cue to action" that triggers the response sequence, either external (i.e., a public interest television warning of the dangers of smoking) or internal (i.e., a health-related symptom) in nature. The critical aspect of the Health Belief Model is that the individual's beliefs are presumed to be modifiable by increasing knowledge and enhancing motivation to action.

Becker and Maiman (1975) revised the Health Belief Model to include three distinct stages, each having several components. The first stage is that of the individual's readiness to undertake particular recommendations, a stage that includes motivation, the value to the individual of reducing the threat posed by the illness, and the subjective probability assigned by the individual to the recommendation's success. The second stage consists of modifying factors, either enabling or blocking in nature, such as demographic variables, the physician–patient interaction, and patient attitudes and prior experiences. The third and last stage consists of the behaviors undertaken in response to the recommendations (not necessarily behaviors that follow the recommendations).

Using this model, counseling psychologists can identify several intervention routes. For example, the nature of the relationship between the physician and the patient can have a significant effect on the patient's "health behaviors," including whether medication is taken as directed and whether modifications in health behaviors are made. As is discussed in a later section of this chapter, certain patterns of communication among physicians and patients appear to be related to patients' satisfaction with the encounter and their subsequent compliance with the prescribed treatment.

The model also suggests the value of educational interventions. As an example, determining that a particular person believes his or her susceptibility to a disease is low when, in fact, it is quite high, would suggest that information should be provided to increase the patient's perceived susceptibility. (It should be noted, however, that giving information is not a singular intervention. The effectiveness of interventions focused on conveying information varies, depending on the nature of the information given to the patient [e.g., perceived severity of disease vs. perceived susceptibility to disease; see DiMatteo & DiNicola, 1982].) Alternatively, if the patient lacks specific cues to action, a behavioral intervention emphasizing environmental planning could assist the patient in rearranging the physical or social environment to increase the presence of relevant stimulus cues.

Although popular in the 1970s and early 1980s, the Health Belief Model is no longer as widely utilized in considering health-related prevention. The model as a whole was directly tested in several large-scale studies and received mixed empirical support (e.g., Becker, Maiman, Kirscht, Haefner, & Drachman, 1977; Langlie, 1977). In this research, health beliefs prior to therapy initiation were not found to predict compliance. However, health beliefs assessed during treatment, reflecting the subjects' experience with treatment, were strongly predictive. It appears that beliefs may become more congruent with compliance as compliance actually occurs. An additional issue is that the model targets a wide range of constructs; recent models of prevention usually consider a narrower range of constructs that can be studied in a more focused way.

Health Locus of Control

The likelihood of engaging in preventive health behavior is a function of many variables, both internal and external to the person, which affect the decision-making process and behavior implementation. One specific aspect of preventive health behavior that is not always considered is individuals' perception of their health as controllable or uncontrollable by themselves.

Health locus of control (Lau & Ware, 1982) is an extension of the construct of locus of control to the health domain. Locus of control was initially defined by Rotter (1966) as the expectancy, developed though prior experience, that one's behavior will bring about certain reinforcements. Applied to health, this construct suggests that persons might expect differential outcomes from health-related behaviors, depending on their beliefs that they have an ability to control their health versus beliefs that health is dependent on various uncontrollable factors such as chance, luck, or powerful others.

There are several components to a health-specific locus of control model. First, persons may expect that health providers can control medical outcomes in the absence of personal control. Such a belief could be considered as "provider control," and might lead to the patient's developing a dependency on medical personnel to deal with health problems. Alternatively, persons might expect that they can themselves exercise control over health outcomes, a belief in "own control." Such persons might be expected to display more independent health-related behaviors. Health might also be considered a series of random events and chance outcomes, in which case no one controls health, a belief that Lau and Ware (1982) labeled "chance health outcomes." Finally, some combination of these beliefs might apply, depending on the individual's valuing of his or her health, the particular disease being considered, and the particular solution being advocated.

What are the implications of the health locus of control model for developing interventions? One obvious implication is to encourage or increase internality (or controllability) of health attitudes. Promoting greater personal responsibility for health can play a critical role in many situations. However, other models of health behavior suggest that locus of control does not operate in a unique manner, but must be considered alongside the value an individual places on health and the larger illness cultural context (McHugh & Vallis, 1986). A second implication is that measures of health locus of control might prove to be an important individual difference variable in assessing treatment effectiveness. It may well be that treatments can be structured in somewhat different ways to accommodate various patients' beliefs regarding control over health.

Applications to Counseling Centers

One location in which counseling psychologists can influence health, including health beliefs and preventive health behaviors, is the college and university counseling center. Although counseling centers have not traditionally emphasized health-related services, these centers come into contact with millions of Americans representing a range of ages and backgrounds, and thus counseling center staff have the opportunity to influence health at a critical juncture in individuals' lives. Stone and Archer (1990) noted that quality of campus life has regained a focus of attention, and the needs of students for increased services targeted to safety, health, economics, and mental health is apparent. There is also increased recognition that health problems identical to those in the general population exist in large proportions on college campus. For example, there appears to be extensive substance abuse on college campuses, and intoxication is likely to lead to failure to exercise other appropriate preventive health behaviors such as condom use during sexual intercourse. Substance abuse is also associated with increased mortality due to violence and motor vehicle accidents.

Further, the AIDS epidemic is likely to increase on campuses. As more students are infected with the AIDS virus, and more publicity is gained, individuals' perceived susceptibility to this disease will increase, and students who desire testing or more general consultation or reassurance may come into counseling centers for assistance.

What form might counseling center interventions take? Perhaps the best way to consider health as a problem focus is to use the "cube" model proposed by Morrill, Oetting, and Hurst (1974), where interventions can be targeted to an individual, a group, or an environment, and delivered through direct contact, consultation, or media. An additional factor is that interventions can be preventive, remedial, or developmental in nature.

Using this model as a foundation for considering health, a student might present himself or herself for counseling with, for example, an eating disorder. Although not exclusively a health problem, there are clear health risks in this disorder, and counseling psychologists treating eating disorders need to be knowledgeable about its health implications. Alternatively, a client may be dealing with a problem that has a health concomitant, although health is not the major focus. An example might be a student who is depressed and doing poorly in his or her studies, and who reports high levels of alcohol use as a coping strategy. In this case, although not the focus of treatment, the counseling intervention can stress the consequences of alcohol abuse and provide the student with a context for exploring this behavior.

Health can also be a focus for programmatic efforts, particularly in a consultative or collaborative mode. Health concerns of students are such a critical problem that more than one campus agency is likely to be dealing with them. Therefore, counseling centers can work with student health, dorm advisors, and/or the student organization office on campus, to sponsor a series of programs on health-related behaviors and problems. Counseling center staff can also consult with faculty and staff, educating them regarding health issues faced by students and appropriate methods of referral.

Counseling centers are well-positioned, by virtue of their historical and current role in student services, to influence the campus system as a whole. Such a systemic approach might emphasize primary prevention, avoiding disease prior to its occurrence. In a given year, a campus-wide focus on prevention of alcohol abuse, for example, would be a means to utilize public health strategies as well as individually targeted strategies.

Future Directions in Research and Practice

In planning interventions, it is important that counseling center staff consider the various components of preventive health. For example, do students possess the relevant knowledge needed to evaluate susceptibility? Is this knowledge influencing their behavior and decision making, or is attention to modifying factors necessary? Counseling centers are in an excellent position not only to deliver services, but also to investigate, in a large-scale way, the influence of such services on the physical health of a defined population. Increased attention to problems of physical health through attention to the promotion of preventive health behaviors is an excellent "match" for the campus environment.

COUNSELING PSYCHOLOGY'S PEDIATRIC ROLE IN CHILDHOOD LEUKEMIA

The counseling psychologist interested in the psychological aspects of health promotion with a pediatric population will find unique challenges and opportunities. When working with children, one must be adept at applying traditional research methodology and psychotherapy interventions to the study and treatment of various medical conditions. In addition, however, one has to be knowledgeable about child development and family systems because, unlike adults, children seldom voluntarily seek out psychology services. As an overall goal, the counseling psychologist attempts to identify psychosocial stressors that can accompany medical conditions and to devise treatment interventions that reduce or prevent physical and psychological suffering. An example of how this goal is achieved can be seen in the treatment of children with leukemia.

Other than accidents, cancer is the most frequent cause of death among children, and approximately 6,000 new cases of childhood cancer are diagnosed annually. The most common form of childhood cancer is leukemia, and the peak age for the diagnosis of juvenile leukemia is age 4. Leukemia once signified certain death, but recent advances in medicine have allowed over half of the afflicted children to eventually be cured. Consequently, childhood leukemia is often a chronic disorder that may require continuous treatment for a period of years (Eiser, 1985; Maul-Mellott & Adams, 1987). The critical phases of the disease have been identified to be diagnosis, treatment, remission, and relapse. During these critical phases, the counseling psychologist can be especially helpful in promoting more adaptive coping. We discuss here the relevant empirical findings and clinical issues that may occur during each of these critical phases for both leukemia patients and their families.

The Child with Diagnosed Leukemia

Receiving the formal diagnosis of leukemia has been reported as the single most distressing phase for children and their families (Chesler & Yoak, 1984). Families are frequently reluctant to inform their children about the ramifications of the diagnosis. However, the general consensus is that children should be told as much as their developmental level allows them to understand (National Cancer Institute, 1982). Spinetta and

Maloney (1975) argued that the majority of children who are not informed about their diagnosis will eventually realize the serious nature of their illness from the sudden changes in their lives and from the attitudes and emotions of their parents. These children usually suspect that something is seriously wrong and feel abandoned or isolated. A study by Slavin, O'Malley, Koocher, and Foster (1982) suggested that the timing of this disclosure may also be important. Children who were told early in the treatment process (within one year) were rated as better adjusted than those who were told later or who were self-informed.

Knowing how children of different ages perceive disease is important when helping them to understand and cope with it. There is a tendency for children to view their disease as a punishment for something that they have done or thought in the past (Maul-Mellott & Adams, 1987). In addition, young children often believe that germs cause all illness. Older children are able to differentiate between symptoms and underlying disease processes, but their understanding is often quite naive as well. It has been observed that, following the initial explanation about the diagnosis, most children will enter into a period of increased receptivity for information about their disease (Culling, 1988). Some children will actually exhibit "cognitive leaps," where their knowledge of the disease greatly exceeds their cognitive capacity in other respects.

Treatments for Leukemia

Children who undergo medical procedures experience considerable anxiety. Therefore, developing interventions that prepare them for these procedures has been a major focus for psychologists working with children, and the research literature, for the most part, has supported the effectiveness of the interventions. Preparatory procedures often involve one or more of the following components: information giving, viewing a peer model's coping skills, and preparatory play (Melamed & Bush, 1985). Information-giving interventions can reduce anxiety by decreasing a child's uncertainty and fostering a trusting relationship between the child and the informant. For example, Fernald and Correy (1981) noted the value of information giving for a group of 3- to 9-year olds having their blood drawn. However, giving information regarding an elective surgery to a group of children under 8 years of age who had had previous surgeries actually increased their behavioral distress and number of health concerns, when compared to children who watched a distracting film (Melamed & Bush, 1985). Often, information is given by watching filmed peer models. In a review of the literature, Kendall and Watson (1981) concluded that peer modeling is the most successful preparatory program for young children, particularly if the coping model initially demonstrates fear and stress, then gradually, through successful coping, overcomes his or her fear and demonstrates mastery. Preparatory play programs, where children are given an opportunity to play with toy instruments and to handle actual instruments, have also been shown to reduce anxiety following hospitalization (Melamed & Bush, 1985).

Current medical treatments for leukemia require children to undergo intensely painful and aversive procedures such as bone marrow aspirations (BMA), chemotherapy, and radiation treatments. BMA is perhaps the most painful procedure of the treatment protocol (Katz & Jay, 1984). In fact, adolescent patients perceive BMA to be more distressing than the disease itself (Zeltzer, Kellerman, Ellenberg, Dash, & Rigler, 1980). BMA is routinely performed in order to determine whether cancer cells are present and, despite the administration of local anesthesia, it produces severe pain. In addition to BMA, children with leukemia must also endure regimens of chemotherapy. Although recent medical practices have attempted to establish minimal therapeutic doses to reduce the severity of side effects, aversive and debilitating side effects such as immuno-suppression and alopecia (hair loss) are still quite common.

As an adjunct to chemotherapy, some children will receive radiation treatments. Radiation that involves the central nervous system (CNS) has been associated with impaired performance on measures of general cognitive ability. Understandably, cognitive deficit resulting from CNS irradiation is a controversial issue. Studies have been conducted using the leukemia patients' healthy siblings or children who received limited radiation treatments for solid tumors as control groups. A recent meta-analysis of 26 controlled studies investigating the effects of radiation treatment suggested that children who receive CNS radiation average a .72 standard deviation (about 11 IQ points) decrement in their expected full-scale IQ scores (Cousens, Waters, Said, & Stevens, 1988). Performance IQ scores may be affected more than verbal IQ scores (Said, Waters, Cousens, & Stevens, 1989), and treatments with children under the age of 5 appear to result in greater deficits (Cousens et al., 1988). Although not enough longitudinal research has been conducted to conclude definitively that these deficits are permanent, Said et al. (1989) presented retrospective data that suggest these deficits are significant for at least 5 years.

In addition to the medical and intellectual side effects of chemotherapy and radiation therapy, these procedures are also capable of producing debilitating psychological side effects. Psychological side effects are presumed to be the result of associative learning (Carey & Burish, 1988) and can be manifested in a variety of symptoms such as irritability, depression, withdrawal, insomnia, anorexia, avoidance, nausea, and vomiting. These side effects are problematic for the children and their families, as well as for treatment teams; children may pose management problems during procedures, fail to comply with the therapeutic regimens, or discontinue treatment altogether (Dolgin, Katz, Doctors, & Siegel, 1986). Consequently, psychologists have used a variety of cognitive and behavioral interventions to alleviate these psychological side effects and to help children cope more effectively.

The most widely investigated intervention with children and adolescents is hypnosis (Carey & Burish, 1988). Hypnosis is a generic term referring to a number of induction procedures that require the child to be completely absorbed in an activity. Unlike adult induction procedures, which typically involve passive images, hypnosis with children uses playful fantasy and physical movement, often with props such as dolls, toys, or picture books (Zeltzer & LeBaron, 1986). Children are considered good candidates for induction procedures because of their vivid imagination and ability to readily move from reality to fantasy.

Zeltzer and colleagues conducted a series of evaluative studies on hypnosis-based treatments in which children either served as their own controls (LeBaron & Zeltzer, 1984; Zeltzer, Kellerman, Ellenberg, & Dash, 1983) or were compared to patients receiving supportive counseling (Zeltzer, LeBaron, & Zeltzer, 1984). Their results suggested that, after one to three training sessions, hypnosis was able to reduce levels of postchemotherapy nausea and vomiting and the severity of symptoms that remained. Further, these benefits continued after the therapist was no longer present.

Another intervention that is beginning to receive attention involves the aid of an external distractor during the procedure, usually achieved by having children play a video game. Distraction has been associated with decreased levels of nausea and anxiety (Redd et al., 1987). Other interventions that have been employed include video modeling of adaptive coping strategies, breathing exercises, and play therapy. Distraction appears to be a common factor in all of these interventions with children.

Interventions that have been successful with adult leukemia patients, but not as yet applied to children in controlled studies, include progressive muscle relaxation training with guided imagery, systematic desensitization, and biofeedback with relaxation training (Carey & Burish, 1988).

Remission

When children enter into remission, they and their families must learn to live with the constant threat of relapse. This uncertainty about the permanence of remission may last for many years, and chronic stress is almost always present. The constant state of fearing relapse has been referred to as the "Damocles syndrome" (Koocher & O'Malley, 1981). Families are often anxious and uncertain about how they should treat their children, and may become overindulgent, overprotective, or relaxed in their discipline. Unfortunately, these types of parent behaviors are often associated with children's behavior problems, and Maguire (1983) noted that children with leukemia are four times as likely to exhibit behavior problems compared to healthy controls. Common behavioral problems include clinging and dependent behaviors, reluctance to sleep alone, and temper tantrums. Perhaps the single most important treatment intervention for children in remission is to send them back to school as quickly as possible (National Cancer Institute, 1982).

A topic of particular interest to counseling psychologists is the career decision making and vocational adjustment of cancer survivors. Zevon, Neubauer, and Green (1988) evaluated the vocational satisfaction of long-term leukemia survivors. Their survivors, now adults, expressed levels of vocational satisfaction and well-being that were similar to controls on standardized measures. In a study of the effects of cancer on adolescent career development, Stern, Norman, and Zevon (1991) reported that adolescent cancer patients were similar to a group of matched controls on dimensions of career maturity, self-image, and perceived social support. The adolescent cancer patients, however, were found to foreclose and commit to a career sooner than controls. Stern et al. (1991) suggested that this early foreclosure does not appear to be detrimental to career pursuits and may reflect the cancer patients' attempts to become more similar to what they consider normal.

Relapse

When a relapse of leukemia occurs, both the children and their families are thrown back onto an "emotional roller coaster." For families that have overrelied on denial, relapse can be especially stressful. Relapse may make children believe that their previous efforts have been in vain, and they may display symptoms of depression, anger, and withdrawal (National Cancer Institute, 1982). Fortunately, these symptoms are often transient and children usually resume active involvement in their treatment. Although as many as 90% of the children who relapse will achieve another remission (Maul-Mellott & Adams, 1987), the threat of death is always present.

In a parallel manner to informing children about their diagnosis, evidence also suggests that children as young as 5 or 6 should be informed about their impending deaths (Spinetta, Rigler, & Karon, 1974). Culling (1988) noted the helpfulness in these discussions of understanding the parents' beliefs about death and incorporating these beliefs into the discussion with children. Obtaining this information will also give parents an opportunity to discuss their concerns and feelings with the counseling psychologist.

Families of Children with Leukemia

A child with leukemia should not be treated in isolation, because children's successful coping and willingness to comply with medical procedures are often determined by how well their families are coping. Upon hearing the diagnosis, a family's initial responses are often shock and numbness. These initial reactions may last for a period of days or for several weeks; when prolonged, the family's ability to participate in treatment decisions may be seriously hampered (Culling, 1988). Parents are forced to undergo a long and often painful process of reconstructing reality for themselves, their children, and their future.

Chesler and Yoak (1984) identified five types of stressors that families encounter:

1. Intellectual stressors, or the requirement to understand a massive amount of complex information regarding their child's disease and treatment;
2. Instrumental stressors, involving the need to plan day-to-day family tasks around the child's disease;
3. Interpersonal stressors, referring to disruption of social relationships;
4. Emotional stressors, which reflect parents' psychological and physical responses to the child's life-threatening illness and their own disrupted routines;
5. Existential stressors, which involve questioning the meaning of life, moral beliefs, or religious faith.

Coping behaviors to counter these stressors include seeking information, religious support, expression of feelings, flexibility in dealing with new tasks, maintaining social relationships, and actively solving problems. During the diagnosis phase, the primary tasks for families are to accept the realities of the disease and its treatments, communicate openly with one another, and begin to implement adaptive coping behaviors (National Cancer Institute, 1982).

These tasks are difficult, and they place stress on both family and marital relationships. In fact, it has been suggested that parents of children with leukemia have higher incidences of marital discord and separation than does the general population (Kaplan, Smith, Grobstein, & Fischman, 1973). Recent studies, however, seem to contradict these earlier conclusions. Chesler and Barbarin (1987), for example, found that 55% of their sample felt more positive toward their spouses after their child's diagnosis. Perhaps these recent findings reflect a lessened pressure on parents, resulting from the increased survival rate of children with leukemia, or the increasing recognition by medical centers that families need psychosocial support.

The siblings of leukemia victims are also at risk for psychosocial difficulties. As many as 50% of the siblings of children with leukemia develop behavioral problems, including somatic complaints, enuresis, school phobias, depression, and dependent behaviors (Culling, 1988). In fact, Spinetta and Deasy-Spinetta (1981) found that, as a group, siblings of children with cancer demonstrated lower adjustment on psychological tests than the cancer patients themselves. Cairns, Clark, Smith, and Lansky (1979) noted that these behavioral problems were especially likely to develop if the siblings perceived their parents as being overinvolved with the patient's care. However, support groups for siblings of leukemia patients have been shown to be effective (Kellerman, Zeltzer, & Ellenberg, 1980) in reducing behavior problems and promoting positive coping strategies at both posttreatment and follow-up assessments.

Treatment

Parents experience considerable stress while observing their children endure painful procedures, such as bone marrow aspirations (Jay, Ozolins, Elliott, & Cadwell, 1983). In response to these concerns, Jay and Elliott (1991) implemented a stress inoculation program for the parents of leukemia patients. Their results demonstrated that parents in the stress inoculation program reported lower anxiety and higher positive self-statement scores than did parents in the control group. Support groups, both professionally led and peer-led, have also become important interventions for parents or primary caregivers. Support groups disseminate information, provide a resource for solving problems, and offer a supportive network. As facilitators, counseling psychologists can convey accurate information, promote adaptive coping, encourage group support, and ensure that the psychosocial needs of all participants are addressed. In addition to group participation, allowing parents and siblings to participate in the child's treatment may be beneficial; activities such as monitoring IVs, attending to the child's hygiene, and feeding are all tasks that parents can and often want to perform.

Remission

Remission has been noted to be a time of mixed feelings for families. Families experience anxiety over the termination of treatment, because they have come to depend on the treatment team for support. The primary coping task for families is to reinvest themselves in relationships outside of the hospital and resume the normal activities of their day-to-day lives (National Cancer Institute, 1982). When parents are apprehensive about discontinuing treatment or allowing their children to resume normal routines, denial or suppression may become an adaptive coping mechanism (Culling, 1988). The counseling psychologist, while acknowledging a family's fears regarding the termination of treatment, should work to decrease the amount of contact with the family at this phase, and to engender reinvolvement in community support networks.

Future Directions in Research and Practice

The impact that a counseling psychologist can have on the treatment of children with chronic diseases, such as leukemia, is substantial. With an understanding of child development, family systems, adaptive coping strategies, and effective therapeutic interventions, the counseling psychologist is capable of providing valuable clinical services to children and their families. Such interventions have been shown to have a positive influence not only while children are being treated, but also well into their remission. Similar long-term benefits are observed for the parents and siblings of these children. As the link between mental and physical health continues to be demonstrated, the importance of counseling psychologists providing clinical services and research in pediatric health care settings will become even more apparent.

Counseling psychologists can also make research contributions to our understanding of childhood leukemia in the areas of pain management, coping facilitation, developmental interventions, and assessment of long-term effects. The pain management procedures described in the literature have been shown to be effective in promoting more adaptive coping during painful medical procedures. Now studies are needed to determine what procedures are most effective for what children, and the long-term effects of these interventions. Much of the research on coping is based on adult models that are applied to children. Researchers need to investigate the unique coping strategies used by children at particular developmental stages and to evaluate the efficacy of training children to use adaptive coping strategies. Finally, researchers must continue to consider the family and its ability to cope as an influential source of variance in overall outcome. More studies such as Jay and Elliott's (1991) stress inoculation procedure for parents need to be conducted.

Counseling psychology's developmental emphasis can also aid the field's understanding of when particular interventions should be applied. The development and utilization of age-appropriate interview devices, in addition to parental and behavioral evaluations, will be important for this area of research. The assessment of long-term morbidity will increase our understanding regarding quality-of-life issues. Studies on the cognitive effects of leukemia treatments, by Cousens et al. (1988), and on vocational planning, by Stern et al. (1991), are promising trends.

CHRONIC PAIN

Chronic pain and its accompanying disability are becoming a health care problem of considerable significance. Low back pain is one of the most common complaints of Western society; estimates suggest that 80% of adults will have significant low back pain during their lifetime (Nachemson, 1976), and about 30% of the population will seek medical care for this problem (Bonica, 1980). Because the majority of occurrences of low back pain resolve in about 6 weeks, most of these cases will not result in appreciable disability. However, although a small minority of acute low back pain cases become cases of chronic low back pain, their impact on the health care system is considerable.

The progress from acute to chronic status among cases of low back pain has been well documented. Bergquist-Ullman and Larsson (1977) found that the following percentages of cases were pain-free at different time intervals: 35% after 1 month, 70% after 2 months, 86% after 3 months, 94% after 6 months, and 96% after 12 months. In their study, only 6 of 184 patients, or 3%, were disabled longer than 12 months. However, given current figures, that 3% translates into an estimated 75,000 workers annually who can be expected to experience a chronic disability from low back pain.

These numbers suggest the immensity of the financial burden associated with chronic low back pain. In 1976, approximately $14 billion were spent on treatment of and compensation for low back injuries in the United States (Akeson & Murphy, 1977). Bonica (1977) calculated that health care costs, disability payments, lost work time, and accompanying litigation totaled $60 billion annually. The current emphasis on rehabilitation of chronic pain cases, and prevention of chronicity among acute pain injuries, is underscored by the fact that about 25% of the cases account for 87% of the costs (Leavitt, Johnston, & Beyer, 1971).

Chronic pain (usually defined as pain of longer than 3 months' duration) is a different problem than acute pain. As Waddell (1987) noted, acute pain is related to peripheral stimulus, nociception (pain stimuli), and tissue damage. Further, the degree and nature of reported pain, illness behavior, and disability are proportional to the physical findings. However, with chronic pain, there is often little relation between reported pain, illness behaviors, disability, and physical findings. Chronic pain becomes increasingly associated with severe and persistent pain reports, "pain behaviors" (e.g., moaning, grimacing), a reduction in activity with a corresponding interference in the completion of normal daily routines, increased use of pain medication, increased emotional disturbance, and disruption of employment and family/marital relationships (Sanders, 1985).

There are many opportunities for intervention by counseling psychologists in this health area, particularly because much intervention is of a short-term nature and emphasizes psychoeducational approaches. A particular strength of counseling psychology in this area is its traditional philosophy of building on strengths and assisting coping efforts. Pain patients resist the notion that the pain is "all in their head," which is often implied by physicians or family members. Rather than diagnosing pathology, the focus on identifying and building on strengths, both individually and within the patients' family and employment systems, is a welcome match for this health care problem. Further, because most chronic pain patients experience employment disruption, career counseling has a definite place in the rehabilitation process.

Evaluating Interventions for Pain

Traditional approaches to treating chronic pain have emphasized a medical model. For example, presumed underlying impairments, such as herniated nucleus pulposus (commonly referred to as a "slipped disc"), are treated with surgery. However, in many cases, surgery fails to improve disability. Surin (1977) studied the total duration of disability from 10 years preoperatively to 10 years postoperatively in 116 patients who had undergone lumbar discectomy. The total number of days of work absence for the group increased continually across the observation period, with no positive effect of surgery on this measure. In addition, failure to achieve a return to work after surgery often precipitates repeated surgery, and the return to work rate among patients who have repeat lumbar surgery is approximately 40% (Lehmann & LaRocca, 1981).

The failure of surgery has been noted for some time. Indeed, studies reported as early as 1975 (Wiltse & Rocchio, 1975) indicated that nonphysical factors—psychological variables in particular—are related to surgical success. Waddell and colleagues have conducted a series of studies (e.g., Waddell, 1987; Waddell, Morris, DiPaola, Bircher, & Finlayson, 1986) demonstrating that surgical decisions may be more influenced by the duration and severity of the patient's pain, the degree of distress manifested by the patient, and the failure of previous treatments than by actual physical indications. Ironically, many of these factors (e.g., anxiety, distress) are negatively correlated with surgical outcomes (Dzioba & Doxey, 1984).

The other traditional treatment method is rehabilitation, usually involving a combination of nonsurgical modalities such as physical therapy, progressive activity, postural training, work hardening, and occupational therapy. Reports of return to work following traditional rehabilitation vary widely, from approximately 35% to upward of 50%, with better outcomes being achieved with more intensive rehabilitation. However, the similarity of low outcome rates between surgery and nonsurgical modalities suggests that other factors account for outcome (Waddell, 1987).

More recently, psychologically based interventions have been investigated as treatments for chronic pain. This focus on the psychological aspects of chronic pain developed out of the changing conceptualization of pain from one that was entirely organic in nature to one that emphasizes pain as a complex phenomenon in which sensory-discriminative, motivational-affective, and cognitive-evaluative components interact (Melzack & Wall, 1965). An additional factor is that the communication of pain influences the experience of pain, and such pain communications appear to be contingently controlled by environmental factors (Fordyce, 1976).

An initial psychologically based approach to treating chronic pain involved the operant modification of pain behaviors (such as prolonged inactivity, overmedication, and verbal expressions of pain) through altering the consequences that follow these behaviors. Thus, operant pain programs systematically reduced pain behaviors by withdrawing staff attention, pain-dependent medication, and the possibility of avoidance of activities and responsibilities. In the place of these pain behaviors, behaviors that are inconsistent with a sick role, such as activity, "up time" out of bed, and exercise, were prompted and reinforced.

A consistent finding in the literature (see Turner & Chapman, 1982a, 1982b, for reviews) is that operant-based rehabilitation programs result in an increase in physical activity and a decrease in medication use. Additionally, return to employment appears to exceed the usual rate for traditional treatments of surgery and rehabilitation. For example, Roberts and Reinhardt (1980) reported a 77% success rate, defined as a return to normal life-style, at 1- and 8-year follow-ups. An additional finding across studies, however, is that indexes of subjective pain experience do not appear to be altered by operant programs.

A second psychologically based treatment for chronic pain has been the use of relaxation training, delivered in variable formats. For example, relaxation training can be: (a) taught as a direct treatment for pain and muscle spasming; (b) accompanied by biofeedback for corrective feedback; (c) delivered entirely in the form of biofeedback, or (d) taught as a coping skill to be applied in daily living situations. The evidence for the effectiveness of relaxation training is mixed. Relaxation accompanied by biofeedback has been demonstrated to be useful for headache pain, but its usefulness for chronic back pain has not been empirically supported. Relaxation taught as a coping skill has been more successful, perhaps because in-vivo use is emphasized. In fact, a recent meta-analysis of nonmedical treatments for chronic pain of all types (Malone & Strube, 1988) concluded that relaxation training demonstrated the highest percentage of improvement among patients.

A third psychological treatment approach has involved altering pain-related cognitions and fostering increased coping responses using cognitive-behavioral intervention models (Turk, Meichenbaum, & Genest, 1983). These cognitive-behavioral treatments incorporate traditional behavioral techniques to change thoughts and attitudes that influence how the patient views the pain stimulus and his or her coping resources and responses. These treatments are based on the assumption that a person's cognitions can serve to exacerbate the subjective experience of pain and to influence the subsequent response to that pain experience. If a patient's cognitions can be altered to allow a more realistic appraisal of both the pain sensation and the available coping resources and responses, then the subjective experience of pain can be reduced and the probability of effective coping can be enhanced (Turk & Rudy, 1986). Specific coping skills that have been used are distraction, imagery, calming or coping self-statements, and relaxation guided by imagery or cognitions. Cognitive-behavioral strategies also teach the patient to discriminate and use physiological signals to initiate coping strategies.

Much of the research on cognitive-behavioral treatments for pain has used laboratory pain analogues (e.g., Horan, Hackett, Buchanan, Stone, & Demchik-Stone, 1977). Under these conditions, cognitive strategies have been demonstrated to be useful for controlling pain. Less research has explored the utility of these strategies for ongoing chronic pain. A notable exception is a study by Turner and Clancy (1988), who compared operant-behavioral and cognitive-behavioral group treatments in the rehabilitation of chronic low back pain. Both treatments were effective compared to a wait-list control on measures of physical disability and psychosocial functioning at both immediate posttesting and 6- and 12-month follow-up assessments. Unfortunately, measures of employment and activities of daily living were not included in the study, so the extent of the treatments' effect on what could be considered actual disability is unknown.

More recently, Altmaier, Lehmann, Russell, Weinstein, and Kao (in press) reported on a randomized, controlled trial of a cognitive-behavioral treatment, including biofeedback and operant conditioning of exercise behaviors, compared to traditional rehabilitation. Both treatments were effective on measures of psychological and physical functioning, and resulted in 80% of patients returning to normal employment or being retrained for new jobs by a 6-month follow-up visit. The active rehabilitation mechanism of these treatments is not clear, although it is hypothesized that providing patients with an array of coping skills to use during painful situations is a primary means of improvement. In support of this contention, gains in self-efficacy during treatment predicted outcome on both physical and psychological dimensions at the 6-month follow-up (Altmaier, Russell, Kao, Lehmann, & Weinstein, 1992).

The area of treatment provision to chronic pain patients is likely to expand in the future, based on evidence that treatment programs that build on psychologically based conceptualizations of pain enhance both vocational and psychosocial functioning. There is also increased interest in developing multidisciplinary programs that incorporate physical therapy, education, and support along with psychological interventions. Another area of growing interest is the prevention of chronic pain. If mechanisms can be identified that are related to an acute condition's becoming a chronic situation, then preventive interventions of varying natures can be developed and evaluated.

Chronic Pain and Families

There is considerable evidence that the patient's family plays a critical role in the patient's experience of chronic pain (see Payne & Norfleet, 1986, and Rowat & Knafl, 1985, for reviews). The family can reinforce pain behaviors, and thus prolong the patient's display of such behaviors and any attendant disability. However, the family can also increase the patient's effective coping efforts, and thus play a facilitative role in recovery. Attention to the family's influence on chronic pain has been the most recent development in research aimed at understanding this disability. Several distinct themes have been identified by Turk, Flor, and Rudy (1987): Do families play an etiological role in the development of chronic pain? Does the family affect the maintenance of chronic pain? Does the family suffer negative effects when there is a family member with chronic pain?

Development of Chronic Pain

There is some evidence that there are "painful" families, that is, families with extensive history of chronic pain episodes. For example, the rate of abdominal pain among parents, siblings, and relatives of children with such pain is up to six times higher than that reported for control groups (Christiansen & Mortensen, 1975). These data may be interpreted in a variety of ways. A genetic perspective would argue that such data reveal a constitutional vulnerability. Research with animals supports such a contention, although the data for humans are inconclusive (Inbal, Devor, Tuchendler, & Lieblich, 1980).

Much of the early literature on pain and families was based on psychoanalytic theory, and argued that pain was a result of psychic pain rooted in family relationships (Knopf, 1935). More recent theorizing, similarly focusing on family interactions, comes from family systems theory. This perspective holds that a person with chronic pain is an expression of dysfunction within the family system. Many of the systems models emphasize unresolved childhood problems as the base of an individual's engaging other family members in the sick role (see Flor & Turk, 1985, for a fuller discussion of the family systems perspective on chronic pain).

Maintenance of Chronic Pain

Research on the role of families in the maintenance of chronic pain has focused primarily on the patient's spouse. Both family systems perspectives and behavioral models have been used to define the role of the spouse in maintaining the chronic pain of the patient. As described above, family systems theories view the family as a system of relationships, with the effective functioning of each member dependent on the effective functioning of other members. Theorists, such as Waring (1977), have argued that seemingly dysfunctional symptoms provide stability for a family and thus are maintained. For example, marital conflict may be avoided by the parents' focusing on a child with chronic pain. Some evidence exists to support this model, but Feuerstein, Sills, and Houle (1985) found that higher levels of pain complaints were associated with increased family independence. Theorists agree that certain constellations of family functioning are characteristic of psychosomatic families (see Minuchin et al., 1975), but empirical tests of these patterns are rare.

An alternate model for understanding the role of the family has been proposed by Fordyce (1976), who suggested that importance be attached to the communication of pain by the patient. This communication, or "pain behavior," is often directed at the family and consists of verbal complaints of pain and suffering, moaning and sighing, postural irregularities, and functional limitations ("downtime"). Fordyce argued that pain behaviors are learned according to principles of operant conditioning and are maintained by reinforcement from family members. Therefore, the frequency of these behaviors can be expected to increase if the patient receives desirable consequences (e.g., attention) or is able to avoid undesirable consequences (e.g., work) upon their performance.

Some evidence demonstrates that spouses do, in fact, serve as discriminative cues for the display of pain behaviors. In a classic study (Block, Kremer, & Gaylor, 1980), pain patients were interviewed about their reported pain levels while being observed by their spouses or by a "neutral observer" (a ward clerk). Patients who reported that their spouses were solicitous to their pain behaviors reported higher levels of pain when being observed by their spouses than by the neutral observer; however, patients with nonsolicitous spouses reported less pain when viewed by the spouse than when observed by the ward clerk. Although this study is suggestive, it relied on self-reported pain only and did not assess whether the presence of the spouse served to elicit actual pain behaviors or communications.

A recent study (Paulsen & Altmaier, 1992) clarified this question in an investigation of actual pain behaviors demonstrated by patients during activities of daily living (i.e., lifting, walking up and down stairs). A differentiation was made in this study between enacted social support and perceived social support. Enacted social support was assessed as the physical support received from the spouse, as might happen when the spouse gets a drink for the patient when the patient is in too much pain to get up from a chair. Perceived social support was measured as the emotional support the pain patient perceives as available from the spouse. Patients who reported higher levels of enacted support from their spouse displayed a greater number of pain behaviors during observation than patients who reported lower levels of enacted support. However, patients who reported higher levels of perceived support displayed fewer pain behaviors in the presence of the spouse than when the spouse was absent.

Including the Family in Treatment

Hudgens (1979) reported a treatment study in which spouses were included as patients in rehabilitation interventions. Spouses (or significant others) of the patients were individually treated for 2 or 3 hours each week of the 8-week inpatient program in which their spouse was participating; the focus of their treatment was the role of pain behavior in the continuation of chronic pain. Later in the program, interviews were held with the patient and spouse, and with the family, to examine and treat family issues concerning the patient's chronic pain. The outcomes of this extended involvement of the family were impressive, with approximately 75% of the patients and families returning to normal levels of functioning on psychological and disability/functional measures.

The involvement of spouses and families, however, has not received unequivocal support. A shorter outpatient cognitive-behavioral program was used by Moore and Chaney (1985) to investigate whether treating patients in couples or by themselves would lead to superior outcomes. Results revealed that both treatments reduced reported pain, spouse-observed pain behaviors, and health care utilization at both immediate and delayed time intervals; however, the results did not favor spouse involvement over treating the patient alone.

Future Directions in Research and Practice

The nature of the support received by the pain patient is critical to understanding the family's influence on rehabilitation. As noted by Altmaier (1987), a spouse or family can function to either impede or promote rehabilitation of chronic pain patients. Several guidelines for intervention may be offered. First, the patient and the family need education concerning the actual limitations that are imposed by the patient's condition. It is likely that some overly solicitous behavior on the part of the family is due to a misunderstanding of the healing period for the injury and an accompanying fear that re-injury might occur. Second, the family needs encouragement and support to assist the patient in using the coping skills he or she is taught during treatment. In the outcome study conducted by Altmaier et al. (in press), spouses were asked to view educational videotapes concerning "myths of pain" and the types of coping responses that were taught during the rehabilitation program. A similar method could be used during any treatment, where spouses and families can be incorporated into the treatment protocol, serving as "partners" in learning and practicing new skills such as relaxation or cognitive restructuring. Third, social support should be conceptualized multidimensionally. Chronic pain researchers and treatment providers must consider the complexity of the relationships among the patient, his or her care providers, and his or her family, in the provision of support. The recent matching model articulated by Cutrona and Russell (1990) provided a valuable means of understanding this complexity.

ALZHEIMER'S DISEASE

Counseling psychologists interested in health promotion are increasingly recognizing the importance of clinical and research involvement with the aged. During the past decade, the literature on this population has proliferated and, in 1986, the American Psychological Association introduced *Psychology and Aging,* a journal dedicated to research with the aged. The recent emphasis on this population is largely due to changing demographic realities. Currently, about 13% of the U.S. population is 65 or older; by the year 2030, this figure is expected to climb to nearly 22%, or over 65 million people

(U.S. Department of Commerce, 1989). The "graying" of America is well-documented, and it is important for counseling psychologists to be prepared to deal with issues related to this growing segment of the population. It is beyond our scope to discuss all of the issues relevant to counseling psychologists' work with the aged; consequently, our discussion is limited to perhaps the greatest threat to the health and psychological well-being of the aged and their families, Alzheimer's disease (AD).

AD has an insidious onset that results in the irreversible deterioration of a person's cognitive, social, and physical functioning. The course of the disease may be from 1 to 15 years, with an average duration of 7 to 8 years (Liston, 1979). The end result has been described as a "persistent vegetative state" eventually leading to death (Walsh & Leonard, 1985). There are no treatments for AD and the exact cause is unknown, although both genetic and environmental factors have been implicated (Kern, 1988). Most of the research on the etiology of AD has produced mixed findings, and there are many methodological problems in the literature; much more etiological work is needed.

The majority of AD victims live in the community (Clark & Rakowski, 1983), although as many as 60% of those in nursing homes may also have AD. It is estimated that there are currently between 2 million and 4 million middle-aged and elderly Americans afflicted with AD (U.S. Office of Technology Assessment, 1987). Recent estimates suggest that 10.3% of all individuals over the age of 65 will develop AD, and the prevalence rate for those over 85 is 47.2% (Evans et al., 1989). These figures are alarming, considering that individuals aged 85 years and older comprise the fastest growing segment of the U.S. population.

Individuals with AD undergo a progressive and unrelenting series of changes. Several descriptions of the deterioration process have been proposed (Reisberg, Ferris, & DeLeon, & Cook, 1982), and in all of these descriptions at least three stages are present. The early stages are usually characterized by memory loss and subtle changes in personality. It is common for the disease to remain undiagnosed during this period (Lovett, 1989). The middle stages are characterized by deficits in judgment, reasoning, abstract thinking, and self-care. Impairments at work and in social functioning become obvious to an objective observer. By the time victims enter the later stages, pervasive deterioration is evident. The loss of bowel or bladder control and of the abilities to walk, talk, or swallow are frequently observed. It is noteworthy that the course of AD is very heterogeneous, and it is impossible to predict the degree or rate of decline for any individual (Mayeux, Stern, & Spanton, 1985). Because AD does not progress in a predictable, uniform manner, these stage models serve primarily as guidelines for effective care planning and interventions.

Counseling Psychology Roles with AD Patients

When working with AD patients, the counseling psychologist may perform three important functions: (a) helping to accurately diagnose AD; (b) evaluating patients periodically, in order to monitor their rate and extent of decline; (c) helping patients and their families to cope.

Diagnosis of AD

Currently, the only way to confirm a diagnosis of AD is through postmortem examination of the cortex. Therefore, diagnosis is most often made by excluding other explanations for the patient's behavior. This process is often a lengthy and frustrating one for patients and their families. Perhaps the most common alternative diagnosis to consider is depression. In fact, 25 to 30% of AD patients meet diagnostic criteria for depression (Lovett, 1989). Depression and memory impairments are frequently the presenting complaints for individuals who are later diagnosed with AD (Brown, Lyon, & Sellers, 1988). Although there are few controlled studies, case studies suggest that antidepressants and psychotherapy may be beneficial for AD patients in the early stages of the disorder. Because of the progressive course of the disease, however, these therapeutic gains are short-lived. Other conditions that need to be ruled out include alcoholism, schizophrenia, metabolic disturbances, neurologic disorders, brain tumors, drug interactions, malnutrition, and acute infections (Benson, 1987). A complete physical and neurological work-up is needed before arriving at a diagnosis of AD.

Ongoing Monitoring

Once the diagnosis is made, an important role for the counseling psychologist is to continue to see the AD patients on a regular basis, to monitor the course of the disease. Evaluations of cognitive, noncognitive, and adaptive behavior functioning are paramount. Researchers are just beginning to search for patterns of cognitive decline that are unique to AD (Nebes, Boller, & Holland, 1986), although cognitive functions that are frequently evaluated include memory, language, attention, and abstract thinking.

Noncognitive function includes affect and personality changes, both of which are extremely common in AD (Fabiszewski, Riley, Berkley, Karner, & Shea, 1988). Frequently noted affective changes include depression, anxiety, impulsiveness, irritability, and lability. Individuals may display sudden temper outbursts or become abusive (Brown et al., 1988). Paranoia is commonly expressed, and the development of delusions and hallucinations may follow.

Changes in adaptive behaviors can be, for caregivers, the most problematic and confusing of all changes. Alzheimer's patients often develop childlike dependence on their caregivers. They may express inappropriate sexual desires, begin to wander, or insist on driving automobiles even though they are incapable of doing so (Brown et al., 1988; Lovett, 1989).

Facilitating Coping Efforts

Available therapeutic interventions for AD patients typically require the involvement of caregivers. A popular therapeutic approach is Reality Orientation (RO; Holden & Woods, 1988). The most common form of RO is a 24-hour system in which patients are reminded of reality cues during every interaction they have with a caregiver. Cues include such information as time of day, month of the year, names of children, or accounts of recent events. RO instruction is also sometimes offered in regular training sessions.

Despite its widespread use, controversy surrounds the therapeutic value of RO (Dietch, Hewett, & Jones, 1989). Woods and Britton (1985) have concluded that RO does improve verbal orientation and cognitive functioning, but other areas of functioning are unaffected. The success of RO interventions may also depend in part on the outcome beliefs of the caregivers (Holden & Woods, 1988). It has been recommended that RO should not be used to orient a person to emotionally charged aspects of reality, such as reminders that a parent is deceased (Brown et al., 1988).

A second intervention is cognitive training, utilizing exercises that challenge various cognitive processes such as memory, logical reasoning, or computation skills. Quayhagen and Quayhagen (1989) showed that a cognitive training program was effective in helping AD patients maintain cognitive and behavioral functioning levels longer than controls, and also had a positive effect on the caregivers' mental health and perceived burden. Other cognitive interventions have included token economy, sensory stimulation, environmental design, art, music, and bibliotherapy (Fraser, 1987). The general consensus is that some benefit results from all of these interventions, but there is little research comparing different types of interventions or assessing their long-term effects.

Treating the Caregivers

The negative consequences of AD are not limited to the insidious incapacitation of the patient; they include the significant psychological, physical, social, and financial burden placed on the caregivers. The majority of AD patients rely on families as their sole sources of support (Toseland & Rossiter, 1989). The risk of caregiver morbidity is so great that caregivers have been referred to as "the hidden patients" (Fengler & Goodrich, 1979). Several informative books have been written describing the stressors of the caregiver experience (Gruetzner, 1988).

Counseling psychologists can play an important role in reducing the caregivers' burden. Work should begin with caregivers at the time of diagnosis, because the patient may not fully appreciate the ramifications of the diagnosis and the caregiver must prepare for the inevitable deterioration. Seltzer, Larkin, and Fabiszewski (1988) recommended a frank discussion about the diagnosis, emphasizing that it is important for caregivers to be told that AD is an irreversible disease.

Numerous studies have investigated factors that contribute to caregiver burden. A frequently investigated factor is the level of the AD patient's impairment. Some studies have found that the more impaired the patients are, the greater the perceived burden (Poulshock & Deimling, 1984); others have failed to show that degree of impairment is a significant influence (Haley, Levine, Brown, & Bartolucci, 1987). Zarit, Todd, and Zarit (1986) actually found an inverse relationship between degree of cognitive impairment and perceived burden.

Another frequently investigated factor is the sex of the caregiver. Stone (1986) noted that 75% of the caregivers are women; further, female caregivers have reported more depression and anxiety than male caregivers (Anthony-Bergstone, Zarit, & Gatz, 1988). It has been demonstrated, however, that men are less willing to admit negative affect (Davies, Priddy, & Tinklenberg, 1986) and are more willing to accept assistance (Pruchno & Resch, 1989). Some additional research has suggested the age of the caregiver as an important factor (Anthony-Bergstone et al., 1988); other studies argue that the quality of the premorbid and present relationship better predicts burden (Pruchno & Resch, 1989).

Interpersonal factors that have been investigated as predictors of burden include centrality of the caregiver/patient relationship (Canter, 1983), race (Mindel, Wright, & Starrett, 1986), and family development (Famighetti, 1986). The influence of social support on coping has also been investigated. For example, Pagel and Becker (1987) found that increased social support was associated with reduced levels of depression for a group of spouse-caregivers. Social support has similarly been associated with increased levels of caregiver life satisfaction (Haley et al., 1987).

Other research has explored methods of reducing caregiver burden. Perhaps the most frequently investigated intervention is support groups. Toseland and Rossiter (1989) reviewed 29 studies and found that the most common goals of such support groups were to provide information, develop a group support system, evaluate the emotional impact of caregiving, discuss self-care, improve interpersonal relations and communication, develop support systems outside the group, and improve home care skills. No single group dealt with all of these themes, and groups differed on how much emphasis was placed on a particular one. Many professionally led groups follow a model outlined by Zarit and Zarit (1982), in which each session lasts two hours. The first hour of every session is devoted to information giving and the second hour is spent on expressing feelings, developing support within the group, addressing specific caregiver concerns, and enhancing caregiving skills.

Although the group experience is frequently viewed by the participants as being very positive, objective measures of outcome are equivocal. For example, Zarit, Anthony, and Boutselis (1987) compared a support group intervention with an individual/family counseling intervention. They found that neither experimental group differed significantly from their wait-list control group on reports of burden or psychiatric symptoms. When studies have employed more restrictive participant selection criteria, however, stronger positive outcomes have been found. Toseland, Rossiter, and Labrecque (1989) evaluated the effectiveness of professionally led and peer-led support groups in which only daughter or daughter-in-law primary caregivers were members. The treatment conditions resulted in significant improvements in members' psychological functioning, support networks, knowledge of support services, and ability to cope with the caregiving role, when compared to the control condition.

Currently, the group literature is plagued with numerous methodological limitations such as small sample sizes; limited use of manipulation checks; participant attrition; use of global change measures; time-limited interventions; and an almost exclusive reliance on white, middle-class participants (Toseland & Rossiter, 1989). More well-controlled cross-sectional and longitudinal studies are needed before definitive conclusions can be drawn about the efficacy of support groups.

A final type of intervention that has been used to reduce burden is respite services (e.g., adult day care, transportation, visiting nurses). Although some have suggested that respite services are helpful in postponing an AD patient's placement in an institution (Lawton, Brody, & Saperstein, 1989), others have found that it postpones placement only if the caregiver is a child of the patient. When caregivers are spouses, placement may even be accelerated (Montgomery & Borgatta, 1989). Like the support group intervention literature, participants' subjective ratings for respite care tend to be quite positive, but outcomes assessed on objective measures are more ambiguous. A major problem for this area of research is getting caregivers to utilize treatment services (Lawton et al., 1989).

Future Directions in Research and Practice

The empirical knowledge base for AD is still in its infancy, and counseling psychologists, with our traditional focus on prevention and rehabilitation, are capable of making substantial contributions in the areas of diagnosis, patient rehabilitation, and caregiver coping. Counseling psychologists who have expertise in neuropsychological assessment can search for patterns of mental decline that predict AD. With much of the research evidence for patient rehabilitation being largely anecdotal, counseling psychologists can determine empirical support for various interventions. Studies on cognitive training (Quayhagen & Quayhagen, 1989) are promising because they demonstrate the efficacy of such interventions with AD patients. Efforts must focus on identifying which interventions are most effective for what types of patients and during which phases of the disease. Caregivers may benefit most from our involvement. With expertise in conducting process and outcome research, we can help determine the efficacy of individual and group therapy. Few studies have investigated process variables such as caregiver, therapist, and patient characteristics. Toseland and Rossiter (1989) identified seven themes of group therapy, and further studies should determine those that are necessary and sufficient. Finally, few studies have investigated coping strategies employed by caregivers and the relationship of these strategies to various kinds of functional and qualitative outcomes. Although AD is a tragic disease, future research efforts may help to significantly reduce both patient and caregiver morbidity.

PROVIDER-PATIENT RELATIONSHIPS

Relationships between health care providers and their patients can be characterized in a number of ways. Health care providers can function as experts, advising patients about the best course of action to ameliorate illness and foster health. Providers can also be educators, teaching patients about disease and health to promote information transfer from provider to patient. Finally, providers can be counselors, engaging patients in a collaborative relationship to solve problems involving emotions, behaviors, and environmental contexts. Ideally, providers function within all of these roles, moving from one perspective to another as the situation demands.

In a classic treatise, Szasz and Hollender (1956) described three basic models of physician–patient relationships, each of which can be related to the roles providers assume. The first and most usual model involves *activity–passivity*, where the patient is the recipient of the physician's efforts. This model characterizes the provider in an expert role. It may be well suited to emergency situations, where immediate action is necessary, but this model does not allow role flexibility in ongoing health provider relationships. A second model is *guidance–cooperation*, where the provider guides and the patient cooperates; Szasz and Hollender recommended this model for acute, symptomatic diseases. Within this model, the expert and educational roles prevail. A third model is that of *mutual participation*, where providers and patients work collaboratively to establish health outcomes for the patient. This model would allow maximum flexibility of behavior in ongoing health relationships, and could contain all three roles as needed. However, as noted by Szasz and Hollander (1956), as well as others, this model has not been widely used in medical encounters.

Our focus in this section of the chapter is on one type of medical provider, the physician. We have chosen to discuss the physician–patient relationship because physicians have been the prevailing force in medical settings and the physician "culture" is predominant (see Altmaier, 1991, for a more complete discussion of the effects of this culture on psychological practice, and Alcorn, 1991, for its history). Further, the bulk of the research regarding the influence of the provider on outcomes has targeted the physician–patient relationship. Our focus is most directed toward the interpersonal aspects of the physician–patient relationship, or those qualities of the physician characterized as "humanistic" (Blurton & Mazzaferri, 1985), such as the abilities to establish rapport, sense patient affect, and communicate on an emotional as well as an informational level. These qualities have recently been brought into focus by the increasing realization that medical care is more than the passive acceptance by the patient of information, medication, or procedures. In fact, during the past decade, there has been increasing recognition that clinical competence extends beyond knowledge to encompass a variety of communication-related skills and perspectives.

Using a Counseling Context for Understanding Medical Encounters

Borrowing our counseling relationship context and using it to conceptualize the physician–patient encounter implies an acceptance of certain assumptions about the nature of the physician–patient relationship and the relevance of a counseling context for this relationship. Specifically, this transfer involves assumptions about the nature of the tasks faced by a physician and a patient, compared to those faced by a counselor and a client. An examination of research on patient–physician relationships and on relevant health outcomes can assist us in determining what transfers to make from a counseling context to a medical context.

What are the expectations that patients bring with them to the physician–patient encounter? In an early study, Falvo and Smith (1983) interviewed an extensive sample of patients concerning different aspects of the physician–patient interaction. Multidimensional scaling procedures employed to analyze the behavioral categories developed from the interviews revealed two dimensions of behavior: general health care delivery and interpersonal communication. More specifically, ineffective interpersonal communication was defined by either the absence of communication (e.g., "The doctor went straight to the problem without greeting me") or a surplus of communication (e.g., "The doctor asked questions that were too personal").

A similar survey (Ware & Snyder, 1975), this time of randomly selected households, revealed that four factors characterized adults' expectations for health care: physician conduct, availability of care, continuity and convenience of care, and access mechanisms. The last three factors pertained to convenience and availability of health care services and will not be further discussed. However, the first factor encompassed many of the attitudes and behaviors that appear to be desirable for effective interpersonal relationships, such as consideration, courtesy, information giving, and thoroughness in information gathering. Ware, Davies-Avery, and Stewart (1978) have since defined this factor as including two distinct aspects: the art of care and the technical quality of care. The former includes such qualities as concern, friendliness, sincerity, and patience; the latter is defined by the provider's being accurate, thorough, and clear in communications.

Similar findings have been noted in a critical incident study defining the interaction between a radiologist and a patient (Morris, Tarico, Smith, Altmaier, & Franken, 1987). In this research, patients were interviewed after a health care interaction, in order to obtain examples of actual interpersonal behaviors that would contribute to either a positive or a negative evaluation of the physician. The behaviors were categorized according to standardized procedures and yielded three dimensions of performance: explanation of procedures and results, interpersonal sensitivity, and attention to patient physical comfort.

Patients' satisfaction with their encounters with physicians has important consequences. One of the primary outcomes that has been investigated within the context of patient satisfaction is patient noncompliance. Lack of cooperation or noncompliance with medical regimens is a major concern, with estimates of noncompliance ranging from 15 to 95%. Most estimates, however, suggest that about one-third of patients fail to comply with the treatment suggested by the physician. Satisfaction has been shown to relate to patient utilization of services (e.g., appointment keeping; DiMatteo, Hays, & Prince, 1986) and, somewhat more weakly, to compliance with treatment directives (Francis, Korsch, & Morris, 1969; Korsch, Gozzi, & Francis, 1968). Such findings suggest that the affective elements of the physician–patient relationship affect patient decision making in critical ways.

How can our own context allow us to make contributions to effective physician performance? One of our contributions may lie in our conceptualization of the client in counseling as an active participant in the encounter. Much of the medical literature views the patient as either a satisfied or a dissatisfied recipient of services rather than within the collaborative model described in the beginning of this section. Thus, a contribution we can make to improving provider–patient relationships is that we understand, and can operationalize, the patient as an active, involved person in the medical process.

This collaborative conceptualization, however, does not directly translate to teaching physicians the type of communication skills that we use in counseling. The counseling context is characterized by longer duration, both within and across sessions, and less immediate resolution of symptomatic complaints. In addition, research (Davis, 1968; Mazzuca, Weinberger, Kurpius, Froehle, & Heister, 1983) has suggested that patient comprehension is negatively related to the types of communication patterns that might be suggested by a "counseling" context, such as empathically acknowledging patient statements. Promoting patient involvement in health care; valuing the humanistic qualities of physicians and the contributions of these qualities to medical care; and viewing "the patient" outside of a "uniformity" assumption (see Kiesler, 1966), in order to respond differentially with both manner and content, are appropriate and reasonable transfers of our counseling context to physician–patient relationships.

Applications of Counseling Psychology to Medical Encounters

Many applications of counseling psychology to the enhancement of medical encounters, and thereby to medical outcomes, could be defined. We have chosen two particular applications that have been well researched and that apply across a variety of health care settings: curriculum innovation, and innovation in the selection and evaluation of physicians.

Interpersonal Skills Curriculum

Kagan and his colleagues at Michigan State University, using Interpersonal Process Recall, made pioneering efforts in the 1960s and 1970s to increase medical students' sensitivity to interpersonal and affective material presented by patients. In their program, medical students received instruction in interviewing skills, practiced new skills on fellow students and on actors serving as patients, and completed several videotaped interviews which were then reviewed with a preceptor. The evidence for the effectiveness of this program (see Kagan, 1984, for review) revealed that the primary outcome for the instruction was that students became more proficient in recognizing and attending to patients' affective responses. An additional conclusion, more supported by anecdotal evidence than by data, was that students became more aware of the influence of emotional processes on physiological ones, a link that presumably might affect their conceptualization of the medical illnesses they would be faced with in their future practices.

The success of this initial program led to a variety of curriculum innovations, most intended to teach specific interpersonal skills such as interviewing. For example, Schnoover, Bassuk, Smith, and Gaskill (1983) described a video-based interpersonal skills training program for medical professionals (e.g., emergency medical technicians, primary care physicians) to improve prehospital care for psychiatric emergencies. Farsad, Galliguez, Chamberlin, and Roghmann (1978) used instruction combined with videotaped review, to improve interviewing skills of pediatrics residents. Their findings demonstrated that the residents became more patient-oriented in their interviews, used more open-ended questions, and provided more support and reassurance as a result of the training.

Similar positive findings are usually noted in evaluations of these instructional packages. Further, in a meta-analysis of an interpersonal skills curriculum, Wolf, Savickas, Saltzman, and Walker (1984) found that the curriculum produced predictable gains on instruments measuring accurate and empathic responses to affective statements. Unfortunately, however, there is little evidence that such gains are maintained over time or are transferred to actual clinical practice.

It is not surprising that recent articles encouraging increased involvement of counseling psychology within health settings (Altmaier, 1987, April; Klippel & DeJoy, 1984) noted the value of providing interpersonal skills training for medical professionals. Such an application allows counseling psychologists to effectively employ their skills in psychoeducation and training. Given the research support for the effectiveness of many such interventions, it is desirable that more attention be given to ways in which both general interpersonal skills, such as interviewing skills, and targeted interpersonal interactions can be improved through training.

Innovative Methods of Selection and Evaluation

As noted earlier, it is important to be able to assess accurately physicians' skills in interpersonal and related areas. Anwar, Bosk, and Greenburg (1981) noted that evaluation of physician performance is not an objective process. Although knowledge can be measured through examinations, and manual and technical skills can be visually assessed, other components of performance do not lend themselves as readily to objective assessment. The literature on resident evaluation (see Lloyd and Langsley, 1986, for a review) notes that, although there is increased demand for accurate evaluation of "noncognitive" performance components, few psychometrically valid and educationally sound measures have been developed. This area of research is ideally suited to the research and assessment backgrounds of counseling psychology. Relevant foci for future research include measuring effective performance and evaluating patient satisfaction and other indexes of physician–patient encounters in areas of interpersonal skills, work attitudes, and personality.

Altmaier and her colleagues have developed a method for defining physician performance and determining the relative importance of noncognitive versus cognitive performance elements in predicting performance. This research began with a job analysis of resident performance (Tarico, Smith, Altmaier, Franken, & VanVelzen, 1984), using faculty physicians as job experts. With a critical incident interview format, categories of performance were labeled and defined as follows:

- Technical skills and abilities included both manual skills and visual perception ability.
- Knowledge covered the resident's knowledge of general science and medicine as well as of radiology.
- Attitudes toward self were defined by behaviors indicating confidence or lack of it, including a recognition of one's limits and the demonstration of insecurity versus comfort in the role of resident.
- Interpersonal skills included communication with patients, staff, and other physicians.
- Conscientiousness described behaviors that indicated thoroughness in work and willingness to expend effort.

- Curiosity described behaviors that indicated the resident sought knowledge because of an intrinsic interest in radiology.

These findings were of interest for two reasons: (a) they demonstrated that categories of performance could be established in an empirical, as opposed to rational, manner, and (b) the distribution of incidents among these categories revealed that the noncognitive categories (i.e., interpersonal skills, attitudes toward self) accounted for the majority of incidents considered critical by staff physicians in the performance of residents.

The broad types of categories have since been replicated in studies of two other types of residencies: pediatrics, a patient care specialty (Altmaier et al., 1990), and obstetrics-gynecology, a surgical specialty (Altmaier, Johnson, Tarico, & Laube, 1988). In addition, categories have been demonstrated to be consistent across several training sites (Altmaier et al., 1989) and to be replicated from the perspective of peer resident physicians as opposed to staff physicians (Tarico, Altmaier, Smith, & Franken, 1986). Taken together, this research further supports the importance, for effective performance, of the types of skills and abilities that might be labeled "noncognitive" in nature—the same aspects of performance earlier referred to as "humanistic." These aspects of performance fit within the art of care, and they may be of most interest to counseling psychologists interested in fostering more effective physician–patient interaction.

This line of research provides an example of the application of behaviorally based methods of defining performance, particularly along dimensions of interest to counseling psychologists, within a medical education setting. Interestingly, the types of behaviors considered critical to success as a medical resident are very similar to those that are critical for success as a psychology intern (Ross & Altmaier, 1990), especially the dimension that balances risking failure with overconfidence concerning limits of training. These parallels further support the potential application of psychology's "perspective" to the improvement of medical encounters through the selection and evaluation of physicians.

Future Directions in Research and Practice

As medicine moves toward greater incorporation of the patients' perspective within medical care, it is increasingly clear that the contributions of counseling psychologists can be pivotal to the medical enterprise. This section has outlined a few of the ways in which counseling psychologists can contribute from the unique aspects of our specialty, but the potential is much greater. Our traditional strength in vocational choice theories can be incorporated to assist in medical specialty choice; our emphasis on normal development and healthy personality can enable better consultation surrounding the course of chronic illness; and our preventive and psychoeducational models are of inestimable value in teaching the types of skills and abilities needed by an array of health providers in situations of illness as well as health promotion.

CONCLUSION

Any single chapter on health applications is inevitably incomplete, and this chapter is no exception. We purposefully omitted discussions of the "tried and true" areas of health applications (e.g., Type A behaviors, obesity, smoking cessation), not because we believe that these areas are unimportant, but because we wanted to explore a broader range of psychological applications in a health care context. We highlighted five diverse areas of health care in which counseling psychologists can make unique contributions:

preventive health, childhood leukemia, chronic back pain among adults, Alzheimer's disease among the aged, and the physician–patient relationship. Discussions for each of these areas focused on the traditional strengths of counseling psychology, such as emphasizing "normal" human development; building on personal strengths; considering vocational concerns; and implementing psychoeducational, preventative, and remediative interventions.

We began this chapter by expressing our hope that the excitement of working in medical settings was "catching." We end by repeating that goal, because it has been our personal experience that this work is indeed challenging and exciting. The research literature demonstrates the efficacy of many of the interventions that we can use for a health care context. Perhaps more importantly, the current emphasis on evaluating clinical outcomes within health services research (Brook, 1989) that includes such desired outcomes as access to care, quality of care, and efficiency of care, highlights the critical importance of the multidisciplinary health-related research that will be conducted in the next several decades. Our research skills and interests and our ability to work collaboratively with other professionals on health care research are in great demand.

REFERENCES

Akeson, W. H., & Murphy, R. W. (1977). Editorial comment: Low back pain. *Clinical Orthopaedics and Related Research, 129,* 2–3.

Alcorn, J. D. (1991). Counseling psychology and health applications. *The Counseling Psychologist, 19,* 325–341.

Altmaier, E. M. (1987, April). *Counseling psychology practice roles in hospital and medical settings.* Invited paper presented at the National Conference for Counseling Psychology, Atlanta, GA.

Altmaier, E. M. (1987). Processes in rehabilitation: A social psychological analysis. In C. D. Stoltenberg, R. Rosenwein, & J. E. Maddux (Eds.), *Social processes in clinical and counseling psychology* (pp. 171–184). New York: Springer-Verlag.

Altmaier, E. M. (1991). Research and practice roles for counseling psychologists in health care settings. *The Counseling Psychologist, 19,* 342–364.

Altmaier, E. M., Johnson, S. R., Tarico, V. S., & Laube, D. (1988). An empirical specification of residency performance dimensions. *Obstetrics and Gynecology, 72,* 126–130.

Altmaier, E. M., Lehmann, T. R., Russell, D. W., Weinstein, J. N., & Kao, C. F. (in press). The effectiveness of psychological interventions for the rehabilitation of low back pain: A randomized controlled trial evaluation. *Pain.*

Altmaier, E. M., McGuinness, G., Wood, P. S., Ross, R. R., Bartley, J., & Smith, W. L. (1990). Defining successful performance among pediatric residents. *Pediatrics, 85,* 139–143.

Altmaier, E. M., Russell, D. W., Kao, C. F., Lehmann, T. R., & Weinstein, J. N. (1992). *Self-efficacy and rehabilitation outcome among chronic low back pain patients.* Manuscript submitted for publication.

Altmaier, E. M., Smith, W., Wood, P., Ross, R., Montgomery, W., Klattee, E., Imray, S., Shields, J., & Franken, E. A. (1989). Cross-institutional stability of behavioral criteria desirable for success in radiology. *Investigative Radiology, 24,* 249–251.

Anthony-Bergstone, C. R., Zarit, S. H., & Gatz, M. (1988). Symptoms of psychological distress among caregivers of dementia patients. *Psychology and Aging, 3,* 245–248.

Anwar, R. A. H., Bosk, C., & Greenberg, A. G. (1981). Resident evaluation: Is it, can it, should it be objective? *Journal of Surgical Research, 30,* 27–41.

Becker, M. H. (1974). The health belief model and sick role behavior. *Health Education Monograph, 2,* 409–419.

Becker, M. H., & Maiman, L. A. (1975). Sociobehavioral determinants of compliance with health and medical care recommendations. *Medical Care, 13,* 10–24.

Becker, M. H., Maiman, L. A., Kirscht, J. P., Haefner, D. P., & Drachman, R. H. (1977). A test of the Health Belief Model in obesity. *Journal of Health and Social Behavior, 18,* 348–366.

Benson, D. F. (1987). Clinical diagnosis of Alzheimer's disease. In G. G. Glenner & R. J. Wurtman (Eds.), *Advancing frontiers in Alzheimer's disease research* (pp. 235–248). Austin, TX: University of Texas Press.

Bergquist-Ullman, M., & Larsson, U. (1977). Acute low back pain in industry. A controlled prospective study with special reference to therapy and confounding factors. *Acta Orthopaedica Scandinavica*, Supp. 170.

Block, A., Kremer, E., & Gaylor, M. (1980). Behavioral treatment for chronic pain: The spouse as a discriminative cue for pain behavior. *Pain, 9,* 243–252.

Blurton, R. R., & Mazzaferri, E. L. (1985). Assessment of interpersonal skills and humanistic qualities in medical residents. *Journal of Medical Education, 60,* 648–650.

Bonica, J. J. (1977). Pain research and therapy: Past and current status and future needs. In L. K. Y. Ng and J. J. Bonica (Eds.), *Pain, discomfort and humanitarian care* (pp. 1–46). New York: Elsevier/North Holland.

Brook, R. H. (1989). Health services research: Is it good for you and me? *Academic Medicine, 64,* 124–130.

Brown, J., Lyon, P. C., & Sellers, T. D. (1988). Caring for the family of caregivers. In L. Volicer, K. Fabiszewski, Y. Rheaume, & K. Lasch (Eds.), *Clinical management of Alzheimer's disease* (pp. 29–41). Rockville, MD: Aspen.

Cairns, N. U., Clark, G. M., Smith, S. D., & Lansky, S. B. (1979). Adaptation of siblings to childhood malignancy. *Journal of Pediatrics, 95,* 484–487.

Califano, J. A. (1986). *America's health care revolution: Who lives? Who dies? Who pays?* New York: Random House.

Canter, M. H. (1983). Strain among caregivers: A study of experience in the United States. *The Gerontologist, 23,* 597–604.

Carey, M. P., & Burish, T. G. (1988). Etiology and treatment of the psychological side effects associated with cancer chemotherapy: A critical review and discussion. *Psychological Bulletin, 104,* 307–325.

Chesler, M. A., & Barbarin, O. A. (1987). *Childhood cancer and the family.* New York: Brunner/Mazel.

Chesler, M. A., & Yoak, M. (1984). Self-help groups for parents of children with cancer. In H. B. Roback (Ed.), *Helping patients and their families cope with medical problems* (pp. 481–526). San Francisco: Jossey-Bass.

Christensen, M. F., & Mortensen, D. (1975). Long-term prognosis in children with recurrent abdominal pain. *Archives of Disease in Childhood, 50,* 110–114.

Clark, N., & Rakowski, W. (1983). Family caregivers of older adults: Improving helping skills. *The Gerontologist, 23,* 597–604.

Cousens, P., Waters, B., Said, J., & Stevens, M. (1988). Cognitive effects of cranial irradiation in leukemia: A survey and meta-analysis. *Journal of Child Psychology and Psychiatry, 29,* 839–852.

Culling, J. (1988). The psychological problems of families of children with cancer. In A. Oakhill (Ed.), *The supportive care of the child with cancer* (pp. 204–237). London: Wright.

Cutrona, C. E., & Russell, D. W. (1990). Type of social support and specific stress: Toward a theory of optimal matching. In B. R. Sarason, I. G. Sarason, and G. R. Pierce (Eds.), *Social support: An interactional view* (pp. 319–366). New York: Wiley.

Davies, H., Priddy, J. M., & Tinklenberg, J. R. (1986). Support groups for male caregivers of Alzheimer's patients. *Clinical Gerontologist, 5,* 385–395.

Dietch, J. T., Hewett, L. J., & Jones, S. (1989). Adverse effects of reality orientation. *Journal of the American Geriatrics Society, 37,* 974–976.

DiMatteo, M. R., & DiNicola, D. D. (1982). *Achieving patient compliance: The psychology of the medical practitioner's role.* New York: Pergamon Press.

DiMatteo, M. R., Hays, R. D., & Prince, L. M. (1986). Relationship of physicians' nonverbal communication skill to patient satisfaction, appointment noncompliance, and physician workload. *Health Psychology, 5,* 581–594.

Dolgin, M. J., Katz, E. R., Doctors, S., & Siegel, S. E. (1986). Caregiver's perceptions of medical compliance in adolescents with cancer. *Journal of Adolescent Health Care, 7,* 22–27.

Dzioba, R. B., & Doxey, N. C. (1984). A prospective investigation into the orthopaedic and psychologic predictors of outcome of first lumbar surgery following industrial injury. *Spine, 9,* 614–623.

Eiser, C. (1985). *The psychology of childhood illness.* New York: Springer-Verlag.

Evans, D. A., Funkenstein, H. H., Albert, M. S., Scherr, P. A., Cook, N. R., Chown, M. J., Hebert, L. E., Hennekens, C. H., & Taylor, J. O. (1989). Prevalence of Alzheimer's disease in a community population of older persons. *Journal of the American Medical Association, 262,* 2551–2556.

Fabiszewski, K. J., Riley, M. E., Berkley, D., Karner, J., & Shea, S. (1988). Management of advanced Alzheimer dementia. In L. Volicer, K. Fabiszewski, Y. Rheaume, & K. Lasch (Eds.), *Clinical management of Alzheimer's disease* (pp. 87–109). Rockville, MD: Aspen.

Falvo, D. R., & Smith, J. K. (1983). Assessing residents' behavioral science skills: Patients' views of physician–patient interaction. *The Journal of Family Practice, 17,* 479–483.

Famighetti, R. A. (1986). Understanding the family coping with Alzheimer's disease: An application of theory to intervention. *Clinical Gerontologist, 5,* 363–384.

Farsad, P., Galliguez, P., Chamberlin, R., & Roghmann, K. (1978). Teaching interviewing skills to pediatric house officers. *Pediatrics, 61,* 384–388.

Fengler, A. P., & Goodrich, N. (1979). Wives of elderly disabled men: The hidden patients. *The Gerontologist, 19,* 175–183.

Fernald, C. D., & Corry, J. J. (1981). Empathic versus directive preparation of children for needles. *Children's Health Care, 10,* 44–47.

Feuerstein, M., Sills, S., & Houle, M. (1985). Environmental stressors and chronic low back pain: Life events, family, and work environment. *Pain, 22,* 295–307.

Flor, H., & Turk, D. C. (1985). Chronic illness in an adult family member: Pain as a prototype. In D. C. Turk and R. D. Kerns (Eds.), *Health, illness, and families* (pp. 255–278). New York: Wiley.

Fordyce, W. E. (1976). *Behavioral methods for chronic pain and illness.* St. Louis: Mosby.

Francis, V., Korsch, B. M., & Morris, M. J. (1969). Gaps in doctor–patient communication: Patients' response to medical advice. *The New England Journal of Medicine, 280,* 535–540.

Fraser, M. (1987). *Dementia: Its nature and management.* Chichester, England: Wiley.

Gruetzner, H. (1988). *Alzheimer's: A caregiver's guide and sourcebook.* New York: Wiley.

Haley, W. E., Levine, E. G., Brown, S. L., & Bartolucci, A. A. (1987). Stress, appraisal, coping, and social support as predictors of adaptational outcome among dementia caregivers. *Psychology and Aging, 2,* 323–330.

Holden, U. P., & Woods, R. T. (1988). *Reality Orientation.* New York: Churchill Livingstone.

Horan, J., Hackett, G., Buchanan, J., Stone, C., & Demchik-Stone, D. (1977). Coping with pain: A component analysis of stress inoculation. *Cognitive Therapy and Research, 1,* 211–221.

Hudgens, A. J. (1979). Family-oriented treatment of chronic pain. *Journal of Marital and Family Therapy, 5,* 67–78.

Inbal, R., Devor, M., Tuchendler, D., & Lieblich, I. (1980). Autonomy following nerve injury: Genetic factors in the development of chronic pain. *Pain, 9,* 327–337.

Jay, S. M., & Elliott, C. H. (1991). *A stress inoculation program for parents of children undergoing painful medical procedures.* Manuscript submitted for publication.

Jay, S. M., Ozolins, M., Elliott, C. H., & Cadwell, S. (1983). Assessment of children's distress during painful medical procedures. *Health Psychology, 2,* 133–147.

Kagan, N. (1984). The physician as therapeutic agent: Innovations in training. In C. Van Dyke, L. Temoshok, & L. Zegans (Eds.), *Emotions in health and illness: Applications to clinical practice* (pp. 209–226). Orlando, FL: Grune & Stratton.

Kaplan, D. M., Smith, A., Grobstein, R., & Fischman, S. E. (1973). Family mediation of stress. *Social Work, 18,* 60–69.

Katz, E. R., & Jay, S. M. (1984). Psychological aspects of cancer in children, adolescents, and their families. *Clinical Psychology Review, 4,* 525–542.

Kellerman, J., Zeltzer, L., & Ellenberg, L. (1980). Psychological effects of illness in adolescence: Anxiety, self-esteem, and perception of control. *Journal of Pediatrics, 97,* 126–131.

Kendall, P. C., & Watson, D. (1981). Psychological preparation for stressful medical procedures. In C. A. Prokop & L. A. Bradley (Eds.), *Medical psychology* (pp. 197–221). New York: Academic Press.

Kern, D. C. (1988). Epidemiology and prevention of Alzheimer's disease. In L. Volicer, K. Fabiszewski, Y. Rheaume, & K. Lasch (Eds.), *Clinical management of Alzheimer's disease* (pp. 1–12). Rockville, MD: Aspen.

Kiesler, D. J. (1966). Some myths of psychotherapy research and the search for a paradigm. *Psychological Bulletin, 65,* 110–136.

Klippel, J. A., & DeJoy, D. M. (1984). Counseling psychology in behavioral medicine and health psychology. *Journal of Counseling Psychology, 31,* 219–227.

Knopf, O. (1935). Preliminary report on personality studies in thirty migraine patients. *Journal of Nervous and Mental Disease, 82,* 270–285, 400–414.

Koocher, G. P., & O'Malley, J. E. (1981). *Damocles syndrome.* New York: McGraw-Hill.

Korsch, B. M., Gozzi, E. K., & Francis, V. (1968). Gaps in doctor–patient communication: Doctor–patient interaction and patient satisfaction. *Pediatrics, 42,* 855–871.

Langlie, J. K. (1977). Social networks, health beliefs, and preventive health behavior. *Journal of Health and Social Behavior, 18,* 244–260.

Lau, R. R., & Ware, J. F. (1982). Refinement in the measurement of health-specific locus-of-control beliefs. *Medical Care, 20,* 77–88.

Lawton, M. P., Brody, E. M., & Saperstein, A. R. (1989). A controlled study of respite services for caregivers of Alzheimer's patients. *The Gerontologist, 29,* 8–16.

Leavitt, S. S., Johnston, T. L., & Beyer, R. D. (1971). The process of recovery: Patterns in industrial back injury. Part 1: Costs and other quantitative measures of effort. *Industrial Medicine, 40*(8), 7–14.

LeBaron, S., & Zeltzer, L. K. (1984). Behavioral intervention for reducing chemotherapy-related nausea and vomiting in adolescents with cancer. *Journal of Adolescent Health Care, 5,* 178–182.

Lehmann, T. R., & LaRocca, H. S. (1981). Repeat lumbar surgery: A review of patients with failure for previous lumbar surgery treated by spinal canal exploration and lumbar spinal fusion. *Spine, 6,* 615–619.

Liston, E. (1979). The clinical phenomenology of presenile dementia: A critical review of the literature. *Journal of Nervous and Mental Disorders, 167,* 329–336.

Lloyd, J. S., & Langsley, D. B. (Eds.). (1986). *How to evaluate residents.* Evanston, IL: American Board of Medical Specialties.

Lovett, S. B. (1989). Process of aging: Enhancement of the later years. In R. A. Winett, A. C. King, & D. G. Altman (Eds.), *Health psychology and public health* (pp. 342–376). New York: Pergamon Press.

Maguire, P. (1983). *The psychological sequelae of childhood leukemia: Recent results in cancer research 83.* Berlin: Springer-Verlag.

Malone, M. D., & Strube, M. J. (1988). Meta-analysis of non-medical treatments for chronic pain. *Pain, 34,* 231–244.

Matarazzo, J. D. (1980). Behavioral health and behavioral medicine. *American Psychologist, 35,* 807–817.

Maul-Mellott, S. K., & Adams, J. N. (1987). *Childhood cancer.* Boston: Jones and Bartlett.

Mayeux, R., Stern, Y., & Spanton, S. (1985). Heterogeneity in dementia of the Alzheimer's type: Evidence of sub-groups. *Neurology, 35,* 453–461.

Mazzuca, S. A., Weinberger, M., Kurpius, D. J., Froehle, T., & Heister, M. (1983). Clinician communication associated with diabetic patients' comprehension of their therapeutic regimen. *Diabetes Care, 6,* 347–350.

McHugh, S., & Vallis, T. M. (1986). *Illness behavior: A multidisciplinary model.* New York: Plenum Press.

Melamed, B. G., & Bush, J. P. (1985). Family factors in children with acute illness. In D. C. Turk & R. D. Kerns (Eds.), *Health, illness, and families* (pp. 183–219). New York: Wiley.

Melzack, R., & Wall, P. D. (1965). Pain mechanism: A new theory. *Science, 150,* 971–979.

Mindel, C. H., Wright, R., & Starrett, R. A. (1986). Informal and formal health and social support systems of black and white elderly: A comparative cost approach. *The Gerontologist, 26,* 279–285.

Minuchin, S., Baker, L., Rosman, B., Liebman, L., Milman, L., & Todd, T. C. (1975). A conceptual model of psychosomatic illness in children: Family organization and family therapy. *Archives of General Psychiatry, 32,* 1031–1038.

Montgomery, R. J., & Borgatta, E. F. (1989). The effects of alternative support strategies on family caregiving. *The Gerontologist, 29,* 457–464.

Moore, J. E., & Chaney, E. F. (1985). Outpatient group treatment of chronic pain: Effects of spouse involvement. *Journal of Clinical and Consulting Psychology, 53,* 326–334.

Morrill, W. E., Oetting, E., & Hurst, J. (1974). Dimensions of counselor functioning. *Personnel and Guidance Journal, 52,* 354–359.

Morris, K. J., Tarico, V. S., Smith, W. L., Altmaier, E. M., & Franken, E. A. (1987). Critical analysis of radiologist–patient interaction. *Radiology, 163,* 565–567.

Nachemson, A. (1976). The lumbar spine: An orthopaedic challenge. *Spine, 1,* 59–71.

National Cancer Institute. (1982). *Coping with cancer* (NIH Publication No. 82-2080). Washington, DC: U.S. Government Printing Office.

Nebes, R. D., Boller, F., & Holland, A. (1986). Use of semantic context by patients with Alzheimer's disease. *Psychology and Aging, 1,* 261–269.

Pagel, M., & Becker, J. (1987). Depressive thinking and depression: Relations with personality and social resources. *Journal of Personality and Social Resources, 52,* 1043–1152.

Paulsen, J., & Altmaier, E. M. (1992). *The effect of perceived social support on the discriminative cue function of spouses for pain behaviors.* Manuscript submitted for publication.

Payne, B., & Norfleet, M. (1986). Chronic pain and the family: A review. *Pain, 26,* 1–22.

Poulshock, C. G., & Deimling, G. T. (1984). Families caring for elders in residence: Issues in the measurement of burden. *Journal of Gerontology, 39,* 230–239.

Pruchno, R. A., & Resch, N. L. (1989). Husbands and wives as caregivers: Antecedents of depression and burden. *The Gerontologist, 29,* 159–165.

Quayhagen, M. P., & Quayhagen, M. (1989). Differential effects of family-based strategies on Alzheimer's disease. *The Gerontologist, 29,* 150–155.

Redd, W. H., Jacobsen, P. B., Die-Trill, M., Dermatis, H., McEvoy, M., & Holland, J. C. (1987). Cognitive/attentional distraction in the control of conditioned nausea in pediatric cancer patients receiving chemotherapy. *Journal of Consulting and Clinical Psychology, 50,* 1018–1029.

Reisberg, B., Ferris, S., DeLeon, M., & Cook, T. (1982). The global deterioration scale of assessment of primary degenerative dementia. *American Journal of Psychiatry, 139,* 1136–1139.

Roberts, A. H., & Reinhardt, L. (1980). The behavioral management of chronic pain: Long-term follow-up with comparison groups. *Pain, 8,* 151–162.

Rosenstock, I. M. (1974). Historical origins of the Health Belief Model. *Health Education Monographs, 2,* 328–335.

Ross, R. R., & Altmaier, E. M. (1990). A job analysis of psychology internships in counseling center settings. *Journal of Counseling Psychology, 37,* 459–464.

Rotter, J. B. (1966). Generalized expectancies for internal versus external control of reinforcement. *Psychological Monographs, 80*(1), No. 609.

Rowat, K. M., & Knapfl, K. A. (1985). Living with chronic pain: The spouse's perspective. *Pain, 23,* 259–271.

Said, J. A., Waters, B., Cousens, P., & Stevens, M. M. (1989). Neuropsychological sequelae of central nervous system prophylaxis in survivors of childhood acute lymphoblastic leukemia. *Journal of Consulting and Clinical Psychology, 57,* 251–256.

Sanders, S. H. (1985). Chronic pain: Conceptualization and epidemiology. *Annals of Behavioral Medicine, 7*(3), 3–5.

Schnoover, S. C., Bassuk, E. L., Smith, R., & Gaskill, D. (1983). The use of videotape programs to teach interpersonal skills. *Journal of Medical Education, 58,* 804–810.

Schofield, W. (1969). The role of psychology in the delivery of health services. *American Psychologist, 24,* 565–584.

Seltzer, B., Larkin, J. P., & Fabiszewski, K. J. (1988). Management of the outpatient with Alzheimer's disease: An interdisciplinary team approach. In L. Volicer, K. Fabiszewski, Y. Rheaume, & K. Lasch (Eds.), *Clinical management of Alzheimer's disease* (pp. 13–28). Rockville, MD: Aspen.

Slavin, L. A., O'Malley, J. E., Koocher, G., & Foster, D. J. (1982). Communication of the cancer diagnosis to a pediatric patient: Impact on long-term adjustment. *American Journal of Psychiatry, 139,* 179–183.

Spinetta, J., & Deasy-Spinetta, P. (Eds.). (1981). *Living with childhood cancer.* St. Louis: Mosby.

Spinetta, J. J., & Maloney, L. J. (1975). Death anxiety in the outpatient leukemic child. *Pediatrics, 56,* 1034–1037.

Spinetta, J. J., Rigler, D., & Karon, M. (1974). Personal space as a measure of a dying child's sense of isolation. *Journal of Consulting and Clinical Psychology, 42,* 751–757.

Stern, M., Norman, S., & Zevon, M. (1991). Career development of adolescent cancer patients: A comparative analysis. *Journal of Counseling Psychology, 38,* 431–439.

Stone, G. L., & Archer, J. (1990). College and university counseling centers in the 1990s: Challenges and limits. *The Counseling Psychologist, 18,* 539–607.

Stone, R. (1986). Caregivers of the frail elderly: A national profile. *Family Caregiving Project.* Rockville, MD: Project Share.

Surin, V. V. (1977). Duration of disability following lumbar disc surgery. *Acta Orthopaedica Scandinavica, 48,* 466–471.

Szasz, T. S., & Hollender, M. H. (1956). The basic models of the doctor–patient relationship. *Archives of Internal Medicine, 97,* 585–592.

Tarico, V. S., Altmaier, E. M., Smith, W. L., & Franken, E. A. (1986). A resident perspective on the radiology residency: The critical incident technique. *Investigative Radiology, 21,* 877–881.

Tarico, V., Smith, W. L., Altmaier, E. M., Franken, E. A., & VanVelzen, D. R. (1984). Critical incident interviewing in evaluation of residency performance. *Radiology, 152,* 327–329.

Thoresen, C. E., & Eagleston, J. R. (1984). Counseling for health. *The Counseling Psychologist, 13,* 15–88.

Thornberry, O. T., Wilson, R. W., & Golden, P. M. (1986). The 1985 Health Promotion and Disease Prevention Survey. *Public Health Report, 101,* 566–570.

Toseland, R. W., & Rossiter, C. M. (1989). Group interventions to support family caregivers: A review and analysis. *The Gerontologist, 29,* 438–448.

Toseland, R. W., Rossiter, C. M., & Labrecque, M. S. (1989). The effectiveness of peer-led and professionally-led groups to support family caregivers. *The Gerontologist, 29,* 465–471.

Turk, D. C., Flor, H., & Rudy, T. E. (1987). Pain and families. I. Etiology, maintenance, and psychosocial impact. *Pain, 30,* 3–27.

Turk, D. C., Meichenbaum, D., & Genest, M. (1983). *Pain and behavioral medicine: A cognitive-behavioral perspective.* New York: Guilford Press.

Turk, D. C., & Rudy, T. E. (1986). Assessment of cognitive factors in chronic pain: A worthwhile enterprise? *Journal of Consulting and Clinical Psychology, 54,* 760–768.

Turner, J. A., & Chapman, C. R. (1982a). Psychological interventions for chronic pain: A critical review. I. Relaxation training and biofeedback. *Pain, 12,* 1–21.

Turner, J. A., & Chapman, C. R. (1982b). Psychological interventions for chronic pain: A critical review. II. Operant conditioning, hypnosis, and cognitive-behavioral therapy. *Pain, 12,* 23–46.

Turner, J. A., & Clancy, S. (1988). Comparison of operant behavioral and cognitive-behavioral group treatment for chronic low back pain. *Journal of Consulting and Clinical Psychology, 56,* 261–266.

U.S. Department of Commerce, Bureau of the Census. (1989). *Statistical abstract of the U.S. 1989* (109th ed.). Washington, DC: U.S. Government Printing Office.

U.S. Office of Technology Assessment. (1987). *Losing a million minds: Confronting the tragedy of Alzheimer's disease and other dementias.* Washington, DC: U.S. Government Printing Office.

Waddell, G. (1987). A new clinical model for the treatment of low back pain. *Spine, 12,* 632–644.

Waddell, G., Morris, E. W., DiPaola, M., Bircher, M., & Finlayson, D. (1986). A concept of illness tested as an improved basis for surgical decisions in low back disorders. *Spine, 11,* 712–719.

Walsh, T., & Leonard, C. (1985). Persistent vegetative state: Extension of the syndrome to include chronic disorders. *Archives of Neurology, 42,* 1045–1047.

Ware, J. E., Davies-Avery, A., & Stewart, A. L. (1978). The measurement and meaning of patient satisfaction. *Health and Medical Care Services Review, 1,* 1–15.

Ware, J. E., & Snyder, M. K. (1975). Dimensions of patient attitudes regarding doctors and medical care services. *Medical Care, 13,* 669–682.

Waring, E. M. (1977). The role of the family in symptom selection and perpetuation in psychosomatic illness. *Psychotherapy Psychosomatics, 28,* 253–259.

Wiltse, L. L., & Rocchio, P. D. (1975). Pre-operative psychological tests and predictors of success of chemonucleolysis in the treatment of the low back syndrome. *Journal of Bone and Joint Surgery, 57A,* 478–483.

Wolf, F. M., Savickas, M. L., Saltzman, G. A., & Walker, M. L. (1984). Meta-analytic evaluation of an interpersonal skills curriculum for medical students: Synthesizing evidence over successive occasions. *Journal of Counseling Psychology, 31,* 253–257.

Woods, R. T., & Britton, P. G. (1985). *Clinical psychology with the elderly.* Rockville, MD: Aspen.

Zarit, S. H., Anthony, C. R., & Boutselis, M. (1987). Interventions with caregivers of dementia patients: Comparison of two approaches. *Psychology and Aging, 2,* 225–232.

Zarit, S. H., Todd, P. A., & Zarit, J. M. (1986). Subjective burden of husbands and wives as caregivers: A longitudinal study. *The Gerontologist, 26,* 160–166.

Zarit, S. H., & Zarit, J. M. (1982). Families under stress: Interventions of caregivers of senile dementia patients. *Psychotherapy: Theory, Research and Practice, 19,* 461–471.

Zeltzer, L., Kellerman, J., Ellenberg, L., & Dash, J. (1983). Hypnosis for reduction of vomiting associated with chemotherapy and disease in adolescents with cancer. *Journal of Adolescent Health Care, 4,* 77–84.

Zeltzer, L., Kellerman, J., Ellenberg, L., Dash, J., & Rigler, D. (1980). Psychologic effects of illness in adolescence: Crucial issues and coping styles. *Journal of Pediatrics, 97,* 132–138.

Zeltzer, L., & LeBaron, S. (1986). Assessment of acute pain and anxiety and chemotherapy related nausea and vomiting in children and adolescents. *Hospice Journal, 2,* 75–98.

Zeltzer, L., LeBaron, S., & Zeltzer, P. (1984). The effectiveness of behavioral intervention for reducing nausea and vomiting in children receiving chemotherapy. *Journal of Clinical Oncology, 2,* 683–690.

Zevon, M., Neubauer, N., & Green, D. (1990). Adjustment and vocational satisfaction of patients treated during childhood or adolescence for acute lymphoblastic leukemia. *American Journal of Pediatric Hematology/Oncology, 12,* 454–461.

CHAPTER 11
RACIAL, ETHNIC, AND CULTURAL VARIABLES IN COUNSELING

DONALD R. ATKINSON
CHALMER E. THOMPSON

Past reviews of cross-cultural counseling research have concluded that (a) racial/ethnic minorities underutilize voluntary mental health services (Leong, 1986; Sattler, 1977); (b) African Americans prefer African American counselors over White American counselors (Atkinson, 1983; Harrison, 1975; Sattler, 1977); (c) findings are mixed regarding racially/ethnically biased clinical diagnosis and treatment (Abramowitz & Murray, 1983; Sattler, 1977); and (d) racial/ethnic minorities are underrepresented in counseling and clinical psychology (Bernal & Padilla, 1982; Russo, Olmedo, Stapp, & Fulcher, 1981).

Earlier reviews also have identified a number of methodological shortcomings of cross-cultural counseling research. Among the approaches frequently criticized are designs in which the client's and the therapist's race or ethnicity is not fully crossed (Sue, 1988), measures that have questionable applicability to counseling (Atkinson, 1985), and subject selections on the basis of accessibility rather than representation (Abramowitz & Murray, 1983; Casas, 1985). Other criticisms point to failure to take intragroup differences (Atkinson, 1983, 1985; Casas, 1985), previous counseling experience (Atkinson, 1983), and socioeconomic variables (Casas, 1985) into account in the research design. A majority of cross-cultural studies to date have also failed to link their hypotheses to an adequate theoretical base (Ponterotto, 1988b), although this is a shortcoming of counseling research in general (Serlin, 1987; Wampold, Davis, & Good, 1990).

Despite these limitations, the counseling profession has learned some very important information from past research about racial/ethnic minority client underutilization of mental health services, underrepresentation in the mental health field, and possible racial/ethnic bias with regard to differential diagnosis and treatment by some clinicians. Studies of underutilization, underrepresentation, and bias, of necessity, have compared data for racial/ethnic minorities to similar data for nonminorities; their findings have important implications for mental health policy. In the first edition of this *Handbook,* Casas (1984) discussed the implications of these findings for professional organizations and governmental agencies, for the recruitment and training of mental health professionals, and for future research. Changes in policy, research, and practice regarding minority populations are still needed (Casas, 1984; Ponterotto & Casas,

1987), but it is important to acknowledge the impact of past research on such issues as ethnic parity in counselor selection, ethnic sensitivity in counselor training, and equity in the provision of counseling services.

Regarding how counseling should proceed in order to produce desirable outcomes with racial/ethnic minority clients, however, past reviews (particularly those based on research prior to 1980) have been relatively unrevealing. We believe that, in order to address this shortcoming, there is a need for more research that examines the effects of client, counselor, and treatment variables on counseling process and outcome *within* racial/ethnic populations. Ponterotto's (1988b) analysis of cross-cultural counseling research published in the *Journal of Counseling Psychology* (*JCP*) from 1976 to 1986 revealed that less than 30% of the studies included intragroup differences as independent variables, and all the studies that did so appeared after 1980. Studies of intergroup differences (in which client or counselor ethnicity serves as the primary independent variable) have provided valuable information, but studies focusing on client variables within a targeted racial/ethnic minority population are needed, to advance theory and counseling practice relative to racial/ethnic minority clients. For example, a study of African American client preferences for counseling styles across types of problems might include racial identity development as an independent variable; such a study may help move us toward understanding "what type of client working with what type of counselor on what type of problem" produces optimal counseling outcome.

We hypothesize that the failure to base research on theory is another reason that past studies and research reviews have shed so little light on how counseling can be effective with ethnic minority clients. Many studies in the past have been based on random speculation or "heartpotheses" (coined by Abramowitz, 1978; hypotheses based on personal conviction and immune to contradicting data). After finding that less than one-third of *JCP* cross-cultural studies tied their research hypotheses to theory, Ponterotto (1988b) concluded that "one of the more critical commentaries on the status of cross-cultural research is that studies for the most part have lacked an overall conceptual framework" (p. 414).

What theories *should* be driving research on racial/ethnic/cultural variables in counseling? Heath, Neimeyer, and Pedersen (1988) recently conducted a Delphi poll in which 53 experts in cross-cultural counseling were asked to predict the future of the field for a 10-year period. With respect to theoretical and empirical publications, the panel predicted a 35% increase in publications related to being bicultural, a 32% increase related to acculturation, a 30% increase related to racial/ethnic identity, and a 20% increase related to client–counselor matching. These predicted areas of increased theoretical and empirical publications actually represent theoretical constructs that began to emerge as the bases of cross-cultural research in the 1980s. Consistent with the panel's prediction for future research and in keeping with our own goal of promoting theory-driven research that examines within-group differences, we have organized the current review under three theoretical constructs: racial identity development, acculturation (including biculturalism), and similarity (client–counselor matching on a variety of variables).

We begin each section with a discussion of the theory from which the construct is taken; a critique of the related research follows, and then a discussion of research implications. We have tried to link research findings to theory, even though the original authors may not have made this connection. Our intent is to suggest lines of theory and research that we hope will promote further investigation. In keeping with the counseling psychology focus of the *Handbook,* only those studies published from 1981 through 1990 that include noninstitutionalized subjects are included in this review.

One more prefatory note. Most earlier reviews of research on racial/ethnic/cultural variables in counseling have identified their subject matter as "cross-cultural" or "multicultural" counseling research. Wherever possible stylistically, we use the more cumbersome but all-encompassing phrase "racial/ethnic/cultural variables in counseling." In doing so, we hope to draw attention to the need for research on these variables even when the counselor and client share the same racial/ethnic heritage.

RACIAL IDENTITY DEVELOPMENT

Theory

According to a growing contingent of scholars, an important factor shaping the personality development of minority group members is racial/ethnic identity. This term refers to a sense of group or collective identity based on one's perception that he or she shares a common racial/ethnic heritage with a particular group (Helms, 1990). In racial/ethnic identity development theory, these perceptions vary according to a stagelike process whereby the individual moves from a deprecating view of self as a racial/ethnic being to a healthy and sound sense of racial/ethnic consciousness. Concurrent with the individual's perceptions and beliefs about self and about those who share common racial/ethnic heritages are perceptions and beliefs about White people, the dominant racial group. Theories of racial/ethnic identity development acknowledge the impact that oppressive forces (i.e., racism and ethnocentrism) have on the psychological development of racial/ethnic minority group men and women. These theories have been developed to explain typological or developmental differences among Black/African Americans (Cross, 1971, 1978; Davidson, 1974; Jackson, 1975; Milliones, 1980; Thomas, 1971; Vontress, 1971), Hispanic Americans (Ruiz & Padilla, 1977), and Chinese Americans (Sue & Sue, 1971). Atkinson, Morten, and Sue (1989) constructed a general model to explicate the identity development of all racial/ethnic minorities.

In our opinion, all these theories of racial/ethnic identity development have important implications for counseling. In the interest of brevity, however, only Cross's (1971, 1978) Black racial identity development (BRID) theory (also termed psychological Nigrescence theory) and recent extensions of this theory by Helms (1984, 1989, 1990) and Parham (1989) will be presented in detail. This theory was selected as an illustration for three reasons. First, in the past decade, the counseling literature has witnessed an increase in the number of experimental studies using this theoretical framework. Although relatively few in number, these studies clearly outnumber the research prompted by other models. Second, recent developments in the theory address the interactive process of the counseling encounter among same- and mixed-race dyads. This movement *away from* an emphasis on the racial minority client in counseling and *toward* the interplay between counselor and client has not been as clearly delineated in other racial/ethnic development theories. Finally, BRID theory is relevant not only to the counseling situation, but also to other activities in which counseling psychologists involve themselves (e.g., research, education, and consultation; see Helms, 1990). We encourage readers to refer to the other identity development theories relative to non-Black racial/ethnic minority groups (Atkinson et al., 1989; Ruiz & Padilla, 1977; Sue & Sue, 1971).

Black Racial Identity Development Theory

Generations of racial/ethnic minority groups have been subjected to oppressive forces in American society. The dehumanization of African American people began with the institution of slavery, continued with Jim Crowism, and manifests itself today in racially motivated violence and covert (and in many cases, institutionalized) forms of racism. The oppression of Black people perpetrated by Whites and by White-dominated institutions has taken many forms throughout the history of the United States. These include formalized and informal methods of subjugation (e.g., establishing "separate but equal" facilities, denying citizenship and voting rights), brutal violence (e.g., lynch mobs, rapes), and other acts that affect the psyche of Black men and women (e.g., the explicit and implicit barring of Blacks from high-level career positions, the omission or distortion of the contributions of non-Whites in American history curricula). These experiences have had an undeniable impact on the psychological development of Black Americans.

Black racial identity development theory posits that Black people proceed through a series of stages in developing racial consciousness and in perceiving the oppressive existence of Black people in America. These stages are: Preencounter, Encounter, Immersion/Emersion, Internalization, and Internalization/Commitment. During the Preencounter stage, the individual thinks, acts, and behaves in ways that reify White people and vilify Black people and Black culture. Having fallen victim to negative racial stereotypes, he or she believes that to be Black is to be "bad" and inferior to Whites and that Whites are a superior race. Behaviorally, the Preencounter person may verbally denounce and/or avoid Black people and Black-owned businesses and institutions, preferring the company of Whites from whom he or she seeks acceptance. Individuals with Preencounter stage attitudes may identify themselves as a "human being" or "an American," rather than as a member of the African American racial/cultural group, in order to assuage discomfort from being associated with the rejected racial group.

The transition from the Preencounter stage to the Encounter stage is stimulated by some significant event or a series of events that shakes the individual's world view. According to Helms (1985), this transition is characterized either by a strong negative experience with White people or a strong positive experience with Black people. Helms later wrote:

> . . . for some people, at some point in their lives, it becomes impossible to deny the reality that they cannot become an accepted part of "the White world." Usually this awareness seems to be aroused by an event(s) in the environment that touches the person's inner core and makes salient the contradiction that no matter how well he or she personally or other Black individuals conform to White standards, most Whites will always perceive him or her as Black and therefore inferior. (1990, p. 25)

A poignantly descriptive, real-life account of this transition was offered by McClain (1983), in an article about her experiences as a *Chicago Tribune* journalist. During Chicago's mayoral race, McClain learned firsthand of her White colleagues' racist attitudes toward Black candidate Harold Washington and, more generally, toward Black people. A troubled McClain (also see Helms, 1990) wrote of her confusion and angry feelings toward her colleagues, as well as her hurt and guilt about her previous world view about Blacks and Whites. According to Parham (1989), this realization phase is experienced by Encounter individuals after the triggering event, and is followed by a second phase "when the person, first cautiously, then definitely decides to develop a Black identity" (p. 189). Once the individual decides to search for Black identity, he or she experiences euphoria and positive self-regard because he or she feels ready to take on an identity that appreciates rather than devalues Blackness.

During the Immersion/Emersion stage, the individual first immerses himself or herself in everything that is perceived as relating to Blackness, in an attempt to rid the self of all traces of the previous identity. Behaviorally, the Immersion phase may be characterized by a withdrawal from interactions with other ethnic groups (particularly Whites), increased participation at predominantly or exclusively Black functions, a newfound interest in the trappings symbolizing Blackness (e.g., hairstyles, clothing, speech) (Parham, 1989), and attempts to "act Black" in order to feel authentic. At the same time, the person rejects White people and White culture. He or she is angry at both Whites, for their role in oppressing Black people, and Blacks who have not recognized racial oppression. A critical component of this first phase of the Immersion/Emersion stage is that the individual's positive acceptance of Blackness is only minimally internalized; he or she has not yet achieved a genuine sense of Blackness.

The Emersion phase of this stage provides the foundation for achieving a more internalized, positive world view of Blackness. The Emersion person engages in activities that allow him or her to explore Black and African culture, to be exposed to the great diversity of Blacks, and to openly discuss matters of race, racism, and racial consciousness in personal encounters and public forums. With these practices, the Emersion person engages in activities that were once avoided but now can create an atmosphere for learning, self-exploration, and an experience of unity with other Blacks.

The Internalization stage is characterized by a resolution of conflict whereby the individual achieves inner security and self-confidence about his or her Blackness (Parham, 1989). He or she internalizes positive acceptance of Blackness and considers the oppression of any group as unjust. The Internalized Black has essentially resolved issues related to the previous stage, in which everything Black was idealized and everything White was deemed evil or wrong. According to Helms (1990):

> Blacks become the primary reference group to which one belongs, though the quality of one's belongingness is no longer externally determined. However, because in developing a stable Black identity the individual can face the world from a position of personal strength, it now becomes possible to renegotiate one's position with respect to Whites and White society. Thus, although the Internalizing person rejects racism and similar forms of oppression, he or she is able to reestablish relationships with individual White associates who merit such relationships and to analyze Whiteness and White culture for its strengths and weaknesses as well. (p. 28)

The second phase of this stage, the Internalization-Commitment phase, was originally conceptualized as a fifth stage by Cross (1971). In this phase, the individual's commitment to eradicating the oppression of all people is behaviorally manifested.

Progression through the stages of racial identity development is a lifelong process. Individuals may go from one stage to the next, or may experience a recycling whereby former stages may be revisited any number of times (Helms, 1985; Parham, 1989). Transition from one stage to the next involves a combination of factors, including personal readiness (i.e., cognitive maturation), prior cultural-socialization experiences, and educational experiences. Stage changes relate generally to oppressive phenomena, but Parham (1989) pointed out that an individual's racial identity is not simply a reaction to oppressive elements in society but is also "actualized through personal thoughts, feelings, and behaviors that are rooted in the values and fabric of Black/African culture itself" (p. 195).

Movement toward an internalized Black identity is equated with the process of self-actualization. Consequently, working through the reality of racism is relevant to developing a more complete sense of self. Until the final stage is reached, persons may experience problems related to their distorted perspectives, including difficulties in interpersonal relationships or possibly in their ability to cope in institutional and environmental contexts (e.g., integrated work environments or academic institutions, all-Black familial occasions). Because of this hypothesized association between racial identity development and mental health, Black racial identity development theorists recommend that therapists learn to assess their clients' racial identity stages. Knowledge of these stages may also better prepare therapists to work with their Black clients.

White Racial Identity Development Theory

According to Helms (1990), White racial identity development refers to the process through which a White person first acknowledges racism, then relinquishes racist attitudes, and, finally, begins to develop a nonracist persona. The five stages of White racial identity are: Contact, Disintegration, Reintegration, Pseudo-Independence, and Autonomy.

During the Contact stage, the individual first becomes aware that Blacks exist. He or she may naively or timidly ignore racial differences or even display "unsophisticated" forms of racism as a result of a norm that either denies or minimizes the existence of non-White people ("I don't' see you as a Black, I see you as a person."). The person enters the Disintegration stage when curiosity about Blacks increases. The Disintegration stage individual becomes very much aware of his or her Whiteness, although this awareness comes with confusion and ambivalence: the person may be learning firsthand about Black people, but he or she is also questioning norms that subtly forbid such interracial interactions from occurring. As a result of this dilemma, "one may overidentify with Blacks, become paternalistic towards Blacks, or retreat into White society" (Carter, 1990b, p. 47).

Entry into the Reintegration stage is prompted when the person feels rejected or alienated, either from Blacks who reject the overidentification and paternalism, or from Whites who do not support the individual's curiosity and interest in interacting interracially. As a result, the person is now able to fully assume a White identity. Instead of facing the dilemmas from the previous stage, however, he or she comes to believe that White people are superior and Black people are inferior. Reintegration people may feel anger and hostility toward Blacks and rely on stereotypes. Further feelings of anger, fear, and/or trepidation are the result.

An event (or events) that is "personally jarring" (Helms, 1990, p. 60) to the individual moves him or her to the Pseudo-Independence stage. During this stage, the person is forced to redefine his or her former positions on race, particularly with his or her "idealized-White–inferior-Black" perspective. The vestiges of anger begin to fade and the person begins to have a sincere acceptance of racial differences and, consequently, to adopt a positive White identity. The individual is likely to intellectualize about racial issues, however, and his or her contacts with Blacks may be few. When these contacts begin to increase, the person enters the Autonomy stage. In this stage, the person internalizes a positive White identity by integrating both an emotional and intellectual appreciation and a respect of racial differences and similarities (Carter, 1990b, p. 47). The individual nurtures his or her newly defined White identity by reconstituting formerly held opinions and biases and by seeking out interracial encounters. Because of the continual need to overcome racism and pervasive racial sentiments in society, completing the goals of this stage is an ongoing process.

The Interaction Model of Counseling

Helms (1984) developed an Interaction Model of Counseling based on the two racial identity development theories just described. When both counselor and client stages of racial consciousness are assessed, four types of relationships are possible: parallel, crossed, progressive, and regressive. When counselors and clients are of the same race, a parallel relationship is one in which the counselor and client are at the same stage of racial consciousness and share the same attitudes about Blacks and Whites (e.g., Preencounter/ Preencounter or Contact/Contact); a crossed relationship is one in which counselor and client are at diametrically opposite stages of racial consciousness, defined as having opposing attitudes about both Blacks and Whites (e.g., Preencounter/Immersion or Reintegration/Autonomy); a progressive relationship is one in which the counselor's stage of racial consciousness is at least one stage more advanced than the client's (e.g., Reintegration/Contact or Immersion/Encounter); a regressive relationship is one in which the client's stage of development is at least one stage more advanced than the counselor's.

When the counselor's and client's races are different, parallel dyads are defined as combinations of stages in which counselors and clients share similar attitudes about Blacks and Whites (e.g., Autonomy/Internalization); crossed dyads involve combinations of stages that are characterized by opposing attitudes toward Blacks and Whites (e.g., Immersion/Reintegration). Each dyad involves two types of attitudes per person (i.e., a general attitude toward Blacks and a general attitude toward Whites). In those instances in which only one type of attitude is similar (or dissimilar), the counseling process will include a blend of the characteristics of each of the stages that are included.

Some examples may be useful. In counseling dyads in which the counselor and client are Black, a client in the Encounter stage may assume that any Black counselor can help him or her resolve the presenting problem (Helms, 1984). This client may feel self-conscious, perhaps even apologizing for being inauthentic as a Black, and may believe that the Black counselor would be disapproving. The Encounter counselor will seek approval from his or her client and, similar to the Encounter client, will be fearful of being viewed as a "fake" or as an inauthentic Black person. In White counseling dyads, issues relating to racial self-acceptance that become manifest during counseling may present themselves differentially according to role (counselor or client) and racial consciousness levels. A Contact client may have tried to satisfy his or her curiosity about Blacks and perhaps suffered negative consequences. The client may come to counseling for a solution or for help in sorting out his or her confused feelings. The Pseudo-Independent counselor who perceives the client as confronting moral dilemmas regarding his or her Whiteness can provide the information and guidance necessary to help the client on these matters. However, as noted earlier, the Pseudo-Independent person tends to intellectualize issues related to race and, as a consequence, may experience difficulty in empathizing with the client. The characteristics and possible outcomes of parallel, crossed, progressive, and regressive relationships for racially similar and mixed dyads are summarized in Table 11.1.

Research

Parham and Helms (1981) developed the Black Racial Identity Attitude Scale (RIAS-B) to measure the attitudinal manifestations of Cross's (1971) first four stages of racial identity development. Current versions of the measure (a long form and a short form) were developed using a highly diverse sample of Black college students. The authors reported good reliability and validity data on these measures.

Table 11.1 Examples of the Four Types of Counseling Relationships Based on Racial Identity Stages

Stages of Identity Counselor's	Client's	Type of Relationship	Common Affective Issues	Counseling Process Counselor/Strategies	Counseling Outcome
			Black Dyads		
1. Preencounter	Preencounter	Parallel	*Anger* about being assigned to a Black person. *Guilt* about negative feelings.	Both will use strategies designed to deny and avoid issues to reinterpret whatever happens in a manner consistent with perceived negative stereotypes.	Client terminates with little symptom remission. Counselor "pushes" client out of counseling.
2. Immersion	Preencounter	Crossed (Progressive)	Counselor may feel angry and *rejecting*; client feels *fearful* and *intimidated*.	General non-acceptance of one another; counselor may be low in empathy, use much advice giving; client is passive and tries not to become involved in the process.	If counselor can act as positive role model, client may develop positive feelings about Blackness; self-esteem is enhanced.
3. Preencounter	Immersion	Regressive (Crossed)	Counselor shares White society's *fear, weariness* and *anxiety*; client displaces *anger*.	Client attempts to *reform counselor*; counselor attempts to avoid issues.	Short relationships; client's anger may be *enhanced*, *counselor's* anxiety may be increased.
4. Encounter	Preencounter	Progressive	Counselor feels *excited* and *apprehensive* about working with Black client; client feels *angry* and *apprehensive* and *distrusting*.	Social discussion in which counselor tries to prove he/she is Black; client tries to prove he/she isn't.	Long relationships if counselor uses enthusiasm to engage client; limited symptom remission if counselor avoids doing therapy.
			White Dyads		
1. Contact	Contact	Parallel	Counselor and client exhibit *curiosity* and *naivete* about racial issues.	Information sharing, avoidance of negative affect related to racial matters.	Discussion of racial issues is aborted because neither knows how to resolve them.

2. Contact	Reintegration	Crossed (Regression)	Mutual *dislike* because they don't empathize with one another's racial attitudes.	Premature termination; client's symptoms may be aggravated because he/she doesn't respect counselor.
3. Autonomous	Disintegration	Progressive	Counselor may be *empathic* and *accepting*; client needs to deal with self-concept issues and confused feelings.	Potential for client insight and knowledge acquisition is good.
4. Disintegration	Autonomous	Regressive	*Friction*; low levels of *empathy* and *understanding*.	Premature termination; client perceives counselor as inexpert.

Mixed Dyads

1. Preencounter	Reintegration	Parallel	Mutual *anxiety*; counselor wants to prove competence; client displaces *anger* previously denied.	Relationship may be long-lasting because it reinforces stereotypes; little symptom remission.
2. Immersion	Reintegration	Crossed	Direct overt expression of *hostility* and *anger* by both.	Short-lived; leaves both feeling frustrated about original beliefs.
3. Internalization	Disintegration	Progressive	Client's *self-concept* issues, feelings of confusion, and helplessness are the focus.	Potential for client cross-racial skill development and improved self-confidence is good.
4. Disintegration	Internalization	Regressive	Counselor experiences *pain* and/or *anxiety* about cross-racial issues.	Premature termination; client will seek counselor more in tune with her/his needs.

Counselor attempts to reeducate each other.

Counselor attempts to encourage self-awareness and understanding of racial dynamics.

Counselor attempts to protect and nurture client inappropriately.

Abusive relationship; client tests and manipulates; counselor is unassertive and task oriented.

Debates; refusal to become involved with one another.

Counselor attempts to model positive adjustment and to elicit denied feelings.

Counselor interacts with undue reserve, uneasiness, and incongruence; client senses counselor's discomfort.

Note: From *Black and White Racial Identity: Theory, Research, and Practice* (pp. 142–143) by J.E. Helms, 1990, New York: Greenwood Press. Copyright 1990 by J. E. Helms. Reprinted by permission of Sage Publications, Inc.

In their first published study using the RIAS, Parham and Helms (1981) asked 52 Black female and 40 Black male college students to complete this measure, in addition to a counselor preference scale and demographic questionnaire. Preference for counselor race was found to be related to racial identity attitudes. Preencounter attitudes were strongly associated with a preference for White counselors; Encounter and Internalization attitudes were most strongly associated with a preference for Black counselors and a rejection of White counselors.

In another study, Parham and Helms (1985b) found self-actualization and affective states to be related to racial identity attitudes. In a sample of 65 male and 101 female Black college students, pro-White–anti-Black (Preencounter) attitudes and pro-Black–anti-White (Immersion) attitudes were inversely associated with mentally healthy self-actualizing tendencies. Encounter attitudes were positively related to self-actualization tendencies and negatively related to feelings of inferiority and anxiety. Using the same sample, Parham and Helms (1985a) also found that racial identity attitudes related to self-esteem, with Preencounter and Immersion attitudes associated with low self-regard, and Encounter attitudes associated with high self-esteem.

Ponterotto, Alexander, and Hinkston (1988) examined the relationship between racial identity development and preferences for counselor characteristics. Using a paired-comparison technique, these authors found that the relationship between racial identity development categories and counselor preferences was not as hypothesized, but concluded that "these differential rankings and percentages . . . are too slight to warrant extended discussion" (p. 180). The authors also acknowledged that their method of assigning subjects to racial identity categories based on peak scores was not consistent with the developmental nature of the construct or with instructions of the developers of the RIAS.

Findings from studies using the RIAS largely support Cross's model as these relate to counseling-related variables. The RIAS has also been used to support Black racial identity development theory with respect to Black students' value orientations (Carter & Helms, 1987) and cognitive styles (Helms & Parham, 1990).

The more recently developed White Racial Identity Attitude Scale (WRIAS; Helms, 1990) has been used to assess Whites' attitudes related to the five stages of White racial identity development. Carter (1990b) examined the relationship between racism and White racial identity attitudes, using the WRIAS among 50 White male and 50 White female college students. He found not only that men and women differed in racial identity attitudes (White men were found to have more dominant Disintegration attitudes than White women, and White women were found to report higher levels of Pseudo-Independence and Autonomy attitudes), but also that racial identity attitudes predicted racist sentiments. For men in his sample, Reintegration attitudes were strongly related to racism, suggesting that the higher the "idealized White–negative Black" attitudes, the more likely they may hold racist attitudes. For women, the higher the Contact attitudes (characterized by racial naïveté), the lower the racist attitudes. Carter (1990b) recommended that future research explore the socialization experiences of women and men to explain these differences in racial attitudes, and that academic institutions formalize interventions for White men and women (perhaps differential interventions) to move them toward greater acceptance of more diverse student populations.

Two studies have explored variables related to Helms's (1984) interaction model. Both studies examined these variables in the context of actual counseling interactions. Carter (1990a) compared the "race perspective" with the "racial identity perspective," to determine which was the better predictor of counseling process variables (i.e., counselor intentions and client reactions). The race perspective assumes that differences that occur in counseling process (and presumably outcome) have to do with the racial compositions of the dyads. Consequently, according to this perspective, differences in counseling process relate solely to the racial composition of the counseling dyad (usually crossed). The racial identity perspective asserts that, regardless of race, the counselor's and client's racial world views (i.e., racial identity stages) have a much stronger impact on counseling process than race. Carter (1990a) examined 10 White counselor–White client dyads, 8 White counselor–Black client dyads, and 4 Black counselor–White client dyads during training workshops and found that counselor usage of intentions and client usage of reactions differed according to the racial composition of the dyads in only two instances. On the other hand, counselors' and clients' racial identity attitudes were related to 16 of the 19 counselor intentions and 12 of the 19 client reactions. Carter's (1990a) findings suggest several ways in which counselors intervene and clients react according to their racial identity attitudes. These findings further suggest that racial identity plays a more significant role than race in client–counselor relationships.

In another study, 20 biracial (White counselor–Black client) dyads were followed for four limited sessions at a college counseling center (Bradby & Helms, 1990). This study examined the influence of clients' racial identity and counselor sensitivity on four dependent measures: client satisfaction with therapy, number of sessions attended, and client- and therapist-reported ideal number of sessions. Encounter and Internalization attitudes, both reflecting biracial acceptance, related positively to satisfaction when Preencounter and Immersion/Emersion attitudes were controlled. An intriguing and incidental finding from this study was that clients with high Preencounter attitudes were likely to be assigned to culturally insensitive counselors. Although it can be speculated that someone may have made these matchings based on assumptions about the needs of Preencounter clients, the authors noted that these pairings leave the client with little or no opportunity to work on his or her issues related to racial identity or racism.

Discussion

To date, BRID theory has generally been supported by the research. The differential world views of Blacks regarding how they perceive themselves and Whites as racial beings contribute to understanding of personality differences and to prediction of some important counseling-related variables. Racial identity attitudes have been shown to relate to differences in self-actualization and affective states, self-esteem, value orientations, preferences for counselor race, and cognitive style. One possible "surprise" from this research is the findings related to Encounter stage attitudes. This stage is characterized by feelings of confusion, guilt, and anger toward the self and toward Whites—variables assumed to be associated with low self-image. Yet, findings show that Encounter attitudes are related to high self-actualization, high self-esteem, and low anxiety. On further examination of Cross's (1971) theory and its extensions, however, it is clear that this transitional stage is comprised of two phases, the latter of which (the awakening phase) appears to be measured by the RIAS, to the neglect of the formative stage.

The RIAS is currently the only instrument used in research on Black racial identity development theory. In its present forms, it assesses the four general attitudes associated with BRID. Expansion of this instrument by developing items to assess the phases within stages may better capture the complexity of this model. In addition to the need for further development of the RIAS, it may be useful to develop other measures of BRID. For example, the development of a structured interview to determine the racial identity stages of the individual as well as the interplay of clients' stage characteristics with their problems could be useful not only as a research aid, but also as a tool for therapists.

Of the studies conducted using BRID theory, all have employed college student samples. Consequently, it is difficult to determine whether the theory or even the RIAS is applicable to other age groups. However, Parham (1989) presented a theoretical explanation of how racial identity stages are cognitively, affectively, and behaviorally expressed by Black persons in varying life stages. Parham's formulations represent fruitful ground for future research in racial identity development among non-college-age adults.

Finally, research to date on White racial identity theory and the counseling interaction model constructed by Helms (1984) suggests they are worthy of further study. Thus far, the studies that have been conducted using these models, although exploratory, have demonstrated their potential usefulness in cross-cultural research and practice.

ACCULTURATION

Theory

According to Keefe (1980), "acculturation is one of those terms all social scientists use although few can agree upon its meanings" (p. 85). Olmedo (1979) referred to acculturation as "one of the more elusive, albeit ubiquitous, constructs in the behavioral sciences" (p. 1061). As with many topics, the more that researchers try to define acculturation, the further we move from a universally acceptable definition of the term. There is general agreement, however, that acculturation is a process of change that occurs when two or more cultures come in contact with each other (Redfield, Linton, & Herskovits, 1936).

Anthropologists and sociologists have studied the process of acculturation for many decades, but their approach has been to focus on the group level of analysis. Psychologists have only recently examined acculturation from the standpoint of psychological adaptation of the individual (Padilla, 1980a). Padilla (1980a) considered acculturation to be "a critical psychological process about which little is yet known" (p. 2) despite the fact that "the literature on acculturation has accumulated since the turn of the century, and today the serious scholar of acculturation has thousands upon thousands of books and articles which must be studied for a complete understanding of the work in the area" (p. 1). He suggested that, although the acculturation process may be somewhat unique to every immigrant group, "many of the psychological processes underlying acculturation are probably similar" (p. 3).

For many years, the primary acculturation model was the assimilation model developed by Park and Burgess (1921) and supported most recently by Chiswick's (1978, 1979) research findings. However, there are several aspects of the assimilation model with which contemporary social scientists disagree. One point of disagreement is whether acculturation of immigrant groups in the United States is a unilateral or bilateral process. Basically, this model proposes that the United States is a melting pot in which immigrant groups contribute elements of their own culture to an evolving U. S. culture (bilateral acculturation). However, most contemporary social scientists define acculturation in the United States as a unilateral process in which immigrant groups adopt the culture of the dominant society while exercising little or no influence on the mainstream culture (Keefe, 1980). Another point of disagreement has to do with the opportunity for complete assimilation. According to the model, complete assimilation usually occurs within three generations after immigration (Neidert & Farley, 1985). However, some critics contend that total assimilation has been limited in the past to European immigrants and that people of color are expected to acculturate but never allowed to completely assimilate (Novack, 1972).

Early in the development of the assimilation model, it was recognized that the acculturation process could be stressful and may result in psychological problems for immigrant groups. Park (1928) introduced the concept of "marginal man" to describe the negative effects of being caught between two cultures. Park (1950) described the marginal person as living in a permanent state of crisis because of an internalized cultural conflict, and suggested that some of the psychological manifestations were "intensified self-consciousness, restlessness, and malaise" (p. 356). According to Stonequist (1961), "the marginal situation produces excessive self-consciousness and race-consciousness" and "'inferiority complexes' are a common affliction" (p. 148). The fact that some individuals function well in two or more cultures, however, leads some critics to question the marginal person concept and the unidimensional view of acculturation (Valentine, 1971). The marginal person concept also has been questioned, because psychological problems that are concomitant with acculturation may be the result of discrimination rather than cultural conflict per se (DeVos, 1980).

In the following sections, we examine further the concepts of unidimensional acculturation and multicultural socialization and the methods of measuring them.

Unidimensional Acculturation

The unidimensional model conceptualizes acculturation along a single linear continuum, with the indigenous culture on one end and dominant American culture on the other. This model assumes that cultural traits (e.g., attitudes, values, behavior) of the indigenous culture are gradually lost while cultural traits of the mainstream society are gradually adopted over time. The degree of acculturation is assumed to be a function of numerous factors, the most prevalent of which is number of generations in the dominant culture.

Several instruments have been developed to measure unidimensional acculturation among various ethnic groups. One of the more commonly used instruments for assessing acculturation among Hispanic Americans is the Acculturation Rating Scale for Mexican Americans (ARSMA; Cuellar, Harris, & Jasso, 1980). The ARSMA, which was partially derived from a larger (126-item) cultural assessment questionnaire, measures acculturation along four dimensions: (a) language familiarity, usage, and preference; (b) ethnic interaction; (c) ethnic identity and generation; and (d) reading, writing, and cultural exposure. It consists of 20 items that are scored on a 5-point Likert scale (1 = Mexican American, 5 = Anglo/English).

Suinn, Rickard-Figueroa, Lew, and Vigil (1987) modeled the Suinn-Lew Asian Self-Identity Acculturation Scale (SL-ASIA) after the ARSMA. The SL-ASIA consists of 21 multiple-choice items covering language (4 items), identity (4 items), friendship (4 items), behaviors (5 items), generation/geographic (3 items), and attitudes (1 item). Each item has five responses ranging from 1 (exclusively Asian, Asian American, or Oriental) to 5 (exclusively Anglo, American, or English). The authors use an item-average for the total score and suggest that the scores be interpreted as representative of three dimensions of acculturation: Asian-identified, bicultural, or Western-identified.

Padilla (1980a, 1980b) developed a model of acculturation suggesting that, even when conceptualized as unidimensional, acculturation may have several threads to it. Padilla's model posits two central concepts, cultural awareness and ethnic loyalty, explained as follows:

Cultural awareness refers to an individual's knowledge of specific cultural material (e.g., language, history, foods) of the cultural group of origin and/or host culture. Ethnic loyalty, on the other hand, refers to the individual's preference of one cultural orientation over another. (1980a, p. 5)

Padilla (1980b) administered a questionnaire consisting of 185 items based on five dimensions important to acculturative change (language familiarity and usage, cultural heritage, ethnic pride and identity, interethnic interaction, and interethnic distance) to 381 Mexican Americans. Factor analysis of the 185 items suggested the instrument actually measured 15 cultural awareness dimensions and 11 ethnic loyalty dimensions, indicating support for Padilla's theory.

Bicultural or Multicultural Socialization

The bicultural socialization model proposed by Valentine (1971) presupposes a dual socialization process for ethnic minority individuals, resulting from simultaneously experiencing enculturation within their own ethnic group culture and being exposed to socialization forces within the majority culture. Instead of a single dimension of acculturation, bicultural socialization can be conceptualized as two continua, one representing low to high levels of commitment to the indigenous culture and one representing low to high levels of commitment to the dominant culture. Similarly, the multidimensional model conceptualizes acculturation along multiple linear continua, with each dimension representative of the cultures to which a person is exposed. One end of each continuum signifies little or no cultural traits, and the other end signifies numerous cultural traits.

According to the bidimensional (or multidimensional) view of acculturation, bicultural persons are distinguishable from marginal persons in terms of how they respond to their socialization in two cultures. A marginal person experiences tension between the two cultures and tends to focus on the conflict of cultural values. As a result, the marginal person may feel little commitment to either. The bicultural individual, on the other hand, is committed to both cultures and selectively embraces those aspects of each culture that are seen as beneficial.

De Anda (1984) identified six factors that she hypothesed help to explain why some individuals and some groups are more successful than others in the process of bicultural socialization. These six factors are:

1. Degree of cultural overlap between the two cultures;
2. Availability of cultural translators, mediators, and models;
3. Amount and type of corrective feedback regarding attempts to produce normative behaviors;
4. Compatibility of the minority individual's conceptual style with the analytical cognitive style valued by the dominant culture;
5. The individual's degree of bilingualism;
6. The degree of dissimilarity in physical appearance between the individual and those representative of the dominant culture.

Several instruments have been developed to measure multidimensional cultural socialization. Ruiz, Casas, and Padilla (1977) proposed a bidimensional model of cultural commitment for Mexican Americans. Basically, the model proposes that a Mexican American has either a weak or a strong commitment to the Mexican American culture *and* either a weak or a strong commitment to the Anglo American culture.

Sanchez and Atkinson (1983) assessed cultural commitment by simply asking Mexican American subjects to indicate their level of commitment (weak or strong) to each of two cultures (Mexican American and Anglo American). Preference for counselor ethnicity and willingness to self-disclose were found to be related to commitment to the Mexican American culture, providing some predictive validation of the cultural commitment model.

Oetting and Beauvais (1991) have proposed a multidimensional model of orthogonal cultural identification in which an individual's identification with two or more cultures is viewed as independent. They assess cultural identification using a combination of items relating to life-styles. For example, respondents indicate whether they "live by or follow the _____ (researcher fills in the cultural group of interest) way of life" (a) a lot, (b) some, (c) not much, or (d) not at all. By asking representatives of a particular racial/ethnic group to respond to these questions with two or more cultures inserted, the researcher can obtain measures of biculturalism, triculturalism, and so on.

Research

It is evident from this discussion of acculturation theory that levels of acculturation differentiate members of an immigrant racial/ethnic group. A number of authors have suggested that mental health problems may result from the acculturation process, for example, for the "marginal person" caught between two cultures. Therefore, the acculturation construct seems particularly applicable to cross-counseling research with Asian Americans and Hispanics, because there are recent immigrants among both of these groups. Surprisingly, however, few studies have examined the effect of this variable on counseling process and outcome.

Three analog studies and one survey study involving Hispanic subjects provide support for a relationship between acculturation and preferences for an ethnically similar counselor, as well as other counseling-related variables. Sanchez and Atkinson (1983), using the Ruiz et al. (1977) model of bicultural socialization, found that a strong commitment to only the Mexican American culture was associated with preference for an ethnically similar counselor and less willingness to self-disclose in counseling. Kunkel (1990) administered the Expectations About Counseling (EAC) form and the ARSMA to Mexican American and Anglo American college students and found a direct and significant relationship between acculturation and expectations. Mexican-oriented respondents had the highest expectations for counselor Directiveness and Empathy; Anglo-oriented respondents had the lowest expectations. Although their results failed to reach traditional levels of significance, Ponce and Atkinson (1989) found a direct relationship between Mexican American acculturation and ratings of counselor credibility.

Four studies (three surveys and one analog study) were found that examined the relationship between acculturation and attitudes toward counseling among Asian Americans. The three survey studies examined the relationship between Asian American acculturation and attitudes toward utilizing counselors for mental health problems. All four of the studies employed the Suinn-Lew Self-Identity Acculturation Scale (SL-ASIA) or a modification of the SL-ASIA as a measure of acculturation.

A survey of Chinese, Japanese, and Korean American college students revealed that, as hypothesized, the most acculturated students were (a) most likely to recognize personal need for professional psychological help, (b) most tolerant of the stigma associated with psychological help, and (c) most open to discussing their problems with a psychologist (Atkinson & Gim, 1989). The results of a subsequent survey of Asian

American students, however, suggested an inverse relationship between acculturation and both the severity of problems the students experienced and their willingness to see a counselor about those problems (Gim, Atkinson, & Whiteley, 1990). The authors proposed that less acculturated Asian Americans may experience greater stress than their more acculturated counterparts; the greater willingness by less acculturated students to see a counselor for these problems, however, was not a hypothesized outcome and appeared to conflict with the Atkinson and Gim (1989) findings. The eight concerns in the latter study included academic or career concerns, health abuse concerns, and financial concerns; the dependent variable in the earlier study had to do with mental illness. It may be that, for problems related to physical health or educational advice, less acculturated Asian Americans are more willing to seek help, and for problems of a psychological nature they are less willing to seek help than are more acculturated Asian Americans.

The same students who responded to the Gim et al. (1990) study were asked to rank counselors/psychologists as help providers from a list of 11 help providers (Atkinson, Whiteley, & Gim, 1990). Less acculturated students ranked counselors/psychologists highest; medium acculturated and more acculturated students gave them lower and lowest rankings, respectively. In relating the results of this study to the Atkinson and Gim (1989) survey, the authors speculated that, although less acculturated students may be less likely than more acculturated students to acknowledge the need for help with a personal problem, because of their cultural values they may prefer to see an expert or person with authority when they are asked to choose among help providers.

The analog study involved exposing Asian Americans of varying levels of acculturation to an audiotaped counseling session in which the counselor was described as either Asian American or "Caucasian American" and portrayed as either culture-sensitive or culture-blind (Gim, Atkinson, & Kim, 1991). Although no main effect was found for acculturation on ratings of perceived counselor credibility, acculturation was a factor in several significant interaction effects. The less acculturated subjects consistently gave their lowest credibility ratings to the culture-blind "Caucasian American" counselor, supporting the hypothesis that ethnic similarity and cultural sensitivity are important issues to less acculturated Asian Americans.

One study was found involving cultural commitment in which Native Americans served as the subject population. Johnson and Lashley (1989) found that students with a strong commitment to Native American culture rated the importance for an ethnically similar counselor higher than did students with a weak commitment to Native American culture. Those with a strong commitment to their indigenous culture also expected more nurturance, facilitative conditions, and counselor expertise than did respondents with a weak commitment. The authors speculated that this may reflect a strong respect for elders (and possibly authority) by students who have a strong commitment to their culture.

Only one study was found in which cultural commitment served as a within-group variable for African Americans. Atkinson, Furlong, and Poston (1986) asked Black college students with either a strong or a weak commitment to Afro-American culture to rank their preferences for counselor characteristics. Few differences were found in the rankings of the two groups.

Discussion

Although few in numbers, these studies suggest that acculturation plays a major role in determining how ethnic minority clients perceive and respond to counseling services.

The results of the four Hispanic studies and the one American Indian study suggest that less acculturated individuals within these populations are less likely to trust an ethnically dissimilar counselor and more likely to express a preference for and a willingness to see an ethnically similar counselor than are more acculturated Hispanic and Native American students. The results of the four studies with Asian American students also document a strong relationship between acculturation and counseling process variables but are more ambiguous regarding the exact nature of the relationship. Some evidence was found that less acculturated Asian Americans were less likely than more acculturated Asian Americans to recognize the need for professional psychological help, tolerate the stigma associated with psychological assistance, and discuss their psychological problems with a psychologist. However, the reverse may be true for concerns perceived as "nonpsychological" in nature. For such concerns as academic or career problems, financial problems, and relationship problems, less acculturated Asian Americans rated the problems as more severe and were more willing to see a counselor than were their more acculturated counterparts. Some evidence also was found that less acculturated Asian Americans express a stronger preference for a racially/ethnically similar counselor who is culturally sensitive than do more acculturated Asian Americans.

Unfortunately, the use of different types of research designs and dependent measures for the Hispanic and Asian American studies make generalizing the impact of acculturation across ethnic groups somewhat problematic. It should be noted that, in the context of this chapter, our use of the acculturation construct assumes that the client or the client's ancestors intentionally migrated to the United States from their country of origin. This is clearly not the case for American Indian or African American people. However, the related construct of biculturalism, which refers to the adoption of aspects of both one's indigenous culture and the dominant culture, may be generalizable across all four racial/ethnic groups discussed in this chapter. We hope that future research will help to determine whether the relationships between acculturation and preference for counselor ethnicity, perceived counselor trustworthiness, willingness to see a counselor, rankings of help providers, perceived severity of problems, and attitudes toward mental health services found in these studies hold across all racial/ethnic minority populations.

SIMILARITY

Theory

The construct of source–receiver similarity is a product of social influence theory that grew out of the attitude change research by Carl Hovland in the 1940s. According to Jones (1985), the research on attitude change spawned by Hovland and his associates "moved from a strangely neglected area to the center stage of social psychology" and "by the end of the 1960s, attitude change took more space in social psychology textbooks than any other topic" (pp. 76–77). However, this turned out to be the high-water mark of attitude change research; research on attitude change faded as a strong interest in cognitive social psychology emerged in the 1970s (Jones, 1985).

Simons, Berkowitz, and Moyer (1970) reviewed the literature on source characteristics and attitude change through the 1960s and developed a tentative theory with important implications for counseling in general and for cross-cultural counseling in particular. These authors articulated a number of propositions around the basic premise that source credibility, attractiveness, and influence are functions of similarity between the source and the receiver. Their review revealed two types of similarity–dissimilarity between sources and receivers: membership-group similarity and attitudinal similarity.

Membership-group similarity includes shared demography, background, or class membership. Included in the membership-group category are racial/ethnic groups; a number of the studies reviewed by Simons et al. (1970) included race or ethnicity as an independent variable. Attitudinal similarity refers to shared interests, feelings, and beliefs. According to Simons et al. (1970), irrelevant similarities are those cited by the source only to gain rapport; relevant similarities are those that are logically related to the proposition being advocated.

The propositions by Simons et al. (1970) that are relevant to the current discussion can be summarized as follows:

1. Receivers judge similar sources as more attractive, expect, and trustworthy than dissimilar sources.

2. Membership-group similarity between source and receiver is a less significant determinant of perceived source attractiveness, expertness, and trustworthiness than is attitudinal similarity.

3. Perceived source expertness and trustworthiness are more significant determinants of source influence than is perceived source attractiveness.

4. Relevant attitudinal similarities between the source and the receiver have positive effects on attitude change; relevant attitudinal dissimilarities have negative effects; irrelevant attitudinal similarities have insignificant effects.

5. The "ideal" source is basically similar to the receiver, the differences tending in the direction of greater source credibility.

6. Attitudinal change on the part of the receiver depends on the extent to which he or she perceives the interpersonal similarities or dissimilarities as having instrumental value.

To the extent that counseling represents a social influence process in which the counselor is attempting to change the attitudes and behavior of the client (Strong, 1968), the Simons et al. (1970) propositions have obvious implications for the counseling process. Further, by substituting counselor for source, client for receiver, and racial/ethnic for membership-group, their propositions can be readily extrapolated to the conditions of multicultural counseling. For example, expressing attitudes similar to the client's would enhance the counselor's influence if those attitudes were judged by the client to be relevant to his or her problem; otherwise, they would have little or no effect. Expressing attitudes dissimilar to the client's could actually reduce the counselor's influence if perceived by the client to be relevant to his or her problem.

If race/ethnicity is relevant to the client's problem, then a racially/ethnically similar counselor who is perceived as expert and trustworthy will exercise greater influence on the client's attitudes than will a racially/ethnicity similar counselor perceived to be inexpert and untrustworthy. If race/ethnicity is irrelevant to the client's problem, then racial/ethnic similarity between the counselor and client should have little effect on attitude change.

This suggests that, ideally, the counselor should be attitudinally and racially/ethnically similar to the client, with any differences being those that increase the counselor's credibility. Examples of differences that increase the counselor's credibility include positive perceptions of ascribed status such as professional competence, training, education, and reputation.

By instrumental value, Simons et al. (1970) mean that "similarity or dissimilarity must be perceived as performing a function for the receiver *in his* (sic) *capacity as a recipient of a particular message"* (emphasis added). Thus, if the attitude expressed by the counselor and/or the racial/ethnic similarity between the counselor and client are not perceived by the client as useful in solving his or her problem, then similarity between the counselor and client on these variables is not likely to affect the outcome of counseling. To the extent that attitudinal and/or racial/ethnic similarity is perceived by the client as useful in solving the problem, however, these similarities will enhance the counselor's influence.

In the following section, we examine some of the research that has directly or indirectly tested these propositions within the multicultural counseling context.

Research

In this section, more than any other, we have taken the liberty of connecting research to theory when the original authors may not have made the same connection. We have focused this part of our review on those studies that have implications for the propositions put forth by Simons et al. (1970), that is, research on counselor and client similarity. Also included in this section are studies related to the constructs of expertness and trustworthiness, constructs that play important roles in the social influence theories of both Strong (1968) and Simons et al. (1970).

Similarity

Racial/Ethnic Similarity. A number of studies have tested the hypothesis that ethnically similar counselors will be perceived as more credible sources of help than will ethnically dissimilar counselors. For most of these studies, the subject population represented a single racial/ethnic group and the ethnicity of the counselor was varied to be either similar or dissimilar to the subjects (in the latter case, the counselor was typically White American). In only a few studies was race/ethnicity completely crossed in the research design.

Five studies involving Hispanic subjects resulted in mostly negative findings regarding the effect of racial/ethnic similarity on counseling process and outcome variables. Le Vine and Franco (1981) reported that ethnic similarity between examiner and subject was not a significant factor in determining preferred topic and target of self-disclosure for Hispanic college students. Atkinson, Ponce, and Martinez (1984) surveyed Mexican American community college students and found no evidence that an ethnically similar counselor was rated as more credible than an ethnically dissimilar counselor. Similarly, Atkinson, Winzelberg, and Holland (1985) found that Anglo American and Mexican American women seeking pregnancy counseling did not differ in their perceived credibility ratings of an ethnically similar or dissimilar counselor. Taussig (1987) examined the records of Mexican American and Anglo American clients of a community mental health center to determine whether they were more likely to keep appointments with an ethnically similar counselor than with an ethnically dissimilar counselor. The results did not support the hypothesized ethnic similarity effect. One study with Hispanics did result in an ethnic similarity effect. Ponce and Atkinson (1989) found that Mexican American community college students gave higher credibility ratings to and were more willing to see a counselor who was described as Mexican American than a counselor who was described as Anglo American.

A number of studies examining the effects of ethnic similarity between counselor and client have been conducted with African American populations, also with equivocal results. Sladen (1982) reported that both Black and White students gave highest counselor empathy ratings, client–counselor attraction and cognitive similarity ratings, and client improvement ratings to racially similar matchings, after reading biographical data about a fictitious counselor and client. Studies by Watkins and Terrell (1988) and Watkins, Terrell, Miller, and Terrell (1989), however, failed to replicate the racial/ethnic similarity effect. Watkins and Terrell (1988) surveyed Black students attending a predominantly Black college and found that their expectations for counseling were not a function of counselor race. Similarly, Watkins et al. (1989) exposed Black college students to descriptions of either a Black or a White counselor and did not find a relationship between counselor race/ethnicity and willingness to see the counselor. One study did find that Black students rated an ethnically dissimilar counselor most attractive (Porche & Banikiotes, 1982). Interestingly, the findings of three studies involving Black and White clients and counselors suggested that Black counselors may be viewed more positively than White counselors by both Black and White college students (Berg & Wright-Buckley, 1988; Green, Cunningham, & Yanico, 1986; Paurohit, Dowd, & Cottingham, 1982).

Only a few studies on racial/ethnic similarity have been conducted with American Indians and Asian Americans. The three studies with American Indians produced mixed results. Dauphinais, Dauphinais, and Rowe (1981), who exposed American Indian college students to a tape-recorded counseling session in which the counselor was introduced as either American Indian or White, found that the counselor received higher credibility ratings when introduced as White. LaFromboise and Dixon (1981) exposed American Indian high school students to several videotaped counseling sessions in which the counselor's race/ethnicity (American Indian or White American) was varied; in this case, however, ratings of counselor trustworthiness were not significantly different because of counselor race. Haviland, Horswill, O'Connell, and Dynneson (1983) surveyed Native American college students and found that both male and female students indicated a strong preference for Native American counselors. In the only study of racial/ethnic similarity involving Asian Americans found for the review period, Gim et al. (1991) exposed Asian American college students to a tape-recorded counseling session in which the counselor was described as either Asian American or "Caucasian American." The students then rated the counselor's credibility. The Asian American counselor was perceived as being both a more credible source of help and a more culturally competent counselor than was the "Caucasian American" counselor.

Four recent studies used a paired comparison survey to examine racial/ethnic group preferences for counselor race/ethnicity simultaneously with preferences for other counselor characteristics (Atkinson et al., 1986; Atkinson, Poston, Furlong, & Mercado, 1989; Bennett & Big Foot, 1991; Ponterotto et al., 1988). Asian American, Black, Mexican American, and White subjects in all four studies all expressed a stronger preference for an ethnically similar counselor over an ethnically dissimilar counselor (when this comparison was singled out for separate analysis). However, in one of the studies involving Black subjects (Atkinson et al., 1986) and in the study involving other racial/ethnic groups (Atkinson, Poston, et al., 1989), subjects also expressed a stronger preference for a counselor who was more educated than, had similar values to, and was older than an ethnically similar counselor, and had a personality similar to their own. In the study by Ponterotto et al. (1988), Black student preference for a racially/ethnically similar counselor ranked second, following preference for a counselor with similar attitude/values. Bennett and Big Foot (1991) replicated these earlier studies with an added dimension. A paired comparison survey similar to those used in the three earlier studies was administered to American Indian and White American students. Participants were asked to express their preference, given two different types of hypothetical problems for which they were seeking help: a personal problem and an academic problem. For an academic problem, the American Indians preferences for an ethnically similar counselor ranked second behind a counselor with more education (for Whites, it ranked sixth). For a personal problem, American Indian preferences for an ethnically similar counselor ranked fourth (for Whites, it ranked fifth).

Attitude Similarity. Six studies were found that examined the relationship between attitude similarity between counselor and client and counseling process variables. All six studies were cited earlier in the section on racial/ethnic similarity.

Porche and Banikiotes (1982) found that counselors portrayed as attitudinally similar were rated more attractive, trustworthy, and expert by Black subjects than were those portrayed as attitudinally dissimilar. In the Atkinson et al. (1984) study, Mexican American subjects expressed less willingness to see the counselor for their own personal concerns if the counselor's attitudes toward acculturation were dissimilar from their attitudes.

The four recent studies using a paired comparison procedure to simultaneously examine preferences for a number of counselor characteristics (Atkinson et al., 1986; Atkinson, Poston, et al., 1989; Bennett & Big Foot, 1991; Ponterotto et al., 1988) all found a preference for counselors with attitudes similar to the respondents' over counselors with dissimilar attitudes. Furthermore, American Indian, Asian American, Black, Mexican American, and White subjects in the four studies all expressed a stronger preference for a counselor with similar attitudes than for an ethnically similar counselor. In fact, a counselor with similar attitudes was ranked as the number-one preference by American Indians, African Americans, and White Americans in three of the studies. (Atkinson, Poston, et al., 1989; Bennett & Big Foot, 1991; Ponterotto et al., 1988), and the second preference by Asian American, Black American, and Mexican American participants in two of the studies (Atkinson et al., 1986; Atkinson, Poston, et al., 1989).

Education Dissimilarity. The Simons et al. (1970) theory predicts that, other things being equal, dissimilarities that enhance source credibility will also enhance the source's influence. The four studies cited in the previous section all provide evidence to support this supposition. In all four studies, a counselor with more education than the respondents was viewed as a more credible source of help than was a counselor with an educational background similar to the respondents'. Furthermore, in all four studies, more education was ranked among the top three preferred counselor characteristics by the various racial/ethnic groups involved in the studies. In the Atkinson et al. (1986) study, African Americans ranked more education as the most important counselor characteristic, a finding that was replicated for Asian Americans and Mexican Americans in a later study (Atkinson, Poston, et al., 1989). In the Ponterotto et al. (1988) study, more education was ranked third, following similar attitudes and similar ethnicity. Interestingly, American Indians in the Bennett and Big Foot (1991) study ranked more education as the number-one counselor characteristic for academic problems but only the eighth for personal problems. The latter finding suggests that American Indians may prefer an expert counselor for academic problems but an attractive counselor for personal problems.

Cultural Mistrust

An essential ingredient in both Simons et al.'s (1970) propositions and Strong's (1968) social influence theory is the construct of trustworthiness. Counselors who are perceived by clients to be trustworthy are hypothesized to be more effective facilitators of behavioral and attitudinal change than are counselors perceived to be untrustworthy.

Among racial/ethnic minority clients, the issue of trust can be particularly problematic for all counselors because they may be perceived as representatives of an oppressive "establishment." White American counselors particularly may be perceived as the perpetrators of past oppression. Thus, trust of White American counselors by racial/ethnic minority clients is a function of social/historical/cultural factors as well as counselor attributes. Terrell and Terrell (1981) labeled the mistrust of Whites among Blacks "cultural mistrust" and developed an inventory, the Cultural Mistrust Inventory (CMI), to measure the construct.

Terrell and Terrell (1984) examined the relationship among counselor race, clients' cultural mistrust levels, and premature termination. They administered the CMI to Black clients who were visiting a community mental health setting and were assigned to either Black or White counselors. As predicted, they found that Black clients with a high level of mistrust who were seen by a White counselor had a significantly higher rate of premature termination from counseling (i.e., the failure to show for a second, scheduled appointment or to contact the facility within three months after the initial interview) than did highly mistrustful Black clients seen by a Black counselor. In a subsequent analog study described in the section on racial/ethnic similarity, Watkins and Terrell (1988) found that highly mistrustful Black students expected a White counselor to be less accepting, trustworthy, and expert than a Black counselor. Similarly, Watkins et al. (1989), also discussed earlier, found that highly mistrustful students given a description of a White counselor rated the counselor less credible and less able to help them with general anxiety, shyness, inferiority feelings, and dating difficulties than did students low in mistrust. Poston, Craine, and Atkinson (1991) gave Black adults using the services of an African-American Community Center a résumé and a letter of application from a White counselor applying for a position with the Center and asked them to rate the counselor's credibility; highly mistrustful participants gave the lowest credibility ratings to the White counselor.

Discussion

This review of cross-cultural research based on constructs from social influence theory suggests that the theory is useful for predicting important counseling process and outcome variables such as client preferences for counselors, perceptions of counselor credibility, expectations for counseling, and incidents of premature termination. As the theory predicts, similar counselors were judged to be more attractive sources of help than were dissimilar counselors, except in the case where membership-group differences involved greater credibility (i.e., more education). In addition, racial/ethnic similarity was found to be a less dependable determinant of perceived counselor attractiveness and credibility than attitudinal similarity. Cultural mistrust was found to be related to perceived counselor credibility, expectations for the success of counseling, willingness to see a counselor, and premature termination, when the counselor was White American. The latter finding supports the tenets of social influence theory but also suggests that cultural mistrust is an important within-group variable that should be taken into account in future cross-cultural counseling research, at least with African American participants.

OBSERVATIONS/CONCLUSIONS

The experts surveyed by Heath et al. (1988) predicted significant increases in research and theory articles based on racial identity development, acculturation (including biculturalism), and client–counselor matching (similarity). This review of cross-cultural counseling process and outcome studies published from 1981 through 1990 confirmed that these constructs have already emerged as the important bases for contemporary cross-cultural counseling research. Further, the current review found that studies linked to these theoretical constructs have produced remarkably consistent results. Earlier reviews often reported conflicting results, presumably attributable in part to research designs that failed to recognize within-group variability, so that conclusions were drawn about all members of a racial/ethnic group when the sample may have been representative of only a small portion of the group. The consistent findings of the recent generation of cross-cultural counseling research help provide a theoretical and empirical foundation on which future theory and research can be built.

In addition to confirming the consistency of these findings, we arrived at several general observations or conclusions as a result of this review. The first observation is that several systematic research programs that are theory-based have emerged during the past 10 years, most notable of which is the research on racial identity development and counseling process conducted by Helms, Parham, and others. Further, recent studies have used a variety of counseling process and outcome measures as dependent variables rather than relying on preference for counselor race as the sole dependent variable.

A second observation is that racial identity development, acculturation, and cultural mistrust are three very important within-group differences that need to be taken into account in future cross-cultural counseling research. To conduct counseling process and outcome research on racial/ethnic/cultural variables in the future without taking these and/or other within-group differences into account would be, in our opinion, a questionable act (the possible exception to this is policy-related research that focuses on *intergroup* differences for comparison purposes). The fact that racial identity development, acculturation, and cultural mistrust play such an important role in client/participant expectations for, and reactions to, counseling reinforces the need for counselors to recognize both cultural influences and individual differences.

A third observation is that the similarity postulates developed by Simons et al. (1970) provide an excellent theoretical base for research on cross-cultural counseling process and outcome. The current review found strong support for the relative influences that Simons et al. hypothesized regarding membership-group and attitude similarity.

A fourth observation is that counselors' racial/ethnic identity development has been ignored by most theorists and researchers. An exception is the BRID theory, which postulates that, in order to develop an effective alliance with Black clients and to work through issues that may relate to clients' racial identity levels, counselors should be at least one stage ahead of their clients, and optimally, at the final stage of development. This notion of counselors' developing racial identity, and thus attaining a commitment to dismantling oppression as it affects all groups, reminds us of the need for psychology professionals to "leave their desks" and assume direct responsibility as change agents rather than simply functioning as purveyors of conventional services in the context of troubled environments. Several counselor training models based on the development of counselor racial consciousness have appeared recently in the literature (Corvin & Wiggins, 1989; Ponterotto, 1988a; Ponterotto & Casas, 1987; Sabnani, Ponterotto, & Borodovsky, 1991).

FUTURE RESEARCH

As we stated in our introduction, we believe more theory-driven research that takes within-group variability into account is needed, in order to advance our knowledge of how best to provide counseling services for racial/ethnic minority clients. We would be disappointed, however, if our efforts in any way encouraged future researchers of racial/ethnic/cultural variables in counseling to limit their research to studies driven by the constructs covered by the preceding review. Presumably, identity development, acculturation, and cultural mistrust are not the only culture-relevant constructs that can be used to identify within-group variance among racial/ethnic minority groups. We also believe that any number of basic psychological constructs could be applied to research on racial/ethnic/cultural variables in counseling.

In the following sections, we briefly discuss some additional research that is needed on racial identity development, acculturation, and social influence, as well as some other theories that could serve as the bases of cross-cultural research. Space does not permit an exhaustive examination of all the relevant theories or even a full discussion of those we do identify. We hope this discussion will stimulate the reader to consider other theoretical possibilities as well.

Our suggestions for future research fall into three categories: research based on the constructs covered in this review, that is, racial identity development, acculturation, and similarity; research based on other constructs identifying within-group differences; and research based on other basic psychological constructs.

Future Research Based on Racial Identity Development, Acculturation, and Social Influence

Although racial identity development, acculturation, and cultural mistrust have emerged in the past 10 years as important constructs for recognizing within-group variability, we still know very little about these constructs—how to measure them, and exactly how they affect counseling process and outcome. Nor do we know how these constructs relate to each other or whether they are equally applicable to all the major racial/ethnic groups. Research is needed to determine whether these constructs are applicable across racial/ethnic groups (and if they are, how they may be manifested in each culture) or are unique to particular cultures.

Currently available instruments intended to measure identity development, acculturation, and cultural mistrust have been designed for specific racial/ethnic groups. Are these instruments measuring orthogonal constructs or are they measuring variations of a common within-group difference? Does Padilla's (1980b) concept of "cultural loyalty," for example, capture some elements of both racial/ethnic identity development and acculturation? Research is needed to determine how best to measure these constructs and to establish the relationship between them.

Research that links racial identity development, acculturation, and similarity to counseling outcome measures is also needed. We simply do not know whether preferences for counselor characteristics, perceived credibility, expectations for counseling, self-disclosure, and some of the other counseling process variables used in cross-cultural counseling research to date are related to counseling outcome. It seems likely that most of the variables that have been studied are related to utilization of services; however, until retention, satisfaction, goal achievement, and other outcome measures are consistently included as dependent variables, we can only speculate about the effect racial identity development, acculturation, and social influence have on counseling outcome. To further our understanding of the dynamics that occur within cross- or same-race counseling dyads, the study of variables related to the quality of interaction between counselor and client (of all races/ethnicities) could provide some extraordinarily insightful data.

With respect to the similarity construct, research is needed to determine which similarities and dissimilarities between the counselor and client are perceived by the client as having instrumental value for resolving which type of problem. Bennett and Big Foot (1991) serve as a model for future research in this area. They had American Indian college students indicate their preferences for a variety of counselor characteristics across two types of problems. Results suggested that students view counselor ethnic similarity and educational dissimilarity as having considerable instrumental value for an academic problem; attitude similarity was perceived as having greater instrumental value for a personal problem. It would be valuable to know whether this relationship holds for American Indian groups other than those surveyed or for other racial/ethnic groups.

A number of other questions about the effects of membership-group and attitude similarities–dissimilarities on client attitudes and behaviors can be generated. Simons et al. (1970) suggested that membership-group similarities play a major role in determining initial perceptions of communicator credibility but, over time, attitude similarities play a greater role. Does racial/ethnic similarity play a less important role and attitude similarity play a more important role in determining perceived counselor credibility as counseling progresses? Is either racial/ethnic or attitudinal similarity related to client compliance with counselor suggestions or other changes in client behavior? Do culturally relevant attitude similarities exert greater influence on the client than culturally irrelevant attitude similarities?

Research that includes within-group variability as an independent variable and that examines factors that contribute to perceived attractiveness, expertness, and trustworthiness could add greatly to our understanding of cross-cultural counseling dynamics. Cultural mistrust, in particular, seems like an important variable, because perceived trustworthiness of the counselor is assumed to be a prerequisite for effective counseling. Is the concept of cultural mistrust, used exclusively to date in studies involving Black subjects, generalizable to other populations?

Future Research Based on Other Constructs Defining Individual Differences

With regard to within-group variability, the question naturally arises as to which constructs (and theories), from the myriad of possible choices, need to be examined in future research on racial/ethnic/cultural variables in counseling. We feel that it is important to identify and include in future research some of the personality constructs that may be a function of the discrimination and oppression experienced by racial/ethnic minorities. Cultural mistrust is an example of a reaction to discrimination and oppression that was covered in the current review.

Bandura's (1982) concept of self-efficacy is another example. It can be hypothesized that systematic discrimination and oppression will affect judgments of ability (Betz & Hackett, 1986). According to Bandura (1982), self-efficacy judgments influence the kinds of activities people engage in, how much effort they will expend in an activity, and how long they will persist when faced with obstacles. Research is needed to determine what role self-efficacy plays in utilization of counseling services, establishment of goals, and counseling process for racial/ethnic minority clients. Research is also needed to determine how counselors can help clients bring their self-efficacy judgments in line with their abilities and how they can help clients overcome environmental constraints that lower expectations of success.

We also believe it is important for future research to examine constructs that are hypothesized to be a function of culture. It remains for cross-cultural psychologists and anthropologists to determine the validity of theories that link cognition, perception, motivation, emotion, memory development, and various other basic processes to culture, but these theories, by their very existence, influence our perceptions of racial/ethnic populations in the United States. By including constructs from these theories in cross-cultural counseling studies, the researcher can help to establish whether the constructs apply to all members of a particular racial/ethnic group and how they relate to counseling process.

Field dependence–independence (Witkin, 1962) is an example of a construct hypothesized to be a function of cultural socialization (Jahoda, 1980). Basically, the theory defines passive, intuitive, spectator learners as field-dependent, and active, hypothesis-testing, participant learners as field-independent (Heesacker, Petty, & Cacioppo, 1983). Although recent research suggests that field independence shows a constant pattern of development across cultures (Carretero, 1982), socialization to a field-dependent learning style is still perceived by many educators as the reason why some racial/ethnic minority children have difficulty learning in traditional school environments (TenHouten, 1989). By including field dependence–independence as a within-group variable, counseling research could help determine within-group variability on this characteristic while relating it to counseling process and outcome. Do some counselors stereotype their ethnic minority clients as field-dependent? If so, how does this affect counseling process and outcome? Are nondirective approaches to counseling more effective with field-independent clients and directive approaches more effective with field-dependent clients? Are field-dependent counselors more effective with field-dependent clients or with field-independent clients?

Locus of control (LOC; Rotter, 1966) is a construct that some researchers believe is a function of culture; others see it as a function of discrimination and oppression. Several studies have produced evidence supporting the hypothesis that expectations of personal control are a function of culture (Reimanis & Posen, 1980; Riordan, 1981). On the other hand, it is possible that racial/ethnic groups who experience systematic discrimination and oppression throughout their formative years may develop an external LOC orientation because, in reality, their lives are under the control of external forces.

Regardless of whether LOC is a function of culture or discrimination, it can by hypothesized that those individuals who develop an external LOC may not perceive counseling as a credible source of help because it assumes that clients can act to change their own future. Clients with an internal LOC presumably are more likely to take action to resolve their problems than are clients with an external orientation. Whether a function of indigenous culture or externally imposed conditions, the locus of control construct could serve as a useful within-group variable for future research on racial/ethnic/cultural variables in counseling. A recent example of how locus of control can be linked conceptually with racial identity development theory was provided by Oler (1989).

These are but a few examples of theory-based constructs that could be used to examine the effects of racial/ethnic within-group differences on counseling process and outcome. Next, we offer some examples of other theoretical constructs that could shape future research on racial/ethnic/cultural variables in counseling.

Other Theoretical Constructs That Could Be Applied to Cross-Cultural Counseling

In our judgment, a number of basic psychological constructs are relevant to multicultural counseling and could serve as the theoretical rationale for future research. (We distinguish between basic psychological constructs, like operant conditioning and cognitive dissonance, which we believe have general application, and theories of personality and psychotherapy, which may not be applicable across cultural groups.) The following are but a few of the constructs that might have application to multicultural counseling research.

Social cognitive theory (Bandura, 1986)—based on the reciprocity of behavior, cognitive and other personal factors, and environmental events as determinants of each other—has obvious implications for cross-cultural counseling research. This model clearly accommodates cultural and ethnic identity influences as determinants of ethnic minority client feelings, cognitions, and behaviors. Social cognitive concepts like social modeling, enactive learning, incentive motivators, and milieu rewards could provide the theoretical bases for cross-cultural counseling research hypotheses. For example, future research might explore whether there are culture-specific incentives that are an effective means of encouraging counseling utilization for clients from some cultures but not others. A related research question is whether racially/ethnically or culturally similar counselors are better reinforcers and/or models of desired client behavior (e.g., self-disclosure) than are dissimilar counselors (see Woods & Zimmer, 1976, for a prototype of this line of research).

Self theories, specifically theories of cognitive consistency and self-esteem, appear to be theoretically relevant to racial/ethnic/cultural issues in counseling (See Chapter 9, by Gibson and Brown, for a more detailed discussion of self theories). Cognitive consistency has to do with "the immediate social situation and the way it is viewed or ordered by the individual participant" (West & Wicklund, 1980). Two cognitive consistency theories, balance theory and cognitive dissonance theory, seem particularly relevant to multicultural counseling research.

Balance theory might have implications for situations where the counselor and client are culturally different and the client is mistrustful of the counselor. According to balance theory (Heider, 1958), if the client receives information that conflicts with his or her perceptions of counselor untrustworthiness (i.e., a respected third person testifies that the counselor is trustworthy), the client will be in a state of imbalance. To achieve balance, the client either will need to change his or her perception of the counselor or discount the third person's testimony. As an example of cross-cultural counseling research based on balance theory, the effects of a variety of third-person testimonies on client perceptions of a culturally different counselor might be examined.

Pedersen (1990) suggested that, although balance is usually defined as the search for an enduring consistency in an otherwise volatile situation, it can also be defined as a tolerance for inconsistency and dissonance rather than for resolving differences: "[B]alance as a construct for multicultural counseling involves the identification of different or even conflicting culturally learned perspectives without necessarily resolving that difference or dissonance in favor of either viewpoint" (p. 552). He provided 10 examples of observable and potentially measurable counseling behaviors based on the construct of balance (e.g., focusing nonjudgmentally on the positive as well as the negative aspects of cultural contact) that provide valuable skills for multicultural counseling. Future research based on consistency theory and the construct of balance might be designed to examine the effects of these behaviors in a multicultural counseling situation.

Cognitive dissonance (Festinger, 1957) also could be used as the basis for cross-cultural counseling research. More recent interpretations of dissonance theory identify it as a consistency theory related to decision making (West & Wicklund, 1980). An individual who makes a decision that is dissonant with previously held opinions, beliefs, or values can reduce the dissonance this creates by adding more consonant cognitions, subtracting dissonant ones, or both. This might apply to situations where the client must decide to seek counseling for a personal problem even though his or her indigenous culture discourages such expression of personal problems. How can the client resolve this dissonance? Can counseling services be structured to reduce dissonance that might arise between a decision to use the services and cultural values opposed to using such services? Can the dissonance be reduced for a low-acculturated client, if the counselor adopts helping strategies from the client's culture?

Attribution theory (Kelley, 1973), conceptually related to some of the theories already discussed, could also provide the basis for future research on cross-cultural counseling. Attribution theory describes the processes by which an individual interprets the causes of particular events (Kelley, 1967). Brickman et al. (1982) derived four models of helping (moral, medical, compensatory, enlightenment) from attributions people make regarding responsibility for a problem and responsibility for a solution to the problem. These models of helping have important implications for counseling when the client and counselor are culturally different and/or make different attributions about the client's responsibility for the problem and for solving the problem. For example, Brickman et al. (1982) hypothesized that "many of the problems characterizing relationships between help givers and help recipients arise from the fact that the two parties are applying models that are out of phase with one another" (p. 375). Parham and McDavis (1987) suggested that, even though many problems experienced by Black men can be attributed to external causes, it is important that counselors support an attribution of internal responsibility for solving the problem (compensatory model). Future research might examine the compatibility of attributions that racial/ethnic minority clients and their counselors make about the causes of client problems and the resolution of these problems.

We believe attributions about the causes of psychological problems deserve special attention. Medical anthropologists have hypothesized that shared beliefs between a healer and patient about the etiology of the patient's health problem play a major role in the healing relationship (Kleinman, 1980; Torrey, 1972). Torrey (1972) provided a poignant example of this phenomenon when applied to psychological problems:

> *A psychoanalyst trying to cure a patient who does not believe in oedipal conflicts and a witchdoctor trying to cure a patient who does not believe in spirit possession will be equally ineffective unless they can persuade the patient to accept their theory of causation. (p. 21)*

Future research might examine the role that culture plays in determining attributions about the causes of psychological problems and how these attributions affect counseling process and outcome.

New developments in social influence theory and research also could be applied to research on racial/ethnic/cultural variables in counseling. The Elaboration Likelihood Model (ELM; Petty & Cacioppo, 1986a, 1986b) has recently emerged as an important model of attitude change in social and counseling psychology research (see Chapter 5, by Heppner and Frazier, for a more detailed discussion of the ELM). Basically, the model hypothesizes two routes to attitude change, the peripheral route and the central route. Persons who lack the motivation or ability to understand a persuasive message tend to rely on such cues as the characteristics of the source or the message, when deciding what attitude to adopt (peripheral route). Persons who have the ability and motivation to consider the true merits of a persuasive message rely on the quality of the message to form an opinion (central route). The central route is posited to elicit more enduring attitude change, which eventually affects behavior; the peripheral route is hypothesized to elicit temporary attitude change that has little effect on behavior.

McNeill and Stoltenberg (1989) discussed how this model expands on Strong's (1968) original theory of social influence processes in counseling and provided an excellent analysis of how it can be applied to counseling research. They discussed three variables—source factors, message factors, and recipient characteristics—that should be taken into account when designing research to test the ELM. According to McNeill and Stoltenberg (1989), source factors (e.g., evidential cues of expertness, attractiveness, and trustworthiness) typically are attended to most in peripheral-route processing; message factors (e.g., strong vs. weak arguments, high vs. low empathy, high vs. low understanding) are attended to in central-route processing. They further suggested that recipient characteristics, including cultural variables, "will interact with the message to influence the type and degree of information processing that occurs" (p. 30).

The ELM could serve as the theoretical base for research on a number of racial/ ethnic/cultural issues in counseling. What source, message, and recipient factors positively affect the counselor's credibility and influence when working with a racial/ethnic minority client? How does the client's stage of racial/ethnic identity development or level of acculturation influence his or her ability to process information from an ethnically similar versus a dissimilar counselor? What can counselors do to optimize a culturally different client's ability to process a persuasive message?

CONCLUDING COMMENTS

Research on racial/ethnic/cultural variables in counseling was in its infancy in the 1970s. Research published during that decade provided us with useful comparative data regarding racial/ethnic minority underutilization of mental health services, differential diagnosis and treatment of racial/ethnic minority clients, and underrepresentation of racial/ethnic minorities in the mental health professions, but offered little information about how counseling should proceed with racial/ethnic minority clients. A second generation of cross-cultural counseling research, produced in the 1980s, began to document within-group variability and to provide some insight into the factors affecting perceptions of counselors and counseling. We believe the next decade will witness a third generation of research on racial/ethnic/cultural variables in counseling, one in which studies will be based solidly on theory and will examine a variety of client, counselor, and treatment variables that affect counseling process and outcome.

A scientific knowledge base grows from systematic programs of research that evolve from theory and that, in turn, provide feedback on which revisions to the theory are based (McBurney, 1983). According to Eiser (1986), "the relationship between experimental or observational evidence on the one hand and theory on the other . . . is one of mutual clarification" (p. 5). We believe that our knowledge about the role of racial/ ethnic/cultural variables in counseling will expand most rapidly if future research evolves from and provides feedback to theory. We further believe that both general psychological constructs and culture-specific constructs can serve as the theoretical bases for research on racial/ethnic/cultural variables in counseling. In the application of general psychological constructs, the challenge is to recognize the role of culture in determining how the construct manifests itself. In the application of culture-specific constructs, the challenge is to recognize variations within the culture.

REFERENCES

Abramowitz, S. I. (1978). Splitting data from theory on the Black patient–White therapist relationship. *American Psychologist, 33,* 957–958.

Abramowitz, S. I., & Murray, J. (1983). Race effects in psychotherapy. In J. Murray & P. R. Abramson (Eds.), *Bias in psychotherapy* (pp. 215–255). New York: Praeger.

Atkinson, D. R. (1983). Ethnic similarity in counseling psychology: A review of research. *The Counseling Psychologist, 11,* 79–92.

Atkinson, D. R. (1985). A meta-review of research on cross-cultural counseling and psychotherapy. *Journal of Multicultural Counseling and Development, 13,* 138–153.

Atkinson, D. R., Furlong, M. J., & Poston, W. C. (1986). Afro-American preferences for counselor characteristics. *Journal of Counseling Psychology, 33,* 326–330.

Atkinson, D. R., & Gim, R. H. (1989). Asian-American cultural identity and attitudes toward mental health services. *Journal of Counseling Psychology, 36,* 209–212.

Atkinson, D. R., Morten, G., & Sue, D. W. (1989). *Counseling American minorities.* Dubuque, IA: Brown.

Atkinson, D. R., Ponce, F. Q., & Martinez, F. M. (1984). Effects of ethnic, sex, and attitude similarity on counselor credibility. *Journal of Counseling Psychology, 31,* 588–590.

Atkinson, D. R., Poston, C. W., Furlong, M. J., & Mercado, P. (1989). Ethnic group preferences for counselor characteristics. *Journal of Counseling Psychology, 36,* 68–72.

Atkinson, D. R., Whiteley, S., & Gim, R. H. (1990). Asian-American acculturation and preferences for help providers. *Journal of College Student Development, 31,* 155–161.

Atkinson, D. R., Winzelberg, A., & Holland, A. (1985). Ethnicity, locus of control for family planning, and pregnancy counselor credibility. *Journal of Counseling Psychology, 32,* 417–421.

Bandura, A. (1982). Self-efficacy mechanism in human agency. *American Psychologist, 37,* 122–147.

Bandura, A. (1986). *Social foundations of thought and action: A social cognitive theory.* Englewoods Cliff, NJ: Prentice-Hall.

Bennett, S., & Big Foot, D. S. (1991). American Indian and White college student preferences for counselor characteristics. *Journal of Counseling Psychology, 38,* 440–445.

Berg, J. H., & Wright-Buckley, C. (1988). Effects of racial similarity and interviewer intimacy in a peer counseling analogue. *Journal of Counseling Psychology, 35,* 377–384.

Bernal, M. E., & Padilla, A. M. (1982). Status of minority curricula and training in clinical psychology. *American Psychologist, 37,* 780–787.

Betz, N. E., & Hackett, G. (1986). Applications of self-efficacy theory to understanding career choice behavior. *Journal of Social and Clinical Psychology, 4,* 279–289.

Bradby, D., & Helms, J. E. (1990). Black racial identity attitudes and White therapist cultural sensitivity in cross-racial therapy dyads: An exploratory study. In J. E. Helms (Ed.), *Black and White racial identity: Theory, research, and practice* (pp. 165–175). Westport, CT: Greenwood Press.

Brickman, P., Rabinowitz, V. C., Karuza, J., Jr., Coates, D., Cohn, E., & Kidder, L. (1982). Models of helping and coping. *American Psychologist, 37,* 368–384.

Carretero, M. (1982). El desarrollo del estilo cognitivo dependencia–independencia de campo (The development of field dependent–independent cognitive style). *Infancia y Aprendizaje, 18* (2), 65–82.

Carter, R. T. (1990a). Does race or racial identity attitudes influence the counseling process in Black and White dyads? In J. E. Helms (Ed.), *Black and White racial identity: Theory, research, and practice* (pp. 145–163). Westport, CT: Greenwood Press.

Carter, R. T. (1990b). The relationship between racism and racial identity among White Americans: An exploratory investigation. *Journal of Counseling and Development, 69,* 46–50.

Carter, R. T., & Helms, J. E. (1987). The relationship between Black value-orientation and racial identity attitudes. *Measurement and Evaluation in Counseling and Development, 19,* 185–195.

Casas, J. M. (1984). Policy, training, and research in counseling psychology: The racial/ethnic minority perspective. In S. D. Brown and R. W. Lent (Eds.), *Handbook of counseling psychology* (pp. 785–831). New York: Wiley.

Casas, J. M. (1985). A reflection on the status of racial/ethnic minority research. *The Counseling Psychologist, 13,* 581–598.

Chiswick, B. R. (1978). The effect of Americanization on the earnings of foreign-born men. *Journal of Population Economy, 86,* 891–921.

Chiswick, B. R. (1979). The economic progress of immigrants: Some apparently universal patterns. In W. Fellner (Ed.), *Contemporary economic problems* (pp. 119–158). Washington: American Enterprise Institute.

Corvin, S. A., & Wiggins, F. (1989). An antiracism training model for White professionals. *Journal of Multicultural Counseling and Development, 17,* 105–114.

Cross, W. E., Jr. (1971). The Negro-to-Black conversion experience: Toward a psychology of Black liberation. *Black World, 20* (9), 12–37.

Cross, W. E., Jr. (1978). The Cross and Thomas models of psychological Nigresence. *Journal of Black Psychology, 5,* 13–19.

Cuellar, I., Harris, L., & Jasso, R. (1980). An acculturation scale for Mexican American normal and clinical populations. *Hispanic Journal of Behavior Science, 2,* 199–217.

Dauphinais, P., Dauphinais, L., & Rowe, W. (1981). Effects of race and communication style on Indian perceptions of counselor effectiveness. *Counselor Education and Supervision, 21,* 72–80.

Davidson, J. P. (1974). *Empirical development of a measure of Black student identity.* (Doctoral dissertation, University of Maryland.) *Dissertation Abstracts International, 35,* 7076-A.

De Anda, D. (1984). Bicultural socialization: Factors affecting the minority experience. *Social Work, 29,* 101–107.

DeVos, G. (1980). Acculturation: Psychological problems. In I. Rossi (Ed.), *People in culture.* New York: Praeger.

Eiser, J. R. (1986). *Social psychology: Attitudes, cognition and social behavior.* New York: Cambridge University Press.

Festinger, L. (1957). *A theory of cognitive dissonance.* Stanford, CA: Stanford University Press.

Gim, R. H., Atkinson, D. R., & Kim, S. J. (1991). Asian American acculturation, counselor ethnicity and cultural sensitivity, and ratings of counselors. *Journal of Counseling Psychology, 38,* 57–62.

Gim, R. H., Atkinson, D. R., & Whiteley, S. (1990). Asian-American acculturation, severity of concerns, and willingness to see a counselor. *Journal of Counseling Psychology, 37,* 281–285.

Green, C. F., Cunningham, J., Yanico, B. J. (1986). Effects of counselor and subject race and counselor physical attractiveness on impressions and expectations of a female counselor. *Journal of Counseling Psychology, 33,* 349–352.

Harrison, D. K. (1975). Race as a counselor–client variable in counseling and psychotherapy: A review of the research. *The Counseling Psychologist, 5*(1), 124–133.

Haviland, M. G., Horswill, R. K., O'Connell, J. J., & Dynneson, V. V. (1983). Native American college students' preference for counselor race and sex and the likelihood of their use of a counseling center. *Journal of Counseling Psychology, 30,* 267–270.

Heath, A. E., Neimeyer, G. J., & Pedersen, P. B. (1988). The future of cross-cultural counseling: A Delphi poll. *Journal of Counseling and Development, 67,* 27–30.

Heesacker, M., Petty, R. E., & Caciopo, J. T. (1983). Field dependence and attitude change: Source credibility can alter persuasion by affecting message-relevant thinking. *Journal of Personality, 51,* 653–666.

Heider, F. (1958). *The psychology of interpersonal relations.* New York: Wiley.

Helms, J. E. (1984). Toward a theoretical explanation of the effects of race on counseling: A Black and White model. *The Counseling Psychologist, 12*(4), 153–165.

Helms, J. E. (1985). Cultural identity in the treatment process. In P. Pedersen (Ed.), *Handbook of cross-cultural counseling and therapy* (pp. 239–245). Westport, CT: Greenwood Press.

Helms, J. E. (1989). Considering some methodological issues in racial identity counseling research. *The Counseling Psychologist, 17,* 227–252.

Helms, J. E. (1990). *Black and White racial identity: Theory, research, and practice.* Westport, CT: Greenwood Press.

Helms, J. E., & Parham, T. A. (1990). The relationship between Black racial identity attitudes and cognitive styles. In J. E. Helms (Ed.), *Black and White racial identity: Theory, research, and practice* (pp. 119–131). Westport, CT: Greenwood Press.

Jackson, B. (1975). Black identity development. *Journal of Educational Diversity, 2,* 19–25.

Jahoda, G. (1980). Theoretical and systematic approaches in cross-cultural psychology. In H. C. Triandis & W. W. Lambert (Eds.), *Handbook of cross-cultural psychology: Perspectives* (Vol. 1, pp. 69–141). Boston: Allyn & Bacon.

Johnson, M. E., & Lashley, K. H. (1989). Influence of Native Americans' cultural commitment on preference for counselor ethnicity and expectations about counseling. *Journal of Multicultural Counseling and Development, 17,* 115–122.

Jones, E. E. (1985). Major developments in social psychology during the past five decades. In G. Lindzey and E. Aronson (Eds.), *The handbook of social psychology* (3rd ed.) (Vol. 1, pp. 47–107). New York: Random House.

Keefe, S. E. (1980). Acculturation and the extended family among urban Mexican Americans. In A. M. Padilla (Ed.), *Acculturation: Theory, models and some new findings* (pp. 85–110). Boulder, CO: Westview Press.

Kelley, H. H. (1967). Attribution theory in social psychology. *Nebraska Symposium on Motivation, 15,* 192–238.

Kelley, H. H. (1973). The processes of casual attribution. *American Psychologist, 28,* 107–128.

Kleinman, A. (1980). *Patients and healers in the context of culture.* Berkeley, CA: University of California Press.

Kunkel, M. A. (1990). Expectations about counseling in relation to acculturation in Mexican-American and Anglo-American student samples. *Journal of Counseling Psychology, 37,* 286–292.

LaFromboise, T. D., & Dixon, D. N. (1981). American Indian perception of trustworthiness in a counseling interview. *Journal of Counseling Psychology, 28,* 135–139.

Leong, F. T. L. (1986). Counseling and psychotherapy with Asian-Americans: Review of the literature. *Journal of Counseling Psychology, 33,* 196–206.

Le Vine, E., & Franco, J. N. (1981). A reassessment of self-disclosure patterns among Anglo-Americans and Hispanics. *Journal of Counseling Psychology, 28,* 522–524.

McBurney, D. H. (1983). *Experimental psychology.* Belmont, CA: Wadsworth.

McClain, L. (1983, July 24). How Chicago taught me to hate Whites. *Washington Post,* C1, C4.

McNeill, B. W., & Stoltenberg, C. D. (1989). Reconceptualizing social influence in counseling: The Elaboration Likelihood Model. *Journal of Counseling Psychology, 36,* 24–33.

Milliones, J. (1980). Construction of a Black consciousness measure: Psychotherapeutic implications. *Psychotherapy: Theory, Research, and Practice, 17*(2), 175–182.

Neidert, L. J., & Farley, R. (1985). Assimilation in the United States: An analysis of ethnic and generation differences in status and achievement. *American Sociological Review, 50,* 840–850.

Novak, M. (1972). *The rise of the unmeltable ethnics.* New York: Macmillan.

Oetting, E. R., & Beauvais, F. (1991). Orthogonal cultural identification theory: The cultural identification of minority adolescents. *International Journal of the Addictions, 25,* 655–685.

Oler, C. H. (1989). Psychotherapy with Black clients' racial identity and locus of control. *Psychotherapy: Theory, Research, and Practice, 26,* 233–241.

Olmedo, E. L. (1979). Acculturation: A psychometric perspective. *American Psychologist, 34,* 1061–1070.

Padilla, A. M. (1980a). *Acculturation: Theory, models and some new findings.* Boulder, CO: Westview Press.

Padilla, A. M. (1980b). The role of cultural awareness and ethnic loyalty in acculturation. In A. M. Padilla (Ed.), *Acculturation: Theory, models and some new findings* (pp. 47–84). Boulder, CO: Westview Press.

Parham, T. A. (1989). Cycles of psychological Nigrescence. *The Counseling Psychologist, 17,* 187–226.

Parham, T. A., & Helms, J. E. (1981). The influence of Black students' racial identity attitudes on preference for counselor's race. *Journal of Counseling Psychology, 28,* 250–257.

Parham, T. A., & Helms, J. E. (1985a). Attitudes of racial identity and self-esteem of Black students: An exploratory investigation. *Journal of College Student Personnel, 26,* 143–146.

Parham, T. A., & Helms, J. E. (1985b). Relation of racial identity attitudes to self-actualization and affective states of Black students. *Journal of Counseling Psychology, 32,* 431–440.

Parham, T. A., & McDavis, R. (1987). Black men, an endangered species: Who's really pulling the trigger? *Journal of Counseling and Development, 66,* 24–27.

Park, R. E. (1928). Human migration and the marginal man. *American Journal of Sociology, 33,* 881–893.

Park, R. E. (1950). *Race and culture.* Glencoe, IL: Free Press.

Park, R. E., & Burgess, E. W. (1921). *Introduction to the science of sociology.* Chicago: University of Chicago Press.

Paurohit, N., Dowd, E. T., & Cottingham, H. F. (1982). The role of verbal and nonverbal cues in the formation of first impressions of Black and White counselors. *Journal of Counseling Psychology, 29,* 371–378.

Pedersen, P. (1990). The constructs of complexity and balance in multicultural counseling theory and practice. *Journal of Counseling and Development, 68,* 550–554.

Petty, R. E. & Cacioppo, J. T. (1968a). *Communication and persuasion: Central and peripheral routes to attitude change.* New York: Springer-Verlag.

Petty, R. E., & Cacioppo, J. T. (1986b). The elaboration likelihood model of persuasion. In L. Berkowitz (Ed.), *Advances in experimental social psychology* (Vol. 19, pp. 123–205). New York: Academic Press.

Ponce, F. Q., & Atkinson, D. R. (1989). Mexican-American acculturation, counselor ethnicity, counseling style, and perceived counselor credibility. *Journal of Counseling Psychology, 36,* 203–208.

Ponterotto, J. G. (1988a). Racial consciousness development among White counselor trainees: A stage model. *Journal of Counseling and Development, 16,* 146–156.

Ponterotto, J. G. (1988b). Racial/ethnic minority research in the *Journal of Counseling Psychology:* A content analysis and methological critique. *Journal of Counseling Psychology, 35,* 410–418.

Ponterotto, J. G., Alexander, C. M., & Hinkston, J. A. (1988). Afro-American preferences for counselor characteristics: A replication and extension. *Journal of Counseling Psychology, 35,* 175–182.

Ponterotto, J. G., & Casas, J. M. (1987). In search of multicultural competence within counselor education programs. *Journal of Counseling and Development, 65,* 430–434.

Porche, L. M., & Banikiotes, P. G. (1982). Racial and attitudinal factors affecting the perceptions of counselors by Black adolescents. *Journal of Counseling Psychology, 29,* 169–174.

Poston, W. S. C., Craine, M., & Atkinson, D. R. (1991). Counselor dissimilarity confrontation, client cultural mistrust, and willingness to self-disclose. *Journal of Multicultural Counseling and Development, 19,* 65–73.

Redfield, R., Linton, R., & Herskovits, M. (1936). Memorandum on the study of acculturation. *American Anthropologist, 37,* 149–152.

Reimanis, G., & Posen, C. F. (1980). Locus of control and anomie in Western and African cultures. *Journal of Social Psychology, 112,* 181–189.

Riordan, Z. V. (1981). Locus of control in South Africa. *Journal of Social Psychology, 115,* 159–168.

Rotter, J. B. (1966). Generalized expectancies for internal versus external locus of reinforcement. *Psychological Monographs, 80,* 1–28.

Ruiz, R. A., Casas, J. M., & Padilla, A. M. (1977). *Cultural relevant behavioristic counseling.* Los Angeles: Spanish-Speaking Mental Health Research Center, University of California.

Ruiz, R. A., & Padilla, A. M. (1977). Counseling Latinos. *Personnel and Guidance Journal, 55,* 401–408.

Russo, N. F., Olmedo, E. L., Stapp, J., & Fulcher, R. (1981). Women and minorities in psychology. *American Psychologist, 36,* 1315–1363.

Sabnani, H. B., Ponterotto, J. G., & Borodovsky, L. G. (1991). White racial identity development and cross-cultural counselor training: A stage model. *The Counseling Psychologist, 19,* 76–99.

Sanchez, A. R., & Atkinson, D. R. (1983). Mexican-American cultural commitment, preference for counselor ethnicity, and willingness to use counseling. *Journal of Counseling Psychology, 30,* 215–220.

Sattler, J. M. (1977). The effects of therapist–client racial similarity. In A. S. Gurman & A. M. Razin (Eds.), *Effective psychotherapy: A handbook of research* (pp. 252–290). New York: Pergamon Press.

Serlin, R. C. (1987). Hypothesis testing, theory building, and the philosophy of science. *Journal of Counseling Psychology, 34,* 365–371.

Simons, H. W., Berkowitz, N. N., & Moyer, R. J. (1970). Similarity, credibility, and attitude change: A review and a theory. *Psychological Bulletin, 73,* 1–16.

Sladen, B. J. (1982). Effects of race and socioeconomic status on the perception of process variables in counseling. *Journal of Counseling Psychology, 29,* 560–566.

Stonequist, E. V. (1961). *The marginal man: A study of personality and culture conflict.* New York: Russell & Russell.

Strong, S. R. (1958). Counseling: An interpersonal influence process. *Journal of Counseling Psychology, 30,* 202–208.

Sue, S. (1988). Psychotherapeutic services for ethnic minorities. Two decades of research findings. *American Psychologist, 43,* 301–308.

Sue, S., & Sue, D. W. (1971). Chinese-American personality and mental health. *Amerasia Journal, 1,* 36–49.

Suinn, R. M., Rickard-Figueroa, K., Lew, S., & Vigil, P. (1987). The Suinn-Lew Asian Self-Identity Acculturation Scale: An initial report. *Educational and Psychological Measurement, 47,* 401–407.

Taussig, I. M. (1987). Comparative responses of Mexican-Americans and Anglo-Americans to early goal setting in a public mental health clinic. *Journal of Counseling Psychology, 34,* 214–217.

TenHouten, W. D. (1989). Application of dual brain theory to cross-cultural studies of cognitive development and education. *Sociological Perspectives, 32,* 153–167.

Terrell, F., & Terrell, S. L. (1981). An inventory to measure cultural mistrust among Blacks. *The Western Journal of Black Studies, 5,* 180–184.

Terrell, F., & Terrell, S. L. (1984). Race of counselor, client sex, cultural mistrust level, and premature termination from counseling among black clients. *Journal of Counseling Psychology, 31,* 371–375.

Thomas, C. (1971). *Boys no more.* Beverly Hills, CA: Glencoe.

Torrey, E. F. (1972). *The mind game: Witchdoctors and psychiatrists.* New York: Emerson Hall.

Valentine, C. A. (1971). Deficit, difference, and bicultural models of Afro-American behavior. *Harvard Educational Review, 41,* 137–157.

Vontress, C. E. (1971). Racial differences: Impediments to rapport. *Journal of Counseling Psychology, 18,* 7–13.

Wampold, B., Davis, B., & Good, R. H., III. (1990). Hypothesis validity of clinical research. *Journal of Counsulting and Clinical Psychology, 58,* 360–367.

Watkins, C. E., & Terrell, F. (1988). Mistrust level and its effects on counseling expectations in Black client–White counselor relationships: An analogue study. *Journal of Counseling Psychology, 35,* 194–197.

Watkins, C. E., Terrell, F., Miller, F. S., & Terrell, S. L. (1989). Cultural mistrust and its effects on expectational variables in Black client–White counselor relationships. *Journal of Counseling Psychology, 36,* 447–450.

West, S. G., & Wicklund, R. A. (1980). *A primer of social psychological theories.* Monterey, CA: Brooks/Cole.

Witkin, H. A. (1962). A cognitive-style approach to cross-cultural research. *International Journal of Psychology, 2,* 233–250.

Woods, E., Jr., & Zimmer, J. M. (1976). Racial effects in counseling-like interviews: An experimental analogue. *Journal of Counseling Psychology, 23,* 527–531.

CHAPTER 12

GENDER AND COUNSELING PSYCHOLOGY: CURRENT KNOWLEDGE AND DIRECTIONS FOR RESEARCH AND SOCIAL ACTION

LUCIA ALBINO GILBERT

The first edition of this *Handbook* included a chapter on counseling women; it appeared in the book's final Part, "Special Issues and Emerging Areas." This edition has a chapter on gender, not counseling women, and the chapter appears not in a final section on special issues but in an early Part devoted to development, prevention, and advocacy. These differences between the two editions of the *Handbook* well reflect the changes in the field during the past decade. We have moved from viewing women and their issues as special to looking at how the social context of women's and men's lives influences their development, choices, and goals (Gelso & Fassinger, 1990). We are broadening explanations of human behavior to consider individual women and men within the social systems in which the two sexes are embedded—and this process very much centers around the concept of gender.

The lives of women and men remain very different, despite women's dramatically increased educational and occupational opportunities. The median income of a college-educated woman, for example, is still about the same as that of high-school-educated men. How can things change so much and still stay so much the same? Sherif (1982) suggested that the answer lies in considerations of gender. Gender, she observed, is not just a property of individuals; it is also a principle of social organization. There is a gendered basis to relationships, social organizations, and institutions, which in turn shapes women's and men's lives.

It is within this larger social reality of women's and men's lives that this chapter considers current knowledge about gender pertinent to the field of counseling psychology and identifies directions for education, research, and social action. The chapter has four main sections. The first section addresses the relevance of gender to counseling psychology. I begin with a brief history of the current interest in gender. Gender bias in both

The author wishes to thank Karen Rossman, Sherwin Davidson, Murray Scher, Gail Hackett, Nancy Betz, Robert Lent, and Steven Brown for their comments on earlier drafts of this chapter. Special appreciation goes to my student, Karen Rossman, who read and reread all the drafts.

practice and research are then addressed in separate subsections; particular attention is given to how gender bias can characterize our research and theory and to emerging theories with regard to gender. In keeping with the educational purposes of the *Handbook,* these as well as later subsections include constructive suggestions and examples.

The second section considers in some depth three specific issues that are associated with gender and are integral to counseling psychology's unique focus on both individual change and social change: (a) men's socialized needs for power, (b) beauty and women's self-concept, and (c) women's and men's multiple role involvement. The reasons for including the first two issues are quite obvious. We are reminded daily that women need to be beautiful and men need to be powerful. Analyses of these concepts are central to understanding the experiences of women and men. Included in these discussions are such topics as rape, sexual harassment, and sexual relations with clients. The third issue, multiple role involvement, was selected because it represents an ever increasing reality for women and men today. Although adults have always fulfilled multiple roles, two roles—family and occupation—were assumed to be incompatible. Such views are undergoing dramatic change and many individuals today assume they can successfully combine work with family. Few would question the relevance of this issue to counseling psychology because of its connection to vocational psychology and career development. It is also clearly related to concepts of gender, as we shall see later. In the discussions about multiple role involvement, particular attention is given to dual-career families.

The last two sections of the chapter identify directions for research and education and for advocacy and social action, respectively. These sections build on the previous two sections and provide specific suggestions for broadening current research methodologies, educational programs, and ways of influencing policy. Examples pertinent to power, beauty, and multiple role involvement are used to illustrate the broader perspectives presented.

Two additional points need to be made here. First, relatively few studies reviewed in preparing the chapter specifically addressed the experiences of racial or ethnic minorities in the United States. Thus, the theory and research presented here predominantly reflect the experiences of Whites, and may have limited applicability to these other populations. Second, the focus on socialization is not intended to deny the role of biological contributors to gender differences, but is based on the premises that females and males are more similar than they are different and that our biological makeup leaves us highly sensitive to shaping by social experiences.

GENDER AND ITS RELEVANCE TO COUNSELING PSYCHOLOGY: FROM "COUNSELING WOMEN" TO CONSIDERATIONS OF GENDER

A Brief History

For some time now, advocates for women's interests within the mental health system and within Division 17 (Counseling Psychology) of the American Psychological Association (APA) specifically have raised objections to sexism in theories about women and in their diagnosis and treatment (Marecek & Hare-Mustin, 1987; Meara & Harmon, 1989). Historically, women were either ignored by social scientists or their experiences and motivations were defined by men (Russett, 1989; Weisstein, 1968). When women were studied, they often were found deficient or lacking in some way (Crawford & Marecek, 1989a). A case in point is the classic study by Broverman, Vogel, Broverman, Clarkson, and Rosenkrantz (1972), which reflected an implicit double standard of mental health for women and men. Mental health professionals described the healthy woman as less independent and rational, and more submissive and childlike, than the healthy man or the healthy adult with sex unspecified.

These early studies and writings, which coincided with the feminist movement in the United States, prompted investigations of bias in research that included (or excluded) women and in the treatment women received from providers of mental health services. The results of these inquiries indicated that women's experiences were not well-represented in psychological theory and research. Moreover, the benefits of the treatment they received came under question (American Psychological Association, 1975; Chesler, 1972). Thus began the development of an extensive body of literature on the psychology of women (Parlee, 1979; Wallston, 1981), the emergence of feminist methodologies (Harding, 1987; Marecek, 1989) and, most recently, the study of the construct of gender (e.g., Crawford & Marecek, 1989a, 1989b; Hare-Mustin & Marecek, 1990).

The Concept of Gender

The conceptual shift from sex to gender represents a somewhat revolutionary change in assumptions about the causes of human behavior and hence in approaches regarding how best to study and understand that behavior (Sherif, 1982; Unger, 1979, 1990). Psychological studies on sex differences historically derived from an internally determined or individual difference perspective, which assumed that the characteristic under study, say assertiveness, reflected an individual's essential nature. But, as Sherif (1982) and others noted, biological sex forms the basis of a social classification system—namely, gender. Viewed from the perspective of gender, many of the traits and behaviors traditionally associated with biological sex are, in effect, constructed by the social reality of individual women and men. Taking the example of assertiveness mentioned above, from a gender perspective women are not less assertive than men by nature, but learn to be less assertive in certain areas because of societal prescriptions and expectations. Not unlike the assumptions underlying counseling psychology as a discipline, the study of gender assumes that human behavior must be studied and understood within the social system in which individual women and men live.

The shift from the term sex to the term gender, then, acknowledges the broader meaning typically associated with one's biological sex. Gender refers not only to biological sex but also to the psychological, social, and cultural features and characteristics that have become strongly associated with the biological categories of female and male.

The growing academic interest in gender studies among American scholars, male and female alike, underscores the importance of gender in current thinking. Moreover, current scholarship focuses on how social norms and institutions influence the psychological development and adjustment of men as well as women (Gilbert, 1987a; Good & Mintz, 1990; Kimmel & Messner, 1989). Attempts to understand the existing inequality related to gender, for example, have led researchers in the areas of men's and women's studies to conceptualize gender not as natural difference but as "constructed power" (Brod, 1987). This notion of constructed power, as we shall see later, becomes important in understanding contemporary male and female behavior in our society.

Gender and Practice: Sex Bias and Sex-Role Stereotyping in Counseling and Psychotherapy with Women—An Overview

Albee (1981) defined sexism as a social condition grounded in false beliefs that, in turn, are rooted in emotional and personal needs. In 1974, the Board of Professional Affairs of the APA, responding to requests from the Committee on Women in Psychology (CWP), established a Task Force to examine "the extent and manner of sex bias and sex-role stereotyping in psychotherapeutic practice as they directly affect women as students, practitioners, and consumers" and to make recommendations based on their findings. The Task Force (American Psychological Association, 1975) identified two underlying problems central to sexism in psychotherapy: values in psychotherapy and therapists' knowledge of psychological processes in women. Four general areas of bias were also identified: fostering of traditional sex roles; bias in expectations and devaluation of women; sexist use of psychoanalytic concepts; and responses to women as sex objects, including seduction of female clients.

Based on its findings, the Task Force concluded that actions were needed to reduce sexism and sex-role stereotyping in psychotherapeutic practice. The final report recommended that specific educational efforts be undertaken with both graduate students and practicing professionals, that theories be examined for sexism, and that sanctions against sexist practice be enforced. A few years later, the Task Force published a set of guidelines for therapy with women (American Psychological Association, 1978). These guidelines emphasized key aspects of the Task Force's findings, namely, that psychologists should be knowledgeable about current research on sex roles and sex-related phenomena, that therapy should not be constricted by sexism or sex-role stereotypes, and that psychologists should recognize the situational and societal conditions that cause psychological difficulties for women.

Since that time, numerous articles, chapters, and books on counseling and therapy with women have further clarified the separate needs and unique struggles of women (Astin, 1985; Betz & Fitzgerald, 1987; Brodsky & Hare-Mustin, 1980; Courtois & O'Neil, 1988; Enns & Hackett, 1990; Hare-Mustin, 1983; Lerner, 1988; Loulan, 1984; Richardson & Johnson, 1984; for earlier published works, see Richardson & Johnson, 1984). Division 17 published a set of "Principles Concerning the Counseling and Psychotherapy of Women," subsequently endorsed by other APA divisions concerned with psychotherapeutic treatment (Ad Hoc Committee on Women, 1979). The background and rationale for each principle, as well as suggestions for implementation, were provided in a later publication (Fitzgerald & Nutt, 1986).

Finally, sexism in the psychotherapeutic treatment of men is receiving increasing attention (O'Neil, 1980, 1982; Robertson & Fitzgerald, 1990; Scher, Stevens, Good, & Eichenfield, 1987). Not unlike the situation with women, the constraints traditionally placed on how men should act were incorporated in theories of and assumptions about "normal" male development.

Emerging Perspectives Related to Gender

Although some writers still question whether controlled research has adequately demonstrated sexism in treatment (Barak & Fisher, 1989), for the most part research in counseling psychology has moved beyond the need to demonstrate sexism and discrimination against women to sophisticated analyses of gender belief systems and organizational factors associated with gender, and their effect on women's and men's behavior (Crawford & Marecek, 1989a; Deaux, 1984, 1985; Mintz & O'Neil, 1990; Wallston, 1987). Illustrations of these kinds of analyses appear in a later section devoted to specific gender issues (e.g., the subsection on men's power includes an analysis of male entitlement and its relation to sexual intimacies between male therapists and female clients).

Key concepts and ideas associated with early feminist therapies also provided a clear recognition of how gender affects individual development and educational processes, including counseling and psychotherapy (Gilbert, 1980). These included the conviction that "the personal is political" (i.e., the experiences clients bring to therapy must be understood and treated within their social and cultural realities); the practice of encouraging women's anger (intended to counter stereotypic views that expect women to accept their lot and be understanding of others); and challenges to psychodynamic theories that viewed women in negative terms (e.g., conceptualizing women's desire for achievement in male-dominated areas as penis envy). Feminist therapies articulated concern about the power that therapists (predominantly men at that time) had over their clients, most of whom were women (Lerman, 1976; Lerner, 1988). Similar kinds of analyses have since been made regarding relationships between educators and their students (e.g., Pope, 1989) and between women in male-dominated settings and their colleagues and supervisors (e.g., Aisenberg & Harrington, 1988)—two areas also central to counseling psychology. Amplification of these points, together with illustrative examples, occurs throughout this chapter and especially in the section that immediately follows.

Gender and Research in Counseling Psychology—An Overview

Among the purposes in evolving feminist approaches to research are facilitating the understanding of women's and men's experiences within their societal context and constructing nonsexist theories of human development. Many social scientists have come to recognize both gender and science as socially constructed categories. In her book, *Reflections on Gender and Science,* Evelyn Fox Keller (1985) stated that "Women, men, and science are created, together, out of a complex dynamic of interwoven cognitive, emotional, and social forces" (p. 4). She saw the task before us as understanding how science has been constructed and then broadening its concepts, methods, and goals.

Gender Bias in Research

Sexism and gender bias characterize psychological research and theory to the extent that unexamined assumptions about the sexes or untested distinctions based on gender enter into the hypotheses, rationale, norms of adjustment, or coverage of the field (McHugh, Koeske, & Frieze, 1986). The purpose of nonsexist research is not the elimination of sex differences but the elimination of "theoryless" quests for sex differences predicated either on unconscious biases about sex differences or on the assumption that a sex difference, found but not hypothesized, reveals unknown truths about women and men.

The scientific literature must adequately and accurately represent the social experiences of women and men. A case in point is spatial relations. Fausto-Sterling (1985), a developmental geneticist, concluded, in her book *Myths of Gender: Biological Theories about Women and Men,* that the disparity between boys and girls on tests of spatial visualizing is small and does not demand explanation by a theory linking the disparity to the chromosomes that determine sex or to a highly speculative theory of sex differences in brain lateralization. Spatial visualization may be an acquired skill, one traditionally fostered among boys who play with blocks and participate in athletic games requiring visual thinking, and traditionally not encouraged among girls. In this example, the notion that men and women must differ could lead researchers to investigation of increasingly complex theories (the quest for sex differences) without first considering more obvious theories that view individuals' capacities as emerging from a web of interactions between the biological being and the social environment.

Hare-Mustin and Marecek (1990) observed that the primary meaning of gender in psychology has been difference. They used the term *alpha bias* to describe the exaggeration of differences that results from the view of male and female as different and opposite and as having mutually exclusive qualities. This world view led to a construction of women and men in which men were always superior, regardless of opposing empirical evidence. Thus, for example, if girls displayed greater quickness than boys in learning material, this was interpreted as proving the shallowness of women's intellectual faculties compared to the slower but surer development of the male mind (Russett, 1989).

McHugh et al. (1986) summarized a comprehensive document, "Guidelines for Nonsexist Research," prepared by a Task Force of Division 35 (Psychology of Women) of the APA. The Task Force identified common areas in which unexamined assumptions about the sexes or untested distinctions based on gender operate. These included excessive confidence in traditional methods of research, bias in explanatory systems, and inappropriate conceptualization and operationalization of variables. Denmark, Russo, Frieze, and Sechzer (1988) further explicated these areas by providing examples and "corrections" pertinent to question formulation, methods and procedures, data analysis, and conclusions drawn from research.

How Bias Can Enter into Research

Four characteristics of traditional psychological research and theory have particular bearing on this chapter's focus on gender and counseling psychology and the view that meaning derives from social experiences. These characteristics are: (a) "context stripping" or the practice of isolating social phenomena from the context in which they typically occur; (b) the focus on intrapsychic and individual variables to explicate and elucidate human behavior; (c) the use of White heterosexual men as the model or standard for adaptive or healthy behavior and psychological functioning; and (d) as mentioned above, the notion of alpha bias proposed by Hare-Mustin and Marecek (1990), which reflects psychology's quest for sex differences. The next section describes these issues in more detail and makes clear how each perpetuates gender bias in counseling psychology. First, however, an example alluded to earlier—assertion training—will serve to illustrate how bias can affect the development of a sizable body of research literature, much of it contributed by counseling psychologists.

Gervasio and Crawford (1989) offered an illuminating critique of the assertiveness literature. They noted that the basic assumption in this literature was the notion that, if women learned to act more assertively, their reality would be different (item (b) above—a focus on individual variables to explain human behavior). Moreover, underlying the empirically based guidelines are values about "healthy" and "adaptive" interpersonal behaviors, which appear to lack sensitivity to women's actual experiences in society (item (a) above—context stripping). The two prevalent values in assertiveness training—masculine stereotypes as norm, and individualism versus interdependence—closely parallel positive stereotypes of masculine behavior (item (c) above—male behavior as the standard). That is, in learning assertive speech and behavior, women are asked to model themselves after men, although women and men live in different social environments and are faced with different types of infringements on their personal rights. Women, for example, are much more likely than men to be sexually harassed, raped, and economically dependent. Thus, although research on assertiveness is for the most part internally valid within its narrow sphere and meets the standards of good experimental research, it lacks external or real-world validity. To be valid in this way, such research must take into account the social context of individuals' lives.

Shift of Focus of Inquiry from Sex to Gender

Historically, researchers generally assumed that women and men differed and that, when both sexes were included in studies of individual differences, tests for sex differences needed no explicit theory. Lack of differences was typically ignored and statistically significant differences were construed as fitting prevailing societal views of women and men. In 1974, Maccoby and Jacklin undertook the enormous task of carefully examining and summarizing the diverse body of psychological literature on sex differences in the areas of cognitive skills, personality traits and dispositions, and social behaviors. These researchers concluded that there was little evidence for objective differences between the sexes, with the possible exceptions of verbal ability, where girls appeared to perform better, and mathematical ability, visual–spatial ability, and aggression, where boys appeared higher.

Later reviews indicated that, even when differences are found, they generally account for less than 5% of the variance (Deaux, 1985) and that differences in cognitive skills have declined over the past two decades as well (Feingold, 1988; Jacklin, 1989). Moreover, statistically significant differences that may favor girls over boys (say, in perceptual speed) or boys over girls (say, in spatial visualization) appear to have little educational significance. Women perform as well as men in high school and college, and increasing numbers of women are completing advanced degrees (U. S. Department of Education, 1989).

Findings such as these, which suggest that women and men are more similar than different in their abilities and skills, stand in marked contrast to the reality of women's and men's lives. Women and men differ enormously in their occupational pursuits and duties, the status of their behaviors and roles, their access to power, their control of resources, and the conditions under which they live (Lott, 1987). One explanation for this large discrepancy between research findings and the day-to-day reality of women's and men's lives is the "context stripping" prevalent in experimental methodologies. That is, the individual differences approach to understanding women's and men's experiences viewed people in isolation from, or stripped of, their social context rather than within their social context. Take the example of leadership, a topic central to career advancement and vocational psychology. In laboratory studies, women and men typically do not differ in abilities and qualities associated with effective leadership (Deaux, 1984, 1985; Riger & Galligan, 1980). In real-world settings, however, significantly more men than women are found in leadership positions (Morrison & Glinow, 1990). The reasons for this discrepancy are complex and involve such *contextual* factors as sex discrimination, perceptions of women's and men's abilities, discomfort with women in leadership positions, inadequate day care, and women's self-efficacy (Morrison & Glinow, 1990; Rose & Larwood, 1988).

Current Theories About How Gender Operates

Psychologists have only recently recognized the pervasive effects of gender (Barnett, Biener, & Baruch, 1987; Deaux, 1985; Eagly & Steffen, 1986; Spence, Deaux, & Helmreich, 1985; Wallston, 1987). Gender beliefs and stereotypes and their concomitant behavioral expectations create self-fulfilling prophecies in interactions such that individuals modify their behavior in response to certain situational cues (Spence et al., 1985). Klein and Willerman (1979) provided a clear illustration of how cues associated with gender affect behavior: women instructed to be as dominant as possible showed comparable responses in their behavior toward either a male or female partner. However, when specific "dominance" instructions were absent, women's behavior differed—lower displays of dominance occurred toward a male than toward a female partner.

In addition, the influence and meaning of gender extend beyond stereotypes and gender beliefs to social structures (Crawford & Marecek, 1989a; Deaux, 1984; Mednick, 1989). As I mentioned in the introduction, gender acts as a pervasive organizer in our culture. Women and men often are divided into different groups because of existing social structures—male CEOs and female executive secretaries; male football players and female cheerleaders. Thus, the focus of our inquiries about gender must not be limited to gender as a static variable but must be broadened to view gender as a principle of social organizations and as a process.

The career choices made by women and men, and the career paths that ensue, provide a pertinent example of process directly relevant to counseling psychology. Although increasing numbers of women are entering the labor force, women and men are typically found in different occupations (Scott, 1982; Spain, 1988) and women continue to earn significantly less than men (U. S. Department of Commerce, Bureau of Labor Statistics, 1989). Positions of power and leadership in organizations are predominantly held by men (Morrison & Glinow, 1990; Rix, 1987). Women now constitute nearly 39% of the professional labor force; but only 3.6% of board directorships and 1.7% of corporate officerships at the Fortune 500 companies are female (Morrison & Glinow, 1990; Wallis, 1989). Recent studies document the difficulty women have in penetrating the "glass ceiling," a barrier so subtle that it is transparent, yet so strong that it prevents women and minorities from moving beyond middle management (McAdoo, 1989; Morrison, White, Velsor, & the Center for Creative Leadership, 1987). (A later section of the chapter provides greater detail about theory and research in which gender is conceptualized as a process.)

THREE SPECIFIC GENDER ISSUES

This section considers in some detail three topics that are inextricably tied to gender and are particularly central to counseling psychology's commitment to facilitating positive human development across the life cycle. These topics are power, beauty, and multiple role involvement. As mentioned in the introduction, power and beauty represent important domains that are typically associated with men and women, respectively. The larger social meaning of these terms, and how this meaning may determine individual behavior, form the content of the subsections that follow. Special attention is given to: implicit views of men and women; sex as a social category; and organizational factors associated with gender, especially opportunity and power. The third topic, multiple role involvement, concerns the dramatic changes that are occurring with regard to work and family. This is a huge and complex literature; my goal here is to identify the aspects of multiple role involvement that are most directly related to gender. Some suggestions for future research are included, but an expanded set of initiatives for research and education is offered in the chapter's final section.

Issue 1. Men's Socialized Needs for Power

Power is often viewed as crucial to men in our culture—power over women, power over other men, power over sons and daughters. Often overlooked, however, is how little power many men have. This subsection considers power relations between the sexes, men's needs for power over women, and the reality of many men's lives. Included are discussions of male entitlement, sex and power, rape, sexual harassment, and sexual relations with clients.

Male Entitlement to Power Over and Dependency on Women

In most cultures, males are more highly valued than females and are superordinate to them. The extent of this differential evaluation may vary, but its result is always to grant men greater power and privilege (Kahn, 1984; Toth, 1982). White men in our culture typically grow up with feelings of confidence and specialness granted them simply because they are born male. This specialness is an essential aspect of male entitlement, which encourages men to feel that what they do or want takes precedence over the needs of women and that their prerogatives should not be questioned. Men may view even small losses of advantage or deference as large threats (Goode, 1982) because their sense of self is so closely tied to their entitlement, especially in relation to women.

Such feelings and behaviors are part of traditional male socialization. Gilmore (1990), an anthropologist, observed that almost nowhere on earth does mere physical maturity make a boy a man. Instead, manhood is earned or proven through an ideology that glorifies toughness, assertiveness, and bravery, and holds these characteristics as the noblest expression of masculine human behavior. Brannon (1985) identified four dimensions of masculinity consistent with this ideology: not being feminine (what Brannon calls "no sissy stuff"); being respected and admired for successful achievement ("the big wheel"); never showing weakness and uncertainty ("the sturdy oak"); and seeking adventure and risk, including the acceptance of violence if necessary ("give 'em hell").

In relations with women, this ideology requires that men be independent and devoid of interpersonal needs. Thus, men were to expect women to provide them with unconditional warmth, sustenance, and love because this was men's prerogative, not a sign of their dependence or interdependence. Women needed men and took care of men in return—this was men's due. As long as the man experienced the caregiving as a "given," he did not have to acknowledge his own neediness (which male socialization denied) or the extent of his dependence on the women in his life. "Sturdy oaks" rely only on themselves and do not need anyone but themselves. Men who internalize such views also must alienate themselves from their own emotions and from the comfort of caregiving (Scher et al., 1987).

Another consequence of this definition of masculinity was to exaggerate female emotional dependency on men while understating male emotional dependency on women (Gilbert, 1987b). Yet another consequence, identified by Pleck (1981), was to construe any dependency men felt toward women as a need for power over women rather than as a need for bonding between equals.

Sex and Power

In an analysis of the effects of men's changing roles, Pleck (1981) identified several psychological sources of men's needs for power over women. Each source relates to male dependency but expresses itself as a power that men attribute to women, which in turn leads men to dominate women. One such source is called masculine-validating power. Through sexual relations with women, men look for validation of themselves as men. A close association between sexual power and manliness pervades American culture (Brod, 1987; Zilbergeld, 1978). The man must be big where it counts, powerful, and able to take charge and successfully orchestrate sexual activities.

Our culture allows men to make their sexual needs explicit because they appear as rights or entitlement divorced from emotional neediness. Women become objects of men's sexual desire. As long as men can experience their sexual needs as simply needs for physical release, they can feel entitled to having women meet their needs. Stiver (1984) described men in therapy who report their yearnings to recapture the ecstatic experience of being enveloped by a woman, while at the same time feeling sexual and powerful.

Thus, some men project on women power that women don't really have—power to make them feel like men. Because men are not supposed to feel dependent, they also may project their own dependency on women. Many men who see women as wanting too much from them may, in fact, themselves desire a great deal of emotional support and understanding from women (Pogrebin, 1983). Women often express men's feelings for them and draw them out (Pleck, 1981).

In summary, the social construction of sexuality as central to masculinity, coupled with men's socialized sense of entitlement, may cause particularly serious difficulties for some men. They may feel entitled to support from women without having to request it. To an extent, this sense of entitlement is based on the assumption that men are superior to women, that women are an underclass with respect to men, and that men are entitled to have women in their lives to serve their needs (Gilbert, 1987b; Pleck, 1981). They may also feel a privileged access to or an ownership of women and their bodies. Horney (1937), for example, described the prerogative of gender—the socially sanctioned right of all males to sexualize all females, regardless of age or status.

According to Horney, women's sexual compliance in situations such as battering and incest is primarily a response of the powerless to the aggression of the powerful. Submission is expressed sexually only when the aggression itself is sexual and demands sexual compliance; submission is a passive attempt to gain safety with a powerful man. This explanation is consistent with the self-reports of female clients who had been in sexual relationships with their male therapists (Pope & Bouhoutsos, 1986). Also pertinent here is assault or rape among male inmates in prisons. Prison rape is generally seen today as an acting-out of power roles within an all-male, authoritarian environment in which those men perceived as weaker are forced to play the role that in the outside world is assigned to women (Brownmiller, 1975).

Men's socialized needs for power can cause difficulties not only for themselves but also for others. Sherif (1982) noted some years ago that a study of the problems associated with the subjection of women is essential to understanding the behavior of both women and men. It is with this intent that the next three subsections are presented. They briefly describe situations that we all find troublesome and that reflect the connection between male sexuality and needs for power over women.

Rape

In recent years, date rape and acquaintance rape have exploded into public consciousness. Recent prevalence figures suggest that 15 to 22% of women have been raped at some point in their lives, many by close acquaintances (Koss & Burkhart, 1989). Romantic partners were implicated in 50 to 57% of sexual assaults reported by college-age and adult women (Koss, 1990). Results from a national sample of over 6,000 women and men enrolled at 32 different colleges and universities across the United States indicated that approximately 54% of college women reported having been sexually victimized some time after they were 14 years old, and 27.5% of the women reported an instance of sexual contact that met the FBI's definition of forcible rape (Koss, Gidycz, &

Wisniewski, 1987). Responses from the men in the sample regarding the frequency of their own sexually aggressive behavior were very similar to the number of times college women in the sample reported being victimized.

Gidycz and Koss (1990) further reported that 1.5% of the 3,187 female respondents in the national survey were victims of group sexual assault. Of these group assaults, 38% were perpetrated by relatives, compared to 18% of the individual sexual assaults, and 39% were perpetrated by strangers (e.g., at fraternity parties), compared to 2% of the individual assaults. Contrary to widely held beliefs, then, the results of this large survey indicate that women are assaulted by a large, diverse pool of men, many of whom are quite highly educated and living quite normal lives. (With regard to domestic violence, it is estimated that up to 1.8 million wives are abused each year; see Courtois & O'Neil, 1988.)

Rape appears to relate to gender in a number of ways. First, as Estrich (1987) pointed out in her well-researched book, *Real Rape: How the Legal System Victimizes Women Who Say No,* simple rape (the legal term for a sexual assault in which the victim knows her assailant and no weapon or overt physical violence is used) embodies a fundamental belief of men in their absolute right to have sex with women they know: their wives, girlfriends, coworkers, or any woman with whom they can claim a prior "socially appropriate" relationship, however brief. According to Estrich, women's right to say no to unwanted sex is circumscribed by male definitions of criminal behavior and by a judicial system that is constructed by men but that denies women's reality in a male-dominated society. For example, the standard for resistance required of rape victims is still defined in male terms. The courts expect that a reasonable woman will fight back like a "real man," an expectation inconsistent with female socialization or the power structure embedded in relations between women and men.

Estrich argued that the focus must be shifted from what is defined or expected as reasonable resistance on the part of women to what is defined as acceptable or reasonable behavior on the part of men. In other words, do we want to continue to view men's behavior in situations of rape as normal, and ignore the violence and entitlement associated with such behavior?

In trying to understand why men rape, Brod (1987) pointed to male socialization patterns in gangs, sports, the military, and fighting, as offering approval of violence. Pollitt (1989) made a similar point:

> What we should be asking is not how the most sensational crimes against women are different from run-of-the-mill threats, rapes, bashings, and murders, but how they are the same. We need to stop thinking of male violence as some kind of freak of nature, like a tornado. Because the thing about tornados is, you can't do anything about them. The onus is on the potential victims to accommodate themselves or stay out of the way. (p. 20)

Many men who rape or batter, particularly within ongoing relationships with women they know, are viewed as good guys who make mistakes. In effect, this distances male violence from the fabric of daily experience by making it seem bizarre or rare when it is actually quite common.

A review of treatment modalities for rape victims and offenders is beyond the scope of this chapter. The interested reader is referred to Koss and Burkhart (1989), who provided a conceptual analysis of rape victimization that subsumes not only the target symptoms that represent the immediate response to rape but also the long-term impact of rape and the process of resolution; and to Courtois and O'Neil (1988), who provided a thoughtful overview of victimization, including its psychological consequences. A primary focus of current research is understanding the long-term cognitive-emotional responses associated with sexual assault. Surveys have revealed that 31 to 48% of rape victims eventually seek professional help, often years after the assault.

Sexual Harassment

Societal attitudes about rape, then, essentially blamed women or excused men for men's violent behavior, and only within the past 10 years have such attitudes been seriously challenged. Similarly, sexual harassment has been taken seriously as an infringement on women's personal rights only within the past decade. Sexual harassment, we now realize, is not about a particular woman, but about views of women; it is not about sexual attraction, but about the abuse of authority and the need to dominate women (Gutek, 1986, 1989).

Sexual harassment varies in severity from very extreme behaviors, such as rape, to mild or even trivial behaviors such as generalized sexist remarks. Till (1980), using a national sample of college women, developed a classification scheme for sexual harassment which Fitzgerald and her coworkers used to devise a Sexual Experiences Questionnaire (SEQ; Fitzgerald, Gold, Ormerod, & Weitzman, 1988). Till's categories included gender harassment (generalized sexist remarks not necessarily designed to elicit a response), seductive behavior (inappropriate but sanction-free advances), sexual bribery (solicitation of sexual activity by promise of reward), sexual threats (coercion of sexual activity by threat of punishment), and sexual imposition, including assault. Studies using the SEQ with faculty and students indicate that women were more likely than men to view less explicitly coercive situations as harassing (Fitzgerald & Ormerod, 1991). Recent prevalence figures suggest that 53% of women have been harassed at some point in their working lives, and about 10% have quit a job because of sexual harassment (Gutek, 1989). Women in nontraditional jobs are especially likely to be harassed.

Because sexual behavior is often viewed as personal, individual, and separate from the effects of organizational structure and societal norms, sexual harassment frequently goes unnoticed or unchallenged. For instance, sexual relationships between students and professors or supervisors occur with some frequency and with little if any negative sanctions for educators (Kitchener, 1989; Robinson & Reid, 1985). In results from a number of recent studies, sexual contact with an educator was reported by 13.6 to 20% of female respondents, and approximately half reported some form of sexual advances or attempted seduction by at least one educator during their years as students (Kitchener, 1989). Over 70% of the respondents in these studies reported feeling that the advances were coercive, and 45% reported that, when they responded negatively to these advances, they received punitive responses from educators which ranged from slight to severe. A sizable percentage of students reported knowing graduate students who dropped out of their graduate programs because of sexual involvement with or sexual advances from a psychology educator. Fitzgerald et al. (1988) found that 25% of the male faculty responding to their survey reported having had a sexual encounter or relationship with a student.

Kitchener (1989), in a thorough review of research in this area, concluded that sexual behavior of male educators with female students often has devastating consequences for the women involved and parallels the pattern of sexual exploitation in therapy associated with gender. "Men put their own needs for power, fulfillment, and acceptance ahead of their responsibility to educate" (p. 7).

Sexual Relationships with Clients

Sexual intimacy between therapists and clients is a serious problem (Pope & Bouhoutsos, 1986). Cases based on violations of Principle 6a (i.e., sexual intimacies with clients are unethical) accounted for 25% of all cases reported to the American Psychological Association (APA) Ethics Committee in 1988—more than twice the number reported for any other category of the ethical principles (American Psychological Association, 1990). Moreover, complaints related to Principle 6a have increased each year since 1979, when sexual intimacies with clients were specifically defined as unethical in the *Ethical Principles of Psychologists* (American Psychological Association, 1981). The professional liability insurance rates of APA's insurance carrier recently doubled because of the cost of the increasing number of malpractice suits involving sexual improprieties (American Psychological Association Insurance Trust, 1990). Malpractice statistics covering the 10-year period from 1976 to 1986 (Fulero, 1986) indicated that sexual violations constituted the largest percentage of any unethical act (18.5% of the cases) and were the most costly (representing 45% of the money paid out). Sex claims remain the biggest problem area in terms of prevalence and cost (APA Insurance Trust, 1990).

The APA's present ethical principle has met resistance within the profession, despite the mounting evidence of the harm such behavior causes to clients (Bates & Brodsky, 1989; Pope & Bouhoutsos, 1986). Some psychologists, for example, conform with Principle 6a only to the extent that their professional practice is not endangered. Thus, they may terminate therapy to pursue a personal relationship and then view themselves as acting ethically. The seriousness of this situation is underscored by a proposed revision of the *Ethical Principles of Psychologists* which says, "It is unethical for a therapist to have sexual intimacies with a current or former client" (Ethical Principles Revised, 1990). This proposed revision would make explicit that sexual intimacies are never acceptable and that engaging in such acts with a former client would constitute unethical professional behavior.

Among therapists, approximately 1 in 10 men, but only 1 in 50 women, have had self-reported erotic contact with clients, nearly all of whom were female (Pope, 1990; Pope & Bouhoutsos, 1986). Female therapists appear to have little need or motivation to be sexually intimate with male clients; the motivations and needs of male therapists vis-à-vis female clients seem stronger. Approximately 90% of reported cases of sexual intimacy involve male therapists and female clients (Pope, 1989). This situation reflects the larger social reality, a manifestation of male and female gender roles.

Gilbert and Scher (1989) analyzed men's socialized entitlement and needs for power over, and dependency on, women in explicating male psychologists' erotic behavior with female clients. They noted that, based on their thorough review of pertinent data, the 10 general themes in cases of sexual intimacy with clients summarized by Pope and Bouhoutsos (1986) all fall under the rubric of male entitlement. Illustrative themes are as follows: the wants and needs of the therapist become the focus of the therapy; the therapist creates and exploits an exaggerated dependence on the part of the client; the therapist uses rationalizations to discount harm to the client. That is, therapists who do not feel dominant or special in their personal lives outside of therapy may look to sexual expression with a female client to maintain their "superior" position. Similarly, their sense of entitlement may lead them to expect women to meet their needs to be dominant. Because female clients may respond in ways that meet the male therapist's needs—a situation made likely by female socialization—the therapist may have little incentive to question his motives.

Suggestions for Research

One general suggestion with regard to men's socialized need for power would be for researchers to reframe dependency as an enhancing rather than as a debilitating quality. Present psychological views of dependency assume that a person with "needs" is lacking in some way and remains unchanged despite interactions with others (i.e., the view that women are basically dependent but men are not). Emerging conceptual views reframe dependency as allowing one to experience one's self as enhanced and empowered through the process of needing others or being able to count on others (e.g., Stiver, 1984). From this perspective, personal well-being becomes enhanced through recognizing the importance of others to one's own sense of self and knowing when particular assistance would be helpful. Findings reported in the social support literature (Brown, Alpert, Lent, Hunt, & Brady, 1988; Gottlieb, 1983) illustrate how certain forms of interdependence can be empowering and worth fostering through interventions.

Such a reconceptualization would be particularly useful in guiding the study of male (in)expressiveness. The theoretical and practical importance of freeing men from emotional restrictions that hinder self-expression and interpersonal dependency has been well articulated (Balswick, 1988). Good, Dell, and Mintz (1989), in a study of college men, found that concerns about expressing emotions were significantly related to negative attitudes toward seeking professional help and to past help-seeking behavior. Werrbach (1989) asked members of Division 17 their perceptions of why men seek therapy and what beliefs and behaviors male clients bring to therapy. The reasons most endorsed by respondents pertained to concerns about sexual functioning and about exhibiting behaviors and interests stereotypically associated with women. The common subset of beliefs viewed as most descriptive of male clients involved issues of power and dominance (e.g., the expectation that women should make them feel more powerful) and restricted emotionality. Cultural proscriptions regarding male expressivity can clearly cause problems for individual men, personally as well as interpersonally. Educational interventions with adolescent boys, men entering relationships, and men rearing children, reframed from the perspective of dependency as empowering, could be beneficial in the development of altered images of oneself as a friend, colleague, lover, and parent.

Issue 2. Beauty and Women's Self-Concept

Traditional sex-role definitions specify different sources of power for women and men. Men derive status and power from wealth, ability, and possessions; women, who are dependent on the men they attract for their status, derive power from physical beauty. This subsection discusses the relation between views of women as dependent on men and women's quest for beauty and thinness.

Reviews of the literature (Attie & Brooks-Gunn, 1987; Polivy & Herman, 1985; Rodin, Silberstein, & Streigel-Moore, 1985) indicate that women more than men spend a great deal of time worrying about their appearance and that concerns about weight and thinness become chronic stressors in many women's lives. In 1985, 46% of adult women across age and race were currently trying to lose weight and 85% of these women were dieting to do so (Attie & Brooks-Gunn, 1987). A 1987 nationwide survey of adolescent health knowledge and behavior, which involved 11,400 eighth and tenth graders in 20 states, found that over 60% of the girls and 28% of the boys had tried dieting during the preceding year (Otten, 1988). Similarly, over half of the white middle-class girls surveyed by Attie and Brooks-Gunn (1989) had been on a diet, usually in the absence of obesity. Thus, women's concerns about weight and thinness are normative.

The endless quests for beauty on the part of many women, not unlike the endless conquests, sexual or otherwise, undertaken by many men to prove their manliness, occur within a cultural and societal context. Two aspects of women's cultural reality have particular relevance here. The first concerns how women become defined in relation to men, and the second, how women learn to live within societal prescriptions for their sex.

The patriarchal ideal of womanhood involved women needing and caring for men. It benefited men to see women as primarily longing to love men and be loved by them, to admire men and serve them and even to pattern themselves after men (Horney, 1937). Early psychological theories of women essentially reflected this patriarchal view (Erikson, 1968). We now realize that women historically admired and served men not because that was their nature, but because tradition and male power shaped their choices and behaviors.

The reality of their situation, in effect, conditioned women to focus their lives around men. Their role was to attract men as life partners and to direct their achievement through their affiliations with their husband and children (Erikson, 1968; Miller, 1976). The more physically attractive women were, the better their chances for being selected by men. The socialization of women centered around what made women desirable to men. Being sexually desired by men became an important component of women's self-concept because women's worth to men was seen in terms of physical characteristics and ability to please, satisfy, and serve men (Westkott, 1986). This oversocialization often resulted in women's assuming dependent stances with men, subordinating themselves to men both in physical and intellectual contexts, and relying on physical beauty to attract and hold on to men (Lerner, 1983).

In Andersen's fable, the old Mother Queen says to the little mermaid: "One must not mind slight inconveniences when one wishes to look well" (Andersen, 1956). Although women today are much less dependent on men economically, notions of what makes women desirable, and why, remain relatively unchanged. That women must suffer to be beautiful still characterizes women's behavior today. As Freedman (1986) made clear in *Beauty Bound,* beauty for women is a double-edged sword. Women are bound on an endless quest that keeps them in bondage. The destructive effects of the ideal of female beauty include damage to women's self-concept and self-esteem, depression, chronic dieting, eating disorders such as bulimia and anorexia nervosa, and the misuse of medical procedures such as cosmetic surgery, liposuction, and estrogen replacement therapy (Freedman, 1986; National Women's Health Network, 1989; Rodin et al., 1985).

Suggestions for Research

Future research efforts should give primary attention to women's quest for physical beauty in the area of thinness. In particular, we need to better understand the process of dieting and how it affects self-perceptions and behavior, both short-term and long-term. Attie and Brooks-Gunn (1987), for example, described the relationship between weight and women's chronic stress. Dieting typically does not result in lower weight, but in fatigue, irritability, chronic hunger, a greater reliance on external guidelines for the regulation of food intake, and "counterregulatory" behaviors, characterized by uncontrollable urges to binge eat. Thus, dieting may cause binging by promoting the adoption of a cognitively regulated, rather than a metabolically regulated, eating style.

By dieting, women are striving relentlessly for a weight or shape that cannot be acquired or maintained—the "beauty bound" described by Freedman (1986). Viewed from this perspective, dieting in the service of the cultural ideal is itself a chronic stressor. "The stereotype of the weight-loss diet as a ticket to self-improvement and stress reduction is a myth" (Attie & Brooks-Gunn, 1987, p. 219). Studies aimed at education and prevention, particularly for adolescent girls, are very much in need. A number of studies link adolescent girls' perceptions of negative body image with a higher likelihood of developing eating problems (Attie & Brooks-Gunn, 1989). Self-reports of college women indicate that 13 to 67% of them engage in binge eating (Attie & Brooks-Gunn, 1987). Like anorexia nervosa, bulimia occurs frequently in weight-preoccupied adolescent and young adult women.

Finally, the role of advertising and the media in creating and reinforcing sex-role stereotypic images of women (and men) needs much more study. The same society that heralds women's diversifying professional accomplishments also presents fashion models chosen to match a template of abnormal thinness, along with new diets to attain it. The message to women is that they must undertake new beauty treatments, new exercise programs, and new diets to hide physical flaws and conceal aging.

Issue 3. Women's and Men's Multiple Role Involvement

This subsection first provides an overview of how women's and men's work and family roles are changing. One type of multiple role involvement is then considered—the heterosexual dual-career family and its several variations. Finally, sources of stress in carrying out multiple roles, which appear related to gender, are discussed. Space does not allow for the fuller consideration of nontraditional pairings such as dual-wage lesbian or gay male couples or of single-parent families. Caution should be used in making generalizations to these and other kinds of nontraditional relationships and situations.

Evidence for Multiple Role Involvement

Women's and men's lives have changed quite dramatically in the past 25 years. Today's young women (aged 25 to 29) are just as likely as young men to have four or more years of college, and more women are in the paid work force than ever before (Spain, 1988). Women now constitute nearly 39% of the professional labor force, compared with 26% in 1960. Current norms not only assume that single and married women and men will work but also consider work as an important component of women's identity (Betz & Fitzgerald, 1987). Today, only 10% of American families fit the traditional model of the two-parent family with children, a wage-earning husband, and a homemaker wife. Even among two-parent families, the proportion of those in which the husband is the only wage earner has dropped to 20%; for minority families, it is even lower (Spain, 1988).

Modifications are also occurring in men's roles, albeit less dramatically than those reported in women's lives. A number of studies indicate that men today base their self-evaluations less on work-related issues, and more on family-related issues, than in previous times (Gilbert, 1985; Pleck, 1985, 1987). Barnett and Baruch (1987) reported that men (and women) who use both employment and family relationships in defining their adult lives experience psychological and physical health benefits. Thus, adult men and women are becoming increasingly similar in the ways they define well-being, although there is still considerable disparity in how roles are actually performed. Wives in dual-earner families, for example, do significantly more of the household work and parenting than do husbands (Pleck, 1985).

Barnett and Baruch (1987) further examined how gender influences involvement in social roles and outcomes of stress and well-being. They identified two hypotheses as underlying the research on gender and involvement in social roles. The "social-role hypothesis" predicts no differences in the nature of social roles. Thus, occupancy of the employment role or spouse role would accrue the same benefits and costs to women and men. In contrast, the second hypothesis—"the sex-role hypothesis"—predicts that the nature of role demands differs by gender, which, in turn, produces differential costs and benefits of role occupancy for women and men.

Available research supports the "sex-role hypothesis." Marriage, for example, appears to benefit men more than women (Bernard, 1982; Thompson & Walker, 1989). More wives than husbands (a) report marital dissatisfaction, frustration, and marital problems; (b) have considered separation or divorce; (c) have regretted their marriages; (d) seek marital counseling; and (e) initiate divorce proceedings. As Bernard (1982) noted, it is not the complaints of wives that demonstrate how damaging marriage can be for women, but rather the poor mental and emotional health of married women compared to married men or unmarried women (Russo, 1986). The overall effects of employment appear more beneficial for men than for women, most likely because men earn more and have more opportunities for advancement, and because women carry more of the home and family responsibilities (Thompson & Walker, 1989; Walker & Wallston, 1985).

The most essential family resource is spouse support—support by the husband for the wife's occupational work and support by the wife for the husband's involvement in parenting and housework (Barnett & Baruch, 1987; Gilbert, 1985). Stress is minimized when the husband has positive attitudes toward the wife's career and involves himself in housework and parenting (Thompson & Walker, 1989). Overall, how roles are combined and the quality of those roles are more important indicators of well-being than is role occupancy per se (Baruch & Barnett, 1987).

The Dual-Career Family

The concern with gender in this chapter makes investigations of the two-career family particularly relevant. Dual-career families are a variation of the nuclear family in which both spouses pursue a lifelong career, relatively uninterrupted, and also establish and develop a family life that often includes children. The uniqueness of the dual-career life-style comes partly from the assumption that the husband and wife both engage in occupational and family work and that they share home and paid work roles in a relatively egalitarian manner. Another important contributor to the uniqueness of this life-style, and one that is often overlooked, is the assumed compatibility of occupational and family systems.

Despite the assumption of egalitarianism, considerable variation exists within the dual-career category (Gilbert, 1985). Some partners achieve a role-sharing marriage; others remain fairly traditional in role behaviors within the home. Useful to understanding this variation is Peplau's (1983) classification of marital roles into three types: traditional, modern, and egalitarian. These three types basically differ on two dimensions—power (the extent to which the husband is more dominant than the wife) and role specialization (the extent of role sharing between the spouses). According to Peplau, "Traditional marriage is based on a form of benevolent male dominance coupled with clearly specialized roles (assigned on the basis of gender). Egalitarian marriage rejects both of these ideas. Modern marriage represents a middle position" (p. 252).

Numerous studies indicate that many dual-career marriages are far from egalitarian (Thompson & Walker, 1989). In an in-depth study of men in dual-career families, Gilbert (1985) found three marital types, which she labeled traditional, participant, and role-sharing, similar to the traditional, modern, and egalitarian types identified by Peplau. In a traditional dual-career family, the responsibility for family work is retained by the woman, who adds the career role to her traditionally held family role. In the participant type, the parenting is shared by the spouses, but the woman retains responsibility for household duties. In this situation, as in the modern marriage identified by Peplau (1983), male dominance is muted and gender-based role specialization is less extensive. In role-sharing dual-career families, both spouses are actively involved in both household duties and parenting. Thus, role sharing in the private lives of heterosexual partners represents the elimination of gender-based role specialization and power associated with male dominance, as evidenced by comparability in such indicators as spouses' salaries, sources of spouse support, and involvement in family responsibilities (Gilbert, 1985). However, because such marriages exist within a larger world of gender inequity, role sharing is still best understood as an ideal rather than as a normative pattern.

Factors influencing the type of marital role pattern adopted in dual-career families can be divided into three major categories: personal factors, relational factors, and environmental factors (Gilbert, 1988; Gilbert & Rachlin, 1987). Personal factors include personality characteristics, attitudes, values, interests, and abilities. Examples of relational factors are sources of power in the relationship (e.g., expert or coercive power) and tasks that need to be done to maintain the family system. Environmental factors refer to the structure of occupations, societal norms and attitudes, and social networks and support systems. Satisfaction with the particular pattern adopted depends on these same factors, as well as on the degree of congruence and mutuality between spouses.

Sources of Stress Related to Gender

One area receiving considerable attention by researchers is *how partners handle home and work roles* and, more particularly, the degree of men's involvement in family work (Crouter, Perry-Jenkins, Huston, & McHale, 1987). Many men advocate equality as an ideal but in reality they may view their work as primary. The emotional support they provide to their spouses and their level of involvement in family work may reflect this view. Needless to say, being a supportive husband or involved father is difficult when doing so is experienced as infringing on a husband's dominance or as interfering with his career ambition.

Men's participation in family work continues to increase, more so in the area of parenting than in the area of household work (Dancer & Gilbert, 1990; Pleck, 1983, 1985, 1987). When both parents of preschoolers are employed, studies indicate that fathers and mothers spend about the same total time in direct interaction with their children as do parents in families in which only the husband is employed (Jump & Haas, 1987; Scarr, Phillips, & McCartney, 1989). Men's involvement in household work, although increasing and significantly higher than that of men in single-wage families, shows a good deal of variation. On the average, wives still do more than husbands, but many husbands do as much as wives and some do more (Gilbert, 1985, 1988; Pleck, 1985). Gilbert (1985) specifically investigated husbands' involvement in housework and parenting in a sample of dual-career families. Spouses in approximately one-third of the sample participated equally in both parenting and household activities; another one-third of the sample participated equally in parenting only. Wives did most of the parenting and household work in the final one-third of the families. Reports from other researchers parallel these findings (Thompson & Walker, 1989).

In families in which wives are employed full-time, their marital satisfaction is highly associated with husbands' involvement in family work and husbands' support for the wives' employment (Baruch & Barnett, 1987). Perry-Jenkins and Crouter (1990) studied the relationship between men's attitudes about the provider role (particularly regarding the issue of who should be responsible for the family's financial security) and their contribution to household work and marital satisfaction. As predicted, husbands having "co-provider" orientations involved themselves more in family work and reported higher marital satisfaction. Thus, men who felt a congruency between their role beliefs and the enactment of roles within the home were more satisfied with their marriage. Husbands in dual-wage families who lack the skills—emotional, behavioral, attitudinal, or otherwise—to involve themselves in family work appear the most distressed (Pleck, 1987).

Child Rearing

This topic is highly investigated. Parenting in our culture is typically equated with mothering. Research initially focused on comparisons of children reared in traditional and dual-wage homes. Results indicated that children are not at added risk if they receive day care instead of parental care for some portion of the day, and that in some ways such children may benefit (Hoffman, 1989; Scarr et al., 1989). Both girls and boys, for example, appear to develop less stereotypic sex role attitudes in day care, and boys from blue-collar families may obtain higher scores on measures of cognitive development and socioemotional adjustment (Hoffman, 1989).

Interest next moved to investigations of the kinds of care provided, definitions of optimal care, and the impact of employers' policies on family life and spouses' well-being (Zedeck & Mosier, 1990). Given current employment benefits and policies, for example, women are better able than men to ask for and receive the accommodations necessary for combining work and family responsibilities (e.g., maternity leaves, flexible schedules). Thus, these policies reflect a traditional workplace culture in which women leave the workplace and men are unencumbered by family responsibilities. As Congresswoman Pat Schroeder (1985) noted, "If the father would want to take off [to stay home with a newborn infant], if he even mentions it, it's like he has lace on his jockey shorts. You don't do that in America" (p. 16).

Generally, role conflict and day-to-day stress associated with parenting are lowest when: (a) employers of both spouses have benefit policies that are family-responsive; (b) one spouse feels he or she will not have to do all the accommodating; (c) husbands make a commitment to involve themselves in parenting; (d) traditional ideas that a child should be reared full-time by the mother are redefined by the spouses; and (e) suitable child care is located (Barnett et al., 1987; Gilbert, 1985, 1988).

Suggestions for Research

One general suggestion would be to focus studies on variables that connect the well-being of individuals in single-parent or dual-earner families to the policies of the workplace. Examples include longitudinal studies exploring the relation between kinds of maternity/paternity leaves used by parents and indexes of family well-being. Investigations of the use of formal and informal paternity leaves are particularly needed (Pleck, 1987). One of the principal longer-term questions in the area of multiple role involvement relates to the shifting of men's roles and self-definitions. For men who want a greater caregiving role, approaches and interventions must be developed to overcome the influences of the workplace and society that discourage and devalue men's involvement with their children. Moreover, because family roles have not been included in the study of men's well-being, we know little about the effects of quality of experience in family roles on men's psychological distress and well being.

DIRECTIONS FOR RESEARCH AND EDUCATION

Thus far, I have described pervasive ways in which societal attitudes, structures, and norms shape the lives of women and men. Many individuals are striving to create new images of themselves as women and men. Counseling psychologists, as educators, advocates, and researchers, can help them to understand how sexism enters into the fabric of their lives and how gender operates within the society to influence their expectations, choices, and accomplishments. This section addresses approaches to research and education, offering broad suggestions in four areas that can then be applied to a number of specific content areas: (a) broadening research methodologies to include contextual models of behavior, (b) studying gender as a process, (c) studying the diversity in women's and men's lives, and (d) incorporating gender into curricula.

Broadening Research Methodologies to Include Interactive and Contextual Models of Human Behavior

Sherif (1979), among others, pointed out that certain beliefs about how to pursue knowledge have made psychological research peculiarly prone to bias in its conception, execution, and interpretation. She identified several problematic beliefs. First, the methodology promoted in psychology rests on the assumption that the causes of events can be determined by breaking events down into their component parts and then studying the interrelationship of the parts, stripped or isolated from their social or cultural context. As a result, "general laws about the relationship among variables are obtained by comparing averages of the responses made by a sizable number of individuals, who are regarded as being without a background, personal history, or gender that might have anything to do with their responses in the situation" (p. 46). Moreover, only one methodology is acceptable: experiments in which certain selected "independent" variables, presumably causative, are manipulated while other possible causes are held constant or controlled. Thus created, the independent variable is somehow regarded as purer, less contaminated by past experiences. Sherif recommended that we broaden the framework within which knowledge is sought and then relate events within that broadened framework through a variety of methods and research techniques.

Many later writers concurred. Keller (1985, p. 177), in describing the past decade of feminist criticism in the natural sciences concluded, "feminist scholars inevitably began to question the gender neutrality of the very criteria defining 'scientific.' . . . Objectivity itself and the mastering of mother nature came under suspicion as androcentric goals." She advocated a reclamation, from within science, of science as a human project, renouncing the division of emotional and intellectual labor that maintains science as a male preserve: "In my vision of science, it is not the taming of nature that is sought, but the taming of hegemony" (p. 178). In describing how science might be different, Keller described the visionary work of Barbara McClintock in the area of classical genetics and cytology. To McClintock, the goal of science was not to predict but to understand; not to have power through manipulation, but to have the power (or empowerment) that results from understanding the world around us and that simultaneously reflects and affirms our connection to the world we are striving to understand.

In a paper written shortly before her untimely death, Sherif (1982) described concepts necessary to understanding women and men in their social context and articulated the relationships among gender, the self-system, reference persons, social power, status, and role relationships. The concept of the self-system summarizes the individual's psychological relationships to significant properties of the social environment, including gender categorization. Social power refers to the control of resources, and status is social position with respect to social power. Reference groups/persons, according to Sherif, serve as tools to trace the links between gender in the self-system and gender in a social context. Study of reference groups and of their norms and values is central to understanding how individuals perceive situations and what they see as salient.

Reference persons and reference groups hold particular importance in Sherif's model. Actual membership in a group makes a difference, but psychological linkage to a group has consequences for an individual's behavior even when one is not a member. Thus, although a woman cannot be a man, she can adopt men as reference persons or groups, which traditional socialization expected women to do and which women entering careers today are often asked to do. Reference persons and groups also help determine what individuals attend to in a situation and how they construe the situation. Social scientists may err in concluding that situational factors or idiographic factors solely determine behavior and overlook conceptual links with reference persons/groups or categories. Thus, in studying the household work and parenting patterns of men and women in dual-career families, we need to find out who the reference persons/groups are for each spouse—their own parents, their colleagues, their employers, their friends, and so on. Those men who typically share household work and parenting with their spouses tend to have family members, colleagues, and friends who support their decisions, and they typically socialize with families who have made similar decisions on how to combine work and family (Gilbert, 1985). Similarly, in investigations of acquaintance rape, it may be useful to explore the reference persons/groups (e.g., peer group, role models from films or television, family members) of the participants.

Further research on structural factors such as power and status is particularly needed. Possibilities include the following.

1. *The power relations among men and between women and men.* Study of this topic would allow for a more differentiated conception of patriarchy (Brod, 1987). We need to understand how society grants certain privileges and advantages to some men over others, and at the same time encourages men to exercise power over women.

2. *Men's response to loss of power over women.* Some women have achieved increased status and economic power. Kahn (1984) and Goode (1982) provided thoughtful analyses of men's response to equality and their loss of power. They identified three important directions for research in this area: the dynamics of power change, the "fear of power loss" for men, and the effects of power abuse. Contrary to societal expectations, many man feel powerless regarding control over resources or their own lives (Goode, 1982).

3. *Influence of power on self-concept.* As noted earlier, women and men continue to differ greatly in their access to power, control of resources, and control over their own bodies. Although we know a good deal about how this affects individuals' mental and physical health, we know much less about how it influences self-systems and role relations.

Studying Gender as a Process

The importance of conceptualizing gender as a process was emphasized earlier. Deaux (1984), building on the arguments of Sherif (1979, 1982), concluded her analysis of a decade's research on gender as follows:

> *Views of gender as a static category must give way, or at least be accompanied by, theories that treat sex-related phenomena as a process—a process that is influenced by individual choices, molded by situational pressures, and ultimately understandable only in the context of social interaction. (p. 115)*

More recently, Deaux and her colleagues proposed a process model of gender in social interaction (Deaux & Major, 1987).

Research summarized by Maccoby (1990) nicely illustrates the usefulness of studying gender as a process. Maccoby and her colleagues were interested in how social interactions influence the way both sexes behave. In a study of 33-month-old children, it was noted that passivity in girls was a function of interaction, not an innate personality trait, as had been presumed. The only time girls in the study stood passively by and watched was when the partner was a boy. A second longitudinal study with 4- and 6-year-old children showed that girls preferred same-sex playmates to other-sex playmates three times as much at age 4 and eleven times as much at age 6. Two factors were proposed as possible explanations: (a) that girls find boys' orientation toward dominance distasteful; (b) that girls have difficulty influencing boys, perhaps because they are reluctant to go against internalized conceptions of appropriate role behavior.

Other studies provide support for these explanations. Maccoby cited a study that found that, when preschool-aged boy–girl pairs were allowed to watch cartoons through a one-person movie viewer, the boys monopolized the viewer when the children were alone. When an adult was present, the girls used the viewer as much as the boys did. A series of studies with college students similarly demonstrated the influence of certain situational constraints on dominance behavior in women. In the first study of this kind, Megargee (1969) paired high and low dominant partners in same- and mixed-sex dyads, and asked them to choose a leader to perform a machine repair task. When leadership was made salient, high dominant individuals assumed the leadership role almost 80% of the time, except when high dominant women were paired with low dominant men. In this pairing, the high dominant female partner became leader only 20% of the time (high dominant women were not paired with high dominant men in the study). Modifications of the task from masculine in nature to being gender-neutral or feminine only moderately increased the percentage of high dominant women willing to take the leadership role when paired with low dominant men.

Building on this work, Davis and Gilbert (1989) included a high–high dominance pairing as well as a two-phase task. Thus, partners in the mixed-sex dyads were classified as high or low in dispositional dominance and grouped into four dominance categories (high–high, low–high, high–low, and low–low). Partners in the dyads first interacted to complete a task and then selected a leader for a second task, the one used by Megargee (1969). Prior task interactions diminished status differences between male and female partners, allowing high dominant women paired with low dominant men to become leader 71% of the time for the second task, far more often than previous studies have found for this pairing. However, high dominant women paired with high dominant men assumed the leadership role only 31% of the time, indicating that their level of dominance expression was influenced by their male partner's dominance level.

As the authors explained, high dominant women might accept the legitimacy of their male partners' assumed power or status and thus assume a follower role.

The following two directions for research involving gender as process are suggested.

1. *Sexual relationships between therapists and clients.* Social interactions and interpersonal expectancies, such as those just described, may provide important insights into the dynamics of situations involving eroticism with clients. As mentioned earlier, approximately 90% of reported cases of sexual intimacy involve male therapists and female clients. Research on interpersonal expectancy indicates that men's expectancies are a more important determinant of the interaction sequence in mixed-sex dyads than are women's, and that women in mixed-sex dyads confirmed men's behavioral expectancies more than men confirmed women's (Christensen & Rosenthal, 1982). Such interpersonal expectancies may derive from gender socialization processes, in particular those articulated by Pleck (1981) and Westkott (1986).

2. *Men as fathers.* When a father is close to his children, how does his participation in child rearing affect his feelings about himself as a man and his children's cognitions about men? Pleck (1987) hypothesized that a father's involvement may be beneficial because it helps revise traditional views of roles. Hoffman (1989) wondered whether the consistent finding that children of employed mothers hold less stereotypic attitudes about sex roles than do children of nonemployed mothers may be partially explained by the parental division of labor vis-à-vis home roles. Two aspects of fathers' behaviors appear relevant here: role modeling and motivations for involvement in home and family roles. That is, the male parent in dual-earner families, not unlike the female parent, may model less stereotypic behavior, which in turn provides the child with alternative images of adult roles and how they can be combined. Thus, children reared in families in which fathers desire active involvement may learn that man can be warm and supportive of others, as well as achieving.

Studying the Diversity in Women's and Men's Lives

There is diversity in the world of women and men, and part of our task as counseling psychologists is to know and understand that variation. That has not been the approach taken in studying women, as Heilbrun (1988) so eloquently described in *Writing a Woman's Life*:

> *Women have long been nameless. They have not been persons. Handed by a father to another man, the husband, they have been objects for circulation, exchanging one name for another. That is why the story of Persephone and Demeter is the story of all women who marry: why death and marriage were the only two possible ends for women in novels, and were frequently the same end. For the young, women died as a subject, ceased as an entity. For this reason, then, women who began to write another story often wrote it under another name. They were inventing something so daring they could not risk, in their own person, the frightful consequences. (p. 121)*

In a now classic article, "Homogenizing the American Woman: The Power of an Unconscious Ideology," Bem and Bem (1970) depicted the difference in how women's and men's lives were approached by social scientists. Men's lives were too varied to be predicted at birth; diversity was anticipated and respected. Women's lives, in contrast, were predictable and thus not necessary to study; all women desired the same goals—

marriage and children. When women were employed, homogeneity again described their choices. Most were clerical workers, nurses, teachers, or service workers.

Although women today clearly have more choices and opportunities than in 1972, the occupational distribution of women within the labor force has changed only slightly over time (Rix, 1987). Clerical jobs account for a larger proportion of employed women now than in 1950. Whereas approximately one in four working women held a secretarial job in 1950, approximately one in three now holds such a position (Spain, 1988). Moreover, women are still depicted as desperate for men. The February 1989 issue of *Cosmopolitan* magazine was on the subject of "How to Attract a Man Like Crazy"; a recent book, *Fringe Benefits* (Gates, 1989), informed women about what occupations were most likely to help them land a husband.

Differences among men have been much more recognized but here, too, cultural proscriptions and androcentric views narrowed and defined areas considered worthy of legitimate inquiry. Earlier theories used White heterosexual middle-class men as the paragon of manliness. The experiences of gay men and men of different ethnic and cultural backgrounds, when considered, were compared to the normative experiences of these men.

Important steps already have been taken to broaden our understanding of the human experience through the inclusion of women and of populations of men often ignored. Examples include research in such areas as menstruation (Golub, 1984), menopause (National Women's Health Network, 1989), sexual expression (Kitzinger, 1983; Loulan, 1984; Zilbergeld, 1978), fathering (Pleck, 1987), ethnicity and cultural diversity (Amaro & Russo, 1987; Atkinson & Hackett, 1988; Franklin, 1984; Hooks, 1981; Staples, 1982) and counseling psychology interventions (Gelso & Fassinger, 1990). Much more research is needed, however. Two suggestions about ways to broaden future research follow.

1. *Broaden models of healthy functioning to include the experiences of groups typically considered deviant.* A case in point is the study of gay men and lesbians. Theories of intimacy, love, and enduring relationships were developed from extant views about women and men in a society organized along gender lines (Eldridge, 1987). Moreover, when researchers studied same-sex relationships, findings from studies with men would often be generalized to women, ignoring gender as a variable. Brown (1989) proposed an alternative model for psychological inquiry based on the experiences of lesbians and gay men. Rather than using heterosexual behaviors as the norm, it might be possible that what is normative, say, for lesbian couples is in fact healthy for any intimate pair. Lesbian dual-career couples, for example, are by and large egalitarian in how they handle household and parenting responsibilities (Eldridge & Gilbert, 1990). Although heterosexual dual-career marriages also are egalitarian in principle, as noted earlier in the chapter, this is not the normative pattern found among families (Gilbert & Rachlin, 1987; Thompson & Walker, 1989).

2. *Broaden the domains of human experiences investigated.* Aspects of the human experience traditionally relegated to women remain underresearched, particularly with regard to men (Shields, 1987). These are the personal, the emotional, and the sexual. The situation with AIDS raises two points in this regard. First, efforts to respond to the homosexual and heterosexual transmission of this disease require more knowledge than we now have about the motivations for men's sexual behavior and its relation to conceptions of masculinity. Do heterosexual and homosexual men learn the same norms for sexual behavior, since there is no anticipatory socialization for homosexuality in our culture (Kimmel & Levine, 1989)? If so, does sexual expression have the same meaning with regard to one's self-concept or does gender make a difference? Second, because AIDS was initially viewed as a homosexually transmitted disease, and many of its victims were men, the strong affection between men become more public and in that sense more known. At the same time, few studies have investigated the affective aspects of male friendships and the nature of emotional connections between men, heterosexual or homosexual. Similarly, few studies have looked at how friendships may function in men's lives.

Incorporating "Gender" into Curricula and Continuing Education Programs

Gender roles and beliefs are salient in the educational and psychotherapeutic processes. All educators and students, therapists and clients, remain profoundly influenced, and to some degree restricted, by their own socialization as women and men. This influence spills over into the process and goals of education. Yet very few APA-approved doctoral programs include courses that specifically address issues of gender in theory, research, and practice. For example, only 9% of the licensed psychologists surveyed by Pope, Keith-Spiegel, and Tabachnick (1986) reported that sexual attraction issues had been given adequate coverage in their graduate training program or internship; 55% indicated that they had received no education on such matters, 24% very little, and 12% only some education.

Of the APA Task Force recommendations (American Psychological Association, 1975), the one concerning sanctions against blatant sexist practices has been implemented, in principle, to the greatest extent (American Psychological Association, 1981; Committee on Women in Psychology, 1989). Since that time, sexual intimacies with clients have been specifically described as unethical conduct in *The Ethical Principles of Psychologists,* although, as we know, sexual contact with clients remains a problem for many psychologists (Pope & Bouhoutsos, 1986). The Task Force recommendations related to educational reform have received less attention both with regard to the content and process of educational programs generally and in the preparation for counseling and psychotherapy specifically. Reports on erotic behavior between male educators and their female students or trainees, noted earlier, reflect the profound insensitivity to gender and power that abounds in educational institutions. Male professors and female students are not individuals making personal choices in a vacuum; they are members of an institution and social system that accord different statuses and privileges based on gender. Several initiatives are needed to change this situation.

1. *Education of educators.* Educators need to evaluate their own attitudes, values, and behaviors with regard to women and men and become educated about the psychology of women, men's and women's changing roles, and the gendered nature of our society. Such education does not simply accrue from involvement in personal and professional relationships with women or men. Educators need to go beyond their own personal views and become familiar with the rich body of literature on gender that has accumulated in the past 20 years (Bronstein & Quina, 1988; Crawford & Marecek, 1989a; Richardson & Johnson, 1984; reference list of this chapter).

2. *Curriculum revision.* Education and training need to be broadened so that psychologists recognize and understand topics such as those discussed in this chapter. The restrictive effects of gender socialization on the lives of individual women and men must be understood by counseling psychologists who are engaged in teaching, research, and/or practice. More attention in coursework should be given to the social construction of gender and how it relates to therapist–client dynamics and the process and goals

of therapy. Publications such as Bronstein and Quina's (1988) *Teaching a Psychology of People: Resources for Gender and Sociocultural Awareness* (available from the APA) and the Federation of Professional Women's (1982) *Women and Psychotherapy: A Consumer Handbook* provide excellent resources for instructors.

Another useful resource is a conceptual model recently described by Good, Gilbert, and Scher (1990). These authors offered a synthesis of feminist therapy and knowledge about gender in their Gender Aware Therapy (GAT). The principles underlying this approach to counseling and behavior include principles discussed in this chapter: viewing gender as an integral aspect of counseling and mental health, considering clients' problems within their societal context, and actively seeking to change gender injustices experienced by women and men. The issues involved in sexual harassment and combining work and family, for example, may differ markedly by gender, and these differences should be appreciated by counselors. A male client who reports sexual harassment from his female boss (an unlikely event) would be expected to present a different set of issues with regard to gender than would a female client in a parallel situation. The same would be true for a male client who was furious about being turned down for a paternity leave (a likely event) versus a female client in a parallel situation.

DIRECTIONS FOR SOCIAL ACTION

Primary prevention often calls for advocacy and social action. Supporting the cause of others is a hallmark of counseling psychology. But "causes" first need to be clarified and framed within a perspective that puts problems in a social framework. Counseling psychologists are in a unique position to help policy makers recognize and understand that the root of many social and individual problems resides in the system and not in the individual who is the identified client or victim. In this final section, three areas related to gender advocacy are described.

Identifying Gender-Related Issues and Biases Inherent in Policy

Psychologists *can* influence public policy when they identify and explicate sex-biased practices in current policy and the real effects of such practices on women's and men's lives. Psychologists, for example, have played an active role in educating policy makers and judicial bodies about the nature of sexual harassment and its effects on women's performance and well-being. An often cited *amicus curiae* brief presented before the U. S. Supreme Court in a case involving sexual harassment was prepared by the APA with assistance from researchers in that area (American Psychological Association, 1988).

Gender-relevant theory and research can also influence child-care policy. Knowledge needs to be conveyed to policy makers about (a) the changing conceptions of gender roles; (b) the need for quality, affordable child care and what such quality care would entail; and (c) the changes needed in the structure of work, to allow both men and women to responsibly and lovingly parent their children (Zigler & Frank, 1988).

As counseling psychologists, we also need to concern ourselves with the bias against women in medical research, which parallels the gender bias in psychological research described earlier. Biomedical research on diseases that affect both women and men typically use only men as subjects, even though results are generalized to women and men (Wolinsky, 1989). The basic research on antidepressants, for example, was performed on male rats to avoid the estrus cycles. The biggest consumers of antidepressants, however, are women.

Finally, we need to continue to counter extant views that, in effect, hold the medical model as the desired model for the treatment of problems associated with physical and psychological health. The bulk of funds available from the National Institutes of Mental Health, for instance, is allocated for research on biomedical factors that reside within the individual. Less funding is earmarked for research that focuses on psychosocial factors such as poverty or chronic physical or emotional abuse (Koss, 1990).

Advocating Sources of Funding That Serve Preventive Purposes

Two of the most striking demographic trends in the United States today are women's increasing poverty and the increasing number of women who are single heads of households (Spain, 1988). Of the population living in poverty, 28% of Whites and 61% of Blacks live in female-headed households. Impoverished women are a high-risk population because they lack supports or resources, experience undue stress, and have reduced access to health services. The problems of these women must be viewed as stressors stemming from the structure of gender (and race) relationships—especially from the lower status, power, and socioeconomic resources held by women—and not simply as deficiencies and inadequacies within these women, which in effect would blame them for their impoverished conditions (National Institute of Mental Health, 1986). Policy makers need our guidance in making possible environments that are conducive to the positive development of these individuals and their children.

Developing Educational Programs That Serve Preventive Purposes

A model program for sexual harassment education was developed by Paludi and her colleagues at Hunter College (Paludi, 1990). This multipronged program involved students, administrators, and professors. Surveys were conducted to document existing problems, and university-wide programs were held to disseminate findings. Students and faculty were educated about the nature of sexual harassment, conversation hours and workshops were conducted with students and faculty, and clear policies were set in place. Other universities have conducted relevant studies and/or have had publicized difficulties on their campuses, and they too have developed new policies; the University of Iowa has adopted an especially clear policy on sexual harassment and consensual relationships. This policy states: "Sexual harassment subverts the mission of the University and threatens the careers, educational experience, and well-being of students, faculty, and staff." The activities and new policies at these major universities may make a positive difference in the developmental experiences of thousands of adolescents and young adults.

CONCLUDING REMARKS

Counseling psychology is unique in its focus on and commitment to both individual change and broad social change. Awareness and understanding of gender as a process and as an organizer of social relations can shape and direct education, research, and treatment, such that the individual issues of women and men can be understood within the context of a society that has denied and, to a large degree, continues to deny women and men equal access to personal, interpersonal, and societal resources. Carolyn Jacklin (1989), a noted scholar in the area of gender, recently concluded: "The times are changing. Change may be occurring too quickly for some, but change is not occurring quickly enough for many girls and boys (and women and men) limited by their gender roles to less than full lives" (p. 132).

REFERENCES

Ad Hoc Committee on Women (Division 17). (1979). Principles concerning the counseling and psychotherapy of women. *The Counseling Psychologist, 8,* 21.

Aisenberg, N., & Harrington, M. (1988). *Women of academe: Outsiders in the sacred grove.* Amherst, MA: University of Massachusetts Press.

Albee, G. W. (1981). The prevention of sexism. *Professional Psychology, 12,* 20–28.

Amaro, H., & Russo, N. F. (1987). Hispanic women and mental health: Contemporary issues in research and practice. *Psychology of Women Quarterly, 11* (Special issue), 391–535.

American Psychological Association. (1975). Report of the Task Force on Sex Bias and Sex-Role Stereotyping in Psychotherapeutic Practice. *American Psychologist, 30,* 1169–1175.

American Psychological Association. (1981). Ethical principles of psychologists (revised). *American Psychologist, 36,* 633–638.

American Psychological Association. (1988). Brief for *amicus curiae,* Supreme Court of the United States, *Price Waterhouse v. Ann B. Hopkins.* (Available from the American Psychological Association, 1200 17th St., NW, Washington, DC 20036.)

American Psychological Association. (1990). Report of the Ethics Committee. *American Psychologist, 45,* 873–874.

American Psychological Association, Task Force on Sex Bias and Sex-Role Stereotyping in Psychotherapeutic Practice. (1978). Guidelines for therapy with women. *American Psychologist, 33,* 1122–1123.

American Psychological Association Insurance Trust. (1990). Letter to members.

Andersen, H. C. (1956). *Andersen's fairy tales.* New York: Doubleday.

Astin, H. S. (1985). The meaning of work in women's lives: A sociopsychological model of career choice and work behavior. *The Counseling Psychologist, 12,* 117–126.

Atkinson, D. R., & Hackett, G. (Eds.). (1988). *Counseling non-ethnic American minorities.* Springfield, IL: Thomas.

Attie, I., & Brooks-Gunn, J. (1987). Weight concerns as chronic stressors in women. In R. C. Barnett, L. Biener, & G. K. Baruch (Eds.), *Gender and stress* (pp. 218–253). New York: Free Press.

Attie, I., & Brooks-Gunn, J. (1989). Development of eating problems in adolescent girls: A longitudinal study. *Developmental Psychology, 25,* 70–79.

Balswick, J. (1988). *The inexpressive male.* Lexington, MA: Lexington Books/Heath.

Barak, A., & Fisher, W. A. (1989). Counselor and therapist gender bias? More questions than answers. *Professional Psychology, 20,* 377–383.

Barnett, R. C., & Baruch, G. K. (1987). Social roles, gender, and psychological distress. In R. C. Barnett, L. Biener, & G. K. Baruch (Eds.), *Gender and stress* (pp. 122–143). New York: Free Press.

Barnett, R. C., Biener, L., & Baruch, G. K. (Eds.). (1987). *Gender and stress.* New York: Free Press.

Baruch, G. K., & Barnett, R. C. (1987). Role quality and psychological well being. In F. Crosby (Ed.), *Spouse, parent, worker* (pp. 63–84). New Haven, CT: Yale University Press.

Bates, C., & Brodsky, A. (1989). *Sex in the therapy hour.* New York: Guilford Press.

Bem, S. L., & Bem, D. J. (1970). Case study of a nonconscious ideology: Training the woman to know her place. In D. J. Bem (Ed.), *Beliefs, attitudes, and human affairs.* Belmont, CA: Brooks/Cole.

Bernard, J. (1982). *The future of marriage.* New Haven, CT: Yale University Press.

Betz, N. E., & Fitzgerald, L. F. (Eds.). (1987). *The career psychology of women.* Orlando, FL: Academic Press.

Brannon, R. (1985). A scale for measuring attitudes about masculinity. In A. Sargent (Ed.), *Beyond sex roles* (pp. 110–116). St. Paul, MN: West Publishing.

Brod, H. (Ed.). (1987). *The making of masculinities—The new men's studies.* Boston: Allen & Unwin.

Brodsky, A., & Hare-Mustin, R. (1980). *Women and psychotherapy: An assessment of research and practice.* New York: Guilford Press.

Bronstein, P., & Quina, K. (Eds.). (1988). *Teaching a psychology of people: Resources for gender and sociocultural awareness.* Washington, DC: American Psychological Association.

Broverman, I. K., Vogel, S. R., Broverman, D. M., Clarkson, F. E., & Rosenkrantz, P. S. (1972). Sex-role stereotypes: A current appraisal. *Journal of Social Issues, 28*(2), 59–78.

Brown, L. S. (1989). New voices, new visions: Toward a lesbian/gay paradigm for psychology. *Psychology of Women Quarterly, 13,* 445–458.

Brown, S. D., Alpert, D., Lent, R. W., Hunt, G., & Brady, T. (1988). Perceived social support among college students: Factor structure of the Social Support Inventory. *Journal of Counseling Psychology, 35,* 472–478.

Brownmiller, S. (1975). *Against our will: Men, women, and rape.* New York: Simon & Schuster.

Chesler, P. (1972). *Women and madness.* Garden City, NY: Doubleday.

Christensen, D., & Rosenthal, R. (1982). Gender and nonverbal decoding skill as determinants of interpersonal expectancy effects. *Journal of Personality and Social Psychology, 42,* 75–87.

Committee on Women in Psychology. (1989). If sex enters into the psychotherapy relationship. *Professional Psychology, 20,* 112–115.

Courtois, C. A., & O'Neil, J. M. (Eds.). (1988). Victimization. *The Counseling Psychologist, 16*(4) (Special issue).

Crawford, M., & Marecek, J. (1989a). Psychology reconstructs the female: 1968–1988. *Psychology of Women Quarterly, 13,* 147–165.

Crawford, M., & Marecek, J. (1989b). Feminist theory, feminist psychology: A bibliography. *Psychology of Women Quarterly, 13,* 477–491.

Crouter, A. C., Perry-Jenkins, M., Huston, T. L., & McHale, S. M. (1987). Processes underlying father involvement in dual-earner and single-earner families. *Developmental Psychology, 23,* 431–440.

Dancer, S. L., & Gilbert, L. A. (1990, June). Participation in family work in dual-career, dual-earner, and traditional families. Paper presented at the annual meeting of the American Psychological Society, Dallas, TX.

Davis, B. M., & Gilbert, L. A. (1989). Effect of dispositional and situational influences on women's dominance expression in mixed-sex dyads. *Journal of Personality and Social Psychology, 57,* 294–300.

Deaux, K. (1984). From individual differences to social categories: Analysis of a decade's research on gender. *American Psychologist, 39,* 105–116.

Deaux, K. (1985). Sex and gender. In L. Porter & M. Rosenzweig (Eds.), *Annual review of psychology 1985* (Vol. 36, pp. 49–81). Palo Alto, CA: Annual Reviews.

Deaux, K., & Major, B. (1987). Putting gender into context: An interactive model of gender-related behavior. *Psychological Review, 94,* 369–389.

Denmark, F., Russo, N. F., Frieze, I. H., & Sechzer, J. A. (1988). Guidelines for avoiding sexism in psychological research. *American Psychologist, 43,* 582–585.

Eagly, A. H., & Steffen, V. J. (1986). Gender and aggressive behavior: A meta-analytic review of the social-psychological literature. *Psychological Bulletin, 100,* 309–330.

Eldridge, N. S. (1987). Gender issues in counseling same-sex couples. *Professional Psychology: Theory and Practice, 18,* 567–572.

Eldridge, N. S., & Gilbert, L. A. (1990). Correlates of relationship satisfaction in lesbian couples. *Psychology of Women Quarterly, 14,* 43–62.

Enns, C. Z., & Hackett, G. (1990). Comparisons of feminist and nonfeminist women's reactions to variants of nonsexist and feminist counseling. *Journal of Counseling Psychology, 37,* 33–40.

Erikson, E. (1968). *Identity, youth, and crisis.* New York: Norton.

Estrich, S. (1987). *Real rape: How the legal system victimizes women who say no.* Cambridge, MA: Harvard University Press.

Ethical Principles Revised. (1990). Comments are sought on proposed revision. *The APA Monitor, 21*(6), 28–32.

Fausto-Sterling, A. (1985). *Myths of gender: Biological theories about men and women.* New York: Basic Books.

Federation of Professional Women. (1982). *Women and psychotherapy: A consumer handbook.* (Available from FOPW, 1825 Connecticut Ave., NW, Suite 403, Washington, DC 20009.)

Feingold, A. (1988). Cognitive gender differences are disappearing. *American Psychologist, 43,* 95–103.

Fitzgerald, L. F., Gold, Y., Ormerod, A. J., & Weitzman, L. (1988). Academic harassment: Sex and denial in scholarly garb. *Psychology of Women Quarterly, 12,* 329–340.

Fitzgerald, L. F., & Nutt, R. (1986). The Division 17 principles concerning the counseling/ psychotherapy of women: Rationale and implementation. *The Counseling Psychologist, 14,* 180–216.

Fitzgerald, L. F., & Ormerod, A. J. (1991). Perceptions of sexual harassment: The influence of gender and academic context. *Psychology of Women Quarterly, 15,* 281–294.

Franklin, C. W., II. (1984). Black male–Black female conflict: Individually caused and culturally nurtured. *Journal of Black Studies, 15,* 139–154.

Freedman, R. (1986). *Beauty bound.* Lexington, MA: Heath.

Fulero, S. (1986). Insurance trust releases malpractice statistics. *The Ohio Psychologist, 33*(1), 18.

Gates, A. (1989). *Fringe benefits.* New York: Dell.

Gelso, C. J., & Fassinger, R. E. (1990). Counseling psychology: Theory and research on interventions. In M. R. Rosenzweig & L. W. Porter (Eds.), *Annual review of psychology* (pp. 355–386). Palo Alto, CA: Annual Reviews.

Gervasio, A. H., & Crawford, M. (1989). Social evaluations of assertiveness: A critique and speech act reformulation. *Psychology of Women Quarterly, 13,* 1–26.

Gidycz, C. A., & Koss, M. P. (1990). A comparison of group and individual sexual assault victims. *Psychology of Women Quarterly, 14,* 325–342.

Gilbert, L. A. (1980). Feminist therapy. In A. M. Brodsky & R. T. Hare-Mustin (Eds.), *Women and psychotherapy: An assessment of research and practice* (pp. 245–265). New York: Guilford Press.

Gilbert, L. A. (1985). *Men in dual-career families: Current realities and future prospects.* Hillsdale, NJ: Erlbaum.

Gilbert, L. A. (Ed.). (1987a). Dual-career families in perspective. *The Counseling Psychologist, 15*(1) (Special issue).

Gilbert, L. A. (1987b). Female and male emotional dependency and its implications for the therapist–client relationship. *Professional Psychology: Research and Practice, 18,* 555–561.

Gilbert, L. A. (1988). Sharing it all: The rewards and struggles of two-career families. New York: Plenum Press.

Gilbert, L. A., & Rachlin, V. (1987). Mental health and psychological functioning of dual-career families. *The Counseling Psychologist, 15,* 7–49.

Gilbert, L. A., & Scher, M. (1989). The power of an unconscious belief: Male entitlement and sexual intimacy with clients. *Professional Practice of Psychology, 8,* 94–108.

Gilmore, D. D. (1990). *Manhood in the making: Cultural concepts of masculinity.* New Haven, CT: Yale University Press.

Golub, S. (Ed.). (1984). Living the curse of menstruation: A feminist appraisal of the influence of menstruation on women's lives. New York: Haworth Press.

Good, G. E., Dell, D. M., & Mintz, L. M. (1989). The male role and gender role conflict: Relationships to help-seeking. *Journal of Counseling Psychology, 36,* 295–300.

Good, G. E., Gilbert, L. A., & Scher, M. (1990). Gender aware therapy: A synthesis of feminist therapy and knowledge about gender. *Journal of Counseling and Development, 68,* 376–380.

Good, G. E., & Mintz, L. M. (1990). Depression and the male gender role. *Journal of Counseling and Development, 68,* 20–30.

Goode, W. J. (1982). Why men resist. In B. Thorne (Ed.), *Rethinking the family: Some feminist questions* (pp. 131–150). White Plains, NY: Longman.

Gottlieb, B. H. (1983). *Social support strategies: Guidelines for mental health practice.* Beverly Hills, CA: Sage.

Gutek, B. A. (1986). *Sex and the workplace.* San Francisco: Jossey-Bass.

Gutek, B. A. (1989, March). Sexual harassment: A source of stress for employed women. Paper presented at the Radcliffe Conference on Women in the 21st Century, Cambridge, MA.

Harding, S. (Ed.). (1987). *Feminism and methodology.* Bloomington, IN: Indiana University Press.

Hare-Mustin, R. T. (1983). An appraisal of the relationship between women and psychotherapy: 80 years after the case of Dora. *American Psychologist, 38,* 593–601.

Hare-Mustin, R. T., & Marecek, J. (1990). *Making a difference: Psychology and the construction of gender.* New Haven, CT: Yale University Press.

Heilbrun, C. G. (1988). *Writing a woman's life.* New York: Ballantine Books.

Hoffman, L. W. (1989). Effects of maternal employment in the two-parent family. *American Psychologist, 44*, 283–292.

Hooks, B. (1981). *Ain't I a woman: Black women and feminism.* Boston, MA: South End Press.

Horney, K. (1937). *The neurotic personality of our time.* New York: Norton.

Jacklin, C. N. (1989). Female and male: Issues of gender. *American Psychologist, 44*, 127–133.

Jump, T. L., & Haas, L. (1987). Fathers in transition: Dual-career fathers' participation in child care. In M. S. Kimmel (Ed.), *Changing men: New directions in research on men and masculinity* (pp. 98–114). Beverly Hills: Sage.

Kahn, A. S. (1984). The power war: Male responses to power loss under equality. *Psychology of Women Quarterly, 8*, 234–247.

Keller, E. F. (1985). *Reflections on gender and science.* New Haven, CT: Yale University Press.

Kimmel, M. S., & Levine, M. P. (1989). Men and AIDS. In M. S. Kimmel & M. A. Messner (Eds.), *Men's lives* (pp. 344–354). New York: Macmillan.

Kimmel, M. S., & Messner, M. A. (Eds.). (1989). *Men's lives.* New York: Macmillan.

Kitchener, K. S. (1989, August). Unethical practices with students: Destroying the myths. Paper presented at the annual meeting of the American Psychological Association, New Orleans, LA.

Kitzinger, S. (1983). *Women's experience of sex.* New York: Penguin Press.

Klein, H. M., & Willerman, L. (1979). Psychological masculinity and femininity and typical and maximal dominance expression in women. *Journal of Personality and Social Psychology, 37*, 2059–2070.

Koss, M. P. (1990). The women's mental health research agency: Violence against women. *American Psychologist, 45*, 374–380.

Koss, M. P., & Burkhart, B. R. (1989). A conceptual analysis of rape victimization. *Psychology of Women Quarterly, 13*, 27–40.

Koss, M. P., Gidycz, C. A., & Wisniewski, N. (1987). The scope of rape: Incidence and prevalence of sexual aggression and victimization in a national sample of higher education students. *Journal of Consulting and Clinical Psychology, 55*, 162–170.

Lerman, H. (1976). What happens in feminist therapy. In S. Cox (Ed.), *Female psychology: The emerging self.* Chicago: Science Research Associates.

Lerner, H. E. (1983). Female dependency in context: Some theoretical and technical considerations. *American Journal of Orthopsychiatry, 53*, 697–705.

Lerner, H. G. (1988). *Women in therapy.* Northvale, NJ: Aronson.

Lott, B. (1987, August). *Masculine, feminine, androgynous, or human?* Paper presented at the meeting of the American Psychological Association, New York.

Loulan, J. (1984). *Lesbian sex.* San Francisco: Spinsters/Aunt Lute.

Maccoby, E. E. (1990). Gender and relationships: A developmental account. *American Psychologist, 45*, 513–520.

Maccoby, E. E., & Jacklin, C. N. (1974). *The psychology of sex differences.* Stanford, CA: Stanford University Press.

Marecek, J. (Ed.). (1989). Theory and method in feminist psychology. *Psychology of Women Quarterly, 13* (Special issue).

Marecek, J., & Hare-Mustin, R. T. (1987, March). *Feminism and therapy: Can this relationship be saved?* Paper presented at the meeting of the American Orthopsychiatric Association, Washington, DC.

McAdoo. (1989, March). Women and work: Climbing the crystal stairs. Paper presented at the Radcliffe Conference on Women in the 21st Century, Cambridge, MA.

McHugh, M. C., Koeske, R. D., & Frieze, I. H. (1986). Issues to consider in conducting nonsexist psychology: A review with recommendations. *American Psychologist, 41*, 879–890.

Meara, N. M., & Harmon, L. W. (1989). Accomplishments and disappointments of the Division 17 Committee on Women, 1970–1987. *The Counseling Psychologist, 17*, 314–331.

Mednick, M. T. (1989). On the politics of psychological constructs: Stop the bandwagon, I want to get off. *American Psychologist, 44*, 1118–1123.

Megargee, E. I. (1969). Influence of sex roles on the manifestation of leadership. *Journal of Applied Psychology, 53,* 377–382.

Miller, J. B. (1976). *Toward a new psychology of women.* Boston: Beacon Press.

Mintz, L. B., & O'Neil, J. M. (1990). Gender roles, sex, and the process of psychotherapy. *Journal of Counseling and Development, 68,* 381–387.

Morrison, A. M., & Glinow, M. V. (1990). Women and minorities in management. *American Psychologist, 45,* 200–208.

Morrison, A. M., White, R. P., Velsor, E. V., & The Center for Creative Leadership. (1987). *Breaking the glass ceiling: Can women reach the top of America's largest corporations?* New York: Addison-Wesley.

National Institute of Mental Health. (1986). Women's mental health: Agenda for research. (Available from the National Institute of Health, 5600 Fishers Lane, Rockville, MD 20857.)

National Women's Health Network. (1989). Taking hormones and women's health. (Available from NWHN, 1325 G St., NW, Washington, DC 20005.)

O'Neil, J. M. (1980). Male sex role conflicts, sexism, and masculinity: Psychological implications for men, women, and the counseling psychologist. *The Counseling Psychologist, 9*(2), 61–80.

O'Neil, J. M. (1982). Gender-role conflict and strain in men's lives. In K. Soloman & N. B. Levy (Eds.), *Men in transition* (pp. 5–44). New York: Plenum Press.

Otten, A. L. (1988, May 22). Surveying teen-agers on health and behavior. *Wall Street Journal,* p. B1.

Paludi, M. (Ed.). (1990). *Ivory power: Sexual harassment on campus.* Albany, NY: State University of New York Press.

Parlee, M. B. (1979). Psychology and women. *Signs, 5,* 121–133.

Peplau, L. A. (1983). Roles and gender. In H. H. Kelley, E. Berscheid, A. Christensen, J. H. Harvey, T. L. Huston, G. Levinger, E. McClintock, L. A. Peplau, & D. R. Peterson (Eds.), *Close relations* (pp. 220–264). New York: Freeman.

Perry-Jenkins, M., & Crouter, A. C. (1990). Men's provider role attitudes: Implications for household work and marital satisfaction. *Journal of Family Issues, 11,* 136–156.

Pleck, J. H. (1981). Men's power with women, other men, and society: A men's movement analysis. In R. A. Lewis (Ed.), *Men in difficult times: Masculinity today and tomorrow* (pp. 234–244). Englewood Cliffs, NJ: Prentice-Hall.

Pleck, J. H. (1983). Husbands' paid work and family roles: Current research issues. In H. Lopata & J. H. Pleck (Eds.), *Research in the interweave of social roles: Jobs and families* (pp. 251–333). Greenwich, CT: JAI Press.

Pleck, J. H. (1985). *Working wives/Working husbands.* Beverly Hills, CA: Sage.

Pleck, J. H. (1987). American fathering in historical perspective. In M. S. Kimmel (Ed.), *Changing men: New directions in research on men and masculinity* (pp. 83–97). Beverly Hills, CA: Sage.

Pogrebin, L. C. (1983). *Family politics: Love and power on an intimate frontier.* New York: McGraw-Hill.

Polivy, J., & Herman, C. P. (1985). Dieting and binging: A causal analysis. *American Psychologist, 40,* 193–201.

Pollitt, K. (1989, June 18). Violence in a man's world. *The New York Times Magazine,* pp. 16–18.

Pope, K. S. (1989). Sexual intimacies between psychologists and their students and supervisees: Research, standards, and professional liability. *Independent Practitioner, 9*(2), 33–41.

Pope, K. S. (1990). Therapist–patient sex as sex abuse: Six scientific, professional, and practical dilemmas in addressing victimization and rehabilitation. *Professional Psychology: Research and Practice, 21,* 227–239.

Pope, K. S., & Bouhoutsos, J. C. (1986). *Sexual intimacy between therapists and patients.* New York: Praeger.

Pope, K. S., Keith-Spiegel, P., & Tabachnick, B. G. (1986). Sexual attraction to clients: The human therapist and the (sometimes) inhuman training system. *American Psychologist, 41,* 147–158.

Richardson, M. S., & Johnson, M. (1984). Counseling women. In S. D. Brown & R. W. Lent (Eds.), *Handbook of counseling psychology* (pp. 832–877). New York: Wiley.

Riger, S., & Galligan, P. (1980). Women in management: An exploration of competing paradigms. *American Psychologist, 35,* 902–910.

Rix, S. E. (Ed.). (1987). *The American woman 1987–88: A report in depth.* New York: Norton.

Robertson, J., & Fitzgerald, L. F. (1990). The (mis)treatment of men: Effects of client gender role and life-style on diagnosis and attribution of pathology. *Journal of Counseling Psychology, 37,* 3–9.

Robinson, W. L., & Reid, P. T. (1985). Sexual intimacies in psychology revisited. *Professional Psychology: Research and Practice, 16,* 512–520.

Rodin, J., Silberstein, L., & Striegel-Moore, R. (1985). Women and weight: A normative discontent. In T. B. Sonderegger (Ed.), *Nebraska symposium on motivation* (pp. 267–307). Lincoln, NE: University of Nebraska Press.

Rose, S., & Larwood, L. (1988). *Women's careers: Pathways and pitfalls.* New York: Praeger.

Russett, C. E. (1989). *Sexual science: The Victorian construction of womanhood.* Cambridge, MA: Harvard University Press.

Russo, N. F. (Ed.). (1986). *A woman's health agenda.* Washington, DC: American Psychological Association.

Scarr, S., Phillips, D., & McCartney, K. (1989). Working mothers and their families. *American Psychologist, 44,* 1402–1409.

Scher, M., Stevens, M., Good, G. E., & Eichenfield, G. (1987). *The handbook of counseling and psychotherapy with men.* Newbury Park, CA: Sage.

Schroeder, P. (1985, December 29). Should leaves for new parents be mandatory? *The New York Times,* p. 16E.

Scott, J. W. (1982). The mechanization of women's work. *Scientific American, 247,* 167–185.

Sherif, C. (1979). Bias in psychology. In J. A. Sherman & E. T. Beck (Eds.), *The prism of sex: Essays in the sociology of knowledge* (pp. 93–133). Madison, WI: University of Wisconsin Press.

Sherif, C. (1982). Needed concepts in the study of gender identity. *Psychology of Women Quarterly, 6,* 375–398.

Shields, S. A. (1987). Women, men, and the dilemma of emotion. In P. Shaver & C. Hendrick (Eds.), *Review of personality and social psychology: Vol. 7. Sex and gender* (pp. 229–250). Beverly Hills, CA: Sage.

Spain, D. (1988, November). Women's demographic past, present, and future. Paper presented at the Radcliffe Conference on Women in the 21st Century, Cambridge, MA.

Spence, J. T., Deaux, K., & Helmreich, R. L. (1985). Sex roles in contemporary American society. In G. Lindzey & E. Aronson (Eds.), *Handbook of social psychology,* (3rd ed.) (Vol. 2, pp. 149–178). Reading, MA: Addison-Wesley.

Staples, R. (1982). *Black masculinity.* San Francisco: Black Scholar Press.

Stiver, I. P. (1984). The meanings of "dependency" in female–male relationships. Stone Center for Developmental Services and Studies. No. 83-07. Wellesley, MA: Wellesley College.

Thompson, L., & Walker, A. J. (1989). Women and men in marriage, work, and parenthood. *Journal of Marriage and the Family, 51,* 845–872.

Till, F. (1980). *Sexual harassment: A report on the sexual harassment of students.* Washington, DC: National Advisory Council on Women's Educational Programs.

Toth, M. A. (1982, April). *The buffalo are gone: The decline of the male prerogative.* Paper presented at the Pacific Sociological Association annual meetings, San Diego, CA.

Unger, R. K. (1979). Toward a redefinition of sex and gender. *American Psychologist, 34,* 1085–1094.

Unger, R. K. (1990). Imperfect reflections of reality. In R. T. Hare-Mustin & J. Marecek (Eds.), *Making a difference: Psychology and the construction of gender.* New Haven, CT: Yale University Press.

U.S. Department of Commerce, Bureau of Labor Statistics. (1989). *Labor force statistics derived from the current population survey: A databook.* Washington, DC: U.S. Government Printing Office.

U.S. Department of Education. (1989). Facts about women and education. Office of Educational Research and Improvement. Washington, DC.

Walker, L. S., & Wallston, B. S. (1985). Social adaptation: A review of dual-earner family literature. In L. L'Abate (Ed.), *Handbook of family psychology* (pp. 698–740). Homewood, IL: Dow Jones-Irwin.

Wallis, C. (1989, December 4). Onward, women. *Time,* pp. 80–89.

Wallston, B. S. (1981). What are the questions in the psychology of women? *Psychology of Women Quarterly, 5,* 597–617.

Wallston, B. S. (1987). Social psychology of women and gender. *Journal of Applied Social Psychology, 17,* 1025–1050.

Weisstein, N. (1968). *Kinder, Kirche, Kuche as scientific law: Psychology constructs the female.* Boston: New England Free Press.

Werrbach, J. (1989). *Psychologists' perceptions of the male gender role and its influence in the psychotherapeutic process with men.* Unpublished doctoral dissertation, University of Texas at Austin.

Westkott, M. (1986). *The feminist legacy of Karen Horney.* New Haven, CT: Yale University Press.

Wolinsky, H. (1989). The bias against women in medical research. *American College of Physicians Observer, 9*(4), 15–18.

Zedeck, S., & Mosier, K. L. (1990). Work in the family and employing organization. *American Psychologist, 45,* 240–251.

Zigler, E. F., & Frank, M. (Eds). (1988). *The parental leave crisis: Toward a national policy.* New Haven, CT: Yale University Press.

Zilbergeld, B. (1978). *Male sexuality.* New York: Bantam Books.

PART THREE
CAREER AND EDUCATIONAL COUNSELING

CHAPTER 13

THEORETICAL ADVANCES AND CURRENT INQUIRY IN CAREER PSYCHOLOGY

GAIL HACKETT
ROBERT W. LENT

The primary goal of this chapter is to examine the empirical status of the major theories of career choice and development. A chapter-length treatment of this voluminous literature requires certain compromises. In particular, we necessarily take a highly selective approach, overviewing research on well-established theories as well as promising newer theoretical developments. Issues of career assessment and intervention are covered in the chapters that follow in this Part of the *Handbook*.

We have further confined our focus primarily to literature appearing in the 1980s, with some exceptions for important works, and we have most thoroughly addressed the theory-based literature since 1983, subsequent to Osipow's most recent edition of *Theories of Career Development* (1983), the *Handbook of Vocational Behavior* (Walsh & Osipow, 1983), and Brown and Brooks' (1984) first edition of *Career Choice and Development*. Our purpose is to update previous major reviews rather than to rehash what others have already covered. We assume that readers have a basic familiarity with the major career theoretical models.

The chapter highlights the following general theoretical perspectives: (a) person–environment interaction approaches, particularly work adjustment theory and Holland's model; (b) developmental theories (Gottfredson, 1981; Super, 1990); (c) social cognitive models, including social learning and self-efficacy theory; and (d) issues of gender and culture/ethnicity in career development. We conclude by commenting on selected conceptual and methodological problems in career psychology and suggesting some future directions for career theorizing and research.

It is important to note that the chapter does not cover sociological perspectives, decision-making models, or personality approaches to career development. Sociological approaches are omitted because of their relative lack of recent empirical activity and their limited counseling implications, although a social systems perspective will be evident in our coverage of gender and ethnicity issues. Decision-making models, although heuristic and relevant to career counseling, do not represent a major career development *theory* per se. We selectively address decision-making issues in the context of reviewing the major theories. Personality theories, such as Roe's (1956) and the psychodynamic perspectives on career development, have simply not garnered much empirical attention of late; the reader is referred to Watkins and Savickas' (1990) recent chapter for coverage of promising directions within this tradition. We offer some comments about the role of personality factors in career development in our concluding section.

PERSON–ENVIRONMENT INTERACTION THEORIES

Several prominent theories conceptualize career development primarily in terms of the fit or match between persons and the salient features of their work or educational environments. In general, good person–environment correspondence is assumed to engender positive outcomes, such as work satisfaction, achievement, and retention, whereas poor correspondence is thought to diminish satisfaction, performance, and job tenure. This "matching persons with jobs" tradition actually extends from vocational psychology's earliest roots (Parsons, 1909) and is synonymous with the ubiquitous, and much debated, "trait and factor" perspective on career behavior (Osipow, 1983). More recently, this approach has been redesignated "person–environment (P–E) fit" (e.g., Rounds & Tracey, 1990), in keeping with the contemporary emphasis within psychology on interactionist conceptions of behavior. This section reviews the two most influential vocational P–E fit theories, those of Dawis and Lofquist (1984) and Holland (1985). (See Chapter 17, by Myers and Cairo, for additional P–E coverage.)

Theory of Work Adjustment

The Theory of Work Adjustment (TWA), stemming from the Work Adjustment Project at the University of Minnesota, debuted in the mid-1960s (Dawis, England, & Lofquist, 1964) and has subsequently been revised and expanded, culminating in its most recent elaboration (Dawis & Lofquist, 1984). TWA holds that individuals are motivated to achieve and maintain *correspondence* (a harmonious relationship) with their work environments. Such correspondence is based on reciprocity, that is, on the individual and the environment meeting each other's requirements. *Work adjustment* is the dynamic process by which persons attain and preserve correspondence with their work environments. Stronger P–E correspondence leads to increased *tenure,* which is the chief outcome of work adjustment. More specifically, tenure depends on both individuals' *satisfaction* with the environment and their *satisfactoriness* in meeting environmental demands. TWA posits two major, complementary sets of constructs to define the P–E relationship, the *work personality* and the *work environment,* each of which is composed of parallel structure and style variables. Given these basic assumptions and concepts, 20 major propositions have been offered to predict work adjustment. Few of these propositions, however, have received sustained empirical attention.

Empirical Base

The Work Adjustment Project is notable for the instrumentation it has developed to operationalize TWA's major variables (e.g., satisfaction, satisfactoriness, work needs/values; see Dawis & Lofquist, 1984), and for the classification schemes it has devised to index qualities of the work environment. Important ancillary work stimulated by TWA has also included exploration of the development and differentiation of vocational needs (Rounds, Dawis, & Lofquist, 1979); study of the factor structure of vocational needs and reinforcers (Doerring, Rhodes, & Kaspin, 1988); and identification of the needs and/or reinforcers of particular occupational groups (Tinsley & Tinsley, 1989).

In exploring research that specifically tested TWA's propositions, we were able to locate relatively few published studies appearing in the past decade. Much of the relevant research fund consists of pre-1980s dissertations, unpublished data, or monographs produced under the aegis of the Work Adjustment Project (for summaries of this work, see Dawis & Lofquist, 1984; Lofquist & Dawis, 1984). Our review emphasizes published studies that were designed to directly test TWA's key propositions. In particular, we will highlight Propositions III and VII, which appear to have attracted the most empirical scrutiny.

Proposition III holds that satisfaction is a function of the correspondence between the worker's values and the reinforcer pattern of the work environment. (TWA conceptualizes values as second-order needs, or the more basic dimensions underlying needs. We will use "values" and "needs" interchangeably in our review; see Chapter 14, by Betz, for a discussion of the dimensionality of needs/values.) Employing a sample of social workers, Tziner (1983) found that job satisfaction was strongly related to the fit between subjects' vocational needs and the rewards of their job. Scarpello and Campbell (1983), studying research and development personnel in two large corporations, reported that the match between individual needs and job rewards predicted satisfaction, although additional variance in satisfaction was explained by subjects' aspiration levels and perceptions of career progression.

Rounds, Dawis, and Lofquist (1987) reported two studies, one using six occupational groups (e.g., salesperson, rehabilitation counselor), and the other containing adults seen in a vocational assessment clinic. Results generally provided support for Proposition III, although the relation of need–reinforcer correspondence to satisfaction was dependent on several factors, such as how correspondence was assessed. Rounds (1990) compared need–reinforcer correspondence with interest congruence, an alternative conceptualization of P–E fit (Holland, 1985), in predicting job satisfaction. Subjects consisted of the adult counselee sample from Rounds et al. (1987). Results indicated that both theoretical fit and indexes were generally predictive of job satisfaction, with the TWA index adding incremental variance beyond interest congruence.

Collectively, these and conceptually related findings (Greenhaus, Seidel, & Marinis, 1983; Vandenberg & Scarpello, 1990) suggest that need–reinforcer correspondence is a good predictor of job satisfaction, but that (a) this prediction can be improved with the addition of non-TWA variables (Rounds, 1990; Scarpello & Campbell, 1983), and (b) the strength of this relation is moderated by measurement considerations and subject gender (Rounds et al., 1987).

TWA's Proposition VII posits that voluntary work termination is inversely related to satisfaction. Scarpello and Campbell (1983) reported that nonsatisfied workers (those exhibiting a poor needs–rewards match) expressed a greater willingness than did satisfied workers to change their occupations. Doerring and Rhodes' (1989) qualitative study of teacher turnover found that career changers linked their departure to job dissatisfaction and poor need–reinforcer correspondence. In an earlier study, Taylor and Weiss (1972) found that satisfaction predicted job defection in a sample of discount store employees. These findings are also consistent with a sizable body of research (employing diverse theoretical models and measures) demonstrating that job satisfaction is negatively related to employee turnover (Lofquist & Dawis, 1984).

Dawis and Lofquist (1984; Lofquist & Dawis, 1984) presented additional evidence bearing on TWA's propositions. However, once again, much of these data were not in published sources and, in several cases, they appeared to emanate from studies that were not designed to directly test TWA's specific propositions. Nevertheless, their general conclusion was that TWA "is a valuable and useful formulation for viewing adjustment to work" (Lofquist & Dawis, 1984, p. 230).

Summary

TWA is, in many respects, an exemplary model. Its authors offer a clear discussion of its assumptions; define its concepts in operational terms; and assemble a coherent, intuitively reasonable set of propositions that specify the relations among the model's constructs and that encompass clinically important outcomes (e.g., work tenure). Further, TWA has spawned a good deal of empirical activity, including a plethora of dissertations, a variety of measurement tools, and an occupational classification system. Such qualities no doubt have spurred one writer to propose TWA as the basis for an integrative framework for vocational psychology (Hesketh, 1985).

Despite these very considerable strengths, however, it is difficult for us to offer a definitive conclusion regarding TWA's empirical adequacy at this time. It is not that the theory has failed to stimulate inquiry or that there is a preponderance of negative findings; rather, much of the inquiry has simply not been directed at the theory's basic propositions. Thus, 25 years after its introduction, the theory's empirical base appears, in certain respects, still to be unevenly constructed. Refined instruments exist and a few propositions (e.g., III and VII) have received at least qualified support, but most of the propositions—particularly those involving personality, environmental, and adjustment style variables—have not yet generated significant research activity.

Several suggestions might be offered to enhance TWA's research base and impact. First, the 20 propositions deserve a more sustained, systematic, and balanced level of inquiry. Second, it seems important to attend to the adequate dissemination of future research findings on TWA, for example, via wide-circulation published sources. Third, although TWA describes work adjustment as a "continuous, dynamic process" and specifies causal relations among key variables (e.g., satisfaction and tenure), researchers have frequently explored static relations among the constructs using designs that do not permit causal inferences. Alternative methods, such as longitudinal and causal modeling designs, might help to elucidate the presumably dynamic interplay of P–E variables fostering person and system change over time. Finally, Dawis and Lofquist (1984) discussed TWA's clinical applicability, for example, to career counseling and retirement adjustment. Research on TWA-derived applied interventions could add a valuable dimension to the theory's empirical base and also provide a useful arena for studying causal relations among its elements (e.g., does improved need–reinforcer correspondence enhance satisfaction?). Rounds and Tracey (1990) cited a number of valuable directions for the extension of trait and factor/P–E models, such as TWA, to career counseling research and practice.

Holland's Theory

John Holland's theory has become, over a 30-year period, the most well-researched and probably the most visible conceptual model emanating from vocational/counseling psychology. First framed in the late 1950s (Holland, 1959), this theory has steadily evolved; to date, it has received five statements, the most recent of which appeared only a few years ago (Holland, 1985). Most counseling psychologists are familiar with Holland's hexagonal model of personality and environmental types, and with the basic assumptions of his theory. However, it will be useful to highlight a few key concepts. *Congruence* refers to the degree of fit between P and E, with more congruent pairings (e.g., a Realistic type in a Realistic setting) assumed to promote favorable outcomes. *Consistency, differentiation,* and *identity* represent three different methods of indexing the same basic concept, that is, the degree to which personalities are well-defined, clear, and focused. Consistency and differentiation are derived from various measures of Holland's types; identity is assessed with an 18-item Identity Scale (Holland, Daiger, & Power, 1980).

Holland has constructed three extensive sets of vocational/educational hypotheses, one each regarding personality types, environmental models, and P–E interaction. Those predictions that have drawn the most inquiry, and around which we have organized our review, include: (a) a person's dominant type or subtype determines the primary direction of vocational and educational choice (e.g., a Realistic/Investigative person will tend to select R/I environments); (b) well-defined persons (those demonstrating high levels of consistency, differentiation, and identity) are more likely both to choose educational/career fields that match their personality and to experience stability of choices; and (c) P–E congruence promotes higher levels of choice stability, achievement, and satisfaction, particularly when well-defined persons are paired with well-defined environments and when persons' educational or intelligence level matches that required by the environment.

Empirical Base

Research on the many facets of Holland's theory has become voluminous. For instance, for his comprehensive review, Holland (1985) located more than 400 relevant studies appearing between 1959 and 1983. There have been other recent reviews of research specifically on the congruence hypothesis (Assouline & Meir, 1987; Spokane, 1985). Our selective review highlights the findings of newer and previously unreviewed studies relating Holland's theory to choice of educational/vocational field, stability of choice, achievement, and satisfaction outcomes.

Holland's hypothesis that personality type determines the primary direction of educational/vocational choice has been a popular topic of inquiry. Studies involving either college students or employed workers have found that types generally aspire to, or inhabit, fields that match their primary interests. For example, in nursing (Hecht, 1980) and premedical (Henry & Bardo, 1987) student samples, a majority of students evidenced primary interest themes that corresponded to theoretical expectations. Similarly, samples of non-college-degreed male (Greenlee, Damarin, & Walsh, 1988) and female (Mazen, 1989) workers tended to occupy work environments that conformed with their predominant interests. However, Heesacker, Elliott, and Howe (1988), in a sample of sewing machine operators, found that subjects' predominant code (Social) did not match that expected by Holland's typology (Conventional).

Another set of studies examined the relation of personality pattern clarity to educational/vocational stability and various other outcomes. Latona (1989) found both person and environment consistency to be unrelated to academic major persistence in college students. Pazy and Zin (1987) found person consistency unrelated to job satisfaction and commitment in employed workers. In contrast, using person differentiation as a clarity index, Erwin (1987) reported a significant, although modest relation to certain achievement and personal development scales in college students; however, differentiation did not relate to career decidedness.

Other studies employing student samples also failed to observe a relation of either person consistency or differentiation to career indecision (Alvi, Khan, & Kirkwood, 1990; Larson, Heppner, Ham, & Dugan, 1988; Lowe, 1981) or vocational maturity

(Guthrie & Herman, 1982). Monahan (1987) did report a significant relation of differentiation to decidedness, but only when employing modified versus traditional differentiation indexes. Holland, Gottfredson, and Baker (1990) found differentiation to relate positively to "coherence of vocational aspirations" in male but not female Navy recruits. Wiggins (1984) reported a positive relation of differentiation to job satisfaction in school counselors, although Gottfredson and Holland (1990) observed that differentiation correlated *negatively* with work satisfaction and persistence in bank tellers. In a methodologically enlightening study, Swanson and Hansen (1986) found that undifferentiated persons may not constitute a unitary group and that failure to account for interest score elevation may obscure meaningful relations.

A number of investigators have begun to study vocational identity, Holland's newest index of person clarity. Studies employing college students have found this scale to be related to career maturity (Fuqua, Seaworth, & Newman, 1987; Leong & Morris, 1989); variety of career options considered (Monahan & Muchinsky, 1985); perceived academic adjustment (Lopez, 1989) but not actual college grades (Lucas, Gysbers, Buescher, & Heppner, 1988); and a host of other developmental, personal, or social adjustment outcomes (Fuqua et al., 1987; Leong & Morris, 1989; Lopez, 1989).

Particularly consistent and generally strong relations have been observed between identity and measures of career decidedness or choice certainty/confidence (Fretz & Leong, 1982; Fuqua et al., 1987; Lucas et al., 1988; Monahan, 1987; Monahan & Muchinsky, 1985). Tinsley, Bowman, and York (1989), in a factor analytic study, have confirmed that identity overlaps substantially with conceptually related constructs assessing career decidedness/choice crystallization. The vocational identity scale has also been used as an outcome measure in several career intervention studies (Remer, O'Neil, & Gohs, 1984). Identity has clearly become a popular research topic but we, like Holland (1985), could not locate published investigations that specifically tested the ability of this construct to forecast vocational stability.

Holland's congruence hypothesis appears to be the most widely studied and debated aspect of his theory in recent years. In a narrative review of the congruence literature, Spokane (1985) reported that most studies found mixed or positive results, although correlations of congruence to dependent measures "rarely exceed .25 to .35." He concluded that, "on balance, congruence is associated with performance, satisfaction and stability" (p. 329), as predicted by Holland. Assouline and Meir (1987) compiled a meta-analytic review of 41 congruence studies. Their findings indicated rather small effect sizes for the relation of congruence to achievement and stability; mean correlations were .06 and .15, respectively. The mean correlation of congruence to satisfaction was .21, but this effect size varied with different congruence indexes and environmental referents. For example, when congruence involved the fit between person and occupational specialty (as opposed to general occupational category), the mean congruence-satisfaction correlation rose steeply to .42.

A number of additional studies of congruence have emerged in recent years. We order them here by the major dependent variables they have employed. The largest category involves congruence in relation to various facets of vocational satisfaction. Several studies reported positive relations between congruence level and job satisfaction (Elton & Smart, 1988; Gottfredson & Holland, 1990; Rounds, 1990) in adult workers, or educational satisfaction (Gade, Fuqua, & Hurlburt, 1988) in students. However, this relation did not materialize in samples of sewing machine operators (Heesacker et al., 1988) or Israeli professionals (Pazy & Zin, 1987). Each of these studies operationalized congruence with respect to global occupational or educational fields. By contrast, a few studies have assessed congruence in novel ways and achieved consistently positive results. For example, Meir (1988) and Meir and Yaari (1988) found stronger congruence–satisfaction relationships when congruence involved the fit between personality type and occupational *specialty* (as opposed to broad occupational category).

Several recent studies examined congruence in relation to achievement and/or stability indexes (Gottfredson & Holland, 1990; Heesacker et al., 1988; Lent, Brown, & Larkin, 1987). Consistent with Assouline and Meir's (1987) review, results of these studies were generally disappointing for the congruence hypothesis. Congruence has also been studied in relation to various other career development criteria such as career maturity and indecision in student samples—again with mixed findings (Guthrie & Herman, 1982; Healy & Mourton, 1985; Lent et al., 1987).

Summary

Holland's theory has had an undeniable impact on vocational psychology. In particular, the theory's relative simplicity and parsimony have made it accessible to both professionals and laypersons; its classification scheme provides a useful framework for organizing information about persons, environments, and their interaction; and Holland's assessment devices (e.g., the Vocational Preference Inventory (VPI) and the Self-Directed Search (SDS)) allow ready quantification of his constructs. Although there has been debate about Holland's measurement strategies and the formal adequacy of his constructs and propositions (Brown, 1987; Holland, 1987a; Weinrach & Srebalus, 1990), the heuristic potential of Holland's theory is evident from its sizable research literature.

On the other hand, research has not been entirely kind to the theory. The one hypothesis that seems to have received the most consistent support involves the prediction that persons tend to select or prefer environments that match their personality types. Supporting Holland's (1985) earlier review, the preponderance of recent evidence does suggest a relationship between Holland's personality types and choice of environment, which generally holds for men, women, majority, and minority subjects in the studies we reviewed. In essence, birds of a feather *do* flock together. However, studies documenting this relationship have sometimes applied liberal match criteria; some samples show theory-discrepant patterns (Heesacker et al., 1988; Mazen, 1989); and even when theory-consistent relations are observed, the designs employed generally do not allow causal interpretations.

Studies on the personality pattern clarity hypotheses have tended to yield disappointing results. As Holland (1985, p. 73) acknowledged, differentiation and consistency have had "a checkered research career—about as many negative as positive findings." Our review corroborates this trend; neither of these constructs has been found uniformly to predict choice stability (the key outcome to which they should, according to theory, relate). Research has yet to explore the relation of vocational identity to choice stability, but emergent findings suggest that this construct correlates with a variety of career and personal development indexes. However, some research indicates a very substantial overlap between identity and certain career decision measures, and evidence for the relation of identity to alternative measures of person clarity, such as differentiation (Monahan, 1987) and vocational aspiration coherence (Holland et al., 1990), is somewhat mixed. Together, these findings may raise questions about the construct validity of identity. In particular, does identity reflect *person clarity* (the degree to which personality patterns are well-defined and focused) or level of *career decidedness*? Are these two constructs discriminable?

Studies of the congruence hypothesis have begun to reveal a fairly consistent pattern, with congruence indexes tending to show small or negligible relations with achievement and stability measures, but somewhat stronger relations with vocational or educational satisfaction. Assouline and Meir's (1987) meta-analysis as well as subsequent research suggest that the largest congruence–satisfaction effect sizes tend to accrue from studies that employ certain methods of indexing congruence. (We will return to this point below.)

In assessing the status of research on his theory, Holland (1985, 1987b) argued that well-designed studies that closely followed his theory and used "potent" P and E variables and "defensible" outcome measures have produced the most findings in support of his theory, whereas studies lacking these qualities have often yielded disconfirmatory results. Unfortunately, organization of the present and previous (Assouline & Meir, 1987; Spokane, 1985) reviews does not permit a clear test of this important point. It would therefore be useful for future meta-analyses of research on Holland's hypotheses to explore study quality or theory "fidelity" as moderators of effect sizes. For example, studies can be rated by judges in terms of the quality of their designs (Multon, Brown, & Lent, 1991) or the degree to which they adequately assess Holland's constructs, enabling an empirical test of whether stronger studies yield stronger independent variable–criterion relationships.

There are a few potentially fruitful directions for further work on Holland's theory. First, given that measurement issues have often plagued research on Holland's constructs, it would be well to consider alternative assessment methods (Gati, 1985; Iachan, 1984; Strahan, 1987) that have been designed to surmount certain problems and that incorporate more information about P and E than do prior indexes. Whether they actually enable stronger tests of Holland's hypotheses, however, is still an open question. Initial findings involving such methods have been mixed (Alvi et al., 1990; Gottfredson & Holland, 1990; Monahan, 1987), and there is need for further work exploring relations between the newer and the traditional indexes and comparing their predictive utility.

Second, there has been a paucity of work exploring interactions among Holland's constructs. For example, although Holland (1985, p. 55) indicated that P–E congruence–criterion relations are "conditioned by the clarity of a person's personality," researchers have only occasionally examined these important moderating conditions (Gottfredson & Holland, 1990; Healy & Mourton, 1985; Pazy & Zin, 1987). Further research elucidating congruence–person clarity interactions may therefore be quite valuable. Relatedly, it would be of value to consider additional moderators of congruence–criterion relationships; for example, recent work suggests that stronger congruence–satisfaction relations may result when the perceived importance of work groups is considered and when congruence is defined in relation to within-occupation specialty fit (e.g., see Meir, 1989).

Third, much more work is needed to assess alternative congruence dimensions and theoretical constructs in relation to Holland's theme congruence. Pervin (1987) observed that "congruence rarely involves a relation between a single motive or personality characteristic and a single dimension of the environment" (p. 229), and Gati (1989) noted that "there are other independent variables which affect the individual's occupational satisfaction, performance, and permanence on the job, in addition to personality and interests" (p. 184). Gati also raised the interesting possibilities that incongruence in certain areas may be compensated for by congruence in other areas and that certain forms of congruence (e.g., interests in Holland's model) may moderate other forms of congruence (e.g., needs in Dawis and Lofquist's).

It is noteworthy that Rounds (1990) found that need–reinforcer correspondence (a TWA fit index) complemented interest congruence in the prediction of job satisfaction. Thus far, there have been very few other studies exploring how Holland's congruence scheme may compare with (or complement) alternative methods of operationalizing congruence (e.g., Meir & Melamed, 1986; Pazy & Zin, 1987) or person variables derived from alternative conceptual frameworks (Lent et al., 1987). Examination of subjective dimensions of P–E fit (Caplan, 1987) and diverse methods of conceptualizing the environment, such as social climate (Moos, 1987), may offer especially promising directions for future research.

Finally, a number of additional research directions have been suggested by other recent writers, such as Holland (1985), Spokane (1985), Gati (1989), and the contributors to the *Journal of Vocational Behavior* special issue on P–E fit (Spokane, 1987). Their collective agenda suggests that Holland's theory, particularly the congruence hypothesis, will generate renewed and sophisticated empirical activity in the years ahead.

DEVELOPMENTAL APPROACHES

Developmental approaches can be distinguished from other career development perspectives by their emphasis on the process of career decision making and their attempts to explain changes in career-related behavior and attitudes over time. The developmental tradition has produced a tremendous amount of research and theorizing. Reviewers have noted problems with the formal adequacy of all the developmental theories, and in fact with vocational theorizing generally (Crites, 1969; Osipow, 1983), but Super's conceptual model has increasingly been viewed as the most comprehensive and promising of the developmental perspectives (Brown, 1990). We focus here on Super's (1980, 1990) updated formulations and on one other important new developmental perspective (Gottfredson, 1981). Vondracek, Lerner, and Schulenberg (1986) also produced an important developmentally based theoretical statement, but their work has not yet garnered sustained inquiry.

Super's Segmental Theory of Career Development

Super's (1953) initial propositions drew heavily from individual differences research, self-concept theory, developmental theory, and occupational sociology. The major concepts included in Super's (1957) early formulations were: (a) *vocational stages;* (b) the *vocational tasks* necessary to successfully negotiate the stages of vocational development; (c) implementation of the *self-concept* as integral to developing a vocational identity; (d) *vocational maturity,* described in terms of both chronological comparisons across individuals and success at negotiating vocational tasks regardless of age; and (e) *career patterns,* that is, the sequencing of jobs.

These concepts remain central to Super's conceptualization, but Super's early propositions have been expanded and revised in several ways (Super, 1990): (a) the potential for recycling through the developmental tasks of various life stages was elaborated (Super, 1984), as were the social and economic forces influencing such recycling; (b) self-concept was broadened to "personal constructs" conceptualized as products of learning; (c) the concept of readiness to cope with developmental tasks, based on level of career maturity, received increased emphasis; (d) the construct of career maturity was defined more fully and the complexities of operationalizing the construct were addressed; and (e) the concept of role salience was introduced in the context of Super's elaboration of the "Life Career Rainbow" (Super, 1980).

Empirical Base

Much of the research bearing on developmental concepts is only loosely tied to Super's propositions, and most of the empirical studies have been conducted outside the framework of Super's theory per se. Consequently, it is difficult to determine the extent to which studies examining variables such as self-concept, career stages, or career exploration have adequately tested Super's propositions. The following is a highly selective, illustrative overview of some of the research trends.

Much of the work on Super's theory has been concerned with the development of measures to assess major constructs. Career maturity, for example, has received a great deal of attention (Crites, 1978; Super, Thompson, Lindeman, Jordaan, & Myers, 1984; Westbrook, 1983), but numerous conceptual and measurement problems remain (see Chapter 14, by Betz). Super and his colleagues have also developed instruments measuring the importance of work values (Super, 1982) and the salience or importance of five major life roles (Nevill & Super, 1986).

Research on adult career concerns has also focused on the measurement of career maturity (Super & Kidd, 1979; Super, Thompson, Lindeman, Myers, & Jordaan, 1985) and career adjustment (Crites, 1990) of adults (see Chapter 14, by Betz), but some studies can be found testing Super's stages in adult populations. For example, Cron, Dubinsky, and Michaels' (1988) findings supported the relationship between career stages and the motivation of salespeople. Studies by Ornstein and her colleagues (Ornstein, Cron, & Slocum, 1989; Ornstein & Isabella, 1990) compared theoretical propositions regarding the life and career stages of Levinson and his colleagues (Levinson, Darrow, Klein, Levinson, & McKee, 1978) and Super (1957); both models received some support but were differentially predictive.

Tests of the role of the self-concept in career development have been supportive of Super's theory (Kidd, 1984). A large body of research also exists on the topic of career exploration, but the results have been equivocal (Blustein, 1990) and sometimes only tangentially related to Super's model. Jepson (1984, p. 205), in a major review of developmental research, noted that "the study of vocational exploratory behavior remains in its infancy despite nearly 20 years of theoretical discussion and research." One of Jepson's (1984) major conclusions was that the evidence did not support the relationships proposed by Super and others between exploratory activity and later career-related outcomes. More recently, attempts have been made to investigate the dimensions of career exploratory behavior predictive of "valued career outcomes" (Blustein, 1988; Blustein, Devenis, & Kidney, 1989; Blustein & Phillips, 1990).

A heavily researched topic within the broad domain of career exploration has been career decision-making processes. Harren (1979) developed a decision-making model based on Tiedeman and O'Hara's (1963) theory, and career maturity scales such as Crites' Career Maturity Inventory (CMI) and Super et al.'s (1981) Career Development Inventory have operationalized career decision-making processes as factors related to career maturity. Much of the work on career decision-making *models* has either not taken place within the context of career development theory per se (Gelatt, 1962) or has been tied to other theoretical orientations, such as social learning theory (Mitchell & Krumboltz, 1984) or Holland's theory (Holland et al., 1980). Career indecision as a factor influencing the decision-making process is clearly relevant to developmental theory, but research on career indecision and indecisiveness has also not been strongly tied to Super's formulations (Phillips & Pazienza, 1988).

Summary

Osipow (1983) concluded that Super's theory was generally supported by the research literature. Super's propositions have not been subjected to direct intensive empirical scrutiny of late, but the research that has appeared, and the indirect evidence from investigations of related concepts, remain generally supportive of some of Super's constructs such as career stages. Results are equivocal with regard to other aspects of the theory, especially the relationship between early exploratory activity and later outcomes.

Super's theory is comprehensive and wide-ranging, perhaps offering a viable framework for integrating the major career development theories (Brown, 1990; Osipow, 1983). Super's work on role salience also represents a major advance, with the potential to shed new light on women's career development, and his recent emphasis on personal constructs allows for more sophisticated representations of the self–environment transaction over time. However, the great breadth of Super's model may be both a strength and a weakness (Brown, 1990). Further, although Super's theoretical revisions consider biological, economic, and social factors a bit more than do previous versions, and the incorporation of learning theory to explain certain aspects of development seems useful, these topics have not yet been fully integrated within the model.

A number of directions for future research and theory development based on Super's model might be pursued. First, the lack of integration among the numerous components of the "archway model" requires attention. We echo Brown's (1990) concern that better integration of the various segments of Super's model is necessary for the continued viability of the theory as well as for guidance of theory-based research. Second, research on developmental concepts, such as career exploration, would benefit if investigators established tighter connections to Super's propositions. Third, continued work on the clarification and measurement of major theoretical constructs seems warranted; in particular, work on career maturity may profit from fresh perspectives (see Chapter 14, by Betz), and Super's revised notion of the self-concept deserves added inquiry.

Finally, it seems important to devote more effort to translating cutting-edge theory, findings, and research methods from developmental psychology to developmental perspectives on career psychology generally, and to Super's theory in particular. Vondracek et al. (1986) noted progress in this direction, but a good deal more work seems necessary. For example, although Super has substantially revised his conceptualization of developmental stages, Vondracek et al. argued that the very notion of stages may be outdated. Further efforts to draw upon, and incorporate, learning theory may also be valuable.

Gottfredson's Developmental Theory of Occupational Aspirations

Originally introduced more than a decade ago, Gottfredson's (1981) theory has received both praise (Brooks, 1990) and severe criticism (Betz & Fitzgerald, 1987), but has only recently been subjected to empirical test. Gottfredson (1981) proposed a stage model of the development of the self-concept. In her view, the self-concept is composed of increasingly differentiated and complex elements over the stages of development. Each element that one incorporates into the self-concept affects not only the self-concept, but also one's perceptions of the range of acceptable occupations. Thus, Gottfredson described a process of increasing circumscription of occupational alternatives.

In Gottfredson's (1981) framework, individuals organize their perceptions of occupations according to cognitive maps of similarities and differences among occupations; thus, preferences for various occupational alternatives reflect the relationship between increasingly complex self-concepts and an individual's occupational images (an alternate term for occupational stereotypes). A person's "zone of acceptable alternatives" is a result of the interaction between preferences and perceptions of accessibility (opportunities and barriers). Gottfredson suggested that the tendency to compromise interests to preserve other, more important aspects of the self-concept might explain some of the anomalous findings with regard to Holland's congruence hypothesis (see the earlier section on P–E fit). Gottfredson (1981) also contended that, once people make compromises, they psychologically adjust to their choices; this adjustment of interests to fit actual choice after job entry may explain the limited relation of interest congruence to job satisfaction in many studies.

Empirical Base

The empirical support for Gottfredson's theory has been mixed; in the past several years, the negative evidence seems to have snowballed. Gottfredson (1981) herself articulated ways in which her propositions could be tested, and researchers have drawn heavily from those suggestions. The process of compromise has received the most empirical attention, but one study has examined the proposed stages of development, and another has investigated the zone of acceptable alternatives.

In a study exploring the process of compromise (Taylor & Pryor, 1985), one of the more intriguing findings was that over half of the sample refused to specify compromise plans. For those students who identified compromise plans, the trend was to make an alternate choice compatible with interests and to sacrifice prestige. The results of this naturalistic investigation suggested that interest, prestige, and sex type all influence both choice and compromise, but that the relative importance of these factors differs from that proposed by Gottfredson, and may vary as a function of gender. Pryor (1987) reported on a follow-up study of the same sample; results of actual choices made 7 months later partially supported Gottfredson's proposals, although, once again, gender differences emerged.

Other investigations have also yielded mixed results regarding Gottfredson's compromise hypotheses. Pryor and Taylor (1986) found that forced compromises involved lowering the prestige level of the compromise alternative rather than sacrificing interests or sex type. Holt (1989) reported that students chose alternatives congruent with occupational interests, but that prestige interacted with interests in the compromise process. Using a "fuzzy logic" rating procedure, Hesketh, Elmslie, and Kaldor (1990) found that, regardless of class background, subjects consistently sacrificed prestige before interests. Hesketh, Durant, and Pryor (1990) found that, under compromise conditions, prestige was more important than sex type in determining choice, and interests were significantly more important than prestige. Leung and Plake (1990) examined Gottfredson's hypotheses concerning compromise, using a different method than those used in earlier studies, but their results also ran counter to theory.

Henderson, Hesketh, and Tuffin's (1988) results indicated that sex typing of occupations occurs earlier than indicated in the theory, and that boys demonstrate more rigidity in sex-typed preferences than do girls. Findings for the impact of socioeconomic background and ability suggest that socioeconomic status (SES) has only an *indirect* influence, through ability, on prestige level of occupational preferences; Gottfredson's theory predicts the opposite pattern. Finally, Leung and Harmon (1990) examined the concept of the zone of acceptable alternatives. Contrary to theory, the area of the zones *increased* with age, up to about late adolescence. Gottfredson's hypotheses regarding the age of sex typing of occupations (6 to 8 years) was not supported, and neither was her proposition that prestige preferences stabilize after the early teenage years. Once again, evidence was found for gender differences in sex typing, with men adhering to more rigid boundaries than women.

Summary

Gottfredson's (1981) theory of occupational aspirations has stimulated much conceptual debate and is now garnering empirical scrutiny. The process of compromise is clearly an important and underresearched topic within career psychology. However, based on recent research, it seems likely that prestige, interests, and sex type of occupations interact more complexly than initially proposed, and probably not in the exact manner specified by Gottfredson. The stage model also seems to require revision, and gender dynamics in the process of compromise warrant much more attention (Leung & Harmon, 1990), as do the interrelations among prestige, interest area, and sex type (Hesketh, Elmslie, & Kaldor, 1990; Leung & Plake, 1990). Further, it seems important to establish the psychometric adequacy and comparability of the various strategies for measuring the compromise process that have appeared in the literature.

SOCIAL COGNITIVE MODELS

The appearance of conceptual models derived from social cognitive theory represents a relatively recent trend in the vocational literature. Previously termed "social learning theory," this approach has been relabeled *social cognitive theory* (Bandura, 1986) to acknowledge that it encompasses psychosocial phenomena, such as motivational and self-regulatory mechanisms, that extend beyond the focus of traditional learning paradigms. Rather than according primary causal status to either person or environmental variables in determining behavior, social cognitive theory espouses a model of *triadic reciprocality* in which behavior, cognitive and other person factors, and environmental events all function as interacting determinants of one another. Although social cognitive theory and the P–E models share an interactional view of career behavior, they differ in important respects. For example, social cognitivists tend to eschew global, trait measures of person attributes (which have been popular with the career P–E models), instead favoring more situational and domain-specific indexes. This section reviews the two major extensions of Bandura's theory to career behavior that have thus far appeared.

Social Learning Theory of Career Decision Making

John Krumboltz and his colleagues provided the initial effort to tailor Bandura's general model to the career domain. Their basic position was first formulated roughly 16 years ago (Krumboltz, Mitchell, & Jones, 1976) and has since received several restatements (e.g., Krumboltz, 1979), although without major modification or extension of the original hypotheses. Krumboltz's theory is directed primarily at explaining how career-relevant preferences and skills are acquired, and how training and career selections are effected and revised.

According to this theory, four categories of factors influence people's career decision paths: (a) *genetic endowment and special abilities,* such as intelligence, (b) *environmental conditions and events,* (c) *learning experiences,* and (d) *task approach skills,* which result from interactions among the first three sets of factors. The effects of these four factors are manifest in several key outcomes: self-observation generalizations, world-view generalizations, task approach skills (which represent both an influence on and an outcome of career development), and entry behaviors. Krumboltz et al. (1976) offered 19 theoretical propositions, organized into three sets, postulating factors that positively and negatively influence the development of career-relevant *preferences, task approach skills,* and *entry behaviors.*

Empirical Base

There have been several reviews of research on Krumboltz and associates' hypotheses (e.g., Krumboltz & Rude, 1981; Mitchell, 1979; Mitchell & Krumboltz, 1990). Reviewers generally acknowledge that many of the social learning hypotheses have not been directly tested, and that their reviews include much research that is relevant to the theory but did not emanate from it. With these caveats in mind, the largest concentration of previously reviewed findings involves the factors that are posited to positively influence career preferences. Mitchell and Krumboltz's (1990) review indicated support for the hypotheses linking positive reinforcement, modeling, and encouragement to the development of vocational preferences. Research on task approach skills has focused mainly on the skill of career information seeking. Mitchell and Krumboltz concluded that, consistent with theory, this skill could be enhanced by direct reinforcement and modeling manipulations. Regarding entry behaviors, Mitchell and Krumboltz cited several studies as demonstrating support for the hypothesis that occupational entry is related to expressed preferences, relevant exposure opportunities, and the match between persons' skills and educational/occupational requirements.

We had difficulty locating additional studies, beyond those included in previous reviews, that sought explicitly to test propositions derived from this model. However, a few studies emanating from related models do provide some corroborating evidence. For example, in a series of experimental studies, Hackett and her colleagues found that success at mathematical and verbal tasks enhanced task interest, and failure experiences diminished task interest (Hackett, Betz, O'Halloran, & Romac, 1990). These results tended to support social learning predictions about the impact of differential reinforcement on preferences. Finally, Krumboltz's general perspective has produced a major prescriptive decision-making model (Mitchell & Krumboltz, 1984), together with instrument development (see Chapter 14, by Betz) and intervention efforts (Mitchell & Krumboltz, 1987).

Summary

Mitchell (1979) concluded her review by noting that "relatively few experimental studies directly relevant to the theory have been conducted. Several of the propositions have fairly strong supporting evidence. Others have no evidence at all or sketchy evidence at best" (p. 64). Even though the ensuing decade had not seen much model-generated research, Mitchell and Krumboltz (1990, p. 177) were more optimistic, concluding "there is considerable evidence to support the processes posited by the theory" in relation to the factors influencing educational/vocational preferences and task approach skills, but noting that there is somewhat less evidence regarding entry behaviors.

Krumboltz's theory provides a useful framework for organizing and explaining certain findings on career preferences, skills, and entry behaviors, and is associated with novel interventions and career simulation activities. However, much of the research cited in earlier reviews was correlational in nature and, therefore, not directly responsive to the theory's causal predictions. The model has not generated much new research on its basic tenets, and, until recently, there has been little effort to expand or modify the theory's propositions. Krumboltz et al. (1976) indicated that "the theory allows for modification by future events. In no sense is it intended as a final statement" (p. 71). Similarly, Mitchell and Krumboltz (1990) observed that the hypotheses they discussed "are only a small sample of those that might be derived from the theory. Much remains to be learned" (p. 177). Despite this flexibility and the addition of several novel concepts (e.g., world-view generalizations) that enhanced its descriptive potential, the basic theory has not evolved appreciably.

At a conceptual level, the theory deals with a valuable, albeit circumscribed, set of outcomes associated with career selection. It may help illuminate the career *choice* process, but, unlike many other career theories, it does not speak directly to such post-entry career development issues as work performance, persistence, and satisfaction. Also, although the model is conceived as relevant to *life-span* career selection issues, its research focus has generally been limited to student populations. Thus, it may be valuable to extend the empirical base to adult workers' decisional concerns (e.g., career change).

It may also be useful for the theory to be updated to encompass recent developments in general social cognitive theory (Bandura, 1986), and to employ conceptual terminology that is consistent with this larger model or accounts more clearly for conceptual disparities. For example, whereas Bandura described self-efficacy as a central cognitive pathway mediating behavior and behavior change, Krumboltz's parallel construct is not postulated to possess such overarching properties. Reconciliation of such differences, and incorporation of additional elements and features (e.g., outcome expectations, self-regulatory and motivational mechanisms, triadic reciprocality) from the larger model, might stimulate novel inquiry, help bridge Krumboltz's model with work on career self-efficacy, and facilitate efforts to generalize recent noncareer social cognitive theory findings to the career domain.

A recent paper by Krumboltz and Nichols (1990) may portend a somewhat different, yet exciting turn for Krumboltz's model. These authors presented Ford's (1987) integrative Living Systems Framework as a broader theoretical context within which Krumboltz's theory might be embedded. Further efforts to explicate the connections between the two systems, and their implications for career-related inquiry, could provide a fruitful new avenue for updating and expanding Krumboltz's theory.

Career Self-Efficacy

Bandura's (1986) recent recasting of social cognitive theory ascribes a central role to *self-efficacy beliefs* in guiding important aspects of psychosocial functioning. He defined self-efficacy (SE) expectations as "people's judgments of their capabilities to organize and execute courses of action required to attain designated types of performances" (p. 391). These expectations were postulated as helping to determine whether a given course of action will be initiated, as well as effort expenditure, persistence, thought patterns, and emotional reactions when confronted by obstacles. Other factors, such as *outcome expectations* (beliefs about the consequences of performance), *performance incentives,* and *environmental support* are also influential in determining behavior, although SE is generally described as the predominant causal mechanism.

In the social cognitive view, SE is not a passive, static trait; rather, it is seen as a dynamic aspect of the self-system that is specific to a given performance domain and that interacts complexly with other person, behavior, and environmental factors. The theory posits that accurate and strong SE expectations are crucial to the initiation and persistence of behavior in all areas of psychosocial functioning.

Recognizing the potential relevance of the SE construct to career development, Hackett and Betz (1981) outlined an extension of social cognitive theory to the career domain. They posited that SE influences the career decisions, achievements, and adjustment behaviors of both men and women, but they stressed SE theory's potential in explaining women's career development. They also offered a variety of specific predictions about the antecedents and consequences of career-related SE beliefs, although these were not organized into a formal set of theoretical propositions. Additional theoretical speculations have been offered in several subsequent papers (Betz & Hackett, 1986; Lent & Hackett, 1987). Most of the research on SE and career behavior that has appeared has addressed three broad topics suggested by Hackett and Betz (1981): (a) the relationship of career SE to career choice and decision making; (b) gender differences in career SE; and (c) efforts to modify SE.

Empirical Base

The literature on career SE has been reviewed recently by Betz and Hackett (1986) and Lent and Hackett (1987). They were generally sanguine about SE's promise in explaining certain career behaviors, but they discussed some important methodological and conceptual considerations and cited a number of overlooked empirical avenues. Several new career SE studies have appeared since these reviews. We highlight them here, along with other previously unreviewed investigations.

The largest subset of new research has explored self-efficacy in relation to career entry behaviors, such as occupational preferences or college performance; many of these same studies have also examined sex differences in SE percepts and/or potential correlates of SE (e.g., vocational interests). Betz and Hackett's (1981) initial investigation in this area has been partially replicated and extended by a number of researchers. Rotberg, Brown, and Ware (1987), studying community college students, reported that expressed interest and SE each predicted range of occupational consideration, and that sex-role orientation was related to SE perceptions. Hannah and Kahn (1989) found that 12th-grade males and females expressed stronger SE for occupations dominated by their own gender, and that efficacy beliefs varied by socioeconomic level, with lower status subjects reporting weaker SE. Matsui, Ikeda, and Ohnishi (1989) found sex differences in the SE ratings of Japanese college students, with women tending to report lower SE than men in male-dominated occupations. Clement (1987), however, found that SE did not contribute significantly to consideration of most male- or female-dominated career fields. Other investigators have reported sex differences in SE relative to specific gender-typed skill domains, such as math (Lapan, Boggs, & Morrill, 1989; Matsui, Matsui, & Ohnishi, 1990) and computer activities (Miura, 1987).

Two recent studies focused specifically on the relationships of SE to inventoried vocational interests. Lent, Brown, and Larkin (1989) found significant relations of SE to corresponding technical/scientific interest scales on the Strong–Campbell Interest Inventory (SCII) and Lapan et al. (1989), using path analyses, reported that math SE beliefs and high school preparation mediated gender differences in investigative and realistic themes on the SCII. Several other investigators have also found at least moderate relations between SE and measures of expressed or inventoried interests (Bores-Rangel, Church, Szendre, & Reeves, 1990; Miura, 1987; Rotberg et al., 1987).

A growing number of studies have explored SE in relation to indexes of career-relevant performance, generally finding that SE is a useful predictor of academic (Bores-Rangel et al., 1990) and analogue-task (Locke, Frederick, Lee, & Bobko, 1984) attainments. SE has also been found to moderate the relationship of aptitude to academic outcomes, with lower aptitude students achieving better grades and persistence if they possessed strong versus weak efficacy percepts (Brown, Lent, & Larkin, 1989). In a meta-analysis of the academic SE literature, Multon et al. (1991) found effect sizes of .38 and .34 for the relation of SE to measures of academic performance and persistence, respectively; this analysis also revealed several moderators of these relationships, such as subject age and achievement level, and the manner in which dependent variables were operationalized.

In addition to postulating relations of SE to occupational consideration and performance, Hackett and Betz (1981) predicted that SE may help explain decision-making outcomes, and several studies have explored this topic. Results generally indicated that higher SE regarding career decision-making skills is associated with less career indecision (Robbins, 1985; Taylor & Popma, 1990); more career exploratory activity (Blustein, 1989); higher levels of cognitive integration (Nevill, Neimeyer, Probert, & Fukuyama, 1986); and greater willingness of women to consider nontraditional (but not traditional) career options (Nevill & Schlecker, 1988). Other relevant studies have found SE measures to relate to college major decision status (Larson et al., 1988) and to course enrollment decisions (Hill, Smith, & Mann, 1987; Miura, 1987).

Hackett and Betz (1981) highlighted the relevance of SE to post-entry career variables, such as adjustment and performance in the workplace. Relevant research has revealed that SE significantly predicts sales performance (Barling & Beattie, 1983), job search success following layoff (Kanfer & Hulin, 1985), and preretirement worry (Fretz, Kluge, Ossana, Jones, & Merikangas, 1989). Two recent studies have explored sex differences in the work task-related SE of university faculty members (Landino & Owen, 1988; Schoen & Winocur, 1988). The SE construct has also been incorporated into recent conceptual models of work motivation and satisfaction (Locke & Latham, 1990) and organizational management (Wood & Bandura, 1989).

A few studies have appeared exploring the effects of intervention on career SE. Frayne and Latham (1987) found that a self-regulatory skills training program for government employees was successful in enhancing both SE regarding job attendance and actual attendance; posttest SE was also predictive of subsequent attendance. Fukuyama, Probert, Neimeyer, Nevill, and Metzler (1988) reported that a computerized career guidance program facilitated changes in decision-making SE and career indecision.

Lent and Hackett (1987) noted that intervention studies are important, in part, because they help to explore causal links between SE and behavior. It is noteworthy, therefore, that several experimental analogue (Hackett et al., 1990) and causal modeling (Hill et al., 1987; Locke et al., 1984) studies have been undertaken; their findings generally support hypothesized directional relations between performance and SE indexes. Investigations of SE in noncareer behavior domains have also corroborated the causal impact of SE on behavior, and behavior on SE (see Bandura, 1986).

Summary

The current review leads us to reaffirm our earlier observation that "there is growing empirical support for the extension of self-efficacy theory to career-relevant behavior" (Lent & Hackett, 1987, p. 362). More specifically, when the present findings are combined with those of previously reviewed studies (Betz & Hackett, 1986; Lent & Hackett, 1987), the following conclusions seem warranted:

1. SE beliefs are generally predictive of career entry indexes, such as range of perceived options, academic achievement and persistence, and career indecision;
2. SE percepts also relate to such important work adjustment outcomes as performance and coping with job loss;
3. Results of intervention, experimental analogue, and causal modeling studies demonstrate directional relations between performance and SE measures;

4. The pattern of relations between SE and alternative constructs, such as vocational interests and self-esteem, generally support the construct validity of SE indexes;

5. Gender differences in SE frequently help explain male–female differences in occupational consideration.

These conclusions must be tempered on several counts. First, not all findings have been supportive. For example, some studies have raised questions about SE's utility in predicting occupational consideration (Clement, 1987), the construct validity of particular SE measures (Robbins, 1985), or the size of SE's incremental contribution to predictive equations after other sources of variance have been controlled (Lent, Brown, & Larkin, 1986). Such anomalous findings impel a consideration of factors—for example, measurement, sampling, or data analytic differences—that may moderate SE effect sizes. Second, relatively few SE intervention or career adjustment studies have been conducted, making inferences about SE in these spheres very tenuous. Third, the gender–SE relationship is not simple or straightforward. Sex differences in SE have been documented with respect to gender-stereotypic tasks and occupational titles, but these differences are often apparent on only a portion of gender-typed items, and they may be offset when males and females possess similar interests or efficacy-relevant experiences (Lent et al., 1989; Schoen & Winocur, 1988). Younger (e.g., 8th and 9th grade) subjects may also be less likely than older students to express gender differences in SE (Post-Kammer & Smith, 1985). Whether societal changes in gender role socialization, the presence of less crystallized efficacy percepts in younger students, or design considerations are the cause remains an open question.

Thus far, Betz and Hackett's (1981) research agenda has received vigorous yet uneven empirical attention, with most studies involving career entry and sex difference issues. This work has been pivotal, but several topics, such as applications to career adjustment and intervention, deserve greater empirical scrutiny. Beyond exploring basic relations between SE and relevant career variables, there is also a need to extend study to more subtle, yet vital questions arising from this model. For example, assuming SE's role in guiding certain career behaviors, it is important to know more about how people construct SE beliefs (Matsui et al., 1990), how these beliefs can best be modified clinically and educationally, and how they may interact with other key person and environmental variables to facilitate or constrain career development.

Only a few years ago, we observed that career SE research had involved a relatively narrow array of career tasks, populations, and environmental contexts, and that most empirical activity had emanated from a small group of researchers (Lent & Hackett, 1987). These comments are clearly less valid at this time, because the past few years have witnessed a growing number of studies by independent research teams, involving diverse subject age groups, cross-cultural and foreign samples, and workplace (as opposed to strictly educational) contexts. This widening scope seems likely to beget yet further research expansion.

GENDER, ETHNICITY, AND CAREER DEVELOPMENT

There is a broad consensus that the effects of gender and ethnicity on career development need to be more fully understood (Osipow, 1983). Debate continues, however, as to whether independent theoretical models of women's and minority career development are needed, or whether these issues can adequately be incorporated into general models of career behavior (Astin, 1984; Betz & Fitzgerald, 1987; Osipow,

1983). Gottfredson (1986) advocated reframing the problem; she suggested that we address risk factors in career choice (e.g., poor education, cultural isolation), rather than focusing on gender or ethnicity per se. Such an approach, she argued, emphasizes concerns that are particularly problematic for certain groups but may also be factors limiting the career development of any individual.

Recent Theoretical Models of Women's Career Development

Focusing on the question of why women frequently achieve below their career potential, Farmer (1976) originally proposed a set of seven internal and external factors that inhibit women's achievement motivation: academic self-confidence, fear of success, vicarious achievement motivation, home–career conflict, myths about women and work, lower risk-taking behavior, and sex-role orientation. Ultimately, her research program culminated in a comprehensive statement of variables influencing both achievement and career motivation (Farmer, 1985). Farmer's model includes background variables (sex, race, age, SES, ability), which are hypothesized to influence personal variables (academic self-esteem, independence, values, and attributions) and environmental variables (parental and teacher support)—all of which, in turn, are hypothesized to influence motivational factors, namely level of aspirations, mastery strivings, and career commitment.

Astin's (1984) sociopsychological model of career choice and work behavior has generated heated debate. Astin (1984) attempted to account for both men's and women's career behavior by proposing a model incorporating basic drives, socialization processes, and structural influences affecting expectations and choices. Specifically, she proposed three basic needs (survival, pleasure, and contribution) that influence peoples' work motivation. These motivations are influenced, according to Astin, by sex-role socialization and the "structure of opportunity," for example, discrimination. Sex-role socialization and the structure of opportunity are seen as being mutually reciprocal, with both influencing expectations and, ultimately, career choice and work behavior.

Betz and Fitzgerald (1987) comprehensively reviewed research on the career psychology of women and summarized the literature by proposing four sets of factors facilitative of women's career choices: (a) individual variables (high ability, liberated sex-role values, instrumentality, androgyny, high self-esteem, strong academic self-concept); (b) background variables (working mother, supportive father, highly educated parents, female role models, work experience as an adolescent, androgynous upbringing); (c) educational variables (higher education, continuation in mathematics, women's schools); and (d) adult life-style variables (late marriage or single, no or few children). Betz and Fitzgerald also proposed a causal ordering of these variables.

Empirical Base

There have been, to our knowledge, no empirical tests of Astin's model, although Astin (1984) identified research in progress. In the most recent published test of Farmer's (1985) model, measures of background, personal, and environmental variables were employed to predict three aspects of achievement motivation. Using both men and women, as well as representative samples of White, Hispanic, Black, and Asian 9th- and 12th-grade students, Farmer (1985) found general support for her model. Separate path analyses indicated that different patterns of variables were influential in predicting each of the three aspects of achievement motivation included in the model (aspirations, mastery, and career commitment). Background variables were the strongest predictors of level of educational and occupational aspirations. Personal variables (especially independence) were most significant in the prediction of mastery motivation. Career motivation was very strongly predicted by personal variables, with background and environmental factors adding some predictive power to the model (Farmer, 1985). Overall, background variables such as sex, race, and socioeconomic status were indirectly predictive of achievement and career motivation. Farmer also found that different patterns existed for girls and boys and for Hispanic and Black girls when compared to White girls.

In addition to the longitudinal nature of her research program and the size and scope of her samples (Farmer, 1980, 1985), another strength of Farmer's research has been her attempt at model construction and testing via causal modeling procedures. On the other hand, although her findings are promising, the amount of variance in the data set explained by her model was modest, suggesting that there are other important factors not accounted for by the model.

Fassinger (1985) employed structural equation modeling procedures to test the Betz and Fitzgerald (1987) model; numerous tests and refinement resulted in a substantially revised version of the model. The revised model employed ability, achievement orientation, and feminist orientation as the independent variables influencing family and career orientation and, ultimately, career choice. Fassinger (1985) noted that feminist orientation was much more strongly predictive of career orientation than was originally suspected. In a second study, Fassinger (1990) tested a revised model, addressing some of the measurement and methodological problems encountered in her 1985 investigation, and also incorporating other theoretical work. Her findings indicated that higher ability levels, in complex interaction with instrumentality and liberal sex-role attitudes, positively influence career orientation and career choice.

Summary

A major problem in assessing the status of theorizing on women's career development is that each model addresses a different dimension of women's career behavior. Farmer (1985) attempted to explain three dimensions of achievement motivation, Astin's (1984) model addressed both career choice and work behavior at a very global level, and Betz and Fitzgerald (1987) identified factors relative to the realism of women's career choices (i.e., choices that are congruent with abilities and interests). On the other hand, this differential focus in theorizing mirrors the state of affairs in career psychology generally, with different theories developed for different purposes (Osipow, 1990).

Despite their different foci, these three conceptual models of women's career development do converge in some important ways. First, Farmer (1985) and Betz and Fitzgerald (1987) emphasized the relevance of "background" factors. Although these factors were conceptualized somewhat differently within each model, there does seem to be agreement that gender, ethnicity, parents' educational and occupational level, and socioeconomic status are important, although probably indirect, determinants of women's achievement-related choices and behaviors. Second, theorists agree that some type of personality or other "internal" traits and attitudes importantly influence women's work-related behavior. Farmer (1985) discussed achievement motivation, Betz and Fitzgerald (1987) and Farmer (1985) addressed academic self-concept and ability, and Astin (1984) proposed three basic needs. Third, socialization influences, whether operationalized as gender-role attitudes, feminist orientation, instrumentality, or androgyny, are generally viewed as crucial (Astin, 1984; Betz & Fitzgerald,

1987; Farmer, 1985). Fourth, there is consensus that cognitive appraisals and expectations need to be included in models of women's career development. Finally, theorists agree that women's career psychology cannot be understood without considering the social context—for example, role models, encouragement, perceived support, discrimination, and occupational sex stereotyping (Betz & Fitzgerald, 1987; Farmer, 1985; Fassinger, 1985).

Research on women's career development will undoubtedly continue to be bifurcated in the near future, with some efforts devoted toward incorporating gender issues into extant theories and others aimed at articulating specialized models of women's career psychology. (Fortunately, the days of studying simple sex differences, uninformed by any theory, seem to be waning.) We see both of these approaches as useful at this stage of inquiry. The former approach serves to enhance the comprehensiveness of the dominant theories, and the latter strategy ensures sustained attention to issues that have typically been neglected in the quest for unisex (or male-oriented) models of career development. Convergence between these two approaches seems likely in the long run. Gottfredson's (1986) focus on common "risk factors" across special groups also seems to be a lead worth pursuing at present, although it is important to consider that a given risk factor may get played out very differently for men and women.

We would like to cite a few additional, more specific conceptual and empirical directions for further work on women's career development. First, the trend toward model building and testing (Farmer, 1985; Fassinger, 1990) represents a significant advance in the literature, and one worth encouraging. However, considerable care must be exercised in designing causal modeling studies and in interpreting their findings. For example, a common problem has been the failure to specify an alternate model or models against which the author's model could be tested. Second, in addition to attending to the differences between men's and women's career patterns, we need to remain sensitive to their commonalities, as well as to the substantial heterogeneity *among* women, owing, for example, to cultural and socioeconomic factors. Third, and relatedly, much more attention to the career development of racial/ethnic minority women is needed.

It seems important for investigations of women's career development to explore, to a much greater degree, the structural and environmental factors that impinge on psychological processes. Attention to sex-role socialization has been valuable, but incorporation of other structural facilitators and barriers may further enhance our understanding of women and work. It is also important to remember that societal changes impact social roles generally, and women's career development in particular (Betz & Fitzgerald, 1987). These shifts may shorten the shelf life of past research findings; they also highlight the need for researchers to attend to current social realities and their interaction with career development processes.

Ethnicity and Career Development

Research on race/ethnicity and career development has fluctuated widely over the years, with quite a bit of activity in the 1970s (Smith, 1983) but comparatively little by the early 1980s (Hackett, Lent, & Greenhaus, 1991). Currently, there seems to be renewed interest in cultural, racial, and ethnic variables in career development, perhaps spurred by belated attention to this topic in the larger counseling literature (see Chapter 11, by Atkinson and Thompson; Helms, 1984; Smith, 1985). The effects of race/ethnicity have been acknowledged within several of the dominant and emerging career development theories (Gottfredson, 1981; Holland, 1985; Krumboltz et al.,

1976; Super, 1990), but have generally not been fully integrated conceptually nor given extensive empirical attention, within these perspectives (Fouad & Hansen, 1987; Gade et al., 1988).

Precursors to Model Building

No comprehensive models of minority career development currently exist, but several recent integrative reviews and conceptual proposals offer the hope of future progress. Cheatham (1990) proposed a model based on the concept of Africentrism, to account for some of the culturally relevant values influencing the career behavior of African Americans. He contrasted Africentric cultural values (affiliation, collectivity, interdependence, and different meanings attached to the value of work) with Eurocentric values characteristic of the dominant U.S. culture, such as competition, individuation, mastery over nature, and rigid adherence to time. Cheatham argued that awareness of such differences would contribute to heightened sensitivity to, and respect for, multicultural diversity. Leonard (1985) also emphasized the influence of cultural values on career development, and discussed problems in applying the concepts of career maturity, career aspirations and expectations, and self-concept theories to the career behavior of Black males.

Arbona (1990) provided an extensive review of Hispanic Americans' career development. The research literature is fragmentary, but she found evidence that middle-class and college-educated Hispanics and Anglos are more similar than different on numerous dimensions. The career-related topics most heavily researched with Hispanics have been occupational aspirations and interest measurement. Research on other topics—for example, the work attitudes, values, and job satisfaction of Hispanics—is virtually nonexistent. Arbona concluded that structural barriers and problems of access rather than interests or aspirations have been the most significant factors affecting occupational mobility among the diverse Hispanic groups. She also presented evidence indicating the cultural heterogeneity of Hispanics and argued for more research examining subgroups of Hispanic Americans, in order to clarify subcultural factors influencing career behavior.

In reviewing the literature on the career development of Asian Americans, Leong (1985) lamented the dearth of empirical research appearing between the early 1970s and mid-1980s. One issue continually raised is how the stereotype of Asian Americans as the "model minority" has masked the very real structural barriers and constraints faced by that diverse group. As identified by Leong, the major variables important to understanding the career development of Asian Americans include social and cultural barriers to occupational aspirations, acculturation and assimilation, occupational values that reflect Asian American cultures, and the personality traits of Asian Americans.

Summary

In addition to the relative absence of theory building and research on cultural influences in career development, the empirical research that does exist often yields conflicting findings (Smith, 1983). Several critical factors appear to have contributed to this situation, such as: (a) the interchangeable use of the terms race, ethnicity, and minority (Smith, 1983, and others noted important distinctions among these terms); (b) the confounding of SES, sex, family background, and race in research designs; (c) the search for simple race differences (usually Black/White) rather than examination of the cultural mechanisms producing observed differences; and (d) lack of attention to cultural heterogeneity within larger ethnic groups (Hispanics, for example, comprise a diverse group of subcultures). In addition to overcoming these conceptual and methodological flaws, theoretical models are needed to guide research on cultural influences in career development. The proposals of Cheatham, Leonard, Leong, and others can serve as a starting point. Finally, we must heed Smith's (1983) call to end the neglect of minority women, and focus increased attention on the interactions of race/ethnicity and gender.

FUTURE DIRECTIONS FOR THEORY AND RESEARCH

Enhancing Theory

We agree with Brown's (1990) assessment that theories of career development are at a relatively low level of scientific development, but we must also acknowledge the considerable advances that have been made in career psychology (Hackett et al., 1991). A number of the theoretical perspectives that have been dominant forces in the past are no longer considered of major importance (Bordin, Nachmann, & Segal, 1963; Ginzberg, Ginsburg, Axelrod, & Herma, 1951; Roe, 1956; Tiedeman & O'Hara, 1963); others have been refined and expanded, and have received renewed attention (Holland, 1985; Super, 1980, 1990); and several newer perspectives have been introduced over the past two decades (Gottfredson, 1981; Krumboltz et al., 1976). Such trends, reflecting movement and vitality in the field, were stimulated by numerous theorists and researchers, past and present, quite apart from the scientific accuracy of their formulations. We focus here on a few possibilities for enhancing further the theoretical base of career development.

Osipow (1990) provided a useful overview of convergences in career theory and identified Holland's approach, social learning perspectives, Super's developmental theory, and work adjustment theory as the major forces in career psychology today. He noted that each of these perspectives addresses, to different degrees and in different ways, the roles of biology, personality, and parental influences on career development. The life-span aspect of career behavior is also generally acknowledged, although only Super highlights particular life stages of career development (Osipow, 1990).

Biology, Personality, and the Family

Biological and genetic factors, although deemed important, are generally considered only peripherally or as uncontrollable influences on career development (Osipow, 1990); this is an area worthy of future conceptual and research attention (Arvey, Bouchard, Segal, & Abraham, 1989). Likewise, although existing personality models of career development have not borne much fruit, we would suggest that personality variables not be altogether abandoned. For example, certain dispositional factors, such as negative affectivity (Brief, Burke, George, Robinson, & Webster, 1988), bear closer scrutiny, as do newer psychodynamic perspectives (e.g., Robbins & Patton, 1985).

The self-concept (Gottfredson, 1981; Super, 1990) may also benefit from renewed consideration, particularly from alternative theoretical perspectives. It is noteworthy that Super has redefined the self-concept within his system to encompass "personal constructs," and has also begun examining role salience and multiple role influences (Super, 1990). Neimeyer and his associates (Neimeyer, 1988) have been studying the development of vocational schemata, and increasingly sophisticated models of the self are being brought to bear on counseling (Mahoney, 1991). Markus and Nurius' (1986) concept of "possible selves," for example, has clear implications for career behavior.

Roe's (1956) theory of early childhood influences on career choice has not fared well, but there are other viable frameworks for conceptualizing family and parental influences on the personality and career development. For example, attachment theory (Bowlby, 1982) has a sound empirical base and addresses some issues that Roe has grappled with; Adlerian approaches (Watkins & Savickas, 1990) consider early recollections and life-style and have direct implications for intervention; and family systems perspectives have also been applied to career development (see Chapter 8, by Lopez).

Life Stages

More work needs to be done in operationalizing the life-span perspective on career development. Super's life-space/life-span model is helpful; so too are the contributions of other developmental life-span theories (Levinson et al., 1978). Writers have repeatedly underscored our neglect of the processes of adult career development and adjustment, but work on that aspect of life-span development seems to be increasing (Hackett et al., 1991). Within the context of developmental models, it seems crucial to begin integrating knowledge of important work/nonwork reciprocities (Tinsley & Tinsley, 1988), as well as research on critical life events and life transitions (see Chapter 9, by Gibson and Brown). More fundamentally, we need to address the issues raised by Vondracek et al. (1986) regarding our very definitions of the term development, and we may also need to consider alternatives to stage conceptions, such as organismic and contextual theories of human development.

Decision-Making Processes

The major theories differ markedly in their conceptualizations of career decision making. Social learning theory specifically emphasizes the decision-making process (Krumboltz et al., 1976); decision making is addressed less explicitly in the other major models. However, even Krumboltz and his colleagues have not fully incorporated advances in basic psychological theory (Bandura, 1986) that may further explicate the complexity of career decision making. Conceptual models developed within social psychology also have promise in expanding our understanding of career decision making. For example, most career theorists seem to assume that information about self and the world of work will be processed objectively by clients. To the contrary, research on human inference processes suggests a variety of cognitive distortions that may bias information processing (see Chapter 5, by Heppner and Frazier).

Theory Testing and Integration

There are important areas of convergence among theories of career development, but there are significant differences as well; many areas of divergence are related to the varying purposes of the theories and the different vocational outcomes they attempt to explain. The significance of each theory, and judgments as to its contributions, must be made within the context of its purposes and goals (Gottfredson, 1983).

We believe it would be useful to continue conceptual and empirical work in pursuit of the varying goals and heterogeneous outcomes reflected in the major theories. However, we must also begin to consolidate our knowledge and to weigh the viability of competing theoretical constructs designed to explain common outcomes such as satisfaction, choice, success, and persistence. Thus, more direct comparisons of theory-based models are needed where different theories predict similar outcomes (Lent et al.,

1987). Meta-analysis (see Assouline & Meir, 1987, on congruence, and Multon et al., 1991, on self-efficacy) also offers a valuable tool for summarizing data on the explanatory or predictive utility of different theoretical constructs.

The time may be ripe for beginning to construct integrative theories that (a) bring together conceptually related constructs (e.g., self-concept, self-efficacy); (b) more fully explain outcomes that are common to a number of career theories (e.g., satisfaction, stability); and (c) account for the relations among seemingly diverse constructs (e.g., self-efficacy, interests, abilities, needs). In attempting an integrative approach to career development, it seems important to consider not only the elements of current vocational theories, but also the value of adopting a multidisciplinary, multilevel view of career behavior (Hackett et al., 1991; Vondracek et al., 1986).

Research Directions

Tying Research to Theory

Reviewers have repeatedly lamented the absence of a strong theoretical focus in much of the field's research (Fitzgerald & Rounds, 1989; Hackett et al., 1991). Some research is totally atheoretical; in other instances, theory is invoked post hoc to justify the study or explain its results (Fitzgerald & Rounds, 1989). Atheoretical research makes it difficult to organize research findings into themes or clusters, delaying aggregation of findings into a coherent knowledge base. Theory-based research, while vital, is not sufficient. *Programmatic* research testing the adequacy and comparative value of career theories is also important. Too many one-shot studies using unique measures compound interpretational difficulties.

Methodological Issues

There have been numerous calls for increasing the diversity of our data-analytic methods. Our ability to test more intricate conceptual models of career development has been limited in the past by the range of analysis options available to researchers. Now, however, highly sophisticated analytic procedures (e.g., causal modeling, multivariate techniques) have been developed and are increasingly being employed by career researchers. These technical advances may eventually enrich our knowledge base, but their very complexity creates problems in their proper use (Fitzgerald & Rounds, 1989).

Career researchers have traditionally relied heavily on quantitative, correlational methods; some of the questions being posed may be better addressed using other types of methods and designs (e.g., experimental, time-series, longitudinal). Further, there has been growing recognition of the potential value of alternate paradigms of inquiry and evolving epistemological views in the larger counseling psychology literature (see Chapter 4, by Borgen, and Chapter 20, by Mahoney and Patterson). These trends may encourage more intensive, qualitative, and contextually sensitive study of career developmental processes.

Intervention Studies

Because as counseling psychologists we are ultimately concerned with the practical application of our theories, we need to expend more effort in systematically deriving and testing theory-driven career interventions. Career interventions have been largely atheoretical (see Chapter 16, by Phillips), with a few notable exceptions such as

Krumboltz's work on cognitive methods (Mitchell & Krumboltz, 1990) and Holland's work on self-help devices (Holland, 1985). This state of affairs stands in sharp contrast to the literature on personal counseling, where most treatments for specific problems are anchored in theory. Crites' (1981) work and Walsh and Osipow's (1990) recent edited book could serve as guides for researchers attempting to develop and test theory-driven interventions.

REFERENCES

Alvi, S. A., Khan, S. B., & Kirkwood, K. J. (1990). A comparison of various indices of differentiation for Holland's model. *Journal of Vocational Behavior, 36,* 147–152.

Arbona, C. (1990). Career counseling research and Hispanics: A review of the literature. *The Counseling Psychologist, 18,* 300–323.

Arvey, R. D., Bouchard, T. J., Segal, N. L., & Abraham, L. M. (1989). Job satisfaction: Environmental and genetic components. *Journal of Applied Psychology, 74,* 187–192.

Assouline, M., & Meir, E. I. (1987). Meta-analysis of the relationship between congruence and well-being measures. *Journal of Vocational Behavior, 31,* 319–332.

Astin, H. S. (1984). The meaning of work in women's lives: A sociopsychological model of career choice and work behavior. *The Counseling Psychologist, 12*(4), 117–126.

Bandura, A. (1986). *Social foundations of thought and action: A social cognitive theory.* Englewood Cliffs, NJ: Prentice-Hall.

Barling, J., & Beattie, R. (1983). Self-efficacy beliefs and sales performance. *Journal of Organizational Behavior Management, 5,* 41–51.

Betz, N. E., & Fitzgerald, L. F. (1987). *The career psychology of women.* San Diego, CA: Academic Press.

Betz, N. E., & Hackett, G. (1981). The relationship of career-related self-efficacy expectations to perceived career options in college women and men. *Journal of Counseling Psychology, 28,* 399–410.

Betz, N. E., & Hackett, G. (1986). Applications of self-efficacy theory to understanding career choice behavior. *Journal of Social and Clinical Psychology, 4,* 279–289.

Blustein, D. L. (1988). A canonical analysis of career choice crystallization and vocational maturity. *Journal of Counseling Psychology, 35,* 294–297.

Blustein, D. L. (1989). The role of goal instability and career self-efficacy in the career exploration process. *Journal of Vocational Behavior, 35,* 194–203.

Blustein, D. L. (1990, April). *Explorations of the career exploration literature: Current status and future directions.* Invited address presented at the annual meeting of the American Educational Research Association, Boston, MA.

Blustein, D. L., Devenis, L. E., & Kidney, B. K. (1989). Relationship between the identity formation process and career development. *Journal of Counseling Psychology, 36,* 196–202.

Blustein, D. L., Ellis, M. V., & Devenis, L. E. (1989). The development and validation of a two-dimensional model of the commitment to career choice processes. *Journal of Vocational Behavior, 35,* 342–378.

Blustein, D. L., & Phillips, S. D. (1990). Relation between ego identity statuses and decision-making styles. *Journal of Counseling Psychology, 37,* 160–168.

Bordin, E. S., Nachmann, B., & Segal, S. J. (1963). An articulated framework for vocational development. *Journal of Counseling Psychology, 10,* 107–116.

Bores-Rangel, E., Church, T. A., Szendre, D., & Reeves, C. (1990). Self-efficacy in relation to occupational consideration and academic performance in high school equivalency students. *Journal of Counseling Psychology, 37,* 407–418.

Bowlby, J. (1982). *Attachment and loss: Vol. 1. Attachment* (2nd ed.). New York: Basic Books.

Brief, A. P., Burke, M. J., George, J. M., Robinson, B. S., & Webster, J. (1988). Should negative affectivity remain an unmeasured variable in the study of job stress? *Journal of Applied Psychology, 73,* 193–198.

Brooks, L., (1990). Recent developments in theory building. In D. Brown, L. Brooks, & Associates, *Career choice and development* (2nd ed.) (pp. 364–394). San Francisco: Jossey-Bass.

Brown, D. (1987). The status of Holland's theory of vocational choice. *Career Development Quarterly, 36,* 13–23.

Brown, D. (1990). Summary, comparison, and critique of the major theories. In D. Brown, L. Brooks, & Associates, *Career choice and development* (2nd ed.) (pp. 338–363). San Francisco: Jossey-Bass.

Brown, D., Brooks, L., & Associates. (1984). *Career choice and development.* San Francisco: Jossey-Bass.

Brown, S. D., Lent, R. W., & Larkin, K. C. (1989). Self-efficacy as a moderator of scholastic aptitude–academic performance relationships. *Journal of Vocational Behavior, 35,* 64–75.

Caplan, R. D. (1987). Person–environment fit theory and organizations: Commensurate dimensions, time perspectives, and mechanisms. *Journal of Vocational Behavior, 31,* 248–267.

Cheatham, H. E. (1990). Africentricity and career development of African Americans. *Career Development Quarterly, 38,* 334–346.

Clement, S. (1987). The self-efficacy expectations and occupational preferences of females and males. *Journal of Occupational Psychology, 60,* 257–265.

Crites, J. O. (1969). *Vocational psychology.* New York: McGraw-Hill.

Crites, J. O. (1978). *Theory and research handbook for the Career Maturity Inventory.* Monterey, CA: CTB/McGraw-Hill.

Crites, J. O. (1981). *Career counseling.* New York: McGraw-Hill.

Crites, J. O. (1990). *Career mastery inventory.* Boulder, CO: Crites Career Consultants, Inc.

Cron, W. L., Dubinsky, A. J., & Michaels, R. E. (1988). The influence of career stages on components of salesperson motivation. *Journal of Marketing, 52,* 78–92.

Dawis, R. V., England, G. W., & Lofquist, L. H. (1964). *A theory of work adjustment. Minnesota studies in vocational rehabilitation.* (Vol. 15). Minneapolis: Department of Psychology, University of Minnesota.

Dawis, R. V., & Lofquist, L. H. (1984). *A psychological theory of work adjustment: An individual differences model and its applications.* Minneapolis: University of Minnesota Press.

Doerring, M., & Rhodes, S. R. (1989). Changing careers: A qualitative study. *Career Development Quarterly, 37,* 316–333.

Doerring, M., Rhodes, S. R., & Kaspin, J. (1988). Factor structure comparison of occupational needs and reinforcers. *Journal of Vocational Behavior, 32,* 127–138.

Elton, C. F., & Smart, J. C. (1988). Extrinsic job satisfaction and person–environment congruence. *Journal of Vocational Behavior, 32,* 226–238.

Erwin, T. D. (1987). The construct validity of Holland's differentiation concept. *Measurement and Evaluation in Counseling and Development, 20,* 106–112.

Farmer, H. S. (1976). What inhibits career and achievement motivation in women? *The Counseling Psychologist, 6*(2), 12–14.

Farmer, H. S. (1980). Environmental, background, and psychological variables related to optimizing achievement and career motivation for high school girls. *Journal of Vocational Behavior, 17,* 58–70.

Farmer, H. S. (1985). Model of career and achievement motivation for women and men. *Journal of Counseling Psychology, 32,* 363–390.

Fassinger, R. E. (1985). A causal model of college women's career choice. *Journal of Vocational Behavior, 27,* 123–153.

Fassinger, R. E. (1990). Causal models of career choice in two samples of college women. *Journal of Vocational Behavior, 36,* 225–248.

Fitzgerald, L. F., & Rounds, J. B. (1989). Vocational behavior, 1988: A critical analysis. *Journal of Vocational Behavior, 35,* 105–163.

Ford, D. H. (1987). *Humans as self-constructing living systems: A developmental perspective on personality and behavior.* Hillsdale, NJ: Erlbaum.

Fouad, N. A., & Hansen, J. C. (1987). Cross-cultural predictive accuracy of the Strong–Campbell Interest Inventory. *Measurement and Evaluation in Guidance and Counseling, 20,* 3–10.

Frayne, C. A., & Latham, G. P. (1987). Application of social learning theory to employee self-management of attendance. *Journal of Applied Psychology, 72,* 287–392.

Fretz, B. R., Kluge, N. A., Ossana, S. M., Jones, S. M., & Merikangas, M. W. (1989). Intervention targets for reducing preretirement anxiety and depression. *Journal of Counseling Psychology, 36,* 301–307.

Fretz, B. R., & Leong, F. T. (1982). Career development status as a predictor of career intervention outcomes. *Journal of Counseling Psychology, 29,* 388–393.

Fukuyama, M. A., Probert, B. S., Neimeyer, G. J., Nevill, D. D., & Metzler, A. E. (1988). Effects of DISCOVER on career self-efficacy and decision making of undergraduates. *Career Development Quarterly, 37,* 56–62.

Fuqua, D. R., Seaworth, T. B., & Newman, J. L. (1987). The relationship of career indecision and anxiety: A multivariate examination. *Journal of Vocational Behavior, 30,* 175–186.

Gade, E., Fuqua, D., & Hurlburt, G. (1988). The relationship of Holland's personality types to educational satisfaction with a Native-American high school population. *Journal of Counseling Psychology, 35,* 183–186.

Gati, I. (1985). Description of alternative measures of the concepts of vocational interest: Crystallization, congruence, and coherence. *Journal of Vocational Behavior, 27,* 37–55.

Gati, I. (1989). Person–environment fit research: Problems and prospects. *Journal of Vocational Behavior, 35,* 181–193.

Gelatt, H. B. (1962). Decision making: A conceptual frame of reference for counseling. *Journal of Counseling Psychology, 9,* 240–245.

Ginzberg, E., Ginsburg, S. W., Axelrod, S., & Herma, J. L. (1951). *Occupational choice: An approach to a general theory.* New York: Columbia University Press.

Gottfredson, G. D., & Holland, J. L. (1990). A longitudinal test of the influence of congruence: Job satisfaction, competency utilization, and counterproductive behavior. *Journal of Counseling Psychology, 37,* 389–398.

Gottfredson, L. S. (1981). Circumscription and compromise: A developmental theory of occupational aspirations [Monograph]. *Journal of Counseling Psychology, 28,* 545–579.

Gottfredson, L. S. (1983). Creating and criticizing theory. *Journal of Vocational Behavior, 23,* 203–212.

Gottfredson, L. S. (1986). Special groups and the beneficial use of vocational interest inventories. In W. B. Walsh & S. H. Osipow (Eds.), *The assessment of interests* (pp. 127–198). Hillsdale, NJ: Erlbaum.

Greenhaus, J. H., Seidel, C., & Marinis, M. (1983). The impact of expectations and values on job attitudes. *Organizational Behavior and Human Performance, 31,* 394–417.

Greenlee, S. P., Damarin, F. L., & Walsh, W. B. (1988). Congruence and differentiation among Black and White males in two non-college-degreed occupations. *Journal of Vocational Behavior, 32,* 298–306.

Guthrie, W. R., & Herman, A. (1982). Vocational maturity and its relationship to Holland's theory of vocational choice. *Journal of Vocational Behavior, 21,* 196–205.

Hackett, G., & Betz, N. E. (1981). A self-efficacy approach to the career development of women. *Journal of Vocational Behavior, 18,* 326–336.

Hackett, G., Betz, N. E., O'Halloran, M. S., & Romac, D. S. (1990). Effects of verbal and mathematics task performance on task and career self-efficacy and interest. *Journal of Counseling Psychology, 37,* 169–177.

Hackett, G., Lent, R. W., & Greenhaus, J. H. (1991). Advances in vocational theory and research: A 20-year retrospective. *Journal of Vocational Behavior, 38,* 3–38.

Hannah, J. S., & Kahn, S. E. (1989). The relationship of socioeconomic status and gender to the occupational choices of grade 12 students. *Journal of Vocational Behavior, 34,* 161–178.

Harren, V. A. (1979). A model of career decision making for college students. *Journal of Vocational Behavior, 14,* 119–133.

Healy, C. C., & Mourton, D. L. (1985). Congruence and vocational identity: Outcomes of career counseling with persuasive power. *Journal of Counseling Psychology, 32,* 441–444.

Hecht, A. B. (1980). Nursing career choice and Holland's theory: Are men and Blacks different? *Journal of Vocational Behavior, 16,* 208–211.

Heesacker, M., Elliott, T. R., & Howe, L. (1988). Does the Holland code predict job satisfaction and productivity in clothing factory workers? *Journal of Counseling Psychology, 35,* 144–148.

Helms, J. E. (1984). Toward a theoretical explanation of the effects of race on counseling: A Black and White model. *The Counseling Psychologist, 12*(4), 153–165.

Henderson, S., Hesketh, B., & Tuffin, K. (1988). A test of Gottfredson's theory of circumscription. *Journal of Vocational Behavior, 32,* 37–48.

Henry, P., & Bardo, H. R. (1987). Expressed occupational choice of nontraditional premedical students as measured by the Self-Directed Search: An investigation of Holland's theory. *Psychological Reports, 60,* 575–581.

Hesketh, B. (1985). In search of a conceptual framework for vocational psychology. *Journal of Counseling and Development, 64,* 26–30.

Hesketh, B., Durant, C., & Pryor, R. (1990). Career compromise: A test of Gottfredson's (1981) theory using a policy-capturing procedure. *Journal of Vocational Behavior, 36,* 97–108.

Hesketh, B., Elmslie, S., & Kaldor, W. (1990). Career compromise: An alternative account to Gottfredson's theory. *Journal of Counseling Psychology, 37,* 49–56.

Hill, T., Smith, N. D., & Mann, M. F. (1987). Role of efficacy expectations in predicting the decision to use advanced technologies: The case of computers. *Journal of Applied Psychology, 72,* 307–313.

Holland, J. L. (1959). A theory of vocational choice. *Journal of Counseling Psychology, 6,* 35–45.

Holland, J. L. (1985). *Making vocational choices: A theory of vocational personalities and work environments* (2nd ed.). Englewood Cliffs, NJ: Prentice-Hall.

Holland, J. L. (1987a). Current status of Holland's theory of careers: Another perspective. *Career Development Quarterly, 36,* 24–30.

Holland, J. L. (1987b). Some speculation about the investigation of person–environment transactions. *Journal of Vocational Behavior, 31,* 337–340.

Holland, J. L., Daiger, D. C., & Power, P. G. (1980). *My Vocational Situation.* Palo Alto, CA: Consulting Psychologists Press.

Holland, J. L., Gottfredson, G. R., & Baker, H. G. (1990). Validity of vocational aspirations and interest inventories: Extended, replicated, and reinterpreted. *Journal of Counseling Psychology, 37,* 337–342.

Holt, P. A. (1989). Differential effects of status and interest in the process of compromise. *Journal of Counseling Psychology, 36,* 42–47.

Iachan, R. (1984). A measure of agreement for use with the Holland classification system. *Journal of Vocational Behavior, 24,* 133–141.

Jepson, D. A. (1984). The developmental perspective on vocational behavior: A review of theory and research. In S. D. Brown & R. W. Lent (Eds.), *Handbook of counseling psychology* (pp. 178–215). New York: Wiley.

Kanfer, R., & Hulin, C. L. (1985). Individual differences in successful job searches following lay-off. *Personnel Psychology, 38,* 835–847.

Kidd, J. M. (1984). The relationship of self and occupational concepts to the occupational preferences of adolescents. *Journal of Vocational Behavior, 24,* 48–65, 315–320.

Krumboltz, J. D. (1979). A social learning theory of career decision making. In A. M. Mitchell, G. B. Jones, & J. D. Krumboltz (Eds.), *Social learning and career decision making* (pp. 19–49). Cranston, RI: Carroll.

Krumboltz, J. D., Mitchell, A. M., & Jones, G. B. (1976). A social learning theory of career selection. *The Counseling Psychologist, 6*(1), 71–81.

Krumboltz, J. D., & Nichols, C. W. (1990). Integrating the social learning theory of career decision making. In W. B. Walsh & S. H. Osipow (Eds.), *Career counseling: Contemporary topics in vocational psychology* (pp. 159–192). Hillsdale, NJ: Erlbaum.

Krumboltz, J. D., & Rude, S. (1981). Behavioral approaches to career counseling. *Behavioral Counseling Quarterly, 1,* 108–120.

Landino, R. A., & Owen, S. V. (1988). Self-efficacy in university faculty. *Journal of Vocational Behavior, 33,* 1–14.

Lapan, R. T., Boggs, K. R., & Morrill, W. H. (1989). Self-efficacy as a mediator of Investigative and Realistic General Occupational Themes on the Strong–Campbell Interest Inventory. *Journal of Counseling Psychology, 36,* 176–182.

Larson, L. M., Heppner, P. P., Ham, T., & Dugan, K. (1988). Investigating multiple subtypes of career indecision through cluster analysis. *Journal of Counseling Psychology, 35,* 439–446.

Latona, J. R. (1989). Consistency of Holland code and its relation to persistence in a college major. *Journal of Vocational Behavior, 34,* 253–265.

Lent, R. W., Brown, S. D., & Larkin, K. C. (1986). Self-efficacy in the prediction of academic performance and perceived career options. *Journal of Counseling Psychology, 33,* 165–169.

Lent, R. W., Brown, S. D., & Larkin, K. C. (1987). Comparison of three theoretically derived variables in predicting career and academic behavior: Self-efficacy, interest congruence, and consequence thinking. *Journal of Counseling Psychology, 34,* 293–298.

Lent, R. W., & Hackett, G. (1987). Career self-efficacy: Empirical status and future directions [Monograph]. *Journal of Vocational Behavior, 30,* 347–382.

Lent, R. W., Larkin, K. C., & Brown, S. D. (1989). Relation of self-efficacy to inventoried vocational interests. *Journal of Vocational Behavior, 34,* 279–288.

Leonard, P. Y. (1985). Vocational theory and the vocational behavior of Black males: An analysis. *Journal of Multicultural Counseling and Development, 13,* 91–105.

Leong, F. T. (1985). Career development of Asian Americans. *Journal of College Student Personnel, 26,* 539–546.

Leong, F. T., & Morris, J. (1989). Assessing the construct validity of Holland, Daiger, and Power's measure of vocational identity. *Measurement and Evaluation in Counseling and Development, 22,* 117–125.

Leung, S. A., & Harmon, L. W. (1990). Individual and sex differences in the zone of acceptable alternatives. *Journal of Counseling Psychology, 37,* 153–159.

Leung, S. A., & Plake, B. S. (1990). A choice dilemma approach for examining the relative importance of sex type and prestige preferences in the process of career choice compromise. *Journal of Counseling Psychology, 37,* 399–406.

Levinson, D. J., Darrow, C., Klein, E., Levinson, M., & McKee, B. (1978). *The seasons of a man's life.* New York: Knopf.

Locke, E. A., Frederick, E., Lee, C., & Bobko, P. (1984). Effect of self-efficacy, goals, and task strategies on task performance. *Journal of Applied Psychology, 69,* 241–251.

Locke, E. A., & Latham, G. P. (1990). Work motivation and satisfaction: Light at the end of the tunnel. *Psychological Science, 1,* 240–246.

Lofquist, L. H., & Dawis, R. V. (1984). Research on work adjustment and satisfaction: Implications for career counseling. In S. D. Brown & R. W. Lent (Eds.), *Handbook of counseling psychology* (pp. 216–237). New York: Wiley.

Lopez, F. G. (1989). Current family dynamics, trait anxiety, and academic adjustment: Test of a family-based model of vocational identity. *Journal of Vocational Behavior, 35,* 76–87.

Lowe, B. (1981). The relationship between vocational interest differentiation and career undecidedness. *Journal of Vocational Behavior, 19,* 346–349.

Lucas, E. B., Gysbers, N. C., Buescher, K. L., & Heppner, P. P. (1988). My Vocational Situation: Normative, psychometric, and comparative data. *Measurement and Evaluation in Counseling and Development, 20,* 162–170.

Mahoney, M. J. (1991). *Human change processes.* New York: Basic Books.

Markus, H., & Nurius, P. (1986). Possible selves. *American Psychologist, 41,* 954–969.

Matsui, T., Ikeda, H., & Ohnishi, R. (1989). Relations of sex-typed socializations to career self-efficacy expectations of college students. *Journal of Vocational Behavior, 35,* 1–16.

Matsui, T., Matsui, K., & Ohnishi, R. (1990). Mechanisms underlying math self-efficacy learning of college students. *Journal of Vocational Behavior, 37,* 225–238.

Mazen, A. M. (1989). Testing an integration of Vroom's instrumental theory and Holland's typology on working women. *Journal of Vocational Behavior, 35,* 327–341.

Meir, E. I. (1988). The need for congruence between within-occupation interests and specialty in mid-career. *Career Development Quarterly, 37,* 63–69.

Meir, E. I. (1989). Integrative elaboration of the congruence theory. *Journal of Vocational Behavior, 35,* 219–230.

Meir, E. I., & Melamed, S. (1986). The accumulation of person–environment congruences and well being. *Journal of Occupational Behavior, 7,* 315–323.

Meir, E. I., & Yaari, Y. (1988). The relationship between congruent specialty choice within occupations and satisfaction. *Journal of Vocational Behavior, 33,* 99–117.

Mitchell, A. M. (1979). Relevant evidence. In A. M. Mitchell, G. B. Jones, & J. D. Krumboltz (Eds.), *Social learning and career decision making* (pp. 50–64). Cranston, RI: Carroll.

Mitchell, L. K., & Krumboltz, J. D. (1984). Research on human decision making: Implications for career decision making and counseling. In S. D. Brown & R. W. Lent (Eds.), *Handbook of counseling psychology* (pp. 238–280). New York: Wiley.

Mitchell, L. K., & Krumboltz, J. D. (1987). The effects of cognitive restructuring and decision-making training on career indecision. *Journal of Counseling and Development, 66,* 171–174.

Mitchell, L. K., & Krumboltz, J. D. (1990). Social learning approach to career decision making: Krumboltz's theory. In D. Brown, L. Brooks, & Associates, *Career choice and development: Applying contemporary theories to practice* (2nd ed.) (pp. 145–196). San Francisco: Jossey-Bass.

Miura, I. T. (1987). The relationship of computer self-efficacy expectations to computer interest and course enrollment in college. *Sex Roles, 16,* 303–311.

Monahan, C. J. (1987). Construct validation of a modified differentiation index. *Journal of Vocational Behavior, 30,* 217–226.

Monahan, C. J., & Muchinsky, P. M. (1985). Intrasubject predictions of vocational preference: Convergent validation via the decision theoretic paradigm. *Journal of Vocational Behavior, 27,* 1–18.

Moos, R. H. (1987). Person–environment congruence in work, school, and health care settings. *Journal of Vocational Behavior, 31,* 231–247.

Multon, K. D., Brown, S. D., & Lent, R. W. (1991). Relation of self-efficacy beliefs to academic outcomes: A meta-analytic investigation, *Journal of Counseling Psychology, 38,* 30–38.

Neimeyer, G. J. (1988). Cognitive integration and differentiation in vocational behavior. *The Counseling Psychologist, 16,* 440–475.

Nevill, D. D., Neimeyer, G. J., Probert, B., & Fukuyama, M. A. (1986). Cognitive structures in vocational information processing and decision making. *Journal of Vocational Behavior, 28,* 110–122.

Nevill, D. D., & Schlecker, D. I. (1988). The relation of self-efficacy and assertiveness to willingness to engage in traditional/nontraditional career activities. *Psychology of Women Quarterly, 12,* 91–98.

Nevill, D. D., & Super, D. E. (1986). *Manual for the salience inventory: Theory, application, and research.* Palo Alto, CA: Consulting Psychologists Press.

Ornstein, S., Cron, W. L., & Slocum, J. W. (1989). Life stage versus career stage: A comparative test of the theories of Levinson and Super. *Journal of Organizational Behavior, 10,* 117–133.

Ornstein, S., & Isabella, L. (1990). Age versus stage models of career attitudes of women: A partial replication and extension. *Journal of Vocational Behavior, 36,* 1–19.

Osipow, S. H. (1983). *Theories of career development* (3rd ed.). Englewood Cliffs, NJ: Prentice-Hall.

Osipow, S. H. (1990). Convergence in theories of career choice and development. Review and project. *Journal of Vocational Behavior, 36,* 122–131.

Parsons, F. (1909). *Choosing a vocation.* Boston: Houghton Mifflin.

Pazy, A., & Zin, R. (1987). A contingency approach to consistency: A challenge to prevalent views. *Journal of Vocational Behavior, 30,* 84–101.

Pervin, L. A. (1987). Person–environment congruence in the light of the person–situation controversy. *Journal of Vocational Behavior, 31,* 222–230.

Phillips, S. D., & Pazienza, N. J. (1988). History and theory of the assessment of career development and decision making. In W. B. Walsh & S. H. Osipow (Eds.), *Career decision making* (pp. 1–31). Hillsdale, NJ: Erlbaum.

Post-Kammer, P., & Smith, P. L. (1985). Sex differences in career self-efficacy, consideration, and interests of eighth and ninth graders. *Journal of Counseling Psychology, 32,* 551–559.

Pryor, R. G. L. (1987). Compromise: The forgotten dimension of career decision making. *British Journal of Guidance and Counselling, 15,* 158–168.

Pryor, R. G. L., & Taylor, N. B. (1986). What would I do if I couldn't do what I wanted to do? Investigating career compromise strategies. *Australian Psychologist, 21,* 363–376.

450 **CAREER AND EDUCATIONAL COUNSELING**

Remer, P., O'Neill, C. D., & Gohs, D. E. (1984). Multiple outcome evaluation of a life-career development course. *Journal of Counseling Psychology, 31,* 532–540.

Robbins, S. B. (1985). Validity estimates for the Career Decision-making Self-efficacy Scale. *Measurement and Evaluation in Counseling and Development, 18,* 64–71.

Robbins, S. B., & Patton, M. J. (1985). Self-psychology and career development: Construction of the superiority and goal instability scales. *Journal of Counseling Psychology, 32,* 221–231.

Roe, A. (1956). *The psychology of occupations.* New York: Wiley.

Rotberg, H. L., Brown, D., & Ware, W. B. (1987). Career self-efficacy expectations and perceived range of career options in community college students. *Journal of Counseling Psychology, 34,* 164–170.

Rounds, J. B. (1990). The comparative and combined utility of work value and interest data in career counseling with adults. *Journal of Vocational Behavior, 37,* 32–45.

Rounds, J. B., Dawis, R. V., & Lofquist, L. H. (1987). Measurement of person–environment fit and prediction of satisfaction in the theory of work adjustment. *Journal of Vocational Behavior, 31,* 297–318.

Rounds, J. B., Dawis, R. V., & Lofquist, L. H. (1979). Life history correlates of vocational needs for a female adult sample. *Journal of Counseling Psychology, 26,* 487–496.

Rounds, J. B., & Tracey, T. J. (1990). From trait-and-factor to person–environment fit counseling: Theory and process. In W. B. Walsh & S. H. Osipow (Eds.), *Career counseling: Contemporary topics in vocational psychology* (pp. 1–44). Hillsdale, NJ: Erlbaum.

Scarpello, V., & Campbell, J. P. (1983). Job satisfaction and the fit between individual needs and organizational rewards. *Journal of Occupational Psychology, 56,* 315–328.

Schoen, L. G., & Winocur, S. (1988). An investigation of the self-efficacy of male and female academics. *Journal of Vocational Behavior, 32,* 307–320.

Smith, E. J. (1983). Issues in racial minorities' career behavior. In W. B. Walsh & S. H. Osipow (Eds.), *Handbook of vocational psychology: Foundations* (Vol. 1, pp. 161–222).

Smith, E. J. (1985). Ethnic minorities: Life stress, social support, and mental health issues. *The Counseling Psychologist, 13,* 537–580.

Spokane, A. R. (1985). A review of research on person–environment congruence in Holland's theory of careers [Monograph]. *Journal of Vocational Behavior, 26,* 306–343.

Spokane, A. R. (1987). Introduction: Conceptual and methodological issues in person–environment fit research. *Journal of Vocational Behavior, 31,* 217–221.

Strahan, R. F. (1987). Measures of consistency for Holland-type codes. *Journal of Vocational Behavior, 31,* 37–44.

Super, D. E. (1953). A theory of vocational development. *American Psychologist, 8,* 185–190.

Super, D. E. (1957). *The psychology of careers.* New York: Harper & Row.

Super, D. E. (1980). A life-span, life-space approach to career development. *Journal of Vocational Behavior, 16,* 282–298.

Super, D. E. (1982). The relative importance of work: Models and measures for meaningful data. *The Counseling Psychologist, 10*(4), 95–103.

Super, D. E. (1984). Career and life development. In D. Brown, L. Brooks, & Associates, *Career choice and development* (pp. 192–234). San Francisco: Jossey-Bass.

Super, D. E. (1990). A life-span, life-space approach to career development. (pp. 197–261). In D. Brown, L. Brooks, & Associates, *Career choice and development* (2nd ed.). San Francisco: Jossey-Bass.

Super, D. E., & Kidd, J. M. (1979). Vocational maturity in adulthood: Toward turning a model into a measure. *Journal of Vocational Behavior, 14,* 255–270.

Super, D. E., Thompson, A. S., Lindeman, R. H., Jordaan, J. P., & Myers, R. A. (1984). *Technical manual for the Career Development Inventory.* Palo Alto, CA: Consulting Psychologists Press.

Super, D. E., Thompson, A. S., Lindeman, R. H., Myers, R. A., & Jordaan, J. P. (1985). *Adult Career Concerns Inventory.* Palo Alto: Consulting Psychologists Press.

Swanson, J. L., & Hansen, J. C. (1986). A clarification of Holland's construct of differentiation: The importance of score elevation. *Journal of Vocational Behavior, 28,* 163–173.

Taylor, K. E., & Weiss, D. J. (1972). Prediction of individual job termination from measured job satisfaction and biographical data. *Journal of Vocational Behavior, 2,* 123–132.

Taylor, K. M., & Popma, J. (1990). An examination of the relationships among career decision-making self-efficacy, career salience, locus of control, and vocational indecision. *Journal of Vocational Behavior, 37,* 17–31.

Taylor, N. B., & Pryor, R. G. (1985). Exploring the process of compromise in career decision making. *Journal of Vocational Behavior, 27,* 171–190.

Tiedeman, D. V., & O'Hara, R. P. (1963). *Career development and adjustment.* New York: College Entrance Examination Board.

Tinsley, H. E. A., Bowman, S. L., & York, D. C. (1989). Career Decision Scale, My Vocational Situation, Vocational Rating Scale, and Decisional Rating Scale: Do they measure the same constructs? *Journal of Counseling Psychology, 36,* 115–120.

Tinsley, H. E. A., & Tinsley, D. J. (1988). An expanded context for the study of career decision making, development, and maturity. In W. B. Walsh & S. H. Osipow (Eds.), *Career decision making* (pp. 213–264). Hillsdale, NJ: Erlbaum.

Tinsley, H. E. A., & Tinsley, D. J. (1989). Reinforcers of the occupation of homemaker: An analysis of the need-gratifying properties of the homemaker occupation across the stages of the homemaker life cycle. *Journal of Counseling Psychology, 36,* 189–195.

Tziner, A. (1983). Correspondence between occupational rewards and occupational needs and work satisfaction: A canonical redundancy analysis. *Journal of Occupational Psychology, 56,* 49–56.

Vandenberg, R. J., & Scarpello, V. (1990). The matching model: An examination of the processes underlying realistic job previews. *Journal of Applied Psychology, 75,* 60–67.

Vondracek, F. W., Lerner, R. M., & Schulenberg, J. E. (1986). *Career development: A life-span developmental approach.* Hillsdale, NJ: Erlbaum.

Walsh, W. B., & Osipow, S. H. (Eds.). (1983). *Handbook of vocational psychology.* Hillsdale, NJ: Erlbaum.

Walsh, W. B., & Osipow, S. H. (Eds.). (1990). *Career counseling: Contemporary topics in vocational psychology.* Hillsdale, NJ: Erlbaum.

Watkins, C. E., & Savickas, M. L. (1990). Psychodynamic career counseling. In W. B. Walsh & S. H. Osipow (Eds.), *Career counseling* (pp. 79–116). Hillsdale, NJ: Erlbaum.

Weinrach, S. G., & Srebalus, D. J. (1990). Holland's theory of careers. In D. Brown, L. Brooks, & Associates, *Career choice and development* (2nd ed.) (pp. 37–67). San Francisco: Jossey-Bass.

Westbrook, B. W. (1983). Career maturity: The concept, the instrument, and the research. In W. B. Walsh & S. H. Osipow (Eds.), *Handbook of vocational psychology: Vol. I* (pp. 263–304). Hillsdale, NJ: Erlbaum.

Wiggins, J. D. (1984). Personality–environmental factors related to job satisfaction of school counselors. *Vocational Guidance Quarterly, 33,* 169–177.

Wood, R., & Bandura, A. (1989). Social cognitive theory of organizational management. *Academy of Management Review, 14,* 361–384.

CHAPTER 14

CAREER ASSESSMENT:
A REVIEW OF CRITICAL ISSUES

NANCY E. BETZ

The topic of career assessment has traditionally generated interest among both researchers and practitioners in counseling psychology, and it continues to be an area characterized by considerable research and development activity. Assessment is an important part of the work of those involved in career counseling and consultation. In addition, measures of important career development concepts are essential to research that expands our understanding of the processes leading to successful career choices and adjustment across the life span.

In considering how to meaningfully discuss this huge topic within the confines of a book chapter, I had to make a number of decisions to delimit both the comprehensiveness and the depth of coverage. I elected, first of all, to focus on current issues in assessment, leaving comprehensive coverage of instruments and their research and counseling uses to the many available sources (see below). Where possible, however, I mention new instruments and revisions of existing instruments so that interested readers are apprised of the most recent additions to our assessment repertoire. Because the chapter focuses on current issues, it assumes, of necessity, a basic familiarity with career development concepts and instruments. Readers lacking this familiarity may wish to consult Walsh and Betz's (1990) *Tests and Assessment* and/or Anastasi's (1988) *Psychological Testing*. Readers interested in more expanded coverage of the use of assessment instruments in career counseling should consult Goldman's (1971) classic *Using Tests in Counseling* or the excellent recent volumes by Watkins and Campbell (*Testing in Counseling Practice,* 1990), Zunker (*Using Assessment Results for Career Development,* 1990), and Spokane (1991).

A second major decision was to focus on developments since the appearance of the first edition of this *Handbook*. Thus, my intentions are to provide an update for the reader that extends but does not supplant the excellent chapters contained in the first edition. Since the earlier *Handbook* appeared, there have been a number of important works related to the topic of career assessment. In particular, Walsh and Osipow have initiated a book series, *Advances in Vocational Psychology*. To date, the series includes *Volume I: The Assessment of Interests (1986), Volume II: Career Decision Making (1988),* and *Volume III: Career Counseling (1990).* A volume covering advances in the career counseling of women is currently in preparation. Readers wishing more depth of coverage on specific topics should consider these sources, as well as Watkins and Campbell (1990) and Walsh and Betz (1990).

In addition, there are several new or revised reference materials. These include the most recent revision of the *Standards for Educational and Psychological Testing* (American Educational Research Association, American Psychological Association, & National Council on Measurement in Education, 1985; "the APA Test Standards") the *Ninth* and *Tenth Mental Measurements Yearbooks* (Mitchell, 1985; and Conoley & Kramer, 1989, respectively); and revisions of *Test Critiques* (Keyser & Sweetland, 1985) and *Tests: A Comprehensive Reference for Assessments in Psychology, Education, and Business* (Sweetland & Keyser, 1986). Finally, in addition to the annual review articles published in the *Journal of Vocational Behavior* (Fitzgerald & Rounds, 1989; Morrow, Mullen, & McElroy, 1990; Phillips, Cairo, Blustein, & Myers, 1988) and, most recently, the *Career Development Quarterly* (Savickas, 1989), two reviews in the *Annual Review of Psychology* (Gelso & Fassinger, 1990; Osipow, 1987a) have appeared since the first *Handbook*.

This chapter is organized into two general areas of assessment in career counseling. The first covers issues in the assessment of traditional individual differences variables, including abilities, interests, needs, and values. The second covers measures of career choice process, including career maturity, career indecision, and career-related cognitions (e.g., self-efficacy expectations).

ISSUES IN ASSESSING INDIVIDUAL DIFFERENCES VARIABLES

The individual differences approach to career assessment stems historically from two areas of psychology: (a) the study and measurement of individual differences, and (b) Frank Parsons' (1909) "matching men and jobs" approach to career choice and guidance. The joining of the concepts and technology of individual differences with matching models of career choice led to "trait-factor" approaches to career development and adjustment. These approaches range from a general emphasis on the use of individual differences variables in selection, placement, and counseling to theories that focus on the correspondence between individuals and vocational environments. More recently, widespread interest in interactionist (person–environment) models of behavior (e.g., Pervin, 1987; Schneider, 1987; Spokane, 1987) has served to continue and broaden this tradition. Attempts to combine trait-factor career counseling with information-processing concepts from cognitive psychology and attitude change concepts from social psychology (Rounds & Tracey, 1990) have even further extended the possible range of trait-factor theories.

Simply stated, the basis of this approach is that: (a) individuals differ in their job-related abilities, interests, needs, and values; (b) jobs/occupational environments differ in the amount and nature of the rewards they offer and in the kinds of demands they make of the employee; and (c) congruence, or "fit," between an individual's characteristics and the characteristics of the job is an important consideration in making good career choices. The important individual differences variables that need to be taken into consideration include abilities and aptitudes (as included, for example, in the Theory of Work Adjustment, Dawis & Lofquist, 1984), vocational interests (e.g., as included in Holland's, 1985, theory), and needs and values (e.g., as included in the Theory of Work Adjustment). Career counselors and researchers should also take into account two of the most basic individual differences variables—gender and racial/ethnic group—because these variables have had massive influence on perceived career options and adjustment through such mechanisms as gender and race segregation, stereotyping, and gender and racial biases in the work world.

Abilities and Aptitudes

Recent Developments

The American College Testing Assessment (ACT) has been revised, providing a somewhat different set of subtests and scores. The subtests include English, Math, Reading, and Science Reasoning (vs. the older Social Science Reading and Natural Science Reading). The Assessment will yield a total of 12 subscores. There are also several relatively new or extensively revised multiple-aptitude batteries, including a revision of the Armed Services Vocational Aptitude Battery (ASVAB) and the relatively new Employee Aptitude Survey and Multidimensional Aptitude Battery (Jackson, 1984).

One especially promising new development is the availability of computer-administered *adaptive* tests, including the DAT-Adaptive, computer-administered adaptive versions of the ASVAB, and the Minnesota Clerical Assessment Battery (Moreno, Wetzel, McBride, & Weiss, 1984; Vale, 1990). An adaptive ability test is one in which examinees receive a set of items "tailored" or customized to their abilities. The computer calculates an estimated ability level following each item or set of items, and then selects from an internal item bank that item or set of items that is closest to (and, therefore, most likely to "refine" or add information to) the calculated ability estimate. In addition to reducing the number of items needed to obtain equally precise ability test scores, adaptive testing limits the extent to which examinees are subject to "failure" experiences because of repeated administrations of test items that are too difficult for them.

Another development having considerable relevance to both research and practice involves the findings that self-estimates of ability vary quite substantially from measured ability. Westbrook, Sanford, Gilleland, Fleenor, and Merwin (1988) and Lowman and Williams (1987) presented data showing inaccuracies of self-estimates of ability. Given the frequent use of such estimates as part of research data and/or as part of the assessment of interests in the Self-Directed Search (SDS, Abilities and Competencies subsections; also see Gottfredson, 1990), caution in such use is suggested.

Issues in Using Aptitude Tests with Racial/Ethnic Minorities

The fundamental issue in using tests with racial/ethnic minority groups is interpretation and use of ability and intelligence test scores. Among Blacks and other U.S. minorities, such as Hispanics and Native Americans, these scores are consistently lower on average than are the average scores of White individuals. Lower scores on such tests have adversely affected minorities' opportunities in higher education and employment and, consequently, constitute a serious barrier to equity in our society. Explanations for these differences imply means of ameliorating them, and two of the most heavily investigated explanations have been test bias and socioeconomic disadvantage.

Readers unfamiliar with concepts of test bias should consult the review by Betz (1990). Test constructors have addressed the problem of content bias by (a) obtaining expert judgments of the degree to which item content is culturally loaded and (b) soliciting item contributions from test professionals representing various cultural groups. The construction of scholastic aptitude and achievement tests is now done by panels of experts, including a representative balance of men and women, racial/ethnic group members, and members of different socioeconomic status (SES) groups. These panel members both contribute items and evaluate the item pool with the objective of minimizing gender, race, cultural, and class bias. Because of widespread criticism on this point, most widely used aptitude tests have been constructed and/or revised with the assistance of minority group experts. Test users and career researchers should evaluate any new test materials with an eye to these considerations.

Studies of possible internal test biases, for example, in factor structure (Humphreys & Taber, 1973; Jensen, 1980), have reported similarity across groups in factor structure and patterns. Studies of other internal characteristics of tests, such as item difficulty and item-total score correlations, have generally shown at least some group differences, but consistent patterns of difference, suggesting test revisions that could reduce race differences, have not yet been found (Cole, 1981). More research comparing tests' internal structural characteristics across groups is needed.

Studies of selection bias suggest that the majority of tests predict about as well for minority group members as they do for majority group members. If anything, use of the overall regression lines leads to overprediction rather than underprediction of the criterion performance of minority group members (Cole, 1981; Hunter, Schmidt, & Hunter, 1979). In general, findings that the use of overall group regression lines benefits Blacks are also true for lower SES groups and, in general, for groups obtaining lower *mean* test scores (see Linn, 1982, for a review of pertinent research). Thus, there is little, if any, evidence that psychological tests discriminate against Blacks in a predictive sense; in fact, the use of total group regression lines is likely in some cases to benefit the Black applicant.

Unfortunately, addressing (and trying to correct) the biases in *tests* has not, nor will it ever, ameliorate the problem of the negative impact that testing has on Blacks and members of other minority groups. In other words, a test can be valid and relatively free of bias, yet still produce scores having negative results for Blacks, for example, scores that lead to the rejection of proportionately more Black than White applicants for a college or a job. Blacks and other minorities are much more likely than Whites to be disadvantaged socioeconomically, which, among other things, may expose them to poorer school systems and deprive them of educational opportunities that would facilitate their performance on standardized tests. Until minority group members have equal economic, educational, and political opportunities throughout their lives, race must be a significant factor in any selection decision.

Operationally, the manuals for tests like the SAT (Scholastic Aptitude Test) and ACT Assessment recommend that test scores be only one of many criteria used in selection, and that institutional diversity should be an objective of the overall admissions policy. It is the responsibility of college and university personnel to develop policies that foster diversity and provide opportunities to underrepresented groups. In fact, most colleges, and graduate and professional schools, are using data that complement test scores in admissions decisions, and test scores may not even be important in many admissions decisions. Kaplan (1982) and Linn (1982) demonstrated that tests like the SAT have very little effect on whether a given individual will go to college. According to Hartnett and Feldnesser (1980), a third of all colleges accept 90% or more of those applying, and only 10% of schools select fewer than 50% of their applicants. Although SATs may be too low for acceptance to Harvard or Princeton, they rarely stand in the way of a college education. Further, many institutions selectively accept and reject people without ever using tests at all (Hartnett & Feldnesser, 1980; Linn, 1982).

As for the use of tests in employment selection, one bitterly discussed issue is the role of "g," or general intelligence, in worker performance. Gottfredson (1986a, 1988) defended use of "g" measures; Prediger (1989) contended that more than "g" is important to job performance. The implications of such discussions are far-reaching: if "g" is all-important, then race differences on measures of "g" have particularly adverse consequences for equality of opportunity.

Regardless of the discussion about the nature and causes of race differences in test performance, most would agree that tests should *not* be the only basis on which to decide access to educational and occupational opportunities in our society. Concerns about past inequities and their possible continuing effects on Blacks and other disadvantaged groups must be part of any decision that controls access to opportunities. Test users must familiarize themselves with the technical and interpretive considerations and cautions necessary in testing minority group members and, most importantly, must confront the inherent contradictions between certain aspects of the institutional value system and the societal value of equal opportunity. It may be valuable to develop decision models that can simultaneously consider quantitative assessment data and institutional objectives of equal opportunity and affirmative action. Also, where possible, tests should serve a developmental function; they can clarify *how* the individual's talents can be further developed and utilized.

For individual counseling, one of the most important things to recall in using ability or aptitude tests with minority group members is the APA Test Standard (1985), which reads: "A test taker's score should not be accepted as a reflection of a lack of ability with respect to the characteristic being tested without alternative explanations for the test taker's inability to perform on that test at that time" (p. 43). In interpreting the ability test scores of a minority group member, the likelihood that the individual has come from a socioeconomically and educationally disadvantaged background *must* be kept in mind. There are many reasons, such as lack of motivation, why students of all races and SES backgrounds might underutilize their intellectual potential, but, because minority students often start with a less advantaged educational background, experiences that can help to enrich that background are vital.

Gender Issues in Aptitude Testing

For women, lower mathematical aptitude scores on tests such as the SAT and Graduate Record Examination (GRE) have deleterious effects on selection and, *especially,* scholarships and financial aid programs in higher education. Some recent research has focused on content biases in tests of mathematics aptitude. For example, predominantly male characters in word problems, sexist language, and sex-biased or stereotypic content have frequently been used (Betz & Fitzgerald, 1987). As an example of the effects of item content, Betz and Hackett (1983) measured the perceived self-efficacy expectations of college women and men with respect to 52 math tasks and problems. As predicted, males reported higher expectations of self-efficacy on 49 of the 52 math- related items, but there were *3 items* on which females reported higher expectations of self-efficacy than males, and those items used stereotypically "female" domains: (a) "Figure out how much material to buy in order to make curtains"; (b) "Estimate your grocery bill in your head as you pick up items"; and (c) "Calculate recipe quantities for a dinner for 41 when the original recipe was for 12 people."

Given these data, one wonders what the effects would be of testing math ability, as well as math self-efficacy, using a more gender-balanced set of items. If the sex differences in self-efficacy expectations can be eliminated by asking questions based on content familiar to women, it seems that ability measurement could also be revised. A similar conclusion has been made by Lunneborg and Lunneborg (1986) in their research exploring experiential bases for the development of spatial ability.

In addition, recent research has strongly suggested that women's performance in college and graduate school is *underpredicted* by their aptitude test scores (Rosser, 1989). In other words, a given SAT score predicts a higher college grade point average (GPA) for a female than a male student, even in math and science courses. One of the results is that women get better grades in college and graduate school than do men, even in science, mathematics, and engineering majors. Thus, use of combined sex selection procedures and/or regression equations using SAT or GRE scores *is* discriminatory against female students, assuming that academic performance is the criterion of interest. Because of the underprediction of females' performance by aptitude test scores, several well-known institutions (e.g., Bates, Bowdoin, and Middlebury colleges) no longer use them in admissions or financial-aid decisions, relying instead on high school grades (see Rosser, 1989).

Even if a test profile is not used in selection, it may be used by a client and counselor to help make educational and career decisions. In this respect, it is vital to recall that we cannot accurately measure an ability, or an interest, if the person's background experience has provided only limited exposure to that domain of competency; again, the APA Test Standard, cautioning against inferences of ability deficit prior to examining other explanations, is relevant. For example, the literature suggests that sex differences in math performance begin to appear only as girls stop taking math, and that the differences disappear when math background is controlled (see Betz & Fitzgerald, 1987, for an extensive review). Although Benbow (1988) has suggested that gender differences in math aptitude exist independent of coursework differences, this view has been contested (Becker & Hedges, 1988; Humphreys, 1988).

There are several ways to address these issues. First, it is critical that counselors, when interpreting differential aptitude test scores (e.g., mathematics vs. verbal ability), remember that gender-role socialization shapes girls and boys differently, that girls are not encouraged to continue taking math, and that girls may need more help in building confidence and reducing anxiety with respect to math. The amount of math taken in high school and college is strongly related to the degree to which educational and career options remain open to the individual. A counselor examining a pattern of aptitude test scores should be particularly sensitive to low tested math aptitude in the context of overall high ability. Other responses include the use of same-sex norms in interpreting ability test scores; advocacy efforts that urge test publishers to include test items representing the experiential backgrounds of both sexes; and cognizance of the overall tendency of females to underutilize their abilities in educational and career pursuits.

Interests

Recent Developments

Recent reviews of the history and future of interest measurement have been provided by Zytowski and Borgen (1983), Hansen (1984), and *The Assessment of Interests,* edited by Walsh and Osipow (1986). Most recently, Watkins and Campbell's (1990) *Testing in Counseling Practice* covered the Strong Interest Inventory, the Kuder Occupational Interest Survey (KOIS), the Career Occupational Preference System (Knapp-Lee, Knapp, & Knapp, 1990) and the Self-Directed Search (Spokane, 1990). Readers wishing more detail should consult these works.

According to Hansen (1984), the field of interest testing has experienced much growth with expanded use of interest inventories, development of new interpretive materials, and testing of new populations. The past few years have seen continued increase in the popularity and use of career guidance instruments in general, including interest inventories. It is estimated that 3.5 million interest inventories are administered each year. The market is a lucrative one, which unfortunately leads to hasty and/or unsophisticated instrument development. The exploding market is also fueled by increasing use of computerized administration and scoring of the inventories, including the development of computer-generated "cookbook" interpretations (Borgen, 1986), similar to those that have been available for years for tests such as the MMPI.

The pace of activity in interest measurement is also reflected in recent revisions of the major interest inventories—the Strong Interest Inventory, the KOIS, the SDS, and the Vocational Preference Inventory (VPI). The Strong Interest Inventory (Hansen & Campbell, 1985) was completely revised in 1985, and summaries of the new version are contained in Hansen (1986, 1990). The current version contains 264 scales; these include 6 General Occupational Theme Scales measuring Holland's Theory, 23 Basic Interest Scales, 207 occupational scales (105 female-normed and 102 male-normed), 2 special scales, and 26 administrative indexes.

The KOIS, Form DD was also revised in 1985 (Zytowski & Kuder, 1986). The revision was summarized by Diamond (1990) and reviewed by Tenopyr (1989) and Herr (1989). The most conspicuous aspect of the revision is a new report form, providing information on four different types of scales: Dependability, Vocational Interest Estimates, Occupations, and College Majors.

The 1985 version of the SDS has been described by Holland and Rayman (1986) and Spokane (1990) and reviewed by Daniels (1989) and Manuele-Adkins (1989). One aspect of the revision was the rewriting of about one-fourth of the items (59 of 228), with the objective of increasing scale validity and reducing age and gender biases. In addition, the Occupations Finder was increased from 500 to 1,156 occupations.

The 1985 revision of the VPI (reviewed by Shepard, 1989b, and Vacc, 1989b) is substantially the same as its 1977 predecessor. It uses 160 occupational titles to yield scores on 11 scales—the 6 Holland themes, plus Self-Control, Masculinity–Femininity, Status, Infrequency, and Acquiescence. The revision involved changing four occupational titles, to reduce weighting of titles toward males. Three new short forms are designed for research on the Holland constructs, although not for counseling use.

As discussed by Borgen (1986), there have also been several more recent additions to the interest inventory market, "beyond the big three" (p. 92). These include:

1. The Career Assessment Inventory (CAI; Johansson, 1982), an adaptation of the Strong Interest Inventory focusing on "nonprofessional" occupations requiring no postsecondary education. The CAI-Enhanced (Johansson, 1986) focuses on careers requiring up to four years of college.

2. The Jackson Vocational Interest Survey (JVIS; Jackson, 1977), which consists of 34 basic interest scales including "work roles" (creative arts, mathematics), "work styles" (e.g., independence, planfulness), and scales such as dominant leadership and stamina, which resemble personality measures. Most notably, the JVIS was constructed to facilitate research on constructs related to career decision making (e.g., interests, work styles) rather than only for use in career counseling. (See Shepard (1989a) for a review.)

3. The Unisex Edition of the ACT Interest Inventory (UNIACT; Lamb & Prediger, 1981), which assesses the 6 Holland themes via 90 items (15 per theme). The 90 items were selected based on minimal response differences between males and females at the item level and the selection, for each scale, of an item set yielding approximate gender balance. The UNIACT is part of the ACT Assessment and

career planning services, and is administered annually to 1.5 million high school and college students and adults.

4. The Vocational Interest Inventory (VII; Lunneborg, 1981), which, like the UNI-ACT, uses minimally sex-restrictive items, that is, items eliciting minimal sex differences in response rates. Like the UNIACT, the VII is based on a well-known vocational taxonomy, in this case Roe's group classification.

Issues in Interest Measurement: Sex Restrictiveness

A comprehensive review of issues regarding sex restrictiveness in interest measurement is beyond the scope of this chapter (readers should consult Betz, 1990, and Walsh & Betz, 1990), but the problem essentially involves the fact that interest inventories have historically yielded different score patterns for men and women and, consequently, suggested a divergent and gender-stereotypic set of occupations to each. For example, because most interest scales are composed of items differentially reflective of the experiences of males versus females (the items "I like to build things with wood" and "I like to take care of children" are illustrative), it is not surprising that, when raw scores or combined sex norms are used, females obtain higher mean scores on the Social, Artistic, and Conventional themes, and males obtain higher mean scores on the Realistic, Investigative, and Enterprising themes (Gottfredson, Holland, & Gottfredson, 1975; Prediger & Hanson, 1976). High scores on the Social and Conventional themes suggest traditionally female occupations involving educational, social welfare, and clerical roles (Holland, 1973, 1985). In contrast, females' lower scores on the Realistic, Investigative, and Enterprising themes result in less frequent suggestion of traditionally male professions—medicine, engineering, science, business management, and the skilled trades (Holland, 1973, 1985).

In response to the criticisms of sex restrictiveness (Diamond, 1975; Tittle & Zytowski, 1978), test developers addressed these issues by combining men's and women's forms (e.g., the Strong Interest Inventory), by eliminating sexist language, and by discussing issues of sex-role socialization in interpretive materials (Association for Measurement and Evaluation in Guidance, Commission on Sex Bias in Measurement, 1977; "the AMEG Commission"). In addition, some test developers focused on reducing the sex-restrictiveness of interest inventory scores through the use of *same-sex normative scores* and/or *sex-balanced items.*

The use of same-sex norms increases the likelihood that the background socialization experiences of the comparison sample are more similar to those of the examinee, and this in turn tends to highlight interests that have developed in spite of the limiting effects of gender-role socialization. Sex-balanced item sets, on the other hand, are constructed to include some items more likely to characterize male sex-role socialization and others more common in female socialization. The desired end result is interest scales on which the sexes obtain similar raw scores. As mentioned, the UNIACT (Lamb & Prediger, 1981) and the revised version of the VII (Lunneborg, 1980, 1981) are based on this strategy of scale construction. On the UNIACT, for example, the Realistic scale contains items pertaining to content areas more often emphasized in female socialization (e.g., sewing and cooking), in addition to items more reflective of males' experiences (e.g., mechanical skills).

Instruments such as the UNIACT and the VII are examples of homogeneous interest scales that result in a more balanced suggestion of occupations to males and females. Some authors (Betz, 1990; Betz & Fitzgerald, 1987) would suggest that, until the gender-role socialization of males and females changes to allow both genders unrestricted access to a full range of experiences relevant to the development of vocational interests (including, for example, science and shop for girls and social skills and home economics for boys), same-sex norms and/or sex-balanced inventory scales should be used to minimize the overdetermining effects of stereotypic socialization practices on subsequent career options. It may be useful to again recall the APA Test Standard, which warned of the danger of interpreting low test scores as indicative of ability deficits prior to exhausting alternative explanations. I would suggest that interpretation of low scores on interest scales as indicative of lack of interest should be deferred until alternative explanations, such as lack of background exposure to a particular area, have been considered.

Other complementary points of view have also been articulated. In a fine review, Gottfredson (1986b) offered a number of suggestions regarding the "science and art of beneficial test usage" (p. 136), with particular reference to "special groups" such as women and ethnic minorities. She noted that the relatively new "special groups" focus in vocational psychology has, appropriately, forced us to consider external constraints to, as well as internal psychological factors in, career development. However, Gottfredson contended that we have focused too much on across-group comparisons of hardships and disadvantages, and less than we need to on the general nature of "risk factors" in career choice and development, and their implications for career counseling. Risk factors discussed by Gottfredson include poor education, low self-esteem, and family responsibilities.

Gottfredson also suggested that inventories should be viewed as treatments that, in part, expand perceived options, and that these treatments are most useful when embedded within a broader career counseling process that recognizes constraints on career choice, for example, those facing women and minorities. Holland (1990) also indicated the importance of interventions for increasing women's competence and self-beliefs in Realistic activities such as mechanical and manual abilities. Betz's (1989) article concerning the null educational environment provided a related philosophical basis for proactive career counseling interventions.

Inventory Use with Minority and Cross-Cultural Clients

It is especially important to validate the use of interest inventories with ethnic minorities in the United States, because these constitute a large potential clientele deserving of unbiased career counseling. The utility of interest inventories cannot be automatically assumed; rather, it needs careful empirical scrutiny. Ponterotto (1988) provided an excellent review of current needs for research on counseling ethnic minorities, and Carter and Swanson (1990) reviewed research regarding the use of the Strong Interest Inventory with Black clients (in a 68-year time period, only 8 studies of the Strong Interest Inventories with Blacks were located). We must redress such omissions.

Examples of recent work include that of Fouad and Hansen on the cross-cultural utility of the Strong Interest Inventories (Fouad, 1984; Fouad, Cudeck, & Hansen, 1984; Fouad & Hansen, 1987). In an important study, for example, their utility with bilingual Hispanic high school students was investigated (Fouad et al., 1984). Gade, Fuqua, and Hurlburt (1988) investigated the validity of Holland's theory among Native American high school students, and Khan, Alvi, Shankat, Hussain, and Bais (1990) examined the utility of the SDS and Holland's theory among Pakistani students.

Research on Holland's Constructs

Hackett and Lent, in Chapter 13, provide a comprehensive discussion of research on Holland's theory, and important recent papers (Gottfredson, 1990; Holland, 1990; Holland & Gottfredson, 1990) have summarized the current state of the theory and needed work in theory development, research, and applications. Thus, my discussion here will only briefly mention research related to the Holland constructs of congruence, differentiation, and consistency. Iachan (1990) proposed several extensions to his widely used congruence index. Strahan (1987) proposed two new measures of consistency for use with Holland codes (consistency is defined as the extent to which an individual's code consists of related versus unrelated scale types (e.g., Realistic/Investigative versus Realistic/Social (RI vs. RS)). Erwin (1987) discussed the construct validity of Holland's concept of differentiation, and Monahan (1987) and Alvi, Khan, and Kirkwood (1990) examined the validity and utility of various indexes of differentiation. Gottfredson (1990), however, noted that those proposing new indexes have yet to demonstrate that they produce outcomes more in accordance with theory than do the old, simpler indexes.

The concept of congruence continues to intrigue researchers. Spokane (1985) reviewed research on person–environment congruence in Holland's theory and, later, edited a special issue of the *Journal of Vocational Behavior* on person–environment theory and research (Spokane, 1987). Articles in this volume included relevant reviews (Pervin, 1987); presentation of supplementary versus complementary models of congruence (Muchinsky & Monahan, 1987); and a study of alternative operationalizations of "correspondence" in the Theory of Work Adjustment and implications for "commensurate measurement," that is, methods allowing persons and environments to be assessed on the same dimensions and units of measurement (Rounds, Dawis, & Lofquist, 1987).

The Structure and Dimensionality of Interests

Another important line of research concerns the structure and dimensionality of interests. Dimensionality issues refer to how *many* basic dimensions of interest to conceptualize and measure. Well-known models include 2 (the World of Work Map; Prediger, 1976), 6 (Holland), 8 (Roe), and 10 (Kuder) dimensions. Issues of structure pertain to how interest dimensions are related to one another. Holland's hexagon is probably the best known structural model, but others include the World of Work Map used in the UNIACT (Prediger, 1976, 1982) and Roe's circular ordering.

Explorations of dimensionality and structure constitute an important challenge to researchers, at least in part because they have implications for the assessment of interests. Itamar Gati and his colleagues (e.g., Gati, 1979; Benyamini & Gati, 1987) have compared hierarchical versus circular models of the structure of interests and have found strong support for a hierarchical ordering based on similarity of "occupational aspects." Other recent work includes that of Lapan, McGrath, and Kaplan (1990) on the factor structure of the SVIB-SCII Basic Interest scales by gender across time; Brookings and Bolton's (1989) examination of the factor structure of the USES Interest Inventory; and Cunningham, Slonaker, and Riegel's (1987) derivation of interest factors from job–analytically based activity preference scales.

Facilitating work on the structure of interests is the increasing availability of a variety of methods of multidimensional scaling (MDS; Fitzgerald & Hubert, 1987). Gati (1979) and his colleagues (Benyamini & Gati, 1987) and Rounds (in press) are among those making use of MDS techniques to explore the structure of interests.

Advances in Theory Development

I would suggest that continuing efforts to understand the structure and dimensionality of interests provide one approach to addressing Borgen's (1986) concern about the lack of theory-based research related to interests, except for that investigating Holland's theory. Borgen noted that interest assessment has been extremely successful and practically useful, but that we still have limited conceptual understanding of the nature of interests as a psychological variable. Borgen recommended more attention to the linkages of interests and personality (as recently exemplified by the study of Costa, McCrae, and Holland, 1984) and to the utility of expressed versus inventoried interests. A recent study by Holland, Gottfredson, and Baker (1990) reported the predictive superiority of occupational aspirations (expressed occupational interests) over measured interests. In addition, I would suggest that one obviously neglected area is that of the development and modifiability of interests. We know very little about how interests develop, about the degree to which they are genetically as well as environmentally based, and about their modifiability. Given such issues as gender differences in interests, and the newer fields of leisure and retirement planning, understanding of how interests can develop and expand throughout the life span would have important counseling implications.

One recent contribution in this area was Barak, Librowsky, and Shiloh's (1989) model proposing three cognitive determinants of interest: perceived abilities, expected success, and anticipated satisfaction. Another approach to this topic integrates Holland's theory with Owens and Schoenfeldt's (1979) work on biodata. Research by Eberhardt and Muchinsky (1982, 1984) demonstrated significant relationships between life-history experiences and vocational interests. Most recently, Smart (1989) used biodata to examine the development of Holland types within individuals. Smart's finding that family background experiences were particularly influential in Holland type development raises the interesting possibility that Roe's theory (based heavily on early family experiences) could be integrated within a larger theoretical framework explaining vocational interest and personality development.

Needs and Values

The third important individual differences variable in career development includes motivational constructs, which have been variously termed needs, values, and preferences. These constructs have been measured by such well-known instruments as the Minnesota Importance Questionnaire (MIQ; Weiss, Dawis, Lofquist, Gay, & Hendel, 1975) and Super's Work Values Inventory (WVI; Super, 1973) and Values Scale (VS; Super & Nevill, 1986b). As will be discussed shortly, there remains much conceptual confusion in this area of measurement.

Recent Developments

One noteworthy new measure is the Work Aspect Preference Scale (WAPS; Pryor, 1983, 1987), which assesses 13 dimensions of work values, each measured by four items. The values are: Independence, Coworkers, Self-Development, Creativity, Money, Life-Style, Prestige, Altruism, Security, Management, Detachment, Physical Activity, and Surroundings. Another important direction involves measuring the importance of career pursuits in relationship to other life domains. Masih (1967) and Greenhaus (1971) can be credited with originating the concept of career salience. Greenhaus's (1971) 27-item measure of career salience has been used extensively, facilitating research on women's career development and dual-career couples over the past two decades (Betz & Fitzgerald, 1987). More recently, Super and Nevill (1986a) developed the Salience Inventory (SI), a 170-item inventory scored for participation in, commitment to, and value expectations of five major life roles: student, worker, homemaker (including spouse and parent), leisurite, and citizen. The respective roles are also referred to in terms of activities: study, work, home and family, leisure, and community service.

Conceptual Issues

One vexing issue facing researchers and counselors is that, even though the concepts of needs, values, and preferences are *defined* differently, they seem to measure an overlapping set of variables. As defined in the Theory of Work Adjustment (Dawis & Lofquist, 1984), "needs are preferences for reinforcers expressed in terms of the relative importance of each reinforcer to the individual" (Rounds, Henley, Dawis, Lofquist, & Weiss, 1981, p. 8). Thus, vocational needs are, ideally, satisfied by reinforcers in the occupational environment. In the theory, values are described as basic dimensions underlying needs, that is, as second-order needs. The concept of work values is exemplified by the work of Super (1973), for whom values were "objectives that one seeks to attain to satisfy a need . . . these are the objectives sought in behavior" (p. 190). Thus, for Super, values are specific objectives designed to satisfy more basic needs, just the opposite of the Theory of Work Adjustment conception. Pryor's (1983) preferences are, essentially, degrees of liking for particular qualities or aspects of the work environment.

The *contrast* in definitions of needs and values is obfuscated by a *similarity* in scale concepts and names. For example, the MIQ (which measures *needs*) and the WVI and VS (measures of *values*) all contain the following scales: Achievement, Creativity, Economic Returns (called Compensation on the MIQ), Security, Social Interaction (Coworkers on the MIQ, and Associates on the WVI), Variety, and Working Conditions (Surroundings on the WVI). In fact, the 21 MIQ and 21 VS scales overlap almost completely. The WAPS also contains several scales that are analogous to those on the MIQ, VS, and WVI—for example, Creativity, Security, and Working Conditions.

The similarity in these measures' component scales is, in one sense, encouraging because it suggests a logical, intuitive convergence on the kinds of things people look for in satisfying work. On the other hand, the law of parsimony is one of the fundamental objectives of scientific progress, and multiple names for a single entity or concept violate this law. Thus, more research investigating the interrelationships of these constructs is needed.

An excellent step in this direction was made by MacNab and Fitzsimmons (1987), who used multitrait–multimethod methodology and confirmatory factor analysis to examine the relationships among eight traits, each of which was measured by four different instruments. The traits—Authority, Coworkers, Creativity, Security, Independence, Altruism, Working Conditions, and Prestige—were contained in one measure of "needs" (the MIQ), two of "values" (the WVI and Values Scale), and one of "preferences" (the WAPS). On the basis of strong evidence for convergent and discriminant validity, the researchers concluded that the four measures were measuring highly similar constructs. A strategy that may provide useful information for the domain of needs and values (as it has for interests) involves investigation of the dimensionality and structure of motivational constructs. Multidimensional scaling, and factor and cluster analysis, may provide valuable analytic methods in this inquiry.

Interests versus Values

A welcome recent trend in research has been the use of both interest and value concepts and measures in the prediction of vocational outcomes. Pryor and Taylor (1986) studied students' preferences for college courses and found that interests were more closely related to preferences than were values. Rounds (1990) studied 187 female and 218 male adult clients for whom Holland General Occupational Themes (GOT) scores (from SCII), MIQ scores, and job satisfaction data were available. The congruence of interests and work environment and the correspondence of needs and reinforcers were used to predict job satisfaction. Results indicated that work value correspondence accounted for a significant proportion of the variance, after controlling for interest congruence; that interest congruence was a better predictor for females than for males; and that there was a moderate relationship between congruence and correspondence among females but not males.

Finally, there is a need for theory and research on the development of individual differences in work needs and work salience; this focus is also needed in the study of vocational interests. One recent contribution was that of Sverko (1989), who proposed a model of the origin of individual differences in the importance attached to work.

Summary

The area of individual differences in vocationally relevant attributes provides a rich array of both concepts and measures. These continue to generate considerable research and test development activity, as well as controversy regarding the fairness and/or appropriateness of particular measures for different genders, racial/ethnic groups, and cultures. Overall, there is need for more work on individual differences variables' (a) applicability across genders, races, and cultures; (b) theoretical linkages; (c) structure and dimensionality, and (d) development and modifiability.

CAREER ASSESSMENT: PROCESS VARIABLES

The preceding section derived from the trait-factor theoretical approach to career psychology. This section has as its basis the developmental theories first postulated in the 1950s with the work of Super (1957) and Ginzberg, Ginsburg, Axelrad, and Herman (1951), and has been enhanced significantly by current interest in what may be termed "career cognitions."

Major tenets of Super's developmental theory were the ideas that vocational development could be conceived as following a series of stages: growth, exploration, establishment, maintenance, and decline. Most significant for the concept of vocational maturity was Super's postulate that each of the vocational life stages presented one or more vocational tasks or challenges which the individual needed to successfully negotiate or master, in order to progress in his/her career development. Two related types of measures emerged from this developmental emphasis. One focused on the individual's possession of the necessary skills, attitudes, and resources to make a good career decision (or, more recently, to successfully master the vocational tasks of adulthood); these can be summarized as measures of career maturity and adjustment. The second measure focused on decisional status and difficulties associated with making a career decision, including measures of career indecision and career-related cognitions such as self-efficacy expectations and irrational beliefs.

Career Maturity and Adjustment

Recent Developments

The oldest and best known measures of career maturity are Crites's Career Maturity Inventory (CMI) and Super's Career Development Inventory (CDI). These instruments were reviewed by Betz (1988) and Savickas (1990), both of whom expressed concern about the internal consistency and test–retest reliability of measures of career maturity, as well as their predictive and construct validity.

Westbrook and his colleagues (Westbrook et al., 1985) took a different approach to the conceptualization and assessment of career maturity. They postulated that the construct of career maturity includes different elements, traits, aspects, or factors, all of which have something in common with each other and with the process of making an "appropriate" career choice. Westbrook et al. (1985) developed new measures of these aspects of career maturity, designed specifically for use with 11th graders. Collectively denoted the Career Planning Questionnaire (CPQ), the battery consists of: (a) Career Decisions, similar to the aims of the Career Decision Scale (CDS; Osipow, Carney, Winer, Yanico, & Koschier, 1976); (b) Career Activities, similar to other measures of career exploratory activities; (c) Career Salience, similar in conception to Greenhaus's (1971) Career Salience Scale and Super and Nevill's (1986b) Salience Inventory; (d) Self-Knowledge, similar to the Self-Appraisal test of the CMI Competencies Test; (e) Career Concerns, similar to the Problem-Solving Test of the CMI Competencies Test and also, in some respects, to the CDS or My Vocational Situation (Holland, Daiger, and Power, 1980); and (f) Knowledge of Career Values, similar to other self-knowledge tests.

Another relatively new instrument is Harren's (1979) Assessment of Career Decision Making (ACDM), a measure of rational, intuitive, and dependent styles of decision making. In addition to these styles, the ACDM also assesses progress in school adjustment, and degree of commitment toward and certainty about major and occupational goals. A manual is available (Buck & Daniels, 1985), and the ACDM was reviewed by Eberhardt (1989) and Vacc (1989a) in the *Tenth Mental Measurements Yearbook*.

Defining Career Maturity

There is a need for investigation of the meaning of the career maturity construct. Westbrook (1983), for example, stated that there is little consensus on (a) the number, names, or organization of dimensions of career maturity; (b) the relative degree of emphasis of scales on cognitive, affective, and psychomotor behavior; (c) whether dimensions postulated should be covered using single- or multi-item scales; or (d) the emphasis on occupational information. The lack of convergent validity among career maturity measures as a group and their typically high correlations with ability measures also lead to confusion about the meaning of the construct.

One of the most useful ways of investigating construct validity involves the construction and evaluation of a nomological network (Cronbach & Meehl, 1955) specifying the system of variables within which a given construct resides. A nomological network is useful for both the evaluation of construct validity and the explication of the *meaning* of the construct (Cronbach & Meehl, 1955). Different researchers may postulate different nomological networks for a construct, and both or all can contribute to understanding. For example, Betz (1988) proposed a model including both antecedents and consequences of career maturity. The antecedent variables included higher versus lower intelligence, which positively influences school performance as well as career maturity;

a construct called "acceptance of middle class values," which Crites (1978) postulated is the explanation for race and SES differences in career maturity; and "extent of career-related experiences during childhood and adolescence," including availability of occupational role models, opportunity to learn about a variety of careers, and work experience.

The use of intelligence as an antecedent would allow the theoretical integration of evidence regarding moderate to high career maturity–intelligence correlations, without necessarily rendering maturity as unnecessary. As long as there are other antecedents to and consequences of career maturity after partialling out intelligence, the construct can be meaningful and important. Betz (1988) noted another advantage of this model: it attempts to explain the development of career maturity by constructs other than age increase. Age alone is atheoretical; that is, it does not imply an underlying psychological process. The question of what it is about the *aging* process that leads to increasing career maturity is a theoretical question.

In Betz's model, the consequences of career maturity include realistic career decisions; consistency of choices over time, field, and level (outcome variables in Crites's theory of career maturity); and, later, indicators of vocational success and satisfaction. Research on this model would add to understanding of the development, as well as the incremental predictive utility, of the career maturity construct.

Alternatively, Savickas (1984) proposed an S–O–R (stimulus–organism–response) framework for the understanding and applied use of variables related to career maturity. In Savickas's conceptualization, vocational development tasks are the stimulus variables, and the measurement objective is to assess the clients' degree of vocational development, also referred to as decisional status. Intervening (organismic) variables are the personal characteristics that determine how effectively individuals respond to the tasks facing them. Intervening variables can be motivational (the CMI—Attitude Scale), structural or cognitive (the CMI—Competencies Scale), and content-related (e.g., interests and values). Finally, response variables are the coping thoughts and behaviors utilized by the individual in response to tasks. Response measures would include the Vocational Exploration Behavior Checklist (Krumboltz & Thoresen, 1964) and the Career Exploration Survey (Stumpf, Colarelli, & Hartman, 1983).

Another useful approach to understanding the career maturity construct involves both rational and analytical studies of its dimensionality. Jepsen (1984) reported a rational clustering of age-related changes in career behavior, culled from the relevant literature. The ten thematic clusters included several that relate to career maturity concepts or measures: vocational choice realism, vocational choice rationale, vocational choice attitudes (the CMI—Attitude Scale), vocational decision-making processes (the ACDM), occupational knowledge, and vocational exploratory behavior (including scales of the ACDM and the CDI). Note that the categories of attitudes, cognitive (occupational knowledge), and psychomotor (exploratory behavior) are all represented, as are several categories not directly associated with existing measures of career maturity.

What is needed now is further understanding of the relationships among these components and, especially, investigation of the incremental contribution, if any, of each component to career maturity criteria. Answers to questions like "Can a measure of cognitive career maturity predict affective and behavioral, as well as cognitive, outcome variables?" and "Is one component of career maturity sufficient to predict major criterion variables, or do we *need* two or more?" are essential to the ultimate goals of parsimony and efficiency in theoretical understanding and applied use of the construct.

Measures of Career Development in Adulthood

One of the most interesting recent developments in the field of career assessment is the application of career developmental concepts to the later (vs. earlier) stages of career development, including the tasks adults face as they progress in the work domain of their lives. As in the assessment of career maturity in adolescence and young adulthood, Super and Crites have taken the leadership roles, developing the Adult Career Concerns Inventory and the Career Mastery Inventory, respectively.

The Adult Career Concerns Inventory (ACCI; Super, Thompson, Lindeman, Myers, & Jordaan, 1985) measures career concerns typical of the Exploration, Establishment, Maintenance, and Disengagement stages of career development, and also assesses the degree to which the individual is considering a career change. A manual now available (Super, Thompson, & Lindeman, 1987) summarizes research to date by the scale developers. Some evidence for validity is provided in the manual and in Halpin, Ralph, and Halpin (1990), but, overall, much more evidence for both predictive and construct validity is needed. Suggested practical uses of the ACCI include needs assessment of adult workers and assessment of career counseling outcome. However, Brown and Rounds (1987) noted that, until adequate norms, more understandable self-scoring procedures, and more information concerning the interpretation of scales and scores are available, the instrument should be used cautiously in counseling.

The Career Mastery Inventory (CMAS; Crites, 1990) assesses mastery of six developmental tasks postulated to be important in the Establishment stage of career development. The scale and the tasks assessed were based on Crites's (1976) Model of Career Adjustment in Early Adulthood and a "diagnostic taxonomy" of career problems among adults (Campbell & Cellini, 1981). The six career developmental tasks are as follows:

1. Organizational adaptability—processes such as becoming socialized in the organization and "learning the ropes";
2. Position performance—learning the content of the job, its duties and responsibilities;
3. Work habits and attitudes—being dependable, having a positive attitude, and being receptive to supervision;
4. Coworker relationships—getting along well with others on the job and dealing effectively with interpersonal conflicts as they arise;
5. Advancement—moving up the organizational ladder;
6. Career choice and plans—looking ahead and planning for the future.

The CMAS is logically appealing, but its widespread use should await the appearance of its forthcoming *Theory and Research Handbook*. The earlier version of the CMAS, the Career Development and Adjustment Inventory, was characterized by low internal consistency values for the individual scales and by low score ceilings, which attenuated the range of scores (Fitzgerald, 1984). On the other hand, encouraging evidence for validity was reported (Fitzgerald, 1984). Savickas, Passen, and Jarjoura (1988), who recently compared the ACCI and CMAS (at that time, the CADI), reported that CMAS scores were related to occupational congruence and job satisfaction, but that the ACCI was not related to coping as postulated. More work on both of these instruments is generally needed.

Classification of Career Stages

Given the importance of understanding adult career development, it is surprising that the measurement of adult career stages has received comparatively little attention; specifically, we lack a reliable and generally agreed-on method of classifying individuals into career stages (Greenhaus & Parasuraman, 1986). A growing body of research has investigated behavioral and attitudinal correlates of career stages (Rabinowitz & Hall, 1981; Slocum & Cron, 1985); yet, as noted by Slocum and Cron (1985), it is difficult to integrate findings across studies when different researchers operationalize career stages in different ways. Further work on the definition of career stages and the conceptualization and measurement of the tasks required to negotiate successive career stages and career transitions would contribute greatly to the field of vocational psychology and career development.

Career Indecision

Recent Developments

Savickas (1989), Slaney (1988), and Sepich (1987) provided excellent reviews of career indecision measures. The oldest and best known measure of career indecision is the Career Decision Scale (CDS; Osipow et al., 1976). A manual for the CDS is available (Osipow, 1987b), as is extensive evidence for the reliability and validity of the CDS (see Osipow, 1987b; Slaney, 1988).

Recent work on the CDS has included continued investigations of its factor structure, with the objective of identifying basic dimensions of indecision. For example, Shimizu, Vondracek, Schulenberg, and Hostetler (1988) reanalyzed data from seven previous studies using oblique rotation, and reported more similarities in the factor structures than those found in previous studies. Further, they replicated their basic findings in a new sample, indicating four factors that they considered to be homogeneous subscales of career indecision: feelings of indecision, relative decidedness but need for reinforcement and support, approach–approach conflict, and internal and external barriers.

Subsequently, Schulenberg, Shimizu, Vondracek, and Hostetler (1988), using confirmatory factor analysis, found a relatively good fit of the four-factor model across four age groups (junior high to high school). Vondracek, Hostetler, Schulenberg, and Shimizu (1990) also examined the usefulness of four linearly independent scales based on the four factors identified by Shimizu et al. (1988). Although the work of the Vondracek/Schulenberg group is noteworthy in terms of its programmatic nature and its focus on elucidating the dimensionality of the CDS, replication of these findings by *other* researchers would increase confidence in the stability of the four-factor structure.

My Vocational Situation (MVS; Holland et al., 1980) includes the Vocational Identity (VI) Scale and two items assessing Occupational Information and Barriers. Lucas, Gysbers, Buescher, and Heppner (1988) collected normative data and examined the psychometric properties of the MVS in samples of college freshmen and adults seeking career counseling. Leong and Morris (1989) administered the MVS, Harren's ACDM, the VPI, the CMI—Attitude Scale, and a measure of Locus of Control, among others, to college students. Results indicated that scores on the MVS-VI scale were: negatively related to social anxiety and tolerance for ambiguity; positively related to the ACDM rational style but negatively related to both the intuitive and dependent styles; and positively related both to Holland's Investigative scale and the CMI—Attitude Scale (48% shared variance between VI and the CMI—Attitude Scale).

Tinsley, Bowman, and York (1989) administered the MVS, CDS, Vocational Rating Scale, and Decisional Rating Scale to college students, and factor-analyzed both scale scores and individual items. The MVS-VI Scale loaded primarily on the first factor, labeled clarity, along with the VRS, DRS, and CDS certainty scales. However, VI also loaded on all three other factors, suggesting its factorial complexity. Hartman, Fuqua, and Jenkins (1988) provided additional evidence for the concurrent validity and scale characteristics of the MVS.

Jones (1989) began work on a revised version of the Vocational Decision Scale (Jones & Chenery, 1980), to be called the Career Decision Profile (CDP). The Decidedness and Comfort scales were increased from one to two items, and seven categories of reasons for career undecidedness were identified a priori and then measured: lack of information, conflict with significant others, lack of information about self, need for cognitive structures relating self to careers, indecisiveness, lack of self-clarity, and choice–work salience. Jones (1989) suggested the usefulness of the CDP in identifying two groups of students who are seldom mentioned in the indecision literature: those who are decided yet not very comfortable with their decision (21% of Jones sample) and those who are undecided but comfortable with that state of affairs (8%). This distinction highlights the fact that decidedness is not always a "good thing" and, conversely, that undecidedness is not always associated with discomfort.

Callahan and Greenhaus (1990) developed a scale to measure career indecision in managers and professionals. Factor analyses of an initial pool of 32 items related to possible sources of indecision revealed seven factors accounting for 54% of the total variance. The factors were: lack of self-information, lack of internal work information, lack of external work information, lack of decision-making self-confidence, decision-making fear and anxiety, nonwork demands, and situational constraints. This effort to acknowledge, conceptualize, and measure the problem of adult career indecision is laudable.

Dimensionality of Career Indecision

Although there is a general consensus that career indecision is multidimensional, there is a lack of agreement concerning both the number and nature of these dimensions. If career indecision is multidimensional, then reliance on an undifferentiated total score is unsatisfactory (Fitzgerald & Rounds, 1989).

In addition to factor analyses of individual scales, studies of the interrelationships among two or more of these scales are now vital to an understanding of the nature and dimensionality of the broader construct of career indecision. Fortunately, several recent studies have examined such relationships. Fuqua, Seaworth, and Newman (1987) conducted canonical and factor analyses of four measures of indecision and four measures of anxiety. The career measures were the CDS, MVS, VDS, and CMI—Attitude Scale. They found *one* canonical root, accounting for 44% of the variance between the "career" set and the anxiety set; a clear two-factor structure (where all the career measures loaded together, as did all the anxiety measures); and high correlations $(r = .80$ to $.85)$ among the CDS, MVS, and VDS, indicating impressive convergent validity for all three measures of indecision.

Fuqua and Newman (1989) examined the interrelationships and factor structure of 13 subscales contained in four measures of career indecision, along with measures of state and trait anxiety. The measures used were the CDS, MVS, CDP, CMI—Attitude

Scale, and State-Trait Anxiety Inventory. Factor 1, accounting for 43% of the total variance, was a decidedness factor that involved some information about both self and occupations. Factor 2 (8% of the variance) was an indecision factor associated with barriers to choice, indecisiveness, lack of clear self-identity, and immaturity. Factor 3, which was somewhat difficult to interpret, seemed to reflect affective *comfort* with the career state; this factor accounted for 5% of the variance. Other interesting findings were that the CDS Indecision Scale loaded significantly (≥ .40) on all three factors, and that the MVS-VI Scale loaded highly on the first two factors. Factors 1 and 2 were both significantly related to anxiety, with higher decidedness associated with less anxiety and more indecision associated with greater anxiety.

As mentioned earlier, Tinsley et al. (1989) factor-analyzed the scale scores and items of the CDS, MVS, VRS, and DRS. Three factors, named crystallization, decision-making obstacles, and indecision, emerged from the factor analyses of the scale scores. Three stable factors emerged from the analyses of items—clarity, certainty, and indecision.

Conceptual Advances

A current area of research interest involves the differentiation of simple indecision from pervasive indecisiveness. Indecision has been viewed as a normal stage of development, which most young adults resolve with relative ease, either with or without counseling or informational assistance (Slaney, 1988). However, there is a subset of young people who have been called "chronically undecided" or "indecisive" (as opposed to undecided) (e.g., Goodstein, 1965). Chronically undecided students are generally found to have less adaptive cognitive and personality characteristics (e.g., external vs. internal locus of control) than do developmentally undecided students (e.g., Holland & Holland, 1977).

Slaney (1988) noted that progress in conceptual understanding is limited by our lack of a measure of indecisiveness that could clearly and consistently differentiate indecisive from undecided students. There have been some promising developments, however. Jones (1989) suggested that the Decisiveness Scale of his newly revised Career Decision Profile (formerly the VDS) may meet this need. Vondracek et al. (1990) concluded that the CDS-based Diffusion Scale may be useful in differentiating indecisiveness from indecision. Serling and Betz (1990) developed a measure of a broad construct called "Fear of Commitment (FOC)," postulated to be a central process separating undecided from indecisive clients. The measure was found to be (a) highly reliable, (b) related to both anxiety and self-esteem, and (c) significantly higher in undecided than in decided (as indicated by the CDS) students. Using number of major changes as a criterion of indecisiveness (the range was 0 to 4), a linear trend in mean FOC scores was observed, even though small sample sizes for those changing majors two or more times prevented group differences from reaching statistical significance. These three approaches may be useful in attempts to distinguish the simply undecided from the chronically indecisive.

An additional conceptual development in the area of career decision making is the work by Blustein, Ellis, and Devenis (1989) on the career developmental task that follows making a career decision, that is, commitment to the career choice. Blustein et al. described the development of a new scale measuring commitment to career choice. Following an extensive literature review, two independent constructs were defined and measured. The first, Vocational Exploration and Commitment (VEC), was defined as reflecting variations in one's commitment to a career choice. The Tendency to Foreclose (TTF) dimension was designed to assess individual differences in how one commits to career choices. Following several interrelated studies (all described in Blustein et al., 1989), the authors concluded that the two constructs have much theoretical, as well as practical, utility. The measure of VEC was strongly related to a measure of career indecision (the VDS), suggesting a common emphasis on the relationship of developmental indecision to an uncommitted, exploratory posture vis à vis career choice.

The TTF construct may be useful in understanding the decided but "uncomfortable" individuals highlighted earlier. One end of the TTF continuum seems to reflect an openness to the experiences that are important to the process of committing to a career choice, and the other end is characterized by a closed, dogmatic, dualistic approach to commitment. The authors suggested that research relating the TTF construct to variables such as breadth of exploratory behaviors, the congruence of choices relative to abilities, interests, and needs, and satisfaction with choices would provide a useful next step.

Career-Related Cognitions

Recent Developments

Consistent with the growth of cognitive and cognitive-behavioral approaches to therapy and advances in the field of cognitive psychology and cognitive science, there has been increased interest in the assessment of career-related cognitions. Cognitive research and assessment can be divided into at least two subareas, one assessing cognitive processes (most notably, information processing), and the other, cognitive *products* or contents (Merluzzi & Boltwood, 1990). The applicability of information-processing approaches to career psychology is in its infancy, and is described in an article by Rounds and Tracey (1990). The cognitive products approach, on the other hand, is now being used in career assessment, particularly in the areas of self-efficacy, outcome expectations, and career beliefs.

Self-Efficacy Expectations

Because self-efficacy in career development is covered extensively in Chapter 13, by Hackett and Lent, and in a review by Lent and Hackett (1987), this discussion will focus only briefly on issues of assessment. The concept of self-efficacy expectations, like that of career beliefs, derives from social learning theory, or, as Bandura (1986) now refers to it, "social cognitive theory." Social cognitive theory refers to aspects of self-referent thought that influence behavior and functioning. Bandura (1977) defined self-efficacy expectations as an individual's beliefs about his or her ability to perform given behaviors. Although the concept of self-efficacy was originally developed by Bandura (1977) for use in the understanding and treatment of phobias, Hackett and Betz (1981) extended self-efficacy to career-related domains, suggesting that this construct might facilitate understanding of career choice behavior. More specifically, they postulated that low expectations of efficacy with respect to traditionally male-dominated career fields could serve as a barrier to women's pursuit of such fields.

In studying self-efficacy in relation to career behavior, decisions about the behavioral domain of interest and about the specificity of behavioral items within that domain must be made. Betz and Hackett (1981) started with a very general assessment of self-efficacy with respect to occupational titles. In the Occupational Self-Efficacy Scale (OSES), subjects were asked to indicate, for 20 occupational titles, whether they felt capable of completing (a) the educational requirements and (b) the job duties of the occupation. Results indicated pervasive and sizable gender differences in self-efficacy as a function of the traditionality of the occupation. Other researchers adapted the general method of assessment for somewhat more particular purposes. For example, Lent, Brown, and Larkin (1984, 1986), who assessed self-efficacy with respect to 15 science and engineering occupations, found the methodology similarly useful.

Occupational self-efficacy is somewhat broader, however, than Bandura's concept would ideally suggest, and researchers have proceeded to attempt to measure more specific career-related domains of behavior. These include Lent et al.'s (1986) measure of self-efficacy with respect to the completion of various "academic milestones" for students in technical programs—for example, "completing the math requirements" and "remaining enrolled in the college of technology." Another is the Mathematics Self-Efficacy Scale (Betz & Hackett, 1983), developed using three types of items: everyday math tasks, math courses, and math problems. Betz and Hackett found large (and predicted) gender differences in math self-efficacy and a significant relationship between math self-efficacy and the selection of science-related majors. Most recently, Osipow and Rooney (1989; Rooney & Osipow, 1992) developed a 230-item task-specific occupational self-efficacy scale using the work groups of the *Dictionary of Occupational Titles*. Evidence for psychometric quality and a four-factor structure accounting for 71% of the variance were reported.

Although occupational, academic, and math self-efficacy can be described as career content domains, Hackett and Betz (1981) also suggested the utility of self-efficacy for understanding career-related process domains, for example, career decision-making behaviors and interviewing skills. For example, Taylor and Betz (1983) developed a measure of career decision-making self-efficacy (CDMSE) and found (as did Taylor & Popma, 1990) that it was highly related to career indecision. Robbins (1985) examined the construct validity of the CDMSE and concluded that it measured a general factor of confidence with respect to making career decisions, rather than measuring self-efficacy with respect to specific decision-making behaviors.

A third area of application suggested by Hackett and Betz (1981) was the career adjustment of adults. Recent studies by Landino and Owen (1988) and Schoen and Winocur (1988) assessed self-efficacy with respect to the job duties of university faculty members. Hackett, Betz, and Doty (1985) outlined the competencies and, thus, the domains of efficacy, that were important to success for professional women.

One of the real advantages of career self-efficacy theory may also be a serious drawback: the requirement of specific measures for each behavior domain of interest. Self-efficacy is conceptualized as a specific rather than a general construct, so its measures must also be specific. This means that there is less evidence for the psychometric quality of individual measures than there is for some (though not all) more general construct measures. There might be some basis to argue that traditional psychometric criteria are less appropriate for "behavioral assessment," and Lent and Hackett (1987) reviewed some arguments for this position. I would agree with Lent and Hackett: even if relaxed standards for test–retest reliability and internal consistency are adopted (for example, if self-efficacy is expected to change over time with experience or intervention and/or if the behavioral domain in question is not postulated to be homogeneous), evidence for discriminant, predictive, and construct validity is necessary. Regarding discriminant validity, it is important that self-efficacy be shown to contribute beyond existing concepts such as global self-esteem or intelligence. Evidence for meaningful relationships to theoretically predicted antecedents and consequents is important to construct validity.

In general, the research reviewed in Chapter 13, by Hackett and Lent, provides support for the utility of the self-efficacy construct. Assessment objectives would be furthered by emphases on validity and on clarifying the generality versus the specificity of the construct.

Outcome Expectations

According to Bandura (1986), judgments of personal efficacy must be distinguished from response–outcome expectations. Perceived self-efficacy is a judgment of one's capability to accomplish a certain level of performance; an outcome expectation is a judgment about the likely consequences of that behavior. Efficacy and outcome expectations are not always the same. For example, a student may judge that completing medical school may lead to a high income (outcome expectation) but may doubt that he or she could complete the math and science needed to be a pre-med major (efficacy expectation). A woman or a minority group member may feel that she or he could complete an MBA (efficacy expectation), but may doubt that she or he would be able to obtain a high-paying job. Although the relationship or interdependence of efficacy and outcome expectations depends on the domain in question, it is important to be able to assess both areas of belief.

In contrast to the extensive interest in the assessment of efficacy expectations, there has been comparatively little work in the assessment of outcome expectations. Siegel, Galassi, and Ware (1985) included a measure of outcome expectations in predicting math performance, but their measure was actually closer to the concept of performance attributions (see Lent & Hackett, 1987). Hackett, Betz, and Casas (1991) utilized a measure of outcome expectations, along with measures of self-efficacy, in their study of women and minority students in a school of engineering. Brooks and Betz (1990) included a measure of instrumentality (a concept of Vroom's 1964 expectancy model of motivation) in their study of the utility of expectancy theory as a predictor of occupational preferences. Strong gender differences in instrumentality (defined as the person's perceptions that a given occupation will bring desired outcomes) as a function of the traditionality of the occupation were reported. These represent a beginning, but more is needed.

Career Beliefs

Another new area in the assessment of career cognitions is the extension of the study of self-relevant cognitions to career beliefs. Based on the classic works of clinical psychologists such as Ellis (1962) and Meichenbaum (1977), the idea that career decision makers might be susceptible to irrational career beliefs emerged. Although several writers have noted the possible impact of irrational, maladaptive, or negative self-beliefs on career choice and decision making (Borders & Archadel, 1987; Lewis & Gilhousen, 1981; Nevo, 1987), there have been few attempts (other than the work on self-efficacy expectations) to assess such beliefs. Krumboltz (1988, in press) developed and recently refined the Career Beliefs Inventory (CBI) to accomplish this objective. Krumboltz's work builds on a 1983 paper in which he suggested that "private rules about the self" (e.g., "I'm not a motivated person") interfere with the career decision-making process. The CBI is "a counseling tool designed to help individuals identify career beliefs that may be blocking them from achieving their career goals" (Krumboltz, in press, p. 1).

Administration of the CBI results in a profile describing the beliefs or assumptions that have influenced the individual's career decision making. The description is organized into sections entitled "My Career Situation Now," "What Seems Necessary for My

Happiness" (e.g., aspirations), "Factors that Influence My Decisions" (e.g., Influence of Others, Personal Responsibility), "Changes I Am Willing to Make" (e.g., relocating), and "Effort I Am Willing to Initiate" (e.g., Self-Improvement, Job Training). Research on the CBI is just beginning and it is described as primarily a counseling tool, but I believe it will be important to distinguish it (at least theoretically) from concepts/measures it seems to resemble—for example, career maturity and indecision.

An important focus in the area of career cognitions is the work of Niemeyer and his colleagues on the assessment of structural features of vocational schemes, that is, integration and differentiation (Neimeyer, 1988, 1989; Neimeyer, Brown, Metzler, Hagnas, & Tanguy, 1989; Neimeyer & Metzler, 1987). Constructs are assessed using the Cognitive Differentiation Grid (CDG; Bodden, 1970) or, more recently, the CDG—Personal (Brown, 1987). The latter requires subjects to formulate their own vocational constructs (vs. having them provided in the original version). Although it has implications for counseling, the assessment of such constructs has thus far primarily involved research on the cognitive bases and/or correlates of vocational decision-making processes.

SUMMARY AND FINAL COMMENTS

One chapter is insufficient to provide a comprehensive discussion of all domains in the field of career assessment. A number of relatively new areas of career assessment have been omitted from this review. For example, the increasing use of computers in career assessment and guidance is discussed by Reckase (1990), Sampson (1990), and Taylor (1988). In the area of adult career development, assessment of occupational stress and coping (Osipow & Spokane, 1987), sexual harassment (Fitzgerald et al., 1988; Fitzgerald & Hesson-McInnis, 1989), leisure experience (Tinsley & Tinsley, 1986), and retirement decision making and adjustment (see Chapter 19, by Tinsley) represent new areas of interest. Readers should consult the resources cited at the beginning of this chapter for further information about these and other topics of interest.

Although the chapter is not a comprehensive review, the issues covered herein represent some of the most important concerns in the field of career assessment, and several basic themes seem to emerge from the topics covered. One recurring and vitally important theme is the need to continue our scrutiny of the differential applicability of career assessment instruments across genders, ethnic/racial groups, and cultures. A second theme is that much work is needed in the explication of constructs and the validation of their measures; a related issue is the need for more work on the dimensionality and structure of vocational concepts. If it were not a hopeless suggestion, I would seriously suggest a moratorium on new instrument development until construct validation procedures using nomological networks (or causal or path models) have been applied to the understanding of existing construct/measure pairings. I would like to see more synthesis and integration, versus continued proliferation of new measures. A third theme is the increase in attention to assessment of career development processes in adults as well as younger people. Work on such constructs as career adjustment, indecision, and career self-efficacy relative to adult career development is to be applauded, and much more is necessary.

Overall, the area of career assessment has both important counseling implications and rich possibilities for expanding our understanding of the processes of vocational choice and adjustment. I recommend special attention to (a) issues of gender and ethnic/racial applicability, (b) studies of construct validity, dimensionality, and structure, and (c) assessment of adult career development processes.

REFERENCES

Alvi, S. A., Khan, S. B., & Kirkwood, K. J. (1990). A comparison of various indices of differentiation for Holland's model. *Journal of Vocational Behavior, 36,* 147–152.

American Educational Research Association, American Psychological Association, & National Council on Measurement in Education. (1985). *Standards for educational and psychological testing.* Washington, DC: American Psychological Association.

Anastasi, A. (1988). *Psychological testing* (6th ed.). New York: Macmillan.

Association for Measurement and Evaluation in Guidance (AMEG), Commission on Sex Bias in Measurement. (1977). A case history of change: A review of responses to the challenge of sex bias in interest inventories. *Measurement and Evaluation in Guidance, 10,* 148–152.

Bandura, A. (1977). Self-efficacy: Toward a unifying theory of behavior change. *Psychological Review, 84,* 191–215.

Bandura, A. (1986). *Social foundations of thought and action.* Englewood Cliffs, NJ: Prentice-Hall.

Barak, A., Librowsky, I., & Shiloh, S. (1989). Cognitive determinants of interests: An extension of a theoretical model and initial empirical examinations. *Journal of Vocational Behavior, 34,* 318–334.

Becker, B. J., & Hedges, L. V. (1988). The effects of selection and variability in studies of gender differences. *Behavioral and Brain Sciences, 11,* 183–185.

Benbow, C. P. (1988). Sex differences in mathematical reasoning ability in intellectually talented preadolescents: Their nature, effects, and possible causes. *Behavioral and Brain Sciences, 11,* 169–183.

Benyamini, Y., & Gati, I. (1987). Perceptions of occupations: Aspects versus dimensions. *Journal of Vocational Behavior, 30,* 309–329.

Betz, N. E. (1988). Advances in the assessment of career development and maturity. In W. B. Walsh & S. H. Osipow (Eds.), *Advances in vocational psychology: Vol. II. Career decision making* (pp. 77–136). Hillsdale, NJ: Erlbaum.

Betz, N. E. (1989). The null environment and women's career development. *The Counseling Psychologist, 17,* 136–144.

Betz, N. E. (1990). Contemporary issues in the use of tests in counseling. In C. E. Watkins, Jr. & V. Campbell (Eds.), *Testing in counseling practice* (pp. 419–450). Hillsdale, NJ: Erlbaum.

Betz, N. E., & Fitzgerald, L. F. (1987). *The career psychology of women.* New York: Academic Press.

Betz, N. E., & Hackett, G. (1981). The relationship of career-related self-efficacy expectations to perceived career options in college women and men. *Journal of Counseling Psychology, 28,* 399–410.

Betz, N. E., & Hackett, G. (1983). The relationship of mathematics self-efficacy expectations to the selection of science-based college majors. *Journal of Vocational Behavior, 23,* 329–345.

Blustein, D. L., Ellis, M. V., & Devenis, L. E. (1989). The development and validation of a two-dimensional model of the commitment to career choices process. *Journal of Vocational Behavior, 35,* 342–378.

Bodden, J. L. (1970). Influence of occupational information giving on cognitive complexity. *Journal of Counseling Psychology, 23,* 280–282.

Borders, L. D., & Archadel, K. A. (1987). Self-beliefs and career counseling. *Journal of Counseling and Development, 14,* 69–79.

Borgen, F. H. (1986). New approaches to the assessment of interests. In W. B. Walsh & S. H. Osipow (Eds.), *Advances in vocational psychology: Vol. I. The assessment of interests* (pp. 83–125). Hillsdale, NJ: Erlbaum.

Brookings, J. B., & Bolton, B. (1989). Factorial validity of the United States Employment Service Interest Inventory. *Journal of Vocational Behavior, 34,* 179–191.

Brooks, L., & Betz, N. E. (1990). Utility of expectancy theory in predicting occupational choices in college students. *Journal of Counseling Psychology, 37,* 57–64.

Brown, M. T. (1987). A comparison of two approaches to the cognitive differentiation grid. *Journal of Vocational Behavior, 30,* 155–166.

Brown, S. D., & Rounds, J. B., Jr. (1987). Review of the Adult Career Concerns Inventory. In D. J. Keyser & R. C. Sweetland (Eds.), *Test critiques: Vol. VII.* Kansas City, MO: Test Corporation of America.

Buck, J. N., & Daniels, M. H. (1985). *Manual for the ACDM.* Los Angeles: Western Psychological Services.

Callahan, G. A., & Greenhaus, J. H. (1990). The career indecision of managers and professionals: Development of a scale and test of a model. *Journal of Vocational Behavior, 37,* 79–103.

Campbell, R. E., & Cellini, J. V. (1981). A diagnostic taxonomy of adult career problems. *Journal of Vocational Behavior, 19,* 175–190.

Carter, R. T., & Swanson, J. L. (1990). The validity of the Strong Interest Inventory with Black Americans: A review of the literature. *Journal of Vocational Behavior, 36,* 195–209.

Cole, N. S. (1981). Bias in testing. *American Psychologist, 36,* 1067–1077.

Conoley, J. C., & Kramer, J. J. (1989). *The tenth mental measurements yearbook.* Lincoln, NE: Buros Institute.

Costa, P. T., Jr., McCrae, R. R., & Holland, J. L. (1984). Personality and vocational interests in an adult sample. *Journal of Applied Psychology, 69,* 390–490.

Crites, J. O. (1976). A comprehensive model of career development in early adulthood. *Journal of Vocational Behavior, 9,* 105–118.

Crites, J. O. (1978). *Career Maturity Inventory: Theory and research handbook* (2nd ed.). Monterey, CA: CTB/McGraw-Hill.

Crites, J. O. (1990). *Career Mastery Inventory.* Boulder, CO: Crites Career Consultants, Inc.

Cronbach, L. J., & Meehl, P. E. (1955). Construct validity in psychological tests. *Psychological Bulletin, 52,* 281–302.

Cunningham, J. W., Slonaker, D. F., & Riegel, N. B. (1987). Interest factors derived from job-analytically based activity preference scales. *Journal of Vocational Behavior, 30,* 270–279.

Daniels, M. H. (1989). Review of the Self-Directed Search. In J. C. Conoley & J. J. Kramer (Eds.), *The tenth mental measurements yearbook.* Lincoln, NE: Buros Institute.

Dawis, R. V., & Lofquist, L. H. (1984). *A psychological theory of work adjustment.* Minneapolis: University of Minnesota Press.

Diamond, E. E. (1975). Guidelines for the assessment of sex bias and sex fairness in career interest inventories. *Measurement and Evaluation in Guidance, 8,* 7–11.

Diamond, E. E. (1990). The Kuder Occupational Interest Survey. In C. E. Watkins & V. L. Campbell (Eds.), *Testing in counseling practice.* (pp. 211–240). Hillsdale, NJ: Erlbaum.

Eberhardt, B. J. (1989). Review of assessment of career decision making. In J. C. Conoley & J. J. Kramer (Eds.), *The tenth mental measurements yearbook.* Lincoln, NE: Buros Institute.

Eberhardt, B. J., & Muchinsky, P. M. (1982). Biodata determinants of vocational typology: An integration of two paradigms. *Journal of Applied Psychology, 67,* 714–727.

Eberhardt, B. J., & Muchinsky, P. M. (1984). Structural validation of Holland's hexagonal model: Vocational classification through the use of biodata. *Journal of Applied Psychology, 69,* 174–181.

Ellis, A. (1962). *Reason and emotion in psychotherapy.* New York: Stuart.

Erwin, T. D. (1987). The construct validity of Holland's differentiation concept. *Measurement and Evaluation in Counseling and Development, 20,* 106–112.

Fitzgerald, L. F. (1984, August). *The developmental process of career adjustment during the establishment stage.* Paper presented at the annual convention of the American Psychological Association, Toronto, Canada.

Fitzgerald, L. F., & Hesson-McInnis, M. (1989). The dimensions of sexual harassment: A structural analysis. *Journal of Vocational Behavior, 35,* 309–326.

Fitzgerald, L. F., & Hubert, L. J. (1987). Multidimensional scaling: Some possibilities for counseling psychology. *Journal of Vocational Behavior, 64,* 469–480.

Fitzgerald, L. F., & Rounds, J. B. (1989). Vocational behavior, 1988: A critical analysis. *Journal of Vocational Behavior, 35,* 105–163.

Fitzgerald, L. F., Shullman, S. L., Bailey, N., Richards, M., Swecker, J., Gold, Y., Omerod, A. J., & Weitzman, L. (1988). The incidence and dimensions of sexual harassment in academia and the workplace. *Journal of Vocational Behavior, 32,* 152–175.

Fouad, N. A. (1984). Comparison of interests across cultures. *Dissertation Abstracts International, 4503A*. (University Microfilms No. 84–13, 777).

Fouad, N. A., Cudeck, R., & Hansen, J. C. (1984). Convergent validity of the Spanish and English forms of the SCII for bilingual Hispanic high school students. *Journal of Counseling Psychology, 31*, 339–348.

Fouad, N. A., & Hansen, J. C. (1987). Cross-cultural predictive accuracy of the Strong–Campbell Interest Inventory. *Measurement and Evaluation in Counseling and Development, 20*, 3–10.

Fuqua, D. R., & Newman, J. L. (1989). An examination of the relations among career subscales. *Journal of Counseling Psychology, 36*, 395–400.

Fuqua, D. R., Seaworth, T. B., & Newman, J. L. (1987). The relationship of career indecision and anxiety: A multivariate examination. *Journal of Vocational Behavior, 30*, 175–186.

Gade, E., Fuqua, D., & Hurlburt, G. (1988). The relationship of Holland's personality types to educational satisfaction with a Native-American high school population. *Journal of Counseling Psychology, 35*, 183–186.

Gati, I. (1979). A hierarchical model for the structure of vocational interests. *Journal of Vocational Behavior, 15*, 90–106.

Gelso, C. J., & Fassinger, R. F. (1990). Counseling psychology: Theory and research on interventions. *Annual Review of Psychology, 41*, 355–386.

Ginzberg, E., Ginsburg, S., Axelrad, J., and Herman, J. (1951). *Occupational choice.* New York: Columbia University Press.

Goldman, L. (1971). *Using tests in counseling* (2nd ed.). Englewood Cliffs, NJ: Prentice-Hall.

Goodstein, L. D. (1965). Behavior theoretical views of counseling. In B. Stefflre (Ed.), *Theories of counseling* (pp. 140–192). New York: McGraw-Hill.

Gottfredson, L. S. (1986a). Societal consequences of the "g" factor in employment. *Journal of Vocational Behavior, 29*, 379–410.

Gottfredson, L. S. (1986b). Special groups and the beneficial use of vocational interest inventories. In W. B. Walsh & S. H. Osipow (Eds.), *Advances in vocational psychology: Vol. 1. The assessment of interests* (pp. 127–198). Hillsdale, NJ: Erlbaum.

Gottfredson, L. S. (1988). Reconsidering fairness: A matter of social and ethical priorities. *Journal of Vocational Behavior, 33*, 293–319.

Gottfredson, G. D. (1990, August). *Applications and research using Holland's theory of careers: Where we would like to be and suggestions for getting there.* Paper presented at the annual meeting of the American Psychological Association, Boston, MA.

Gottfredson, G. D., Holland, J. L., & Gottfredson, L. S. (1975). The relation of vocational aspirations and assessments to employment realities. *Journal of Vocational Behavior, 7*, 135–148.

Greenhaus, J. H. (1971). An investigation of the role of career salience in vocational behavior. *Journal of Vocational Behavior, 1*, 209–216.

Greenhaus, J. H., & Parasuraman, S. (1986). Vocational and organizational behavior, 1985: A review. *Journal of Vocational Behavior, 29*, 115–176.

Hackett, G., & Betz, N. E. (1981). A self-efficacy approach to the career development of women. *Journal of Vocational Behavior, 18*, 326–339.

Hackett, G., Betz, N. E., & Casas, M. (1991). *Self-efficacy expectations and performance of women and minority students in a school of engineering.* Unpublished manuscript.

Hackett, G., Betz, N. E., & Doty, M. D. (1985). The development of a taxonomy of career competencies for professional women. *Sex Roles, 12*, 393–409.

Halpin, G., Ralph, J., & Halpin, G. (1990). The Adult Career Concerns Inventory: Reliability and validity. *Measurement and Evaluation in Counseling and Development, 22*, 196–202.

Hansen, J. C. (1984). The measurement of vocational interests: Issues and future directions. In S. D. Brown & R. W. Lent (Eds.), *Handbook of counseling psychology* (pp. 99–136). New York: Wiley.

Hansen, J. C. (1986). Strong Vocational Interest Blank/Strong–Campbell Interest Inventory. In W. B. Walsh and S. H. Osipow (Eds.), *Advances in vocational psychology: Vol. I. The assessment of interests* (pp. 1–30). Hillsdale, NJ: Erlbaum.

Hansen, J. C. (1990). Interpretation of the Strong Interest Inventory. In C. E. Watkins & V. L. Campbell (Eds.), *Testing in counseling practice* (pp. 177–210). Hillsdale, NJ: Erlbaum.

Hansen, J. C., & Campbell, D. P. (1985). *Manual for the Strong–Campbell Interest Inventory* (4th ed.). Palo Alto, CA: Consulting Psychologists Press.

Harren, V. A. (1979). A model of career decision making for college students. *Journal of Vocational Behavior, 14,* 119–133.

Hartman, B. W., Fuqua, D. R., & Jenkins, S. J. (1988). Multivariate generalizability analysis of three measures of career indecision. *Educational and Psychological Measurement, 48,* 61–68.

Hartnett, R. T., & Feldnesser, R. A. (1980). College admissions testing and the myth of selectivity. *AAHE Bulletin, 32,* 3–6.

Herr, C. L. (1989). Review of the Kuder Occupational Interest Survey. In J. C. Conoley and J. J. Kramer (Eds.), *The tenth mental measurements yearbook.* Lincoln, NE: Buros Institute.

Holland, J. L. (1973). *Making vocational choices: A theory of careers.* Englewood Cliffs, NJ: Prentice-Hall.

Holland, J. L. (1985). *Making vocational choices: A theory of vocational personalities and work environments* (2nd ed.) Englewood Cliffs, NJ: Prentice-Hall.

Holland, J. L. (1990, August). *Applications and research using Holland's theory of careers: Where are we now?* Paper presented at the annual meeting of the American Psychological Association, Boston, MA.

Holland, J. L., Daiger, D. C., & Power, P. G. (1980). *My Vocational Situation.* Palo Alto, CA: Consulting Psychologists Press.

Holland, J. L., & Gottfredson, G. D. (1990). *An annotated bibliography for Holland's theory of vocational personalities and work environments.* Baltimore, MD: Johns Hopkins University.

Holland, J. L., Gottfredson, G. D., & Baker, H. G. (1990). Validity of vocational aspirations and interest inventories: Extended, replicated, and reinterpreted. *Journal of Counseling Psychology, 37,* 337–342.

Holland, J. L., & Holland, J. E. (1977). Vocational indecision: More evidence and speculation. *Journal of Counseling Psychology, 24,* 404–414.

Holland, J. L., & Rayman, J. R. (1986). The Self-Directed Search. In W. B. Walsh & S. H. Osipow (Eds.), *Advances in vocational psychology: Vol. I. The assessment of interests* (pp. 55–82) Hillsdale, NJ: Erlbaum.

Humphreys, L. G. (1988). Sex differences in variability may be more important than sex differences in means. *Behavioral and Brain Sciences, 11,* 195–196.

Humphreys, L. G., & Taber, T. (1973). Ability factors as a function of advantaged and disadvantaged groups. *Journal of Educational Measurement, 10,* 107–115.

Hunter, J. E., Schmidt, F. L., & Hunter, R. (1979). Differential validity of employment tests by race: A comprehensive review and analysis. *Psychological Bulletin, 86,* 721–735.

Iachan, R. (1990). Some extensions of the Iachan congruence index. *Journal of Vocational Behavior, 36,* 176–180.

Jackson, D. N. (1977). *Manual for the Jackson Vocational Interest Survey.* Port Huron, MI: Research Psychologists Press.

Jackson, D. N. (1984). *Multidimensional Aptitude Battery manual.* Port Huron, MI: Research Psychologists Press.

Jensen, A. R. (1980). *Bias in mental testing.* New York: Free Press.

Jepsen, D. A. (1984). The developmental perspective on vocational behavior: A review of theory and research: In S. D. Brown & R. W. Lent (Eds.), *Handbook of counseling psychology* (pp. 178–215). New York: Wiley.

Johansson, C. B. (1982). *Manual for the Career Assessment Inventory* (2nd ed.). Minneapolis: National Computer Systems.

Johansson, C. B. (1986). *Career Assessment Inventory: The enhanced version.* Minneapolis: National Computer Systems.

Jones, L. K. (1989). Measuring a three-dimensional construct of career indecision among college students: A revision of the Vocational Decision Scale—The Career Decision Profile. *Journal of Counseling Psychology, 36,* 477–486.

Jones, L. K., & Chenery, M. F. (1980). Multiple subtypes among vocationally undecided college students: A model and assessment instrument. *Journal of Counseling Psychology, 27,* 469–477.

Kaplan, R. M. (1982). Nader's raid on the testing industry: Is it in the best interests of the consumer? *American Psychologist, 37,* 15–23.

Keyser, D. J., & Sweetland, R. C. (Eds.). (1985). *Test critiques, Vol. II.* Kansas City, MO: Test Corporation of America.

Khan, S. B., Alvi, S. A., Shankat, N., Hussain, M. A., & Bais, T. (1990). A study of the validity of Holland's theory in a non-Western culture. *Journal of Vocational Behavior, 36,* 132–146.

Knapp-Lee, L., Knapp, L., & Knapp, R. (1990). A complete career guidance system. In C. E. Watkins & V. L. Campbell (Eds.), *Testing in counseling practice* (pp. 241–284). Hillsdale, NJ: Erlbaum.

Krumboltz, J. D. (1983). *Private rules in career decision making.* Columbus, OH: National Center for Research in Vocational Education.

Krumboltz, J. D. (1988). *Career Beliefs Inventory.* Palo Alto, CA: Consulting Psychologists Press.

Krumboltz, J. D. (in press). *Manual for the Career Beliefs Inventory.* Palo Alto, CA: Consulting Psychologists Press.

Krumboltz, J. D., & Thoresen, C. E. (1964). The effect of behavioral counseling in group and individual settings on information-seeking behavior. *Journal of Counseling Psychology, 11,* 324–333.

Lamb, R. R., & Prediger, D. J. (1981). *Technical report for the unisex edition of the ACT Interest Inventory (UNIACT).* Iowa City, IA: American College Testing Program.

Landino, R. A., & Owen, S. V. (1988). Self-efficacy in university faculty. *Journal of Vocational Behavior, 33,* 1–14.

Lapan, R. T., McGrath, E., & Kaplan, D. (1990). Factor structure of the basic interest scales by gender across time. *Journal of Counseling Psychology, 37,* 216–222.

Lent, R. W., Brown, S. D., & Larkin, K. C. (1984). Relation of self-efficacy expectations to academic achievement and persistence. *Journal of Counseling Psychology, 31,* 356–362.

Lent, R. W., Brown, S. D., & Larkin, K. C. (1986). Self-efficacy in the prediction of academic success and perceived career options. *Journal of Counseling Psychology, 33,* 265–269.

Lent, R. W., & Hackett, G. (1987). Career self-efficacy: Empirical status and future directions. *Journal of Vocational Behavior, 30,* 347–382.

Leong, F. T. L., & Morris, J. (1989). Assessing the construct validity of Holland, Daiger, & Power's measure of vocational identity. *Measurement and Evaluation in Counseling and Development, 22,* 117–125.

Lewis, R. A., & Gilhousen, M. R. (1981). Myths of career development: A cognitive approach to vocational counseling. *Personal and Guidance Journal, 59,* 296–299.

Linn, R. L. (1982). Admissions testing on trial. *American Psychologist, 37,* 279–291.

Lowman, R. L., & Williams, R. E. (1987). Validity of self-ratings of abilities and competencies. *Journal of Vocational Behavior, 31,* 1–13.

Lucas, E. B., Gysbers, N. C., Buescher, K. L., & Heppner, P. P. (1988). My Vocational Situation: Normative, psychometric, and comparative data. *Measurement and Evaluation in Counseling and Development, 21,* 162–170.

Lunneborg, P. W. (1980). Reducing sex bias in interest measurement at the item level. *Journal of Vocational Behavior, 16,* 226–234.

Lunneborg, P. W. (1981). *The Vocational Interest Inventory manual.* Los Angeles: Western Psychological Services.

Lunneborg, P. W., & Lunneborg, C. E. (1986). Everyday Spatial Activities Test for studying differential experience and vocational behavior. *Journal of Vocational Behavior, 28,* 135–141.

MacNab, D., & Fitzsimmons, G. W. (1987). A multitrait–multimethod study of work-related needs, values, and preferences. *Journal of Vocational Behavior, 30,* 1–15.

Manuele-Adkins, R. (1989). Review of the SDS. In J. C. Conoley & J. J. Kramer (Eds.), *The tenth mental measurements yearbook.* Lincoln, NE: Buros Institute.

Masih, C. R. (1967). Career saliency and its relation to certain needs, interests, and job values. *Personnel and Guidance Journal, 45,* 653–658.

Meichenbaum, D. (1977). *Cognitive behavior modification.* New York: Plenum Press.

Merluzzi, T. V., & Boltwood, M. D. (1990). Cognitive and behavioral assessment. In C. E. Watkins, Jr. & V. L. Campbell (Eds.), *Testing in counseling practice* (pp. 135–176). Hillsdale, NJ: Erlbaum.

Mitchell, J. V., Jr. (Ed.). (1985). *The ninth mental measurements yearbook.* Highland Park, NJ: Gryphon Press.

Monahan, C. J. (1987). Construct validation of a modified differentiation index. *Journal of Vocational Behavior, 30,* 217–226.

Moreno, K. E., Wetzel, C. D., McBride, J. R., & Weiss, D. J. (1984). Relationship between corresponding ASVAB and computerized adaptive testing (AT) subtests. *Applied Psychological Measurement, 8,* 155–163.

Morrow, P. C., Mullen, E. J., & McElroy, J. C. (1990). Vocational behavior 1989: The year in review. *Journal of Vocational Behavior, 37,* 121–195.

Muchinsky, P. M., & Monahan, C. J. (1987). What is person–environment congruence? Supplementary versus complementary models of fit. *Journal of Vocational Behavior, 31,* 268–277.

Neimeyer, G. J. (1988). Cognitive differentiation and integration in vocational behavior. *The Counseling Psychologist, 16,* 440–475.

Neimeyer, G. J. (1989). Applications of repertory grids to vocational assessment. *Journal of Counseling and Development, 67,* 585–589.

Neimeyer, G. J., Brown, M., Metzler, A. E., Hagnas, C., & Tanguy, M. (1989). The impact of sex, sex-role orientation, and construct type on vocational differentiation, integration, and conflict. *Journal of Vocational Behavior, 34,* 236–251.

Neimeyer, G. J., and Metzler, A. (1987). The development of vocational schemas. *Journal of Vocational Behavior, 30,* 16–32.

Nevo, O. (1987). Irrational expectations in career counseling and their confronting arguments. *Career Development Quarterly, 35,* 1239–1250.

Osipow, S. H. (1987a). Counseling psychology: Theory, research, and practice in career counseling. *Annual Review of Psychology, 38,* 257–278.

Osipow, S. H. (1987b). *Manual for the Career Decision Scale.* Odessa, FL: Psychological Assessment Resources.

Osipow, S. H., Carney, C. G., Winer, J. L., Yanico, B., & Koschier, M. (1976). *The Career Decision Scale* (3rd ed., rev.). Columbus, OH: Marathon Consulting Press.

Osipow, S. H., & Rooney, R. A. (1989). *Task-Specific Occupational Self-Efficacy Scale.* Authors: Columbus, OH.

Osipow, S., & Spokane, A. (1987). *Occupational Stress Inventory.* Odessa, FL: Psychological Assessment Resources.

Owens, W. A., & Schoenfeldt, L. F. (1979). Toward a classification of persons. *Journal of Applied Psychology, 65,* 569–607.

Parsons, F. (1909). *Choosing a vocation.* Boston: Houghton Mifflin.

Pervin, L. A. (1987). Person–environment congruence in the light of the person–situation controversy. *Journal of Vocational Behavior, 31,* 222–230.

Phillips, S. D., Cairo, P. C., Blustein, D. L., & Myers, R. A. (1988). Career development and vocational behavior, 1987: A review. *Journal of Vocational Behavior, 33,* 119–184.

Ponterotto, J. G. (1988). Racial/ethnic minority research in the Journal of Counseling Psychology: A content analysis and methodological critique. *Journal of Counseling Psychology, 35,* 410–418.

Prediger, D. P. (1976). A World of Work map for career exploration. *Vocational Guidance Quarterly, 24,* 198–208.

Prediger, D. P. (1982). Dimensions underlying Holland's hexagon: Missing link between interests and occupations? *Journal of Vocational Behavior, 21,* 259–287.

Prediger, D. J. (1989). Ability differences across occupations: More than *g. Journal of Vocational Behavior, 34,* 1–27.

Prediger, D. P., & Hanson, G. R. (1976). A theory of career applied to men and women: Analysis of implicit assumptions. *Journal of Vocational Behavior, 8,* 167–184.

Pryor, R. G. L. (1983). *Manual for the Work Aspects Preference Scale.* Melbourne, Australia: Australian Council for Educational Research.

Pryor, R. G. L. (1987). Differences among differences: In search of general work preference dimensions. *American Psychologist, 72,* 426–433.

Pryor, R. L., & Taylor, N. B. (1986). On combining scores from interest and value measures for counseling. *The Vocational Guidance Quarterly, 34,* 178–187.

Rabinowitz, S., & Hall, T. (1981). Changing correlates of job involvement in three career stages. *Journal of Vocational Behavior, 18*, 138–144.

Reckase, M. D. (1990). Introduction to the special issue on computerized testing. *Measurement and Evaluation in Counseling and Development, 23*, 1–2.

Robbins, S. B. (1985). Validity estimates for the career decision-making self-efficacy scale. *Measurement and Evaluation in Counseling and Development*, 64–71.

Rooney, R. A., & Osipow, S. H. (1992). Task-specific occupational self-efficacy: The development and validation of a prototypic scale. *Journal of Vocational Behavior, 40*.

Rosser, P. (1989). *The SAT gender gap.* Washington, DC: Center for Women Policy Studies.

Rounds, J. B. (1990). The comparative and combined utility of work value and interest data in career counseling with adults. *Journal of Vocational Behavior, 37*, 32–45.

Rounds, J. B. (in press). Vocational interests: Evaluating structural hypotheses. In R. V. Dawis & D. Lubinsky (Eds.), *Individual differences and assessment.* Minneapolis: University of Minnesota Press.

Rounds, J. B., Dawis, R. V., & Lofquist, L. L. (1987). Measurement of person–environment fit and prediction of satisfaction in the theory of work adjustment. *Journal of Vocational Behavior, 31*, 297–318.

Rounds, J. B., Jr., Henley, G. A., Dawis, R. V., Lofquist, L. H., & Weiss, D. J. (1981). *Manual for the Minnesota Importance Questionnaire.* Minneapolis: Vocational Psychology Research, University of Minnesota.

Rounds, J. B., & Tracey, T. J. (1990). From trait-factor to person–environment fit counseling: Theory and process. In W. B. Walsh & S. H. Osipow (Eds.), *Advances in vocational psychology: Vol. III. Career counseling.* Hillsdale, NJ: Erlbaum.

Sampson, J. P., Jr. (1990). Computer applications and issues in using tests in counseling. In C. E. Watkins, Jr. & V. L. Campbell (Eds.), *Testing in counseling practice* (pp. 451–474). Hillsdale, NJ: Erlbaum.

Savickas, M. L. (1984). Career maturity: The construct and its measurement. *The Vocational Guidance Quarterly, 32*, 222–231.

Savickas, M. (1989). Annual review: Practice and research in career counseling and development, 1988. *Career Development Quarterly, 38*.

Savickas, M. (1990). Career choice process scales. In C. E. Watkins, Jr. & V. L. Campbell (Eds.), *Testing in counseling practice.* Hillsdale, NJ: Erlbaum.

Savickas, M. L., Passen, A. J., & Jarjoura, D. G. (1988). Career concern and coping as indicators of adult vocational development. *Journal of Vocational Behavior, 33*, 82–98.

Schneider, B. (1987). E = f(P, B): The road to a radical approach to person–environment fit. *Journal of Vocational Behavior, 31*, 353–361.

Schoen, L. G., & Winocur, S. (1988). An investigation of the self-efficacy of male and female academics. *Journal of Vocational Behavior, 32*, 307–320.

Schulenberg, J. E., Shimizu, K., Vondracek, F. W., & Hostetler, M. (1988). Factorial invariance of career indecision dimensions across junior high and high school males and females. *Journal of Vocational Behavior, 33*, 63–81.

Sepich, R. T. (1987). A review of the correlates and measurements of career indecision. *Journal of Counseling and Development, 14*, 8–23.

Serling, D. A., & Betz, N. E. (1990). Development and evaluation of a measure of fear of commitment. *Journal of Counseling Psychology, 37*, 91–97.

Shepard, J. W. (1989a). Review of the Jackson Vocational Interest Survey. In J. C. Conoley & J. J. Kramer (Eds.), *Tenth mental measurements yearbook.* Lincoln, NE: Buros Institute.

Shepard, J. W. (1989b). Review of the Vocational Preference Inventory. In J. C. Conoley & J. J. Kramer (Eds.), *Tenth mental measurements yearbook.* Lincoln, NE: Buros Institute.

Shimizu, K., Vondracek, F. W., Schulenberg, J. E., & Hostetler, M. (1988). The factor structure of the CDS: Similarities across studies. *Journal of Vocational Behavior, 32*, 213–225.

Siegel, R. G., Galassi, J. P., & Ware, W. B. (1985). A comparison of two models for predicting math performance: Social learning versus math aptitude-anxiety. *Journal of Counseling Psychology, 32*, 531–538.

Slaney, R. B. (1988). The assessment of career decision making. In W. B. Walsh & S. H. Osipow (Eds.), *Advances in vocational psychology: Vol. II. Career decision making* (pp. 33–76). Hillsdale, NJ: Erlbaum.

Slocum, J. W., Jr., & Cron, W. L. (1985). Job attitudes and performance during three career stages. *Journal of Vocational Behavior, 26,* 126–145.

Smart, J. C. (1989). Life history influences on Holland vocational type development. *Journal of Vocational Behavior, 34,* 67–87.

Spokane, A. R. (1985). A review of research on person–environment congruence in Holland's theory of careers. *Journal of Vocational Behavior, 26,* 306–343.

Spokane, A. R. (1987). Conceptual and methodological issues in person–environment research. *Journal of Vocational Behavior, 31,* 217–221.

Spokane, A. R. (1990). Self-guided interest inventories as career interventions: The Self-Directed Search. In C. E. Watkins & V. L. Campbell (Eds.), *Testing in counseling practice* (pp. 285–316). Hillsdale, NJ: Erlbaum.

Spokane, A. R. (1991). *Career intervention.* Englewood Cliffs, NJ: Prentice-Hall.

Strahan, R. F. (1987). Measures of consistency for Holland-type codes. *Journal of Vocational Behavior, 31,* 37–44.

Stumpf, S. A., Colarelli, S. M., & Hartman, K. (1983). Development of the Career Exploration Survey (CES). *Journal of Vocational Behavior, 2,* 191–226.

Super, D. E. (1957). *The psychology of careers.* New York: Harper & Row.

Super, D. E. (1973). The Work Values Inventory. In D. G. Zytowski (Ed.), *Contemporary approaches to interest measurement.* Minneapolis: University of Minnesota Press.

Super, D. E., & Nevill, D. D. (1986a). *The Salience Inventory.* Palo Alto, CA: Consulting Psychologists Press.

Super, D. E., & Nevill, D. D. (1986b). *The Values Scale.* Palo Alto, CA: Consulting Psychologists Press.

Super, D. E., Thompson, A. S., & Lindeman, R. H. (1987). *Manual for the ACCI.* Palo Alto, CA: Consulting Psychologists Press.

Super, D. E., Thompson, A. S., Lindeman, R. H., Myers, R. A., & Jordaan, J. P. (1985). *Adult Career Concerns Inventory.* Palo Alto, CA: Consulting Psychologists Press.

Sverko, B. (1989). Origin of individual differences in importance attached to work: A model and a contribution to its evaluation. *Journal of Vocational Behavior, 34,* 28–39.

Sweetland, R. C., & Keyser, D. J. (Eds.). (1986). *Tests: A comprehensive reference for assessments in psychology, education, and business* (2nd ed.). Kansas City, MO: Test Corporation of America.

Taylor, K. M. (1988). Advances in career planning systems. In W. B. Walsh and S. H. Osipow (Eds.), *Advances in vocational psychology: Vol. II. Career decision making* (pp. 137–212). Hillsdale, NJ: Erlbaum.

Taylor, K. M., & Betz, N. E. (1983). Applications of self-efficacy theory to the understanding and treatment of career indecision. *Journal of Vocational Behavior, 22,* 63–81.

Taylor, K. M., & Popma, J. (1990). An examination of the relationships among career decision-making self-efficacy, career salience, locus of control, and vocational indecision. *Journal of Vocational Behavior, 37,* 17–31.

Tenopyr, M. (1989). Review of the KOIS, Form DD. In J. C. Conoley & J. J. Kramer (Eds.), *Tenth mental measurements yearbook.* Lincoln, NE: Buros Institute.

Tinsley, H. E. A., Bowman, S. L., & York, D. C. (1989). CDS, MVS, Vocational Rating Scale, and Decisional Rating Scale: Do they measure the same thing? *Journal of Counseling Psychology, 36,* 115–120.

Tinsley, H. E. A., & Tinsley, D. J. (1986). A theory of the attributes, benefits, and causes of leisure experience. *Leisure Sciences, 8,* 1–45.

Tittle, C. K., & Zytowski, D. G. (Eds.). (1978). *Sex fair interest measurement: Research and implications.* Washington, DC: National Institute of Education.

Vacc, N. (1989a). Review of the assessment of career decision making. In J. C. Conoley & J. J. Kramer (Eds.), *Tenth mental measurements yearbook.* Lincoln, NE: Buros Institute.

Vacc, N. (1989b). Review of the Vocational Preference Inventory. In J. C. Conoley & J. J. Kramer (Eds.), *Tenth mental measurements yearbook*. Lincoln, NE: Buros Institute.

Vale, D. C. (1990). The Minnesota Clerical Assessment Battery: An application of computerized testing to business. *Measurement and Evaluation in Counseling and Development, 23,* 11–20.

Vondracek, F. W., Hostetler, M., Schulenberg, J. E., & Shimizu, K. (1990). Dimensions of career indecision. *Journal of Counseling Psychology, 37,* 98–106.

Vroom, V. H. (1964). *Work and motivation*. New York: Wiley.

Walsh, W. B., & Betz, N. E. (1990). *Tests and assessment* (2nd ed.). Englewood Cliffs, NJ: Prentice-Hall.

Walsh, S. H., & Osipow, S. H. (Eds.). (1986). *Advances in vocational psychology: Vol. I. The assessment of interests*. Hillsdale, NJ: Erlbaum.

Walsh, S. H., & Osipow, S. H. (Eds.). (1988). *Advances in vocational psychology: Vol. II. Career Decision making*. Hillsdale, NJ: Erlbaum.

Walsh, W. B., & Osipow, S. H. (Eds.). (1990). *Advances in vocational psychology: Vol. III. Career counseling*. Hillsdale, NJ: Erlbaum.

Watkins, C. E., Jr., & Campbell, V. L. (Eds.). (1990). *Testing in counseling practice*. Hillsdale, NJ: Erlbaum.

Weiss, D. J., Dawis, R. V., Lofquist, L. L., Gay, E., & Hendel, D. D. (1975). *The Minnesota Importance Questionnaire*. Minneapolis: University of Minnesota, Work Adjustment Project.

Westbrook, B. W. (1983). Career maturity: The concept, the instrument, and the research. In W. B. Walsh & S. H. Osipow (Eds.), *Handbook of vocational psychology: Vol. I. Foundations* (pp. 263–301). Hillsdale, NJ: Erlbaum.

Westbrook, B. W., Sanford, E. E., Gilleland, J., Fleenor, J., & Merwin, G. (1988). Career maturity in grade 9: The relationship between accuracy of self-appraisal and ability to appraise the career-relevant capabilities of others. *Journal of Vocational Behavior, 32,* 269–283.

Westbrook, B. W., Sanford, E. E., O'Neal, P., Horne, D. F., Fleenor, J., & Garren, R. (1985). Predictive and construct validity of six experimental measures of career maturity. *Journal of Vocational Behavior, 27,* 338–355.

Zunker, V. G. (1990). *Using assessment results for career development* (3rd ed.). Pacific Grove, CA: Brooks/Cole.

Zytowski, D. G., & Borgen, F. (1983). Assessment. In W. B. Walsh & S. H. Osipow (Eds.), *Handbook of vocational psychology: Vol. II. Applications* (pp. 5–40). Hillsdale, NJ: Erlbaum.

Zytowski, D. G., & Kuder, F. (1986). Advances in the Kuder Occupational Interest Survey. In W. B. Walsh & S. H. Osipow (Eds.), *Advances in vocational psychology: Vol. I. The assessment of interests*. Hillsdale, NJ: Erlbaum.

CHAPTER 15

ACADEMIC ADJUSTMENT OF COLLEGE STUDENTS: ASSESSMENT AND COUNSELING

RICHARD K. RUSSELL
TRENT A. PETRIE

Since its inception, the historical development of counseling psychology has been marked by numerous changes. Debates over issues of professional identity and the role of the counseling psychologist have been ongoing, particularly over the past 20 years (Whiteley, 1984). Throughout this process of transition, one theme has remained constant—the role of counseling psychologists in helping students adjust to the demands, pressures, and challenges of college life. From the early work of Parsons and the development of the vocational guidance movement through the expansion of university counseling centers following World War II, counseling psychologists have been in the forefront in providing both vocational and personal counseling services to college students. By 1968, almost two-thirds of counseling psychologists reported being employed in some type of educational setting, in teaching, service, and/or administrative roles (Jordaan, Myers, Layton & Morgan, 1968). Recent figures on job placements for counseling psychologists indicate that, in 1989, approximately 40% of new Ph.D.s began employment in some type of educational institution, with counseling centers representing the single largest employer for these graduates (Council of Counseling Psychology Training Programs, 1990).

The role that counseling psychologists adopt in working with issues related to academic adjustment fits well within the functions of practice first outlined by Hahn (1955). These include working with reasonably well-adjusted clients on issues involving attitude change, values clarification, and personal growth. Hahn (1955) also noted that counseling psychologists were the most well-trained professionals to work with persons experiencing difficulties that were educational and/or vocational in focus. Finally, counseling psychologists emphasize the clients' psychological strengths and personal/social resources in dealing with problems, rather than adhering to a more diagnostic or remedial perspective.

Implicit in this discussion is the belief that counseling psychologists should be trained to be firmly grounded in issues relevant to the academic adjustment of college students. The purpose of this chapter is to examine the factors that influence this adjustment process. Because the subject of academic adjustment is so diverse, we have developed an organizational structure to serve as a guide through the plethora of research investigations that comprise this topic.

ACADEMIC ADJUSTMENT AND SUCCESS:
AN ORGANIZING MODEL

An overview of the model from which this chapter will present information on counseling for academic adjustment is illustrated in Figure 15.1. The subject matter has been divided into three main sections: Factors Predictive of Academic Adjustment and Success; Academic Adjustment Outcome Variables; and Interventions. Each of these sections is subdivided into content areas, as shown in Figure 15.1. The organization of this review is conceptually similar to Lazarus's (1976) model of the BASIC ID. A fundamental premise of both the Lazarus model and the one presented here is that each of the domains or factors needs to be systematically evaluated to assess the students' strengths and weaknesses. When assessments and/or interventions are directed at only one or two content areas, the possibility exists that significant material will be overlooked, which may influence the outcome of counseling. By evaluating strengths and weaknesses within each content area, a more complete picture of the students' level of functioning can be determined, leading to a more balanced intervention program.

The section on Factors Predictive of Academic Adjustment and Success is divided into three major content areas, each representing a significant domain of inquiry when working with students on issues related to academic adjustment. The three types of factors to be reviewed are: academic, social/environmental, and personality. A fourth factor dealing with career issues and their relationship to academic adjustment and success has not been included in this review because of space limitations. (See Chapter 13, by Hackett and Lent, and Chapter 16, by Phillips, for relevant coverage.)

Any discussion of factors predicting academic adjustment must include consideration of how the terms "academic success" and/or "academic adjustment" are operationally defined. As Figure 15.1 illustrates, the Academic Adjustment Outcome Variables section has been divided into three domains: academic performance, social adjustment, and personal adjustment.

The Interventions section examines treatment techniques and interventions designed to facilitate the process of academic adjustment and success. In Figure 15.1, this domain has been divided into two categories: counseling or skill-focused interventions, and program or institution-focused interventions.

Before examining the literature on academic adjustment and success, it should be noted that certain decision rules were applied in synthesizing the research. First, most of the studies have been drawn from journal articles published since 1980. Second, because of space limitations, certain subject areas have been excluded from this review. As noted, this chapter will not examine the relationship between career factors and academic outcome. An additional content area not included concerns the unique needs of special populations of students. A third decision rule has been to emphasize those factors that are in some way manipulable—those that counselors have the potential to influence or change. Topics such as self-efficacy, study skills, social support, and family interactions, for example, represent variables that influence academic adjustment and are subject to change through the counseling process. Conversely, factors such as high school academic performance, socioeconomic status, and personality traits are much less amenable to change, even though they may be related to academic performance.

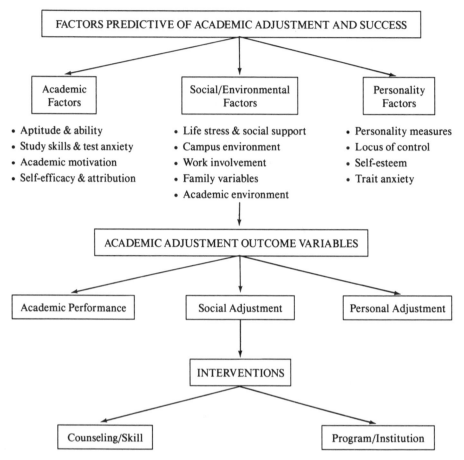

Figure 15.1 Organizing model.

FACTORS PREDICTIVE OF ACADEMIC ADJUSTMENT AND SUCCESS

Academic Factors

Any exploration of the factors influencing a student's adjustment to college must consider a number of variables related to academic performance. The subsections included in this discussion of academic factors are: aptitude and ability variables, study skills and test anxiety, academic motivation, and self-efficacy expectations and effort attributions.

Aptitude and Ability Variables

In assessing a student's academic adjustment, it is imperative that consideration be given to prior high school academic performance, as well as scores received on college admissions tests. Several authors have noted that high school grade point average (GPA) and test scores from the Scholastic Aptitude Test (SAT) and American College Testing Program (ACT) appear to comprise the best predictors of college academic success (Malloch & Michael, 1981; Mathiasen, 1985; Weitzman, 1982). In a review article exploring various predictors of college academic achievement, Mathiasen (1985) observed that, although factors such as study skills, motivation, and certain personality traits all correlated with academic success, high school grades and test scores maintained the strongest predictive relationship to college GPA. Similarly, Neely (1977) found that the best predictors of college graduation were high school GPA, high school class rank, and composite ACT score. Additional attempts to predict college academic success have focused on specific subject matter abilities and their relationship to academic success. For example, Waits and Demana (1988) reported a strong positive relationship between math skills of entering college students and subsequent graduation rates. Blustein et al. (1986) and Royer, Abranovic, and Sinatra (1987) noted significant correlations between reading comprehension ability and college GPA.

Study Skills and Test Anxiety

Factors such as high school academic performance and standardized test scores have demonstrated positive correlations with college GPA and graduation rates, but these relationships are far from perfect. Many students who succeed academically in high school and perform well on entrance exams do not show similar patterns of success in college. Conversely, there are many students who perform at a marginal level in high school, yet respond very well to the academic demands of the college experience.

One area to be considered when assessing a student's potential for academic success is study skills and attitudes (Mathiasen, 1985). Several authors have noted that a significant positive relationship exists between self-reported study skills and college GPA (Allen, Lerner, Hinrichsen, 1972; Cappella, Wagner, Kusmierz, 1982). Cappella et al. (1982), for example, reported a correlation of .46 between scores on the Survey of Study Habits and Attitudes (SSHA) and cumulative GPA. Lin and McKeachie (1970) found that study skills made an independent contribution to academic achievement beyond that of aptitude measures such as SAT scores, and that this relationship was stronger for the females than for the males in their sample.

Gadzella, Ginther, and Williamson (1987) examined the relationship between study skills and the ability to process information deeply. Depth of processing referred to differences in learning style; deep processors were those who developed a thorough understanding of the material, and shallow processors were those who emphasized rote learning of specific knowledge. The results indicated that the ability to process information deeply correlated significantly (though modestly) with study effectiveness and GPA.

Several investigators have examined the relationship between knowledge of study skills, test anxiety, and academic performance (Brown & Nelson, 1983; Bruch, Pearl, & Giordiano, 1986; Naveh-Benjamin, McKeachie, and Lin, 1987). Brown and Nelson (1983) employed a 2 × 2 factorial design in which two levels of test anxiety were crossed with two levels of academic performance. The results indicated that students in the high academic performance groups (e.g., those with high grades) scored higher on measures of academic skills than did students in the low groups, regardless of their reported level of test anxiety. Although high levels of test anxiety were associated with various indexes of cognitive and somatic distress, actual academic performance was related to differences in study and test-taking skills. The authors noted that efforts to improve the academic performance of unsuccessful, test-anxious students should include interventions focusing on the development of effective study behaviors. Bruch et al. (1986) employed a similar design, crossing levels of academic performance with high and low test anxiety. These authors found that deficits in academic skills led to poor performance. Students with high GPAs demonstrated a greater knowledge of effective test-taking skills and employed learning strategies that led to deep rather than superficial levels of information processing.

Naveh-Benjamin et al. (1987) also examined the relationship among academic performance, study skills, and test anxiety, and reported that there appear to be two types of test-anxious students. The first type are those with effective study skills who have sufficient knowledge of the subject when entering the exam situation. For these students, the experience of test anxiety leads to task-irrelevant responses in the exam situation itself which, in turn, lead to performance deficits. These students' problem becomes one of information retrieval in the evaluative setting. In contrast, the second type of test-anxious students are those who lack adequate study skills and therefore have difficulty with organizing and encoding relevant information. These findings suggest that intervention programs need to be developed to address the unique needs of these two types of test-anxious students. The first type of test-anxious student would likely benefit from anxiety-management treatment strategies designed to reduce the worry and emotionality components of test anxiety; the second type may benefit from these interventions as well, but also requires the development of effective study behaviors and test-taking skills to facilitate both information encoding and retrieval.

Academic Motivation

The relationship between academic achievement motivation and success in college has been examined by several investigators (Baker & Sryk, 1984; Edwards & Waters, 1981; Neumann, Finaly, & Reichel, 1988). Edwards and Waters (1981), for example, found that achievement motivation moderated the relationship between academic ability and GPA, with high-motivation students obtaining stronger ability–GPA relations and showing more persistence in their academic efforts.

Neumann et al. (1988) noted that the construct of achievement motivation is comprised of two dimensions: goal-directedness and personal excellence. Goal-directedness refers to an individual's desire to accomplish important tasks, and is related to factors such as persistence, planning ability, and action orientation. Personal excellence is conceptualized as the need to excel, and includes measures of the individual's aspiration level, risk-taking behaviors, and locus of control. Neumann et al. (1988) found moderate positive relations between most aspects of achievement motivation and measures of college success, such as grades, involvement, and commitment.

Hollenbeck, Williams, and Klein (1989) examined the relationship among need for achievement, locus of control, and commitment to difficult goals. Although a significant relationship was not observed between the measure of need for achievement and GPA, a significant positive correlation was reported for goal commitment and GPA ($r = .36$). The results also revealed that individuals high in need for achievement demonstrated a higher commitment to difficult goals than did those low in need for achievement. Locus of control also was observed to be positively related to goal commitment, such that individuals with an internal orientation and high need for achievement were more likely to commit to difficult goals.

One methodological difficulty that exists throughout the literature on academic motivation and college success is the lack of a standardized operational definition of the motivation construct. Typically, academic motivation is assessed by paper-and-pencil instruments that vary from study to study, making it difficult to compare findings across investigations.

Self-Efficacy Expectations and Effort Attributions

Self-efficacy theory, as developed by Bandura (1977, 1982), is an attempt to explain behavior change from a cognitive-behavioral perspective. Within this model, self-efficacy refers to a person's belief about his or her ability to successfully perform a given task or behavior. It is hypothesized that self-efficacy expectations influence a person's choice of behavioral settings and activities, and the degree of persistence that person will demonstrate when confronted with obstacles or aversive consequences (Lent, Brown, & Larkin, 1984). Early research on self-efficacy theory examined applications to pseudo-clinical problems such as snake phobias (Bandura & Adams, 1977) and social skill development (Moe & Zeiss, 1982). Other researchers have explored the usefulness of the theory in explaining vocational behavior and academic achievement. For a detailed examination of the application of self-efficacy theory to academic and career-relevant behaviors, the reader is referred to a review of this topic by Lent and Hackett (1987), and to Chapter 13, by Hackett and Lent.

Lent et al. (1984) examined the relationship between self-efficacy beliefs and academic success and persistence in a sample of college students who were considering careers in science and engineering. Their findings revealed that students reporting high self-efficacy for educational requirements generally achieved higher grades and demonstrated greater persistence than those reporting low self-efficacy.

In an effort to extend the findings of their previous investigation, Lent, Brown, and Larkin (1986) examined the degree to which measures of self-efficacy, ability, achievement, and interest could serve as predictors of academic success and persistence. Hierarchical regression analyses were used, and the results indicated that both math PSAT scores and high school rank made significant contributions to the variance in GPA; in addition, self-efficacy accounted for a significant portion of the variance in the prediction of GPA. For the measure of academic persistence, it was found that high school rank and self-efficacy were the only predictors making significant contributions to the regression equation. In a related study, Lent, Brown, and Larkin (1987) examined the relative contribution of self-efficacy, interest congruence, and consequence thinking in predicting grades and persistence in technical/scientific majors. The pattern of results was consistent with their earlier investigation, in that self-efficacy was found to be the most useful of the three variables in predicting grades and academic persistence.

O'Brien, Brown, and Lent (1990) explored the relationship of aptitude–efficacy congruence to academic achievement in a sample of underprepared, at-risk college students. Based on self-efficacy theory, the authors hypothesized that students who either greatly overestimated or underestimated their academic ability would perform less well than students for whom the efficacy-aptitude relationship was congruent. The results supported these predictions, revealing that self-efficacy beliefs most facilitative of academic performance are those that are relatively congruent with a student's ability.

Multon, Brown, and Lent (1991) conducted a meta-analytic investigation on the relation of self-efficacy beliefs to academic performance and persistence. From a sample of 39 studies in the meta-analysis, Multon et al. (1991) found support for the facilitating relationship of self-efficacy beliefs to both academic performance and persistence, with effect size estimates of .38 for performance and .34 for persistence.

Investigations into the relationship between *effort attributions* and academic outcome have been based primarily on the model of achievement motivation developed by Weiner (1979, 1985). Basic to this model is the assumption that individuals seek to identify the causes of both their successes and failures on achievement-related tasks. According to Weiner, these causal attributions for performance can be described along the dimensions of locus (internal/external), stability (stable/unstable), and controllability (controllable/uncontrollable). When success or failure is attributed to ability or effort, it is seen as an internal attribution; attributions to task difficulty or luck are seen as external. When successful performance is attributed to the stable, internal factor of ability, it should lead to increased expectancy for success in the future. Effort attributions for success are seen as less stable than ability attributions, yet should serve to enhance self-esteem and future effort expenditure, thereby enhancing performance. Ideally, future success is most facilitated by a combination of ability and effort attributions for success. In the academic realm, persistence and future performance are likely to be enhanced when students are able to attribute their prior successes to both aptitude and hard work (Platt, 1988).

In the case of failure experiences, expectancies for future success are lowered most dramatically when failure is attributed to a stable cause such as ability. Conversely, when failure is attributed to the unstable, internal factor of effort, expectancies for future task success are less strongly influenced. Blaming failure on a lack of effort may induce guilt feelings, but effort is seen as a controllable factor that can be increased on subsequent tasks.

Several investigators have examined the effects of causal attributions on the motivation and academic performance of college students. Powers, Douglas, Cool, and Gose (1985) studied the relationship between attributions for success and failure and achievement motivation in a sample of academically talented high school students. Effort attributions for both success and failure were significantly correlated with achievement motivation in expected ways. Platt (1988) explored the effects of attributions for high school success on academic self-concept and predicted effort in college among first-term students. In general, results were consistent with Weiner's attributional model: ability and effort attributions were found to contribute to academic self-concept; ability alone influenced expectancy; and effort alone contributed to predicted effort in college. Interestingly, although the measures of attribution did not directly influence GPA, the intervening variables of expectancy and predicted effort were found to have significant effects on GPA.

In a study investigating the role of failure attributions on subsequent attitude and performance measures, Clifford (1986) explored the effects of attributing failure to effort versus strategy. According to Clifford, attributing failure to deficits in preparation strategy may allow students to avoid the negative effects of either ability or effort attributions. That is, strategy attributions may allow the individual to avoid the guilt typically associated with not trying (i.e., effort attribution), and to avoid feeling incapable or inadequate (i.e., ability attribution). Strategy attributions also may enable the student to turn failure experiences into problem-solving situations, as the person seeks to identify more effective strategies for the future. The results of Clifford's (1986) study supported the prediction that strategy attributions for academic failure would lead to more positive and constructive judgments than would effort attributions.

Social/Environmental Factors

Several researchers have noted that social and environmental factors (e.g., family, campus environment, peers) appear to play an important role in a student's academic adjustment and success. In fact, the inclusion of the social domain is supported by previous research concerning the etiology of underachievement. In a comprehensive summary of the literature, Zilli (1971) indicated that multiple factors need to be considered, to adequately explain underachievement. Of the nine etiological factors suggested by Zilli (1971), six concerned variables related to family, peer, or school environment. In this section, social/environmental factors will be considered under the domains of: (a) life stress and social support, (b) campus environment, (c) work involvement, (d) family variables, and (e) academic environment variables.

Life Stress and Social Support

Over the past 30 years, researchers have examined the relationship between *life stress* and the onset of various physical and psychological illnesses in college and general populations (Brown & Siegel, 1988; Rahe, 1972; Sarason, Johnson & Siegel, 1978; Suls & Mullin, 1981). Life stress research with college students has also been extended to include the non-health-related area of academic performance and success. Harris (1973) retrospectively investigated the relationship between life stress and academic performance in first-year college students. Controlling for entrance examination scores, Harris (1973) reported that students with lower GPAs experienced significantly more life stress during the preceding year than those with higher GPAs.

De Meuse (1985), who also examined the effects of life stress on academic success, found that life stress was negatively related to academic success in the classroom, with low-stress students performing better across six indexes of classroom performance. Garrity and Ries (1985) corroborated the findings of Harris (1973) and De Meuse (1985) by demonstrating that recent negative life events were inversely correlated with college grades. They found no evidence, however, to support the contention that physical illness mediated the life stress–academic performance relationship.

In another retrospective study, Wildman (1978) found that the life stress–academic performance relationship was governed by a threshold effect. College students' performances suffered significantly only after they had experienced at least 10 independent negative life events. Citing the limitations of retrospective designs, Lloyd, Alexander, Rice, and Greenfield (1980) utilized a prospective methodology in reexamining and extending the research questions proposed by Wildman (1978). Lloyd et al. (1980) substantiated Wildman's findings by demonstrating that a threshold effect occurs when individuals have experienced 12 independent life events.

Although a number of studies have demonstrated the beneficial effects of peer and familial *social support* on physical and psychological health (Brown, Alpert, Lent, Hunt, & Brady, 1988; Cohen & Hoberman, 1983; Cutrona, 1986; Sarason, Sarason, Potter & Antoni, 1985; Thoits, 1982), few studies have investigated the direct or buffering effects of social support on academic performance. In a health-related study of college students, Jemmott and Magliore (1988) examined the effects of academic stress and social support on antibody production for defense against acute upper respiratory tract infections. They found that students who reported more satisfaction with their social support produced higher levels of antibodies than those who reported less satisfaction, and that this relationship existed during academically stressful and less stressful periods of time. This finding suggests that social support might influence academic performance indirectly by reducing a student's risk for illness.

Okun, Sandler, and Baumann (1988) examined the buffering and boosting effects of social support on quality of academic life in community college students. They found that positive school events, when supported by teachers and family members, improved the quality of the students' academic lives. For negative life events, social support provided by teachers and family members buffered the life stress–academic quality relationship. Students who experienced negative life events and were unsupported perceived the quality of their academic life to be lower than those who were supported.

Campus Environment

Several researchers have recognized the individual and interactional influences of the environment on various aspects of individuals' behavior (Bandura, 1978; Holland, 1973; Moos, 1976; Pervin, 1968, 1977). For university students, campus environments have been operationalized and investigated in a variety of ways. One variable that has received attention is the location of the student's residence. Specifically, what are the differential effects associated with on-campus versus at-home living? In a summary of previous research, Pascarella (1985) indicated that students residing on campus expressed more satisfaction with college, had higher levels of self-esteem and educational aspirations, and were more likely to remain in school than were commuter students. Pascarella (1985) also concluded that living on campus indirectly influenced the students' intellectual and interpersonal self-concepts by positively affecting social interactions with peers and faculty. Janosik, Creamer, and Cross (1988) found that higher levels of self-reported sense of competence were associated with student living environments that provided emotional support, minimal competition, and a high degree of involvement in self-governance.

Extending the definition of campus environment beyond place of residence, Pascarella (1984) examined the effects of the academic and social press of the institution on educational aspirations. He found that college environment indirectly influenced educational aspirations through its effects on the students' interactions with faculty. In general, easy access to faculty increased a student's level of academic aspirations, although this relation was moderated somewhat by student gender and academic selectivity of the college.

Several studies have examined the effects of student involvement in programs and activities on the campus. For example, Evanoski (1988) found that students who were active in campus volunteer programs reported higher levels of self-esteem and more positive feelings about school experiences than those who did not participate. Feltz and Weiss (1984) found that, regardless of the type of extracurricular activity, increased levels of involvement were related to increased academic achievement in female students. These studies, and those presented above, suggest that the campus environment is a complex, dynamic entity with the potential to influence students' academic success and adjustment. It appears that students might increase their positive academic experiences by becoming more involved in their campus community and, particularly, by interacting socially with peers and faculty. For a more thorough discussion of interactional theories and environmental assessment and intervention, see Huebner and Corazzini (1984).

Work Involvement

Because of financial need, many students obtain employment at some time during their tenure at a college or university. The press for students to work during school has prompted researchers to investigate the relationship between student nonacademic workloads and academic performance. Henke, Lyons, and Krachenberg (1987) reported that no relationship existed between measures of workload and second-semester GPA or first- and second-semester grades in an accounting class. A small but significant negative relationship, however, was found for workload and first-semester GPA. The findings from this study, and those reported in Lyons, Krachenberg, and Henke's (1986) review, suggest that increased hours of outside employment may be detrimental to academic performance, although more refined research needs to be conducted in this area before any definitive conclusions can be reached.

Family Variables

Studies examining the relationship between *socioeconomic status* (SES) and indicators of academic achievement and adjustment have been equivocal. Barney, Fredericks, Fredericks, and Robinson (1987) found that success in the first two years of college or business school was unrelated to social class, and Webb (1986) also reported no relationship between SES factors and academic achievement. Other researchers, however, have noted a positive relationship between SES variables and measures of academic success and adjustment. Carpenter and Western (1982) found that social origins (e.g., high-income family) had direct and mediated effects on academic aspirations. In their 18-year longitudinal study, Alwin and Thornton (1984) found that SES variables were related positively to academic achievement, and that this relationship was strongest when SES variables from early in the individual's life were considered. In his sociological analysis of first-year college students, Hearn (1984) eloquently summarized the effects of socioeconomic status by stating that ". . . in the high school to college transition, the academically and socioeconomically 'rich' become richer (i.e., attend schools having superior intellectual and material resources) while the academically and socioeconomically 'poor' become poorer" (p. 28).

Manski and Wise (1983) found that *parents' education level* had a positive relation to their children's applying to college, and that this relationship existed even when the children's class rank and SAT scores were held constant. In their survey of high school seniors who already had been admitted to a university, MacDermott, Conn, and Owen (1987) reported that: (a) parents who had attended college assumed their children also would attend; (b) parents who had not attended college did not assume their children would attend, and their children ultimately considered fewer schools as options; and (c) children whose parents did not attend college were likely to visit schools alone, and were more concerned about the availability of financial aid and the cost of tuition than were children of parents who did attend college.

Several researchers have identified the *family structure* as a variable that influences students' achievement and adjustment in school. Using group discussions, Gurman (1970) examined the interactional patterns of male high school students and their parents, to determine the role of the family in creating and sustaining underachievement. From these discussions, five conflictual themes emerged. For example, underachieving students believed their parents were concerned more with grades than with their general development; their parents claimed to be more concerned with their children's inner happiness. Baker (1975) identified several family interactional patterns that might contribute to the development of underachievement.

The transition from high school to college may also be influenced by the structure of the family system. To determine the effects of family structure on psychological separation and adjustment to college, Lopez, Campbell, and Watkins (1988) examined the responses of over 500 undergraduates from intact families. For male students, parent marital distress and poorly defined familial boundaries were associated with conflicted, distant relationships with parents; for females, parent marital distress and poor family structure were associated with conflicted and dependent parent–child relations. (See Chapter 8, by Lopez, for a more thorough discussion of family variables.)

The cognitive development and academic growth of children are influenced by siblings as well as parents. Irish (1964) noted that siblings have direct and important effects on one another in their roles as socializer, teacher, and role model. The investigation into the relationship between *birth order* and academic and intellectual development, however, has tended to be indirect. Most researchers have attempted to identify sibling effects by focusing primarily on the effects of birth order and/or family size.

The results of birth order research have not been consistent, but Cicirelli (1978) concluded that decrements in students' academic ability and achievement tend to occur as: (a) family size increases, (b) birth order position increases, and (c) spacing (i.e., time) between children decreases. An attempt to bring order and clarity to birth order research was made by Zajonc and colleagues in their development of the confluence model (Zajonc, 1983; Zajonc, Markus, & Markus, 1979). This model is represented by a mathematical equation, which is used to quantify the intellectual growth of children at any point in their lives. Central to the model is the idea that a child's cognitive development is influenced primarily by the intellectual environment of the family, and that this intellectual environment is a dynamic entity that changes with the addition of each new child. Although a full review of the model and relevant research is beyond the scope of this chapter, it is important to note that studies incorporating this perspective have been relatively successful in predicting individual cases (Berbaum & Moreland, 1980) and sociological trends (Zajonc, 1986). (For a comprehensive review of the confluence model, see Zajonc, 1983; Zajonc et al., 1979).

Academic Environment Variables

A university's academic environment, which is determined by several variables, can affect students' academic achievements and preferences. Similar to other person–environment fit theories, college fit theory suggests that the greater the congruence between the student's values, goals, and attitudes and those of the college, the greater the likelihood that the student will remain in the college (Taylor & Whetstone, 1983). Using a sample of successful and unsuccessful students, Taylor and Whetstone (1983) found support for the validity of college fit theory. To assess the effectiveness of three different types of universities—research, graduate, and teaching—Kleeman and Richardson (1985) surveyed students to determine what they felt were the most important functions of a university and how well their schools achieved these goals. Students across all three types of schools indicated that the following domains or activities were the most important: (a) programs and services for students, (b) offerings of graduate programs, and (c) quality of research and teaching. Unfortunately, evaluations of how well schools achieved these "most" important functions indicated that students felt their institutions were doing a poor job.

Personality Factors

This section reviews some of the major findings linking personality to academic adjustment. For organizational purposes, four subsections examine (a) standardized personality measures, (b) locus of control, (c) self-esteem, and (d) trait anxiety.

Standardized Personality Measures

Much of the early research in this area focused on correlations between standardized personality tests and academic success as measured by GPA. The California Psychological Inventory (CPI) has been particularly popular; several investigators have examined the relationships between CPI subscale scores and college grades. For example, Holland (1959) correlated CPI scales with first-year college GPA in a sample of National Merit Scholarship finalists. He found that the CPI scales were better predictors of GPA than were SAT scores, but this result was undoubtedly due to the restricted range of SAT scores in his academically elite sample.

Stroup (1970) compared the relative strength of CPI–GPA versus SAT–GPA correlations in a more diverse sample of college students than the one used by Holland (1959). The results indicated that the SAT Math *and* SAT Verbal scores were more highly correlated with GPA than any single CPI scale. However, the strongest predictive relationship was achieved by combining SAT scores with selected scales from the CPI. Rutowski and Domino (1975) found that the CPI scales correlated with a measure of study habits and attitudes.

More recently, Gough and Lanning (1986) attempted to examine the relationship between the CPI and three indexes of academic success: one course grade, the two-year GPA, or the four-year GPA. Multiple regression analyses produced a single equation for both sexes that included the following six scales from the CPI: Wb (Sense of Well-Being), Re (Responsibility), Gi (Good Impression), Ai (Achievement via Independence), Ie (Intellectual Efficiency), and Py (Psychological-Mindedness). Scores computed from the equation using these six scales were found to correlate .31 with GPA.

Karnes, Chauvin, and Trant (1984) examined the relationship between personality factors, as measured by the Sixteen Personality Factors Questionnaire, and ACT scores in a sample of college honor students. Results indicated a number of significant correlations between the factors of the 16 PF and the ACT subscales. The ACT composite score was found to be positively correlated with measures of emotional stability and enthusiasm, and negatively correlated with timidity, although the size of the correlations was rather modest.

Locus of Control

To identify relationships between specific personality characteristics and academic performance, several investigators have focused on the construct of locus of control (Brown & Strickland, 1972; Warehime, 1972). Intuitively, it might be expected that students who score on the internal end of the internal–external continuum would be more successful academically because internals believe that reinforcements (i.e., grades) are contingent on their own ability and effort. Conversely, externals might be expected to perform less well because they believe that reinforcement is a function of uncontrolled forces such as powerful others, luck, chance, or fate. In general, studies correlating GPA with locus of control have reported correlation coefficients that are statistically significant, yet small in magnitude. For example, Prociuk and Breen (1974) and Traub (1982) found correlations, respectively, of .28 and .18 between measures of internality and college grades.

Rotter (1966) pointed out that any general measure of control beliefs is not likely to show a strong relationship with measures in a specific content area, such as academic performance. Thus, several investigators have sought to identify mediating variables that might explain the ways in which locus of control influences academic behavior. Prociuk and Breen (1974), for example, found a relation between locus of control and study habits and attitudes. Crump, Hickson, and Laman (1985) and Gadzella, Williamson, and Ginther (1985) reported that internal attributions are associated with positive self-concept. In neither study, however, was a significant relationship observed between locus of control and GPA. Although previous research had found a significant relationship between self-concept and academic achievement (Caplin, 1968; Gadzella & Williamson, 1984), the direct link between locus of control and academic performance remains weak at best. Other studies noted positive relationships between internality and (a) information-seeking behavior (Prociuk & Breen, 1977), (b) need for achievement (Trice, 1985), and (c) academic retention (Bers, 1986).

Self-Esteem

Several investigators have explored the possible relationship between self-esteem and academic performance (Prager, 1983; Prager & Freeman, 1979). In general, these studies have concluded that, although self-esteem may correlate with constructs such as level of educational aspiration or expectancy for success, any direct relationship between self-esteem and academic performance is minimal. Prager and Freeman (1979), for example, found that self-esteem was related to students' level of degree aspiration, but the correlation between GPA and self-esteem was insignificant. Burke, Midkiff, and Williams (1985) investigated the role of self-esteem in students' affective reactions to either success or failure academic outcomes. They found that students with positive self-concepts tended to internalize success more (and failure less) than did students with negative self-concepts.

Trait Anxiety

Trait anxiety is defined as representing relatively stable individual differences in anxiety proneness (Spielberger, 1972). State anxiety is viewed as a much more transitory emotional condition that is triggered by various environmental stimuli. The relationship between personality traits and states is such that the stronger a particular trait, the more probable it is that a person will experience the corresponding emotional state in a variety of situations (Spielberger, 1972).

Early research on trait anxiety suggested that individuals with high trait anxiety tend to be more self-preoccupied and self-deprecatory (Sarason, 1960), and to experience a high fear of failure (Atkinson, 1964). The extensive literature on test anxiety has demonstrated that persons with high state (i.e., test-specific) anxiety experience performance deficits in the exam situation (Sarason, 1961; Spielberger, 1972). In contrast to the many studies examining the relationship between test anxiety and academic performance, relatively few investigations have explored the possible link between trait anxiety and academic adjustment.

Schreiber (1985) examined the relationship between trait anxiety and academic performance. Using the Cattell Anxiety Scale as a measure of trait anxiety and course grades to index academic performance, Schreiber found that students with high anxiety scores performed significantly better than those with low scores. Unfortunately, this study did not determine whether a curvilinear relationship exists between trait anxiety and exam performance. (Based on the classic Yerkes–Dodson Law (Yerkes & Dodson, 1908), a prediction might be made that students with extremely low or extremely high levels of trait anxiety would perform less well than those with more moderate scores.)

ACADEMIC ADJUSTMENT OUTCOME VARIABLES

This section presents a brief examination of some of the key issues involved in the assessment of academic adjustment and success outcomes. In the original organizational model presented in Figure 15.1, the outcome domain is divided into three general categories: academic performance, social adjustment, and personal adjustment.

Academic Performance

The majority of research studies examining academic adjustment employ outcome criteria selected from the academic performance domain. Measures within this category frequently are more readily defined, more objective, and easier to obtain than are measures assessing personal and/or social adjustment. The two most common outcome criteria in this category are: (a) academic grades and (b) graduation rate or progress-toward-degree.

The use of course grades as a measure of academic adjustment and success is not surprising, because typically we consider successful students to be those who perform well academically. Presumably, students who excel in terms of grade point average are those who will be the most competitive for quality jobs and additional graduate or professional education. Unfortunately, the literature on academic adjustment appears to be remiss in two important ways. First, there has been an overreliance on the use of course grades or grade point average as a measure of academic outcome. These measures represent valid, relevant assessments of academic performance, but too many studies have relied on them as the *only* measure of outcome. Just as therapeutic outcome needs to be assessed multidimensionally, so too do we need to expand the range of outcome variables employed in the assessment of academic adjustment. For example, assessing social and/or personal adjustment along with grades may help to provide a more thorough assessment of outcome.

A second problem is that many studies operationalize the grade criterion so narrowly as to severely restrict the external validity of their findings. It may be useful to conceptualize the grade criterion as falling on a continuum ranging from general to specific. At the more general end of the continuum are investigations that utilize cumulative GPA derived over a 2- or 4-year period as a measure of academic outcome. In contrast, studies at the narrow end of the continuum define outcome as a grade on a specific test or in a single course. Perhaps the most common measure of academic outcome in the literature is the use of first-term GPA as the criterion variable. The studies that are most limited in terms of external validity are those in which the assessment of outcome is restricted to a single variable (e.g., grades) and narrowly defined (e.g., test score).

Some investigations employ graduation rates as an outcome measure. These studies track students' progress over varying intervals to determine whether they continue in school and/or graduate or are near graduation by the end of the time period. The advantage inherent in this type of outcome measure is that it provides a more stable evaluation of academic performance when compared to a single course grade or a one-term GPA assessment. An important concern when graduation rate is studied over longer (e.g., 4-year) time intervals is that of missing data, because of student dropout or transfer. In particular, it becomes very difficult to categorize dropouts either as academic failures or successes. Many academically successful students choose to transfer schools or are forced to interrupt their studies for a variety of reasons that are unrelated to their academic functioning. These individuals might not meet the goal of graduation in a 4-to-5-year period, but it would be a mistake to identify them as unsuccessful.

Undoubtedly, many investigators have chosen to utilize single-criterion outcome measures, such as course grades or a one-term GPA, in part because of the practical and conceptual difficulties in employing more long-term assessments of outcome. Nevertheless, researchers should attempt to expand the range of outcome measures whenever possible.

Social and Personal Adjustment

The social adjustment outcome domain focuses on the student's interpersonal level of functioning. Ideally, the college experience not only enhances students' academic knowledge, but also refines their ability to relate effectively with others. Outcome measures that fall within the social adjustment category include indexes of moral and ethical development, maturity, and leadership abilities. Assessment of these variables is often difficult, particularly if the researcher is examining change in a longitudinal design that may require monitoring students over a 3-to-4-year period. Some of these difficulties can be overcome by comparing already existing groups (e.g., first-year vs. fourth-year students) on certain measures, but operationalizing constructs within this domain tends to be more complex than measuring performance in the academic realm.

The personal adjustment outcome category emphasizes the assessment of intrapersonal functioning. Examples of variables within this domain include: (a) personality measures derived from standardized assessment instruments (e.g., CPI, MMPI); (b) indexes of state and trait anxiety, including test anxiety; and (c) subjective measures of satisfaction regarding the college experience. As was true of social adjustment variables, the assessment of change in personal adjustment involves a number of complexities, both in terms of operationalizing constructs adequately and in the data collection process.

INTERVENTIONS

As is evident from the previous sections in this chapter, the problems students face in adjusting to college are numerous and varied. Many students, particularly those considered to be "high-risk," often are inadequately prepared to face the rigorous psychological, emotional, and academic realities of higher education (Francis, McDaniel, & Doyle, 1987). A result of this inadequate preparation is an attrition rate of up to 40% by the third year of school (Scherer & Wygant, 1982). Included among the many reasons students might not reach their junior year of college are: (a) academic skills deficiencies, (b) an inability to effectively manage time, (c) a feeling of isolation and lack of support in the new environment, and/or (d) the absence of defined academic or career goals (Scherer & Wygant, 1982).

Interventions that have been proposed and implemented to assist high-risk students have been as varied as the predisposing factors outlined above. Although three categories of adjustment factors have been outlined in this chapter, most intervention studies are multidimensional in nature and often incorporate several of these domains.

For organizational purposes, we therefore will consider intervention studies according to the structure or type of intervention employed, as opposed to the specific category or outcome measure targeted. Specifically, interventions will be subdivided into two major categories: counseling/skill-focused and program/institution-focused. Counseling/skill-focused interventions are those that have been directed at improving identifiable skills (e.g., coping with anxiety) or have been provided within the context of individual or group counseling. Program/institution-focused interventions are those that are programmatic in nature (e.g., a multidimensional study skills class) or have been implemented and supported at a university/institutional level.

Counseling/Skill-Focused Procedures

Anxieties, both general and specific, have been identified as underlying factors in high-risk students, and thus have been targeted for intervention. Although Russell and colleagues (Russell & Lent, 1982; Russell, Miller, & June, 1975; Russell, Wise & Stratoudakis, 1976) demonstrated the efficacy of behavioral interventions (e.g., systematic desensitization, cue-controlled relaxation) in the reduction of self-report anxiety levels, the effectiveness of these treatment strategies relative to academic performance has not been established. To determine whether behavioral therapies were a necessary component of a successful intervention, Lent and Russell (1978) examined the combined effectiveness of cue-controlled desensitization and study skills training in the treatment of test anxiety. They found that students from the combined treatment condition demonstrated lower levels of anxiety than study-skills-only or no-treatment students, and higher levels of academic performance than did no-treatment controls. Lent and Russell (1978) concluded that a combined approach was most effective in treating test-anxious students.

Dendato and Diener (1986) examined the combined and independent effects of cognitive/relaxation training and study skills training on the anxiety levels and academic performance of test-anxious students. They found that the combined treatment condition was more effective in improving anxiety levels and academic scores than either method alone or no treatment. Similarly, Williams, Decker, and Libassi (1983) found that students participating in an academic skills/stress management training group had higher GPAs and fewer symptoms of stress than those in a study-skills-only group. Smith, Arnkoff, and Wright (1990) found that cognitive-attentional, cognitive skills, and social learning processes all were important in explaining academic performance and test anxiety, supporting the utility of multimodal counseling interventions for modifying academic performance.

Hudesman, Avramides, Loveday, Wendell, and Griemsmann (1986) compared the impact of structured and nondirective counseling styles on the academic performance of high-risk students. In the structured condition, students initially completed detailed counseling contracts concerning specific academic recommendations in collaboration with their counselor. Counselors were actively involved in reviewing and discussing the students' progress, their compliance with the contract, and nonacademic issues that might be affecting their functioning. In contrast, students in the nondirective condition met with a counselor who allowed each student to be self-directing. Results indicated that students in the structured condition had higher GPAs than those in the nondirective condition at the end of the first semester, although these improvements were not maintained in subsequent semesters.

Francis, McDaniel, and Doyle (1987) examined the effects of two different group counseling approaches on communication patterns, study habits, and academic achievement. In one group, students were counseled in attending and clarifying communication skills. In the other group, students were offered traditional, academically oriented counseling (e.g., course scheduling). Students in the communication skills group demonstrated higher GPAs than those in the other group, and significantly improved their interpersonal communication skills.

Program/Institution-Focused Procedures

This section examines large-scale academic interventions that are part of a university's structure. Summer orientation programs represent one type of intervention program that has received attention in the literature. Using volunteer, high-risk students, Scherer and Wygant (1982) investigated the effects of a multidimensional orientation program that focused on basic academic skills (e.g., math, writing), career planning, general life skills, and familiarity with the university. Following the completion of the program, students reported higher educational aspirations and adjustment to college. After three consecutive quarters, Scherer and Wygant found that 75% of the participating students remained enrolled in the university. Bron and Gordon (1986) examined the efficacy of a voluntary orientation program that focused on helping first-year students achieve competencies in academic, social, career, personal, and environmental areas. They found that participating students had higher GPAs and lower attrition rates than nonparticipating students.

Another type of institutionally based intervention is the academic support/enrichment program, which students complete concurrently with other academic courses. In terms of content and general purpose, these interventions are very similar to the summer orientation programs. Landworth and Hepworth (1984), who compared the academic performances of high-risk students who had participated in an enrichment program with two sets of high-risk control students, found that participants received higher grades than nonparticipants; however, positive effects were not maintained in subsequent quarters.

Behrman, Dark, and Paul (1984) compared the long-term effectiveness of a structured multicomponent study skills intervention against a nontreated control after 1 and 3 years. The study skills course focused on skills such as note taking, time management, and test taking. After 1 year, study skills students evidenced higher GPAs than did nonparticipants; after 3 years, the former demonstrated higher levels of retention.

Other studies also have demonstrated short- and long-term benefits of academic support programs. In an examination of a comprehensive academic support program for high-risk students, Abrams and Jernigan (1984) found that those who actively participated in the program benefited most and enjoyed the greatest academic success. In fact, students' willingness to seek assistance from tutors and instructors was a better predictor of first-semester academic success than were entrance examination scores or high school grades. Patrick, Furlow, and Donovan (1988) developed and evaluated a multidisciplinary academic support program for first-year students. The program emphasized study skills, decision making, career and educational planning, and academic advising. In comparison with a no-treatment control group, Patrick et al. found that participants scored higher GPAs and had lower attrition rates, which were maintained after 2 years. For examples of successful academic support programs for minority, older, and commuter students, see Sharkey et al., (1987), and Smith and McMillon (1986).

Other forms of institutional interventions have involved variations in curriculum and teaching style. Hendel (1985) compared the effects of individualized and structured curricula on the academic performance of college students. He found that students in individualized programs reported significantly higher levels of satisfaction with college than did students from structured programs, although no differences existed between the two groups on academic performance and persistence. Rysberg (1986) found that students enrolled in a less traditionally taught class (involving unit testing to mastery, and proctors) achieved higher class grades, rated the class more positively, and remained in the class longer than did students taught through a more standard, lecture-based approach. Another instructor-related intervention concerns the use of progress reports and ongoing monitoring of student academic performance. Burke, Cartwright, and Morris (1986) examined the effects of faculty progress reports on the retention of first-year students. The progress reports were designed to identify those students who were performing poorly, notify them of their status, and encourage them to seek additional assistance from instructors or other personnel. Results indicated that participating students evidenced improved GPAs.

To determine the overall effectiveness of academic programs for high-risk and disadvantaged students, Kulik, Kulik, and Schwalb (1983) performed a meta-analysis on 60 intervention studies, noting that the most commonly assessed outcomes were academic achievement and persistence in school. They found that the majority of the intervention programs (a) had positive effects on level of academic achievement (e.g., GPA) and (b) increased the retention rate of students in comparison to control groups. Kulik et al. also found that the most effective intervention programs for high-risk students were study and reading skills courses, counseling sessions, and comprehensive support services. Overall, intervention programs were most effective when introduced early in the students' educational career.

IMPLICATIONS FOR COUNSELING AND RESEARCH

The conceptual model presented in Figure 15.1 divides the broad topic of academic adjustment into three primary domains. This division has been somewhat arbitrary, but it should serve to guide both research and practice on issues related to academic effectiveness. Even though a particular domain may have special relevance for a given research question or client concern, it is important to consider all three categories in obtaining an accurate assessment of the issues involved.

In comparing the three domains, it is not surprising that academic factors such as aptitude, study skills, achievement motivation, and self-efficacy demonstrate consistent relation with academic outcome variables (e.g., course grades, GPA). The other domains also play an important role in college adjustment, but their relation to specific measures of academic performance appears less direct. For example, although certain personality measures (e.g., locus of control) correlate with performance indexes such as college GPA, these relationships tend to be rather weak. A similar pattern of results holds true regarding social/environmental variables. These findings are not surprising, given that the measures drawn from these domains are conceptually broader and more distal from specific measures of academic performance. It is to be expected, for example, that high school GPA would more accurately predict college grades than would measures of personality type or socioeconomic status. Nonetheless, it is valuable to assess these "nonacademic" variables, particularly when the criteria for academic adjustment include students' intrapersonal and social development.

A Proposed Assessment Scheme

Consistent with the multimodal perspective suggested by Lazarus's (1976) BASIC ID, efforts to improve a student's level of academic functioning require accurate assessments of both *strengths* and *weaknesses* across all three domains. A specific factor may be particularly relevant for a given individual, but an initial survey across all categories provides a more global conceptualization of the client. The following outline exemplifies some of the key issues and questions to be examined in the assessment phase. This outline is not intended to be exhaustive; rather, it is designed to provide a framework to guide the interviewer across each of the three domains.

I. Academic Factors

    A. Current Academic Performance

        What is the student's college GPA? Have there been significant increases or decreases in GPA recently? How is the student currently performing on course exams, quizzes, papers? Does the student demonstrate particular strengths or weaknesses in specific content areas?

    B. High School Performance

        What were the student's high school GPA and class rank? Are standardized test scores available? What was the nature of the student's high school curriculum, especially in core courses such as math and English?

    C. Study Skills

        How much time does the student spend studying, and what is the estimated quality of that study time? How does the student take course notes, and does he or she appear to engage in any adaptive or maladaptive test-taking behaviors?

    D. Self-Efficacy

        What is the student's general level of academic self-efficacy? Does this vary depending on course content?

II. Social/Environmental Factors

    A. Life Stress

        Has the student been exposed to significant life stressors in the past 6 months to 1 year? What is the nature of the student's support system, including family, peers, and teachers?

    B. Family Structure

        What is the parental educational level and overall socioeconomic status? What is the family's general level of psychological functioning? If dysfunctional patterns do appear to exist, to what extent does the student continue to be a part of these?

    C. Campus Environment

        Does the student live on or off campus? Does the student live in a dormitory, an apartment, or with parents? What is the level of the student's involvement in campus extracurricular activities? To what extent does the student interact with college faculty?

    D. Financial/Work Considerations

        Is the student experiencing financial pressures associated with attending college? How stressful does the student evaluate these pressures? Does the student hold a job while attending school? How many hours per week? Does the job involve on-campus work-study or off-campus employment?

III. Personality Factors

    A. Standardized Personality Tests

        If test data are available, how does the student score on scales assessing responsibility, independence, and achievement motivation? Does the student appear to be internal or external on the dimension of locus of control?

B. Self-Esteem and Anxiety

What is the student's general level of self-esteem? How does the student make attributions for success and failure experiences? Does the student report high levels of trait anxiety? What type of coping strategies does the student use in anxiety-arousing situations?

This outline is intended to serve as an illustration of the range of issues that require examination when counseling a student on academic effectiveness. Knowledge of a student's high school academic performance is important information, even though there is nothing that can be done in counseling to change that record. Information regarding high school grades, class rank, and test scores may be helpful in identifying a student's strengths or in anticipating problem areas that might benefit from proactive interventions. Knowledge of areas such as study skills and behaviors, family dynamics, career decision status, and social support network may have more direct and immediate implications for treatment. By surveying the student's level of functioning across all domains, it becomes feasible to prioritize intervention strategies. In this way, a more planful, systematic, multidimensional intervention program can be developed to guide both the student and counselor through the treatment process.

Directions for Future Research

In keeping with the multidimensional focus of this chapter, the following suggestions for future research are organized around the three major factors predictive of academic success. In addition, some general suggestions are offered concerning the evaluation and implementation of intervention programs as well as the measurement of outcome variables.

Academic Factors

Several areas warrant further investigation within this domain, but two seem particularly noteworthy. First, continued study in the areas of self-efficacy and effort attribution seems promising. Because self-efficacy beliefs have been related positively to academic performance and persistence, it appears that the development and evaluation of intervention strategies to enhance students' academic self-efficacy would be especially worthwhile.

Second, now that two distinct types of test-anxious students have been identified (Naveh-Benjamin et al., 1987), methods for accurately assessing and treating the two groups should be examined. Researchers might well focus on determining the relative frequency of each test-anxious group, and the specific interventions that would be most effective with these students.

Social/Environmental Factors

The two major areas where additional research appears warranted are: (a) life stress and social support, and (b) campus environment "fit." The negative life stress–academic performance relationship has been established within the general college population; future studies might examine whether this relationship exists within specific subgroups of students who are known to be academically "at-risk" (e.g., athletes). Research investigating the moderating effects of social support on the life stress–academic performance relationship would be another area of focus. An examination of the relative effects of varying social support levels on a student's vulnerability to negative life stress seems particularly important. To avoid the methodological inadequacies of previous retrospective studies, future life stress research would benefit by incorporating prospective designs.

For the issue of campus environment "fit," researchers might try to further delineate the environments that are most conducive to the adjustment and success to college students. Specifically, it would be important to determine the relative benefits of living on vs. off campus, and how students' living environments affect their involvement in campus activities. In addition, because the benefits of students' interacting with each other and with faculty have been noted, future research might focus on the development and evaluation of interventions aimed at increasing students' levels of involvement with campus programs, faculty, and peers.

Personality Factors

Within this domain, additional research examining the effects of personality variables appears warranted. Although previous research has found certain personality measures to be related to academic performance, the strength of these relationships generally has been weak. Future research might do well to focus on the effects of personality variables, in conjunction with other nonpersonality variables, on students' academic adjustment. For example, it would be useful to determine the potential moderating effects of personality measures (e.g., locus of control, trait anxiety) on the life stress–academic performance relationship. Because the global measure of locus of control has been shown to be weakly related to academic outcome, researchers might develop and evaluate more specific measures of control, such as students' perceived control. These specific control measures might prove to be more strongly related to academic outcomes and, thus, may provide a better means for predicting academic success.

Interventions and Outcome Measures: Final Comments

The following comments represent some general suggestions for future research on issues relevant to academic adjustment:

1. It will be important to continue to develop and evaluate counseling/skill-focused as well as program/institution-focused intervention programs, particularly for high-risk groups such as students of color and athletes.
2. To validly assess the efficacy of intervention programs, evaluation studies need to be more rigorous in the inclusion of appropriate control groups within their methodologies.
3. An expansion of academic outcome measures beyond the current reliance on GPA is needed, to strengthen the external validity of the studies in this area.
4. It is essential for researchers to move beyond the traditional, academically focused measures and consider variables from the social/environmental and personality domains. In light of the various factors presented in this chapter, it will be important for specific models of academic adjustment to be developed and directly tested via methods such as causal modeling.

REFERENCES

Abrams, H. G., & Jernigan, L. P. (1984). Academic support services and success of high-risk college students. *American Educational Research Journal, 21,* 261–274.

Allen, G. J., Lerner, W. M., & Hinrichsen, J. J. (1972). Study behaviors and their relationships to test anxiety and academic performance. *Psychological Reports, 30,* 407–410.

Alwin, D. F., & Thornton, A. (1984). Family origins and the schooling process: Early versus late influence of parental characteristics. *American Sociological Review, 49,* 784–802.

Atkinson, J. W. (1964). *An introduction to motivation.* Princeton, NJ: Van Nostrand Reinhold.

Baker, H. S. (1975). Academic freedom: A structural approach. *Journal of the American College Health Association, 24,* 4–7.

Baker, R. W., & Siryk, B. (1984). Measuring academic motivation of matriculating college freshmen. *Journal of College Student Personnel, 25,* 459–464.

Bandura, A. (1977). Self-efficacy: Toward a unifying theory of behavior change. *Psychological Review, 84,* 191–215.

Bandura, A. (1978). The self system in reciprocal determinism. *American Psychologist, 33,* 344–359.

Bandura, A. (1982). Self-efficacy mechanism in human agency. *American Psychologist, 37,* 122–147.

Bandura, A., & Adams, N. E. (1977). Analysis of self-efficacy theory of behavioral change. *Cognitive Therapy and Research, 1,* 287–308.

Barney, J. A., Fredericks, J., Fredericks, M., & Robinson, P. (1987). Relationship between social class, ACT scores, SAT scores and academic achievement of business students: A comparison. *College Student Journal, 21,* 395–401.

Behrman, J. A., Dark, V. J., & Paul, S. C. (1984). The effects of a structured learning-skills intervention on long-term academic performance. *Journal of College Student Personnel, 25,* 326–331.

Berbaum, M. L., & Moreland, R. L. (1980). Intellectual development within the family: A new application of the confluence model. *Developmental Psychology, 16,* 506–515.

Bers, T. H. (1986). Confidence, commitment, and academic performance and retention of community college students. *Community/Junior College Quarterly, 10,* 35–57.

Blustein, D. L., Judd, T. P., Krom, J., Viniar, B., Padilla, E., Wedemeyer, R., & Williams, D. (1986). Identifying predictors of academic performance of community college students. *Journal of College Student Personnel, 27,* 242–249.

Bron, G. D., & Gordon, M. P. (1986). Impact of an orientation center on grade point average and attrition. *College Student Journal, 20,* 242–246.

Brown, J. C., & Strickland, B. R. (1972). Belief in internal–external control of reinforcement and participation in college activities. *Journal of Consulting and Clinical Psychology, 38,* 148.

Brown, J. D., & Siegel, J. M. (1988). Attributions for negative life events and depression: The role of perceived control. *Journal of Personality and Social Psychology, 54,* 316–322.

Brown, S. D., Alpert, D., Lent, R. W., Hunt, G., & Brady, T. (1988). Perceived social support among college students: Factor structure of the Social Support Inventory. *Journal of Counseling Psychology, 35,* 472–478.

Brown, S. D., & Nelson, T. L. (1983). Beyond the uniformity myth: A comparison of academically successful and unsuccessful test-anxious college students. *Journal of Counseling Psychology, 30,* 367–374.

Bruch, M. A., Pearl, L., & Giordano, S. (1986). Differences in the cognitive processes of academically successful and unsuccessful test-anxious students. *Journal of Counseling Psychology, 33,* 217–219.

Burke, J., Cartwright, N., & Morris, E. (1986). Progress reports: Improving freshman retention. *Journal of College Student Personnel, 27,* 462–464.

Burke, J. P., Midkiff, R. M., & Williams, R. V. (1985). The role of self-esteem in affective reactions to achievement-related situations. *Educational and Psychological Research, 5,* 191–203.

Capella, B. J., Wagner, M., & Kusmierz, J. A. (1982). Relation of study habits and attitudes to academic performance. *Psychological Reports, 50,* 593–594.

Caplin, M. D. (1968). The relationship between self-concept and academic achievement. *Journal of Experimental Education, 37,* 13–16.

Carpenter, P. G., & Western, J. S. (1982). Aspirations for higher education. *The Australian Journal of Education, 26,* 266–278.

Cicirelli, V. G. (1978). The relationship of sibling structure to intellectual abilities and achievement. *Review of Educational Research, 48,* 365–379.

Clifford, M. M. (1986). The comparative effects of strategy and effort attributions. *British Journal of Educational Psychology, 56,* 75–83.

Cohen, S., & Hoberman, H. M. (1983). Positive events and social support as buffers of life change stress. *Journal of Applied Social Psychology, 13,* 99–125.

Council of Counseling Psychology Training Programs (1990, August). *1990 Survey of counseling psychology doctoral training programs.* Paper presented at the annual convention of the American Psychological Association, Boston, MA.

Crump, B. R., Hickson, J. H., & Laman, A. (1985). Relationship of locus of control to achievement and self-concept in education majors. *Psychological Reports, 57,* 1055–1060.

Cutrona, C. E. (1986). Objective determinants of perceived social support. *Journal of Personality and Social Psychology, 50,* 349–355.

De Meuse, K. P. (1985, Fall). The life events stress–performance linkage: An exploratory study. *Journal of Human Stress,* 35–40.

Dendato, K. M., & Diener, D. (1986). Effectiveness of cognitive/relaxation therapy and study-skills training in reducing self-reported anxiety and improving the academic performance of test-anxious students. *Journal of Counseling Psychology, 33,* 131–135.

Edwards, J. E., & Waters, L. K. (1981). Moderating effect of achievement motivation and locus of control on the relationship between academic ability and academic performance. *Educational and Psychological Measurement, 41,* 585–587.

Evanoski, P. O. (1988). An assessment of the impact of helping on the helper for college students. *College Student Journal, 22,* 2–10.

Feltz, D. L., & Weiss, M. R. (1984). The impact of girls' interscholastic sport participation on academic orientation. *Research Quarterly for Exercise and Sport, 55,* 332–339.

Francis, K. X., McDaniel, M., & Doyle, R. E. (1987). Training in role communication skills: Effect of interpersonal and academic skills of high-risk freshmen. *Journal of College Student Personnel, 28,* 151–156.

Gadzella, B. M., Ginther, D. W., & Williamson, J. D. (1987). Study skills, learning processes and academic achievement. *Psychological Reports, 61,* 167–172.

Gadzella, B. M., & Williamson, J. D. (1984). Study skills, self-concepts, and academic achievement. *Psychological Reports, 54,* 923–929.

Gadzella, B. M., Williamson, J. D., & Ginther, D. W. (1985). Correlations of self-concept with locus of control and academic performance. *Perceptual and Motor Skills, 61,* 639–645.

Garrity, T. F., & Ries, J. B. (1985, Fall). Health status as a mediating factor in the life change–academic performance relationship. *Journal of Human Stress,* 118–124.

Gough, H. G., & Lanning, K. (1986). Predicting grades in college from the California Psychological Inventory. *Educational and Psychological Measurement, 46,* 205–213.

Gurman, A. S. (1970). The role of the family in underachievement. *Journal of School Psychology, 8,* 48–53.

Hahn, M. E. (1955). Counseling psychology, *American Psychologist, 10,* 279–282.

Harris, P. W. (1973). *The relationship of life change to academic performance among selected college freshmen at varying levels of college readiness.* (Doctoral dissertation, East Texas State University, 1972). *Dissertation Abstracts International, 33,* 6665A–6666A. (University Microfilms No. 73.14285)

Hearn, J. C. (1984). The relative roles of academic, ascribed, and socioeconomic characteristics in college destinations. *Sociology of Education, 57,* 22–30.

Hendel, D. D. (1985). Effects of individualized and structured college curricula on students' performance and satisfaction. *American Educational Research Journal, 22,* 117–122.

Henke, J. W., Lyons, T. F., & Krachenberg, A. R. (1987). Measuring students' workload: A new perspective. *Psychological Reports, 60,* 667–670.

Holland, J. L. (1959). The prediction of college grades from the California Psychological Inventory and the Scholastic Aptitude Test. *Journal of Educational Psychology, 50,* 135–142.

Holland, J. L. (1973). *Making vocational choices: A theory of careers.* Englewood Cliffs, NJ: Prentice-Hall.

Hollenbeck, J. R., Williams, C. R., & Klein, H. J. (1989). An empirical examination of the antecedents of commitment to difficult goals. *Journal of Applied Psychology, 74,* 18–73.

Hudesman, J., Avramides, B., Loveday, C., Wendell, A., & Griemsmann, R. (1986, September). Impact of counseling style on the academic performance of college students in special programs. *Journal of College Student Personnel,* 394–399.

Huebner, L. A., & Corazzini, J. G. (1984). Environmental assessment and intervention. In S. D. Brown & R. W. Lent (Eds.), *Handbook of counseling psychology.* New York: Wiley.

Irish, D. P. (1964). Sibling interactions: A neglected aspect in family life research. *Social Forces, 42,* 279–288.

Janosik, S., Creamer, D. G., & Cross, L. H. (1988). The relationship of residence halls' student-environment fit and sense of competence. *Journal of College Student Development, 29,* 320–326.

Jemmott, J. B., & Magliore, K. (1988). Academic stress, social support, and secretory immunoglobin A. *Journal of Personality and Social Psychology, 55,* 803–810.

Jordaan, J. P., Myers, R. A., Layton, W. C., & Morgan, H. H. (1968). *The counseling psychologist.* Washington, DC: American Psychological Association. Also in J. M. Whiteley (Ed.). (1980). *The history of counseling psychology* (pp. 179–195). Monterey, CA: Brooks/Cole.

Karnes, F. A., Chauvin, J. C., & Trant, T. J. (1984). Comparisons of personality factors and American College Test scores for university honor students, *Educational and Psychological Research, 4,* 111–114.

Kleeman, G. L., & Richardson, R. C. (1985). Student characteristics and perceptions of university effectiveness. *The Review of Higher Education, 9,* 5–20.

Kulik, C. C., Kulik, J. A., & Shwalb, B. J. (1983). College programs for high risk and disadvantaged students: A meta-analysis of findings. *Review of Educational Research, 53,* 397–414.

Landworth, S., & Hepworth, D. (1984). Support systems for high-risk college students: Findings and issues. *College and University, 59,* 119–128.

Lazarus, A. (1976). *Multi-modal behavior therapy.* New York: Springer.

Lent, R. W., Brown, S. D., & Larkin, K. C. (1984). Relation of self-efficacy expectations to academic achievement and persistence. *Journal of Counseling Psychology, 31,* 356–362.

Lent, R. W., Brown, S. D., & Larkin, K. C. (1986). Self-efficacy in the prediction of academic performance and perceived career options. *Journal of Counseling Psychology, 33,* 265–269.

Lent, R. W., Brown, S. D., & Larkin, K. C. (1987). Comparison of three theoretically derived variables in predicting career and academic behavior: Self-efficacy, interest congruence, and consequence thinking. *Journal of Counseling Psychology, 34,* 293–298.

Lent, R. W., & Hackett, G. (1987). Career self-efficacy: Empirical status and future directions. *Journal of Vocational Behavior, 30,* 347–382.

Lent, R. W., & Russell, R. K. (1978). Treatment of test anxiety by cue-controlled desensitization and study-skills training. *Journal of Counseling Psychology, 25,* 217–224.

Lin, Y. G., & McKeachie, W. J. (1970). Aptitude, anxiety, study habits, and academic achievement. *Journal of Counseling Psychology, 17,* 306–309.

Lloyd, C., Alexander, A. A., Rice, D. G., & Greenfield, N. S. (1980, Fall). Life events as predictors of academic performance. *Journal of Human Stress,* 15–25.

Lopez, F. G., Campbell, V. L., & Watkins, C. E. (1988). Family structure, psychological separation, and college adjustment: A canonical analysis and cross-validation. *Journal of Counseling Psychology, 35,* 402–409.

Lyons, T. F., Krachenberg, A. R., & Henke, J. W. (1986). Academic performance and work: Methodological critique and review. *Social and Behavioral Sciences Documents, 16,* 17.

MacDermott, K. G., Conn, P. A., & Owen, J. W. (1987, Spring). The influence of parental education level on college choice. *Journal of College Admissions,* 3–10.

Malloch, D. C., & Michael, W. B. (1981). Predicting student grade point average at a community college: SAT, ACT scores, and measures of motivation. *Educational and Psychological Measurement, 41,* 1127–1135.

Manski, C. F., & Wise, D. A. (1983). *College choice in America.* Cambridge, MA: Harvard University Press.

Mathiasen, R. E. (1984). Predicting college academic achievement: A research review. *College Student Journal, 18,* 380–386.

Moe, K. O., & Zeiss, A. M. (1982). Measuring self-efficacy expectations for social skills: A methodological inquiry. *Cognitive Therapy and Research, 6,* 191–205.

Moos, R. H. (1976). *The human context.* New York: Wiley.

Multon, K. D., Brown, S. D., & Lent, R. W. (1991). Relation of self-efficacy beliefs to academic outcomes: A meta-analytic investigation. *Journal of Counseling Psychology, 38,* 30–39.

Naveh-Benjamin, M., McKeachie, W. J., & Lin, Y. J. (1987). Two types of test-anxious students: Support for an information processing model. *Journal of Educational Psychology, 79,* 131–136.

Neely, R. (1977). Discriminant analysis for prediction of college graduation. *Educational and Psychological Measurement, 37,* 965–970.

Neumann, Y., Finaly, E., & Reichel, A. (1988). Achievement motivation factors and students' college outcomes. *Psychological Reports, 62,* 555–560.

O'Brien, K. M., Brown, S. D., & Lent, R. W. (1990, August). *The effect of aptitude-efficacy congruence on academic performance.* Paper presented at the annual convention of the American Psychological Association, Boston, MA.

Okun, M. A., Sandler, I. N., & Baumann, D. J. (1988). Buffer and booster effects as event-support transactions. *American Journal of Community Psychology, 16,* 435–443.

Pascarella, E. T. (1984). College environmental influences on students' educational aspirations. *Journal of Higher Education, 55,* 751–771.

Pascarella, E. T. (1985). The influence of on-campus living versus commuting to college on intellectual and interpersonal self-concept. *Journal of College Student Personnel, 26,* 292–299.

Patrick, J., Furlow, J. W., & Donovan, S. (1988). Using a comprehensive academic intervention program in the retention of high-risk students. *NACADA Journal, 8,* 29–34.

Pervin, L. A. (1968). Performance and satisfaction as a function of individual–environment fit. *Psychological Bulletin, 69,* 56–68.

Pervin, L. A. (1977). The representative design in person–situation research. In D. Magnusson & N. S. Endler (Eds.), *Personality at the crossroads: Current issues in interactional psychology.* Hillsdale, NJ: Erlbaum.

Platt, C. W. (1988). Effects of causal attributions for success on first-term college performance: A covariance structure model. *Journal of Educational Psychology, 80,* 569–578.

Powers, S., Douglas, P., Cool, B. A., & Gose, K. F. (1985). Achievement motivation and attributions for success and failure. *Psychological Reports, 57,* 751–754.

Prager, K. J. (1983). Educational aspirations and self-esteem in returning and traditional community college students. *Journal of College Student Personnel, 24,* 144–147.

Prager, K. J., & Freeman, A. (1979). Self-esteem, academic competence, educational aspiration and curriculum choice of urban community college students. *Journal of College Student Personnel, 5,* 392–397.

Prociuk, T. J., & Breen, L. J. (1974). Locus of control, study habits and attitudes, and college academic performance. *Journal of Psychology, 88,* 91–95.

Prociuk, T. J., & Breen, L. J. (1977). Internal–external locus of control and information-seeking in a college academic situation. *Journal of Social Psychology, 101,* 309–310.

Rahe, R. H. (1972). Subjects' recent life changes and their near-future illness susceptibility. *Advances in Psychosomatic Medicine, 8,* 2–19.

Rotter, J. B. (1966). Generalized expectancies for internal versus external control of reinforcement. *Psychological Monographs, 80,* (609).

Royer, J. M., Abranovic, W. A., & Sinatra, G. M. (1987). Using entering reading comprehension performance as a predictor of performance in college classes. *Journal of Educational Psychology, 79,* 19–26.

Russell, R. K., & Lent, R. W. (1982). Cue-controlled relaxation and systematic desensitization versus nonspecific factors in treating test anxiety. *Journal of Counseling Psychology, 29,* 100–103.

Russell, R. K., Miller, D. E., & June, L. N. (1975). A comparison between group systematic desensitization and cue-controlled relaxation in the treatment of test anxiety. *Behavior Therapy, 6,* 172–177.

Russell, R. K., Wise, F., & Stratoudakis, J. P. (1976). Treatment of test anxiety by cue-controlled relaxation and systematic desensitization. *Journal of Counseling Psychology, 23,* 563–566.

Rutkowski, K., & Domino, G. (1975). Interrelationship of study skills and personality variables in college students. *Journal of Educational Psychology, 67,* 784–789.

Rysberg, J. A. (1986). Effects of modifying instruction in a college classroom. *Psychological Reports, 58,* 965–966.

Sarason, I. G. (1960). Empirical findings and theoretical problems in the use of anxiety scales. *Psychological Bulletin, 57,* 403–415.

Sarason, I. G. (1961). The effects of anxiety and threat on the solution of a difficult task. *Journal of Abnormal and Social Psychology, 62,* 165–168.

Sarason, I. G., Johnson, J. H., & Siegel, J. M. (1978). Assessing the impact of life change: Development of the Life Experiences Survey. *Journal of Consulting and Clinical Psychology, 46,* 932–946.

Sarason, I. G., Sarason, B. R., Potter, E. H., & Antoni, M. H. (1985). Life events, social support, and illness. *Psychosomatic Medicine, 47,* 156–163.

Scherer, C., & Wygant, N. S. (1982). Sound beginnings support freshmen transition into university life. *Journal of College Student Personnel, 23,* 378–383.

Schreiber, E. H. (1985). Cattell Anxiety Scale in predicting college students' achievement. *Psychological Reports, 56,* 567–570.

Sharkey, S. J., Bischoff, P. M., Echols, D., Morrison, C., Northman, E. A., Liebman, A., & Steele, B. (1987). Pioneer programs for retaining "at-risk" students. *New Directions for Higher Education, 15,* 61–86.

Smith, A. L., & McMillon, H. G. (1986). Counselors as educational facilitators. *Journal of Multi-Cultural Counseling and Development, 14,* 167–176.

Smith, R. J., Arnkoff, D. B., & Wright, T. L. (1990). Test anxiety and academic competence: A comparison of alternative models. *Journal of Counseling Psychology, 37,* 313–321.

Spielberger, C. D. (1972). Anxiety as an emotional state. In C. D. Spielberger (Ed.), *Anxiety: Current trends in theory and research.* New York: Academic Press.

Stroup, A. L. (1970). The prediction of academic performance from personality and aptitude variables. *Journal of Experimental Education, 38,* 83–86.

Suls, J., & Mullin, B. (1981, June). Life events, perceived control and illness: The role of uncertainty. *Journal of Human Stress,* 30–34.

Taylor, R. G., & Whetstone, R. D. (1983). The college-fit theory and engineering students. *Measurement and Evaluation in Guidance, 15,* 267–273.

Thoits, P. A. (1982). Conceptual, methodological, and theoretical problems in studying social support as a buffer against life stress. *Journal of Health and Social Behavior, 32,* 329–337.

Traub, G. S. (1982). Relationship between locus of control and grade point average in freshmen college students. *Psychological Reports, 50,* 1294.

Trice, A. D. (1985). An academic locus of control scale for college students. *Perceptual and Motor Skills, 61,* 1043–1046.

Waits, B. K., & Demana, F. (1988). Relationship between mathematics skills of entering students and their success in college. *The School Counselor, 35,* 307–310.

Warehime, R. G. (1972). Generalized expectancy for locus of control and academic performance. *Psychological Reports, 30,* 314.

Webb, G. (1986). Factors affecting achievement in the University of Cambridge GCE A-level geography examination. *Educational Research, 28,* 132–138.

Weiner, B. (1979). A theory of motivation for some classroom experiences. *Journal of Educational Psychology, 71,* 3–25.

Weiner, B. (1985). An attributional theory of achievement motivation. *Psychological Review, 92,* 548–573.

Weitzman, R. A. (1982). The prediction of college achievement by the SAT and the high school record. *Journal of Educational Measurement, 19,* 179–191.

Whiteley, J. M. (1984). A historical perspective on the development of counseling psychology as a profession. In S. D. Brown & R. W. Lent (Eds.), *Handbook of counseling psychology.* New York: Wiley.

Wildman, R. C. (1978). Life change with college grades as a role performance variable. *Social Psychology, 41,* 34–46.

Williams, J. M., Decker, T. W., & Libassi, A. (1983). The impact of stress management training on the academic performance of low-achieving college students. *Journal of College Student Personnel, 24,* 491–494.

Yerkes, R. M., & Dodson, J. D. (1908). The relation of strength of stimulus to rapidity of habit-formation. *Journal of Comparative Neurological Psychology, 18,* 459–482.

Zajonc, R. B. (1983). Validating the confluence model. *Psychological Bulletin, 93,* 457–480.

Zajonc, R. B. (1986). The decline and rise of scholastic aptitude scores. *American Psychologist, 41,* 862–867.

Zajonc, R. B., Markus, H., & Markus, G. B. (1979). The birth order puzzle. *Journal of Personality and Social Psychology, 37,* 1325–1341.

Zilli, M. B. (1971). Reasons why the gifted adolescent underachieves and some implications of guidance and counseling to this problem. *Gifted Child Quarterly, 15,* 279–292.

CHAPTER 16
CAREER COUNSELING: CHOICE AND IMPLEMENTATION

SUSAN D. PHILLIPS

Questions about how an individual prepares for, selects, and functions in the world of work have been of considerable interest to the field of counseling psychology. Theoretical and empirical contributions have illuminated the complexities of occupational choice and career development for nearly a century. Similarly, recognizing the complexities of functioning in the work domain, practitioners have developed broader and more varied strategies for intervention. Where career counseling might once have been considered a fairly short and simple endeavor, it has clearly expanded to such a multi-faceted scope that Osipow (1982) suggested that it defied clear definition.

Regardless of the difficulty in defining what career counseling is, there is considerable evidence that it works. The evidence accumulated over many decades, with many different intervention strategies, and for many different populations, is reassuring: what career counselors do, helps. This conclusion was drawn by a number of previous reviewers (Fretz, 1981; Holland, Magoon, & Spokane, 1981; Krumboltz, Becker-Haven, & Burnett, 1979; Myers, 1971, 1986), and was recently refined by the observation that some of our career intervention efforts may be more helpful than others (Oliver & Spokane, 1988; Spokane & Oliver, 1983).

Although it seems clear that our efforts generally produce positive outcomes, there has been less attention to the question of whether what we are able to do is what needs to be done. The approach of the present review, therefore, is to focus on what needs to be done and, from that vantage point, to consider the evidence about what we are able to do. In defining what needs to be done, there can be little argument with the notion that the ideal is problem-free choosing. More specifically, the "ideal" might be portrayed as follows: the individual has a clearly defined self, is ready to choose, approaches and proceeds well through the decision-making process, arrives at an appropriate and satisfying choice to which he or she can commit, and easily implements that choice. In the following review, each component of the "ideal" (self-definition, readiness, decision making, choice and commitment, and implementation) is addressed separately. Such partitioning should not suggest that the phenomena are indeed separate in reality. On the contrary, in practice, they are likely to be experienced as highly interrelated and continuous.

Consistent with the general approach outlined above, theoretical prepositions and empirical evidence for each component are reviewed first, to provide a view of relevant factors and potential problems to be considered in attempting intervention. A practical perspective is taken next, including a review of assessment strategies and intervention efforts relevant to each component. Finally, drawing on the theoretical and practical review, suggestions are offered for future practice and research.

SELF-DEFINITION

Following Super's (1953) assertion that "the process of vocational development is essentially that of developing and implementing a self concept" (p. 190), there has been little argument with the notion that a critical element in occupational choice is the development of a clearly defined self. That is, consideration of what occupation to pursue must necessarily be preceded by a period of self-development and self-definition. An extended discussion of the development of the self is beyond the scope of this chapter; however, questions about how an individual forms a clear definition of self are addressed below.

Theoretical Perspectives

Beyond Super's initial theoretical statements about the role of self-concept in vocational behavior, there are a number of theoretical perspectives on self-definition. In his own subsequent writings, Super (1963) described self-concept formation as essentially a process of exploration, self-differentiation, identification, role playing, and reality testing. These various activities, undertaken on a lifelong basis, serve to establish for the individual a sense of identity that includes elements of both uniqueness and similarity to others. This sense of identity, once translated into occupational terms, functions as the basis for one's occupational choices. Jordaan (1963) further elaborated those activities that would enable an individual to "try out" various definitions of self and to refine various self-views. In short, exploration—that set of activities, undertaken intentionally or otherwise, that elicits information about one's self—was seen as the primary vehicle for self-concept formation. Such self-exploration, in concert with exploration of occupational environments, was presumed to yield a host of desirable vocational outcomes.

Although the contributions of Super and his colleagues are those most closely associated with self-concept development, the notion of self-definition is evident in a variety of major theories of vocational behavior. This is particularly true for those models in which the "how" and "why" of choosing are emphasized. For example, Tiedeman and O'Hara's (1963) model of career decision making considers self-definition as crucial. In a related model, Harren (1979) specifically designated two aspects of self-definition—identify and self-esteem—as critical decision-maker characteristics.

In other models of process, self-definition and self-evaluation are less clearly distinguished. For example, in Krumboltz, Mitchell, and Jones's (1976) social learning model, the learning mechanisms by which one acquires self-definition are described. According to this perspective, it is through various associative and instrumental learning experiences that one observes oneself and consequently acquires generalized evaluations about who one is. These self-observation generalizations, then, serve, together with other factors, to determine subsequent action. Drawing from a related theoretical basis, Hackett and Betz (1981) delineated the acquisition and role of self-referent thought in the vocational domain. In this social cognitive model, self-efficacy expectations are derived from several sources (such as past performance or observational learning) and, in turn, form the basis for an individual's judgments about capabilities with respect to future career behaviors.

The notion of self-definition is also evident in those models that focus on *what is chosen* (rather than how choice is made). Thus, although Holland's (1985a) model is most widely known for its typology of persons and environments, it also offered the constructs of consistency (the degree of relatedness among aspects of an individual's personality) and differentiation (the extent to which an individual's personality is clearly defined) as indirect estimates of self-definition. Holland also described the construct of identity as "the possession of a clear and stable picture of one's goals, interests, and talents" (1985a, p. 5), and as a factor implicated in the predictability of vocational choice.

Taken together, these theoretical perspectives would suggest that self-definition is a critical element in vocational behavior, and that the process of defining oneself proceeds, intentionally or otherwise, through exploration of and interaction with various aspects of the environment. Despite the evident importance of self-definition and some broadly consistent views on how it is acquired, much of the research relevant to self-concept and vocational behavior has focused on the implications of self-definition. However, there is some evidence about what factors facilitate or hinder self-definition, driven by the general hypothesis that there should be some self-definitional consequences of various exploratory or interactional events. For example, in circumscribed investigations of the impact of exploration on self-definition, support was found for the notion that those undergraduates who had engaged in vocational exploration would have more certain self-concepts (Arnold & Masterson, 1987), and that during the school-to-work transition for graduate and undergraduate students, some job-specific forms of exploration lead to greater self-concept crystallization (Taylor, 1985).

A different method of approaching this general hypothesis is seen in the social learning literature. As noted above, various experiences and interactions are thought to account for an individual's self-view. In studying the acquisition of self-efficacy expectations, Hackett and colleagues (Campbell & Hackett, 1986; Hackett & Betz, 1984; Hackett & Campbell, 1987) documented that success or failure in the performance of a task can affect self-view formation.

Recently, a second hypothesis has emerged concerning the formation of a self-concept. Given that the theoretical models noted above were drawn, in part, from an examination of literature in more general domains of behavior, some investigators have suggested that it would be profitable to study other kinds of development in concert with vocational development. Based on the notion that self-definition occurs in many different domains of functioning and that the process of self-definition in these various domains may not be isolated, several investigations have attempted to trace self-definition across developmental domains, seeking evidence that self-definitional movement in one domain is associated with advances in self-definition in other domains. Savickas (1985), for example, documented a relationship between ego identity development and vocational identity, and Blustein, Devenis, and Kidney (1989) found an association between vocational exploration and ego identity status.

Practical Perspectives

Although empirical evidence about how self-definition evolves is far from conclusive, the applied literature has provided a number of avenues for detecting and solving self-definitional problems. Reviewed below are strategies for assessment and intervention in the area of self-definition.

Assessment

Detecting problems—or improvements—in self-definition requires that information be obtained about what the individual knows about his or her own characteristics. This type of information has been elicited in a number of ways, the most common of which in the intervention literature involves use of the Identity Scale of My Vocational Situation (MVS; Holland, Daiger, & Power, 1980). This is a self-report instrument that assesses the extent to which the respondent holds clear and stable views about himself or herself in the vocational domain. A similar measure is the Vocational Rating Scale, assessing self-concept crystallization (Barrett & Tinsley, 1977a). Another commonly used measure of self-definition is the Self Appraisal subscale of the Career Maturity Inventory Competence Test (CMI; Crites, 1978), which provides a view of the individual's ability to appraise the characteristics of described *others*. Other, less widely used techniques for self-definition assessment include indexes of the accuracy of self-knowledge that are derived from discrepancies between subjective and objective ratings of various characteristics (Oliver, 1978).

Intervention

As one might expect, given the general theory outlined above, intervention strategies aimed at change in self-definition would likely entail the deliberate exposure of individuals to information and/or experiences from which greater knowledge or clarity about their own characteristics can be derived. A number of such interventions have been attempted, and they vary in scope, duration, and target population.

Of the intervention strategies documented, some are quite brief and circumscribed. For example, Flake, Roach, and Stenning (1975) demonstrated that a brief three-session individual counseling intervention entailing little more than test interpretation produced significant gains in self-appraisal for 10th graders. It would appear from these results that the provision of even a minimal amount of self-information serves to alter self-definition.

Not all brief attempts to supply self-information have been uniformly successful, however. Slaney and Dickson (1985) failed to find consistent changes in the identity of reentry women, following various card sort interventions. With a similar population, Slaney and Lewis (1986) found no differential identity improvements between a card sort procedure and an interpretive report of the Strong–Campbell Interest Inventory (SCII; Campbell, 1974). Further, no differential identity improvements among college students were found by Hoffman, Spokane, and Magoon (1981) in their study of different levels of counselor contact when obtaining SCII profile results.

Some differential benefits of brief interventions have been documented on the basis of the characteristics of the individual. Kivlighan and Shapiro (1987) demonstrated that the self-administered Vocational Exploration and Insight Kit (Holland et al., 1982) had a more beneficial impact on the vocational identities of college students with less people-oriented interests than on those of their more people-oriented peers.

The effects of several more comprehensive interventions have also been documented, offered typically in a group or class format. These widely studied, "standard issue" interventions are more extensive in terms of content and amount of contact. In terms of content, although each has some unique features, all include some form of self-assessment and feedback, information about specific and general aspects of the world of work, and advice on how career decisions are made. In terms of contact, these range from approximately 15 hours of intervention over the span of 5 weeks to nearly 3 hours a week over a 16-week semester. These efforts have produced significant improvements in various aspects of self-definition for college students (Ganster & Lovell, 1978; Johnson, Smither, & Holland, 1981; Lent, Larkin, & Hasegawa, 1986;

Rayman, Bernard, Holland, & Barnett, 1983; Remer, O'Neill, & Gohs, 1984; Ware, 1985).

Similar gains have been documented with younger individuals. Yates, Johnson, and Johnson (1979) were able to enhance self-appraisal among 8th- and 9th-grade students involved in a vocational exploration group, and Wiggins and Moody (1981) demonstrated that those classes in which self-information was provided (e.g., through testing and follow-up interpretation and exercises) were more effective in producing identity improvements among high school seniors than were those classes in which occupational information alone was provided. As with the more circumscribed interventions, not all of the comprehensive efforts have been successful. For example, Pavlak and Kammer (1985) were unable to produce changes in self-appraisal among delinquent adolescent males.

Finally, the question of whether a more comprehensive intervention is necessary was partially addressed by Babcock and Kaufman (1976), who found greater improvement in self-knowledge for college females following a 7-week comprehensive course than following brief individual counseling.

Implications

Given that the literature on career-related self-definition does not yet provide a precise explanation of self-definition or a prescription for intervention, several directions for the future can be suggested. First, based on current knowledge, a practitioner would be well-advised to use one of the more comprehensive intervention strategies to effect self-definitional gain. At present, the brief or self-directed strategies would appear to be reliably effective only for a small segment of the client population, although this is an area deserving further study.

Second, an increased number of intervention studies specifically directed toward self-definition would be particularly useful. Further, given the little sure help that is available for those clients whose vocational lives are complicated by particular barriers (such as delinquency or reentry), new strategies will need to be developed and tested in future investigations. Also of interest would be studies on the effects of prevention efforts aimed at providing younger individuals with adequate and accurate interactions with the environment.

Finally, it is important to enhance the knowledge base from which interventions are designed. Given the critical nature of self-definition in setting the stage for subsequent vocational events, it is somewhat surprising that there has not been more investigation of how self-definition evolves. More empirical information is needed on how a self-concept is formed. In this regard, as Grotevant (1986) pointed out, it is unfortunate that the study of identity development has been undertaken without attention to the particular developmental processes that occur in different content domains. Further, although much of the theoretical work suggests that self-definition is an ongoing process, the ensuing research has focused only on youth. Future research might study self-definitional changes later in life. If it is the case that exploration of and interaction with the environment serves as the impetus for self-definitional change, one might expect that such later events as work-force entry would have self-definitional consequences.

READINESS TO CHOOSE

To be "ready" to choose means more than simply arriving at a point where a choice is necessary. Just as enrolling in an advanced course requires prior mastery of basic elements, making a decision involves various prerequisites. In the following review, the concept of readiness to choose is addressed, along with its "prerequisites."

Theoretical Perspectives

The concept of "readiness" emerged from the basic notion that vocational choices should be seen not as single, point-in-time events, but rather as the result of previous processes and as the precursors of future processes (Jordaan, 1974; Super, 1953, 1957). Such a notion suggests a developmental view in which previous events might make one more or less ready to cope with subsequent ones.

Super (1953, 1957, 1963) proposed such a view, drawing on the concept of life stages as an organizing framework. In his model, vocational development can be conceived of as occurring in the context of five major life stages, each of which imposes certain developmental tasks that require mastery prior to movement to the next stage. The concept of "readiness" in this model implies that one has adequately negotiated previous life tasks and thus has acquired the requisite attitudes and skills necessary to take on present and future life tasks. The term "vocational maturity" was used to indicate the individual's "readiness to cope with the development tasks of one's life stage, to make socially required career decisions, and to cope appropriately with the tasks with which society confronts the developing youth and adult" (Super & Jordaan, 1973, p. 4). Given that each life stage imposes a different set of tasks, a new set of attitudes and behaviors is required at subsequent stages, and it is through the acquisition of these attitudes and behaviors that an individual becomes "ready."

This initial theoretical framework has generated an enormous number of conceptual and empirical avenues. An exhaustive review of this literature is not possible here; however, a selective summary of three general avenues is provided below.

The Construct and Measurement of Vocational Maturity

Many investigators have sought to elaborate the precise elements of readiness and to develop assessment devices to measure these elements. The majority of these efforts have focused on readiness at the exploration stage of development. The work of major contributors in this area is briefly summarized below; for a more complete review and critique of these efforts, the reader is referred to Betz (1988), Westbrook (1983), Super (1974), and Crites (1973).

The work of Super and his colleagues (Jordaan & Heyde, 1979; Super et al., 1957; Super & Overstreet, 1960) was conducted in the context of the Career Pattern Study—a 20-year longitudinal investigation of the career development of 8th- and 9th-grade males. Over the course of this study, attempts were made to specify, revise, and validate the concept of vocational maturity. A number of different elements of maturity were considered at various points in the investigation; the most recent model contains attitudinal and cognitive components derived from five basic elements: planfulness, exploration, information, decision making, and reality orientation (Super, 1983).

In response to the array of conceptual and operational definitions of vocational maturity, Crites offered both a critique of existing formulations (1961) and a new model of the structure of maturity (1965). In his hierarchical model, two primary factors—career-choice content and career-choice process—were posited. In terms of content, the realism and consistency of choices were considered central; in terms of process, various attitudes (decisiveness, involvement, independence, orientation, and compromise) and competencies (self-appraisal, occupational information, goal selection, planning, and problem solving) were required. Westbrook and his colleagues also emphasized the importance of being able to acquire and use information in occupational decision making. The work of Westbrook and Parry-Hill (1973) and Westbrook and Mastie (1974) focused on the cognitive components of vocational maturity.

Inquiry about vocational maturity has provided a broad view of what constitutes "readiness," at least as it applies to the exploration stage of development. (Although, theoretically, the concept of readiness is applicable throughout the life span, it is less well developed and elaborated for other life stages.) To be ready, or vocationally mature, at the exploration stage entails the acquisition of (a) facilitative attitudes that orient one toward being involved in planning and exploring one's own occupational future; (b) information about self, occupations, and participation in the world of work; and (c) competencies to put all available information together into a decision and implementation plan.

Causes and Consequences of Vocational Maturity

This avenue of investigation, reflecting the need for studying developmental phenomena longitudinally, is marked more by neglect than contribution. Theoretically derivable postulates about causes and consequences of developmental readiness have yet to be subjected to empirical test. For example, as implied in the summary offered above, current readiness is based, in part, on successful completion of the tasks of the previous life stage. In other words, present maturity should be preceded by past maturity, and future maturity should be predictable from present maturity.

Despite the logic of this assertion, it has received little scrutiny. However, the results of the Career Pattern study (Jordaan & Heyde, 1979; Super et al., 1957; Super & Overstreet, 1960) and the Career Development Study (Gribbons & Lohnes, 1968, 1982) have provided some (albeit equivocal) information that the subsequent display of mature coping behaviors is related to the earlier demonstration of selected elements of vocational maturity. In addition, the notion that being mature—engaging in stage-appropriate behavior—should lead to desirable vocational outcomes other than future developmental preparedness has been seriously neglected. The relevant findings were summarized by Super (1985), who reviewed a number of published and unpublished analyses of Career Pattern Study data and concluded that an individual's vocational outcomes (e.g., attained status, job and career satisfaction, occupational advancement) are indeed partially traceable to adolescent maturity.

Correlates of Maturity

Numerous studies have documented the correlates of readiness; this has been the favored avenue for investigation. Maturity has been related to such constructs as locus of control, decision-making ability and style, self-concept crystallization, cognitive complexity, and a host of other psychological variables (see Osipow, 1983). Although these investigations elaborate the characteristics of the individual who is ready to choose, vocational maturity has also been found to relate to variables with which there should be no association. In a review of the theoretical and assessment status of vocational maturity, Westbrook (1983) noted that there are alarmingly high correlations between maturity and intellectual ability, gender, and ethnic background. Whether these relationships reflect the realities of development or are artifacts of measurement remains a question for further investigation.

Practical Perspectives

The theoretical and empirical perspectives outlined above clearly suggest that readiness to choose results from the mastery of previous and current developmental tasks. The detection of and interventions for readiness problems largely follow this developmental prescription.

Assessment

As noted above, there are a variety of methods available for detecting problems in readiness. Because these have been the subject of two exhaustive critiques (Betz, 1988; Westbrook, 1983), only the most commonly used measures in the intervention literature are mentioned here.

Corresponding to Super's model of vocational maturity, the Career Development Inventory (CDI; Super, Thompson, Lindeman, Jordaan, & Myers, 1981) provides a five-scale measure of readiness. The five elements are: planning, exploration, world-of-work information, decision making, and knowledge of preferred occupation. A portion of Crites's two-factor model is assessed by the CMI (Crites, 1978). In this measure, only the process factor is considered, including a scale to assess the attitudinal dimension and five scales to assess the competency dimension.

Intervention

Readiness—either in the composite form known as vocational maturity, or in the various specific elements that comprise maturity—has been an extremely popular target for career intervention. Attempts to produce comparative gains in this area are reviewed below, grouped by the nature of the comparison (e.g., treatment vs. no treatment, alternate forms of treatment, and attribute-treatment interactions). Within each group, differences in scope, duration, and target population are noted.

Given the many components and measures of maturity, dependent variables are designated as "attitudes" or "competencies," to simplify the description of gains. That is, the attitudinal domain (regardless of how measured) will refer to those attitudes that orient the individual toward resolving various career tasks (e.g., planfulness), and the competency domain (again, regardless of how measured) will refer to various knowledge sets or skills (e.g., acquired information). Excluded from consideration are those studies aimed at self-definition (reviewed earlier), and exploratory behavior and decision making (reviewed in the next section).

Treatment versus No Treatment. In recognition of readiness as a multidimensional phenomenon, most intervention strategies are of the comprehensive variety and contain similar content. That is, regardless of the specific format or focus, most include some form of self- and world-of-work information, together with decision-making guidance. These comprehensive strategies have been largely effective for participants, relative to their untreated counterparts. A number of these efforts have been directed at adolescent participants. For example, Yates et al. (1979) found immediate and longer-term (Johnson, Johnson, & Yates, 1981) attitudinal and competency gains in 8th and 9th graders, following participation in a vocational exploration group. Pavlak and Kammer's (1985) group efforts with delinquent adolescents were not similarly successful. However, Egner and Jackson (1978) found attitudinal gains for their 11th-grade academic-track students.

Intervention programs with a more specialized focus or format have also been effective for adolescents: Laskin and Palmo (1983) documented gains in planfulness (but not in other attitudinal elements or competencies) among 11th graders, following participation in a program focused on decision making. A similar pattern of gains was seen following 10th graders' use of a computer-based educational and career exploration system (Myers, Lindeman, Thompson, & Patrick, 1975). Flake et al.'s (1975) brief individual counseling intervention was effective in producing attitudinal gains in their 10th-grade participants, as was Savickas's (1990) teach-the-test course strategy. Finally, in a particularly novel approach, Palmer and Cochran (1988) demonstrated that maturational gains in 10th- and 11th-graders could be achieved by training parents in how to facilitate their children's career planning and development.

The effectiveness of treatment relative to no treatment has also been studied within the college population. Semester-long courses, or more limited contact groups that had similar content, have produced attitudinal gains (Carver & Smart, 1985; Knickerbocker & Davidshofer, 1978; Sherry & Staley, 1984). However, not all attempts have produced gains in the competency (Ware, 1985) and attitudinal (Mencke & Cochran, 1974) domains. As with the precollege population, strategies with a specialized focus have also been effective. For example, Bartsch and Hackett (1979) evaluated the effects of a course that, in addition to the standard components, emphasized personal responsibility. They found no significant impact on locus of control, but they documented treatment effects for various career attitudes and competencies. Lent et al.'s (1986) course, designed specifically for science and engineering students, produced gains in the competency domain. Finally, Ganster and Lovell (1978) found gains in both attitudes and overall competencies, following a college course in which all self and work information was Holland-coded.

Alternate Forms of Treatment.   Given the general effectiveness of treatment when compared to no treatment, other investigators have compared the effects of different treatments. For example, Babcock and Kaufman (1976) found a comprehensive college course more effective than limited individual counseling or no treatment, in fostering readiness in both domains. Stonewater and Daniels (1983) found superior attitudinal gains (specifically, in the development of autonomy and purpose) in a comprehensive course based on Harren's (1979) model relative to a career information class. Jepsen, Dustin, and Miars (1982) demonstrated greater attitudinal gains by training in problem solving than by guided field trips.

A number of comparative studies have failed to reveal differential effects of interventions that have similar content but vary in format. For example, Glaize and Myrick (1984) found comparable attitudinal gains among 11th graders using DISCOVER and those participating in a vocational exploration group, and Davis and Horne (1986) found no differences in the attitudinal gains achieved by those enrolled in a college course versus those exposed to the same content through small group counseling. No differential attitudinal gains were found for college students based on whether their career-planning course was supplemented with a computer-assisted guidance system (Garis & Niles, 1990). Jepsen et al. (1982) found comparable attitudinal gains resulting from cognitive and behavioral methods of problem-solving training.

There is also some evidence that different content can foster equivalent gain. For example, Rodriguez and Blocher (1988) found comparable gains for Puerto Rican college women enrolled in a course designed to enhance the life skills of disadvantaged individuals and those enrolled in a traditional comprehensive career course. Further, comparing groups that focused on career information and decision making with others that targeted self-growth, Perovich and Mierzwa (1980) found no differential gains in attitudinal or competency domains. Finally, no significant differential gains in competencies relative to world-of-work information and goal selection were obtained by high school students who visited various work sites and received occupational information versus those receiving information only (Yongue, Todd, & Burton, 1981).

Attribute-Treatment Interactions.   Given the lack of consistent differences between alternate forms of treatment, a third kind of investigation has considered the possible interaction between individual and treatment characteristics. These studies provide a view of what type of treatment might be most effective for what kind of client. Among college students, Kivlighan, Hageseth, Tipton, and McGovern (1981) found that matching the format of the intervention (interactional vs. individual) to the personality type of the individual (social and enterprising types vs. realistic and investigative types) was more effective than mismatching in producing attitudinal gains, and Rubinton (1980) showed that such gains could also be achieved by matching the focus of the intervention to the corresponding decisional style of the individual. Robbins and Tucker (1986) found attitudinal gains when those high in goal instability were involved in an interactional (as opposed to self-directed) workshop. Schenk, Johnston, and Jacobsen (1979) demonstrated that maturational gains following group participation were greater for college students with undifferentiated or inconsistent interest profiles than for those with clearer interest profiles. However, Warner and Jepsen (1979) did not find differential gains when the conceptual level of high school students was matched to the level of structure in a workshop experience.

Implications

Readiness has been the subject of extensive study in both theoretical and practical efforts, and, although much work remains for the future, it appears that most interventions that have been studied are more effective than no treatment. However, it is difficult to draw more refined conclusions. For example, there is no clear evidence that the various treatments affect attitudinal and competency domains differentially; indeed, this notion has been barely subjected to study. Further, definitive decisions about treatment based solely on differences in format, method, or even content would not be well founded from the current literature. Somewhat more promising, however, is the growing evidence that differential treatment decisions can be made if the developmental or personality characteristics of the participant are taken into account.

Future investigations might well attempt to clarify the contradictory findings about content and format, perhaps yielding a more precise view of how successful treatments work. Attribute–treatment interaction investigations also continue to be warranted. In addition, the success of some of the less intensive and direct interventions (Flake et at., 1975; Palmer & Cochran, 1988) raises some interesting new questions about "how much" and "to whom" intervention should be given to effect desired gain. Finally, and despite Myers's (1971) and Oliver's (1978) advocacy for short-term outcome evaluation, one cannot help but wonder what happens in the long run for these readiness-improved clients.

From a theoretical perspective, it would be particularly useful to determine more precisely the elements of vocational maturity and to study the role of such characteristics as gender and ethnicity in the acquisition and measurement of those elements. Further, the question of long-term consequences of vocational maturity needs to be addressed. Does vocational maturity (and all of the intervention efforts that can enhance it) actually lead to desirable outcomes?

DECISION-MAKING PROCESS

In the ideal circumstance, individuals are well-prepared, in terms of self-definition and readiness, to engage in the decision-making process. Such prior preparation can be considered to provide the general substrate underlying the more specific task of decision making. Hence, where the preceding sections focused on more global phenomena, this section highlights the specific process of deciding.

Theoretical Perspectives

Given the centrality of decision making to nearly every aspect of human functioning, a number of models of the process of deciding have been proposed in an attempt to understand and improve decision making. With respect to the vocational domain of functioning, some of these models are extremely comprehensive, incorporating developmental and contextual dimensions; some provide detail about what elements or steps are necessary in arriving at a choice; and others focus narrowly on the precise mechanisms by which alternatives are (or should be) evaluated. To provide a general picture of the important aspects of the decision-making process, a sampling of each kind of model is provided here. For a comprehensive review and analysis of available models, the reader may want to consult Jepsen and Dilley (1974), Pitz and Harren (1980), and Mitchell and Krumboltz (1984).

Tiedeman (1961) was among the first to articulate a comprehensive model of the career decision-making process. He provided a view of decision making as a sequence of stages that occurs before and after a particular alternative is implemented. The preimplementation stages involve awareness and information gathering, the emergence of specific alternatives, selection of one alternative, and specifying how the choice will be implemented. Based in part on this model, Harren (1979) drew a broader picture of the decision-making process, placing it in the context of individual, developmental, and contextual factors. The sequence of decision making, according to this model, begins with awareness of an impending decision, proceeds through stages of planning (gathering and weighing information) and commitment (selecting an alternative to which a commitment can be made), and concludes with implementation. Factors thought to influence progress through this sequence include individual differences (e.g., decision-making style and self-concept), developmental progress, and the contextual factors that surround the decision (e.g., time pressures and the involvement of others).

In addition to comprehensive models of the career decision-making process, other models have been offered to elaborate the necessary elements or steps involved in arriving at a choice. Perhaps the most widely known example is Krumboltz and Hamel's (1977) DECIDES model. This model portrays a rational sequence of steps beginning with Defining the problem and Establishing an action plan; proceeding through Clarifying values, Identifying alternatives, and Discovering probable outcomes; and concluding with Eliminating alternatives systematically and Starting action.

The Krumboltz model was devised explicitly for use in career counseling efforts; other models developed outside the vocational domain also have relevance for career decision making. Janis and Mann (1977), for example, offered an extensive analysis of the elements of "vigilant information processing." According to this model, quality decision making depends on a thorough review of objectives and values relevant to the decision and of alternatives and their likely consequences. Potentially relevant or new information is used to reevaluate alternatives before a final course of action is selected, and detailed plans are made for implementing the chosen course of action. Finally, from the perspective of decisions as problems to be solved, the problem-solving model provided by D'Zurilla and Goldfried (1971) suggests a series of problem-solving steps beginning with an orientation to and definition of the problem situation, proceeding through generating and evaluating alternatives, and concluding with verifying the choice.

A variety of more focused models has been offered; these models elaborate the precise mechanisms by which alternatives are evaluated for ultimate selection. Among these, most have endorsed an "expected utility" perspective (Pitz & Harren, 1980), in which the best alternative is identified by evaluating each of the available alternatives on the basis of a combination of its desirability and probability of outcome. In contrast to the expected utility perspective, Gati (1986) suggested that an acceptable array of alternatives could be arrived at by a sequential process of evaluation and elimination. In this model, alternatives are either eliminated or retained for further consideration, depending on the extent to which they satisfy criteria identified as most important, next most important, and so on.

As is evident, the array of models that have been applied to career decision making is quite diverse. In general, however, these views portray the decision-making process as following a logical sequence that involves the identification, exploration, and evaluation of alternatives, and the selection (and implementation) of a single alternative. Given this general view of the process, empirical efforts have been directed toward identifying factors that might lead to "better" decisions. One relevant approach has focused on individual differences that are likely to affect the entire decision-making process. Decision-making styles have become recognized as an influential set of factors (see Phillips & Pazienza, 1988, for a review), and some fairly consistent relationships have been observed between the use of different styles and progress in career decision making. For example, those using a more rational, planful style were found to be more likely to approach, rather than avoid, problems (Phillips, Pazienza, & Ferrin, 1984) and to progress through the process (Harren, Kass, Tinsley, & Moreland, 1978), compared to those relying on more impulsive or dependent styles.

Another strategy for identifying factors involved in "good" decisions has emphasized the role of selected components of the decision-making process. For example, the models outlined above consider information an essential component in the decision-making process. Thus, information-seeking and exploratory activity that results in acquiring relevant information has become a factor of interest. Although this factor has been frequently studied as a target of intervention, little is known about whether engaging in exploration or acquiring information is indeed associated with "better" decision making. Of the available evidence, some is positive. Defining "better" as resulting in a choice that is congruent with one's interests, Grotevant, Cooper, and Kramer (1986) provided some support for the importance of exploration. Similarly, Krumboltz, Rude, Mitchell, Hammel, and Kinnier (1982) found that they could distinguish "good" from "poor" decision makers (thus classified by the extent to which the selected option matched the decider's values) on the basis of a persistent and focused information-seeking strategy. However, no distinction could be made on the basis of volume or kind of information sought. Further, using decisional progress as a criterion, Phillips and Strohmer (1983) failed to find evidence to support the necessity of obtaining occupational information.

A second component in the decision-making process that has received attention involves the evaluation of identified alternatives in light of the acquired information.

Because such an evaluation would seem to require the decider to retain and process a considerable volume of information, variations in cognitive processes and structures have been of interest. From the process perspective, Blustein and Strohmer (1987) found evidence of biased hypothesis-testing strategies in evaluating occupational alternatives, and Gati and Tikotzki (1989) suggested that evaluative processes are operative when decision makers engage in selective exploration. From a structural perspective, the differentiation and integration of an individual's cognitive system have been shown to play a significant role in the evaluation of occupational alternatives (see Niemeyer, 1988, for a review of this literature).

Practical Perspectives

The array of decision-making models has provided the basis for a variety of strategies to detect and resolve decision-making problems. These strategies are derived from a number of perspectives, ranging from a global view of decisional progress to a more detailed view of selected elements within the decision-making process.

Assessment

A variety of methods of assessing problems in decision making has been offered in the intervention literature. From the perspective of overall decisional progress, for example, Harren's (1985) Assessment of Career Decision Making (ACDM) provides an index of the extent to which an individual has progressed through the stages of decision making with respect to three decision-making tasks (choice of school, major, and occupation).

Other devices provide a view of possible deficits in decision-making skill or knowledge of the principles of decision making. These devices typically examine the individual's ability to select an appropriate alternative for a fictitious other—for example, the Goal Selection scale of the CMI; the Decision Making scale of the CDI; the Career Decision Making Skills Assessment Instrument (Educational Testing Service, 1977); other variants require individuals to engage in a simulated decision-making task for themselves—for example, Krumboltz et al.'s (1979) Career Decision Simulation.

Assessment of the particular components of decision making may assist in identifying specific problematic areas. In this vein, evaluation of the quantity and quality of considered alternatives (Dixon, Heppner, Petersen, & Ronning, 1979) may be useful. Similarly, exploration is easily assessed through simple checklists or estimates of the frequency or variety of information-seeking behaviors (e.g., the Vocational Exploration Behavior Checklist described by Krumboltz and Thoresen, 1964; the Career Exploration scale of the CDI), or through more formal assessment of the various components of the exploration process. In this regard, the Career Exploration Survey (Stumpf, Collarelli, & Hartman, 1983) offers a method of tapping not only what and how exploration regarding self and world of work has been undertaken, but also individual beliefs about and reactions to the exploration process. With respect to evaluation of alternatives, Jepsen and Grove (1986) devised a method to evaluate the complexity with which an individual is considering his or her choices, and a number of strategies for evaluating the structure of an individual's cognitive system are available (Niemeyer, 1988). Some caution is necessary when using these component indexes, given the lack of conclusive information about what level or kind of these components is essential for optimal decision making.

Intervention

As was the case with readiness to choose, there have been a number of successful strategies to improve decision making. The interventions reviewed below are organized according to the way in which decision-making improvement was defined.

Decisional Progress. The first group of efforts was aimed at global gains in decisional progress (roughly defined as movement through Tiedeman's (1961) stages of decision making). The majority of these interventions targeted college students and were of the comprehensive group or academic class variety. Similar to those noted in earlier sections of this chapter, these treatments provided opportunities for self-assessment, occupational exploration, and instruction and practice in decision making and planning. Greater decisional progress following such intervention has been repeatedly documented (Barker, 1981; Berman, Gelso, Greenfeig, & Hirsch, 1977; Cochran, Hetherington, & Strand, 1980; Evans & Rector, 1978; Remer et al., 1984). An intervention of more limited contact, however, has also proven effective. Cochran, Hoffman, Strand, and Warren (1977) found significant gains in college major choice progress following a 3-hour use of a computer-assisted guidance system.

Knowledge of Decision-Making Principles. Another set of studies targeted gains in general knowledge of decision-making or problem-solving principles. The assumption here is that knowing the principles—and even being able to apply them in standardized decision-making situations—increases the likelihood of making one's own decisions well. As noted earlier, interventions aimed at readiness contain evidence that knowledge of decision making (one element of maturity) has been improved following class or group participation (Egner & Jackson, 1978; Ganster & Lovell, 1978; Jepsen et al., 1982; Laskin & Palmo, 1983; Perovich & Mierzwa, 1980; Schenck et al., 1979; Yates et al., 1979).

However, other efforts specifically designed to increase knowledge have been less successful. Knowledge of the principles of rational decision making as applied to hypothetical situations was not improved by a cognitive restructuring or a decision-making intervention (Mitchell & Krumboltz, 1987), nor by 90-minute instruction in rational decision making (Krumboltz, Scherba, Hamel, & Mitchell, 1982). Interventions focused on problem-solving training (Dixon et al., 1979; Mendonca & Seiss, 1976) also failed to improve responses to selected problem situations. However, the brief instruction in rational decision making noted above did produce improvement for participants who did not previously display a rational decision-making style (Krumboltz, Kinnier, Rude, Scherba, & Hamel, 1986).

Array of Alternatives. Based on the notion that poorer decisions may result from restricted alternatives, several interventions have sought to improve the array of considered alternatives. Two such efforts from the problem-solving perspective are notable. Mendonca and Seiss (1976) found that involvement in problem-solving training (either alone or in combination with an anxiety management component) produced greater generation of alternatives than did involvement in a discussion placebo comparison group. Relatedly, Dixon et al. (1979) found that an intensive problem-solving training intervention enhanced the quality of alternatives. Further, investigations of the effects of various testing procedures have suggested that simply stimulating awareness of available occupational alternatives (as is done in the Self Directed Search (SDS; Holland, 1977), for example) increases the number that one considers (Takai & Holland, 1979;

Talbot & Birk, 1979; Zener & Schnuelle, 1976). Decreases, however, have also been found following similar procedures (Atanasoff & Slaney, 1980). Given that the subjects displaying this decrease also showed gains on other indexes, it is questionable to assume that an increased array of alternatives is always beneficial.

Exploration. Given the presumed importance of information in decision making, increasing exploratory activities has been an extremely popular focus of intervention. A wide variety of intervention strategies has been successful in this regard. Considered from the perspective of exploration as one element of vocational maturity, several of the interventions revealing gains in readiness also show improvements in exploration following group or class-participation (Laskin & Palmo, 1983; Lent et al., 1986; Mencke & Cochran, 1974; Perovich & Mierzwa, 1980; Schenck et al., 1979) or a computer-assisted exploration system (Myers et al., 1975). Other comprehensive interventions have also produced gains in information-seeking activity (Prediger & Noeth, 1979; Remer et al., 1984). In a novel approach to promoting such activity following the provision of various stimulus materials, Lazarick, Fishbein, Loiello, and Howard (1988) demonstrated that exploration could be promoted or inhibited simply by asking participants to explore or, alternately, to refrain.

Increases in exploration have also been documented following self- or counselor-administered vocational interest tests. For example, although no increased information-seeking behavior occurred following administration of the SDS or VPI to high school students (Zener & Schnuelle, 1976), college students receiving SCII results in a variety of formats (Atanasoff & Slaney, 1980; Hoffman et al., 1981) or completing a vocational card sort (Cooper, 1976) did increase their exploratory activity. Relatedly, Jones, Gorman, and Schroeder (1989) found greater exploration following use of the Career Key (a self-guided assessment device with direct links to occupational information; Jones, 1987) than following use of the SDS.

As with the interventions of readiness, a number of investigators have studied whether different intervention strategies would produce different gains in exploratory activity. For example, Mendonca and Seiss's (1976) anxiety management training, alone and in combination with problem-solving training, was more effective in increasing exploration than was problem-solving training alone. Mitchell and Krumboltz (1987) found comparable exploratory gains for those involved in a cognitive restructuring versus a decision-making intervention; however, only the restructuring group maintained its gains 1 month after treatment. Comparing cognitively and behaviorally focused problem-solving training, Jepsen et al. (1982) found both to be equally effective (and better than a control) in increasing exploration. Also equally effective were 15-hour and 30-hour career planning groups (McAuliffe & Fredrickson, 1990). Minimal differences in information seeking were found following reinforcement versus modeling plus reinforcement counseling, although either was more effective than less behaviorally oriented alternatives (Fisher, Reardon, & Burck, 1976; Krumboltz & Schroeder, 1965; Krumboltz & Thoresen, 1964). Finally, further evidence in support of considering attributes in treatment decisions was provided by Kivlighan et al. (1981) and Robbins and Tucker (1986), who found enhanced information seeking among participants whose personality type was matched with type of treatment (interactional vs. individual).

Evaluation. The final element of decision making—that of evaluating the alternatives—has received far less attention in the literature. In one study, Warner and Jepsen (1979) found, unexpectedly, that a greater degree of choice basis complexity could be achieved by those higher in conceptual level who had participated in a career counseling workshop that was more, rather than less, structured.

Implications

Given the multitude of ways that decision making has been conceptualized and the frequency and variety of interventions in this area, the available literature provides many practical implications. For gain in decisional progress or knowledge of decision-making principles, exposure to the standard contents of the more comprehensive intervention strategies (even in computerized form) is recommended. More limited and focused instruction appears less effective for most participants. In terms of various elements of the decision-making process, clients can increase the array of alternatives they consider with minimal suggestion to do so; however, a better quality of alternatives might require more intensive intervention. In addition, it appears that it is fairly easy to increase exploratory behavior. Even without the comprehensiveness of a course, the power of behavioral reinforcement, or the precision of an attribute-tailored intervention, simple exposure to materials that might stimulate curiosity, coupled with a directive to explore, may suffice. However, some cognitive change (Mitchell & Krumboltz, 1987) might be necessary to sustain exploratory gains on a longer-term basis.

Given the generally convincing findings of previous intervention studies, further treatment research efforts would be well directed toward asking more refined questions and toward filling in the understudied gaps. For example, knowledge of rational principles can be increased and elements of the decision-making process can be enhanced, but it is not clear how this knowledge or enhancement actually benefits the individual. Interventions to assist in the weighing and evaluating of real alternatives are quite scarce; attention to treatment strategies for this aspect of the process is needed.

Along more theoretical lines, decision-making models generally provide a number of discrete elements that might be targets for intervention (such as the array of alternatives, exploration, or evaluation of alternatives); however, it is not known how variations in these elements affect the decision-making process or outcome. To evaluate the adequacy of such elements as treatment targets, it would be useful to know their relationship to other aspects of choosing (such as indecision, congruence, or satisfaction). Such knowledge would allow useful answers to such questions as "Is more information always better?" or "How appropriate is it for someone nearing commitment to be encouraged to generate a wider array of alternatives?"

Finally, much remains unknown about how decisions are actually made. In particular, the processing of information and the weighing of alternatives in the course of arriving at a choice are rich and underinvestigated areas for study. Attempts to integrate the cognitive and career decision-making literatures have been promising and have provided the suggestion that good decision making may not be as complex, objective, or rational as one might like to believe. Gelatt (1989) offered an interesting challenge to the prevailing (and his own prior (1962)) view that decision making should be an entirely rational process. His argument for "positive uncertainty" may well provide the basis for the future inclusion of other, nonrational factors as acceptable elements of a prescriptive model of decision making.

CHOICE AND COMMITMENT

A number of significant elements are involved in the task of choosing prior to the point of choice. Self-definition, readiness to choose, and engaging in the decision-making process are necessary but not sufficient to complete the task. A choice must be arrived at—a single, preferably satisfying alternative must be selected. This choice may not be permanent, but it must be one to which the individual can commit sufficiently to pursue its implementation.

Theoretical Perspectives

Addressing vocational choice per se is a tradition of long standing in counseling psychology. Stemming from Parsons' (1909) assertion that a wise choice is one in which reasoning is applied to the relationship between knowledge of self and knowledge of the world of work, there is a rich history of prescriptive principles about choice. A broad view of the prevailing prescription and explanation is succinctly summarized in the assertion that "people search for environments that will let them exercise their skills and abilities, express their attitudes and values, and take on agreeable problems and roles" (Holland, 1985a, p. 4).

The notion that an individual's choice should be in agreement with his or her characteristics—variously termed "fit," "match," "correspondence," or "congruence"—is endorsed by a variety of theoretical models. Variations in the details and consequences of congruence have been addressed by a number of writers from the structural and/or interactional perspective (Spokane, 1987). However, Holland's (1985a) theory is probably the most widely known. Although his model extends beyond choice per se, he offers the persuasive argument that choice is a function of personality, and, further, that satisfactory and stable vocational outcomes are dependent on congruent choices (in which one's personality and work environment match). The advocacy for choices based on fit is also evident in developmental and process-oriented writings. Super (1953), for example, pointed to the differential suitability of individuals for occupations and argued that work and life satisfactions are dependent on the extent to which an adequate outlet is located for these individual differences.

Different theories consider different characteristics as critical in defining the congruence of a choice (e.g., interests, values, personality, abilities). However, there is little disagreement with the basic premise that the alternative selected will be most satisfying if it is congruent with individual characteristics. With some exceptions, the evidence suggests that individuals who make congruent choices do indeed experience a number of more favorable outcomes (see Spokane, 1985, for a review of this research from the perspective of Holland's model).

Given the apparent value of congruent choices, it is important to ask why some individuals do not select congruent alternatives and, further, why others have difficulty in arriving at a choice of any kind. Four perspectives on choice problems are evident in the literature. The first perspective on these questions is derived from the general endorsement of Parsons' (1909) dictum and, consequently, of the necessity to have an adequate fund of knowledge as the basis for choice. Hence, a lack of clarity and of knowledge of one's relevant characteristics would likely prohibit the selection of a congruent alternative, as would lack of information about the corresponding characteristics of various work environments. Such a perspective underscores the importance of the phases of choosing that were detailed in earlier segments of this chapter.

A second perspective arises from speculation and evidence that choice difficulties may stem from factors other than those outlined by Parsons (1909). Some identified factors are individual characteristics (e.g., self-esteem, motivation) that impose limitations on the capacity on inclination to accurately appraise self and world of work. The work of Barrett and Tinsley (1977b) on the relation of self-esteem and self-concept crystallization is of particular note here. Also relevant are contextual or group factors that reduce an individual's capacity to select a satisfying alternative. Specifically, the role of social context in development and learning has been highlighted in two recent portrayals of choice. Gottfredson (1981) argued that the development of a self-concept includes the successive incorporation of various socially relevant dimensions (such as gender and socioeconomic status) that serve to circumscribe the considered array of alternatives before the individual is capable of considering more unique characteristics (such as interests). The effect of this circumscription process is that, ultimately, "congruent" choices are made only after a number of potentially viable alternatives have been eliminated on the basis of gender and socioeconomic status. Similar limitations are notable from the social learning perspective. Hackett and Betz (1981) argued that the socialization and learning histories of women fail to provide avenues through which strong career-related self-efficacy expectations are acquired. In the absence of such expectations, alternatives that might well be congruent with individual talents or capabilities are eliminated from consideration. An excellent review of the relevant empirical literature is provided by Lent and Hackett (1987).

The third perspective on choice problems considers the developmental or dispositional status of those who are undecided. Early work on indecision attempted to distinguish between decided and undecided individuals; subsequent efforts have recognized the developmental appropriateness, for some individuals, of being undecided (Holland & Holland, 1977; Salomone, 1982). Further, given the many reasons one could have for being undecided, a number of authors have attempted to delineate the various possible components of indecision (see Slaney, 1988, for a thorough review). These efforts have been largely driven by the desire to develop an accurate and comprehensive method of assessing degree and kind of indecision. They have produced a number of measurement devices (reviewed below) and have prompted a great deal of controversy about the dimensions of indecision (e.g., within a single measure—Vondracek, Hostetler, Schulenberg, & Shimizu, 1990; across several measures—Tinsley, Bowman, & York, 1989). In a related line of study, several investigators have illuminated various kinds of indecision through association with other aspects of functioning (e.g., anxiety—Fuqua, Seaworth, & Newman, 1987; career planning and problem solving—Larson, Heppner, Ham, & Dugan, 1988).

The final perspective on problems of choice stems from the notion that the choice process extends beyond becoming "decided." Although several writers (Harren, 1979; Super, 1957) have suggested that individuals must arrive eventually at a firm sense of commitment to their choice, little other theoretical or empirical attention has been directed toward this aspect of choice. Two recent and promising exceptions have attempted to address this void. Blustein, Ellis, and Devenis (1989) offered a model of the commitment to career choice process and highlighted the possibility that individual differences in the tendency to foreclose may alter the commitment process. From a different perspective, Serling and Betz (1990) suggested that fear of commitment, defined as a dispositional "reduced ability to make important decisions due to perceptions of negative outcomes after decisions" (p. 91), may underlie the problems in choice experienced by indecisive individuals.

Practical Perspectives

As evident from the theoretical and empirical perspectives, choice and commitment processes are far from simple. A variety of factors may be implicated in an individual's ability to select an alternative. Further, even if an alternative is selected, it may be incongruent with individual characteristics and may fail to be accompanied by adequate commitment. Practical attention to detecting and solving the array of potential problems in choice and commitment is reviewed below.

Assessment

Detection of problems in choice and commitment includes strategies that are designed to (a) evaluate the nature of the choice, (b) assess problems associated with the process of becoming decided, and (c) detect problems in commitment.

Of those related to the nature of the choice, assessment of congruence, or the "fit" of individual and choice characteristics, is the most prominent. A variety of systems is available for assessing congruence from the perspective of Holland's (1985a) model. These systems entail appraisal of individual and choice (preference or actual environmental) characteristics, and calculation of an index of agreement. Spokane (1985) offered a thorough review of the available indexes and calculation methods. In addition to congruence, the nature of a choice may be evaluated for "appropriateness" on other dimensions. Indeed, prior to the past two decades, dimensions such as education, achievements, or aptitudes served as the basis for expert determination of the adequacy of "fit" between individual characteristics and the selected alternative (Oliver, 1978). As a more subjective index of "fit," an individual's satisfaction with choice is often used to detect problems in the nature of the choice.

Of those strategies designed to evaluate problems in the process of becoming decided, the simplest index is merely the assessment of the presence of a choice and the certainty with which a particular choice is held. However, given the questionable meaning of "certainty" and the potentially temporary nature of the choice, measures that offer more detailed information are preferable. One such device is the Occupational Alternatives Questionnaire (Zener & Schnuelle, 1976), which provides an indication of the extent to which a "first choice" has been selected, with or without other alternatives still being considered.

Offering a more detailed view of the potential causes of problems in deciding is the popular Career Decision Scale (Osipow, Carney, Winer, Yanico, & Koshier, 1980), which provides a global index of indecision, including items related to antecedents such as lack of structure and confidence, multiple interests, and external barriers. Also frequently used is Holland et al.'s (1980) My Vocational Situation (MVS), which contains indexes of problems in identity, needed information, and personal or environmental barriers. More recently available are the Career Decision Profile (Jones, 1989), which assesses level of decidedness, comfort with decisional status, and reasons for decisional status (including lack of self-clarity, lack of information, indecisiveness, and choice–work salience), and the Career Factors Inventory (Chartrand, Robbins, Morrill, & Boggs, 1990), which measures need for career information, need for self-knowledge, career choice anxiety, and generalized indecisiveness.

Detection of problems in commitment has been made possible recently by the introduction of two new instruments. Serling and Betz (1990) developed the Fear of Commitment Scale, which focuses on a variety of anticipated negative consequences of deciding. Blustein et al. (1989) provided the Commitment to Career Choices Scale, which evaluates both progress in the commitment process and the individual's tendency to foreclose.

Intervention

There are two major targets for intervention with respect to choice and commitment. The first of these stems from the prescription to choose an alternative that is congruent or at least satisfying to the chooser. The second focuses on certainty and indecision.

Congruence and Satisfaction.   Given the ingredients of a congruent choice, a logical intervention strategy would be to provide individuals with the opportunity to appraise and categorize their own characteristics and then provide them with information about various alternatives, similarly coded. Such an "appraisal-and-information" strategy is evident in the studies of the effects of various forms of test administration and interpretation, particularly using the Self-Directed Search (SDS; Holland, 1977). Zener and Schnuelle (1976) demonstrated the general effectiveness of this strategy in their study of gains following administration of the SDS, the Vocational Preference Inventory (VPI; Holland, 1985b), or no treatment. Both SDS and VPI takers were more satisfied with their current choices than were those receiving no treatment, and SDS takers showed more congruent choices following treatment than did VPI takers.

Given the success of the SDS, other investigators pursued variations in how or to whom the SDS is presented, and found essentially no differential satisfaction gains based on order of presentation or provision of instructions or supplementary material (Holland, Takai, Gottfredson, & Hanau, 1978), and no differential congruence gains based on test-taker characteristics such as consistency, differentiation, ability, achievement, or gender (Schaeffer, 1976). Fretz and Leong (1982) suggested that the effectiveness of the SDS might be predicated on the individual's career development status. Although they found little support for this notion for males, congruence and satisfaction with choice following administration of the SDS for females were predictable from such variables as identity and level of indecision.

The appraisal-and-information strategy is also evident in studies of gains following administration of other assessment devices, with similarly limited findings of differential impact. For example, no differential gains in congruence were found based on the amount of counselor contact in receiving SCII results (Hoffman et al., 1981). Slaney and Lewis (1986) found no differential gains in congruence or satisfaction for undecided reentry women following completion of the SCII versus a vocational card sort. Further, undecided reentry women were less satisfied with their career plans and less congruent than were decided women, regardless of variations in the vocational card sort treatment (Slaney & Dickson, 1985).

Other interventions that offer more comprehensive coverage of appraisal and information have also been shown to produce gains in congruence and satisfaction. With respect to congruence, Prediger and Noeth (1979) documented gains among their 9th-grade female participants following a brief group treatment that entailed interest assessment and interpretation, information about occupational groups and career planning, and information about resources for exploration. Mencke and Cochran (1974) found that college students in a treatment that included taking the SDS, studying case materials, and participating in a structured workshop were more congruent than controls after treatment. A less extensive attempt to produce congruence was unsuccessful, however. Malett, Spokane, and Vance (1978) found no differences in congruence between undergraduate controls and those who had taken the SDS and had received instruction and encouragement about exploring occupations. With respect to satisfaction with choice, Snodgrass and Healy (1979) found significant gains using an individual counseling treatment, and McAuliffe and Fredrickson (1990) reported greater satisfaction following a 30-hour versus a 15-hour career planning group.

Certainty and Indecision.   The second major target for intervention has been certainty and indecision. In addition to the interventions involving self-definition (reviewed earlier), the effectiveness of several brief as well as more comprehensive treatment strategies has been investigated with regard to increasing certainty and decreasing indecision. Among the briefer strategies (primarily involving test administration and interpretation), limited evidence of success is available. McGowan (1977) found that a treatment entailing administration of the SDS and provision of occupational information was effective in reducing the number of high school students who remained undecided. No differential gains in decidedness were found for reentry women in Slaney and Lewis's (1986) comparison study of the effects of the SCII and a vocational card sort.

More promising results have been observed with more comprehensive treatments. Using a college class as a general intervention strategy, Rubinton (1980) found gains in certainty among all treated participants, regardless of the match between individual decision-making style and format of intervention. Similarly, Carver and Smart (1985), Lent et al. (1986), and Savickas (1990) documented that their class-based interventions were effective in reducing indecision. Career-planning assignments embedded in a business course reduced indecision for upper-level college students (Quinn & Lewis, 1989). Davis and Horne (1986) found that class and small-group participation were equally effective in reducing indecision for college students. A brief career workshop based on social influence theory reduced indecision regardless of participant motivation (Dorn, 1989). Use of the DISCOVER computer system provided gains in decidedness among undergraduates (Fukuyama, Probert, Niemeyer, Nevill, & Metzler, 1988) and high school students (Glaize & Myrick, 1984) relative to no treatment. Gains attributable to DISCOVER were also equivalent to those demonstrated by participants in a vocational exploration group (Glaize & Myrick, 1984). However, gains due to use of a computer-assisted guidance system alone may not be comparable to those achieved when the computer supplements a career-planning course (Garis & Niles, 1990).

In terms of individual counseling efforts, Snodgrass and Healy's (1979) procedures produced no gains in certainty relative to pretreatment. Comparing individual and group methods, Cooper (1986) found no evidence of differential effectiveness. Barak and Friedkes (1981) demonstrated that the effectiveness of intervention was mediated by the type of indecision problem. Their findings suggested that, regardless of individual versus group format or method of test interpretation, greater gains in confidence were made by those undergraduates who were anxious and needed information about themselves in relation to the world of work than by those who experienced external barriers or who suffered from personal conflict.

Implications

Questions of choice and commitment have received considerable attention in the counseling psychology literature. For the practitioner, this attention has yielded results with varying degrees of clarity. Most convincing is the evidence about promoting congruence. Spokane et al.'s findings to the contrary, the selection of a satisfying and congruent alternative would appear to be easily encouraged by any of a number of variations on the "appraisal-and-information" strategy. However, some caution in this prescription is warranted for female clients. Considerably less convincing is the evidence regarding indecision, which appears to require a more comprehensive intervention. However, there is no clear evidence that the format of the treatment effort matters, and merely a preliminary hint that treatment effectiveness might depend on the reasons for an undecided status. Finally, very little is known about how commitment to choice can be fostered.

Future practical and theoretical efforts should address the deficit in knowledge about what to do for career indecision problems. First, much of the literature on indecision to date has approached the topic as if it were merely a measurement problem. The attempts of Larson et al. (1988), Savickas and Jarjoura (1991), and Lucas and Epperson

(1990) to identify functional differences within the undecided population are commendable exceptions. More conceptual and theoretical efforts in this direction would be beneficial. Second, it would be extremely useful if, based on such efforts, some uniform and measurable diagnostic scheme emerged from the literature. In its most desirable form, such a scheme would detail the various kinds and causes of indecision in theoretically meaningful and operationally definable ways. Finally, the often voiced plea to refrain from client uniformity myths should be addressed. Barak and Freidkes (1981) have made a promising start; future efforts should continue in this direction.

Beyond needed research on indecision, there have been promising recent efforts in developing models and measures of commitment. It is to be hoped that these will be pursued. Finally, given that the phase of choice and commitment can be considered to represent a culmination of all prior phases, investigation of how the prior tasks of self-definition, readiness, and decision making are reflected in choice and commitment would also be welcome additions to the literature.

IMPLEMENTATION

Implementation is the point at which individual preferences and workplace realities meet. With the implementation of the selected alternative, the tasks of choosing are complete and the tasks of adjustment to the consequences of choice begin. Thus, implementation represents a critical phase in the evolution of vocational choice.

Theoretical Perspectives

Despite the critical and recurrent role of implementation in an individual's development, both theory and research on this topic have been limited, at least from the counseling psychology perspective. Major theorists in career development clearly recognize that implementation must occur, but largely emphasize intraindividual choice development rather than the concrete and practical realities of implementing that choice. Thus, little theoretical attention has been directed at the actual activities and events associated with translating a selected alternative into a workplace reality, or toward the potential impact of prior phases of choosing on this final phase. Although job search and employment interviewing are the subjects of vigorous investigation by scholars in such fields as labor economics and personnel psychology, this work offers limited guidance to the task of career counseling. There are, however, a few broad, counseling-relevant perspectives on implementation that can be identified.

The first such perspective reflects the prevailing view that, when confronted with the task of finding a suitable way to implement one's preference, it is best to proceed in a systematic and methodical manner, being as resourceful and as logically evaluative as possible. Such a view parallels recommendations noted earlier about decision making and problem solving, and is reflected in popular approaches to implementation behavior (Bolles, 1990). Whether the realities of implementation are adequately described by this view was the subject of an investigation by Rynes and Lawler (1983). In studying how individuals function in a job search situation, they found little support for an objective model of search motivation. Rather, their findings suggested that individual differences in circumstance and personality might be a better avenue for study.

The second perspective emerges from several subsequent investigations on individual differences in implementation, which have supported Rynes and Lawler's suggestion. For example, differences in the nature of an individual's job search have been traced to such factors as self-esteem (Ellis & Taylor, 1983), locus of control (Friedrich,

1987), and behavioral intention (Vinokur & Caplan, 1987). Interview experiences and actual employment offers would appear to be partly dependent on such factors as confidence, self-efficacy expectations, and coping strategies (Kanfer & Hulin, 1985; Stumpf, Brief & Hartman, 1987).

Two studies of individual differences are particularly noteworthy in that they attempt to establish a direct link between individual career development variables and implementation events. Taylor (1985) suggested that self- and occupational knowledge might play a critical role in the school-to-work transition. She found that the receipt of job offers upon graduation was predicted by levels of self- and occupational knowledge. The level of knowledge, in turn, was predicted by the individual's exploratory behavior. The benefits of career exploration activity were also evident in the investigation of interview readiness and performance conducted by Stumpf, Austin, and Hartman (1984). Results from this study suggested that, although prior exploration did not predict interview outcome, it was predictive of both subjective interview readiness and objective ratings of interview performance.

A third perspective is evident in those investigations that have tested the utility of practical advice about how to conduct a job search and behave in a job interview. Allen and Keaveny (1980) studied the benefits of using formal (e.g., ads) versus informal (e.g., personal contacts) sources of information about job opportunities. Despite recommendations in the popular press and previous empirical studies on informal sources (Granovetter, 1974; Irish, 1987), these investigators found that more favorable employment outcomes were obtained by those who used formal job sources. Focusing on popular recommendations about interview behavior, Cianni-Surridge and Horan (1983) questioned the wisdom of assertiveness. They found that some frequently advocated behaviors might well be adaptive, but others might be quite dysfunctional.

Practical Perspectives

Although theoretical understanding of the problems of implementation has been limited, considerably greater attention has been directed at practical issues.

Assessment

The assessment of problems in implementation has received relatively little attention, although this has not impeded study of implementation interventions. Given the practical nature of this phase of the choice process, most assessment approaches focus on behavioral indicators (such as obtaining a job) or ratings of job-seeking or interviewing skills. Recent exceptions were provided by Heimberg, Keller, and Peca-Baker (1986), who drew on a social–evaluative anxiety perspective to develop a measure of positive and negative self-statements likely to occur during a job interview, and by Jones and Pinkney (1989), who devised a measure of sources of interview anxiety.

Interventions

Interventions designed to prevent or solve implementation problems have emerged from views of (a) job finding as requiring a set of instrumental search behaviors, and (b) the interview as an interaction requiring a particular set of social, self-presentational skills.

Search. Efforts to improve an individual's search for and pursuit of job opportunities have ranged from simple didactic presentation of necessary job search skills to more intensive and comprehensive procedures. Of the purely didactic methods, it appears that self-directed learning is a reasonably effective approach. A self-instruction package of written and audiotaped components was found effective in improving individuals' understanding of the steps in obtaining a job and their confidence in job search skills (Jacobson, 1984). A similar self-instruction method was found to be a necessary supplement to basic lecture and discussion (Arthur & Ebbers, 1981). In addition to exclusively didactic presentations of job search skills, several intervention efforts have offered practice components. For example, Matthews, Damron, and Yuen (1985) combined lecture and discussion of job-seeking skills with opportunities for practice and feedback in the context of a semester-long college seminar, and found significant improvement in a variety of job search skills.

By far the most popular, and perhaps most potent, intervention in job search has been variations on the intensive and comprehensive "Job Club" method (Azrin, Flores, & Kaplan, 1975). Based on the notion that job finding requires an array of complex skills that are best learned in a structured and intensive format, this method includes skill acquisition, rehearsal, and maintenance, and attends to both motivational and environmental obstacles. The intervention is conducted on a daily basis until a job is obtained, and participants receive detailed assistance in generating and pursuing job leads. Evidence of the effectiveness of the "Job Club" method, based on such indicators as obtaining employment, latency of job finding, and the salary and level of the obtained job, has been impressive (Azrin et al., 1975; Azrin, Philip, Thienes-Hontos, & Besalel, 1980, 1981).

The intensity and comprehensiveness of the "Job Club" method has stimulated inquiry about the effectiveness of its separate components. Chandler (1984) found similarly positive outcomes from participation in an abbreviated (e.g., twice a week) version of the "Job Club." Focusing on the supportive versus directive elements of the method, Keller, Glauber, and Snyder (1983) demonstrated that a nondirective, supportive intervention was about as effective as no treatment, and that self-set goals for gain were more likely to be achieved when the counselor actively focused on behavioral skill acquisition or alteration of dysfunctional cognitions. Azrin, Besalel, Wisotzek, McMorrow, and Bechtel (1982) studied the didactic versus rehearsal components of the method. Although, as noted above, didactic presentation of job search skills appears to be an effective method of intervention, Azrin et al. (1982) demonstrated that instruction alone is less effective than when combined with behavioral practice.

Self-Presentation.   Efforts to improve self-presentation have emphasized enhancing the individual's ability to interact in the context of a job interview. A variety of behavioral methods has been found successful in improving interview behaviors and in increasing the likelihood of job offers.

Much of this work has involved skills training approaches for individuals likely to be "at risk" in an interview situation, such as unemployed adults (Matthews, 1984), disadvantaged individuals (Barbee & Keil, 1973), retarded adolescents (Kelly, Wildman, & Berler, 1980), and individuals who have a psychiatric or rehabilitative history (Furman, Geller, Simon, & Kelly, 1979; Kelly, Laughlin, Claiborne, & Patterson, 1979; Stevens & Tornarzky, 1976; Stone & Geppert, 1979). The majority of these efforts focus on either entry or reentry into the labor market, although some seek to facilitate advancement from a current position (e.g., Campion & Campion, 1987).

The relative benefits of different components or methods of interview skills training have received attention in a number of studies. For example, Austin and Grant (1981) identified first-generation college students as an "at risk" population, and examined the relative effects of five different instructional strategies. One group received only a basic treatment of didactic instruction and role play; the remaining groups also participated in various supplementary modeling and rehearsal components. Compared to no treatment, all treated groups showed improvements in assertiveness and overall interview performance; differences among the treated groups were minimal.

Although Austin and Grant's findings suggested that more comprehensive treatment may be unnecessary, Speas (1979) found that a comprehensive training package was essential for another "at risk" group. Speas compared several methods of interview training for a sample of prerelease prisoners. On ratings of various behaviors during a simulated interview, only those methods that included at least modeling and role play opportunities emerged as consistently more effective than no treatment. Further, on ratings of behavior during actual interviews and probability of hiring following the interviews, only the most comprehensive method (including modeling, role play, and videotaped feedback) emerged as more effective than no treatment.

Hollandsworth, Dressel, and Stevens (1977) compared behavioral methods of improving interviewing skills with traditional lecture/discussion methods among college seniors. Using simulated videotaped interviews before and after treatment, they found the behavioral group better on some indexes and the lecture group better on others. On the basis of their results, they recommended a combined approach to interview training, and offered evidence of the social validity to counselors and clients of such an approach (Hollandsworth & Sandifer, 1979).

Much of the interview training effort in the literature has sought to demonstrate the effectiveness of various "standard" behavioral methods. There has also been some effort to test the efficacy of methods based on a refined learning model. For example, Harrison et al. (1983) noted that most attempts to enhance social skills have involved attention only to strengthening behaviors that have already been acquired and stored, and suggested that enhancing acquisition and storage per se would yield greater skill acquisition. To test this notion, they offered either a standard modeling and role play intervention focusing on interview skills alone; or the standard treatment with (a) a cognitive map of the modeled behavior (to enhance acquisition), (b) a symbolic encoding mechanism (to enhance storage recall), or (c) both the map and the encoding mechanism. Following treatment, those who had received one of the enhanced treatments showed significantly greater interview proficiency.

A few interview skill interventions have been based on other, nonbehavioral orientations. For example, suggesting that the central task in the job interview is one of persuasion, Wild and Kerr (1984) used a social influence model to increase the persuasion skills of high school students. Another approach to the interview situation was suggested by Riggio and Throckmorton (1987), who compared didactic interview training emphasizing common interview errors (e.g., giving vague responses) with a no-treatment control. In a posttreatment mock interview, however, the treated participants made as many errors as did their untreated counterparts.

The vast majority of intervention efforts have selected the interview situation as the critical point of self-preservation; however, there has also been some study of self-presentational skills prior to the point of interview. For example, focusing on the presentation of self in written form, Knouse, Tauber, and Skonieczka (1979) found that instruction in skill identification enhanced ability to list detailed job skills. Attempts to improve self-presentation in written application materials (Matthews & Fawcett, 1984) and in telephone contacts (Harris, Prue, Brubaker & Rychtarik, 1986) have also been successful.

Implications

The theoretical contributions to problems of implementation provide limited suggestions for the practitioner. However, implications from treatment studies are quite straightforward and can be regarded with some degree of confidence. In particular, the "Job Club" method, even in abbreviated form, has been found effective in facilitating job search, and comprehensive behavioral treatments have also been effective in improving self-presentational skills. Because this area of inquiry has been largely neglected in the counseling psychology literature, further study of implementation phenomena is clearly desirable. In particular, the relationship of the earlier reviewed aspects of choosing (and of treatments to facilitate them) to problems of implementation should be explored. The importance of such exploration is evident in the common observation that those who search for and obtain jobs include the unclear, the unready, the undecided, and the uncommitted.

CONCLUSION

This chapter has reviewed the literature concerning five components of the process of choosing, with an emphasis on theoretical understanding of each component and on strategies for detecting and solving problems. On a general level, it may be concluded that our theoretical and empirical base has contributed well to the treatment of problems in choosing. At a more specific level, however, there are some rather serious gaps identifiable from the present review, including several areas about which we know little (e.g., self-definition and commitment), and others for which our repertoire of successful treatments needs refinement (e.g., indecision). In addition, our knowledge is limited about the process of career counseling and about what counselors and clients actually do when not under study, although some promising efforts have recently appeared (Nevo, 1990; Spokane & Hawks, 1990; Watkins, Savickas, Brizzi, & Manus, 1990).

Although there is an impressive body of literature available to assist those involved in career counseling efforts, intervention studies represent only a small portion of this literature. Further, such interventions are rarely directed toward an assessed client need, and most have emphasized the general effects of various intervention strategies. Such a global approach does not inform treatment decisions about which ingredients are the critical agents of change for which individuals. As in Rounds and Tinsley's (1984) review and recommendations, this continues to be *the* crucial area for future career intervention research.

The relative absence of specifically tailored interventions highlights another direction for future contributions. This void seems due, in part, to the lack of a readily usable diagnostic system and the consequent failure of investigators to evaluate client need adequately. Attention to the call of several previous reviewers (Holland et al., 1981; Myers, 1986; Oliver & Spokane, 1988; Rounds & Tinsley, 1984) to generate and use such a system is of critical necessity in future investigations. The absence of specificity in treatment research may be seen to imply that it is more important to evaluate what we prefer to do than it is to do what clients need.

In closing, it is useful to reconsider some of the recommendations of earlier reviewers. First, in spite of an increased number of attribute-interaction studies since the time of Fretz's (1981) call, progress in this regard is slow. Another call for such study appeared in the first edition of this *Handbook* (Rounds & Tinsley, 1984) and warrants repetition here. Second, the numerous recommendations about the use of multiple and reliable outcome measures have received only a moderate amount of attention. The current review would suggest that conceptual precision and meaning should also receive priority in the selection of evaluative criteria. Finally, the bulk of the literature—of either the theoretical or the practical variety—attends primarily to problems and solutions associated with readiness, decision making, and choice. Although problems of self-definition have been the subject of renewed interest, problems of implementation appear to have been largely abandoned by counseling psychologists. It is hoped that greater balance among these problem areas will emerge in future work.

REFERENCES

Allen, R. E., & Keaveny, T. J. (1980). The relative effectiveness of alternative job sources. *Journal of Vocational Behavior, 16,* 18–32.

Arnold, J., & Masterson, A. (1987). Self-concept certainty, career exploration and readiness for career decision-making amongst undergraduate students. *British Journal of Guidance and Counselling, 15,* 92–96.

Arthur, J. V., & Ebbers, L. H. (1981). Using learning packages to develop job-search readiness. *Journal of College Student Personnel, 22,* 125–129.

Atanasoff, G. E., & Slaney, R. B. (1980). Three approaches to counselor-free career exploration among college women. *Journal of Counseling Psychology, 27,* 332–339.

Austin, M. F., & Grant, T. N. (1981). Interview training for college students disadvantaged in the labor market: Comparison of five instructional techniques. *Journal of Counseling Psychology, 28,* 72–75.

Azrin, N. H., Besalel, V. A., Wisotzek, I., McMorrow, M., & Bechtel, R. (1982). Behavioral supervision versus informational counseling of job seeking in the Job Club. *Rehabilitation Counseling Bulletin, 25,* 212–218.

Azrin, N. H., Flores, T., & Kaplan, S. J. (1975). Job-Finding Club: A group-assisted program for obtaining employment. *Behaviour Research and Therapy, 13,* 17–27.

Azrin, N. H., Philip, R. A., Thienes-Hontos, P., & Besalel, V. A. (1980). Comparative evaluation of the Job Club program with welfare recipients. *Journal of Vocational Behavior, 16,* 133–145.

Azrin, N. H., Philip, R. A., Thienes-Hontos, P., & Besalel, V. A. (1981). Follow-up on welfare benefits received by Job Club clients. *Journal of Vocational Behavior, 18,* 253–254.

Babcock, R. J., & Kaufman, M. A. (1976). Effectiveness of a career course. *Vocational Guidance Quarterly, 24,* 261–266.

Barak, A., & Friedkes, R. (1981). The mediating effects of career indecision subtypes on career-counseling effectiveness. *Journal of Vocational Behavior, 20,* 120–128.

Barbee, J. R., & Keil, E. C. (1973). Experimental techniques of job interview training for the disadvantaged. *Journal of Applied Psychology, 58,* 209–213.

Barker, S. B. (1981). An evaluation of the effectiveness of a college career guidance course. *Journal of College Student Personnel, 22,* 354–358.

Barrett, T. C., & Tinsley, H. E. A. (1977a). Measuring vocational self-concept crystallization. *Journal of Vocational Behavior, 11,* 305–313.

Barrett, T. C., & Tinsley, H. E. A. (1977b). Vocational self-concept crystallization and vocational indecision. *Journal of Counseling Psychology, 24,* 301–307.

Bartsch, K., & Hackett, G. (1979). Effect of a decision-making course on locus of control, conceptualization, and career planning. *Journal of College Student Personnel, 20,* 230–235.

Berman, M. R., Gelso, C. J., Greenfeig, B. R., & Hirsch, R. (1977). The efficacy of supportive learning environments for returning women: An empirical evaluation. *Journal of Counseling Psychology, 24,* 324–331.

Betz, N. E. (1988). The assessment of career development and maturity. In W. B. Walsh & S. H. Osipow (Eds.), *Career decision making* (pp. 77–136). Hillsdale, NJ: Erlbaum.

Blustein, D. L., Devenis, L. E., & Kidney, B. (1989). Relationship between the identity formation process and career development. *Journal of Counseling Psychology, 36,* 196–202.

Blustein, D. L., Ellis, M. V., & Devenis, L. E. (1989). The development and validation of a two-dimensional model of the commitment to career choices process [Monograph]. *Journal of Vocational Behavior, 35,* 342–378.

Blustein, D. L., & Strohmer, D. C. (1987). Vocational hypothesis testing in career decision making. *Journal of Vocational Behavior, 31,* 45–62.

Bolles, R. N. (1990). *The 1990 what color is your parachute.* Berkeley, CA: Ten Speed Press.

Campbell, D. P. (1974). *SVIB–SCII manual.* Stanford, CA: Stanford University Press.

Campbell, N. K., & Hackett, G. (1986). The effects of mathematics task performance on math self-efficacy and task interest. *Journal of Vocational Behavior, 28,* 149–162.

Campion, M. A., & Campion, J. E. (1987). Evaluation of an interviewee skills training program in a natural field experiment. *Personnel Psychology, 40,* 675–691.

Carver, D. S., & Smart, D. W. (1985). The effects of a career and self-exploration course for undecided freshmen. *Journal of College Student Personnel, 26,* 37–43.

Chandler, A. L. (1984). Using an abbreviated Job Club program in a job service setting. *Journal of Employment Counseling, 21,* 98–102.

Chartrand, J. M., Robbins, S. B., Morrill, W. H., & Boggs, K. (1990). Development and validation of the Career Factors Inventory. *Journal of Counseling Psychology, 37,* 491–501.

Cianni-Surridge, M., & Horan, J. J. (1983). On the wisdom of assertive job-seeking behavior. *Journal of Counseling Psychology, 30,* 209–214.

Cochran, D. J., Hetherington, C., & Strand, K. H. (1980). Career choice class: Caviar or caveat. *Journal of College Student Personnel, 21,* 402–406.

Cochran, D. J., Hoffman, S. D., Strand, K. H., & Warren, P. M. (1977). Effects of client/computer interaction on career decision-making processes. *Journal of Counseling Psychology, 24,* 308–312.

Cooper, J. F. (1976). Comparative impact of the SCII and the Vocational Card Sort on career salience and career exploration of women. *Journal of Counseling Psychology, 23,* 348–352.

Cooper, S. E. (1986). The effects of group and individual vocational counseling on career indecision and personal indecisiveness. *Journal of College Student Personnel, 27,* 39–42.

Crites, J. O. (1961). A model for the measurement of vocational maturity. *Journal of Counseling Psychology, 8,* 255–259.

Crites, J. O. (1965). Measurement of vocational maturity in adolescence: I. Attitude Test of the Vocational Development Inventory. *Psychological Monographs, 79*(2; No. 595).

Crites, J. O. (1973). *Theory and research handbook for the Career Maturity Inventory.* Monterey, CA: CTB/McGraw-Hill.

Crites, J. O. (1978). *The Career Maturity Inventory.* Monterey, CA: CTB/McGraw-Hill.

Davis, R., & Horne, A. (1986). The effect of small-group counseling and a career course on career decidedness and maturity. *Vocational Guidance Quarterly, 34,* 255–262.

Dixon, D. N., Heppner, P. P., Petersen, C. H., & Ronning, R. R. (1979). Problem solving workshop training. *Journal of Counseling Psychology, 26,* 133–139.

Dorn, F. J. (1989). An examination of client motivation and career certainty. *Journal of College Student Development, 30,* 237–241.

D'Zurilla, T. J., & Goldfried, M. R. (1971). Problem solving and behavior modification. *Journal of Abnormal Psychology, 78,* 107–126.

Educational Testing Service (1977). *Career skills assessment program.* Princeton, NJ: Author.

Egner, J. R., & Jackson, D. J. (1978). Effectiveness of a counseling intervention program for teaching career decision making skills. *Journal of Counseling Psychology, 25,* 45–52.

Ellis, R. A., & Taylor, M. S. (1983). Role of self-esteem within the job search process. *Journal of Applied Psychology, 68,* 632–640.

Evans, J. R., & Rector, A. P. (1978). Evaluation of a college course in career decision making. *Journal of College Student Personnel, 19,* 163–168.

Fisher, T. J., Reardon, R. C., & Burck, H. D. (1976). Increasing information-seeking behavior with a model-reinforced videotape. *Journal of Counseling Psychology, 23,* 234–238.

Flake, M. H., Roach, A. J., & Stenning, W. F. (1975). Effects of short-term counseling on career maturity of tenth-grade students. *Journal of Vocational Behavior, 6,* 73–80.

Fretz, B. R. (1981). Evaluating the effectiveness of career interventions [Monograph]. *Journal of Counseling Psychology, 28,* 77–90.

Fretz, B. R., & Leong, F. T. L. (1982). Career development status as a predictor of career intervention outcomes. *Journal of Counseling Psychology, 29,* 388–393.

Friedrich, J. R. (1987). Perceived control and decision making in a job hunting context. *Basic and Applied Social Psychology, 8,* 163–176.

Fukuyama, M. A., Probert, B. S., Neimeyer, G. J., Nevill, D. D., & Metzler, A. E. (1988). Effects of DISCOVER on career self-efficacy and decision making of undergraduates. *Career Development Quarterly, 37,* 56–62.

Fuqua, D. R., Seaworth, T. B., & Newman, J. L. (1987). The relationship of career indecision and anxiety: A multivariate examination. *Journal of Vocational Behavior, 30,* 175–186.

Furman, W., Geller, M., Simon, S. J., & Kelley, J. A. (1979). The use of a behavioral rehearsal procedure for teaching job-interviewing skills to psychiatric patients. *Behavior Therapy, 10,* 157–167.

Ganster, D. C., & Lovell, J. E. (1978). An evaluation of a career development seminar using Crites' CMI. *Journal of Vocational Behavior, 13,* 172–180.

Garis, J. W., & Niles, S. G. (1990). The separate and combined effects of SIGI or DISCOVER and a career planning course on undecided university students. *Career Development Quarterly, 38,* 261–274.

Gati, I. (1986). Making career decisions—a sequential elimination approach. *Journal of Counseling Psychology, 33,* 408–417.

Gati, I., & Tikotzki, Y. (1989). Strategies for collection and processing of occupational information in making career decisions. *Journal of Counseling Psychology, 36,* 430–439.

Gelatt, H. B. (1962). Decision making. A conceptual frame of reference for counseling. *Journal of Counseling Psychology, 9,* 240–245.

Gelatt, H. B. (1989). Positive uncertainty: A new decision-making framework for counseling. *Journal of Counseling Psychology, 36,* 252–256.

Glaize, D. L., & Myrick, R. D. (1984). Interpersonal groups or computers? A study of career maturity and career decidedness. *Vocational Guidance Quarterly, 32,* 168–172.

Gottfredson, L. S. (1981). Circumscription and compromise: A developmental theory of occupational aspirations. *Journal of Counseling Psychology, 28,* 545–579.

Granovetter, M. S. (1974). *Getting a job: A study of contacts and careers.* Cambridge, MA: Harvard University Press.

Gribbons, W. D., & Lohnes, P. (1968). *Emerging careers.* New York: Teachers College Press.

Gribbons, W. D., & Lohnes, P. (1982). *Careers in theory and experience.* Albany, NY: State University of New York Press.

Grotevant, H. D. (1986). Assessment of identity development: Current issues and future directions. *Journal of Adolescent Research, 1,* 175–182.

Grotevant, H. D., Cooper, C. R., & Kramer, K. (1986). Exploration as a predictor of congruence in adolescents' career choices. *Journal of Vocational Behavior, 29,* 201–215.

Hackett, G., & Betz, N. E. (1981). A self-efficacy approach to the career development of women. *Journal of Vocational Behavior, 18,* 326–339.

Hackett, G., & Betz, N. E. (1984, April). *Gender differences in the effects of relevant and irrelevant task failure on mathematics self-efficacy expectations.* Paper presented at the annual meeting of the American Educational Research Association, New Orleans, LA.

Hackett, G., & Campbell, N. (1987). Task self-efficacy and task interest as a function of performance on a gender neutral task. *Journal of Vocational Behavior, 30,* 203–215.

Harren, V. A. (1979). A model of career decision making for college students. *Journal of Vocational Behavior, 14,* 119–133.

Harren, V. A. (1985). *Assessment of Career Decision Making.* Los Angeles: Western Psychological Services.

Harren, V. A., Kass, R. A., Tinsley, H. E. A., & Moreland, J. R. (1978). Influence of sex role attitudes and cognitive styles on career decision making. *Journal of Counseling Psychology, 25,* 390–398.

Harris, J. K., Prue, D. M., Brubaker, R. G., & Rychtarik, R. G. (1986). Training alcoholics in telephone skills for contacting potential employers. *Journal of Employment Counseling, 23,* 146–155.

Harrison, R. P., Horan, J. J., Torretti, W., Gamble, K., Terzella, J., & Weir, E. (1983). Separate and combined effects of a cognitive map and a symbolic code in the learning of a modeled social skill (job interviewing). *Journal of Counseling Psychology, 30,* 499–505.

Heimberg, R. G., Keller, K. E., & Peca-Baker, T. (1986). Cognitive assessment of social-evaluative anxiety in the job interview: Job Interview Self-Statement Schedule. *Journal of Counseling Psychology, 33,* 190–195.

Hoffman, M. A., Spokane, A. R., & Magoon, T. M. (1981). Effects of feedback mode on counseling outcomes using the Strong–Campbell Interest Inventory: Does the counselor really matter? *Journal of Counseling Psychology, 28,* 119–125.

Holland, J. L. (1977). *The Self-Directed Search: A guide to educational and vocational planning.* Palo Alto, CA: Consulting Psychologists Press.

Holland, J. L. (1985a). *Making vocational choices* (2nd ed.). Englewood Cliffs, NJ: Prentice-Hall.

Holland, J. L. (1985b). *Vocational Preference Inventory.* Odessa, FL: Psychological Assessment Resources.

Holland, J. L., Birk, J. M., Cooper, J. F., Dewey, C. R., Dolliver, R. H., Takai, R., & Tyler, L. E. (1982). *The Vocational Exploration and Insight Kit.* Palo Alto, CA: Consulting Psychologists Press.

Holland, J. L., Daiger, D. C., & Power, P. G. (1980). *My Vocational Situation.* Palo Alto, CA: Consulting Psychologists Press.

Holland, J. L., & Holland, J. E. (1977). Vocational indecision: More evidence and speculation. *Journal of Counseling Psychology, 24,* 404–414.

Holland, J. L., Magoon, T. M., & Spokane, A. R. (1981). Counseling psychology: Career interventions, research and theory. *Annual Review of Psychology, 32,* 279–305.

Holland, J. L., Takai, R., Gottfredson, G. D., & Hanau, C. (1978). A multivariate analysis of the effects of the Self-Directed Search on high school girls. *Journal of Counseling Psychology, 25,* 384–389.

Hollandsworth, J. G., Dressel, M. E., & Stevens, J. (1977). Use of behavioral versus traditional procedures for increasing job interview skills. *Journal of Counseling Psychology, 24,* 503–510.

Hollandsworth, J. G., & Sandifer, B. A. (1979). Behavioral training for increasing effective job-interview skills: Follow-up and evaluation. *Journal of Counseling Psychology, 26,* 448–450.

Irish, R. (1987). *Go hire yourself an employer.* New York: Doubleday.

Jacobson, T. J. (1984). Self-directed job search training in occupational classes. *Journal of Employment Counseling, 21,* 117–125.

Janis, I. L., & Mann, L. (1977). *Decision making.* New York: Free Press.

Jepsen, D. A., & Dilley, J. S. (1974). Vocational decision-making models: A review and comparative analysis. *Review of Educational Research, 44,* 331–349.

Jepsen, D. A., Dustin, R., & Miars, R. (1982). The effects of problem-solving training on adolescents' career exploration and career decision making. *Personnel and Guidance Journal, 60,* 149–153.

Jepsen, D. A., & Grove, W. M. (1986). Generalizability of Vocational Decision-Making Questionnaire scales. *Measurement and Evaluation in Counseling and Development, 19,* 67–76.

Johnson, J. J., Smither, R., & Holland, J. L. (1981). Evaluating vocational interventions: A tale of two career development seminars. *Journal of Counseling Psychology, 28,* 180–183.

Johnson, N., Johnson, J., & Yates, C. (1981). A 6-month follow-up on the effects of the vocational exploration group on career maturity. *Journal of Counseling Psychology, 28,* 70–71.

Jones, D. B., & Pinkney, J. W. (1989). An exploratory assessment of the sources of job-interviewing anxiety in college students. *Journal of College Student Development, 30,* 553–560.

Jones, L. K. (1987). *The Career Key.* Chicago: Furguson.

Jones, L. K. (1989). Measuring a three-dimensional construct of career indecision among college students: A revision of the Vocational Decision Scale—The Career Decision Profile. *Journal of Counseling Psychology, 36,* 477–486.

Jones, L. K., Gorman, S., & Schroeder, C. G. (1989). A comparison between the SDS and the Career Key among career undecided college students. *Career Development Quarterly, 37,* 334–344.

Jordaan, J. P. (1963). Exploratory behavior: The formation of self and occupational concepts. In D. E. Super, R. Starishevsky, N. Matlin, & J. P. Jordaan (Eds.), *Career development: Self concept theory* (pp. 42–78). New York: College Entrance Examination Board.

Jordaan, J. P. (1974). Life stages as organizing modes of career development. In E. L. Herr (Ed.), *Vocational guidance and human development* (pp. 263–295). Boston: Houghton Mifflin.

Jordaan, J. P., & Heyde, M. B. (1979). *Vocational maturity during the high-school years.* New York: Teachers College Press.

Kanfer, R., & Hulin, C. L. (1985). Individual differences in successful job searches following lay-off. *Personnel Psychology, 38,* 835–847.

Keller, K. E., Glauber, D., & Snyder, J. (1983). Beliefs-focused and skills-focused employment interventions for women. *Journal of Employment Counseling, 20,* 163–168.

Kelly, J. A., Laughlin, C., Claiborne, M., & Patterson, J. (1979). A group procedure for teaching job interviewing skills to formerly hospitalized psychiatric patients. *Behavior Therapy, 10,* 299–310.

Kelly, J. A., Wildman, B. G., & Berler, E. S. (1980). Small group behavioral training to improve the job interview skills repertoire of mildly retarded adolescents. *Journal of Applied Behavior Analysis, 13,* 461–471.

Kivlighan, D. M., Hageseth, J. A., Tipton, R. M., & McGovern, T. V. (1981). Effects of matching treatment approaches and personality types in group vocational counseling. *Journal of Counseling Psychology, 28,* 315–320.

Kivlighan, D. M., & Shapiro, R. (1987). Holland type as a predictor of benefit from self-help career counseling. *Journal of Counseling Psychology, 34,* 326–329.

Knickerbocker, B., & Davidshofer, C. (1978). Attitudinal outcomes of the life planning workshop. *Journal of Counseling Psychology, 25,* 103–109.

Knouse, S. B., Tauber, R. T., & Skonieczka, K. (1979). The effects of one-session training on résumé writing skills. *Vocational Guidance Quarterly, 27,* 326–333.

Krumboltz, J. D., Becker-Haven, J. F., & Burnett, K. F. (1979). Counseling psychology. *Annual Review of Psychology, 30,* 555–602.

Krumboltz, J. D., & Hamel, D. A. (1977). *Guide to career decision making skills.* New York: College Entrance Examination Board.

Krumboltz, J. D., Kinnier, R. T., Rude, S. S., Scherba, D. S., & Hamel, D. A. (1986). Teaching a rational approach to career decision making: Who benefits most? *Journal of Vocational Behavior, 29,* 1–6.

Krumboltz, J. D., Mitchell, A. M., & Jones, G. B. (1976). A social learning theory of career selection. *The Counseling Psychologist, 6,*(1), 71–80.

Krumboltz, J. D., Rude, S. S., Mitchell, L. K., Hamel, D. A., & Kinnier, R. T. (1982). Behaviors associated with "good" and "poor" outcomes in a simulated career decision. *Journal of Vocational Behavior, 21,* 349–358.

Krumboltz, J. D., Scherba, D. S., Hamel, D. A., & Mitchell, L. K. (1982). Effect of training in rational decision making on the quality of simulated career decisions. *Journal of Counseling Psychology, 29,* 618–625.

Krumboltz, J. D., Scherba, D. S., Hamel, D. A., Mitchell, L., Rude, S., & Kinnier, R. (1979). *The effect of alternate career decision making strategies on the quality of resulting decisions.* Final report. Stanford, CA: Stanford University. (ERIC Document Reproduction Service No. 195 824).

Krumboltz, J. D., & Schroeder, W. W. (1965). Promoting career planning through reinforcement. *Personnel and Guidance Journal, 11,* 19–26.

Krumboltz, J. D., & Thoresen, C. E. (1964). The effect of behavioral counseling in group and individual settings on information-seeking behavior. *Journal of Counseling Psychology, 11,* 324–333.

Larson, L. M., Heppner, P. P., Ham, T., & Dugan, K. (1988). Investigating multiple subtypes of career indecision through cluster analysis. *Journal of Counseling Psychology, 35,* 439–446.

Laskin, S. B., & Palmo, A. J. (1983). The effect of Decisions and Outcomes on the career maturity of high school students. *Journal of Vocational Behavior, 23,* 22–34.

Lazarick, D. L., Fishbein, S. S., Loiello, M. A., & Howard, G. S. (1988). Practical investigations of volition. *Journal of Counseling Psychology, 35,* 15–26.

Lent, R. W., & Hackett, G. (1987). Career self-efficacy: Empirical status and future directions [Monograph]. *Journal of Vocational Behavior, 30,* 347–382.

Lent, R. W., Larkin, K. C., & Hasegawa, C. S. (1986). Effects of a "focused interest" career course approach for college students. *Vocational Guidance Quarterly, 34,* 151–159.

Lucas, M. S., & Epperson, D. L. (1990). Types of vocational undecidedness: A replication and refinement. *Journal of Counseling Psychology, 37,* 382–388.

Malett, S. D., Spokane, A. R., & Vance, F. L. (1978). Effects of vocationally relevant information on the expressed and measured interests of freshman males. *Journal of Counseling Psychology, 25,* 292–298.

Matthews, R. M. (1984). Teaching employment interview skills to unemployed adults. *Journal of Employment Counseling, 21,* 156–161.

Matthews, R. M., Damron, W. S., & Yuen, C. K. (1985). A seminar in job finding skills. *Journal of Employment Counseling, 22,* 170–173.

Matthews, R. M., & Fawcett, S. B. (1984). Building the capacities of job candidates through behavioral instruction. *Journal of Community Psychology, 12,* 123–129.

McAuliffe, G. J., & Fredrickson, R. (1990). The effects of program length and participant characteristics on group career-counseling outcomes. *Journal of Employment Counseling, 27,* 19–22.

McGowan, A. S. (1977). Vocational maturity and anxiety among vocationally undecided and indecisive students. *Journal of Vocational Behavior, 10,* 196–204.

Mencke, R. A., & Cochran, D. J. (1974). Impact of a counseling outreach workshop on vocational development. *Journal of Counseling Psychology, 21,* 185–190.

Mendonca, J. D., & Seiss, T. F. (1976). Counseling for indecisiveness: Problem-solving and anxiety management training. *Journal of Counseling Psychology, 23,* 339–347.

Mitchell, L. K. & Krumboltz, J. D. (1984). Research on human decision making: Implications for career decision making and counseling. In S. D. Brown & R. W. Lent (Eds.), *Handbook of counseling psychology* (pp. 238–282). New York: Wiley.

Mitchell, L. K., & Krumboltz, J. D. (1987). The effects of cognitive restructuring and decision-making training on career indecision. *Journal of Counseling and Development, 66,* 171–174.

Myers, R. A. (1971). Research on educational and vocational counseling. In A. E. Bergin & S. L. Garfield (Eds.), *Handbook of psychotherapy and behavior change: An empirical analysis* (pp. 863–891). New York: Wiley.

Myers, R. A. (1986). Research on educational and vocational counseling. In S. L. Garfield & A. E. Bergin (Eds.), *Handbook of psychotherapy and behavior change: An empirical analysis* (pp. 715–738). New York: Wiley.

Myers, R. A., Lindeman, R. H., Thompson, A. S., & Patrick, T. A. (1975). Effects of Educational and Career Exploration System on vocational maturity. *Journal of Vocational Behavior, 6,* 245–254.

Neimeyer, G. J. (1988). Cognitive integration and differentiation in vocational behavior. *The Counseling Psychologist, 16,* 440–475.

Nevo, O. (1990). Career counseling from the counselee perspective: Analysis of feedback questionnaires. *Career Development Quarterly, 38,* 314–324.

Oliver, L. W. (1978). *Outcome measures for career counseling research* (Technical Paper 316). Alexandria, VA: U. S. Army Research Institute for the Behavioral and Social Sciences.

Oliver, L. W., & Spokane, A. R. (1988). Career-intervention outcome: What contributes to client gain? *Journal of Counseling Psychology, 35,* 447–462.

Osipow, S. H. (1982). Research in career counseling: An analysis of issues and problems. *The Counseling Psychologist, 10*(4), 27–36.

Osipow, S. H. (1983). *Theories of career development* (3rd ed.). Englewood Cliffs, NJ: Prentice-Hall.

Osipow, S. H., Carney, C. G., Winer, J. L., Yanico, B., & Koshier, M. J. (1980). *The Career Decision Scale* (3rd ed.). Columbus, OH: Marathon Consulting Press.

Palmer, S., & Cochran, L. (1988). Parents as agents of career development. *Journal of Counseling Psychology, 35,* 71–76.

Parsons, F. (1909). *Choosing a vocation.* Boston: Houghton Mifflin.

Pavlak, M. F., & Kammer, P. P. (1985). The effects of a career guidance program on the career maturity and self concept of delinquent youth. *Journal of Vocational Behavior, 26,* 41–54.

Phillips, S. D., & Pazienza, N. J. (1988). History and theory of the assessment of career development and decision making. In W. B. Walsh & S. H. Osipow (Eds.), *Career decision making* (pp. 1–32). Hillsdale, NJ: Erlbaum.

Phillips, S. D., Pazienza, N. J., & Ferrin, H. H. (1984). Decision-making styles and problem-solving appraisal. *Journal of Counseling Psychology, 31,* 497–502.

Phillips, S. D., & Strohmer, D. C. (1983). Vocationally mature coping strategies and progress in the decision-making process: A canonical analysis. *Journal of Counseling Psychology, 30*, 395–402.

Perovich, G. M., & Mierzwa, J. A. (1980). Group facilitation of vocational maturity and self esteem in college students. *Journal of College Student Personnel, 21*, 206–211.

Pitz, G. F., & Harren, V. A. (1980). An analysis of career decision making from the point of view of information processing and decision theory. *Journal of Vocational Behavior, 16*, 320–346.

Prediger, D. J., & Noeth, R. J. (1979). Effectiveness of a brief counseling intervention in stimulating vocational exploration. *Journal of Vocational Behavior, 14*, 352–368.

Quinn, M. T., & Lewis, R. J. (1989). An attempt to measure a career planning intervention in a traditional course. *Journal of College Student Development, 30*, 371–372.

Rayman, J. R., Bernard, C. B., Holland, J. L., & Barnett, D. C. (1983). The effects of a career course on undecided college students. *Journal of Vocational Behavior, 23*, 346–355.

Remer, P., O'Neill, C. D., & Gohs, D. E. (1984). Multiple outcome evaluation of a life-career development course. *Journal of Counseling Psychology, 31*, 532–540.

Riggio, R. E., & Throckmorton, B. (1987). Effects of prior training and verbal errors on students' performance in job interviews. *Journal of Employment Counseling, 24*, 10–16.

Robbins, S., & Tucker, K. (1986). Relation of goal instability and interactional career counseling workshops. *Journal of Counseling Psychology, 33*, 418–424.

Rodriguez, M., & Blocher, D. (1988). A comparison of two approaches to enhancing career maturity in Puerto Rican college women. *Journal of Counseling Psychology, 35*, 275–280.

Rounds, J. B., & Tinsley, H. E. A. (1984). Diagnosis and treatment of vocational problems. In S. D. Brown & R. W. Lent (Eds.), *Handbook of counseling psychology* (pp. 137–177). New York: Wiley.

Rubinton, N. (1980). Instruction in career decision making and decision-making styles. *Journal of Counseling Psychology, 27*, 581–588.

Rynes, S., & Lawler, J. (1983). A policy-capturing investigation of the role of expectancies in decisions to pursue job alternatives. *Journal of Applied Psychology, 68*, 620–631.

Salamone, P. R. (1982). Difficult cases in career counseling: II—The indecisive client. *Personnel and Guidance Journal, 60*, 496–500.

Savickas, M. L. (1985). Identity in vocational development. *Journal of Vocational Behavior, 27*, 329–337.

Savickas, M. L. (1990). The Career Decision-Making Course: Description and field test. *Career Development Quarterly, 38*, 275–284.

Savickas, M. L., & Jarjoura, D. (1991). The Career Decision Scale as a type indicator. *Journal of Counseling Psychology, 38*, 85–90.

Schaeffer, B. E. (1976). Holland's SDS: Is its effectiveness contingent upon selected variables? *Journal of Vocational Behavior, 8*, 113–123.

Schenck, G. E., Johnston, J. A., & Jacobsen, K. (1979). The influence of a career group experience on the vocational maturity of college students. *Journal of Vocational Behavior, 14*, 284–296.

Serling, D. A., & Betz, N. E. (1990). Development and evaluation of a measure of fear of commitment. *Journal of Counseling Psychology, 37*, 91–97.

Sherry, P., & Staley, K. (1984). Career exploration groups: An outcome study. *Journal of College Student Personnel, 25*, 155–159.

Slaney, R. B. (1988). The assessment of career decision making. In W. B. Walsh & S. H. Osipow (Eds.), *Career decision making* (pp. 33–76). Hillsdale, NJ: Erlbaum.

Slaney, R. B., & Dickson, R. D. (1985). Relation of career indecision to career exploration with reentry women: A treatment and follow-up study. *Journal of Counseling Psychology, 32*, 355–362.

Slaney, R. B., & Lewis, E. T. (1986). Effects of career exploration on career undecided reentry women: An intervention and follow-up study. *Journal of Vocational Behavior, 28*, 97–109.

Snodgrass, G., & Healy, C. C. (1979). Developing a replicable career decision-making counseling procedure. *Journal of Counseling Psychology, 26*, 210–216.

Speas, C. M. (1979). Job-seeking interview skills training: A comparison of four instructional techniques. *Journal of Counseling Psychology, 26*, 405–412.

Spokane, A. R. (1985). A review of research on person–environment congruence in Holland's theory of careers [Monograph]. *Journal of Vocational Behavior, 26*, 306–343.

Spokane, A. R. (1987). Conceptual and methodological issues in person–environment fit research [Special issue]. *Journal of Vocational Behavior, 31*(3).

Spokane, A. R., & Hawks, B. K. (1990). Annual review: Practice and research in career counseling and development, 1989. *Career Development Quarterly, 39,* 98–128.

Spokane, A. R., & Oliver, L. W. (1983). The outcomes of vocational intervention. In W. B. Walsh & S. H. Osipow (Eds.), *Handbook of vocational psychology: Vol. 2. Applications* (pp. 99–136). Hillsdale, NJ: Erlbaum.

Stevens, W., & Tornatzky, L. (1976). The effects of a job-interview skills workshop on drug-abuse clients. *Journal of Employment Counseling, 13,* 156–163.

Stone, C. I., & Geppert, C C. (1979). Job-interviewing skills training: An empirical investigation of two methods. *Rehabilitation Counseling Bulletin, 22,* 396–401.

Stonewater, J. K., & Daniels, M. H. (1983). Psychosocial and cognitive development in a career decision-making course. *Journal of College Student Personnel, 24,* 403–410.

Stumpf, S. A., Austin, E. J., & Hartman, K. (1984). The impact of career exploration and interview readiness on interview performance and outcomes. *Journal of Vocational Behavior, 24,* 221–235.

Stumpf, S. A., Brief, A. P., & Hartman, K. (1987). Self-efficacy expectations and coping with career-related events. *Journal of Vocational Behavior, 31,* 91–108.

Stumpf, S. A., Collarelli, S. M., & Hartman, K. (1983). Development of the Career Exploration Survey (CES). *Journal of Vocational Behavior, 22,* 191–226.

Super, D. E. (1953). A theory of vocational development. *American Psychologist, 8,* 185–190.

Super, D. E. (1957). *The psychology of careers.* New York: Harper & Row.

Super, D. E. (1963). Toward making self-concept theory operational. In D. E. Super, R. Starishevsky, N. Matlin, & J. P. Jordaan (Eds.), *Career development: Self concept theory* (pp. 17–32). New York: College Entrance Examination Board.

Super, D. E. (Ed.). (1974). *Measuring vocational maturity for counseling and evaluation.* Washington, DC: American Personnel and Guidance Association.

Super, D. E. (1983). Assessment in career guidance: Toward truly developmental counseling. *Personnel and Guidance Journal, 61,* 555–562.

Super, D. E. (1985). Coming of age in Middletown. *American Psychologist, 40,* 405–414.

Super, D. E., Crites, J. O., Hummel, R. C., Moser, H. P., Overstreet, P. L., & Warnath, C. F. (1957). *Vocational development: A framework for research.* New York: Teachers College Press.

Super, D. E., & Jordaan, J. P. (1973). Career development theory. *British Journal of Guidance and Counselling, 1,* 3–16.

Super, D. E., & Overstreet, P. L. (1960). *The vocational maturity of ninth grade boys.* New York: Teachers College Press.

Super, D. E., Thompson, A. S., Lindeman, R. H., Jordaan, J. P., & Myers, R. A. (1981). *Career Development Inventory.* Palo Alto, CA: Consulting Psychologists Press.

Takai, R., & Holland, J. L. (1979). Comparison of the Vocational Card Sort, the SDS, and the Vocational Exploration and Insight Kit. *Vocational Guidance Quarterly, 27,* 312–318.

Talbot, D. B., & Birk, J. M. (1979). Does the Vocational Exploration and Insight Kit equal the sum of its parts? A comparison study. *Journal of Counseling Psychology, 26,* 359–362.

Taylor, M. S. (1985). The roles of occupational self knowledge and vocational self concept crystallization in students' school-to-work transition. *Journal of Counseling Psychology, 32,* 539–550.

Tiedeman, D. V. (1961). Decisions and vocational development: A paradigm and its implications. *Personnel and Guidance Journal, 40,* 15–21.

Tiedeman, D. V., & O'Hara, R. P. (1963). *Career development: Choice and adjustment.* New York: College Entrance Examination Board.

Tinsley, H. E. A., Bowman, S. L., & York, D. C. (1989). Career Decision Scale, My Vocational Situation, Vocational Rating Scale, and Decisional Rating Scale: Do they measure the same constructs? *Journal of Counseling Psychology, 36,* 115–120.

Vinokur, A., & Caplan, R. D. (1987). Attitudes and social support: Determinants of job-seeking behavior and well-being among the unemployed. *Journal of Applied Social Psychology, 17,* 1007–1024.

Vondracek, F. W., Hostetler, M., Schulenberg, J. E., & Shimizu, K. (1990). Dimensions of career indecision. *Journal of Counseling Psychology, 37,* 98–106.

Ware, M. E. (1985). Assessing a career development course for upper level college students. *Journal of College Student Personnel, 26,* 152–155.

Warner, S. G., & Jepsen, D. A. (1979). Differential effects of conceptual level and group counseling format on adolescent career decision-making processes. *Journal of Counseling Psychology, 26,* 497–503.

Watkins, C. E., Savickas, M. L., Brizzi, J., & Manus, M. (1990). Effects of counselor response behavior on clients' impressions during vocational counseling. *Journal of Counseling Psychology, 37,* 138–142.

Westbrook, B. W. (1983). Career maturity: The concept, the instrument, and the research. In W. B. Walsh & S. H. Osipow (Eds.), *Handbook of vocational psychology: Vol. 1. Foundation* (pp. 263–304). Hillsdale, NJ: Erlbaum.

Westbrook, B. W., & Mastie, M. M. (1974). The Cognitive Vocational Maturity Test. In D. E. Super (Ed.), *Measuring vocational maturity for counseling and evaluation* (pp. 41–50). Washington, DC: American Personnel and Guidance Association.

Westbrook, B. W., & Parry-Hill, J. W., Jr. (1973). The measurement of cognitive vocational maturity. *Journal of Vocational Behavior, 3,* 239–252.

Wiggins, J. D., & Moody, A. (1981). A field-based comparison of four career exploration approaches. *Vocational Guidance Quarterly, 30,* 15–20.

Wild, B. K., & Kerr, B. A. (1984). Training adolescent job-seekers in persuasion skills. *Vocational Guidance Quarterly, 33,* 63–69.

Yates, C., Johnson, N., & Johnson, J. (1979). Effects of the use of the Vocational Exploration Group on career maturity. *Journal of Counseling Psychology, 26,* 368–370.

Yongue, I. T., Todd, R. M., & Burton, J. K. (1981). The effects of didactic classroom instruction versus field exposure on career maturity. *Journal of Vocational Behavior, 19,* 369–373.

Zener, T. B., & Schnuelle, L. (1976). Effects of the Self-Directed Search on high school students. *Journal of Counseling Psychology, 23,* 353–359.

CHAPTER 17
COUNSELING AND CAREER ADJUSTMENT

ROGER A. MYERS
PETER C. CAIRO

In his thoughtful treatise on the history of applied psychology, Donald Napoli (1981) argued persuasively that, in order to establish psychology as a profession, psychologists had convinced America that they—and they alone—were specialists in *adjustment*. Whereas curing the mentally ill was considered the province of medicine and educating children belonged to educators, psychologists made the case for their utility in promoting adjustment to parents, to educators, and to businesspeople. Napoli noted:

> *And beyond the logical argument—written between the lines of the textbooks and popular manuals—was a vision of a better America, a well adjusted society in which social utility merged with personal fulfillment to provide a satisfactory life for all. (p. 31)*

Although they acknowledged the importance of the family and the schools in promoting adjustment, applied psychologists recognized that the most important arena for adjustment was the workplace. Finding the right job was of particular importance, and the emerging insights of individual differences and of vocational guidance armed psychologists well to assist in this critical life task. Adjusting to one's job meant feeling enthusiastic about it, becoming deeply involved in it, and enjoying the physical and mental health that satisfactory job performance promoted. The concentration on adjustment to work not only served the cause of individual welfare but also enhanced the purposes of employers. The notion that a happy worker was a productive worker was easily accepted, as was the notion that well-adjusted workers helped create vigorous and successful organizations.

The acceptance and growth of applied psychology, especially after World War II, provided the backdrop for the emergence of counseling psychology as a specialty and for the logical assumption that, among the several important functions of that specialty, attention to work adjustment was especially salient.

Nevertheless, it is difficult to reckon how much counseling psychologists, under the banner of their specialty, do in fact devote their attention and their energies to the human problems of adjustment to work. Toomer (1982) provided data to suggest that, although many counseling psychologists expressed an interest in expanding their work to business and industry, only about 3% of his sample were currently employed therein.

Another 8% listed consulting as their primary work setting, and presumably some of them were involved in work adjustment interventions.

Osipow (1982) was firmly convinced that the level of workplace activity among counseling psychologists was not very high, and expressed his dismay that "counseling applications to industry have been ignored for so long" (p. 19). Seeing involvement in the world of work as a logical role for the specialty, Osipow asserted that the role has not been fulfilled. As possible reasons for this gap, he cited negative attitudes of managers toward counseling, relationships to other psychological specialties, and shortcomings in the training of counseling psychologists.

Not everyone agrees with Osipow's reasons for counseling psychologists' neglect of the workplace, but no one disputes his assertion that the neglect is characteristic of the specialty. Alarms have been sounded (Savickas, 1990) to call attention to the danger that issues of adjustment to work may be fading rapidly from the attention and interest of counseling psychologists. The frequently cited work of Fitzgerald and Osipow (1988) and Watkins, Lopez, Campbell, and Himmell (1986) supports the suspicion that such danger exists, especially among the younger members of the specialty.

However, the agendum has not faded completely. Some counseling psychologists do focus on adjustment to work and do, in fact, direct that focus to the organizations in which people implement their career choices (Gavin, 1982; Lacey, 1982; Minatoya, 1982; Ridley & Hellervik, 1982; Stark & Romans, 1982; Stern, 1982; Wilbur & Vermilyea, 1982). As Blustein (1990) and Fouad (1990) pointed out, research and publication in vocational psychology are increasing rapidly, signaling a rise in interest in the realities of life at work among psychologists and other social scientists. Furthermore, Chapter 18, by Gerstein and Shullman, cites ample reasons for optimism and proposes means for turning the optimism into future reality.

This apparent paradox results from three conditions. The first is the obvious fact that the interests and skills of counseling psychologists are demonstrably relevant to concerns about adjustment to work. Stark and Romans (1982) put it succinctly:

> Much of the subject matter of counseling psychology is transferable to business and industry: career development, assessment, androgogy (adult learning theory), psychology of individuals, and group dynamics. Topical concerns to which counseling psychologists have applied these theories are equally important to organizations: crisis intervention, stress management, alcoholism, grief . . ., burnout, and self-actualization. Skills and personal qualities that counseling psychologists have developed . . . are valued by business and industry: problem analysis, individual and group process skills, program design (interventions), objectivity, and empathy. (p. 45)

The second condition contributing to the paradox is the increased enlightenment within organizations—public as well as private—regarding the needs that psychology can help to satisfy. Toomer (1982) listed medical functions, equal employment opportunity issues, labor relations, training, and employee assistance programs among the many functions to which the counseling psychologist can contribute within organizations. As counselor/therapist, trainer/educator, organizational specialist, researcher/program evaluator, selection/promotion expert, and human resource manager, the counseling psychologist (as Toomer would have it) plays a variety of roles of increasing importance in the workplace.

The third condition that contributes to the paradoxical situation of increased interest in vocational psychology and progressive neglect of adjustment to work among counseling psychologists is the fact that the work of counseling psychologists in organizations is not recognizable as distinct from the work of practitioners and scientists from other specialties. Industrial/organizational psychologists, clinical psychologists, social workers, organizational behavior specialists, educators, and others, all contribute to the inquiry and constructive action designed to understand and improve the adjustment of employed adults. It is possible to create specialty categories for research reviews (Hackett, Lent, and Greenhaus (1991) did it brilliantly), but that which is unique to counseling psychologists is difficult and perhaps impossible to discern. Just as remedial psychotherapy is one of the functions of psychiatrists, counseling psychologists, clinical psychologists, counselors, social workers, and others, so is understanding and improving work adjustment the legitimate activity of many professional specialties.

In recognition of this absence of boundaries, this chapter has been organized to present what is known about adjustment to work and how counseling psychologists, among others, can and do contribute to the process of that adjustment. Claims of unique insights and special capacities creep in at various points in what follows; the reader is cautioned to bear in mind that those insights and capacities are not the province of counseling psychologists solely.

We begin with a consideration of adjustment to work as it is currently examined, noting how attempts to understand such adjustment are limited by opportunities for inquiry and by the traditions of psychology in the workplace. Attitudes about working and easily observable responses to work are then considered. Next follows a treatment of issues that emerge when things at work change. The second major section deals with the perplexing relationship between work and the rest of life, including the difficulties of separating work from that which is not work and understanding the relationship between the two. In the third section, we consider recent documentation of how the themes and principles of counseling psychology have been applied to promoting adjustment to work, career, and life. The final section provides our views of the current state of the enterprise and some prescriptive notions on what the future might bring.

ADJUSTMENT TO WORK

A career, as has been widely acknowledged, is substantially more than the work one does for pay. It includes the early recognition that adults work, fantasies about the kind of work one might do as an adult, preferences among the kinds of work available, preparation for working, securing positions in the work force, combining work with the personal and situational changes of life, and reflecting on work after one has ceased to engage in it. As a concept, it is a frame for thinking about the productive aspects of life and how productive behavior mingles with other thoughts, feelings, and attitudes about life. Nevertheless, within this robust and comprehensive understanding of what constitutes a career is an explicit awareness of the importance of paid work as a major source of variance in career adjustment.

Most of what we regard as insight about career adjustment we extrapolate from what has been learned about individuals' attitudinal reactions and behavioral responses to the circumstances of their paid work. All too often, although not always, these learnings result from observations of individuals in their current work positions—the specific set of tasks assigned to them at a specified time within an identifiable organization. Most of these observations are taken at a single point in time or at a few points in time that are close together. There are exceptions, but they are rare (Howard & Bray, 1988; Schein, 1978; Super, 1980).

A major portion of the observations on which we depend for understanding career adjustment are reactive, resulting from asking workers to reply to questions they might not have asked themselves: How satisfied are you with your supervision? Do you expect to be promoted? How likely are you to leave this organization? The questions arise from the intentions of the investigators, not from the interests or concerns of the respondents. Much is learned by this method, but its limits are obvious. Furthermore, such reactive observations are, according to the traditions of inquiry in psychology, aggregated in order to represent the regularities and commonalities of experience among workers. These regularities and commonalities inform us about general conditions and about antecedents, concomitants, and sequels of the conditions, but leave as uninformed as to the individual levels and styles of adjustment.

In general, we cannot be sanguine about the state of knowledge about career adjustment, despite its current popularity both inside and outside the private sector of the economy. Reactions and responses of workers to their current positions are reasonably well-charted; the problems of entering a position and changing positions have attracted some attention; interest in integrating paid work with the rest of one's life experiences is emerging; and interventions intended to enhance career adjustment are in evidence. Yet, as in all the realms of constructive action we engage in, counseling psychologists must be tolerant of a sequence in which practice precedes inquiry rather than following it. Without such tolerance, counseling psychologists are highly likely to suffer the pangs of poor person–environment fit.

Attitudes About Work

Research on workers' evaluative, hedonic reactions to the work in which they are engaged constitutes a large portion of the literature of organizational behavior and industrial/ organizational psychology. Schneider (1985) suggested three hypotheses for why this is so. One hypothesis is that work attitudes are relatively easy to study. Another is that they represent an important outcome of organizational life. The third is that they give promise—sometimes realized—of being effective predictors of important behaviors.

Attitudes about work are evoked and collected under a wide variety of labels. Included among these labels are job satisfaction, job involvement, work involvement, organizational commitment, role ambiguity, stress, and burnout. For the purposes of this chapter, we will maintain that each of these labels designates a subset of the category called *attitudes about work*. The inclusion of stress and burnout in this category may well raise eyebrows in some learned circles. Nevertheless, it seems reasonable to assert that the act of identifying tension-creating circumstances in one's work and the act of admitting to feelings of alienation are not characteristically different from the acts of expressing one's pleasure (or lack of it) with the conditions of work or of pledging one's loyalty to one's employer. This is especially true when all such acts are performed with a pencil and a questionnaire.

Not everyone would agree with our clustering of these constructs. In fact, substantial scholarly activity is devoted to the argument and the demonstration that the various concepts are not redundant. For example, Brooke, Russell, and Price (1988) provided factor-analytic evidence that the employees of a VA medical center were able to distinguish among how much they liked their jobs (satisfaction), how absorbed or preoccupied they were with them (job involvement), and how much loyalty they felt toward their employer (organizational commitment). Misra, Kanungo, von Rosensteil, and Stuhler (1985) reported results that demonstrated that job involvement and work involvement bore different relationships to satisfaction and that the phenomenon generalized across two cultures. Warrenfeltz (1986) was also able to show differentiation between job involvement (which was manipulable) and work involvement (which was more enduring). Morrow and McElroy (1986) countered assertions that approaches to work commitment were redundant, and Wiley (1987) reported that job and family role conflicts correlated negatively with satisfaction and positively with job involvement and organizational commitment.

Additional attempts at conceptual clarity have been focused on organizational commitment (Kemery, Mossholder, & Bedeian, 1987; McGee & Ford, 1987; Reichers, 1985), job involvement (Blau, 1985a; Verma & Upadhyay, 1986), and burnout (Blostein, Eldridge, Kilty, & Richardson, 1985–86; Maslach & Jackson, 1984). Brief, Burke, and George (1988) suggested that an unrecognized moderator, negative affectivity, has been ignored in stress research, and Kanungo (1986) argued that assumptions about the relation of work attitudes to productivity need to be questioned.

Whether the various subcategories of attitudes about work are conceptually distinct, completely redundant, or somewhere in between is of little moment for this chapter. It is worth noting, however, that correlations among them are difficult to interpret in the absence of a comprehensive theory (Morrow, 1983) and, whatever the correlations, redundancy may be presumed in the absence of a competing hypothesis (Schneider, 1985).

Worker Characteristics

Attempts to identify concomitants of work attitudes among the personal characteristics of the workers have provided the challenge for much of the contemporary research. Positive relationships that have been demonstrated include: commitment with locus of control (Blau, 1985b; Luthans, Baack, & Taylor, 1987); job satisfaction with self-esteem (Sekaran, 1986a) and occupational membership (Malinowska, 1987); and burnout with problem-solving style (Veninga, 1983) and personality type (Nagy & Davis, 1985; Nowack, 1987). McNeely (1987) found that Black and White human service workers were similar to each other and different from Hispanics with regard to what predicted job satisfaction and job stress. Sahni and Chadha (1987) found that job involvement was positively related to ambiguity tolerance for Indian supervisors and to locus of control for their British counterparts. Luthans, McCaul, and Dodd (1985) challenged recent conventional wisdom with findings that suggested that: (a) U.S. workers had higher levels of organizational commitment than Japanese and Korean workers, and (b) nationality accounted for a small portion of the variance in levels of commitment. Gomez-Mejia (1984) demonstrated that cultural factors influence work attitudes less for managers than for workers in samples from 20 countries.

Although the positive relationship between the age of the worker and attitudes about work has been demonstrated frequently (e.g., Lee & Wilbur, 1985; Lindstrom, 1988; McNeely, 1988), a few recent studies provide contradictory results (Hanlon, 1986; Mount, 1984). Pond and Geyer (1987) interpreted their data to show that age was an important modifier of the relationship between job characteristics and positive attitudes. Mottaz (1987) and White and Spector (1987) saw in their data reasons to argue that job characteristics were important modifiers of the relationship between age and positive attitudes.

In the face of the evidence, it is difficult to deny that personality, ethnicity, national origin, and age are related to the ways in which workers react to their work. It is even more difficult to fashion useful generalizations about what worker characteristics influence or predispose what kinds of reactions. Much of the quest for such generalities rides on correlational data—albeit multivariate and complex—and the progress is impeded by the absence of causal models and integrating theories. Yet, the assertion that individual characteristics are irrelevant to work adjustment is so blatantly counterintuitive that one must applaud the investigative efforts to date and hope for better methods and models.

Characteristics of Work

A highly plausible and much favored strategic research hypothesis is that the conditions of one's work are important determinants of one's work attitudes. Positive attitudes have been shown to covary with pay, promotional prospects, social rewards, the nature of supervision, physical conditions of work, the opportunity to use one's skills and abilities, and a wide variety of other issues (Locke, 1976). The research of Hackman and Oldham (1976) and their subsequent book (1980) on job design did much to focus interest and research activity on this topic. Their proposition, called Job Characteristics Model, was that five job characteristics strongly influence worker motivation and work attitudes. These characteristics are: skill variety, task identity, task significance, autonomy, and feedback. The model has been subjected to theoretical criticism (Salancik & Pfeffer, 1977), but it has been the stimulus for considerable research activity and for the search for alternate construction of the conditions–attitudes relationship.

Recent research on job conditions continues to support the notion that they are important covariates of work attitudes. Knoop (1986) demonstrated that worker characteristics did not influence positive attitudes of secondary school teachers, but job conditions—especially participation in decision making—did. Jans's (1985) data also emphasized the importance of participation in decision making, but Cotton, Vollrath, and Froggatt (1988) cautioned that the nature of the opportunities for participation was important—that is, informal participation and employee ownership help but short-term participation is ineffective. The importance of opportunities for personal and professional development was demonstrated by Penn, Romano, and Foat (198) and by Sherman (1986), and the importance of competence as a mediator between stressful work conditions and negative work attitudes was upheld by Jayaratne and Chess (1986).

Leiter and Maslach (1988) related pleasant and unpleasant communication patterns on the job to negative work attitudes, and Leiter (1988) showed that negative work attitudes were accompanied by communication patterns that lacked informal, supportive relationships with coworkers. Skaret and Bruning (1986) showed that the relationship between leader behavior and positive attitudes was moderated by the workers' attitudes about their work groups. Evidence that job characteristics were more influential than worker characteristics was provided by Glisson and Durick (1988) and Mottaz (1988).

Some recent attention has been focused on the importance of the organization in which one's job exists. Zahra (1984) concluded that organizational factors were more important than worker characteristics in influencing work attitudes, but Angle and Perry (1983) found that both were influential. Leigh, Lucas, and Woodman (1988) suggested that organizational issues combined with job characteristics to influence work attitudes, and Dean, Ferris, and Konstans (1988) reported that organizational issues were important when workers' expectations were not met, but less so when they were.

Interaction Conditions

Concerns about the consequences of the interaction between characteristics of the worker and characteristics of the work are as venerable as concerns about work itself. Plato seems to have anticipated—and probably inspired—Frank Parsons by observing that "more will be accomplished, and better, and with more ease, if every man does what he is best fitted to do, and nothing else." Munsterberg (1913) is usually credited with introducing the concept of worker–job match to American psychology, thus providing an important impetus to what we now know as applied psychology. Contemporary attention to this issue, especially among counseling psychologists, is referred to as *person–environment fit.*

The theoretical contributions of Lofquist and Dawis (1969) (see also Dawis & Lofquist, 1984) and of Holland (1973, 1985) have done much to stimulate research and scholarship on the intricacies of person–environment fit. Representing, as they do, the modern refinements of trait-and-factor theory, the works of these theorists have generated numbers of studies that are truly impressive. Expanded interest in the topic is exhibited in a comprehensive treatment of the conceptual and methodological complexities of fit in a special issue of the *Journal of Vocational Behavior* ("Conceptual and methodological issues," 1987) and by Chapter 13, by Hackett and Lent.

As a concomitant of work attitudes, person–environment fit has attracted the attention of contemporary researchers. Inspired by Lofquist and Dawis's Work Adjustment Theory, Elizur and Tziner (1977) demonstrated that correspondence between worker needs and job rewards was correlated with work attitudes: the greater the correspondence, the more positive the attitudes. Recognizing that the correlation between such correspondence and satisfaction was not high, Scarpello and Campbell (1983) interviewed 185 workers in two multinational corporations, with a view toward understanding "off-quadrant" cases—for example, those with good needs–rewards match and low satisfaction. Their results convinced them that level of aspiration and views of career progression added to the fit–satisfaction relationship.

In a longitudinal study, Swaney and Prediger (1985) found a modest significant relationship between Holland-type congruence (interest–occupation fit) and work satisfaction, modified by variables of interest clarity, career salience, and valuing interesting work. Elton and Smart (1988), who identified congruence of interests for college freshmen with the jobs they held 9 years later, further established the congruence–satisfaction link over time. Blau (1987) showed that fit was related to job involvement but not to organizational commitment for nurses, and Burke and Deszca (1988) found that fit was related to stress, burnout, and satisfaction among police workers. In what is perhaps the most sophisticated test of the fit–attitudes relationship, Meir and Yaari (1988) demonstrated that, for a sample of engineers, physicians, nurses, teachers, police officers, biologists, lawyers, and psychologists, person–environment fit for specialties within occupations was a better predictor of satisfaction than was the person–occupation fit. Meir and Melamed (1986) showed that adding congruence measures for avocational interests and for skill utilization increased the predictive power of the occupational fit variable.

Responses to Work

In addition to reactive, evaluative attitudes about work, adjustment to work is represented by behavioral responses to the job. There is a general interest in the positive responses of workers, but organizational psychologists have concentrated far more investigative energy on their negative responses, especially the withdrawal responses of lateness, absenteeism, and turnover. (Withdrawal responses are problems for organizations to solve if organizational goals are to be pursued in optimal fashion.) Understanding, predicting, and eliminating withdrawal responses stand as important contributions applied psychologists might make toward the vision of fulfilled workers contributing to social utility through the production of goods and/or the provision of services.

From the perspective of the counseling psychologist interested in career adjustment, the failure of an individual to meet expectations that have been mutually agreed on and the act of canceling a social contract with an employer represent career decisions that have meaning, even though they do not necessarily signal problems in the career process. Insight into that meaning requires some understanding of the antecedents and concomitants of such decisions.

Absenteeism

According to Staw (1984), early notions about absence from work held that such withdrawal behavior was a direct consequence of negative work attitudes. Locke's (1976) review established the validity of these notions, but the correlations between work attitudes and measures of absenteeism were sufficiently low to suggest that other influences were at work. Although some recent studies (Blau, 1986; Scott & Taylor, 1985) continued to produce the expected attitude–absenteeism relationship, others (Ivancevich, 1985; Martin & Miller, 1986; Tziner & Vardi, 1984) did not. Hackett and Guion (1985) offered methodological criticisms that help to explain why research has not settled the issue: measures of absenteeism vary in reliability; voluntary absenteeism may be different from the involuntary kind; and much of the research does not consider the perceptions of the workers.

As one might expect, absenteeism has been shown to be related to various aspects of employee health (Leigh, 1985, 1986; Parkes, 1987) and to the nature and extent of nonwork stresses and obligations (Smulders, 1983), especially parenting young children. A number of investigators have also argued that organizational culture plays a larger role in promoting absenteeism than do worker characteristics (Arsenault & Dolan, 1983; Farrell & Stamm, 1988; Nicholson & Johns, 1985). Kopelman (1986) and Moch and Fitzgibbons (1985) provided reasons to question the automatic assumption that work absence has a negative effect on productivity.

Largely because of the work of Steers and Rhodes (1978) and Morgan and Herman (1976), contemporary approaches to the understanding of absence from work focus on the effects of both worker characteristics and environmental influences on the individual's decision to show up or stay away. Such approaches concentrate on the kinds of individual decisions that workers make as their careers unfold, bringing the concerns of organizational psychologists closer to those of the counseling psychologist. Missing from current understanding of the phenomenon are insights about the meaning of work absence over the span of a career.

Turnover

Although it is difficult to ascertain precisely the career implications of absence from work, the act of quitting one's job is clearly a career event of considerable importance. Through the lenses of the counseling psychologist, the anticipation of paid work, the preparation for it, and the instrumental behaviors required to secure it appear as processes and events of major concern. The decision to leave a position in the work force once it has been secured is no less important. As an individual moves from forming an occupational preference to making an occupational choice to implementing that choice, there is no doubt that the phenomena observed are the stuff of which careers are made. An implemented choice abandoned represents an event that must be considered critical to the course of a life of productive behavior. How do people make such decisions? What conditions influence the probabilities? What are the consequences?

For organizational psychologists, with few exceptions (Dalton, Krackhardt, & Porter, 1981; Dalton & Todor, 1979; Staw, 1980), individuals who leave an employer represent a problem to be solved. The costs of recruitment, training, and work disruption are real and can be substantial. As a result, attempts to understand and minimize the decision to quit are plentiful in the literature on life at work.

Most of the research on turnover has sprung from the rational decision-making mode proposed by March and Simon (1958) and Mobley (1977). The model posits that working conditions affect attitudes about work (e.g., job satisfaction), which give rise to (a) thoughts of quitting, (b) assessment of the utility of searching for alternatives, (c) search behavior, (d) the comparison of available alternatives to the present job, (e) intentions to stay or leave, and (f) the act itself. Decades of research have established that attitudes about work are related to turnover (Barber, 1986; DeCotiis & Summers, 1987; Mayes & Ganster, 1988) and to intentions to quit (Lachman & Aranya, 1986; Lee, 1988; Williams & Hazer, 1986). The demonstrated relationships are sufficiently small to confirm March and Simon's (1958) early insight that negative attitudes about one's job might well stimulate thoughts of quitting, but other issues influence that decision, such as job market conditions (Carsten & Spector, 1987; Hui, 1988) and perceptions of career equity (Mobley, 1982).

Coping with Change

As in all other arenas, life at work includes changes that provide a variety of challenges for the worker during the course of a career. Among these challenges are the problems of initial entry to an organization, changes of status and position within the organization, departure from the organization, and—for some—the revision of an implemented occupational choice. Currently referred to as *transitions,* these changes in the circumstances of one's work life represent decisions individuals make about their careers and reactions to the decisions that influential others make for them. From an individual's point of view, little is known about the determinants of these processes of deciding and reacting. However, because aggregated individual transitions create challenges for employing organizations, those who study organizations have begun to devote attention to them.

Entry

Considering the costs, to both the individual and the organization, that result when one is hired and quickly becomes dissatisfied and/or proves unsatisfactory, it is not surprising that attempts to understand the problems of entry have attracted attention. Unmet expectations for either the worker or the employer can influence performance, work attitudes, and withdrawal behaviors. In general, the research on entry has focused on what organizations do to forestall negative posthiring effects (Van Maanen, 1976). Considerable attention has been devoted to the effectiveness of having the employer deal in an honest way with the potential employee through the use of realistic job previews (Breaugh, 1983; Wanous, 1975). More recent attacks on the problem have added some concerns about what the new worker brings to the transaction to the traditional concerns about what the employer does to socialize him or her (Nicholson, 1984). For example, Jones (1986) demonstrated that self-efficacy played a role in determining the reactions of newcomers to institutionalized versus individualized socialization efforts, and Colarelli, Dean, and Konstans (1987) concluded that both organizational and individual characteristics differentially influenced the attitudes and behaviors of newcomers. Of the many concomitants identified with satisfactory entry to the work situation, social support on the job emerges as one of the most important

(Fisher, 1985; Pearson, 1982), especially when the new worker seeks it in an active way (Feldman & Brett, 1983).

Changes in Status

Empirical research has uncovered little about changes in status or position at work. However, the obvious relevance of such changes for the human drama has attracted considerable attention and evoked a fair measure of speculation and advice. For example, the perils of *technological change* for the worker have recently been considered by Majchrzak and Cotton (1988), Carlopio (1988), and Shenkar (1988), all of whom advise that dire consequences for workers are present and special measures to help them adapt are needed. Decades after Goldner's (1965) treatment of the problem of downward movement in occupational level (i.e., *demotion*), new interest in this topic and new advice about its handling have begun to appear (Isabella & Hall, 1984; Minor, Slade, & Myers, 1991). A recent study even provided evidence that engineers and managers would accept demotions as an alternative to leaving the organization, and offered advice as to how organizations could present demotions as not only palatable but also career-enhancing (Hall & Isabella, 1985).

Although it is not, strictly speaking, a change in work status, the condition in which one becomes aware that expectations for promotion are no longer realistic qualifies as a transition of considerable psychological consequence. Referred to in the literature as *plateauing,* this condition has attracted what appears to be exaggerated attention in recent years, for a variety of demographic, economic, and social reasons. The assumption underlying the perception of plateauing is that a career consists of a series of positions within an organization, which one occupies in a sequence; this sequence leads to progressive (and, presumably, continuous) upward mobility. When upward mobility is no longer likely, one is said to have "plateaued." Given the pyramidal structure of most organizations, with fewer opportunities at each higher level, reaching a plateau in organizational level is inevitable. Nevertheless, the nature of aspirations among those who ascend to managerial positions seems to predispose a negative psychological event—or stage—in which one faces the probability that further upward mobility will not occur.

As with most of the changes in work status, worker perceptions of and reactions to plateauing are not well documented. Stout, Slocum, and Cron (1988) provided data to suggest that the longer one is on a plateau, the more negative one's work attitudes become. Howard and Bray (1980) found that most managers in their longitudinal study adjusted to their career plateaus without difficulty. Patterson, Sutton, and Schuttenberg (1987) reported that university professors who perceived themselves to be on a plateau felt as productive and as accomplished as those who did not see themselves on a plateau. Tausky and Dubin (1965) concluded that only about 10% of the managers they studied were concerned about plateaus in their career planning.

Ference, Stoner, and Warren (1977) provided a thoughtful view of the plateau phenomenon by distinguishing between plateaued employees whose work performance is less than satisfactory—called "deadwood"—and those whose work performance remains high—the "solid citizens." The investigators called attention to the fact that most employers neglect the solid citizens, who represent a cadre of stable, tenured employees essential to effective organizational functioning. Such neglect incurs the risk of turning solid citizens into deadwood. Dawson (1983) has recommended that organizations recognize the increasing frequency of the career plateau and respond by encouraging employee interest in career changes, increasing recognition rituals for solid citizens, and sponsoring nonwork activities that promote individual development.

No change in status at work is as painful and disruptive as involuntary *job loss*. As worldwide economic conditions change for the worse and employers—both public and private—exercise their option to improve efficiency and enhance profitability by reducing labor costs (euphemistically called "downsizing"), vast numbers of individual careers are affected. Research on the effects of job loss on career behavior is scarce, but the negative consequences for physical and psychological well-being have been documented for decades (Bakke, 1933; Brenner, 1976; Cohn, 1978; Dooley & Catalano, 1980; Eisenberg & Lazarsfeld, 1938; Feather & Davenport, 1981; Komarovsky, 1940; Stokes & Cochrane, 1984; Wedderburn, 1964). Contemporary interest in the individual dilemma created by job loss includes continued concern for the negative emotional reactions of terminated (Gummer, 1987; Harrick, Hansel, & Schutzius, 1982; Jones, 1979) and displaced (Benesch, 1986) workers. Mallinckrodt and Fretz (1988) demonstrated the importance of social support in mediating the impact of job loss, and others have offered advice about how psychologists can best help individual workers (Gordus, 1986) and organizations (Latack & Dozier, 1986) deal with job loss in more humane ways. Brown and Heath (1984) provided a thoughtful model for enhancing an individual's capacity to cope with critical life events, such as job loss, by concentrating on self-efficacy; Kanfer and Hulin (1985) demonstrated that self-efficacy is an important component of successful job search behavior among the unemployed. Some researchers have studied the effects of layoffs on "survivors"—those who have not been laid off (Brockner, Grover, & Blonder, 1988; Cooper-Schneider, 1989).

Although job loss has not generated much research on the consequences of this kind of discontinuity for career adjustment, it has provided career opportunities for counseling psychologists in "outplacement" services. Such services, almost always provided by the employer doing the terminating, are designed to influence the career transition by promoting self-insight, increasing awareness of the opportunity structure, and teaching job search behaviors. The effectiveness of such services has yet to be documented, but the career opportunities for counseling psychologists—and, more and more, clinical psychologists—are already apparent.

Changing Occupations

It would be difficult to find a single person who endorses it, but the myth of stability within a career remains amazingly durable (Rothstein, 1980). The notion that an occupation, once chosen, remains an occupation for life remains a part of our national folklore. Less pervasive but equally durable is the idea that a career takes place within a single organization. These myths have never held for large portions of the population, yet deviation from the putative norm attracted the attention of researchers and practitioners during the 1970s and 1980s. The relatively affluent conditions of those decades provided ample opportunity for leaving one's occupation and entering another, and for changing employers. The increased insights about adult development and the heightened sensitivity to the changes experienced in "mid-life" surely helped to designate occupational change as a topic worthy of study.

As with many newly emerging areas of inquiry, definitions and boundaries have not been consensually validated. Hence, some researchers write of career change as if any change of position, job, occupation, or organization were a change *of* career rather than a change *in* career. Others write about *second* careers, ignoring the accepted convention that a career is a sequence of activities related to productive behavior that occurs during the course of one's life, making a second career a logical impossibility within a single lifetime.

Despite this lack of clarity, substantial work has been devoted to understanding what happens when an individual decides to change occupations and therefore bring about changes in position, employer, location, and/or other factors. One popular research strategy is based on the assumption that people who change occupations are characteristically different from those who do not. For example, Vaitenas and Wiener (1977) showed that the changers they studied were more maladjusted, had more fear of failure, and were lower in congruity, differentiation, and consistency than nonchangers. The same investigators (Wiener & Vaitenas, 1977) related changing to personality traits of ascendancy, dominance, responsibility, endurance, and order, as well as person–occupation fit. Gilkison and Drummond (1988) found changers-in-training to be high in self-esteem, self-confidence, and achievement motivation. Although group differences between changers and nonchangers have been demonstrated, it is clear that the observed differences are specific to the samples studied, all of which appear to be of the convenience type.

Another popular research strategy is based on the extension of models constructed to explain organizational turnover. For a variety of reasons, negative work attitudes develop and, depending on the availability of alternative possibilities and other constraints, a decision to make a change is undertaken. The importance of the nature of the alternative opportunities available was emphasized in studies by Collins (1983) and Rothstein (1980), both of whom argued that the opportunity structure plays a larger role in the decisions than is usually acknowledged. The importance of decision-making style was addressed by Armstrong (1981), who found reason to advocate rational (vs. incremental) decision making, and by Perosa and Perosa (1983), who demonstrated efficacy for two decision-making models.

Dissatisfaction with current occupation as a motivator for change has been demonstrated for social workers (Herrick, Takagi, Coleman, & Morgan, 1983), nurses (Lane, Mathews, & Presholdt, 1988), and clinical psychologists (Coche & Coche, 1986). But, for many changers, such dissatisfaction is best explained by the personal changes one undergoes at mid-life. At that life stage—variously defined—values change and the previously satisfactory occupation no longer satisfies the new value set (Hill & Miller, 1981; Thomas, 1977, 1979). The assumption that the degree of postchange satisfaction, which is frequently reported, will be explained by a better person–occupation fit has been challenged. Thomas and Robbins (1979) reported that most of their mid-life changers did not move to occupations more congruent with their personalities. Furthermore, those who did change to more congruent occupations were not more satisfied with the move than those who did not. The consequences of mid-life changes for the changers' families, most of which are easily anticipated, have been studied by Henton, Russell, and Koval (1983) and by Entine (1984).

Conclusion

Counseling psychologists cannot ignore or even neglect the stern reality that the events of a career unfold in sequences that are characterized by both regularities and discontinuities. Patterns in these events are identifiable and useful, but each career includes its measure of interruptions and perturbations. This dynamic tension between stability and change in the course of a life at work enriches the challenge for those who strive to help others anticipate career decisions, make and implement those decisions, and adjust to their consequences. Perhaps Super (1985), who is often misconstrued as having placed too much emphasis on the stability side of the dilemma, has put it best:

> *The fact that one can identify a maxicycle of growth, exploration, establishment, maintenance, and decline through which many people progress in a common sequence should not hide the facts that some people never cease exploring, that some drift, and that some are destabilized by accident, illness, war, politics, recessions, and their own personal development as interests change and values shift with age and experience. . . . Careers have minicycles within the maxicycle. (p. 407)*

The work of organizational psychologists and other students of work has served to enlighten us about a wide variety of career discontinuities. However, implications for assisting individuals are few and far between.

CAREER ADJUSTMENT AND LIFE ADJUSTMENT

Considering the large proportion of one's waking hours that is spent preparing for work, getting to work, working, getting home from work, and negotiating the boundaries between work and other pursuits, it is tempting to regard work as life. Considering the large proportion of one's life that is spent anticipating, preparing for, enacting, and reflecting upon a career, it is tempting to regard a career as a life. Yet, everyone understands that working is but a part—albeit a large part—of living and that a career is but a part—no matter how important a part—of a life. Other experiences are enabled by, are inhibited by, surround, intrude upon, and otherwise interact with the experiences of life at work. Ancient philosophers and contemporary psychologists remind us that, in work, we establish our identity, implement our self-referent fantasies, expiate our guilt, pay homage to our deities, reenact early family dramas, develop the capacity for intimacy, escape from unwanted intimacies, satisfy neurotic and healthy cravings, insulate ourselves from pain, and pursue our own demise. Making a life while making a living stands for each of us as the developmental meta-task that transcends all life's stages and endures all pretension to "having it made."

For some, the problem is relatively simple: Work is an unpleasant necessity that provides the means for enjoying what life is really about. It must be suffered and, as long as the suffering produces the wherewithal, the prize is worth the price. For others, there is nothing but work; nonwork experiences, obligations, and entitlements are merely incidental to the essence of being—or becoming—who one is at work. But, for most, the expectation is that the manner in which the career role is enacted will influence, and be influenced by, the other roles that constitute a life (Super, 1980).

Attempts to understand the intricacies of this influence process have occupied a variety of investigators from several specialty areas. Almost without exception, the crucial data are measures of satisfaction with work and satisfaction with life. Therefore, as was true with attitudes about work, the available insights are derived from reactive, hedonic self-reports.

Quality of Life

The affluence of American society since World War II and the heightened awareness of dissatisfaction in the presence of such affluence have brought the phrase *quality of life* to the fore as part of everyday language. The idea that one might have a good job, a nice home, a sympathetic spouse, and children with naturally straight teeth and still not be happy is now common in our social discourse. An apparent rise in teleological thinking about work—itself probably a product of sustained affluence—has further emphasized the wisdom of asking oneself from time to time: "All things considered, how am I?"

For the purposes of disciplined inquiry, what is meant by quality of life must be explicit and agreed upon. Rice (1984) provided the most adequate definition available to date:

> The quality of life is the degree to which the experience of an individual's life satisfies that individual's wants and needs (both physical and psychological). (p. 157)

Rice recognized that conceptual distinctions could be made between objective quality of life—that is, meeting specified standards by verifiable conditions—and perceived quality of life, but he also recognized that what we have learned about quality of life (QL) has been based on data representing the set of affective beliefs one holds about one's life, i.e., perceived QL.

For our immediate purposes, it is useful to think about how work contributes to one's perceptions of QL and how work coexists with nonwork in the processes of influencing it. In the absence of comprehensive theory, three rather vague hypotheses have guided much of the research on this issue. The *spillover* hypothesis suggests that affective reactions to work carry over to the rest of one's activities, creating a similarity in reactions to work and nonwork. The *compensation* hypothesis suggests that individuals seek nonwork activities that provide for needs not satisfied at work, leading to dissimilar reactions to the two spheres of experience. The *segmentation* hypothesis suggests that reactions to work and nonwork are unrelated, because of the separate nature of the classes of experience as they are ordered in our society or the individual's efforts to keep them separate. Rice's (1984) review of all reported relationships through 1979 persuaded him that "no one of these hypotheses has received consistent and unambiguous empirical support" (p. 162).

Job Satisfaction and Life Satisfaction

Despite the lack of consistent support for the explanatory hypotheses linking satisfaction with work to satisfaction with life, the appealing logic that the two are related has been a stimulus for many investigators. Rice, Near, and Hunt (1980) identified 23 studies of the phenomenon containing 379 empirical relationships between job satisfaction and life satisfaction. Nearly all of the reported relationships were positive, and most were statistically significant. The mean and median of the observed correlations were .31, estimating that about 10% of the common variance was accounted for. An analysis of the studies reported from 1939 to 1979 revealed no temporal influences, despite speculations about changes in the work ethic and work orientation over time.

Since Rice's review, many investigators have continued to support the conclusion that the two realms of satisfaction are related (Arias, 1984; Blase & Pajak, 1986; DeJong & Verhage, 1985, 1987; Greenhaus, Bedeian, & Mossholder, 1987; Kopelman, Greenhaus, & Connolly, 1983; Mykletun, 1984; Wiener, Muczyk, & Gable, 1987), and to explore in detail the complexities of the relationship. Many of the investigators have focused on facets of job satisfaction instead of global satisfaction, and on domains of life satisfaction as distinct from overall life satisfaction. No major conceptual gains have resulted, but some interesting suggestions have emerged. The general puzzlement over why the relationship between satisfaction with work and satisfaction with life is so low has led to speculation that there may be powerful suppresser variables that are masking what are really greater amounts of shared variance. However, Rice's (1984) analysis convinced him that the magnitude of the observed relationship is not suppressed.

The notion that different subgroups will produce different relationships has also been an attractive one. In fact, Rice et al. (1980) did find patterns of stronger relationships for males than for females. However, Kavanagh and Halpern (1977) demonstrated that such findings can be confounded by occupational level. Brief and Hollenbeck (1985) also showed that occupational level was an important moderator. Gender per se does not seem to be an important moderator (Beutell & O'Hare, 1987; Sekaran, 1986b), but there is growing evidence that career orientation is (Beutell & Greenhaus, 1982; Peitromonaco, Manis, & Markus, 1987; Pryor & Reeves, 1982; Sekaran, 1986b; Steiner & Truxillo, 1987). Keller (1987) found no subgroup differences in life–work satisfaction among White, Hispanic, and Black Americans, and Mexican nationals; but two studies demonstrated that, among Hispanics, the degree of acculturation played an important role (Hawkes, Guagnano, Smith, & Forest, 1984; Lang, Munoz, Bernal, & Sorenson, 1982). Attempts to identify social class (Ferree, 1984) and educational level (King & Hautaluoma, 1987) as moderators were unsuccessful.

Although the search for subgroup differences that moderate the work satisfaction–life satisfaction relationship continues (Morrow, Mullen, & McElroy, 1990) and shows signs of accelerating, the question of whether different subgroups can be reliably expected to experience these satisfactions differently is far from settled. Two issues cloud the picture and inhibit confidence: sampling and statistical analysis. Most investigators use samples of convenience rather than probability samples, and few investigators put the suspected moderator to the rigorous test of demonstrating unique variance. Only Rice (1984) and his colleagues avoided these pitfalls. Their conclusion is that the relationship between job satisfaction and life satisfaction is not moderated by demographic characteristics or by individual differences in work salience. The rigor and comprehensiveness of Rice's work argue strongly for his view on this important question. Furthermore, he concluded from his work that, when job satisfaction and life satisfaction are measured reliably, the correlation between them is nearly .50, accounting for about 25% of the common variance.

Work, Nonwork, and Life Satisfaction

There is little doubt that satisfaction with life is related to satisfaction with work, but it is equally apparent that life circumstances other than those at work contribute in powerful ways. In fact, the convention of separating work and nonwork in seeking to understand satisfaction with life is more of a pedagogical device than an accurate representation of human phenomenology. Near, Smith, Rice, and Hunt (1984) illustrated this point with their analysis of a large-scale quality of employment survey. They concluded that: (a) job satisfaction explains less variance in life satisfaction than does satisfaction with nonwork conditions; (b) job satisfaction and working conditions combined explain less variance in life satisfaction than do nonwork satisfaction and living conditions combined; (c) job satisfaction and nonwork satisfaction explain more variance in life satisfaction than do working conditions and living conditions combined; and (d) living conditions explain a significant portion of the variance in job satisfaction, and working conditions explain a significant portion of the variance in nonwork satisfaction. Boundaries between what is work and what is not do exist in time and place, but the existence of such boundaries in the human experience does not seem likely. Near and her colleagues are not alone in their recognition of the importance of nonwork conditions (Bergermaier, Borg, & Champoux,

1984), nor in their appreciation of the complexities of the patterns of satisfactions (Linn, Yager, Cope, & Leake, 1986; Shaffer, 1987).

No area of inquiry has attracted more attention in recent years than that having to do with being both a worker and a family member. The variety of ways in which these two roles enable each other, conflict, evoke coping strategies, and otherwise influence the quality of life are among the most lively topics of research and scholarship in the entire career arena (e.g., Gilbert & Rachlin, 1987; Thompson & Walker, 1989). There seems to be little doubt that the work stresses experienced by one spouse are influential in the life satisfaction of the other (Bamberg, Ruckert, & Udris, 1986; Burke, 1982) and that support from the nonworking spouse is facilitative of the well-being of the other (Bambert et al., 1986; Ladewig & McGee, 1986). When both spouses work, the problems of balancing roles and sharing chores become magnified. The simple fact that wives work has been shown to have a negative effect on the life satisfaction of their husbands (Staines, Pottick, & Fudge, 1985, 1986).

The presence of children complicates the satisfaction picture for both spouses (Amaro, Russo, & Johnson, 1987; Googins & Burden, 1987; Holtzman & Gilbert, 1987; Lewis & Cooper, 1987; Sund & Ostwald, 1985), but not necessarily for the children (Knaub, 1986). Husbands and wives seem to react differently to the stresses of the multiple roles (Sekaran, 1983, 1984, 1985), although, for both, nonwork issues contribute more to overall life satisfaction.

FACILITATING CAREER ADJUSTMENT IN THE WORKPLACE

The extensive research on the antecedents and correlates of career adjustment has not led to comparable diligence in investigating the effects of methods to promote it. The literature is replete with prescriptive and descriptive approaches for facilitating work adjustment, but few studies have examined the impact of these interventions on the populations they are intended to serve. This shortcoming, although noteworthy, is not surprising. Interventions in the workplace are often provided by professionals who lack the requisite skills and training to conduct well-conceived studies of their impact. Furthermore, rewards and recognition for human services in most organizational settings are typically unconnected to actual effects, and are more directly linked to good intentions and the ability to elicit self-reported satisfaction from their target populations. Thus, for example, efforts to promote career self-awareness are judged on the basis of employees' *reporting* greater insight rather than on demonstrable evidence of having actually achieved it.

This is not to say that the literature is devoid of important contributions to our understanding of what works, what doesn't, and what might. This section focuses on three types of interventions: those that facilitate aspects of career development, those addressing employee personal problems, and those specifically targeted toward helping individuals cope with stress and burnout. The latter could more appropriately be considered a subcategory of "personal problems," but is handled separately here because of the considerable attention it has received in the literature.

Included here are only those interventions associated with the workplace. One could argue, quite correctly, that there are many services available to individuals outside of their work setting that can influence career adjustment. It is not unreasonable to assume that individuals who seek personal counseling or psychotherapy from a private practitioner may receive help on issues at least indirectly related to their success and satisfaction at work. Such interventions, however, are outside the scope of this chapter.

Career Counseling and Development

The recent surge in the popularity of programs intended to promote the career development of individuals at work is well documented (Gutteridge, 1986; Gutteridge & Otte, 1983; Keller & Piotrowski, 1987). Career development interventions remain popular in enlightened organizations because they are seen as having the potential to meet both organizational and individual needs. The benefits for organizations, it is assumed, are the enhancement of employee performance and satisfaction, reduction of turnover and absenteeism, and the opportunity to optimize individual talents. For the individual, efforts to enhance career development are seen as having the potential to influence the overall quality of their work lives.

A fundamental tenet in career development strategies is that, ultimately, each individual is responsible for his or her own career. However, equally important to the success of career interventions in the workplace is the recognition that individual initiative to achieve increased success and satisfaction is quickly stifled if the environment (i.e., the organization) does not provide the support necessary to reinforce employee actions.

This recognition, that career adjustment is a function of both individual and organizational characteristics, has led to models of organizational career systems. Schein (1978) proposed a model based on the notion that traditional organizational human resource activities, such as recruitment, performance appraisal, training and development, must be congruent with both organizational needs and individual needs, in order to both maximize organizational effectiveness and enhance individual satisfaction. Leibowitz, Farren, and Kaye (1986) described a comprehensive approach for developing career systems that includes assessing individual and organizational needs, designing intervention strategies, integrating new activities with existing approaches, ensuring organizational commitment, and evaluating effectiveness.

These models typically include a description of specific practices necessary to promote organizational careers. Gutteridge (1986) distinguished between *career management processes* and *career planning.* The former are traditional human resource activities intended primarily to serve the needs of the organization, such as those described above. The latter focuses on the individual's need to choose appropriate jobs and engage in career self-development. Gutteridge suggested that effective career systems must incorporate the following tools and techniques: (a) self-assessment activities, such as career planning workshops and career workbooks; (b) individual counseling by personnel staff, professional counselors, or managers; (c) internal labor market information, typically communicated through job posting, skills inventories, career ladders/paths, and/or career resource centers; (d) organizational potential assessment processes such as assessment centers, promotability forecasts, succession planning, and/or psychological testing; and (e) development programs, such as job rotations, training programs, external seminars, tuition reimbursement/educational assistance, supervisor training in career counseling, dual-career programs, and mentoring systems.

Despite efforts to prescribe the appropriate conditions necessary to promote career development, there is a wide gap between what is desired and what is practiced. Noting inconsistencies in what is generally termed *career planning,* Brooks (1984) nevertheless identified several commonalities. Individual career planning in the workplace generally includes some method of fostering individual self-assessment, career exploration, occupational choice, goal setting, and planning; the intention to bring about movement and growth; and the belief that career planning interventions are useful at various points throughout one's life.

Career development interventions are not necessarily targeted toward individuals' experiencing problems in work adjustment. In many cases, in fact, career development activities are made available to well-adjusted employees who are expected to benefit from the opportunity to acquire the skills and attitudes necessary to manage future opportunities more effectively. However, in addition to what might be considered a "generic" approach to helping individuals with their career development and planning, some programs have been developed for populations considered to have special needs, for example, entry-level employees (Baker & Berry, 1987), plateaued workers (Bardwick, 1986), midcareer changers (Brown, 1981; Heald, 1977; Isaacson, 1981; Talley, 1982; Thomas & Shepher, 1975), and terminated employees receiving outplacement counseling (Burdett, 1988).

No subgroup of the working population has attracted more attention than women. The extensive literature on this subgroup better summarized elsewhere (Heilman, 1983; Kanter, 1979; Morrison, White, & Van Velsor, 1987; Terborg, 1977). However, it is worth noting that societal attitudes toward women seeking careers, sex-role stereotyping, parental influences, and dual-career couple dilemmas are all believed to trigger role conflicts and self-defeating behaviors that set women apart from their male counterparts (Borman, 1986). This has led some researchers to the conclusion that women require a variety of techniques for assessment, goal setting, and intervention, in addition to the more traditional methods of promoting career choice and work adjustment (Fee-Fulkerson, 1988; Richman, 1988).

Personal Counseling

The problem of substance abuse in the workplace has long been a concern of employers. Decades ago, employers recognized that alcoholism among workers led to increased turnover, work-related accidents, loss of productivity, absenteeism, and increased health care costs (Steele, 1989). This recognition led to the emergence of Employee Assistance Programs (EAPs)—services provided to employees who required help in dealing with their problem drinking.

In recent years, EAPs have been expanded to help employees cope with a wider range of personal and emotional problems. Trice and Beyer (1984) traced the EAP movement from the early, job-based, alcoholism treatment programs to the present. For example, helping employees cope with problems of drug abuse has become increasingly important over the past two decades and is now a major emphasis in EAPs (Backer, 1988b). O'Hara and Backer (1989) identified and analyzed 35 studies on workplace drug abuse programs, drug-testing programs, incidence of drug use in the workplace, and treatment-strategy effectiveness.

The types of problems that fall under the purview of EAPs are not limited to substance abuse (McClellan & Miller, 1988). Employees with mental health, financial, marital, eldercare, legal, and other personal problems unrelated to alcohol or other drugs are often referred to EAPs. Backer (1988a) described the role of worksite programs in helping employees with the range of problems associated with AIDS. Anderson and Stark (1985) presented a proposal for how EAPs could help with the stress associated with relocation. The common theme that unites these disparate problems is the employee and his or her job performance; that is, EAPs are an employer's response to helping troubled employees with problems that have had a direct or indirect effect on their job performance.

EAP services take various forms, including direct in-house services, referrals to community agencies, and contracts for services with outside consultants or companies.

Services may be sponsored by the organization itself or by unions serving the workers employed by the organization. The type of service offered is generally determined by available resources, number of employees, the extent to which services are available in the community, and the organization's policy regarding its own responsibility for helping troubled employees.

Employees' managers play a key role in the success of EAPs. Recommendations abound for the role that managers should play in helping employees with personal problems. Some advocate that managers should provide coaching themselves; others insist that the manager's role is simply to identify the problem and make the appropriate referral for professional help. Some empirical data suggest that a technique referred to as "constructive confrontation" has been found to be an effective means for supervisors to help employees with their problems. This approach involves supervisors' confronting employees with evidence of unsatisfactory job performance, coaching them on ways to improve, urging them to use EAPs, and emphasizing the consequences of continued poor performance (Sonnenstuhl, 1989). Gerstein, Eichenhofer, and Bayer (1989) found a relationship between constructive confrontation training and industrial supervisors' recognition of impaired employees. On the other hand, Groeneveld and Shain (1985) observed that many, if not most, supervisors are unskilled in the appropriate techniques for helping their troubled employees. In all cases, however, the supervisor's response must be driven by observed performance problems on the job.

Rigorous and empirically sound evaluations of EAPs' effectiveness are rare. However, Steele and Hubbard (1985) did examine the relationships among organizational style, perceptions of the extent of substance abuse, and the structure and process of EAPs among a random sample of employees from seven corporations. Organizational climate and satisfaction were inversely related to the extent of substance abuse in the workplace; the majority of employees were unaware of EAP policies and procedures; and EAPs tended to be poorly integrated with organizations' administrative hierarchy. This last finding is consistent with Sonnenstuhl's (1989) observation that increased cooperation and integration of EAPs with health promotion and quality-of-work/life programs is necessary for effective management of alcohol problems. Despite the absence of research, EAPs remain widely regarded as critical elements of an organization's efforts to help workers resolve their personal problems and return to productive employment.

EAPs, by definition, identify the employee as "the problem." Some observers have reasonably asserted that characteristics of the workplace may cause, or at least predispose, some individuals to become problems. Trice and Sonnenstuhl (1988), in a thoughtful review of work culture perspectives, argued that administrative and occupational subcultures establish norms for alcohol use. For example, disciplinary policies, workplace conditions (e.g., boredom, overload), and/or workplace alienation may cause distress, which employees seek to relieve through drinking. They presented implications for future research and guidelines for reducing risk factors associated with alcoholism.

Stress/Burnout Interventions

The literature on stress in the workplace and the numerous ways to confront it has increased dramatically in recent years. Just what constitutes stress and/or burnout and how they differ are matters of continuing debate. Numerous interventions exist to try to reduce the stress/burnout of employees. Jaffe, Scott, and Orioli (1986) attempted to categorize the various types of stress interventions. They identified five: educational/awareness building; assessment-focused; skill building (focused on relaxation, coping, and interpersonal skills); therapeutic/counseling; and organizational/environmental change.

Research on the effects of various stress management approaches has produced conflicting results. Ivancevich and Matteson (1986) correctly observed that, despite public perceptions, stress management interventions in the workplace that have incorporated well-designed evaluations have rarely been attempted. Nevertheless, several studies pointing to the potential effect of well-designed stress management programs have been conducted. Higgins (1986) compared the effectiveness of two multicomponent programs: (a) combined progressive relaxation and systematic desensitization, and (b) a program involved with offering instruction in time management, rational-emotive therapy, and assertiveness training. No differences were found between the programs; both led to significant decreases in emotional exhaustion and personal strain. Bruning and Frew (1987) also compared three types of interventions (i.e., management skills training, relaxation, and meditation) and found that each led to decreases in pulse rate and systolic blood pressure. Relaxation and biofeedback techniques have also been related to lower absenteeism and higher attendance (Murphy & Sorenson, 1988), less self-reported psychological and physical strain, and higher job satisfaction (Orpen, 1984). These results are promising, but Ivancevich and Matteson's call for more and better investigations of stress management interventions remains salient. This is especially true in light of the rapid proliferation of approaches that claim to have an impact.

CONCLUSIONS

The achievements of psychologists devoted to understanding people at work are substantial. Activity in this arena has increased dramatically in recent years, as has the concern of some portion of the counseling psychology specialty for contributing to our understanding of the antecedents, concomitants, and sequels of success and satisfaction at work. However, as Hackett et al. (1991) pointed out, counseling researchers have largely overlooked career adjustment as an object of inquiry, focusing instead on issues of career entry. Furthermore, practitioners in organizational settings attend to matters of career adjustment mainly at circumscribed time segments such as transitions (entry, retirement) and crises (burnout, separation). Even programs labeled career development in the most sophisticated organizations focus on limited points in the lives of the worker rather than on the course of a working life. We are forced to conclude, therefore, that the concept of career as a lifelong process does not serve as a guide for either research or practice. The reasons for this are clearly understood, but they remain as impediments to fuller understanding of life at work and to better designs for interventions to improve it.

It remains for future researchers to press opportunities to make observations of people at work in longer time segments. Although it seems unlikely that many investigators will enjoy the luxury of a 20-year study such as the one Howard and Bray (1988) reported, some will find openings to make observations over time, at repeated times, and/or with overlapping cohorts. Such openings are much more likely to occur if investigators propose their studies with expanded time sequences in the first place. The acceptance rate for such proposals within organizations will not be as high as for "running a quick survey," but it is not likely to be zero. Contemporary managers are much more likely to think in developmental terms than were their predecessors and much more confident about the value of career research for their enterprises.

The preponderance of research on work attitudes poses an interesting challenge for researchers of the future. The advantages of the job satisfaction survey and the organizational commitment questionnaire are obvious, but the limits of the insights they provide are equally apparent. The value of aggregated, reactive, hedonic responses cannot be denied; however, other insights would surely emerge from examining how workers construe themselves at work, how those constructs change, how they differ from worker to worker, how they fit with self-constructs when one is not at work, and so on. Hackett et al. (1991) were cautiously optimistic about how emerging cognitive perspectives might assist in this kind of inquiry, yet they recognized that such work is in its preliminary stages. Even if they are based on cognitive theories, the invention of methods for observing the phenomenology of self-at-work in ways that are not constrained by the researcher's favorite technology would add to the understanding of career adjustment in important ways. It remains to be seen whether cognitive schemata will fulfill their promise, whether personal constructs (Kelly, 1955) will return to favor, or whether new methods and techniques will be created. Progress in any such direction will add texture to the fabric that has been woven from the work attitudes research and further enable students of career adjustment.

It is encouraging to observe the growing interest in how experiences at work relate to other experiences of life. Although that line of inquiry is limited by the same observation technologies that limit the research on work attitudes, it represents an important expansion of what are considered data of merit in career adjustment. The relationship of work satisfaction to life satisfaction has long seemed an obvious—if foreboding—topic for students of careers. Rice et al. (1980) helped to make it less foreboding. The research tasks for the future are to transcend the limitations of method—the single time slice, the one-item scale—and expand the operational definitions of the principal variables. Of all of the items on the agenda for future research on career adjustment, this one seems the most doable and the one most worth doing.

There is no longer any doubt that counseling interventions in the workplace are seen as appropriate, have been eagerly sought by organizations, and are widely accepted. The conditions that led to Osipow's (1982) observation about counseling psychologists' neglect of that setting have changed, in less than a decade, sufficiently to encourage Gerstein and Shullman to predict, in Chapter 18, that counseling interventions in organizations may well stimulate the creation of a subspecialty within counseling psychology. The rapid growth of professional literature on psychological interventions in organizations gives testimony to the fact that considerable interest exists and that those who are interested are eager to communicate about their experiences to their intellectual peers. It is particularly interesting to observe the way in which EAPs, which were created to help with worker problems of alcohol abuse, have expanded in scope to the current state of "broad brush" counseling services that are available to employees regardless of the source of their need for service. In some ways, this expansion parallels the transformation of the university counseling centers of the 1940s from vocational guidance services for World War II veterans to the comprehensive student development centers of today. The lesson may well be that, once counseling services are established in a new setting, acceptance grows and the appreciation of their value leads to expansion of their functions well beyond the original intent.

Of special importance to counseling psychologists are the growth and acceptance of career development services within organizations. The origins of the EAP can be traced to labor unions, recovering alcoholics, and social workers; the roots of career development programs and services rest undeniably in the soil of counseling psychology. The recognition of the need for them, the principles that guide their design, and, in many cases, the people who provide them are of and from the specialty. No other psychological specialty and no other mental health profession possessed the interest, the theories, or the techniques to introduce career development services to organizations and to establish them in their currently secure positions. The shortcomings in our understanding of the concepts that make up career adjustment are cause for considerable humility, but our success at making career services available in the workplace permit no small amount of pride.

We noted earlier that research on the efficacy of psychological interventions in organizations is either nonexistent or badly flawed, and we offered some suggestions for why this is so. Although we regard this as a natural state of affairs, it is not a necessary one. The fact that officers of organizations do not need to publish peer-reviewed research to be retained and promoted depresses the probability that rigorous outcome research will flow from them. The fact that most organizations exist in a competitive atmosphere depresses the probability that rigorous evaluative research, once done, would be shared with competitors. But rigorous evaluative research has been done on some topics and put into the public domain by academics who collaborate with organizations and by organizational officers who seek acceptance and prestige from their fellow professionals. Volumes of research on work attitudes, work withdrawal behaviors, and similar topics have been produced and published. Our point is that the scarcity of well-done research on the impact of counseling interventions within organizations results from the newness of the phenomenon. We fully anticipate that when counseling interventions in organizations are firmly established and considered to be indispensable components of adequate organizations, evaluations of interventions will begin to appear and rapidly increase in rigor. The opportunities for the researchers of the future will, we suspect, be rich for those who pursue program evaluation and treatment-outcome paradigms. In the not too distant future, it will be as easy to study the effects of counseling in an EAP as it is now to study the same phenomenon in a university counseling center. Someday, it will be as easy to study the sequels of a career planning program in an organization as it is now to study one in a community college.

REFERENCES

Amaro, H., Russo, N. F., & Johnson, J. (1987). Family and work predictors of psychological well-being among Hispanic women professionals. *Psychology of Women Quarterly, 121,* 505–521.

Anderson, C., & Stark, C. (1985). Emerging issues from job relocation in the high-tech field: Implications for Employee Assistance Programs. *Employee Assistance Quarterly, 1,* 37–54.

Angle, H. L., & Perry, J. L. (1983). Organizational commitment: Individual and organizational influences. *Work and Occupations, 10,* 123–146.

Arias, G. F. (1984). Some organizational factors and psychological quality of life. *Organization Development Journal, 2,* 2–3.

Arsenault, A., & Dolan, S. (1983). The role of personality, occupation, and organization in understanding the relationship between job stress, performance, and absenteeism, *Journal of Occupational Psychology, 56,* 227–240.

Backer, T. E. (1988a). Managing AIDS at work: Psychology's role. *American Psychologist, 43,* 983–987.

Backer, T. E. (1988b). Workplace drug abuse problems: Consultation issues and opportunities. *Consultation: An International Journal, 7,* 216–227.

Baker, H. G., & Berry, V. M. (1987). Processes and advantages of entry-level career counseling. *Personnel Journal, 66,* 111–121.

Bakke, E. W. (1933). *The unemployed man.* London: Nisbet.

Bamberg, E., Ruckert, D., & Udris, I. (1986). Interactive effects of social support from wife, non-work activities and blue-collar occupational stress. *International Review of Applied Psychology, 35,* 297–413.

Barber, G. (1986). Correlates of job satisfaction among human service workers. *Administration in Social Work, 10,* 25–38.

Bardwick, J. (1986). *The plateauing trap.* Toronto: Bantam.

Benesch, K. F. (1986). The displaced farmer: Career counseling concerns. *Career Development Quarterly, 35,* 7–13.

Bergermaier, R., Borg, I., & Champoux, J. E. (1984). Structural relationships among facets of work, nonwork, and general well-being. *Work and Occupations, 11,* 163–181.

Beutell, N. J., & Greenhaus, J. H. (1982). Interrole conflict among married women: The influence of husband and wife characteristics on conflict and coping behavior. *Journal of Vocational Behavior, 21,* 99–110.

Beutell, N. J., & O'Hare, M. M. (1987). Work–nonwork conflict among MBA's: Sex differences in role stressors and life satisfaction. *Work and Stress, 1,* 35–41.

Blase, J. J., & Pajak, E. F. (1986). The impact of teachers' work life on personal life: A qualitative analysis. *Alberta Journal of Educational Research, 32,* 307–322.

Blau, G. J. (1985a). A multiple study investigation of the dimensionality of job involvement. *Journal of Vocational Behavior, 27,* 19–36.

Blau, G. J. (1985b). The measurement and prediction of career commitment. *Journal of Occupational Psychology, 58,* 227–288.

Blau, G. J. (1986). Job involvement and organizational commitment as interactive predictors of tardiness and absenteeism. *Journal of Management, 12,* 577–584.

Blau, G. J. (1987). Using a person–environment fit model to predict job involvement and organizational commitment. *Journal of Vocational Behavior, 30,* 240–257.

Blostein, S., Eldridge, W., Kilty, K., & Richardson, V. (1985-86). A multidimensional analysis of the concept of burnout. *Employee Assistance Quarterly, 1,* 55–66.

Blustein, D. L. (1990, August). *Vocational realm of counseling psychology.* Paper presented at the annual meeting of the American Psychological Association, Boston, MA.

Borman, C. A. (1986). The career development of women: Helping Cinderella lose her complex. *The Journal of Career Development, 12,* 250–261.

Breaugh, J. A. (1983). Realistic job previews: A critical appraisal and future directions. *Academy of Management Review, 8,* 612–619.

Brenner, M. H. (1976). *Estimating the social costs of national economic policy: Implications for mental and physical health, and criminal aggression.* Library of Congress, Congressional Research Service. Washington, DC: U.S. Government Printing Office.

Brief, A. P., Burke, M. J., & George, J. M. (1988). Should negative affectivity remain an unmeasured variable in the study of job stress? *Journal of Applied Psychology, 73,* 193–198.

Brief, A. P., & Hollenbeck, J. R. (1985). Work and the quality of life. *Instructional Journal of Psychology, 20,* 199–206.

Brockner, J., Grover, S. H., & Blonder, M. D. (1988). Predictors of survivors' job involvement following layoffs: A field study. *Journal of Applied Psychology, 73,* 436–442.

Brooke, P. P., Jr., Russell, D. W., & Price, J. L. (1988). Discriminant validation of measures of job satisfaction, job involvement, and organizational commitment. *Journal of Applied Psychology, 73,* 139–145.

Brooks, L. (1984). Career planning programs in the workplace. In D. Brown & L. Brooks (Eds.), *Career choice and development* (pp. 388–405). San Francisco: Jossey-Bass.

Brown, D. (1981). Emerging models of career development groups for persons at midlife. *Vocational Guidance Quarterly, 29,* 232–340.

Brown, S. D., & Heath, R. (1984). Coping with critical life events: An integrative cognitive-behavioral model for research and practice. In S. D. Brown & R. W. Lent (Eds.), *Handbook of counseling psychology* (pp. 545–578). New York: Wiley.

Bruning, N. S., & Frew, D. R. (1987). The effects of exercise, relaxation, and management skills training on psychological stress indicators: A field experiment. *Journal of Applied Psychology, 72,* 515–521.

Burdett, J. O. (1988). Easing the way out. *Personnel Administration, 33,* 157–166.

Burke, R. J. (1982). Occupational demands on administrators and spouses' satisfaction and well-being. *Psychological Reports, 51,* 823–836.

Burke, R. H., & Deszca, G. (1988). Career orientations, satisfaction and health among police officers: Some consequences of person–job misfit. *Psychological Reports, 62,* 639–649.

Carlopio, J. (1988). A history of social psychological reactions to new technology. *Journal of Occupational Psychology, 61,* 67–77.

Carsten, J. M., & Spector, P. E. (1987). Unemployment, job satisfaction, and employee turnover: A meta-analytic test of the Muchinsky model. *Journal of Applied Psychology, 72,* 374–381.

Coche, J. M., & Coche, E. (1986). Leaving the institutional setting to enter private practice: A mid-life crisis resolution. *Psychotherapy in Private Practice, 4*(3), 43–50.

Cohn, R. M. (1978). The effect of employment status change on self attitudes. *Social Psychology, 41,* 81–93.

Colarelli, S. M., Dean, R. A., & Konstans, C. (1987). Comparative effects of personal and situational influences on job outcomes of new professionals. *Journal of Applied Psychology, 72,* 558–566.

Collins, A. (1983). A mid-career perspective on the opportunity-structure/occupational-choice debate. *British Journal of Guidance and Counselling, 11,* 52–67.

Conceptual and methodological issues in person–environment fit research. (1987). *Journal of Vocational Behavior, 31*(3) [Special issue].

Cooper-Schneider, R. (1989). *An analysis of survivors' reactions to layoffs based on psychological theories of justice, organizational commitment, job insecurity, and corporate culture.* Unpublished doctoral dissertation, Columbia University, New York.

Cotton, J. L., Vollrath, D. A., & Froggatt, K. L. (1988). Employee participation: Diverse forms and different outcomes. *Academy of Management Review, 13,* 8–22.

Dalton, D. R., Krackhardt, D. M., & Porter, L. W. (1981). Functional turnover: An empirical assessment. *Journal of Applied Psychology, 66,* 716–721.

Dalton, D. R., & Todor, W. D. (1979). Turnover turned over: An expanded and positive perspective. *Academy of Management Review, 4,* 225–235.

Dawis, R. V., & Lofquist, L. H. (1984). *A psychological theory of work adjustment.* Minneapolis, MN: University of Minnesota Press.

Dawson, C. M. (1983). Will career plateauing become a bigger problem? *Personnel Journal, 62,* 78–81.

Dean, R. A., Ferris, K. R., & Konstans, C. (1988). Occupational reality shock and organizational commitment: Evidence from the accounting profession. *Accounting, Organizations and Society, 13,* 235–250.

DeCotiis, T. A., & Summers, T. P. (1987). A path analysis of a model of the antecedents and consequences of organizational commitment. *Human Relations, 40,* 445–470.

DeJong, R. D., & Verhage, J. (1985). Quality of life and depression: Research and implications for O.D. practice. *Organization Development Journal, 3*(4), 27–29.

DeJong, R. D., & Verhage, J. (1987). Quality of life and depression in entrepreneurs and managers. *Journal of Human Behavior and Learning, 4*(2), 46–53.

Dooley, D., & Catalano, R. (1980). Economic change as a cause of behavioral disorder. *Psychological Bulletin, 87,* 450–468.

Eisenberg, P., & Lazarsfeld, P. F. (1938). The psychological effects of unemployment. *Psychological Bulletin, 35,* 358–390.

Elizur, D., & Tziner, A. (1977). Vocational needs, job rewards, and satisfaction: A canonical analysis. *Journal of Vocational Behavior, 10,* 205–211.

Elton, C. F., & Smart, J. C. (1988). Extrinsic job satisfaction and person–environment congruence. *Journal of Vocational Behavior, 32,* 226–238.

Entine, A. D. (1984). Voluntary mid-life career change: Family effects. *Family Therapy Collections, 10,* 72–80.

Farrell, D., & Stamm, C. L. (1988). Meta-analysis of the correlates of employee absence. *Human Relations, 41,* 211–227.

Feather, N. J., & Davenport, P. R. (1981). Unemployment and depressive affect: A motivational and attributional analysis. *Journal of Personality and Social Psychology, 41,* 422–436.

Fee-Fulkerson, K. (1988). Changing canoes in white water: Counseling women in successful careers they dislike. *Journal of Career Development, 14,* 249–258.

Feldman, D. C., & Brett, J. M. (1983). Coping with new jobs: A comparative study of new hires and job changers. *Academy of Management Journal, 26,* 258–272.

Ference, T. P., Stoner, J. S. F., & Warren, E. K. (1977). Managing the career plateau. *Academy of Management Review, 2,* 602–612.

Ferree, M. M. (1984). Class, housework, and happiness: Women's work and life satisfaction. *Sex Roles, 11,* 1057–1074.

Fisher, C. D. (1985). Social support and adjustment to work: A longitudinal study. *Journal of Management, 11*(3), 39–53.

Fitzgerald, L. F., & Osipow, S. H. (1988). We have seen the future, but is it us? The vocational aspirations of graduate students in counseling psychology. *Professional Psychology: Research and Practice, 19,* 575–583.

Fouad, N. A. (1990, August). *The challenges of vocational psychology.* Paper presented at the annual meeting of the American Psychological Association, Boston, MA.

Gavin, J. (1982). A "Change of Heart" is not enough. *The Counseling Psychologist, 11*(3), 29–30.

Gerstein, L. H., Eichenhofer, D. J., & Bayer, G. A. (1989). EAP referral training and supervisors' beliefs about troubled workers. *Employee Assistance Quarterly, 4,* 15–30.

Gilbert, L. A., & Rachlin, V. (1987). Mental health and psychological functioning of dual-career families. *The Counseling Psychologist, 15,* 7–49.

Gilkison, B., & Drummond, R. J. (1988). Academic self-concept of older adults in career transition. *Journal of Employment Counseling, 25,* 24–29.

Glisson, C., & Durick, M. (1988). Predictors of job satisfaction and organizational commitment in human service organizations. *Administrative Science Quarterly, 33,* 61–81.

Goldner, G. H. (1965). Demotion in industrial management. American *Sociological Review, 30,* 714–724.

Gomez-Mejia, L. R. (1984). Effect of occupation on task related, contextual, and job involvement orientation: A cross-cultural perspective. *Academy of Management Journal, 27,* 706–720.

Googins, B., & Burden, D. (1987). Vulnerability of working parents: Balancing work and home roles. *Social Work, 32,* 295–300.

Gordus, J. P. (1986). Coping with involuntary job loss and building a new career: Workers' problems and career professionals' challenges. *Journal of Career Development, 12,* 316–326.

Greenhaus, J. H., Bedeian, A. G., & Mossholder, K. W. (1987). Work experience, job performance, and feelings of personal and family well-being. *Journal of Vocational Behavior, 31,* 200–215.

Groenveld, J., & Shain, M. (1985). The effect of corrective interviews with alcoholic dependent employees: A study of 37 supervisor–subordinate dyads. *Employee Assistance Quarterly, 1,* 63–73.

Gummer, B. (1987). Organizational puerperium: Employee leavings and heavings. *Administration in Social Work, 11,* 81–94.

Gutteridge, T. G. (1986). Organizational and career development systems: The state of the practice. In D. T. Hall and Associates, *Career development in organizations* (pp. 50–94). San Francisco: Jossey-Bass.

Gutteridge, T. G., & Otte, F. L. (1983). Organizational and career development: What's going on out there? *Training and Development Journal, 37,* 22–26.

Hackett, G., Lent, R. W., & Greenhaus, J. H. (1991). Advances in vocational theory and research: A 20-year perspective. *Journal of Vocational Behavior, 38,* 3–38.

Hackett, R. D., & Guion, R. M. (1985). A reevaluation of the absenteeism–job satisfaction relationship. *Organizational Behavior and Human Decision Processes, 35,* 340–381.

Hackman, J. R., & Oldham, G. R. (1976). Motivation through the design of work: Test of a theory. *Organizational Behavior and Human Performance, 126,* 250–279.

Hackman, J. R., & Oldham, G. R. (1980). *Work redesign.* Reading, MA: Addison-Wesley.

Hall, D. T., & Isabella, L. A. (1985). Downward movement and career development. *Organizational Dynamics, 14,* 5–23.

Hanlon, M. D. (1986). Age and commitment to work: a literature review and multivariate analysis. *Research on Aging, 8,* 289–316.

Harrick, E. J., Hansel, M., & Schutzius, R. E. (1982). Outplacement training: Process, content, and attitudes. *Training and Development Journal, 36,* 78–85.

Hawkes, G. R., Guagnano, G. A., Smith, J. W., & Forest, M. K. (1984). The influence of work and nonwork factors on job satisfaction for Mexican-American male workers. *Rural Sociology, 49*, 117–126.

Heald, J. E. (1977). Mid-life career influence. *Vocational Guidance Quarterly, 25,* 309–312.

Heilman, M. E. (1983). Sex bias in work settings: The lack of fit model. *Research in Organizational Behavior, 5,* 269–298.

Henton, J. M., Russell, R., & Koval, J. E. (1983). Spousal perceptions of midlife career change. *Personnel and Guidance Journal, 61,* 287–291.

Herrick, J., Takagi, C. Y., Coleman, R., & Morgan, L. J. (1983). Social workers who left the profession: An exploratory study. *Journal of Sociology and Social Welfare, 10,* 78–94.

Higgins, N. C. (1986). Occupational stress and working women: The effectiveness of two stress reduction programs. *Journal of Vocational Behavior, 29,* 66–78.

Hill, R. E., & Miller, E. L. (1981). Job change and the middle seasons of a man's life. *Academy of Management Journal, 24,* 114–127.

Holland, J. L. (1973). *Making vocational choices: A theory of careers.* Englewood Cliffs: NJ: Prentice-Hall.

Holland, J. L. (1985). *Making vocational choices: A theory of vocational personalities and work environments* (2nd ed.). Englewood Cliffs, NJ: Prentice-Hall.

Holtzman, E. H., & Gilbert, L. A. (1987). Social support networks for parenting and psychological well-being among dual-earner Mexican-American families. *Journal of Community Psychology, 15,* 176–186.

Howard, A., & Bray, D. W. (1980, September). *Career motivation in midlife managers.* Paper presented at the American Psychological Association Convention, Montreal, Canada.

Howard, A., & Bray, D. W. (1988). *Managerial lives in transition: Advancing age and changing times.* New York: Guilford Press.

Hui, C. H. (1988). Impacts of objective and subjective labour market conditions on employee turnover. *Journal of Occupational Psychology, 61,* 211–219.

Isaacson, L. E. (1981). Counseling male mid-life career changes. *Vocational Guidance Quarterly, 29,* 324–331.

Isabella, L., & Hall, D. T. (1984). Demotions and career growth. *Training and Development Journal, 38*(4), 62–64.

Ivancevich, J. M. (1985). Predicting absenteeism from prior absence and work attitudes. *Academy of Management Journal, 28,* 219–228.

Ivancevich, J. M., & Matteson, M. T. (1986). Organizational level stress management interventions: A review and recommendations. *Journal of Organizational Behavior Management, 8,* 229–248.

Jaffe, D. T., Scott, C. D., & Orioli, E. M. (1986). Stress management: Programs and prospects. *American Journal of Health Promotion, 1,* 29–37.

Jans, N. A. (1985). Organizational factors in work involvement. *Organizational Behavior and Human Decision Processes, 35,* 382–396.

Jayaratne, S., & Chess, W. A. (1986). Job stress, job deficit, emotional support, and competence: Their relationship to burnout. *Journal of Applied Social Sciences, 10,* 135–155.

Jones, G. R. (1986). Socialization tactics, self-efficacy, and newcomers' adjustments to organization. *Academy of Management Journal, 29,* 262–279.

Jones, W. H. (1979). Grief and involuntary career change: Its implications for counseling. *Vocational Guidance Quarterly, 27,* 196–201.

Kanfer, R., & Hulin, C. L. (1985). Individual differences in successful job search following layoff. *Personnel Psychology, 38,* 835–847.

Kanter, R. M. (1979). Differential access to opportunity and power. In R. Alvarez (Ed.), *Discrimination in organizations* (pp. 55–68). San Francisco: Jossey-Bass.

Kanungo, R. N. (1986). Productivity, satisfaction and involvement: A brief note on some conceptual issues. *International Journal of Manpower, 7*(5), 8–12.

Kavanagh, M. J., & Halpern, M. (1977). The impact of job level and sex differences on the relationship between job and life satisfaction. *Academy of Management Journal, 20,* 66–73.

Keller, J., & Piotrowski, C. (1987). Career development programs in Fortune 500 firms. *Psychological Reports, 61,* 920–922.

Keller, R. T. (1987). Cross-cultural influences on work and nonwork contributions to quality of life. *Group and Organizational Studies, 12,* 304–318.

Kelly, G. A. (1955). *The psychology of personal constructs.* New York: Norton.

Kemery, E. R., Mossholder, K. W., & Bedeian, A. G. (1987). Role stress, physical symptomatology, and turnover intentions: A causal analysis of three alternative specifications. *Journal of Occupational Behaviour, 8,* 11–23.

King, W. L., & Hautaluoma, J. E. (1987). Comparison of job satisfaction, life satisfaction, and performance of overeducated and other workers. *Journal of Social Psychology, 127,* 421–433.

Knaub, P. K. (1986). Growing up in a dual-career family: The children's perceptions. *Family Relations Journal of Applied Family and Child Studies, 35,* 431–437.

Knoop, R. (1986). Job involvement: An elusive concept. *Psychological Reports, 59,* 451–456.

Komarovsky, M. (1940). *The unemployed man and his family.* New York: Dryden.

Kopelman, R. E. (1986). Alternate work schedules and productivity: A review of evidence. *National Productivity Review, 5,* 150–165.

Kopelman, R. E., Greenhaus, J. H., & Connolly, T. F. (1983). A model of work, family, and interrole conflict: A construct validation study. *Organizational Behavior and Human Performance, 32,* 198–215.

Lacey, D. W. (1982). Industrial counseling psychologists. *The Counseling Psychologist, 11*(3), 49–51.

Lachman, R., & Aranya, N. (1986). Job attitudes and turnover intentions among professionals in different work settings. *Organization Studies, 7,* 279–293.

Ladewig, B. H., & McGee, G. W. (1986). Occupational commitment, a supportive family environment, and marital adjustment: Development and estimation of a model. *Journal of Marriage and the Family, 48,* 821–829.

Lane, I. M., Mathews, R. C., & Presholdt, P. H. (1988). Determinants of nurses' intentions to leave their profession. *Journal of Organizational Behavior, 9,* 367–372.

Lang, J. G., Munoz, R. F., Bernal, G., & Sorenson, J. L. (1982). Quality of life and psychological well being in a bicultural Latino community. *Hispanic Journal of Behavioral Sciences, 4,* 433–450.

Latack, J. C., & Dozier, J. B. (1986). After the ax falls: Job loss as a career transition. *Academy of Management Review, 11,* 375–392.

Lee, R., & Wilbur, E. R. (1985). Age, education, job tenure, salary, job characteristics, and job satisfaction: A multivariate analysis. *Human Relations, 38,* 781–791.

Lee, T. W. (1988). How job dissatisfaction leads to employee turnover. *Journal of Business and Psychology, 2,* 263–271.

Leibowitz, Z., Farren, C., & Kaye, B. L. (1986). *Designing career development systems.* San Francisco: Jossey-Bass.

Leigh, J. H., Lucas, G. H., & Woodman, R. W. (1988). The effects of perceived organizational factors on roll stress–job attitude relationships. *Journal of Management, 14,* 41–58.

Leigh, J. P. (1986). Correlates of absence from work due to illness. *Human Relations, 39,* 81–100.

Leigh, J. P. (1985). The effects of unemployment and business cycle on absenteeism. *Journal of Economics and Business, 37,* 159–170.

Leiter, M. P. (1988). Burnout as a function of communication patterns: A study of a multidisciplinary mental health team. *Group and Organizational Studies, 13,* 111–128.

Leiter, M. P., & Maslach, C. (1988). The impact of interpersonal environment on burnout and organizational commitment. *Journal of Organizational Behavior, 9,* 297–308.

Lewis, S. N., & Cooper, G. L. (1987). Stress in two-earner couples and stage in the life cycle. *Journal of Occupational Psychology, 60,* 289–303.

Lindstrom, K. (1988). Age-related differences in job characteristics and in their relation to job satisfaction. *Scandinavian Journal of Work, Environment and Health, 14* (Suppl. 1), 24–26.

Linn, L. S., Yager, J., Cope, D. W., & Leake, B. (1986). Factors associated with life satisfaction among practicing internists, *Medical Care, 24,* 830–837.

Locke, E. A. (1976). The nature and causes of job satisfaction. In M. D. Dannette (Ed.), *Handbook of industrial and organizational psychology.* Chicago: Rand McNally.

Lofquist, L. H., & Dawis, R. V. (1969). *Adjustment to work.* New York: Appleton-Century-Crofts.

Lofquist, L. H., & Dawis, R. V. (1984). Research on work adjustment and satisfaction: Implications for career counseling. In S. D. Brown & R. W. Lent (Eds.), *Handbook of counseling psychology*, (pp. 216–237). New York: Wiley.

Luthans, F., Baack, D., & Taylor, L. (1987). Organizational commitment: Analysis of antecedents. *Human Relations, 40*, 219–235.

Luthans, F., McCaul, H. S., & Dodd, N. G. (1985). Organizational commitment: A comparison of American, Japanese, and Korean employees. *Academy of Management Journal, 28*, 213–219.

Majchrzak, A., & Cotton, J. (1988). A longitudinal study of adjustment to technological change: From mass to computer-automated batch production. *Journal of Occupational Psychology, 61*, 43–66.

Mallinckrodt, B., & Fretz, B. R. (1988). Social support and the impact of job loss on older professionals. *Journal of Counseling Psychology, 35*, 281–286.

Malinowska, T. E. (1987). Complex measures of satisfaction/dissatisfaction among professionals. *Social Indicators Research, 19*, 451–473.

March, J., & Simon, H. A. (1958). *Organizations*. New York: Wiley.

Martin, J. K., & Miller, G. A. (1986). Job satisfaction and absenteeism: Organizational, individual, and job-related correlates. *Work and Occupations, 13*, 33–46.

Maslach, C., & Jackson, S. E. (1984). Burnout in organizational settings. *Applied Social Psychology Annual, 5*, 133–153.

Mayes, B. T., & Ganster, D. C. (1988). Exit and voice: A test of hypotheses based on fight/flight responses to job stress. *Journal of Organizational Behavior, 9*, 199–216.

McClellan, K., & Miller, R. E. (1988). EAPs in transition: Purpose and scope of services. *Employee Assistance Quarterly, 3*, 25–42.

McGee, G. W., & Ford, R. D. (1987). Two (or more?) dimensions of organizational commitment: Reexamination of the affective and continuance commitment scales. *Journal of Applied Psychology, 72*, 638–641.

McNeely, R. L. (1987). Predictors of job satisfaction among three racial/ethnic groups of professional female human service workers. *Journal of Sociology and Social Welfare, 14*, 115–136.

McNeely, R. L. (1988). Age and job satisfaction in human service employment. *Gerontologist, 28*, 163–168.

Meir, E. I., & Melamed, S. (1986). The accumulation of person–environment congruences and well-being. *Journal of Occupational Behaviour, 7*, 315–323.

Meir, E. I., & Yaari, Y. (1988). The relationship between congruent specialty choice within occupations and satisfaction. *Journal of Vocational Behavior, 33*, 99–117.

Minatoya, L. Y. (1982). Comments on counseling psychology. *The Counseling Psychologist, 11*(3), 27–28.

Minor, F. J., Slade, L. A., & Myers, R. A. (1991). Career transitions in changing times. In R. F. Morrison & J. Adams (Eds.), *Contemporary career development issues, practices and voids* (pp. 109–119). Hillsdale, NJ: Erlbaum.

Misra, S., Kanungo, R. N., von Rosensteil, L., & Stuhler, E. A. (1985). The motivational formulation of job and work involvement: A cross-national study. *Human Relations, 38*, 501–518.

Mobley, W. H. (1977). Intermediate linkages in the relationship between job satisfaction and turnover. *Journal of Applied Psychology, 62*, 237–240.

Mobley, W. H. (1982). *Employee turnover in organizations*. Reading, MA: Addison-Wesley.

Moch, M. K., & Fitzgibbons, D. E. (1985). The relationship between absenteeism and production efficiency: An empirical assessment. *Journal of Occupational Psychology, 58*, 39–47.

Morgan, L. G., & Herman, J. B. (1976). Perceived consequences of absenteeism, *Journal of Applied Psychology, 61*, 738–742.

Morrison, A. M., White, R. P., & Von Velsor, E. (1987). *Breaking the glass ceiling: Can women reach the top of America's largest corporations?* Reading, MA: Addison-Wesley.

Morrow, P. C. (1983). Concept redundancy in organizational research: The case of work commitment. *Academy of Management Review, 8*, 486–500.

Morrow, P. C., & McElroy, J. C. (1986). On assessing measures of work commitment. *Journal of Occupational Behaviour, 7*, 139–145.

Morrow, P. C., Mullen, E. J., & McElroy, J. C. (1990). Vocational behavior in 1989: The year in review. *Journal of Vocational Behavior, 37,* 121–195.

Mottaz, C. J. (1987). Age and work satisfaction. *Work and Occupations, 14,* 387–409.

Mottaz, C. J. (1988). Determinants of organizational commitment. *Human Relations, 41,* 467–482.

Mount, M. K. (1984). Managerial career stage and facets of job satisfaction. *Journal of Vocational Behavior, 24,* 340–354.

Munsterberg, H. (1913). *Psychology and industrial efficiency.* Boston: Houghton Mifflin.

Murphy, L. R., & Sorenson, S. (1988). Employee behaviors before and after stress management. *Journal of Organizational Behavior, 9,* 173–182.

Mykletun, R. J. (1984). Teacher stress: Perceived and objective sources, and quality of life. *Scandinavian Journal of Educational Research, 28,* 17–45.

Nagy, S., & Davis, L. G. (1985). Burnout: A comparative analysis of personality and environmental variables. *Psychological Reports, 57,* 1319–1326.

Napoli, D. S. (1981). *Architects of adjustment. The history of the psychological profession in the United States.* Port Washington, NY: Kennikat Press.

Near, J. P., Smith, C. A., Rice, R. W., & Hunt, R. G. (1984). A comparison of work and nonwork predictors of life satisfaction. *Academy of Management Journal, 27,* 184–190.

Nicholson, N. (1984). A theory of work role transitions. *Administrative Science Quarterly, 29,* 172–191.

Nicholson, N., & Johns, G. (1985). The absence culture and the psychological contract: Who's in control of absence? *Academy of Management Review, 10,* 397–407.

Nowack, K. M. (1987). Health habits, Type A behavior and job burnout. *Work and Stress, 1,* 135–142.

O'Hara, K., & Backer, T. E. (1989). Index of research studies on workplace drug abuse and EAPs. *Employee Assistance Quarterly, 4,* 79–100.

Orpen, C. (1984). Managerial stress, relaxation and performance. *Journal of Management Development, 3,* 34–47.

Osipow, S. H. (1982). Counseling psychology: Applications in the world of work. *The Counseling Psychologist, 10*(3), 19–25.

Parkes, K. R. (1987). Relative weight, smoking, and mental health as a predictor of sickness and absence from work. *Journal of Applied Psychology, 72,* 275–286.

Patterson, L. E., Sutton, R. E., & Schuttenberg, E. M. (1987). Plateaued careers, productivity, and career satisfaction of college of education faculty. *Career Development Quarterly, 35,* 197–205.

Pearson, J. M. (1982). The transition into a new job: Tasks, problems, and outcomes. *Personnel Journal, 61,* 286–290.

Penn, M., Romano, J. L., & Foat, D. (1988). The relationship between job satisfaction and burnout: A study of human service professionals, *Administration in Mental Health, 15,* 157–165.

Perosa, S. L., & Perosa, L. M. (1983). The midcareer crisis: A description of the psychological dynamics of transition and adaptation. *Vocational Guidance Quarterly, 32,* 69–79.

Peitromonaco, P. R., Manis, J., & Markus, H. (1987). The relationship of employment to self-perception of well-being in women: A cognitive analysis. *Sex Roles, 17,* 467–477.

Pond, S. B., & Geyer, P. D. (1987). Employee age as a modifier of the relationship between perceived work alternatives and job satisfaction. *Journal of Applied Psychology, 72,* 552–557.

Pryor, M. G., & Reeves, J. B. (1982). Male and female patterns of work opportunity structure and life satisfaction. *International Journal of Women's Studies, 5,* 215–226.

Reichers, A. E. (1985). A review and reconceptualization of organizational commitment. *Academy of Management Review, 10,* 465–476.

Rice, R. W. (1984). Organizational work and the overall quality of life. *Applied Social Psychological Annual, 5,* 155–178.

Rice, R. W., Near, J. P., & Hunt, R. G. (1980). The job-satisfaction/life-satisfaction relationship: A review of empirical research. *Basic and Applied Social Psychology, 1,* 337–364.

Richman, D. R. (1988). Cognitive career counseling for women. *Journal for Rational-Emotive Therapy, 6,* 50–65.

Ridley, C. R., & Hellervik, L. W. (1982). Counseling psychology in the corporate environment. *The Counseling Psychologist, 11*(3), 53–54.

Rothstein, W. G. (1980). The significance of occupations in work careers: An empirical and theoretical review. *Journal of Vocational Behavior, 17*, 328–343.

Sahni, V. B., & Chadha, N. K. (1987). Psychological factors in job involvement: A cross cultural study. *Indian Journal of Behaviours, 11*(4), 17–22.

Salancik, G. R., & Pfeffer, J. (1977). An examination of need satisfaction models of job attitudes. *Administrative Science Quarterly, 22*, 427–456.

Savickas, M. L. (1990, August). *Career development at the crossroads: Current concerns and future directions.* Symposium conducted at the meeting of the American Psychological Association, Boston, MA.

Scarpello, V., & Campbell, J. P. (1983). Job satisfaction and the fit between individual needs and organizational rewards. *Journal of Occupational Psychology, 56*, 315–328.

Schein, E. H. (1978). *Career dynamics: Matching individual and organizational needs.* Reading, MA: Addison-Wesley.

Schneider, B. (1985). Organizational behavior. *Annual Review of Psychology, 36*, 573–611.

Scott, K. D., & Taylor, G. S. (1985). An examination of conflicting findings on the relationship between job satisfaction and absenteeism: a meta-analysis. *Academy of Management Journal, 28*, 599–612.

Sekaran, V. (1983). Factors influencing the quality of life in dual career families. *Journal of Occupational Psychology, 56*, 161–174.

Sekaran, V. (1984). Job and life satisfactions experienced by dual-career family members. *Journal of Psychological Researchers, 28*, 139–144.

Sekaran, V. (1985). The paths to mental health: An exploratory study of husbands and wives in dual-career families. *Journal of Occupational Psychology, 58*, 129–137.

Sekaran, V. (1986a). Self-esteem and sense of competence as moderators of the job satisfaction of professionals in dual career couples. *Journal of Occupational Behaviour, 7*, 341–344.

Sekaran, V. (1986b). Significant differences in quality-of-life factors and their correlates: A function of differences in career orientation or gender? *Sex Roles, 14*, 261–279.

Shaffer, G. S. (1987). Patterns of work and nonwork satisfaction. *Journal of Applied Psychology, 72*, 115–124.

Shenkar, O. (1988). Robotics: A challenge for occupational psychology. *Journal of Occupational Psychology, 61*, 103–112.

Sherman, J. D. (1986). The relationship between factors in the work environment and turnover. *IEEE Transactions on Engineering Management, 33*, 72–78.

Skaret, D. J., & Bruning, N. S. (1986). Attitudes about the work group: An added moderator of the relationship between leader behavior and job satisfaction. *Group and Organizational Studies, 11*, 254–279.

Smulders, P. G. (1983). Personal, nonwork and work characteristics in male and female absence behavior. *Journal of Occupational Behaviour, 4*, 285–295.

Sonnenstuhl, W. J. (1989). Reaching the impaired professional: Applying findings from organizational and occupational research. *Journal of Drug Issues, 19*, 533–539.

Staines, G. L., Pottick, K. J., & Fudge, D. A. (1985). The effect of wives' employment on husbands' job and life satisfaction. *Psychology of Women Quarterly, 9*, 419–423.

Staines, G. L., Pottick, K. J., & Fudge, D. A. (1986). Wives' employment and husbands' attitudes toward work and life. *Journal of Applied Psychology, 71*, 118–128.

Stark, S., & Romans, S. (1982). Business and industry: How do you get there? *The Counseling Psychologist, 11*(3), 45–47.

Staw, B. M. (1980). The consequences of turnover. *Journal of Occupational Behaviour, 1*, 253–273.

Staw, B. M. (1984). Organizational behavior: A review and reformulation of the field's outcome variables. *Annual Review of Psychology, 35*, 627–666.

Steele, P. D. (1989). A history of job-based alcoholism programs: 1955–1972. *Journal of Drug Issues, 129*, 511–532.

Steele, P. D., & Hubbard, R. L. (1985). Management styles, perceptions of substance abuse, and employee assistance programs in organizations. *Journal of Applied Behavioral Science, 21*, 271–286.

Steers, R. M., & Rhodes, S. R. (1978). Major influences on employee attendance: A process model. *Journal of Applied Psychology, 63*, 391–407.

Steiner, D. D., & Truxillo, D. M. (1987). Another look at the job satisfaction—life satisfaction relationship: A test of the disaggregation hypothesis. *Journal of Occupational Behaviour, 8,* 71–77.

Stern, L. R. (1982). Response commentary on business and industry. *The Counseling Psychologist, 11*(3), 37–38.

Stokes, G., & Cochrane, R. (1984). Psychological effects of unemployment and redundancy. *Journal of Occupational Psychology, 57*(4), 309–322.

Stout, S. K., Slocum, J. W., & Cron, W. L. (1988). Dynamics of the career plateauing process. *Journal of Vocational Behavior, 32,* 74–91.

Sund, K., & Ostwald, S. K. (1985). Dual-earner families' stress levels, and personal and life-style related variables. *Nursing Research, 34,* 357–361.

Super, D. E. (1980). A life-span, life-space approach to career development. *Journal of Vocational Behavior, 13,* 282–298.

Super, D. E. (1985). Coming of age in Middletown: Careers in the making. *American Psychologist, 40,* 405–414.

Swaney, K., & Prediger, D. (1985). The relationship between interest–occupation congruence and job satisfaction. *Journal of Vocational Behavior, 26,* 13–24.

Talley, W. M. (1982). Practical considerations relative to mid-life career counseling. *Canadian Counsellor, 16,* 225–230.

Tausky, C. T., & Dubin, R. (1965). Career anchorage: Managerial mobility motivations. *American Sociological Review, 30,* 725–735.

Terborg, J. R. (1977). Women in management: A research review. *Journal of Applied Psychology, 62,* 647–664.

Thomas, L. E. (1977). Mid-career changes: Self-selected or externally mandated? *Vocational Guidance Quarterly, 25,* 320–328.

Thomas, L. E. (1979). Causes of mid-life change from high-status careers. *Vocational Guidance Quarterly, 27,* 202–208.

Thomas, L. E., & Robbins, P. I. (1979). Personality and work environment congruence of mid-life career changes. *Journal of Occupational Psychology, 52,* 177–183.

Thomas, L. E., & Shepher, J. (1975). Why study mid-life career change? *Vocational Guidance Quarterly, 24,* 37–40.

Thompson, L., & Walker, A. J. (1989). Gender in families: Women and men in marriage, work, and parenthood. *Journal of Marriage and the Family, 51,* 845–871.

Toomer, J. E. (1982). Counseling psychologists in business and industry. *The Counseling Psychologist, 10*(3), 9–18.

Trice, H. M., & Beyer, J. M. (1984). Employee assistance programs: Blending performance-oriented and humanitarian ideologies to assist emotionally disturbed employees. *Research in Community and Mental Health, 4,* 245–297.

Trice, H. M., & Sonnenstuhl, W. J. (1988). Drinking behaviors and risk factors related to the workplace: Implications for research and prevention. *Journal of Applied Behavior Science, 24,* 327–346.

Tziner, A. E., & Vardi, Y. (1984). Work satisfaction and absenteeism among social workers: The role of altruistic values. *Work and Occupations, 11,* 461–470.

Vaitenas, R., & Wiener, Y. (1977). Developmental, emotional, and interest factors in voluntary mid-career changes. *Journal of Vocational Behavior, 11,* 291–304.

Van Maanen, J. (1976). Breaking in: Socialization at work. In R. Dubin (Ed.), *Handbook of work, organization, and society.* Chicago: Rand McNally.

Veninga, R. L. (1983). Burnout and personality. *Clinical Gerontologist, 2,* 61–63.

Verma, O. P., & Upadhyay, S. N. (1986). Organizational commitment, job involvement and job satisfaction. *Indian Journal of Current Psychological Research, 1,* 24–31.

Wanous, J. P. (1975). Tell it like it is at realistic job previews. *Personnel, 52,* 50–60.

Warrenfeltz, R. B. (1986). Toward a developmental model of work involvement: An integration of the investment, normative and motivational models (commitment, job satisfaction, alienation). *Dissertation Abstracts International, 47,* 08B.

Watkins, C. E., Lopez, F. G., Campbell, V. L., & Himmell, C. D. (1986). Contemporary counseling psychology: Results of a national survey. *Journal of Counseling Psychology, 33,* 301–309.

Wedderburn, D. (1964). *White collar redundancy: A case study.* Cambridge, MA: Cambridge University Press.

White, A. T., & Spector, P. E. (1987). An investigation of age-related factors in the age-job satisfaction relationship. *Psychology and Aging, 2,* 261–265.

Wiener, Y., Muczyk, J. P., & Gable, M. (1987). Relationships between work commitments and experience of personal well-being *Psychological Reports, 60,* 459–466.

Wiener, Y., & Vaitenas, R. (1977). Personality correlates of voluntary mid-career change in enterprising occupations. *Journal of Applied Psychology, 62,* 706–712.

Wilbur, C. S., & Vermilyea, C. J. (1982). Some business advice to counseling psychologists. *The Counseling Psychologist, 11*(3), 31–32.

Wiley, D. L. (1987). The relationship between work/nonwork role conflict and job-related outcomes: Some unanticipated findings. *Journal of Management, 13,* 467–472.

Williams, L. H., & Hazer, J. T. (1986). Antecedents and consequences of satisfaction and commitment in turnover models: A reanalysis using latent variable structure equation methods. *Journal of Applied Psychology, 71,* 219–231.

Zahra, S. A. (1984). Antecedents and consequences of organizational commitment: An integrative approach. *Akron Business and Economic Review, 15*(3), 26–32.

CHAPTER 18

COUNSELING PSYCHOLOGY AND THE WORKPLACE: THE EMERGENCE OF ORGANIZATIONAL COUNSELING PSYCHOLOGY

LAWRENCE H. GERSTEIN
SANDRA L. SHULLMAN

Everybody seems to be encouraging us to proceed in expanding the opportunities and skills of Counseling Psychologists for industrial and business settings. I say, let's get on with it! (Osipow, 1982a, p. 55)

In recent years, there has been a rapid increase in the roles, functions, and scope of counseling psychology's practice. Although many members of our profession continue to practice in settings that have an educational or clinical emphasis, a growing number have moved to corporate, industrial, and other types of organizational settings. The resulting changes in role expectations and conceptions of practice and research have been addressed only sporadically in the literature. In response to this shortcoming, this chapter explores current and potential contributions of counseling psychologists interested in the workplace. We briefly examine economic, cultural, and technical changes in our society, and the effects of these changes on contextual shifts in the workplace and on the provision of social services offered in this setting. Current roles of counseling psychologists affiliated with business and organizational settings are highlighted. We also present a conceptual framework for a new subspecialty in our profession—organizational counseling psychology—and outline a research agenda based on this framework. Finally, we highlight a curriculum designed to prepare predoctoral and postdoctoral counseling psychologists for entry into business and organizational settings.

The authors share equal responsibility for this chapter. We appreciate the editorial and library assistance of Colleen Brown, Patricia Brown, Daniel Moore, Karen Novak, and William Valutis. Portions of this chapter were completed while Lawrence Gerstein was a Visiting Scholar in the Counseling Psychology Program, Department of Psychology, The Ohio State University.

581

BRIEF HISTORY OF COUNSELING PSYCHOLOGY IN BUSINESS AND ORGANIZATIONAL SETTINGS

Early Roots in the Workplace

Counseling psychology's involvement in business and organizational settings traces its roots to Frank Parsons and the vocational guidance movement. This movement focused on efficient selection and placement of persons in jobs and on protection of the economic stability of society in the early 1900s (Whitely, 1984). In 1913, individuals connected with this movement formed the first professional organization designed to represent their shared interests, the National Vocational Guidance Association (now named the National Career Development Association).

Vocational guidance programs were initially constructed to address the difficulties of child labor and the entry of youth into the labor market (Hoppock, 1950; cited in Blum & Balinsky, 1951). Industrial mental hygiene programs, also appearing at the beginning of this century, were often staffed by social workers, psychiatrists, and industrial psychologists (Gavin, 1982). In 1914, the first industrially based counseling program for adults was established at the Ford Motor Company (Bellows, 1961). A mental health program, comprised of various helping professionals, including psychologists, was also introduced at R. H. Macy and Company in the early part of the century. This program offered assistance with different types of legal, financial, and personal problems (Dunnette & Kirchner, 1965).

Following the advances in vocational services subsequent to World War I and the Great Depression, innovative programs were established in the early 1940s at the Hawthorne Plant of Western Electric and at the Prudential Insurance Company. These programs addressed workers' morale and job satisfaction problems (Dunnette & Kirchner, 1965; Levinson, 1983). World War II had a major impact on the provision of vocational services to veterans and other adults (Blum & Balinsky, 1951; Whitely, 1984).

The more formal recognition of counseling psychology as a distinct specialty of the American Psychological Association occurred in 1951. Prior to this recognition, Division 17 was (in 1944) called the Division of Personnel Psychologists. One of the original purposes of Division 17 was "to extend the application of the methods and techniques of psychology to counseling and guidance in educational, vocational, and personal adjustment, whether in educational institutions, *industrial or business enterprises* [emphasis added], governmental agencies, or in private practice" (cited in Whitely, 1984, p. 11).

Counseling Psychology and the Workplace: 1950–1990

During the 1950s and 1960s, counseling psychology as a profession continued its involvement in personnel issues and the broader issues of vocational choice and development. Emphasis on industrial settings was reiterated in the 1956 Report on Counseling Psychology as a Specialty (cited in Thompson & Super, 1964) and at the Greyston Conference in 1964. One important function of counseling psychologists identified at this conference was "coordination and administration of programmatic activities within the job settings and related agencies" (The Conference Report, cited in Thompson & Super, 1964, p. 14). In 1965, Dunnette and Kirchner published *Psychology Applied to Industry,* a book that included a chapter on counseling in industry. In 1971, the *Journal of Vocational Behavior* was established by counseling psychologists to publish research of interest to counseling and industrial/organizational (I/O) psychologists. More recently, Osipow and Toomer (1982) edited an issue of *The Counseling Psychologist* entirely focused on counseling psychology in business and industry. This issue presented numerous suggestions for expanding the opportunities and skills of counseling psychologists in business and industrial settings.

Trends Affecting Counseling Psychology in the Workplace

The work of counseling psychologists affiliated with the workplace may look very different 20 years from now. During the past 20 years, major changes significantly affected the world of work, and it is expected that the nature and rate of change will continue.

A Service-Based Economy

One of the dramatic changes occurring presently and projected to continue beyond the year 2000 involves the transformation of the United States to a service-based economy. The service sector now accounts for more than 68% of the U.S. gross national product and at least 71% of U.S. employment (Quinn & Gagnon, 1986). Although the services sector of the economy has grown tremendously, there have not been comparable gains in productivity. Thus, organizations will continue seeking new strategies to spur productivity.

Internationalization of the Marketplace

Another dramatic change during the past 20 years has been the internationalization of the marketplace (Cascio, 1986). A significant portion of the profits and jobs created can be directly attributed to U.S. companies doing business overseas. Further, by the year 2000, we can expect a slowdown in the growth of the U.S. work force to its slowest rate since the 1930s (Rauch, 1989). Finally, the demographics of the U.S. workplace are rapidly changing and will result in a strikingly different work force by the year 2000 (Offermann & Gowing, 1990).

Acquisitions, Divestitures, and Mergers

Beyond these broad changes, a number of other significant changes are occurring that will directly affect the future work of counseling psychologists in the workplace. For example, acquisitions, divestitures, and mergers have been rapidly increasing (Fulmer & Gilkey, 1988; Ropp, 1987). Downsizing approaches such as natural attrition, layoffs, early retirement, shortened workweeks, and job transfers have been increasingly used as organizational management strategies. During the next 20 years, career development opportunities and programs will be dramatically affected by technological, organizational, and individual responses to strategies like downsizing (London & Stumpf, 1986). Traditional views of career choice, development, and adjustment will need to incorporate these critical factors into both theory building and the design of interventions.

High-Technology/"High-Touch" Approaches

Another major change affecting counseling psychologists is the use of high-technology or "high-touch" approaches. It is expected that office automation strategies will result in radical modifications in organizational communications. Further, through teleworking strategies, the ability to work at locations other than traditional office settings may change the basic assumptions about "going to work" (Turnage, 1990). For counseling psychologists, the onslaught of high-technology environments will modify both the nature of jobs and how the job world is defined. The resulting individual, career, and organizational growth and development issues will need to be addressed (Shullman & Carder, 1983).

Work Force Diversity

It is projected that one-third of the new entrants into the work force between now and the year 2000 will be persons of color (Johnson & Packer, 1987), more than half of whom were raised in poverty (Horowitz & O'Brien, 1989). Such trends emphasize the need to retrain persons of color for new occupations (Offermann & Gowing, 1990) and to address the issue of diversity itself. Solomon (1989) suggested that work force diversity training will emerge as the next critical step after equal employment opportunity and affirmative action. Persons of color and women are underrepresented in middle management and virtually absent from boardrooms and positions of corporate leadership (Morrison & Von Glinow, 1990; Offermann & Gowing, 1990). Thus, counseling psychologists must be ready to build models and interventions that focus on a culturally diverse work force, and that address values and conflicts arising from individual differences.

Roles of Women, Families, and Work

Concerns regarding child care, health benefits, flexible working hours, and geographic mobility have increased substantially as more single-parent families, women, and dual-career couples have become part of the work force (Zedeck & Mosier, 1990). Counseling psychologists must increasingly focus on the complex set of issues involved in balancing work and family commitments in today's and tomorrow's world of work. The stress generated by such concerns is already a major focus in counseling, especially in corporate Employee Assistance Programs (EAPs) (Zedeck & Mosier, 1990).

Professionalization of the Work Force

The professionalization of the work force will likely result in a changing array of responses and services provided to employees. It is estimated that 20% of the U.S. work force will soon be professional workers and that most of these employees will work in the service sector of the economy (Raulin, 1988). This segment of the work force will be a highly educated group with heightened expectations for quality-of-work-life issues and sensitivity to career development issues.

Expanded Training in the Workplace

It also appears that training in the workplace will become a critical means of maintaining a competitive edge in areas of productivity, innovation, and creativity (Mone, 1988). On-the-job training will be necessary to integrate increasing numbers of both unskilled youth and professional personnel into the work force of the future (Goldstein & Gilliam, 1990), and evaluation research will be needed to assess the effectiveness of this training.

Mental Health Services: Shifts in Responsibility and Context

Perhaps the most significant trend affecting counseling psychologists and other helping professionals has been the movement of mental health and other health initiatives toward the corporate sector. Roman (1981) suggested that the work organization represents the "last frontier for the delivery of mental health and substance abuse services" (p. 12). With the corporate sector now paying at least half of the country's health care bills (Farkas, 1989), emphasis on health care cost reduction has focused increasingly on prevention and development rather than remediation (Kurpius, 1985). Healthy employees are seen as more productive and less expensive to maintain in the workplace (Cohen, 1985).

With the rising emphasis on prevention and development as cost containment strategies, there has also come an increasing demand for mental health and counseling services (Lewis & Lewis, 1986). Many organizations are now offering services, through EAPs, to deal with career, job performance, or personal concerns. Various psychological interventions are being used more frequently at the workplace, to alter life-style behaviors such as exercise patterns, smoking, drinking, and improper diet (Cohen, 1985). Substantial research has suggested that the inclusion of mental health benefits into traditional insurance plans and corporate health maintenance provider programs results in reduced hospital costs (Toomer, 1982).

The corporate view is perhaps reflective of general changes in cultural attitudes about health. Employees are bringing to the workplace an increased sensitivity to personal health and fitness and a greater readiness to address substance abuse and mental health concerns (Roman & Blum, 1988). Thus, general health promotion and wellness programs, and corporate-sponsored counseling programs like EAPs, are increasing in frequency and acceptance, resulting in a critical intersection between the workplace and health care institutions and providers.

CURRENT AND POTENTIAL ROLES FOR COUNSELING PSYCHOLOGISTS IN THE WORKPLACE

Types of Work Settings

Traditionally, counseling psychologists have practiced in a variety of educational, health care, and private practice settings. In recent years, as psychology has moved more extensively into the workplace, counseling psychologists have often found themselves in less traditional work settings. For example, increasing numbers of counseling psychologists are affiliated with organizations that provide employee assistance and managed care services to businesses as external vendors. Others are employed in training and consulting organizations—again, providing these services as external vendors—or work directly in business organizations. Some provide training, programming, and counseling as part of a centralized human resources effort. Others are employed as internal consultants, helping to resolve organizational and work group issues. Virtually all types of industries and businesses now utilize psychologists, and counseling psychologists can be found in most of these organizations.

Roles and Functions

Historically, I/O psychologists, social workers, management specialists, occupational nurses, and physicians were the primary helping professionals offering services to employees and organizations in need. Table 18.1 shows that this is no longer the case; 10 groups of professionals perform mental health functions in 10 broad programmatic areas. Although the 10 professional groups depicted in Table 18.1 share common interests in addressing individual and organizational needs, the philosophical foundations of

Table 18.1 Current Roles and Functions of Helping Professionals in Business and Organizational Settings

	Types of Helping Professionals									
	1	2	3	4	5	6	7	8	9	10
Functions	I/O Psychologist	Counseling Psychologist	Clinical Psychologist	Social Psychologist	Social Worker	Mental Health Counselor	Mgmt. Specialist	Health Educator	Nurse	Medical Doctor
HUMAN RESOURCES										
Job Characteristics										
Job Classifications	X						X			
Job Analysis	X						X			
Salary Decisions	X						X			
Benefits	X						X			
Recruitment	X	X	X		X	X	X			
Selection	X	X	X		X	X	X			
Human Resources Mgmt./Planning	X									
Executive Screening	X	X	X							
Assessment Centers	X	X	X							
Placement	X	X	X		X	X	X			
Human Factors	X									
Performance Appraisals	X									
Job Design	X									
Job Redesign	X									
Staffing Requirements Planning	X						X			
Transfer Evaluations	X						X			
Workers' Compensation	X						X			
Training										
Team Building	X			X			X			
Leadership Development	X			X			X			
Human Relations Training	X	X	X		X	X	X			
Executive Coaching	X	X	X		X	X	X			
Worker Literacy	X						X			
Career Development										
Career Mgmt. & Planning		X				X				

Job Enrichment		X				X				
Leisure		X				X		X		
Outplacement	X	X			X	X	X			
Retirement		X			X	X				
Organizational Dynamics										
Organizational Diagnosis	X			X			X			
Organizational Development	X						X			
Consultation	X	X	X	X			X			
Evaluation										
Surveys	X	X	X	X			X			
Needs Assessment	X	X	X	X			X			
EQUAL EMPLOYMENT OPPORTUNITY PROGRAMS										
Counseling	X	X	X		X	X				
Consultation	X				X		X			
Evaluation	X						X			
Expert Witness	X				X		X			
Program Administration	X				X		X			
EMPLOYEE ASSISTANCE PROGRAMS										
Assessment & Diagnosis					X	X		X	X	
Short-Term Counseling					X	X		X	X	
Long-Term Counseling					X	X		X	X	
Case Management					X	X		X	X	
Community Referrals					X	X		X	X	
Staff Training					X	X	X	X	X	
Community Outreach					X	X	X	X	X	
Evaluation					X		X			
Program Administration					X	X	X	X	X	X
WELLNESS PROGRAMS										
Health Appraisals								X	X	X

Types of Helping Professionals

Functions	1 I/O Psychologist	2 Counseling Psychologist	3 Clinical Psychologist	4 Social Psychologist	5 Social Worker	6 Mental Health Counselor	7 Mgmt. Specialist	8 Health Educator	9 Nurse	10 Medical Doctor
Prevention Programs					X			X	X	X
Health Promotion					X			X	X	X
Program Administration					X		X	X	X	X
MEDICAL PROGRAMS										
Assessment & Diagnosis								X	X	X
Treatment & Prevention								X	X	X
Drug Screening								X	X	X
SAFETY PROGRAMS										
Health-Protective Worksites	X			X			X	X	X	X
Safety & Human Behavior	X			X			X	X	X	X
Fitness for Duty	X							X	X	X
Accident Investigations	X							X	X	X
OSHA & ERISA Regulations	X						X	X	X	X
Training	X			X			X	X	X	X
Program Administration	X						X	X	X	X
LABOR RELATIONS										
Collective Bargaining	X				X		X			
Arbitration	X				X		X			
Grievances	X				X		X			
Training	X				X		X			
Sexual Harassment	X	X	X		X		X			

MARKETING DEPARTMENT

Product Development	X		X			
Product Distribution	X		X			
Pricing	X					
Communications	X					

RESEARCH & DEVELOPMENT

Policy Development	X	X	X			
Program Development	X	X	X			
Program Evaluation	X	X	X			
Environmental Design	X	X				
Systems Design	X	X	X			
Research	X	X	X			

MISCELLANEOUS

Succession Planning	X	X				
Mergers	X	X				
Downsizing	X	X				
Community Outreach	X	X	X	X	X	X

Note: An *x* indicates a competency, assuming appropriate coursework and training experiences.

their respective interventions differ. For example, providers affiliated with psychology are directed by the scientist-professional model of practice, whereas social workers and mental health counselors rely more heavily on a practitioner-scientist framework.

Not surprisingly, I/O psychologists and management specialists continue to be more involved in activities related to job characteristics and organizational dynamics than are other professional groups (Phillips, Cairo, Blustein, & Meyers, 1988). Counseling psychologists and mental health counselors, by contrast, are more likely to provide career services than are other professionals (Gerstein & Bayer, 1990, 1991). Based on our review of the literature and experience, we found that, of the major functions itemized in Table 18.1, counseling psychologists are engaged to a significant degree in only three areas: human resources, equal employment opportunity programs, and community outreach.

Human Resources

The major function of counseling psychologists in the workplace is the provision of human resources services. Human resources traditionally was dominated by I/O psychologists and management specialists, but counseling psychologists have begun recently to provide training, career development, organizational interventions, and evaluation services. With their long tradition of research in vocational selection and adjustment, counseling psychologists have focused on the interaction between workers' characteristics and those of the work environment, recognizing that job success and satisfaction may be affected by worker–environment congruence (see Chapter 13, by Hackett & Lent).

Executive screening and assessment centers are specific applications of this general developmental, holistic, interactional approach to career development. In executive screening, specific leadership characteristics and skills are defined, and procedures are developed, including traditional testing methods, to identify a pool of candidates who possess the necessary behaviors. Perhaps the best known technology for examining management characteristics of candidates is the assessment center (Moses & Byham, 1977). In this approach, appropriate skill dimensions are identified and candidates experience a series of highly structured simulations and complete assessment instruments that are evaluated by trained multiple raters. The assessment center method has been used for job selection and for personal/professional development purposes.

The placement function, from a counseling psychology perspective, is viewed as an attempt to match employees' skills and experiences with jobs that are congruent with their profile. To achieve such congruence, the person needs to be assessed for available knowledge, skills, values, and abilities. The job environment must be assessed along similar dimensions. The design of such assessments requires a strong background in ability, aptitude, value, and interest measurement—areas in which most counseling psychologists have a great deal of preparation.

In terms of training, counseling psychologists have been particularly active in human relations programs and executive coaching. Human relations training involves teaching basic interpersonal and communications skills to employees, managers, and executives. Such training helps workers to learn to function together more effectively. The fact that over 80% of managerial and executive jobs are executed through verbal communication (Mintzberg, 1973) underlines the importance of effective communication skills to organizations. Participation in other kinds of training programs (e.g., leadership training) has been found to be associated with decreased absenteeism (Frayne & Latham, 1987), improved occupational safety (Reber & Wallin, 1984), increased productivity (Lefkowitz, 1970), and more effective work-related judgments (Gaeth & Shanteau, 1984).

Executive coaching involves helping high-level managers to work effectively with intact groups and preparing these persons for key leadership events. Such leadership events may include critical performance appraisal and management challenges (e.g., coping with organizational downsizing, acquisition, or implementation of new services). In high-technology organizations, for instance, key executives may have moved up through the organization quickly because of their outstanding technical skills. Executive coaching may entail helping such executives to view work group issues strategically and dynamically.

Counseling psychologists have long been engaged in a variety of career development areas (Cairo, 1983; Toomer, 1982). Career management and career planning activities involve the examination of job possibilities from the perspective of the organization (career management) and the individual (career planning). Many larger corporations have established fairly extensive career development programs (Gutteridge & Otte, 1983; Sonnenfeld, 1984). Organizations also utilize psychologists to assist with job design (e.g., job enrichment), so that valuable personnel remain stimulated and productive. Some job enrichment activities include job rotation, internships, formal or informal coursework, and personal development planning as part of annual goal setting. In recent years, as part of career development and wellness efforts, many organizations have also begun to focus on leisure planning.

With the massive transition to a service-based economy over the past 15 years, outplacement concerns have grown rapidly. Outplacement involves helping people who no longer have a viable role within an organization to secure positions elsewhere. Often, the need for outplacement services results from shifts in product or service goals, reductions in force as cost-cutting measures, downsizing for efficiency, or unanticipated job obsolescence. At times, outplacement may also involve placing key managers or technical workers in new companies as part of formal separation or termination agreements. The process of helping persons under extreme stress to use effective problem-solving skills to secure new employment taps a wide range of issues long focused on by counseling psychologists (Osipow, 1979).

Another contribution of counseling psychologists to the workplace is also related to career development—namely, retirement planning. With the rising number of people close to retirement age and the emergence of "baby boomers'" planning for their future retirement, the issue of retirement at both the individual and organizational levels has become critical. Some organizations use retirement options as a means of reduction in work force without layoffs. Many psychologists assist people with preretirement planning, to help the person and the organization make realistic financial and life-style projections (see Chapter 19, by Tinsley and Schwendener-Holt).

As Table 18.1 suggests, counseling psychologists are currently not highly involved in organizational dynamics. Organizational diagnosis and development have been traditionally the domain of I/O psychologists and management specialists; however, some counseling psychologists are being called on to apply their group process expertise to work-group situations. Table 18.1 indicates that counseling psychologists have used their skills in a wide range of evaluative situations, such as conducting organizational surveys and needs assessments.

Equal Employment Opportunity Programs

Counseling psychology has historically had a limited role in organizational affirmative action programming, but many counseling psychologists have been involved with such programming on an individual process level. More recently, counseling psychologists have pursued systemic issues such as diversity training and sexual harassment in the workplace (Shullman, 1990), and it appears that increasing numbers of counseling psychologists will move into consultative roles with regard to affirmative action and equal employment opportunity programming. Also, a greater number of persons in our profession will be asked to provide expert testimony on issues involving diversity or harassment (Shullman, 1990).

Employee Assistance Programs (EAPs)

Some counseling psychologists have recently become involved in the provision and evaluation of employee assistance services at the workplace. The roles and functions connected with EAPs are very compatible with mainstream counseling psychology practice: assessment and diagnosis, short- and long-term counseling, case management, community referrals, staff training, community outreach, program evaluation, and administration (Gerstein & Bayer, 1990, 1991). In one counseling psychology practice, employee assistance programming is conceptualized as involving multiple client foci: the individual EAP client *and* the organization. In that practice, positions are structured to make sure each client focus has a primary service provider or client advocate (Shullman, 1989).

Wellness, Medical, and Safety Programs

A substantial number of counseling psychologists are involved in what has been termed "health psychology" (see Chapter 10, by Altmaier and Johnson), but, as shown in Table 18.1, counseling psychologists have generally not been affiliated with workplace wellness, medical, and safety programs. Wellness programming, defined to include both physical and psychological wellness, involves such roles and functions as health appraisal administration, conduct of prevention training programs and health promotion activities (e.g., stress management), and program administration.

As displayed in Table 18.1, organizational medical programs have typically been staffed by medical personnel, who do assessment and diagnosis, treatment and prevention programs, and drug screening. With a background in effective behavioral and cognitive treatment strategies, counseling psychologists could play key roles in drug treatment and prevention programs in organizational settings. Likewise, although occupational safety programs have traditionally been the domain of I/O psychologists, social workers, management specialists, and medical personnel, counseling psychologists could make critical contributions to these programs. Historically, safety programs focused on modifying health-endangering aspects of the physical environment. More recently, occupational safety programs have broadened their focus to encompass healthy worksites, the interaction between safety and human behavior, the assessment of fitness for duty, accident investigations, complying with a broad array of OSHA (Occupational Safety and Health Act) and ERISA (Employment Retirement Income Security Act) regulations, and safety training programs.

Labor Relations

Labor relations activities have been the almost exclusive domain of management specialists, I/O psychologists, social workers, and attorneys. (See Table 18.1.) Traditional labor relations functions include collective bargaining, arbitration, grievances, and training. By definition, many of the basic labor relations activities have been rooted in adversarial assumptions about the roles of management and labor. However, partly because of economic shifts, more emphasis is now being placed on new models of workplace problem solving and conflict resolution. Traditional training, which stressed labor rule compliance, is now shifting its emphasis to enhancing supervisory interpersonal skills. Counseling psychology, with its focus on small-group problem solving and the establishment of effective interpersonal relationships, can make an important contribution to this new perspective on labor relations practice.

Marketing Department Activities

Most counseling psychologists would consider involvement in marketing-related activities as pure professional anathema. However, in addition to fairly traditional marketing functions such as product development, product distribution, pricing, and communications, the shift to a service economy has created a major need to develop and maintain effective service relationships between consumers and organizations (Kennedy, 1989). Increasing emphasis is being placed on needs assessment and relationship development activities, and marketing communications are now central to the delivery of most organizational services. Kennedy (1989) observed that counseling psychologists may contribute substantially to these new services.

Research and Development

Roles and functions of professionals engaged in organizational research and development traditionally have involved policy development, program development and evaluation, environmental design, systems design, and coordination of research. Historically, as displayed in Table 18.1, these roles have been the domains of I/O and social psychologists and management specialists. As we discuss later, counseling psychologists with a process orientation could assist in environmental design, program evaluation, and systems design.

Diversity and the Delivery of Organizational Services

As mentioned earlier, diversity will become an operating principle in the workplace by the year 2000. There will be a major shift in the basic demographic composition of the work force, which will bring poverty-related issues more directly into the workplace itself. Also, minority persons will disproportionately experience technical obsolescence, and there will be a great need to help all workers learn to function in culturally diverse work settings. Because few organizations have truly addressed the scope of the diversity issue, there will likely be a premium on professionals who can promote effective work relations among culturally diverse individuals.

THE ORGANIZATION AS CLIENT: CONCEPTUAL AND APPLIED CONSIDERATIONS

In the previous section, we discussed counseling psychology's current and potential contributions to the business community. It is our belief that, in the near future, members of our profession will become more involved in business and organizational settings. Not only will they assist individual workers in their career adjustment and development, but they will also intervene at the systems level to help organizations develop and prosper financially and in terms of human resources utilization. Before discussing how this might be accomplished, we define in Table 18.2 some important concepts often associatedwith organizations. These definitions are critical to providing a framework for possible future organizational roles for counseling psychologists. The following sections highlight some intervention activities associated with a few of these terms.

Table 18.2   Glossary of Organizational Terms

ORGANIZATION   The rational coordination of the activities of a number of people for the achievement of some common explicit purpose or goal, through division of labor and function, and through a hierarchy of authority and responsibility (Schein, 1970, p.9).

ORGANIZATIONAL SYSTEM   A view of an organization as a complex set of interrelated elements called a system. The organizational system contains different components or elements (people, technology, organizational structure, etc.), and these components or elements are related. The organization includes both social components and subsystems (people, relationships, behavior, structures) and technical components and subsystems (technology, capital, etc.). For the system to function productively, it must be involved with other organizations or individuals, such as suppliers, customers, competitors, government regulators, etc. (Nadler, 1977, pp. 8–9).

ORGANIZATIONAL STRUCTURE   How tasks are to be allocated, who reports to whom, and the formal coordinating mechanisms and interacting patterns that will be followed (Robbins, 1990, p. 5).

ORGANIZATIONAL ENVIRONMENT   Essentially, the general environment— economic factors, political conditions, the social milieu, the legal structure, the ecological situation, and cultural conditions. The general environment encompasses conditions that may have an impact on the organization, but their relevance is not overtly clear. The specific environment is that part of the environment that is directly relevant to the organization in achieving its goals (Robbins, 1990, p. 206).

ORGANIZATIONAL CULTURE   (a) A pattern of basic assumptions, (b) invented, discovered, or developed by a given group (c) as it learns to cope with its problems of external adaptation and internal integration, (d) that has worked well enough to be considered valid and, therefore, (e) to be taught to new members as (f) the correct way to perceive, think, and feel in relation to those problems (Schein, 1990, p. 111).

ORGANIZATIONAL CLIMATE   A set of attributes that can be perceived about a particular organization and/or its subsystems, and that may be induced from the way the organization and/or its subsystems deal with members and the environment (Hellriegel & Slocum, 1974, p. 256). Psychological climates are the meanings an individual attaches to a work context; organizational climates are the summated, averaged meanings that people attach to a particular feature of the setting (Schneider & Reichers, 1983, p. 21).

ORGANIZATIONAL CITIZENSHIP BEHAVIOR   An individual's discretionary behavior; not directly or explicitly recognized by the formal reward system. In the aggregate, it promotes the effective functioning of the organization (Organ, 1988, p. 4).

ORGANIZATIONAL COMMUNICATION   The display and interpretation of messages among communication units that are part of a particular organization. An organization is comprised of communication units relating hierarchically to each other and functioning in an environment (Pace & Faules, 1989, p. 20).

ORGANIZATIONAL DESIGN   The formal system of communication, authority, and responsibility that management creates to help achieve organizational goals (Hellriegel et al., 1983, p. 311).

ORGANIZATIONAL BEHAVIOR   A systematic attempt to understand the behavior of people in organizations (Hellriegel et al., 1983, p. 5).

Table 18.2 *(Continued)*

ORGANIZATIONAL THEORY   The discipline that studies the structure and design of organizations (Robbins, 1990, p. 7).

ORGANIZATIONAL DEVELOPMENT   A distinct area within the field of organizational science that focuses on the planned and controlled change of organizations in desired directions (Vecchio, 1988, p. 509).

ORGANIZATIONAL CHANGE   An intentional attempt by an organization to influence the status quo of itself or of any other organization (Hellriegel et al., 1983, p. 517).

CHANGE AGENTS   Those in power and those who wish either to replace or constrain those in power (Katz & Kahn, 1978, p. 679); typically, senior executives, managers of major units within the organization, internal staff-development specialists, powerful lower-level employees, and consultants brought in from the outside (Robbins, 1990, p. 388).

ORGANIZATIONAL DIAGNOSIS   A process, based on behavioral science theory, for publicly entering a human system, collecting valid data about human experiences with that system, and feeding that information back to the system to promote increased understanding of the system by its members (Alderfer, 1980, p. 459).

HUMAN RESOURCES PLANNING   The process by which the need for and the internal availability of human resources for some future time period are estimated; also includes the personnel action plans required to fulfill the net staffing requirements and to achieve the organization's staffing objectives (Gutteridge, 1986, p. 52).

HUMAN RESOURCES MANAGEMENT   A systematic effort to ensure an effective interface between an organization's human resources and its internal and external environment (Gutteridge, 1986, p. 52).

CAREER PLANNING   A deliberate sequence and process of determining one's own career-related interests, values, and skills; assessing career options; deciding on a course of action; and designing a meaningful, realistic career plan (Leibowitz & Schlossberg, 1981, pp. 72–73).

ORGANIZATIONAL CAREER DEVELOPMENT   The outcomes emanating from the interaction of individual career-planning and institutional career-management processes (Gutteridge, 1986, p. 54).

CAREER MANAGEMENT   Maximization of the fit between the employee's objectives and the work opportunities available in the organization (Scarpello & Ledvinka, 1988, p. 10).

CAREER DEVELOPMENT SYSTEM   An organized and planned effort, comprised of structures, activities, or processes, which results in a "mutual plotting" effort between employees and the organization (Leibowitz & Schlossberg, 1981, p. 72).

CONSULTATION   A major vehicle for bringing needed knowledge and services to modern work organizations (Gallessich, 1985, p. 336) by seeking assistance from a consultant, in order to identify or clarify a concern or problem and to consider the options available for problem resolution (Wynne, McDaniel, & Weber, 1986, p. 8).

Note: Definitions of these terms were paraphrased from the sources cited.

Organizational Change and Development Strategies

As is apparent in Table 18.2, organizations are multidimensional, complex, and dynamic. Their complexity can easily complicate the planning and implementing of strategies designed to bring about organizational change. However, various organizational change (OC) and organizational development (OD) strategies are available to facilitate modifications in an organization's behavior. The most frequently used OC and OD strategies, or the variables that serve as the targets of change, can be grouped into four categories: people, structure, technology, and task or human resources management.

People Strategies

The goal of this technique of organizational change is to modify the behaviors, values, attitudes, and interpersonal relationships of employees. This approach is often implemented in such a way that power is redistributed among the organization's workers—for instance, by supporting independent decision-making and opening up communication networks (Hellriegel, Slocum, & Woodman, 1983). Examples of this approach are: conducting and giving feedback on surveys; team building; sensitivity training; and process consultation.

The *survey approach* takes an action–research perspective in carrying out data collection and feedback. The main purpose of this approach is to encourage staff to discuss common problems and, in so doing, enhance relationships between people and departments. Thus, a specific organizational change is not planned during the feedback session, but the expectation is that change will occur because of the interdepartmental discussions that are structured around the obtained results (Hellriegel et al., 1983).

In this model, change is a cyclical process that involves collaboration between OD consultants and organizational members. There are seven main steps: problem identification, consultation with a consultant, data gathering and preliminary diagnosis, feedback to the key client or group, joint diagnosis of the problem, action, and data gathering after action (Huse & Cummings, 1985). In reviewing research on the effectiveness of the survey approach, Hellriegel et al. (1983) concluded that this approach increases the influence of front-line staff and managerial personnel, and improves staff members' problem-solving and decision-making abilities.

Team building "is an effort in which a team studies its own process (how they work together) and takes some action steps to create a climate in which team members' energies are directed toward problem-solving and maximizing the use of all team members' resources in this process" (Hanson & Lubin, 1986, p. 28). Changes in the work group's functioning are thought to result from having the team focus on: (a) setting goals/priorities; (b) analyzing and allocating work tasks; (c) assessing how the team functions; and/or (d) examining relationships among team members (Hellriegel et al., 1983). Briefly, the team building cycle typically includes six steps: problem identification, data collection, diagnosis, action planning, implementation of a plan, and evaluation (Hellriegel et al., 1983).

Although team development interventions enhance communication and group cohesion (De Meuse & Liebowitz, 1981), research on the effect of this intervention on work performance and financial savings has yielded mixed results (Woodman & Sherwood, 1980). In a review of 13 studies, Sundstrom, De Meuse, and Futrell (1990) found that performance improved in 4 of 9 cases, and communication and cohesion were enhanced in 8 of 10 studies that used interpersonal approaches. Other reviews of research

on team building have reached similar conclusions, suggesting that it positively influences job performance and reduces costs about 50% of the time (Nicholas, 1982; Porras
& Berg, 1978a). Most research on this intervention, however, has focused on group
members' feelings and attitudes, has made assessments over brief time periods, and has
ignored the influence of confounding variables (e.g., effects of other approaches) (Huse
& Cummings, 1985).

In many ways, the goal of *sensitivity training* is similar to team building; that is, it
strives to enhance and/or change the relationships among work group members. Sensitivity training or T-groups are different, however, in that their focus is on improving
social skills rather than on individual or group productivity. Research suggests that,
when effective, this type of training leads to changes in employees' self-awareness,
sensitivity to others (Vecchio, 1988), flexibility in roles, openness, and communication
skills (Campbell & Dunnette, 1968). However, effects of sensitivity training on the
organization seem to be inconsistent (Nicholas, 1982; Porras & Berg, 1978a). In fact, in
reviewing numerous studies, Campbell and Dunnette (1968) concluded there is little
evidence that this type of training has any long-term effect on organizational performance. These authors also raised questions about the scientific rigor of the research
paradigms used.

Process consultation is another example of a people-oriented organizational change
approach. This technique is constructed to assist "members of an organization [to]
perceive, understand, and act upon process events that occur in their work environments" (Schein, 1969, p. 9). Process events are defined as the process by which work is
accomplished in groups and in the organization. Process consultation is carried out by a
consultant who assists employees and work groups in assessing the process events that
occur as they strive toward task goals. Because this form of consultation focuses on
interpersonal, group, and intergroup processes, it is not surprising that it is designed to
address communication patterns, leadership styles, group roles and norms, decision-
making and problem-solving styles, and conflict resolution (Hellriegel et al., 1983).

There are data suggesting that process consultation does change attitudes, values,
interpersonal skills, norms, and cohesiveness (Kaplan, 1979a), but there is very little
research supporting its effect on task performance (Huse & Cummings, 1985). A review
of studies indicated, however, that it is difficult to assess the impact of this intervention
on work performance (Kaplan, 1979b). In fact, most investigators have not gathered
performance data, but rather have relied on self-report measures (Huse & Cummings,
1985). Porras and Berg (1978b) discovered, for instance, that of 160 evaluations involving OD consultations, only 35 employed quantitative data (self-report and performance). Finally, in her review, Gallessich (1985) concluded that consultation is effective
50 to 80% of the time. However, she was cautious about this finding because of the
subjective measures used. More detailed discussion of various research issues and
questions related to process consultation can be found in the July 1985 issue of *The
Counseling Psychologist* and in Dustin and Blocher (1984).

Structure Strategies

The second major category of strategies constructed to facilitate organizational change
involves the structure approach. This strategy targets modifications in the distribution
of authority, alterations in the managerial hierarchy, allocation of reinforcement, and
changes in job positions, departments, and/or divisions (Robbins, 1990). As such, this
intervention attempts to alter the organization's internal structure. An example of this
strategy would be decentralization of the organization's decision-making polices, which

would result in giving each manager and unit more autonomy and power (Hellriegel et al., 1983). Robbins (1990) reviewed the strengths and weaknesses of various organizational structures and their impact on employee and group behavior.

Technology Strategies

The third strategy for organizational change, the technological intervention approach, "focuses mainly on problem-solving mechanisms and the processes by which an organization generates and adopts new problem-solving methods" (Hellriegel et al., 1983, p. 537). This strategy is used to modify work flow among units, information systems, and the assessment of particular jobs. Basically, this is done in order to link people with technology. Research on technostructural approaches indicates that these strategies have a long-lasting, positive effect on the organization and employees, but they might not lead to increased worker commitment or competence (Macy, Hurts, Izumi, Norton, & Smith, 1986).

Task Strategies

The last strategy for bringing about organizational change uses the task or human resources management approach. Task interventions attempt to integrate workers into the organization. They also target a worker's job performance (Hellriegel et al., 1983) through, for instance, career planning and development programs and stress management programs. Frequently, combinations of task and technological approaches are utilized, because the variables targeted by these interventions are usually highly interrelated. In general, four methods are employed to foster changes in tasks and in the organization's technology: job design, sociotechnical systems, management by objectives (MBO), and reward systems.

Job design involves a systematic restructuring in how work is performed. The objective is to enhance employees' involvement, motivation, and work efficiency. Job design includes job enrichment programs, job rotation, job engineering, and behavioral types of change programs (Hellriegel et al., 1983). Participation in such programs appears to improve the quality of employees' products, but there is inconsistent evidence that these programs lead to strong gains in productivity (Organ & Bateman, 1991).

Sociotechnical systems are also systematic restructuring approaches, but they focus on modifying the technical and social features of the organization such that the relationship between the two is strengthened. This modification is typically accomplished by redesigning how work is done, and by changing technical and interpersonal features of the organization. The ultimate goal of this strategy is to increase the organization's effectiveness (Hellriegel et al., 1983). Research supports this goal: use of this approach has led to decreases in absences and turnover, increases in cooperation (Pasmore & Sherwood, 1978), and enhanced productivity and cost savings (Pasmore & King, 1978).

In comparison to a sociotechnical approach, *MBO* involves managers and their staff in a mutually agreed-on goal-setting process aimed at satisfactory work performance and personal development. This approach requires that managers and their subordinates arrive at jointly endorsed realistic change objectives (Hellriegel et al., 1983). A review of the methods employed in 185 studies indicated that the effectiveness of MBO varied as a function of the quality of the method used (Kondrasuk,

1981). Less sophisticated research procedures resulted in positive findings. Some studies have reported that MBO can enhance productivity (Raia, 1965), but others have concluded that the benefits are short-lived (Ivancevich, 1972) and are not linked to financial gains (Mucyzk, 1978). Based on their literature review, Huse and Bowditch (1977) argued that MBO programs could be helpful if properly constructed and implemented.

The last kind of strategy designed to foster changes in tasks and in the organization's technology is the implementation or modification of a *reward system*. Research suggests that various types of reward systems (e.g., skill-based pay plans, all-salaried work force, lump-sum salary increases, performance-based pay systems, gain sharing) can be implemented to foster changes in the performance of employees (e.g., decreases in absenteeism and turnover, enhanced performance), work groups, and organizations (Huse & Cummings, 1985).

The four types of interventions just presented have often been associated with quality of work life (QWL) programs. According to DuBrin (1988), QWL "is the extent to which employees are able to satisfy important needs through their work experiences, with particular emphasis on participating in important decisions about their work" (p. 401). No specific interventions are connected with QWL programs; the overall objective is to improve the organizational work climate and employees' involvement and satisfaction with their jobs (Vecchio, 1988). To accomplish this, change agents frequently rely on job redesign programs, sociotechnical systems, MBO, and innovative reward systems. Research on QWL programs has resulted in a mixture of findings. Participation in these programs has been linked with lowered absenteeism, but it has not led to improved job productivity (enhanced quality or quantity) (Katz, Kochan, & Weber, 1985), job satisfaction, or motivational potential (Ondrack & Evans, 1986).

Regardless of the overall strategy (i.e., people, structure, technology, or task) used to bring about organizational change, it appears that, to be effective, this change process must follow three steps outlined by Lewin (1951). The first step is known as unfreezing: the change agent(s) attempts to overcome the individual and group pressures of resistance to change. To achieve this step, one can try to shift behavior away from the status quo (the driving forces), decrease restraining forces that block movement from the equilibrium, or rely on some combination of these forces. Once this step is accomplished, it is possible for the change agent(s) to implement the desired change or to move the organization to a new state (the second step). After the change has been successfully implemented, it is important for the change agent(s) to ensure that the new situation persists over time. This third step, the process of stabilizing change by balancing the driving and restraining forces, is known as refreezing (Robbins, 1990). The successful implementation of an organizational change strategy is aided by understanding of fundamental social psychological theories of group dynamics (e.g., group development, cohesiveness, group think, coalitions, norms, roles, leadership styles) (Shaw, 1981).

APPLICATIONS OF PERSON–ENVIRONMENT INTERACTION

In addition to concepts of change, development, and prevention, a significant theoretical component of the practice of counseling psychology in organizational settings is represented by theories of person–environment interaction. Recent approaches to organizational practice and research reflect a reemergence of interactionism versus earlier emphases on personalism and situationism (Huebner & Corazzini, 1984).

Models of Interactionism

Interactionism focuses on variations in behavior that result from transactions between individual and situational variables, rather than either class of factors alone. In earlier writings, many psychologists discussed the importance of the interaction between personal and situational variables (Lewin, 1936; Murray, 1938). Most psychologists, however, continued to debate the relative merits of the person versus the situation until the 1960s and 1970s, when interactionist concepts reemerged as a major focus (Mischel, 1977). Walsh (1973) reviewed five broad-based models of person–environment interaction. Others (see Chapter 13, by Hackett and Lent; Schneider, 1987; Spokane, 1987) added significant new concepts or perspectives to the interactionist framework.

Behavior Setting Approach

Barker (1968) posited that environments select and shape the actions of individuals and that, through standing patterns of behavior, termed behavior settings, individuals within the same environment will act in similar ways. Barker did not focus on the individuals' perception and ascribed meaning of what was observed in the environment; rather, emphasis was placed on those aspects of the environment that visibly affected individual behavior (Huebner & Corazzini, 1984). Originally, it was assumed that behavior settings had singularly large power over individuals; however, other research has demonstrated that factors such as physical size of the setting, number of essential functions within the setting, and the number of individuals within the setting have significant impact on behavior (Wicker, 1973; Willems, 1969).

Need-Press Theory

Stern (1970) expanded the work of Lewin (1936) and Murray (1938). Stern viewed the investigation of person and environment as requiring study of covarying parts of one event or situation. He talked about person variables in terms of needs (self-reports), and environmental variables in terms of press (total of self-reports by all individuals). Behavioral outcomes in a given environment were viewed as a function of the level of congruence between needs and press, or between explicit and implicit press (stated vs. perceived environmental purposes and behavioral rules).

Transactional Approach

Pervin (1968) focused on the extent to which individuals subjectively fit with their interpersonal and physical environments. His basic tenet was that individual performance and satisfaction are better in environments where the discrepancy between perceptions of actual self and ideal self is reduced (Huebner & Corazzini, 1984).

Human Aggregate Approaches

These approaches define an environment in terms of the collective characteristics of its inhabitants. Perhaps the work of Holland (1985) is most representative of this approach. He described six personality types based on vocational preference, and six corresponding occupational environments comprised of people in those designated vocational areas. Holland postulated that individuals search for occupational environments congruent with their personalities, and that such congruence leads to more positive outcomes, such as vocational stability, performance, and satisfaction. He further argued that individuals whose personality patterns were more consistent and more highly differentiated from other personality patterns experienced greater stability and satisfaction (see Chapter 13, by Hackett and Lent; Huebner & Corazzini, 1984).

Social Climate Models

Moos (1976) viewed behavior as a function of the social climate, which he defined as the collective subjective perceptions of the environment and reported behaviors within that context. Moos postulated that the perceived social climate, as a set of environmental variables, had a major impact on individual behavior. Moos's work on social climate in many ways parallels efforts in I/O psychology to examine organizational climate, defined by Schneider and Reichers (1983) as "summated, average meanings that people attach to a particular feature of the setting" (p. 21). Moos and others identified three broad dimensions of social climate: (a) relationships (how people relate); (b) personal development (opportunities for enhanced self-esteem); and (c) system maintenance and system change (how orderly, responsive to change, clear in expectations, and in control the organization is seen to be) (Huebner & Corazzini, 1984; Insel & Moos, 1974; Moos & Van Doort, 1979).

Other Significant Concepts and Approaches

Several others have contributed to a better understanding of the individual and situational factors related to variability in behavior. Mischel (1976) presented a conceptualization of why environments vary in the amount of influence they have over individual behavior. Basically, he hypothesized that, when environmental attributes have minimal effect, it is because individual attributes are present that strongly affect behavior. Millon (1981), taking a somewhat different approach, emphasized the consistency of certain primary individual characteristics that appear to differentially resist the influence of environmental factors, depending on the individual. Millon argued that each individual has certain traits that are highly resistant to environmental influence and other traits that are easily affected by situational factors. Millon (1981) referred to stable and consistent individual characteristics as "personality" (p. 23).

In a number of thorough analyses of concepts of organizational climate, Schneider and Reichers (1983) concluded that climates emerge out of the interactions that members of a work group have with each other. These researchers identified three major views of organizational climate. The first, termed the structuralist approach, assumes that the meanings that individuals give to organizational practices, procedures, and events follows from the actual events themselves. According to this perspective, organizational climates vary as a function of differences in organizational structure variables.

In contrast, the second approach emphasizes the meaning that individuals ascribe to organizational events (Schneider, 1987; Schneider & Reichers, 1983). This process involves an attraction–selection–attrition (ASA) cycle. One of Schneider's (1987) major propositions is that "attraction to an organization, selection by it, and attrition from it yield particular kinds of persons in an organization. These people determine organizational behavior" (p. 441). Schneider (1987) viewed this ASA approach as a way to understand the genesis of both organizational climate (how the organization functions) and culture (why the organization does what it does).

The third viewpoint of organizational climate discussed by Schneider and Reichers (1983) is the symbolic interactionist approach. This perspective places the meaning of events within the interaction between people rather than within the people or the events themselves. This approach also places heavy emphasis on interactions during a new-comer's initial socialization period and stresses the importance of group membership in determining why organizational climates vary among groups. The symbolic interac-tionist viewpoint specifies the nature and content of interactions that result in particu-lar organizational climates. Schneider and Reichers (1983) concluded that "while some researchers have hypothesized the importance of a statistical interaction between per-sons and situations, the symbolic interactionist approach maintains that people in communicative interactions with each other, respond to, define, and interpret elements of the situations in particular ways. These characteristic modes of interpretation and definition form distinct subgroup climates within organizations" (p. 33).

Shullman (1988) introduced the idea of a *calculus of person–environment interaction,* asserting that behavior is a function of two simultaneously and continually changing sets of variables—a set of person/individual variables and a set of environmental/situational variables. She posited that, in addition to the traditional emphasis on the individual and the impact of other people, the incorporation of variables such as technology, physical plant, and policies into a definition of the situation could help bring the practice of counseling psychology into line with the needs of organizations.

Counseling Psychology and Interactionist Models: A Theoretical Interface

Much has been written in recent years about the application of interactionist assump-tions to the practice of counseling psychology, but actual attempts to apply such models systematically have been limited (Claiborn & Lichtenberg, 1989; Hackett, Lent, & Greenhaus, 1991; Shullman, 1989). In fact, virtually all model projects and applica-tions of interactionist approaches have taken place in the context of educational set-tings, emphasizing the campus ecology perspective. Campus ecology, a spin-off of social ecology (Hobbs, 1966; Paul & Huebner, 1977), was an attempt to apply human/ social ecology concepts to student affairs work with students on college and university campuses.

Oetting (1967) suggested that counselors focus their developmental roles on the students and the institution. He encouraged counselors to help students learn how to manage in their environments and to actually create change within their own environ-ments as a goal of growth and development. Morrill and others (Morrill & Hurst, 1971; Morrill, Oetting, & Hurst, 1974) defined three potential roles for the counseling psy-chologist from an interactionist perspective: "to contribute to, support, modify and enhance the learning environment; to facilitate maximum utilization of the learning environment by students; and to study the student, the learning environment and inter-action as a means of providing the necessary data base for the implementation of roles one and two" (Morrill & Hurst, 1971, p. 5).

Morrill and others also broadened the definition of target client populations by including all students, not just those in obvious need of assistance, and advocated professional activity designed to understand the interaction of the student with the campus. They encouraged counselors to leave their offices and become more directly involved in environmental assessment as part of their work with individuals. This strong emphasis on the environment and environmental design roles was further elabo-rated by other writers (Conyne, 1980; Huebner & Corazzini, 1978; Western Interstate Commission for Higher Education, 1973).

Banning and Kaiser (1974) identified three levels of intervention for counseling psychologists in university settings: (a) macrodesigns directed at large numbers of students; (b) microdesigns directed at specific subgroups within the larger population; and (c) life-space designs directed at matching individual students to environments. Treadway (1979) used a macrodesign approach to identify positive aspects of the campus environment and barriers to student development. Based on this project, a number of policy and structural changes were made within the university environment. In contrast, Daher, Corazzini, and McKinnon (1977) used a microdesign approach to develop, implement, and evaluate programs for facilitating students' adjustment to their housing environments.

In essence, it appears that counseling psychologists have effectively applied interactionist concepts to educational settings. Coupled with an emphasis on development, prevention, and health, counseling psychologists have demonstrated that interactionist approaches can make valuable contributions to at least one environmental setting (universities) and the individuals who inhabit it.

The Emergence of Organizational Counseling Psychology as a Subspecialty

Despite the above advances in interactionist models, the practice of counseling psychology has, by and large, continued to heavily emphasize the individual. Although there have been interactionist interventions in university settings, counseling psychologists have virtually ignored using such interventions in other contexts. There are no obvious reasons why a developmental, preventive, health-oriented interactionist approach could not be applied to a variety of organizational settings in the public and private domain. What is required to do this is a focus on interventions on multiple levels of organizational behavior: the individual, the small subgroup, and the larger work environment. This involves examining characteristics and processes of organizational and individual change so that the impact of their interaction can be determined.

Some might argue that such an investigation overlaps with the work of our colleagues in other disciplines. We believe counseling psychologists with organizational perspectives can bring a unique viewpoint to those very organizations, a framework rooted in a fluid conceptualization of the person–environment interaction. Traditionally, MBAs and, to a large degree, I/O psychologists have interpreted person–environment interaction as Behavior = $f(P \times E)$. In general, they have examined issues such as organizational structure and function, and have emphasized a position that addresses what the organization can do to motivate the individual to get the job done. Implicit in this orientation is the concept of the organization as client—the organization as initiator and actor, and the individual as receiver and pawn. When interaction happens here, the cause and effect of this transaction stem from the E (organizational environment), which continuously influences the p (person).

By contrast, clinical psychologists and many counseling psychologists have traditionally expressed the person–environment interaction as Behavior = $f(P \times E)$. They have examined what the individual does to adjust to or control the environment, or, at times, they have explored what is wrong with the person. Historically, emphasis has been placed on either getting P in sync with the existing e, or getting P to operate as if there were infinite choices and predictable consequences.

From our perspective, what has been missing is an emphasis on the $\times$, the dynamic nature of the interaction between the person and the environment. It is not that the interaction has been ignored, but rather that it has been viewed as making fixed or little contribution to variance in behavior. One solution to this dilemma is to initiate a subspecialty within counseling psychology that investigates the calculus of person–environment interactions between two sets of simultaneously and continuously changing sets of variables, P and E. We would call this subspecialty organizational counseling psychology (OCP). We view counseling psychology as being theoretically comfortable with concepts such as simultaneous, continuous, healthy, developmental change—change as a natural, predictable part of individual, group, and organizational life cycles at various levels of complexity. The focus of OCP would be on Behavior = f (P × E), where the individual and organization are in dynamic relation, and *both* P and E are accorded important causal status.

We believe that OCP can emphasize the process of change and how individuals, subgroups, and organizations interact to create and manage positive or negative change experiences. More specifically, we define OCP as a subspecialty in counseling psychology that endorses a multidisciplinary theoretical and applied approach to conceptualizing, investigating, and assisting organizations or businesses and their staff members. This systemic approach is based on the translation and integration of principles, philosophies, and intervention strategies linked with counseling, I/O, social, and community psychology, and other social sciences (e.g., sociology, anthropology, economics, and management).

ORGANIZATIONAL RESEARCH: COUNSELING PSYCHOLOGISTS' ROLE AS SCIENTISTS

We contend that, if counseling psychologists want to enhance their role in providing and evaluating services in the workplace, it is imperative that they continue to adhere to the scientist-professional model that serves as the foundation for our discipline (Meara et al., 1988). This model can effectively guide the actions of counseling psychologists who are drawn to this setting. This organizational environment also offers us a rich source of empirical and experiential data that can be used to refine and strengthen our theoretical, methodological, and therapeutic paradigms.

Before mentioning some possible lines of research that might be pursued in the business arena, we discuss here some basic theoretical issues. As with any other area of research, counseling psychologists who pursue science in the workplace must first observe a phenomenon; identify a need for examining it further; locate, if possible, a theoretical framework to systematically guide the potential investigation and explain the phenomenon; devise a research question or hypothesis; and construct the best possible methodology to study the behavior(s) of interest.

In terms of a theoretical framework, we concur, in general, with Fitzgerald and Rounds (1989), who called for more theory-driven research; Hackett et al. (1991), who encouraged research based on an integration of organizational and counseling psychology; and Weiss (1989), who argued that psychologists conducting research in the workplace should translate basic theories of social, learning, developmental, and experimental psychology to the organizational context. Weiss's thesis is based on the assumption that, for the most part, our current organizational and individual models of behavior are homogeneous; they explain a small subset of human actions in specific settings and lack external validity. In contrast, Weiss claimed that basic theories of psychology are heterogeneous, explaining a host of behaviors across a variety of contexts; thus, they are rich in external validity. Weiss recommended that organizational researchers rely on these theories when operationally defining and investigating constructs and behaviors relevant to the workplace, thereby enhancing our understanding of the principles and dynamics underlying human and organizational behavior.

Although we agree with Weiss's basic premise, we recommend the integration of counseling psychology-derived constructs with basic theories of intrapersonal, interpersonal, and group behavior. For instance, our comprehension of interpersonal relationships at work might be expanded by testing models that join together social psychological explanations of social support with theories of career development and work adjustment.

There are many options for counseling psychologists who want to pursue research in the workplace. The following sections highlight some general topics that seem particularly relevant to the counseling psychology-organizational interface—studies on EAPs, career development programs, multicultural diversity in the workplace, wellness, and organizational behavior. (See Chapter 17, by Myers and Cairo, for suggestions about research on work adjustment.)

Employee Assistance Programs (EAPs)

EAPs are relatively new (they emerged in the past 20 years) to the workplace and the mental health delivery system. Therefore, there are still numerous programmatic and conceptual issues that need to be resolved and investigated. In fact, given the enormous growth rate of EAPs (12,000 + currently), there has been a dearth of research on various aspects of these programs. Additionally, most previous studies were driven by sociological rather than psychological concepts and methodologies (Gerstein, 1990; Gerstein & Bayer, 1990, 1991).

One area that merits further consideration is how helping occurs in the workplace. Although there is a social psychological model designed to explain this phenomenon (Bystander-Equity Model of Workplace Helping Behavior; Bayer & Gerstein, 1988) and research supports this paradigm (Gerstein, 1990; Gerstein & Bayer, 1991), there remains a need to investigate what type of assistance is offered to various kinds of impaired workers (e.g., substance abusers, persons with family problems), when and how frequently it is offered, and by whom. For instance, it is unclear whether racial differences are linked with the identification and helping of workers, particularly when the potential helper and employee are of different ethnic origins. Obtaining data on this issue is extremely important, given predictions about the multicultural makeup of our future work environments. It is also unclear what role the helper's and troubled employee's sex plays in the assistance process. Again, this topic is of considerable importance, given women's increasing presence in managerial positions in which they oversee male and female staff members.

To date, there has been no research on various actions that supervisors and peers might take with workers who display career development, work adjustment, and/or occupational mental health problems. Thus, it is unknown whether employees who exhibit these difficulties get referred to the EAP, and, if they do, it is uncertain how they are viewed (e.g., diagnosed) and treated.

A growing body of literature now suggests that most persons seek EAP services on their own rather than as a result of referral. This literature, however, is replete with conceptual and methodological problems. Therefore, further studies are needed to examine how and when employees decide to obtain services, what factors shape these decisions, and what can be done to ready these individuals for treatment. More importantly, theoretical models must be designed to explain concepts and structures associated with the self-diagnosis and referral processes. Social psychological models of reactance, motivation, compliance, and person perception might be adapted to frame these processes.

Models are also needed to guide research on the short- and long-term effectiveness of EAP interventions. EAPs are set up to serve workers whose job performance has been impaired, but there is little systematic data on whether, after receiving services, these persons function more effectively on their jobs and elsewhere. Surprisingly, there is also a paucity of data (Amaral & Kelly, 1989; Bruhnsen & DuBuc, 1988; Mahoney & Smith, 1989) on the financial costs and benefits of offering these programs. Models designed to explain a variety of outcomes (e.g., financial, psychological, vocational) resulting from EAP interventions are needed, as are studies constructed to test these models. EAPs have much to gain from comprehensive program evaluation efforts. (For a discussion of various program evaluation techniques that are applicable to the workplace, see Sloan, Gruman, & Allegrante, 1987.) EAPs can also benefit from research on how to optimally train employee assistance staff members and from projects that investigate the types of professionals (e.g., mental health counselors, psychologists) best suited for various occupational roles (e.g., crisis workers, trainers, program evaluators) found in these programs.

Adult Career Development and Intervention Programs

A second general area of research that counseling psychologists interested in the workplace might pursue is how adults adjust to work, develop in their careers, and make vocational decisions. Although there are models in the literature that discuss these issues (e.g., Campbell & Heffernan, 1983; Crites, 1986; Hall, 1986; Lofquist & Dawis, 1984; Schein, 1981; Super, 1980), these paradigms need to be refined, expanded, and more thoroughly tested (Greenhaus & Parasuraman, 1986; Hall & Lerner, 1980; Chapter 17, by Myers and Cairo). For instance, the stages of adult development, especially vocational development, must be further operationalized, particularly with respect to the career development of women, persons of color, and individuals in nonprofessional jobs.

Assessment devices constructed specifically to evaluate the behaviors, interests, skills, attitudes, values, aptitudes, and decision-making styles of adults across different stages of vocational development are needed as well. Skill development and career enhancement programs designed to assist adults at various stages of development should also be constructed and tested for their effect on participants' decision-making abilities, job satisfaction, career advancement, and successful transition to different developmental stages (Cairo, 1983; Hall & Lerner, 1980; Super & Hall, 1978). To date, there have been few well-designed studies that have evaluated the effectiveness of career planning and development programs, how employees perceive participation in these programs, and how financial costs and benefits are influenced by participation in these programs (see Chapter 17, by Myers and Cairo; Scarpello & Ledvinka, 1988). In fact, in reviewing 30 studies, Cairo (1983) concluded that there was very little empirical data on the effectiveness or availability of counseling programs in industry. He also claimed that there were many serious conceptual and methodological problems with those studies that had been conducted. Moravec (1982) indicated, however, that career development programs could be cost-effective and helpful to employees and organizations, if properly planned and implemented.

There is a dearth of data on the overall effectiveness of career development programs in the workplace, but there is research on highly specialized programs targeted to change particular vocational behaviors. Participation in programs designed to reduce career plateauing, for example, has been found to be positively related to promotions, performance, and perceived marketability (Stout, Slocum, & Cron, 1988). Further, persons who were exposed to "realistic job previews" had a higher likelihood of staying on the job and were more satisfied with their positions (Wanous, 1980). A meta-analysis of job previews also indicated that participation in these programs resulted in reductions in job turnover (McEvoy & Cascio, 1985).

Providing midcareer managers with counseling also appears to be an effective career intervention (Hall & Hall, 1976), as is mentoring persons at every career stage (Kram, 1985). Mentored individuals feel more satisfied, perceive more job mobility, and expect more promotions and recognition (Fagenson, 1989). Finally, a review of longitudinal research suggested that career progress was linked with participation in management training programs (Wakabayashi, Graen, Graen, & Graen, 1988).

Along with investigating the effectiveness of comprehensive career development programs, it would also be useful to examine the impact of different organizational activities on employees' behavior (Hall & Lerner, 1980). Additional research is needed as well to explore various aspects of how organizations recruit, select, and integrate top executives (succession planning) into the organizational culture (Hall, 1986). Results of each of these efforts might lead to workers' experiencing more challenging and rewarding jobs over the course of their careers.

A related issue that warrants further investigation is the long-term effect of services offered through assessment centers. To date, meta-analytic results on the effectiveness of these programs with respect to future managerial performance and progress are inconsistent (Dobson & Williams, 1989; Gaugler, Rosenthal, Thornton, & Bentson, 1987; Hunter & Hunter, 1984). Some researchers have discovered that assessment center participation was predictive of later job performance (Bray & Grant, 1966; Klimoski & Brickner, 1987; Noe & Steffy, 1987); others either failed to find this association (Turnage & Muchinsky, 1984) or found that subordinate ratings were better and less expensive predictors on some criteria (McEvoy & Beatty, 1989).

Low correlations also have been discovered among involvement in these centers, role playing, and on-the-job training (Pynes & Bernardin, 1989). Questions about the construct validity of assessment center procedures have been raised as well (Klimoski & Brickner, 1987), leading some researchers to conclude that various methods result in different findings (Bycio, Alvares, & Hahn, 1987). Questions also remain about the effectiveness of executive coaching on job placement, adjustment, and development. To date, there is no research on this topic.

Another area of research that organizational counseling psychology might pursue is the effectiveness of outplacement counseling. One author claimed that outplacement counseling succeeds frequently (over 90% placement rates) in helping workers find jobs (Henriksen, 1982); others have observed that such success rates are based on anecdotal support (Roscow & Zager, 1984).

A very important topic deserving of our attention is the interface between the career needs of organizations and their employees (Granrose & Portwood, 1987; London & Stumpf, 1986). As yet, it is still relatively unclear how an organization's development and an employee's development influence each other. Models that integrate concepts from organizational (e.g., organizational culture, managerial structures), social (e.g., group behavior, reward structures), and vocational psychology (e.g., work adjustment, job satisfaction) could help illuminate this interaction. Evaluation devices based on these models could also be used to assist in long-range planning designed to maximize the needs of the organization and its staff.

Cultural Diversity

One can only speculate about what kinds of issues will arise as our work force becomes more diverse in terms of race, sex, nationality, and other factors (e.g., persons with physical and/or behavioral impairments). Even so, there are some predictable topics that could be researched. For example, the norms, roles, expectations, values, behaviors, and dynamics involved in the socialization and maintenance processes of multicultural work groups could be investigated, as could the effects of culturally diverse groups on individual and work-unit job performance. Other topics include: (a) design and evaluation of training programs to enhance communication and respect among culturally diverse employees; (b) examination of the effects of tokenism, affirmative action, and discrimination (including reverse discrimination) on employee behaviors and attitudes (Greenhaus & Parasuraman, 1986); (c) investigation of the association between employees' sex and management styles, decision-making, communication skills, and the formation and maintenance of supervisor–subordinate and peer–peer relationships; (d) ways in which work and family expectations and accomplishments of women might affect the career roles and values of future generations of males and females; (e) long-term influences of dual-career couples/families on parental and offspring roles, work and life satisfaction, and job performance (see Chapter 12, by Gilbert); and (f) preparation of counseling professionals, so that they can offer preventive and remedial services to multicultural employees and work groups.

Workplace Wellness and Stress Management Programs

As noted earlier, workplace wellness programs are on the rise, serving important functions for organizations and individuals. It has been discovered that participation in comprehensive wellness and fitness programs leads to overall improvements (Bly, Jones, & Richardson, 1986; Bowne, Russell, Morgan, Optenberg, & Clarke, 1984), including enhanced fitness, reductions in coronary risk factors (Wilbur, 1983), decreased health care costs (Bly et al., 1986; Warner, Wickizer, Wolfe, Schildroth, & Samuelson, 1988), lowered absenteeism (Bowne et al., 1984), and improved job performance (Bernacki & Baun, 1984). Similar results have been found when investigating the effects of stress management programs on employee behaviors (Everly & Feldman, 1985; Hollander & Lengermann, 1988).

Although these findings are encouraging, more recent reviews indicated that many of these projects involved interventions and outcomes for individuals and not organizations, thereby ignoring situational variables (Ivancevich, Matteson, Freedman, & Phillips, 1990). The research methodology used in these studies has also been described as less than ideal (DeFrank & Cooper, 1987; Ivancevich & Matteson, 1986; Murphy, 1986).

Beyond addressing these shortcomings, there are some other worksite wellness or stress issues that counseling psychologists might investigate. In particular, the following questions could be explored in empirical studies:

1. What are the long-term effects of worksite wellness programs on the vocational behavior of employed individuals and future generations of employees?
2. Will members of our work force, as a result of participating in these programs, be less competitive, more successful, and more invested in their jobs?
3. What effect will these programs have on the family, the community, and a worker's spiritual growth?
4. How will involvement in these programs influence the quality of goods and services produced?
5. What are the psychological ramifications for employees and organizations, if employers continue to carry the monetary burden of providing these programs? What will happen if this burden is placed on the worker?

To pursue research on these questions and others related to worksite wellness and stress management programs, it will be necessary to synthesize theoretical models and methodological technologies tied to health, business, vocational psychology, and social psychology. (For a detailed description of types of worksite wellness programs, see Gebhardt and Crump (1990); for a conceptual model to offer worksite stress management programs, see Ivancevich et al. (1990).)

Organizational Behavior

Although organizational behavior is typically the province of I/O psychologists, members of our profession can offer a slightly different perspective, particularly if they adopt the Behavior = f (P × E) model described earlier. For example, instruments are needed to assess organizational culture, climate, and citizenship behavior from a developmental perspective. This perspective can serve as the foundation for measures designed to evaluate an individual's and a work group's job performance. It would also be helpful to identify and investigate the stages of development for work teams (Sundstrom et al., 1990). Theoretical models that explain the link between modifications in an organization's structure and workers' adjustment are needed as well. These models might focus, for instance, on the effects that mergers, downsizing, and participatory decision-making have on worker stability, job commitment and satisfaction, and career development (e.g., recruitment, advancement, and retirement).

Organizations would also benefit from models and research projects that explain interdepartmental communication structures and their effect on job performance; models that identify networking variables that influence interdepartment activities; studies that can assist administrators in the construction and implementation of comprehensive human resource systems; and projects that evaluate and facilitate an organization's and its workers' capacity for change (Jackson & Schuler, 1990). As yet, we know very little about the process of organizational change and its influence on people and organizations.

PREPARING ORGANIZATIONAL COUNSELING PSYCHOLOGISTS: THE CAREER NEEDS OF STUDENTS AND PRACTICING PROFESSIONALS

Since its inception, leaders of counseling psychology have discussed how to train graduate students to practice in business and organizational settings. Four basic training models have been mentioned but are only briefly described in the literature (Osipow, 1982b). The first suggests that a new specialty in this area be offered within the counseling psychology program; the second argues for students to complete a business or I/O specialization outside of the program but as a part of their doctoral studies. The third model recommends that a subspecialty be made available in the program; this model requires the development of a few new courses and the infusion of information on business and organizational settings in the existing doctoral curriculum. The fourth model suggests that persons interested in this area of practice receive training (e.g., participation in continuing education classes, workshops, and institutes; work experiences) after earning their doctorate. We contend that training programs should be designed for both students and doctoral-level professionals who want to affiliate with businesses. Each group can benefit from experiences and courses that address their needs and competencies.

Training for Business Settings: A Survey of Counseling Psychology Programs

To determine how many counseling psychology programs are currently preparing students to practice in business and organizational settings and the types of programs being offered, we constructed a 34-item survey and mailed it (Spring 1990) to each Training Director affiliated with the Council of Counseling Psychology Training Programs. Our sample consisted of 71 doctoral-level training programs. (Most of these programs were APA-approved (88%).) After two follow-up letters, we received 42 usable responses (59% return rate).

As shown in Table 18.3, 9 programs (21% of the total responses) offered a subspecialty in business and organizational settings. Typically, this subspecialty was named some variation of "Organizational Consultation" ($n = 4$). One program labeled the subspecialty "Counseling in Business and Industry." Of the remaining 33 programs that responded to our survey, 7 (17%) permitted their students to complete a specialization in business and organizational settings in another department or program (e.g., management); 4 (10%) reported that their students took business courses (without a specialty); and 22 (52%) indicated no subspecialty in this area and no student enrollment in business classes. Thus, 38% of the responding programs offered students an opportunity to specialize in business and organizational settings, a finding that is somewhat consistent with a survey conducted in 1985 (Foley & Redfering, 1987). Moreover, 48% of the programs in the current survey reported some association with business classes. It should also be noted that 50% of respondents mentioned that the topic of counseling psychology in business and organizational settings was addressed in their curricula.

Table 18.3 also presents data on respondents' perceptions of the percentage of students involved in specialty training for the workplace. Extrapolating from these data, it appears that 13% of counseling psychology students were enrolled in a curriculum that prepared them to practice in business environments. Further, according to the 42 respondents, 16% of the graduate students in their programs were interested in these settings—a result that is fairly similar to Fitzgerald and Osipow's (1988) findings. Our respondents also reported that 4% of their graduates were currently affiliated with the business community.

When respondents were asked how many of their faculty had expertise in counseling psychology in business and organizational settings, most stated one or none, depending on whether their program offered a subspecialty in business settings. This finding is also reflected in respondents' beliefs about what factors inhibit and contribute to students' pursuing an interest in business and organizational settings. Our data suggest that faculty interest may be a major factor. Other obstacles mentioned by the respondents (e.g., inflexible curriculum, unavailable courses, focus of the program), for the most part, result from the structure of the curriculum offered. In contrast, factors that frequently facilitate this pursuit included student interest, the financial rewards and opportunities of this setting, career opportunities, and students' business background.

Overall, the results of our survey were quite encouraging. Many counseling psychology training programs are introducing students to, or preparing them to practice in, business and organizational work environments. It does seem, however, that many programs lack faculty with interest in this area and/or, because of curriculum requirements, are unable or unwilling to offer this subspecialty.

Table 18.3 Descriptive Data on Counseling Psychology Programs That Train Students for Business and Organizational Settings

Variables	Percent of Programs		Percent of Students Enrolled		Number of Faculty with Expertise		Total Faculty		Percent of Students Interested	
	Mn	Sd	Mn	Sd	Mn	Sd	Mn	Sd	Mn	Sd
Programs with subspecialty[a] (n = 9)	21		9	5.1	1	.87	7	2.1	8	4.3
Ball State Univ.										
Columbia Univ.										
Kent State Univ.										
Michigan State Univ.										
Ohio State Univ.										
Univ. of Illinois										
Univ. of Kentucky										
Univ. of Texas—Austin										
Univ. of Utah										
Subspecialty elsewhere[b] (n = 7)	17		5	7.6	.9	.90	6	1.3	8	7.6
Indiana Univ.										
Loyola Univ.—Chicago										
Univ. of Florida										
Univ. of Iowa										
Univ. of Minnesota-Psy										
Univ. of Oregon										
Univ. of Southern Calif										
Only business classes[c] (n = 4)	10		8	5.4	1	1.4	9	2.5	5	4.4
Boston College										
Univ. of Georgia										
Univ. of Kansas										
Univ. of Pittsburgh										
No focus (n = 22)	52				.3	.66	7	1.8	4	5.2

Note: Total n = 42. In some instances, figures are based on lower n's. Mn = mean; Sd = standard deviation.

[a]These programs offer some type of subspecialty in counseling psychology in business and organizational settings in their curriculum.

[b]These programs permit their students to complete a subspecialty in business/organizational settings in another department/program.

[c]These programs do not offer a specialty, but students do take business classes.

Skills of Counseling Psychologists in Business and Organizational Settings

Historically, a number of authors have discussed the competencies and knowledge needed by counseling and other psychologists to practice effectively in business environments (Beer & Walton, 1990; Cristiani & Cristiani, 1979; Foley & Redfering, 1979; Gerstein & Cholofsky, 1986; Leonard, 1977; Lewis & Lewis, 1986; McLagan, 1983; Myers, 1982; Oberer & Lee, 1986; Offermann & Gowing, 1990; Osipow, 1982b; Schein, 1990; Toomer, 1982). Table 18.4 synthesizes the areas of expertise that we and others believe are important for organizational counseling psychologists to possess.

Curriculum for Predoctoral Specialization in Counseling and Business

Given the competencies listed in Table 18.4, it behooves counseling psychology programs to carefully select students who are interested in specializing in business and organizational settings. Persons who complete coursework in business, anthropology, or sociology would seem suited for this subspecialty, as would individuals with a business background or a special interest in adult career development (Stark & Romans, 1982). Regardless of their background, these students should exhibit strong conceptual, methodological, and human relations skills.

The training model we propose offers students a specialization in business and organizational settings within the counseling psychology program. It is critical, however, given the interdisciplinary foundation of the competencies mentioned previously, that strong bridges be established with other departments (e.g., business, sociology) on the university campus. The basic objective of this training program is to prepare scientist-professionals to function as service providers, trainers, program designers, program evaluators, administrators, consultants, and/or researchers in business and organizational settings. In addition, the program is constructed to ready graduates to pursue academic careers with these settings as their major empirical focus.

Our proposed 4-year curriculum is designed so that students complete a sequence of psychology (e.g., I/O, community), business (e.g., management, human resources, organizational development), and other (e.g., occupational sociology, field research methods) courses within a 3-year period, followed by a 1-year full-time internship. Rather than discuss each class included in our proposed curriculum, we present here an overview of two new counseling psychology courses, as well as the practica and internship experience.

Table 18.4 Necessary Knowledge and Skills for Organizational Counseling Psychologists

ADULT DEVELOPMENT   Understanding models of adult development and how to apply these models in the workplace in order to teach adults the acquisition and maintenance of skills.

CAREER DEVELOPMENT   Comprehending models of adult career development, work adjustment, job analysis, and job satisfaction, and models of organizational career development. Using instruments to assess these concepts. Designing adult and organizational career development programs and interventions.

ORGANIZATIONAL BEHAVIOR   Knowing models of organizational development, structure, dynamics, culture, climate, human resources management, personnel practices, EAPs, and training. Conducting organizational assessments.

Table 18.4 (*Continued*)

GROUP BEHAVIOR   Understanding social psychological models of group behavior and how to apply methodologies to assess and change group dynamics.

WELLNESS   Grasping models of worksite wellness programs. Implementing health promotion and intervention strategies.

INTERDISCIPLINARY MODELS OF BEHAVIOR   Familiarity with concepts and research techniques advocated by the various social sciences (e.g., sociology, anthropology, economics, political science) and other disciplines in psychology (e.g., community, developmental, and I/O psychology).

SYSTEMS   Comprehending various systemic models and social structures. Using technologies designed to assess systemic concepts.

FOUNDATIONS OF BUSINESS   Knowing basic principles of management, economics, accounting, and marketing. Being aware of business strategies and philosophies, and characteristics of the workplace and the economy (national and international). Preparing cost-benefit analyses, and budgets. Performing strategic planning.

ETHICS   Understanding competencies and responsibilities and how they relate to ethical standards endorsed by psychologists and the business community.

CONCEPTUAL MODEL BUILDING   Thinking creatively and logically. Being able to identify, evaluate, and use a host of ideas and observations. Employing these skills to build and test useful and acceptable models and interventions.

RELATIONSHIP BUILDING   Establishing and maintaining effective relationships with a broad range of individuals and groups, including executives and staff members. Exhibiting strong human relations skills. Capable of negotiating, delegating, influencing, and sharing feedback with others.

COMMUNICATIONS   Speaking the language of business and communicating effectively. Translating science and theory into understandable terms and practice. Having marketing competencies. Preparing appropriate and creative reports that achieve objectives. Employing audio-visual technologies to communicate information effectively. Achieving proficiency in using computers.

PROBLEM SOLVING   Comprehending and implementing various problem-solving models.

COUNSELING INTERVENTIONS   Knowing and employing a variety of models of brief counseling and group counseling. Being able to assist multiculturally diverse individuals and groups. Developing and implementing preventive and remedial programs. Using a host of assessment devices.

PROGRAM EVALUATION   Understanding models of program evaluation. Performing program evaluations and preparing recommendations.

RESEARCH   Constructing, choosing, and employing field methodologies and quantitative and qualitative statistical approaches. Interpreting and communicating findings.

CONSULTATION   Comprehending and using models and methods of consultation.

Note: The skills and knowledge areas presented are *not* ordered in terms of their importance. Competent organizational counseling psychologists exhibit some degree of proficiency in each of the 17 areas. These professionals are not expected to display a high degree of expertise in every area.

The proposed new course in OCP is intended to cover the following topics: (a) the history of counseling psychology in business and organizational settings; (b) the vocational behavior of adults (e.g., career development, work adjustment, job satisfaction); (c) vocational assessment strategies used with adults (e.g., instruments, assessment centers); (d) the career development of organizations; (e) models and technologies of consultation and program evaluation; (f) worksite wellness and safety programs; (g) EAPs; (h) research issues and questions of interest; and (i) trade publications important to the business community (e.g., *Wall Street Journal*). This course would provide students with a strong conceptual foundation and some of the research and applied skills they will need to function as organizational counseling psychologists.

The proposed new Seminar in Counseling Psychology in Business and Organizational Settings is also intended to teach students research and applied skills. The overall objective of this course, however, is to provide a forum for critical thinking and the integration of concepts and methodologies advocated by the various social sciences. In addition, this course teaches students how to translate principles (e.g., models of human development and health) and philosophies (e.g., focus on strengths, the importance of relationships) of counseling psychology to the workplace. Ethical issues related to functioning as a scientist-professional in the workplace are examined as well.

During their first practicum, students would be expected to spend 10 to 15 hours per week in a human resources unit (e.g., personnel, EAP, wellness) linked with an organization or business. This placement ought to provide students with an opportunity (e.g., through job shadowing) to learn how the unit and organization operate. It should also offer them a chance to do direct service (e.g., counseling) with employees, under the supervision of a licensed psychologist. The second practicum would also require students to spend 10 to 15 hours per week in a human resources unit. We recommend that this be the same unit that the student was placed in during the first practicum. Students should gain further experience as direct service providers and should begin to use their program development, evaluation, and budgeting skills throughout the course of this placement.

The skills just mentioned should be used and refined during the 1-year internship. In addition, students should be expected to develop some administrative, supervisory, and training skills. We know of only one APA-accredited internship in a business setting (Contact Inc., an EAP located in Tempe, Arizona); we generally recommend that students select APA-accredited sites that interface with businesses and/or that offer extensive community outreach and evaluation services to adults and large groups.

Postdoctoral Curriculum in Organizational Counseling Psychology

In practice, the current structure of predoctoral training programs typically precludes the depth of study required to help new professionals adequately address the challenges of practicing in organizational settings. Thus, postdoctoral preparation may be a more realistic goal for adequate training in OCP. Perhaps the most comprehensive postdoctoral program to date for counseling psychologists in the workplace has been designed by Carder and Bender (1989). In this program, the core skills acquired in counseling psychology are considered as the foundation for more advanced work. The components of this 40-week training experience include didactic seminars, individual and group supervision, and practica projects or placements. The curriculum has seven major areas: (a) overview of organizational development and human resources consultation (historical roots and assumptions of OD); (b) understanding of organizations (overview of theories of management, culture, and reward systems); (c) organizational diagnosis; (d) interventions (human resources models, and individual- and group-oriented techniques); (e) large systems (information on organizational structure, design, and change); (f) evaluation of organizational development efforts (theories and methods); and (g) practice of organizational consultation (ethics, creating a practice).

Carder and Bender (1989) identified several student and supervisory issues that need to be addressed during training. For students, they noted that postgraduate trainees experience a sense of "starting over" and initially display a lack of confidence in being able to apply their previous training to organizational situations. There are also external realities, such as financial and career status, with which to contend. Carder and Bender perceived postdoctoral trainees as struggling with a redefinition of the client while they are engaged in organizational work. These struggles involve conceptual, ethical, and practical dilemmas as well as threats to the trainee's professional self-concept.

A major supervisory issue involves a shift in focus in the supervisory relationship, with increasing emphasis on the content of the organizational intervention and the application of theory and models. For some, this represents a significant departure from a primary focus on the relationship between the supervisor and the trainee. Carder and Bender's (1989) program emphasizes the need to use multiple supervisors who themselves have made the career transition from traditional counseling psychology to full-time organizational work. Carder and Bender argued that supervisors should have had training in their supervisory roles, noting that the successful application of counseling psychology in organizational settings no more assures the development of good supervisory skills than does counseling ability assure the development of good clinical supervisory skills. They concluded that postdoctoral training models may provide the most viable option for preparing counseling psychologists for work in organizational settings.

ETHICAL ISSUES FOR THE ORGANIZATIONAL COUNSELING PSYCHOLOGIST

The practice of OCP involves an elaborate set of ethical issues. With a more complex definition of the helping relationship, there are major issues surrounding how professionals perform their roles with organization members. Carder and Bender (1989) cited the problem of defining the client as one of the most challenging for the organizational practitioner. Also, there is potential for misconduct and abuse of clients inherent in any helping relationship, particularly as client relationships become more multifaceted (Huse & Cummings, 1985). At times, the needs of the larger organization may appear to conflict with those of specific individuals within the organization. Further, there are predictable ethical dilemmas that emerge as a result of organizational practice.

Confidentiality, Use of Information, and Boundaries of Analysis

Organizational practitioners invariably obtain great quantities of information. Knowing when and how to use particular information is essential. It is also critical to be clear about the conditions under which the information is obtained and how the organization and/or individuals treat such information. There can be pressure to share information in organizational settings, to enhance the perceived power of the intervener (Huse & Cummings, 1985). Inappropriate information sharing, however, although well intended, may harm individuals, work groups, or the organization as a whole. A related dilemma involves being asked for information that is obtained inadvertently as part of a data-gathering effort. If such information reflects poorly on certain respondents, for example, the organizational practitioner can be in a great bind about how to proceed.

Choice of Intervention and Scope of Competence

The choice of an organizational intervention is based on some level of organizational diagnosis and assessment. To a large extent, both the diagnosis and the choice of intervention are linked closely to the values and beliefs of the individual organizational practitioner. If the initial assessment does not include a realistic appraisal of environmental readiness to engage in certain interventions, or other such contextual factors, then the organization may experience extreme resistance and conflict related to intervention efforts. Further, if the organizational practitioner selects a strategy beyond the scope of individual competence, then the organization may end up dedicating time, money, and valuable human resources to misguided efforts.

Consent and Informed Choice

Many roles and functions of organizational practitioners involve procedures that should require the consent of participating individuals and work groups. Even when participants give consent to participate in organizational interventions, they may not have sufficient knowledge about approaches and procedures to truly give informed consent. Organizations and managers may state that employees have the option to refuse to participate, but perceived coercion can be involved. This situation can result from perceptions of how the organization or particular managers privately view lack of participation in activities sanctioned by the organization.

Client Manipulation and Withholding of Services

It may be argued that any organizational intervention designed to change participant behavior in and of itself constitutes client manipulation. Further, it is conceivable that no organizational program or intervention exists that does not involve some level of client manipulation (Huse & Cummings, 1985). One rule of thumb used by many organizational practitioners is to keep all programs, processes, and information collected as open as possible, to minimize manipulative professional behavior (Huse & Cummings, 1985).

Perhaps one of the greatest dilemmas for organizational practitioners rests in deciding how and whether to be involved in various organizational interventions. If certain programs are to take place anyway, it could be argued that the practitioner has an obligation to constructively assist the organization (Argyris, 1961). This issue may be particularly critical if the practitioner already has established an ongoing working relationship with the organizational client (Huse & Cummings, 1985).

The issues just mentioned represent only a small but significant sample of the ethical concerns and dilemmas involved in organizational practice and research. It is clear that, as the complexity of organizations increases, the potential for ethical dilemmas also increases considerably. The Ethical Guidelines of the American Psychological Association (APA, 1990) may be inadequate to deal with many of the organizational dilemmas that can emerge. Therefore, organizational counseling psychologists must be particularly vigilant to ethical binds occurring in the workplace.

CONCLUSION

Different groups—organizations, employees, and scientific communities—can potentially benefit from the contributions of organizational counseling psychologists. At this time, the business community is much more inclined to value its human resources. It is widely understood that investing in human resources can reduce insurance claims and the use of other benefits. Moreover, to compete successfully in the international and national marketplaces, it is recognized that the needs of workers must be addressed, and an environment that fosters growth, creativity, cooperation, respect, and productivity must be created and maintained. Preparing counseling psychologists to function as scientist-professionals in the workplace can contribute to this overall objective. Specifically, counseling psychologists could help organizations to: (a) decrease job turnover; (b) increase job involvement; (c) facilitate communication between and within departments; (d) clarify the mission of departments and the organization as a whole; (e) assist in establishing mid-range and long-term goals; (f) improve psychological reward structures; (g) identify strengths and weaknesses in the organizational structure; (h) improve the corporate culture and climate; (i) enhance services provided to consumers; (j) attract new corporate clients (e.g., results of program evaluation studies can be used as a marketing tool); and (k) strengthen the organization's relationship with the academic community. The benefits to organizations, in both human and financial terms, are apparent.

Employees can also profit from an increased presence of counseling psychologists in the workplace. For instance, counseling or consulting interventions can be used to restructure the work environment so that employees experience greater job satisfaction, better morale, more involvement in corporate decisions, and a greater commitment to the organization's mission. Revisions to this environment could also lead to increases in employee benefits, more promotions, facilitation of worker transitions in and out of the organization, and reductions in stress, discrimination, and accidents. Overall, such outcomes can improve the "fit" among the employee, his or her job, and the work environment. This, in turn, can significantly elevate a person's quality of work life.

It can be argued that counseling psychology as a discipline would be enriched through greater involvement in the workplace. This setting provides an excellent medium for synthesizing our interests in vocational behavior, mental health, and education. Moreover, our science base could be expanded. For example, models of human development, wellness, leisure, family life, cultural diversity, and group behavior may be extended to investigate vocational behavior across the adult life span. This expansion could enhance the generalizability of our theories, because data would be gathered on multiculturally diverse adults in their natural environment. The realism of our research would be strengthened, and there could be a greater likelihood of changing individual and group behavior. Further, our opportunities for data sites and grant funding would be expanded.

Exposure to organizational research might also enhance graduate students' desire to pursue empirical activities. Most of our students have a strong motivation to contribute to society in some tangible fashion. Because of this, it is not surprising that they are often "turned off" by laboratory studies that do not focus on issues that they consider to be important to society and human welfare. Action research conducted in the workplace, however, does not suffer from mundane realism. If carried out properly, including appropriate recommendations to the organization being served, such research can have an immediate, long-term, and positive effect on individuals and organizations. Thus, organizational research can provide students with a clearer appreciation of how science is relevant to practice, and may enhance their identification with the scientist-professional model.

In conclusion, we strongly contend that counseling psychologists, as scientists and practitioners, can make a unique contribution to the workplace. Many different types of social scientists have recognized the urgency of providing a variety of mental health, career, and organizational services at the workplace. In fact, a recent issue of the *American Psychologist* (February, 1990) detailed how psychologists could contribute to this setting. Surprisingly, the role of counseling psychologists in this setting was mentioned only once (Ilgen, 1990). Moreover, this author presented a narrow view of our role and placed greater emphasis on the contributions that I/O psychologists could make to organizations. It is hoped that counseling psychologists will become more actively involved in the development, provision, administration, and evaluation of organizational and individual services offered at the worksite. We agree with Dunnette and Kirchner (1965), who stated over 25 years ago that "it is unlikely that counseling will disappear from the industrial scene" (p. 98). We are also quite certain that members of our profession have much more to contribute through the practice of organizational counseling psychology. Counseling psychologists who bring their expertise and traditions to the workplace (emphasizing applied developmental and holistic practice, the person–environment interaction, applications of career development and small-group processes, and the scientist-professional model) will find that the workplace will not only be responsive, but may actually change as a result of their efforts.

REFERENCES

Alderfer, C. (1980). The methodology of organizational diagnosis. *Professional Psychology, 11,* 459–468.

Amaral, T., & Kelly, M. (1989, October). *EAP cost–benefits analysis: Exploring assumptions.* Paper presented at the annual meeting of the Employee Assistance Professionals Association, Baltimore, MD.

American Psychological Association. (1990). Ethical principles of psychologists. *American Psychologist, 45,* 390–395.

American Psychologist. (1990). *45*(2), 95–283. [Special issue: Organizational Psychology]

Argyris, C. (1961, Fall). Explorations in consulting–client relationships. *Human Organizations, 20,* 121–133.

Banning, J., & Kaiser, L. (1974). An ecological perspective and model for campus design. In C. Parker (Ed.), Thirty-six faces of counseling. *Personnel & Guidance Journal, 52,* 370–375.

Barker, R. (1968). *Ecological psychology: Concepts and methods for studying the environment of human behavior.* Stanford, CA: Stanford University Press.

Bayer, G., & Gerstein, L. (1988). An adaptation of models of prosocial behavior to supervisor interventions with troubled employees. *Journal of Applied Social Psychology, 18,* 23–37.

Beer, M., & Walton, E. (1990). Developing the competitive organization. *American Psychologist, 45,* 154–161.

Bellows, R. (1961). *Psychology of personnel in business and industry.* Englewood Cliffs, NJ: Prentice-Hall.

Bernacki, E., & Baun, W. (1984). The relationship of job performance to exercise adherence in a corporate fitness program. *Journal of Occupational Medicine, 26,* 529–531.

Blum, M., & Balinsky, B. (1951). *Counseling and psychotherapy.* Englewood Cliffs, NJ: Prentice-Hall.

Bly, J., Jones, R., & Richardson, T. (1986). Impact of worksite health promotion on health care costs and utilization: Evaluation of Johnson & Johnson's live for life program. *Journal of the American Medical Association, 256,* 3235–3240.

Bowne, D., Russell, M., Morgan, M., Optenberg, S., & Clarke, A. (1984). Reduced disability and health care costs in an industrial fitness program. *Journal of Occupational Medicine, 26,* 809–816.

Bray, D., & Grant, D. (1966). The assessment center in the measurement of potential for business management. *Psychological Monographs, 80*(625), 25.

Bruhnsen, K., & DuBuc, L. (1988). A cost–benefit analysis of the University of Michigan Medical Center's EAP. *ALMACAN, 18*(8), 28–30.

Bycio, P., Alvares, K., & Hahn, J. (1987). Situational specificity in assessment center ratings: A confirmatory factor analysis. *Journal of Applied Psychology, 72,* 463–474.

Cairo, P. (1983). Counseling in industry: A selected review of the literature. *Personnel Psychology, 36,* 1–18.

Campbell, J., & Dunnette, M. (1968). Effectiveness of T-group experiences in managerial training and development. *Psychological Bulletin, 20,* 73–104.

Campbell, R., & Heffernan, J. (1983). Adult vocational behavior. In W. Walsh & S. Osipow (Eds.), *Handbook of vocational psychology: Volume 1. Foundations* (pp. 223–260). Hillsdale, NJ: Erlbaum.

Carder, C., & Bender, L. (1989). *A training model for counseling psychologists in the workplace.* Paper presented at the annual meeting of the American Psychological Association, New Orleans, LA.

Cascio, W. (1986). *Managing human resources.* New York: McGraw-Hill.

Claiborn, C., & Lichtenberg, J. (1989). Interactional counseling. *The Counseling Psychologist, 17,* 355–453.

Cohen, W. (1985). Health promotion in the workplace: A prescription for good health. *American Psychologist, 40,* 213–216.

Conyne, R. (1980). Toward primary prevention: An evaluation research approach for college counselors. *Journal of College Student Personnel, 21,* 426–431.

Cristiani, T., & Cristiani, M. (1979). The application of counseling skills in the business and industrial setting. *Personnel & Guidance Journal, 58,* 166–169.

Crites, J. (1986). Appraising adults' career capabilities: Ability, interest, and personality. In Z. Leibowitz & D. Lea (Eds.), *Adult career development: Concepts, issues, & practices* (pp. 63–83). Alexandria, VA: AACD Press.

Daher, D., Corazzini, J., & McKinnon, R. (1977). An environmental redesign program for residence halls. *Journal of College Student Personnel, 18,* 11–15.

DeFrank, R., & Cooper, C. (1987). Worksite management interventions: Their effectiveness and conceptualization. *Journal of Managerial Psychology, 2,* 4–10.

De Meuse, K., & Liebowitz, S. (1981). An empirical analysis of team-building research. *Group & Organization Studies, 6,* 357–378.

Dobson, P., & Williams, A. (1989). The validation of the selection of male British army officers. *Journal of Occupational Psychology, 62,* 313–325.

DuBrin, A. (1988). *Human relations: A job-oriented approach.* Englewood Cliffs, NJ: Prentice-Hall.

Dunnette, M., & Kirchner, W. (1965). *Psychology applied to industry.* New York: Appleton-Century-Crofts.

Dustin, D., & Blocher, D. (1984). Theories and models of consultation. In S. Brown & R. Lent (Eds.), *Handbook of counseling psychology* (pp. 751–781). New York: Wiley.

Everly, G., Feldman, R. (Eds.). (1985). *Occupational health promotion: Health behavior in the workplace.* New York: Wiley.

Fagenson, E. (1989). The mentor advantage: Perceived career/job experiences of protégés versus non-protégés. *Journal of Organizational Behavior, 10,* 309–320.

Farkas, G. (1989). The impact of federal rehabilitation laws on the expanding role of Employee Assistance Programs in business and industry. *American Psychologist, 44,* 1482–1490.

Fitzgerald, L., & Osipow, S. (1988). We have seen the future, but is it us? The vocational aspirations of graduate students in counseling psychology. *Professional Psychology: Research & Practice, 19,* 575–583.

Fitzgerald, L., & Rounds, J. (1989). Vocational Behavior, 1988: A critical analysis. *Journal of Vocational Behavior, 35,* 105–163.

Foley, R., & Redfering, D. (1987). Bridging the gap between counseling psychologists and organization development consultants. *Journal of Business & Psychology, 2,* 160–170.

Frayne, C., & Latham, G. (1987). Application of social learning theory to employee self-management of attendance. *Journal of Applied Psychology, 72,* 387–392.

Fulmer, R., & Gilkey, R. (1988). Blending corporate families: Management and organizational development in a postmerger environment. *Academy of Management Executives, 2,* 275–283.

Gaeth, G., & Shanteau, J. (1984). Reducing the influence of irrelevant information on experienced decision makers. *Organizational Behavior & Human Performance, 33*, 263–282.

Gallessich, J. (1985). Toward a meta-theory of consultation. *The Counseling Psychologist, 13*, 336–354.

Gaugler, B., Rosenthal, D., Thornton, G., & Bentson, C. (1987). Meta-analysis of assessment center validity. *Journal of Applied Psychology, 72*, 493–511.

Gavin, J. (1982). A change of heart is not enough. *The Counseling Psychologist, 10*(3), 29–30.

Gebhardt, D., & Crump, C. (1990). Employee fitness and wellness programs in the workplace. *American Psychologist, 45*, 262–272.

Gerstein, L. (1990). The Bystander-Equity Model of Supervisory Helping Behavior: Past and future research on the prevention of employee problems. In P. Roman (Ed.), *Alcohol problem intervention in the workplace: Employee Assistance Programs and strategic alternatives* (pp. 203–225). Westport, CT: Quorum.

Gerstein, L., & Bayer, G. (1990). Counseling psychology and Employee Assistance Programs: Previous obstacles and potential contributions. *Journal of Business and Psychology, 5*, 101–111.

Gerstein, L., & Bayer, G. (1991). Counseling and the Bystander-Equity Model of Supervisory Helping Behavior: Directions for EAP research. *Journal of Counseling and Development, 69*, 241–247.

Gerstein, M., & Chalofsky, N. (1986). Training professionals for career development responsibilities in business and industry. In Z. Leibowitz & D. Lea (Eds.), *Adult career development: Concepts, issues, & practices* (pp. 310–323). Alexandria, VA: AACD Press.

Goldstein, I., & Gilliam, P. (1990). Training system issues in the year 2000. *American Psychologist, 45*, 134–143.

Granrose, C., & Portwood, J. (1987). Matching individual career plans and organizational career management. *Academy of Management Journal, 4*, 699–720.

Greenhaus, J., & Parasuraman, S. (1986). Vocational and organizational behavior, 1985: A review. *Journal of Vocational Behavior, 29*, 115–176.

Gutteridge, T. (1986). Organizational career development systems: The state of the practice. In D. Hall (Ed.), *Career development in organizations* (pp. 50–94). San Francisco: Jossey-Bass.

Gutteridge, T., & Otte, F. (1983). Organizational and career development: What's going on out there? *Training & Development Journal, 37*, 22–26.

Hackett, G., Lent, R., & Greenhaus, J. (1991). Advances in vocational theory and research: A 20-year retrospective. *Journal of Vocational Behavior, 38*, 3–38.

Hall, D. (Ed.). (1986). *Career development in organizations*. San Francisco: Jossey-Bass.

Hall, D., & Hall, F. (1976, Summer). What's new in career management. *Organization Dynamics*, 21–27.

Hall, D., & Lerner, P. (1980). Career development in work organizations: Research and practice. *Professional Psychology, 11*, 428–435.

Hanson, P., & Lubin, B. (1986, Spring). Team building as group development. *Organization Development Journal*, 27–35.

Hellriegel, D., & Slocum, J. (1974). Organizational climate: Measure, research, and contingencies. *Academy of Management Journal, 17*, 255–280.

Hellriegel, D., Slocum, J., & Woodman, R. (1983). *Organizational behavior*. St. Paul, MN: West.

Henriksen, D. (1982, August). Outplacement: Program guidelines that ensure success. *Personnel Journal*, 583–589.

Hobbs, N. (1966). Helping disturbed children: Psychological and ecological strategies. *American Psychologist, 21*, 1105–1115.

Holland, J. (1985). *Making vocational choices: A theory of vocational personalities and work environments*. Englewood Cliffs, NJ: Prentice-Hall.

Hollander, R., & Lengermann, J. (1988). Corporate characteristics and worksite health promotion programs: Survey findings from Fortune 500 companies. *Social Science & Medicine, 26*, 491–501.

Hoppock, R. (1950). Presidential address, 1950. *Occupations, 28*, 497–499.

Horowitz, F., & O'Brien, M. (1989). In the interest of the nation: A reflective essay on the state of our knowledge and the challenges before us. *American Psychologist, 44*, 441–445.

Huebner, L., & Corazzini, J. (1978). Ecomapping: A dynamic model for intentional campus design. *JSAS Catalog of Selected Documents in Psychology, 8*(1), 9.

Huebner, L., & Corazzini, J. (1984). Environmental assessment and intervention. In S. Brown & R. Lent (Eds.), *Handbook of counseling psychology* (pp. 579–621). New York: Wiley.

Hunter, J., & Hunter, R. (1984). Validity and utility of alternative predictors of job performance. *Psychological Bulletin, 76,* 72–93.

Huse, E., & Bowditch, J. (1977). *Behavior in organizations: A systems approach to organizing* (2nd ed.). Reading, MA: Addison-Wesley.

Huse, E., & Cummings, T. (1985). *Organization development and change.* St. Paul, MN: West.

Ilgen, D. (1990). Health issues at work: Opportunities for Industrial/Organizational psychology. *American Psychologist, 45,* 273–283.

Insel, P., & Moos, R. (1974). Psychological environments: Expanding the scope of human ecology. *American Psychologist, 29,* 179–186.

Ivancevich, J. (1972). A longitudinal assessment of management by objectives. *Administrative Science Quarterly, 17,* 126–138.

Ivancevich, J., & Matteson, M. (1986). Organizational level stress management interventions: Review and recommendations. *Journal of Organizational Behavior & Management, 8,* 229–248.

Ivancevich, J., Matteson, M., Freedman, S., & Phillips, J. (1990). Worksite stress management interventions. *American Psychologist, 45,* 252–261.

Jackson, S., & Schuler, R. (1990). Human resource planning. *American Psychologist, 45,* 223–239.

Johnson, W., & Packer, A. (1987). *Workforce 2000: Work and workers for the twenty-first century.* Indianapolis, IN: Hudson Institute.

Kaplan, R. (1979a). The utility of maintaining relationships openly: An experimental study. *Journal of Applied Behavioral Science, 15,* 41–59.

Kaplan, R. (1979b). The conspicuous absence of evidence that process consultation enhances task performance. *Journal of Applied Behavioral Science, 15,* 346–360.

Katz, D., & Kahn, R. (1978). *The social psychology of organizations* (2nd ed.). New York: Wiley.

Katz, H., Kochan, T., & Weber, M. (1985). Assessing the effects of industrial relations systems and efforts to improve the quality of working life on organizational effectiveness. *Academy of Management Journal, 28,* 509–526.

Kennedy, S. (1989, August). *A new marketing mix: Applying counseling psychology in the field of business marketing.* Paper presented at the annual meeting of the American Psychological Association, New Orleans, LA.

Klimoski, R., & Brickner, M. (1987). Why do assessment centers work? The puzzle of assessment center validity. *Personnel Psychology, 40,* 243–260.

Kondrasuk, J. (1981). Studies in MBO effectiveness. *Academy of Management Review, 6,* 419–430.

Kram, K. (1985). *Mentoring at work.* Glenview, IL: Scott, Foresman.

Kurpius, D. (1985). Consultation interventions: Successes, failures, and proposals. *The Counseling Psychologist, 13,* 368–389.

Lefkowitz, J. (1970). Effect of training on the productivity and tenure of sewing machine operators. *Journal of Applied Psychology, 54,* 81–86.

Leibowitz, Z., & Schlossberg, N. (1981, July). Training managers for their role in a career development system. *Training & Development Journal,* 72–79.

Leonard, M. (1977). The counseling psychologist as an organizational consultant. *The Counseling Psychologist, 7*(2), 73–77.

Levinson, H. (1983). Clinical psychology in organizational practice. In J. Manuso (Ed.), *Occupational clinical psychology* (pp. 7–13). New York: Praeger.

Lewin, K. (1936). *Principles of topological psychology.* New York: McGraw-Hill.

Lewin, K. (1951). *Field theory in social science.* New York: Harper & Row.

Lewis, J., & Lewis, M. (1986). *Counseling programs for employees in the workplace.* Monterey, CA: Brooks/Cole.

Lofquist, L., & Dawis, R. (1984). Research on work adjustment and satisfaction: Implications for career counseling. In S. Brown & R. Lent (Eds.), *Handbook of counseling psychology* (pp. 216–237). New York: Wiley.

London, M., & Stumpf, S. (1986). Individual and organizational career development in changing times. In D. Hall (Ed.), *Career development in organizations* (pp. 21–49). San Francisco: Jossey-Bass.

Macy, B., Hurts, C., Izumi, H., Norton, L., & Smith, R. (1986, August). *Meta-analysis of United States empirical organizational change and work innovation field experiments: Methodology and preliminary results.* Paper presented at the meeting of the National Academy of Management, Chicago, IL.

Mahoney, J., & Smith, D. (1989, October). *Employee Assistance Program financial offset study.* Paper presented at the annual meeting of the Employee Assistance Professionals Association, Baltimore, MD.

McEvoy, G., & Beatty, R. (1989). Assessment centers and subordinate appraisals of managers: A seven-year examination of predictive validity. *Personnel Psychology, 42,* 37–52.

McEvoy, G., & Cascio, W. (1985). Strategies for reducing employee turnover: A meta-analysis. *Journal of Applied Psychology, 70,* 342–353.

McLagan, P. (1983). *Training and development competencies.* Washington, DC: American Society for Training and Development.

Meara, N., Schmidt, L., Carrington, C., Davis, K., Dixon, D., Fretz, B., Myers, R., Ridley, C., & Suinn, R. (1988). Training and accreditation in counseling psychology. *The Counseling Psychologist, 16,* 366–384.

Millon, T. (1981). *Disorders of personality.* New York: Wiley.

Mintzberg, H. (1973). *The nature of managerial work.* New York: Harper & Row.

Mischel, W. (1976). *Introduction to personality* (2nd ed.). New York: Holt, Rinehart, & Winston.

Mischel, W. (1977). On the future of personality measurement. *American Psychologist, 32,* 246–254.

Mone, E. (1988). Training managers to be developers. In M. London & E. Mone (Eds.), *Career growth and human resource strategies* (pp. 207–225). Westport, CN: Quorum.

Moos, R. (1976). *The human context: Environmental determinants of behavior.* New York: Wiley.

Moos, R., & Van Dort, B. (1979). Student physical symptoms and the social climate of college living groups. *American Journal of Community Psychology, 7,* 31–45.

Moravec, M. (1982). A cost-effective career planning program requires a strategy. *Personnel Administrator, 27,* 28–32.

Morrill, W., & Hurst, J. (1971). A preventive and developmental role for the college counselor. *The Counseling Psychologist, 2*(4), 90–95.

Morrill, W., Oetting, E., & Hurst, J. (1974). Dimensions of counselor functioning. *Personnel & Guidance Journal, 52,* 354–360.

Morrison, A., & Von Glinow, M. (1990). Women and minorities in management. *American Psychologist, 45,* 200–208.

Moses, J., & Byham, W. (Eds.). (1977). *Applying the assessment center method.* New York: Pergamon Press.

Muczyk, J. (1978). A controlled field experiment of measuring the impact of MBO on performance data. *Journal of Management Studies, 15,* 318–319.

Murphy, L. (1986). A review of organizational stress management research: Methodological considerations. *Journal of Occupational Behavior Management, 8,* 215–228.

Murray, H. (1938). *Explorations in personality.* New York: Oxford University Press.

Myers, R. (1982). Education and training—The next decade. *The Counseling Psychologist, 10*(2), 39–44.

Nadler, D. (1977). *Feedback and organizational development: Using data-based methods.* Reading, MA: Addison-Wesley.

Nicholas, J. (1982, October). The comparative impact of organization development interventions on hard criteria measures. *Academy of Management Review,* 531–542.

Noe, R., & Steffy, B. (1987). The influence of individual characteristics and assessment center evaluation on career exploration behavior and job involvement. *Journal of Vocational Behavior, 30,* 187–202.

Oberer, D., & Lee, S. (1986). The counseling psychologist in business and industry: Ethical concerns. *Journal of Business & Psychology, 1,* 148–162.

Oetting, E. (1967). A developmental definition of counseling psychology. *Journal of Counseling Psychology, 14,* 382–385.

Offermann, L., & Gowing, M. (1990). Organizations of the future. *American Psychologist, 45,* 95–108.

Ondrack, D., & Evans, M. (1986). Job enrichment and job satisfaction in quality of work life and nonquality of working life work sites. *Human Relations, 39,* 871–889.

Organ, D. (1988). *Organizational citizenship behavior: The gold soldier syndrome.* Lexington, MA: Lexington Books.

Organ, D., & Bateman, T. (1991). *Organizational behavior* (4th ed.). Homewood, IL: Irwin.

Osipow, S. (1979). Occupational mental health: Another role for counseling psychologists. *The Counseling Psychologist, 8*(1), 65–69.

Osipow. S. (1982a). A rejoinder for the counseling psychologist. *The Counseling Psychologist, 10*(3), 55.

Osipow, S. (1982b). Counseling psychology: Applications in the world of work. *The Counseling Psychologist, 10*(3), 19–25.

Osipow, S., & Toomer, J. (1982). Counseling psychology in business and industry. *The Counseling Psychologist, 10*(3), 3–55.

Pace, R., & Faules, D. (1989). *Organizational communication.* Englewood Cliffs, NJ: Prentice-Hall.

Pasmore, W., & King, D. (1978). Understanding organizational change: A comparative study of multifaceted interventions. *Journal of Applied Behavioral Science, 14,* 455–468.

Pasmore, W., & Sherwood, J. (1978). *Sociotechnical systems: A sourcebook.* La Jolla, CA: University Associates.

Paul, S., & Huebner, L. (1977). *Multiple perspectives: Intervening with people and their contextual systems.* Unpublished manuscript, University of Missouri, Columbia, MO.

Pervin, L. (1968). Performance and satisfaction as a function of individual–environment fit. *Psychological Bulletin, 69,* 56–58.

Phillips, S., Cairo, P., Blustein, D., & Myers, R. (1988). Career development and vocational behavior, 1987: A review. *Journal of Vocational Behavior, 33,* 119–184.

Porras, J., & Berg, P. (1978a, April). The impact of organization development. *Academy of Management Review,* 249–266.

Porras, J., & Berg, P. (1978b). Evaluation methodology in organization development: An analysis and critique. *Journal of Applied Behavioral Science, 14,* 151–174.

Pynes, J., & Bernardin, H. (1989). Predictive validity of an entry-level police officer assessment center. *Journal of Applied Psychology, 74,* 831–833.

Quinn, J., & Gagnon, C. (1986, November–December). Will services follow manufacturing into decline? *Harvard Business Review,* 95–103.

Raia, A. (1965). Goal setting and self-control: An empirical study. *Journal of Management Studies, 2,* 34–53.

Rauch, J. (1989, August). Kids as capital. *The Atlantic.* 56–61.

Raulin, J. (1988). The role of the human resource professional in managing other salaried professionals. In M. London & E. Mone (Eds.), *Career growth and human resource strategies* (pp. 271–288). Westport, CT: Quorum.

Reber, R., & Wallin, J. (1984). The effects of training, goal setting and knowledge of results on safe behavior: A component analysis. *Academy of Management Review, 27,* 544–560.

Robbins, S. (1990). *Organization theory: Structure, design, and applications.* Englewood Cliffs, NJ: Prentice-Hall.

Roman, P. (1981). *Prevention and health promotion programming for work organizations: Employee Assistance Program experience.* PRN Monograph, Prevention Resources Project, Northern Illinois University, DeKalb, IL.

Roman, P., & Blum, T. (1988). Formal intervention in employee health: Comparisons of the nature and structure of Employee Assistance Programs and Health Promotion Programs. *Social Science Medicine, 26,* 503–514.

Ropp, K. (1987, February). Restructuring: Survival of the fittest. *Personnel Administrator,* 45–47.

Roscow, J., & Zager, R. (1984). *Employment security in a free economy.* New York: Pergamon Press.

Scarpello, V., & Ledvinka, J. (1988). *Personnel/human resource management: Environments and functions.* Boston, MA: PWS-Kent.

Schein, E. (1969). *Process consultation: Its role in organization development.* Reading, MA: Addison-Wesley.

Schein, E. (1970). *Organizational psychology.* Englewood Cliffs, NJ: Prentice-Hall.

Schein, E. (1981). The individual, the organization, and the career. In H. Montross & C. Shinkman (Eds.), *Career development in the 1980s: Theory and practice* (pp. 259–276). Springfield, IL: Thomas.

Schein, E. (1990). Organizational culture. *American Psychologist, 45,* 109–119.

Schneider, B. (1987). E = f(P, B): The road to a radical approach to person–environment fit. *Journal of Vocational Behavior, 31,* 353–361.

Schneider, B., & Reichers, A. (1983). On the etiology of climates. *Personnel Psychology, 36,* 19–39.

Shaw, M. (1981). *Group dynamics* (3rd ed.). New York: McGraw-Hill.

Shullman, S. (1988, August). *Dilemmas of a scientist-practitioner.* Paper presented at the annual meeting of the American Psychological Association, Atlanta, GA.

Shullman, S. (1989, August). *Conceptual models, counseling psychology, and the workplace.* Paper presented at the annual meeting of the American Psychological Association, New Orleans, LA.

Shullman, S. (1990, August). *Dealing with workplace sexual harassment: Educating the workplace.* Chair of Symposium presented at the annual meeting of the American Psychological Association, Boston, MA.

Shullman, S., & Carder, C. (1983). Vocational psychology in industrial settings. In W. Walsh & S. Osipow (Eds.), *Handbook of vocational psychology* (Vol. 2, pp. 141–179). Hillsdale, NJ: Erlbaum.

Sloan, R., Gruman, J., & Allegrante, J. (1987). *Investing in employee health.* San Francisco: Jossey-Bass.

Solomon, C. (1989, August). The corporate response to work force diversity. *Personnel Journal,* 43–53.

Sonnenfeld, J. (1984). *Managing career systems: Channeling the flow of executive careers.* Homewood, IL: Irwin.

Spokane, A. (1987). Conceptual and methodological issues in person–environment fit research. *Journal of Vocational Behavior, 31,* 217–221.

Stark, S., & Romans, S. (1982). Business and industry: How do you get there? *The Counseling Psychologist, 10*(3), 45–47.

Stern, G. (1970). *People in context: Measuring person–environment congruence in education and industry.* New York: Wiley.

Stout, S., Slocum, J., & Cron, W. (1988). Dynamics of the career plateauing process. *Journal of Vocational Behavior, 32,* 74–91.

Sundstrom, E., DeMeuse, K., & Futrell, D. (1990). Work teams: Applications and effectiveness. *American Psychologist, 45,* 120–133.

Super, D. (1980). A life-span, life-space approach to career development. *Journal of Vocational Behavior, 16,* 282–298.

Super, D., & Hall, D. (1978). Career development: Exploration and planning. *Annual Review of Psychology, 29,* 333–372.

The Counseling Psychologist, (1985) *13*(3), 333–476. [Special issue: Consultation]

Thompson, A., & Super, D. (Eds.). (1964). *The professional preparation of counseling psychologists.* New York: Bureau of Publications, Teachers College, Columbia University.

Toomer, J. (1982). Counseling psychologists in business and industry. *The Counseling Psychologist, 10*(3), 9–18.

Treadway, D. (1979). Use of campus-wide ecosystem surveys to monitor a changing situation. In L. Huebner (Ed.), *New directions for student services: Redesigning campus environments.* San Francisco: Jossey-Bass.

Turnage, J. (1990). The challenge of new workplace technology for psychology. *American Psychologist, 45,* 171–178.

Turnage, J., & Muchinsky, P. (1984). A comparison of the predictive validity of assessment center evaluations versus traditional measures in forecasting supervisory job performance:

Interpretive implications of criterion distortion for the assessment paradigm. *Journal of Applied Psychology, 69,* 595–602.

Vecchio, R. (1988). *Organizational behavior.* New York: Dryden.

Wakabayashi, M., Graen, G., Graen, M., & Graen, M. (1988). Japanese management progress: Mobility into middle management. *Journal of Applied Psychology, 73,* 217–227.

Walsh, W. (1973). *Theories of person–environment interaction: Implications for the college student.* Iowa City, IA: The American College Testing Program.

Wanous, J. (1980). *Organizational entry.* Reading, MA: Addison-Wesley.

Warner, K., Wickizer, T., Wolfe, R., Schildroth, J., & Samuelson, M. (1988). Economic implications of workplace health promotion programs: Review of the literature. *Journal of Occupational Medicine, 30,* 106–112.

Weiss, H. (1989, May). *What is "basic research" in organizational psychology?* Paper presented at the annual meeting of the Midwestern Psychological Association, Chicago, IL.

Western Interstate Commission for Higher Education. (1973). *The ecosystem model: Designing campus environments.* Boulder, CO: Author.

Whitely, J. (1984). Counseling psychology: A historical perspective. *The Counseling Psychologist, 12*(1), 2–109.

Wicker, A. (1973). Undermanning theory and research: Implications for the study of psychological and behavioral effects of excess populations. *Representative Research in Social Psychology, 4,* 190–191.

Wilbur, C. (1983). The Johnson & Johnson program. *Preventive Medicine, 12,* 672–681.

Willems, E. (1969). Planning a rationale for naturalistic research. In E. Willems & H. Raush (Eds.), *Naturalistic viewpoints in psychological research.* New York: Holt, Rinehart & Winston.

Woodman, R., & Sherwood, J. (1980). The role of team development in organizational effectiveness. *Psychological Bulletin, 88,* 166–186.

Wynne, L., McDaniel, S., & Weber, T. (Eds.). (1986). *Systems consultation: A new perspective for family therapy.* New York: Guilford Press.

Zedeck, S., & Mosier, K. (1990). Work in the family and employing organization. *American Psychologist, 45,* 240–251.

CHAPTER 19
RETIREMENT AND LEISURE

DIANE J. TINSLEY
MARY J. SCHWENDENER-HOLT

This chapter provides an overview of retirement as an aspect of human development. Theoretical conceptualizations of retirement that have influenced research and practice are reviewed, and their relevance to counseling psychologists is discussed. Increased leisure is one of the major consequences of retirement, so those aspects of leisure theory, research, and practice most pertinent to retirement are reviewed briefly. Our views regarding the current state of knowledge are expressed, and the development of retirement and leisure counseling, counseling issues, and types of interventions are reviewed. Finally, we present our recommendations for research and practice.

Our view of retirement emphasizes developmental theory as a conceptual framework. Given this emphasis, a more complete understanding of the ideas in this chapter will be gained by reviewing other chapters in this *Handbook*. Specifically, we anticipate that readers will gain a more complete understanding of retirement by attempting to relate the material in this chapter to the information appearing in Chapter 7, by Fassinger and Schlossberg, on theoretical advances in life-span development; Chapter 8, by Lopez, on the promotion of psychological individuation and identity development; Chapter 9, by Gibson and Brown, on counseling for life transitions; Chapter 10, by Altmaier and Johnson, on health promotion and disease prevention; and Chapter 17, by Myers and Cairo, on counseling for career adjustment and change.

The proportion of Americans over 50 continues to increase as individuals live longer and as the baby boom generation moves through middle adulthood (Kiefer, 1986; London, 1990). Despite the recognition of the importance of retirement and leisure by some counseling psychologists, career counseling remains somewhat focused on attempts to improve the assessment of vocational constructs and the development of models for facilitating career decision making (Hackett, Lent, & Greenhaus, 1991). Counseling psychologists who recognize the importance of retirement and leisure roles in this life-span approach and integrate the use of these constructs within their practice will find themselves prepared to deal effectively with a growing proportion of Americans.

RETIREMENT

Statistics on Aging

Several changes in American society suggest the need for increased attention to the roles fulfilled by older people. As medical science and technology become more advanced and life-styles become more healthy, people will live longer, leading to a larger elderly population. At present, the life expectancy is 78 years for men and 83 years for women. In 1986, Kieffer reported that 90% of people over age 65 were not working and a large percentage of persons aged 55 to 64 (33% of men and 66% of women) were not working. As a consequence, a greater proportion of adulthood will be focused on leisure roles. An even more rapid increase in the proportion of the population 65 years of age and older is expected between the years 2010 and 2020 (Kiefer, 1986). About 13% of our population will be 65 years and older in the year 2000; that proportion will increase to 21% by the year 2030. Social, economic, leisure, employment, and other psychological issues of concern to older Americans are growing in importance with this increase in the number of elderly (London & Greller, 1991). Adult developmental models can provide a comprehensive framework within which to view older persons' development, understand their needs, and enhance their well-being.

Public Policy and the Elderly

Policy toward older Americans is influenced by social attitudes toward the aged. Until recently, rejection of the elderly had been widespread and youth had been glorified. This view has been common in counseling psychology, where the ideal client has long been regarded as YAVIS (i.e., young, attractive, verbal, intelligent, and social; Scofield, 1964). Recently, attempts have been made to meet the needs of the elderly, eliminate the effects of age discrimination, and effect social change (Merikanges & Fretz, 1986). Continued progress is needed so that older individuals are accepted and more integrated into society. Changing individuals' ageist attitudes and governments' policies could contribute to more socially responsible attitudes toward older individuals (London & Greller, 1991). Currently, governmental policy is primarily directed toward meeting the financial expense of basic health care. Overall policy has not focused sufficiently on the social, intellectual, and self-actualization needs of older Americans.

Odell (1980) described an example of governmental policy that creates a cultural bind for retirees. According to the Judeo-Christian work ethic, people older than age 18 should be working contributing members of society. However, social security benefits and some employees' pension plans encourage individuals to retire at an earlier age than is physically or intellectually necessary; social security wealth is greatest if collected beginning at age 62. The longer individuals wait to begin receiving benefits, the less money they receive from social security. In this manner, the current social security system provides disincentives to continue working (Boaz, 1987).

Essentially, current governmental and business policies amount to age discrimination. Levine (1980) identified four models of age discrimination in employment. In the *economic-rational decision-making model,* corporate policies regarding age are determined by the economics of the workplace. These policies often involve assumptions that elderly workers are more highly paid but less effective than younger workers, and that turnover in the employee pool is positive. In the *minor group competitions model,* elderly workers are seen as competing with middle-aged and young workers for limited numbers of jobs. Perhaps the most humanistic model is the *time preference model,* which assumes that we treat elderly Americans as future images of ourselves. Unfortunately, however, short-term interests often assume more importance than long-term interests. Finally, psychodynamic theorists suggested a *stereotyping model* in which intergenerational conflicts are seen as the primary factor in age discrimination. Some of our stereotyping of the elderly may be traceable to fear of death and dying and to the fact that retirement is a reminder of each individual's own mortality.

Historical Perspective

Retirement is a relatively new phenomenon. An individual's time was once divided into work time (secular time) and sacred time. A change of perception occurred with industrial development; time came to be viewed as divided into work time and rest or leisure time (Tinsley & Tinsley, 1988). Work time is measured by the clock and must be filled completely. Nonwork time has often been seen as a time when individuals satisfy needs not gratified by work and replenish their energy for work (Grossin, 1986). This dichotomy can be seen in the residual and discretionary time views of leisure that prevailed until the early 1980s (Tinsley & Tinsley, 1988). The residual time perspective advanced by Brightbill (1960) defined leisure as the time remaining to the individual after the time required for existence (e.g., eating, sleeping, meeting biological needs) and subsistence (i.e., working at a job) are subtracted. A similar view of leisure is the notion of leisure as discretionary time (Dumazedier, 1967). This perspective emphasizes the freedom or discretion of the individual to choose activity for that time. Like the residual definition of leisure, however, an individual's discretionary time is usually defined as the time remaining after the existence and subsistence needs of the person have been met. Following these definitions, retirement can be viewed primarily as leisure time.

Streib and Schneider (1971) identified three conditions that must be present in society, for retirement to occur: (a) individuals must live long enough to retire, a condition recently satisfied with improved health care; (b) the economy must be able to function efficiently without older workers' contributions; (c) pensions and other financial retirement plans must exist for retirees' financial support.

The need for social security was realized during the 1930s depression, when increases in the life span (enabling older people to continue working) combined with a decline in employment opportunities (preventing younger people from finding jobs). The objectives of social security were: to provide a dignified retirement for workers over 65, to provide a socially acceptable means of removing older workers from the work force, and to relieve employers of their obligations to tenured, highly paid employees (Cahill & Salomone, 1987). The Social Security Act of 1935 established the policy that workers covered are entitled to retirement benefits. It also limited their earning power: workers lose social security benefits if they earn more than a set minimum after retiring (Kouri, 1986). In recent years, the declining birth rate and the large number of retired persons have placed a strain on the social security system and have begun to cause a shortage of skilled workers (London & Greller, 1991). A 1983 amendment to the Social Security Act will delay an individual's retirement benefits until age 66 in 2009, and until age 67 in 2027. The amendment also reduced the benefits an individual can collect at age 62 to 75%, and gave incentives for an individual to continue to work (Boaz, 1987). Overall, however, social security and most private pension plans reduce financial rewards to individuals who continue working after meeting eligibility for benefits. Those who work past an eligibility point are penalized by the equivalent of a pay cut (Quinn, Burkhauser, & Myers, 1990).

Definitions of Retirement

Like leisure, retirement has been defined in a variety of ways. Palmore (1965) defined retirement in terms of time spent working. Others have defined a retired person as one who is not gainfully employed full-time and receives at least some retirement pension benefits as a result of prior employment (Schulz & Ewen, 1988). Traditionally, retirement has been defined as the cessation of full-time occupational activity (Kasiworm & Wetzel, 1981). There are several problems with these definitions. Presently, the traditional definition is not applicable for many groups, as will be described more thoroughly in the section on individual differences in retirement. This definition simplistically dichotomizes individuals as workers and nonworkers (Kasiworm & Wetzel, 1981), a dichotomy reminiscent of earlier definitions of leisure in which activities were viewed simplistically as work or leisure. Other definitions consider multiple aspects of retirement, including retirement as a process, as a role, or as a phase of life occurring after years of work or after children have grown (Palmore, Burchett, Fillenbaum, George, & Wallman, 1985). For example, Atchley (1979) defined retirement as a reduction in hours and weeks employed, receipt of a majority of income from pensions or retirement plans, and/or individuals' subjective assessment of themselves as retired.

Until recently, retirement could be described as a forced withdrawal from the labor market for most individuals qualifying for social security benefits. Since the federal government abolished mandatory retirement in 1986, however, retirement has become an organizational behavior that is a voluntary choice for nearly all American workers (Hanisch & Hulin, 1990). As such, retirement is classified within a broader frame of reference that includes other employee decisions such as absenteeism, tardiness, and psychological withdrawal from work.

We do not believe that there is one definition of retirement that is more appropriate than others. We believe that simplistic definitions have hindered our understanding of some Americans in middle to late adulthood. The use of different definitions in research can be confusing and may make it difficult to generalize the results obtained across different studies. This concern is especially problematic because the research literature on retirement is multidisciplinary and still at a very early stage of development.

Theories of Retirement

A number of theories of retirement have been described in the professional literature. Several have been formulated in reaction to one another and are briefly summarized here. Counseling psychologists should become aware of this literature because, although it has not been central to counseling psychology, it provides a relevant background for those engaged in developing theory and providing retirement and leisure counseling interventions. The theories described represent cultural values that are more representative of certain groups of Americans than of others. As beliefs held by particular groups, these societal norms may contribute to an individual's sense of life satisfaction, personal growth, and self-actualization.

Disengagement Theory

One of the earliest theories of retirement is disengagement theory (Cummings & Henry, 1961), which conceptualized retirement as a mutual withdrawal of the older individual and society from each other. Cummings (1975) argued that, as individuals grow older, they prefer to interact with fewer people and begin to withdraw from a variety of interpersonal situations such as work. As individuals withdraw from roles, they are less likely to seek out or to be sought after for new roles (Cummings, 1975; Markson, 1975). In one of the first studies exploring the specific leisure activities of older adults, Cowgill and Baulch (1962) reported that home- and family-centered activities dominated. According to disengagement theory, this withdrawal allows older persons to become introspective and prepare for death (Riddick & Daniel, 1984). Disengagement was believed to protect society from the disruptions that the death of integral members of society would cause (Cummings & Henry, 1961; Gordon, 1975).

Originally, disengagement was thought to be inevitable for all individuals (Cummings & Henry, 1961). Metropolous (1980) suggested that disengagement is an option chosen by some elderly Americans because of their personality and physical characteristics. Alternatively, some elderly persons may continue to be engaged or may reengage with society by changing careers or doing volunteer work. Metropolous viewed disengagement as positive for those who choose it.

Several criticisms of disengagement theory exist. Cath (1975) argued that disengagement theory ignores genetic, environmental, social, and economic forces. Levin and Levin (1980) rejected disengagement theory as ageist, because it focuses on individual withdrawal and ignores the social forces that combine to force elderly individuals to withdraw. Gordon (1975) suggested that disengagement theory lacks breadth as a general theory of normative aging, although it may be useful to explain the disengagement of some individuals. In addition to these criticisms, we disagree with the view that retirees who are primarily involved in their own leisure are disengaged from society. In general, empirical studies have failed to support this theory (Edwards & Klemmack, 1973; Gordon, 1975; Lemon, Bengston, & Peterson, 1972).

Crisis Theory

The underlying assumption of crisis theory is that life events such as retirement involve great amounts of stress, causing loss of self-esteem, withdrawal, decline, and depression (Palmore, Cleveland, Nowlin, Ranm, & Siegler, 1979). Crisis theorists generally assume an individual's work identity to be the most salient and important part of identity. Loss of work role is seen to imply loss of ability to perform, which leads to loss of status, self-respect, and identity (Palmore et al., 1985). According to crisis theorists, the occupational role promotes a sense of self and, thereby, life satisfaction (Bell, 1978).

Research has found little empirical support for crisis theory (Bell, 1975, 1978; Palmore et al., 1979). Studies of crisis theory have found a decline in life satisfaction soon after retirement, but they have not found the significant role disruption expected. No relation has been found between commitment to work and negative change in life situation postretirement. Palmore (1979) suggested that crisis theory may apply only to individuals with poor psychological, physical, and social resources, which make their adjustment to retirement more difficult. In fact, individuals strongly committed to work before retirement did not show negative changes in life situation (Bell, 1978), and they were less inclined to return to work than were other retirees. Bell (1975) argued that crisis theory may not be relevant in cases where the work role is not a central part of the individual's identity.

Continuity Theory

Continuity theory was developed in reaction to crisis theory. Rosow (1963) argued that adjustments in old age are continuations of previous life patterns, and Bell (1978) described a relatively stable pattern of role behavior that develops across the life span and continues into retirement. Work role is only one of several roles on which persons base their identity. According to continuity theory, people turn to other roles, particularly leisure roles, to maintain identity upon retirement (Atchley, 1980). Therefore, their identity is not totally disrupted by the loss of the work role when they retire (Kaiser, Peters, & Babcheck, 1982; McPherson & Guppy, 1979; Mobily, 1984). Criticisms of continuity theory focus on its failure to consider changes in income, social resources, and interpersonal interactions that often occur upon retirement (Kaiser et al., 1982; Palmore et al., 1985).

Activity Theory

Initially formulated by Burgess (1960), activity theory is probably the most popular theory of retirement. Individuals with a large number of roles are believed to be better equipped to cope with the loss of a single role, and interpersonal activity is regarded as a key feature of successful retirement. New activities may compensate for roles that are lost as the individual ages. Leisure values are seen as replacing work values in maintaining activity level (Neulinger, 1981).

Several studies have found support for activity theory (Dorfman, Kohout, & Heckert, 1985; Palmore et al., 1979; Romsa, Bandy, & Blenman, 1985). Most of these studies found participation in organizations and activities to be positively related to life satisfaction and high morale after retirement. For example, Tinsley, Colbs, Teaff, and Kaufman (1987) found evidence confirming the importance of interpersonal relations in the leisure activities of the elderly. In contrast, Lemon et al. (1972) did not find support for the hypotheses that greater activity leads to greater satisfaction and greater role loss leads to greater dissatisfaction. These authors suggested that the linear model of greater activity leading to enhanced self-concept and life satisfaction was not complex enough. This research is described in more detail in the section reviewing the effects of retirement on the individual.

Developmental Theory

Atchley (1977) conceptualized retirement as a process that occurs in five stages. The first is the *preretirement* stage, in which an awareness of the future retirement develops and individuals may begin to plan for retirement by attending programs, reading, initiating financial planning, and identifying role models. Atchley suggested that proximity to retirement (not age) is the key to retirement preparation in this stage. The second phase is the *honeymoon,* which occurs just after retirement, when retirees feel euphoria and enjoy their new freedom. The third phase involves *disenchantment,* as individuals deal with concerns such as the inadequacy of their pensions and the loss of social contacts. The fourth stage, one of *reorientation and stability,* involves individuals' acceptance of retirement and establishment of alternative life-styles. The fifth stage involves the *termination* of retirement through reentry into the workplace or death. Atchley (1977) believed that dramatic changes in one's self-identity are not inevitable and that leisure can be one of the greatest sources of continuity across the life span.

Some research has supported the existence of a developmental process of retirement, although it is not clear that this process conforms to Atchley's five-stage model (Evans, Ekerdt, & Bosse, 1985; Keating & Marshall, 1980). Ash (1966) found that individuals' attitudes toward retirement became more negative as they approached retirement. Atchley and Robinson (1982) found that temporal distance before or after retirement was unrelated to attitudes toward retirement. Beck (1982) found no support for the honeymoon phase. Fretz, Kluge, Ossana, Jones, and Merikangas (1989) found no support for Atchley's five-stage model. Their results showed that the best predictors of anxiety and depression among individuals planning to retire were a low sense of self-efficacy about being able to deal effectively with retirement and a low level of planfulness.

Hatcher (1988) studied individuals 45 to 64 years old who accepted an early retirement option from an organization where many had worked since attending college. She suggested that, because 64% worked at least part-time at another job, these individuals did not define themselves as retired, in a cultural sense, but rather as no longer working for their former employer. She recommended that, because early retirement offers are likely to continue as the baby boomers provide large numbers of employees, additional research is needed.

Summary

Criticisms have been leveled at the preceding theories for their narrowness and their failure to account for the influences of income, health, attitudes, and perceptions on retirement (Riddick, 1985b; Romsa et al., 1985). These theories have assumed the centrality of the occupational role for all individuals. They may also be ageist in their assumptions of decline (London & Greller, 1991) and their acquiescence to social forces impelling elderly Americans to withdraw from society (Rosen & Jerdee, 1988). Case study evidence indicates that withdrawal is not inevitable (Berman, 1989; Shneidman, 1989).

We need new theories of retirement that incorporate individual differences and the meaning of different roles and take into account the physical, financial, and social situations of retiring individuals. An individual's socialization history and perception of retirement are important aspects to include in retirement theory. We need to consider the social environment's effect on retired Americans.

Perhaps some of these needs can be met by using relevant career and adult development theories. Although not specifically career-related, the developmental theories of Levinson, Gould, and Neugarten are relevant because of their life-span approach and their focus on stages and transitions through the life cycle (see Chapter 7, by Fassinger and Schlossberg). The applicability of the "theory of work adjustment" to retirement and to leisure environment was described in one of the earliest treatises recommending that leisure should be analyzed using the same perspectives as were applied to work (Lofquist & Dawis, 1969).

Holland's concept of person–environment congruence is relevant to selecting volunteer work environments and leisure activities, and his typology recently has been extended to leisure activities. Holmberg, Rosen, and Holland (1990) and Tinsley and Tinsley (1988) examined the relations of the needs gratified by leisure activities to Holland's typology. Krumboltz's emphasis on the environment and social learning process provides a context not available in other theories. Bandura's (1977) notion of self-efficacy is relevant to individuals' levels of anxiety and depression in adjusting to retirement, as shown by Fretz et al. (1989). Despite their general applicability to retirement issues, however, career development theories in counseling psychology have tended to focus disproportionately on issues of career choice, while neglecting work and retirement adjustment processes (Hackett et al., 1991; Tinsley & Tinsley, 1988).

Individual Differences in Retirement

Women's Retirement

Information is less available on women's retirement than on men's (Hayes & Deren, 1990). One factor contributing to this lack of research on women's retirement is that many women were not employed outside the home until recently. For years, retirement was believed to contribute to a dramatic shift in life roles for men but not for women. Because it was assumed that work identity was secondary to family roles for women, retirement from work was believed to have little effect on women's identity (Riddick, 1985a). Another assumption was that women's social support networks were primarily outside the workplace. These beliefs were supported by early studies suggesting that retirement had no effect on women's psychological function or adjustment (Kasiworm & Wetzel, 1981). Keith (1985) found that women who were single because of widowhood, divorce, or separation were more vulnerable to stress upon retiring, and more in need of planning ahead for retirement, than female workers who had never been married. Moreover, Secombe and Lee (1986) found no support for the hypothesis that retirement was less stressful for women than for men. In fact, they found that women reported somewhat lower levels of life satisfaction than did men.

Traditional definitions of work and work patterns used in researching men's retirement do not fit well for women (Belgrave, 1989). Richardson (1970) argued that career should be defined more broadly to include traditional roles of spouse and parent as well as that of worker. Women who have worked in the home, in the family business, or on the farm have been considered as nonworking (Kasiworm & Wetzel, 1981). Other women's patterns of part-time work or entry–reentry into the work force have been considered as nonwork patterns. Women themselves differ in the ways they define retirement, causing greater confusion (Belgrave, 1989).

Some research has studied the process of women's retirement. For example, Gigy (1985) reported that 21% of women retired spontaneously with little or no overall plan, and 68% developed a plan for retirement. Most were concerned about financial problems (62%), although 25% of the sample reported no worries about retirement. Gigy concluded that women have as much or more difficulty thinking about retirement as do their male counterparts.

DeRenzo (1990) studied a group of wives of retired military officers. She stated that specific research efforts need to be completed because military personnel retire earlier than civilians, which means that most wives are still rearing children during the retirement process. Other special characteristics include the unique social networks and frequent moves for military families, compared to civilians. DeRenzo wrote that little research is available regarding the effects of retirement on the family, and little attention has been focused on military wives. She found that social interaction and the personality variable of neuroticism were both significant predictors of well-being for wives who were involved with their husbands in planning for retirement.

A second area of research concerns women's adjustment to retirement. Fox (1977) found that changes after retirement included a reduction of income, loss of social contacts, and changes in women's perceptions of health. Fox concluded that these changes contributed to women's decreased psychological well-being. These results were supported by Secombe and Lee (1986), who found lowered levels of life satisfaction among the retired women they studied, compared with the retired men.

Tinsley et al. (1987) found that women over 65 who were of lower economic status and low morale reported companionship to be the principal psychological need gratified by their leisure experiences. These results suggested that the retired elderly are especially vulnerable to loneliness, but the number of friends a person has is less related to loneliness than is the lack of relationships of mutual sharing. Another important need gratified by leisure experiences was the need for power—contradicting disengagement theory, which states that retirement and increasing age are associated with an increasing orientation toward home-based, passive activities. Neuh (1990) found positive self-image and flexible attitudes to be related to positive adjustment to retirement for a sample of 120 women who were contacted through senior citizen centers.

Research on women's life satisfaction after retirement has compared working women, retired women, and nonworkers. Results are mixed. Fox (1977) reported that retired women had lower morale than older working women. Jaslow (1976) and Riddick (1985a) found that both retired women and homemakers reported lower life satisfaction than did employed women. Holahan (1981) found that homemakers were equally satisfied, compared to retired or working women. Riddick and Daniel (1984) found that homemakers were more satisfied than retired women. The number and amount of leisure activities were related to life satisfaction, but income was a confounding factor. As income increased, both participation in leisure activities and satisfaction increased. Riddick and Daniel (1984) concluded that retirement may contribute to more disequilibrium among women than assumed previously.

A third focus of research has compared women's and men's retirement. Several gender differences have been reported for retirees. Atchley (1976) found that women were more active than men as they aged. Because of the difference in life expectancy, women live longer after retirement and are more likely to live without a spouse after retirement than are men (Kasiworm & Wetzel, 1981). Kaye and Monk (1984) reported that former women educators spent more time engaging in social and recreational pursuits than their male counterparts, who continued to participate in more work-oriented activities after retirement. Women are less financially prepared for retirement, and, therefore, more likely to have smaller pensions and less insurance than men (Behling & Merves, 1985). Tinsley et al. (1987) found that women were more likely than men to report the gratification of their needs for companionship and recognition through leisure activities.

Because attention has increasingly been directed toward understanding women's work and life patterns in the past decade, it is imperative to study women's retirement rather than to continue ignoring women or assuming the applicability of findings obtained using male samples. Pertinent topics for future research include the circumstances under which retirement may be more or less disruptive for women than for men, and how the patterns of life roles affect retirement across the life span for women and men. New ways of viewing career and life patterns and new conceptualizations of retirement are needed to guide future research.

Racial and Ethnic Group Retirement

The elderly White population is expected to increase 22.7% by the year 2000; the number of Black aged will increase by 45.6% by that year (Markides & Mindel, 1987). Very little research, however, has examined retirement among racial and ethnic minority groups. A low degree of agreement exists concerning the effects of retirement on White males, but there is even less information about members of other racial and ethnic groups. Most of what is known about the effects of retirement on these groups reveals more about the effects of socioeconomic status on retirement than those of race or ethnicity (Behling & Merves, 1985; Clemente & Sauer, 1974; Markides & Mindel, 1987).

Several problems are apparent in the research on the retirement of ethnic groups (Markides & Mindel, 1987). Most of the assessment instruments used in retirement research were developed and standardized on White populations, making their applicability to non-White individuals suspect. Much research has failed to separate ethnic differences from social class differences—an important problem in all cross-cultural research, because a large percentage of non-White individuals are of lower socioeconomic status. Another issue concerns cross-cultural differences in the nature and definition of retirement. Gibson (1987) suggested that retirement for Whites is subjectively based on work status, source of income, or perception of disability. Personal definitions of retirement for members of some other racial and ethnic groups may be complicated by the fact that many ethnic elderly rely on part-time work for old-age income. Jackson and Gibson (1985) found that elderly Blacks who did not define themselves as retired were more likely to have been part-time workers throughout their lifetime and to be still working part-time.

The theories of retirement reviewed earlier grew out of White middle-class perspectives and were not intended to apply to elderly Black or other ethnic minority individuals (Manuel, 1982; Markides & Mindel, 1987; Rey, 1982). One relevant theoretical notion is that of double jeopardy theory, which hypothesizes an additive effect of race/ethnicity and age for non-White retirees (Dowd & Bengston, 1978). Markides and Mindel (1987) suggested that gender and social class may also contribute additively to one's level of disadvantage in retirement. Thus, older, ethnic females of lower socioeconomic status have the greatest disadvantage, and younger, White, middle-class males are most advantaged. Dowd and Bengston (1978) found that the income and health inequalities experienced by middle-aged African Americans and Hispanics became more pronounced as they aged, supporting the double jeopardy theory. Other studies found mixed results. In summary, it is important to understand that ethnic minority elderly are less likely to have adequate education, money, housing, or health to ensure a high level of satisfaction during retirement. At the same time, however, they are more likely to experience discrimination and other difficulties in receiving social services (Ego, 1983; Manuel, 1982).

African Americans and Mexican Americans.   Individuals' patterns of preretirement income and employment history influence their sources and amount of retirement income, thereby influencing the course of their retirement. Black and Hispanic persons are underrepresented in higher paying jobs that are covered by social security or private pension programs; consequently, these individuals are without adequate retirement income (Rhodes, 1982). Richardson and Kilty (1989) found that a greater percentage of Black professionals (76.1%) were expecting to receive social security income, compared with Whites (65.6%), suggesting that Black professionals are still less represented by private pension plans than are White professionals. Because low-wage jobs are less stable, those who hold them are more likely to become unemployed. Until recently, an employee had to work at the same firm for 10 to 20 years *and* reach a certain age, before qualifying for a pension. Thus, even when African American or Hispanic individuals held jobs covered by private pension programs, they often did not work long enough to qualify for pensions. As a result, 43% of White workers were covered by a pension plan and only 20% of Black workers were so covered (Rhodes, 1982). McVeigh (1980) argued that many Black workers lack the time and financial resources needed for retirement planning. Belgrave (1988) found that, for her sample of White and Black women, ages 62 to 66, the Black women were more likely to have worked throughout most of their adult lives, were more likely to be eligible for pensions, but were less likely to have retired than White women.

Black individuals are more likely to experience sporadic work patterns, low levels of income, and restriction to unstable, low-paying jobs that offer few benefits and no pensions or only low social security benefits. They, therefore, must gain a greater proportion of their retirement income from continued part-time work or other nonretirement sources. Like Black workers, Mexican Americans traditionally have worked as unskilled laborers. Their occupations pay low wages and provide few benefits, pensions, or chances for upward mobility. Retirement for Mexican Americans takes the form of a gradual withdrawal from work, in which brief periods of unemployment grow longer and longer until the individual is no longer employed (Markides & Mindel, 1987). Because of their lack of savings and pension, retired Mexican Americans have much less retirement income than retired White workers. In addition to social security, they rely on part-time work for income, creating uncertainty as to whether the individual is actually retired (Gibson, 1987). Dichotomous definitions of retirement, which classify all individuals as working or retired, are not adequate in representing the many variations of retirement among minority group members.

McVeigh (1980) found that Black couples had about 50% of the income of White couples upon retirement. About 13% of White elderly persons were classified below the poverty level; 35% of Blacks and 26% of Hispanics were below the poverty level. Nevertheless, Rhodes (1982) found that Black retirees were more satisfied with their retirement than were a comparable sample of White individuals. Rhodes concluded that Blacks' previously frugal life-style enabled them to cope with retirement (and the lower income that comes with it) more effectively. Jackson (1980) argued that Whites have a harder time adjusting to retirement because their reduction in income is greater than that of many ethnic group individuals. Others have suggested that retirement is less disruptive and less stressful for many members of minority racial and ethnic groups because they often hold jobs that are less intrinsically meaningful and, therefore, they are often less invested in the work role than are their White counterparts. Markides and Mindel (1987) countered that White retirees are better off after the initial shock of retirement, because they have more educational and financial resources. We think that it is sometimes difficult to interpret these research results because the research was undertaken within a society that holds stereotypes and overgeneralizations regarding racial and ethnic minority groups.

Sauer (1977) found that health and participation in solitary activities were major predictors of life satisfaction for Blacks and Whites older than 65 years. Black persons were more likely than Whites to retire because of poor health, a factor that has a large negative effect on adjustment to retirement. Whites had significant interactions among family, gender, and morale that were not present for Blacks. Geist (1981) found religion to be an important factor in the satisfaction of Black individuals; White individuals relied on family for satisfaction.

Asian Americans. Nineteenth-century Chinese immigrants worked primarily as skilled and unskilled laborers, upon arriving in this country. After the completion of the transcontinental railroad, many Chinese Americans lived together in "Chinatown" communities and entered occupations that served these communities. By the 1960s and 1970s, Chinese Americans had the highest proportion of persons employed in professional and technical occupations of any non-White ethnic group in this country (Markides & Mindel, 1987). Much of the move to professional and technical careers has occurred because of the emphasis placed on education in the Chinese American community. Because of intense acculturation pressure, Markides and Mindel (1987) concluded, retirement for Chinese Americans is much like that of White Americans. Chang (1977) reported that Chinese Americans were facing more disappointment and disillusionment because the younger generation was less committed to support of their elderly.

The Japanese American culture has also stressed education. Salaries for Japanese Americans may not be as high as those of similarly employed White Americans, but most Japanese Americans have savings or family financial support for their elderly years (Markides & Mindel, 1987). Because of acculturation, however, the traditional roles of the elderly as ceremonial and religious leaders in the community have eroded.

Markides and Mindel (1987) believed that, with the disappearance of these traditional roles, the retirement life faced by Japanese retirees is much different from that of their parents and grandparents and more like that of White Americans.

As counseling psychologists become more sensitive to issues of cross-cultural counseling, we may well learn to identify a number of culturally different groups among the more general classification of Asian Americans.

Native Americans.   One of the least researched racial/ethnic groups probably is Native Americans. With the loss of their lands, Native Americans were reduced to poverty and have tended to hold low-level occupations. Older people were respected and revered for their wisdom, in the original tribes. No abrupt change of work roles occurred around 65 years; older persons were expected to be productive, to lead, to educate, and to advise (Markides & Mindel, 1987). In Native American terms, old age is not defined by years but rather in terms of the individual's ability to contribute to the community (Markides & Mindel, 1987). Montana's state plan for elderly American Indians has defined old age as 45 years, because of the groups' extreme economic problems, health problems, and median life expectancy (Solomon, 1979). With the imposition of White values and attitudes on Native Americans, older individuals lost the respected position and prestige associated with their age. Most older Native Americans have not worked at jobs that qualify them for pensions, social security, or other retirement benefits (Markides & Mindel, 1987). Life for these elderly is impoverished. The pattern is changing, however; younger individuals are leaving their reservations. As change occurs, middle-aged Native Americans who have worked and will retire outside the reservation will have few role models to help them prepare for their elderly years.

Effects of Retirement

Research on the effects of retirement has been broad-based but generally atheoretical. Much of the research has described negative effects assumed to accompany the drastic change in individuals' life situations. Research has found retirees to have less income, a greater incidence of physical and mental illness, lower self-esteem, and less happiness with their life situations. Almost all of this research has been cross-sectional, however, and investigators have not controlled for the preretirement status of retirees (Palmore et al., 1985). Controlling for preretirement characteristics such as health and SES may mitigate some negative consequences often attributed to retirement (Sauer, 1977). Because research generally has not considered the possible effects of cultural norms, interpretations are confounded by societal expectations that retirees will be less healthy and less active than younger persons. With these limitations in mind, we review here the literature on the effects of retirement.

Physical Health and Life Expectancy

For years, Americans have assumed that retirement reduces physical health and life expectancy (Bosse, Aldwin, Levinson, & Ekerdt, 1987). Several early studies reported negative effects of retirement on the health of retirees (Haynes, McMichael, & Tyroler, 1978), but retirement has been found to have little or no effect on the health of retirees when preretirement health is controlled (Bosse et al., 1987; Ekerdt, 1987; Montgomery & Borgatta, 1987; Palmore, Fillenbaum, & George, 1984). Interestingly, Ekerdt, Bosse, and LoCastro (1983) found a perception of health improvement after retirement. About one-third of their subjects perceived that retirement had a positive effect on their health, suggesting that the removal of job-related stress and dissatisfying work conditions might lead to the perception of improved health and greater vitality on the part of retirees.

The stereotypes regarding the relations between retirement and health may exist for several reasons. People tend to retire because of poor health, making poor health a cause rather than an effect of retirement. Other explanations may be retirees' exaggerating health problems, retirees' taking on a "sick role" to justify being retired, and cultural expectations of health deterioration in old age (Bosse et al., 1987). Nevertheless, there is little empirical support for the belief that retirement has negative effects on individuals' physical health. To the contrary, retirees may experience an improvement in health, when their previous occupations had placed them in physically or psychologically stressful situations (Ekerdt, 1987; Montgomery & Borgatta, 1987).

Mental Health and Identity

Another common assumption is that retirement negatively affects mental health (Montgomery & Borgatta, 1987). Popular culture assumes that people who work gain much of their identity from their work (Mutran & Reitzes, 1981). The results of research are mixed. Studies by Atchley (1971) and Mutran and Reitzes (1981) found that retirees' identities were not disrupted by loss of their work role. Bosse et al. (1987) found that retirees reported more psychological symptoms than nonretirees, even after preretirement health was controlled, but they were unable to determine the causal direction of this relation. Bosse et al. (1987) and Seccombe and Lee (1986) suggested that the lack of status, responsibility, work identity, contact with peers, activities, and income that often accompanies retirement may cause mental health problems in retirement.

Research on the relation between leisure and mental health provides evidence that individuals who meet their needs through leisure have better mental health than those who do not. For example, Havighurst (1957) and Havighurst and Feigenbaum (1959) reported a significant relation between personality and life-style, with individuals' high personal adjustment being positively associated with a tendency to spend a greater amount of time in leisure activities. Among middle-aged subjects, good personal adjustment was associated with participation in leisure activities characterized by autonomy, creativity, enjoyment, novelty, prestige, vitality, and expansion of interests. Pfeiffer and Davis (1971) reported evidence that depression and suicide rates reached a peak for women between 46 and 55 years old, the time at which they reported having too little free time. Lewissohn and Graf (1973) reported that the number of pleasant activities a person experienced was associated with mood. In particular, people who were depressed engaged in a smaller number of pleasant activities. Csikszentmihalyi (1975) deprived subjects of all voluntary noninstrumental activities for 48 hours. Participants reported a great deal of irritability and feelings of constraint and isolation after only 24 hours under these conditions. The great majority of subjects reported detrimental effects in mood, self-concept, and some performance factors. Tiger (1979) reported that leisure activities/experiences give an individual increased feelings of optimism.

Some evidence suggests that personal identity is not as singularly determined by work identity as was previously believed. Neulinger (1971) reported that people's conceptions of work were unrelated to their mental health, but that persons having good personality integration engaged in more meaningful and enjoyable leisure participation than did persons with poor personality integration. Spreitzer and Snyder (1983) investigated the attitudes of runners, racquetball players, and the general population toward work and leisure. About half (48%) of the runners and racquetball players agreed with the statement "You would get a better understanding of me through my leisure activities than through my work" (p. 36). A majority of the general population (61%) agreed with "My personal identity is realized more in my work than in my leisure activities" (p. 36), but the runners (38%) and racquetball players (42%) were less likely to agree. These results reveal a significant relation between personal identity and leisure activity participation.

Research evidence suggests that leisure attitudes and leisure participation are related to mental health and personal identity, but several problems are endemic to research in this area. First, mental health is a complex construct. Whatever operational definition is used, it is likely that some important aspects of mental health will be missed. The best solution to this problem may well be the use of multiple indexes of mental health. Second, most of the studies reported have been correlational in nature. Longitudinal data collection procedures and time-series analyses are needed, to determine the relations among retirement, leisure experiences, and mental health. Third, age discrimination should be studied as a contributor to mental illness in the elderly population. At present, it cannot be assumed that retirement per se causes mental illness or psychological difficulties. The effects of environmental characteristics such as ageist stereotypes need to be taken into account.

Life Satisfaction

The largest body of research on the effects of retirement involves life satisfaction or morale. Many researchers have assumed that work is the greatest source of personal satisfaction, self-expression, and creative outlet for men (Conner, Dorfman, & Tompkins, 1985), but not for women (Belgrave, 1989). Stull (1988) found that husbands and wives had different predictors of happiness in retirement. Bishop, Epstein, Baldwin, and Miller (1988) found husbands' morale was most strongly associated with health, SES, and income; wives' morale was most strongly associated with family functioning and less with health and SES. Thus, it is assumed that the loss of work identity causes a decrease in men's life satisfaction. The probable gender bias in the assumptions made and research questions addressed has been discussed in the section on individual differences toward retirement. The research in this section focuses primarily on the retirement satisfaction of men.

Research on the effects of retirement on life satisfaction has produced inconsistent results. Some early studies documented a decrease in life satisfaction (Kimmel et al., 1978). Others found retirees to be more satisfied with life than nonretired workers (Pollman, 1971), and still others found retirement to have no effect on life satisfaction (Beck, 1982; George & Maddox, 1977; Palmore et al., 1984). Researchers have subsequently begun to study individual characteristics—health, SES, social support, educational levels, preretirement occupational levels, activity levels, leisure satisfaction, and religious beliefs—as ways to understand changes in postretirement life satisfaction (Palmore & Kivett, 1977; Steinkamp & Kelly, 1985).

Numerous studies have found SES to relate positively to life satisfaction in retirement (Beck, 1982; Dorfman & Hill, 1986; Edwards & Klemmack, 1973; Kimmel et al., 1978; Markides & Mindel, 1987; Palmore, 1979; Riddick & Daniel, 1984; Szinovacz, 1987). Individuals with higher SES are relatively free from major financial difficulties, enabling them to retire in more physical comfort. The greater the income, the greater is retirees' satisfaction with retirement (Seccombe & Lee, 1986).

Physical health (Beck, 1982; Conner et al., 1985; Dorfman & Hill, 1986; Kimmel et al., 1978; Palmore, 1979) and social activity (Dorfman et all., 1985; Dorfman & Maffett, 1987; Romsa et al., 1985) have been found to be important factors associated with life satisfaction in retirement. As with SES and income, the better the health of the retired individuals, the greater is their satisfaction with retirement. Social activity studies have examined retired individuals' social support networks, friendships, volunteer activities, and informal social contacts. For example, Tinsley et al. (1987) found the need for companionship was one of three psychological needs gratified through leisure activity participation by older women. Related studies on the effects of marriage, divorce, and widowhood have found that social involvement is an important factor in retirement satisfaction (Beck, 1982; Palmore, 1979; Seccombe & Lee, 1986).

Activity is one of the primary variables that has been related to life satisfaction. Bultena and Wood (1970) reported that retirement community residents who were most involved in leisure activities also tended to have a more favorable outlook on their life situations. Bley, Goodman, Dye, and Harel (1972) reported regular participation in an organized leisure program to be significantly related to high morale and life satisfaction among older Americans. Erratic participation was related to low scores on satisfaction measures. Using a sample of volunteers from senior citizen centers, Ray (1979) found significant relations between life satisfaction and activity, health, leisure activities, and social contacts. He found no significant relation between activity breadth or frequency and life satisfaction.

Guinn (1980) reported significant relations between leisure activity participation and life satisfaction for 406 elderly tourists. Ragheb and Griffith (1982) surveyed 565 persons, 55 years of age and older, regarding their participation in eight categories of leisure activities. Total leisure participation ($r = .34$) and total leisure satisfaction ($r = .53$) correlated significantly with life satisfaction. In order of importance, Riddick and Daniel (1984) found life satisfaction to be influenced by leisure roles, income, health problems, and employment background for a sample of 1,102 older women. Steinkamp and Kelly (1985) investigated the effects of motivational orientations on levels of leisure activity and life satisfaction among 217 people between the ages of 40 to 89 years. The results indicated that challenge seeking, concern with recognition and reward, and family focus were systematically related to life satisfaction among these older men and women. Tinsley et al. (1987) found the psychological benefits obtained from leisure activity participation to be related to morale for a sample of 1,449 persons in the age range of 55 to 75 years. Leisure satisfaction is an important factor in influencing retirees' experiences of retirement satisfaction.

The results of studies relating measures of religious beliefs to life satisfaction for the elderly are mixed. Pargament (1987) summarized the information about the relations between religious attitudes and well-being for older adults. Although he indicated that the findings of cross-sectional studies contradict each other, religious belief and religious participation were related to feelings of well-being among the elderly. He noted that, among all the variables, only health status accounted for more variance in life satisfaction than religion among the elderly. Worthington (1989) made a further distinction between individuals pursuing religion for extrinsic or intrinsic rewards. After reviewing relevant research, he concluded that religion per se has little effect on mental health. However, he found that intrinsic religion (religion pursued for its own sake) is correlated with positive mental health; extrinsic religion (religion adopted as a means to achieve other ends) is not.

Other factors associated with greater life satisfaction in retirement include preretirement occupational level (Dorfman & Hill, 1986; Kremer, 1985; Seccombe & Lee, 1986), educational level (Kimmel et al., 1978; Kremer, 1985; Seccombe & Lee, 1986) and voluntary versus involuntary retirement (Beck, 1982; Kimmel et al., 1978). It is difficult to summarize the broad range of studies that have investigated the life satisfaction of elderly individuals, because so many results are inconsistent. Many variables have been found to relate to satisfaction in retirement; health status, SES, and activity levels have shown the most consistent results. People with a high level of income are more likely to have worked in healthier work conditions, have higher educational and occupational levels, have more money and time to spend on leisure activities, and are more likely to have exercised choice in the decision to retire. It is imperative, therefore, to control for health status, SES, and activity level when studying the life satisfaction of retired individuals.

Counseling Practice

This section summarizes the development of retirement and leisure counseling, issues to consider in counseling, and counseling interventions. Research on attitudes toward retirement is also briefly summarized.

Attitudes Toward Retirement

Researchers and theorists have long believed that preretirement beliefs affect adjustment to retirement (Thompson & Streib, 1958). For example, Neulinger (1981) suggested that individuals' leisure attitudes and values influence their likelihood of accepting a leisure role after retirement. Neulinger argued that a strong work ethic (i.e., valuing work for its own sake) contributes to an attitude of guilt and shame among individuals who are not gainfully employed. In place of the work ethic, Neulinger (1981) called for a leisure ethic that would emphasize the expression and actualization of one's potential through leisure.

Much of the retirement literature has focused on the effects of retirement on individuals; some attention has also been given to the adjustment of individuals to retirement. In that regard, leisure competence may have a causal influence on adjustment to retirement. White (1976) described competence as a universal need of individuals to expand boundaries, to investigate the world, and to achieve mastery. According to White, the subjective state of competence is more important than objective assessments of fitness or ability. The move from incompetence to competence is usually made by changing oneself, by pursuing and learning new skills, and by altering one's environment. Individuals can be extremely vulnerable at times of transition and change. Tedrick (1983) and Peacock and Talley (1985) viewed developing leisure competence as a concern of individuals of all ages, but particularly as individuals prepare for retirement and during their retirement years.

Early research into attitudes toward retirement assumed that workers' degree of commitment and involvement in work would influence attitudes toward retirement (Glamser, 1976; Goudy, Powers, & Keith, 1975). Friedmann and Havighurst (1954) found that individuals highly committed to work were unwilling to retire. Saleh and Otis (1963) found that dissatisfied workers looked forward to retirement. Fillenbaum (1971b) found that attitudes toward retirement are affected by work commitment when the worker is in a high-status career or when the work role is the central organizing factor in the individual's life. In a study of 300 police officers, Forcese and Cooper (1985) found that those officers who were most detached (least emotionally committed to their jobs) had the most positive attitudes toward retirement. Other studies found no relation between career involvement and attitudes toward retirement (Poitrenaud, Vallery-Masson, Valleron, Demeestere, & Liam, 1979).

Several studies highlighted the importance of financial resources in attitudes toward retirement (Evans et al., 1985; Glamser, 1981b; Kilty & Behling, 1985; Poitrenaud et al., 1979). Jacobson (1974) found that finances influenced willingness to retire for 89% of his sample who were reluctant to retire. The perception that they would be unable to manage financially if they retired kept them in the work force. Other factors that have been linked to attitude toward retirement are health (Evans et al., 1985; Poitrenaud et al., 1979), level of social and leisure activity (Cox & Bhak, 1979; Evans et al., 1985; Kilty & Behling, 1985), time to retirement (Evans et al., 1985), and occupational status (Evans et al., 1985; Kilty & Behling, 1985). Good health and higher levels of social activity were related to positive views of retirement, and high occupational status and high degree of career independence were related to negative views of retirement.

Development of Retirement and Leisure Counseling

Over the past several decades, descriptions of a wide variety of models for preretirement, retirement, and leisure planning or counseling have appeared in the literature. Although many of these have been described as leisure interventions or avocational counseling, they have direct application in retirement counseling. For example, some of the more ambitious programs have been designed explicitly for use in retirement counseling (Loesch & Wheeler, 1982; Myers, 1984; Overs, Taylor, & Adkins, 1974; Overs, Taylor, Cassell, & Chernov, 1977). Applications of these models, and efforts to evaluate their efficacy, have occurred specifically with retired Americans.

To some extent, retirement counseling shares its intellectual heritage with career and leisure counseling. Rehabilitation and parks and recreation programs were influential in the development of early leisure counseling models; industrial and organizational psychology programs have been more associated with retirement planning and counseling models. Both retirement and leisure counseling are influenced by recent developments in career counseling.

Retirement counseling and planning began at several universities in the 1950s and 1960s (Brache & Hunter, 1990). It was believed that dispersing information about retirement through these programs would minimize social, emotional, and practical problems in retirement (Dennis, 1986). Initially, interventions were limited to a coverage of financial matters, pension plans, insurance, and benefits, and they highlighted such topics as social security, Medicare, taxes, death benefits, and estate planning (Comrie, 1985; Prentis, 1980).

Many early leisure models represent a relatively general adaptation of a counseling or educational guidance paradigm. Some of these so-called counseling models are little more than descriptions of specific counseling techniques that could be applied in retirement or leisure interventions. Still others consist essentially of relatively general attempts to adopt a mainstream counseling paradigm to leisure counseling. For example, Gunn and Peterson (1978) developed an approach to leisure based on transactional analysis, gestalt awareness, and systems theory (Gunn, 1976, 1978). Dickason (1972) proposed a model that included elements of client-centered and behavioral approaches. Rule and Stewart (1977) used an Adlerian approach to describe how early childhood concerns could be dealt with in leisure counseling. Montagnes (1977) applied reality therapy principles, and Orthner and Herron (1984) outlined a family systems approach to leisure counseling.

The need for more comprehensive approaches extending beyond financial planning has been recognized, and more comprehensive retirement and leisure counseling models have been suggested fairly recently (Blocher & Siegal, 1984; Loesch & Wheeler, 1982; McDowell, 1981; Myers, 1984; Overs et al., 1974; Overs et al., 1977; Schlossberg, 1984; Tinsley & Tinsley, 1982). These models represent significant advances over earlier retirement and leisure counseling approaches, in their overall flexibility in conceptualizing the goals of counseling, their focus on the total individual, and their attention to the counseling relationship. These more comprehensive programs are becoming more common in large organizations (Greenhaus, 1987; Russell, 1991). By one estimate, however, only 30% of the retirement counseling programs are comprehensive in nature (Atchley, 1987).

Counseling Issues

The multiple problems involved in retirement and leisure counseling and the development of multiple approaches to treatment make it difficult to summarize existing models; however, retirement, career, and leisure counseling are intended to help relatively normal individuals make personally satisfying decisions concerning the fulfillment of their life roles. Proponents of retirement and leisure counseling believe they can help individuals increase their self-esteem, facilitate personal adjustment, improve overall life satisfaction, and promote self-actualization. These comprehensive retirement and leisure counseling models emphasize the establishment of a counseling relationship that embodies the facilitative conditions. Furthermore, these comprehensive retirement and leisure counseling models emphasize a concern for the total individual rather than focusing only on the problems of retirement finances, leisure, or activity choice.

There is considerable agreement in the literature regarding the issues to be included in retirement and leisure counseling. The emphasis may vary, however, given the theoretical orientation of the counseling psychologist and the particular needs of the individual, couple, family, or group seeking services. The following discussion focuses on some issues having more unique relevance to retirement and leisure counseling. Overlap among the issues is apparent, but we believe that the inclusion of the separate issues can facilitate client understanding, the determination of specific treatment strategies, and the accomplishment of specific counseling goals.

Transition to Retirement.   As a transition, retirement requires change and adjustment, and may be accompanied by anxiety, depression (Fretz et al., 1989; Schlossberg, 1984), or crisis (Zawada & Walz, 1979). The retirement transition differs for each individual and provides opportunities for counselors to facilitate the transition, to assist individuals to successfully manage life transitions, and to encourage further growth (Brache & Hunter, 1990; Riker & Myers, 1990). More about transitions in general is available in Chapter 7, by Fassinger and Schlossberg, Chapter 9, by Gibson and Brown, and Chapter 16, by Phillips.

Social Attitudes.   Another important issue in retirement and leisure counseling is the effect of social attitudes concerning retirement and aging on clients (Brache & Hunter, 1990; Hartford, 1984; J. A. Peterson, 1984; Riker & Myers, 1990). Our society's work ethic and the negative connotations concerning nonworkers can combine with pervasive ageism to lead to a lack of self-confidence and low self-esteem for retirees. These factors may combine to cause retirees to question their usefulness and the meaningfulness of their lives (J. A. Peterson, 1984). Thus, counseling psychologists need to be alert to the possible effects of negative stereotyping and ageism on their clients. Because of our culture's discrimination toward the aged, it may be important to discuss self-esteem and self-confidence issues (Kouri, 1986; Riker & Myers, 1990; Sommerstein, 1986).

Relationships.   Relationship issues may be salient for clients, their partners, and their extended families. Bradford (1979) believed that increases in the amount of time spent together, the lack of challenges that tie a couple together, and previous problems in the relationship, which become magnified by retirement, are common issues for retirees. Changes in the relationship, caused by changes in work roles, may necessitate a renegotiation of other roles (Brache & Hunter, 1990; Bradford & Bradford, 1979). For example, many couples need to make a thorough review of their relationship. They may need to learn new patterns of living together. Issues of territoriality may need to be addressed. The effects of retirement on partners may include fear for themselves and their partners and a worsening of previous problems because of living in close quarters. Relationship counseling that focuses on expectations for retirement, sensitivity to the needs of the other, communication skills, conflict resolution, and resolution of any issues from previous times in the relationship is important (Bradford & Bradford, 1979).

It may be important for couples to be involved in preretirement counseling together (Hartford, 1984); children and other extended family members might be included, if they are involved with the retirees on a regular basis. Counseling psychologists can work with individuals to assess their social network for strengths and weaknesses, and they can help them to extend and improve their support networks (Riker & Myers, 1990).

Vocational and Avocational Issues. Some of the career choice issues that confront young clients (e.g., unfamiliarity with the world of work, lack of self-knowledge, inadequate decision-making skills) also confront older clients and retirees (Overs et al., 1977). Work interests may be important when clients are considering self-employment, part-time employment, and volunteer positions. Harris (1981) found that a third of retired older Americans would return to part-time or full-time work, if given the opportunity, and 45% of the people over 65 reported they had not wanted to retire in the first place. This corresponds with other research showing that 50% of retired workers reported returning to work voluntarily (Minkler, 1981). Rather than continuing to view retirement as an irreversible decision, we need to think of individuals as having multiple roles, which they may emphasize to different degrees across the life span. Some elderly individuals would want to keep working for financial reasons or for the intrinsic value of work activities to their mental health and life satisfaction. Counseling interventions with older individuals will probably be more successful if the complexity of retirement is understood and taken into account. Counseling psychologists may need to assist in identifying client skills that can be transferred to new activities, to help clarify individuals' values (Sommerstein, 1986), to assess vocational and avocational interests, needs, and abilities (Overs et al., 1974; Overs et al., 1977), and to help with goal setting and decision making (Cahill & Salomone, 1987).

Loss and Death. Clients experience losses when they face endings of jobs, reduction of income, and changes in job-related relationships. These losses may be compounded by losses of friends and family through death. The elderly may experience losses of belonging, achievement, territory, power, support network, productivity, and industry, which were formerly met through work (Bradford, 1979; Riker & Myers, 1990). The social losses may be especially poignant as retirees struggle with the loss of work-related friendships. Typically, as the status of *worker* disappears, so do the relationships that go along with the job (J. A. Peterson, 1984). It may, therefore, be important for counseling psychologists to allow clients to grieve these losses and to help them make plans for continuing their lives.

Special issues of loss and death may exist because of the age and physical health of retirees. For example, retirees may want to discuss their feelings about their age and their impending death (Hornstein & Wapner, 1985; Riker & Myers, 1990; Sommerstein, 1986).

Anxieties about death and dying may enter into retirement counseling whether expressed or not (J. A. Peterson, 1984). Death needs to be dealt with, both objectively and emotionally. Failure to help clients with these major issues leaves them unresolved.

Spiritual Development.   We want to emphasize that retirement is a time for challenge and for new beginnings, as individuals find themselves less constrained by responsibilities such as paid employment and raising a family. Retirement can provide opportunities to continue to learn, to create, and to share with others. The importance, for individuals, of continuing to develop their personal interpretation of the underlying meaning of life should not be ignored or overlooked.

Fiske and Chiriboga (1990) reported on a 12-year longitudinal study that examined the personality traits, gender, social factors, and stressors influencing development during late adolescence, young adulthood, early middle age, and late middle age. They reported an increased concern with religion and spirituality for individuals in the oldest group, reflected in many facets of the individuals' lives. Despite this evidence, however, counseling psychologists have given little attention to the spiritual identity of older Americans.

A continuing challenge for people in retirement is to seek validation of themselves within their overall world view. Individuals' value systems develop over the years in relation to job, family, friends, leisure, and community involvements. Spiritual beliefs are an important part of individuals' overall value systems. Although spiritual development is a lifelong process, it often assumes new significance for elderly Americans. For these individuals, spiritual development seems to center around their efforts to make sense of themselves within the world and in relation to a higher purpose.

A focus on spirituality allows individuals to use energy for personal growth and the creation of hope for everlasting life. Individuals may strengthen their trust in themselves and continue their personal development, despite the loss of physical and intellectual capacities and increasing feelings of isolation. Erikson (1963) described some of the concerns of this stage of development in his treatment of the individual's struggle to achieve ego integrity versus despair. Worthington (1989) expanded on these ideas, suggesting that the limitations of age require individuals to realize that they are more than what they have accomplished. According to Worthington, the losses of old age are ways of letting go of the false securities of life. By letting go, individuals are free to live more fully in the present and to transcend barriers that they believed held them captive within their physical beings. Challenges of old age can change a person's religious faith. For many retired individuals, these concerns may be of central importance.

Types of Interventions

Tinsley and Tinsley (1981, 1984) proposed a two-dimensional classification scheme for leisure interventions that is applicable to retirement interventions. They noted that helping relationships vary, from those that are primarily information giving, to those that involve counseling. The goals of the interventions also vary, from a narrow, atheoretical focus on helping the individual to make specific decisions, to the more general goal of facilitating the individual's personal growth. The result is a classification system that distinguishes among retirement and leisure education, retirement and leisure guidance, retirement and leisure decision making, and retirement and leisure counseling.

Retirement and Leisure Education.   The primary nature of these types of interventions is one of information giving. For example, Neulinger (1981) stressed that the primary function of leisure education is to make individuals aware of the nature of the leisure experience and the conditions that need to occur to experience leisure. J. A. Peterson (1984) emphasized that the goal of retirement education is the imparting of factual information. Thus, educational approaches generally involve helping relationships in which the emphasis is primarily on attaining new information in a cognitive manner.

Most preretirement education programs consist of 10 to 12 hours of meetings, presented in a 3-day workshop, in 2-to-3-hour meetings spread over 3 to 4 weeks, or in 1-hour meetings spread over a 10-to-12-week period (D. A. Peterson, 1984). Employees and their spouses are invited to attend. The format consists of presentations, lectures, and group discussions. Standard topics covered generally include financial planning, health and wellness, insurance, living arrangements, consumer information, legal issues, leisure activities, and aging (Manion, 1981; D. A. Peterson, 1984). Often, these programs are sponsored by employers and involve presentations by experts trained to conduct retirement education seminars. Atchley (1987) suggested that 70% of retirement planning programs are of this type. Riker and Myers (1990) gave descriptions of such programs at Atlantic Richfield, Polaroid Corporation, Florida Power, and Kimberly Clark.

Several writers have proposed a life-span approach to retirement education and planning. Lieberman and Lieberman (1983) and Singleton (1985) argued that children need to be taught to think about and plan for retirement while in grade school. Because our ideas of leisure are formed at an early age, Singleton (1985) suggested that leisure education in youth will help individuals to incorporate healthy living and leisure into their life-style and form a foundation for later retirement. Riker and Myers (1990) identified the undergraduate years as the proper time to begin developing financial plans, leisure interests, and a positive attitude concerning retirement and aging. Quirk (1976) proposed that preretirement education and planning need to begin in young adulthood; others argue that education about retirement needs to begin at least 10 to 15 years before anticipated retirement.

Danish, D'Augelli, and Ginsberg (1984), noting that the concept of retirement has been almost entirely associated with old age, discussed retirement problems for many athletes. Because there frequently are no organized levels of activity for college athletes, Danish et al. raised the possibility of issues for college athletes as well as for professional athletes. Danish and Hale (1983) described the design of a course to improve the development of athletes; it specifically included the topic of retirement for athletes. In a fashion similar to that used for career life planning, the athletes examined needs being met through their sport and considered alternative activities to pursue subsequent to their retirement from college sports.

Hayes and Deren (1990) identified five characteristics of innovative programming for preretirement education for women: (a) the programs are designed to be sensitive to the women they serve; (b) the facilitators are similar to the participants and have received specialized training to understand culture and class differences among the participants; (c) the programs are designed to be comprehensive in scope, but begin by presenting basic information; (d) the importance of the emotional and social aspects of the planning is emphasized; and (e) peer support is considered essential.

A major grant from the Department of Health and Human Services, Administration on Aging, provided funding to develop preretirement planning programs specifically for women (Hayes & Deren, 1990). The programs were developed to help women communicate concerns to their spouses, understand changing aspects of their marriages, and learn to negotiate strategies for resolving conflicts. Topics covered included women as caretakers and their role overload; building relationships; and achieving positive mental health.

After conducting a needs assessment, Houlihan and Caraballo (1990) developed an educational preretirement planning model for women, specifically designed for workers in the service sector, health care, blue-collar jobs, and human services. They were concerned that the services be affordable and accessible, and they marketed them through organizations in which the women were already affiliated.

Others have published collections of exercises designed for use in retirement and leisure interventions (Godbey, 1981; Kimeldorf, 1989; Stumbo & Thompson, 1986; Witt, Campbell, & Witt, 1975), many of which are very similar to self-exploration activities used in career counseling.

The expansion of electronic media has opened new avenues for preretirement education. Currently, preretirement educators are discovering what can be done with videos and television. Brache and Hunter (1990) described a Massachusetts program called "Elderview," which is carried on cable-TV and is useful in retirement education. Preretirement education has also expanded to the self-help book market. These books are primarily informational, often containing worksheets for budgeting, rough drafts of wills, and information for evaluating potential retirement communities (American Association for Retired Persons, 1988; Brown, 1988; Dickenson, 1984; Palder, 1989).

Retirement and Leisure Guidance.   Models that rely primarily on information-giving techniques and are primarily intended to help the client make a specific decision are guidance models. Like educational models, guidance models emphasize an information-giving relationship. In contrast, however, guidance models focus very narrowly and atheoretically on helping the client make a specific decision. The focus of the relationship is quite specific. Although some concern may be expressed for establishing a good interpersonal relationship, the relationship is clearly of secondary importance. Tinsley and Tinsley (1981) gave examples of these models.

Retirement and Leisure Decision Making.   The main focus of these approaches is on helping clients obtain the information necessary to make a decision. Unlike the guidance models, however, the goals of these models are conceptualized more broadly and the affective qualities of the relationship are important. Consequently, these models indicate a greater awareness of the psychological complexity of the decision-making process.

The most extensively applied and evaluated retirement/leisure decision-making model reported in the literature is that developed by Overs and his associates (Magulski, Faull, & Rutkowski, 1977; Overs et al., 1974; Overs et al., 1977; Wilson, Mirenda, & Rutkowski, 1975). Their model differs from most other decision-making approaches in its overall flexibility in conceptualizing goals, its focus on the total individual, and its attention to the helping relationship. In most respects, the core elements follow the trait-and-factor paradigm of learning about the individual, learning about the environment, studying the relation between the individual and the environment, and recommending suitable leisure activities. Despite this emphasis, a large share of the work with clients was devoted to personal adjustment counseling. Often, clients had to work through problems of life adjustment before they were ready to consider avocational choice. A variety of personal and emotional problems on the part of clients were addressed, the most common being depression and stress. Attention is given to the relationship between the counselor and client and to establishing the facilitative conditions.

Retirement and Leisure Counseling. Retirement and leisure counseling models emphasize the establishment of a counseling relationship that embodies the facilitative conditions. Furthermore, retirement and leisure counseling emphasizes a concern for the total individual rather than focusing on only a limited problem. The goal of retirement counseling is to contribute to the personal growth of the individual rather than to assist in making a specific decision.

A program called Retirement Options (Green, 1979), directed toward emotional issues, includes family members in a multigenerational approach to preretirement counseling. The goals of this program include helping families gain an awareness of their perceptions about retirement, helping retirees and their children explore their feelings about retirement, and sensitizing participants to their stereotypes about retirement. In this program, the retirees and their children are divided into two groups. Each group is given a retirement scenario and asked to make decisions for the retirees in the scenario. The two groups are then combined for discussion of the rationale, emotions, and values that motivated their decisions. Topics discussed include relationships, living arrangements, time issues, and the accompanying emotions.

Johnson and Riker (1982) enumerated the following goals of preretirement counseling: (a) problem resolution; (b) behavioral change and redirection of maladaptive responses; (c) help in decision making, integration, and adjustment; (d) promotion of positive mental health; (e) increase in personal effectiveness; (f) instruction about the aging process and its effects, to aid individuals in accepting these changes in themselves; and (g) development of self-advocacy within individuals. In contrast to the educational focus on information dissemination, counseling emphasizes the helping relationship.

Loesch and Wheeler (1982) proposed a seven-step model of leisure counseling for use with older individuals. The first step, determining the need for counseling, is often done through informal assessment. The second step is to evaluate individuals' current leisure satisfaction, to determine whether leisure counseling is needed. Determining an appropriate counseling orientation; performing a comprehensive evaluation of the person's affective, behavioral, and cognitive functioning; and determining the goals of leisure counseling are the next steps. The identification of those leisure activities that can contribute most to life satisfaction, and the selection of leisure activities that will help the person change in desired ways, such as developing an improved self-concept, are examples of leisure counseling goals. Leisure counseling concludes with the determination of the most appropriate leisure activities for the client, and an evaluation of the process.

According to J. A. Peterson (1984), retirement counseling involves imparting the same information as retirement education but with a focus on the individuals' emotional responses to the information and to the prospect of retirement itself. In retirement counseling, the focus is on the anxiety and emotions of participants in response to the presentations, and the attitudes and adjustment of participants as they ready themselves for retirement. J. A. Peterson (1984) believed retirement counseling is most effective when it encourages participants to express, confront, and work through their emotions. Presentation of factual information without emotional debriefing is, according to Peterson, of little use, because individuals' emotional responses will obscure the factual information. J. A. Peterson (1984) advocated the use of group discussions that encourage expression of feelings. Group leaders should expect to encounter deep emotions and need to be comfortable with these emotions.

Orthner and Herron (1984) worked from the premise that most leisure behavior is learned and occurs within the family context. Therefore, it is important to understand the shared leisure experiences of the family and not just those of particular individuals in the family. Leisure problems within families vary considerably and may involve relational enmeshment, relational differentiation, activity addiction, and incongruent activity preferences.

Tinsley and Tinsley (1984) believed that effective retirement and leisure counselors differ from other counselors in several important respects. Most relevant to this discussion is the emphasis on counselors' understanding that the creative use of multiple roles is necessary to the realization of individuals' full potential. This philosophy is revolutionary to many clients. The work ethic has been so deeply ingrained in our value system that many persons feel guilty when they are not working. This issue may be especially salient when individuals are planning for or adjusting to retirement.

Research on Retirement and Leisure Interventions

Although retirement planning is now available through many outlets, very few people actually plan for their retirement (Behling & Merves, 1985; Kragie, Gerstein, & Lichtman, 1989; Prentis, 1980; Singleton, 1985). Estimated rates of retirement planning range from 28% (Fillenbaum, 1971a) to 42% (Prentis, 1980). Beck (1982) reported that only about 4 to 8% of men 60 years and older participate in formal retirement preparation programs. Singleton (1985) estimated that most people spend more time planning a 2-week vacation than a 15-year retirement. Retirement planning is particularly absent for women and racial/ethnic group members (Behling & Merves, 1985). Negative connotations of retirement (e.g., negative associations with mortality, loss of role in society) may be important reasons for this widespread lack of planning (Atchley, 1980).

Several researchers have investigated factors that influence persons to become involved in preretirement programs. Age is an obvious factor that has been found to be related to participation in retirement planning. The older individuals are, the more likely they are to have thought about retirement or to have begun planning for their retirement (Evans et al., 1985; Fillenbaum, 1971a; Prentis, 1980). Atchley (1977) believed that proximity to retirement rather than age per se is a greater determinant of participation in preretirement planning. Educational level has been found to be positively related to retirement planning, and occupational level is inversely related (Fillenbaum, 1971a; Prentis, 1980).

Some studies have investigated the impact of retirement planning programs. In one study, subjects reported increased feelings of competence, adequacy, financial ability, and personal worth after a 14-hour lecture and discussion series (Charles, 1971). Individuals reported an increase in thoughts about leisure activities and a decrease in concern with legal planning and the need for employment during retirement. Tiberi, Boyack, and Kerschner (1978) investigated facilitated interaction programs, semistructured discussions, formal presentations, and individual resource centers. They found different models to be differentially effective in influencing behavior, information acquisition, or attitudes. Facilitated interaction programs and formal presentations were found to yield the largest increase in information, and facilitated interaction and semistructured discussion were most effective for changing preretirement behaviors. In general, information-giving models appeared less effective than models that helped preretirees to deal with their emotions about retirement. While not specifically evaluating retirement or leisure counseling interventions, Wellman and McCormack (1984) concluded that results for individual counseling with elderly clients are comparable with results available for younger clients.

In a study of group versus individual retirement programs, Glamser and DeJong (1975) found group discussion to be most effective in increasing knowledge of retirement issues and feelings of preparedness while decreasing uncertainty about the future. In a 6-year follow-up, Glamser (1981a) found no difference between the groups in their postretirement adjustment. He suggested that the most important effects of preretirement programs occur in the form of alleviation of anxiety and uncertainty about retirement, through knowledge and emotional support. Thus, it may be important to shift the focus of preretirement programs toward concentration on the emotions associated with the transition to retirement, and to be less concerned with imparting information.

RECOMMENDATIONS

Research

We believe that four considerations must be addressed successfully, to conduct meaningful research on retirement. First, a realistic definition of retirement must be used. The need for further conceptual development is clear, but investigators must select their definition carefully and report the definition used. Research comparing results obtained using different definitions will also help to illuminate this issue. Second, investigators must control for socioeconomic status in retirement research. As we have seen in this chapter, differences in the health, mental health, and life satisfaction of retirees are confounded by differences in socioeconomic status. Third, it is important to look at the total life of the retiree, including work and leisure roles, caregiving and receiving roles, and other social and instrumental roles. Finally, we believe research on retirement needs to be more theory-based and to use more sophisticated data-analytic techniques. Longitudinal studies are needed, to help provide an overall view of the relations among work, leisure, nonwork, and retirement. We encourage researchers to make more use of qualitative analyses in studying the concepts that underlie leisure, work, and retirement. It is important to investigate the validity of some of the theories that we have outlined in this chapter.

These four considerations are important in all research on retirement. Of importance to us is that a substantial portion of the research effort be directed to studying previously neglected segments of our society, such as women, racial and ethnic groups, and the economically disadvantaged. Examining retirement as it occurs for these groups will provide insights into issues such as the definition of retirement and the effects of socioeconomic status. Work is experienced differently by the corporate executive, the homemaker, the pipefitter, and the custodian; so too, retirement is a multifaceted aspect of life. We believe that it holds different meanings for various segments of our society and is experienced differently by members of each segment. Counseling psychologists need to attend to the complex and essentially pluralistic nature of retirement and be guided by our openness to change.

Attention needs to be given to evaluating retirement and leisure interventions. Fretz's (1981) observation that we need to be much more explicit in describing what we do with clients is germane in considering research on retirement and leisure interventions. Counseling varies along a number of dimensions. We cannot completely understand which outcomes are likely related to what methods of intervention, until we can describe these dimensions.

Several other interesting and potentially important research issues would involve investigating the influence of social and cultural variables on outcomes of retirement and leisure counseling. For example, investigators could study the effects of counselor stereotypes on counseling outcome. Or, investigators might determine the effects of partner or extended family involvement on counseling outcome. Another type of research might investigate how specific interventions such as emotional debriefing influence the effectiveness of retirement and leisure education.

The issues that need investigation for understanding leisure and quality of life are too numerous to list. Our own list of high-priority research issues reveals our belief that leisure is an important aspect of life for all persons. We believe research is needed on the meaning of leisure and free time for special groups such as the unemployed, students, and retired individuals, and on the relations between leisure behavior and personal adjustment. We believe that it is important to examine the intrinsic and extrinsic rewards experienced in such diverse areas as work, leisure, religion, and retirement. The development of instruments to measure important constructs such as the psychological benefits of leisure is a promising area to pursue. Further assessment of older persons is needed, particularly in terms of their attitudes and retirement maturity. It is also important to investigate the validity of scales for older Americans. In one recent study (Smith and Robbins, 1988), the investigators modified an instrument to assess its validity for retirement-age adults. They determined that the modified measure of goal stability predicted adjustment. Identification of the components of life satisfaction in later years is important. We need to improve the measurement of important constructs such as perceived social competence, leisure participation, leisure satisfaction, and overall quality of life.

Practice

Improved training of new professionals is important in counseling psychology, if we are to improve the quality of retirement and leisure counseling. It is our belief, however, that this training should not focus on special techniques. Instead, we encourage training that focuses on providing counseling psychologists with an understanding of and sensitivity to the special aspects of life that support and challenge older Americans. These include issues of loss and death, to be sure; but they also include the many other topics covered in this chapter, such as ageism and discrimination, vocational and leisure issues, spiritual development, physical and mental health, and life satisfaction.

Training is important to help counselors overcome potential age biases and gain an understanding of the aged. Salisbury (1975) found that only 6% of the 304 counselor education programs surveyed offered an elective course on aging, and none of these programs required such a course. Myers (1983) found that 37% of the programs surveyed offered a course incorporating some information about the aged. Myers (1983) and Salisbury (1975) both noted the emphasis counseling psychology has placed on training students to work with college-age clients, to the neglect of older clients. Once counselors are trained to understand the aging process, they could be instrumental in developing life-span, personal, and vocational counseling programs for older adults (Bradford, 1979; McVeigh, 1980; Olsen & Robbins, 1986). More focus on gerontological course offerings and more encouragement of counseling psychology students to study gerontology are needed.

Recruitment of bicultural, bilingual students for admission to our training programs deserves special attention. As we discuss potential age and cultural biases, we can make a commitment to work toward equality of opportunities for all Americans. We can learn to act in more socially responsible ways toward elderly Americans from diverse backgrounds. We can influence the socialization process of the younger generations to value diversity and promote socially responsible behavior.

Hartford (1990) suggested several content areas in the curriculum to train effective retirement counselors. Counselors working in the retirement area need to be aware of social policy (i.e., legislation and law regarding retirement), the resources available to older Americans, and how to access these resources (Hartford, 1990; Riker & Myers, 1990). Retirement counselors also need a working knowledge of the biology, physiology, psychology, and sociology of aging (Brache & Hunter, 1990). As is already clear, counseling psychologists need to have strong clinical skills for working with retirees, their partners, and families. These skills will probably include the ability to conduct individual and group counseling, establish and maintain rapport, and conduct retirement counseling so that each individual gains from the experience (Hunter, 1980). Assessment, evaluation, and planning skills are also important (Brache & Hunter, 1990; Riker & Myers, 1990).

Brammer (1984) analyzed counseling theories, such as person-centered, existential, and cognitive-behavioral, with the intent of helping counseling psychologists become more flexible in counseling the elderly. Although not specifically referring to retirement or leisure counseling, Brammer's analysis can be useful for client conceptualization and treatment planning regarding the themes or issues of such counseling described earlier.

Counseling psychologists interested in helping older Americans who live in community residential settings may adapt models developed on college campuses, which focus on wellness and recreation programming to facilitate human development (Krivoski & Warner, 1986).

CONCLUDING REMARKS

The inclusion of this chapter on retirement and leisure in the *Handbook of Counseling Psychology* illustrates a recognition of the need for counseling psychologists to increase their understanding of middle and late adulthood and of the need to incorporate retirement and leisure as topics of central importance to counseling psychologists. The primary focus of this chapter has been on retirement and leisure as they relate to the later stages of life, but these topics need not be conceived of as relevant only during the later years of life. The importance of understanding retirement and leisure issues across the life span must be given a high priority by counseling psychologists.

A variety of barriers can exclude older individuals from satisfying participation in life and continued personal growth. Some of the barriers include societal attitudes and stereotypes. Our society values the work ethic, conspicuous consumption, and youth and physical prowess. Counseling psychologists can take an active role in educating the public about the realities of retirement and old age and in challenging stereotypes and ageism when they occur. We need a more progressive value base that goes beyond the competition for scarce resources and survival of the most fit to one of greater recognition and valuing of diversity and the potential for self-actualization for all Americans. Counseling psychologists can also become stronger advocates for the improvement of the social and psychological environment of all Americans. We can continue to identify and challenge the myths that older Americans are of no further usefulness to themselves or society and that they are a burden to abide until death. We believe that society has the current technology and human resources to make great strides in providing equal opportunities to all Americans to continue to develop their potential in old age. We can, therefore, combat the ageism of the public, of employers, and of retirees themselves (Cahill & Salomone, 1987). Furthermore, counseling psychologists need to be aware of their own attitudes and biases against older Americans and work to resolve those issues.

We see a number of barriers to gaining an increased understanding of retirement. The development of a more complete understanding of retirement has been hindered by a tendency to accept simple-minded definitions of retirement used in everyday language. Given our historical review of retirement, we can see that the construct developed primarily from a White male perspective. Often viewed as a just reward for job services rendered, required retirement also minimized the disruption that occurs when workers leave the work force because of actual performance deficits, death, and physical/mental disabilities.

The residual definition of leisure provides one good example of how limiting a simple definition of a construct can be. The significant influence of leisure on the physical health, mental health, life satisfaction, and personal growth of the individual was not appreciated as long as investigators thought of leisure simply as time other than work. The holistic view of leisure advocated by Tinsley and Tinsley (1988) emphasizes leisure as an important area of study in its own right. The consequences of this expanded view can be the scientific study of the causes, attributes, and benefits of leisure experience, and an examination of the scope and diversity of leisure experiences. Research on retirement would benefit from a similar broadening of the conceptualization of retirement. It is important to continue to expand our understanding of the meanings of retirement and leisure for various individuals across the life span, so that diverse meanings can be integrated into a comprehensive understanding of the total life-span development.

It is our view that the constructs of retirement and leisure are beginning to receive well-deserved attention within counseling psychology. An earlier neglect, resulting in part from the societal value placed on the work ethic, conspicuous consumption, and youth, is being replaced by a curious interest and well-disciplined efforts to increase our understanding and improve counseling psychologists' practice. Although relatively little theory development has occurred pertaining to these constructs and our knowledge base regarding retirement and leisure are currently inadequate, we predict that, during the 1990s, counseling psychologists will directly engage in efforts to improve the quality of life of older Americans. We are learning that individual differences abound during the retirement years; it is equally important for counseling psychologists in practice to take into account the different needs of the elderly. We need to consider how our current representations of elderly Americans continue to restrict their roles in society today. Counseling psychologists can assist older Americans to value themselves, to continue contributing to their communities and the world, and to seek new and deeper meaning in their lives.

Even as older Americans face challenges that they cannot directly control, they can strive to help each other. Americans can be responsible and self-directed to promote their own and others' balanced, personal development throughout their life span. We believe that Americans will be able to promote a new world order that truly values individual diversity. We can create a unity of purpose in helping others and can reduce the impact of prejudice and discrimination on others' lives. We can create a unity of purpose. In today's world, the constructs of retirement, leisure, and creativity seem especially important as we support and challenge each other throughout the cycle of life.

REFERENCES

American Association for Retired Persons. (1988). *How to plan your successful retirement.* Glenview, IL: Scott, Foresman.

Ash, P. (1966). Pre-retirement counseling. *The Gerontologist, 6,* 97–99, 127.

Atchley, R. C. (1971). Retirement and leisure participation: Continuity or crisis? *The Gerontologist, 11*, 13–17.

Atchley, R. C. (1976). Selected social and psychological differences between men and women in later life. *Journal of Gerontology, 31*, 204–211.

Atchley, R. C. (1977). *The social forces in later life: An introduction to social gerontology.* Belmont, CA: Wadsworth.

Atchley, R. C. (1979). Issues in retirement research. *The Gerontologist, 19*, 44–54.

Atchley, R. C. (1980). *The social forces in later life.* Belmont, CA: Wadsworth.

Atchley, R. C. (1987). *Aging: Continuity and change (2nd ed.).* Belmont, CA: Wadsworth.

Atchley, R. C., & Robinson, J. L. (1982). Attitudes toward retirement and distance from the event. *Research on Aging, 4*, 299–313.

Bandura, A. (1977). Self-efficacy: Toward a unifying theory of behavioral change. *Psychological Review, 84*, 191–215.

Beck, S. (1982). Adjustment to and satisfaction with retirement. *Journal of Gerontology, 37*, 616–624.

Behling, J. H., & Merves, E. S. (1985). Pre-retirement attitudes and financial preparedness: A cross cultural and gender analysis. *Journal of Sociology and Social Welfare, 12*, 113–128.

Belgrave, L. L. (1988). The effects of race differences in work history, work attitudes, economic resources, and health on retirement. *Research on Aging, 10*, 383–398.

Belgrave, L. L. (1989). Understanding women's retirement. *Generations, 13*, 49–52.

Bell, B. D. (1975). The limitations of crisis theory as an explanatory mechanism in social gerontology. *International Journal of Aging and Human Development, 6*, 153–169.

Bell, B. D. (1978). Life satisfaction and occupational retirement: Beyond the impact year. *International Journal of Aging and Human Development, 9*, 31–50.

Berman, P. L. (Ed.). (1989). *The courage to grow old.* New York: Ballantine.

Bishop, D. S., Epstein, N. B., Baldwin, L. M., & Miller, J. W. (1988). Older couples: The effect of health, retirement, and family functioning on morale. *Family Systems Medicine, 6*, 238–247.

Bley, G., Goodman, M., Dye, D., & Harel, B. (1972). Characteristics of aged participants and non-participants in age-segregated leisure program. *Gerontologist, 12*, 368–370.

Blocher, D. H., & Siegal, R. (1984). Toward a cognitive development theory of leisure and work. In E. T. Dowd (Ed.), *Leisure counseling: Concepts and applications* (pp. 52–59). Springfield, IL: Thomas.

Boaz, R. F. (1987). The 1983 amendments to the Social Security Act: Will they delay retirement? A summary of the evidence. *The Gerontologist, 27*, 151–155.

Bosse, R., Aldwin, C. M., Levenson, M. R., & Ekerdt, D. J. (1987). Mental health differences among retirees to workers: Findings from the normative aging study. *Psychology of Aging, 2*, 383–389.

Brache, C. I., & Hunter, W. W. (1990). Leadership training for retirement education. In R. H. Shernan & D. B. Lumsden (Eds.), *Introduction to education gerontology* (pp. 269–293). New York: Hemisphere.

Bradford, L. P. (1979). Emotional problems in retirement and what can be done. *Group and Organizational Studies, 4*, 429–439.

Bradford, L. P., & Bradford, M. I. (1979). *Retirement: Coping with emotional upheavals.* Chicago: Nelson-Hall.

Brammer, L. M. (1984). Counseling theory and the older adult. *The Counseling Psychologist, 12*(2), 29–37.

Brightbill, C. K. (1960). *The challenge of leisure.* Englewood Cliffs, NJ: Prentice-Hall.

Brown, P. F. (1988). *From here to retirement: Planning now for the rest of your life.* Waco, TX: Word Books.

Bultena, G., & Wood, V. (1970). Leisure orientation and recreational activities of retirement community residents. *Journal of Leisure Research, 2*, 3–15.

Burgess, E. W. (1960). *Aging in Western societies.* Chicago: University of Chicago Press.

Cahill, M., & Salomone, P. R. (1987). Career counseling for work life extension: Integrating the older worker into the labor force. *Career Development Quarterly, 35*, 188–196.

Cath, S. H. (1975). The orchestration of disengagement. *International Journal of Aging and Human Development, 6*, 199–213.

Chang, P. (1977). Working with the elderly Asians. In B. L. Newsome (Ed.), *Insights on the minority elderly.* Washington, DC: National Center on the Black Aged.

Charles, D. C. (1971). The effect of participation in a pre-retirement program. *The Gerontologist, 11,* 24–28.

Clemente, F., & Sauer, W. J. (1974). Race and morale of the urban aged. *The Gerontologist, 14,* 342–344.

Comrie, S. M. (1985). Training: Teach employees to approach retirement as a new career. *Personnel Journal, 64*(8), 106–108.

Conner, K. A., Dorfman, L. T., & Tompkins, J. B. (1985). Life satisfaction of retired professors: The contribution of work, health, income, and length of retirement. *Educational Gerontology, 11,* 337–347.

Cowgill, D., & Baulch, N. (1962). The use of leisure time by older people. *The Gerontologist, 2,* 47–50.

Cox, H., & Bhak, A. (1970). Symbolic interactions and retirement adjustment: An empirical assessment. *International Journal of Aging and Human Development, 9,* 279–286.

Csikszentmihalyi, M. (1975). *Beyond boredom and anxiety: The experience of play in work and games.* San Francisco: Jossey-Bass.

Cummings, E. (1975). Engagement with an old theory. *International Journal of Aging and Human Development, 6,* 187–191.

Cummings, E., & Henry, W. (1961). *Growing old.* New York: Basic Books.

Danish, S. J., D'Augelli, A. R., & Ginsberg, M. R. (1984). Life development intervention: Promotion of mental health through the development of competence. In S. D. Brown and R. W. Lent (Eds.), *Handbook of counseling psychology.* New York: Wiley.

Danish, S. J., & Hale, B. D. (1983). Sport psychology: Teaching skills to athletes and coaches. *Journal of Physical Education, Recreation and Dance, 54*(8), 11–12, 80–81.

Dennis, H. (1986). Retirement preparation programs: Issues in planning and selection. *Journal of Career Development, 13*(2), 30–38.

DeRenzo, E. D. (1990). Pre-retirement planning among wives of retired military officers. In C. Hayes & J. Deren (Eds.), *Pre-retirement planning for women: Program design and research.* New York: Springer.

Dickason, J. G. (1972). Approaches and techniques of recreation counseling. *Therapeutic Recreation Journal, 6*(2), 74–78.

Dickenson, P. A. (1984). *The complete retirement planning book.* New York: Dutton.

Dorfman, L. T., & Hill, E. A. (1986). Rural housewives and retirement: Joint decision-making matters. *Family Relations, 35,* 507–514.

Dorfman, L. T., Kahout, F. J., & Heckert, D. A. (1985). Retirement satisfaction in the rural elderly. *Research on Aging, 7,* 577–599.

Dorfman, L. T., & Maffett, M. M. (1987). Retirement satisfaction in married and widowed rural women. *The Gerontologist, 27,* 215–221.

Dowd, J. J., & Bengston, V. L. (1978). Aging in minority populations: An examination of the double jeopardy hypothesis. *Journal of Gerontology, 33,* 427–436.

Dumazedier, T. (1967). *Toward a society of leisure.* New York: Free Press.

Edwards, J. N., & Klemmack, D. L. (1973). Correlates of life satisfaction: A re-examination. *Journal of Gerontology, 28,* 497–502.

Ego, M. (1983). The urgent need for humanistic delivery of leisure services to the minority elderly. *Leisure and aging.* Alexandria, VA: National Recreation and Park Association.

Ekerdt, D. J. (1987). Why the notion persists that retirement harms health. *The Gerontologist, 27,* 454–457.

Ekerdt, D. J., Bosse, R., & LoCastro, J. S. (1983). Claims that retirement improves health. *Journal of Gerontology, 38,* 231–236.

Erikson, E. K. (1963). *Childhood and society.* New York: Norton.

Evans, L., Ekerdt, D. J., & Bosse, R. (1985). Proximity to retirement and anticipatory involvement: Findings from the normative aging study. *Journal of Gerontology, 40,* 368–374.

Fillenbaum, G. G. (1971a). Retirement planning programs: At what age, and for whom? *The Gerontologist, 11,* 33–36.

Fillenbaum, G. G. (1971b). On the relation between attitude to work and attitude to retirement. *Journal of Gerontology, 26,* 244–248.

Fiske, M., & Chiriboga, D. A. (1990). *Continuity and change in adult life.* San Francisco: Jossey-Bass.

Forcese, D., & Cooper, J. (1985). Police retirement: Career succession or obsolescence? *Canadian Police Journal, 9,* 413–424.

Fox, J. F. (1977). Effects of retirement and former work life on women's adaptations in old age. *Journal of Gerontology, 32,* 196–202.

Fretz, B. R. (1981). Evaluating the effectiveness of career interventions. *Journal of Counseling Psychology Monograph, 28,* 77–90.

Fretz, B. R., Kluge, N. A., Ossana, S. M., Jones, S. M., & Merikangas, M. W. (1989). Intervention targets for reducing preretirement anxiety and depression. *Journal of Counseling Psychology, 36,* 301–307.

Friedmann, E., & Havighurst, R. J. (1954). *The meaning of work and retirement.* Chicago: University of Chicago Press.

Geist, H. (1981). *Psychological aspects of the aging process with sociological implications.* New York: Krieger.

George, L. K., & Maddox, G. L. (1977). Subjective adaptation to loss of the work role: A longitudinal study. *Journal of Gerontology, 32,* 456–462.

Gibson, R. C. (1987). Reconceptualizing retirement for Black Americans. *The Gerontologist, 27,* 691–698.

Gigy, L. L. (1985). Pre-retired and retired women's attitudes toward retirement. *International Journal of Aging and Human Development, 22,* 31–44.

Glamser, F. D. (1976). Determinants of a positive attitude toward retirement. *Journal of Gerontology, 31,* 104–107.

Glamser, F. D. (1981a). The impact of retirement programs on the retirement experience. *Journal of Gerontology, 36,* 244–250.

Glamser, F. D. (1981b). Predictors of retirement attitudes. *Aging and Work, 4,* 23–29.

Glamser, F. D., & DeJong, G. F. (1975). The efficacy of present preparation process for industrial workers. *Journal of Gerontology, 30,* 595–600.

Godbey, G. (1981). *Leisure in your life: An exploration.* New York: Saunders.

Gordon, J. B. (1975). A disengaged look at disengagement theory. *International Journal of Aging and Human Development, 6,* 215–227.

Goudy, W. J., Powers, E. A., & Keith, P. (1975). Work and retirement: A test of attitudinal relationships. *Journal of Gerontology, 30,* 193–198.

Green, L. (1979). *Retirement options: A gerontological simulation. Leader's manual.* Ann Arbor, MI: Institute of Gerontology, University of Michigan.

Greenhaus, J. H. (1987). *Career management.* Hinsdale, IL: Dryden.

Grossin, W. (1986). The relationship between work time and free time to the meaning of retirement. *Leisure Studies, 5,* 91–101.

Guinn, R. (1980). Elderly recreational vehicle tourists: Life satisfaction correlates of leisure satisfaction. *Journal of Leisure Research, 12,* 198–204.

Gunn, S. L. (1976). Leisure counseling: An analysis of play behavior and attitudes using transactional analysis and gestalt awareness. In G. Rob & G. Hitzhusen (Eds.), *Expanding horizons in therapeutic recreation III.* Columbia, MO: University of Missouri Press.

Gunn, S. L. (1978). Structural analysis of play behavior: Pathological implications. In D. J. Brademas (Ed.), *New thoughts on leisure.* Champaign, IL: University of Illinois.

Gunn, S. L., & Peterson, C. A. (1978). *Therapeutic recreation program design: Principles and procedures.* Englewood Cliffs, NJ: Prentice-Hall.

Hackett, G., Lent, R. W., & Greenhaus, J. H. (1991). Advances in vocational theory and research: A 20-year retrospective. *Journal of Vocational Behavior, 38,* 3–38.

Hanisch, K. A., & Hulin, C. L. (1990). Job attitudes and organizational withdrawal: An examination of retirement and other voluntary withdrawal behaviors. *Journal of Vocational Behavior, 37,* 60–78.

Harris, L., & Associates, Inc. (1981). *Aging in the eighties: America in transition.* Washington, DC: National Council on the Aging.

Hartford, M. E. (1984). Self-inventory for planning. In H. Dennis (Ed.), *Retirement preparation: What retirement specialists need to know*. Lexington, MA: Lexington Books.

Hartford, M. E. (1990). Career education for the preparation of practitioners in gerontology with special reference to adult education. In R. H. Sherhan & D. B. Lumsden (Eds.), *Introduction to educational gerontology*. New York: Hemisphere.

Hatcher, M. A. (1988). What happens to the early retiree? *Career Development Quarterly, 37*, 184–190.

Havighurst, R. J. (1957). The leisure activities of the middle aged. *American Journal of Sociology, 63*, 152–162.

Havighurst, R. J., & Feigenbaum, K. (1959). Leisure and life style. *American Journal of Sociology, 64*, 396–405.

Hayes, C. L., & Deren, J. M. (Eds.). (1990). *Pre-retirement planning for women: Program design and research*. New York: Springer.

Haynes, S. G., McMichael, A. J., & Tyroler, H. A. (1978). Survival after early and normal retirement. *Journal of Gerontology, 33*, 269–278.

Holahan, C. K. (1981). Lifetime achievement patterns, retirement, and life satisfaction of gifted aged women. *Journal of Gerontology, 36*, 741–749.

Holmberg, K., Rosen, D., & Holland, J. L. (1990). *The Leisure Activities Finder*. Odessa, FL: Psychological Assessment Resources.

Hornstein, G. A., & Wapner, S. (1985). Modes of experiencing and adapting to retirement. *International Journal of Aging and Human Development, 21*, 291–315.

Houlihan, P., & Caraballa, E. (1990). Women and retirement planning: The development of Future Connections, Inc. In C. L. Hayes & J. M. Deren (Eds.), *Pre-retirement planning for women: Program design and research* (pp. 63–76). New York: Springer.

Hunter, W. W. (1980). *Preretirement Education Leader's Manual*. Ann Arbor, MI: Institute of Gerontology, University of Michigan.

Jackson, J. J. (1980). *Minorities and aging*. Belmont, CA: Wadsworth.

Jackson, J. S., & Gibson, R. C. (1985). Work and retirement among Black elderly. In Z. Blau (Ed.), *Current perspectives on aging and the life cycle*. Greenwich, CT: JAI Press.

Jacobson, D. (1974). Rejection of the retiree role: A study of female industrial workers in their 50's. *Human Relations, 27*, 477–492.

Jaslow, P. (1976). Employment, retirement and morale among older women. *Journal of Gerontology, 31*, 212–218.

Johnson, R. P., & Riker, H. C. (1982). Counselors' goals and roles in assisting older persons. *American Mental Health Counselors Association Journal, 4*, 30–40.

Kaiser, M. A., Peters, G. R., & Babcheck, N. (1982). When priests retire. *The Gerontologist, 22*, 89–94.

Kasiworm, L., & Wetzel, J. W. (1981). Women and retirement: Evolving issues for future research and education intervention. *Educational Gerontology, 7*, 299–314.

Kaye, L. W., & Monk, A. (1984). Sex role traditions and retirement from academe. *The Gerontologist, 24*, 420–426.

Keating, N., & Marshall, J. (1980). The process of retirement: The rural self employed. *The Gerontologist, 20*, 437–443.

Keith, P. M. (1985). Work, retirement, and well-being among unmarried men and women. *The Gerontologist, 25*, 410–416.

Kieffer, J. A. (1986). Kicking the premature retirement habit. *Journal of Career Development, 13*(2), 39–51.

Kilty, K. M., & Behling, J. H. (1985). Predicting the retirement intentions and attitudes of professional workers. *Journal of Gerontology, 40*, 219–227.

Kimeldorf, M. (1989). *Pathways to leisure*. Bloomington, IL: Meridian.

Kimmel, D. C., Price, K. F., & Walker, J. W. (1978). Retirement choice and retirement satisfaction. *Journal of Gerontology, 33*, 575–585.

Kouri, M. K. (1986). A life design process for older adults. *Journal of Career Development, 13*(2), 6–13.

Kragie, E. R., Gerstein, M., & Lichtman, M. (1989). Do Americans plan for retirement? Some recent trends. *The Career Development Quarterly, 37,* 232-239.

Kremer, Y. (1985). Predictors of retirement satisfaction: A path model. *International Journal of Aging and Human Development, 20,* 113-121.

Krivoski, J. F., & Warner, M. J. (1986). Implementing strategies for high-level wellness programs in student housing. *New Directions for Student Services, 34,* 53-66.

Lemon, B. W., Bengston, V. L., & Peterson, J. A. (1972). An exploration of the activity theory of aging: Activity types and life satisfaction among in-movers to a retirement community. *Journal of Gerontology, 27,* 511-523.

Levin, J., & Levin, W. C. (1980). *Ageism: Prejudice and discrimination against the elderly.* Belmont, CA: Wadsworth.

Levine, M. (1980). Four models for age/work policy research. *The Gerontologist, 20,* 561-574.

Lewissohn, P., & Graf, M. (1973). Pleasant activities and depression. *Journal of Consulting and Clinical Psychology, 41,* 261-268.

Lieberman, L., & Lieberman, L. (1983). The second career concept. *Aging and Work, 6,* 277-289.

Loesch, L. C., & Wheeler, P. T. (1982). *Principles of leisure counseling.* Minneapolis, MN: Education Media Corp.

Lofquist, L. H., & Dawis, R. V. (1969). *Adjustment to work.* New York: Appleton-Century-Crofts.

London, M. (1990). Enhancing career motivation in late career. *Journal of Organizational Change Management, 3*(2), 58-71.

London, M., & Greller, M. M. (1991). Demographic trends and vocational behavior: A twenty-year retrospective and agenda for the 1990s. *Journal of Vocational Behavior, 38,* 125-164.

Magulski, M., Faull, V. H., & Rutkowski, B. (1977). The Milwaukee leisure counseling model. *Journal of Physical Education and Recreation, 48*(4), 49-50.

Manion, V. V. (1981). *Preretirement education and counseling.* Ann Arbor, MI: ERIC/CAPS.

Manuel, R. C. (1982). The study of the minority aged in historical perspective. In R. C. Manuel (Ed.), *Minority aging: Sociological and social psychological issues.* Westport, CT: Greenwood Press.

Markides, K. S., & Mindel, C. H. (1987). *Aging and ethnicity.* Berkeley, CA: Sage.

Markson, E. W. (1975). Disengagement theory revisited. *International Journal of Aging and Development, 6,* 183-186.

McDowell, C. F., Jr. (1981). Leisure: Consciousness, well-being, and counseling. *The Counseling Psychologist, 9*(3), 3-31.

McPherson, B., & Guppy, N. (1979). Pre-retirement life-style and the degree of planning for retirement. *Journal of Gerontology, 34,* 254-263.

McVeigh, F. J. (1980). Mandatory vs. flexible retirement and the functions of counseling. *Canadian Counselor, 14,* 102-109.

Merikanges, M. W., & Fretz, B. R. (1986). Pre-retirement programming. In Z. Leibowitz & D. Lea (Eds.), *Adult career development: Concepts, issues and practices.* Alexandria, VA: American Association for Counseling and Development.

Metropolous, N. D. (1980). The retirement years: Disengagement or reengagement? *Lifelong Learning: The Adult Years, 4*(4), 12-15.

Minkler, M. (1981). Research on the health effects of retirement: An uncertain legacy. *Journal of Health and Social Behavior, 22,* 117-130.

Mobily, K. (1984). Leisure and retirement: The need for leisure counseling. *Physical Educator, 41*(1), 6-15.

Montagnes, J. M. (1977). Reality therapy approach to leisure counseling. In A. Epperson, P. A. Witt, & G. Hitzhusen (Eds.), *Leisure counseling: An aspect of leisure education* (pp. 149-160). Springfield, IL: Thomas.

Montgomery, R. J. W., & Borgatta, E. J. (1987). Plausible theories to the development of scientific theory: The case of aging research. *Research on Aging, 8,* 586-608.

Mutran, E., & Reitzes, D. C. (1981). Retirement, identity to well-being. Realignment of role relationships. *Journal of Gerontology, 36,* 733-740.

Myers, J. E. (1983). Gerontological counseling training: The state of the art. *Personnel and Guidance Journal, 61,* 398-400.

Myers, J. E. (1984). Leisure counseling for older people. In E. T. Dowd (Ed.), *Leisure counseling: Concepts and applications* (pp. 157–177). Springfield, IL: Thomas.

Neuh, H. P. (1990). Predictions of adjustment in retirement of women. In C. Hayes & J. Deren (Eds.), *Pre-retirement planning for women: Program design and research* (pp. 133–150). New York: Springer.

Neulinger, J. (1971). Leisure and mental health: A study in a program of leisure research. *Pacific Sociological Review, 14,* 288–300.

Neulinger, J. (1981). *To leisure: An introduction.* Boston: Allyn & Bacon.

Odell, C. E. (1980). Employment counseling for the elderly: Legislative history and outlook. *Journal of Employment Counseling, 17,* 57–67.

Olsen, S. K., & Robbins, S. B. (1986). Guidelines for the development and evaluation of career services for the older adult. *Journal of Career Development, 13*(2), 63–73.

Orthner, D. K., & Herron, R. W. (1984). Leisure counseling for families. In E. T. Dowd (Ed.), *Leisure counseling: Concepts and applications* (pp. 178–197). Springfield, IL: Thomas.

Overs, R. P., Taylor, S., & Adkins, C. (1974). *Avocational counseling in Milwaukee.* Final report on project H233466, No. 50, Curative Workshop of Milwaukee, WI.

Overs, R. P., Taylor, S., Cassell, E., & Chernov, M. (1977). *Avocational counseling for the elderly.* Sussex, WI: Avocational Counseling Research.

Palder, E. L. (1989). *The retirement sourcebook: Your complete guide to health, leisure and consumer information.* Woodbine House.

Palmore, E. B. (1965). Differences in the retirement patterns of men and women. *The Gerontologist, 5,* 4–8.

Palmore, E. B. (1979). Predictors of successful aging. *The Gerontologist, 19,* 427–432.

Palmore, E. B., Burchett, B. M., Fillenbaum, G. G., George, L. K., & Wallman, L. M. (1985). *Retirement: Causes and consequences.* New York: Springer.

Palmore, E., Cleveland, W. P., Nowlin, J. B., Ranm, D., & Siegler, I. C. (1979). Stress to adaptation in later life. *Journal of Gerontology, 34,* 841–851.

Palmore, E. B., Fillenbaum, G. G., & George, L. K. (1984). Consequences of retirement. *Journal of Gerontology, 39,* 109–116.

Palmore, E., & Kivett, V. (1977). Change in life satisfaction: A longitudinal study of persons aged 46–70. *Journal of Gerontology, 32,* 311–316.

Pargament, K. I. (1987, August). *God help me: Towards a theoretical framework of coping for the psychology of religion.* Paper presented at the annual meeting of the American Psychological Association, New York.

Peacock, E. W., & Talley, W. M. (1985). Developing leisure competence: A goal for late adulthood. *Educational Gerontology, 11,* 261–276.

Peterson, D. A. (1984). Instruction in retirement preparation programs. In H. Dennis (Ed.), *Retirement preparation: What retirement specialists need to know.* Lexington, MA: Lexington Books.

Peterson, J. A. (1984). Preretirement counseling. In H. Dennis (Ed.), *Retirement preparation: What retirement specialists need to know.* Lexington, MA: Lexington Books.

Pfeiffer, E., & Davis, G. (1971). The use of leisure time in middle life. *The Gerontologist, 11,* 187–195.

Poituenaud, J., Vallery-Massan, J., Valleran, A. J., Demeestere, M., & Liam, M. R. (1979). Factors related to attitude toward retirement among French pre-retired managers and top executives. *Journal of Gerontology, 34,* 723–727.

Pollman, W. A. (1971). Early retirement: Relationship to variation in life satisfaction. *The Gerontologist, 11,* 43–47.

Prentis, R. S. (1980). White-collar working women's perception of retirement. *The Gerontologist, 20,* 90–95.

Quinn, J. F., Burkhauser, R. V., & Myers, D. A. (1990). *Passing the torch: The influence of economic incentives on work and retirement.* Kalamazoo, MI: Upjohn Institute for Employment Research.

Quirk, D. A. (1976). Is aging here to stay? Life-span opportunities for the older adult. *Personnel and Guidance Journal, 55,* 140–143.

Ragheb, M. G. & Griffith, C. A. (1982). The contribution of leisure participation and leisure satisfaction to life satisfaction of older persons. *Journal of Leisure Research, 14*, 295–306.

Ray, R. O. (1979). Life satisfaction and activity involvement: Implications for leisure service. *Journal of Leisure Research, 11*, 112–119.

Rey, A. B. (1982). Activity to disengagement: Theoretical orientations in social gerontology to minority aging. In R. C. Manuel (Ed.), *Minority aging: Sociological and social psychological issues.* Westport, CT: Greenwood Press.

Rhodes, L. (1982). Retirement, economics, and the minority aged. In R. C. Manuel (Ed.), *Minority aging: Sociological and social psychological issues.* Westport, CT: Greenwood Press.

Richardson, M. S. (1970). Toward an expanded view of careers. *The Counseling Psychologist, 8*(1), 34–35.

Richardson, V., & Kilty, K. M. (1989). Retirement financial planning among black professionals. *The Gerontologist, 29*, 32–37.

Riddick, C. L. (1985a). Life satisfaction for older female homemakers, retirees, and workers. *Research on Aging, 7*, 383–393.

Riddick, C. L. (1985b). Life satisfaction determinants of older males and females. *Leisure Sciences, 7*, 47–63.

Riddick, C. L., & Daniel, S. N. (1984). The relative contributions of leisure activities and other factors to the mental health of older women. *Journal of Leisure Research, 16*, 136–148.

Riker, H. C., & Myers, J. E. (1990). *Retirement counseling: A practical guide for action.* New York: Hemisphere.

Romsa, G., Bandy, P., & Blenman, M. (1985). Modeling retirees' life satisfaction levels: The role of recreational, life cycle, and socio-environmental elements. *Journal of Leisure Research, 17*, 29–39.

Rosen, B., & Jerdee, T. (1988). Managing older workers' careers. *Research in Personnel and Human Resources Management, 6*, 37–74.

Rosow, O. (1963). *Socialization to old age.* Berkeley, CA: Wadsworth.

Rule, W. R., & Stewart, M. W. (1977). Enhancing leisure counseling using an Adlerian technique. *Therapeutic Recreation Journal, 11*(3), 87–93.

Russell, J. E. A. (1991). Career development interventions in organizations. *Journal of Vocational Behavior, 38*, 237–287.

Saleh, S. D., & Otis, J. L. (1963). Sources of job satisfaction and their effects on attitude toward retirement. *Journal of Industrial Psychology, 1*, 101–106.

Salisbury, H. (1975). Counseling the elderly: A neglected area in counselor education and supervision. *Counselor Education and Supervision, 14*, 237–238.

Sauer, W. (1977). Morale of the urban aged: A regression analysis of race. *Journal of Gerontology, 35*, 600–608.

Schlossberg, N. K. (1984). *Counseling adults in transition.* New York: Springer.

Schulz, R., & Ewen, R. B. (1988). *Adult development and aging: Myths and emerging realities.* New York: Macmillan.

Scofield, W. (1964). *Psychotherapy: The process of friendship.* Englewood Cliffs, NJ: Prentice-Hall.

Seccombe, K., & Lee, G. R. (1986). Gender differences in retirement satisfaction and its antecedents. *Research on Aging, 8*, 426–440.

Shneidman, E. (1989). The Indian summer of life: A preliminary study of septuagenarians. *American Psychologist, 44*, 684–694.

Singleton, J. F. (1985). Retirement: Its effects on the individual. *Activities, Adaptation, and Aging, 6*(4), 1–7.

Smith, L. C., & Robbins, S. B. (1988). Validity of the goal instability scale (modified) as a predictor of adjustment in retirement-age adults. *Journal of Counseling Psychology, 35*, 325–329.

Solomon, C. (1979). Elderly non-whites: Unique situations and concerns. In M. L. Ganikos, K. A. Grady, & J. B. Olson (Eds.), *Counseling the aged: A training syllabus for educators.* Washington, DC: American Personnel and Guidance Association.

Sommerstein, J. C. (1986). Assessing the older worker: The career counselor's dilemma. *Journal of Career Development, 13*(2), 52–56.

Spreitzer, E., & Snyder, E. E. (1983). Correlates of participation in adult recreational sports. *Journal of Leisure Research, 15,* 27–38.

Steinkamp, M. W., & Kelly, J. R. (1985). Relationships among motivational orientation, level of leisure activity, and life satisfaction in older men and women. *Journal of Psychology, 119,* 509–520.

Streib, G., & Schneider, G. (1971). *Retirement in American society.* Ithaca, NY: Cornell University Press.

Stull, D. E. (1988). A dyadic approach to predicting well being in later life. *Research on Aging, 10,* 81–101.

Stumbo, N. J., & Thompson, M. S. (1986). *Leisure education: A manual of activities and resources.* Peoria, IL: Central Illinois Center for Independent Living and Easter Seal Center, Inc.

Szinovacz, M. (1987). Preferred retirement timing and retirement satisfaction in women. *International Journal of Aging and Human Development, 24,* 301–317.

Tedrick, T. (1983). Leisure competency: A goal for aging Americans in the eighties. In *Aging and Leisure* (pp. 87–91). Alexandria, VA: National Recreation and Park Association.

Thompson, W. E., & Streib, G. F. (1958). Situational determinants: Health and economic deprivation in retirement. *Journal of Social Issues, 14*(2), 18–34.

Tiberi, D. M., Boyack, V. L., & Kerschner, P. A. (1978). A comparative analysis of retirement education models. *Educational Gerontology, 3,* 355–374.

Tiger, L. (1979). *Optimism: The biology of hope.* New York: Simon & Schuster.

Tinsley, H. E. A., Colbs, S. L., Teaff, J. D., & Kaufman, N. (1987). The relationship of age, gender, health, and economic status to the psychological benefits older persons report from participation in leisure activities. *Leisure Sciences, 9,* 53–65.

Tinsley, H. E. A., & Tinsley, D. J. (1981). An analysis of leisure counseling models. *The Counseling Psychologist, 9*(3), 45–54.

Tinsley, H. E. A., & Tinsley, D. J. (1982). A holistic model of leisure counseling. *Journal of Leisure Research, 14,* 100–116.

Tinsley, H. E. A., & Tinsley, D. J. (1984). Leisure counseling models. In E. T. Dowd (Ed.), *Leisure counseling: Concepts and applications* (pp. 80–96). Springfield, IL: Thomas.

Tinsley, H. E. A., & Tinsley, D. J. (1988). An expanded context for the study of career decision-making, development, and maturity. In W. B. Walsh & S. H. Osipow (Eds.), *Career decision making.* Hillsdale, NJ: Erlbaum.

Wellman, F. E., & McCormack, J. (1984). Counseling with older persons: A review of outcome research. *The Counseling Psychologist, 12*(2), 81–96.

White, R. (1976). Strategies of adaptation: An attempt at systematic description. In R. H. Moos (Ed.), *Human adaptation: Coping with life crises.* Lexington, MA: Heath.

Wilson, G. T., Mirenda, J. J., & Rutkowski, B. A. (1975). Milwaukee leisure counseling model. *Journal of Leisurability, 2,* 11–17.

Witt, J., Campbell, M., & Witt, P. (1979). *A manual of therapeutic group activities for leisure education.* Washington, DC: Hawkins.

Worthington, E. L., Jr. (1989). Religious faith across the life span: Implications for counseling and research. *The Counseling Psychologist, 17,* 555–612.

Zawada, M. A., & Walz, G. R. (1979). *Counseling adults.* Ann Arbor, MI: ERIC/CAPS.

PART FOUR

PERSONAL AND INTERPERSONAL COUNSELING

CHAPTER 20

CHANGING THEORIES OF CHANGE: RECENT DEVELOPMENTS IN COUNSELING

MICHAEL J. MAHONEY
KATHLEEN McCRAY PATTERSON

In this last decade of the century, we have reached a pivotal period in the history of ideas. World events leave little doubt that we are not just on the cusp of change: we are living it. Decisions that are made (or not made) and actions that are taken (or not taken) in the next few decades will have special impact on the quality of life for ourselves, our children, and our children's children. The times are clearly changing, and, with them, people and the planet.

At this critical juncture in history, it is important for us as helping professionals to examine our beliefs about human change. Our efforts to understand and to help others are inseparable from our assumptions about human change processes. Some of these assumptions lie deeply buried in cultural, social, ideological, and personal histories. For us as individuals, it is critically important that we expand our beliefs in each of these areas and that we critically examine them for unwarranted biases and limiting preconceptions.

Our theories carry with them assumptions about human nature and the possibility of change. These "hidden human images" are seldom clearly stated (Friedman, 1974). Rather, they are tacit and generative rules that we use in constructing our experience. These implicit human images make up:

> the hidden ground in which literature, philosophy, psychotherapy, religion, and social thought all meet. The human image might well be called the matrix from which each of these fields emerges, which they continue to embody within them, and which continues to bind them together in essential ways. (Friedman, 1974, p. 10)

These tacit rules influence our understanding and facilitation of human development in ways that we are only beginning to appreciate. For us as professional counselors, such rules can limit not only our sense of who and how we (and our clients) are in the present, but also our sense of who and how we and they can (and cannot) be in the future. What is important here is not the relative validity of these views so much as our recognition of the role they play in influencing our practice as counselors. It is especially important that we be sensitive to any cultural-ethnic and gender-role biases that may be inherent in these theories. As both researchers and practitioners, we must ask ourselves: "What are the implications of this theory or therapy? What possibilities does it allow for human change? Will it serve to empower or disempower this particular client? Does it treat this client not only with empathy and positive regard but also with respect for her or his cultural heritage, individual uniqueness, and social embeddedness?"

Given this responsibility, it should be acknowledged that this is both a challenging and exciting time to be teaching, training, and practicing in the field of counseling psychology. In the first half of this century, there were basically three varieties of psychological services: behavioral, humanistic-existential, and psychoanalytic. There are now an estimated 400 varieties of psychotherapy. As professional psychologists, we are faced with multiple conceptualizations of what it means to be human, how humans change, and what we can do to facilitate this process. In the midst of this complexity, professional identity is not easily established. Graduate students are particularly vulnerable to feeling bewildered by a diverse and sometimes contradictory array of theories and concepts.

In this chapter, we address some of these issues and discuss the perplexities that they can engender. We begin by briefly reviewing theories of change in psychology, focusing particularly on the cognitive revolution and its implications for the theory and practice of counseling and psychotherapy. We then look at the international movement toward transtheoretical convergence in psychology. Next, the beliefs and practices of U.S. psychologists are examined in terms of shifts in the relative popularity of theories, and changing beliefs about psychological development and optimal counseling practice. Finally, we address current issues and future directions within the field, including the need for reuniting scientists and practitioners and for developing more adequate research methodologies.

THE FIRST FOUR "FORCES" IN PSYCHOLOGY

It may be helpful to briefly review the first four forces in psychology, in terms of their assumptions about human change and its processes. Any such condensation necessarily involves simplifications, and all simplifications are oversimplifications (Whitehead, 1957). Some generalizations about these theoretical perspectives and their basic assumptions are, however, warranted. Table 20.1 offers a condensation of our best effort at such generalizations.

Psychoanalytic theory is often considered the First Force in psychology because of both its early appearance and its initial theoretical dominance (Freud, 1953–1966; Hilgard, 1987; Mahoney, 1991). Central to psychoanalytic theory is a belief in the power of unconscious forces and biological impulses (sex, aggression, and death). Its view of human nature is basically negative, because these impulses are felt to be fundamentally in conflict with "civilization." Traditionally, psychoanalytic theory holds that humans have little ability to change after the sixth year. In psychodynamic therapy, the role of the therapist is to act as a "blank screen" on which clients can project and "transfer" feelings and attitudes associated with significant others, primarily their parents. Of primary concern to the therapist are the internal processes of the client, who changes via the emotionally charged "reliving" and "undoing" of past experiences as well as the insights developed in the context of the transference provided by the therapeutic relationship.

More recently, some neodynamic theorists have portrayed human nature in a more positive light and with greater potential for change. A primary departure has been the greater emphasis on the power and the autonomy of the ego, the self-in-relationship, and an acknowledgment that self-system needs must be balanced with social responsibility (Wachtel, 1987; Young-Eisendrath & Hall, 1987).

The Second Force in psychology developed most visibly in the United States, where many pioneers in the social sciences had followed the lead of the physical sciences in embracing positivism and objectivity as explicit ideals. By self-proclamation, behaviorism became *the* scientific psychology, changing the focus of study from the mind and unconscious processes of the client to only those behaviors that could be directly observed (Watson, 1913, 1924). What went on within the "black box" of the human mind was considered unknowable, and its study became largely taboo. Behaviorism did, however, bring with it a sense of optimism in that it considered the human organism at birth a *tabula rasa* with virtually limitless, life-long plasticity. It was believed that any behavior could be changed, once the determinants of that behavior were identified and the proper conditioning or counterconditioning methods were employed. Little thought was given to the therapeutic relationship or to the personal qualities of the therapist, who was considered a neutral and objective technician.

Both the psychodynamic and behavioral schools of thought were self-limiting in their decision to focus on only part of the human organism. Behaviorists looked only at observable, external events; psychoanalysts were concerned only with internal events. The limitation of each became apparent in the inability of psychoanalysis to institute behavioral change and the ability of behaviorism to change behavior only within limited contexts (Mahoney & Gabriel, 1987).

What these theories did have in common was a linear, unidirectional model of causality. The client's behavior, thought, and affect were construed as being fully determined—by intrapsychic forces in psychoanalysis and by environmental forces in behaviorism. In neither perspective was the client seen as interactive and interdependent with his or her environment.

With the advent of World War II came the development of a Third Force in psychology—existentialism in Europe and humanistic psychology in the United States. Although rooted in the psychoanalytic tradition, humanistic and existential perspectives generally took a positive view of human nature. Humans were considered to possess extensive possibilities for change through social, scientific, and symbolic teachings. The therapist was seen neither as a blank screen nor as a technician, but rather as an active participant in therapy whose own psychological development (or lack of same) could directly influence the client. Rogers (1957) proposed three necessary conditions for a helping relationship: congruence of the therapist, empathy of the therapist toward the client, and unconditional positive regard for the client by the therapist. In general, humanistic and existential therapies are thought by behaviorists to be too soft and lacking in scientific rigor (Skinner, 1987). Modern humanistic and existential perspectives tend to be blended and often combine phenomenological (experiential) elements.

There has been great sibling rivalry among these three forces, each claiming to have exclusive rights to the answers. Until the past decade, there has been little movement toward integration or even communication among them.

Between 1955 and 1965, there began to be a conceptual shift in all areas of psychology. This shift, which has been called the "cognitive revolution," entailed the reemergence of cognition as a legitimate domain of scientific inquiry. Cognitive theories began to dominate research on learning, memory, personality, motivation, and social psychology. Using a broad approach to knowing systems and processes, cognitive science tends to be interdisciplinary, uniting the fields of cognitive psychology, linguistics, communications science, biological psychology, anthropology, and philosophy. The cognitive

Table 20.1 Theoretical Views on Selected Issues in Psychological Change

Theory	Version	Human Nature	Plasticity	Power	Self	Adaptation	Change Process
Psychoanalytic	Orthodox	Fundamentally negative; dominated by biological impulses (e.g., sex and aggression).	Very limited after sixth year.	Psychic determinism makes the individual primarily an effect, rather than cause, in development.	Equated with "ego," the "reality" checker that coordinates id and superego.	The progressive domination of ego (and superego) over id.	Emotionally charged "reliving" and "undoing" combine with insight in the social context of transference.
	Neodynamic	Neutral to positive; self and social needs can transcend biological.	Limited but not insignificant.	A sense of power can develop if needs for other people are balanced with needs for separation and individuation.	The separate-but-related individual 'self' is the central point of differentiation from orthodox psychoanalysis.	The ongoing dynamic balance of self-system integrity and social sensitivity/responsibility.	"Corrective emotional experiences" override deficient or dysfunctional lessons about the integrity of self and social system.
Behavioral	Radical	Neutral to negative; human nature is biological conditionability.	Virtually unlimited and lifelong.	All power for change rests in power to change environmental contingencies.	A mentalistic concept devoid of meaning.	Behavioral conformity to environmental contingencies.	Conditioning (classical and operant).
	Liberal	Neutral to positive; human nature is not a central topic.	Considerable, but sometimes limited by genetic variables and learning history.	Variable, depending on individual's skills in "behavioral self-management."	A problematic domain in which the subject and object of "behavior technology" are the same.	Compliance with environmental and "self-regulated" contingencies.	Conditioning, with "covert" or private events involved in chained associations.

Humanistic	Naturalist	Neutral to positive; emphasizes the "natural science" analysis of human characteristics.	Considerable, with emphasis on social, symbolic, and scientific teachings.	Considerable, usually via rational reflection and social reform.	An important domain dictated by the social context of human development.	The balancing of individual and collective needs.	Reason (scientific) combined with social influence.
	Spiritualist	Positive, with some varieties linking human nature with godliness.	Virtually infinite; perhaps immortal.	Extensive, although many individuals fail to appreciate or exercise their own potential.	An important domain, with "local self" reflecting a universal "larger Self."	The integration of individual and collective expressions of Being.	Spiritual experiences "awaken" the individual to greater meanings and potentials.
Cognitive	Rationalist	Neutral to positive; intellect and reason elevate humanity over other life forms.	Virtually infinite within the limits of reason.	Extensive, via "rational restructuring" of personal meanings.	An important domain of reflective "self-talk."	Rational compliance with existing rules for survival.	Rational restructuring.
	Constructivist	Neutral to positive; emphasis is on lifelong *activity*.	Considerable, but with individual limits.	Considerable within the contexts that constrain individual development.	An essential domain of development that constrains all others.	The ongoing coordination of individual activity with changing opportunities and constraints.	"Deep structure" differentiation results from trial and error efforts to maintain or regain dynamic equilibrium.

revolution has emphasized a determinism that is reciprocal and interactive rather than linear and unidirectional. It has created a climate in which it is possible to consider the influence of both private events and environmental factors on human performance (Mahoney & Lyddon, 1988).

The cognitive revolution has had an impact on the practice of counseling and psychotherapy. Many researchers and practitioners have turned to cognitive science to find models and constructs to assist them in their understanding of the development and organization of an individual's knowledge and experience patterns. Early cognitive therapies (for example, Albert Ellis's 1962 Rational-Emotive Therapy (RET)) generally regarded human plasticity in a way that was similar to behaviorism, believing that the human capacity for change is virtually limitless. This change was accomplished by the directed use of "self-talk," leading to rational restructuring of personal meanings within the context of established social norms.

EVOLUTIONS AND REVOLUTIONS

The number of cognitive therapies has grown from three in 1970 (George Kelly's 1955 personal construct psychology, Ellis's 1962 RET, and Aaron T. Beck's 1970 cognitive therapy) to 20 distinguishable forms of cognitive therapy today (Mahoney & Lyddon, 1988). This growth and proliferation of cognitive therapies is a reflection of the evolution that has gone on within cognitive science, where there have been at least three major theoretical developments in the past quarter-century: information processing, connectionism, and constructivism.

Information Processing

The first major development in the cognitive revolution was the emergence of information-processing models throughout the 1950s and 1960s. These models, the first scientific alternatives to the mediational models based on classical learning theories, made quite a splash in the field of experimental psychology. They argued that learning and memory involve the acquisition and storage of information in much the same manner that a computer is programmed. Information-processing models were ultimately found to be very limited in scope, because of their overemphasis on computer metaphors and their inability to deal with processes other than computation (Mahoney, 1991).

Connectionism

The second major theoretical development was and is that of connectionism. It differentiated itself from information processing in three ways. First, it shifted from computers to biological studies of the nervous system as sources of metaphors for its models. Second, it rejected exclusively linear or serial processing in favor of the parallel processing possible with the greater power and flexibility of modern super-computers. Instead of assuming that learning is nothing but a sequencing of information or computer programs, connectionists argued that many different forms of processing could be going on at the same time. Third, connectionism acknowledged the existence of "subsymbolic" processes or "deep structures" that cannot be expressed explicitly in symbolic form. Although connectionist models have been undoubtedly more powerful than their information-processing predecessors, some problems may persist in that they are still excessively tied to computational logic (Mahoney, 1991). Connectionists have only partially abandoned the computer metaphor, and some experts believe that they need to look at alternate ways of modeling the activities of the nervous system.

Constructivism

The third major theoretical development in cognitive science has been constructivism, which has presented alternative views in theories about knowledge (epistemology), theories about reality (ontology), and theories of causation (causality). The basic tenet of constructivism is that "humans actively construct the realities to which they respond." From a constructivist viewpoint, human knowing is a process of "meaning making" by which personal experiences are ordered and organized. Thus, constructivism implicitly challenges the assumption that sensory experience reflects the existence of a single, stable, external reality. This does not mean that clients' problems are necessarily "all in their head," however. A person who fears rejection, for example, may be less inclined to meet or interact with others, thereby co-creating a psychological "distance" that may constitute a self-fulfilling prophecy. Constructivist theory distinguishes between the validity of an idea (its approximation to reality) and the viability of an idea (its functional utility). It also questions whether human thought can be separated from action and feeling in any meaningful way (Mahoney, 1988a).

Constructivist theory has three basic components:

1. Proactive cognition—the notion that all human knowing is active, anticipatory, and constructive;
2. Self-organizing processes—the idea that all learning and knowing is comprised of complex developmental and dynamic processes through which the self is organized;
3. Primacy of structure—the assumption that all knowing involves tacit, unconscious, or deep structures.

These components are grounded in several recent developments in cognitive science: motor metatheories, evolutionary epistemology, and autopoiesis.

In contrast to the traditional model of the nervous system, in which the organism passively awaits impinging external stimuli and then reacts through the motor system:

What the motor metatheory asserts is that there is no sharp separation between sensory and motor components of the nervous system which can be made on functional grounds, and that the mental or cognitive realm is intrinsically motoric, like all the nervous system. (Weimer, 1977, p. 272)

Motor metatheories add the idea of feedforward systems to the feedback mechanism introduced by the information-processing model. The implication of this addition is that the human brain is not the reactive organ that it has been assumed to be for so long. Rather than registering and retaining accurate copies of external reality, the human brain actively participates in the construction of reality by selectively attending to and interpreting stimuli. Humans are interacting with their environment at the same time that they are construing and constructing it.

Not only do humans interact with their environment, but they also expend a good deal of energy, in terms of neurochemical activity, interacting with themselves. External stimulation is not the "cause" of neurochemical activity. Rather, this stimulation joins the continually generated activity of the nervous system. Sensory neurons (from which we get information about the world "outside") comprise only .001% of all neurons and interneurons in the human nervous system. There are ten times more motor neurons than sensory neurons, and an amazing 10,000 interneurons (which connect only with other neurons) for each motor neuron. Thus, much of the activity of the human nervous system can be considered self-referencing.

A self-organizing system is one that has the capacity to transform its basic structure and functions when they are sufficiently challenged. Episodes of disorder or disequilibrium are both unavoidable and necessary, because they allow such a system to reorganize in a more viable fashion. From this viewpoint, all knowing, learning, and memory can be seen as attempts by the brain and the body to organize and to reorganize their constructions of experience and action.

Autopoiesis is the process by which a living system incessantly organizes and reorganizes itself in order to maintain itself and its viability as a system (Jantsch, 1980; Maturana & Varela, 1987; Varela, 1979). This process allows the system to keep a sense of itself as a coherent entity in the face of both changes within itself and interactions with an ever changing environment. The processes of assimilation and accommodation as described by Piaget (1970, 1981) are examples of autopoietic activities. New information can be assimilated into the existing system if it is sufficiently congruent with constructs that are already operating. If not, the system must modify itself in a way that allows for the accommodation of the new information. Thus, the processes by which we maintain stability and the processes by which we change are part of the same dynamic system.

Evolutionary epistemology is the study of systems of knowing and the way in which they have developed over time (Campbell, 1974; Radnitzky & Bartley, 1987). The assumption is that knowledge has evolved along with other aspects of life. This idea is evidenced in MacLean's (1973) model of the triune brain, which posits the human brain not as a single, unitary organ but as at least three partially independent brains that have evolved during the course of human development. These brains are the reptilian, the paleomammalian or limbic system, and the bicameral neocortex.

The reptilian brain is the oldest from an evolutionary perspective. It consists of the brain stem (fundamentally an enlargement of the neural tube) and controls the most basic, primitive, and vital life processes such as breathing and movement. Directly above the reptilian brain is the paleomammalian brain or the limbic system, which is concerned with basic emotional processes. Seated on top of both of these brains is the neocortex, considered by some the "crowning achievement" of human evolution. The neocortex emerged with the development of bipedalism in higher primates. It is important to realize that the reptilian brain was not replaced or usurped by the mammalian brains. Its functions were not subsumed by the "higher" brains sitting on top of it. It continues to function today as it has for millions of years. In addition to this simultaneous vertical organization of the brain, the neocortex in humans has differentiated horizontally by the process of the lateralization of the left and right hemispheres such that each hemisphere exhibits specialized functions.

All learning and knowing involves processes that are beyond conscious knowledge. These processes are referred to as "deep structures" or "tacit knowing." The contents of our conscious experience are constrained but not specified by these processes. Polanyi's work (1958) demonstrates that "tacit knowing is more fundamental than explicit knowing: we can know more than we can tell and we can tell nothing without relying on our awareness of things we may not be able to tell." An example of this is any activity that requires skill. It is generally easier to perform certain acts, such as hitting a ball or recognizing the voice of a friend, than it is to explain how to carry out these activities.

Deep structures are not the subconscious process of psychoanalytic theory. Rather than subconscious, these processes are considered by Hayek (1967, 1978) to be "'superconscious' because they govern the conscious processes without appearing in them" (1978, p. 45).

There are four proposed core themes of tacit knowing (Mahoney, 1991). These should be considered not as discrete categories but as actively interdependent processes:

1. Valence or value—concerned with motivation and emotion;
2. Meaning or reality—concerned with order and stability;
3. Personal identity—concerned with self and integrity;
4. Power—concerned with control and ability.

Because our perceptions are necessarily filtered through such processes, they often reflect more about us than about the event that occasioned them. This can be seen clearly in the example of ambiguous stimuli, which can be either visual, as in projective tests or in the art work of M. C. Escher, or verbal. Consider the sentence "Visiting relatives can be fun." The sense you make from it will depend on your mindset in regard to relatives (would you rather see them at their home or your own?) as well as your recent experiences. It is important to remember that the different possible connotations of words and symbols are not only individually but also culturally determined.

Because all knowing is considered to be both personal and participatory, the client must necessarily be an active, knowing participant in the therapeutic process (Mahoney, 1988b). In contrast to the extremely limited possibility for change posited by the psychoanalysts and the limitless possibilities of the behaviorists, according to constructivist theory, humans exhibit some plasticity but not limitless pliability. Core beliefs or assumptions (regarding reality, identity, power/control, and values) are the least amenable to change.

Problems are considered discrepancies between the client's current capabilities and the demands placed on him or her by the environment (physiologically, interpersonally, and intrapersonally). Problems are thus valuable sources of information about the limits of the client's constructions about self, the world, and the relationship between the two. What is considered problematic today might well have been the best possible adaptation of the client at an earlier time. When constructs change during the process of therapy, what is desirable is not that the client's constructs be shaped to a closer approximation of the therapist's view of external reality, but that they become more viable and adaptive within the client's world.

From a constructivist perspective, resistance is regarded as a natural self-protective process that keeps the system from changing too much or too soon. It is generally more effective to work with this resistance than against it. Periods of apparent disorder and emotional intensity are inherent in psychological development, which is a complex, nonlinear, oscillative process. Thus, development can be conceptualized as a spiral rather than as a smooth and neat accumulation of steps leading to some desired outcome or final "cure." Relapse and regression are indications that the client has reached his or her limit of current (but by no means permanent) capacities for change.

It is important that therapy not focus exclusively on behavior, cognition, or affect, but that it recognize that each contributes to the unique being of the client as a whole. Emotions, in particular, are not considered problems to be routed out but, rather, primitive and powerful knowing processes that need to be experienced, responsibly expressed, and explored. Emotional experience, behavioral enactment, and insight may all combine to facilitate transformations of personal meaning.

The therapeutic relationship provides a safe and caring base from which the client can safely and responsibly explore novel ways of being with self and the world. Rather than concentrating on what the therapist does to the client, there is increased focus on what the client does to and with the self. It is thus important to respect individual differences and the social and cultural context the client brings into counseling, and to realize that any changes that occur in therapy will impact on both the client's relationship with self and the client's relationships with significant others.

Perhaps unintentionally, constructivist metatheory has managed to incorporate certain aspects of other major forces in psychology. It shares with the First Force (psychoanalysis) the notion of unconscious structures, even though the hypothesized content and function of these structures are not identical. Common with the Second Force (behaviorism) is the emphasis on activity as implied by motor metatheory. As do many Third Force (existential and humanistic) theorists, constructivists embrace an appreciation for the client as a whole being. These commonalities are just one sign of the movement toward integration and convergence that is being made in the midst of the baffling array of systems of therapy abounding in psychology today (Goldfried, 1982).

THE CONVERGENCE MOVEMENT

There have been many indications that psychology as a field has begun to move in a direction of theoretical integration or convergence. In Vienna, in 1982, the theme of the world congress of the Society for Individual Psychology was "the contact of Individual Psychology with other approaches." To promote this contact, representatives from all major forms of psychotherapy were invited. This led to the opening of a valuable and, some would say, long overdue dialogue on the nature of human nature and the helping professions. A year later, in Bogotá, Colombia, there was a similar happening. Once again, dialogue was initiated among representatives of diverse systems of therapy at an International Congress on the Convergence of Psychotherapies.

In the United States, there have also been movements to examine the possibility of integration and convergence in the field of psychology. What began as an informal network of scholars in 1980 developed into the Society for the Exploration of Psychotherapy Integration (SEPI), which held its first congress in 1985. These events are among the many signs that psychotherapy and psychology are in the throes of major change. It is perhaps a sign of growing maturity in the discipline that professionals with diverse training experience and theoretical outlooks can now acknowledge areas of similarity and agreement (Norcross, 1986, 1987). Recent surveys of U.S. psychologists also suggest a growing acceptance of eclecticism and substantial agreement about basic principles and practices of counseling and psychotherapy.

The Changing Popularity of Theories

There are further indications of convergence in the way that psychologists identify themselves and in how they conceptualize human development and psychotherapy. Figure 20.1 presents a summary of the results of 15 surveys of the theoretical orientation of psychologists, conducted between 1953 and 1988 (Mahoney, 1991).

In general, there has been a decrease in the relative proportion of psychodynamic therapists and an increase in eclectic therapists, with as many as 60% of respondents choosing that label for themselves. Of note also is the steady increase, between 1975 and

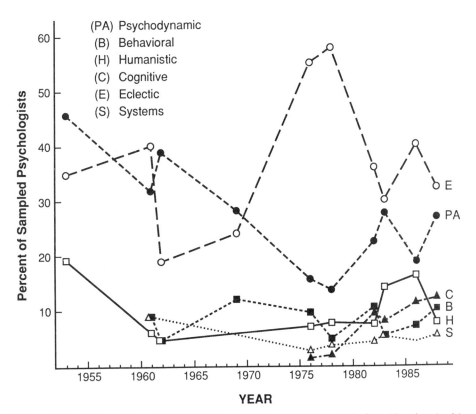

Figure 20.1 Primary theoretical orientations of U.S. clinical psychologists. (Reprinted with permission from Mahoney, 1991.)

1988, of those identifying themselves as cognitive therapists. The field is changing, theoretical alliances are shifting, new perspectives are emerging, and—perhaps—meanings of terms may be undergoing changes.

Beliefs About Psychological Development

A 1989 study looked at areas of convergence and divergence among psychologists on the topics of what psychological change is and how this change is brought about (Mahoney, Norcross, Prochaska, & Missar, 1989). Surveyed were 1,000 randomly selected clinical psychologists belonging to Division 12 (Clinical) of the American Psychological Association. Among the 61% who returned the survey, theoretical orientations were reported as: psychodynamic (24%), behavioral (14%), humanistic-existential (10%), eclectic (32%), and cognitive (12%). Of those sampled, 23% were female and 6% non-White, which is consonant with Division 12 membership for these groups.

Across orientations, respondents concurred that *exploration of novelty* and *risk taking* (Figure 20.2) are often central to individual psychological development. They agreed that this change can also involve the elimination of old habits and/or ideas.

A second component on which there was strong transtheoretical convergence was *self-system development* (Figure 20.3). Across orientations, there was 80% consensus

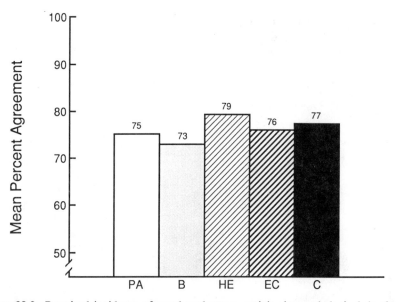

Figure 20.2 Perceived incidence of novel exploratory activity in psychological development. (Reprinted with permission from Mahoney, 1991.)

that (a) psychological development includes increased tolerance for ambiguity, increased self-reliance and self-awareness, and increased psychological flexibility and resilience, and that (b) these changes are "facilitated by a safe and caring relationship." Behaviorists did, however, see increased self-awareness and increased tolerance for other people as less central to psychological development than did their nonbehavioral colleagues.

In general, the respondents in this survey agreed that personal psychological development often entails feelings of depression and anxiety as well as feelings of excitement and joy. They also concurred that resistance to change is a common phenomenon. Feelings were recognized as being less amenable to change than thoughts. There was also modest agreement that, for some people, psychological growth is accompanied by the experience of feeling out of control and by episodes of "sensed unreality."

The only area in which there was considerable divergence was in "difficulty of change." Overall behaviorists thought that change was less difficult to achieve than did practitioners of other orientations (Figure 20.4). Among the other four groups, there was agreement that "episodes of emotional intensity, resistance and nonlinear progress" are often part of psychological change. The exception to this finding was that, if behaviorists had been in therapy themselves, they tended to recognize change as harder to accomplish.

In general, this study affirmed the convergence of beliefs about the nature of psychological change. The findings reflect several themes that have appeared in recent work on personal psychological development which may allude to the beginnings of an integrative transtheoretical approach in psychology (Goldfried, 1982; Prochaska, 1984).

The first theme is an appreciation for the difficulty of change—especially in the area of such core ordering processes as value, reality, identity, and power. These core processes are strongly affected early in the life cycle by powerful and recurrent emotional experiences, particularly with significant others. There is a growing recognition that

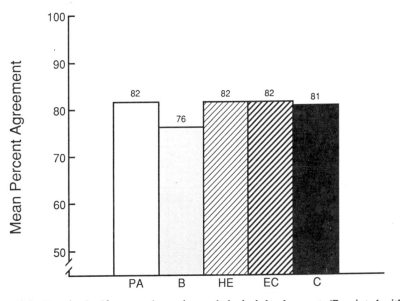

Figure 20.3 Perceived self-system change in psychological development. (Reprinted with permission from Mahoney, 1991.)

psychological change is rarely a quick, easy, and painless process. Rather, we are coming to the increasing realization that, although personal problems can be improved, they can seldom be eradicated completely.

There has also been an increased recognition of emotions as powerful knowing processes that are extensively involved in psychological change as well as in the development of a sense of self (Greenberg & Safran, 1987; Mahoney, 1991). For this reason, significant psychological change is frequently accompanied by emotional intensity, instability, and distress.

Emotional development has been found to be intimately related to cognitive development during all phases of the human life cycle, from the cradle to the grave. There is considerable involvement of emotions in perception, learning, and memory, although much of this involvement is at an unconscious (tacit) level. Emotional processes have also been found to be extensively involved in the focusing of attention; the "negative" emotions of anger, anxiety, and depression may be especially potent in this regard. These negative emotions tend to be associated with impaired performance as well as with diminished curiosity and exploratory activity.

Because of their biochemical and neurophysiological foundations, emotional processes are intrinsically related to other psychological processes that affect the individual's health, such as immune system functioning and stress level. The behavioral expression of emotions is integral to their experience and to interpersonal communication, especially in the deep emotional bonding that occurs first in the parent–child relationship and later in intimate relationships.

Another emergent theme has been the importance of novel experience in all learning, especially in the realm of psychological development. An individual who is feeling depressed, anxious, or vulnerable in any way will tend to avoid rather than seek novel experiences. Active exploration has also been considered important, especially in the

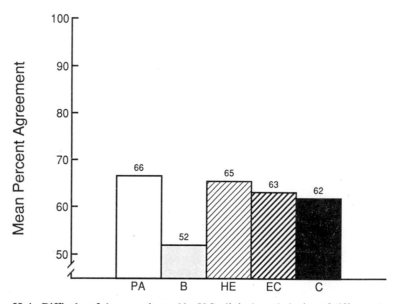

Figure 20.4   Difficulty of change estimated by U.S. clinical psychologists of different theoretical orientations. (Reprinted with permission from Mahoney, 1991.)

area of the development of identity and the study of the self. There are actually two components to active exploration. The first is an openness to experiences, especially to those experiences that are often avoided because they are intensely emotional and/or novel. The second component involves the attainment of a sense of balance between what can be considered "learned helplessness" (a lack of willingness to try anything to change one's situation) and "learned restlessness" (a preoccupation with efforts to control or to change one's situation; Fogle, 1978).

A final point is that the above-mentioned experiences and explorations are most likely to occur in an environment that the individual considers both safe and familiar. Change is facilitated by the presence of a "secure base," like that provided by a stable and caring family or by other intimate relationships, including a relationship with a "sensitive, self-aware, and still developing counselor" (Mahoney et al., 1989).

Beliefs About Optimal Counseling Practice

A second aspect of the above-mentioned Division 12 study was the consideration of the question of "how" people change. One area of general agreement among practitioners was that optimal psychotherapy includes encouragement of self-exploration (Figure 20.5). Over 80% agreed that, to be optimally helpful, a psychotherapist will "help clients clarify thoughts and feelings, encourage self-examination, foster hope or faith, focus on current concerns, offer general support and encouragement, and verbally reinforce appropriate client changes" (Mahoney et al., 1989, p. 259).

There were, however, areas in which there was evidence of divergence in terms of practice. Behaviorists were significantly less inclined than other practitioners to engage clients in "consciousness raising" activities (Prochaska, 1984). They were less likely to invite clients to express emotions and were also less likely to be reflective, to offer

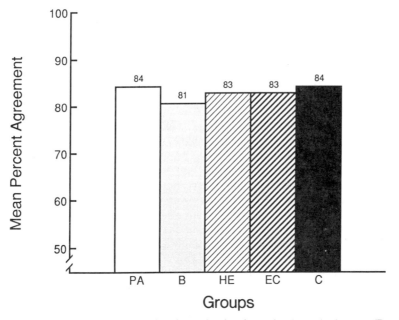

Figure 20.5 Perceived importance of self-examination in optimal psychotherapy. (Reprinted with permission from Mahoney, 1991.)

interpretations, and to help clients clarify either thoughts or feelings. They were, however, more likely to use behavioral assignments than other practitioners. In contrast (but not surprisingly), psychodynamic therapists were significantly less in favor of the therapist self-disclosing, confronting, encouraging, or giving information to the client. Psychodynamic therapists were more in favor than other respondents of offering interpretations to the client as well as concentrating on the client's family background and childhood experiences.

There was also divergence between those practitioners who had been in therapy themselves and those who had not. Significantly more therapists identifying themselves as psychodynamic, humanistic, or eclectic had been in therapy, compared with those who considered themselves behaviorists or cognitive therapists. Those who had been in therapy recognized, to a significant extent, the value of "active risk-taking, resilience, and novel experience" in personal development. They were also more likely to allow that, during the course of their own psychological growth and development, there had been times when they had felt "out-of-control" or "stuck." Regardless of orientation, those who had experienced therapy themselves tended to acknowledge the importance of disputing irrational beliefs, imparting pertinent information, sharing feelings and self-disclosures, and encouraging physical activities such as exercise, in addition to therapy.

In contrast, those respondents who had had no experience as clients in therapy considered themselves to be less reluctant or resistant to change, less inclined to feel "out-of-control" or to have experienced "episodes of 'sensed' unreality," and more evenly consistent in their own growth and progress than were psychotherapy clients. In general, they characterized their own development as less arduous and anguishing than that of their clients. There is no way to determine from these data whether these answers are an accurate presentation of the respondents' perceptions of themselves or whether they reflect the way respondents thought they "should be."

Respondents tended to diverge on the definition of what constitutes optimal counseling practices and techniques, but they converged on the characteristics that constitute psychological change. Change was seen as a difficult, emotional process that is expedited by the active exploration of novel situations and is best carried out in a safe, familiar, nurturing environment. Given the divergence of theories of counseling and the proliferation of information in this field, it is important to remember Hebb's (1975) remarks that the half-life of knowledge in psychology is probably about 5 years; that is, every 5 years, about half the facts are outdated or recognized to be inaccurate. Because of this impending obsolescence, the memorizing of facts is less important to us as practitioners and researchers than is the cultivation of skills that will allow us to continue reviewing our own development and assumptions. In a sense, our capabilities as counseling psychologists depend on our own psychological growth as evidenced in our ability to be openly self-examining, to tolerate ambiguity, and to question not only our answers but also our questions (Masterpasqua, 1989).

An area in which there has been considerable convergence is the increasing recognition of the importance of relationships, both with self and others, in human growth and development. The work of feminist theorists (Gilligan, 1982; Miller, 1976) and attachment theorists (Ainsworth, 1989; Belsky & Nezworski, 1987; Bowlby, 1988) has emphasized the interdependence of interpersonal relationships and personal psychological development.

These important relationships include those not only with significant people in the client's daily life but also with the therapist. The robustness of the evidence for the importance of the therapeutic alliance is unusual in the field of psychotherapy research (Greenberg & Pinsoff, 1986). This alliance has been examined and measured by a variety of researchers, in numerous ways. Bordin (1975, 1979) described this alliance as a synergistic combination of the relationship between counselor and client, and the tasks and goals of therapy. This conceptualization acknowledges the fact that therapeutic techniques can be effectively employed only within the matrix of a well-functioning therapeutic relationship. Bergin and Lambert (1978) reported technique to be less important to successful psychotherapy outcome than either client variables or therapist variables. Likewise, in a recent review of four major psychotherapy research projects, therapist variables were found to be eight times more influential than treatment techniques (Lambert, 1989).

Implications for Counseling

The optimal therapeutic relationship is one that is secure, developmentally flexible, fundamentally caring, and conducive to active exploratory behavior on the part of the client. It provides a secure base from which the client can investigate both familiar and unfamiliar ways of being with self, with others, and with the world. The following general principles, drawn from Mahoney (1991), reflect our current understanding of the optimal counseling process. Optimal counseling:

1. Is uniquely individual, respecting the client's diversity in terms of sex, ethnicity, sexual orientation, and disabilities, as well as the biological, cultural, social, interpersonal, spiritual, and religious matrix in which he or she lives.

2. Attends first to issues that are most urgent.

3. Offers a safe base to the client by providing an environment that is gently, patiently, and consistently nurturing.

4. Contains three important elements: the *relationship* between counselor and client; the *rationale* for therapy, which provides the metaphor for change; and *rituals,* which are both personally and affectively meaningful to the client (Frank, 1985).

5. Is assisted by a counselor who both respects and understands the client's personal phenomenology.

6. Is aided by a counselor who is able to model psychological health, well-being, and resilience while still accepting his or her own humanness.

7. Is facilitated by the self-care of a counselor who is both willing and able to seek and accept help from others.

8. Encourages the exploration and expression, by the client, of the full range of emotions in a context that is both self-caring and socially responsible.

9. Works *with* rather than *against* the client's resistances.

10. Seeks to empower the client, by showing respect for his or her individual right to privacy and resilience.

11. Involves an intimate, nonsexual relationship between the counselor and the client, in which the client's needs come before those of the counselor.

12. Fosters compassion, forgiveness, and love within both the client and the counselor, for themselves and for others.

13. Recognizes and respects the ultimate right and responsibility of each individual to make his or her own choices, as much as is humanly possible.

14. Stresses the desirability of "primary prevention" over "corrective intervention."

CHANGES IN CHANGE AGENTS AND METHODS

A recent survey of both researchers and practitioners corroborated the extent of the importance of client, therapist, and relationship factors in the counseling process (Mahoney & Craine, 1991). Members of the Society for Psychotherapy Research and the Society for the Exploration of Psychotherapy Integration were asked to rate the importance to successful psychotherapy outcome of various factors, both as they currently perceive them and as they remembered perceiving them when they first began their practice. Client's social support, therapist's personality, the therapeutic relationship, client's self-esteem, therapist's experience, and client's motivation (in descending order; see Figure 20.6) were all considered more influential than was originally believed by the respondents. Predominant was the theme of the client's relationships—with the therapist, with self, and with supportive others outside therapy. A second theme concerned those things that the therapist brings to therapy, in terms of personality and experience.

What is of particular interest here is that the therapist's theoretical orientation was not among the therapist variables that were deemed significant. In fact, it was number-one among the items that were rated as *less* important; others included the client's intelligence and the length of therapy (Figure 20.6). Another intriguing finding from this survey was that the magnitude of therapists' changes in therapeutic factors perceived to be influential was predicted both by the number of years that they had been practicing and by the number of hours that they themselves had spent as clients in therapy (Figure 20.7).

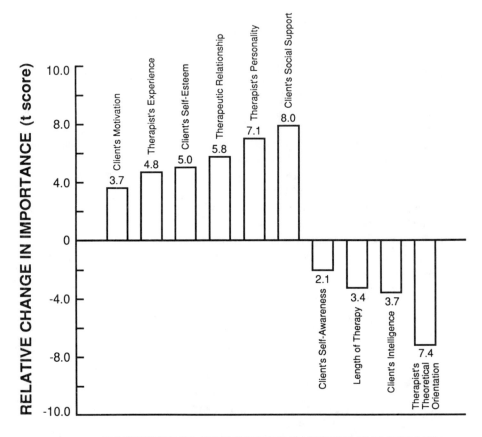

FACTORS IN SUCCESSFUL PSYCHOTHERAPY

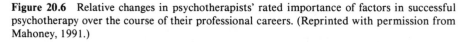

Figure 20.6 Relative changes in psychotherapists' rated importance of factors in successful psychotherapy over the course of their professional careers. (Reprinted with permission from Mahoney, 1991.)

Despite the evidence that specific therapy techniques are not the most influential factor in the outcome of therapy, as judged both by the research (Bergin & Lambert, 1978; Lambert, 1989) and by practitioners (Mahoney & Craine, 1991), much of the psychotherapy research over the past decade has focused on techniques (Lambert, 1989). Although therapist variables have been considered important (again, both through research findings and through the opinions of practitioners), many psychotherapy outcome research designs have treated these variables as "error" variance rather than as a significantly influential component of the process of therapy.

There is an obvious need for the study of therapist variables, although there are problems inherent in this type of research. For one thing, such research has little appeal to many researchers (and funding agencies) from a theoretical standpoint, because it is not involved in proving the efficacy of one type of treatment over another. Also problematic is the possible embarrassment (at the very least) to a practitioner who is found to be less than optimally helpful or, possibly, even damaging to clients. It could be

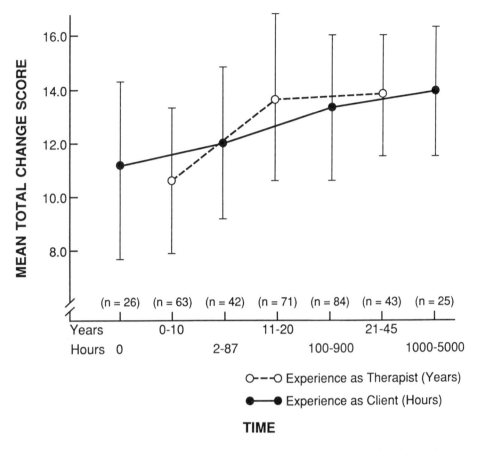

Figure 20.7 Total belief change over the course of a professional career as related to levels and types of experiences. (Reprinted with permission from Mahoney, 1991.)

difficult to find practitioners who are willing to participate in research that focuses on them rather than on their techniques. Finally, there is the ethical dilemma that would confront the researcher if a certain therapist were found to be ineffective or psychonoxious (Lambert, 1989). The need for a clearer understanding of therapist variables and their influence on the counseling process remains, however. Among those variables that warrant research interest in the years to come are the therapist's social support system, the therapist's comfort and competence in relating to intense emotions (of clients and self), and the therapist's ability to negotiate "boundary" issues (and "psychological distance") in his or her ongoing emotional attachments and separations (e.g., within and between sessions, among different clients, and over the course of long-term counseling).

Many factors have contributed to the growing recognition of the need to integrate psychotherapy process and outcome research (Greenberg & Pinsoff, 1986). Among them is the above-mentioned awareness of the importance of both client and therapist variables in the counseling process. This awareness has led to an acknowledgment of the importance of the interaction between the client and the counselor, who are both acting and interacting, not only as members of the counseling dyad but also as members of numerous other systems of family, friends, work, and community.

In the past, much research has been based on a nonparticipant observer model's confirming a bias against the participant observer model. However, new self-report instruments have been developed that possess greater predictive validity of the outcome than do other measures completed by a nonparticipant observer (Greenberg & Pinsoff, 1986). That is, the counselor's and client's evaluations of their own and each other's experience may be more helpful and predictive than are the "detached" ratings of a third person observing them on videotape.

In the past decade, there have been important advances in methods of studying the process of change in counseling (see Chapter 3, by Wampold and Poulin) as well as improvements in video- and audiotape recording technology. These enhancements allow for the observation of many facets of the therapeutic process that were previously difficult to access: verbal and nonverbal communication, counselor–client relationship, and episodes or events in and across sessions.

It is beginning to be recognized that the notion that there is a final, definitive outcome ("and they all lived happily ever after") to therapy is a myth. Rather than one big outcome to therapy, there is actually a succession of many little outcomes during the process of therapy. These outcomes can occur at any point in time—during the therapy hour or after the therapy hour is over (Greenberg & Pinsoff, 1986). Often, life changes begun in therapy come to fruition only after the formal process of therapy has terminated.

Finally, there is the concept of the "event-in-context": "nothing can be known or ultimately even exists outside the context in which it occurs" (Greenberg & Pinsoff, 1986). The implication is that research cannot focus solely on isolated events in therapy but must also take into consideration what has happened to the client in her or his world outside the confines of the therapy hour.

ISSUES AND FUTURE DIRECTIONS

Until recently, research in counseling psychology has been based on a positivistic, reductionistic methodology of experimental inquiry. This basis is changing, however. The following general trends are beginning to emerge in psychology:

1. A decline in authority-based theories of knowing or epistemologies;
2. An abandonment of the assumption that humans are passive organisms whose actions are solely reactions to environmental stimuli;
3. An abandonment of a mechanistic, billiard-ball determinism in favor of complex, participatory models of reciprocal determinism between an organism and its environment;
4. An abandonment of the search for a "prime mover" among behavior, affect, and cognition;
5. A recognition of the necessity of regarding an organism in its entirety;
6. An acknowledgment of the psychological aspects of all knowing.

Within counseling psychology itself, a variety of factors has contributed to the perceived need for alternative research paradigms. One is the concern that research become more relevant to and more widely used by practicing counseling psychologists. There is hope that this might help to bridge what appears to some as an ever widening gap between scientists and practitioners (Hoshmand, 1989). Studies have found that practitioners tend to view conversations with colleagues (Cohen, Sargent, & Sechrest, 1986) and their own experiences with clients (Morrow-Bradley & Elliott, 1986) as more valuable resources than research. Practitioners have been especially critical of research that overlooks the complexity inherent in the therapeutic environment (Morrow-Bradley & Elliott, 1986). Others have expressed concern that some of the most urgent problems facing our society are seldom researched because the questions that need to be asked cannot be addressed through current research paradigms (Holland, 1986). Instead, trivial but more readily doable research takes its place. Through the sponsorship of two task forces that have investigated these issues, counseling psychology has taken leadership in both recognizing and acting on the need for more viable research paradigms (Hoshmand, 1989).

There is also a need to reconcile the rival metatheories within psychology that led to a split, in 1988, between scientists and practitioners. The need for counseling psychology as a discipline to be open to new ways of knowing and understanding is based on more than theoretical reasons; it is also a reflection of the increasing acknowledgment of the need to show respect for the diversity among researchers, practitioners, clients, and subjects of experiments. We must expand the paradigms available to us, in order to study the concerns of diverse populations. We must ask ourselves, both as scientists and practitioners: "What are the implications of this theory or therapy? Is it sensitive to issues of diversity? In what ways do its constructions limit the potential or possibility of change in the client-subject? How does it empower the client?"

The American Psychological Association Ad Hoc Committee on Nonsexist Research (Denmark, Russo, Frieze, & Secher, 1988) reported that gender bias has affected all stages of research in psychology, from question formulation, research methodology, data analysis, and interpretation, to conclusions. Bias in research is in no way limited solely to sex bias. It can also occur in terms of ethnicity, race, sexual orientation, socioeconomic status, and disability.

By relying heavily on the use of readily available subject pools of undergraduate psychology students, academic psychology has often been criticized as being a psychology of college sophomores. Indeed, the subjects of experiments have often been almost exclusively white, male, and middle-class. For example, Kohlberg's (1981) often cited study of moral development in students used only white males as subjects (Gilligan, 1982). When Kohlberg's criteria were applied to women, the latter were found to be deficient in moral development. Gilligan, in her own study, found that the moral development of women is different from that of men but certainly not deficient. Gilligan's work has emphasized the necessity of recognizing that there are at least two paths of moral development that can be considered complementary rather than contradictory. It is probable that this point would be missed if moral development were viewed as a single hierarchical process, leading to only one possible outcome. We need to go much further toward studying diverse populations and taking care not to generalize universal human principles from one small segment of the population.

There is warrant for the development of alternate research paradigms on epistemological, conceptual-empirical, and ideological grounds (Hoshmand, 1989; also see Chapter 4, by Borgen). In the realms of both the philosophy of science and the psychology of ideas, we are now beginning to appreciate the extent to which meaning is a function of context. In the domain of research, this context must necessarily include the observer, with his or her mental constructions. The assumption of the positivistic model—that the scientist can be a totally objective observer—is being called into question. Indeed, we are beginning to realize the extent to which all our scientific "facts" are really artifacts of the questions that we ask and the ways in which we ask them. Scientific advances rarely consist of only "correct" answers to particular questions. Rather, they more frequently provide inducement for a change in the type and substance of questions that are asked.

Hayek (1979) defined an age of superstition as a time when "people imagine that they know more than they do (p. 176)." Perhaps we have been guilty in this century of imagining that we know more than we actually do in the area of complex psychological phenomena. Further, it has been argued conceptually and empirically that traditional methods of inquiry have narrowed the range of questions that can be researched by the precise standards of measurement and objectifying operations they require. Given the new developments in cognitive science—motor metatheories and their emphasis on feedforward mechanisms—new models are needed to adequately describe such self-constructing living systems. Empirical support can be found in systems theory and phenomenology, which allow for the significance both of context and of the reciprocal interaction of the researcher and the subject of research (Ford, 1987). Ideological arguments acknowledge that paradigms have both descriptive and prescriptive power. Thus, there is need for more collaborative models that empower the subject.

Hoshmand (1989) defined a research paradigm as "a system of inquiry with its particular epistemological and ideological foundations, conceptual assumptions, and methodological standards and procedures" (p. 12). Alternate research paradigms tend to view knowledge in a way that is both experiential and practical. Presently, there is a variety of classifications for such paradigms. There are, however, some commonalities of purpose, mode of inquiry (including researcher's roles and attitudes), structure and process of inquiry, strategies for collecting and analyzing data, and procedural rules and standards of knowledge that distinguish these paradigms from traditional research paradigms (Hoshmand, 1989).

Alternate research paradigms can be considered *interpretive* in that their purpose is the study of meanings. This exploration of the meaning of human experience is carried out by an investigator who is personally involved and who uses this involvement heuristically. Thus, the inquiry is highly personal and social, with more emphasis on description and discovery than on the testing and verification of theory.

These paradigms acknowledge the *role of the researcher* as an instrument of the research. In this "open, reflective, and sometimes atheoretical" mode, the researcher sometimes will treat the subject as a co-investigator who possesses meaningful ideas both about the questions to be asked and the interpretations made of their experience. Thus, the researcher places himself or herself in a role that is more egalitarian and respectful to the client than has often been found in traditional research procedures. Such an attitude toward the subjects of counseling process research has implications for the way such research is then put into practice. The client would be regarded as a collaborator in therapy, not as an object to be acted upon by the therapist.

To facilitate discovery, the *process of inquiry* is one that is open to feedback and modification as research progresses, rather than being fixed in an established linear sequence. The structure of such an experiment is also subject to change from subject to subject, because of the interactive involvement of subject and researcher.

Strategies for data collection have tended to be naturalistic and/or qualitative, borrowing from linguistics (hermeneutics), anthropology (participant observer), and philosophy (phenomenology). There is an attempt to find patterns of meaning by analyzing content and themes of the text. Such methods and procedures are still in a state of development.

CONCLUDING REMARKS

We have come full circle. We began by suggesting the need for examination of our beliefs about human change processes—those beliefs that are both explicit and implicit in our theories. We have moved through the diversity in the history of theories of human change to the current international movement toward convergence both in theory and in practice. We have looked at current beliefs and practices of psychologists in this country and reflected on future directions both in research and practice. If nothing else, we hope that we have demonstrated that there are no single, simple, easy answers for understanding the complexity of human life and change processes.

In the end, we were brought back to the research paradigms used by the counseling psychologist. As professional caregivers, our personal values figure extensively in our choice of theory, methodology, and research topics, as well as in the services that we provide. For this reason, we must continually explore and expand our assumptions about human change processes. Finally, we hope we have emphasized the importance of human relationships to human growth and change. The quality of the helping relationship is constrained by the quality of life of the people involved—especially the quality of their relationships with self and with others.

REFERENCES

Ainsworth, M. D. S. (1989). Attachments beyond infancy. *American Psychologist, 44,* 709–716.

Beck, A. T. (1970). Cognitive therapy: Nature and relation to behavior therapy. *Behavior Therapy, 1,* 184–200.

Bergin, A. E., & Lambert, M. J. (1978). The evaluation of therapeutic outcomes. In S. L. Garfield & A. E. Bergin (Eds.), *Handbook of psychotherapy and behavior change* (2nd ed.) (pp. 139–189). New York: Wiley.

Belsky, J., & Nezworski, M. T. (1987). *Clinical implications of attachment.* Hillsdale, NJ: Erlbaum.

Borden, E. S. (1975, April). *The generalizability of the psychoanalytic concept of the working alliance.* Paper presented at the Society for Psychotherapy Research, Denver, CO.

Borden, E. S. (1979). The generalizability of the psychoanalytic concept of the working alliance. *Psychotherapy: Theory, Research and Practice, 16,* 252–260.

Bowlby, J. (1988). The origins of attachment theory. In J. Bowlby (Ed.), *A secure base* (pp. 20–38). New York: Basic Books.

Campbell, D. T. (1974). Evolutionary epistemology. In P. A. Schilpp (Ed.), *The philosophy of Karl Popper* (Vol. 14, I & II, pp. 413–463). La Salle, IL: Open Court Publishing.

Cohen, L. H., Sargent, M. M., & Sechest, L. B. (1986). Use of psychotherapy research by professional psychologists. *American Psychologist, 41,* 198–206.

Denmark, F., Russo, N. F., Frieze, I. H., & Sechzer, J. A. (1988). Guidelines for avoiding sexism in psychological research. *American Psychologist, 43,* 582–585.

Ellis, A. (1962). *Reason and emotion in psychotherapy.* New York: Stuart.

Fogle, D. O. (1978). Learned helplessness and learned restlessness. *Psychotherapy, 15,* 39–47.

Ford, D. H. (1987). *Humans as self-constructing living systems: A developmental perspective on behavior and personality.* Hillsdale, NJ: Erlbaum.

Frank, J. D. (1985). Therapeutic components shared by all psychotherapies. In M. J. Mahoney & A. Freeman (Eds.), *Cognition and psychotherapy* (pp. 49–79). New York: Plenum Press.

Friedman, M. (1974). *The hidden human image.* New York: Dell.

Freud, S. (1953-1966). J. Strachey (Ed. and Trans.), *The standard edition of the complete psychological works of Sigmund Freud* (Vols. 1–23). London: Hogarth Press.

Gilligan, C. (1982). *In a different voice: Psychological theory and women's development.* Cambridge, MA: Harvard University Press.

Goldfried, M. R. (1982). *Converging themes in psychotherapy.* New York: Springer.

Greenberg, L. S., & Pinsoff, W. (Eds.). (1986). *The psychotherapeutic process.* New York: Guilford Press.

Greenberg, L. S., & Safran, J. D. (1987). *Emotions in psychotherapy: Affect, cognition, and the process of change.* New York: Guilford Press.

Hayek, F. A. (1967). *Studies in philosophy, politics, and economics.* Chicago: University of Chicago Press.

Hayek, F. A. (1978). *New studies in philosophy, politics, economics, and the history of ideas.* Chicago: University of Chicago Press.

Hayek, F. A. (1979). *Law, legislation and liberty: Vol. 3. The political order of a free people.* Chicago: University of Chicago Press.

Hebb, D. O. (1975). Science and the world of imagination. *Canadian Psychology, 16,* 4–11.

Hilgard, E. R. (1987). *Psychology in America: An historical survey.* San Diego, CA: Harcourt Brace Jovanovich.

Holland, J. L. (1986). Planning for alternative futures. In J. M. Whitely, N. Kagan, L. W. Harmon, B. R. Fretz, & F. Y. Tanney (Eds.), *The coming decade in counseling psychology.* Schenectady, NY: Character Research Press.

Hoshmand, L. L. S. T. (1989). Alternate research paradigms: A review and teaching proposal. *The Counseling Psychologist, 17,* 3–79.

Jantsch, E. (1980). *The self-organizing universe.* New York: Pergamon.

Kelly, G. A. (1955). *The psychology of personal constructs.* New York: Norton.

Kohlberg, L. (1981). *The philosophy of moral development.* San Francisco: Harper & Row.

Lambert, M. J. (1989). The individual therapist's contribution to psychotherapy process and outcome. *Clinical Psychology Review, 9,* 469–485.

MacLean, P. D. (1973). *A triune concept of the brain and behavior.* Toronto: University of Toronto Press.

Mahoney, M. J. (1988a). Constructive metatheory: I. Basic features and historical foundations. *International Journal of Personal Construct Psychology, 1,* 1–35.

Mahoney, M. J. (1988b). Constructive metatheory: II. Implications for psychotherapy. *International Journal of Personal Construct Psychology, 1,* 299–315.

Mahoney, M. J. (1991). *Human change processes.* New York: Basic Books.

Mahoney, M. J., & Craine, M. (1991). Changing beliefs of psychotherapy experts. *Journal of Psychotherapy Integration, 1,* 207–221.

Mahoney, M. J., & Gabriel, T. J. (1987). Psychotherapy and the cognitive sciences: An evolving alliance. *Journal of Cognitive Psychotherapy: An International Quarterly, 1,* 29–59.

Mahoney, M. J., & Lyddon, W. J. (1988). Recent developments in cognitive approaches to counseling and psychotherapy. *The Counseling Psychologist, 16,* 190–234.

Mahoney, M. J., Norcross, J. C., Prochaska, J. O., & Missar, C. D. (1989). Psychological development and optimal psychotherapy: Converging perspectives among clinical psychologists. *Journal of Integrative and Eclectic Psychotherapy, 8,* 251–263.

Masterpasqua, F. (1989). A competence paradigm for psychological practice. *American Psychologist, 44,* 1366–1371.

Maturana, H. R., & Varela, F. G. (1987). *The tree of knowledge: The biological roots of human understanding.* Boston: Shambala Publications.

Miller, J. B. (1976). *Toward a new psychology of women.* Boston: Beacon Press.

Morrow-Bradley, C., & Elliot, R. (1986). Utilization of psychotherapy research by practicing psychotherapists. *American Psychologist, 41,* 188–197.

Norcross, J. C. (Ed.). (1986). *Handbook of eclectic psychotherapy.* New York: Brunner/Mazel.

Norcross, J. C. (Ed.). (1987). *Casebook of eclectic psychotherapy.* New York: Brunner/Mazel.

Piaget, J. (1970). *Psychology and epistemology: Toward a theory of knowledge.* New York: Viking.

Piaget, J. (1981). *Intelligence and affectivity: Their relationship during child development.* Palo Alto, CA: Annual Review.

Polanyi, M. (1958). *Personal knowledge: Towards a postcritical philosophy.* Chicago: University of Chicago Press.

Prochaska, J. O. (1984). *Systems of psychotherapy: A transtheoretical analysis.* Homeland, IL: Dorsey Press.

Radnitzky, G., & Bartley, W. W. (Eds.). (1987). *Evolutionary epistemology, theory of rationality, and the sociology of knowledge.* La Salle, IL: Open Court Publishing.

Rogers, C. R. (1957). The necessary and sufficient conditions of therapeutic personality change. *Journal of Consulting Psychology, 21,* 95–103.

Skinner, B. F. (1987). What happened to psychology as the science of behavior? *American Psychologist, 42,* 780–786.

Varela, F. J. (1979). *Principle of biological autonomy.* New York: Elsevier North Holland.

Wachtel, P. L. (1987). *Action and insight.* New York: Guilford Press.

Watson, J. B. (1913). Psychology as the behaviorist views it. *Psychological Review, 20,* 158–177.

Watson, J. B. (1924). *Behaviorism.* Chicago: University of Chicago Press.

Weimer, W. B. (1977). A conceptual framework for cognitive psychology: Motor theories of mind. In R. Shaw & J. Bransford (Eds.), *Perceiving, acting, and knowing* (pp. 267–311). Hillsdale, NJ: Erlbaum.

Whitehead, A. N. (1957). *Process and reality.* New York: Macmillan.

Young-Eisendrath, P., & Hall, J. A. (1987). *The book of the self: Person, pretext, and process.* New York: New York University Press.

CHAPTER 21

DEPRESSION ASSESSMENT AND INTERVENTION: CURRENT STATUS AND FUTURE DIRECTIONS

KATHLEEN McNAMARA

Depression was recognized as a clinical syndrome as early as 1033 B.C. The Old Testament provides, in the book of Job, King Saul's description of recurrent symptoms of depression and suicidal thoughts. The first clinical description of melancholia, however, is credited to Hippocrates, who, in the fourth century B.C., suggested that depression was attributable to brain pathology. Although Hippocrates believed a preponderance of black bile in the brain was the primary cause of melancholia, he recognized the influence of environment and emotional stress on both the body and mind. He rejected the earlier torturous practices designed to exorcise demons and, instead, prescribed sobriety, tranquility, nutrition, and sexual abstinence. The demise of the Greco-Roman civilization at the end of the fifth century A.D. brought the collapse of the Hippocratic view of depression as a scientifically understandable and treatable syndrome.

In the Middle Ages, the treatment of depression was brought under the jurisdiction of priests, who viewed the afflicted individual as a sinner possessed by the devil. The depressed individual (usually a female) was perceived as either unwillingly possessed by Satan or willfully doing his bidding. The depressive was often believed to be a witch or heretic. Historically, depression in women was viewed as hysteria, a disease of the hypothetical "wandering womb," arising ostensibly from disturbed sexual function. It was believed to be best treated by compression of the ovaries or by uterine surgery. Some believe this idea persists today, citing as evidence the current frequency with which hysterectomies are performed when depression is a symptom in menopausal women.

In the late 1800s, Emil Kraepelin, a German physician, argued for the classification of mental illness based on the identification of causal factors, clinical course, and outcome. His own diagnostic criteria emphasized somatogenic factors and became the basis for contemporary classification schemas. Adolph Meyer, a dominant figure in American psychiatry in the early 1900s, developed the psychobiologic concept of reactive depressions, rather than the Kraepelian disease entities. Meyer was responsible for replacing the term melancholia with the term depression and for paving the way for psychosocial views of depression.

Despite depression's long history, debate continues over its etiology and appropriate treatment. Some authorities contend that depression is primarily biological in origin; others just as adamantly argue that social and psychogenic factors are at the root of most depressions. Undoubtedly, our current views of depression and procedures for assisting depressed individuals are as hampered by our culture-bound views of mental health and limited etiological knowledge as previous theories have been.

SYMPTOMS OF DEPRESSION

Depression ranges from the common "blues" to severe despair. Feelings of sadness are the hallmark of depression; however, some individuals may consciously conceal depressed affect and others may unconsciously deny feelings of sadness. Individuals who do not readily express depressed affect may be experiencing what is commonly referred to as "masked depression." When depression is masked, well-timed probing can usually reveal the dysphoric mood, which often includes feelings of anxiety, guilt, and resentment.

In addition to the emotional components, depression is characterized by difficulties with concentration, decision making, and problem solving. Pessimistic thoughts about the world, oneself, and the future are not only symptoms of depression but have been casually linked to the disorder. These negative thoughts, like depressed affect, may be fully and easily disclosed by the depressed client or they may require elicitation by the counselor. Irrational beliefs and thoughts of helplessness, hopelessness, and worthlessness are important to assess, in order to understand the client's world view and to assess suicide lethality.

When the depression is more serious, behavioral and physical symptoms are manifested. Social withdrawal is a typical behavior found in depressed individuals, and some depressives become dependent on significant others. Crying, inactivity, and loss of concern for physical appearance are signs of more serious depressions. Some individuals become retarded in their motor responses and show reduced speech and slowed body movements.

Physical or vegetative signs are commonly associated with serious depression, but can also be experienced by some individuals in moderate depressions. These symptoms usually include loss of appetite and inability to sleep, although the opposite conditions can sometimes occur. Muscle aches, headaches, and sex-drive disturbance are also commonly associated with depression. Fatigue is almost always present.

These symptoms are the common features that define the term depression. However, when a client presents with these complaints, it is encumbent on the counselor to assess the severity and type of depression present, in order to effectively assist the client. Until recently, it was assumed that there was a single, underlying cause of depressive disorders and that, if this could be understood and agreed on, then a single effective method of treatment could be derived. This assumption of homogeneity with regard to the affective disorders has been more or less abandoned as a result of recent biological investigations and treatment outcome studies, which have demonstrated that the affective disorders are heterogeneous with regard to both biology and treatment response (Craighead, 1980; Rush, 1982).

Although depression is now considered to be a final common pathway through which various psychogenetic and biochemical imbalances may be expressed, there is considerable controversy regarding the classification of depression. Indeed, some humanistic-existential theorists would offer justification for not using a nosological system at all. In cases of serious depression, however, and when the risk of suicide associated with depression is considered, the need for accurate differential diagnosis and informed treatment selection becomes paramount.

Traditionally, counseling psychologists have steered away from medical–clinical diagnostic systems that focus on identifying psychopathology (Ivey, 1976; Morrill, Oetting, & Hurst, 1974; Osipow, Cohen, Jenkins, & Dostal, 1979; Super, 1955). Some writers (Tyler, 1972) have advocated assessing individuals as "whole persons," identifying their assets, and using these assets to compensate for areas of weaknesses. Without arguing the relative merits of counseling versus clinical orientations, it is important to accurately assess depressive disorders in order to know which clients are good candidates for counseling and when medical consultation and possible referral are indicated. Because of the heterogeneous nature of depression, it is essential that collaboration occur between medically trained practitioners and counseling practitioners. To illustrate, Rush (1982) pointed to the example of bipolar depressions, which can be and often are misdiagnosed as nonendogenous depression. The client may describe life experiences that are causing depressive symptoms and not report significant vegetative signs. The counselor may expect counseling methods to be effective alone, even though bipolar depressions have not been found to respond well to various psychotherapeutic approaches. If the counselor is not knowledgeable about depression, the client's failure to respond to counseling might be interpreted as "resistance," and referral for pharmacological treatment—the treatment of choice for manic depression—will not occur.

CLASSIFICATION OF DEPRESSION

DSM-III-R (American Psychiatric Association, 1987) departed significantly from the classification schema that had been used for the depressive disorders in DSM-III. The term Mood Disorders is now used in place of Affective Disorders, and these disorders are subclassified into the Bipolar and the Depressive Disorders. The Bipolar Disorders include Bipolar Disorder, which is marked by one or more manic episodes, and Cyclothymia, which includes numerous episodes of both hypomanic (less severe manic symptoms) and depressive symptoms. The Depressive Disorders include Major Depression, in which one or more major depressive episodes have occurred, and Dysthymia, which is marked by a more or less chronic state of depressed mood for at least 2 years and which does not meet the criteria for Major Depression.

The reader is referred to DSM-III-R for a detailed description of the diagnostic criteria for each of these disorders. The major features of the Depressive Disorders are summarized here, along with a summary of the diagnostic features of Adjustment Disorder with depressed mood, a diagnostic label that may be applied to a substantial portion of individuals seeking counseling for depression. For these individuals, the counseling approaches reviewed in this chapter may be appropriate.

MAJOR DEPRESSION

The key feature of Major Depression is one or more episodes of depressed mood or loss of interest or pleasure in most activities for a period of at least 2 weeks, without a history of manic or hypomanic episodes. Other symptoms commonly presented include weight loss or gain, sleep disturbance, psychomotor agitation and retardation, fatigue, sense of worthlessness, impaired ability to concentrate or make decisions, and suicidal ideation. Major Depression may occur as a single episode with complete recovery to normal functioning, but, for 50% of those who have a single episode, another major depressive episode will eventually occur. At that point, the disorder is considered to be recurrent (American Psychiatric Association, 1987). Recurrent Major Depression may occur in episodes separated by many years of more or less healthy functioning, or the episodes may occur in clusters or with increasing frequency with age. Most individuals experience relief between episodes, with periods of normal healthy functioning; for 20 to 35% of individuals with Recurrent Major Depression, the course is chronic, with considerable social, occupational, and familial impairment.

A Major Depression may occur in a seasonal pattern in which there is a regular temporal relationship between the onset of the depression and a particular 60-day period or the remission of the depression within a particular 60-day period. For example, an individual may experience the regular appearance of depression between the beginning of October and the end of November, or the disappearance of depression for a similarly discrete 60-day period. The seasonal pattern is ruled out if the period of depression is associated with an obvious psychosocial stressor, such as regularly being unemployed in the winter or the anniversary of the death of a loved one.

Major Depression is considered to be the leading mental health problem in the United States, and it may be the most lethal, given its association with suicide. It is estimated that 9 to 26% of females and 5 to 12% of males will experience a Major Depressive Disorder sometime in their lives and that 4.5 to 9.3% of females and 2.3 to 3.2% of males currently have the disorder.

DYSTHYMIA

Dysthymia, sometimes referred to as Depressive Personality or Depressive Neurosis, usually begins between childhood and young adulthood, without a clear onset. The pattern of this disorder is chronic, and individuals with dysthymia can simultaneously experience a Major Depression, a condition sometimes referred to as "Double Depression."

Dysthymia is characterized by the chronicity of the depressive syndrome rather than the severity of symptoms. The DSM-III-R criteria for Dysthymia require the presence of depressive symptoms for at least 2 years, with periods of remission lasting no longer than 2 months. Dysthymia may be a consequence of another primary disorder such as Anorexia Nervosa or Psychoactive Substance Dependence, or it may exist apart from other disorders. Dysthymia is considered to be "primary type" when it exists alone and "secondary type" when it is related to a preexisting disorder.

Dysthymia is common among adults and is more common for females than for males. In children, Dysthymia is seen equally frequently in both sexes. Hospitalization is rarely indicated unless there is a superimposed Major Depression or suicidal behavior is evident. Impairment in social and occupational functioning is usually mild to moderate because the depressive symptoms are not severe. However, individuals with Dysthymia may be at greater risk of developing a drug dependency stemming from the depressive's attempt to control symptoms with alcohol or drugs (American Psychiatric Association, 1987).

Adjustment Disorder with Depressed Mood

Adjustment Disorder is the diagnosis given when an individual is experiencing a maladaptive reaction to a psychosocial stressor or stressors (e.g., divorce, occupational problems, discordant familial relationships, getting married, going to school, chronic illness, retirement). The maladaptive reaction includes either impairment in occupational or social functioning or symptoms that are in excess of a normal and expectable reaction to the stressor(s). Adjustment Disorder with depressed mood is diagnosed when the individual experiences predominantly depressive symptoms such as depressed mood, tearfulness, feelings of hopelessness, lethargy, and low self-esteem. By definition, the disorder begins within 3 months of the onset of a stressor and lasts no longer than 6 months. If the symptoms of Adjustment Disorder with depressed mood last longer than 6 months, then a change in diagnosis is warranted, possibly to Major Depression. This chapter critically reviews current assessment methods and comparative outcome studies on depression. Later, suggestions will be made for future research efforts in this area, and implications for practitioners will be discussed.

DEPRESSION ASSESSMENT

Depression has been measured in a variety of ways, with some methods focusing on the global construct of depression and others measuring specific aspects of the syndrome. Unfortunately, the current available depression assessment devices are of limited value when diagnosing depressing types. Differential diagnosis depends mainly on the counselor's knowledge of the differential criteria of the depression types and his or her ability to match interview data with the correct diagnosis. The specific depression measures can be useful in identifying specific deficits that may become targets of treatment, but even these measures are of little use in making differential diagnosis according to DSM-III-R criteria. In this section, the global and specific self-report measures that are currently available are reviewed with regard to content, usage, and psychometric properties. Interview and observational methods are also discussed. The methods reviewed here are limited to those that are used with adults.

Global Self-Report Measures

MMPI Depression Scale

The Minnesota Multiphasic Personality Inventory (MMPI; Hathaway & McKinley, 1951) contains a 60-item true–false depression scale (MMPI-D) that has been widely used both clinically and as a screening instrument for selecting depressed samples for research purposes. The MMPI-D scale is the most widely used psychodiagnostic instrument available and one of the most widely studied psychometrically. The scale has been used frequently to define depressed populations and to measure therapeutic outcome. It is a useful measure for comparison across studies. The recently revised MMPI-2 possesses very similar reliabilities for each scale, and the factor structure of the two versions is virtually the same (Graham, 1990).

The measure is of limited value in terms of its ability to identify specific targets for treatment and psychometrically, there are weaknesses that limit its usefulness. The MMPI was designed to measure a broad range of psychopathology, with the profile of scores across all clinical scales (not a score on a single scale) serving as the basis for clinical diagnosis (Dahlstrom, Welsh, & Dahlstrom, 1972). Many of the depression scale items also appear on the other clinical scales, thus limiting the discriminant validity of the measure. Individuals with various psychological problems may have elevations on the depression scale, a status that usually coincides with clinical evaluations on other scales.

Another limitation involves the internal consistency of the measure. Factor analyses have demonstrated that the MMPI-D scale is a multidimensional scale containing some factors that are not reliably associated with depression (Comrey, 1957; Harris & Lingoes, 1955).

Beck Depression Inventory

The Beck Depression Inventory (BDI; Beck, Ward, Mendelson, Mock, & Erbaugh, 1961) is a 21-item multiple-choice inventory that measures depression severity. Each item consists of 4 or 5 statements (listed in order of symptom severity) selected from among the following categories: mood, pessimism, crying, guilt, self-hate, irritability, social withdrawal, work inhibition, sleep and appetite disturbance, and loss of libido.

Test–retest reliability has been reported as .75 after 1 month (Rehm, 1976) and .74 after 3 months (Miller & Seligman, 1973). Construct validity has been supported by a number of investigations (Beck & Beamesderfer, 1974), and Beck (1972) has reported high discriminant validity, finding a .72 correlation between the BDI and clinical ratings of depression, and a .14 correlation between the BDI and clinical ratings of anxiety.

The BDI appears to be the best measure of global depression symptoms currently available. It is simple to administer and is widely used, making comparisons across studies possible. It is the instrument of choice for screening depressed individuals and measuring pre- and posttherapy outcome, given its ease of administration and psychometric strengths. Limitations of the measure include what some believe is a cognitive emphasis consistent with Beck's cognitive view of depression (Schwab, Bialow, & Holzer, 1976), at the expense of assessing symptoms from other theoretical views of depression. In addition, the measure assesses only general symptoms of depression and is of limited utility in identifying specific problematic thoughts or behaviors for intervention.

Center for Epidemiological Studies — Depression Scale

The CES-D (Radloff, 1977) was developed by the Center for Epidemiological Studies, at the National Institute of Mental Health. The measure was developed to assess depressive symptomatology for survey purposes, not as a diagnostic tool or measure of depression severity. The scale contains 20 items, consisting of statements referring to specific depressive symptoms. The scale emphasizes depressed affect, but cognitive, behavioral, somatic, and social functioning are also tapped.

This instrument has very good psychometric properties (Craig & Van Natta, 1976; Radloff, 1977; Weissman et al., 1977; Weissman, Prusoff, & Newberry, 1975). Radloff (1977) reported that interitem correlations are relatively low (not surprising for a scale of this kind); however, item–scale correlations are moderate. Test–retest reliability across 2- to 8-week intervals are moderate (.57 over several assessments), and correlations across longer intervals taper off to .32 at the 1-year test–retest period.

The CES-D has been found to discriminate between clinical and normal populations, to differentiate between acute and nonacute depressed subgroups, and to reflect changes with clinical improvements (Craig & Van Natta, 1976; Weissman et al., 1975; Weissman et al., 1977). The CES-D does not discriminate between subtypes of depressives (primary vs. secondary), nor does it appear to adequately discriminate depression from anxiety (Craig & Van Natta, 1976; Weissman, Sholomskas, Pottenger, Prusoff, & Locke, 1977).

Although the CES-D stresses affective symptomatology, it is a good device for measuring global depression. Unlike most other measures that focus on the individual's current functioning, the CES-D focuses on a 1-week time frame that should be considered when determining its suitability for specific uses. Because this instrument has not been used widely in treatment outcome studies, it is less useful as an outcome measure for comparability purposes.

Specific Self-Report Measures

Specific self-report measures in depression assessment have become popular for two reasons. First, specific measures of constructs believed to underlie depression can be tapped for diagnostic purposes and measurement of specific treatment outcomes. Second, these measures may be used for testing theories of depression. Given the multidimensional aspects of depression and the various deficits believed to underlie it, a set of specific devices should be included in an assessment battery for depression, in order to isolate specific deficits in functioning.

Automatic Thoughts Questionnaire

The Automatic Thoughts Questionnaire (ATQ; Hollon & Kendall, 1980) is a measure of depressogenic thoughts. The 30-item questionnaire was developed by having college students report their thoughts in recent sad situations. Items that discriminated between psychometrically identified depressed and nondepressed students were selected.

The ATQ possesses good internal consistency (Dobson & Breiter, 1983; Harrell & Ryon, 1983) and correlates with global measures of depression. Studies indicate that the ATQ also discriminates depressed from nondepressed clinical and normal controls (Dobson & Shaw, 1986; Eaves & Rush, 1984; Harrell & Ryon, 1983; Hollon, Kendall, & Lumry, 1986; Ross, Gottfredson, Christensen, & Weaver, 1986). The ATQ appears to covary with depression level (DeRubeis, Hollon, Evans, & Tuason, 1985; Hollon et al., 1986), and change on the ATQ occurs following various cognitive and noncognitive intervention approaches (DeRubeis et al., 1985; Simons, Garfield, & Murphy, 1984).

Dysfunctional Attitudes Scale

The Dysfunctional Attitudes Scale (DAS; Weissman & Beck, 1978) is a 40-item measure of attitudes and beliefs believed to be held by individuals prone to depression. Unlike the ATQ, which measures surface-level, depression-evoking thoughts, the DAS is intended to capture certain beliefs that place an individual at risk for depression when faced with life stress (e.g., "I am nothing if a person I love doesn't love me"; "I cannot be happy unless most people I know admire me").

The DAS (a) has high internal consistency (alpha = .90) and good stability ($r = .73$ over 6 weeks) (Oliver & Baumgart, 1985); (b) has been found to differentiate between depressed subjects and normal and clinical controls (Eaves & Rush, 1984; Hamilton & Abramson, 1983); and (c) evidences moderate ($r = .36$) correlations with global measures of depression (Oliver & Baumgart, 1985), suggesting that not all depressives hold dysfunctional attitudes and that individuals may hold dysfunctional attitudes without experiencing depression.

The DAS may be differentially affected by different forms of treatment, although the data are inconclusive (Simons et al., 1984; DeRubeis et al., 1985). There is some evidence that the measure may predict relapse following treatment (Evans et al., 1985; Rush, Weissenberger, & Eaves, 1986). Wise and Barnes (1986) found in a nonclinical sample that the DAS interacted with recent life stress to predict level of depression; however, no interaction was found in a clinical sample, although main effects were evidenced for both dysfunctional attitudes and life stress.

The DAS is a psychometrically adequate measure of attitudes believed to underlie depression. It is of limited usefulness as an outcome measure, unless subjects are screened on the basis of elevated DAS scores, because the correlation between the DAS and global depression is low. More study of normal subjects evidencing high DAS scores and of their propensity for developing depression needs to be done, to assess the construct validity of this measure.

Attributional Style Questionnaire

The Attributional Style Questionnaire (ASQ; Seligman, Abramson, Semmel, & Von Baeyer, 1979) was derived from the attributional reformulation of the learned helplessness theory of depression (Abramson, Seligman, & Teasdale, 1978). The measure consists of 12 vignettes, 6 describing positive outcomes and 6 describing negative outcomes. Some vignettes deal with achievement-related themes and others deal with interpersonal themes. Respondents identify one major cause (a free response) and then rate that cause on four 7-point dimensions: internal–external, global–specific, stable–unstable, and importance. Theoretically, internal, global, and stable causal attributions for important negative outcomes contribute to the development of depression.

Although it is often noted that this device is confusing to subjects, the psychometric indexes are generally adequate (Peterson et al., 1982). The measure appears to discriminate depressed from nondepressed psychiatric controls (Eaves & Rush, 1984; Hamilton & Abramson, 1983; Persons & Rao, 1985), although Miller, Klee, and Norman (1982) reported a null effect. In all of these studies, a subset of depressed patients (not all) were found to exhibit depressogenic attributional styles, although few of the nondepressed controls did so.

The ASQ appears to be a potentially useful predictor of relapse (Evans et al., 1985), although its usefulness as an outcome measure is more limited (DeRubeis et al., 1985). The measure seems to be most useful in theory-testing research.

Pleasant Events Schedule

The Pleasant Events Schedule (PES; MacPhillamy & Lewinsohn, 1974, 1976) is based on Lewinsohn's theoretical model of depression, which construes depression as resulting from insufficient amounts of response-contingent positive reinforcement. The PES is designed to assess the amount of external positive reinforcement that an individual receives.

The PES consists of 320 positive events. The respondent indicates how frequently each event has occurred in the past 30 days. In addition, the respondent indicates how pleasant each event was (or would have been, if it had occurred). Three scores are then derived: the activity level, the sum of the frequency ratings; the Reinforcement Potential, the sum of the pleasantness ratings; and Obtained Reinforcement, a multiplicative product of the frequency and pleasantness ratings.

The PES appears to possess sound psychometric properties. Internal consistency of the measure is very high, with alpha coefficients reported at .96, .98, and .97 for the three scores, and test–retest reliabilities over a 4-to-8-week period reported at .85, .66 and .72 for the three respective scores (Macphillamy & Lewinsohn, 1972). MacPhillamy and Lewinsohn (1974, 1976) reported validity data showing that all three scores distinguished depressed individuals from both clinical and normal controls. These data must be viewed cautiously, however. A recent article by Evans (1991) discussed the prevalent use of inappropriate statistical techniques when analyzing multiplicative composites. The potential misuse of statistical analyses of the PES cross-product score raises questions regarding the validity of the previous tests of psychometric properties and warrants careful scrutiny in future research.

The PES is a behavioral measure that has utility as a diagnostic tool, an outcome measure, and a therapeutic device. The drawbacks of this measure include its lengthiness and the possibility of depressive distortion in the reporting of events.

Interview Devices

The Hamilton Rating Scale

The Hamilton Rating Scale (HRS; Hamilton, 1960) was developed as a survey of depressive symptoms. It was designed originally to assess depression severity for drug treatment outcome studies. The scale emphasizes somatic complaints but also includes behavioral, cognitive, and affective symptoms. The 17 symptoms are rated on either a 3- or a 5-point scale, and assessment of these symptoms is based on information obtained via interview, observations, input from relatives, and records (Hamilton, 1960). Scores on the HRS are derived by totaling two independent ratings of each of the 17 symptoms. If only one rater is used, then the score is doubled for comparability.

Means for different samples have been reported by various researchers; however, no normative or cutoff scores have been determined. Rehm (1987), who cited means from various studies using diverse populations, indicated that inpatient depressives typically score around 32 to 42; depressed outpatients, between 24 and 27; and normals, as low as 6.2.

Psychometric data indicate adequate internal consistency (Rehm & O'Hara, 1985) and item-total correlations ranging from .21 to .67 in one study (Rehm & O'Hara, 1985) and .45 to .78 in another (Schwab, 1976). Interrater reliabilities have been reported as very high in a number of studies (Rehm, 1987).

The HRS differentiates between clinical and normal populations and between depressed and nondepressed psychiatric groups (Weissman, Sholomskas, Pottenger, Prusoff, & Locke, 1977). The HRS has been sensitive to therapeutic changes in depression level (Green, Aleser, Stone, & Seifert, 1975; Knesevich, Biggs, Clayton, & Ziegler, 1977) and has been used widely in pharmacological and psychotherapy outcome studies.

The HRS has accumulated psychometric evidence to indicate that it possesses good validity and reliability, and its popularity as an interview rating scale for use in outcome studies has earned it a central place in depression assessment (Rehm, 1987). The instrument emphasizes somatic symptoms, which limits its utility as a change measure with less severe depressives, and, despite reports of excellent interrater reliability, it is somewhat unclear how consistently the ratings are determined, given the allowable variety of methods for obtaining clinical information.

Schedule for Affective Disorders and Schizophrenia

The Schedule for Affective Disorders and Schizophrenia (SADS; Endicott & Spitzer, 1978) is a semistructured interview device for collecting standardized classifications based on the Research Diagnostic Criteria (RDC; Spitzer, Endicott, & Robins, 1975; 1978), a listing developed to establish standardized, operational criteria in order to improve the homogeneity of subject selection in research. The RDC is an extension of the Feighner diagnostic criteria (Feighner et al., 1972) and many of these criteria were incorporated into the criteria set forth in the DSM-III and DSM-III-R.

The SADS is a complex and lengthy interview schedule that requires the expertise of professionals who have considerable knowledge of psychopathology. The 1978 version of the SADS is 78 pages long, takes between 1 and 2 hours to complete, and requires computer scoring. There is no manual available for the SADS. The SADS is designed to enable the interviewer to quantify symptoms and level of functioning in terms of the past week, the peak of the current episode, and historically throughout the individual's life. The schedule covers symptoms related to affective disturbance, including depression, mania, and thinking disturbances.

Interrater reliabilities based on joint interviews with 150 subjects ranged from .82 to .99, and Cronbach alpha indexes of internal consistency ranged from .47 to .97, according to data provided by the NIMH collaborative program on the psychobiology of depression (Rehm, 1987). Concurrent validity has been established with adequate correlations with other measures of psychopathology (Endicott & Spitzer, 1978).

The SADS is a sophisticated interview rating device that has caught the attention of clinical and behavioral researchers. More psychometric data are needed, however, to more fully establish its validity and reliability. Its lengthiness and complexity diminish its usefulness for smaller-scale research studies, for in-office use, and for use by professionals who lack a sophisticated knowledge of psychopathology.

Diagnostic Interview Schedule

The Diagnostic Interview Schedule (DIS; Robins, Helzer, Crougham, & Ratliff, 1981) was developed for large-scale epidemiological studies. This device is a highly structured interview schedule that can be administered by professionals who do not have extensive knowledge of psychopathology. All questions and probes are specified, and a probe flow chart enables interviewers to assess severity of symptoms and to evaluate alternate explanations for symptoms. The DIS is designed to measure severity, frequency, and distribution over time of depressive symptoms. A computer program determines whether diagnostic criteria have been met according to the Feighner criteria, the RDC, and the DSM-III. Although reports have been made of DIS's use in large studies (Eaton et al., 1984; Meyers et al., 1984; Regier et al., 1984), scant data have been reported on the psychometrics of this device.

In general, DIS appears to be a very promising research tool, pending further evidence of its psychometric soundness. According to Rehm (1987), the DIS may replace the SADS as the preferred research instrument for diagnosis in the future, particularly because of its ease of administration relative to the SADS. A shortcoming of this device, and of the SADS, is that it may not be a feasible measure to use in smaller studies with less severe depressives, or in practice, given the need for computer scoring and extensive structured interviewing.

Observation Methods

Overt Verbal Behaviors

Many studies have found differences between depressives and normal controls in verbal-interactive behaviors. For example, Coyne (1976) found in telephone interviews that depressives differed significantly from nondepressed persons in terms of time spent talking about self versus others, and Andreason and Pfohl (1976) reported depression-associated differences in use of power, overstatement, and achievement words. Hinchliffe, Lancashire, and Roberts (1970, 1971) found differences on personal references, negators, direct references, expression of feelings, nonpersonal references, speech rate, eye contact, and gaze duration. These studies point to the potential importance of assessing verbal behavior in depressives.

Lewinsohn and his associates have developed a method for coding verbal communication based on the formulation of depression as a social skills deficit (Lewinsohn, Weinstein, & Alper, 1970; Libet & Lewinsohn, 1973; Libet, Lewinsohn, & Javorek, 1973). Verbal behaviors measured include: (a) total among of behavior emitted by the depressive and directed toward the depressive; (b) use of positive and negative responses by the depressive; (c) interpersonal efficiency ratio, defined as the number of verbal behaviors directed toward the depressive divided by the number of verbal behaviors emitted; and (d) range of interaction with others. Libet and Lewinsohn (1973) reported interrater reliabilities ranging from .63 to .99.

McLean, Ogston, and Grauer (1973) used a simplified version of Lewinsohn's coding system to code positive and negative initiations and reactions, and reported high interrater agreement using this method. They also reported positive changes on this measure, following intervention relative to placebo controls. Fuchs and Rehm (1977), reporting on a method of simply counting verbal statements made in a therapy group of depressed subjects, stated that this method was sensitive to pre- and posttherapy changes, relative to placebo controls. Rehm, Fuchs, Roth, Kornblith, & Romano (1979) found that negative self-references and negative references to others significantly decreased relative to controls, following a group intervention. Rehm et al. (1981) found that expressivity and latency were positively affected by Rehm's self-control treatment for depression.

Overt Motor Behaviors

Assessment of overt motor behaviors has revealed differences between depressed and nondepressed groups. Williams, Barlow, and Agras (1972) found that a composite measure of talking, smiling, motor activity, and time out of room every half-hour, for 10 depressed inpatients (used as a single behavioral measure), correlated .71 with the Hamilton Rating Scale and .67 with the Beck Depression Inventory. Furthermore, for 5 patients, improvement on this measure was a better predictor of posthospitalization improvement than either the Beck Depression Inventory or the Hamilton Rating Scale. Hersen, Eisler, Alford, and Agras (1973), using single-subject reversal designs, found that 3 inpatients under a token economy system also showed improvement on this behavioral measure.

Fisch, Frey, and Hirshrunner (1983) reported on a complex behavior observation system that was used with 13 depressed individuals at admission and discharge from the hospital. Percentage of time in motion, simultaneous movements, and rapidity of start and stop of actions were calculated using a time-series coding of body movements in half-second intervals of 3-minute segments. Time in motion and rapidity of actions were found to be increased at hospital discharge, although there were large individual differences. Simultaneous movements were found to be correlated with doctors' ratings of depression.

The observational methods of depression assessment reviewed above are the least developed area of depression assessment. Much research is needed in this area, to provide the standardization, replication, and psychometric data necessary to make these measures of significant utility in a depression assessment battery. Currently, these measures are generally used only for research purposes, although there is potential for future therapeutic use because these measures aim to identify specific aspects of depressive behaviors that can become the target of intervention.

DEPRESSION INTERVENTIONS

Numerous theoretical and therapeutic approaches to depression have been proposed, and each has at least some research to support its theoretical tenets and treatment efficacy. It is impossible in a single chapter to delve in detail into the theoretical conceptualizations of each model and to review all recent studies pertaining to each model. Instead, an overview of each theoretical model is provided, followed by an exploration of the general status of comparative treatment outcome research for depression.

Cognitive-Behavioral Approaches

Beck's Cognitive Theory

Beck's cognitive theory of depression (1967, 1974, 1976; Beck, Rush, Shaw, & Emery, 1979) conceptualizes depression as a disturbance in cognition where depressed affect emanates from a distorted, negatively biased view of oneself, the world in general, and the future. Beck has focused his attention on the cognitive disturbances that he believes influence these depressive manifestations. Beck is clear in his postulation that cognitions cause and maintain depression.

Beck proposed that a set of assumptions or cognitive schemata develops in childhood and accounts for an individual's basic view of self, the world, and the future. These schemata provide the grounds for healthy functioning or may create a vulnerability to depression or other psychological disturbance. Depressed individuals are hypothesized to engage in systematic errors in thinking, which support and sustain underlying dysfunctional schemata. These errors include overgeneralization, magnification and minimization, personalization, selective abstraction, and arbitrary inference (Beck, 1976).

Cognitive schemata may remain dormant, and an individual's evaluation of situations and events may be realistic, until a particular stressor or a set of stressors occurs and activates the long dormant constellation of thoughts that make up the cognitive schema. As the depression develops, the individual begins to have difficulty evaluating objective reality and to engage in the errors in thinking noted above. As the depression increases in severity, the depressive accepts his or her negative self-statements and may be unwilling, or unable, to evaluate the self or the situation realistically without professional intervention.

Cognitive therapy (see Beck et al., 1979, for a detailed description of how to implement cognitive therapy) involves establishing a collaborative relationship between the counselor and the client. Clients are provided with an explanation of depression, according to Beck's cognitive theory, and are taught to recognize the association between dysfunctional thinking and their affect and behavior. Then, cognitive therapy techniques are presented to train the client to identify, evaluate, and correct faulty thinking.

Cognitive therapy relies on behavioral homework assignments, particularly with more severe depressives, to encourage activity and to provide material for discussion about the relationship between beliefs and actual capabilities. Whatever the outcome of the various behavioral assignments, the focus is on the individual's expectations and assumptions about self, the world, and the future.

Cognitive therapy emphasizes the importance of assisting the client in self-assessing the accuracy of his or her thinking. Avoiding making judgments about the accuracy of the client's perceptions, the therapist asks *the client* to judge the correctness of the assumption and encourages a focus on factual information about the event.

Cognitive therapy is brief (approximately 20 sessions) and goal-oriented, and the counselor is active and directive. The therapy is intended to achieve rapid relief of symptoms and prevention of recurrence.

The Learned Helplessness Model

In 1975, Martin Seligman proposed the original learned helplessness theory of depression which was reformulated in 1978 by Abramson, Seligman, and Teasdale. The original theory proposed (a) that depression results from a belief that one cannot control important outcomes in life and (b) that such a belief is sufficient to produce the motivational, behavioral, and ultimately vegetative symptoms of depression.

The reformulated model of learned helplessness emphasized that the causal attributions people make in helpless situations are critical to a vulnerability to depression. Specifically, the reformulated model described three dimensions along which attributions may occur: internal–external, stable–unstable, and global–specific. Attributions about important negative outcomes that are internal, stable, and global are postulated to be most depression-inducing. Attributing lack of control to internal factors presumably leads to lowered self-esteem, whereas attribution to external factors does not. Lack of control attributable to stable factors is hypothesized to lead to the expectation of uncontrollability in future situations, and attributions that are global are hypothesized to lead to the expectation of uncontrollability across various situations. For example, if a prospective graduate student performs poorly on the Graduate Record Examination, and makes the attribution "I am stupid" (internal, stable, and global attribution), the student is likely to experience depression and lowered self-esteem. If the student attributes the poor outcome to more transient and situational factors (e.g., "I was sick that day" or "I didn't prepare for it"), depression and lowered self-esteem would not be expected.

The learned helplessness model does not offer a specific treatment package, although therapeutic strategies have been suggested. Beach, Abramson, and Levine (1981) made four suggestions regarding intervention for depression based on the reformulated learned helplessness model: (a) the expectation of no control over important outcomes should be challenged: (b) a shift from unrealistic goals to realistic goals should be facilitated; (c) the importance of unattainable goals should be decreased; and (d) the expectation that other people have control over important goals, whereas the client does not, needs to be reversed. These recommendations were based on the inference that individuals who have certain cognitive biases are likely to possess a cognitive style that predisposes them to be depressive. Particular examples are biases toward (a) judging that outcomes are uncontrollable; (b) attributing negative outcomes to internal, stable, and global factors; and (c) subscribing to unrealistic and unattainable goals and viewing these goals as important (Beach et al., 1981). Beck's cognitive therapy, although based on a different cognitive emphasis, is not incompatible with achieving the goals outlined above.

Lewinsohn's Behavioral Model

Lewinsohn's behavioral model of depression emphasizes the role of reinforcement in the development and maintenance of depression. Lewinsohn (1974) proposed that a low rate of response-contingent reinforcement is likely to produce depression. The quality of person–environment interactions is emphasized in this theory, with interactions that lead to positive outcomes (making the person feel good) constituting positive reinforcement.

When the behavior of depressed individuals does not lead to positive reinforcement, the behavior tends to extinguish, and the passivity characteristic of depressives develops. Furthermore, the lack of rewarding interactions causes the feelings of sadness. A high rate of punishing experiences may also cause depression. When person–environment interactions are aversive (i.e., distressing, unpleasant, upsetting), depression may ensue.

Lewinsohn stated that there are three general reasons why a person may experience low rates of positive reinforcement or high rates of punishment. First, the immediate environment may have few available positive reinforcers or many punishing aspects. Lewinsohn referred to this as low *availability* of reinforcers. Second, the individual may lack the skills necessary to elicit positive reinforcement or to cope with aversive events (*skill deficits*). Third, the *potency* of previous positively reinforcing experiences may be reduced and/or the impact of punishing experiences may be heightened.

Therapy for depression, based on this model, is straightforward. Treatment aims to increase the rate of positively reinforcing interactions with the environment and to decrease the rate of punishing interactions, in terms of both quantity and quality. After an initial screening phase to determine whether an individual is suffering from depression, Lewinsohn advocates the extensive use of the Pleasant and Unpleasant Events Schedules to pinpoint specific person–environment interactions related to the individual's depression. A personal activity schedule is constructed from 80 items that the client has rated as most pleasant and frequent and 80 items that the client has rated as most unpleasant and frequent. Lewinsohn and Amenson (1978) developed an Activity Schedule that may be used for most individuals. It contains items that are commonly endorsed in individualized lists.

After completing this stage of "functional analysis," clients are instructed to monitor daily both their moods and the occurrence of the pleasant and unpleasant activities. Over the course of treatment, the therapist employs a variety of tactics designed to change the client's environmental conditions, to teach depressed individuals skills necessary for changing problematic interactions, and to enhance pleasantness and decrease aversiveness of person–environment interactions. These tactics include relaxation, assertiveness, contingency management, time management, goal setting, cognitive skills training to cope with aversive events, and social skills training.

Lewinsohn's behavioral treatment for depression is highly goal-oriented and educational in its emphasis. Little emphasis is placed on the therapeutic relationship per se. In addition, little, if any, focus is placed on the client's history or subjective experience. Heavy and almost exclusive emphasis is placed on changing the client's specific behaviors to alter dysphoric mood.

Rehm's Self-Control Model

Rehm's (1977) self-control theory of depression is based on Kanfer's (1970, 1971) more general self-control theory. This model suggests that depressed persons have specific deficits in self-control behavior. Self-control behavior is construed in terms of self-monitoring, self-evaluation, and self-reinforcement phases. Rehm suggests that two deficits in each phase are characteristic of depressives. In the self-monitoring phase, depressed individuals are hypothesized to attend to negative events to the exclusion of positive events and to attend to immediate consequences of behaviors as opposed to delayed consequences. In the self-evaluation phase, depressives are hypothesized to set stringent self-evaluative criteria for their behavior and to make self-attributional errors consistent with expectations of a negative outcome. In the self-reinforcement phase, depressives are hypothesized to self-administer insufficient rewards as well as excessive punishments.

Self-control therapy attempts to remedy the various deficits specified by the model. Like other cognitive-behavioral models, the self-control program is generally didactic in nature. The client is presented with a rationale for each segment of the program, and behavioral exercises are used to facilitate changes. Rehm has implemented the self-control program in a group format that usually includes 6 to 12 weekly 90-minute sessions.

The program begins with the counselor's presenting the self-control theory of depression and emphasizing that mood is related to activity and that positive mood changes will occur if positive activities are increased. As in Lewinsohn's program, clients are asked to record daily mood and daily participation in positive activities, to illustrate the relationship between mood and activity level. Participants are taught to differentiate short-term from long-term or delayed effects of various activities, particularly when the positive consequences of an activity may not be realized immediately. Participants self-monitor in daily logs the delayed effects of at least one positive activity per day. A series of similar exercises is presented to deal with the hypothesized self-evaluation deficits. Specifically, participants learn to define reasonable, attainable goals and to break larger goals into subgoals. To address inaccurate attributions, participants are presented with information about how depressives tend to distort the attributions for positive and negative outcomes. To modify this distortion, clients are asked to self-monitor estimates of personal responsibility (percentages) for various positive and negative events each day. Self-reinforcement exercises aim to increase the participant's use of contingent self-reward. Participants make lists of positive self-statements and overt rewards that can be used to reward themselves for efforts in working toward their goals.

Rehm et al. (1981) pointed out that the structure and group format of the self-control program frequently lead clients to refer to the program as a "class" rather than to think of it as a form of psychotherapy. He also noted that clients have been critical of the emphasis on positive activities and self-reinforcement, with some expressing the view that not enough attention is paid to real problems and truly aversive situations. Furthermore, some clients have felt that the program teaches a self-centered and hedonistic approach to human interaction. Despite these criticisms, Rehm et al. (1981) indicated that most participants find the program to be flexible, practical, and useful in various circumstances.

Interpersonal Therapy

Interpersonal therapy for depression has evolved over years of clinical practice and research at the New Haven–Boston Collaborative Depression Project. Klerman and Weissman have been the primary figures associated with this approach to the conceptualization and treatment of depression. Interpersonal therapy is derived from various theoretical sources, particularly the work of Harry Stack Sullivan and his theory of interpersonal relations, and John Bowlby's attachment theory. Interpersonal therapy, which is based on the premise that depression derives from problems in social roles and interpersonal relations, hypothesizes that vulnerability to depression occurs when strong attachments do not develop early in life.

Although interpersonal therapy acknowledges early developmental experiences as key to adult patterns of interpersonal relationships and vulnerability to depression, the focus of therapeutic intervention is on current interpersonal relationships, not the reconstruction of early experiences. Interpersonal therapy was developed as a short-term psychotherapy aimed primarily at symptom reduction and improved interpersonal functioning. Furthermore, this model assumes that the client's family of origin will be reflected in current interpersonal attitudes and behavior. Interpersonal therapy is commonly employed in conjunction with psychopharmacologic approaches, to help alleviate symptoms more rapidly. A detailed description of the techniques of interpersonal therapy is available in a manual prepared by Klerman, Rounsaville, Chevron, Neu, and Weissman (1979).

Interpersonal therapy focuses on four major interpersonal problem areas commonly presented by depressed individuals: grief, interpersonal role disputes, role transitions, and interpersonal deficits. These problem areas are not considered to be mutually exclusive; a combination of problems in several areas may be present, or one particular area may become the focus of treatment.

In cases of depression in which an abnormal grief reaction appears to be the primary cause, interpersonal therapy focuses on encouraging the client to think about the loss and the events surrounding it, and to explore feelings associated with the death, such as shame and helplessness for not being able to prevent the death, rage or guilt, or fear of repetition of the event. Interpersonal therapy emphasizes reconstructing the client's relationship with the deceased, in order to determine what conflicts may have been present in the relationship that are inhibiting the expression of normal grief. As the client becomes less invested in continuing an abnormal grief process, active encouragement to consider new relationships and activities takes place.

In the case of interpersonal role disputes, clients display a loss of self-esteem stemming from nonreciprocal expectations about a significant relationship. The conflicts can be overt or covert. The general goals of interpersonal therapy when the focus is a role dispute are to help the client identify the dispute, to decide on a plan of action, and to encourage modification of communication patterns or reassess expectations in order to bring about a resolution. Improvements in role disputes may result from behavioral changes by the client (or the significant other), attitude changes by the client, or a satisfactory dissolution of the relationship. The general treatment strategy is to help clients understand how nonreciprocal role expectations relate to the dispute and how the dispute relates to the current depressed state. Attempts are made to discover parallels in previous relationships and to determine how disputes are perpetuated.

Depressions associated with role transition occur when individuals experience difficulty adjusting to and coping with life changes. Often, the role transition is associated with a feeling of loss even when the loss is not readily apparent, such as the loss of freedom associated with the birth of a child. The general goals of treatment for depression associated with role transitions are to enable the client to view the life change in a more positive manner and to restore self-esteem by developing mastery vis-à-vis the demands of the new role. The therapeutic focus is similar to that of grief work, whereby the counselor facilitates the patient's realistic evaluation of what has been lost, encourages the appropriate expression of affect, and helps the client develop a support system and a repertoire of social skills needed for the new role.

When the depressive presents with a history of impoverished social relationships involving few lasting social or intimate relationships, the key aspect of the depression is viewed as social isolation. Therapy focuses on an analysis of past relationships, the relationship with the therapist, and the formation of new relationships. Techniques to improve communication are commonly employed, including role playing to improve social skills.

Psychodynamic Therapy

Arieti and Bemporad (1978) provided an extensive review of the literature on depression from the psychoanalytic perspective, and Strupp, Sandell, Waterhouse, O'Malley, and Anderson (1982) described short-term psychodynamic therapy for depression. Without delving into the early psychoanalytic views of depression and the evolution of psychoanalytic thought regarding the eitology and treatment of depression, the current major psychodynamic concepts of depression are reviewed here.

According to Bemporad (1978), depression is viewed as a problem of disturbed interpersonal relations. The predisposition and origin of depressive disorders are hypothesized to stem from disappointments with significant others in early childhood, which lead to pervasive ambivalence in all relationships. Depression is seen as a problem in adaptive functioning that reflects a disparity between the actual state of self and a desired ego ideal. The depressive experiences a conflict between feelings of helplessness (an activation of a potent childhood state) and extremely high aspirations that the depressive is unable to fulfill. Psychodynamic theory suggests that early experiences of deprivation or loss trigger feelings of anger and rage that, because of the child's dependency, could not be directed outward and, instead, became internalized and directed against the self.

This conceptualization of depression is not fundamentally different from that which might be used to describe a variety of other problems from the psychodynamic perspective. Thus, the psychodynamic approach does not yield a differential treatment prescription for depression. The psychodynamic therapist aims to strengthen the client's adaptive capacities or "ego strength," thereby reducing depressive symptoms.

The psychodynamic technique for facilitating change involves two major components. First, the therapist encourages the development of an interpersonal relationship that will enable the client to experience the conflict that exists between oneself and other people in the therapeutic relationship ("transference"). Second, the therapist provides understanding and emotional support, as well as insight into maladaptive relationship patterns. The treatment process occurs in four stages (Zalden, 1982): "primary resistance," "treatment resistance," "termination resistance," and "termination resolution." In the initial phase, the client resists acknowledgment of the pain of initial parental separation and ambivalence toward one's parents. In addition, the client may remain distanced from the therapist, in order to prevent a painful repetition of the early parental attachment and subsequent disappointment or loss. The therapist aims to build the therapeutic alliance while challenging the client's defenses during this initial phase.

In the second phase, the client resists the therapeutic process, out of fear of too much self-exposure to the newly cathected therapist. In this stage, the therapist actively confronts and clarifies this situation and interprets past and present behavior patterns. Clients are encouraged to fully experience the resistance and to avoid repression of feelings, especially anger. As clients experience the expression without retaliation from the therapist, a corrective emotional experience occurs. At this point, the client, now more open, is able to see maladaptive behavior patterns in other relationships and to make necessary changes to reduce ambivalence in those relationships.

Termination resistance occurs when the client senses impending termination. Sometimes this is manifested in self-distancing from the therapist and self-isolation socially. This phase calls for additional confrontation and interpretation on the part of the therapist, and acknowledgment by the client of feelings regarding termination. Termination resolution involves appropriately "grieving" the loss of the therapist and connecting this experience to earlier parental loss, with the goal of experiencing the termination without ambivalence.

Although psychodynamic approaches typically aim for personality reconstruction as opposed to symptom reduction, the briefer psychodynamic models are not intended to produce such deep-seated characterological changes. Rather, their focus has been on improved interpersonal behavior, daily functioning, and symptom reduction, attained via insight and the working through of transference. The briefer psychodynamic approaches to depression allow for empirical comparisons with the other modes of treatment reviewed earlier and provide an insight-oriented approach for those individuals who strongly resist more behaviorally oriented programs.

TREATMENT EFFECTIVENESS

Given the diverse approaches to the conceptualization and treatment of depression, the question of relative efficacy naturally arises. This review is restricted to comparative studies, because of space limitations. Far more research has been conducted examining the efficacy of the cognitive-behavioral treatments, compared to the interpersonal model or psychodynamic model. Therefore, evaluation of the cognitive-behavioral therapies is disproportionately represented in this review.

Taylor and Marshall (1977) compared cognitive therapy to Lewinsohn's (1974) behavioral model and created a third treatment that combined these two approaches. Twenty-eight mildly-to-moderately depressed volunteers were randomly assigned to one of the three active treatments or to a wait-list control. At posttest, all three active treatments showed significantly more improvement than controls on the Beck Depression Inventory (BDI; Beck, Ward, Mendelson, Mock, & Erbaugh, 1961), another self-report depression scale, and a self-esteem index. There were no significant differences between the cognitive therapy alone and the behavioral intervention alone, although the combined treatment generally surpassed the individual treatments both at posttest and follow-up.

In a similar study, Shaw (1977) contrasted Beck's cognitive approach and Lewinsohn's behavioral approach, with attention (nondirective) and wait-list (no treatment) control conditions. Screening criteria and dependent measures for the 32 subjects were a score of 18 or higher on the BDI and independent observer ratings of at least mild depression on two scales, including the Hamilton Rating Scale for Depression (HRSD; Hamilton, 1960). At posttest evaluation, cognitive therapy generally produced significant improvement on the BDI and HRSD, relative to the behavioral, nondirective, and wait-list control treatments. The behavioral treatment produced significant improvement over the wait-list control but was not superior to the nondirective condition. At a 1-month follow-up, the superiority of the cognitive treatment over the behavioral treatment eroded; no follow-up data were obtained on the control subjects.

Hodgson (1981) compared interpersonal skills training with a cognitive treatment program under either "massed" or "distributed" conditions. Thirty-eight subjects were assigned into groups of 9 or 10, matched on the basis of age, gender, depression level, and intellectual capacity. Both treatments were significantly superior to no treatment on the Self-Rating Depression Scale (SDS; Zung, 1965) and on Lubin's (1965) Depression Adjective Checklist (DACL). Interpersonal skills training (combined over massed and distributed groups) was significantly more effective than the cognitive treatment on the SDS but not on the DACL. At 1 month follow-up, however, the relative advantages of the interpersonal skills training had disappeared. Interestingly, interpersonal skills training produced a superior effect on an index of social functioning, and the massed group profited most from interpersonal skills training. Unfortunately, the study did not include dependent measures designed to tap specific cognitive improvements.

Zeiss, Lewinsohn, and Munoz (1979) examined the impact of three separate approaches to depression on outcome measures keyed to the respective treatments. Interpersonal skills training was expected to positively influence the Interpersonal Events Schedule, as well as ratings of verbal behavior and social skills; a pleasant activities treatment was presumed to change scores on the Pleasant Events Schedule; cognitive therapy was hypothesized to lower depression as measured by several cognitive indexes. The study used multiple therapists and stringent subject-screening criteria. At posttest, wholesale improvements over time emerged on the specific measures, as well as on the MMPI-D scale. Unfortunately, however, none of the active treatments had differential impact on any measure relative to delayed treatment control conditions. The authors suggested that their extensive contact with the control subjects may have washed out possible differences. Low statistical power also hampered the possibility of uncovering differential effects.

In a related study, Rehm et al. (1979) compared self-control therapy to assertiveness training after a delayed treatment control session of 6 weeks. Depression was assessed at pretherapy, the initial session, posttherapy, and follow-up, using a variety of global depression measures, videotape ratings of overt-motor behavior associated with depression, self-control attitudes and beliefs, and assertiveness. Results suggested that self-control therapy was more effective on the global measures of depression, assertion training was more effective on measures of assertion, and self-control therapy was superior on at least one measure of self-control.

Wilson, Goldin, and Charbonneau-Powis (1983) examined the impact of cognitive and behavior therapy on treatment-related target areas. Twenty-five subjects were randomly assigned to one of the two active treatments or to a wait-list control and were assessed on a variety of cognitive and behavioral measures in addition to global measures of depression. At posttest, the active treatments showed superior improvement on the global measures of depression relative to controls; however, there were no significant differences between the cognitive and behavior therapies. On the target-area measures, the active treatments again showed significantly more improvement than controls, but there were no significant differences between the active treatments of any of the treatment-specific measures at either posttest or 5-month follow-up.

The failure to find differences between the cognitive and behavioral treatments on the treatment-specific measures raises the possibility that the therapists failed to administer the two treatments in a sufficiently distinct manner. Without conducting independent variable manipulation checks, it remains unknown whether the therapists adhered to the treatment manuals. However, it may be that low statistical power (8 subjects per treatment) simply prevented the detection of significant differences that might have existed. Furthermore, given the absence of a nonspecific control condition, the influence of nonspecific factors cannot be dismissed as an explanation of the improvements made by subjects in these treatments.

DiMascio et al. (1979) studied the differential effects of interpersonal psychotherapy and pharmacotherapy with acutely depressed outpatients. Eighty-one subjects were randomly assigned to one of four conditions: (a) 16 weeks of psychotherapy, which focused on the interpersonal or social context of depression; (b) 100 to 200 mg of amitriptyline, which was stabilized over a 3-week period and maintained for 12 weeks; (c) 16 weeks of treatment combining drugs and psychotherapy; or (d) nonscheduled treatment control, which allowed subjects to contact a psychiatrist whenever they felt a need for assistance. If the patient's needs were of sufficient intensity, a 50-minute support session was scheduled. Any subject who required more than one support session per month was dropped from the study. Subjects were assessed after 1, 4, 8, 12, and 16 weeks by a clinical evaluator blind to the subjects' treatment condition and by the patient's treating psychiatrist on the HRSD and another rating scale. The combined treatment produced the most overall symptom reduction, psychotherapy alone and pharmacotherapy alone were about equal, and the nonscheduled treatment produced the lease effect. In terms of differential effects, it was found that pharmacotherapy had its effect mainly on the vegetative symptoms—sleep disturbance, somatic complaints, and appetite. Effects of psychotherapy were mainly on depressed mood, suicidal ideation, work and interests, and guilt. The researchers concluded that, for patients who show marked vegetative complaints, particularly sleep disturbance, pharmacotherapy may be most useful; for patients whose emotional complaints and mood disturbance override the somatic symptoms, psychotherapy may be more useful.

Comparative treatment outcome studies published after 1980 have tended to focus on treatment-specific effects, in an attempt to isolate mechanisms of change as well as reductions in general depression symptoms. Each theoretical model emphasizes different therapeutic deficits or targets in the treatment of depression, and the 1980s were marked by a surge of attention focused on matching specific deficits with specific treatments or examining specific outcomes produced by specific treatments.

A study by Rude (1986) examined responses to behavioral assertion training compared to a cognitive self-control treatment as a function of depressed clients' relative strength in the corresponding skill areas at pretreatment. Rude predicted that reductions in depression would be greater for treated subjects relative to wait-list controls and that those initially deficient in a skill would obtain maximum benefits from the treatment targeting that skill deficit. Results revealed the effectiveness of a combined assertion skill–cognitive treatment on global depression (BDI) relative to controls; however, neither cognitive nor assertion skill level predicted response to the treatments. The combined treatment also improved cognitive self-control relative to controls, but did not affect assertion skill.

McNamara and Horan (1986) attempted to identify the treatment-specific outcomes of Beck's (cognitive) and Lewinsohn's (behavioral) treatments for depression. They found that cognitive therapy produced a consistent and durable impact on a battery of measures reflecting cognitive manifestations of depression as well as one behavioral measure. The behavioral treatment failed to produce similar impact on the behavioral measures. All treatment conditions, including the high-demand control (nondirective counseling), produced significant reductions in global depression scores, with the cognitive and behavioral treatments generally yielding superior reductions relative to the nondirective condition.

In another comparative study, Thompson, Gallagher, and Breckenridge (1987) reported no differential treatment effects for cognitive therapy, behavior therapy, and short-term psychodynamic therapy relative to a delayed-treatment condition with depressed elderly persons who met the criteria for Major Depressive Disorder. Results indicated that 52% of the 91 subjects were in remission and 18% showed significant improvement at posttreatment, although 30% were clear treatment failures, still meeting the criteria for Major Depressive Disorder. This study employed global measures of depression as well as specific measures reflecting treatment approach, but no differential effects emerged on any measure.

Heiby (1986) examined the effects of treatment matched or unmatched to presenting deficits in either social skills or self-control skills. Although only four cases were used in this crossover treatment design, matched treatment was more effective than unmatched treatment in alleviating global depression and skill deficits.

Rehm, Kaslow, and Rabin (1987) employed a sample of 104 depressed women to examine the relative efficacy of three versions of their self-control therapy program. They found that each of their behavioral, cognitive, and combined conditions improved significantly on general depression, but there were no between-group differences.

There was also no evidence of differential treatment outcome as a function of initial status on pretreatment measures.

SUMMARY AND CRITIQUE

Earlier studies (Hodgson, 1981; Shaw, 1977; Taylor & Marshall, 1977) provided seminal knowledge on the treatment of depression but exhibited a number of serious methodological flaws. First, all three studies used a single experimenter to administer the treatments, and, in the Shaw and Hodgson studies, a single counseling group represented each treatment condition. Second, each study used global measures of depression, with the exception of one interpersonal skills measure included in the Hodgson study. Without measuring specific skills, behaviors, or thoughts to reflect the specific content of the treatment administered, the differential effect on the targeted behaviors addressed by each treatment is unknown. By examining the differential effects of the treatments, the particular mechanisms of change of the separate treatments may be revealed. Clarification of *how* the separate approaches evoke change has implications for the suitability of a given treatment for a given client or type of depression. Hollon (1981) noted that mechanisms of action—that is, those processes presumed to be central to the change process—may be independent of global treatment outcome. Therefore, various approaches to depression intervention may be effective in reducing depressive symptoms, but how those reductions are produced remains unknown without evidence of differential mechanisms of change.

In addition to the possibility that examining specific effects may aid in the determination of the suitability of certain treatments for certain individuals, the "construct validity" of the treatments themselves may be established by evaluating treatments on specific measures. That is, it can be revealed whether the treatments are actually affecting the specific skills, behaviors, or thoughts that the treatments are theoretically designed to address.

Comparative outcome studies conducted in the late 1970s and beyond (DiMascio et al., 1979; Heiby, 1986; McNamara & Horan, 1986, Thompson et al., 1987; Rehm et al., 1979; Rude 1986; Wilson et al., 1983; Zeiss et al., 1979) showed a concerted effort to measure the specific targets of different treatments. The findings were mixed. Five studies (Rehm et al., 1979; Rude, 1986; Thompson et al., 1987; Wilson et al., 1983; Zeiss et al., 1979) failed to find differential treatment effects, even on measures specifically keyed to those treatments; two studies (McNamara & Horan, 1986; Rehm et al., 1977) found partial support for differential effectiveness of treatments; and two studies (DiMascio et al., 1979; Heiby, 1986) reported clear differential effects.

Methodologically, great improvements have been seen in the conduct of most of these studies. Multiple therapists or therapy groups are included; sufficient sample sizes are used, to increase statistical power; and specific dependent measures are used. The failure to find consistent differential effects to elucidate mechanisms of change has, thus, been disappointing. Several possible explanations for this might be posited.

First, failure to find consistent and clear support for differential treatment effects might be construed as failure to support the construct validity of the treatment under scrutiny. That is, perhaps the theoretical construct being measured is simply invalid. A second possibility regards our ability to measure the constructs hypothesized to produce change. To date, the specific measures of thoughts, behaviors, and attitudes have not been as well developed as are the global measures of depression symptomatology (see Chapter 19, by Tinsley, for a discussion of important measurement issues).

Comparing various measures utilized to tap theoretical constructs of different treatments can be problematic, because the formats and time frames of the measures vary a great deal. Third, the global depression measures yield simple severity scores rather than subscale scores for specific sets of symptoms or subtypes of depression based on the various theoretical models. The latter would greatly enhance our ability to evaluate treatments more precisely and, ultimately, to match clients to particular treatments.

Rehm et al. (1987) suggested that the lack of specificity of treatment effects may indicate that various treatments are effective in relieving depression for reasons other than the validity of their separate theoretical rationales. Specifically, Rehm et al. noted several features that are shared by the major models of treatment for depression. One is the explicit delivery of rationales for treatment with clear conceptualizations of the causes, maintenance, and methods of change. Another is that the cognitive-behavioral approaches, in particular, are all highly structured approaches with specific steps to be followed by the client in order to reduce depressive symptoms. Even the interpersonal and newer short-term psychodynamic approaches propose a specific process that needs to occur to remedy the client's dysphoria. The cognitive-behavioral approaches also share the common features of having clients perform certain behaviors and self-monitor so as to provide direct feedback about positive changes. The extent to which these "common factors" in treatment approach impact their efficacy is unknown. Highlen and Hill (1984) addressed this issue as occurring in comparative psychotherapy research in general (see Chapter 20, by Mahoney); depression treatment research appears to be plagued with these potentially powerful but difficult to assess factors as well.

FUTURE RESEARCH DIRECTIONS

In the area of depression assessment, the global measures of depression lack subscales, which would be highly useful diagnostically to identify depression subtypes or specific deficits to be targeted in treatment. The currently available measures emphasize different symptoms, and all of them neglect interpersonal symptoms. Further, the interview devices, also used to measure global depression, are useful in assessing depression severity and making appropriate diagnostic decisions (resulting in homogeneous research samples), but they are still in need of supporting psychometric data, and the best methods are lengthy and difficult to employ. Some promising innovations include the development of subscales for the Schedule for Affective Disorders and the appearance of a Diagnostic Interview Schedule that is more easily administered.

The area most in need of attention involves further development and refinement of specific measures for the purposes of differential treatment. Current measures have been developed to assess specific constructs, but they are not comparable in terms of format or time reference (Rehm, 1987). There is also a need for a systematic assessment battery covering important deficits in a similar fashion across perspectives.

In the area of treatment outcome research, the most pressing need is to identify predictors of treatment response and relapse. A related concern involves identifying outcome indicators for a specific type of psychotherapy. To date, psychological measures do not yet indicate which type of depression will respond better to behavioral methods as opposed to cognitive, interpersonal, or psychodynamic treatments. One approach to dealing with these issues is to conduct psychometric research to identify depression subtypes that can be matched to specific psychotherapies. Another approach is to identify the mechanisms of change for the separate approaches to treatment. Efforts to identify subtypes and isolate mechanisms of change have yielded disappointing results thus far. Perhaps we are at a crossroads where it must be decided whether more effort should be made to isolate independent–dependent variable relationships with more stringently controlled studies and improved measures, or to abandon this approach altogether.

It is probably premature to suggest a radical shift in our efforts to examine the "construct validity" of depression interventions. Some recommendations for the future direction of this line of research, however, are in order. First, it is imperative that dependent measures be closely linked to the treatment strategy under investigation. Second, treatments under evaluation need to be administered in a manner that maximizes their conceptual distinctions to such a degree that their differences may be detected. Third, given the current state of affairs with regard to assessment, multiple measures of a specific construct are necessary. Fourth, therapists administering treatments in experimental studies typically administer each of the different modes of treatment to eliminate a therapist confound; however, therapists may not be equally committed to or competent in the administration of disparate approaches. Therefore, the therapist's implementation of and attitude toward each approach should be evaluated. In addition, subjects' preferences for and reactions to different methods of treatment ought to be solicited, to determine the relationship between these subject variables and treatment outcome.

IMPLICATIONS FOR PRACTICE

Working with depressed clients can be difficult and draining for practitioners, not only because of the pessimism and dysphoria of the client, but because of the lack of clear-cut prescriptions for intervention. On the bright side, the literature seems to indicate that various short-term approaches are effective in alleviating depression, although it is still unknown which approach is best for which client.

Practitioners who counsel depressed individuals must be familiar with the diagnostic classifications of depressions, particularly regarding the bipolar–nonbipolar distinction. Individuals evidencing symptoms of bipolar depression should be referred for consideration for pharmacological treatment. Any depression of significant intensity should be medically evaluated to rule out organic causes, particularly if onset is sudden, severe, and without a clear psychosocial trigger. If vegetative signs are prominent, pharmacological intervention is likely to be effective.

The intervention literature suggests that various approaches to depression treatment are effective in alleviating symptoms. Therefore, the practitioner may develop competence on the model that most closely matches his or her general theoretical orientation and feel confident that his or her approach to cases of depression is likely to be successful on average. On the other hand, given the current status of the outcome research, a purist approach to treatment may not be totally justified. Despite the tendency to be wary of eclectic approaches, the heterogeneity of depression may justify a theoretically eclectic approach to treatment, emphasizing the theoretical constructs that apply most directly to the presenting concerns of the client.

Empirical findings that deserve particular attention by practitioners are the relationships found between depression and dysfunctional thought processes, low activity levels, and interpersonal difficulties. Regardless of theoretical orientation, depressed clients generally seem to need assistance in these three areas.

Dialogue between researchers and practitioners is needed to enhance the efforts of both endeavors. As predictors of treatment response are identified, practitioners will need to adjust their conceptual mindset and therapeutic approaches accordingly, in order to be most helpful to their clients. Likewise, researchers need to stay abreast of the insights and successes that occur in the practice of psychotherapy.

REFERENCES

Abramson, L. Y., Seligman, M. E. P., & Teasdale, J. (1978). Learned helplessness in humans. Critique and reformulation. *Journal of Abnormal Psychology, 87,* 49–74.

American Psychiatric Association. (1987). *Diagnostic and statistical manual of mental disorders* (3rd ed. rev.). Washington, DC: Author.

Andreasen, N. J. C., & Pfohl, B. (1976). Linguistic analysis of speech in affective disorders. *Archives of General Psychiatry, 33,* 1361–1367.

Arieti, S., & Bemporad, J. (1978). *Severe and mild depression.* New York: Basic Books.

Beach, S. R. H., Abramson, L. Y., & Levine, F. M. (1981). Attributional reformulation of learned helplessness and depression: Therapeutic implications. In J. F. Clarkin & H. I. Glazer (Eds.), *Depression: Behavioral and directive intervention strategies.* New York: Garland.

Beck, A., Ward, C., Mendelson, M., Mock, J., & Esbaugh, J. (1961). An inventory for measuring depression. *Archives of General Psychiatry, 4,* 561–571.

Beck, A. T. (1967). *Depression: Clinical, experimental, & theoretical aspects.* New York: Hoebes.

Beck, A. T. (1972). *Depression: Causes and treatment.* Philadelphia: University of Pennsylvania Press.

Beck, A. T. (1974). The development of depression: A cognitive model. In R. Friedman & M. Katz (Eds.), *Psychology of depression: Contemporary theory and research.* Washington, DC: Winston & Wiley.

Beck, A. T. (1976). *Cognitive therapy and the emotional disorders.* New York: International Universities Press.

Beck, A. T., & Beamesderfer, A. (1974). Assessment of depression: The Depression Inventory. In P. Pichot (Ed.), *Psychological measurements in psychopharmacology. Modern problems in pharmacopsychiatry, Vol. 7.* Basel, Switzerland: Parisi Kasger.

Beck, A. T., Rush, A. J., Shaw, B. F., & Emery, G. (1979). *Cognitive therapy of depression.* New York: Guilford Press.

Bemporad, J. (1978). Critical review of the major concepts of depression. In S. Arieti & J. Bemporad (Eds.), *Severe and mild depression.* New York: Basic Books.

Comrey, A. (1957). A factor analysis of items on the MMPI depression scale. *Educational and Psychological Measurement, 17,* 578–585.

Coyne, J. C. (1976). Depression and the response of others. *Journal of Abnormal Psychology, 85,* 186–193.

Craig, T. J., & Van Natta, P. A. (1976). Presence and persistence of depressive symptoms in patient and community populations. *American Journal of Psychiatry, 133,* 1426–1429.

Craighead, W. E. (1980). Away from a unitary model of depression. *Behavior Therapy, 11,* 122–128.

Dahlstrom, W., Welsh, G., & Dahlstrom, L. (1972). *An MMPI handbook,* Vol. I. Minneapolis: University of Minnesota Press.

DeRubeis, R. J., Hollon, S. D., Evans, M. D., & Tuason, V. B. (1985). *Components and mechanisms in cognitive therapy and pharmacotherapy for depression: III. Process of change in the CPT project.* Unpublished manuscript, University of Minnesota and the St. Paul-Ramsey Medical Center, Minneapolis-St. Paul, MN.

DiMascio, A., Weissman, M., Prusoff, B. A., Neu, C., Zwilling, M., & Klerman, G. L. (1979). Differential symptom reduction by drugs and psychotherapy in acute depression. *Archives of General Psychiatry, 36,* 1450–1456.

Dobson, K. S., & Breiter, H. J. (1983). Cognitive assessment of depression: Reliability and validity of three measures. *Journal of Abnormal Psychology, 92,* 107–109.

Dobson, K. S., & Shaw, B. F. (1986). Cognitive assessment with major depressive disorders. *Cognitive Therapy and Research, 10,* 13–29.

Eaton, W. W., Holzer, C. E., Van Korff, M., Anthony, J. C., Helzer, J. E., George, L., Burnam, M. A., Boyd, J. H., Kessler, L. G., & Locke, B. Z. (1984). The design of the epidemiological catchment area surveys. *Archives of General Psychiatry, 41,* 942–948.

Eaves, G., & Rush, A. J. (1984). Cognitive patterns in symptomatic and remitted unipolar major depression. *Journal of Abnormal Psychology, 93,* 31–40.

Endicott, J., & Spitzer, R. L. (1978). A diagnostic interview: The schedule for affective disorders and schizophrenia. *Archives of General Psychiatry, 35,* 837–844.

Evans, M. G. (1991). The problem of analyzing multiplicatives composites: Interactions revisited. *American Psychologist, 46,* 6–15.

Feighner, J. P., Robins, E., Guze, S., Woodruff, R. A., Winokur, G., & Munoz, R. (1972). Diagnostic criteria for use in psychiatric research. *Archives of General Psychiatry, 26,* 57–63.

Fisch, H. U., Frey, S., & Hirshrunner, H. P. (1983). Analyzing non-verbal behavior in depression. *Journal of Abnormal Psychology, 92,* 307–318.

Fuchs, C. Z., & Rehm, L. P. (1977). A self-control behavior therapy program for depression. *Journal of Consulting and Clinical Psychology, 45,* 206–215.

Graham, J. R. (1990, August). Congruence between MMPI and MMPI-2 code types. *MMPI-2 News and Profiles,* pp. 1–2, 12.

Green, B. L., Aleser, G. C., Stone, W. N., & Siefert, R. F. (1975). Relationships among diverse measures of psychotherapy outcome. *Journal of Consulting and Clinical Psychology, 43,* 689–699.

Hamilton, E. W., & Abramson, L. Y. (1983). Cognitive patterns and major depressive disorders: A longitudinal study in a hospital setting. *Journal of Abnormal Psychology, 92,* 173–184.

Hamilton, M. (1960). A rating scale for depression. *Journal of Neurology, Neurosurgery and Psychiatry, 23,* 56–61.

Harrell, T. H., & Ryon, N. B. (1983). Cognitive behavioral assessment of depression: Clinical validation of the Automatic Thoughts Questionnaire. *Journal of Consulting and Clinical Psychology, 51,* 721–725.

Harris, R. E., & Lingoes, J. C. (1955). *Subscales for the MMPI: An aid to profile interpretations.* Unpublished manuscript, The Langley Porter Neuropsychiatric Institute.

Hathaway, S. R., & McKinley, J. C. (1951). *MMPI manual* (rev.). New York: The Psychological Corporation.

Heiby, E. M. (1986). Social versus self-control skills deficits in four cases of depression. *Behavior Therapy, 17,* 158–169.

Hersen, M., Eisler, R. M., Alford, G. S., & Agras, W. S. (1973). Effects of token economy on neurotic depression: An experimental analysis. *Behavioral Therapy, 4,* 392–397.

Highlen, P. S., & Hill, C. E. (1984). Factors affecting client change in individual counseling: Current status and theoretical speculations. In S. D. Brown and R. W. Lent (Eds.), *Handbook of counseling psychology,* New York: Wiley.

Hinchliffe, M., Lancashire, M., & Roberts, F. J. (1970). Eye contact and depression: A preliminary report. *British Journal of Psychiatry, 117,* 571–572.

Hinchliffe, M., Lancashire, M., & Roberts, F. J. (1971). Depression: Defense mechanisms in speech. *British Journal of Psychiatry, 118,* 471–472.

Hodgson, J. W. (1981). Cognitive versus behavioral–interpersonal approaches to the group treatment of depressed college students. *Journal of Counseling Psychology, 28,* 243–249.

Hollon, S. (1981). Comparisons and combinations with alternative approaches. In L. P. Rehm (Ed.), *Behavior therapy for depression.* New York: Academic Press.

Hollon, S. D., & Kendall, P. C. (1980). Cognitive self-statements in depression: Development of an automatic thoughts questionnaire. *Cognitive Therapy and Research, 4,* 383–397.

Hollon, S. D., Kendall, P. C., Lumry, A. (1986). Specificity of depressotypic cognitions in clinical depression. *Journal of Abnormal Psychology, 95,* 52–59.

Ivey, A. (1976). Counseling psychology, the psychoeducator model and the future. *The Counseling Psychologist, 6,* 72–75.

Kanfer, F. H. (1970). Self-monitoring: Methodological limitations and clinical applications. *Journal of Consulting and Clinical Psychology, 35,* 148–152.

Kanfer, F. H. (1971). The maintenance of behavior by self-generated stimuli and reinforcement. In A. Jacobs & L. B. Sachs (Eds.), *The psychology of private events. Perspectives on covert response systems.* New York: Academic Press.

Klerman, G. L., Rounsaville, B., Chevron, E., Neu, C., & Weissman, M. M. (1979). *Manual for short-term interpersonal psychotherapy (IPT) of depression.* Unpublished manuscript.

Knesevich, J. W., Biggs, J. T., Clayton, P. J., & Ziegler, V. E. (1977). Validity of the Hamilton Rating Scale for Depression. *British Journal of Psychiatry, 131,* 49–52.

Lewinsohn, P. M. (1974). A behavioral approach to depression. In R. J. Friedman & M. M. Katz (Eds.), *The psychology of depression: Contemporary theory and research,* Washington, DC: Winston.

Lewinsohn, P. M. (1976). Activity schedules in treatment of depression. In J. D. Krumboltz & C. E. Thoresen (Eds.), *Counseling methods.* New York: Holt, Rinehart and Winston.

Lewinsohn, P. M., & Amenson, C. (1978). Some relationships between pleasant and unpleasant mood related activities and depression. *Journal of Abnormal Psychology, 87,* 644–654.

Lewinsohn, P. M., Weinstein, M. S., & Alper, T. (1970). A behavioral approach to the group treatment of depressed persons: Methodological contribution. *Journal of Clinical Psychology, 26,* 525–532.

Libet, J., & Lewinsohn, P. M. (1973). The concept of social skill with special reference to the behavior of depressed persons. *Journal of Consulting and Clinical Psychology, 40,* 304–312.

Libet, J., Lewinsohn, P. M., & Javorek, F. (1973). *The construct of social skill: An empirical study of several measures on temporal stability, internal structure, validity, and structural generalizability.* Unpublished manuscript, University of Oregon, Eugene, OR.

Lubin, B. (1965). Adjectives check lists for measurement of depression. *Archieves of General Psychiatry, 12,* 57–62.

MacPhillamy, D. J., & Lewinsohn, P. M. (1972). *The measurement of reinforcing events.* Paper presented at the 80th Annual Convention of the APA, Honolulu, HI.

MacPhillamy, D. J., & Lewinsohn, P. M. (1974). Depression as a function of levels of desired and obtained pleasure. *Journal of Abnormal Psychology, 83,* 651–657.

MacPhillamy, D. J., & Lewinsohn, P. M. (1976). *Manual for the Pleasant Events Schedule.* Unpublished manuscript, University of Oregon, Eugene, OR.

McLean, P. D., Ogston, K., & Grauer, L. (1973). A behavioral approach to the treatment of depression. *Journal of Behavior Therapy and Experimental Psychiatry, 4,* 323–330.

McNamara, K., & Horan, J. J. (1986). Experimental construct validity in the evaluation of cognitive and behavioral treatments for depression. *Journal of Counseling Psychology, 33,* 23–30.

Miller, I. W., Klee, S. H., & Norman, W. H. (1982). Depressed and nondepressed inpatients' cognitions of hypothetical events, experimental tasks, and stressful life events. *Journal of Abnormal Psychology, 91,* 78–81.

Miller, W. R., & Seligman, M. E. P. (1973). Depression and the perception of reinforcement. *Journal of Abnormal Psychology, 82,* 62–73.

Morrill, W. H., Oetting, E. R., & Hurst, J. C. (1974). Dimensions of counselor functioning. *Personal and Guidance Journal, 56,* 354–356.

Meyers, J. K., Weissman, M. M., Tischler, G. L., Holzer, C. E., Leat, P. J., Orvaschel, H., Anthony, J. C., Boyd, J. H. Burke, J. D., Kramer, M., & Stoltzman, R. (1984). Six-month prevalence of psychiatric disorders in three communities. *Archives of General Psychiatry, 41,* 959–970.

Oliver, J. M., & Baumgart, E. P. (1985). The Dysfunctional Attitudes Scale: Psychometric properties and relation to depression in an unselected adult population. *Cognitive Therapy and Research, 9,* 161–167.

Osipow, S. H. J., Cohen, W., Jenkins, J., Dostal, J. (1979). Clinical versus counseling psychology: Is there a real difference? *Professional Psychology, 10,* 149–153.

Persons, J. B., & Rao, P. A. (1985). Longitudinal studies of cognitions, life events, and depression in psychiatric inpatients. *Journal of Abnormal Psychology, 94,* 51–63.

Peterson, C., Semmel, A., von Baeyer, C., Abramson, L. Y., Metalsky, G. E., & Seligman, M. E. P. (1982). The Attributional Style Questionnaire. *Cognitive Therapy and Research, 6,* 287–299.

Radloff, L. S. (1977). The CES-D Scale: A self-report depression scale for research in the general population. *Applied Psychological Measurement, 1,* 385–401.

Regier, D. A., Meyers, J. K., Kramer, M., Robins, L. N., Blazer, D. G., Haugh, R. L., Eaton, W. W., & Locke, B. Z. (1984). The NIMH epidemiologic catchment area program. *Archives of General Psychiatry, 41,* 934–941.

Rehm, L. (1976). Assessment of depression. In M. Hersen & A. S. Bellack (Eds.), *Behavioral assessment: A practical handbook.* New York: Pergamon Press.

Rehm, L. P. (1977). A self-control model of depression. *Behavior Therapy, 8,* 787–804.

Rehm, L. P. (1987). The measurement of behavioral aspects of depression. In A. J. Marsella, R. Hirschfeld, & M. Katz (Eds.), *The measurement of depression: Clinical, biological, psychological and psychosocial perspectives.* New York: Guilford Press.

Rehm, L. P., Fuchs, C. Z., Roth, D. M., Kornblith, S. J., & Romano, J. (1979). A comparison of self-control and social skill treatments of depression. *Behavior Therapy, 10,* 429–442.

Rehm, L. P., Kaslow, N. J., & Rabin, A. S. (1987). Cognitive and behavioral targets in a self-control therapy program for depression. *Journal of Consulting and Clinical Psychology, 55,* 60–67.

Rehm, L. P., Kornblith, S. J., O'Hara, M. W., Lamparski, D. M., Romano, J. M., & Volkin, J. (1981). An evaluation of major elements in a self-control therapy program for depression. *Behavior Modification, 5,* 459–490.

Rehm, L. P., & O'Hara, M. W. (1985). Item characteristics of the Hamilton Rating Scale for Depression. *Journal of Psychiatric Research, 19,* 31–41.

Robins, L. N., Helzer, J. E., Crougham, J., & Ratliff, K. (1981). National Institute of Mental Health diagnostic interview schedule. *Archives of General Psychiatry, 38,* 381–389.

Ross, S. M., Gottfredson, D. K., Christensen, P., & Weaver, R. (1986). Cognitive self-statements in depression: Findings across clinical populations. *Cognitive Therapy and Research, 10,* 159–165.

Rude, S. (1986). Relative benefits of assertion or cognitive self-control treatment for depression as a function of proficiency in each domain. *Journal of Consulting and Clinical Psychology, 54,* 390–394.

Rush, A. J. (1982). *Short-term psychotherapies for depression.* New York: Guilford Press.

Rush, A. J., Weissenberger, J., & Eaves, G. (1986). Do thinking patterns predict depressive symptoms? *Cognitive Therapy and Research, 10,* 225–235.

Schwab, J. J., Blalow, M. R., & Holzer, C. E. (1976). A comparison of two rating scales for depression. *Journal of Clinical Psychology, 23,* 94–96.

Seligman, M. E. P., Abramson, L. Y., Semmel, A., & Von Baeyer, C. (1979). Depressive attributional style. *Journal of Abnormal Psychology, 88,* 242–247.

Shaw, B. F. (1977). Comparison of cognitive therapy and behavior therapy in the treatment of depression. *Journal of Consulting and Clinical Psychology, 4,* 543–551.

Simons, A. D., Garfield, S. L., & Murphy, G. E. (1984). The process of change in cognitive therapy and pharmacotherapy for depression. *Archives of General Psychiatry, 41,* 45–51.

Spitzer, R. L., Endicott, J., & Robins, E. (1975). Research diagnostic criteria. *Psychopharmacologia Bulletin, 11,* 22–25.

Spitzer, R. L., Endicott, J., & Robins, E. (1978). Research diagnostic criteria: Rationale and reliability. *Archives of General Psychiatry, 36,* 773–782.

Strupp, H. H., Sandell, J. A., Waterhouse, G. J., O'Malley, S. S., & Anderson, J. L. (1982). Psychodynamic therapy: Theory and research. In A. J. Rush (Ed.), *Short-term psychotherapies for depression.* New York: Guilford Press.

Super, D. E. (1955). Transition: From vocational guidance to counseling psychology. *Journal of Counseling Psychology, 2,* 3–9.

Taylor, F. G., & Marshall, W. L. (1977). Experimental analysis of a cognitive-behavioral therapy for depression. *Cognitive Therapy and Research,* 59–72.

Thompson, L. W., Gallagher, D., & Breckenridge, J. S. (1987). Comparative effectiveness of psychotherapies for depressed elders. *Journal of Consulting & Clinical Psychology, 55,* 385–390.

Tyler, L. E. (1972). Reflections on counseling psychology. *The Counseling Psychologist, 3,* 6–11.

Weissman, A., & Beck, A. T. (1978, November). *Development and validation of the Dysfunctional Attitude Scale (DAS).* Paper presented at the 12th annual meeting of the Association for the Advancement of Behavior Therapy, Chicago, IL.

Weissman, M. M., Pottenger, M., Kleber, H., Ruben, H. L., Williams, D., & Thompson, W. (1977). Symptom patterns in primary and secondary depression. *Archives of General Psychiatry, 34,* 854–862.

Weissman, M. M., Prusoff, B. A., & Newberry, P. (1975). *Comparison of CES-D, Zung Self-Rating Depression Scale, and Beck Depression Inventory.* Progress Report, Yale University, New Haven, CT.

Weissman, M. M., Sholomskas, D., Pottenger, M., Prusoff, B. A., & Locke, B. Z. (1977). Assessing depressive symptoms in five psychiatric populations: A validation study. *American Journal of Epidemiology, 10b,* 203–214.

Williams, J. G., Barlow, D. H., & Agras, W. S. (1972). Behavioral measurement of severe depression. *Archives of General Psychiatry, 27,* 330–333.

Wilson, P. H., Goldin, J. C., & Charbonneau-Powis, M. (1983). Comparative efficacy of behavioral and cognitive treatments of depression. *Cognitive Therapy and Research, 7,* 111–124.

Wise, E. H., & Barnes, D. R. (1986). The relationship among life events, dysfunctional attitudes, and depression. *Cognitive Therapy and Research, 10,* 257–266.

Zaiden, J. (1982). Psychodynamic therapy: Clinical applications. In A. J. Rush (Ed.), *Short-term psychotherapies for depression.* New York: Guilford Press.

Zeiss, A. M., Lewinsohn, P. M., & Munoz, R. F. (1979). Nonspecific improvement effects in depression using interpersonal, cognitive, and pleasant events focused treatments. *Journal of Consulting and Clinical Psychology, 47,* 427–439.

Zung, W. K. (1965). A self-rating depression scale. *Archives of General Psychiatry, 13,* 508–516.

CHAPTER 22
COUNSELING FOR ANXIETY MANAGEMENT

JERRY L. DEFFENBACHER

Anxiety is a ubiquitous experience. Humans are neurologically "hard wired" to experience anxiety and express it through primitive survival strategies of the "fight–flight–freeze–faint" reactions (Beck & Emery, 1985). These mechanisms developed for coping with physically threatening environments and may still have adaptive value in confronting real or potential physical dangers (e.g., lowered blood pressure, after an injury, can prevent extensive bleeding; autonomic arousal mobilizes escape). These once adaptive mechanisms, however, often go awry in our complex psychosocial environments, and anxiety may become attached to innocuous or minimally threatening events.

The costs of such maladaptive anxiety are quite high. At low levels, anxiety may be motivating and attention-focusing; at higher levels, it may become debilitating. The personal and social costs of a housebound agoraphobic are obvious, but the costs of less severe anxiety reactions are also high. For example, test anxiety can interfere with classroom and aptitude test performance (e.g., Deffenbacher, 1977a, 1986; Sarason, 1972), cause lower self-esteem, contribute to academic dropout, and limit educational and vocational development. Speech anxiety contributes to lower grades and higher dropout (Paul, 1968) and to restricted vocational choice (Daly & McCroskey, 1975). Fear of potential negative outcomes is one of the most frequent reasons given by cancer patients for not engaging in early diagnostic testing (Henderson, 1966), even for cancers such as breast cancer, where patients are competent in self-examination procedures (Magery, Todd, & Blizard, 1977). Estimates (which most likely are underestimates because they do not include surveys of subclinical anxieties) suggest that anxiety disorders are the most frequent type of psychiatric disorder, afflicting 8 to 15% of the U. S. population (National Institute of Mental Health, 1985). Anxiety, therefore, is a significant problem because it reaches levels that interfere with personal, social, educational, vocational, and/or health adjustment of large numbers of people.

The nature and reduction of interfering anxiety are the focus of this chapter. These are expansive topics, and numerous books and articles are devoted to them. This chapter is, therefore, necessarily broad in scope and surveys a number of issues related to the conceptualization, assessment, and treatment of anxiety. It begins by overviewing the nature of anxiety in terms of expression in three major response systems—affective-physiological, cognitive-perceptual, and somatic-behavioral. Next, a general, descriptive organization of anxiety concerns is presented. This is followed by an overview of assessment methodologies and a discussion of issues that should be assessed prior to selecting anxiety as the target of intervention. Major anxiety reduction strategies are then reviewed. Theory and procedures are briefly described, and a small number of outcome studies are summarized to reflect the effectiveness and range of application of interventions. One important type of intervention—use of psychotropic medications— is not reviewed, because of space limitations. Readers are referred to Taylor and Arnow (1988) for excellent coverage of common anxiolytic medications and their interface with counseling and psychotherapy. The chapter concludes with discussion of several issues that are important to both research and practice.

THE NATURE OF ANXIETY

In general, anxiety is an aversive emotional experience that motivates individuals to move away from, remove, or control the source of anxiety. It is marked by subjective feelings of tension and fear, increased physiological arousal, perceptions of danger and risk, decreased cognitive and behavioral performance, and/or avoidance and escape. Anxiety, however, does not involve a perfect synchrony in all aspects of experience. To the contrary, anxiety is an inference or conclusion based on information in three loosely correlated response domains—the affective-physiological, cognitive-perceptual, and somatic-behavioral (Beck & Emery, 1985; Deffenbacher & Suinn, 1982; Lang, Levin, Miller, & Kozak, 1983). Each domain may be subdivided further, suggesting that the basis for inferring that anxiety is present varies across people and within persons over time.

Affective-Physiological Response Domain

The affective-physiological domain may be involved in any of three ways. The individual may report subjective feelings of anxiety (e.g., tension, dread, fear, nervousness, edginess). He or she may experience heightened autonomic arousal. Many physical symptoms reflect sympathetic arousal of the "fight or flight" reaction (e.g., increased heart rate, rapid breathing, blushing). Sometimes overlooked is parasympathetic arousal involved in the "faint or freeze" reaction (Beck & Emery, 1985) (e.g., dizziness, feeling faint or weak, nausea, frequent urge to urinate). The individual may also experience an increase in or exacerbation of anxiety-related psychophysiological disorders (e.g., tension or migraine headaches, ulcerative gastrointestinal conditions, sleep onset insomnia), even though he or she may be unaware of heightened arousal.

Cognitive-Perceptual Response Domain

Anxiety may also be inferred from many cognitive and perceptual processes. For example, the person may report sensory-perceptual distortions of nonpsychotic proportions (e.g., feelings of unreality, objects appearing blurred or distant, the environment seeming somehow unusual). A related element is the spectator role: the person describes the situation as if he or she were an observer, rather than a participant in his or her own experience. In addition to being common experiences in panic and posttraumatic stress disorders, these distortions, particularly the spectator role, have been related to anxiety in sexual dysfunctions (Masters & Johnson, 1970), athletic performance (Mahoney & Avener, 1977), and test taking (Wine, 1980). Anxiety may also be reflected in attentional processes. For some individuals, attention does not seem under their control (e.g., dazed, unable to concentrate). Others report narrowed attention wherein they focus only on anxiety-arousing stimuli and are unable to shift attention to task-oriented cues (Beck & Emery, 1985; Sarason, 1972).

Anxious individuals are acutely sensitive and responsive to "danger" cues, whether objectively dangerous or not. The nature of danger depends heavily on the individual's vulnerabilities or what Beck and Emery (1985) called the vulnerability mode. For example, panicked (Rapee, Ancis, & Barlow, 1988), agoraphobic (McNalley & Lorenz, 1987), and posttraumatic stress disordered (McNalley et al., 1987) individuals are overly and selectively attentive to their physiological states. Socially anxious persons are very sensitive to feedback about their behavior and to possible negative evaluation by others (Beck & Emery, 1985). Danger cues may include one's own thoughts and urges (in obsessive-compulsive disorders) or one's worries (in generalized anxiety disorder). The nature of the vulnerability mode is fairly specific to each anxiety concern. For example, Hope, Rapee, Heimberg, and Dombeck (1990) found that social phobics were hypervigilant to social-evaluative, but not physical threat cues, whereas panic disordered individuals showed the reverse pattern.

Whatever the danger cues, anxious individuals have their perceptual-attentional processes tuned to real and potential harm, leading them to overperceive danger and, conversely, underperceive safety cues such as internal and external support, evidence of positive coping, and intrapersonal and environmental resources for threat prevention and coping (Barlow & Cerny, 1988; Beck & Emery, 1985). Having once overpredicted danger and experienced anxiety, anxious individuals are reluctant to risk being unprepared again and continue to overpredict threat and anxiety (Rachman & Bichard, 1988). Only after repeated disconfirmations of their anxiety do they adjust their expectations and reduce vigilance for their danger cues.

Cognitive performance and information processing (i.e., associations made to, interpretations made of, and operations performed on information) may reflect anxiety. For example, anxious individuals show greater difficulty in learning (e.g., Sarason, 1972) and memory encoding (Mueller, 1980). Memory decoding and retrieval may also reveal interference, such as when a speech-anxious individual forgets portions of a well-rehearsed speech. However, anxious individuals do not appear to show the mood-congruent recall bias (i.e., greater recall of anxiety-related, self-referent associations) so often seen in depression (Moog & Mathews, 1990). Cognitive performance may also be impaired. For example, test-anxious individuals perform more poorly under social-evaluative conditions (e.g., difficult, competitive, or timed tasks) than they do under less evaluative circumstances (Deffenbacher, 1978; Sarason, 1972). Anxious individuals may also reveal stereotypical, compulsive approaches to problem solving (i.e., the person perseverates on certain strategies to the exclusion of others, even though he or she demonstrates flexible problem solving under nontaxing circumstances). For example, test-anxious individuals performing under evaluative conditions on laboratory tasks (Deffenbacher, 1978; Deffenbacher & Hazaleus, 1985) and classroom exams (Deffenbacher, 1986) have difficulty leaving unsolved problems, terminating ineffective strategies, and moving efficiently through the task.

Information processing of anxious individuals also reflects a number of errors and distortions (Beck, 1976; Beck & Emery, 1985)—errors that are accepted as real and are maintained despite objective evidence to the contrary. For example, anxious individuals often catastrophize and dwell on possible disaster (Beck, 1976; Beck & Emery, 1985; Ellis, 1962); in some cases, they envision outcomes that go beyond any realistic worst-case scenario. Not all catastrophies are verbally mediated. Many anxious individuals experience catastrophic images, of which they are often unaware, as part of information processing (Beck & Emery, 1985; Beck, Laude, & Bohnert, 1974; Hibbert, 1984). These visual and somatic images (e.g., flashbacks to trauma; or an image of falling, in acrophobia) involve imminent harm and become part of the internal stimuli for arousal.

Anxious individuals also tend to make negative, inaccurate attributions and interpretations (Beck, 1976; Beck & Emery, 1985). Common cues are given idiosyncratic, dangerous meanings (e.g., heart palpitations mean a heart attack), and more probable, benign interpretations are overlooked.

Another characteristic of anxious thinking is its dichotomous nature, especially where danger is involved. Situations are coded as either safe or unsafe. Anxiety is often reflected in the individual's rigid personal and situational rules, assumptions, and beliefs, such as "I can't confront my fear" or "Panic means I am going crazy and will lose control." Beliefs and expectations about situations tend to guide approach behavior (Bandura, 1977), and assumptions made by anxious persons tend to be absolutistic (Beck, 1976; Ellis, 1962; Zwemer & Deffenbacher, 1984). Such assumptions increase the sense of danger because they carry an implied catastrophe, enhance preoccupation with real or potential negative events, and undercut coping and self-efficacy.

Cognitive processes may also reflect avoidant, escapist, and defensive maneuvers suggestive of anxiety. A common example of cognitive avoidance is distraction: the individual engages in activities that keep attention away from threatening topics. Some individuals consciously distract themselves; others immerse themselves in cognitively demanding activities in order to avoid thinking about or dealing with threat. When threatened, they may also engage in cognitive escape. Cognitive rituals in obsessive-compulsives are clear examples of this escape, but rituals are often found in other anxiety disorders (e.g., panicked individuals and social phobics often employ cognitive routines when they experience arousal and danger cues). Worry may serve as a cognitive avoidance or escape function in that, at least temporarily, it narrows the stimulus field, thereby reducing the range of threat cues, offering a sense of control over the situation (Deffenbacher & Suinn, 1987), and bypassing the experience of anxiety imagery (Borkovec & Inz, 1990). Many defense mechanisms (e.g., denial, intellectualization, rationalization) are cognitive strategies that help to avoid, escape, or partially neutralize internal or external threat.

Somatic-Behavioral Response Domain

The somatic-behavioral domain (i.e., voluntary musculature and overt behavior) also contains many indexes of anxiety. For example, the person may experience heightened muscle tension (e.g., general tension; specific areas of tension, such as the neck; muscle cramping; bruxism). Muscle tension may reach levels that directly interfere with performance (e.g., speech dysfluencies). In other cases, the source of anxiety interference is not clear, but deterioration of behavior (e.g., a skilled performer missing well-rehearsed moves) is noted. Whatever the source, overt behavior provides one of the most obvious means for inferring that anxiety is present.

As with cognitive performance, overt behavior may also show behavioral constriction, rigidity, and compulsivity; that is, the individual behaves repetitively in rigid and stereotypical ways, even though feedback suggests that the behavior is ineffective. Attempts to interrupt this behavior often only increase tension and the felt need to perform the behavior. Compulsive rituals are perhaps the clearest example; however, lower-level compulsivity and rigidity are seen in many anxiety problems. Anxiety may also be inferred from off-task behavior (i.e., not task-centered), which may represent direct or implicit attempts to escape or to cope, albeit ineffectively. For example, test-anxious students spend more time glancing away from evaluative tasks (Nottleman & Hill, 1977) and engaging in off-task behavior (looking at the clock or around the room) (Deffenbacher, 1978, 1986) than do nonanxious students.

Avoidance and escape are hallmarks of many anxiety problems. An individual may work to prevent contact with a situation (avoid) or to remove himself or herself (escape). Avoidance and escape can be highly active (e.g., the person physically moves away) or more passive (e.g., a shy individual does not maintain eye contact). Regardless of form, such behaviors are designed to remove or reduce exposure to threatening stimuli. Phobias are perhaps the clearest example of avoidance and escape, but many subtle or less obvious avoidance and escape behaviors are involved in other anxiety disorders.

AN ORGANIZATION OF ANXIETY CONCERNS

Anxiety problems can be understood and classified, in part, by the response domains involved and their intensity at the moment and over time. A further element needed to describe anxiety is the source of the anxiety reactions. In some cases, relatively clear external events, current or past, elicit anxiety; in others, anxiety stems more from within the individual (e.g., in response to thoughts, memories, images, and physiological arousal), giving the appearance that anxiety is unprovoked. These elements are combined in this discussion, to organize client anxiety concerns, and reference is made to DSM-III-R (American Psychiatric Association, 1987) anxiety disorders. Less extreme examples are also described, because they are frequent client problems seen by counseling psychologists.

Short-Term Anxiety in Response to Identifiable Stressors

Many people experience anxiety when facing difficult transitory situations, decisions, or life tasks. Anxiety may also occur in response to unusual or traumatic stressors such as being a victim of violence or disaster. If the intensity of the anxiety in response to external stressors or the degree of interference with functioning is more than that experienced by the average individual, the person may be judged as experiencing an adjustment disorder with anxious mood. If anxiety is mixed with other emotions such as anger or depression, adjustment disorder with mixed emotional features is appropriate. If anxiety is even more intense or is severely debilitating, the person may be judged as experiencing acute posttraumatic stress disorder (PTSD).

Long-Term Anxiety in Response to Identifiable Stressors

Mild anxiety may persist for some time after trauma, without the degree of arousal or interference becoming intrusive. However, if significant anxiety persists for long periods of time, chronic PTSD is probable. This form of PTSD is marked by: (a) reexperiencing the trauma through intrusive memories, dreams, feelings of trauma reenactment, and/or distress when confronted with cues of the trauma; (b) avoidance of thoughts, situations, and memories of the trauma and/or general numbing of responsiveness, reflected in decreased interest in significant activities, feelings of estrangement or detachment, restricted range of affect, and/or a sense of foreshortened future; and (c) persistent symptoms of arousal (American Psychiatric Association, 1987).

Chronic PTSD typically refers to chronic anxiety experienced in relation to a definable trauma. But what of significant lingering anxiety stemming from failure to resolve developmental tasks? For example, counseling psychologists often see individuals who suffer chronic anxiety and indecision concerning careers, are anxious about separating from family of origin, or are chronically anxious from failure to find meaning in life. These are individuals for whom there is often no clear DSM-III-R diagnosis. Might they be considered to suffer chronic PTSD, which is milder in intensity and in which the traumatic event is one or more failed developmental tasks? Experiences seem parallel. They often show: (a) a worrisome and conflictual preoccupation with the developmental content, and considerable distress when confronted with cues of unresolved developmental issues; (b) avoidance of and indecision about developmental tasks, and/or numbing of responsiveness reflected in feelings of detachment, estrangement, and restricted affect; and (c) persistent mild symptoms of arousal. Although these thoughts are speculative, they are an example of the reconceptualization of anxieties frequently seen in counseling. Such reconceptualization may bring research paradigms from other areas to aid our understanding of these anxieties and may facilitate application of alternative strategies to them.

Social-Evaluative Anxieties

For some individuals, real or potential evaluation elicits significant emotional and physiological arousal and significant impairment of cognitive and behavioral performance. Although multiple response domains are involved, social-evaluative anxieties show distinctive cognitive involvement (Beck & Emery, 1985; Buss, 1980; Schlenker & Leary, 1982). Specifically, social-evaluatively anxious individuals are preoccupied with what others may think of them. They selectively attend to and interpret cues of real or potential negative evaluation and believe that their behavior or other characteristics could lead to rejection, humiliation, or embarrassment. They catastrophize the importance of evaluation, employ unrealistic performance standards, and make negative attributions and interpretations in social interactions. Heightened arousal and avoidance of evaluative situations follow from these cognitive dimensions.

If severe, these characteristics form a social phobia (i.e., persistent, irrational fear of and desire to avoid one or more situations in which the person may be evaluated, such as a public speaking engagement), but many people suffer from subclinical social-evaluative anxieties as well. The situational range of some social phobias is relatively circumscribed, involving one or two contexts. For others, the problem is pervasive and diffuse, with the individual being generally timid and shy and virtually needing to be guaranteed of social acceptance.

Other Situational Anxieties

This residual group of situational anxieties does not stem from social evaluation or agoraphobia. Many people become somewhat anxious, but endure certain situations such as driving, heights, or dental visits. Others become very emotionally and physiologically aroused when confronted with such situations, and actively avoid or escape them if possible, thus meeting DSM-III-R criteria for simple phobias.

Worrying and Chronic Anxiety

Problem solving (i.e., defining the source of threat, generating and evaluating possible response options, implementing and evaluating effective solutions) can be very adaptive in dealing with threatening stimuli. Worry resembles problem solving that is fixed at the problem identification stage (Borkovec, 1985); that is, worry involves cognitively turning over negative events and outcomes and asking serial what-if questions without following through to the development, implementation, and evaluation of quality plans. Nearly everybody worries on occasion, but some people are chronic worriers. They spend unusual amounts of mental activity processing real and possible negative outcomes, with their worries often becoming more and more unrealistic and improbable. The heightened sense of danger elicits chronic, moderate tension. Such processes may reach levels sufficient for generalized anxiety disorder (GAD) (i.e., worrying unrealistically about two or more life circumstances and experiencing six or more signs of motor tension, autonomic arousal, or vigilance and scanning).

Although significant emotional-physiological involvement is present, cognitive aspects predominate in GAD (Beck & Emery, 1985; Deffenbacher & Suinn, 1987; Taylor & Arnow, 1988). For example, intrusive, seemingly credible, negative thoughts precede arousal in GAD, whereas attention to physical feelings tends to precipitate panic (Hibbert, 1984). Verbal thought processes rather than imagery processes seem to predominate in GAD (Borkovec & Inz, 1990). Further, the process of worrying may, at least momentarily, lower arousal by interrupting information processing (Borkovec & Hu, 1990), allowing cognitive avoidance of anxiety imagery (Borkovec & Inz, 1990), functioning as a mental ritual, or enabling partial problem solving, which returns a sense of control (Deffenbacher & Suinn, 1987).

Obsessions and Compulsions

Occasionally, nearly everyone experiences unwanted negative thoughts and engages in ritualistic behavior. For some individuals, the frequency and negativity (e.g., fears of contamination, harm to others, sexually unthinkable acts) of the thoughts (obsessions) lead to ritualized behaviors (compulsions) that partially neutralize the content of the obsession. The obsessive-compulsive is cognitively preoccupied with dangerous thoughts, images, urges, and fears, and the cognitive processes in obsessive-compulsive disorder (OCD) reflect dramatic overestimations of dangerous or unpleasant outcomes, rigidity, perfectionism, doubting, and an inordinate need for control (Carr, 1974; McFall & Wollersheim, 1979; Steketee & Foa, 1985). Performance of the compulsion lowers tension, avoids or escapes negative mental events, and/or provides "safety signals" that return a sense of control (Emmelkamp, 1987; Steketee & Foa, 1985).

Panic and Its Consequences

Some individuals have relatively frequent, intense anxiety attacks. If the person experiences at least four intense physiological or cognitive symptoms at least four times in a 4-week period or has an intense fear of such attacks, a DSM-III-R panic disorder diagnosis is warranted. Phenomologically, panic seems to strike without warning. However, investigations (Barlow & Cerny, 1988; Beck et al., 1974; Hibbert, 1984) suggest that panic-disordered individuals are very sensitive to and make catastrophic interpretations of their physiological arousal and/or have vivid, catastrophic images preceding panic. Panic is an intensely aversive experience, and many individuals quickly develop a "fear of fear" (i.e., a fear of experiencing the intense somatic component of panics) (Barlow & Cerny, 1988; Goldstein & Chambless, 1978). Panic also is perceived as unavoidable. Some individuals, however, come to believe that if they could stay in "safe" places and avoid situations that elicit arousal, then they could avoid or reduce the probability of panic. This is what happens to individuals who develop agoraphobia. Home becomes a safe place, and they leave only when they can take safety with them in the form of reliable others who can take care of them in the event of a panic or other calamity.

This section, in outlining a descriptive organization of anxiety concerns, has suggested that anxiety problems can be organized by: (a) the dominant response domains involved; (b) the intensity and patterning of response involvement; and (c) the internal and external events that trigger anxiety. These are primary dimensions that counselors need to assess, in order to understand and conceptualize clients' anxieties and to develop effective interventions.

ASSESSMENT OF ANXIETY

Counselors need a quality information base from which to draw conclusions about which domains are most involved in anxiety and how they link together. This is the enterprise of assessment. Assessment is not a formal, static task; it is a dynamic, continuous process unfolding over time. New information leads to probes for more data, and intervention successes and failures provide more information, each potentially altering conceptualization. Some commonly employed assessment strategies for anxiety are described in this section.

Interviewing

Interviewing is a most basic means of acquiring information. A style of open-ended, thematic interviewing can be highly facilitative. The counselor begins the interview with an open-ended inquiry, allowing the client to describe anxiety in his or her own words. As the client describes the relevant experience, the counselor uses affect and content reflections and summaries to communicate and check understanding. This is followed by additional open-ended inquiries that explore the area more or shift to another dimension, still in the client's own words. The process is thematic in that the counselor systematically explores major themes and response domains. Using this interview style, the counselor also solicits concrete examples and follows them sequentially, to clarify general themes and provide richer detail. These processes are recycled until a clear picture of the client's anxiety is developed.

Interviews need not always be with the client. Although confidentiality and informed consent must be addressed, interviews with significant others may provide relevant information. Others may describe situational triggers and patterns of behavior or coping assets of which the client is unaware.

Thematic, open-ended interviews can be supplemented and expanded by structured interviews using a series of questions designed to explore possible anxiety disorders. When key questions indicate anxiety, this area is explored in more depth through a series of follow-up questions. One of the most extensive and reliable structured interview formats is the Anxiety Disorders Interview Schedule—Revised (ADIS-R; DiNardo, O'Brien, Barlow, Waddell, & Blanchard, 1983). The ADIS-R is linked conceptually to anxiety disorders in DSM-III-R, and each anxiety disorder has one or more key questions related to it. If key questions are answered affirmatively, then the interviewer pursues a series of structured, sequential, often closed-ended (e.g., presence or absence of symptom) or rating (e.g., symptom intensity ratings) type questions.

Self-Report Inventories

The number of self-report anxiety inventories is voluminous, preventing a comprehensive review; the interested reader may therefore wish to consult standard test reviews as well as reviews in articles, books, and chapters on particular types of anxiety.

Anxiety inventories can be employed to: (a) provide a quick screening of range and intensity of anxiety concerns, potentially identifying anxiety issues not previously covered; (b) understand client anxiety normatively by comparison to group data; (c) understand anxiety idiographically by exploring individual items and response patterns and by using items as stimuli for further inquiry; and (d) aid in case conceptualization when questionnaire data are integrated with other information.

Some scales—for example, anxiety scales from the MMPI-2 (Butcher, Dahlstrom, Graham, Tellegren, & Kaemmer, 1989) or the Trait Anxiety Inventory (Spielberger, Gorsuch, & Lushene, 1970)—provide information on general anxiety level. Others, such as the Fear Inventory (Wolpe, 1982) and Fear Questionnaire (Marks & Mathews, 1979), list many potentially anxiety-provoking situations and provide a quick screening device. Additionally, factor-analytic studies have generated meaningful subscales (e.g., agoraphobia, blood-injury, and social anxiety subscales of the Fear Questionnaire) for some of these inventories. Other scales are situation-specific, assessing anxiety in specific contexts. For example, there are reliable scales for test anxiety (Sarason, 1972), speech anxiety (Paul, 1966), fear of negative evaluation (Watson & Friend, 1969), and dental fear (Kleinknecht & Bernstein, 1978).

Anxiety response domain assessment has also received attention in self-report inventories. For example, the Cognitive-Somatic Anxiety Questionnaire (Schwartz, Davidson, & Goleman, 1978) separates general emotional-physiological and cognitive response tendencies, and the Anxiety Symptom Questionnaire (Lehrer & Woolfolk, 1982) measures these two domains as well as behavioral avoidance tendencies. Other scales assess response dimensions in specific anxiety-arousing situations. For example, the Social Interaction Self-Statement Test (Glass, Merluzzi, Biever, & Larsen, 1982) assesses cognitive elements of heterosocial anxiety; the Test Anxiety Inventory (Spielberger, 1980) measures emotional and cognitive elements of test anxiety; and the Body Sensations and Agoraphobic Cognitions Questionnaire (Chambless, Caputo, Bright, & Gallagher, 1984) includes emotional-physiological and cognitive elements of agoraphobia.

Self-Monitoring (SM)

Having clients track anxiety in the natural environment is an excellent way of supplementing other sources of information. Self-monitoring (SM) provides a concrete, current data base and helps to increase the client's awareness of his or her experience.

SM is based on client cooperation and compliance; noncompliance compromises the reliability of SM data. Several procedures enhance compliance with SM (Barlow, Hayes, & Nelson, 1984; Meichenbaum & Turk, 1987). First, SM is best when it emerges collaboratively, rather than directively from the counselor (Meichenbaum & Deffenbacher, 1988); that is, if the counselor assists the client in suggesting and developing SM, compliance and involvement increase. Further, it is suggested that the counselor and client collaboratively develop recording systems on the spot, rather than having them pulled from the counselor's desk. Second, SM should begin with simple tasks (Deffenbacher, 1981). Because SM is an unusual activity for most clients, SM complexity increases confusion about what is to be done and generates an onerous feeling, both of which increase noncompliance. Adding SM behaviors over time decreases these problems. Third, it is important to review and discuss SM. Review provides the opportunity for detailed, corrective feedback on the completeness and accuracy of SM; for addressing problems; and for positive support of SM and its relevance to treatment. Fourth, where feasible, counselors can review SM prior to the session. This communicates that the counselor does his or her homework, and enhances an active, collaborative working alliance. Finally, SM methods should be tailored to the client's specific concerns. Logs and notebooks are common, excellent methods; however, particular clients may profit from other SM methods (e.g., a client who worries incessantly might carry a tape recorder and dictate thoughts as they are happening).

Simulation and In Vivo Enactment

Clients may be asked to approach anxiety-arousing situations in real life or simulations (e.g., an agoraphobic might be asked to go to a local market and return with a loaf of bread). The client may go alone, or the counselor may accompany him or her. The client completes as much of the task as possible, and various response dimensions (e.g., approach behavior, self-efficacy predictions, physiological arousal) may be noted. This type of assessment can also be facilitated by structured recall procedures. For example, a speech-anxious client might be videotaped giving a speech. The tape can be replayed and stopped at different places to allow the client to describe thoughts, feelings, urges, and other experiences. Although there may be distortion in recall, detailed cross-sectional slices of experience can be gained from a complex sequence of experience.

The counseling interview itself may be a kind of enactment process; client anxieties may manifest themselves during an interview that has not been structured formally to have that result. For example, the counselor may notice that a client blushes (physiological) and stutters (behavioral) when approaching a topic and then appears to intellectualize (cognitive defense) about it. Such observations provide information and hypotheses about the nature and extent of anxiety.

Imagery Recall

Some anxiety-arousing situations are difficult to arrange in vivo. For example, the situation may not be current (PTSD), may be prohibited for ethical reasons (sexual activities), or may present other logistical difficulties. However, if the client has experienced the situation, then imagery may be used to facilitate recall. For example, the counselor might ask the client to close his or her eyes and recall the event. The structure of the recall may vary considerably. For example, the client may remain quiet throughout the visualization and then describe experiences afterward, or the client may visualize segments of the experience, stopping between segments for counselor inquiry. Although there may be some distortion in recall and some potential for cognitive avoidance of anxiety-arousing material, imagery recall can be of assistance in exploring material that might otherwise be difficult to assess.

Physiological Recording

Physiological recording can clarify autonomic and somatic arousal. Repeated measurement of arousal at resting-level periods provides baseline information and an estimation of chronic physiological tension. Physiological recording can be combined with in vivo enactment or imagery recall procedures. For example, veterans with PTSD may recall images of combat experience while being monitored physiologically. Clients also can employ some physiological recording on an SM basis (e.g., an individual with GAD may use portable units to record finger temperature or blood pressure, when worrying or feeling tense). Although access to sophisticated recording equipment may be difficult for many counselors, relatively low-cost equipment for heart rate, blood pressure, and skin temperature assessment is now available.

Archival Data

Naturally occurring records provide an often overlooked source of data. These records are as variable as clients, but counselors should inquire about them. For example, exams of test-anxious individuals might be acquired and explored for signs of anxiety and test-taking strategies. Dentists, doctors, or school personnel may have recorded observations that are relevant. Clients sometimes have relevant diaries or letters that describe their experiences, or occasionally, home movies of relevant events.

In summary, potential sources of assessment data are quite varied. Assessment ideally should be tailored to the client's concerns and should involve ongoing, multidomain indexes that employ a variety of strategies to map the nature and interrelationship among anxiety components. However, a number of other issues also should receive assessment attention, prior to intervention.

Assessment of Anxiety Mimics, Consequences, and Correlates

A variety of issues may contribute to anxiety or may be intertwined with anxiety, thereby influencing conceptualization and intervention design. Thorough assessment may profitably address issues such as the following.

Does apparent anxiety stem from a biological cause? What appear as anxiety symptoms may actually be physical symptoms of diseases that mimic anxiety. For example, shortness of breath might be due to asthma or cardiovascular problems; heart palpitations or elevated heart rate might stem from a prolapsed mitral valve. Side effects of prescription or nonprescription drugs, such as aspirin, caffeine, and nicotine, can also mimic or exacerbate anxiety responses. When anxiety is already present, medical conditions and drugs may exacerbate it. It is valuable for clients to have a thorough medical evaluation, to rule out the more common possibilities. It is also useful for counselors to assess prescription and nonprescription drugs for possible self-medication, anxiety-simulating side effects, and anxiety symptoms due to withdrawal.

Is anxiety a result of another problem? Anxiety may be a natural outcome of other problems such as marital friction, financial strain, or decisions such as choosing a college major. Additionally, anxiety may stem from information and skill deficits such as poor study and test-taking skills. Anxiety, although very real, is secondary to these stressful situations or skill deficits, and interventions aimed at resolving those issues will typically dissipate the anxiety. Anxiety reduction interventions may still be relevant, but they become ancillary to interventions designed to alleviate the primary problem.

Is anxiety a covariate or part of another problem? Anxiety may stand alone or be mixed with other psychological difficulties. Alcohol and drug abuse is a common example. Alcohol and other drugs have anxiolytic properties, and clients may abuse them to self-medicate or may have drug abuse as a coexisting problem. For example, alcohol abuse and dependence are significant problems for social phobics (Munjack & Moss, 1981; Mullaney & Trippett, 1979; Taylor & Arnow, 1988). Depression is another common covarying problem (American Psychiatric Association, 1987). Depression, and its relationship to anxiety, needs careful assessment to judge suicide risk and design treatment. Additionally, in severe anxiety disorders such as panic attacks, agoraphobia, OCD, and PTSD, depression may deepen over the course of intervention (Barlow & Cerny, 1988; Taylor & Arnow, 1988), requiring monitoring of depression and possible switch of intervention format. Anger is another potential covarying problem. High-anger clients were found to be generally anxious (Deffenbacher, Demm, & Brandon, 1986; Hazaleus & Deffenbacher, 1986), suggesting that some generally anxious clients are also highly angry. Psychosis is also associated with anxiety. Anxiety is a common symptom of schizophrenia generally and is part of the prodromal and active psychotic phases in particular. Hence, it is important to assess current functioning and client and family history of psychotic problems. A final example is that of personality disorders. For example, agoraphobia is associated with personality disorders, especially avoidant and dependent types (Mavissakalian & Hamann, 1986).

In summary, even though anxiety is manifest, it may be secondary to other problems or may result from a biological process. Careful assessment of such possibilities is required, to determine whether anxiety reduction strategies are indicated. Other problems may need to be the prime focus of intervention or to be taken into account in planning and implementing anxiety intervention.

INTERVENTION FOR ANXIETY REDUCTION

Theoretically, at least, interventions address some response elements of anxiety over others. Although an intervention may target one area, it may be effective for other reasons, or its effects may be mediated through or interact with other response channels. With this caveat in mind, interventions are outlined here in terms of theoretical targets of intervention.

Environmental Change Interventions

If certain situations elicit anxiety, then anxiety could be lowered if anxiety-arousing stimuli were removed or reduced (i.e., the environment is made less threatening).

Consultation and Environmental Redesign

A widely recommended role for counseling psychologists is that of consultant and environmental redesigner (Huebner & Corazzini, 1984). In this role, counselors survey users of an environment and identify anxiety-arousing situations and populations at risk. Having located sources contributing to anxiety, they offer consultation to influence that environment. Plans for environmental redesign are developed, implemented, and evaluated. This process is recycled until anxiety is reduced or eliminated. Then, plans are made for maintenance of environmental change and/or follow-up programming.

Consultation and environmental redesign can have positive effects (Daher, Corazzini, & McKinnon, 1977). Some limitations, however, may exist when applying this strategy to anxiety reduction (Deffenbacher, 1977b). First, some sources of anxiety (e.g., traumatic imagery and exaggerated performance demands) exist primarily within the individual, not the environment. Redesigning the environment may do little to reduce anxiety because the remedy misses the internal source. Second, if the environment has meaningful, potentially negative consequences connected to it (e.g., placement based on an entrance test), it may be very difficult to reduce significantly its anxiety-arousing capacity. Third, there is no guarantee of transfer of anxiety reduction effects. Redesigning one environment does not ensure that similar environments will also change or that individuals will be able to carry over effects into other anxiety-arousing situations. Finally, there may be unexpected side effects of redesign. Reducing anxiety for some persons may inadvertently increase anxiety or other adverse consequences for others. For example, some environmental conditions that enhance the performance of highly test-anxious students may lower the performance of less test-anxious students (e.g., Sarason, 1972).

Stimulus Control

At an individual level, anxiety might be controlled if the individual removes or avoids anxiety-arousing stimuli. However, this is not feasible in many cases, and avoidance is often part of the problem (i.e., the person is already avoiding important situations).

At first glance, stimulus control strategies appear to have little relevance to anxiety reduction. Borkovec (Borkovec, Robinson, Pruzinsky, & DePree, 1983; Borkovec, Wilkinson, Folensbee, & Lerman, 1983), however, described an intriguing application. He suggested that worry is a poorly controlled habit with many internal and external factors triggering it. Consequently, worry may be pervasive and chronic (i.e., worry is under poor stimulus control). Worrying clients might, therefore, reduce worry and associated tension if they delayed worry until a specific time and place (i.e., brought worry under tighter stimulus control).

Clients who reported worry as a personal problem and who reported worrying 50% of the day were trained in a four-step, stimulus control intervention in a 1-hour group session. First, they established a daily half-hour worry period at the same time and place. Second, they identified and monitored negative worry thoughts and discriminated these from pleasant and task-relevant thoughts. Third, when they became aware of worry, they were to postpone the worry until the appointed time and to redirect attention to the task at hand. Fourth, during the worry period, they were to worry intensely about their negative thoughts and engage in problem solving to eliminate worrisome issues. After 4 weeks, stimulus control subjects reported less time worrying and reduced levels of unrealistic worry, compared to control subjects.

In a second study, stimulus control was modified by dropping instructions for problem solving and by having individuals worry either (a) mentally or (b) in writing. Subjects in both stimulus control conditions reduced worry and general tension more than controls and did not differ from one another. In a third study, these two conditions were compared to a relaxation placebo. At posttreatment and 6-month follow-up, stimulus control subjects reported less worry than relaxation subjects, even though the relaxation condition was credible and promoted positive treatment expectations.

Although the mechanisms of change are unclear in these studies, chronic worriers lessened their tendencies to ruminate negatively and, in some cases, their general tension as well. These findings suggest that stimulus control may be applicable to chronic worry and tension, GAD, and ruminative processes in pervasive social phobias and OCD. It may be useful for practitioners and researchers to adapt and evaluate such procedures. For example, the initial structuring of the worry period might remain the same, but the period could become a time to apply skills such as applied relaxation, cognitive restructuring, or covert behavioral rehearsal. Alternatively, the strategy might be applied to other response domains (e.g., a designated procrastination period).

Affective-Physiological Interventions

A number of interventions target heightened emotional and physiological arousal, on the theory that they directly reduce arousal and its motivational influence on escape and avoidance behavior and promote a spread of effects to other domains. Theoretically, these interventions are most appropriate when anxiety is inferred from problems in the affective-physiological domain, such as increased muscle tension, perseverative attention to arousal, behavioral disruption caused by heightened arousal rather than skill deficit, and cognitive and behavioral avoidance and escape motivated by arousal reduction. The most well-researched strategies in this group include systematic desensitization, self-managed relaxation coping skill interventions, and exposure.

Systematic Desensitization (SD)

A counterconditioning model is the basis of systematic desensitization (SD) (Wolpe, 1958, 1982). Specifically, if stimuli that elicit anxiety are paired with a response that neurologically inhibits fear, those stimuli lose their anxiety-arousing capacity. Any anxiety-antagonistic response (e.g., playfulness, assertiveness) might be employed, but relaxation is typically used because it is easy to teach to clients and applicable across different fears. Progressive relaxation training (Bernstein & Borkovec, 1973; Wolpe, 1982) is most often employed, although other methods such as biofeedback and autogenic relaxation may be used. In most SD formats (see Deffenbacher & Suinn, 1988; and Wolpe, 1982, for greater detail), clients are trained first in relaxation. Then, anxiety-arousing stimuli are defined and arranged hierarchically in small steps, according to their anxiety-arousing capacity. Starting with the least fearful situation, clients are exposed to the situation while in a relaxed state. When the first situation has been associated repeatedly with relaxation, the next situation is presented in a similar manner. This process is repeated until the hierarchy is completed and relaxation has been paired with all stimuli. Should a client become anxious at any point, exposure to the anxiety-arousing stimuli is stopped, relaxation is reestablished, and then the client is reexposed to the situation until relaxation predominates over tension.

In vivo SD applies this process with a hierarchy composed of real-life situations (e.g., different driving activities for fear of driving, or distance above the ground for acrophobia). Typically, the counselor accompanies the client; however, in certain cases (e.g., sexual anxieties), clients may self-administer in vivo SD, with the counselor acting as a consultant about structuring and repeating steps. In vivo SD is the treatment of choice if desensitization is chosen (Deffenbacher & Suinn, 1988; Wolpe, 1982). It minimizes transfer problems because naturalistic stimuli are employed, and self-efficacy may increase more rapidly as direct behavioral feedback in feared situations is acquired. Logistically, however, in vivo SD may be difficult to employ if the counselor is unable to control presentation of stimuli hierarchically, as is often the case with many performance, social, and sexual interactions.

Imaginal SD overcomes difficulties in controlling and presenting stimuli by having clients visualize hierarchy scenes. Scenes are typically visualized for approximately 30 seconds while the client remains relaxed. When the scene has been presented in this fashion two to four times in a row without anxiety, the next scene is introduced. The process is repeated until the hierarchy is completed. Life experience with feared situations is monitored to evaluate transfer to the external environment.

Variants of SD have been developed to increase efficiency. For example, SD may be employed with groups of 6 to 10 clients who have the same fear. A group variant involving individual hierarchy construction and group relaxation training and scene presentation (Deffenbacher, 1976) allows different fears to be treated in the same group. SD can also be self-administered or presented via audiotape for common anxieties such as speech or test anxiety (Crouse, Deffenbacher, & Frost, 1985; Donner & Guerney, 1969). The latter two approaches are very flexible, but are plagued by problems of attrition and compliance (Rosen, 1987). Thus, self-administered and automated SD are best saved for very reliable clients, for situations difficult for counselor-administered SD, and for repetition of procedures completed within sessions.

The effects of SD are well-documented (see Deffenbacher & Suinn, 1988; and Wolpe, 1982, for reviews). In an exceptionally well-designed study with speech-anxious college students, Paul (1966) compared individual imaginal SD with individual psychotherapy, an attention placebo, and a no-treatment control. SD led to greater reduction of general, emotional, behavioral, and physiological indexes of speech anxiety than did individual counseling, which, in general, was superior to the untreated control. SD subjects also reported less general anxiety than controls. A 2-year follow-up (Paul, 1967) revealed that SD subjects continued to report less speech and test anxiety than individual therapy and control subjects, and less general anxiety and greater extroversion than controls. In the same series of studies, group SD (Paul & Shannon, 1966) was as effective as individual SD and more effective than individual therapy and control conditions, for speech and general anxiety reduction. Further, group SD subjects' grades were one full point higher (3.56 vs. 2.57) than those of the control subjects. A 2-year follow-up (Paul, 1968) revealed maintenance of test and speech anxiety reduction relative to other conditions, and impressive differences in grade (3.53 vs. 2.41) and drop-out rate (10% vs. 60%), compared to untreated controls.

Overall, SD is effective for a wide range of phobias, such as acrophobia (Pendleton & Higgins, 1983) and agoraphobia (James, Hampton, & Larsen, 1983); for situational anxieties such as test (Deffenbacher & Shelton, 1978), speech (Paul, 1966), and math (Suinn & Richardson, 1971) anxieties; for anxiety-related problems such as nightmares (Miller & DiPalto, 1983); and for aversion reactions such as anticipatory nausea and chemotherapy reactions (Morrow, 1986). SD is particularly appropriate for conditions of high emotional-physiological arousal triggered by clear environmental stimuli. SD may also be useful for clients who have passive counselor-directed notions of intervention and/or very low self-efficacy expectations for tolerating anxiety arousal (Deffenbacher & Suinn, 1988). The high degree of counselor control of procedures, the small steps involved, and the minimal exposure to anxiety arousal may maximize compliance and minimize resistance and premature termination in such clients.

SD is not appropriate where external, anxiety-arousing stimuli cannot be identified and organized into a graded hierarchy. SD is, therefore, not very useful in the treatment of panic, OCD (Steketee & Foa, 1985), GAD (Deffenbacher & Suinn, 1987), and some social-evaluative anxieties (Beck & Emery, 1985; Malkiewich & Merluzzi, 1980), because many of the cues for such problems are internal. SD, like other relaxation interventions, may also be problematic for individuals who develop relaxation-induced anxiety (i.e., increased anxiety when relaxing), although this can be remediated through changed relaxation format, repetition of relaxation, and counterdemand instructions (Deffenbacher & Suinn, 1987; Heide & Borkovec, 1984).

Self-Managed Relaxation Coping Skills

Several interventions develop relaxation coping skills for anxiety reduction (i.e., they train clients to become aware of the internal cues of anxiety arousal and to apply specific relaxation skills when those cues are perceived). Although programs differ in how they develop relaxation coping skills, they share elements in common. First, their rationale frames intervention as an active, self-control process that trains clients to reduce anxiety by recognizing tension and applying relaxation. Second, they train not only basic progressive relaxation, but also specific relaxation coping skills. Third, they emphasize increased sensitivity to internal cues of anxiety arousal and the use of these cues to initiate relaxation. Discrimination of internal cues of anxiety arousal may be achieved by focusing on tension during relaxation training, by self-monitoring anxiety reactions, and/or by attending to anxiety aroused during sessions. Fourth, anxiety is induced within sessions to provide practice in becoming aware of arousal and relaxing it away. Fifth, graded homework assignments are used to transfer coping skills and consolidate external application (i.e., as anxiety control is demonstrated within sessions, skills are transferred via homework).

Given this overview of commonalities, several self-managed relaxation coping skills programs are described briefly here. Then, examples of outcome research supporting relaxation coping skill interventions are provided. A detailed comparison of self-managed relaxation procedures can be found in Deffenbacher and Suinn (1982), and more extensive reviews of outcome research appear in Barrios and Shigetomi (1979), Deffenbacher and Suinn (1982), Denney (1980), and Ost (1987).

Cue-controlled relaxation (CCR) (e.g., Russell, Miller, & June, 1975; Russell & Wise, 1976) involves pairing a cue word (e.g., "calm" or "relax") or phrase (e.g., "calm control") with relaxation. Theoretically, the cue is classically conditioned to relaxation such that presentation of the cue should elicit relaxation, providing clients with a way of self-initiating relaxation when feeling tense. Initially, the counselor presents the cue in synchrony with the client's exhalation. After 10 to 20 counselor-assisted pairings, clients are instructed to continue the process by focusing on their breathing and subvocally presenting the cue as they exhale. Clients practice CCR at home and use it to control anxiety. Efforts to control anxiety are discussed, and CCR training is repeated within sessions. Initial CCR applications did not involve anxiety arousal and control within sessions. Subsequently, in cue-controlled SD (Lent & Russell, 1978), the issue of anxiety control within sessions was addressed, and CCR was employed to cope with anxiety induced from hierarchy items.

Self-control desensitization (SCD), developed by Goldfried (1971), brought self-control modifications to SD. For example, to maximize the range of situations in which relaxation skills are applied, hierarchies include different anxiety-arousing themes, instead of the monothematic hierarchies of SD. Clients are trained in coping skills of CCR, relaxation without tension (i.e., focusing on letting tension release from muscles without tensing them), and breathing-cued relaxation (i.e., relaxing on each deep exhalation for 3 to 5 breaths). During scene presentation, clients are instructed to cope with anxiety arousal using their relaxation skills (i.e., scenes are used to provide opportunities to experience arousal and actively reduce it). As clients cope more rapidly and easily, the next scene from the hierarchy is introduced, providing coping with increasing levels of anxiety.

Anxiety management training (AMT) (Suinn, 1986; Suinn & Deffenbacher, 1988; Suinn & Richardson, 1971) develops relaxation coping skills of relaxation without tension (i.e., focusing on and releasing muscles without tensing them), breathing-cued relaxation, and relaxation imagery (i.e., visualizing a specific, relaxing image from past experience). After clients learn these coping skills, a period of guided training in anxiety arousal and reduction begins. Clients develop two moderately and two highly anxiety-arousing scenes from personal experience. These images contain as much situational, cognitive, emotional, physiological, and behavioral detail as possible, so that anxiety may be reexperienced. Starting with moderate scenes in early sessions and moving to more intense scenes a few sessions later, clients visualize a scene, experience anxiety arousal, and then initiate relaxation coping skills to reduce anxiety. Initially, the counselor assists in reinstating relaxation, but, as client proficiency increases, counselor assistance is faded.

Relaxation as self-control (RSC) (Deffenbacher & Snyder, 1976) trains clients in a number of relaxation coping skills (e.g., CCR, relaxation without tension, relaxation imagery, breathing-cued relaxation, unobtrusive tension exercises for key muscle areas). After practicing them for 3 to 4 weeks, clients identify their most effective coping skills and write out a set of self-instructions with which to initiate them. After approximately four sessions, clients are exposed to anxiety via simulated or real-life experiences and employ their relaxation skills to reduce tension. For example, a group of speech-anxious subjects might give short speeches. The individual giving the speech relaxes away tension while giving the speech; others relax tension while waiting for their turn or for the opportunity to ask a question.

Outcome research on self-managed relaxation interventions is generally positive. For example, CCR significantly lowered self-reports of test (Russell et al., 1975; Russell, Wise, & Stratoudakis, 1976) and speech (Russell & Wise, 1976) anxieties in college students, and did not differ significantly from SD. Few CCR studies (Deffenbacher & Suinn, 1982) evidenced nontargeted or general anxiety reduction, suggesting that full coping skill effects were not being achieved and that CCR might not be a sufficient general treatment (Grimm, 1980). The addition of active coping training within sessions in the cue-controlled SD format (Lent & Russell, 1978) appeared to remedy this problem. However, this procedure might as easily be considered a variant of SCD.

Outcomes for other self-managed relaxation coping skills programs are positive and appear roughly equivalent. For example, Deffenbacher and Payne (1977) found SCD and RSC equally effective in lowering targeted communication apprehension and nontargeted fear of negative evaluation, and in increasing assertiveness in teacher trainees. Similar results were found for test anxiety (Deffenbacher, Mathis, & Michaels, 1979; Snyder & Deffenbacher, 1977); SCD and RSC lowered targeted test and nontargeted general anxiety in college students, compared to controls. Although no performance differences were found in analog testing in either study, RSC subjects had higher psychology grades than controls in the one study in which grades were explored (Deffenbacher et al., 1979). A 1-year follow-up of the Deffenbacher et al. (1979) study (Deffenbacher & Michaels, 1980) revealed maintenance of targeted and nontargeted anxiety reduction for both SCD and RSC.

In initial studies of AMT (Richardson & Suinn, 1973; Suinn & Richardson, 1971) AMT lowered math and test anxieties, improved math performance, and was as effective as SD. AMT and SD reduced test and general anxiety in college counseling center clients (Deffenbacher & Shelton, 1978). However, at 1-month follow-up, AMT was superior on general anxiety reduction. Deffenbacher, Michaels, Michaels, and Daley (1980) reported equivalent test and general anxiety reduction for AMT and SCD, and 15-month follow-up (Deffenbacher & Michaels, 1981a) revealed maintenance of these effects compared to controls. Although analog test performance was not affected, subjects receiving AMT or SCD had higher psychology grades than did control subjects. Deffenbacher, Michaels, Daley, and Michaels (1980) employed AMT in either homogeneous groups or mixed groups of test- and speech-anxious students. Both formats reduced targeted and general anxiety relative to controls, and some clients fared better in mixed groups. Test, speech, and general anxiety reductions were maintained at 1-year follow-up (Deffenbacher & Michaels, 1981b). Cragan and Deffenbacher (1984) compared AMT and RSC with generally anxious medical outpatients, many of whom would have met GAD criteria, and found not only reduction of general anxiety and tension, but also reduction of nontargeted depression and hostility. A 1-month follow-up revealed maintenance of targeted and nontargeted gains and lower resting heart rates for RSC subjects than for AMT or control clients. Other studies have shown AMT to be effective in the reduction of agoraphobia (Jannoun, Munby, Catalan, & Gelder, 1980) and general anxiety (Daley, Bloom, Deffenbacher, & Stewart, 1983; Hutchings,

Denney, Basgall, & Houston, 1980). Hutchings et al. (1980) also showed reductions in worrisome cognitions and maintenance of general anxiety reduction at 1-year follow-up.

In summary, self-relaxation coping skills interventions are effective with situational anxieties, multiple sources of anxiety, and, with the possible exception of CCR, general anxiety without clear situational referents. They also appear effective with social-evaluative anxiety, but perhaps not as effective as cognitive interventions (Kanter & Goldfried, 1979; Shahar & Merbaum, 1981). They can be adapted to the emotional-physiological component of other anxiety disorders such as panics (Barlow & Cerny, 1988).

At a practice level, it may not be easy to select among these interventions. Procedurally, CCR is the least complex. However, some evidence (Deffenbacher & Suinn, 1982; Grimm, 1980) suggests that CCR is not maximally effective and that it should be used as one of several relaxation coping skills presented to clients as part of more comprehensive self-control training. RSC might be best employed with situation-specific anxieties, because it employs simulations and real-life situations for training. It may maximize transfer and self-efficacy because coping skill is applied in realistic situations. Although it may be difficult to arrange some stimuli (e.g., flashbacks in PTSD, or worry in GAD), RSC has been successfully adapted to groups of clients who have diverse sources of anxiety and stress (Cragan & Deffenbacher, 1984). SCD might be particularly appropriate when a cluster of clear environmental precipitants of anxiety can be arranged hierarchically. AMT has perhaps the greatest flexibility. It can be applied to both clear situational anxieties and tensional states without clear precipitants. All that is needed is that the client be able to generate anxiety arousal from recalling past events. Further, it can be employed in small groups for general anxiety (e.g., Daley et al., 1983) or for clients with differing sources of anxiety (Cragan & Deffenbacher, 1984), because anxiety scenes do not have to be thematic or shared, as they do in SD or SCD. Use of AMT in large group or workshop formats, however, may not be optimal; Daley et al. (1983) found AMT effective in small, but not large groups.

Exposure

This treatment involves exposing the client to anxiety cues and preventing escape and avoidance (e.g., an obsessive-compulsive with a cleaning compulsion touches dirt and is not allowed to wash for several hours), theoretically facilitating extinction and habituation of arousal. Other response domains, in addition to the affective-physiological, may be affected, because the motivational base for avoidance is removed, approach behavior is enhanced, and cognitive processes (e.g., self-efficacy) are altered.

A central issue is whether exposure should involve graded, hierarchically arranged stimuli or only the most anxiety-arousing stimuli. Graduated exposure (GE) moves at the client's pace, encouraging habituation to greater anxiety over time; flooding subjects the individual to high levels of anxiety from the start. Theoretical and applied research (Michelson, 1987) favors GE because increased exposure, rather than intense emotional-physiological arousal per se, appears to be the critical factor in habituation. Practically, GE minimizes aversiveness and related problems such as premature termination, noncompliance, and resistance because GE does not greatly outstrip the client's sense of control. Research suggests that, whenever possible, exposure should be graduated (Michelson, 1987).

Literature reviews on exposure interventions (e.g., Emmelkamp, 1987; Michelson, 1987; Steketee & Foa, 1985) suggest that several procedural factors maximize therapeutic outcome for GE. First, sessions lasting from 1½ to 3 hours maximize consolidation of habituation across domains and are preferred to sessions of shorter length. Second, multiple sessions per week, at least initially, facilitate progress. Third, in general, in vivo GE is preferable to imaginal GE. It is as effective or more effective than imaginal GE, bypasses difficulties in developing and controlling imagery, and minimizes problems in transfer to the external environment. Imaginal GE may be employed when it is difficult to arrange external stimuli, when feared stimuli are images, and/or as a rehearsal process for in vivo GE. Fourth, counselor-administered GE may be most effective, at least initially. Although self-directed GE is more economical, counselor-assisted GE generally leads to greater anxiety reduction (Mavissakalian & Michelson, 1984; Michelson, 1987). Fifth, where feasible, GE may work well in a group composed of similar clients, because group support and reinforcement may facilitate greater exposure within sessions. Group members can also provide supportive suggestions and coping alternatives and can buddy up for repeated exposures between sessions.

Outcome research generally supports the efficacy of exposure interventions. For example, Solyom, Shurgar, Bryntwick, and Solyom (1973) employed exposure, SD, aversion relief, and group counseling with airplane phobics. They found exposure to be as effective as SD and aversion relief and more effective than group counseling, in reducing fear of flying. Ost, Lindahl, Sterner, and Jerremalm (1984) found GE to be as effective as or more effective than applied relaxation, in the reduction of blood phobias. Ost, Johansson, and Jerremalm (1982), who replicated these outcomes with claustrophobics, found evidence supporting matching intervention to dominant response characteristics (i.e., applied relaxation was better for physiological arousal, whereas GE was superior for behavioral avoidance). Biran and Wilson (1981), working with clients who had differing phobias, found that exposure and cognitive restructuring were equally effective in reducing phobias, but self-efficacy was enhanced more by GE. Exposure was also as effective as SCD in the reduction of speech anxiety (Goldfried & Goldfried, 1977). Several studies with agoraphobia (Chambless, Foa, Groves, & Goldstein, 1982; Emmelkamp, 1974; Emmelkamp & Mersch, 1982; Emmelkamp & Wessels, 1975) showed exposure interventions to be as effective as or more effective than drug interventions and psychological interventions such as cognitive restructuring. Positive effects have also been found with OCD. For example, Rachman et al. (1979) compared exposure and relaxation interventions with and without drugs and found the psychological interventions to be the most effective treatment ingredients.

In summary, exposure tends to be as effective as or more effective than other anxiety interventions. However, dropout, noncompliance, and other problems may be greater for exposure than for other interventions (Michelson, 1987), suggesting that other treatment elements may also be needed.

Cognitive Interventions

Cognitive interventions are intended to correct biased information processing and distortions of perception and interpretation. Although cognitive interventions differ procedurally, they share the rationale that dysfunctional cognitions bias the individual toward an enhanced sense of danger and subsequent arousal, disrupted cognitive and behavioral processes, and cognitive and behavioral avoidance, escape, and defensiveness. Therefore, cognitive processes are their primary targets.

Three of the major, empirically validated cognitive interventions—rational-emotive therapy, cognitive therapy, and cognitive modification—are described here. This overview is followed by a brief review of outcome research relevant to cognitive approaches.

Rational-Emotive Therapy (RET)

A biosocial theory of personality is the basis for rational-emotive therapy (RET) (Ellis, 1962). Specifically, humans are viewed as biologically susceptible to developing dysfunctional rules (irrational beliefs) for living, especially in early development. Such beliefs are often modeled and reinforced socially, making them even more deeply ingrained. Even though these beliefs are philosophically, scientifically, and logically unsound, individuals unthinkingly employ them to make sense out of the world and to structure their responses to it.

According to Ellis, an activating event (A) triggers combinations of rational and irrational beliefs (B), which largely determine the nature of emotional and behavioral consequences (C). If healthy, reality-based, rational beliefs are present, the individual will feel and behave appropriately. If irrational beliefs predominate, exaggerated emotions and self-defeating behavior are likely to occur. Ellis further asserted that emotional disturbances such as anxiety stem from two primary irrational processes or tendencies: to elevate human desires (e.g., *wanting* to be liked or to do well) into absolute dictates (e.g., *having* to be liked or to perform perfectly), and to catastrophize the consequences of these dictates' not being met (e.g., terrible, awful, and devastating, instead of sad, disappointing, and unfortunate).

RET is a highly cognitive, active, directive counseling strategy that directly attacks irrational beliefs. RET counselors quickly communicate the RET model of emotional disturbance (i.e., emotional and behavioral disturbances stem from clients' indoctrinating themselves with magical, illogical beliefs) and begin pointing out beliefs inherent in the client's problems and interactions with the counselor. In a deductive fashion, using logical and empirical arguments, the counselor vigorously disputes the client's beliefs. Clients are repeatedly confronted with evidence of their beliefs and pressed to replace them with realistic, logical interpretations. This focus on altering beliefs and developing functional behavior is extended through a variety of homework (e.g., A-B-C analysis and disputation during the week), bibliotherapy (reading RET or other material), audiovisual (e.g., listening to session tapes), humorous (e.g., exaggeration of catastrophization), and behavioral (e.g., rehearsal of assertion) activities. RET attempts not only to develop rational-cognitive processes and appropriate behavior, but also to instill a general method of identifying and disputing beliefs and generating new behavior.

RET is conducted both individually and in groups. Groups, often composed of members with prior individual RET, enable members to offer one another additional rational arguments, support for and feedback on behavioral and risk-taking activities, and encouragement for completing homework exercises. Group RET has also been adapted for individuals who share a common anxiety.

Cognitive Therapy (CT)

Like RET, cognitive therapy (CT) (Beck, 1976; Beck & Emery, 1985) focuses on the cognitive domain; however, CT departs significantly in theory and intervention style. CT points to a biological basis for anxiety disorders, but suggests they are caused by primitive response systems' being triggered inappropriately by an exaggerated sense of danger. RET suggests that a few beliefs underlie nearly all psychological disturbances; CT considers cognitive dysfunction to be a more complex phenomenon. Beck maintained that: (a) many different distortions of cognitive content (e.g., absolute demands, and magnified, catastrophic implications) and cognitive process (e.g., selective abstraction of negative cues out of context, and misattribution of dangerous meanings to nondangerous events) contribute to anxiety; (b) certain profiles of distortions underlie specific disorders (e.g., catastrophic interpretations of bodily and mental experiences for panic disorders, and negative view of self, world, and future for depression); and (c) cognitive distortions may be more situation-specific than RET constructs. Thus, CT assumes individually unique patterns of cognitive distortions that must be assessed and targeted for intervention.

CT and RET both emphasize personal, empirical, scientific processes. RET employs a rational, deductive approach; CT emphasizes a more experimental, inductive strategy marked by four characteristics:

1. CT counselors form a warm, supportive relationship with clients.
2. The counselors enjoin clients in a collaborative empiricism; client and counselor work together to understand the nature of problems, determine goals of treatment, and treat anxiety experiences as hypotheses to be tested, rather than as facts.
3. CT uses Socratic questioning to assist clients in identifying important assumptions and images, assessing their meaning, exploring the logical limits and consequences of cognitions, and considering alternative ways of thinking about and dealing with events.
4. The Socratic process is extended through behavioral experiments. The counselor and client develop a series of experiences that is intended to lead to change in perspective and skill.

Thus, CT does not exhort clients to develop new cognitions; rather, it encourages clients to collect and use information and experiences to develop a more realistic perspective of self and the world.

Beck and Emery (1985) described an extensive array of CT techniques for anxiety reduction. For example, in addressing distorted cognitions via Socratic questioning, they suggested three general types of questions. First, clients explore their logic (e.g., "What is your evidence for that?"). As this process unfolds, clients engage in behavioral experiments that provide relevant evidence in response to the questions (e.g., engaging in self-disclosure and seeing whether it leads to rejection). Second, they explore different perspectives (e.g., "What are other ways of looking at that?"). Clients are encouraged to develop and evaluate many different interpretations and attributions and then to evaluate them behaviorally (e.g., a speech-anxious person interviews others, to determine their thoughts when they observe someone who is anxious while speaking, and finds others are empathic, not rejecting). Third, they explore implied catastrophies (e.g., "And then what would happen?" or "So what if the worst happened?" or a similar series of questions). When limits of negativity are pushed, clients often indicate that they can cope. Plans and skills for coping are then rehearsed and employed in the external world.

Anxiety-arousing imagery is addressed in a fashion similar to that used with verbal cognitions. Clients are also assisted in ways of modifying images (e.g., turning off the image and refocusing on the external environment, substituting coping imagery). Affective and behavioral components are addressed, as are cognitions that interfere with change, and clients are encouraged to accept some uncomfortable feelings and less than ideal behavior. These efforts are followed by behavioral experiments such as exposure in small steps to feared situations, development of relaxation skills, and activity schedules for anxiety-related tasks.

Cognitive Modification (CM)

Although cognitive modification (CM) typically is part of stress inoculation training (SIT) (Meichenbaum, 1985; Meichenbaum & Deffenbacher, 1988), it has been employed alone. CM follows the three-phase model of SIT. In the *educational phase,* collaborative assessment takes place, and clients are informed of the importance of cognitive components of anxiety. CM is described as involving restructuring of distorted cognitions and task-irrelevant self-instruction. Thus, clients are trained in task-relevant self-instruction that focuses on the task and brings extant coping capacities to bear, as well as in cognitive restructuring. In the *rehearsal phase,* clients develop both counterreponses to dysfunctional cognitions and appropriate, task-oriented self-instruction. The general style of intervention parallels CT: the counselor employs Socratic methods and modeling to assist clients. Once developed, these new responses are practiced via graded imagery. As anxiety reduction is evidenced within sessions, clients move to the *external application phase,* in which skills are rehearsed in simulated and real-life situations. Cognitive self-instruction is modified until clients can focus on and cope with anxiety-arousing situations.

Overall, cognitive approaches have been applied effectively for anxiety reduction. For example, Warren, Smith, and Velten (1984) compared RET to rational-emotive imagery (REI) (an RET variant that uses imagery to rehearse rational alternatives), relationship counseling, and control conditions for interpersonal anxiety in adolescents. RET and REI reduced self-report and sociometric indexes of social anxiety more than the control, but were not significantly different from relationship counseling. With socially anxious college students, systematic rational restructuring (SSR), another RET variant employing an imaginal hierarchy to rehearse restructuring, effectively reduced social anxiety compared to controls and was superior to self-managed relaxation methods on some anxiety measures (Kanter & Goldfried, 1979; Shahar & Merbaum, 1981). Similar effects have been found for adult social phobics (Emmelkamp, Mersch, Vissia, & van der Helm, 1985), among whom generally equivalent effects were found for group RET, CM, and in vivo GE. RET and REI also significantly lowered global anxiety in generally anxious community mental health center clients (Lipsky, Kassinove, & Miller, 1980). In working with OCD, Emmelkamp, Visser, and Hoekstra (1988) demonstrated individual RET and GE to be effective in reducing obsessive-compulsive problems and social anxiety. RET, however, was superior in reducing depression. Results for both conditions were maintained at 6-month follow-up.

Several studies with social-evaluative anxieties in college students have revealed positive effects for cognitive interventions. For example, CM and SD both reduced speech anxiety relative to a control group, but only CM evidenced nontargeted anxiety reduction (Meichenbaum, Gilmore, & Fedoravicius, 1971). Holroyd (1976) found that CM reduced test anxiety and improved grades and performance on an analog test, and that effects for CM were superior to those of SD, a combination of SD and CM, and a pseudotherapy control on a number of variables. Findings were similar for music performance anxiety; CM and behavioral rehearsal were superior to controls, but CM was superior to behavioral rehearsal on some anxiety measures (Kendrick, Craig, Lawson, & Davidson, 1982). Two studies with test anxiety (Deffenbacher & Hahnloser, 1981; Finger & Galassi, 1977) and another with speech anxiety (Altmaier, Ross, Leary, & Thornbrough, 1982) revealed that CM was as effective as relaxation coping skills and the combination of CM and relaxation coping skills in the reduction of targeted anxieties. Finally, group RET and CM promoted equivalent reductions in test anxiety and improved performance on analog tasks compared to controls, and anxiety reduction was maintained at 8-month follow-up (Wise & Haynes, 1983).

In sum, cognitive strategies show promise and have proven as effective as alternative interventions. Although cognitive interventions may be appropriate for many anxiety concerns, they are particularly relevant to social phobias (Beck & Emery, 1985) and GAD (Deffenbacher & Suinn, 1987), which show distinctive cognitive involvement. Unfortunately, there is little research that suggests for whom and for what problems the more confrontational, deductive approach of RET or the more Socratic, inductive approach of CT or CM is more effective.

Behavioral Intervention

The interventions reviewed in this section seek to enhance requisite approach behaviors and/or task skills. They may reduce anxiety directly, by increasing behavioral competence, approach behavior, self-efficacy, and positive reinforcement, and indirectly, by changing emotions resulting from positive interactions with the environment.

Modeling

Modeling involves exposure to individuals who interact competently with an anxiety-arousing situation. It can be conducted symbolically (e.g., clients view a movie in which a youngster overcomes surgical anxiety), overtly (e.g., the counselor models an approach and supports clients through the modeled steps), or covertly (e.g., clients visualize a model or self engaging in approach or new skills). Whatever the format, modeling programs typically include several common steps. First, clients receive realistic information about feared situations, to correct misinformation, unrealistic appraisals, and false attributions, and to prompt coping cognitions and behaviors in the client's repertoire. Second, the counselor (or others) models an approach to and has contact with the fear situation, copes with it, and does not experience adverse consequences. Third, the client is encouraged to interact gradually with the anxiety-arousing situation. The counselor supports the client verbally and by close proximity. Response induction aids (e.g., a client wears gloves before bare-hand contact with a feared object) may be employed. Fourth, as competency and self-efficacy increase and emotional arousal decreases, independent approach is encouraged, although the counselor may be present as a consultant. Finally, self-directed practice alone, in varied situations, is undertaken to maximize self-efficacy and transfer.

Modeling is effective for situational anxieties. For example, Ladouceur (1983) found participant modeling effective with adults whose lives were restricted by phobias of dogs or cats; the addition of CM did not add to treatment effects. Williams, Dooseman, and Kleifeld (1984) demonstrated that modeling was superior to GE in restoring approach and lowering anxiety in adults who were afraid of driving or of heights. Covert modeling has also been employed successfully. For example, Kazdin (1974) found that covert modeling enhanced assertive refusal, an anxiety-related behavior for many clients. In subsequent studies (Kazdin, 1976, 1979a, 1979b), covert modeling effects were enhanced by use of multiple models, positive response consequences to models, generation of verbal summaries of modeled behavior, and elaboration of modeled scenes.

Symbolic modeling also has achieved positive results. For example, children who were facing elective surgery and saw a movie of a boy coping with surgery revealed less anxiety and problematic behavior pre- and postoperatively than did children who saw a film of a nature trip (Melamed & Siegel, 1975). Another study (Klingman, Melamed,

Cuthbert, & Hermecz, 1984) employed a film to model controlled breathing and distracting imagery, to reduce fear of dental injections. One group of dental phobic children saw the movie; another group saw the movie and had the opportunity to practice strategies. Both were effective, but the practice group was less anxious and more cooperative. Shaw and Thoreson (1974) found video modeling equal to SD and better than placebo and control conditions in reducing dental anxiety.

Other Skill Training Approaches

Study skills, social skills, and assertiveness training are among the other skill-building approaches that target the behavioral domain on the assumption that anxiety results from a skill deficit. Although programs differ in content and methodology, they tend to share common elements. They describe, model, and discuss component skills. Elemental skills are then role-played or rehearsed, with coaching and feedback from the counselor. Rehearsal continues until clients consolidate skill components fluidly, comfortably, and reliably. Clients then practice in a variety of situations so that they can enact skills under novel conditions. General guidelines for behavior are abstracted, to aid clients in adapting and modifying skills in the future. Finally, as skills are demonstrated within sessions, homework extends application externally. Successes are reviewed and rewarded, difficulties are clarified, and new responses are rehearsed and tried again in vivo.

Several studies have found skill building successful with anxious, unskilled groups. For example, Bander, Russell, and Zamostny (1982) compared mathematics study skills training, CCR, and a combined group to an untreated control. Study skills improved math anxiety and performance; CCR and combined conditions reduced test anxiety. Study skills programs have not always proven effective for test anxiety, however (Dendato & Diener, 1986; Harris & Johnson, 1980). Gormally, Varvil-Weld, Raphael, and Sipps (1981) compared a social skills-building group, a CM group, and a combined group to a control, in treating socially anxious college males. All three groups improved in assertiveness and reduced social anxiety compared to the control. Stravynski, Marks, and Yule (1982) employed a social skills program with and without CM for anxious psychiatric outpatients. Social skills training lowered anxiety, depression, and isolation, and improved social activities and relationships at work. Social skills effects were not enhanced by the addition of CM. Ost, Jerremalm, and Johansson (1981) found social skills training and applied relaxation effective for social phobias. However, client characteristics × treatment condition findings revealed that relaxation was more effective for clients who reacted more physiologically, and social skills training worked best for clients who showed more behavioral problems.

In summary, interventions targeting approach behavior or skills enhancement have shown positive results. Overt modeling procedures for approach behavior are very effective but are limited to situational anxieties where anxiety-arousing stimuli can be arranged and controlled. Covert modeling procedures may bypass this constraint and extend the range of modeling applications by presenting situations imaginally. Symbolic modeling has potential in preparing individuals to deal with predictable but unavoidable stressors, such as medical and dental procedures. Rehearsing modeled skills may enhance these effects. Skills-building programs have generally proven effective with anxious, unskilled clients and should be considered when assessment suggests skill deficits are contributing to anxiety reactions.

Combined Interventions

Many approaches reviewed previously are actually multichannel interventions, even though they theoretically target one domain primarily. Stress inoculation training (Meichenbaum, 1985; Meichenbaum & Deffenbacher, 1988), however, specifically targets multiple elements of anxiety.

Stress Inoculation Training (SIT)

Three interlocking phases are involved in stress inoculation training (SIT). In *education,* the counselor and client form a warm, collaborative, Socratic relationship, much as in CT. In a largely inductive manner, an assessment of anxiety concerns is undertaken. Clients are assisted to reconceptualize anxiety in more benign ways, rather than as uncontrollable, overwhelming, victimizing conditions. Intervention strategies are linked to this emergent conceptualization (e.g., relaxation for heightened arousal, cognitive restructuring for dysfunctional attitudes, problem solving and task-oriented self-instruction for worry, and skills training for behavioral deficits). The counselor and client collaboratively develop treatment plans, which are phrased in the client's language, metaphors, and examples.

Rehearsal is an outgrowth of the education phase and involves training and rehearsal of intervention components. Initial rehearsal often involves imaginal scenes and is extended into low-arousal in vivo situations via homework. Needed coping skills vary widely and are individually tailored to the assessment. Four classes of coping skills are commonly employed in SIT (see Meichenbaum & Deffenbacher, 1988, for examples). First, applied relaxation coping skills are developed, much as they are in AMT or SCD. When relaxation coping skills are well-rehearsed, clients may develop a set of self-instructions with which to self-prompt relaxation. Second, cognitive restructuring, which is very similar to CT, is effected. Through collaborative interactions, clients identify and modify dysfunctional self-dialogue, images, cognitive processes, and schemata. Third, problem-solving skills and task-oriented self-instruction are added when clients are deficient in breaking down anxiety arousal and working through a series of steps. Fourth, self-reward and self-efficacy skills are encouraged, to provide clients with the means to nurture and maintain coping efforts.

The third phase, *application and follow-through,* ensures transfer and maintenance of coping skills. Anxiety-arousing imagery, simulations, and graduated in vivo exposure are employed to elicit anxiety, which is controlled through coping skills application. Coping skills are revised as needed and are transferred to external environments through homework and experiments. Maintenance and relapse prevention receive direct attention (e.g., clients are encouraged to expect anxiety in the future and to view it as an opportunity to continue to employ coping skills). Later sessions are often spaced more than a week apart, to consolidate external application. Booster sessions at intervals of 1, 3, 6, and 12 months are often included, to promote continued coping and to work through difficulties encountered.

SIT has been employed successfully both individually and in groups (see Meichenbaum, 1985; and Meichenbaum & Deffenbacher, 1988, for reviews of outcome literature). For example, in the initial study of SIT with test-anxious college students (Meichenbaum, 1972), group SIT and SD were superior to a control on measures of trait and state test-anxiety reduction. On some anxiety measures, SIT was also superior to SD. Furthermore, SIT led to higher grades than SD which, in turn, was superior to the control. SIT and skills training were also more effective than a control in reducing speech anxiety in college students (Fremouw & Zitter, 1978). In a study with social phobics, Butler, Cullington, Munby, Amies, and Gelder (1984) found SIT and GE more effective than a control in reducing social anxiety, general anxiety, and depression. SIT revealed significantly better results than GE on several measures, especially at 6-month follow-up. In working with chronically anxious community volunteers, Long (1984) found that SIT effectively lowered state and trait anxiety and increased self-efficacy compared to controls. Elective surgery patients receiving SIT, compared to a control, reported less pre- and postsurgery anxiety and pain, had better postsurgery adjustment, and tended to take less pain medication and to be discharged earlier (Wells, Howard, Nowlin, & Vargas, 1986).

SIT has also proven useful for developmental and vocational stress. For example, SIT reduced attrition rates in a practical nursing program (Wernick, 1984) and increased coping, self-efficacy, and rational beliefs in stressed high school seniors who were undergoing a developmental transition (Jason & Burrows, 1983). In two studies of stressed public school teachers (Forman, 1982; Sharp & Forman, 1985), SIT increased self-efficacy and general coping, and lowered teaching and general anxiety better than a control and as well as a child management training intervention.

Finally, in a series of component analyses with test (Deffenbacher & Hahnloser, 1981), speech (Altmaier et al., 1982), and music performance (Sweeney & Horan, 1982) anxieties, SIT was found to be more effective than controls and at least as effective as relaxation and cognitive treatment components.

Other Combined Interventions

Many other interventions (see studies reviewed earlier) represent a successful combination of treatment components. For example, Dendato and Diener (1986) compared SIT, study skills training, a combined condition, and a control for test-anxious college students. Study skills training produced no effects; SIT and the combined treatment reduced test anxiety; but only the combined group improved grades. Lent and Russell (1978) found similar results for the combination of study skills with SD or cue-controlled SD. Study skills alone was relatively ineffective, but the combined condition reduced test and general anxiety and improved grades. Harris and Johnson (1980) found a combination of covert modeling and study skills to be as effective as SCD in reducing test anxiety, but reported that the combined condition improved performance, whereas SCD and study skills groups showed no academic improvement, and the control group's performance deteriorated. Haynes-Clements and Avery (1984) combined CM and social skills training to reduce social anxiety and increase social participation in shy individuals. Emmelkamp and Felten (1985) found a combination of CM and GE superior to GE for acrophobia. Brown (1980) provided either a multicomponent coping skills program (combining relaxation, anxiety management, social skills, and reinforcement training) or group counseling to anxious community mental health center clients. Coping skills clients reported less anxiety and more assertiveness and were less likely to be hospitalized in the next year than were group counseling clients.

Because interventions targeting multiple sites of anxiety are frequently effective, and in some cases somewhat more effective than singular interventions (Deffenbacher & Hahnloser, 1981; Lent & Russell, 1978; Meichenbaum, 1972; Sweeney & Horan, 1982), it is tempting to conclude that "more is better." However, several caveats should be noted. First, the appearance of increased effectiveness for multicomponent treatments may be an artifact of incomplete assessment and poor matching of treatments to client characteristics. Thus, a heterogeneous intervention may unsystematically, but fortuitously, match diverse treatment components to different clients. Second, at a practical level, adding more elements may weaken the strength of individual components; group and workshop formats may be particularly vulnerable to this problem. As more intervention components are introduced, practice and follow-through activities may suffer. Third, clients may see intervention components as irrelevant or misplaced for them. This view may increase resistance, noncompliance, and, potentially, premature termination. Multifaceted interventions should therefore be based on careful individual assessment.

RECOMMENDATIONS FOR PRACTICE AND RESEARCH

In writing a chapter such as this one, important issues and themes begin to emerge and crystallize. The chapter concludes by proposing six of these themes as recommendations for action for those involved in counseling for anxiety management. These are issues to which, I believe, we should attend in our research and practice, in order to increase our understanding of anxiety concerns, sharpen our interventions, improve our service delivery, and broaden our efforts to underserved groups.

1. Attend to the Therapeutic Relationship

Intervention for anxiety reduction, regardless of its specific format, should be imbedded in a positive, therapeutic relationship. For some readers, this recommendation may appear so obvious that it does not seem to need mention. However, three related but different issues suggest that it must continue to receive attention in counseling anxious clients. First, relationship factors such as warmth, friendliness, empathy, and congruence have been found important in maximizing the effects of SD and GE (Morris & Suckerman, 1974; Ryan & Moses, 1979). Presumably, these factors potentiate effects of other interventions as well. Second, anxious clients often have a relief-oriented agenda, which may be at odds with the growth, self-exploration, or historical exploration agendas of some counselors. Care should be devoted to the development of a working alliance in which client and counselor share a common definition of problems and approaches and minimize dysfunctional interactions in pursuit of different goals. Third, research on exposure (Gustavsson, Jansson, Jerremalm, & Ost, 1985; Rabavilas, Boulougouris, & Perissaki, 1979) suggests that counselors who are more explicit and encouraging and less negotiative and permissive achieve better results. Thus, counselors are encouraged to develop positive working alliances without encouraging unproductive dependency, and to adopt an explicit, encouraging style that does not encourage avoidance.

These recommendations have both obvious and not so obvious implications for training and supervision. Programs should train students in quality relationship skills and their use with anxious clients. However, less obvious is a need to address a particular kind of countertransference. Specifically, many counselors may adopt passive strategies because they are uncomfortable with client anxiety arousal or are anxious inquiring about or doing certain things. For example, I nearly aborted the following intervention because of my own anxiety and embarrassment. A panic disorder client strongly feared the reactions of others (e.g., rejecting comments and looks of disgust) if she panicked. We decided to see what would happen if we went to a cafeteria, where I would act as if I were having a panic attack and she would observe from a few tables away. I had to deal with my concerns about looking foolish, before we could proceed. Subsequently, I sat alone at a table, began to shake visibly, and in a loud voice said, "Oh, no! I'm having a panic attack." Two bystanders expressed concern and offered to help, and others looked concerned, all of which were helpful observations to the client. Counselors may defend their avoidance; I could have done so. But how often do supervisors press counselors to explore anxiety about encouraging clients to experience anxiety or about counselor behaviors needed for efficacious intervention?

Research should explore relationship and process dimensions that are predictive or facilitative of successful outcome. For example, research on the working alliance could focus on anxiety reduction and explore dimensions of productive and unproductive working alliances. A great deal of work needs to be done in this broad area; such work might fruitfully blend the research skills of those focused on outcome assessment with the skills of those studying process variables.

2. Target Interventions to Salient Elements of Anxiety

As outlined earlier, clients differ on the nature and predominance of emotional, physiological, cognitive, and behavioral involvement. Practitioners might carefully assess these dimensions and target interventions to them. Multifaceted anxiety interventions, referrals, and other forms of intervention are often appropriate, but should flow from a careful mapping of the contributors to and the nature of anxiety.

This recommendation may seem to contradict the many studies showing that interventions based on diverse theories have similar effects. Several recent studies, however, suggest that, although many interventions are generally effective, inattention to individual differences may mask more powerful findings. Treatments may be even more effective if targeted to individual response profiles. For example, Norton and Johnson (1983) found meditation more effective for clients who showed greater cognitive involvement, while relaxation was superior for more somatic reactions. Studies by Ost and his colleagues (Jerremalm, Jansson, & Ost, 1986; Ost et al., 1981, 1982; Ost, Jerremalm, & Jansson, 1984), with simple phobias, social phobias, and agoraphobia, showed that physiological responders were helped more by relaxation interventions; cognitive reactors, by CM; and behavioral responders, by GE or social skills training. Safran et al. (1980) also reported evidence of treatment consonance: low-anxiety, unassertive clients did equally well with behavioral rehearsal or cognitive approaches, but high-anxiety clients showed greater effects on behavioral and cognitive measures with behavioral and cognitive interventions, respectively. Gormally et al. (1981) and Altmaier et al. (1982) also have found greatest cognitive change in conditions with a cognitive component. Michelson (1986) classified agoraphobics as cognitive, behavioral, or physiological responders and found greatest effects with consonant interventions (i.e., paradoxical intention, GE, and relaxation, respectively). Thus, effects appear to be enhanced if interventions are targeted specifically to individual differences in anxiety.

Much research is still needed to identify which intervention is best for which client with which kind of anxiety experience. Such research can be facilitated in two significant ways. First, designs should include at least one measure from each major response domain. This allows not only comprehensive evaluation of outcome, but also evaluation of whether interventions achieve greatest effects in consonant domains. If sample sizes are sufficiently large, meaningful subgroups of reactors can be defined after the fact, to see whether they responded differentially to treatment. Second, different reactor groups can be defined prior to intervention and assigned to consonant or nonconsonant treatments, to evaluate matching directly. Over time, research of either type should increase understanding of and assessment strategies for identifying and targeting important individual differences.

3. Include Exposure and Active Anxiety Management

Most effective interventions include some type of exposure. Although exposure alone is effective, it may lead to resistance and avoidance, including dropping out of counseling. The recommendation, therefore, is that counselors include *graduated* exposure to anxiety-arousing situations or material, and provide clients with practice in applying insights or skills gained in counseling (i.e., active anxiety management). In most cases, extension of exposure to real-life circumstances should receive attention before termination. Graduated exposure (i.e., starting with less anxiety-arousing exposure and greater counselor support) generally appears most effective. Because low self-efficacy may interfere with exposure (Bandura, 1977), counselors should explicitly assess client efficacy predictions. As a rough rule of thumb, clients who estimate chances of success at less than 70% are at risk for aborting effort (Taylor & Arnow, 1988). When low efficacy estimates are discovered, it may be helpful to assist clients to reassess efficacy and/or structure intermediate exposure to tasks at which client efficacy predictions are higher.

Research should continue to study exposure and active anxiety management directly. For example, studies can compare outcomes of interventions that vary in degree of exposure. Outcome measures should be broadly based and should include anxiety reduction in daily life or anxiety-relevant life circumstances, because effects of exposure are most likely to be found on these dimensions. Follow-up is also needed; some effects may be delayed. Situational or issue-specific self-efficacy measures should be included, to evaluate whether exposure increases self-efficacy as theorized.

4. Attend to Maintenance and Relapse Prevention

Some anxious clients experience anxiety reduction during counseling, but later reexperience anxiety. New life stressors may be present for some, but, for others, insights and skills gained in counseling have been abandoned. Counselors may take a number of steps to prevent relapse (Deffenbacher & Suinn, 1982, 1987; Meichenbaum, 1985; Meichenbaum & Turk, 1987). In particular, these recommendations may be helpful. (a) Alert clients to the possibility of relapse, discuss how they will conceptualize it if it happens, and make concrete plans for dealing with it. Simulating relapse and having clients practice coping with it are also desirable. (b) Encourage continued self-monitoring of anxiety and coping efforts and scheduling of specific times for review and maintenance planning. (c) Vary exposure and application systematically, across diverse anxiety-arousing circumstances. This increases generalized self-efficacy and coping capacities, to combat relapse. (d) Lengthen the time interval between sessions toward the end of counseling. This provides opportunities to deal with relapse during counseling. (e) Build in follow-up or planned booster sessions. For example, sessions might be scheduled at 3-month intervals for a year postcounseling, or clients can have scheduled phone or written contact with the counselor, to support management and trouble-shoot problems.

Two basic research agendas are needed in this area (Galassi & Galassi, 1984). First, there is a primary need for long-term follow-up studies. Without these studies, we cannot establish maintenance effects, much less study factors that enhance or interfere with them. The absence of follow-up may also lead to erroneous conclusions. Several studies reviewed earlier revealed different findings at follow-up than at posttreatment. Had conclusions been drawn at posttreatment assessment, the power of some interventions would have been overestimated, whereas others, particularly cognitive and self-control interventions, would have been underestimated. Long-term follow-up studies should also attempt to correlate process or client variables (e.g., self-efficacy ratings, faithfulness in completing homework, relationship factors) with maintenance, to identify factors that enhance or deter maintenance. Second, relapse prevention strategies could be manipulated and studied directly. For example, interventions with and without relapse prevention efforts (e.g., booster sessions) can be compared. Alternatively, different relapse prevention strategies (e.g., booster sessions vs. written contracts) can be compared.

5. Develop and Evaluate Anxiety Reduction Strategies for Diverse Populations

As was evident in writing this chapter, and as noted by Casas (1988), nearly all published anxiety reduction studies are based on white, predominantly middle-class populations from Canada, the United States, and northern European countries. Although exceptions exist (Morse, 1983), very little is known about the anxiety experiences of clients of diverse ethnic, religious, cultural, and other backgrounds, and the adaptation of anxiety reduction principles to these populations.

Quite simply, it is time to address these issues. Practitioners must remain culturally sensitive to clients of diverse backgrounds, in order to understand the nature and meaning of their anxiety and to intervene in culturally appropriate ways. Researchers must include diversity more frequently in their studies. Such factors must be related to the epidemiology, experience, and expression of anxiety in different populations. Finally, culturally sensitive strategies for assessing and relieving anxiety must be developed and evaluated.

6. Evaluate Anxiety Reduction Efforts

When initial assessment suggests that certain anxiety dimensions are important, practitioners might monitor those dimensions continuously. Monitoring provides information for designing effective intervention and for modifying or terminating ineffective efforts. Thus, case monitoring and evaluation are important parts of competent and ethical practice.

Researchers, too, need to continue evaluation efforts. Combining a number of prior recommendations, outcome research, wherever possible, should contain: (a) multichannel assessment of anxiety; (b) short-term (1 to 6 months) and long-term (6 to 24 months) follow-up; (c) measures of situational and general self-efficacy; (d) correlation of process and individual difference variables with outcome, to clarify facilitators of and impediments to anxiety reduction; (e) measures of nontargeted outcomes (e.g., anger, depression, social skills, self-esteem), to assess generalization and breadth of treatment effects; and (f) large sample sizes, to allow adequate study of different treatments that have some therapeutic effect.

Especially needed are large, multisite, collaborative studies that identify anxious clients according to some consistent criteria and then intervene with promising alternative interventions that address different anxiety components. Multiple sites allow for the large sample sizes necessary for meaningful between-group comparisons; for exploration of individual difference, diversity, and process variables related to outcome; and for high external validity, because many different counselor and client populations are sampled. Smaller substudies might be built into some of the trials as well.

Such research would be a challenging but rewarding undertaking, and counseling psychology is in an excellent position to respond to this challenge (Deffenbacher, 1985). We have strong connections with college and university counseling centers nationally and, potentially, internationally. These centers exist in environments that are at least somewhat supportive of research and that have significant numbers of anxious individuals and trained counselors. A collaborative network of participating centers could be identified. A core group of researchers could meet, potentially at APA or AACD conventions, and outline assessment and treatment protocols. Training could then extend to identified center staff who would execute the project at the collaborative sites. External funding may be necessary for such an endeavor, but counseling psychologists could be in one of the best positions, among all professionals, to establish such collaborative research. Are we ready for the challenge?

REFERENCES

Altmaier, E. M., Ross, L. L., Leary, M. R., & Thornbrough, M. (1982). Matching stress inoculation treatment components to client's anxiety mode. *Journal of Counseling Psychology, 29,* 331–334.

American Psychiatric Association. (1987). *Diagnostic and statistical manual of mental disorders* (3rd ed. rev.). Washington, DC: Author.

Bander, R. S., Russell, R. K., & Zamostny, K. P. (1982). A comparison of cue-controlled relaxation and study skills counseling in the treatment of mathematics anxiety. *Journal of Educational Psychology, 74,* 96–103.

Bandura, A. (1977). Self-efficacy: Toward a unifying theory of behavior change. *Psychological Review, 84,* 191–215.

Barlow, D. H., & Cerny, J. A. (1988). *Psychological treatment of panic.* New York: Guilford Press.

Barlow, D. H., Hayes, S. C., & Nelson, R. O. (1984). *The scientist-practitioner: Research and accountability in clinical and educational settings.* New York: Pergamon Press.

Barrios, B. A., & Shigetomi, C. C. (1979). Coping-skills training for the management of anxiety: A critical review. *Behavior Therapy, 10,* 491–522.

Beck, A. T. (1976). *Cognitive therapy and the emotional disorders.* New York: International Universities Press.

Beck, A. T., & Emery, G. (1985). *Anxiety disorders and phobias.* New York: Basic Books.

Beck, A. T., Laude, R., & Bohnert, M. (1974). Ideational components of anxiety neurosis. *Archives of General Psychiatry, 31,* 319–325.

Bernstein, D. A., & Borkovec, T. D. (1973). *Progressive relaxation training: A manual for the helping professions.* Champaign, IL: Research Press.

Biran, M., & Wilson, G. T. (1981). Treatment of phobic disorders using cognitive and exposure methods: A self-efficacy analysis. *Journal of Consulting and Clinical Psychology, 49,* 886–899.

Borkovec, T. D. (1985). Worry: A potentially valuable concept. *Behaviour Research and Therapy, 23,* 481–482.

Borkovec, T. D., & Hu, S. (1990). The effect of worry on cardiovascular response to phobic imagery. *Behaviour Research and Therapy, 28,* 69–73.

Borkovec, T. D., & Inz, J. (1990). The nature of worry in generalized anxiety disorder: A predominance of thought activity. *Behaviour Research and Therapy, 28,* 153–158.

Borkovec, T. D., Robinson, E., Pruzinsky, T., & DePree, J. (1983). Preliminary exploration of worry: Some characteristics and processes. *Behaviour Research and Therapy, 21,* 9–16.

Borkovec, T. D., Wilkinson, L., Folensbee, R., & Lerman, C. (1983). Stimulus control applications to the treatment of worry. *Behaviour Research and Therapy, 21,* 247–251.

Brown, S. D. (1980). Coping skills training: An evaluation of a psychoeducational program in a community mental health setting. *Journal of Counseling Psychology, 27,* 340–345.

Buss, A. H. (1980). *Self-consciousness and social anxiety.* San Francisco: Freeman.

Butcher, J. N., Dahlstrom, W. G., Graham, J. R., Tellegren, A., & Kaemmer, B. (1989). *Manual for administration and scoring Minnesota Multiphasic Personality Inventory—2.* Minneapolis, MN: University of Minnesota Press.

Butler, G., Cullington, A., Munby, M., Amies, P., & Gelder, M. (1984). Exposure and anxiety management in the treatment of social phobia. *Journal of Consulting and Clinical Psychology, 52,* 642–650.

Carr, A. T. (1974). Compulsive neurosis: A review of the literature. *Psychological Bulletin, 81,* 311–318.

Casas, J. M. (1988). Cognitive behavioral approaches: A minority perspective. *The Counseling Psychologist, 16,* 106–110.

Chambless, D. L., Caputo, G. C., Bright, P., & Gallagher, R. (1984). Assessment of fear of fear in agoraphobics: The body sensations questionnaire and the agoraphobic cognitions questionnaire. *Journal of Consulting and Clinical Psychology, 52,* 1090–1097.

Chambless, D. L., Foa, E. B., Groves, G. A., & Goldstein, A. J. (1982). Exposure and communication training in the treatment of agoraphobia. *Behaviour Research and Therapy, 20,* 219–232.

Cragan, M. K., & Deffenbacher, J. L. (1984). Anxiety management training and relaxation as self-control in the treatment of generalized anxiety in medical outpatients. *Journal of Counseling Psychology, 31,* 123–131.

Crouse, R. H., Deffenbacher, J. L., & Frost, G. A. (1985). Desensitization for students with different sources and experiences of test anxiety. *Journal of College Student Personnel, 26,* 315–318.

Daher, D. M., Corazzini, J. G., & McKinnon, R. D. (1977). An environmental redesign program for residence halls. *Journal of College Student Development, 18,* 11–15.

Daley, P. C., Bloom, L. J., Deffenbacher, J. L., & Stewart, R. (1983). Treatment effectiveness of anxiety management training in small and large group formats. *Journal of Counseling Psychology, 30,* 104–107.

Daly, J. A., & McCroskey, J. C. (1975). Occupational desirability and choices as a function of communication apprehension. *Journal of Counseling Psychology, 22,* 309–313.

Deffenbacher, J. L. (1976). Group desensitization of dissimilar anxieties. *Community Mental Health Journal, 12,* 263–266.

Deffenbacher, J. L. (1977a). Relationship of worry and emotionality to performance on the Miller Analogies Test. *Journal of Educational Psychology, 69,* 191–195.

Deffenbacher, J. L. (1977b). Test anxiety: The problem and possible responses. *Canadian Counsellor, 11,* 59–64.

Deffenbacher, J. L. (1978). Worry, emotionality and task-generated interference in test anxiety: An empirical test of attentional theory. *Journal of Educational Psychology, 70,* 248–254.

Deffenbacher, J. L. (1981). Anxiety. In J. L. Shelton & R. L. Levy (Eds.), *Behavioral assignments and treatment compliance: A handbook of clinical strategies* (pp. 93–109). Champaign, IL: Research Press.

Deffenbacher, J. L. (1985). A cognitive-behavioral response and a modest proposal. *The Counseling Psychologist, 13,* 261–269.

Deffenbacher, J. L. (1986). Cognitive and physiological components of test anxiety in real-life exams. *Cognitive Therapy and Research, 10,* 635–644.

Deffenbacher, J. L., Demm, P. M., & Brandon, A. D. (1986). High general anger: Correlates and treatment. *Behaviour Research and Therapy, 24,* 481–489.

Deffenbacher, J. L., & Hahnloser, R. M. (1981). Cognitive and relaxation coping skills in stress inoculation. *Cognitive Therapy and Research, 5,* 211–215.

Deffenbacher, J. L., & Hazaleus, S. L. (1985). Cognitive, emotional, and physiological components of test anxiety. *Cognitive Therapy and Research, 9,* 169–180.

Deffenbacher, J. L., Mathis, H., & Michaels, A. C. (1979). Two self-control procedures in the reduction of targeted and nontargeted anxieties. *Journal of Counseling Psychology, 26,* 120–127.

Deffenbacher, J. L., & Michaels, A. C. (1980). Two self-control procedures in the reduction of targeted and nontargeted anxieties—A year later. *Journal of Counseling Psychology, 27,* 9–15.

Deffenbacher, J. L., & Michaels, A. C. (1981a). Anxiety management training and self-control desensitization—15 months later. *Journal of Counseling Psychology, 28,* 459–462.

Deffenbacher, J. L., & Michaels, A. C. (1981b). A twelve-month follow-up of homogeneous and heterogeneous anxiety management training. *Journal of Counseling Psychology, 28,* 463–466.

Deffenbacher, J. L., Michaels, A. C., Daley, P. C., & Michaels, T. (1980). A comparison of homogeneous and heterogeneous anxiety management training. *Journal of Counseling Psychology, 27,* 630–634.

Deffenbacher, J. L., Michaels, A. C., Michaels, T., & Daley, P. C. (1980). Comparison of anxiety management training and self-control desensitization. *Journal of Counseling Psychology, 27,* 232–239.

Deffenbacher, J. L., & Payne, D. M. J. (1977). Two procedures for relaxation as self-control in the treatment of communication apprehension. *Journal of Counseling Psychology, 24,* 255–258.

Deffenbacher, J. L., & Shelton, J. L. (1978). A comparison of anxiety management training and desensitization in reducing test and other anxieties. *Journal of Counseling Psychology, 25,* 277–282.

Deffenbacher, J. L., & Snyder, A. L. (1976). Relaxation as self-control in treatment of test and other anxieties. *Psychological Reports, 39,* 379–385.

Deffenbacher, J. L., & Suinn, R. M. (1982). The self-control of anxiety. In P. Karoly & F. Kanfer (Eds.), *Self-management and behavior change from theory to practice* (pp. 393–442). New York: Pergamon Press.

Deffenbacher, J. L., & Suinn, R. M. (1987). Generalized anxiety syndrome. In L. Michelson & L. M. Ascher (Eds.), *Anxiety and stress disorders* (pp. 332–360). New York: Guilford Press.

Deffenbacher, J. L., & Suinn, R. M. (1988). Systematic desensitization and the reduction of anxiety. *The Counseling Psychologist, 16,* 9–30.

Dendato, K. M., & Diener, D. (1986). Effectiveness of cognitive/relaxation therapy and study-skills training in reducing self-reported anxiety and improving academic performance of test-anxious students. *Journal of Counseling Psychology, 33,* 131–135.

Denney, D. (1980). Self-control approaches to the treatment of test anxiety. In I. G. Sarason (Ed.), *Test anxiety: Theory, research, and application* (pp. 209–243). Hillsdale, NJ: Erlbaum.

DiNardo, P. A., O'Brien, G. T., Barlow, D. H., Waddell, M. T., & Blanchard, E. (1983). Reliability of DSM-III anxiety disorder categories using a new structured interview. *Archives of General Psychiatry, 40,* 1070–1078.

Donner, I., & Guerney, B. (1969). Automated group desensitization for test anxiety. *Behaviour Research and Therapy, 7,* 1–13.

Ellis, A. (1962). *Reason and emotion in psychotherapy.* New York: Lyle Stuart.

Emmelkamp, P. M. G. (1984). Self-observation versus flooding in the treatment of agoraphobia. *Behaviour Research and Therapy, 12,* 229–237.

Emmelkamp, P. M. G. (1987). Obsessive-compulsive disorders. In L. Michelson & L. M. Ascher (Eds.), *Anxiety and stress disorders* (pp. 310–331). New York: Guilford Press.

Emmelkamp, P. M. G., & Felten, M. (1985). The process of exposure in vivo: Cognitive and physiological changes during treatment of acrophobia. *Behaviour Research and Therapy, 23,* 219–223.

Emmelkamp, P. M. G., & Mersch, P. (1982). Cognition and exposure in vivo in the treatment of agoraphobia: Short-term and delayed effects. *Cognitive Therapy and Research, 6,* 77–88.

Emmelkamp, P. M. G., Mersch, P., Vissia, E., & van der Helm, M. (1985). Social phobia: A comparative evaluation of cognitive and behavioral interventions. *Behaviour Research and Therapy, 23,* 365–369.

Emmelkamp, P. M. G., Visser, S., & Hoekstra, R. J. (1988). Cognitive therapy vs. exposure in vivo in the treatment of obsessive-compulsives. *Cognitive Therapy and Research, 12,* 103–114.

Emmelkamp, P. M. G., & Wessels, H. (1975). Flooding in imagination versus flooding in vivo: A comparison with agoraphobics. *Behaviour Research and Therapy, 13,* 7–15.

Fremouw, W. J., & Zitter, R. E. (1978). A comparison of skill training and cognitive restructuring relaxation for the treatment of speech anxiety. *Behavior Therapy, 9,* 248–259.

Finger, R., & Galassi, J. P. (1977). Effects of modifying cognitive versus emotionality response in the treatment of test anxiety. *Journal of Consulting and Clinical Psychology, 45,* 280–287.

Forman, S. G. (1982). Stress management for teachers: A cognitive-behavioral program. *Journal of School Psychology, 20,* 180–187.

Galassi, J. P., & Galassi, M. D. (1984). Promoting transfer and maintenance of counseling outcomes: How do we do it and how do we study it? In S. D. Brown & R. W. Lent (Eds.), *Handbook of counseling psychology* (pp. 397–434). New York: Wiley.

Glass, C. R., Merluzzi, T. V., Biever, J. L., & Larsen, K. H. (1982). Cognitive assessment of social anxiety: Development and validation of a self-statement questionnaire. *Cognitive Therapy and Research, 6,* 37–55.

Goldfried, M. R. (1971). Systematic desensitization as training in self-control. *Journal of Consulting and Clinical Psychology, 37,* 228–234.

Goldfried, M. R., & Goldfried, A. P. (1977). Importance of hierarchy content in the self-control of anxiety. *Journal of Consulting and Clinical Psychology, 45,* 124–134.

Goldstein, A. J., & Chambless, D. L. (1978). A reanalysis of agoraphobia. *Behavior Therapy, 9,* 47–59.

Gormally, J., Varvil-Weld, D., Raphael, R., & Sipps, G. (1981). Treatment of socially anxious college men using cognitive counseling and skill training. *Journal of Counseling Psychology, 28,* 177–187.

Grimm, L. G. (1980). The evidence for cue-controlled relaxation. *Behavior Therapy, 11,* 283–293.

Gustavsson, B., Jansson, L., Jerremalm, A., & Ost, L. (1985). Therapist behaviors during exposure treatments of agoraphobia. *Behavior Modification, 9,* 491–504.

Harris, G., & Johnson, S. B. (1980). Comparison of individualized convert modeling, self-control desensitization, and study skills for alleviation of test anxiety. *Journal of Consulting and Clinical Psychology, 48,* 186–194.

Haynes-Clements, L. A., & Avery, A. W. (1984). A cognitive-behavioral approach to social skills training with shy persons. *Journal of Consulting and Clinical Psychology, 40,* 710–713.

Hazaleus, S. L., & Deffenbacher, J. L. (1986). Relaxation and cognitive treatments of anger. *Journal of Consulting and Clinical Psychology, 54,* 222–226.

Heide, F., & Borkovec, T. (1984). Relaxation induced anxiety: Mechanisms and theoretical implications. *Behaviour Research and Therapy, 22,* 1–12.

Henderson, J. G. (1966). Denial and repression as factors in the delay of patients with cancer presenting themselves to the physician. *Annals of the New York Academy of Sciences, 125,* 856–864.

Hibbert, G. A. (1984). Ideational components of anxiety: Their origin and content. *British Journal of Psychiatry, 144,* 618–624.

Holroyd, K. A. (1976). Cognition and desensitization in the group treatment of test anxiety. *Journal of Consulting and Clinical Psychology, 44,* 991–1001.

Hope, D. A., Rapee, R. M., Heimberg, R. G., & Dombeck, M. J. (1990). Representations of self in social phobia: Vulnerability to social threat. *Cognitive Therapy and Research, 14,* 177–190.

Huebner, L. A., & Corazinni, J. G. (1984). Environmental assessment and intervention. In S. D. Brown & R. W. Lent (Eds.), *Handbook of counseling psychology* (pp. 579–621). New York: Wiley.

Hutchings, D., Denney, D., Basgall, J., & Houston, B. (1980). Anxiety management and applied relaxation in reducing general anxiety. *Behaviour Research and Therapy, 18,* 181–190.

James, J. E., Hampton, B. A. M., & Larsen, S. A. (1983). The relative efficacy of imaginal and in vivo desensitization in the treatment of agoraphobia. *Journal of Behavior Therapy and Experimental Psychiatry, 14,* 203–207.

Jannoun, L., Munby, M., Catalan, J., & Gelder, M. G. (1980). A home-based treatment program for agoraphobia: Replication and controlled evaluation. *Behavior Therapy, 11,* 294–305.

Jason, L. A., & Burrows, B. (1983). Transition training for high school seniors. *Cognitive Therapy and Research, 7,* 79–92.

Jerremalm, A., Jansson, L., & Ost, L. (1986). Cognitive and physiological reactivity and the effects of different behavioral methods in the treatment of social phobia. *Behaviour Research and Therapy, 24,* 171–180.

Kanter, N. J., & Goldfried, M. R. (1979). Relative effectiveness of rational restructuring and self-control desensitization in the reduction of interpersonal anxiety. *Behavior Therapy, 10,* 472–790.

Kazdin, A. E. (1974). Effects of covert modeling and model reinforcement on assertive behavior. *Journal of Abnormal Psychology, 33,* 240–252.

Kazdin, A. E. (1976). Effects of covert modeling, multiple models, and model reinforcement on assertive behavior. *Behavior Therapy, 7,* 211–222.

Kazdin, A. E. (1979a). Effects of covert modeling and coding of modeled stimuli on assertive behavior. *Behaviour Research and Therapy, 17,* 53–61.

Kazdin, A. E. (1979b). Imagery elaboration and self-efficacy in the covert modeling treatment of unassertive behavior. *Journal of Consulting and Clinical Psychology, 47,* 725–733.

Kendrick, M. J., Graig, K. D., Lawson, D. M., & Davidson, P. O. (1982). Cognitive and behavioral therapy for musical-performance anxiety. *Journal of Consulting and Clinical Psychology, 50,* 353–362.

Kleinknecht, R. A., & Bernstein, D. A. (1978). The assessment of dental fear. *Behavior Therapy, 22,* 465–469.

Klingman, A., Melamed, B. G., Cuthbert, M. I., & Hermecz, D. A. (1984). Effects of participant modeling on information acquisition and skill utilization. *Journal of Consulting and Clinical Psychology, 52,* 414–421.

Ladouceur, R. L. (1983). Participant modeling with or without cognitive treatment for phobias. *Journal of Consulting and Clinical Psychology, 51,* 942–944.

Lang, P., Levin, D., Miller, G., & Kozak, M. (1983). Fear behavior, fear imagery, and the psychophysiology of emotion: The problem of affective response integration. *Journal of Abnormal Psychology, 92,* 276–306.

Leher, P. M., & Woolfolk, R. L. (1982). Self-report assessment of anxiety: Somatic, cognitive and behavioral modalities. *Behavioral Assessment, 4,* 167–177.

Lent, R. W., & Russell, R. K. (1978). Treatment of test anxiety by cue-controlled desensitization and study-skills training. *Journal of Counseling Psychology, 25,* 217–224.

Lipsky, M., Kassinove, H., & Miller, N. (1980). Effects of rational-emotive imagery on the emotional adjustment of community mental health center patients. *Journal of Consulting and Clinical Psychology, 48,* 366–374.

Long, B. C. (1984). Aerobic conditioning and stress inoculation: A comparison of stress management interventions. *Cognitive Therapy and Research, 8,* 517–542.

Magerey, C., Todd, P., & Blizard, P. (1977). Psychological factors influencing delay and breast self-examination in women with symptoms of breast cancer. *Social Science and Medicine, 11,* 229–232.

Mahoney, M. J., & Avener, M. (1977). Psychology of the elite athlete: An exploratory study. *Cognitive Therapy and Research, 1,* 135–141.

Malkiewich, I. E., & Merluzzi, T. V. (1980). Rational restructuring versus desensitization with clients of diverse conceptual levels. A test of client treatment matching model. *Journal of Counseling Psychology, 27,* 453–461.

Marks, I. M., & Mathews, A. M. (1979). Brief standard self-rating for phobic patients. *Behaviour Research and Therapy, 17,* 263–267.

Masters, W. H., & Johnson, V. E. (1970). *Human sexual inadequacy.* Boston: Little, Brown.

Mavissakalian, M., & Hamann, M. S. (1986). DSM-III personality disorder in agoraphobia. *Comprehensive Psychiatry, 27,* 471–479.

Mavissakalian, M., & Michelson, L. (1984). The role of self-directed in vivo exposure in behavioral and pharmacological treatments of agoraphobia. *Behavior Therapy, 14,* 506–519.

McFall, M. E., & Wollersheim, J. P. (1979). Obsessive-compulsive neurosis: A cognitive-behavioral formulation and approach to treatment. *Cognitive Therapy and Research, 3,* 333–348.

McNalley, R. J., & Lorenz, M. (1987). Anxiety sensitivity in agoraphobics. *Journal of Behavior Therapy and Experimental Psychiatry, 18,* 3–11.

McNalley, R. J., Luedke, D. L., Besyner, J. K., Peterson, R. A., Bohm, K., & Lips, O. J. (1987). Sensitivity to stress-relevant stimuli in posttraumatic stress. *Journal of Anxiety Disorders, 1,* 105–116.

Meichenbaum, D. H. (1972). Cognitive modification of test-anxious college students. *Journal of Consulting and Clinical Psychology, 39,* 370–380.

Meichenbaum, D. H. (1985). *Stress inoculation training.* New York: Pergamon Press.

Meichenbaum, D. H., & Deffenbacher, J. L. (1988). Stress inoculation training. *The Counseling Psychologist, 16,* 69–90.

Meichenbaum, D. H., Gilmore, J. B., & Fedoravicius, A. (1971). Group insight versus group desensitization in treating speech anxiety. *Journal of Consulting and Clinical Psychology, 36,* 410–421.

Meichenbaum, D., & Turk, D. C. (1987). *Facilitating treatment adherence.* New York: Plenum Press.

Melamed, B., & Siegel, L. (1975). Reduction of anxiety in children facing hospitalization and surgery by use of filmed modeling. *Journal of Consulting and Clinical Psychology, 43,* 511–521.

Michelson, L. (1986). Treatment consonance and response profiles in agoraphobics: The role of individual differences in cognitive, behavioral and physiological treatments. *Behaviour Research and Therapy, 24,* 263–275.

Michelson, L. (1987). Cognitive-behavioral assessment and treatment of agoraphobia. In L. Michelson & L. M. Ascher (Eds.), *Anxiety and stress disorders* (pp. 213–279). New York: Guilford Press.

Miller, W. R., & DiPilato, M. (1983). Treatment of nightmares via relaxation and desensitization: A controlled evaluation. *Journal of Consulting and Clinical Psychology, 51,* 870–877.

Moog, K., & Mathews, A. (1990). Is there a self-referent mood-congruent recall bias in anxiety? *Behaviour Research and Therapy, 28,* 90–92.

Morris, R., & Suckerman, K. (1974). Therapist warmth as a factor in automated desensitization. *Journal of Consulting and Clinical Psychology, 42,* 244–250.

Morrow, G. R. (1986). Effects of the cognitive hierarchy in systematic desensitization treatment of anticipatory nausea in cancer patients: A component comparison with relaxation only, counseling, and no treatment. *Cognitive Research and Therapy, 10,* 421–446.

Morse, R. N. (1983). Test anxiety reduction workshops for black college students. *Journal of College Student Development, 24,* 567–568.

Mueller, J. H. (1980). Test anxiety and the encoding and retrieval of information. In I. G. Sarason (Ed.), *Test anxiety: Theory, research, and applications* (pp. 63–86). Hillsdale, NJ: Erlbaum.

Mullaney, J. A., & Trippett, C. J. (1979). Alcohol dependence and phobias: Clinical description and relevance. *British Journal of Psychiatry, 135,* 565–573.

Munjack, D. J., & Moss, H. B. (1981). Affective disorders and alcoholism in families of agoraphobics. *Archives of General Psychiatry, 38,* 869–871.

National Institute of Mental Health. (1985). *Mental Health, United States, 1985.* Washington, DC: U.S. Government Printing Office.

Norton, J. R., & Johnson, W. E. (1983). A comparison of two relaxation procedures for reducing cognitive and somatic anxiety. *Journal of Behavior Therapy and Experimental Psychiatry, 14,* 209–214.

Nottleman, E. D., & Hill, K. T. (1977). Test anxiety and off-task behavior in evaluative situations. *Child Development, 48,* 225–231.

Ost, L. (1987). Applied relaxation: Description of a coping technique and review of controlled studies. *Behaviour Research and Therapy, 25,* 397–409.

Ost, L., Jerremalm, A., & Jansson, L. (1984). Individual response patterns and the effects of different behavioral methods in the treatment of agoraphobia. *Behaviour Research and Therapy, 22,* 697–707.

Ost, L., Jerremalm, A., & Johansson, J. (1981). Individual response patterns and the effects of behavioral methods in the treatment of social phobia. *Behaviour Research and Therapy, 19,* 1–16.

Ost, L., Johansson, J., & Jerremalm, A. (1982). Individual response patterns and the effects of behavioral methods in the treatment of claustrophobia. *Behaviour Research and Therapy, 20,* 445–460.

Ost, L., Lindahl, I., Sterner, U., & Jerremalm, A. (1984). Exposure in vivo vs. applied relaxation in the treatment of blood phobia. *Behaviour Research and Therapy, 22,* 205–216.

Paul, G. L. (1966). *Insight vs. desensitization in psychotherapy.* Stanford, CA: Stanford University Press.

Paul, G. L. (1967). Insight versus desensitization in psychotherapy two years after termination. *Journal of Consulting Psychology, 31,* 333–348.

Paul, G. L. (1968). A two year follow-up of systematic desensitization in therapy groups. *Journal of Abnormal Psychology, 73,* 119–130.

Paul, G. L., & Shannon, D. L. (1966). Treatment of anxiety through systematic desensitization in therapy groups. *Journal of Abnormal Psychology, 72,* 124–135.

Pendleton, M. G., & Higgins, R. I. (1983). A comparison of negative practice and systematic desensitization in the treatment of acrophobia. *Journal of Behavior Therapy and Experimental Psychiatry, 14,* 317–323.

Rabavilas, A. D., Boulougouris, J. C., & Perissaki, H. (1979). Therapist qualities related to outcome with exposure in vivo in neurotic patients. *Journal of Behavior Therapy and Experimental Psychiatry, 10,* 293–294.

Rachman, S., & Bichard, S. (1988). The overprediction of fear. *Clinical Psychology Review, 8,* 303–313.

Rachman, S., Cobb, J., Grey, S., McDonald, B., Mawson, D., Sartory, G., & Stern, R. (1979). The behavioral treatment of obsessional-compulsive disorders with and without clomipramine. *Behaviour Research and Therapy, 17,* 467–478.

Rapee, R. M., Ancis, J. R., & Barlow, D. H. (1988). Emotional reactions to physiological sensations: Panic disorder patients and non-clinical subjects. *Behaviour Research and Therapy, 26,* 265–269.

Richardson, F., & Suinn, R. (1973). A comparison of traditional systematic desensitization, accelerated massed desensitization, and anxiety management training in the treatment of mathematics anxiety. *Behavior Therapy, 4,* 212–218.

Rosen, G. M. (1987). Self-help treatment books and the commercialism of psychotherapy. *American Psychologist, 42,* 46–51.

Russell, R. K., Miller, D. E., & June, L. N. (1975). A comparison between group systematic desensitization and cue-controlled relaxation in the treatment of test anxiety. *Behavior Therapy, 6,* 172–177.

Russell, R. K., & Wise, F. (1976). Treatment of speech anxiety by cue-controlled relaxation and desensitization with professional and paraprofessional counselors. *Journal of Counseling Psychology, 23,* 583–586.

Russell, R. K., Wise, F., & Stratoudakis, J. P. (1976). Treatment of test anxiety by cue-controlled relaxation and systematic desensitization. *Journal of Counseling Psychology, 23,* 563–566.

Ryan, V. L., & Moses, J. A. (1979). Therapist warmth and status in the systematic desensitization of test anxiety. *Psychotherapy: Theory, Research and Practice, 16,* 178–184.

Safran, J. D., Alden, L. E., & Davidson, P. O. (1980). Client anxiety level as a moderator variable in assertion training. *Cognitive Therapy and Research, 4,* 189–200.

Sarason, I. G. (1972). Experimental approach to test anxiety: Attention and the use of information. In C. D. Spielberger (Ed.), *Anxiety: Current trends in theory and research* (Vol. 2 pp. 383–403). New York: Academic Press.

Schlenker, R. B., & Leary, M. R. (1982). Social anxiety and self-presentation: A conceptualization and model. *Psychological Bulletin, 92,* 641–669.

Schwartz, G. E., Davidson, R. J., & Goleman, D. J. (1978). Patterning of cognitive and somatic processes in self-regulation of anxiety: Effects of meditation versus exercise. *Psychosomatic Medicine, 40,* 321–328.

Shahar, A., & Merbaum, M. (1981). The interaction between subject characteristics and self-control procedures in the treatment of interpersonal anxiety. *Cognitive Therapy and Research, 5,* 221–224.

Sharp, J. J., & Forman, S. G. (1985). A comparison of two approaches to anxiety management for teachers. *Behavior Therapy, 16,* 370–383.

Shaw, D. W., & Thoreson, C. E. (1974). Effects of modeling and desensitization in reducing dental phobia. *Journal of Counseling Psychology, 21,* 415–420.

Solyom, L., Shurgar, R., Bryntwick, S., & Solyom, C. (1973). Treatment of fear of flying. *American Journal of Psychiatry, 130,* 423–427.

Snyder, A. L., & Deffenbacher, J. L. (1977). A comparison of relaxation as self-control and systematic desensitization in the treatment of test anxiety. *Journal of Consulting and Clinical Psychology, 45,* 1202–1203.

Spielberger, C. D. (1980). *The Test Anxiety Inventory.* Palo Alto, CA: Consulting Psychologists Press.

Spielberger, C. D., Gorsuch, R., & Lushene, R. (1970). *Manual for the State-Trait Anxiety Inventory.* Palo Alto, CA: Consulting Psychologists Press.

Steketee, G., & Foa, E. B. (1985). Obsessive-compulsive disorder. In D. H. Barlow (Ed.), *Clinical handbook of psychological disorders* (pp. 69–144). New York: Guilford Press.

Stravynski, A., Marks, I. M., & Yule, W. (1982). Social skills problems in neurotic outpatients. *Archives of General Psychiatry, 39,* 1378–1385.

Suinn, R. (1986). *Manual: Anxiety management training (AMT).* Fort Collins, CO: Rocky Mountain Behavioral Science Institute.

Suinn, R. M., & Deffenbacher, J. L. (1988). Anxiety management training. *The Counseling Psychologist, 16,* 31–49.

Suinn, R., & Richardson, F. (1971). Anxiety management training: A non-specific behavior therapy program for anxiety control. *Behavior Therapy, 2,* 498–512.

Sweeney, G. A., & Horan, J. J. (1982). Separate and combined effects of cue-controlled relaxation and cognitive restructuring in treatment of musical performance anxiety. *Journal of Counseling Psychology, 29,* 486–497.

Taylor, C. B., & Arnow, B. (1988). *The nature and treatment of anxiety disorders.* New York: Free Press.

Warren, R., Smith, G., & Velten, E. (1984). Rational-emotive therapy and the reduction of interpersonal anxiety in junior high school students. *Adolescence, 19,* 893–902.

Watson, D., & Friend, R. (1969). Measurement of social-evaluative anxiety. *Journal of Consulting and Clinical Psychology, 33,* 448–457.

Wells, J. K., Howard, G. S., Nowlin, W. F., & Vargas, M. J. (1986). Presurgical anxiety and postsurgical pain and adjustment: Effects of a stress inoculation procedure. *Journal of Consulting and Clinical Psychology, 54,* 831–835.

Wernick, R. L. (1984). Stress management with practical nursing students. *Cognitive Therapy and Research, 8,* 543–550.

Williams, S. L., Dooseman, G., & Kleifeld, E. (1984). Comparative effectiveness of guided mastery and exposure treatments for intractable phobias. *Journal of Consulting and Clinical Psychology, 52,* 505–518.

Wine, J. D. (1980). Cognitive-attentional theory of test anxiety. In I. G. Sarason (Ed.), *Test anxiety: Theory, research, and applications* (pp. 349–385). Hillsdale, NJ: Erlbaum.

Wise, E. H., & Haynes, S. N. (1983). Cognitive treatment of test anxiety: Rational restructuring versus attentional training. *Cognitive Therapy and Research, 7,* 69–77.

Wolpe, J. (1958). *Psychotherapy by reciprocal inhibition.* Stanford, CA: Stanford University Press.

Wolpe, J. (1982). *The practice of behavior therapy* (3rd ed.). New York: Pergamon Press.

Zwemer, W. A., & Deffenbacher, J. L. (1984). Irrational beliefs, anger and anxiety. *Journal of Counseling Psychology, 31,* 391–393.

CHAPTER 23

COUNSELING WITH SOCIAL INTERACTION PROBLEMS: ASSERTION AND SOCIAL ANXIETY

JOHN P. GALASSI
MONROE A. BRUCH

This chapter is concerned with counseling for social interaction problems. These problems are referred to by a variety of labels: communication apprehension, heterosocial anxiety, nonassertiveness, reticence, shyness, social anxiety, social skill deficits, social incompetence, social phobia, and unwillingness to communicate. They also include such diverse phenomena as difficulty dating, talking to authority figures, meeting people for the first time, urinating in public restrooms, writing or speaking in public, and refusing unreasonable requests. Fundamental is the experience of anxiety or presence of deficient performance, or both, while in a situation that includes at least one other person. The literature on these problems is vast, frequently confusing, and rapidly growing.

In this chapter, we provide an overview of what is known about these problems and their treatment. Included is a discussion of how they are manifested and how they have been conceptualized. Prominent theoretical formulations and empirical findings relevant to causation and maintenance are presented, and the status of alternative treatment interventions is reviewed.

The focus here is on problems in what Leary (1983) termed *contingent* as opposed to *noncontingent* social interactions. In noncontingent interactions, an individual's behavior is governed more by his or her own plans than by the reactions of others. Contingent interactions, on the other hand, involve guiding one's responses not only by personal plans, but, more importantly, adjusting one's responses continuously to the moment-to-moment reactions of others in the situation. Shyness and nonassertion represent problems with contingent social interactions; public speaking difficulty represents a noncontingent social interaction problem. Leary believed that *interaction anxiety* is engendered in contingent social interactions, and *audience anxiety* arises from noncontingent interactions. Although both forms of anxiety are viewed as arising from a single source—a concern with how one is appearing to others—different situational and dispositional antecedents and consequences may be involved in the two types of problems. Regardless of the role that anxiety may or may not subsequently be shown to play in these problems, the contingent–noncontingent conceptual distinction seems to be useful.

This chapter focuses on problems in contingent social interactions; assertion, shyness, and social phobia are used to illustrate such problems. In addition, the chapter concentrates primarily on those instances that occur in a dyadic or small-group context and involve verbal interactions between adolescents or adults.

CONCEPTUALIZATION

Assertion

Assertion (assertiveness) is a construct that originated from clinical practice and research in behavior therapy, and is, by far, the most researched and referenced of the constructs in this chapter. Moreover, many of the therapeutic techniques used in assertion training have found more widespread application in the broader area of social skills training as well as in the treatment of shyness, social anxiety, and social phobia in particular. In a number of instances, the techniques have been directly transferred or only slightly modified.

Unlike social anxiety, data about the incidence of nonassertion are difficult to find. Discounting the popularized accounts of the 1970s, which linked assertion with the women's movement and portrayed it as a need of women generally, researchers commonly set statistical cutoffs for assertion. Individuals who scored more than one standard deviation below the normative mean on a validated, global self-report measure of assertiveness were often considered to be appropriate candidates for assertion training. Thus, approximately 16% of the population was implicitly viewed as displaying global nonassertion. Moreover, this statistical cutoff received some empirical support from studies showing that individuals who sought counseling scored about one standard deviation below the normative mean on global assertion measures and displayed other characteristics similar to clinical populations (Berrier, Galassi, & Mullinix, 1981; Galassi, Berrier, & Mullinix, 1982; Gay, Hollandsworth, & Galassi, 1975). In addition, other individuals might demonstrate nonassertion in a more limited range of situations with only certain behaviors (e.g., refusal assertion), thereby increasing the number who had at least some assertion problems.

The manner in which nonassertive behavior is manifested has been studied in role play or contrived situations across a variety of populations such as college students and hospitalized psychiatric patients. Typically, the less assertive subjects differ from their more assertive peers by displaying less eye contact or gazing, more objective and subjectively rated anxiety, less appropriate verbal content, more compliance with unreasonable requests, fewer requests for behavior change, fewer smiles during commendatory assertion, less loudness and affect, longer response latency, less overall assertiveness, and, in the case of inpatients, shorter speech duration (see Galassi, Galassi, & Fulkerson, 1984; Galassi, Galassi, & Vedder, 1981; St. Lawrence, 1987, for reviews). Although women were portrayed as less assertive than men by the popularized accounts in the 1970s, most of the empirical studies have yielded equivocal findings or suggested that gender differences were not marked (Galassi et al. 1984). Nevertheless, there is evidence that assertive behavior is evaluated more negatively when demonstrated by women than by men (Kelly, Kern, Kirkley, Patterson, & Keane, 1980; Romano & Bellack, 1980; Rose & Tryon, 1979), and that men behave least assertively to a woman who both appears and behaves in a stereotypically sex-typed fashion (Hess & Bornstein, 1979). Moreover, androgynous and masculine women were found to be more assertive than feminine and undifferentiated women (Rodriguez, Nietzel, & Berzins, 1980), suggesting that sex-role and appearance factors may be more important than gender per se for women.

Conceptualization of assertive behavior was initially influenced by trait personality conceptions, as Wolpe (1958) built on Salter's work on the excitatory and inhibitory personality. Moreover, Alberti and Emmons's (1970) classic book, *Your Perfect Right*, illustrated nonassertive, assertive, and aggressive behavior—terms that frequently have been used as global descriptors for individuals rather than as characteristics of situational behaviors.

The assertion construct has also been plagued by unresolved definitional problems. Galassi et al. (1981), who called for abandoning the construct as outmoded, identified at least six basic definitional approaches. As originally defined by Wolpe, assertion was broadly conceived, it overlapped with aggression, and it was related to anxiety. The word assertive ". . . refers not only to more or less aggressive behavior, but also to the outward expression of friendly, affectionate, and other nonanxious feelings" (Wolpe, 1958, p. 114) and is ". . . the proper expression of any emotion other than anxiety toward another person" (Wolpe, 1973, p. 81). Other definitions have limited assertion to saying no or standing up for legitimate rights (Lazarus, 1971), and have emphasized its functional properties in problem solving (Heimberg, Montgomery, Madsen, & Heimberg, 1977) or gaining reinforcement (Rich & Schroeder, 1976), and the antecedent and consequent obligations in interactions (Rakos, 1979).

Probably the most common conceptualization, however, is of a series of learned, situation-specific behaviors (Eisler, Hersen, & Miller, 1973). Of the constructs discussed in this chapter, assertion is the one in which situational influences have received the most attention. Galassi and Galassi (1978), for example, stated that ". . . an adequate conceptualization involves the specification of . . . a behavioral dimension (behaviors), a persons dimension (persons), and a situations dimension (situations) within a cultural or subcultural context" (p. 17). Standing up for one's rights; initiating and refusing requests; giving and receiving compliments; initiating, maintaining, and terminating conversations; expressing love and affection; expressing personal opinions, including disagreement; and expressing justified anger and annoyance are all examples of the behavioral dimensions, which, in turn are expressed through complex, integrated sets of verbal and nonverbal responses. Friends and acquaintances (same and opposite sex), spouse or boyfriend/girlfriend, parents and family, authority figures, strangers and business relations are examples of the persons dimension. The situations dimension may be subdivided according to public versus private, or in a variety of other ways.

Evidence for a situation-specific conceptualization has derived from at least three types of data. First, factor-analytic studies of assertion self-report measures (Galassi & Galassi, 1980; Henderson & Furnham, 1983; Nevid & Rathus, 1979) have repeatedly yielded multiple factors rather than a single large, common factor, as would be predicted by a trait perspective. Moreover, each factor accounts for a modest amount of common variance and reflects behavioral and/or situational influences. Futch, Scheirer, and Lisman (1982), who took exception to this argument, noted that a trait label's capacity to be divided into subcomponents does not preclude the utility of trait considerations if the subcomponents demonstrate predictive utility across situations. A second source of support is the common finding that the results of assertion training have failed to generalize to improvement in untrained response or situation classes (Kirschner, 1976; McFall & Lillesand, 1971; Young, Rimm, & Kennedy, 1973). If assertion is indeed situation-specific, it can be argued that treatment generalization should not be expected. As has been discussed elsewhere (Galassi et al., 1981; St. Lawrence, 1987), however, lack of generalization may well reflect inadequate treatment rather than a situation-specific construct. Finally, the results of numerous studies with both hospitalized (Eisler, Hersen, Miller, & Blanchard, 1975; Hersen, Bellack, &

Turner, 1978) and nonhospitalized (Pitcher & Meikle, 1980; Skillings, Hersen, Bellack, & Becker, 1978) individuals indicate that a variety of verbal and nonverbal components of assertion reflect cross-situational variability. In these studies, subjects were frequently divided into high–low assertion groups and asked to role-play a variety of situations. The situation-specific conclusions drawn from such studies are somewhat surprising, however, because they typically demonstrate effects attributable to person, situation, and person × situation interactions, and more clearly support an interactionist (Kirschner & Galassi, 1983) rather than a purely situational view of assertion.

Social Anxiety

Social anxiety is a generic term that covers a variety of anxiety-eliciting situations and subsequent behavioral consequences that vary in the degree to which they impair a person's functioning. In this chapter, we discuss the problems of shyness and social phobia. Although these problems differ in important ways, they also share some antecedents, and thus, for the sake of our discussion, are organized under the rubric of social anxiety.

Shyness

Shyness is the ordinary language term most often used to label one's feelings of anxiousness and inhibition in social situations. It is frequently experienced; more than 80% of 5,000 people surveyed by Zimbardo (1977) reported being shy at some point in their lives. Although the percentages vary as a function of culture, Zimbardo (1986) reported a figure of 40% (plus or minus 3%) as a reliable index of current dispositional shyness; a similar percentage reporting being formerly shy, and 15% were situationally shy.

By psychological standards, shyness represents a rather "fuzzy" construct. Its origin in ordinary language has created debate about the precise nature of shyness as a construct (Cheek & Watson, 1989). This debate stems from Harris's (1984) charge that psychologists have superimposed their operational definitions on laypersons and instead should devote more attention to laypersons' accounts of their shyness experience. As Harris (1984) argued, "It is nonsense for psychologists to borrow a term from the layperson and then construct a definition of that term which enables them to subsequently inform the layperson that they are using the term incorrectly" (p. 174). Although professionals are free to create their own definitions, it is undeniable that there are overlapping constructs in the social anxiety literature.

Leary (1986) noted 14 different definitions of shyness, which he classified into three categories. The first category emphasized the subjective experience of shyness (feelings of apprehension in social situations), or what Leary believed should be labeled social anxiety. The second category was concerned with behavioral inhibition, reticence, and social avoidance or "acting shy." A third category, the optimal conceptualization of shyness, according to Leary, included both subjective apprehension and behavioral inhibition and defined *shyness* as ". . . an affective-behavioral syndrome characterized by social anxiety and interpersonal inhibition that results from the prospect or presence of interpersonal evaluation" (Leary, 1986, p. 30).

Although Leary acknowledged that the anxiety and behavioral components are imperfectly correlated, it is such attempts to categorize the key aspects of shyness that have provoked controversy. Cheek and Watson (1989) criticized Leary's definition as too restrictive and inflexible, because cognitive and somatic components are combined under the affective part of the definition. Also, they argued that there is evidence that some people who label themselves as shy do not show any signs of behavioral inhibition, although they often think that others perceive them as lacking in social skills. In the spirit of Harris's (1984) challenge, Cheek and Watson (1989) assessed the degree to which people who label themselves as shy report experiencing any or all of the three most agreed-on symptoms of shyness: somatic arousal, negative cognition, and behavioral inhibition. They found that, among a sample of 187 adult women, 43% experienced symptoms from only one shyness component category, 37% reported symptoms from two categories, and 12% mentioned symptoms from all three categories. However, of equal importance was the fact that not all participants provided responses that fit one of the three component categories, suggesting that people focus on a variety of response consequences when defining their shyness problem.

From their survey and other research, Cheek and Melchior (1990) defined shyness as the tendency to feel tense, worried, and/or behave awkwardly when anticipating or engaging in social interactions, especially with unfamiliar others of the opposite sex. This definition is consistent with results from a recent laboratory study in which shy and nonshy subjects engaged in a conversation with an opposite-sex stranger. Specifically, Bruch, Gorsky, Collins, and Berger (1989a) found that shys evidenced a greater increase in heart rate, more worrisome thoughts, and more behavioral dysfunction (e.g., gaze aversion, nervous laughter, less talking) during the interaction. Furthermore, although each of these components was correlated with shyness, they were minimally correlated with each other, suggesting variability among shy persons' manifestation of each component.

Differences in definition notwithstanding, contemporary research on shyness (Jones, Cheek, & Briggs, 1986) has shown three general trends. The first involves efforts to distinguish shyness from related constructs such as introversion. In contrast to shyness, introversion entails an inward intellectual focus, a preference for solitude, and an ability to interact with others when necessary. Consistent with this conceptualization, Briggs (1988) used four different shyness scales and found that these scales correlated on average $-.40$ with Eysenck's introversion–extroversion scale and $+.40$ with the neuroticism scale. Furthermore, shyness is not the same as low sociability, which is defined as a preference for not affiliating with others. Research indicates that the average correlation between shyness and various measures of sociability ranges from $-.30$ to $-.54$ (Bruch et al., 1989a), thus supporting this distinction.

A second trend involves attempts to distinguish among person, situation, and person $\times$ situation aspects of shyness. Little research has been conducted on situational factors in shyness. Russell, Cutrona, and Jones (1986) reported on research in which a measure of shyness situations was developed, and the separate and interactive effects of person and situation influences were compared. Results from their work revealed that both person and situation variance influenced subjects' negative affect and subjective perceptions in social situations, but there was no evidence of a significant interaction. These findings were the first to show that situational factors can predict consequences of shyness on a level similar to measures of dispositional shyness.

A third trend focuses on how shyness develops and whether there are distinct subtypes of shyness. Buss (1980, 1986) proposed a distinction between early developing, *fearful* shyness and later developing, *self-conscious* shyness. The fearful type begins prior to formation of a child's self-concept, or before age 5, and may involve a genetically acquired component of fearfulness. The stimuli that elicit this type of shyness include novel social situations, and Buss believed that the child's emotional reactivity predisposes him or her to acquire fear responses to such social situations.

This conditioning process leads to the individual's associating certain types of people and situations with the threat of negative evaluation.

Buss's self-conscious subtype does not involve fearfulness but evidences an excessive concern with how other people will evaluate the public self. It first appears around age 6, when the cognitive self begins to develop, and it peaks between ages 14 and 17, as adolescents confront their cognitive egocentrism (the "imaginary audience" phenomenon; see Elkind & Bowen, 1979) and identity tasks. In contrast to the fearfulness and somatic arousal associated with fearful shyness, the self-conscious type involves cognitive responses involving anxious self-preoccupation.

Two studies that provided findings relevant to Buss's subtype distinctions (Bruch, Giordano, & Pearl, 1986; Cheek, Carpentieri, Smith, Rierdan, & Koff, 1986) showed that: (a) 36% of current shy respondents reported that they had been shy since early childhood; (b) fearful shyness appears to be more enduring, because 75% of those who said they had been shy as long as they could remember were currently shy, while only 50% of those reporting shyness as starting in late childhood were currently shy; and (c) fearful types reported more physiological arousal than self-conscious types.

Social Phobia

Social phobia was first described by Marks (1970) in the late 1960s, but it received little attention in the United States until the publication of the DSM-III in 1980. Social phobia is defined in DSM-III-R as a "persistent fear of one or more situations in which the person is exposed to possible scrutiny by others and fears that he or she may do something or act in a way that will be humiliating or embarrassing" (American Psychiatric Association, 1987, p. 241). DSM-III-R includes additional criteria specifying that social phobia may be manifested as a *generalized type* (in which the individual fears most or all social situations) or as a fear in a specific situation where the person is observed by others (e.g., public speaking).

Although the problems of social phobia and shyness share the common antecedent of fear of negative evaluation, it is important to understand their distinctions. Bruch (1989) and Turner and Beidel (1989) suggested that shy and social phobic individuals are similar in their cognitive and affective responses but appear to differ in their behavioral reactions. According to Cheek and Melchior (1990), the behavioral component of shyness involves quietness, awkwardness in verbal and nonverbal responses, and inhibition rather than spontaneity in social interaction. Shyness is an approach–avoidance conflict in which the person desires social contact but becomes inhibited because of the threat of others' scrutiny. Social phobia, a more pervasive pattern of social avoidance, can result in substantial impairment in a person's educational, occupational, and social functioning (Turner & Beidel, 1989).

Another difference is in the course taken by some forms of shyness and social phobia. For example, discrete social phobias such as fear and avoidance of public restrooms and writing in public involve situations that do not typically elicit apprehension in shy persons. Buss (1986) indicated that a substantial number of shy people experience the onset of their symptoms in late childhood, a time when the child begins to differentiate between self and others' perceptions, but that shyness disappears by about age 16, when the adolescent learns to judge the veracity of others' feedback. Such a pattern differs markedly from evidence that symptom onset for social phobia occurs in midadolescence (Ost, 1987).

Is a social phobic someone who is extremely shy? Given current evidence, the answer to this question is probably yes. Specifically, it appears that people who meet criteria for social phobia—generalized type are individuals who evidence developmental histories that are indicative of Buss's (1980, 1986) *fearful* shyness subtype. Bruch and Heimberg (1990) found that, in retrospective reports, generalized as compared to nongeneralized social phobics (e.g., fear of public speaking only) indicated that: (a) they currently perceived themselves as shy and their shyness started prior to elementary school age; (b) many more people labeled them as shy throughout their life; (c) they perceived themselves as more shy than their peers; and (d) they dated less frequently. Generalized types also reported that their family unit was less involved in social and community activities, which is a child-rearing characteristic that Buss (1986) believed maintains fearful shyness. Because the developmental histories of social phobia and shyness show some overlap, subsequent sections of this chapter combine the presentation of information under the generic term of social anxiety. However, throughout our presentation, we will continue to distinguish between these two syndromes and will note limitations in generalizing findings from one area to the other.

Social phobia is estimated to affect about 2% of the general population, and from 8 to 12% of the persons seeking treatment at anxiety disorder clinics receive a primary diagnosis of social phobia (Turner & Beidel, 1989). In terms of demographic characteristics, Amies, Gelder, and Shaw (1983) and Ost (1987) reported that social phobia occurs approximately equally in males and females and typically has an onset in mid-adolescence. They also found that social phobics are less likely to be married, and are more likely to come from a higher socioeconomic class and to present for treatment in their early 30s.

With regard to symptoms, social phobia has been distinguished from other anxiety disorders in a number of ways. However, because similarities exist between social phobia and panic disorder with avoidance (i.e., agoraphobia), much of the evidence is based on comparisons with this particular disorder. According to Amies et al. (1983), social phobics are more likely to report somatic symptoms that are visible to others (e.g., trembling hands, twitching muscle, and blushing); agoraphobics are more likely to report somatic symptoms involving weakness in the limbs, difficulty breathing, dizziness, and fainting. Similarly, Gorman and Gorman (1987) noted the presence of a specific subset of autonomic symptoms (i.e., palpitations, trembling, sweating) that were more unique to social phobics. Such somatic arousal patterns seem consistent with the types of negative cognitions that differentiate social phobics from agoraphobics. An individual in the former category would be concerned that someone will notice these somatic reactions and think poorly of him or her as a result. The agoraphobic's concern focuses on the physical consequences of the symptoms; these persons report thoughts such as "I am going to pass out," "I will have a heart attack," and "I will not be able to control myself."

In recent years, research on social phobia has begun to focus on potential etiological factors and on identifying differences between generalized and nongeneralized subtypes. In the case of etiological factors, Reich and Yates (1988) found the frequency of social phobia in the relatives of diagnosed social phobics to be higher than in the families of panic disorder patients. In another study, Bruch, Heimberg, Berger, and Collins (1989b) compared the retrospective reports of social phobics and agoraphobics and found that the former group perceived their mother as more avoidant of social phobic situations and, hence, likely to have met criteria for social phobia. Also, in terms of child-rearing practices, social phobics, in contrast to agoraphobics, believed that their parents (a) isolated them from normal social situations, (b) overemphasized the opinions of others regarding appearance and mannerisms, and (c) de-emphasized family involvement in social and community activities.

Finally, with regard to differences between subtypes, Heimberg, Hope, Dodge, and Becker (1989) compared generalized social phobics to social phobic clients whose fears were restricted to public speaking situations. The groups were compared on self-report and behavioral measures while engaged in an individually relevant fear situation. The two groups did not differ on measures involving fear of evaluation and scrutiny by others. However, interviewers rated the generalized social phobics as more impaired in life functions, and observers perceived them as more anxious and less skilled in their behavioral performance than were those with public speaking fears. Moreover, the two groups showed a substantial difference in heart-rate patterns during their individualized behavioral simulation tasks. Generalized types showed a small, consistent increase in reactivity (3 to 6 bpm) over the course of the simulation; public speakers showed a drastic and immediate surge of heart rate (20 bpm) that subsided only gradually. Generalized types might have reacted similarly if exposed to a public speaking situation, but these situations are typically less relevant to their presenting concerns. These findings, together with Bruch and Heimberg's (1990) data on developmental differences in social phobia subtypes, suggest that this topic should continue to receive research attention.

CONTROLLING AND MAINTAINING FACTORS

Assertion

Three major theoretical models—anxiety inhibition, skills deficits, and cognitive differences (deficits)—have guided research and practice with regard to controlling and maintaining factors in assertion, and each model has received some empirical support (Galassi et al., 1981, 1984; Heimberg & Becker, 1981; St. Lawrence, 1987; Stefanek & Eisler, 1983). We briefly review here the major tenets of each, with special emphasis on the cognitive differences model, the most recently developed of the three. The interested reader is referred to the previously cited sources for additional discussion of the models and related research.

The Anxiety Inhibition Model

The anxiety or response inhibition model had its beginnings in the conditioned reflex therapy of Andrew Salter (1949), who viewed excitatory and inhibitory personalities as naturally behaving differently in social situations. Salter essentially endorsed a trait conception of behavior in social situations. Wolpe (1958), who built on Salter's work, adopted the term assertive and viewed nonassertive behavior as primarily the result of anxiety conditioned in social situations. The presence of high levels of conditioned neurotic anxiety blocks the expression of assertive behavior. Similarly, strong assertive tendencies can (reciprocally) inhibit weaker conditioned anxiety responses. Effecting change with clients who had assertion deficits was conceptualized primarily as repeatedly inducing them, through behavior rehearsal, to behave assertively in a succession of situations in which their tendency toward assertion was always more potent than the anxiety they experienced. By maintaining this relationship, the bond between the social stimuli and the anxiety and nonassertiveness that they elicited was seen as being weakened (reciprocally inhibited) and ultimately deconditioned. The principles of operant conditioning and modeling were also viewed as playing a role in Wolpe's theory, but anxiety assumed the causal role in nonassertive behavior because the presence of anxiety inhibited the expression of assertive or more adaptive behavior.

The Skills Deficit Model

Proposed by McFall and his colleagues (McFall, 1976; McFall & Lillesand, 1971; McFall & Marston, 1970), this model portrays nonassertive behavior as resulting from a skills deficit. If an individual fails to behave assertively, it is because the skills necessary for competent performance are absent from his or her behavioral repertoire. The individual has not learned how to behave assertively. If anxiety is present, it is a consequence rather than a cause of behavior. Thus, both anxiety and nonassertive behavior are by-products of skills deficits. If the individual processed the absent skill, he or she would behave assertively. Therapy therefore consists of teaching the component skills required for assertion, through such methods as behavior rehearsal, instructions, modeling, coaching, and feedback. Once these skills are learned, it is assumed, anxiety and nonassertion will be replaced by assertion. Other assumptions of the model include: (a) reinforcement is important to the development and maintenance of assertive behavior, and, once learned, assertive behavior will be maintained by naturally occurring consequences; (b) the response components (e.g., eye contact) that comprise assertive behavior are largely independent and must be treated separately; and (c) assertive behavior is situation-specific and training in one situation is not likely to result in improved performance in an unrelated situation (Heimberg & Becker, 1981).

The Cognitive Differences Model

Some of the more recent research has been concerned with the role of cognitions in mediating assertive behavior. From a cognitive perspective, assertion deficits are neither the result of conditioned social anxiety nor a deficit in performance capability. Rather, they are a function of cognitive excesses or deficits in self-statements, irrational beliefs, anticipation and valuing of consequences, knowledge of appropriate behavior, faulty problem solving, limited ability to read and process social cues, and so forth. These cognitive differences are presumed to mediate the anxiety responses and deficient social performance of individuals who exhibit assertion deficits.

The precise interplay among cognitions, cognitive processes, and overt behavior is complex and, to date, has never been clearly and comprehensively articulated. As such, the term cognitive differences model is used somewhat liberally (Galassi et al., 1984; Heimberg & Becker, 1981; Stefanek & Eisler, 1983) to encompass a number of loosely related studies concerned with the relationship between assorted cognitive phenomena and assertive behavior. Our approach here is to review a few influential studies in three major areas—cognitive content, cognitive processing, and cognitive structure. These three somewhat arbitrary and overlapping divisions constitute a useful way of organizing the research in this area.

Cognitive content refers to the ongoing, ever changing subject matter of an individual's internal dialogue as he or she proceeds through daily activities. It includes such phenomena as self-statements and irrational beliefs and is influenced by a variety of factors, including situational variables. Cognitive processing refers to a person's customary manner of making decisions and evaluating and processing information. Cognitive structure refers to a hypothetical, relatively enduring representation of a person's past experiences in a particular area; the person draws on this representation in order to perceive and process future events within that area.

Cognitive Content. A study by Schwartz and Gottman (1976) on self-statements has been among the most influential with respect to the potential mediating function of cognitive content in assertive behavior. To better understand the relationship among overt behavior, cognitions, and physiological arousal, Schwartz and Gottman conducted a task analysis of refusal responses. Groups of differentially assertive individuals were compared on (a) knowledge (one type of cognitive content) of an assertive response (ability to write a response), (b) ability to articulate an oral response within a safe situation (model for a friend what to say), (c) ability to perform in a direct interaction role play, and (d) self-statements (the major cognitive content focus of the study) as measured by endorsement of 16 facilitating and 16 inhibiting self-statements for refusal behavior. "I was thinking that there doesn't seem to be a good reason why I should say yes" and "I was thinking that I would get embarrassed if I refused" represent examples of facilitating (positive) and inhibiting (negative) self-statements, respectively. It was believed that knowledge of a competent response was prerequisite to articulating or performing effectively and that physiological arousal and cognitions may intervene to affect terminal role-play performance.

Moderate and low assertives were found to be less able than high assertives to perform adequately in the direct role-play situation. These findings, coupled with the fact that low assertives reported significantly higher self-perceived tension than moderate and high assertives and significantly less positive and more negative self-statements, led Schwartz and Gottman to comment that ". . . the most likely source of nonassertiveness in low-assertive subjects could be related to the nature of their cognitive positive and negative self-statements" (p. 918). In fact, whereas the high and moderate groups each had significantly more positive than negative self-statements, the low assertive group did not differ on number of positive and negative statements. Moreover, more assertive subjects tended to describe their pattern of thoughts as either positive thoughts followed by positive thoughts (unshaken confidence) or negative thoughts followed by positive thoughts (coping); less assertive subjects were as likely to have negative thoughts followed by negative thoughts (unshaken doubt) or positive thoughts followed by negative thoughts (giving up) as they were to have the more positive sequences. Thus, nonassertives were described as experiencing an "internal dialogue of conflict" (p. 919).

Subsequent research (Bruch, 1981; Heimberg, Chiauzzi, Becker, & Madrazo-Peterson, 1983; Pitcher & Meikle, 1980), for the most part, has replicated the self-statement findings with refusal behavior, but Bruch (1981) found that high assertives had greater knowledge and more ability in the hypothetical situations. Using the self-statements (negative self-image/fear of being disliked and other-directed vs. self-directed self-statements) that Schwartz and Gottman (1976) found to best distinguish high and low assertives, Pitcher and Meikle (1980) replicated the earlier findings, showing that concerns about being disliked, negative self-image, and other-directed self-statements were characteristic of nonassertives. In addition, self-statements correlated with other self-report measures of assertion but not with behavioral measures in negative situations. In positive assertion situations (e.g., complimenting, expressing feelings), self-statements and behavioral measures were correlated, although self-statements revealed no group differences.

Heimberg et al. (1983) tested the generality of Schwartz and Gottman's findings with college students, normal adults, and psychiatric inpatients. Nonassertives reported a greater frequency of negative self-statements than assertives, regardless of their psychiatric or student status. High assertives also had higher difference (positive–negative self-statement) scores, suggesting less internal conflict. Patients had the lowest difference scores (most internal conflict). Positive self-statements, however, did not differentiate level of assertion. Heimberg et al. interpreted their findings as support for Kendall and Hollon's (1981) notion of "the power of non-negative thinking."

In somewhat related research, Alden and Safran (1978) reported that high scorers on a measure of irrational beliefs (especially perfectionistic standards and overconcern for others) were less assertive on a variety of measures, even though they did not differ on knowledge of appropriate behavior. Moreover, Lohr and Bonge (1982) reported that low assertiveness was associated with demand for approval, high self-expectations, problem avoidance, and the total score on the Irrational Beliefs Test.

Cognitive Processes.   One of the most comprehensive cognitive process models tested was in analogue research by Chiauzzi and Heimberg (1986). Adopting the five-stage problem-solving model of D'Zurilla and Goldfried (1971), they performed three experiments to investigate assertive and nonassertive subjects' evaluation of the legitimacy (reasonableness) of requests, perceived ability to respond to requests, and the factors that influenced the responses that subjects selected. Subjects viewed videotapes of refusal requests that had been demonstrated empirically to vary on legitimacy (low, moderate, and high). Legitimacy of request influenced several of the variables. Moreover, assertive subjects rated requests as significantly less reasonable for low and moderate legitimacy situations and rated themselves as significantly more able to make any effective response in the low legitimacy situations. Assertive and nonassertive subjects did not differ on the number of response alternatives that they generated for the situations, but assertive subjects perceived themselves as more able to perform effective responses and expected a greater likelihood of possible outcomes.

Taken together, the results strongly suggest that high and low assertive subjects differ in problem solving with respect to situational (legitimacy) and self-related judgments. With respect to the D'Zurilla and Goldfried model, differences occur in stages 1 (problem orientation—recognizing the presence of an interpersonal problem), 2 (problem definition and formulation—assessing resources and formulating a goal), and 4 (decision making—assessing alternative responses vis-à-vis expected and desired outcomes), but not in stage 3 (generating response alternative). Differences in stage 5 (solution and implementation/verification) were not tested.

Sparked by Fiedler and Beach (1978), a number of studies have investigated the role of evaluative processes with respect to the probability and/or desirability of anticipated consequences for assertive behavior. In the Fiedler and Beach study, college students were presented with scenes in which unreasonable requests were made. High and low scorers on intention to refuse a request differed in their assessment of the probabilities that good and bad consequences would occur but not in their evaluations of the favorableness of those consequences. Thus, the nonassertives viewed the negative consequences as more likely if they refused and the positive consequences more likely if they complied, and assertives showed the opposite pattern.

In related research with psychiatric patients, Eisler, Fredriksen, and Peterson (1978) found that high assertive patients expected more favorable consequences for assertion than low assertive patients. Kuperminc and Heimberg (1983) criticized the Fiedler and Beach study on a number of methodological grounds, including failure to rate the utility (desirability) of consequences following each scene and selection of subjects based on self-report measures alone. Their replication effort largely supported the previous differences with respect to probabilities. In addition, however, they found that assertive subjects rated the positive consequences of refusal as more desirable and the negative consequences of compliance as more undesirable than did nonassertive subjects. Thus, the decision to behave assertively (especially for refusal situations) would appear to be influenced by evaluations of both the desirability and probability of favorable and unfavorable outcomes for assertive and nonassertive behavior.

A study by Josefowitz (1989) suggested a possible contributing mechanism for these differential expectations. High and low assertive women were asked to imagine refusing requests and were then shown three different photographs (smiling, slightly distressed, and very distressed) of the other person's reactions to the refusal. In viewing the smiling person, low assertives saw significantly more negative emotion and less positive emotion than high assertives. No other differences were obtained. Thus, high and low assertives differ not only in expectations regarding probable consequences and rated desirability of these consequences, but also in the way in which they perceive or process others' reactions to their behavior. It may well be that the processing of emotional reactions leads to subsequent differences in expectations regarding likely consequences and their desirability. Moreover, Josefowitz speculated that perception of the low assertives may, in fact, be more accurate because a smiling response to a refusal seems ingenuine and could be perceived as an attempt to conceal a negative emotion by the recipient of the refusal.

The fact that assertive behavior is viewed in complex and not always positive ways is well established in the literature. Assertion is frequently viewed as less likable, considerate, and desirable than more passive responses. Studies on perceptions of assertive behavior were most recently reviewed by Delamater and McNamara (1986), who noted that factors such as sex, empathy, assertiveness level, race, and situation-specific variables appear to moderate the perceptions of assertiveness and its social impact, making it difficult to arrive at conclusive generalizations. However, among the conclusions they did reach are the following: (a) unassertive, assertive, and aggressive individuals are likely to evaluate perceived consequences and their desirability in different ways, resulting in different decisions regarding how to respond; (b) results concerning the effects of the sex of the respondent are inconclusive, with a major uncontrolled variable being subjects' attitudes toward women's roles in society; (c) adding an empathy component (an expression of concern/understanding for the other person's feelings) to assertive responses tends to minimize negative reactions; (d) racial and cross-cultural differences in assertive behavior exist, suggesting different standards of behavioral appropriateness.

Attributional processes may also play a role in assertive behavior. Alden (1984) provided assertive and nonassertive females with either positive or negative feedback on their performance on a social interaction task (getting to know a stranger). Assertives attributed positive outcomes more internally than negative outcomes, whereas no attributional differences occurred for nonassertives as a function of positive or negative feedback. Assertive subjects rated positive feedback as more accurate than negative feedback; nonassertives rated both types of feedback equally. Nonassertives also rated themselves as less confident prior to the interaction and as performing more poorly. In addition, nonassertives attributed both positive and negative outcomes (feedback) to more stable factors than did assertives, suggesting that they expected factors that influence social interactions to be resistant to change. Alden (1984) compared these results to those for depressives (Raps, Peterson, Reinhard, Abramson, & Seligman, 1982), who appear to possess a negative set or cognitive style that buffers them against positive outcomes.

Cognitive Structure. Investigations of the relation between hypothesized cognitive structures and assertive behavior have been limited. However, Bruch and colleagues (Bruch, Heisler, & Conroy, 1981; Bruch, Kaflowitz, & Berger, 1988) have explored the role of two cognitive structures, conceptual complexity and self schemata for assertiveness.

Conceptual complexity (CC) refers to the number and interrelatedness of rules or schemata used for discriminating, encoding, and retrieving information about the social environment (Bruch et al., 1981) and represents an information-processing style (e.g., abstract vs. concrete). According to Schroder, Driver, and Streufert (1967), highly conceptually complex individuals can make finer discriminations of situational attributes and view situations from multiple perspectives; rely more on internally developed standards for problem solving; and possess more integrative schemata, thereby increasing tolerance for conflict. Bruch (1981) reported that higher assertives were more conceptually complex—as measured by performance on a semiprojective measure, the Paragraph Completion Method—than were low assertives. Moreover, in a pair of experiments (Bruch et al., 1981), high CC subjects demonstrated greater knowledge of assertive behavior, better oral delivery skill, more obligation (i.e., consideration for the needs of others) statements, and fewer negative statements than did low CC subjects. High CC subjects also were more assertive in extended interaction tests (better able to refuse multiple requests) and more flexible in sex-role orientation. Moreover, conceptual complexity appeared to be more critical for performance in complex social situations because differences between high and low CC subjects on simple situations were neither predicted nor found, but were evident, as predicted, in the more difficult situations.

"A schema refers to a cognitive representation on one's past experiences in a given domain of behavior, which serves to assist individuals in constructing their perception of events within that domain" (Bruch et al., 1988, p. 424). Self-schemata are presumed to guide processing of social information relevant to the self. Bruch et al. (1988) examined the influence of a self-schema for assertion in two studies. Based on endorsement of seven pairs of bipolar adjectives that reflected assertion, subjects were characterized as schematics or aschematics. Schematics endorsed the adjective *assertive,* and four of the six related adjectives, as being both highly self-descriptive and important. In contrast, aschematics had mid-range endorsement ratings on both importance and self-description.

In the first study, an assertion self-schema appeared to facilitate greater retrieval of assertion-relevant stimuli because schematics remembered significantly more assertion-related adjectives in an incidental recall task but did not differ from aschematics on recall of adjectives in domains unrelated to assertion. In the second study, it was demonstrated that the possession of a self-schema could influence information processing on tasks known to be critical to effective performance. On a series of tasks, assertion schematics differed from aschematics in a variety of ways: (a) they recalled more past instances of assertive behavior; (b) they were more certain that they would behave assertively in situations in which assertion was appropriate *as well as* in situations in which compromise was more appropriate; (c) they were more likely to judge moderately legitimate (ambiguous) requests as more unreasonable; and (d) when asked to generate expected consequences for assertion, they focused more on self than on other-person consequences. In essence, possession of an assertion self-schema influenced (biased) recall, behavioral intention, and perception related to social situations.

Social Anxiety

Antecedents of Social Anxiety

Research on antecedents of social anxiety has focused on inherited potentials, family characteristics, and developmental experiences that make one vulnerable to acquiring social fears. It should not be assumed, however, that there is a single, common pathway to the development of social anxiety nor a continuity between childhood shyness and adult social anxiety. Evidence for the genetic transmission of shyness is found in work by Plomin and Daniels (1986) and Kagan and Reznick (1986). Plomin and Daniels (1986) reviewed 17 twin studies that evaluated the heritabiity of shyness based on ratings of apprehension toward strangers. Without exception, monozygotic twins evidenced significantly higher correlations on measures of shyness than did dizygotic twins.

Because twin studies can only assume that cohorts share the same environment, Daniels and Plomin (1985) employed a full adoption design to study the heritability of shyness. Their results showed both a genetic and an environmental influence. A reliable relationship was found between biological mothers' self-report of social reticence and adoptive parents' ratings of adoptees' shyness 1 year after placement. Relative to the environmental influence, ratings of children's shyness by both adoptive and biological parent caretakers was inversely related to scores on the Personal Growth subscales of the Family Environment Scale (Moos, 1986). Such findings suggest that shy mothers avoid exposing themselves and their children to varied social activities, thereby perpetuating their child's social fears.

Despite evidence of maternal transmission of shyness, it is important to specify characteristics that may be markers of social fear. Kagan and Reznick's (1986) research on children's behavioral inhibition may be relevant to this question, because their work focused on physiological correlates of inhibition that imply a genetic influence. They found that inhibited children had higher and less variable heart rates than uninhibited children in laboratory testing situations, which suggests that inhibited children have lower thresholds of excitability in their limbic system structures. Consistent with this hypothesis was the fact that inhibited children also showed larger pupillary dilation and higher cortisol levels, both of which implicate the limbic system and hypothalamus.

Research on family antecedents of social anxiety has implicated two characteristics: parental child-rearing practices and sibling relationships. Most of the research on child-rearing has been conducted with social phobics and involves retrospective reports of parental behaviors during formative years. In one study, Parker (1979) found that social phobics perceived both of their parents as high on overprotection and low on emotional support, in contrast to controls. Arrindell et al. (1989) likewise noted that social phobics perceived their parents as overprotective and nonemotional, but also found that social phobics, compared to agoraphobics, perceived their parents as more rejecting and less consistent in rewarding their children's behavior.

One problem with this research is the lack of a conceptual rationale as to why certain parenting approaches are more associated with one type of anxiety disorder and not others. For instance, Buss (1980, 1986) advanced hypotheses about how certain child-rearing behaviors may contribute to shyness. According to him, one practice that may foster fear of negative evaluation is parental emphasis on proper grooming and manners. This practice presumably stems from a parent's concern about the opinions of others regarding appropriate social decorum in children. If parents repeatedly remind their children of how others are examining their behavior, such admonitions may contribute to development of shyness because the child may seek to avoid the scrutiny of others. Moreover, Buss (1980) contended that isolating the child from the social contact and de-emphasis of family social activities restricts opportunities for the acquisition of social skills and extinction of social fears. As noted earlier, Bruch et al. (1989b) compared groups of social phobics and agoraphobics on measures of three child-rearing practices (i.e., isolation, concern about the opinions of others, and family sociability) and found that social phobics were significantly higher on the first two and lower on the third, thus supporting Buss's hypotheses.

For sibling relationships, Zimbardo (1977) presented data suggesting that ordinal position may be a factor in the etiology of shyness. His data revealed that there was a greater tendency for single and firstborn children to be shy, and he offered two reasons for this finding. First, because parents set higher expectations for firstborn than for younger children, social evaluative concerns are more likely to develop for the firstborn. Second, because later-born children are at a power disadvantage deriving from their subordinate status, they must acquire more social skills to negotiate their needs. Asendorpf (1986) found that mothers' reports of their children's shyness were greatest for single children, followed by firstborn, middle, and, finally, last-borns. Because shyness ratings were uncorrelated with age, social status, and number of siblings, Asendorpf reasoned that the role of birth order may be to induce younger children to interact more with older siblings, thereby acquiring social skills and reducing shyness—a conclusion similar to Zimbardo's.

The most neglected area of research on the etiology of social anxiety is the effect that changes in physical, cognitive, and social development may have on the individual. No developmental studies have focused exclusively on the characteristic of shyness, but some related research appears to hold implications for shyness. One area involves the development of peer group status and the phenomenon known as peer neglect. Based on the peer nomination technique, the neglected child is defined as neither disliked nor liked, in contrast to the popular child (i.e., highly liked and not disliked) or the controversial child (i.e., both highly liked and disliked). Coie, Dodge, and Coppotelli (1982) found that shy children were most frequently classified as *neglected*. Although this status does not always persist over lengthy time intervals, Gilmartin's (1987) study of extremely shy men provided data consistent with the peer neglect notion. He found that shy (in contrast to nonshy) men were 70% more likely to report being the last chosen when drawing sides for baseball and other games, as well as being assigned insignificant roles in these activities.

Another developmental factor may be the occurrence of acute self-consciousness in early adolescence. According to Buss (1980, 1986) and Cheek et al. (1986), this anxious self-preoccupation is due to the occurrence of three processes: onset of puberty, entering new situations (e.g., junior high school), and the onset of formal operations thinking (i.e., distinguishing the perspectives of others from self-view). These processes may be critical, because they provide opportunities for scrutiny by others. In the case of formal operations thinking, the individual is in a stage of cognitive development where one has to distinguish between what is important to the self and what is of interest to others (Elkind & Bowen, 1979). Consequently, some adolescents may come to doubt previously unquestioned views about themselves and begin to imagine that others are viewing them more negatively.

Components that Maintain Social Anxiety

The definition of social anxiety as the tendency to feel tense, to worry, and to manifest awkward behavior has led to the study of somatic, behavioral, and cognitive response components. Conceptually, these three components are potential coeffects of antecedent phobic stimuli. Although individuals differ in their manifestation of one or more of these components, an understanding of the role that each plays is important.

Because anxiety, by definition, is accompanied by arousal of the sympathetic nervous system, the *somatic component* is considered to be an involuntary response. When a socially anxious person feels evaluated, the somatic symptoms almost always include tachycardia, sweating, and trembling. A review of the few studies that have included physiological assessments of social anxious people verifies that they are more aroused than their nonanxious counterparts, but only to a small degree (Beidel, Turner, & Dancer, 1985; Bruch et al., 1989a; Turner, Beidel, & Larkin, 1986). This research also shows that physiological differences are situation-specific, occurring more consistently in opposite-sex interactions than in same-sex interactions. Furthermore, in the study by Turner et al. (1986), socially anxious undergraduates and social phobics were compared, and, although both differed from nonanxious controls, they did not differ from each other in physiological arousal.

If the amount of arousal experienced by socially anxious persons is not so great, why are these symptoms problematic? One answer may be that socially anxious persons take longer to habituate to their arousal during an interaction, perhaps because of genetic and/or learned differences. Beidel et al. (1985) presented evidence to support this notion, but subsequent research has not replicated their finding. A second answer may be that socially anxious people overattend to their somatic arousal, and thereby raise concerns that others will notice their nervousness. In fact, Johanssen and Ost (1982) found that social phobics, compared to claustrophobic patients, showed a greater relation between self-perceived arousal and actual heart rate in a fear-relevant situation, suggesting that socially anxious individuals are particularly sensitive to physiological changes.

Because nervousness can be associated with low self-confidence or incompetence, changes in somatic arousal may signal a person that he or she will not be able to prevent the nervousness from being noticed by others. Consequently, the role that autonomic arousal plays may not arise from the aversiveness of the symptoms per se but in the tendency for these symptoms to cue dysfunctional cognitions. McEwan and Devins (1983) found that undergraduates who were high in both social anxiety and somatic arousal, in contrast to subjects who were high only in social anxiety, believed that their nervous behaviors were more visible than was reported by acquaintances. Bruch et al. (1989a) extended this research by having visibility ratings collected after an unstructured, videotaped interaction. This procedure allowed for an absolute standard against which to compare visibility ratings of subjects and their partner. Results showed that socially anxious persons overestimated the visibility of their nervousness relative to both their partner's ratings and videotaped evidence. In addition, visibility ratings were correlated with negative cognitions but not with heart rate, suggesting that what people think about their arousal rather than arousal per se played a more critical role.

In contrast to somatic arousal, the *behavioral component* of social anxiety involves responses that a person engages in voluntarily to cope with social difficulties. Essentially, the behavioral component refers to the presence of verbal and motor behaviors that signify inhibition or the actual avoidance of feared situations. However, Leary (1986) argued that inhibited behavior needs to be defined by recording both the *presence* of disaffiliative behaviors (e.g., gaze aversion) as well as the *absence* of responses that the person intended to engage in during the interaction. Leary's point is important because research with shy and social phobic persons suggests that actual avoidance of situations is infrequent. Instead, because of career and family responsibilities, socially anxious persons often enter fearful situations but suffer through them with great discomfort. Although a strong desire to avoid may remain, a variety of factors ultimately determines any decision to avoid. Consequently, a more meaningful way of conceptualizing the behavioral component may involve the types of dysfunctional behaviors used to minimize distress in the feared situation.

The previous discussion raises questions about the role of behavioral components in the maintenance of social anxiety. From a behavioral perspective, somatic anxiety is regarded as negative reinforcement for engaging in social interaction; thus, when one inhibits their interaction, they remove this aversive stimulus. In contrast, social psychological approaches, such as Schlenker and Leary's (1982) self-presentational model, suggest that, if the person does not expect to receive the reactions he or she desires, then goal attainment is impossible and the person inhibits further interaction to retain his or her status and prevent further social costs. Regardless of theoretical perspective, it appears that behavioral inhibition serves to minimize any anticipated or real distress that can occur in social situations. Unfortunately, such behaviors may create misimpressions or leave the individual feeling inadequate and guilty. For example, Leary (1983) suggested that gaze aversion serves both to shut out the stimuli that evoke somatic symptoms (e.g., not seeing others' facial expressions) and to decrease the chances that others will engage the person in conversation (people usually establish eye contact before addressing others). The drawback to this behavior is that people find others more interesting and attractive when they maintain eye contact during an interaction.

With regard to the *cognitive component* of social anxiety, the cognitive variables receiving significant attention in recent years (Arnkoff & Glass, 1989) include: self-statement patterns, attributions, and cognitive schemata. Self-statements are defined as "positive" if they facilitate effective or successful social interactions and "negative" if they appear to inhibit effective interaction. To date, substantial research shows that socially anxious persons report significantly more negative than positive self-statements when anticipating and actually engaging in a social interaction. Although not surprising, this finding is important to the extent that it relates to particular dysfunctional behaviors. For instance, in a study by Mandel and Shrauger (1980), male subjects were asked to read and concentrate on a list of self-statements that were either self-enhancing or self-critical; subsequently, the extent of their approach to a female peer was unobtrusively assessed. Subjects who received the self-critical statements took longer to initiate conversation and spent less time interacting than subjects who read self-enhancing statements.

A few studies have used unstructured measures to collect self-statements (i.e., thought-listing procedure) and have assessed the focus of thoughts as well as the valence. The assumption is that negative evaluative concerns should lead to a disproportionately greater focus on self than on others. Although results supporting this notion are mixed, there may be another reason to evaluate the target of subjects' self-statements. Beck and Emery (1985) postulated that one tendency of socially anxious persons is to overevaluate the qualities of others (e.g., attractiveness, competence) relative to oneself. As a result, individuals may increase their anxiety by attending to personal qualities of the other person rather than the task at hand.

In a provocative study, Mahone (1989) tested this notion with socially anxious and nonanxious college men who reported their self-statements after viewing a photograph of an attractive female student they were about to meet. Using a thought-listing procedure, subjects were instructed to describe any thoughts they had about self and about the woman as they anticipated having a conversation. Order of administration of self or other thought listing was counterbalanced and proved to be unrelated to criterion measures. Based on a multivariate analysis, Mahone found that percent of negative thoughts of self was associated with (a) lower self-efficacy ratings collected prior to the conversation and (b) greater report of anxiety at the end of the conversation. After controlling for thoughts of self, the analysis revealed that percent of positive other thoughts (e.g., "She seems very poised") was related to greater behavioral anxiety (e.g., gaze aversion) during the conversation but unrelated to self-efficacy and subjective anxiety. These results suggest that the focus of one's thoughts may trigger additional concerns, which may exacerbate the number of symptoms that occur (e.g., cognitive plus behavioral).

In terms of attributional tendencies, Arkin, Appelman, and Berger (1980) found that socially anxious persons reverse the attributional pattern known as "the self-serving bias." This bias involves the tendency to assume more personal responsibility for successful outcomes and to explain failures by situational factors. Instead, Arkin et al. (1980) revealed that socially anxious compared to nonanxious subjects attributed more personal responsibility to themselves when socially unsuccessful. Andersen and Arnoult (1985) analyzed the types of attributional dimensions (e.g., locus, stability) that were related to social anxiety compared to depression and loneliness. They found that, for shy persons, controllability (i.e., one's control over the causal factor) was more salient than locus, stability, and globality. The latter finding is interesting, given the socially anxious person's concern with not emitting behaviors that will cause embarrassment. Leary, Atherton, Hill, and Hur (1986) examined subjects' attributional tendencies regarding their feelings of nervousness in social situations and the degree to which particular attributions related to their report of social avoidance and inhibition. Their results indicated that, when nervousness was attributed to characterological factors such as limited social ability, subjects reported greater inhibition and avoidance. Because attributions are hypothesized to affect behavior through their influence on expectancies for future success, it appears from these findings that socially anxious persons are likely to become pessimistic about their chances of obtaining social rewards.

Unlike self-statements and attributions, cognitive schemata are studied using methods that do not depend on the individual's awareness of his or her cognitive activity. Because it is recognized that people do not have access to some cognitive processes, the schema construct might facilitate an understanding of the information processing of socially anxious persons. The Stroop color-naming task has been used to demonstrate the existence of a cognitive schema of vigilance for social threat stimuli. In the original Stroop task, subjects are asked to name the ink colors while trying to ignore the printed color name (e.g., "red" printed in green ink). Because subjects' response time is much longer for color names than for neutral stimuli, it appears that these increased latencies are attributable to semantic processing of color-named words despite instructions to ignore the printed color name.

Hope, Rapee, Heimberg, and Dombeck (1990) used a modified Stroop task to test whether social phobics were hypervigilant to social-evaluative threat cues. In their study, social phobics and panic disorder patients named the ink color of words related to social threat (e.g., foolish) and physical threat (e.g., stroke), as well as neutral control words. Consistent with their hypotheses, results showed that: (a) social phobics produced longer color-naming latencies for social threat words compared to control words, (b) panickers produced longer latencies for physical threat words compared to control words, and (c) neither group evidenced increased latencies for the nonrelevant threat words. As Hope et al. (1990) indicated, their data support Beck and Emery's (1985) hypothesis that social phobics have specific schemata that facilitate processing of cues relevant to their perceived vulnerability. Thus, for the social phobic, one or two speech dysfluencies may be more salient than five minutes of fluent speech, because the former are more extensively processed and remembered.

Consequences of Social Anxiety

Apart from the dysfunctional cognitive, somatic, and behavioral responses that occur in social interactions, social anxiety has been associated with a number of life adjustment problems. Research on the maladaptive consequences of shyness has generally focused on three areas that are reviewed here: loneliness, sexual behavior, and career adjustment.

Loneliness. Given their difficulties in initiating and maintaining conversations with others, it is reasonable to expect that socially anxious persons would be more lonely than nonanxious persons. Relative to this hypothesis, Cheek and Busch (1981) had shy and nonshy college students complete a loneliness scale during the first week and again just prior to the end of a semester. As expected, shys reported being more lonely than nonshys both at the beginning and the end of the semester. However, because loneliness can have multiple determinants, Bruch, Kaflowitz, and Pearl (1988) used a hierarchical regression design to evaluate the relative contribution of shyness to loneliness in undergraduate women. It was hypothesized that the influence of attribution style, self-disclosure, and perspective-taking ability would be mediated by shyness and social skills deficits, because the latter are more primary inhibitors of affiliation with others. Results indicated that shyness was the sole mediator of other variables' association with loneliness, except that lower levels of self-disclosure added a unique increment to predicting loneliness scores. Thus, it appears that the socially anxious person's tendency to disaffiliate from his or her peers can lead to feelings of loneliness.

Alternatively, Leary (1983) speculated that, because shy people tend to be viewed less positively by others, they may be more lonely because others are less likely to seek their company. Jones and Carpenter (1986) presented evidence consistent with this notion. In one study, they had undergraduate subjects bring their best friend with them to a testing session at which both completed a similar set of measures. Correlations between ratings of friendship dimensions (e.g., easy to talk to) and the shyness of the person being rated revealed a number of interesting patterns. For example, males rated shy male friends as less fun and shy female friends as less likable, less sensitive, and less physically attractive. Women rated shy male friends as less warm, less similar, and less likable, whereas they rated shy female friends as less happy, less affectionate, and less easy to talk to. These results do not mean that socially anxious people are without friends, but they suggest that their friendships are hampered by a diminished quality on such relationship dimensions as understanding, cooperation, and support.

Sexual Behavior. Although it is recognized that cross-sex interactions are anxiety-provoking for most people, these interactions are particularly difficult and frequently avoided by socially anxious persons. Not only does such avoidance limit opportunities to develop comfort in casual interactions, but it also limits opportunities for satisfying sexual experiences. Sexual encounters engender evaluative concerns, because of their ambiguous nature and emphasis on performance. Therefore, it seems unlikely that people who experience anxiety in mundane encounters will initiate or respond to sexual overtures in an effective manner.

The first research to shed light on the sexual behavior of shy persons was Leary and Dobbins's (1983) study of the sexual experiences of 260 single undergraduates. Compared with nonanxious subjects, socially anxious students were less sexually experienced, had had fewer sexual partners, were less likely to engage in oral sex, and reported a higher incidence of sexual dysfunctions. Also, social anxiety was related to contraceptive use among women but not among men. Although both anxious and nonanxious women were equally likely to use contraception, they differed in the types of birth control used. Nonanxious women were much more likely to use the pill; anxious women indicated that their partner used a condom the last time they had sex.

Leary and Dobbins's (1983) findings led Bruch and Hynes (1987) to predict that shyness would be inversely related to initiating discussion about birth control, communicating effectively about birth control, and using more effective contraceptive methods. For a woman's first intercourse experience, analysis showed that shyness was negatively correlated with discussing birth control prior to sex, with the woman's rating of her partner's effectiveness in discussing birth control, and with the effectiveness of the contraceptive method used. Further, based on women's report about recent sexual relationships, shyness was inversely related to whether the woman initiated discussion about birth control, her partner's communication effectiveness, and the effectiveness of the method for subsequent sexual relations with the same partner. These results suggest that socially anxious persons' evaluative concerns may impede their willingness to acknowledge that they are sexually active and to consult with health care providers to secure effective birth control materials. In addition, anxious women appeared to have difficulty establishing an open atmosphere with their partner, in which they discussed birth control problems and alternatives.

Career Adjustment.   Because many occupations require employees to interact with others or speak in front of groups, social anxiety may relate to the acquisition of particular vocational interests, the proper choice of a career, and effective functioning in one's job. Regarding career development, Phillips and Bruch (1988) evaluated the relation between shyness and a number of important career development behaviors. Their results indicated that shy, as compared to nonshy, undergraduates of both genders were less likely to express interest in interpersonally oriented careers (i.e., Holland's Social and Enterprising types) and engaged in fewer career information-seeking activities (e.g., talking to friends who work in a career field that is of interest). In addition, shy men and women scored lower on a career decidedness scale, and shy men were the least likely to expect that assertive job interview behaviors would lead to favorable evaluations from employers.

With respect to adult career behavior, Caspi, Elder, and Bem (1988) reported results from a 30-year study of the life-course sequelae of childhood shyness. Their most striking finding about men who were shy as children was that they delayed marrying, becoming fathers, and establishing stable careers (i.e., careers in which they held a functionally related job for at least 6 years). Further, they found that shyness alone and not in combination with other dysfunctional characteristics (e.g., aggression) accounted for later career entry, underachievement in career activities, and greater career instability during midlife years (ages 30 to 40). Unlike their male counterparts, women with a childhood history of shyness were not delayed or off-time in marrying or starting families, compared with nonshy women in the cohort. This result was not surprising: the subjects were in their adult years during a time that emphasized traditional sex roles. Consequently, women's career patterns were assessed by examining the timing and duration of periods in and out of the labor force, from before marriage through midlife. Caspi et al. (1988) found that women with a childhood history of shyness were more likely than nonshy women (56% vs. 36%) either to have no work history at all, or to terminate employment at marriage or childbirth and not reenter the labor force.

TREATMENT

Assertion

As developed historically, interventions for assertion deficits often involved a variety of treatment components packaged together in assorted ways, depending on whether the therapist/investigator was influenced by an anxiety reduction, skills deficit, cognitive deficit, or some combined conceptual model. Many of these interventions were subsequently adopted or modified for use in treating social anxiety. Some of the most common intervention components included behavioral rehearsal, modeling, reinforcement, relaxation, audio- or videotape feedback, therapist coaching, cognitive restructuring or other cognitive change techniques, role reversal, self-evaluation, group discussions, therapist exhortations, homework assignments, bibliotherapy, and training in nonverbal expression (Galassi & Galassi, 1978).

Overall, the majority of research in this area has been concerned with answering one of three questions:

1. Is assertion training effective as compared to a no-treatment or other control group?
2. What contributions do different components (e.g., rehearsal vs. modeling) make to effective treatment?
3. Is a cognitive treatment better than a skills-based treatment or does it add appreciably to a skill-based treatment?

As has been noted previously (Galassi et al., 1981; Galassi & Galassi, 1978), a variety of methodological limitations have complicated cross-study comparisons, including differences in the populations studied, length of treatment, components of treatment, response classes treated (e.g., refusals), subjects' initial level of difficulty with assertion, failure to screen subjects, type of study (analogue or clinical), and differences in assessment procedures used. Nevertheless, a number of tentative conclusions were drawn by several reviewers (Galassi et al., 1981, 1984; Galassi & Galassi, 1978; Rich & Schroeder, 1976; Stefanek & Eisler, 1983), and these are briefly summarized and illustrated here.

The Treatment Package Approach

The first "objective" appraisal of assertion training was conducted by Lazarus (1966), who was both the therapist and the investigator in the study. Lazarus "demonstrated" the effectiveness of assertion training based on behavior rehearsal, compared to direct advice and nondirective therapy, with neurotic outpatients.

Since that time, the effectiveness of assertion training packages, which typically include behavior rehearsal, has been evaluated compared to no-treatment or other types of control groups, primarily with two populations: college students and hospitalized psychiatric patients. Demonstrations of effectiveness have usually been provided by (a) self-report measures of assertion and anxiety and (b) behavioral observation measures based on performance in analogue role-play situations in laboratory settings, staged interactions in lab or waiting-room encounters, or contrived in vivo encounters (e.g., telephone refusal situations). Overall, research has tended to support the effectiveness of these treatment packages, especially for college students.

Research by Galassi and colleagues (Galassi, Galassi, & Litz, 1974; Galassi, Kostka, & Galassi, 1975) exemplifies this approach. Galassi et al. (1974) administered to college students 12 hours of group treatment using a comprehensive package consisting of behavior rehearsal, modeling, coaching, peer and videotape feedback, homework, bibliotherapy, trainer exhortation, and peer group support. The students scored 1 to 1 1/2 standard deviations below the mean on a validated, self-report measure of assertion. The study employed a Solomon four-group design, to allow for detection of pretest and pretest-by-treatment interaction effects. Following treatment, significant differences were found between experimental and control group subjects on self-report measures of anxiety and assertion and on several behavioral measures (eye contact, assertive content, and length of scene, but not response latency) in untrained role-play situations. Some pretest effects were also evident for several of the variables. At a 1-year follow-up (Galassi et al., 1975), significant experimental–control group differences were still evident for the two self-report measures and for two (assertive content and scene length) of the three behavioral measures.

The Components Approach

Another body of research has been concerned with the differential effectiveness of various components of the training packages. Unfortunately, a number of problems are encountered in comparing these studies, including (a) the same named components are not identical from study to study; (b) variation in response classes, dependent variables, and/or subject populations have resulted in conflicting findings; and (c) there is a lack of statistical power to detect differential component effects (Galassi et al., 1981; Galassi & Galassi, 1978). Nevertheless, some general trends and tentative conclusions appear warranted.

Early research in the area focused on the effectiveness of behavior rehearsal and on what components were added above and beyond behavior rehearsal; later research began with a modeling base. Behavior rehearsal involves repeated practice of situational behavior, which often is preceded by instructions about how to behave and/or followed by performance feedback. Modeling involves observing another individual perform the behavior and observing the consequences the performance produces. It appears that effective treatment packages can be based on either foundation (Galassi et al., 1984), as is illustrated by research by McFall and by Kazdin and Eisler.

McFall and Marston (1970) found that overt behavior rehearsal was effective in increasing assertive behavior in college students and that taped (audio or video) performance feedback and self-evaluation did not significantly augment effectiveness. In a subsequent study, McFall and Lillesand (1971) reported that a covert (an imaginal) rehearsal treatment that included modeling and coaching regarding what makes a good response produced significantly greater improvement on a number of measures of refusal behavior than did a similar overt rehearsal group. Unfortunately, the overt group also received performance feedback, which makes the results difficult to interpret. Correcting for this problem, McFall and Twentyman (1973) investigated the contribution of rehearsal, modeling, and coaching in a series of experiments. Rehearsal and coaching both made significant additive contributions, but modeling added little to the effects of rehearsal alone or rehearsal plus coaching. In addition, there were no differences due to type of rehearsal—covert, overt, or combined.

In a series of studies, Kazdin (1974, 1975, 1976a, 1976b, 1979a, 1979b) studied the effects of covert modeling and additional intervention components. Kazdin (1974), for example, found that covert modeling was effective in increasing refusal responses in college students as compared to no-model and no-treatment control groups, and that reinforcement of the model enhanced the effects on a few of the variables. In subsequent studies, it was shown that: imagining several models led to greater changes than imagining a single model; favorable model consequences enhanced performance; gains transferred to novel role-playing situations; and gains were maintained on self-report follow-up measures 4 months later. Moreover, generating verbal summary codes of imagined assertive responses to aid memory and subsequent retrieval enhanced modeling effects, as did allowing subjects to elaborate the imagery of modeling scenes.

Eisler and colleagues (Eisler, Blanchard, Fitts, & Williams, 1978; Eisler, Hersen, & Miller, 1973; Hersen, Eisler, Miller, Johnson, & Pinkston, 1973) studied the effects of overt modeling plus practice, with psychiatric patients. Eisler et al. (1973) found that this condition was more effective in increasing assertive behavior than either a practice-alone or a test–retest control group. Hersen et al. (1973) reported that modeling plus practice and instructions was significantly more effective on a number of variables than were modeling plus practice, practice-alone, instructions-alone, or test–retest control groups. Instructions proved the most effective component in increasing loudness, and modeling plus practice was most effective in changing compliance behavior. These results suggest that intervention components may be differentially effective with different verbal and nonverbal behaviors. Eisler et al. (1978) investigated the effects of adding modeling to social skills training (behavior rehearsal, coaching, feedback) with schizophrenic and nonpsychotic patients. Modeling was necessary for improving the performance of schizophrenics, particularly with respect to delivery style, but was unnecessary or even detrimental for nonpsychotics.

In summary, it appears that effective assertion training packages can be constructed based on either a modeling or a behavior rehearsal foundation. The additive effects of components to these basic packages are a function of a variety of factors, such as the specific component, what is already in the package, the population (e.g., psychotic or not), and the verbal or nonverbal behavior to be changed. The interested reader is referred to the previously cited reviews for additional details.

The Cognitive Approach

Not surprisingly, a number of studies have investigated the effectiveness of a cognitive approach to assertion training based on the assumption that cognitive deficits mediate unskilled, anxious (nonassertive) behavior. Thus, dysfunctional cognitions or cognitive processes and their correction are the focus of treatment. For the most part, these studies reflect the influence of Ellis and Meichenbaum, because the treatments typically have been concerned with identifying and disputing irrational beliefs or with substituting positive, coping self-statements for negative self-statements.

Four basic research approaches have predominated: (a) comparisons of a cognitive or cognitive-behavioral treatment with a control group (Craighead, 1979; McIntyre, Jeffrey, & McIntyre, 1984); (b) comparisons of a cognitive treatment with a behavioral treatment (Alden, Safran, & Weideman, 1978; Safran, Alden, & Davidson, 1980; Stoppard & Henri, 1987); (c) investigations of the additive effects of a cognitive component to an existing behavioral treatment (Hammen, Jacobs, Mayol, & Cochran, 1980; Wolfe & Fodor, 1977); and (d) comparisons of a combined cognitive-behavioral treatment to simpler cognitive-only and behavioral-only treatments (Kaplan, 1982; Linehan, Goldfried, & Goldfried, 1979). Unfortunately, a variety of methodological weaknesses have plagued research in this area—failure to screen subjects on assertion measures, use of subjects scoring at or above the mean on assertion, failure to demonstrate the presence of assertion-relevant cognitive deficits prior to training, failure to measure cognitions directly tied to assertion, low statistical power, and infrequent follow-up assessment (Galassi et al., 1981, 1984; Stefanek & Eisler, 1983).

A few examples, however, will provide the reader with a sense of research in this area. In an interesting recent study, Stoppard and Henri (1987) investigated the effects of cognitive and behavioral assertion training (AT) within a matching context. Conceptual level (CL; discussed in an earlier section on cognitive processes and assertion) was the matching variable. In accordance with conceptual systems theory (Harvey, Hunt, & Schroeder, 1961), it was hypothesized that low-CL clients who received behavioral AT (high structure) would make greater gains in assertiveness and express greater satisfaction with counseling than low-CL clients who received cognitive AT (low structure). Moreover, high-CL clients who received cognitive AT (low structure) were expected to make greater gains and to be more satisfied than high-CL clients who received behavioral AT (high structure). Following four 2-hour treatment sessions led by the same counselor, subjects in the behavioral and cognitive groups did not differ from each other. Moreover, only limited support for the matching hypothesis was obtained on a few variables. Low-CL clients in the behavioral (high structure) AT group showed more improvement in verbal content during role playing and evaluated the counselor as more expert and trustworthy than did low-CL clients in the cognitive group. No matching effects were obtained for high-CL clients.

Hammen et al. (1980) compared the effectiveness of an 8-week skills training program (behavior rehearsal, instructions, coaching, modeling, group and trainer feedback, praise, homework assignments, and discrimination of unassertive, assertive, and aggressive behavior) to a cognitive-behavioral treatment (skills training plus cognitive restructuring based on Ellis and Meichenbaum) with students high and low in dysfunctional cognitions, as measured by the Dysfunctional Attitude Scale. The subjects were nonstudent adults. Results indicated that the training groups were significantly more effective than a wait-list control group but not different from each other across most dependent measures. The skills group, however, significantly outperformed the cognitive-behavioral group on a goal attainment scale, and the cognitive-behavioral group did significantly better on a measure of behavioral compliance. No differential generalization effects were evident for the two groups. Moreover, level of dysfunctional attitude did not interact with type of treatment, although individuals who had less dysfunctional cognitions showed more improvement across most measures than those who had more dysfunctional cognitions. Thus, cognitions may be important in predicting outcome or amount of treatment needed but not type of treatment needed.

The fact that cognitions correlate with outcome has also been demonstrated by Lee (1983). In an assertion training program with college students, she found that self-efficacy measures (self-beliefs that one can perform a given behavior) predicted subsequent behavioral performance. Contrary to Bandura's (1977) theory, however, self-efficacy measures were less accurate than behavioral measures in predicting subsequent behavior.

Kaplan (1982) compared cognitive assertion training, behavioral assertion training, cognitive-behavioral assertion training, and a self-awareness training control group with nonassertive college students over 8 weeks (1½ hours per week) of training and 3- and 6-month follow-ups. Cognitive assertion training included eliciting and challenging irrational beliefs, coping (emotive imagery and relaxation), and self-instructional skills, whereas behavioral assertion training relied on behavior rehearsal, modeling, coaching, and feedback. The self-awareness treatment consisted of structured experiences in human relations, and values clarification to facilitate self-awareness and sharing of feelings among group members. A variety of self-report and behavioral measures, including a situational test of assertion cognitions and two unobtrusive measures were used to assess outcome. In general, the three treatment groups were more effective in increasing assertive behavior than the self-awareness control group, but did not differ from each other. Moreover, a greater number of significant differences emerged between the combined treatment group and the self-awareness control group than between any other treatment group and the control group.

Overall, the conclusions reached in earlier reviews (Galassi et al., 1981, 1984; Stefanek & Eisler, 1983) still appear applicable. Although there is some support for the effectiveness of cognitive and cognitive-behavioral assertion treatments, "we lack solid evidence that cognitively based assertion treatments are superior to more traditional behaviorally based treatments, that they add appreciably to behaviorally based treatments, or that they enhance maintenance" (Galassi et al., 1984, p. 368). "On the other hand, the statement that behavioral skills approaches add little to the efficacy of cognitive approaches would seem just as valid . . . ." (Stefanek & Eisler, 1983, p. 310). It is difficult to explain the lack of differential treatment effects. Low statistical power, insufficient or inadequate training, the multifaceted nature of treatments, and a common treatment mechanism (e.g., self-efficacy or outcome expectations) are among the explanations that have been posed (Stefanek & Eisler, 1983). In contrast, the potential of cognitive variables (e.g., conceptual complexity, dysfunctional attitudes, self-efficacy) as predictors of treatment or differential treatment responsiveness is suggestive and worth pursuing in future research concerned with interpersonal interactions and social performance.

Social Anxiety

Counselors have only recently developed systematic treatment strategies for the problems of shyness and social phobia. There have been several recent reviews of the differential effectiveness of various intervention procedures for shyness and social phobia (Alden & Cappe, 1986; Glass & Shea, 1986; Haemmerlie & Montgomery, 1986; Heimberg, 1989). Because no single approach has emerged as the treatment of choice, the purpose of the present section is to provide a brief overview of the procedures being used and the issues that need further investigation. This overview does not discuss recent advances in pharmacological therapy for some types of social phobia, which may be found in Levin, Schneier, and Liebowitz (1989).

Social Skills Training

Early formulations of social anxiety problems emphasized a skills-deficit hypothesis suggesting that anxious persons lacked the requisite interpersonal skills to function effectively in various social situations. Thus, social skills treatments utilizing modeling, rehearsal, and feedback for acquisition of important microresponses (e.g., eye contact) seemed appropriate. However, subsequent research showed that this treatment was not superior to other approaches, because many clients already possessed requisite skills. Consequently, Alden and Cappe (1986) proposed a redefinition of skills training procedures that focuses more on the dyadic communication process in which clients become active listeners, empathic responders, and reciprocal self-disclosers. In the only study to test the validity of their approach, Cappe and Alden (1986) found that the skills treatment, compared to an exposure-alone treatment, increased shy adult clients' report of participation and comfort in outside social activities. However, judges' ratings did not support Cappe and Alden's (1986) hypothesis that the skills treatment would shift the shy clients' attentional focus to the task, thereby reducing their self-consciousness.

Relaxation Strategies

The use of applied relaxation techniques in which the individual practices tension reduction during role-played social interactions, and then follows this up with in vivo practice, has received some attention. This procedure is presumed to be effective for persons who experience a significant amount of somatic arousal, which inhibits their utilization of social skills. Unfortunately, as Heimberg (1989) noted, the few studies that employed this technique with social phobics showed mixed results. It may be useful to develop a reliable means for classifying clients as "somatic reactors," to determine whether relaxation is particularly effective with this type of socially anxious person.

Exposure

It is well recognized that the most effective treatment for phobic anxiety of any kind is exposure (Butler, 1989). Although the mechanisms by which exposure achieves its effect are not well understood, the use of graduated, repeated, and prolonged exposure trials reduces subjective anxiety and avoidance in virtually all anxiety problems. Social phobia, unlike other phobias, creates some difficulties in the application of exposure techniques. For example, exposure tasks cannot always be graduated and prolonged because social situations are highly variable and have their own intrinsic time limit. Nonetheless, Butler (1989) described a number of tactics for increasing the effectiveness of exposure, such as being more active in a conversation so as not to be a passive participant, and repeating a series of brief exposure situations that focus on a theme (e.g., center of attention), in order to produce a more prolonged exposure experience. As reported by Heimberg (1989), studies employing exposure procedures have shown the most consistent results in ameliorating some aspects of social phobia. However, in several studies, exposure treatments had little impact on cognitive measures and showed some deterioration between posttreatment and follow-up assessment on behavioral and cognitive aspects of anxiety. This pattern suggests that exposure may work best in combination with other techniques, an issue we will return to shortly.

For shy undergraduates, Haemmerlie and Montgomery (1986) developed an exposure-like procedure called the *biased interaction technique,* in which students participate in multiple interactions that have been structured unobtrusively to ensure a positive experience. Designed for problems of dating anxiety, the treatment consists of two sets of six 12-minute interactions with different men or women who have been simply instructed to be friendly and initiate conversation. Results from three studies indicated that the procedure led to a significant reduction in self-reported social anxiety and, in one study, 6-month follow-up data revealed reduced subjective anxiety and report of more frequent dating. Unfortunately, subjects in these studies were not informed until after their exposure that the interactions were positively biased, and, in the one study with follow-up data, were not informed that they were even being treated. Consequently, it is unclear whether informing subjects about the interactions reduced the long-term effectiveness of this treatment.

Cognitive Treatment

Both Heimberg (1989) and Glass and Shea (1986) discussed a number of studies that employed various aspects of cognitive restructuring in treating shy and social phobic adolescents and adults. In general, cognitive techniques evidenced some effectiveness. Heimberg's (1989) analysis suggests, however, that this approach is most effective when integrated with exposure procedures (i.e., having clients learn and practice cognitive restructuring routines during an exposure task). In Heimberg et al.'s (1990) cognitive-behavioral group treatment, clients learned to identify their automatic thoughts relative to a feared situation. In turn, thoughts were analyzed for their underlying distortions (e.g., emotional reasoning, mindreading) and then disputed (e.g., What evidence do I have?). Rational responses were taught to help clients cope with their automatic thoughts, and these rational responses were practiced in both laboratory exposure tasks and in vivo homework assignments. Heimberg et al.'s (1990) data support the efficacy of this treatment relative to a credible educational-supportive condition, particularly on indexes of cognitive change that persisted over a 6-month follow-up.

What can be concluded from recent reviews of the effectiveness of various treatments for shyness and social phobia? First, it appears that social skills and relaxation strategies might be most beneficial for clients with particular dysfunctional characteristics (e.g., deficient social skills, intense levels of somatic arousal), although there is a need to examine the treatment effectiveness further as a function of client characteristics. For example, might generalized social phobics benefit more from social skills training or shy persons with limited impairment benefit more from exposure with cognitive restructuring? Second, as Heimberg (1989) argued, it is important that future studies address the mechanisms by which specific treatments achieve their effect on social anxiety problems. Cognitive treatments have shown long-term impact on reducing fear of negative evaluation, but other mechanisms, such as reduced self-consciousness, should be considered. In this regard, self-efficacy beliefs might be important, because results from some cognitive treatments show a reduction in avoidance behavior despite continued arousal, suggesting that clients no longer interpret their nervousness as debilitating. Finally, the impact of parameters such as group versus individual treatment and the existence of a social support system on treatment outcome requires study. Such factors have unique relevance to the problem of social anxiety.

CONCLUSIONS

It has been just over 30 years since Wolpe (1958) published his landmark work on assertiveness training and just over 20 years since the first empirical studies by Marks (1970) and McFall and Marston (1970) on social phobia and assertiveness, respectively. Much has been learned about the development, maintenance, and modification of what we have called social interaction problems, in this short time.

The "early" work on assertion has resulted in many important contributions. The assertion construct and the literature it has engendered have clearly taught us the significance of situational influences on social behavior, spawned important theoretical models concerning the factors that control and maintain social interaction problems, and produced a significant body of research about the effective treatment of these problems.

For the practicing counselor, the assertion literature has produced a number of useful, validated assessment tools, including self-report measures of assertion frequency and comfort as well as behavioral role-play tests and cognitive measures (Galassi et al., 1981, 1984; St. Lawrence, 1987). Moreover, from these, a relatively clear picture of assertive and nonassertive functioning has emerged. This picture, in turn, has treatment-related implications for the counselor with respect to the benchmarks or indexes of competent client social performance. Behaviorally, less assertive individuals differ from their more assertive counterparts in displaying less eye contact or gazing (similar to shys and social phobics), more objective and subjectively rated anxiety, less appropriate verbal content, more compliance to unreasonable requests, fewer requests for behavior change, fewer smiles during commendatory assertion, less loudness and affect, and longer response latency.

In addition, research suggests that the counselor will encounter important differences in cognitive functioning between individuals displaying assertion deficits and those who do not. Notably, the internal dialogue of clients with assertion deficits (and social anxiety) is one of conflict between negative and positive self-statements, whereas positive self-statements predominate in other individuals. In addition, as with the social phobic, the internal dialogue is characterized by perfectionist standards, overconcern for others, concern about being disliked, self-image, and other-directed thoughts. Differences in cognitive processing, notably in problem solving and attributions, are also evident. Individuals exhibiting assertion deficits (a) view requests from others as more legitimate (i.e, perceive less of a problem); (b) see themselves as less able to perform effective responses; (c) view negative consequences as more likely and undesirable for refusal behavior, and positive consequences as more likely and desirable for acquiescence (the opposite of the pattern of their more assertive peers); and (d) attribute social outcomes to more stable factors, suggesting that they expect social interactions to be resistant to change. Finally, individuals with assertion deficits appear to be less cognitively complex which, in turn, is adversely related to their ability to perform effectively in more difficult social situations.

All of these cognitive differences would seem to strongly suggest that counselors should employ exclusively cognitively-oriented treatments for clients with assertion deficits. Although there certainly are data supporting the effectiveness of these treatments as compared to no-treatment and other types of control groups, there appears to be no reason to favor cognitive treatments over behavioral treatments or to believe that a cognitive treatment adds appreciably to the effects of a behavioral treatment or vice versa. Moreover, there does not even appear to be a basis for concluding that cognitive and behavioral treatments have different response-specific effects, with cognitive treatments effecting change only (or even maximally) on cognitive variables and behavioral treatments on behavioral variables. On the other hand, cognitive variables may have an important role to play in predicting overall response to treatment, because cognitive complexity, dysfunctional attitudes, and self-efficacy have all shown some promise in that regard.

With respect to treatment effectiveness in general, the assertion literature represents a somewhat confusing state of affairs for the researcher, but a rather rich and informative one for the counselor. On the one hand, we know very little about the effective underlying mechanism(s) of change in these treatments and have little empirical basis for matching treatment components with client characteristics. Both of these are situations that are all too common in counseling and psychotherapy research and that represent important areas for future research. On the other hand, the practicing counselor can feel confident that various treatment packages, including those based on behavior rehearsal, modeling, and cognitive components, have been shown to effect change in clients who have assertion deficits, and that there is some evidence that this change can be maintained for a year or more.

At the same time, the literature has shown that the counselor should not expect wide generalization of treatment effects across response classes (e.g., from refusal behavior to commendatory assertion) and needs to intervene with clients in a situation- and response-specific manner. Finally, the literature has demonstrated that, depending on a variety of variables, assertion is not always positively perceived but that teaching clients to include an empathic component in their responses will help to forestall or minimize negative reactions from others.

In addition to the specific contributions mentioned above, the assertion literature has influenced and paved the way for many of the current emphases and directions in recent research and practice with social interaction problems. At this time, however, it would appear that the interest in assertion, as well as what it has to offer to the future understanding and treatment of social interaction problems, has peaked.

In contrast, it would appear that interest in social anxiety and in the potential contribution that research on this construct has to make is still on the rise. This research already has much to offer to the practicing counselor who is confronted with a socially anxious client. With respect to assessment and diagnosis, this phase of intervention is best conceptualized from a person–situation perspective, similar to assertion. Because social anxiety problems involve multiple response components that occur in relation to situation-eliciting cues, it is important to identify those situations that are most troublesome and to assess what cognitive, somatic, and/or behavioral consequences occur. Having the client construct a hierarchy of problem situations may reveal common themes (e.g., being the center of attention). In turn, the client's cognitive representation of these situational cues should always be evaluated along with any physiological and behavioral responses. Even for the client who insists that he or she does not think about anything but only feels his or her heart racing when conversing with someone of the opposite sex, there is a cognitive component. For this client, it might involve the thought of "If I show the true me, he or she will be turned off."

Differential diagnosis is also important in establishing the degree of impairment caused by the client's interaction problems. Many clients may report substantial feelings of shyness and/or great discomfort in situations involving members of the opposite sex, but show little impairment in other daily functioning. Such problems require attention, to prevent the individual from becoming more dysfunctional (e.g., more avoidant of those situations) and to facilitate more optimal adjustment (e.g., greater confidence in job role). However, it is important to consider whether a client meets DSM-III-R criteria for social phobia. If so, does the client meet criteria for the subtype of generalized or nongeneralized? In the former case, there is greater certainty that the individual will have difficulty in assertiveness, social, and public-speaking situations. In the latter case, the person may be comfortable asserting himself or herself with sales clerks and may enjoy attending parties, but may become highly anxious in meetings, especially if called on to speak.

Given the evidence for the central role that cognitive variables play in social anxiety, treatment procedures should be operationalized to target cognitive components as well as other factors (e.g., behavioral inhibition). Consequently, whether the focus is on irrational beliefs that limit awareness or somatic arousal that occurs in the presence of situational cues, both conditions contain cognitive elements that need to be addressed. In the former case, cognitive therapy techniques might be used to identify and modify dysfunctional beliefs. However, in the second case, relaxation training paired with a cognitive-plus-exposure procedure may lead to a more adaptive interpretation of one's arousal and subsequent coping. Despite the absence of substantial treatment outcome results, the evidence reviewed suggests that a multiple-treatment-components approach tailored to the unique situational difficulties of a given client should produce observable changes.

Although much has already been learned from social anxiety research, many questions still remain to be answered. Among the most prominent of these are the following: (a) What familial and developmental antecedents are associated with particular subtypes of shyness and social phobia? (b) What dysfunctional cognitive mechanisms are crucial for maintaining problems of social anxiety? and (c) What mechanisms are responsible for treatment improvement relative to different social anxiety problems?

With the emphasis on developmental, genetic, social, and psychological influences that has typified this area—coupled with its tie to the widely accepted DSM-III-R classification system—social anxiety is likely to continue to attract a very broad audience of researchers from a variety of academic and professional disciplines. We feel optimistic that such multidisciplinary involvement can only enrich and enhance our knowledge in this area. At the same time, it is important that we not forget the knowledge acquired from the earlier assertion research and continue to recognize the importance of such factors as situational influences on behavior and the need for clear specification of treatment components in outcome research. As we shift our focus to social anxiety, we need to accommodate, not relearn, what we already know.

REFERENCES

Alberti, R. E., & Emmons, M. L. (1970). *Your perfect right: A guide to assertive behavior.* San Luis Obispo, CA: Impact.

Alden, L. (1984). An attributional analysis of assertiveness. *Cognitive Therapy and Research, 8,* 607–618.

Alden, L., & Cappe, R. (1986). Interpersonal process training for shy clients. In W. H. Jones, J. M. Cheek, & S. R. Briggs (Eds.), *Shyness: Perspectives on research and treatment* (pp. 343–355). New York: Plenum Press.

Alden, L., & Safran, J. (1978). Irrational beliefs and nonassertive behavior. *Cognitive Therapy and Research, 2,* 357–364.

Alden, L., Safran, J., & Weideman, R. (1978). A comparison of cognitive and skills training strategies in the treatment of unassertive clients. *Behavior Therapy, 9,* 843–846.

American Psychiatric Association. (1987). *Diagnostic and statistical manual of mental disorders* (3rd ed.). Washington, DC: Author.

Amies, P. L., Gelder, M. G., & Shaw, P. M. (1983). Social phobia: A comparative clinical study. *British Journal of Psychiatry, 142,* 147–179.

Anderson, C. A., & Arnoult, L. H. (1985). Attributional style and everyday problems in living: Depression, loneliness, and shyness. *Social Cognition, 3,* 16–35.

Arkin, R. M., Appelman, A. J., & Berger, J. M. (1980). Social anxiety, self-presentation, and the self-serving bias in causal attribution. *Journal of Personality and Social Psychology, 38,* 23–35.

Arnkoff, D. B., & Glass, C. R. (1989). Cognitive assessment in social anxiety and social phobia. *Clinical Psychology Review, 9,* 61–74.

Arrindell, W. A., Kwee, M. G. T., Methorst, G. J., Van Der Ende, J., Pol, E., & Moritz, B. J. M. (1989). Perceived parental rearing styles of agoraphobic and socially phobic in-patients. *British Journal of Psychiatry, 155,* 526–535.

Asendorpf, J. B. (1986). Shyness in middle and late childhood. In W. H. Jones, J. M. Cheek, & S. R. Briggs (Eds.), *Shyness: Perspectives on research and treatment* (pp. 91–103). New York: Plenum Press.

Bandura, A. (1977). Self-efficacy: Toward a unifying theory of behavior change. *Psychological Review, 84,* 191–215.

Beck, A. T., & Emery, G. (1985). *Anxiety disorders and phobias: A cognitive perspective.* New York: Basic Books.

Beidel, D. C., Turner, S. M., & Dancer, C. (1985). Physiological, cognitive, and behavioral aspects of social anxiety. *Behaviour Research and Therapy, 23,* 109–117.

Berrier, G. D., Galassi, J. P., & Mullinix, S. D. (1981). A comparison of matched clinical and analogue subjects on variables pertinent to the treatment of assertion deficits. *Journal of Consulting and Clinical Psychology, 49,* 980–981.

Briggs, S. R. (1988). Shyness: Introversion or neuroticism? *Journal of Research in Personality, 22,* 290–307.

Bruch, M. A. (1981). A task analysis of assertive behavior revisited: Replication and extension. *Behavior Therapy, 12,* 217–230.

Bruch, M. A. (1989). Familial and developmental antecedents of social phobia: Issues and findings. *Clinical Psychology Review, 9,* 34–47.

Bruch, M. A., Giordano, S., & Pearl, L. (1986). Differences between fearful and self-conscious shy subtypes in background and current adjustment. *Journal of Research in Personality, 20,* 172–186.

Bruch, M. A., Gorsky, J. M., Collins, T. M., & Berger, P. A. (1989a). Shyness and sociability reexamined: A multicomponent analysis. *Journal of Personality and Social Psychology, 57,* 904–915.

Bruch, M. A., & Heimberg, R. G. (1990). *Social phobia subtype and differences in early parental and personal characteristics.* Manuscript in preparation.

Bruch, M. A., Heimberg, R. G., Berger, P., & Collins, T. M. (1989b). Social phobia and perceptions of early parental and personal characteristics. *Anxiety Research: An International Journal, 2,* 57–65.

Bruch, M. A., Heisler, B. D., & Conroy, C. G. (1981). Effects of conceptual complexity on assertive behavior. *Journal of Counseling Psychology, 28,* 377–385.

Bruch, M. A., & Hynes, M. J. (1987). Heterosocial anxiety and contraceptive behavior. *Journal of Research in Personality, 21,* 343–360.

Bruch, M. A., Kaflowitz, N. G., & Berger, P. (1988). Self-schema for assertiveness: Extending the validity of the self-schema construct. *Journal of Research in Personality, 22,* 424–444.

Bruch, M. A., Kaflowitz, N. G., & Pearl, L. (1988). Mediated and nonmediated relationships of personality components to loneliness. *Journal of Social and Clinical Psychology, 6,* 462–471.

Buss, A. H. (1980). *Self-consciousness and social anxiety.* San Francisco: Freeman.

Buss, A. H. (1986). A theory of shyness. In W. H. Jones, J. M. Cheek, & S. R. Briggs (Eds.), *Shyness: Perspectives on research and treatment* (pp. 39–46). New York: Plenum Press.

Butler, G. (1989). Issues in the application of cognitive and behavioral strategies to the treatment of social phobia. *Clinical Psychology Review, 9,* 91–106.

Cappe, R. F., & Alden, L. E. (1986). A comparison of treatment strategies for clients functionally impaired by extreme shyness and social avoidance. *Journal of Consulting and Clinical Psychology, 54,* 796–801.

Caspi, A., Elder, G. H., & Bem, D. J. (1988). Moving away from the world: Life-course patterns of shy children. *Developmental Psychology, 24,* 824–831.

Cheek, J. M., & Busch, C. M. (1981). The influence of shyness on loneliness in a new situation. *Personality and Social Psychology Bulletin, 7,* 572–577.

Cheek, J. M., Carpentieri, A. M., Smith, T. G., Rierdan, J., & Koff, E. (1986). Adolescent shyness. In W. H. Jones, J. M. Cheek, & S. R. Briggs (Eds.), *Shyness: Perspectives on research and treatment* (pp. 105–115). New York: Plenum Press.

Cheek, J. M., & Melchior, L. A. (1990). Shyness, self-esteem, and self-consciousness. In H. Leitenberg (Ed.), *Handbook of social and evaluation anxiety* (pp. 47–82). New York: Plenum Press.

Cheek, J. M., & Watson, A. K. (1989). The definition of shyness: Psychological imperialism or construct validity? *Journal of Social Behavior and Personality, 4,* 85–95.

Chiauzzi, E., & Heimberg, R. G. (1986). Legitimacy of request and social problem solving. *Behavior Modification, 10,* 3–18.

Coie, J. D., Dodge, K. A., & Coppotelli, H. (1982). Dimensions and types of social status: A cross-age perspective. *Developmental Psychology, 18,* 557–570.

Craighead, L. W. (1979). Self-instructional training for assertive refusal behavior. *Behavior Therapy, 10,* 529–542.

Curran, J. P., Wallander, J. L., & Fischetti, M. (1980). The importance of behavioral and cognitive factors in heterosexual-social anxiety. *Journal of Personality, 48,* 285–292.

Daniels, D., & Plomin, R. (1985). Origins of individual differences in infant shyness. *Developmental Psychology, 21,* 118–121.

Delamater, R. J., & McNamara, J. R. (1986). The social impact of assertiveness: Research findings and clinical implications. *Behavior Modification, 2,* 139–158.

D'Zurilla, T. J., & Goldfried, M. R. (1971). Problem solving and behavior modification. *Journal of Abnormal Psychology, 78,* 107–126.

Eisler, R. M., Blanchard, E. B., Fitts, H., & Williams, J. G. (1978). Social skill training with and without modeling for schizophrenic and non-psychotic hospitalized psychiatric patients. *Behavior Modification, 2,* 147–172.

Eisler, R. M., Frederiksen, L. W., & Peterson, G. L. (1978). The relationship of cognitive variables to the expression of assertiveness. *Behavior Therapy, 9,* 419–427.

Eisler, R. M., Hersen, M., & Miller, P. M. (1973). Effects of modeling on components of assertive behavior. *Journal of Behavior Therapy and Experimental Psychiatry, 4,* 1–6.

Eisler, R. M., Hersen, M., Miller, P. M., & Blanchard, E. B. (1975). Situational determinants of assertive behavior. *Journal of Consulting and Clinical Psychology, 42,* 330–340.

Elkind, D., & Bowen, R. (1979). Imaginary audience behavior in children and adolescents. *Developmental Psychology, 15,* 38–44.

Fiedler, D., & Beach, L. R. (1978). On the decision to be assertive. *Journal of Consulting and Clinical Psychology, 46,* 537–546.

Futch, E. J., Scheirer, C. J., & Lisman, S. A. (1982). Factor analyzing a scale of assertiveness: A critique and demonstration. *Behavior Modification, 6,* 23–43.

Galassi, J. P., Berrier, B. D., & Mullinix, S. D. (1982). The appropriateness of using statistically selected college students as analogues to adult clinical subjects: A preliminary comparison on measures of psychological adjustment. *The Behavior Therapist, 5,* 179–180.

Galassi, M. D., & Galassi, J. P. (1978). Assertion: A critical review. *Psychotherapy: Theory, Research, and Practice, 15,* 16–29.

Galassi, M. D., & Galassi, J. P. (1980). Similarities and differences between two assertion measures: Factor analysis of the College Self-Expression Scale and the Rathus Assertiveness Schedule. *Behavioral Assessment, 2,* 43–57.

Galassi, J. P., Galassi, M. D., & Fulkerson, K. (1984). Assertion training in theory and practice: An update. In C. M. Franks (Ed.), *New developments in practical behavior therapy: From research to clinical application* (pp. 319–376). New York: Haworth Press.

Galassi, J. P., Galassi, M. D., & Litz, C. M. (1974). Assertive training in groups using videofeedback. *Journal of Counseling Psychology, 21,* 390–394.

Galassi, J. P., Galassi, M. D., & Vedder, M. J. (1981). Perspectives on assertion as a social skills model. In J. D. Wine & M. D. Smye (Eds.), *Social competence* (pp. 287–345). New York: Guilford Press.

Galassi, J. P., Kostka, M. P., & Galassi, M. D. (1975). Assertive training: A one-year follow-up. *Journal of Counseling Psychology, 22,* 451–452.

Gay, M. L., Hollandsworth, J. G., Jr., & Galassi, J. P. (1975). An assertiveness inventory for adults. *Journal of Counseling Psychology, 22,* 340–344.

Gilmartin, B. G. (1987). Peer group antecedents of severe love-shyness in males. *Journal of Personality, 55,* 467–489.

Glass, C. R., & Shea, C. A. (1986). Cognitive therapy for shyness and social anxiety. In W. H. Jones, J. M. Cheek, & S. R. Briggs (Eds.), *Shyness: Perspectives on research and treatment* (pp. 315–327). New York: Plenum Press.

Gorman, J. M., & Gorman, L. K. (1987). Drug treatment of social phobia. *Journal of Affective Disorders, 13,* 183–192.

Haemmerlie, F. M., & Montgomery, R. L. (1986). Self-perception theory and the treatment of shyness. In W. H. Jones, J. M. Cheek, & S. R. Briggs (Eds.), *Shyness: Perspectives on research and treatment* (pp. 329–342). New York: Plenum Press.

Hammen, C. L., Jacobs, M., Mayol, A., & Cochran, S. C. (1980). Dysfunctional cognitions and the effectiveness of skills and cognitive-behavioral assertion training. *Journal of Consulting and Clinical Psychology, 48,* 685–695.

Harris, P. R. (1984). Shyness and psychological imperialism: On the dangers of ignoring the ordinary language roots of the terms we deal with. *European Journal of Social Psychology, 14,* 169–181.

Harvey, O. J., Hunt, D. E., & Schroeder, H. M. (1961). *Conceptual systems and personality organization.* New York: Wiley.

Heimberg, R. G. (1989). Cognitive and behavioral treatments for social phobia: A critical analysis. *Clinical Psychology Review, 9,* 107–128.

Heimberg, R. G., & Becker, R. E. (1981). Cognitive and behavioral models of assertive behavior: Review, analysis and integration. *Clinical Psychology Review, 1,* 353–371.

Heimberg, R. G., & Chiauzzi, E. J., Becker, R. E., & Madrazo-Peterson, R. (1983). Cognitive mediation of assertive behavior: An analysis of the self-statement patterns of college students, psychiatric patients, and normal adults. *Cognitive Therapy and Research, 7,* 455–464.

Heimberg, R. G., Dodge, C. S., Hope, D. A., Kennedy, C. R., & Zollo, L. J. (1990). Cognitive behavioral group treatment for social phobia: Comparison to a credible placebo control. *Cognitive Therapy and Research, 14,* 177–189.

Heimberg, R. G., Hope, D. A., Dodge, C. S., & Becker, R. E. (1989). DSM-III-R subtypes of social phobia: Comparison of generalized social phobics and public speaking phobics. *Journal of Nervous and Mental Diseases, 178,* 172–179.

Heimberg, R. G., Montgomery, D., Madsen, C. H., & Heimberg, J. S. (1977). Assertion training: A review of the literature. *Behavior Therapy, 8,* 953–971.

Henderson, M., & Furnham, A. (1983). Dimensions of assertiveness. Factor analysis of five assertion inventories. *Journal of Behavior Therapy and Experimental Psychiatry, 14,* 223–231.

Hersen, M., Bellack, A. S., & Turner, S. M. (1978). Assessment of assertiveness in female psychiatric patients: Motor and autonomic measures. *Journal of Behavior Therapy, 17,* 63–69.

Hersen, M., Eisler, R. M., Miller, P. M., Johnson, M. B., & Pinkston, S. G. (1973). Effects of practice, instructions, and modeling on components of assertive behavior. *Behaviour Research and Therapy, 11,* 443–451.

Hess, E. P., & Bornstein, P. H. (1979). Perceived sex-role attitudes in self and others as a determinant of differential assertiveness in college males. *Cognitive Therapy and Research, 3,* 155–159.

Hope, D. A., Rapee, R. M., Heimberg, R. G., & Dombeck, M. J. (1990). Representations of the self in social phobia: Vulnerability to social threat. *Cognitive Therapy and Research, 14,* 177–189.

Johanssen, J., & Ost, L. (1982). Perception of autonomic reactions and actual heart rate in phobic patients. *Journal of Behavioral Assessment, 4,* 133–143.

Jones, W. H., & Carpenter, B. N. (1986). Shyness, social behavior, and relationships. In W. H. Jones, J. M. Cheek, & S. R. Briggs (Eds.), *Shyness: Perspectives on research and treatment* (pp. 227–238). New York: Plenum Press.

Jones, W. H., Cheek, J. M., & Briggs, S. R. (Eds.). (1986). *Shyness: Perspectives on research and treatment.* New York: Plenum Press.

Josefowitz, N. (1989). How unassertive women perceive emotional expressions. *Canadian Journal of Behavioral Science, 21,* 239–245.

Kagan, J., & Reznick, S. J. (1986). Shyness and temperament. In W. H. Jones, J. M. Cheek, & S. R. Briggs (Eds.), *Shyness: Perspectives on research and treatment* (pp. 81–90). New York: Plenum Press.

Kaplan, D. A. (1982). Behavioral, cognitive, and behavioral-cognitive approaches to group assertion training therapy. *Cognitive Therapy and Research, 6,* 301–314.

Kazdin, A. E. (1974). Effects of covert modeling and model reinforcement on assertive behavior. *Journal of Abnormal Psychology, 33,* 240–252.

Kazdin, A. E. (1975). Covert modeling, imagery assessment, and assertive behavior. *Journal of Consulting and Clinical Psychology, 43,* 716–724.

Kazdin, A. E. (1976a). Assessment of imagery during covert modeling of assertive behavior. *Journal of Behavior Therapy and Experimental Psychiatry, 7,* 213–219.

Kazdin, A. E. (1976b). Effects of covert modeling, multiple models, and model reinforcement on assertive behavior. *Behavior Therapy, 7,* 211–222.

Kazdin, A. E. (1979a). Effects of covert modeling and coding of modeled stimuli on assertive behavior. *Behaviour Research and Therapy, 17,* 53–61.

Kazdin, A. E. (1979b). Imagery elaboration and self-efficacy in the covert modeling treatment of unassertive behavior. *Journal of Consulting and Clinical Psychology, 47,* 725–733.

Kelly, J. A., Kern, J. M., Kirkley, G. B., Patterson, J. N., & Keane, T. M. (1980). Reactions to assertive versus unassertive behavior. Differential effects for males and females and implications for assertiveness training. *Behavior Therapy, 11,* 670–682.

Kendall, P. C., & Hollon, S. D. (1981). Assessing self-reference speech: Methods in the measurement of self-statements. In P. C. Kendall & S. D. Hollon (Eds.). *Assessment strategies for cognitive-behavioral interventions.* New York: Academic Press.

Kirschner, N. M. (1976). Generalization of behaviorally oriented assertive training. *Psychological Record, 26,* 117–125.

Kirschner, S. M., & Galassi, J. P. (1983). Person, situational, and interactional influences on assertive behavior. *Journal of Counseling Psychology, 30,* 355–360.

Kuperminc, M., & Heimberg, R. G. (1983). Consequence probability and utility as factors in the decision to behave assertively. *Behavior Therapy, 14,* 637–646.

Lazarus, A. A. (1966). Behavior rehearsal vs. non-directive therapy vs. advice in effecting behavior change. *Behaviour Research and Therapy, 4,* 209–212.

Lazarus, A. A. (1971). *Behavior therapy and beyond.* New York: McGraw-Hill.

Leary, M. R. (1983). *Understanding social anxiety.* Beverly Hills: Sage.

Leary, M. R. (1986). Affective and behavioral components of shyness. In W. H. Jones, J. M. Cheek, & S. R. Briggs (Eds.), *Shyness: Perspectives on research and treatment* (pp. 27–38). New York: Plenum Press.

Leary, M. R., Atherton, S. C., Hill, S., & Hur, C. (1986). Attributional mediators of social inhibition and avoidance. *Journal of Personality, 54,* 704–716.

Leary, M. R., & Dobbins, S. E. (1983). Social anxiety, sexual behavior, and contraceptive use. *Journal of Personality and Social Psychology, 45,* 1347–1354.

Lee, C. (1983). Self-efficacy and behaviour as predictors of subsequent behaviour in an assertiveness training program. *Behaviour Research and Therapy, 21,* 225–232.

Levin, A. P., Schneier, F. R., & Liebowitz, M. R. (1989). Social phobia: Biology and pharmacology. *Clinical Psychology Review, 9,* 129–140.

Linehan, M. M., Goldfried, M. R., & Goldfried, A. P. (1979). Assertion therapy: Skill training or cognitive restructuring. *Behavior Therapy, 10,* 371–378.

Lohr, J. M., & Bonge, D. (1982). Relationships between assertiveness and factorially validated measures of irrational beliefs. *Cognitive Therapy and Research, 6,* 353–356.

Mahone, E. M. (1989). *Self-other discrepancy in social anxiety.* Unpublished doctoral dissertation, The University at Albany, State University of New York.

Mandel, N. M., & Shrauger, J. S. (1980). The effects of self-evaluative statements on heterosocial approach in shy and nonshy males. *Cognitive Therapy and Research, 4,* 369–381.

Marks, I. M. (1970). The classification of phobic disorders. *British Journal of Psychiatry, 16,* 377–386.

McEwen, K. L., & Devins, G. M. (1983). Is increased arousal in social anxiety noticed by others? *Journal of Abnormal Psychology, 92,* 417–421.

McFall, R. M. (1976). Behavioral training: A skill-acquisition approach to clinical problems. In J. T. Spence, R. C. Carson, & J. W. Thibaut (Eds.), *Behavioral approaches to therapy* (pp. 227–259). Morristown, NJ: General Learning Press.

McFall, R. M., & Lillesand, D. B. (1971). Behavior rehearsal with modeling and coaching in assertion training. *Journal of Abnormal Psychology, 77,* 313–323.

McFall, R. M., & Marston, A. R. (1970). An experimental investigation of behavior rehearsal in assertive training. *Journal of Abnormal Psychology, 76,* 313–323.

McFall, R. M., & Twentyman, C. T. (1973). Four experiments on the relative contributions of rehearsal, modeling, and coaching to assertion training. *Journal of Abnormal Psychology, 81,* 199–218.

McIntyre, T. J., Jeffrey, D. B., & McIntyre, S. L. (1984). Assertion training: The effectiveness of a comprehensive cognitive-behavioral treatment package with professional nurses. *Behaviour Research and Therapy, 22,* 311–318.

Moos, R. H. (1986). *Family Environment Scale.* Palo Alto, CA: Consulting Psychologists Press.

Nevid, J. S., & Rathus, S. A. (1979). Factor analysis of the Rathus Assertiveness Schedule with a college population. *Journal of Behavior Therapy and Experimental Psychiatry, 10,* 21–24.

Ost, L. (1987). Age of onset of different phobias. *Journal of Abnormal Psychology, 96,* 223–229.

Parker, G. (1979). Reported parental characteristics of agoraphobics and social phobics. *British Journal of Psychiatry, 135,* 550–560.

Phillips, S. D., & Bruch, M. A. (1988). Shyness and dysfunction in career development. *Journal of Counseling Psychology, 35,* 159–165.

Pitcher, S. W., & Meikle, S. (1980). The topography of assertive behavior in positive and negative situations. *Behavior Therapy, 5,* 375–388.

Plomin, R., & Daniels, D. (1986). Genetics and shyness. In W. H. Jones, J. M. Cheek, & S. R. Briggs (Eds.), *Shyness: Perspectives on research and treatment* (pp. 63–90). New York: Plenum Press.

Rakos, R. F. (1979). Content consideration in the distinction between assertive and aggressive behavior. *Psychological Reports, 44,* 767–773.

Raps, C., Peterson, C., Reinhard, K., Abramson, L., & Seligman, M. (1982). Attributional style among depressed patients. *Journal of Abnormal Psychology, 91,* 102–108.

Reich, J., & Yates, W. (1988). Family history of psychiatric disorders in social phobia. *Comprehensive Psychiatry, 29,* 72–75.

Rich, A. R., & Schroeder, H. E. (1976). Research issues in assertiveness training. *Psychological Bulletin, 83,* 1084–1096.

Rodriguez, R., Nietzel, M. T., & Berzins, J. I. (1980). Sex-role orientation and assertiveness among female college students. *Behavior Therapy, 11,* 353–366.

Romano, J. M., & Bellack, A. S. (1980). Social validation of a component model of assertive behavior. *Journal of Consulting and Clinical Psychology, 48,* 478–490.

Rose, Y. J., & Tryon, W. W. (1979). Judgments of assertive behavior as a function of speech loudness, latency, content, gestures, inflection, and sex. *Behavior Modification, 3,* 112–123.

Russell, D., Cutrona, C., & Jones, W. G. (1986). A trait-situational analysis of shyness. In W. H. Jones, J. M. Cheek, & S. R. Briggs (Eds.), *Shyness: Perspectives on research and treatment* (pp. 238–249). New York: Plenum Press.

Safran, J. D., Alden, L. E., & Davidson, P. O. (1980). Client anxiety level as a moderator variable in assertion training. *Cognitive Therapy and Research, 4,* 189–200.

St. Lawrence, J. S. (1987). Assessment of assertion. In M. Hersen, R. M. Eisler, & P. M. Miller (Eds.), *Progress in behavior modification* (Vol. 21, pp. 152–190). New York: Academic Press.

Salter, A. (1949). *Conditioned reflex therapy.* New York: Capricorn.

Schlenker, B. R., & Leary, M. R. (1982). Social anxiety and self-presentation: A conceptualization and model. *Psychological Bulletin, 92,* 641–669.

Schroder, H. M., Driver, M. J., & Streufert, O. (1967). *Human information processing.* New York: Holt, Rinehart and Winston.

Schwartz, R. M., & Gottman, J. M. (1976). Toward a task analysis of assertive behavior. *Journal of Consulting and Clinical Psychology, 44,* 910–920.

Skillings, R. E., Hersen, M., Bellack, A. S., & Becker, M. P. (1978). Relationship of specific and global measures of assertion in college females. *Journal of Clinical Psychology, 34,* 346–353.

Stefanek, M. E., & Eisler, R. M. (1983). The current status of cognitive variables in assertiveness training. In M. Hersen, R. M. Eisler, & P. M. Miller (Eds.), *Progress in behavior modification* (Vol. 15, pp. 277–319). New York: Academic Press.

Stoppard, J. M., & Henri, G. S. (1987). Conceptual level matching and effects of assertion training. *Journal of Counseling Psychology, 34,* 55–61.

Turner, S. M., & Beidel, D. C. (1989). Social phobia: Clinical syndrome, diagnosis, and comorbidity. *Clinical Psychology Review, 9,* 3–18.

Turner, S. M., Beidel, D. C., & Larkin, K. T. (1986). Situational determinants of social anxiety in clinic and non-clinic samples: Physiological and cognitive correlates. *Behaviour Research and Therapy, 24,* 56–64.

Wolfe, J. L., & Fodor, I. G. (1977). Modifying assertive behavior in women: A comparison of three approaches. *Behavior Therapy, 8,* 567–574.

Wolpe, J. (1958). *Psychotherapy by reciprocal inhibition.* Stanford, CA: Stanford University Press.

Wolpe, J. (1973). *The practice of behavior therapy* (2nd ed.). New York: Pergamon Press.

Young, E. R., Rimm, D. C., & Kennedy, T. D. (1973). An experimental investigation of modeling and verbal reinforcement in the modification of assertive behavior. *Behaviour Research and Therapy, 11,* 317–319.

Zimbardo, P. G. (1977). *Shyness: What is it and what to do about it.* Reading, MA: Addison-Wesley.

Zimbardo, P. G. (1986). The Stanford Shyness Project. In W. H. Jones, J. M. Cheek, & S. R. Briggs (Eds.), *Shyness: Perspectives on research and treatment* (pp. 17–25). New York: Plenum Press.

CHAPTER 24
COUNSELING PSYCHOLOGY PERSPECTIVES ON THE PROBLEM OF SUBSTANCE ABUSE

CHRISTINE M. OLSON
JOHN J. HORAN
JOAN POLANSKY

SUBSTANCE ABUSE: WHAT IS THE PROBLEM?
WHY SHOULD COUNSELING PSYCHOLOGY BE INVOLVED?

Civil libertarians have long argued that the problem of drug abuse in our culture is largely one of our own making. By restricting the availability of a given substance, we increase its market value, create an underground culture of users not amenable to help and suppliers not subject to taxation, and damage our law-enforcement structure by draining its resources and exposing its personnel to overwhelmingly lucrative, but corrupt, alternatives.

Despite the fact that the civil libertarian case for decriminalization has been increasingly embraced by major conservative theorists such as William Buckley and Milton Friedman, President George Bush's continuing escalation of the war on drugs designates the casual user as another member of the enemy within. Given that half of our nation's high school seniors have smoked marijuana (Johnston, Bachman, & O'Malley, 1989), the new battle front portends to be wide indeed.

The case for decriminalization has been eloquently presented elsewhere (Nadelmann, 1989; Trebach, 1988); we will return to it at the close of this chapter. Regardless of its merits on other grounds, decriminalization will not solve the problem of substance abuse any more than repeal of Prohibition eliminated alcoholism. Portions of the sociopolitical problem we now experience would remain long after enforcement and incarceration costs, for example, were no longer an issue. This chapter is concerned with those aspects of the problem that exist now and would likely continue under conditions of decriminalization.

We would prefer to define the problem of substance abuse strictly in terms of tissue damage and sustained psychological dysfunction (the latter needing thorough operationalization). Although the hazard potential of most drugs when taken infrequently at

Preparation of this manuscript was supported in part by Project REAL (Regional Educational Action Labs) and by the Sally M. Berridge Foundation.

a very low dosage level has not been clearly established, there is general consensus about the deleterious effects of prolonged heavy consumption.

The problem of substance abuse can be clarified further through a secondary analysis of survey research findings. Contrary to opinions frequently expressed in the media, "use" and "abuse" are not synonyms. Data on high school seniors updated yearly by Johnston and his associates (1989), for example, show that students commonly experiment with drugs (47.2% have tried marijuana, and 12.1%, cocaine); however, the numbers of students currently involved with these substances on a monthly or daily basis are substantially and progressively smaller.

Even though these latter percentages are relatively tiny (2.7% for marijuana and 0.2% for cocaine), they are not trivial; when extrapolated nationwide, they indicate that large numbers of youths are heavily involved with drugs. Nevertheless, the current patterns of drug use reported by Johnston and his associates are consistent with data from a 20-year longitudinal study by Baumrind (1990), which rendered erroneous the popular impression that experimentation invariably leads to habit formation and poly-drug addiction. Indeed, Shedler and Block (1990) showed that abstainers, heavy users, and experimenters represent distinct diagnostic categories, with the latter displaying the highest personal-social competence. Such findings provide a focus for this chapter. We concern ourselves here with the etiology, assessment, prevention, and treatment of *chronic* use, given that exploratory forays with a number of substances are well within the limits of normality (if not legality).

Before proceeding further, however, we wish to note with some bewilderment the relative lack of attention given to the topic of substance abuse in the counseling psychology literature. We found a flurry of articles on substance abuse published in the *Journal of Counseling Psychology* during the early 1970s, but, in the latter part of that decade and on through the 1980s, the publication frequency of such manuscripts dropped to about once every three years. Moreover, not a single manuscript in *The Counseling Psychologist,* a journal published by Division 17 of the APA, has ever focused on the topic of substance abuse. Conversely, other related professional societies, such as the Association for Advancement of Behavior Therapy and the Association for Counseling and Development, have devoted considerable journal space to drug use.

How can this be? There can be little doubt that a literature on preventive interventions applied to normal individuals is well within the bailiwick of counseling psychology (Fretz, 1982; Ivey, 1980; Sprinthal, 1990). The casual use of certain illegal drugs can hardly be called abnormal; if one includes alcohol and tobacco in our compendium of problematic products, the phenomenon of which we speak becomes a majority experience. Even if, for the sake of argument, we relegate the subtopic of "inpatient care of the chronically addicted" to clinical psychology, we are still perplexed that the growing body of literature relevant to the prevention of drug abuse is not finding its way into counseling psychology journals. We are pleased that the editors of this *Handbook* have designated substance abuse as a topic of special interest to counseling psychology. We would hope that the literature of counseling psychology will follow suit and provide increasing coverage of new data-based developments in this field.

Our chapter is divided into four sections of somewhat uneven length and depth. We open with a discussion of the etiology of substance abuse. There is no dearth of data here, but, given the correlational nature of most projects, many insights must be considered speculative. The second section focuses on assessment; it includes a brief description of the ambiguities within the popularly used DSM-III-R diagnostic system and offers an alternative framework for classifying the goals of intervention. We then review the prevention-programming and addictions-treatment literatures, and conclude with a brief discussion of public policy formation.

Throughout the chapter, we provide special attention to the topics of cigarettes and alcohol, given that they are the most widely abused drugs among adults and adolescents in the United States (Johnston et al., 1989; Spieger & Harford, 1987). Indeed, cigarette smoking is the foremost preventable cause of death in America (Califano, 1979), and the health cost associated with alcohol abuse, estimated at $100 billion per year, dwarfs that of all illegal drugs combined (Nadelmann, 1989).

THE ETIOLOGY OF SUBSTANCE ABUSE

For a variety of reasons, any discussion of the etiology of substance abuse must remain somewhat speculative. In the first place, the accumulated data are frequently retrospective in nature; that is, they are gathered after (often, long after) drug use has begun. Thus, it is difficult to sort out the potential causes for taking drugs from the possible effects of having consumed them. For example, does low self-esteem produce or result from drug abuse? Or, do both variables derive from poor social skills?

Well-controlled cross-sectional designs such as those cited by Block, Block, and Keys (1988) and Kandel (1980) can increase confidence in our etiological suppositions, as can longitudinal research that examines the relationships between personal-social variables and *subsequent* drug use (Baumrind, 1990; Shedler & Block, 1990). However, exemplary longitudinal projects are rare and, in any event, do not fully establish causality; there is no methodological substitute for the inability of researchers to randomly assign individuals to the personal-social variables presumably leading to substance abuse.

Yet another obstacle to the construction of a consensually validated etiological theory stems from the manner in which drugs may be classified. For example, some researchers study only alcoholism; others may study more than one drug but categorize them in idiosyncratic ways. Moreover, researchers differ widely in their definition of terms. Some define "abuse" as a single exploratory puff on a pipe full of marijuana; others restrict the term's meaning to chronic addiction. Only the most confirmed optimist would expect to find stable predictors in the wake of shifting criterion variables. Given related issues such as the differing availabilities of certain drugs and the disparate social sanctions their use may engender (e.g., tobacco vs. heroin), useful etiological theory may need to be drug-specific.

Because of the foregoing difficulties, our goals here are rather modest. We begin with a review of general behavioral factors that undergird most etiological frameworks, including classical decision theory. Although decision theory can be invoked to support the use of information-based programming (the most common prevention modality of the past two decades), it has not yet been embellished to include more recently published behavioral correlates which, at least theoretically, contribute to the initiation and maintenance of drug use. We examine a number of these correlates in closer detail and briefly review the purported biological determinants of alcoholism, before concluding with a summary of Marlatt's comprehensive etiological framework.

General Behavioral Factors

The sources of reinforcement for taking drugs were catalogued long ago on a theoretical level by Cahoon and Cosby (1972), Horan (1973), and Miller (1973). For example, both physiological positive reinforcement (euphoria) and social positive reinforcement (enhanced peer status) may occur after drug use. Moreover, modeling is an efficient substitute for trial-and-error learning; we need not experience social reinforcement directly, but rather can readily learn about whatever payoffs exist from watching the behavior of others.

Positive reinforcement may act along or in conjunction with negative reinforcement; in other words, one might use drugs because of the "reward" that follows or the "pain" that precedes taking them. Negative reinforcement, likewise, may be physiological or social, as in warding off a withdrawal reaction or escaping from a noxious home, school, or vocational life. A vicious cycle can easily develop: continual use of drugs usually produces a worsening of one's physical and social condition, which then may be followed by more and more relief-seeking (drug-taking) behavior.

Many current etiological models of substance abuse ultimately derive from one or more of these elementary behavioral factors. For example, the "peer cluster theory" of Oetting and Beauvais (1987) and Lichtenstein's (1982) "natural history of a smoker's career" paid considerable homage to social reinforcement as a precursor to substance abuse. Similarly, escape from ghetto stressors and/or other untoward life events were prominent features of frameworks developed by Lex (1987), Lisansky-Gomberg (1987), Morales (1984), and Rhodes and Jason (1990).

In more recent years, these behavioral factors have been given a "cognitive" overlay. It has been argued, for example, that substance abusers differ from users (e.g., social drinkers) both in their (faulty) beliefs about potential benefits of the drug and in their ability to cope with the stress of everyday life (Abrams & Niaura, 1987; Cooper, Russell, & George, 1988; George & Marlatt, 1983; Wilson, 1987). Etiological models and consequent intervention paradigms have become increasingly cognitive and complex.

Many counseling psychologists are familiar with the cognitive-behavioral components of classical decision theory applied to the field of career development (Katz, 1966); however, they may not be aware that classical decision theory provides the basis for an etiological model of substance abuse essential to the logic of information-based prevention programming.

Classical Decision Theory and Drug Use

The behavioral factors underlying drug use, mentioned above, fit rather comfortably into a classical-decision-theory framework (Broadhurst, 1976; Horan, 1979; Mausner, 1973). In its simplest form, classical decision theory posits that our choice of a given activity rests on the cornerstone concepts of value and probability.

Subjective values are known as utilities and (like reinforcers) may be positive or negative in nature. Indulging in or abstaining from drugs, for example, will result in a variety of utilities. Depending on the particular peer group, drug abstinence might be met with approval or ridicule. Similarly, the physical effects of drug consumption might be perceived as pleasant or aversive. Utilities can be quantified in such a way as to imply that one alternative may be far more desirable than another. If peer approval is important to us and our peer group abhors the use of drugs, and if we perceive the effects of a particular drug to be unpleasant, our choice is obvious. Our choice is much less obvious if our peer group advocates the use of drugs. In this case, our decision would rest on the magnitudes we attach to peer approval and physical comfort.

The foregoing example presumes that the probabilities of the relevant utilities are certain (i.e., equal to 1.0). In many decisions, however, the probabilities of the various utilities accruing are much less than inevitable. For example, "getting caught" with drugs by parents or police might be perceived as quite horrible. However, in a given situation, the odds of this occurring might be very slight. Classical decision theory thus suggests that, in choice situations, we select the alternative with the highest subjectively expected utility (SEU). In other words, we qualify our utilities with an estimation of how likely they are to be realized if we implement a given alternative. In deciding whether to smoke marijuana on a given occasion, for example, we would: (a) identify the possible positive and negative utilities; (b) weight them (e.g., on a 1-to-10 scale); (c) multiply each utility score by each probability "guesstimate"; and finally (d) select the alternative with the highest perceived payoff (total SEU value).

Although classical decision theory does not proclaim that everyone purposefully goes through the foregoing mental gymnastics prior to choosing, the mathematical relationships involved are good predictors of which alternative we will eventually select (Bauman, 1980). Curiously enough, classical decision theory not only accounts for what we in fact do; it also has strong implications for what we *ought* to do. Whenever the former does not correspond with the latter, factors such as irrational utilities or inaccurate probability information can usually be found lurking in the background.

Unfortunately, classical decision theory has not evolved to accommodate newly emerging etiological data in the substance abuse field. How, for example, do faulty child-rearing practices contribute to the development of irrational utilities, and what can be done to remediate such irrationality? Consequently, in the behaviorally oriented substance abuse literature, classical decision theory is far less popular than the more ambitious formulations of others (Marlatt, 1978). Let us now turn to a number of environmental and individual correlates on which more complex etiological models may be built.

Environmental and Individual Correlates

Environmental correlates refer to the influences of family, peers, and availability. A wide variety of *family* variables apparently contribute to substance abuse by children and adolescents. These include rather obvious factors such as parents' favorable attitudes or actual use of drugs by parents (Barnes & Welte, 1986; Harford, 1984; Harford & Grant, 1986; Kandel & Adler, 1982; Newcomb & Bentler, 1988; Newcomb, Chou, Bentler, & Huba, 1988) and more circuitous influences such as the absence of perceived parental support, excessive permissiveness, chaotic living conditions, family disruption through divorce or separation, and inconsistent parenting styles (Block, Block, & Keyes, 1988; Kovach & Glickman, 1986). Interestingly, disruption per se may be less important when strong mutual attachments exist between parents and their offspring (Hawkins, Lishner, Catalano, & Howard, 1986). Moreover, Baumrind's (1990) data indicate that the presence of such attachments, along with coherent and consistent parenting styles, is "protective" against substance abuse. As the adolescent matures, the influence of family variables wanes and that of the peer group becomes primary, peaking between the ages of 18 and 21 (Harford, 1984; Kandel, 1980; Kandel & Adler, 1982).

Peer group variables are consistently predictive of substance use (Newcomb et al., 1988; Newcomb & Bentler, 1986), undoubtedly through modeling and social reinforcement processes (Harford & Grant, 1986). Indeed, the power of these processes has been experimentally demonstrated on alcohol consumption (Dericco & Garlington, 1977) and in the formation of expressed drug attitudes (Stone & Shute, 1977). Additionally, there appear to be "drug-specific" peer subcultures that engage in, for example, alcohol or marijuana, and eschew the use of other substances (Spieger & Harford, 1987).

Availability is also associated with increased consumption of various substances (Spieger & Harford, 1987). For example, living in college dormitories precipitates more drug use than does living with one's parents, presumably because of decreased opportunity at home (Bachman, O'Malley, & Johnston, 1984). Moreover, Helzer's (1987) review of large-scale epidemiological studies in many countries supports the notion that increased availability of alcohol contributes to alcohol-related problems and morbidity rates.

Individual correlates of substance abuse include gender, personality, and cognitive motivations. The role of *gender* is relatively straightforward; male adolescents abuse more substances, especially alcohol and marijuana, than females (Barnes & Welte, 1986; Newcomb et al., 1988; Newcomb, Fahy, & Skager, 1986); however, this is no longer the case for tobacco (Kandel, 1980). Although males and females self-report similar reasons for using drugs (Johnston & O'Malley, 1986), females appear to be more vulnerable to peer and family influences (Kandel, 1986).

Personality variables related to substance abuse have received considerable attention over the past decade (Block et al., 1988). Many researchers believe there is no evidence for a unitary "addictive personality" (Kandel, 1980, 1986; Nathan & Lansky, 1978; Spieger & Harford, 1987); yet, Shedler and Block's (1990) exemplary study of 101 young adults tracked from preschool to 18 years of age would seem to suggest otherwise. The study sorted abstainers, experimenters, and abusers into distinct diagnostic categories and concluded that the latter "were maladjusted, showing a distinct personality syndrome marked by interpersonal alienation, poor impulse control, and manifest emotional distress." Moreover, differences among these categories "could be traced to the earliest years of childhood and related to the quality of parenting received" (p. 612).

In any event, there is little consensus in the research community about which personality variables contribute to substance abuse. Some argue that there are very few personality precursors, with the most prominent being unconventionality or nonconformity with adult societal expectations (Baumrind, 1990); others posit characteristics such as sensation seeking (Hawkins et al., 1986), depressed mood (Kashani, Keller, Solomon, Reid & Mazzola, 1985), and low self-esteem (Hawkins et al., 1986). Still others believe that personality determinants vary with the type of drug abused and the gender of the abuser; for example, personality correlates suggested for marijuana use include rebelliousness, nontraditional values, de-emphasis on achievement, and self-centeredness, and those for other drugs include distancing and distrustfulness (for females), and aggressiveness (for males) (Block et al., 1988). Baumrind (1990) concluded that any role played by personality characteristics is overshadowed by the family variables discussed earlier.

Cognitive variables such as self-reported motivations or reasons for substance use have important intervention implications, given their high correlations with actual substance use and the fact that they may differentiate type of substance used, frequency of use, age of user, and state of use (initiation vs. maintenance). For example, reported motivations for alcohol and marijuana abuse include "getting away from problems," and those for cocaine and amphetamines involve "staying alert and awake." Moreover, "self-medicating" motives increase with consumption frequency and age of the abuser; in contrast, younger adolescents and infrequent users commonly cite social cohesion as a reason for use (Baumrind, 1990; Hawkins et al., 1986; Johnston & O'Malley, 1986; Kovach & Glickman, 1986; Newcomb & Bentler, 1986, 1988; Newcomb et al., 1988).

Biological Determinants of Alcoholism

Research on the biological determinants of alcoholism flows from the assumption that variability in the use and abuse of alcohol arises from genetic and environmental factors and their interactions (Searles, 1988). Four methods of inquiry are typically used: family history (consanguinity), twin, adoption, and, more recently, high-risk-group studies.

Family, twin, and adoption studies have shown a definite "familial" nature to the development of alcoholism, but the relative influence of genetic and environmental factors has not been established. Some reports suggest genetic "links" (Blum et al., 1990; Goodwin, Schulsinger, Hermansen, Guze, & Winokur, 1973; Kaij, 1960); others demonstrate little or no such influence (see Murray, Clifford, & Gurling, 1983, for an extensive review). The lack of consistency here may well be a function of numerous conceptual and methodological flaws. These include, for example, inaccurate determination of zygosity, inadequate diagnostic criteria, inappropriate samples, and poor operational definitions of environmental factors (Helzer, 1987; Murray et al., 1983; Searles, 1988). Nevertheless, this line of research does suggest that males have a higher vulnerability for the development of alcoholism than females (Saunders & Williams, 1983). Prior to a recent report indicating the possible presence of a genetic marker for some forms of alcoholism (Blum et al., 1990), no other study has found any biological marker(s) exclusively responsible for the development of alcoholism (Reed, 1985; Stabenau, 1985; Swinson, 1983).

High-risk-group research rests on an investigative strategy that identifies nonalcoholic individuals who have a family history of alcohol abuse, matches them with a control group having no such family history, and compares these groups on a variety of responses to alcohol ingestion. Emerging differences would presumably serve as "markers" for genetically controlled mechanisms contributing to alcohol abuse. For example, sons of alcoholics rate themselves as less intoxicated and demonstrate smaller decrements in cognitive performance than sons of nonalcoholics, even when there are no significant differences in time to reach peak blood-alcohol-concentration (BAC) levels (Schuckit, 1981). Moreover, on electrophysiological measures, sons of alcoholics demonstrate less alpha wave activity compared to sons of nonalcoholics, suggesting that ethanol may have different reinforcing effects on individuals at high risk for alcoholism (Schuckit, 1987).

It is often the case that investigators report more variability within the groups than between them, on biochemical, neuropsychological, and electrophysiological responses to alcohol ingestion and subsequent susceptibility to alcohol-related problems. Nevertheless, because previous attempts to find a genetic marker solely responsible for predisposing a given population to alcohol abuse have not been especially fruitful, high-risk-group research has become increasingly prominent (Schuckit, 1987).

The Marlatt Model

Marlatt's evolving biopsychosocial model of the addiction process incorporates many of the above-mentioned etiological correlates in an attempt to account for the initiation, maintenance, and change of substance abuse behavior (Marlatt, 1978; Marlatt, Baer, Donovan, & Kivlahan, 1988). The *initiation* stage includes both genetic and social factors that place one at risk for addiction. For example, high levels of acetaldehyde may protect against the development of alcoholism in Asians, whereas peer drug use, poor self-esteem, and/or parental sociopathy may predispose anyone to becoming an addict. The *transition and maintenance* stage explains the passage from social to deviant usage patterns. The pharmacological effects of the drug, the person's psychological set, and a complex system of physical and social stimuli that comprise the setting in which the drug is consumed are all involved. *Initiation of the change process* begins as individuals become increasingly aware of the difficulties that drugs have produced in their lives.

These negative consequences underlie self-change attempts and/or the seeking of treatment. The success of the *active change process* (or treatment) is influenced by characteristics of both the patient and the program and whether the two are appropriately matched. Finally, *maintenance of successful change* primarily involves relapse prevention efforts imbued with the recognition that single lapses are highly probable. We will move on to the topic of intervention (prevention and treatment) after covering how substance abuse is assessed.

THE ASSESSMENT OF SUBSTANCE ABUSE

In professional practice, diagnostic judgments about children and adults are, unfortunately, often made with an eye to third-party payments rather than to clinical reality. For example, the determination of whether an individual is to be labeled as suffering from "depression" or "substance abuse" may well depend on which subsequent treatment program is likely to be better funded by the individual's insurance company.

The DSM-III-R (American Psychiatric Association, 1987) is frequently used in facilities that treat substance abusers. Although, when appropriately deployed, it does permit some degree of specificity, such as the classification of individuals by drug category and level of use (dependence or abuse), this particular approach to assessment is not especially helpful for quantifying the possible goals of various approaches to intervention (Niaura & Nathan, 1987). These goals can be crudely classified along three dimensions: relevance, assessment method, and success criteria. The following discussions examine each of these dimensions in turn.

Relevance

Most professionals in the field agree that the reduction of drug abuse behavior is their *raison d'être*. There is a temporal dimension to behavior as an evaluation criterion: treatment programs are designed with the intent of reducing *current* substance abuse; prevention programs focus on *future* abuse by psychologically "inoculating" uninvolved youths against some of the etiological variables discussed earlier. Most work with children is preventive in nature, which has helped fuel the development of moderating and alternative outcome variables having wide-ranging relevance. A number of substance abuse intervention programs, for example, attempt to modify drug attitudes or drug knowledge in addition to drug behavior. The guiding rationale for this activity—that both antidrug attitudes and increased knowledge about drugs ultimately will manifest themselves in lowered levels of substance abuse behavior—is implied by recent research on the cognitive etiological correlates discussed earlier.

Because attitude scales are typically more malleable than usage indexes, they offer the researcher a potential consolation prize when no changes occur in the behavioral data. Gains in drug knowledge are likewise relatively easy to effect. However, the relationship between drug knowledge and drug use is extremely complex. Although certain subsets of the knowledge variable may inhibit drug use, other subsets—such as familiarity with drug jargon—may result from or covary with drug consumption (Horan & Harrison, 1981).

Drug attitudes and knowledge would seem to fit rather comfortably in the construct known as "outcome expectations" in Bandura's (1986) self-efficacy theory. Etiological research has shown that outcome expectations such as "smoking marijuana will enhance my sexual appeal and ability" are potent predictors of drug use (Cooper et al., 1988; George & Marlatt, 1983). Moreover, Fishbein and Ajzen's (1975) empirically based "theory of reasoned action," which incorporates perceived outcomes as a critical predictor variable, has recently been extended to address drug use (Fishbein & Middlestadt, 1987). At present, however, we are unaware of any experimental study that either designates outcome expectations as a moderator variable or uses an outcome-expectations measure to assess program success.

The attempt to evaluate prevention programs with behavioral data poses several thorny methodological problems. For example, because such programs are conceptually focused on youth who are not (yet) abusing drugs, long-range follow-ups are required before the behavioral data reach a magnitude that can be meaningfully analyzed. Attitude and knowledge scales provide a quick posttest analysis of program efficacy. Questionnaires that tap drug usage on a tentative or hypothetical basis can also yield preliminary feedback. For example, after participating in a prevention program, respondents might be asked if they *would* consume a particular product rather than how often they have done so in the past (Horan & Williams, 1975, 1982). It might be argued, of course, that such data are more indicative of transient attitudes than actual behavior.

Measures of social skills may be highly appropriate to drug abuse assessment and program evaluation. Etiological research has linked social skills deficiencies to the development of substance abuse. Because increasing one's interpersonal competence has been *experimentally* shown to contribute to the amelioration or prevention of a drug problem (Botvin, Renick, & Baker, 1983; Horan & Williams, 1982; Van Hasselt, Hersen, & Milliones, 1978), the relevance of social skills measures is clear (as long as the content of the intervention program addresses social skills development).

The case for including measures of other etiological variables in assessment batteries is less convincing. Some biological and sociological correlates, for example, are simply not malleable, nor would data derived from them suggest differential interventions. Although certain family variables, such as parental drug use, have been linked to the development of substance abuse in offspring (Barnes & Welte, 1986; Baumrind, 1990; Harford & Grant, 1986), real change on these indexes may lie outside the scope of possible interventions at hand. If one has the resources to conduct intensive family-based interventions, then all relevant moderating variables in the family should be assessed.

Finally, we note with some dismay that the typical drug abuse prevention project over the past 15 years is more likely to have been evaluated with measures of self-acceptance than with surveys of subsequent drug use. Such measures could certainly supplement a drug use assessment battery; indeed, their use would even be warranted, given convincing etiological data and relevance to the intervention deployed. Unfortunately, their ubiquitous adoption signals the fact that many evaluators have abandoned the task of gathering behavioral data—the most convincing index of success.

In sum, a growing body of literature is calling for a multifaceted assessment of substance abuse problems (Emrick & Hansen, 1983; Nathan & Skinsted, 1987; Wanberg & Horn, 1983). We concur; however, the relevance of a given assessment device would seem to hinge on its strength as an etiological correlate, its malleability and/or its capacity for dictating differential treatment, and, finally, its theoretical link to the content of the intervention. A very strong case can be made for inclusion of social skills measures, given their experimentally demonstrated stature as moderators of substance abuse.

Assessment Method

Drug abuse variables can also be classified according to their method of assessment. For example, data may be derived from self-report, other-report, unobtrusive observations, and/or physiological monitoring. Although any drug-related outcome can be assessed using multiple methods, our primary concern here is with substance abuse behavior.

Self-reported drug use is the most common form of assessment. Oetting and Beauvais (1990) concluded that self-report data in national surveys are reasonably reliable. In program evaluation, however, this data collection method is inherently vulnerable to questions of validity. Different self-report procedures, for example, produce different levels of candor, suggesting that some subjects deny or minimize their use of drugs in order to avoid even the slightest possibility of legal entanglements (Horan, Westcott, Vetovich, & Swisher, 1974). A wide variety of other factors, including the characteristics of survey administrators, can produce variability in subjects' willingness to acknowledge drug use (Foy, Cline, & Laasi, 1987; McClary & Lubin, 1987).

There are probably as many specific self-report devices available for assessing drug and alcohol abuse as there are studies of the problem. However, several cautions are in order. For example, item structures such as "Have you ever . . ." or "How often do you consume *x* drug?" are useless as posttest gauges of program efficacy because they address behaviors concurrent or even prior to treatment. Rewording such items is tricky. Moreover, the authors of drug use behavioral logs inevitably categorize the substances and consumption frequencies in idiosyncratic ways. We would urge program evaluators to give serious thought to adopting the widely understood organizational framework used by Johnston and his colleagues (1989) in their annual national surveys; doing so would enhance the replicability and comparability of findings in this field.

The Johnston framework is useful for determining the self-reported frequencies of consumption of many drugs. In contrast, the Michigan Alcohol Screening Test (MAST; Selzer, 1971) is a rapid and inexpensive device for assessing alcohol-related problems per se. Despite some classification error troubles (e.g., "false positives" for low-socioeconomic-status (SES) clients), the MAST has demonstrated reasonable validity and reliability. Additionally, the Alcohol Use Inventory (AUI; Horn, Wanberg, & Foster, 1983) has received some acclaim as a multivariate, differential-diagnostic instrument (Emrick & Hansen, 1983; Jacobson, 1983). State-of-the-art reviews of alcohol assessment devices have been published elsewhere (Davidson, 1987; Foy et al., 1987; Jacobson, 1983; Midanik, 1988).

Attempting to confirm self-report data by questioning those residing in the home (*other-report*) can increase one's confidence in the data or even provide an alternate measure (Foy et al., 1987; Midanik, 1988). However, significant others are also quite capable of distorting the truth, and, even if they are predisposed to veracity, the validity of their answers depends on whether they have a pipeline to the subject's private consummatory behavior. Chamberlain and Patterson (1984) noted, however, that parental observations implying substance abuse (e.g., finding money missing, noticing alcohol or marijuana odors, discovering drug paraphernalia) may be as valuable as witnessing actual use, when evaluating the accuracy of other measures. Moreover, Ciminero and Drabman (1977) suggested that the validity and reliability of interviews can be improved by soliciting only recent information and by encouraging the expression of all events in precise behavioral terms.

Unobtrusive behavioral measures of the sort described by Webb, Campbell, Schwartz, and Sechrest (1966) (e.g., tallying liquor bottles in trash cans, after-hours searches of student lockers) would undoubtedly resolve some of the problems with self-report. However, many of these procedures are, at least, costly and cumbersome and, at most, repugnant and illegal (Flygare, 1979). Currently, the art of unobtrusive drug behavior assessment remains impractical.

Biochemical analyses of bodily products, such as breath, saliva, blood, or urine, are highly touted methods for verifying drug use. Their limitations, however, have not received widespread publicity. To preclude the possibility of switching samples, for example, athletes in a number of international competitions are required to stand nude in the center of a room as they urinate into a specimen jar in front of witnesses. Some have found the experience disconcerting enough to inhibit micturating for several hours (Mahoney, 1989). Moreover, although breath and saliva tests routinely pose no similar problems, many subjects will balk at having blood samples drawn, especially if such monitoring is required on a regular basis.

Once obtained, biochemical samples are still vulnerable to confounding by the subject (e.g., dietary habits, use of patent or prescribed medicines, or consumption of "masking" agents) and by the laboratory (e.g., careless or poorly trained technicians). Metabolic differences may also lead to erroneous conclusions (Skinner, 1984). The half-life of the product being monitored poses another set of problems. If brief, abstaining for a day or two will result in a spuriously low reading; if long, traces may be present months after subjects validly report they have stopped. No test is perfectly reliable, anyway, even under ideal conditions.

Despite the foregoing problems, biochemical collaboration of self-report data is of utmost importance in the context of research on addictions treatment. Moreover, in certain situations, self-report data must be validated with biochemical assays. For example, when prosecuting drunk drivers, law enforcement personnel frequently rely on legal definitions of intoxication expressed in terms of blood-alcohol concentration; and the Food and Drug Administration requires urinanalysis testing on a regular basis for addicts enrolled in methadone maintenance programs (Edwards, 1972; Goldstein & Brown, 1969; Miller, Hersen, Eisler, & Watts, 1974; Trellis, Smith, Alston, & Siassi, 1975).

Apart from the utility of biochemical assays in their own right, their use probably increases the accuracy of self-report measures via something akin to the "bogus-pipeline" effect (Midanik, 1988). Simply put, subjects are less likely to fib in the face of perceived objective evidence. Most work with children and adolescents, however, is school-based and prevention-oriented. Although biochemical monitoring can be routinely embedded in medical, military, or penal settings, its application elsewhere may elicit objections grounded in the Constitution and Bill of Rights. Except for a few endeavors targeting smoking behavior, no drug prevention program, to our knowledge, has even been evaluated with biochemically verified self-report data.

Success Criteria

The final assessment dimension is the definition of program success, which presumably ought to be the mirror image of what constitutes the clinical problem. Decreased consumption frequency (evidenced by self-report and/or lowered quantities of targeted biochemical compounds) is a consensually validated objective. Documenting improvements on the other variables in a multifaceted assessment battery (e.g., social skills and/or decision-making ability) is also important in terms of guiding future research. For example, if measured drug abuse has declined in the absence of improvements on targeted decision-making skills, then experimental construct validity has not been demonstrated (Cook & Campbell, 1979; McNamara & Horan, 1986). The program may have worked, but not for the reasons proffered.

In the case of cigarette smoking, abstinence provides the most meaningful test of treatment efficacy. Complete elimination of the habit is the goal sought by most smokers undergoing treatment—a wise choice, given that those who simply reduce their consumption level eventually return to baseline (Lichtenstein & Danaher, 1976). Incidentally, from a research standpoint, abstinence is easier to verify than lowered levels of use in self-reports, other-reports, and biological assays. For example, expired-air samples taken from nonsmokers and those who have successfully quit will typically yield carbon monoxide concentrations in the range of 0 to 3 parts per million (ppm); smokers, on the other hand, can readily be spotted from samples in the range of 20 to 80 ppm. An individual smoker's decrease from, say, 70 to 60 ppm does not necessarily indicate a reliable diminution in real-life smoking behavior (Horan, Hackett, & Linberg, 1978).

Perfect abstinence (i.e., zero consumption over time) is readily understood, but researchers do not treat "blemished" abstinence (e.g., a single consumption episode in a follow-up period) with consistency. Moreover, given the epidemiological normalcy of experimentation with some substances, it is difficult to argue that perfect abstinence from all other drugs is either desirable and/or attainable. The concept of "controlled drinking," for example, has been defended as a viable outcome in the treatment of alcoholism, albeit not without controversy (Marlatt, 1983; Miller & Caddy, 1977).

INTERVENTION

Practitioners in the drug abuse field usually function in one of three roles: (a) prevention, (b) crisis intervention, or (c) treatment of the addicted. The majority of drug abuse work with children and adolescents falls within the *prevention* category. Drug education and drug abuse prevention are essentially interchangeable descriptors for intervention activities directed toward general audiences who are not (yet) using drugs. The emphasis is on the avoidance of future use rather than on the reduction of present consumption.

Crisis intervention usually occupies a very short period between that point in time when prevention has failed and treatment begins. Crisis intervention includes specific activities, such as "telephone hotline" work with highly anxious callers and emergency-room management of barbiturate comas. This subset of the drug abuse field lies outside the scope of our chapter.

Addictions treatment unequivocally involves the reduction of drug consumption. Depending on the particular substance being abused and/or the theoretical orientation of the program, this goal is accomplished either directly or through moderator variables. We view exploratory drug use as relevant to prevention activities. Our discussion of treatment refers exclusively to the chronic drug abuser.

Prevention

There is an enormous body of literature on how to prevent substance abuse. Between January 1987 and September 1991, for example, the *Psychological Abstracts* data base (i.e., PsycLIT) offered 304 citations using the descriptors "drug abuse" and "prevention"; these are but a small subset of 12,575 references having to do with drugs.

Much of this literature (and that of the preceding decade), however, is of relatively little use to practitioners seeking to discover and employ empirically verified prevention programs. Horan and Harrison's (1981) review, for example, found only 26 published references that included drug-related outcome measures. Moreover, only a third of these studies used random assignment to experimental conditions, the main requirement of true experimentation. Also, some projects were apparently conducted in the absence of a coherent theoretical base, and most were not replicable because of the undefined or undefinable nature of the independent variable. Furthermore, data-analysis errors seemed to be the norm rather than the exception. Finally, "prevention," by definition, implies a reduced probability of future substance abuse; yet only 4 of the 26 projects in the Horan and Harrison (1981) review included any sort of follow-up evaluation effort.

Schaps, DiBartolo, Moskowitz, Palley, and Churgin (1981) located 75 citable projects (of which 69% were unpublished) and expressed similar dismay about poor design quality in the literature. Their exhaustive review identified 10 kinds of intervention strategies: information, persuasion, affective-skill, affective-experiential, counseling, tutoring/teaching, peer group, family, program development, and alternatives. Only 10 studies met their minimal criteria for design quality and service delivery intensity; of these, only 2 showed an impact on drug use. Given that this exhaustive compilation of 75 documents contained 127 evaluated programs, the fact that 2 should emerge as promising is not surprising and, indeed, might be expected by chance alone.

More recent authors have bemoaned the continuing lack of empirical rigor in the literature (Botvin, 1985, 1986; Flay, 1985; Noel & McCrady, 1984), and meta-analytic reviews (Bangert-Drowns, 1988; Rundall & Bruvold, 1988; Tobler, 1986) underscore the difficulty investigators have faced in producing meaningful changes on behavioral data. False starts and failures, however, vastly outnumber breakthroughs in all areas of scientific inquiry. Newly emerging theory and data appear quite promising. We take a second look here at information-based programming, a much maligned strategy, before focusing on psychosocial approaches to intervention.

Information-Based Programming

Information-based programming is the most common (yet one of the most controversial) prevention modalities that has been deployed over the past two decades. The logic of this approach can ultimately be traced to classical decision theory, described earlier. Essentially, information-based programming rests on the assumption that, if we provide our youth with an awareness of the dangerous consequences of drug use (negative utilities) and indicate to them that these consequences are highly probable, the drug avoidance option is virtually assured. No rational person would select an alternative with a comparably low SEU value.

From an empirical standpoint, Horan and Harrison's (1981) review indicated that, compared to no-treatment control groups, information-based programming can raise drug knowledge levels (as measured by achievement tests keyed to the particular program). Such findings are hardly noteworthy, given that we might expect parallel outcomes from any curriculum in math or spelling.

Despite the historical failure of information-based programming to meaningfully alter attitudes and drug use behavior, we believe that this approach has been unfairly treated by researchers and reviewers. In the first place, the links between classical decision theory and the intervention materials per se are rarely if ever articulated; the programs simply do not adequately represent the theoretical model. Moreover, information-based curricula are inevitably saturated with distorted "facts" about the consequences of drug use (a phenomenon that has made student skepticism a serious obstacle to program evaluation). Trebach (1988), for example, reported that "despite being told that our children were dying in droves from crack overdoses . . . the total of all known deaths from all forms of cocaine and crack abuse among children (ages 10–17) was seven in 1985" (p. 6). (About the same number of children die yearly from ingestion of toy balloons.)

We wonder if the purported failure of information-based programming might be attributable to implementation inadequacies rather than to deficiencies in the conceptual basis of the approach. What, for example, is more responsible for the well-known decline in cigarette use among physicians than the dispassionate data presented in the Surgeon General's reports on smoking and health? Distorting the facts about drugs to student audiences, however noble one's intentions, is empirically impotent (Kovach & Glickman, 1986; Stainback & Rogers, 1983) and educationally abhorrent.

Psychosocial Change Approaches

In the years following the Horan and Harrison (1981) and Schaps et al. (1981) reviews, a growing bank of evidence accumulated in favor of psychosocial change approaches to prevention. Assertiveness is among the most basic and relevant of these skills. The "Just Say No!" campaign, for example, owes its uncited theoretical base to the assertion training literature. Saying "No" presumes that one has reasons for saying "No," as well as the personal-social competence to do so; unfortunately, many youths do not have these resources, and would presumably profit more from focused training than from slogans. Horan and Williams (1982), for example, found less substance use during a 3-year follow-up period for junior high students who received a fully articulated assertion training treatment in comparison to students in a placebo control condition.

As a drug abuse prevention strategy, assertion training rests on the etiological assumption that many youths, who would otherwise abstain from taking drugs, reluctantly imbibe because they lack the social skills necessary to extricate themselves from peer-group situations in which drug use is imminent. SEUs other than those pertaining to peer approval–disapproval are relevant to drug decisions. For example, the potential user also may estimate (however crudely) the probabilities of euphoric and adverse physiological consequences. Thus, the role of assertion training is limited to shoring up the possibility of free choice. Following such training, youths could still decide to take drugs (on the basis of other SEUs), but in so doing they would not be capitulating to peer pressure because they would have the competence to decline drug consumption without losing face.

In the Horan and Williams (1982) study, 72 nonassertive junior high students were randomly assigned to assertion training, to placebo discussions on peer pressure, or to no treatment. At posttest, compared to control subjects, the experimental students showed highly significant gains on behavioral and psychometric measures of assertiveness, as well as decreased willingness to use alcohol and marijuana. At a 3-year follow-up, these students continued to display higher levels of assertiveness and less drug use.

In this study, the role of assertion training was limited to that of fostering the competence to say "No" in peer pressure situations focused on drug use. More elaborate social skills programs have been designed and evaluated by other researchers, with similar positive effects. In theory, improved social skills should result in greater control over (and reinforcement derived from) one's environment, the lack of which figures heavily in the Marlatt et al. (1988) etiological formulation.

Botvin and his colleagues (Botvin, Baker, Renick, Filazzola, & Botvin, 1984; Botvin, Renick, & Baker, 1983) developed and tested a 20-session cognitive-behavioral "life skills" curriculum that included instructional units on drug use, decision making, media influences, self-improvement, coping with anxiety, and four different types of social skills (communication, overcoming shyness, boy–girl relationships, and assertiveness). In the 1984 large-scale implementation of their program, involving 1,311 junior high students from 10 schools, significant effects on the use of tobacco, alcohol, and marijuana were produced using carefully selected and closely supervised older peers from the 10th and 11th grades to implement the treatment. Whereas a teacher-led version of their program produced significant effects with students in the 1983 study, it failed to do so in the 1984 evaluation. The authors suggested that the problem may have been caused by "implementation failure" on the part of the teachers. They successfully attended to this problem in a more recent large-scale field test involving 4,466 students and two methods of teacher training (Botvin, Baker, Dusenbury, Tortu, & Botvin, 1990). Although the particular social skills curricula developed by various authors differ in some respects, and although the outcomes produced by a given research team are not always consistent from one study to the next, current data (Best, Thompson, Santi, Smith, & Brown, 1988; Botvin, 1983, 1985, 1986; Flay, 1985; McAlister, 1983; Pentz, 1983) clearly indicate that comprehensive social skills programs are the most defensible choice for preventing substance abuse among our nation's youth.

By including instructional modules on decision making and on coping with anxiety, the Botvin program went far beyond the boundaries of traditional social skills training—hence the more inclusive "psychosocial skills" nomenclature. Many contemporary investigators endorse such multifaceted curricula; "acquisition-oriented" approaches to prevention are those in which interventions are directly linked to additional etiological factors (Chassin, Presson, & Sherman, 1985).

Nevertheless, the problem of exporting effective programs to the practitioner community continues to vex us as researchers, as does the ever present burden of cost-benefit analysis. Professional labor-intensive programs, or those requiring a high level of expertise to implement, will rarely escape a dusty bookshelf destiny. Although the general strategies of assertion training and other psychosocial skills interventions are within the bailiwick of many mental health practitioners, there are fine nuances that may not be in the professional public domain.

One possible solution to the exportability problem is to package the intervention materials in such a way that they can be property delivered to large audiences by individuals with highly variable knowledge and skills in the substance abuse field. Videotaped and/or computer-based treatments, for example, can be efficiently delivered to entire school populations at minimal cost. Unfortunately, most of the intervention materials already committed to a self-contained media format are commercial productions that were never subjected to empirical scrutiny at any point in their development. A few have been experimentally evaluated by independent researchers (Horan et al., 1989). Others, such as a series of videotapes funded by the National Institute of Education, await controlled study.

Project D.A.R.E. (drug abuse resistance education), currently under nationwide implementation by local law enforcement agencies, is a notable exception to the self-contained-packaging approach; the contents are linked to the literatures of decision making and assertion training. The D.A.R.E. curriculum targets 5th and 6th graders who receive a total of 17 lessons, each lasting from 45 to 60 minutes. Police officers, rather than classroom teachers, provide the instruction.

The exponential growth of Project D.A.R.E. is truly remarkable, given its labor-intensive requirements. It was first piloted in Los Angeles during 1983 and vanguard efforts are now emerging in virtually every state. In some metropolitan regions, the majority of targeted youth have already received this intervention. It is also remarkable that so many school systems have unhesitatingly opened their doors and allocated the necessary 17 hours of classroom times. Unfortunately, implementation efforts have far outstripped those directed toward evaluation. Although anecdotal evidence abounds, and some project materials imply significant pre–post gains on a variety of indexes, we have not been able to locate adequately controlled experimental data indicative of the D.A.R.E. intervention's impact on decision-making and refusal skills, much less consummatory behavior (but see DeJong, 1987).

There is certainly intuitive appeal for further development of comprehensive psy-chosocial skills approaches to prevention, whether implemented by professionals in the substance abuse field, regular classroom teachers, self-contained media, or police offi-cers. Others urge drawing on human resources from an even broader socialcultural realm, such as parents and members of the community (Forman & Linney, 1988; Perry & Jessor, 1985; Rhodes & Jason, 1988). The general consensus of our discipline is that the causes of substance abuse are multivariate; thus, the logic of comprehensive treat-ment is to blanket all possible etiological facets with all potential remedies. This makes sense for those individuals who have deficiencies in all curricular areas. We believe it is inefficient, however, for subsets of the target audience whose susceptibilities to substance abuse are more circumscribed and homogeneous. As an alternative to the ever expanding comprehensive curriculum approach, we hope the future will reveal a diagnosis/prevention system from which subjects could be shunted only to those inter-vention modules of highest relevance. The time saved from the delivery and receipt of irrelevant instruction could more appropriately be spent, for example, in ensuring mastery of the relevant skills.

Treatment

Exploratory use of cigarettes, alcohol, and certain illegal drugs is well within the boundaries of statistical and psychological normality (Baumrind, 1990; Shedler & Block, 1990). Even though consumption has occurred, there is no real evidence of a clinical problem; thus, interventions more intensive than the large-scale prevention approaches described above (i.e., providing information and promoting psychosocial skills) would be neither appropriate nor cost-beneficial. Chronic use of drugs, however, is another matter. Addictions treatment usually requires a far more extensive scope and budget than are needed for drug abuse prevention. We begin our review of the relevant treatment literature with the relatively circumscribed problem of cigarette addiction, and then move on to other substance abuses, including alcoholism. We conclude this section with a brief discussion of pharmacological adjuncts to treatment.

Treatment of Cigarette Addiction

Many treatments for cigarette addiction have been subjected to reasonably rigorous em-pirical scrutiny. Three aversion-conditioning strategies (rapid smoking, focused smok-ing, and smoke holding) stand out as primary ingredients in comprehensive treatment programs. *Rapid smoking* was first described by Lublin (1969), although Lichtenstein and his associates are credited with most of the procedural refinement and validation (Lichtenstein & Rodrigues, 1977). Rapid smoking essentially consists of having cigarette users take a normal inhalation every 6 seconds until they are no longer able to do so. The procedure induces physiological discomfort through bodily absorption of greatly in-creased quantities of tobacco smoke, which contains particularly reactive ingredients like nicotine and carbon monoxide. Because larger doses of these compounds can strain one's cardiovascular system, the technique should only be employed in consultation with a cardiologist (Linberg, Horan, Hodgson, & Buskirk, 1982).

Focused smoking (Hackett & Horan, 1978, 1979) and normal-paced aversive smok-ing (NAPS; Danaher & Lichtenstein, 1978) are risk-free alternatives to rapid smoking. Although independently conceived, both techniques have evolved in such a way as to permit a common description. Essentially, clients sit facing a blank wall and smoke at their normal rate while being cued by the counselor to focus on the discomforts of smoking, for example, bad taste, burning in the throat, and feelings of light-headedness and nausea. *Smoke holding* is another less risky alternative; clients breathe normally through their noses but hold smoke in their mouths for 30 seconds and concentrate on unpleasant sensations.

Although early research found these aversion techniques to be quite successful when deployed alone, Schwartz's (1987) review of 883 references suggests that they ought to be embedded in comprehensive programs containing additional strategies for *self-management* and *relapse prevention*. The former includes, for example, self-monitoring, stimulus control, and contingency contracting; the latter, social support, coping skills, and cognitive restructuring about abstinence violations.

Treatment of Substance Abuse in General

The classic comprehensive behavioral approach to addictions treatment (Miller & Eisler, 1977) includes three generic objectives: (a) decrease the immediate reinforcing properties of drugs through, for example, aversion therapies and medications such as methadone; (b) teach alternative behaviors; and (c) rearrange the environment so that reinforcement occurs for being "off" drugs. Marlatt's model (Marlatt & Donovan, 1981) also implies the need for problem-solving skills and cognitive restructuring. The latter is employed to challenge erroneous beliefs about the effects of drugs. As might be expected, all of the individual ingredients of the psychosocial approaches to prevention discussed earlier are theoretically relevant to addictions treatment as well (Battjes, 1985; Botvin, 1986; Hansen, 1988; Stitzer, Bigelow, & McCaul, 1985). For example, because peer involvement and "self-medication" (i.e., decreasing negative affect) are frequently cited etiological correlates, training in psychosocial skills would presumably enhance social ease and reduce psychological distress (Newcomb et al., 1988).

Other approaches to addictions treatment include Pentecostal Protestantism (U.S. Department of Health and Human Services, 1980) and self-help derivatives of Alcoholics Anonymous. Although behavior principles are rarely if ever articulated in these literatures, they are nevertheless discernible:

> *A behavioral analysis shows that these groups provide a potently reinforcing group atmosphere which does not tolerate drug or alcohol abuse. New, more adaptive patterns of behavior are encouraged and reinforced through group approval and increased status within the group. Drinking buddies and addicted friends are replaced with more appropriate role models exhibiting complete abstinence. The fact that the "helping agents" were once abusers of drugs or alcohol and therefore represent successful coping models may foster imitation of their behavior and enhance their reinforcing value. (Miller & Eisler, 1977, p. 392)*

Regardless of its theoretical basis, most of the addictions treatment literature involves adults or at least older adolescents. Although the problem of youthful addiction may seem ubiquitous, controlled research on the effectiveness of specific treatment programs for young addicts is rare (Nathan & Skinsted, 1987). Studies that do appear in print frequently suffer from methodological inadequacies. The Teen Challenge program, for example, reported striking differences between graduates of their facilities and comparison groups on substance abuse indexes (U.S. Department of Health and Human Services, 1980). However, because (a) their program requires that participants be heterosexual, free of emotional disturbance, and willing to give up TV, radio, and recordings and become "born again" Christians, and (b) their comparison groups consisted of dropouts of their program, their data are difficult to interpret. The conventional canons of evaluation require that dropouts and success cases be combined and contrasted against subjects in alternative or control treatments initially formed by random assignment. By analogy, one cannot claim success for a surgical procedure using those who died on the operating table as a control group!

There are, moreover, conceptual difficulties with extrapolating the logic and data implications of adult treatment downward to the youthful addict. Treatment programs for adults are not always well-suited for teens. The consequences of substance abuse, for example, differ with age. Adults suffer more tangible health and material losses and are more likely to have been arrested or jailed; youths experience more familial friction and are more likely to have attempted suicide (Griswold-Ezekoye, Kumpfer, & Bukoski, 1986; Spieger & Harford, 1987).

Adult and youthful addicts, however, do share at least one thing in common. Treatment facilities and philosophies have evolved (i.e., exploded) well beyond their research base. In the practitioner community, one typically finds three types of facilities: (a) inpatient, (b) outpatient, and (c) residential. *Inpatient* facilities usually provide hospital detoxification and other supportive services to long-term chronic abusers and those at medical risk from an overdose (Rhodes & Jason, 1988). Their fees are inevitably high relative to other available programs (Griswold-Ezekoye et al., 1986). *Outpatient* facilities (e.g., "drop-in" centers, family service agencies, individual and group counseling centers) receive the majority of youthful referrals who are presumably, but not necessarily, less at-risk than those requiring inpatient or residential treatment (Rhodes & Jason, 1988). *Residential* (nonmedical) facilities are usually less costly than inpatient treatment centers; thus, those serviced are more likely to have a low level of education, to have been referred by the criminal justice system, to have had previous drug abuse treatment, and to be poly-drug users (Griswold-Ezekoye et al., 1986). Residents are usually required to participate in therapeutic activities and are expected to share "household" responsibilities.

The practitioner literature unequivocally recommends that, upon discharge from an inpatient or residential facility, recovering addicts receive some form of aftercare services, to prevent relapse. Intuitively, it would be difficult to disagree, but, in truth, data are relatively sparse on the differential efficacy of such services, on methods for appropriately matching people to different aftercare programs, or on the effectiveness of such services compared to no treatment at all. The practitioner literature is also replete with recommendations for various therapeutic interventions used in the foregoing facilities. In addition to the generic behavioral and psychosocial rationales discussed above, endorsements for family therapy and reality therapy are common. Despite the etiological link between family variables and substance abuse, most of the research on family treatment strategies (e.g., parenting training) suffers from multiple confounding variables (Moskowitz, 1985). Likewise, studies evaluating the effects of reality therapy (Glasser, 1969) on substance abuse have methodological shortcomings that preclude meaningful interpretations of their results (Rhodes & Jason, 1988).

Treatment of Alcoholism in Particular

The foregoing comments on the treatment of substance abuse in general apply to alcoholism as well. Nevertheless, several additional remarks are warranted. Miller and Hester (1986) reviewed 26 controlled studies and reported that inpatient services were not significantly more effective than outpatient services, and that the outcome of alcoholism treatment is more likely to be influenced by the content of the interventions than by the settings in which they are offered. They noted that inpatient per-capita treatment costs commonly range between $4,000 and $15,000 (in 1979 dollars), whereas outpatient services are available for less than 10% of that amount, "even if delivered by fully credentialed professionals at prevailing private practice rates" (p. 802). They also bemoaned the fact that empirically supported treatment methods such as Azrin's community reinforcement approach remain virtually unused in standard treatment.

Azrin's program (Azrin, 1976; Azrin, Sisson, Meyers, & Godley, 1982; Hunt & Azrin, 1973; Sisson & Azrin, 1986) originally began with four treatment components: (a) placement in full-time, steady, satisfying, and well-paying jobs; (b) marriage and family counseling aimed at becoming more pleasurably and continually involved in family activities; (c) establishment of a social club for abstinent members that includes enjoyable social events and support, particularly during evening hours and on weekends; and (d) gradual engagement in pleasurable hobbies and recreational activities that provide alternatives to drinking. Hunt and Azrin (1973) reported that, compared to a matched control group admitted for treatment at a state hospital, their four-component program produced significant decrements in drinking, unemployment, time away from home, and institutionalization—and these benefits endured over a 6-month follow-up period.

Subsequent modifications to the program included the addition of a buddy system, a daily report procedure, group counseling, and a special social motivation module to ensure self-administration of Disulfiram. Azrin (1976) reported similar results, stable over a 2-year period. More recently, Sisson and Azrin (1986) evaluated methods for teaching family members of problem drinkers how to minimize their own distress, reduce their own drinking, increase the motivation of the alcoholic family member to obtain formal treatment, and assist in the treatment regimen. Their results suggest that teaching concerned family members appropriate reinforcement procedures can lead even unmotivated alcoholics to begin formal treatment. We share Miller and Hester's (1986) dismay that Azrin's long-standing and demonstrably effective program lies far outside the mainstream of standard treatment practice.

Pharmacological Adjuncts to Treatment

The rationale for using pharmacological adjuncts in the treatment of substance abuse derives in part from experimental studies showing that animals self-administer the same types of drugs that humans abuse (Johanson & deWit, 1989). Because, compared to human beings, the learning history of an animal is subject to infinitely greater degrees of inspection and control, it is relatively easy to demonstrate that the animal's addiction arises from the reinforcing properties of the drug (Bigelow, Stitzer, & Liebson, 1984). These properties include, for example, those that produce euphoria when the substance is consumed and those that ward off an aversive withdrawal reaction when the substance is not available. Hence, two classes of drugs used in pharmacological treatments have developed: *antagonists* avert the reinforcing properties of drugs by inhibiting the neurotransmitter effects on the postsynaptic cell; *agonists* facilitate the neurotransmitter effects and mimic the substance being abused, thus eliminating the need for it (Carlson, 1988).

Unlike that of experimental animals, the drug-taking behavior of humans is inevitably under the control of social-reinforcement variables, in addition to the physiologically reinforcing properties of the drug. Thus, pharmacological products are usually viewed as adjuncts to treatment rather than as treatments per se. Most pharmacological adjuncts are specific to the type of substance that is being abused; within a given abuse category, different pharmacological adjuncts may be directed toward different objectives. For example, Chlordiazepoxide is a new drug relevant to the alcohol detoxification process; it purportedly prevents withdrawal symptoms from occurring. Antabuse, on the other hand, produces severe nausea if followed by alcohol ingestion; it has been used in aversion therapy for alcoholics for many years. With heroin addicts, methadone arguably is the adjunct of choice (Dole & Nyswander, 1965; Schuster, 1986). Other pharmacological adjuncts to the treatment of opiate addiction include Naltrexone, an antagonist that purportedly inhibits the reinforcing properties of opiates, and Buprenorphine, a mixed agonist–antagonist that is said to prevent withdrawal and simultaneously block the opiate's reinforcing properties

Nicotine gum has been shown to be a reasonably effective adjunct in research on comprehensive smoking-treatment programs (Lam, Sze, Sacks, & Chalmers, 1987). Data supporting its use in general medical practice, however, are less convincing (Russell, Merriman, Stapleton, & Taylor, 1983).

Cessation of marijuana use is not known to produce a withdrawal reaction; recent descriptions of a cocaine withdrawal syndrome must be considered as preliminary (Kleber & Gawin, 1986). Although no specific pharmacological adjuncts have been developed to assist in treating the abuse of either drug, antidepressants are sometimes prescribed for the depression that may occur after quitting the use of cocaine.

Given recent success in immunizing animals against the reinforcing properties of drugs, some researchers are hoping to replicate the procedure with humans (Schuster, 1986). Once developed, the serum antibodies would be effective only against the drug targeted by the inoculation. In view of our current low level of precision in predicting which children will grow up and abuse what drug, the inevitability of toxic consequences resulting from widespread inoculation efforts raises serious ethical concerns.

Pharmacological adjuncts are not commonly used with children and adolescents, except in circumscribed ways such as in the practice of emergency-room medicine. Little is known about the short- and long-term effects of these drugs on younger patients. All pharmacological adjuncts have side effects: Antabuse, for example, may produce heart failure in certain individuals, following as little as 2 drinks. Some treatment adjuncts generally considered safe for adults, such as methadone, are not recommended for children because adequate research remains to be conducted before proper dosage can be prescribed.

PUBLIC POLICY FORMATION

In addition to prevention, crisis intervention, and treatment, a fourth professional role has emerged in recent years—that of public policy formation. This role encompasses at least three phenomena: media interventions, political action groups, and legislation. Although the profession of counseling psychology has traditionally had little input in public policy formation, the potential impact of this role on our clients and, indeed, on the quality of our lives, is too great to ignore. If the practice of our professional is guided by empirical data, should not those data steer public policy as well?

Media Interventions

During the early 1980s, the National Institute on Drug Abuse (NIDA) sponsored the "Just Say No!" advertising campaign, presumably geared toward arming youths with refusal skills akin to those targeted by assertion training programs. Later, the National Broadcasting Corporation (NBC), borrowing a NIDA slogan, aired public service announcements featuring popular actors as role models exclaiming "Don't be a dope" when it comes to using drugs; the U.S. Department of Transportation mounted a television campaign featuring the music of Michael Jackson, to discourage teenagers from drinking an driving. More recently, the National Institute of Education funded the development of videotapes that serve as self-contained drug-abuse-prevention treatments capable of prime-time broadcast or showings in public schools. There is also a popular television spot commercial likening a frying egg to "your brain on drugs." That message and similar others are delivered to us by corporate America, which, in April 1987, formed the Media–Advertising Partnership for a Drug-Free America.

Experimental evaluations of media interventions in natural settings, such as commercial television, are problematic. How, for example, does one engineer a randomly assigned control group that does not observe a television spot commercial in the middle of "L. A. Law"? Nevertheless, replicable research can be embedded in analog settings, such as cable-TV instruction in public schools. Moreover, the messages themselves are easily improved, and, given their extraordinary ability to reach large audiences, their cost-benefit potential is vastly superior to labor-intensive traditional approaches.

Media interventions are quite capable of being developed from a coherent theoretical base in, for example, the social skills and vicarious learning literatures. Unfortunately, most of the media interventions we have reviewed seem to derive from the filmmaker's art rather than from social science research. Many rely exclusively on scare tactics; some contain outright distortions of facts, reminiscent of 1970s drug *mis*education. In the words of Yogi Berra, "It seems like *déjà vu* all over again!" Schilling and McAlister (1990) note that most spots say what not to do, rather than model the complex behaviors needed to handle high-risk situations. We concur. If counseling psychology science ever becomes imbued with media practice, we look forward to an accumulating bank of efficacy data.

Political Action Groups

The continuing national tragedy of alcohol-related automobile fatalities has received enormous public attention, largely due to the efforts of grass-roots organizations such as Mothers Against Drunk Driving (MADD) and Students Against Driving Drunk (SADD). Their influence has been felt in at least two ways. First, they have pressured legislators to effect changes in law and judges to respond in a consistent manner. Second, they have contributed to the development of a media-supported social ethic wherein having "one for the road" is increasingly viewed as irresponsible if not criminal on the part of both host and driver. Indeed, major breweries have even begun to model responsible drinking in their television commercials (e.g., "It's the right beer . . . but definitely not now!").

Although a cynic might suggest that the social consciousness of breweries ultimately derives from the tenacity of political action groups who are quite capable of launching an effort to ban beer commercials on TV, other corporations have behaved in a less self-interested manner. Nike commercials, for example, frequently feature high-status role models promoting antidrug messages as well as athletic shoes.

One interesting convergence between political action groups and the media involved the now-ended television series "Dallas," once notorious for depicting capricious consumption of alcohol. In response to public criticism, Dallas actors and actresses began routinely to model requests for alternative beverages or to simply say "No thanks" when offered a drink (Schilling & McAlister, 1990). Should counseling psychology lend its weight to such causes? We think so. Seemingly small socially responsible changes brought about by political action groups have the potential to favorably impact vast numbers of clients and potential clients.

Legislation

Tobacco has been the target of increased legislative activity at both the national and local levels. For example, in 1984, cigarette manufacturers were required to rotate four new and harsher warnings on cigarette packs, stating the specific hazards of cigarette smoking. Similar action taken in Sweden apparently resulted in a significant decline in smoking, especially among teenagers (Bayh & Neumeyer, 1984). Moreover, to protect bystanders from the dangers of sidestream inhalation, smoking has become subject to increasing prohibitions in airplane flights, areas of public assembly, restaurants, and workplace environments.

Alcohol has also been subject to increased restriction, at least by teenagers. In response to the youth movement of the late 1960s and early 1970s, 29 states lowered their minimum legal drinking age; this action was followed by an increase in alcohol-related traffic fatalities that did not occur in other states (Smart & Goodstadt, 1977; Williams, Rich, Zador, & Robertson, 1975). Nine states that subsequently raised their minimum age showed a corresponding decline in traffic fatalities (Williams, Zador, Harris, & Karpf, 1983). Findings such as these were presented at congressional hearings (*Congressional Record,* June 26, 1984), and, in July 1984, legislation was passed that threatened states with loss of federal highway construction funds if they did not comply with a nationwide minimum drinking age of 21. The states were offered incentive grants if they (a) enacted tougher laws against driving under the influence of alcohol and/or other drugs, (b) computerized their traffic records to determine accident locations and identify problem drivers, and (c) created research and rehabilitation programs.

Although we strongly favor any legislative action to reduce the annual carnage on our highways (half as many Americans are killed *each* year in alcohol-related traffic accidents as were killed in *all* the years of the Vietnam War), we are somewhat perplexed that Breathalyzers remain instruments of enforcement rather than education and treatment as well. California, for example, has stiffened its legal definition of intoxication from .1% blood-alcohol concentration (BAC) to .08%; yet, few readers of this chapter have any idea what either percentage "feels like," and routinely make decisions about drinking and driving without adequate knowledge. We would like to see Breathalyzers become as common as toasters in restaurants and homes. Beyond that, we wonder whether teaching individuals to relate their subjective experience to objective BACs has any implications for intervention.

We opened this chapter with a discussion of decriminalization, and end now in the same domain. It is important to understand that decriminalization embodies multiple meanings. For example, the libertarian perspective (complete removal of all criminal sanctions and taxation of any resulting commercial enterprise) differs *in extremis* from another decriminalization viewpoint that distribution ought to be subject to the same constraints as methadone. Our own view occupies the "middle ground" described by Nadelmann (1989): we should do everything possible to discourage the production, sale, and abuse of all illegal drugs (as well as alcohol and tobacco) short of criminalization, and transfer government resources from antidrug law enforcement to drug prevention and treatment.

A full discussion of decriminalization would take us well beyond the confines of this chapter. Suffice it to say that our current laws do not seem to have a deterrent value; indeed, the proportion of admissions to American federal prisons for drug law violations has increased from 22% in 1980 to 34% in 1986 (Hogan, 1988), and is expected to reach 50% by 1998 (Nadelmann, 1989). Moreover, fears that drug abuse will rise as a consequence of repealing our drug laws are not substantiated by data from either the British or Dutch experiences. For example, the Dutch found substantial *decreases* in marijuana use and in the number of new addicts, following the decision in 1976 to stop enforcing certain drug-possession laws (Kupfer, 1988).

We urge counseling psychologists to become informed on the concepts and data behind the various decriminalization alternatives. Nadelmann's (1989) exceptionally cogent review and synthesis of the issues should be required reading for politicians and students in our field. Additional information may be obtained from the Drug Policy Foundation (Suite 400, 4801 Massachusetts Avenue, N.W., Washington DC, 20016; tel. 202-895-1634). Our decades-long "war on drugs" has proved to be a costly national disaster. There are data-based alternatives that demand a closer look.

REFERENCES

Abrams, D. B., & Niaura, R. S. (1987). Social learning theory. In H. T. Blane & K. E. Leonard (Eds.), *Psychological theories of drinking and alcoholism* (pp. 131–178). New York: Guilford Press.

American Psychiatric Association. (1987). *Diagnostic and statistical manual of mental disorders* (3rd ed. rev.). Washington, DC: Author.

Azrin, N. H. (1976). Improvements in the community-reinforcement approach to alcoholism. *Behavior Research and Therapy, 14,* 339–348.

Azrin, N. H., Sisson, R. W., Meyers, R., & Godley, M. (1982). Alcoholism treatment by Disulfiram and community reinforcement therapy. *Journal of Behavior Therapy and Experimental Psychiatry, 13,* 105–112.

Bachman, J. G., O'Malley, P. M., & Johnston, L. D. (1984). Drug use among young adults: The impacts of role status and social environment. *Journal of Personality and Social Psychology, 47,* 629–645.

Bandura, A. (1986). *Social foundations of thought and action: A social cognitive theory.* Englewood Cliffs, NJ: Prentice-Hall.

Bangert-Drowns, R. L. (1988). The effects of school-based substance abuse education—A meta-analysis. *Journal of Drug Education, 18,* 243–265.

Barnes, G. M., & Welte, J. W. (1986). Patterns and predictors of alcohol use among 7–12th grade students in New York State. *Journal of Studies on Alcohol, 47,* 53–62.

Battjes, R. J. (1985). Prevention of adolescent substance abuse. *The International Journal of the Addictions, 20,* 1113–1134.

Bauman, K. E. (1980). *Predicting adolescent drug use: The utility structure and marijuana.* New York: Praeger.

Baumrind, D. (1990, February). *Types of adolescent substance users: Antecedent and concurrent family and personality influences.* Paper presented for the Department of Psychology, Arizona State University, Tempe, AZ.

Bayh, B., & Neumeyer, D. B. (1984, September 10). Four-warninged is forearmed. *The New York Times,* A21.

Best, J. A., Thompson, S. M., Santi, E. A., Smith, K., & Brown, K. S. (1988). Preventing cigarette smoking among school children. *Annual Review of Public Health, 9,* 161–201.

Bigelow, G. E., Stitzer, M. L., & Liebson, I. A. (1984). Behavioral intervention techniques in drug abuse treatment: Summary of discussion. In M. L. Grabowski, M. L. Stitzer, & J. E. Henningfield (Eds.), *Behavioral intervention techniques in drug abuse treatment* (pp. 147–156). (NIDA Research Monograph Series 46.) Rockville, MD: U.S. Government Printing Office.

Block, J., Block, J., & Keyes, S. (1988). Longitudinally foretelling drug usage in adolescence: Early childhood personality and environmental precursors. *Child Development, 59,* 336–355.

Blum, K., Noble, E. P., Sheridan, P. J., Montgomery, A., Ritchie, T., Jagadeeswaran, P., Nogami, H., Briggs, A. H., & Cohn, J. B. (1990). Allelic association of human dopamine D2 receptor gene in alcoholism. *Journal of American Medical Association, 263,* 2055–2059.

Botvin, G. J. (1983). Prevention of adolescent substance abuse through the development of personal and social competence. In T. J. Glynn, C. G. Leukefeld, & J. P. Ludford (Eds.), *Preventing adolescent drug abuse: Intervention strategies* (pp. 115–140). (NIDA Research Monograph Series 47.) Washington, DC: U.S. Government Printing Office.

Botvin, G. J. (1985). The Life Skills Training Program as a health promotion strategy: Theoretical issues and empirical findings. *Special Services in the Schools, 1,* 9–23.

Botvin, G. J. (1986). Substance abuse prevention research: Recent developments and future directions. *Journal of School Health, 56,* 369–374.

Botvin, G. J., Baker, E., Dusenbury, L., Tortu, S., & Botvin, E. (1990). Preventing adolescent drug abuse through a multimodal cognitive-behavioral approach: Results of a 3-year study. *Journal of Consulting and Clinical Psychology, 58,* 437–446.

Botvin, G. J,. Baker, E., Renick, N. L., Filazzola, A. D., & Botvin, E. M. (1984). A cognitive-behavioral approach to substance abuse prevention. *Addictive Behaviors, 9,* 137–147.

Botvin, G. J., Renick, N. L, & Baker, E. (1983). The effects of scheduling format and booster sessions on a broad-spectrum psychosocial smoking prevention program. *Journal of Behavioral Medicine, 6,* 359–379.

Broadhurst, A. (1976). Applications of the psychology of decisions. In M. P. Feldman & A. Broadhurst, (Eds.), *Theoretical and experimental bases of the behavior therapies.* Chichester, England: Wiley.

Cahoon, D. D., & Cosby, C. C. (1972). A learning approach to chronic drug use: Sources of reinforcement. *Behavior therapy, 3,* 64–71.

Califano, J. A. (1979). The secretary's foreword. In U.S. Public Health Service, *Smoking and health: A report of the surgeon general.* (Department of Health, Education & Welfare, U.S. Public Health Service Publication No. 79-50066). Washington, DC: U.S. Government Printing Office.

Carlson, N. R. (1988). *Foundations of physiological psychology.* Boston: Allyn & Bacon.

Chamberlain, P., & Patterson, G. R. (1984). Aggressive behavior in middle childhood. In D. Shaffer, A. A. Ehrhardt, & L. L. Greenhill (Eds.), *The clinical guide to child psychiatry* (pp. 229–250). New York: Free Press.

Chassin, L. A., Presson, C. C., & Sherman, S. J. (1985). Stepping backward in order to step forward: An acquisition-oriented approach to primary prevention. *Journal of Consulting and Clinical Psychology, 53,* 612–622.

Ciminero, A. R., & Drabman, R. S. (1977). Current developments in behavioral assessment. In B. B. Lahey & A. E. Kazdin (Eds.), *Advances in clinical child psychology* (Vol. 1). New York: Plenum Press.

Cook, T. D., & Campbell, D. T. (1979). *Quasi-experimentation: Design and analysis issues for field settings.* Chicago: Rand McNally.

Cooper, M. L., Russell, M., & George, W. H. (1988). Coping, expectancies, and alcohol abuse: A test of social learning formulations. *Journal of Abnormal Psychology, 97,* 218–230.

Danaher, B. G., & Lichtenstein, E. (1978). *How to become an ex-smoker.* Englewood Cliffs, NJ: Prentice-Hall.

Davidson, R. (1987). Assessment of the alcohol dependence syndrome: A review of self-report screening questionnaires. *British Journal of Clinical Psychology, 26,* 243–255.

DeJong, W. (1987). A short-term evaluation of Project D.A.R.E.: Preliminary indications of effectiveness. *Journal of Drug Education, 17,* 279–295.

Dericco, D. A., & Garlington, W. K. (1977). The effect of modeling and disclosure of experimenter's intent on drinking rate of college students. *Addictive Behaviors, 2,* 135–139.

Dole, U. P., & Nyswander, M. (1965). Narcotic blockade. *Archives of Internal Medicine, 118,* 304–309.

Edwards, C. C. (1972). Conditions for investigational use of methadone for maintenance programs for narcotic addicts. *Federal Register, 35,* 9014–9015.

Emrick, C. D., & Hansen, J. (1983). Assertions regarding effectiveness of treatment for alcoholism. *American Psychologist, 38,* 1078–1088.

Fishbein, M., & Ajzen, I. (1975). *Belief, attitude, intention, and behavior: An introduction to theory and research.* Boston: Addison-Wesley.

Fishbein, M., Middlestadt, S. E. (1987). Using the theory of reasoned action to develop educational interventions: Applications to illicit drug use. *Health Education Research, 2,* 361–371.

Flay, B. R. (1985). Psychosocial approaches to smoking prevention: A review of findings. *Health Psychology, 4,* 449–488.

Flygare, T. J. (1979). Detecting drugs in school: The legality of scent dogs and strip searches. *Phi Delta Kappan, 61,* 280–281.

Forman, S. G., & Linney, J. A. (1988). School-based prevention of adolescent substance abuse: Programs, implementation and future directions. *School Psychology Review, 17,* 550–558.

Foy, D. W., Cline, K. A., Laasi, N. (1987). Assessment of alcohol and drug abuse. In T. D. Nirenberg and S. A. Maisto (Eds.), *Developments in the assessment and treatment of addictive behaviors* (pp. 89–114). Norwood, NJ: ABLEX.

Fretz, B. R. (1982). Perspective and definitions. *The Counseling Psychologist, 10*(2), 15–20.

George, W. H., & Marlatt, G. A. (1983). Alcoholism: The evolution of a behavioral perspective. In M. Galanter (Ed.), *Recent developments in alcoholism: Vol. 1* (pp. 105–137). New York: Plenum Press.

Glasser, W. (1969). *Reality therapy.* New York: Harper & Row.

Goldstein, A., & Brown, B. W. (1969). Urine testing schedules in methadone maintenance treatment of heroin addiction. *Journal of the American Medical Association, 214,* 311–315.

Goodwin, D. W., Schulsinger, F., Hermansen, L., Guze, S. B., & Winokur, G. (1973). Alcohol problems in adoptees raised apart from biological parents. *Archives of General Psychiatry, 31,* 164–169.

Griswold-Ezekoye, A., Kumpfer, K. L., & Bukoski, W. J. (1986). Childhood and chemical abuse: Prevention and intervention. *Journal of Children in Contemporary Society, 18,* 231–248.

Hackett, G., & Horan, J. J. (1978). focused smoking: An unequivocally safe alternative to rapid smoking. *Journal of Drug Education, 8,* 261–266.

Hackett, G., & Horan, J. J. (1979). Partial component analysis of a comprehensive smoking program. *Addictive Behaviors, 4,* 259–262.

Hanse, W. B. (1988). Effective school-based approaches to drug abuse prevention. *Educational Leadership, 45,* 9–14.

Harford, T. C. (1984). Situational factors in drinking: A developmental perspective on drinking contexts. In P. M. Miller & T. D. Nirenberg (Eds.), *Prevention of alcohol abuse* (pp. 119–160). New York: Plenum Press.

Harford, T. C., & Grant, B. F. (1986). Psychosocial factors in adolescent drinking contexts. *Journal of Studies on Alcohol, 48,* 551–557.

Hawkins, J. D., Lishner, D. M., Catalano, R. F., & Howard, M. O. (1986). Childhood predictors of adolescent substance abuse: Toward an empirically grounded theory. *Journal of Children in Contemporary Society, 18,* 11–48.

Helzer, J. E. (1987). Epidemiology of alcoholism. *Journal of Consulting and Clinical Psychology, 55,* 284–292.

Hogan, H. L. (1988). *Drug legalization: Pro and con.* (Congressional Research Service Report for Congress.) Washington, DC: The Library of Congress.

Horan, J. J. (1973). Preventing drug abuse through behavior change technology. *Journal of the Student Personnel Association for Teacher Education (SPATE), 11,* 145–152.

Horan, J. J. (1979). *Counseling for effective decision making: A cognitive behavioral perspective.* North Scituate, MA: Duxbury Press.

Horan, J. J., Hackett, G., & Linberg, S. (1978). Factors to consider when using expired-air carbon monoxide in smoking assessment. *Addictive Behaviors, 3,* 25–28.

Horan, J. J., & Harrison, R. P. (1981). Drug abuse by children and adolescents: Perspectives on incidence, etiology, assessment, and prevention programming. In B. B. Lahey, & A. E. Kazdin (Eds.), *Advances in clinical child psychology* (Vol. 4, pp. 283–330). New York: Plenum Press.

Horan, J. J., Robinson, S. E., Olson, C. M., Cusumano, J. A., Bourgard, L. L., Adler, R. L., Vaughan, S. M., & McWhirter, E. H. (1989, April). *Effects of two computer based interventions on adolescent smoking and drinking.* Paper presented at the annual meeting of the American Educational Research Association, San Francisco, CA.

Horan, J. J., Westcott, T. B., Vetovich, C., & Swisher, J. D. (1974). Drug usage: An experimental comparison of three assessment conditions. *Psychological Reports, 35,* 211–215.

Horan, J. J., & Williams, J. M. (1975). The tentative drug use scale: A quick and relatively problem-free outcome measure for drug abuse prevention projects. *Journal of Drug Education, 5,* 91–94.

Horan, J. J., & Williams, J. M. (1982). Longitudinal study of assertion training as a drug abuse prevention strategy. *American Educational Research Journal, 19,* 341–351.

Horn, J. L., Wanberg, K. W., & Foster, F. M. (1983). *Guidelines for understanding alcohol use and abuse: The Alcohol Use Inventory (AUI).* Baltimore, MD: PsychSystems.

Hunt, G. M., & Azrin, N. H. (1973). A community-reinforcement approach to alcoholism. *Behavior Research and Therapy, 11,* 91–104.

Ivey, A. E. (1980). Counseling 2000: Time to take charge! *The Counseling Psychologist, 8*(4), 12–15.

Jacobson, G. R. (1983). Detection, assessment, and diagnosis of alcoholism. In M. Galanter (Ed.), *Recent developments in alcoholism* (pp. 377–411). New York: Plenum Press.

Johanson, C. E., & deWit, H. (1989). The use of choice procedures for assessing the reinforcing properties of drugs in humans. In M. W. Fishman & N. K. Mello (Eds.), *Testing for use liability of drugs in humans* (pp. 171–210). (NIDA Research Monograph 92.) Rockville, MD: U.S. Government Printing Office.

Johnston, L., Bachman, J., & O'Malley, P. (1989, February 28). Press release, University of Michigan, Ann Arbor, MI.

Johnston, L., & O'Malley, P. (1986). Why do the nation's students use drugs and alcohol? Self-reported reasons from nine national surveys. *The Journal of Drug Issues, 16,* 29–66.

Kaij, L. (1960). *Alcoholism in twins.* Stockholm, Sweden: Almqvist and Wilson.

Kandel, D. B. (1980). Drug and drinking behavior among youth. *Annual Review of Sociology, 6,* 235–285.

Kandel, D. B. (1986). Processes of peer influences in adolescence. In R. K. Silbereisen, K. Eyferth, and G. Rudinger (Eds.), *Development as action in context* (pp. 203–228). Heidelberg, Germany: Springer-Verlag.

Kandel, D. B., & Adler, I. (1982). Socialization into marijuana use among French adolescents: A cross-cultural comparison with the United States. *Journal of Health and Social Behavior, 23,* 295–309.

Kashani, J. H., Keller, M. B., Solomon, N., Reid, J. C., & Mazzola, D. (1985). Double depression in adolescent substance users. *Journal of Affective Disorders, 8,* 153–157.

Katz, M. (1966). A model of guidance for career decision making. *Vocational Guidance Quarterly, 15,* 2–10.

Kleber, H., & Gawin, F. (1986). Cocaine. In A. J. Frances & R. G. Hales (Eds.), *Psychiatry update annual review: Vol. 5* (pp. 160–185). Washington DC: American Psychiatric Press.

Kovach, J. A., & Glickman, N. W. (1986). Levels and psychosocial correlates of adolescent drug use. *Journal of Youth and Adolescence, 15,* 61–77.

Kupfer, A. (1988, June 20). What to do about drugs? *Fortune,* 39–41.

Lam, W., Sze, P. C., Sacks, H. S., & Chalmers, T. C. (1987). Meta-analysis of randomized controlled trials of nicotine chewing gum. *Lancet 2,* 27–30.

Lex, B. W. (1987). Review of alcohol problems in ethnic minority groups. *Journal of Consulting and Clinical Psychology, 55,* 293–300.

Lichtenstein, E. (1982). The smoking problem: A behavioral perspective. *Journal of Consulting and Clinical Psychology, 50,* 804–819.

Lichtenstein, E., & Danaher, B. G. (1976). Modification of smoking behavior: A critical analysis of theory, research, and practice. In M. Hersen, M. Eisler, & P. M. Miller (Eds.), *Progress in behavior modification* (Vol. 3, pp. 79–132). New York: Academic Press.

Lichtenstein, E., & Rodrigues, M. P. (1977). Long-term effects of rapid smoking treatment for dependent cigarette smokers. *Addictive Behaviors, 2,* 109–112.

Linberg, S. E., Horan, J. J., Hodgson, J. E., & Buskirk, E. R. (1982). Some physiological consequences of the rapid smoking treatment for cigarette addiction. *Archives of Environmental Health, 37,* 92–98.

Lisansky-Gomberg, E. S. (1987). Drug and alcohol problems of elderly persons. In T. D. Nirenberg & S. A. Maisto (Eds.), *Developments in the treatment and assessment of addictive behaviors* (pp. 319–338). Norwood, NJ: ABLEX.

Lublin, I. (1969). Principles governing the choice of unconditioned stimuli in aversive conditioning. In R. D. Rubin & C. M. Franks (Eds.), *Advances in behavior therapy 1968.* New York: Wiley.

Mahoney, M. J. (1989). Personal communication.

Marlatt, G. A. (1983). The controlled drinking controversy: A commentary. *American Psychologist, 38,* 1097–1110.

Marlatt, G. A. (1978). Craving for alcohol, loss of control, and relapse: A cognitive-behavioral analysis. In P. E. Nathan, G. A. Marlatt, & T. Loberg (Eds.), *Alcoholism: New directions in behavioral research and treatment* (pp. 271–314). New York: Plenum Press.

Marlatt, G. A., Baer, J. S., Donovan, D. M., & Kivlahan, D. R. (1988). Addictive behaviors: Etiology and treatment. *Annual Review of Psychology, 39,* 223–252.

Marlatt, G. A., & Donovan, D. M. (1981). Alcoholism and drug dependence: Cognitive social-learning factors in addictive behaviors. In W. E. Craighead, A. E. Kazdin, & M. J. Mahoney (Eds.), *Behavior modification: Principles, issues, and applications* (2nd ed.) (pp. 264–285). Boston: Houghton Mifflin.

Mausner, B. (1973). An ecological view of cigarette smoking. *Journal of Abnormal Psychology, 81,* 115–126.

McAlister, A. L. (1983). Social-psychological approaches. In T. J. Glynn, C. G. Leukefeld, & J. P. Ludford (Eds.), *Preventing adolescent drug abuse: Intervention strategies* (pp. 36–50). (NIDA Research Monograph 47.) Washington, DC: U.S. Government Printing Office.

McClary, S., & Lubin, B. (1987). Effects of type of examiner, sex, and year in school on self-report of drug use by high school students. *Journal of Drug Education, 15,* 49–55.

McNamara, K., & Horan, J. J. (1986). Experimental construct validity in the evaluation of cognitive and behavioral treatments for depression. *Journal of Counseling Psychology, 33,* 23–30.

Midanik, L. T. (1988). Validity of self-reported alcohol use: A literature review and assessment. *British Journal of Addiction, 83,* 1019–1029.

Miller, P. M. (1973). Behavioral treatment of drug addiction: A review. *International Journal of the Addictions, 8,* 511–519.

Miller, P. M., & Eisler, R. M. (1977). Alcohol and drug abuse. In W. E. Craighead, A. E. Kazdin, & M. J. Mahoney (Eds.), *Behavior modification: Principles, issues, and applications* (pp. 376–393). Boston: Houghton Mifflin.

Miller, P. M., Hersen, M., Eisler, R. M., & Watts, J. G. (1974). Contingent reinforcement of lowered blood/alcohol levels in an outpatient chronic alcoholic. *Behaviour Research and Therapy, 12,* 261–263.

Miller, W. R., & Caddy, G. R. (1977). Abstinence and controlled drinking in the treatment of problem drinkers. *Journal of Studies on Alcoholism, 38,* 986–1003.

Miller, W. R., & Hester, R. K. (1986). Inpatient alcoholism treatment. Who benefits. *American Psychologist, 41,* 794–805.

Morales, A. (1984). Substance abuse and Mexican-American youth: An overview. *Journal of Drug Issues, 14,* 297–311.

Moskowitz, J. M. (1985). Evaluating the effects of parent groups on the correlates of adolescent substance abuse. *Journal of Psychoactive Drugs, 17,* 173–178.

Murray, R. M., Clifford, C. A., & Gurling, H. M. D. (1983). Twin and adoption studies. In M. Galanter (Ed.), *Recent developments in alcoholism* (pp. 25–48). New York: Plenum Press.

Nadelmann, E. A. (1989). *Science, 245,* 939–947.

Nathan, P. E., & Lansky, D. (1978). Common methodological problems in research on the addictions. *Journal of Consulting and Clinical Psychology, 39,* 713–726.

Nathan, P. E., & Skinsted, A. (1987). Outcomes of treatment for alcohol problems: Current methods, problems, and results. *American Psychologist, 55,* 332–340.

Newcomb, M. D., & Bentler, P. M. (1986). Substance use and ethnicity: Differential impact of peer and adult models. *The Journal of Psychology, 120,* 83–95.

Newcomb, M. D., & Bentler, P. M. (1988). The impact of family context, deviant attitudes, and emotional distress on adolescent drug use: Longitudinal latent-variable analysis of mothers and their children. *Journal of Research in Personality, 22,* 154–176.

Newcomb, M. D., Chou, C. C., Bentler, P. M., & Huba, G. J. (1988). Cognitive motivations for drug use among adolescents: Longitudinal tests of gender differences and predictors of change in drug use. *Journal of Counseling Psychology, 35,* 426–438.

Newcomb, M. D., Fahy, B. N, Skager, R. (1988). Correlates of cocaine use among adolescents. *The Journal of Drug Issues, 18,* 327–354.

Niaura, R. A., & Nathan, P. E. (1987). DSM-III and the addictive behaviors. In T. D. Nirenberg & S. A. Maisto (Eds.), *Developments in the assessment and treatment of addictive behaviors* (pp. 31–48). Norwood, NJ: ABLEX.

Noel, N. E., & McCrady, B. S. (1984). Target populations for alcohol abuse prevention. In P. M. Miller & T. D. Nirenberg (Eds.), *Prevention of alcohol abuse* (pp. 55–93). New York: Plenum Press.

Oetting, E. R., & Beauvais, F. (1987). Peer cluster theory, socialization characteristics, and adolescent drug use: A path analysis. *Journal of Counseling Psychology, 34,* 205–213.

Oetting, E. R., & Beauvais, F. (1990). Adolescent drug use: Findings of national and local surveys. *Journal of Consulting and Clinical Psychology, 58,* 385–394.

Pentz, M. A. (1983). Prevention of adolescent substance abuse through social skill development. In T. J. Glynn, C. G. Leukefeld, & J. P. Ludford (Eds.). *Preventing adolescent drug abuse: Intervention strategies* (pp. 36–50). (NIDA Research Monograph 47.) Washington, DC: U.S. Government Printing Office.

Perry, L. P., & Jessor, R. (1985). The concept of health promotion and the prevention of adolescent drug abuse. *Health Education Quarterly, 12,* 169–184.

Reed, I. E. (1985). Ethnic differences in alcohol use, abuse, and sensitivity: A review with genetic interpretation. *Social Biology, 32,* 143–145.

Rhodes, J., & Jason, L. A. (1988). *Preventing substance abuse among children and adolescents.* New York: Pergamon Press.

Rhodes, J., & Jason, L. A. (1990). A social stress model of substance abuse. *Journal of Consulting and Clinical Psychology, 58,* 395–401.

Rundall, T. G., & Bruvold, W. H. (1988). A meta-analysis of school-based smoking and alcohol use prevention programs. *Health Education Quarterly, 15,* 317–334.

Russell, M. A. H., Merriman, R., Stapleton, J., & Taylor, W. (1983). Effects of nicotine chewing gum as an adjunct to general practitioner's advice against smoking. *British Medical Journal, 278,* 1782–1785.

Saunders, J. B., & Williams, R. (1983). The genetics of alcoholism: Is there an inherited susceptibility to alcohol related problems? *Alcohol and Alcoholism, 18,* 189–217.

Schaps, E., DiBartolo, R., Moskowitz, J., Palley, C. S., & Churgin, S. (1981). A review of 127 drug abuse prevention program evaluations. *Journal of Drug Issues, 11,* 17–44.

Schilling, R. F., & McAlister, A. L. (1990). Preventing drug use in adolescents through media interventions. *Journal of Consulting and Clinical Psychology, 58,* 416–424.

Schuckit, M. A. (1981). Twin studies on substance abuse. In L. Gedda, P. Parisi, & W. Nance (Eds.), *Twin research 3: Epidemiological and clinical studies* (pp. 61–70). New York: Alan R. Liss.

Schuckit, M. A. (1987). Biological vulnerability to alcoholism. *Journal of Consulting and Clinical Psychology, 55,* 301–309.

Schuster, C. R. (1986). Implications for treatment of drug dependence. In S. R. Goldberg & I. P. Stolerman (Eds.), *Behavioral analysis of drug dependence* (pp. 357–385). New York: Academic Press.

Schwartz, J. L. (1987). *Review and evaluation of smoking cessation methods: The United States and Canada, 1978–1985.* Division of Cancer Prevention and Control, National Cancer Institute, Public Health Service (NIH Publication #87-2940), Bethesda, MD.

Searles, J. S. (1988). The role of genetics in the pathogenesis of alcoholism. *Journal of Abnormal Psychology, 97,* 153–167.

Selzer, M. L. (1971). The Michigan Alcoholism Screening Test: The quest for a new diagnostic instrument. *American Journal of Psychiatry, 127,* 89–94.

Shedler, J., & Block, J. (1990). Adolescent drug use and psychological health: A longitudinal inquiry. *American Psychology, 45,* 612–630.

Sisson, R. W., & Azrin, N. H. (1986). Family-member involvement to initiate and promote treatment of problem drinkers. *Journal of Behavior Therapy and Experimental Psychiatry, 17,* 15–21.

Skinner, H. A. (1984). Assessing alcohol use by patients in treatment. In R. G. Smart, H. D. Cappell, F. B. Glaser, Y. Israel, H. Kalant, R. E. Popham, W. Schmidt, & E. M. Sellers (Eds.), *Research advances in alcohol and drug problems* (Vol. 8, pp. 183–207). New York: Plenum Press.

Smart, R. G., & Goodstadt, M. S. (1977). Effects of reducing the legal alcohol purchasing age on drinking related problems: A review of empirical studies. *Journal of Studies on Alcohol, 38,* 1313–1323.

Spieger, D. L., & Harford, T. C. (1987). Addictive behaviors among youth. In T. D. Nirenberg & S. A. Maisto (Eds.), *Developments in the assessment and treatment of addictive behaviors* (pp. 305–318). Norwood, NJ: ABLEX.

Sprinthal, N. (1990). Counseling psychology from Greystone to Atlanta: On the road to Armageddon. *The Counseling Psychologist, 18,* 455–463.

Stabenau, J. R. (1985). Heredity and alcohol abuse: Implications for clinical application. *Social-Biology, 35,* 297–319.

Stainback, R. D., & Rogers, R. W. (1983). Identifying effective components of alcohol abuse prevention programs: Effects of fear appeals, message style, and source expertise. *The International Journal of the Addictions, 18,* 393–405.

Stitzer, M. L., Bigelow, G. E., & McCaul, E. (1985). Behavior therapy in drug abuse treatment: Review and evaluation. In R. S. Ashery (Ed.), *Progress in the development of cost-effective treatment for drug abusers* (Research monograph 58).

Stone, C. I., & Shute, R. (1977). Persuader sex differences and peer pressure effects on attitudes toward drug abuse. *American Journal of Drug and Alcohol Abuse, 4,* 55–64.

Swinson, R. P. (1983). Genetic markers and alcoholism. In M. Galenter (Ed.), *Recent developments in alcoholism* (pp. 9–24). New York: Plenum Press.

Tobler, N. S. (1986). Meta-analysis of 143 adolescent drug prevention programs: Quantitative outcome results of program participants compared to a control or comparison group. *Journal of Drug Issues, 16,* 537–567.

Trebach, A. S (1988, August). *Tough choices: The practical politics of drug policy reform.* Paper presented at the Drug Policy Workshop, Baltimore, MD.

Trellis, E. S., Smith, F. F., Alston, D. C., & Siassi, I. (1975). The pitfalls of urine surveillance: The role of research in evaluation and remedy. *Addictive Behaviors, 1,* 83–88.

U.S. Department of Health and Human Services. (1980). *An evaluation of the Teen Challenge treatment program.* (National Institute on Drug Abuse Services Report.) Washington, DC: U.S. Government Printing Office.

Van Hasselt, V. B., Hersen, M., & Milliones, J. (1978). Social skills training for alcoholics and drug addicts: A review. *Addictive Behaviors, 3,* 221–233.

Wanberg, K. W. & Horn, J. L. (1983). Assessment of alcohol use with multi-dimensional concepts and measures. *American Psychologist, 38,* 1055–1069.

Webb, E. J., Campbell, D. T., Schwartz, R. D., & Sechrest, L. (1966). *Unobtrusive measures: Nonreactive research in the social sciences.* Chicago: Rand McNally.

Williams, A. F., Rich, R. F., Zador, P. L, & Robertson, L. S. (1975). The legal minimum drinking age and fatal motor crashes. *Journal of Legal Studies, 4,* 219–239.

Williams, A. F., Zador, P. L., Harris, S. S., & Karpf, R. S. (1983). The effect of raising the legal minimum drinking age on involvement in fatal crashes. *Journal of Legal Studies, 12,* 169–179.

Wilson, G. T. (1987). Cognitive studies in alcoholism. *Journal of Consulting and Clinical Psychology, 55,* 325–331.

AUTHOR INDEX

SUBJECT INDEX